STOPPING THE VIOLENCE

CREATE, ENHANCE, AND MAINTAIN HARMONY

JOSEPH ALEXANDER BAILEY II, MD FACS

Member of the clinical faculty at the UCR/UCLA Division of
Biomedical Sciences at the University of California, Riverside

ABOUT THE COVER

Ma'at (pronounced "Ma aut"—derived from "Maa", the measure of a cubit)—is the central moral and spiritual theme in the Traditional African approach to life. Ma'at is the Spiritual Elements in action—i.e. Unconditional Love, Truth, Reality, and the Natural. Ma'at's origin dates to ?20,000 BC, following Very Ancient African priest-astronomers charting of the stars and planets by devising units of measurements (e.g. arithmetic and geometry) based upon the observed periodicity of astronomic events. These measurements so matched the Celestial Order as to itself amount to a revelation regarding the organizing principles by which Ancient Africans (e.g. the Dogon and Woyo) realized and recognized its own latent harmony. So wondrous were the cycles of Celestial Bodies--and their ever greater, more majestic, and infinitely widening cycles—that African Sages inferred laws by which gods came into being and then disappeared. These laws were "hooked" up to their new mathematical insights and into the earlier-known mystery of biological death and regeneration. Thought to arise from the lunar rhythm of the womb (i.e. the Great Mother) as a result of Cosmic Order, the goddess Ma'at emerged through a mathematical law. Besides being a model on how to Live Life, she crystallized the "Big Picture" Seed, Pattern, and Vision of Divine Cosmic Order. By putting pertinent mathematical connections into philosophical words, African Sages formulated Ma'at laws.

Ma'at was personified as holding the Ankh cross, a symbol of the heka Aung (i.e. magic power) in one hand and the Papyrus scepter (representing the book of Law) in the other. On her head rests the feather—her main symbol. She was next designated as the feminine counterpart of Tehuti (god-man of Wisdom)--and was viewed as a correspondent between the Earth and Celestial realms. In the Book of Ptah-hotep (?4599-4402 BC)—the oldest complete Sebait (or Books of Wise Instruction which also contained Ancient African Moral Philosophy)—the concept of Ma'at is introduced as an intimate link with the Ultimate Divine Plan Ideal. To this end, Ma'at's name became associated with the idea of Truth, Righteousness, and Order—with what concerns respect, levelness, genuineness, uprightness, and with the world steadfast and in equilibrium. This meant Ma'at became an unalterable connection of measurement for Social and Spiritual order—by the relationship between one human being and another—between humankind and the gods—and serving to bridge humankind and the Living Dead. All of this was an elaboration on the meaning that any human, by being *made in the Image of God,* was naturally imparted with *Dignity* (inherent worthiness incapable of being diminished).

The creation, enhancement, and maintenance of Dignity were comprised of the *Twelve African Cardinal Virtues*--pathways symbolizing the highest of human excellence—Propriety (be in accordance with the fitting and appropriate), Balance, Order, Truth, Harmony, Peace and Tranquility, Fellowship, Justice, Rightness, Straightness or Righteousness, and Reciprocity ("the reward of one whose acts consist in the fact that one will act for her/him" in doing good). Modeling a Rightness path of standards, filters, measures, and guides to a thriving, more meaningful and rewarding life, and Happiness was called "*The Way*" of Ma'at. These twelve were fashioned into 42 laws governing "the Way" of living—and also for criteria in the Hall of Justice to weigh and measure the deceased life's beliefs and actions on the "*Day of Judgment*". The Judgment included first the deceased having to pass the Negative Confessions or Declarations of Innocence or the 42 Admonitions of Ma'at. Next, the deceased's "Heart"/ab was placed on one Balance

Scale pan and Ma'at's feather on the other--Truth's lightness being the standard against which initiates' Will (i.e. "Hearts") were weighed. This was followed by judging the Soul. The determination was based on living by a standard imposed by ones essential divine nature—i.e. staying within and living life out of the Spiritual Elements since one could not claim to have done Right Living if there had been inconsistency at every moral choice crossroad.

The original essence of Ma'at and the Weighing of the Soul was laid out in Ancient Egyptian hieroglyphics. This summarized the wisdom recorded millennia earlier on temples, tombs, coffins, papyruses, and oral teachings pertaining to African Spiritual Literature. The purpose was to encourage spiritual liberation, awakening, or revivification (give new life to) in order to elevate from ordinary human consciousness and mortality up to Cosmic Consciousness and immortality. Although Ancient Africans discovered and codified mechanical, physics, chemistry, and other academia, their focus was on the patterns governing people's day to day existence and spiritual development. Rightness' Twelve African Cardinal Virtues implied each human has an obligation, duty, and responsibility to pursue them as goals. This stemmed from defining the Divine and the Natural ingredients for Human Ideals as: social right relations with and interaction behaviors toward people—with personal behavior—with Nature—and with the Divine. To follow the Ma'at Way is the path to a successful life—preparing and qualifying one to cross the great abysm in the Afterlife so as to bathe in the divine powers at ones appropriate Ari (i.e. Karmatic) level. Because the supreme law governing humans' divinity is centered on a Free Will to choose, the knowledge of the law is conveyed to one in such a manner that allows one the freedom to follow or reject it. Ancient Africans said such happens via human's Ma'at faculty deeply buried in the Spirit of the mid-function of the Right Brain.

It has the capability of communicating to ones mind the working of forces that maintain Order of ones physiological and mental functions. Ma'at itself is a projection of the forces that inter-relate the various functions of the body into a human's awareness. The perfect harmony existing between these various functions is Truth and Reality. One can intuit from this faculty and experience the urge to live by the Spiritual Elements—the Human Ideal in Life Living according to the laws of ones indwelling Divine Consciousness—i.e. the "Soul Sunshine" of ones Private Self. They defined *Intuiting* as seeking the Will of God through ones 'Self' (Divine Consciousness—a human's "First Wisdom") so as to experience ones own true nature. From resultant Insights, *Intuitive Inductions* (inferring general principles from particular facts present in the Cosmic Order) are done. This means making compatible imaginative leaps to discover unrealized realities--i.e. the taking of Leaps from facts of Reality into realms dealing with corresponding Unrealized Realities. The revealed Ma'at Principles are absorbed into ones mind to guide thinking and thereby be led "instinctively" to the apprehension of Truth for its application on any "Branch" of the "Truth Tree"--perhaps of a premise or to do what is Right, even if it puts one at a disadvantage and ones opponent at an advantage. One can thereby live in harmony with all things because all things in the Cosmos are functions within a system. Examples include giving Unconditional Love without seeking anything in return or making available needed entities of life in spite of the needy refusing them.

The components on the Cover indicate the major aspects of how to get out of a mindset of Violence and return to the Spiritual Elements stream in order to swim through the course of ones life. The Sankofa Process starts it by reviewing Ancient African *Wisdom* (derived from deep experiences and realizations about them) of Tehuti so as to extract pertinent principles to put ones present life in Order. The switch over process is spurred by a *Self-Declaration* ("Nothing will stop me from becoming my Highest Self"). However, all switching Self-Declarations demand paying a high price. At first, it seems things will get worse--but that worsening is simply the process of getting rid of all that is contributing to Violence applied to oneself and to others. To best solve ones major problems, ones skilled Critically Thinking Intellect partners with the Spiritual Emotions (i.e. Pre-Birth Emotions) emanating from ones "Heart." The ingredients needed to harmoniously fit together ones newly fashioned Human Ideal Goals into a workable plan is by Ma'at's 12 virtues. The correctness and effectiveness of ones time, energy, and efforts are determined by one gradually experiencing in ones Private Selfhood the essential "5Ss" (safety, security, self-confidence, strength, and stability) so as to move confidently into a thriving future and be happy in the process of simply doing Right Life Living.

Ref. Ani, 2003; Wells-Wilbon.Cover design is by Sharon Bingaman R.N.

PREFACE

As a boy, my all-Black community in Wilson and Greensboro, North Carolina was like "the eye of a storm"—meaning it was filled with peaceful, cooperative, and wonderful people. This image came to me from an ex-Slave, one of my newspaper customers, telling me the "eye" symbolized Unconditional Love while the storm was anything and everything that attacked its expressions. Thereafter, being perplexed about the nature of Unconditional Love, I looked for metaphors to help explain it. One came that evening. While bathing in the bathtub, I noticed the soap bubbles constantly changing figures in their ever evolving new combinations of colors. Both patterns, stemming from a series of reflections, designed a "movie" of beautiful effects. Yet, there was no change in the soap bubbl es' ingredients themselves. In Grade school, I had fun playing with a kaleidoscope (a tube containing small brightly colored pieces of glass). While slowly turn it and looking into the peephole, several images of fragments of glass fashioned intriguing optical effects. These effects were made because the image formed in one of its mirrors was also reflected by another, and in turn, that reflected image was reflected--and so on. Yet, there was no change in the fragments of glass themselves.

In high school, I learned a Rainbow is composed of sunlight broken up in the air into red, orange, yellow, green, blue, indigo, and violet tiny drops of rain. Each drop acts like a small *Prism* (a three-sided piece of glass that, when held up to sunlight, is a rainbow maker). Combined, these colored rain drop components are a *Spectrum* (like Ma'at displays = Unconditional Love). In college, we students were told each drop of dew has a reflection of all the other drops on a spider web and each drop, in turn, is reflected in all the others--implying one drop needs all other drops to be whole. As with any human, each drop is vital and all other drops depend upon it. During adulthood, studying Ancient African Philosophy, I realized soap bubbles, Rainbows, and dew drops share correspondence features. Their endless respective combinations and repetition displays emanate from a tiny few principles--all apparently coming from the same "Oneness" source—each being Unconditional Love patterns!

This insight led me to remember another ex-Slave telling me that each God-made pattern possesses a drop of the Cosmic Intelligence--each drop corresponds to all other drops--and all the drops conform to the plan of the Cosmic Intelligence (called God). Hence, people who choose to live in the kernel of the "eye" of the storm continually experience the vigor and freshness contained in Unconditional Love's immediate sense experiences. Such experiences are like *Magic*" in that *things once joined or which have been in contact continue to act on each other* at a distance after the social interaction has ended. By being part of that, as the community newspaper boy, enabled me to see a correspondence in how humans and Nature are interrelated and interconnected—a correspondence I internalized to cultivate my talents into a "ME/WE" Mission—better put by the Black Church as: "Lifting [Others] while Climbing [towards ones Highest or Divinity Self]. Besides, experiencing what Unconditional Love is all about (from my family and my community, which included Ex-Slaves), as a gardener I gained an intimacy with Nature which paved the path for me to follow African Tradition.

Nature's and humans' harmonious "ME/WE" interdependence is how Unconditional Love came to be known to me—and life does not get any better than that. However, my observations suggest that Unconditional Love is unknown to the vast majority of the World Crowd and that is, I believe, the "bottom-line" cause of

Violence. Hence, *to return to Unconditional Love is the way to end Violence.* To elaborate, surrounding this "eye" kernel of my boyhood community was hostile White people exhibiting all forms of terrorism, including lynching and killing Black People just "for sport." Black People reacted by huddling together in hopes of gaining mutual protection. Meanwhile, they kept busy instilling Manners into all of us Black youth and prompting us to be successful "for your race." It was within and out of this setting that I was reared.

Nevertheless, subtle changes began after World War II because more and more Black People embraced European philosophies and traits at the expense of African Tradition themes--escalating rapidly with and following the 1960s Black Power movement. During this time I was intensely pursuing my career education and training in order to become an Orthopaedic Surgeon. While having to fight racism "Alligators" at every step, "ME/WE" remained a vital conceptual link in my development chain. For example, at almost "giving up" times, my all-Black Community's: "Succeed for your race" admonition would suddenly pop up and push me to continue to stay in the "Alligator's mouth" because its insides contained necessary ingredients for my progress.

By contrast, reflecting a correspondence from our Enslaved African American Ancestors having had the "Spirit" beaten out of them by conspiracy racist practices, current racism did the same to most of my Black youth peers. Although scattered on an assortment of paths, some being predisposed to violence, a common display of their loss of Spiritual Courage was to shun facing any problem when an opportunity to "Escape" arose. The reasoning was that since they had nothing, not handling significant emergencies would give no worse results. Yet, the price paid for each "Escape" prevented "learning from the struggle" the skills to handle increasingly bigger up-coming problems. The consequences of such ongoing neglect compounded their problems into vicious cycles of ever increasing daily living survival difficulties. Societal hostility left them meager alternatives for survival.

Suddenly, in Black communities, there appeared "out of nowhere" train box cars and numerous duffle bags loaded with free "street" drugs and guns—both generating problems of untold magnitude. "Crack" cocaine usage exploded in the 1970s-1980s—leading to "street" drug addiction "Escapes" to "get away from it all" as well as to "Black-on-Black" Violence. Both invited a "war on drugs"—itself causing crime to explode until the 1990s. Hence, prisons were quickly over-populated.

Two early contributions from my Mother which put me on a different course was first drilling into me to stay aware of my birth gift of Selfhood Greatness. Perhaps this was what was behind her second contribution of saying, whenever I brought her one of my creative works, "Son, you can do better." My reaction was not to get hurt emotions but, because of feeling Selfhood Great, to go back to the 'drawing board' and see how to improve my creation. That attitude was vital to help me keep going in my medical practice. In the face of ever present "Alligators," I had no alternative but to be self-reliant as an "Isolated Individualist"—and always strive for perfection. Such was transferrable in frustrating efforts to help struggling Black People. Most problematic are those with violent tendencies from minds turned "Inside-Out"—meaning they are against their own Survival, Self-Protection, and Self-Preservation so as to fight any efforts, including mine, specifically intended to help them thrive.

But my lifetime personal experiences with them, and particularly since the 1970s, lets me know their displays of self-violence and/or violence applied to others is not out of hatred, as with European Brutes. Instead, it is out of Extreme Despair and Desperation. I am convinced that the overwhelming majority would immediately convert into "Right" Life Living if they could reasonably take care of their Physical and Spiritual (not religious) Human Nature Needs. Still, this is only one thread in a spider web symbolizing today's violence. The "spider" weaving that thread is Brute European males who attack the Spiritual Elements. These *Brutes will never change.* Since they control the world and the minds of most in the world crowd, in order to Stop the Violence necessitates Black People get out from under Satanists' influences. The "What to do" for Black People to become free of Brute European male influence is not difficult to determine. Such Europeans have nothing Black People need to model—no mindsets or lifestyle or possessions--no standards, values, guides, filters, or measures—no philosophies or ways of thinking or forms of entertainment—no ways of dealing with people or Nature. Thus, they ought to be completely disregarded, especially since their source of existence is so victimizing to Black People. Black People already have everything they need to return to their natural Selfhood Greatness state. It simply needs scholarly organized, workable applications.

The overriding self-healing management principle is the *Sankofa Concept*: Establishing Trust in ones Selfhood by returning to philosophical building blocks of African Tradition. This is the source of Wisdom for serving as a guide for fashioning a sound present daily living so as to properly move into a thriving future. Yet, the "How to get free" so as to be able to return to African Tradition's "How Shall I Live?" principles is extremely complex and difficult. One reason is that most struggling Black People's mindsets are "Inside-Out". Another is that most successful Black People have adopted European Individualism customs of "every man for himself". Both reasons combine to ensure Black People will not easily come together and do what it takes to return to the super-brilliant state of thriving and happiness that characterized our Ancient African Ancestors. Still, as Mother use to say: "It is better to light a candle than curse the Darkness". Thus, the purpose of this book is to serve as a "candle" inside the "Dark Side" of life called Violence. Hopefully some leader of the future will use this "candle" to start a "fire" that lights up Black People to see the wisdom of returning to Ancient African paths which are Certain to lead to successful lives. Certainty comes from proven African Tradition success for tens of thousands of years. By contrast, European ways have never been successful in bringing peace to the world—not even for six months.

What gives rise to Violence originates in a Supernatural (i.e. Fantasy) realm out of Brute Brains. Satanist rules, designed in a fantasy Supernatural realm to operate in the Physical World through violence, deception, and excitement, are devoid of anything Spiritual or Metaphysical, except for being shrewdly used as tools to confuse and control the minds of the naïve. An example is Europeans using their Supernatural God to falsely be the same as the Spiritual God of African Tradition. Within this context and out of necessity, the majority of this book's discussions deal with the Supernatural—how its Codes are used to do what it does and how its practices appear in camouflage forms.

CHAPTER I -- "BIG PICTURE" OF VIOLENCE starts with what is Ma'at Right Life Living for purposes of comparing it with a life of Violence. It discusses how making a voluntary choice to give up the mindset each human was given at birth leads to the causes, paths, effects of Violence

CHAPTER II -- INDIFFERENCE/HATE/EVIL/SADISM VIOLENCES are reflections of ones mind being turned "Inside-Out". How this is done, as stated in Chapter I, leads to elaborating on what each is about. People with this mindset have devised their own "Hall of Infamy" and aspire to do what it takes to be inducted into it.

CHAPTER III -- "NORMAL VARIANT" CROWD VIOLENT IMAGES are from European minds whose intent is to program their "Troops" to join in bringing about pain, suffering, and death to innocent people unlike them. This is done as a "sporting" adventure which is filled with excitement.

CHAPTER IV -- EUROPEAN MANHOOD is subdivided into "gentlemen" (who are socialized to believe they are superior to all others) as well as white collar workers and the lower classes who must assume the role of a Superiority Complex. Yet, all are burdened with being Self-Unknown and with Self-Hate. Oddly, they pride themselves on being "Individualists" and yet are dependent on following the same philosophy of life which prevents independent thought and actions that are unapproved by the Supernatural cult. If they do not "follow the leader," they are ostracized and isolated. Their power comes, not from within, but by the GUN and their Network.

CHAPTER V -- AFRICAN AMERICAN SLAVERY has no Humankind equal in its "here and now" horribleness done to the minds, emotions, bodies, spirits, family, social, traditions, customs, and other aspects of each Enslaved. Also, just as horrible is what the effects of slavery and racism have done to these same Selfhood parts of all Black Americans as well as Africans in Africa and the diaspora.

CHAPTER VI -- BLACK PEOPLE'S PARA-SLAVERY DESPAIR emphasizes the Brain Switch from a balanced brain usage of each Enslaved over to functioning primarily out of their Emergency Fight-Flight-Fright-Funk brain. The usage for each brain pattern has Extreme Despair as its Background for fashioning their varied forms of Life Living.

CHAPTER VII -- "KILLER" POLICE constitute any philosophically oriented European, regardless of "race" or uniform, who has selected Black People or Amerindians or Hispanics as their scapegoat targets. They believe these need to be killed so as to make it safe for the "White race".

CHAPTER VIII -- VICTIMS OF VIOLENT MINDS are any under the influence of Predators, regardless of "race" or gender or class. It can range from gross overt violence, to tempered to masked to concealed to Microaggression (e.g. flying the Confederate Flag on college campuses; or telling a Black person she has good diction, implying that other Blacks do not because the "White way is the Right way"). Those little things lead Whites to develop Chimera images of Black People and to react violently.

CHAPTER IX -- CASTLES OF CONSCIOUSNESS are vitally important because the Consciousness one chooses to use sets the pattern for ones philosophy of life and determines what one focuses on. People do not appreciate that this is a "Seed" to which the primary attention is to be paid, rather than starting with "Leaves" of the problem. For example, to speak of teaching police how to speak to Black People as a way to improve community relations completely omits the fact that the Consciousness of "Killer" police is about their own self-hatred projected as racism and generating a need to "kill." Thus, when the opportunity presents itself, there will probably be another dead unarmed Black person.

CHAPTER X -- BLACK GANG ICON IMAGES seem to differ significantly from the Chimera Images associated with the European "Killer" police *"Phantasmagoria"* Killing process done for "sport." Instead, they are more of a Self-Image nature whose payload message is focused on Respect and Disrespect as well as survival.

CHAPTER XI -- BLACK AMERICAN GANGS are replicas of Black youth's interpretations of the way European male gangs are set up and run—but under the circumstances available to these youth. However, their Consciousness Background reasons for being in gangs differs greatly and they are not as wed to violence for its own sake as are European males. Whereas Black youth's destruction of fellow Blacks is at a local level, European Satanists' destruction is for all of Black People, and to get those same Black victims to defend the Satanists against Blacks trying to help bring peace.

CHAPTER XII -- WOMEN & VIOLENCE share many similarities with Black male gang members and much of the information presented in this book is interchangeable.

CHAPTER XIII -- NATURE/MA'AT MANAGING OF VIOLENCE are the models for Stopping The Violence. Such is illustrated by the Bailey Farm at the conclusion of this book.

What stimulated my need to write this book has come from an ongoing shocking experience that compared to my boyhood days there seems to have been a steady escalation of hatred and displays of violence throughout the world in general and among people in my environmental area in particular. I believe much of this is do to ignorance on the part of the afflicted World Crowd who has no concept of being led by Satanists—the very ones who remain vigilant in promoting Violence among everybody. Violence is the "divine and conquer" tool that provides them with the ability to control the World Crowd's minds, money, and scarce desired possessions. The benefits for Satanists is to boost their fragile "little god" sense to hide their self-hate and "faceless" hatred of everybody. Verification is by means of complete controlling power, all of the riches, and being above the Rules for Right Life Living.

Profound Appreciation goes to Sharon Bingaman R.N. for helping with research, proof reading many parts, and all of the illustrations, including the Cover.

Joseph A. Bailey II, MD, FACS
7/22/15

TABLE OF CONTENTS

FIGURES

CHAPTER I

VIOLENCE IS CAUSED

BY

DISREGARDING UNCONDITIONAL LOVE

"BIG PICTURE" OF VIOLENCE

The "Big Picture" is the gist of the totality essentials of a "Thing." *The "Big Picture" of African Traditions' Right Life Living is to stay within and evolve out of the Spiritual Elements of Unconditional Love, Truth, Reality, and the Natural.* The "Big Picture" of Violence is the gist of anything about Life Living contrary to the Spiritual Elements. "*Gist*" is a fuzzy mental representation of the general meaning of or the "how to do" of something significant. This may include the conveying of an experience; state of an association of Ideas; or about things done. A Very Ancient African analogy for "Gist" is the Halo—i.e. the semi-transparent envelope of its Star--and consisting of the radiant aura of that Star's character. When, they said, one finds a Star filled with the Spiritual Elements, one has discovered ones "*Lucky Star*"—the Star serving to provide the inner Selfhood luminescence to guide one through life. However, to become attached to anything short of the Spiritual Elements is to be forever under the influence of a "*Disaster Star*"—an influence causing one to cling to it.

The Halo of either a "Lucky Star" or of a "Disaster Star"—by symbolizing a Star's "What it is"--represents an *Icon Image* (an essence visual image). A "Lucky Star's" Halo--consisting of the reflected essence of the "Lucky Star" as well as emanating its Divine Message--was thought of as a "store-house" for the Star's Message from God. Thus, the Icon Image of a "Lucky Star" was Personified as the *Goddess Ma'at*. To be a representative of the "Lucky Star's" essence and to live by its Divine Message were what characterized the Principles of Ma'at (i.e. the Spiritual Elements in daily living action). Similar reflections on a "Disaster Star" were features of everything to be avoided in daily living since Violence comes from being the essence of and/or following the dictates of the "Diaster Star" as well as using its ingredients for ones Life Living standard, guide, filter, and measure.

The use of such Affect Symbolic Imagery as the "Lucky Star" and "Diaster Star" enabled Ancient African Sages to make the gist of the Principles of Cosmic Knowledge understandable to African People. Spiritual "*Principles*," by being pieces of the Spiritual Elements in varying combinations, are unchanging Essence realities of Cosmic Knowledge--possessing *Certainty* because they cannot be broken down any further. These Principles were said to also be housed in the Lucky Star's *Iconic Store*. Insight into the message of the "Lucky Star" (or any like-kind Spiritual Symbol) is gained by *Intuiting* it—a process which disregards any human layered boundaries on the boundless or disregards any limitations placed on the essentials. The extracted Knowledge conveys a realistic, truthful, and vivid clear sense of the indescribable Essence. Such paves the way for sound reasoning for life-shaping or life-changing decisions and solutions. Thus, a *Spiritual "Big Picture"* or Halo or Spiritual Icon Image is the abstract or abstraction gist of the wholism essentials of Cosmic Knowledge, as conveyed by the metaphoric use of Affect Symbolic Imagery (Bailey, Teaching Black Youth).

An illustrative example of how to image a Spiritual or a Violence (fig. 1) "Big Picture" is the "*Tree Concept*," whose essentials are its "Seed" (its essence) as well as its Roots, Trunk, Branches, Leaves, and Fruit, as discussed below. The *Violence "Seed"* appears from choosing flow in a stream of life outside of Unconditional Love, Truth, Reality, and/or the Natural. Correction for this choice and actions of Ignorance, as Ancient Africans termed it, is to embrace the "Tree's" *Spiritual Element "Seed"*. The actuality of that "Seed" being composed purely of the Spiritual Elements necessarily means it is God-made. The Spiritual Element "Seed," out of which the Ma'at Big Picture is made, consists of a treasury of meanings, standards, guides, filters, and measures for use in daily living--and as long as one stays in that stream of flow throughout life, one will thrive and be Happy. The Base upon which any Spiritual "Seed" is fashioned is Unconditional Love, the metaphorical "*Spiritual Anchor*" for any aspect of Ma'at Life Living. By being of a God-made Spiritual Source means the "Anchor" for any Spiritual "Seed" is eternal, unchanging, permanent, stationary, and sound.

The Spiritual "Big Picture" is subdivided into a microcosm ('little world') of its Cosmic macrocosm ('big world'). The macrocosm is the Cosmic Organism, orchestrated by God's Cosmic Mind. Similarly, a human, representing the microcosm, is given a Soul consisting of the "Spark of God" out of which emerge Ma'at Principles devised within the Cosmic Organism. Put another way, by each human's Private Selfhood being of a God-made possessor of a Spiritual Soul "Seed" (i.e. made from a "Spark" of God) implies a Private Selfhood "Anchoring" that is empowered with the "5Ss"—Safety, Security, Self-Confidence (i.e. Sureness), Strength, and Stability.

Both macrocosm and microcosm Spiritual *Anchors* ('a crook or hook') are like the weights holding a ship in place under varying extremes of conditions. Examples of how different types of ship anchors are used for different purposes include: those lowered into the seabed to hold the vessel in a particular place and prevent it from drifting--those that keep the vessel from moving from place to place--those that float while a ship is going along to keep it on course in a heavy sea; those used by a small boat when landing through surf to prevent its being pushed sideways. All of these are made from some type of material which, in ancient times, consisted of large stones, baskets full of stones, sacks filled with sand, logs of wood loaded with lead and, in modern times, of various types of metal.

HUMANS MA'AT "BIG PICTURE"

A human's Private Selfhood "Anchor" is what is perfect for activities of daily living. It is an 'invisible eternal Anchor' called Ma'at in African Tradition. Ma'at reflects Spiritual Elements displays of the Soul/"Self" in evolution. The "Big Picture" of Ma'at (discussed in "About The Cover") is understood by grasping the subject by its underlying Principles. Ma'at implies one may feel safe by staying within the crowd but, as ships are safe in harbor, that is not what ships or humans are for. The Courage powering Ma'at is naturally displayed by those who retain contact with the Source of their Souls. That God-Source is the furnisher of a first and continuous supply of everything needed to live within the "Big Picture" of Ma'at. To illustrate, the bull's eye of the Archery Pad (fig. 7) equates to the Source within ones Soul while the rest of the Pad equates to the "Big Picture" of how one deals with all of ones birth gifts. These gifts are all one needs to have a thriving and happy life. Inside that "Source" can be discovered the inner factors that unify things within the issue at hand. That unification is based upon the mutual relationships and interdependence of things with each other and the whole.

DETERMINING TRUTH: Foundational to being in the right flow of the Truth is to be aware that the Spiritual God elaborated on in the Ancient African Bible is not to be confused with the Supernatural "God" advocated by Europeans. To be aware of the Divine Unity underlying Ma'at ingredients enables one to see the whole—i.e. the "Big Picture" and its "Seed". *Determining the harmonious underlying interdependence and interrelationship between ingredients in a situation--both with each other and with the whole--is to arrive at the Truth.* Verification of having grasped the Truth of the "Seed" is when all the ingredients and their products conform to the Spiritual Elements. The way Ancient Africans put this is by the *Law of Holonomy*: The whole is inside the Seed; the whole is contained in each of the Seed's manifested parts; and the Seed is found throughout the whole. This Law is the essence of the "Tree Concept". The "Seed" is what the Tree is before it came into Being. So, to discover if something is "Good" or "Bad," focus on its "Seed" and disregard its Roots, Trunk, Branches, Leaves, and/or Fruit until its nature is determined. This process, opposite to what most people do, is fundamental to knowing what to choose at the crossroad of a life-shaping or life-changing decision.

DETERMINING "THE BEST": Specifically for the Good, if there is more than one Spiritual Elements Source for a situation—each capable of giving rise to an association which forms the Good, then an essential of seeing "the Big Picture" is to determine what is likely to be the best of all viable options—e.g. what is most practical for people involved and the situation at hand—which, of course, may change with each situation. Otherwise, the criteria of THE BEST is: *the one that has longest stood the test of time; that has produced the greatest success agreed upon as beneficial by all Sages of all cultures through the ages; and that has brought the longest and greatest degree of happiness when internalized by anyone anywhere.*

DETERMINING WHAT TO DO: Humans have the obligation, duty, and responsibility to make discernments of how to stay inside the Spiritual Elements as a way of life—and how to learn and master the Ma'at wholistic way of life so as to keep producing Truths compatible with Divine Law. "*Obligation*" is a naturally occurring binding promise to take the steps necessary for Caring and Compassion. This means there is no problem too great to undertake managing--even if it has never been done before or has never seen nor heard of before. "*Duty*" is doing the tasks which have to be done without consideration of fame, money, status, or even appreciation (which best comes from pride in ones work). Two of its features are: first, take care of other people's things better than if they were yours; second, stay in people contact without needing something. "*Responsibility*" is shouldering the consequences for anything not properly done or that is left undone but should have been done in accordance with ones obligation. Always do the job right and strive for perfection.

MA'AT BACKGROUND LEADING TO "RIGHT" LIVING: The first of two situations concerning African Tradition's mythological concept of Cosmic Creation deals with Metaphysical Order; the second with Metaphysical Disorder (a break in the integrity of Ma'at). Ancient Africans conceived of the newly forming Cosmos as being surrounded on its outside by Disorder--existing at the beginning of time and thus present before humans appeared in the Cosmos. Metaphysical Disorder is amoral but has the potential to be cultivated by any human into a False Self and anti-Ma'at state.

African Sages said God was situated in "The Other World" at the time of spilling metaphorical Waters into what would become the finite Cosmos. Those Waters, called the Ocean of Nun (OON), contained a special kind of Order. Its resting Energy and Matter, despite having no form and being undefined and undifferentiated, still were *not disordered*--a state called *CHAOS*. Imagine this OON--with its contents of the Spiritual Elements--flowing throughout the entire Cosmos, around and into every nook and cranny of each of God's creatures and creations. Out of the OON comes the etymology of Ma'at, suggesting an evolutionary order from a physical concept of straightness, evenness, levelness, correctness onward to embrace the Metaphysical concepts of Rightness of "Things"--Righteousness and Lawfulness of the Natural and Social Order (Karanga, p6, 374). *Ma'at's Seven Cardinal Virtues are: Truth, Justice, Propriety, Harmony, Balance, Reciprocity, and Order.*

These were all personified in the mythological African goddess Ma'at, the image of which is used to give people and "Things" direction within the Spiritual Elements and serve as a defense against Secular Chaos in Nature and society. The "Self" as the orchestrator of ones Selfhood—the staying within and operating out of the Spiritual Elements flow—the "ME/WE"--all represent individual "Anchors." They are indivisible and function as a unity in creating, enhancing, and maintaining Harmony, Coherence, Consistency, Compatibility, Balance, Endurance, Connectedness, and an Unchanging Sameness, in spite of an individual's Uniqueness in composition and in Patterns of presentation in daily living. Ma'at is the Human Ideal core for the interrelated ethical, social, religious, political, and natural order for all real aspects of the Cosmos. Each human is given the Free Will to determine what to Cause out of ones Real or False Self. Real Self people Climb towards their own Highest (Divinity) Selves while Lifting others to do the same.

FIGURE 1

"ME/WE" OF MA'AT: Every human Chooses to Cause Effects or that human reaps Causes from ones Choices that lead to Effects. All Effects have Consequences leading to a "Big Picture" of Results. The purpose of Ma'at Life Living is to have constructive Results for oneself as well as for others. The features of Ma'at needed to make this happen are present in "ME/WE" Form (fig. 1)—a Form present in ones Soul and in ones Cosmic Organism pre-birth residence—a Form manifested in ones Earth World Selfhood as long as one remains in the "Ma'at" flow. Every living human is a Spiritual Cosmic Organism Caused Real Self and is thus given all the ingredients at birth to have a "ME/WE" beneficial Effect in the Earth World—an Effect that is about "lifting others towards a Ma'at life as one is climbing there". To stay within the Spiritual Elements means those Effects will naturally deliver Consequences benefitting the "ME/WE". But first, one must maintain ones own health and "5Ss" (Safety, Security, Sureness, Strength, and Stability) before trying to help others. Yet, everything one does in preparation to be personally sound can also be shared, at some later time, to benefit the "WE."

My "ME/WE" comes from my enjoying learning so I can share it with others. Personally, I believe the European "Golden Rule"—"do unto others as you would have them do unto you"--is quite limited. People who truly need help do not respond to situations or the way to handle situations as I do. For me to be efficient and effective requires knowing how they evolved so as to gain an idea of how they think. The trick, which I have not mastered, is to provide them with what they really, really need and to find a way to present it that they will accept. My attempts have not met with success but I must keep trying because my Mission says that is the right thing to do. My hurt emotions and continual defeats are not important in the "Big Picture" of my Mission. For the present I simply make the information available and hope a leader will arise who is willing to translate the messages relayed to me from my Spiritual Entourage.

HUMANS PATH TO VIOLENCE

A *Secular "Big Picture"* is a fuzzy mental representation—i.e. a picture, image, likeness, figure, drawing, portrait--reflecting the general meaning of information or experience of a situation. It may or may not have an anchor and if an anchor is present, it may or may not be appropriate. This corresponds to the 1762 European idiom: a *"Bird's Eye"* view which implies only an aerial, wide angle cursory view that gives a gist of what is extracted without indicating its source. One is on the path of Metaphysical Disorder when clutching an unseen Source or a flawed Source or fails to have a source for what is seen. This is because fundamental to discerning Good from Bad 'payload' messages contained in a "Thing" is to determine its "Seed"—its essence when it came into Being—the Spiritual, Secular, or Supernatural Source for that "Seed"—and the good or bad nature of that Seed. Any Spiritual Seed is the ultimate best. Otherwise, any impurities—even what "SEEMS right"--in the "Seed" will display in its Roots, Trunk, Branches, Leaves, and Fruit. Furthermore, if that "Seed" has impurities or absent Spiritual Elements, it is human-made and not to be accepted into ones Selfhood.

However, by Unconditional Love being the Base of the human Soul naturally means one has the freedom to choose to remain in the Selfhood Greatness Real Self state of ones birth or to deviate from ones Real Self. Real Self people are aware of being a vital part of a multiplicity of real things in the Cosmos and that multiplicity can be telescoped into a Divine Unity (fig. 11)—meaning God underlies the entire process. Hence, one is interconnected to all that make up the Cosmic Organism and, as a result, one is supplied with everything needed to have a Human Ideal life. Anything which breaks the integrity of ones luminous clarity and complete Certainty of that awareness is Metaphysical Disorder which automatically dissolves the Selfhood "5Ss" innate in every human at birth. The resultant wobbly state of Selfhood instability leads to doubts--and doubts cause mistakes and errors—repeated and uncorrected mistakes and errors lead into a vicious cycle of feeling unsafe, insecure, powerless—for which one seeks protection in the External World.

FALSE SELF CREATION: Much of the problem leading Real Self people to switch to a False Self (fig. 4, 15) is the fact that outside of those reared in African Tradition, none have ever been taught the Truth about anything—or at least not the complete Truth. Reasons include that those teachers know nothing about the Truth—are not interested in knowing the Truth—do not want the public to know the Truth— and do all they can to keep the public from knowing the Truth because the Truth would destroy all of the propaganda these teachers use to control the public's minds. Satanists are dedicated to attacking the Truth and doing whatever is opposite to it. In other words, Truth is contrary to all of what they are trying to accomplish because the Truth will set one free. A False Self develops as one starts disregarding ones Interconnection (i.e. all Cosmic Organism things work interdependently) so as to *narrow the focus of ones Consciousness to ones own Selfhood—called an Ego*. This puts one on the Metaphorical DISORDER path, being outside the boundaries of Ma'at.

That narrowing Consciousness focus into Self-Absorption makes for untrue Ego beliefs—e.g. being Separate from every human and everything in Nature—beliefs which cause one to be ever on the lookout for trouble pertaining to ones self-preservation, self-protection, and even survival—beliefs about "Me at war with Them." The path of manifestations derived from ones False Self begins with the disavowal of virtues—e.g. permitting flaws in self-control, good disposition, truthfulness, contentment. Such deviations may be spurred by clinging to only having the gist of something—a clinging which guides one into habits of "Picking and Choosing" or getting only "Bits and Pieces"—first about the difficult, despite its vital information. One then focuses only on what generates "Excitement"—desiring pertinent information for living only on a "need to know" basis. To worsen matters, "Disordered Selfhoods" pay attention only to getting the gist of what it takes to get through the moment--sufficient to get an answer that is "good enough" or "Almost" or "SEEMS" right.

AT THE CROSSROAD OF MA'AT AND VIOLENCE: To assess the "Big Picture" of the Bad, like the subject of "Violence," is to seek the essence (what it was when it came into Being) of its nature (fig. 3). If it does not "Feel Right"—it is not what it ought to be--a clue of disharmony lurking. If one is in sufficient contact with ones Real Self, then an intense analysis of that disharmonious situation is done. The "Big Picture" of this analysis goes like this. Since "Violence" is incompatible with the God-made Spiritual Elements, it must be human-made. Thus, the "Big Picture" of Violence consists of its human-made Source ("Seed")—a Choice. The "Seed" produces a "Thing" which generates a Cause(s) ("Roots") capable of designing Effects ("Trunk"). Out of Effects come Consequences ("Branches") compatible with the Disposition of what was in the Cause of the "Thing." Those Consequences manifest as "Leaves" on a Tree. The totality of the Consequences are the "Fruit"—i.e. the Results of the "Seed". Results show in ones Lifestyle and lead to ones Destiny. In short, *the "Big Picture" of Violence stems from the human-made Seed of Bad Thoughts—Thoughts against the Spiritual Elements—Thoughts filled with any aspects of the Indifference/Hate/Evil/Sadism Complex (IHES)—Thoughts which have a ripple effect into every aspect of ones own life as well as the lives under ones influence.* It is at this point that one can make a volitional ("I will") choice to use ones Brain/Mind to self-correct so as to proceed down the Ma'at Stream, or to step out of Metaphysical Disorder into the Violence Stream.

HUMANS' BRAINS

Medical literature says the brain is Triune (3 brains in one). However, my research indicates a Quintaune Brain (5 brains-in-one). To elaborate, the human brain (and spinal cord) is like an ice cream cone containing three scoops of ice cream. The top scoop is chocolate, representing the *Thinking Brain* portion—the Cerebral Cortex, half being unprogrammed and if done properly, has unlimited potential for increasing their brain power. Its prefrontal lobes are what enable humans to exercise Will Power, to manifest insight, and exhibit Selfless Service. It is able to control ones animal brains. Failure to develop it causes problematic behaviors featured by the "Crowd". The middle scoop is strawberry, representing the Emotional Brain. The scoop on top of the cone is a twirl of three colors, representing the *Ancient Brain*. My research has subdivided it into the Instinct (black), Omnibus (red), and Brute (vanilla) Brains. Specifically, the subdivision of the Ancient Brain called: (a) the Instinct Brain is purely made up of involuntary reflexes, as with the newborn's startle reflex, and for emergency Survival without thought.; (b) the Omnibus Brain is about Self-Protection with thought; and (c) the Brute Brain started out in evolution as self-protective before it was taken over by those humans possessing a Satanist nature. Furthermore, the *Instinct Brain* is associated with the "Alarm Centers" of Fear and Rage (fig. 2). To a somewhat lesser degree, so is the *Omnibus Brain*. The *Brute Brain* is of a different breed within this family of five, accounting for evil and sadistic deeds.

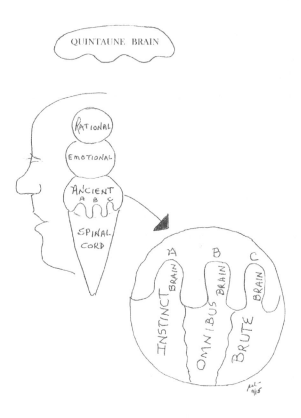

FIGURE 2

Despite its different colors, the three parts of the Ancient Brain have features somewhat in common, perhaps like three children in the same family but each being quite distinct from the other two. For example, although the Ancient Brain is the home of those functions involved in survival, self-protection, and self-preservation, how those functions are carried out is specific to each of the three parts. Second, the Ancient Brain works automatically (e.g. heartbeat, breathing, and digestion of food). Third, being in a constant state of alertness it always concerns the "here and now." Fourth, it is the home of obsessions, compulsions, and habits--thereby making it *homeostatic* (the natural movement toward equilibrium and away from change) and resistant to change. But certain features are more pronounced in the Brute Brain as, for example, total selfishness, a lack of concern for others, and being devoid of morals. All three subdivisions of the Ancient Brain have connections with the Emotional and Rational Brains and combine variously with one or both. Although the Instinct and Omnibus Brains are like marriage partners, the Brute Brain is not an ally with either.

BRUTE BRAINS--THE SOURCE OF VIOLENCE: All humans, said Ancient Africans, possess at birth *anti-Spiritual Elements Contingent Potential Possibility Genes which they metaphorically termed the god Set.* Those of the lowest of their Lower (animalistic) Self nature have activated their "god Set" genetics and display them as a mask of self-confidence and greatness with a reality of arrogance and aggression to conceal a sense of deep insecurity and inferiority. Then their Egos make up evil Supernatural *Contingent entities* (an image of something either having no real existence or exists incompletely) to act in a manner similar to a human's DNA. For example, the Ego chooses to activate certain "Set genes," which activate certain Brute Brain displays. Suppose this is the "Indifference" to humans "anti-Spiritual Elements gene," which is then stimulated to come into existence as a Contingent entity. But as one progresses from a Transitional Brute to a Peripheral Brute, the "Hate and Evil Genes" have their tensions released. Core Brutes add the release of "Sadism Genes." All feel free to display violence and the owner sees that as the ultimate in "Manhood"--thus qualifying him to be an "Alpha Male" candidate. Brutes feature a willingness to fight aggressively, physically or kill, if need be, for what they have and want as well as maintain or elevate their status. They must give the appearance of showing no Fear in carrying out their "Manhood" aggression and exhibit European type courage, as opposed to African Type Courage.

A reason Ancient Africans brilliantly elaborated on the metaphorical god Set, who represents what the Brute Brain is about, was to use it as a standard for what is not to be done in daily living for those aiming to reach the Heaven Afterlife. They said Evil is interwoven with the animal portions of human's brains—the product of allowing the animal faculties to be in charge and control of ones think, feel, say, and do expressions—determining likes/dislikes, pleasure/repulsions in dealing with things of the External World. After symbolizing Evil by the serpent Apep (i.e. the Ancient Brain and borrowed into the European Bible as the serpent Nachash that caused the fall of Adam and Eve) and a pig symbolizing the god Set (i.e. the Mammalian or Emotional Brain), they added that a main purpose of the Rational Brain is to curb the animalistic behavior of both the Brute and the Emotional Brains. However, in order for the Cerebral Cortex to achieve its most efficient and effective controlling aspects or preventing detrimental functions necessitates it be cultivated—and that requires the knowledge found in the Ancient African Bible concerning the Cosmic Mind being the orchestrator of ones Selfhood. Making victims suffer is how Satanists and their Brute followers derive "Sick Pleasure". In the process, the damage caused to the Selfhood of each victim adversely affects every aspect of their thinking abilities, despite many being quite intelligent. Damaged thinking also affects every aspect of ones activities of daily living. Satanists are dedicated to destroying their victims or keeping their victims down. They are vigilant in stirring up trouble to get victims to fight themselves. Lower Self people live in a Delusional world--a contingent one they have made up from bits and pieces to form a collage Contingent Being out of their imagination, from what peers do, and from what is fed to them by Satanists. Their ever ready state of alarm to possible Destructive or "In Danger" situations cause an Amorphous (formless) sense of *Frustration* about nothing in particular.

By European males choosing to not use their Right Brains (as a reflection of its "feminine" features not being "manly"), they have promoted their Left Brains to make them extroverted, hence materialistic, individualistic, and anti-Spiritual Elements oriented—all inside the Brute Brain/Old Mammalian Brain wrappings. Here, "*Extroverting*" implies both needing the External World for approval as well as gathering what is cherished in the External World as ones standards, guides, and filters. This automatically means such people are insecure and are unable to do volitional thinking. Brute Brain's "Me, Me, Me" fantasy is all about survival, self-protection, and self-preservation by any means necessary--accounting for clinging to evil and sadistic deeds. The *Brute Greedy Mindset*--a mindset consisting of a glob of reality + distortion + fantasy--a mindset using Fear as a Weapon to stimulate aggression so as to gain power and control over others as well as engage in "exciting entertainment" by applying Kill/Take/Destroy/Dominate/Oppression as a lifestyle.

Three messages Brutes advertise world-wide is that the "Good Life" for those like them is to be secured through the avoidance or elimination of challenges, solving things by a "quick fix" while, for those unlike them, that a terrible life with pain, suffering, and bad emotions is "unavoidable." This is in direct contrast to Ancient Africans who said to immediately and willingly accept challenges in life as a way to return to calmness and peace as well as the exercise involved in handling the challenges is the way to build the skills of the Frontal Lobe and its companions which, in turn, is a path to spiritual evolution. The principle is the same as in body building. The excitement they require is what gave rise to the Western idea of the *Heroic Style*—violent things made vivid in "short and sweet" episodes like auto racing, bungie jumping provide an adrenaline rush which activates the functions of their Left Brains, particularly finding "pleasure" in Kill/Take/Destroy/Dominate/Oppress aggressions, as indicated by "high fiving" after killing even unarmed peaceful people.

Since the Left Brain works like a calculator, such users are analytical (separating things that belong together, as women from men—humans from Nature—Colored Peoples from White people—religion from government, science, education, philosophy (unless it gives them an unfair advantage to do so). Yet, their analytical skills are unable to do any more than grasp the outer side of where compared Things differ. Also, they are unable to see the hidden inner aspect or any Base/Foundation underlying the situation. This leaves them, not as creative thinkers but, at best, Patterned Thinking innovators directing attention to what is of an anti-Spiritual Elements nature. This prevents them from seeing any 'big picture'. Instead, they only work within Brute Brain characteristics—thus preventing them from distinguishing right/wrong, good/bad, appropriate/inappropriate.

By eliminating their Right Brain, their Self-Images are built within the confines of their Material World animalistic self. That automatically separates them from God and all of God's creatures and creations. Lacking Knowledge from within, they rely on the Supernatural and Physical world for information about Material Things. This makes for realistic, distorted, fantasy, and opportunists Fears as well as "Facts". They use themselves as "The Standard" to judge everything and everybody.

ANCIENT BRAIN FEATURES: Despite the unique differences of the Instinct, Omnibus, or Brute Brains, they share the Ancient Brain's "sameness" features of: (I) Total Selfishness; (II) lack of concern for others; (III) Obsessions/Compulsions; (IV) total focus on the 'here and now'; (V) No desire to learn; (VI) No striving for improvement; (VII) Devoid of Morals; (VIII) Constant state of Alertness; (IX) Resistant to Change; (X) excess Chemical and Psychophysical Effects; and (XI) Survival, Self-Protection, and Self-Preservation--whether real and natural, a distortion of reality, or fantasy of the intentional or unintentional type.

STEPPING INTO THE VIOLENCE STREAM: Violence can be spurred to *Begin* when anti-Spiritual Elements reign; where thought and rational communication have broken down; from bad misinterpretations out of ones memory; from disharmony going on inside ones Selfhood; from embracing Satanists influences from ones interpretations of the monitored feedback one gets from ones Crowd; from something triggering ones "Raw Nerve" senses; from chronic and extreme desperation and frustration; from being socialized into violence; or from adopting and imitating violent patterns of others. Regardless of what broke up the integrity of ones awareness of being interconnected with the Cosmic Organism, that "Thing" accelerated ones disavowal of virtues. Next, stepping outside the flow of virtues puts one on the path of Vices. In following that path, one goes from Mild, to Slight, to Moderate, to Extreme distances from Ma'at, fashioning compatible False Self masks and masquerades for living (fig. 4, 15). Manifestations show in such things as loudness, rapacity, covetousness, and resentment--all introductions to the realm of Violence.

Violence is *Generated*: (1) by oneself to act on oneself directly, or by invitation, or by passive acceptance or by an "I'll Show You"; (2) by oneself to act ugly on God's creatures and creations; (3) by others who seek out violence as self-punishment for wrongs or as a test of strength; (4) by others who find benefit in violating God's creatures and creations; and (5) by those seeking adventure and "excitement." For one to submit to violence needlessly is to be attacked more often because it is easy.

CONCEPTS OF VIOLENCE

"Violence," as I define it, is any threat to--or disturbance caused by an attack on—or the destruction of the Spiritual Elements—whether in the form of the spiritual, emotional, mental, physical, social, financial, or what is materially meaningful. "Violence," said Ancient Africans, "is a disease of the Soul." This means it is opposite Maa—the true--the real--the just--that which conforms to the orderliness of the Cosmos. Moral equivalents of *Maa are the Good, the Beautiful, the Beneficial (nefer)*. The Middle English (1066-1500) word "*Violent*" originally meant marked or powerful destructive stresses or uncontrolled physical forces--implying those organized at the top cause a "trickle down" to individual violence at the bottom. In European psychological literature, "Violence" represents the extreme pole of the *Aggressive Spectrum* of behavior--characterized by an explosive, sudden quality—and incorporating the use of force to threaten, disturb, injure, or destroy something (e.g. a person(s), object, organization). For example, a Revolution is an insurrection, an act of violence by which one class overthrows another. Yet, *Micro-Aggressions* are forms of Psychic Cumulative Micro-traumas.

Violence is *Displayed* in manipulating and maneuvering Indifference/Hate/Evil/Sadism—the IHES Complex ingredients--into various forms. Briefly, these include: Indifference (disregard, neglect, abandon), Hate (think the worst about), Evilness (break the hated person in some way), and Sadism (go beyond the extremes of cruelty). Violent *Effects* cause partial or complete *Impairment* (decrease in the "5Ss"—*safety, security, self-confidence, stability, and strength*) manifesting in the limiting functions of the body, mind, spirit, abilities, or potential possibilities for success personally, socially, financially, in ones career, or pertaining to ones Mission. Invariably, when one has adopted a False Self and thus is in a Self-Unknown state, adverse progression is engaged in. Such is evident by what one does to oneself; what one does to others; what one allows one to do to oneself; and what one invites to enter oneself. These Effects may cause one to change ones course in life for the worst or cause one to shift into a Self-Absorbed state and become involved in Inner World and/or External World vicious cycles.

VIOLENCE CONSEQUENCES: When only Violence is floodlighted, it is extremely hard to see the "Right" almost hidden in the shadows. Violent Consequences are an *Expansive Synthesis* resulting from somethings happening as a result of something having branched out of a given Effect. When gathered together, the *Resultant Disability* ('not able') is greater than the sum of each when added together. Violence is not the problem that ought to draw the spotlight. Instead, it is the consequences of violence that require immediate attention. Examples are aloneness, shame, guilt, insecurity, incompetence, and 'giving up". Such Consequences affect every product aspect of ones Selfhood and lifestyle—riddling both with Flaws, as in being shoddy, weak, inadequate, limited, defective, incomplete; non-pertinent; not of keystone importance; facades; confusingly directed or headed; placed on improper planes of existence; improperly arranged or combined; deceiving; in conflict; evilly misinterpreted; racially/ethnocentrically biased and prejudiced; injustice; in conflict; and/or mostly simply wrong! A consequence of violence is that when one is despised and hated by others while in a setting of being bombarded by the instruments of violence, one is likely to resort to hatred as a means of salvaging a sense of Self, no matter how fragmented (fig.3).

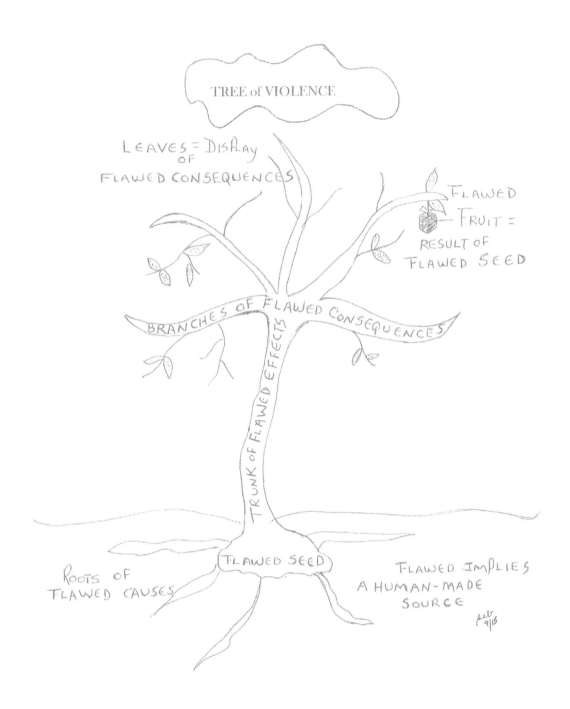

FIGURE 3

FALSE SELF FORMS OF VIOLENT MINDS

A False Self, by definition, means one does not know who one is. Because Unconditional Love's nature includes that of absolute Freedom, every human has the Free Will to choose any way to live that is outside the Spiritual Elements flow and even its opposite, which is called Satanism. To deviate from the Spiritual Elements to the tiniest of the Mildest degree is to enter into Metaphysical Disorder. With this entrance, two things happen. First, there is an automatic replacement of ones Real Self with ones self-designed False Self, orchestrated by an unreality Contingent Being called an Ego. Second, this entrance is a prelude to some form of violence. At this point one can easily step back into the stream flow of the Spiritual Elements. Or, one can choose to walk away from the Spiritual Elements stream and head toward destruction—perhaps to oneself and/or to others—perhaps concerning not reaching ones potential or preventing others from reaching their potential—perhaps to do damage which leaves oneself and/or others worse off than prior to what was badly expressed or done. These represent Mild, Slight, Moderate, and Extreme degrees of Ego (fig. 4, 15).

Similarly, Violence *Character Flaws Ratings* are Mild, Slight, Moderate, Extreme, and Normal Variant. In all, Violence *Character Flaws* stem from any given Cause (e.g. trauma) which leads to an Effect (impairments). That Effect, in turn, is pregnant with Consequences of the Cause and the sum of these Effects and Consequences is called a Resultant Disability. An example is ones Character flaws showing as un-realness, disorder, incorrectness, deceit, greed, rapacity, aggression, baseness, and crime—all aspects of violence because they imply choice, decision, and will for which one must bear moral responsibility if they have a Conscience. Brutes lack a Conscience. Those who make peaceful revolution impossible will make violent revolution inevitable. Regardless of its nature, nothing good ever comes out of violence and nothing violent ever lasts. Let us look closer.

Three *Causes* of Violence are: First is the "*Big Bang*" *Trauma*—some significant blow to ones mind, body, and/or spirit that is sudden usurpations which leaves a permanent wound called a mental "*Raw Nerve.*" Second is *Cumulative Trauma* (also called Continuing small Traumas, Micro-Aggressions, and Accumulative Micro-trauma) which leave multiple 'little wounds' that are resistant to healing. Cumulative (Latin, cumulus, heap or piled—like cumulus clouds) traumas are typically occasional, intermittent, or recurrent instead of continual. They may be gradual and silent encroachments stemming from violent powers. Third, is being *Socialized* into a False Self—by those of the upper class having a Superiority Complex—or by those of middle or lower classes who have an Inferiority Complex but adopt a Superiority Complex. If either form of Trauma or Socialization leads one to disconnect from the environment and "everybody," one has entered a Self-Unknown state, meaning all of ones thoughts and rational communications have broken down and one has lost connection with ones original Collective Unconscious. Thus, one adopts a Contingent Consciousness.

SELF-UNKNOWN LEADS TO A FALSE SELF: Ancient African Sages said "Knowing" of ones Selfhood is present at birth—that every divine and earthly Cosmic (i.e. Real) creature ultimately arose from God's androgynic protoplast—that all initially resided together and interdependently in a "Virtual" boundary-less, undefined, and undifferentiated—but not *disordered*—state inside unformed Matter situated in infinite space. By each human containing a 'drop' of the Cosmic Mind—i.e. ones "Self" (the absolutely unchanging "sameness" of ones Selfhood) meant/means the Real Self of the newborn has knowledge of the entire Cosmos. This Cosmic Knowledge--the 'Self's' *Ultimate Background*—provides every Private Self "tool" needed for one to have a thriving and happy life. To illustrate why I research thoroughly words whose meanings I think I already know, "Unknown" was one of those words.

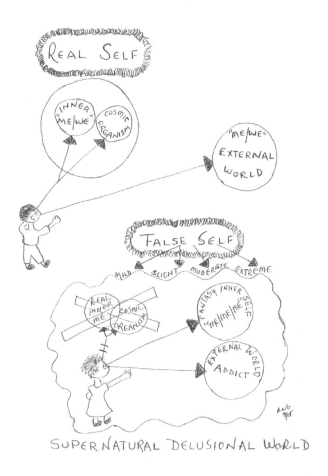

FIGURE 4

The word "Unknown" is an "*Umbrella*" term. "Umbrella" designates: (1) something of a "Like-Kind" nature in "Like-Kind" Things; (2) that all share ideas, concepts and/or features having application on more than one Cosmic plane of existence; and (3) each plane of existence is unique and operating under its own rules. An analogy is that of many chicks--possessing the same "Genetics" but each with unique features—and all hiding under the wings of their mother. Very Ancient Africans entered the Cosmic Unknown by following brilliantly done astro-mathematical scientific investigations and then determined certain fixed Laws (i.e. Truths) in the Cosmos from which they made Inferences. One is that the One Universal Spiritual High God--not the Supernatural God of Europeans--resides in the all Black Amenta. Although, they said, God is Unknowable, still God is known by God's manifestations—a process which began with the pouring out of God's Mind, the primal waters called the Ocean of Nun. The contents of the Nun consist of the Spiritual Elements—Unconditional Love, Truth, Reality, and the Natural. This Subjective Realm is called the "Void" because of its "Nothingness" in the African sense of the non-material existence of Cosmic Nun "Things"—meaning its reality is in a "virtual" (boundary-less) state of potential possibilities, without objects and without forms—a "no-thing" condition. Despite the Subjective Realm being Unknown to almost all humans, cultivated and disciplined human minds can become acquainted with it by being in a "Hetep" state (a Kamitic word for a state of unshakable inner peace and bliss coming from appreciation for ones blessings). Since it is situated in a human's Divine Consciousness, "Hetep" is the Ultimate in "inner" peace. Once in the "Void"--this "Nothingness"--the human Selfhood is bathed with the greatest power possible.

Just as there are different waves in the ocean, all possessing the "Genetics" of the ocean while each wave is unique, there are different planes of reality existence with the same "Genetics" and each with uniqueness. This means all Cosmic planes are linked with those of another in their essence and in their ultimate significance. Thus, to know any given aspect on any given plane means one has a "sense" of what is on the other planes, despite those planes being otherwise Unknown. Ancient Africans used gods/goddesses to personify attributes of a given plane and thereby convey the mathematically derived significance of each Metaphysical plane. *Metaphysical* (the Spiritual Elements displays away from the Physical Realm) implies any natural phenomenon or the occurrence of any event doing so without human participation. Besides, none could have occurred differently and none could have failed to occur. So Unknown are these planes to the human mind (in the sense of 'unfamiliar') as to be thought of as vague, lofty, and not down to Earth. To elaborate, because of the *Order and consistent Patterns underlying natural events,* Mathematics allows assessments which give rise to mental items having significant worth, value, or meaning. The appropriate prioritization of Thoughts for a given issue provides the clearness and the Order to lay out paths for the "Rightness" of choices, decisions, and solutions that apply to Unknowns having Correspondence with the Known. Thus, based upon derived Circumstantial Evidence and Inferences, Ancient African Sages said with Certainty that: *Nature is the God Substance the Cosmic Spirit impregnates into the essence of God's creatures and creations. They deemed Nature to be the home of God's Laws; the source of humans' wisdom*--and that Nature and humans are an indivisible unity, like two sides of a coin.

Of concern here is the Unknown of "*Who am I?*"—*an awareness or unawareness of which is at the bottom of all the mysteries of ones think, feel, say, act, and react aspects of ones life itself and what one employs concerning "Life-Living."* The African Tradition answer to "Who am I?" is the permanently enduring birth-gift of the "Spark of God" contained in ones Divine Consciousness—i.e. the "Self". Through such capacities as delight and wonder, every human newborn knows this. However, since each human has a Free Will to institute a coup d'etat—i.e. a sudden and violent over-throw of this governing "Spark of God"—it can be replaced with an Ego supreme authority. From ones False Self then being fashioned by unreal aspects and by operating out of an unreal realm of existence, ones Ego absolutely establishes an Unknown "Who am I?" state. As long as ones False Self orchestrates ones life, ones self-identity can never be known nor ever ascertained—a lost Soul!

So, "*Self-Unknown*" itself means not recognized as a fact or as an individual; not discovered; not apprehended mentally and thus unidentified; unaware that ones spiritual sense is aware of oneself as well as one having clouded out ones own material senses of awareness; an ultimate reality experienced incompletely in terms of Images and Symbols inadequate to its true nature. To lack an established or normal status, makes one mysterious or a secret to oneself because of ignorance and that unfamiliarity causes a sense of strangeness. It is like being "X"—one of the last letters in the alphabet or at the end of the line of Humanity. The result of Self-Unknowing is the think, feel, say, and do things of ones "Living Life"—some to an excess, others to an insufficiency—yet still hidden, obscure, and debatable. It is Self-Unknowing that wedges apart ones Talents and ones Motivation. In short, one cannot solve or even enter into any profound aspect of life without being a whole entity.

But what part of the brain does one use upon stepping into ones Self-Unknown mind? Since the living human mind is never inactive, perhaps one sees or experiences: (1) *Hallucinations* (wander in mind)—creations from existing, visible objects and incorporating other memories to form frightening Contingent Beings that seem real; (2) *Illusions*—misinterpretations of sense-impressions; (3) a *Kaleidoscope or variety of colors*—produced by, say, a type of people—and then, as a result, producing a symmetrical set of images that trigger self-induced "*Situational Epilepsy*" type mental disturbance as, for example, in the Brute Brain. Such Effects generate a sense of being among uncertainties, doubts, mysteries unprovoked by fact or reason and a craving to understand the nonexistent that is both within and without of oneself. The consequence may be resultant Supernatural voices or visions that inspire doing something dangerous to oneself and/or to others.

FALSE SELF CATEGORIES: Any one who has chosen to give up being his/her Real Self automatically enters into a False Self state—a state of the Unknown. For all humans, the *Unknown* can be imaged as an Icon symbol consisting of a collage of an Association of Ideas--Ideas one has no concept about, is somehow remotely acquainted, and/or one has made-up and repeated so often as for it to seem real. This Icon Symbol's bits and pieces thus carry the potential for being about the Normal, Misfits, and Miscellaneous. Any of these "as is" or any which undergo a 'mutation' might form a "*Normal Variant*." This lies between Normal and Abnormal but is not sufficiently different from either to be called one or the other. In medicine, clinical pathological manifestations are generally not present when the "Normal Variant" is closer to the Normal than to the abnormal. Yet, considerable confusion can exist as the "Normal Variant" approaches the Abnormal pathological state. For example, the "Normal Variant" of ones genetically derived bunion (and thus unlikely to cause symptoms, despite its increased susceptibility to do so) can be carelessly and wrongly designated to be the cause of ones foot pain. Violence, the essence of war, is the quest for identity as a result of one feeling "Self-Unknown" which, in return, causes one to feel incompetent to the point that violence is the last refuge. That is why Ancient Africans wrote on their temple walls: "Man, Know Thyself."

Rankings are determined by each person's assessment and by the Effects, Consequences, and Results what they do have on others of an "Indifference/Hate/Evil/Sadism (IHES) Complex nature.

Mild False Selves have an "unbudded" IHES Complex, featuring Deception and Simple Assertive Understatements. For example, Al Capone (1899-1947) said you can get a lot more done with a kind word and a gun, that with a kind word alone.

Slight False Selves' IHES Complex is in the "budding" stage--being about subtle Aggression—as seen in "Conditional" Love or Belonging. Both are geared to what one will not receive that one desires if one does not "go along to get along." For gang members, violence is a cleansing force—freeing them of their problematic sense of self-worth and self-value—from despair and inaction—as well as makes them fearless, which restores self-respect. Yet, very effective destruction can be done by violence masquerading as 'love.' *Slight* is types include such Deceitful violence as sending Black children to get a college degree but then not being able to get a job.

Slight-to-Moderate False Selves' IHES refers to more advanced deceitful violence is in passing off their "Democracy" to represent majority rule when it is actually a State that recognizes the subjection of the minority to the majority—i.e. the systematic use of violence by one class against the other—by one part of the population against another.

Moderate False Selves' have flowering IHES into every conceivable Category. Their use of force is not necessarily physical but is directed to overcoming resistance from others. It is usually associated with intimidations like anger, indifference, rage, and possibly hate.

Extreme False Selves' violence is any Sadism. Their "Seed" of violence comes out of its organization by Satanists at the top and that filters down to individualized violence settings at the bottom, thereby accounting for today's Black-on-Black Violence.

SELF-UNKNOWING MAKES ONE MEAN: Ones *Real Self* provides Spiritual Elements type Wisdom which imparts a *real* Self-Identity. But a *False Self* "Clouds" over ones birth-gift "Soul Sunshine," causing one to lose contact with who one is as a human. That philosophically puts one outside the Natural Cosmos + establishes a Self-Unknowing + causes a loss of courage and the "5Ss" (which only comes from having a true sense of Selfhood Greatness). Resultant self-doubt automatically places boundaries on ones own Self-Trust in times of threats, disturbances, or destructions. Not knowing who one is *disconnects one from all there is in ones environment and in the Cosmos*—a disconnection making for a "me vs. everything else" mindset—a mindset of overflowing Hate-full-ness. Such Supernatural mindsets that now think "Inside-Out" see no alternative but to be aggressive against "everything else" before "everything else" can push me around." For example, if "Black" is "everything else," then I must fight "Black" and win before "Black" attacks me. By Self-Unknowing also being rooted in an occult mythological context, all of this is serious business and for which there is no time to relax from "war" and have fun. Because an "Inside-Out" mindset operates out of a fantasy (fig. 5) "Air Castle," it fashions Delusions (believing what is not real and not believing what is real). Thus, all of its thinking patterns are confused, in conflict, and follow no order. To get through life they fashion "*Simultaneous opposites*" to live by—meaning hypocrisy seems natural, even if one contradicts oneself in the same breath—as done by politicians.

They can only extend guarded trust to like-kind people who do not like each other. This dates to ancient Aryans who would fight each other to pass the time of day. But they immediately stopped and joined forces to attack and rob the rich or to prevent losses of ill-gotten gains (those stolen from others). Together, they create in their own image a Contingent god who embodies their beliefs. So as to have some semblance of order, they all act in conformity to their cult. Hence, these "Individualists" are always in the dilemma of having to act out of conformity—a situation calling for partial trust in ones cult members and the cult's doctrines—but staying suspicious of both. Such is exhibited by all of today's Republicans voting to repeal the law of Obamacare—and doing it 60+ times—and with no power to change this law. They give up all independent thought so as to blend into each other's ways of think, feel, say, and do expressions, for these unhappy people are all they have. Their power is exerted, not by personal power, but rather by the GUN. This is the composition of the hypocritical state of each saying: "I am my own man"!!! Such "Inside-Out" thinking is simplified by all cult members seeing things in definite "Either/Or" and "All-or-None" terms; simultaneously "oppose/favor not just one but all"; believing there is no "Right" way other than what they think, feel, say, and do. From being mad with life's history as well as hating themselves and "everyone else", their presumed remedy is to select an enemy and destroy it so as to get momentary relief from causing misery to others. Many Europeans look at dark-skinned people and their achievements with extreme envy. Then they engage in *Reaction Formation*—the converting of something extremely desired but wholly unattainable into something discredited and despised. The world's top tennis player, Serena Williams, always receives a barrage of hateful insults.

That *Envy Insults* are a pattern of Self-Unknowing people is illustrated by the Italian Vespucci (1451-1512) who gave his name of Amerigo to the New World as America. He borrowed labels of Jews as the ultimate racist metaphor for greed, cunning, super-human sexual powers, and malevolent Christ-killer. He then assigned such labels—e.g. savages, infidels, and cannibals--to Amerindians and Africans, including the cultured Moors in Spain and Portugal. Europeans (e.g. Freyre) who wrote/write about slavery in romantic and racist statements but disguised as liberal and enlightened scholarship have typically and stupidly implied: (1) Enslaved Africans took to slavery "like birds take to the air"; (2) the Enslaved were happy because they kept their music, dance, and song alive; and (3) they could be civilized by whips, chains, and forced labor and racism. To expose such "Inside-Out" thinking, Frobenius (1550) said: "Africans and Mexican Indians were civilized to the marrow of their bones—the idea of the barbaric Negro is a European invention." jabaileymd.com

EXPLORING THE MYSTERIOUS SELF-UNKNOWN

Self-UnKnowing from any cause leads one into the only other option of reaching into mysterious "Supernatural" realms to make-up ridiculous substitutes for knowledge. By using erroneous presumptions of who one imagines oneself to be, each establishes personal Icon Images to serve as ones standard, guide, filter, measure for dealing with the 'here and now.' What is imagined is a mere enumeration of disjointed things falsely believed to have a necessary sequence. When one does not know much about oneself, one can only attack others. To live out of the birth-gift of ones Real Self is to be completely "Alive" to ones Spiritual Elements (Unconditional Love, Truth, Reality, and the Natural) essence. This means ones inherent Wisdom has two categories of "Life-Living" Instinct Tools. First is ones *Spiritual* intuitive realization of ones own Being/Spirit lying beyond ones thoughts. Its instinct tools enable *assessments of mysterious "Things" in Unseen Realms of existence—e.g. what it is, what belongs to it, what is revealed by it, what it does, and how it appears.* Resultant conclusions serve as then knowing how to fashion harmonious 'big picture' relationships to the common things of life.

Second is the *Collective Unconscious* (Supra-conscious, Universal Spirit, Impersonal or Transpersonal Unconsciousness; Epic Memory) acquired inheritance 'instinct' tools. As described by Ancient Africans, its memory bank contents of depository forms of Archetypes (African, Seed) are of ones most remote Ancestors' Spiritual experiences and wisdom—those representing the Cosmic Organism's reality, stability, absoluteness, universality, and permanent Truths for all time—those serving as the foundation for Earth World "Right Living" inside a connected and unified Wholism. When tuned into them, they are conceived as *Primordial Images*—also called Dominants, Imago's, Mythological Images, Icon Behavior Patterns—i.e. root displays of the Cosmic Mind acting in fashioning patterns or being models for the production of *Prototypes* (created Spiritual Elements manifestations which, in turn, create like-kind things).

In other words, in Real Self people, both the Archetypes and Prototypes each, by themselves, reproduce themselves, to become the thing each makes so as to help shape how one thinks, feels, expresses, acts, and reacts in accordance with the Cosmic Organism. This Spiritual Archetype which imparts a Cosmic Mind Disposition into ones Conscience, enables it to assess the good or bad presentation of every deed or temper in life as being in harmony or in disharmony. Similarly, though every human's Collective Unconscious exists whether perceived by a given human or not and its manifestations are responsible for what occurs in the material world, both it and ones Spiritual Archetypes effects can be "Clouded" out by ones Free Will choice to do so. The trade-off for giving up ones complete "Aliveness" inherent in being ones Real Self is to step into a "blankness"—a mystery—an Unknown. This means ones understanding of profound answers to profound questions is buried, in a manner simulating being in a coma—a state of profound unconsciousness from which one is, in that mindset, incapable of being aroused.

An ancient self-induced state idea leading into Self-Unknowing was that of an overpowering mental mighty wave force rolling into ones mental thinking paths--sending its power through, around, over, and under the mind so as to envelop and overwhelm all sides and thus burying everything along the way. Hence, the over-spreading hurricane-like force; the crushing weight; and the cutting off of the mind's thinking supply lines suffocated and made useless ones mind—like a "zombie." An early alternative cause for Self-Unknowing was bad energy pumping into ones mind and swelling up into the shape of a bowl to such an extent that the bowl would turn upside down and/or inside-out. These would prevent ones mind from seeing the sun's brightness and thereafter one would look over everything in a gloomy way. Being overturned covered up any bright and clear thinking.

FANTASY: Although the Old French word "*Speculation*" ('spy out') has wide-ranging and conflicting meanings, its dominant dictionary sense is the propounding of theories and making generalizations around them--both based upon many assumptions for which proof is not possible. In taking advantage of this confusion, attorneys in the Medico-Legal courtroom tried to trick me: "Doctor, didn't you arrive at your conclusions by speculation?" When this first happened in my capacity as an Independent Medical Examiner for the state of California, I said "yes!" Smugly, in his closing argument he told the judge my opinions were on the 'Guessing' ['no calculations'] end of the "Speculation Scale"—implying my opinions were merely Fantasy ('unreal'—only in my imagination).

Actually, it was *a priori reasoning*—carefully studying minute case details + my education, training, and experience + relying on African Tradition's *Subjective Science* tools—i.e. Observation, Reflection, "Pure" Feelings, Productive Imagination, Contemplation, Inductive and Deductive Inferences, and Common Sense—to make inferences in arriving at circumstantial evidence and judgments. This highly abstract Thinking method had been developed during my specialized training in Medical Genetics and Birth Defects. Of course, "*Fantasy*" (Greek, 'make visible as how things seem'; appearance; what is sensed; apparition; perception)—by meaning the capacity to form Images and even Hallucinations ('astray thoughts')—is a phantom and has no solid base in reality. This 'inability to distinguish Fantasy from Reality' vignette points out how people daily use Fantasy in "SEEMS" right and "ALMOST" enough situations to deceive others and to deceive themselves by 'self-talk'.

Fetuses in the mother's womb have sense organs that respond to few stimuli, and then for only a short duration. Following birth, they learn to respond to increasingly larger numbers of stimuli. Hence, they emerge gradually from their Inner World isolation while getting oriented to the External World. Assuming these stimuli are met in a satisfying manner, they crave more and more out-going activity and that stimulates them to personally develop fantasy in Play at two levels. First is using *Role Playing* to act out what they have developed with their imagination and this cultivates *a true respect for the fascinating art of Magic*, no matter what its nature. By participating in such fantasy, they script being the "star" in settings as they desire. This puts their minds in a 'Supernatural box' that sprouted inside a 'Natural World Imagination box.' Second, they Play with their make-believe situation by '*Acting As If*' what they have fantasized is an actual and already existing reality.

This develops a tool of *Fantasy for linking with other people's Fantasies*. However, at any point following birth, if the evolution from "Fetuses' Inner World Isolation" is unsatisfying, they learn to focus on stimuli which leads inwardly to "Air Castle" fantasies. Whether satisfactory or not, Fantasies are mainly Right Brain functions, persisting variously in everyone throughout life. Fantasy is a consciousness form lying between ordinary thought processes and an uncontrolled state of awareness--a form of Imaginative thinking (itself is a brain faculty) controlled more by the Magical Thinking (also a brain faculty) of ones wishes, motives, and emotions than by conditions of the External World—a form of treating events in a manner the rational mind considers impossible or highly unlikely.

Fantasy enables one to dissolve boundaries between unrelated things, to put boundaries on the boundless, and to declare bounded things (e.g. physical and social world laws) as boundless—all for the purpose of making people and events appear as one wishes. The free play of associations between ideas far removed from the realistic realm gives rise to *Fancy* and that is what creates the "*larger than life*" aspect which characterizes the Supernatural. To be distinguished is the brilliant "*Productive Creative Imagination.*" It consists of a flowing visual stream of dramatic sequences--as Images, Metaphors, Symbols, Icons—each forming major parts of ones internal world of experiencing. *Magical Thinking* orchestrated Fantasy is Imagination working freely within normal guide-lines while flowing along like a stream. Hence, ones mind is released from all parameters of the

Natural World and thereby allowing ones Fantasy Imagination to roam about. Still, ones mind is usually subtly guided somewhat by Unconscious urges, concerns, and memories. jabaileymd.com

THE OCCULT--"SOIL" OF VIOLENCE: The term "*Occultism*" ("to conceal"; hidden; mysterious and inscrutable) is about the Unknown and yet believing in something, or experiencing something, beyond the realm of the five senses. Religion, Mysticism, and Magic all sprang from the same basic "Non-Rational" sense of the Unseen aspects of the Cosmos. Similar to the way a radio might pick up some unknown station, Primitive Africans sensed and "picked-up" sudden 'feelings' floating all around them and perceived certain of those accidental glimpses had 'meaning' going beyond everyday banality or the commonplace. This is like when the Magical Thinking of the 'human radio set' (the brain's pineal gland) tunes into unknown reality vibrations. These bits and pieces were meshed together into certain patterns of 'meaning' and collectively they became known as ingredients of the Occult ('the unknown, the hidden). Subtle Vibrations, which I have experienced all of my life, impart a sense of "Aliveness". Perhaps those who experience boredom are simply ignorant of the meaning of these vibrations or have pulled down their 'senses shade' so as to be cut off from them.

Nevertheless, evolution that leads to insights into Magical Thinking and Magical Practices that follow laws of the Cosmos can conceivably encourage the good Spirits that lead to Religion, Mysticism, and Magic based upon the Spiritual Elements. All that needs to be done is to cultivate vibrational 'meanings' about things already there—and with the sense of great Awe and Fascination serving as Metaphysical verification. This route of the Occult Cultivation is done by the pursuit of reality through intuition aided by intellect and the observations of the Law of Correspondence. This led to the Occult Sciences of African Tradition which focused on the secrets of Nature—physical and psychic, mental and spiritual—called Hermetic (the Greek name for the African Tehuti) and Esoteric Sciences. They cannot be appreciated by the selfish educated classes, nor understood by the uneducated.

African Sages had to hide them from those who might misuse them for their own profit and thus turn the divine science into Black Magic. The Occult Science facts are of so abstruse a nature that in most cases no words exist in European languages to express them. Such is a different experience from those who merely engage in Fantasy because that lacks an instinctual basis. Although Fantasy in children is a normal part of Imagination, those who live out of their False Self carry Fantasy into the Indifference/Hate/Evil/Sadism (IHES) Complex. That Complex leads to the use of destructive forces—necessitating the cooperation of victims--which benefit those (e.g. "*Sorcerers*") bent on having self-interest gains or to do harm to victims. From early in human history they have engaged in witchcraft, lycanthropy, and vampirism; have been the historical instigators of Spiritualism, ghosts, and Poltergeists. IHES Fantasy led to the development of things of torture and creations, like Satan and Hell—both described as part of religion in Dante's Inferno--and 'man's downfall' leading to Sin resulting from the inherent evil in people.

European medieval Occult concept properties included only those reveal-able by "sham" experimentation. The Alchemists, Astrologers, Seers, Sorcerers, Magicians as well as the pseudo-Occult Sciences of Witchcraft, Vodun, and Numerology—all embraced these concepts. They were under the assumption that the secrets of Nature have relations which once revealed will confer great power. These beliefs were in conflict with orthodox theology and their work was termed "*Occultism*."

Modern Occultism began with C18 beliefs in Animal Magnetism; C19 beliefs in Spiritualism (the dead manifesting through mediums), and C20, beliefs in Mental Telepathy. All of these, which are outside Natural World laws, are Supernatural, with advocates saying they are mysterious powers that can be controlled, influenced, or used through hidden, secret methods using "*Non-Rational*" thinking (which is undefined). This began from the belief that the secrets of Nature must be guessed—like a riddle (an indication that they were obviously unaware of Ancient African Astro-Mathematics and Objective Sciences). To solve their ignorance they elevated those they believed to be in possession of peculiar powers that were able to penetrate the secrets of hidden forces. There were all sorts of "Miracles"—e.g. instant transfer of a message from distant places or answers to sealed questions placed in a shrine—but all were proven to be accomplished by fraud. Supernatural manifestations attributed to the European God are not considered part of the occult.

FASCINATION WITH THE OCCULT: Within the Occult some of what there is to believe in is the very best of what exists in life while some are of the very worst of what exists. For Ancient Africans, the very worst—i.e. anti-Spiritual Elements, anti-humaneness, anti-Nature, and anti-God—was believed to be the result of Ignorance. They symbolized these principles of evil in the Ancient African Bible using the god Set. Millennia later Set became the basis of the Christian Satan--an evil metaphysical entity honored with a superhuman status; an opposing reality to God (a form of idolatry) and a user of *blasphemy* (false statements, problem creators, hypocrisy, or done out of self-interest). Their featured character is compassionless and cold; planners of evil deception; and manipulators of things to gain power and control. For these same worst aspects, Europeans have used the very common term "*Dark Side*" and attribute them to the Devil. African Tradition never considered Set as a devil and never saw him as the source of evil itself (until the late Dynastic Period which was when the Jewish people were living in Egypt). Western religious traditions relate the problem of evil to a movement away from virtue under the influence of a demon (the devil) and thereby assigning blame to an outside force which, of course, allows people with poor moral development to shirk responsibility for their actions.

The African concept of what orthodox Western religions call evil relates adversity to passion and a movement away from virtue—and thereby retaining human responsibility. In other words, according to African Tradition one has the ability to overcome ones "Dark" side. What fails to be emphasized is the Ancient Egyptian teaching that Satan is ultimately subject to God. Otherwise, if Satan were the true adversary of God this would mean that God is not omnipotent because there is a Being who can limit God's power. For those who did not believe in God, such a concept was "*Fascinating*"--a concept carrying some powerful or irresistible influence on the affections or passions to such a degree as to lead one to be bewitched, enamored, or enraptured.

A Fascination mindset dates to early childhood, with self-perceptions of being pleasantly or disagreeably controlled magically and by omnipotence inside the world of fairy tales. Here, they believe in compelling fairies, magicians, or gods who can cast spells over little children for good or evil. In ancient times many people were captivated, as if under a hypnotic influence by sorcery and necromancy. What was so attractive was followers' beliefs that Satan could wield supreme power over the entire universe. Thus, to absorb the halo of Satan would enable them to become "little gods." It is the hope of obtaining limitless power which spurs them on so as to get pleasure from the exercise of power. To this end, Brutes exalt dominance, cruelty, hatred, lust, all fierce and hard emotions while scorning kindness, humility, sympathy, compassion, self-sacrifice, and the Spiritual Elements. They take a double-edged attitude to their own activities, convincing themselves that their intention to kill or terrify is the highest good while simultaneously wriggling with glee at their own delicious evilness.

They are totally dedicated to the complete reversal of the accepted rules of society but demand victims follow their rules. The Americas were set up by Europeans using the mindset and practices of Satanism, and this continues in full force to this day. Many naïve and oppressed people have been and remain excited by Brutes power and attractive appearances; are allured through the passions or affections to absorb Satanism's halo effects which fashions an "*Awe*" mindset--a complete mind blank occurring either then or sometime later once the realization had set in--geared to believing in magical things; and readily revising existing mental schemas to assimilate something novel. Such "Fascination," as if one is stunned to such an extent as to have an arrests of ones will power. The stunning force is an irresistible attraction, as if under a magical spell, that does not delight. In other words, evil must be understood as the actions of people who either use their Brute brains or are ignorant of the higher spiritual reality within themselves (egoism) based upon fear, pride, anger, hatred, greed, lust, envy, jealousy, etc. These destroy ones Soul while knowledge of ones Self (Aset) restores it to its true nature.

BRUTES SELF-UNKNOWING: The idea that Europeans' Self-Unknowing has the adverse greatest impact on the world came to me in the middle of a week-long attempt to discover the beginnings of Europeans and, from being unsuccessful, recalling Sharon Bingaman's quote: "The more you don't know about us, the better off we are". At the end of that week there was the pervading idea that there were four initial causes of primitive Europeans not knowing who they were and the resultant detachment from their Real Self were: (1) the Free Will choice to adopt a False Self (Ego); (2) to power their "Life-Living" using their Brute Brains; (3) not believing in the Spiritual and Supernatural; and (4) not knowing and not caring about who were their ultimate ancestors or their origin—i.e. the 'that they ever existed' or from where they came or when. Suppose a today's European is asked: "Where did your original ancestors come from?" The answer will probably be: "From Europe." Q: "But since European Geneticists say all humans originated out of Africa, where did those European ancestors come from"? A: agree with the Geneticists, research the subject (and likely find conflicting information), or to deny it. If there is the deliberately denying of the reality of their ultimate ancestral origins being Africans, then there is no origin they can pin down that will truthfully answer the question. Thus, they immediately enter the realm of the Self-Unknown without keys to open any of its doors and no tools to cut out windows in order to see. Not struggling in order to find a way out means one is like an entangled Slave to the Mysteriousness of ones Ignorance.

There is nothing in the Self-Unknown or in any aspect of its mysteries to rationalize. Instead, to be awed by the "Nothing" of what ones mind Imagines things to be, is all there is. The *"Awe" is because of what is upside down and "inside out."* For example, in the Natural Cosmos the way to have happiness is to look within for ways to use ones Talents in a "ME/WE" manner and doing that to perfection, regardless of the outcome. This is associated with simple tastes, striving for Spiritual "Aliveness," benefitting from hard work, and liking the companies of others. Instead, what one sees in the Self-Unknown is "ME" only; getting others to do ones work; having elaborate and ostentatious tastes; striving for acquired emotional "Excitement"; cunningly planning how to control others; and deceptively designing what is to their disadvantage in order to give oneself an unfair advantage.

Recognition of the mental stretching required to gain these External World acquisitions and indulge ones Lower (animalistic) Self Passions and Fetters causes one to: (1) immediately become self-absorbed; (2) shift to *Impulsive Superficial Reflections* about who one thinks one is and who one desires to become; (3) form an Icon Image of a Superiority Complex; and (4) focus on ways to improve on the variety of methods and degrees to manifest Kill/Take/Destroy/Dominate in order to acquire ones goals. Rather than thinking rationally, one uses ones imagination to generate Icon Images that match the conditions one deals with on a daily basis. Hence, actions are founded on Brute Non-rationalism (emotions orchestrated by Left Brain thinking). The absence of the Right Brain input means there is Indifference to all non-cult members. Still for having given up one Real Self and its "5Ss" leads them to be Fear-Based. Hence their intense propensity for emulation of idols and an alertness to all.

Self-UnKnowers from any cause have no other way of getting out of the Unknown except by reaching into mysterious "Supernatural" realms by seeking out like-kind others afflicted with the insecurity of not knowing who they are. By so doing they experience themselves in terms of each other and together fashion a dogma of shared values and beliefs which the entire cult lives up to and uses as standards, guides, filters, and measures for daily living. By being strategically located in all aspects of society, there is a collective Omnipresence—i.e. present everywhere simultaneously. Out of that cult and personal combination each establishes an imagined erroneous but presumed personal Icon Image of superiority. Next, one lives up to ones personal Icon Image of being superior by attacking scapegoats. A typical trigger for such attacks by "Killer" police is dark skin color.

This color is like the psychedelic effect that triggers an echo to expand ones consciousness through greater awareness of the senses and emotional feelings as well as to reveal ones Unconscious motivations. Both effects of the trigger color are vividly expressed symbolically. Its bold abstract emotive sense plays daily like a tape recorder and thus causes a Conditioned Response to the Trigger color. This plus an obsession to be honored by ones cult members are greatly contributory to "Killer" police's needless killings of unarmed Black People.

"DARK SIDE" BRUTE MINDSETS

"Dark Side" refers to those minds devoted to thinking about and perfecting and displaying inside the range of the Secular and the Supernatural every degree of the IHES Complex—i.e. Indifference, Hate, Evilness, Sadism in order to adversely affect victims. *"Dark Side"* people's Divine Consciousness and Divine Spirit are so far away from their awareness as for them to be anti-Spiritual Elements advocates. This has dominated the European mindset from primitive times to the present. This was particularly prominent during Europe's "Dark Ages" (i.e. early Middle Ages)—starting after the Fall of Rome and featuring 600 years of Godless behavior where ignorance and barbarism prevailed. Ones "Dark Side" mind spotlights human emotions generated by ones fantasy life and the nature of ones fantasies thereby spur powerful effects bodily, intellectually, emotionally, spiritually, and per-ceptually—each capable of influencing--by shaping or blocking--every aspect of ones life. One is so immersed in mental entanglements as to prevent the ability to run away, leaving one with no choice but to *"Escape"* ('throw off restraint') into *"self-delusions"*—the deeming of oneself to be who one is not so as to avoid facing who one really is.

Hiding from any of these aspects about oneself by Denials is a *Self-Scam*. It concerns ones 'self-talk' answers that cannot come to grips with ones true emotions and reality limitations, flaws, inadequacies. Yet, Denials can bring temporary satisfaction. Yet, it is associated with a loss of ones inherent "5Ss"—safety, security, sureness, strength, and stability. Whatever caused those losses (e.g. "I'm not good enough" about something) forms a "Raw Nerve" one must hide from the External World as well as from oneself. Even then, the "Hiding" uses up so much energy and generates so much inner turmoil as to urge one to "Escape" from reality. That is the primary goal and the chief result of Fantasy. Fantasy's actions are like the finger of a clock—running, while still at home, the great circuit of ill and/or relief. Such a state indicates one is unable to consistently stay within the Magic Circle of Reality—a sign of Selfhood weakness—and indicates one has entered the Supernatural realm. To be repeatedly outside the Magic Circle of Reality allows that Supernatural "Air Castle" companionship to be an outlet for *Frustrations*. But the consequence is to be thrown into mental disorder, bewilderment, and Confusion (pour together; mix together; fail to distinguish) as to tangle oneself into a Delusional Mindset. Such weakness causes ones mental ingredients to run into extremes—"Too Much/Too Little"—about them-selves and about aspects of the External World.

Some of the most powerful and dangerous emotions (e.g. envy, greed) derive their primary nourishment from a source so trivial as living inside "extremes" and this invariably leads to the IHES complex. This com-bination of unhealthy mental features designs "Dark Side" Fantasies—some being in the form of Icon Images related to oneself and certain others. *Images* are patterns of forms and figures endowed with a unity, a message having a 'payload,' and an obscureness from its remoteness to impart fascination. Although the Image may be formed from a collage of things, as with melody, the whole—the visual synthesis--is greater than the sum of its parts being, in a sense, the origin of and justification for the Icon aspect. Together, they elevate the core of the 'payload' into the language of the incomprehensible so it can be understood by its mere presence "saying everything". Its impact stirs ones "Dark Side" Fantasies to bud into a dispositional thought and perhaps erupt into action.

The "Dark Side" Fantasy Icon Images become ones intimate companion that replace reason and reality. Fantasy Icon Images cause one to consciously choose an Inferiority Complex (as displayed by being a follower) or a Superiority Complex (as displayed by self-grandiosity/*Narcissism* in fantasy with an excessive need for admiration). Either lead one to over-compensate for ones secret doubts pertaining to the "5Ss"; to continuously fortify ones "Raw Nerve"; to roam so freely as to ensure there is no place in this home for Pleasure in life.

CLASSIFICATION OF BRUTES: The European "Air Castle" Supernatural Military Order features all humans arranged and combined in a row or series--and designated by grade, class, rank, sequence, or in-group closeness. "*Rules*" are autocratically determined to serve as pattern for governing procedures or conduct by laying down laws to which others are bound. Personal insecurities force them to come up with rigid rules. Since clinging to Fear necessitates defensiveness, there are desperate struggles to prove ones power is the greatest--thus necessitating making wrong those not in agreement and needing to pay a harsh penalty. Rules are enforced by the GUN. All "troops" must play the game the way the rules are set up--and unique rules operate on a given rung of the Military Order Ladder.

They orchestrate these Rules to be a competitive act of "I must win at all costs." These "Troops" comply from a sense of inferiority, a lack of "5Ss," and their Selfhood Greatness loss of awareness of their birth gift of, Control of everybody's minds can be done no other way than by Deception and Rules of a Military Order nature. Yet, the more rigid the Rules applied to victims on the lowest rungs of the Military Order Ladder, the further each is pushed away from personal freedom and therefore ones Real Self. This *chain-of-command* is best illustrated with the Archery Pad Concept (fig. 7):

Group I--Core Brutes-- Satanists—are situated in the bull's eyes since they are the most evil and sadistic of the amoral. Group IA are Socialized Brutes while Group IB are Self-declared out of an Inferiority Complex so as to be a "fraternal twin" of Group IA. Group IA (Socialized Brutes) were/are likely to have always been the ones to set up Order within a military Rule system that generates the IHES complex.

Group II--Peripheral Brutes are the same as Group I except for possessing periodic faint morals. They are located in the first ring around the bull's eye.

Group III--Transitional Brutes, situated outside the circles and checkered throughout the Archery Pad but yet are close-by to those inside the circles. They are sometimes bothered by a conscience for doing evil deeds.

Group IV--Brute Imitators (e.g. the "Baddest Dudes" of Black gangs) draw "this and that" from Types A, B, and C.

Group V—The Supernatural "Troops" are indoctrinated to believe that whatever their chosen values--consciously/subconsciously, rationally/irrationally—are right and moral. Hence, they are guided by chance emotions and whims, not by ones mind. They feature Hedonism—the doctrine that good is whatever gives one pleasure and therefore, pleasure is the standard for morality. Education for those outside the cult is only to be about deliberately breeding helplessness, resignation, and self-pity so that the result is a lethargic group of victims. Since the Supernatural mind is not able to compete with Rational Thinkers, cult members seek to deprive, of great fear and envy, "those favored by Nature"—i.e. the talented, the intelligent, the creative—out their success and rewards, of benefits, and of achievements created by personal attributes and virtues. By honoring victims for only engaging in sports or entertainment helps finish off the crippling of the "Inside-Out" minds and ensures there will be no cognitive development. In order to maintain their stereotypical picture of the worse features which characterize victims, they prominently display in television and stage programs the incompetent, the stupid, the slothful, and those of the "Streets" as representatives of their victim group.

Discussion: Group I's success in controlling "Troops" and "Victims" derives from the maxim: to persuade good and moral potential "Troops" to do evil, it is not necessary to first persuade them to become evil. Instead, it is only necessary to teach them that they are doing good. Notice how Black gangs have imitated these practices. Groups II, III, and IV take orders from Group I and see that the Brute Rules are enforced. They are intent on being "right" at all costs, for to be wrong in action is viewed as a danger to their lives and thus unfit for existence. This makes for a life of chronic imaginary fears. Regardless of action types, at their extremes they are equally devastating. Their system control exists because of Evil and it persists by Evil. Violence is employed to maintain it and all violence involves criminality. Punishment for violating Rules include being: ignored; reprimanded; demeaned; fined; burdened with stoppage or forfeiture of pay or beneficial programs; demoted; discharged; being placed under close (restrained) or open (confined) arrest; penal servitude for life; or death. Soldiers, policemen, and jailers; knives clubs, and batons; and fetters, isolation, and stereotypes are instruments for inflicting pain. They also ensure the rest of the people who follow do not know any other way.

VIOLENCE PRACTICES OF EUROPEAN MALES

Much of Europe and western Asia, from as far back as 130,000 BC, was inhabited by Neanderthals or Neandertals who existed in Europe as late as 30,000 BC. Nevertheless, it is said they were replaced by anatomically modern humans, Cro-Magnoid Homo Sapiens, who began to appear in Europe c45,000 years ago. Given that the two hominid species likely co-existed in Europe, anthropologists wondered whether the two interacted. Yet, the question is: "where did they come from?" They did not know and most of their today's descendants still do not know. The effect of one not knowing who is ones own Selfhood is, as one saying goes: " by one having both feet firmly planted in the air, one can busily saw air in order to anchor, form, and build a castle around ones feet." However, that "Air Castle" is so rickety—so weak—as to be like a shaky shanty. They thereby become Unstable Introverts (e.g. unsociable, pessimistic, rigid, moody) or Unstable Extroverts (e.g. touchy, aggressive, excitable, and changeable).

ORIGINAL FALSE SELF DEVELOPMENT: The Ice Age's (Glacial or Pleistocene Period) great ice sheets, up to a mile thick, covered 8,000,000 square miles of the earth's surface—but not in sunny Africa when, in 200,000 BC, the first humans appeared on East Africa's beautiful, snow-capped Rwenzori ("rainmaker") Mountains between Uganda and the Republic of Congo--called the Mountain of the Moon. No doubt this was the true Garden of Eden referred to in the European Bible because there was a plentiful food supply and pleasant equatorial climate, despite it being in the Ice Age elsewhere in the world. Then they migrated towards the shoreline of Ethiopia's Afar and fashioned what is now known as the *Cradle of Humankind*. But the focus here is on Europeans' earth arrival in 45,000 BC. At that time there was not much more than such large animals as mammoths, the mastodon, the glyptodont, and the woolly rhinoceros. All were available for food supply. This was followed by a complicated demographic which included many successive periods of population growth--but initially and mainly Africans in Africa. These Paleolithic populations created sophisticated inventions and left evidence of their advanced culture in the cave paintings of southern France, dating to at least 30,000 BC. Geneticists say northern Europe was populated by the migration of a very small number of modern humans who left the center of the Great

Lakes of eastern Africa about 50,000 years ago. These Grimaldi Negroids moved up through northern Africa into Europe to become, many believe, the Aurignacian foundations (c45,000 BC) of the various European "races."

Of greater importance is their bringing of a more advanced and inventive culture--things which ensured their survival—rafts, crude clothing, stone tools, weapons and traps, the wheel, pottery, the marked stick for measuring, and ways of making fire. Over the next 20,000 years they transformed into White people--e.g. Aryan, Alpine, and Slavic (Diop, *African Origins* p260; King, *Africa* p57; Bynum *African Unconscious*). During this Ice Age, the "Ice People" (e.g. Scandinavians, Germans, and Southern Russians) who lived in the region of the Baltic Sea encountered fierce weather in the Eurasian Steppes (vast treeless grasslands from the icy cold in winter). The barrenness of those regions and the lack of riches within the soil all fashioned a setting of the necessity for basic survival (Asante, "Afro-centricity," p81) and striving for security. At that time, the Ice Age environment ensured the land was minimally productive of food and other such essentials required for survival. The Realistic Scarcity that initially led to survival by "any means necessary"--because the world was viewed as hostile to them—was compatible with "the First Law of Nature".

By these Eurasians also lacking other environmental advantages of necessities for life, made it easy to develop a 'second nature' mindset of Scarcity. *Scarcity* implies insufficient resources to supply everyone's needs and wants and the reaction to the need for "Scarcity" essentials led individuals and their nomadic tribes to rob and kill neighbors so as to acquire what they needed to live. However, when applied where survival was not the issue meant they had shifted into a "False Self" (i.e. Ego). As a result they developed such behaviors into 'second nature' experiences and the associated competitive actions became *Conditioned Responses* of using 'any means necessary'. Those who did this best were able to survive Scarcity (Bailey: *Post-Traumatic Distress Syndrome in Black Americans*). Fears related to this Background Consciousness of Scarcity is seen today. For example, most salesmen speak rapidly and with a high-voice of anxiety to tell you to "hurray and buy this before its too late or before its all gone"; "this is the last chance"; "there are only two days left".

PRIMITIVE EUROPEAN WARRIORS: The C14 Old French word "Warrior" (one who wages war) means an experienced fighting soldier. For those who make war, better things do not exist for them--for this is where they show the "primitive" masculinities of courage, strength, and virility. Each battle is an opportunity to reclaim and prize these. Primitive European warriors' battles were initially oriented to overcoming their human nature Scarcity needs. Eventually, they expanded to embrace their concept of happenings in those Unseen Realms influencing their existence--concepts manifesting in a mainly religious to a mainly violence range. Varied subdivisions were involved in local battles or in '*Shamanism*' (those thought to have visions and to perform healing) or in hierarchical organizations. But common to each form, regardless of its nature, was the '*Charismatic*' (Greek, favor or grace) leader—spotlighting powers demonstrated to be an irresistible self-interest force in human affairs. One form was "*Religious Warriors*" who engaged in sacrifices as the root of their religious rituals. Overtime, Sacrifice was a collective celebration that ritually undermined the prohibition or taboo on murder, especially of relatives and kinfolk. However, in the big picture, sacrifice as a collective ritual, obscured the origins of religious practices by resorting to actual murder and physical violence.

Another but somewhat later form, "*Battle Warriors*," turned their individuality completely over to their leadership and lived by the code: "I will always place my mission first; I will never accept defeat; I will never quit; I will never leave a fallen comrade" (Samet, *Armed Forces & Society, 2005*). Honor, the first of their two obsessive concerns, was deemed inseparable from external measures and spoils. For example, there was no grander or nobler prospect for exhibiting an "honorific trophy" than to carry home the bloody armor stripped from an enemy's back. Yet, generating an even greater share of honor was being able to display enemies' heads. Failure to obtain, or retain, such treasures following battle brought with it a corresponding shame. A second obsession was with each fellow fallen soldier thereby becoming the momentary object of a new frenzy from the rest of the Troops. Fellow warriors would strip off his armor before starting to drag the corpse back into their lines. Often this was done at the expense of losing sight of both tactical and larger strategic aims, thereby allowing the enemy to regroup and charge again. Primitive/Ancient codes of loyalty and honor manifested themselves nowhere more clearly than in a steadfast determination to protect the body from the enemy, even at the loss of ones own life.

Homer put this into words by indicating: "he corpse acquires a value independent of its armor--becoming a tactical objective on the battlefield—the vehicle through which one retains nobility." The imperative to retrieve a fallen comrade's body from the field regardless of tactical cost also suggested the *preeminence of the dead over the living*. Warriors of the Classical period somewhat altered these patterns. While fighting for countless reasons, they continued to emphasize primitive warfare's centrality of the dead body by taking honor in its possession and returning home with it. This satisfied many things for fellow warriors to see and admire: loyalty, fear, vengeance, and honor. By contrast, whereas the body is real, the principles behind humanitarian intervention, peacekeeping, and pursuing terror seemed far more elusive. Nevertheless, there was an expansion of their actions in two parts.

One is that rather than being a mere reflection of the customary practice regarding retrieval and identification of battlefield dead, the return of corpses in itself was tantamount to an acknowledgment of victory, defeat, or stalemate. Another was that they fought most frequently and most desperately to preserve the honor of the living. In Biblical times, a central OT Icon Image for the nature and activity of the Jewish God is that of being the divine warrior (Exod. 15:3; Isa. 42:13; Psalm 24:8). Although this "man of war" image did not conform to European Christianity's dogma about God as love, there has been the ever presence of a fusion in Christianity of violence and the sacred in institutional forms. Examples are plentiful in history—e.g. the C11-C13 AD Crusades; the C13-C19 Inquisition (gaining confessions through torture for unjust trials); and Middle Ages Feudalism, where religion provided an institutional check on interpersonal violence by integrating the warrior into society.

PRIMITIVE WARRING SURVIVAL WAYS: From their beginnings, European tribes constantly warred against each other—over "anything" or for "no reason." With any ethnic group out to destroy the other, wars in the Steppes (grasslands) were fought with "Inflamed Raw Nerve" vengeance. While on conquests of weaker neighbors, ongoing food scarcity in northern Europe caused primitive Europeans to have a nomadic, hunting lifestyle. Of course, there was an absence of political authority; the lack of society principles and cohesiveness geared to a common purpose; and gods were made in the warriors' images. Victims of vicious Kill/Take/Destroy/Dominate methods of these European Warriors were "Awed" and readily accepted being "inferiors." Meanwhile, these Warrior barbarians treasured their tools of war above all else, often endowing them with Supernatural power. Many legends tell of swords inhabited by demons, or acting as agents of gods who they fashioned into Contingent Beings to personify all the: (1) pride (arrogance), (2) wrath (great anger), (3) envy, (4) lust, (5) gluttony, and (6) avarice (covetousness, greediness) they believed in.

Throughout the Ice Age, Scarcity remained the keystone problem. Following the end of the Ice Age in 12,500 BC their Supernatural Realm was perceived as non-sensory, non-rational, non-definable, and non-identifiable inside a reality whose realm is not natural as humans live in and yet is superior to it. This Delusional World they lived in was 'second nature'. All its perceptions were culturally transmitted into today's descendants. *After African women originated agricultural practices in c20,000 BC, these spread widely outside Africa.*

Although it took time for certain primitive Middle Eastern nomadic hunter-gatherers to learn farming, many of them--appearing to have shared the same culture and similar physical traits--immigrated into Europe, spread out in nomadic bands, and traded with each other over vast distances. By forming a bridge for movement back and forth between these areas, residents of the Middle East traced their ancestry to both Africa and Europe. Some say Aryans originated this way c12,000 BC in Iran. Others say they came from Central Asia. The Aryans' Patriarchal (literally "the rule of the fathers") evil practices as warring semi-nomads were in full force at least by 2300 BC. Nevertheless, consisting of bands of tribes, they spoke a somewhat common language; possessed a similar social structure; and practiced a like-kind religion. Contrary to popular belief, they were not a race. Besides, they were quite a dumb people. Greed, spurring fighting as a normal daily occurrence, was the keystone solution. Yet certain groups would stop fighting each other and join forces if attacked by a commonly disliked outsider. Rather than these enmities and rivalries being a unity, they formed look-alikes of unity--i.e. Alliance, Coalition, and Liaison connections.

Joining only temporary allowed for fighting units changing combinations--units who otherwise remained dissimilar, distinct, and individualistic. Such *Civility* patterns—doing the proper thing for the group out of: "every man for himself" self-interest—is seen today (e.g. in political and legal systems). Then these Brutes' (part of a larger group now known as Indo-Europeans)--who lived in the grasslands of Eastern Europe, north of the Black and Caspian Seas and in the region of south Russia and Turkestan--started migrating "everywhere." In successive waves by c2000 BC--from central Asia, South Russia, and Turkestan--the horse riding Aryans spread throughout such places as Syria, Israel, Iran, Mesopotamia (Sumeria, Iraq), Persia, the Balkan Peninsula, and Asia Minor (an expanded Turkey). Note that many of these areas, and particularly around the Mediterranean Sea, were originally Black populations. Along the way--while settling in Iran, Mesopotamia, Persia, Asia Minor, Greece, Rome, Germany, Britain, and India--they devastated peaceful peoples.

Aryans set up caste systems consisting of priests, warriors, kings, traders, farmers, laborers, artisans, and servants (who were forbidden to mix with the higher castes); then invaded India c1700 BC and colonized the Punjab region of Northwest India; plundered the rich cities of the Indus valley civilizations while absorbing much of the culture. While setting up caste systems (e.g. in India), they assumed positions of kings, priests, warriors, artisans, and traders--implanting the mental orientation of prejudices; the practices of discriminatory Caste Systems (the rigid and permanent separation of groups of people in society); and the self-declaration of being noble (!) compared to the Slaves they captured and a superior people (!!!). They were known to be needlessly destructive; to drink the blood of the enemy they killed; have sex with their mothers, sisters, and animals; to eat their dead fathers; and to grab hold of any trivial matter so as to fight, even friends--and without regard for their own lives or the lives of those close to them. Their superiority was in making, and using, tools for Kill/Take/Destroy/Dominate in continual wars.

Still, to hide their ever present and overwhelming inferiority complex, they routinely stole the intellectual property of their Colored victims and claimed it as their own creations. As savages, Aryans destroyed as much as possible of the long established high civilizations of Black or Brown people—e.g. literature, craftsmanship, architecture, art, and various other cultural and civilization achievements. This situation caused them to fear White or Yellow strangers and thus to react to their made-up fear with Kill/Take/Destroy/Dominate aggression. By allowing their manufactured "*Scarcity Legend Symbol*" to orchestrate their lives, racism was deemed necessary among those unlike them, and dissention among those like them. Xenophobia (fearful of strangers), a dulling of their senses, and a war oriented disposition became entrenched traits of European cultures (Diop in Ani p304).

Since Primitive Europeans were "living on the edge" to survive--with each greedily grabbing-- this raises a moral dilemma issue. Were these practices a display of constructive survival which justified Greed and Kill/

Take/Destroy/Dominate/Oppress? Or, did they conform to the European concepts of the "Seven Deadly Sins" drawn from the twelve tormentors of the Egyptian Tehuti (Hermes, ?12,500 BC) provided the model for Pope Gregory in C6 to declared Arrogance to be one of the Seven Deadly Sins. He said it is a serious moral offense and a source for the other six sins. Associated with them are Fetters (e.g. hatred, fear, lies, and jealousy) and Self-Absorption (e.g. maladaptive "Me, Me" first Individualism). These vices, producers of evil and hatred are present in any form of evil.

The Old English word "*Pride*" may have arisen from the appearance of a group of lions. Later it was applied to humans who demonstrated a lofty and arrogant assumption of superiority--called "puffed up" self-esteem. This image came from the hot air smoke produced from fireplaces--"hot air" that was like the ranting and raving seen in the boastful and the conceited--"hot air" that was like what "lifted up" their balloon wrapping of smoke. Back then, smoke was often associated with Fools as well as present in those who are quarreling, jealous, angry, slandering, or gossiping. So "puffed up" did these prideful people become that their delusions and thoughts of grandeur caused them to be considered as today's equivalent of mild paranoid psychotics. The boastful and the conceited were condemned during Biblical Times because both draw one away from godliness; generate stubbornness; and march one into the destruction of others and of themselves. In the Bible, Psalm 73 depicts the character of the arrogant: "From their callous hearts come iniquity; the evil conceits of their minds know no limits. They scoff, and speak with malice; in their arrogance they threaten oppression. Their mouths lay claim to heaven, and their tongues take possession of the earth."

However, by the time the Ice Age was over and their actual "Survival *Greed*" was no longer needed, Greedy pursuits had become "second nature," despite the lack of environmental Scarcity. Excuses were manufactured so as to keep getting significantly more than was needed via Kill/Take/Destroy/Dominate--the only methods they knew. Furthermore, greed never allows one to think one has enough. That means: (a) one stays in a miserable state of unhappiness; (b) the "Seven Deadly Sins" are rationalized into being "the right thing to do"; (c) greed demands segregation and deception out of (d) constant fear of retaliation from victims or (e) from having ones ill-gotten gains "stolen." A "second nature" of Greed first means using ones Brute Brain as a way of life--characteristically manifesting traits similar to psychopaths. But the difference is Brutes' causes derive from a philosophical "Inside-Out" amoral worldview. There is a sincere belief that what the world Sages agree to as Right is just the opposite. For example, they simply do not care about enhancing the suffering of the truly needy and, in fact, gain "sick" pleasure from contributing to it.

Second, there is problematic functioning of these Brutes' brain chemistry in the processing of Oxytocin--which normally causes people to be moral. Third, Kill/Take/Destroy is "sick" pleasure which, like winning, becomes addicting. During Biblical times, "Greed" was on lists with murder, adultery, and malice (Mk. 7:22). Because desire for riches or possessions take first place in the greedy person's heart, greed is equated with idolatry (Col. 3:5). "Living on the edge" with respect to survival is not a justifiable excuse because it simply means one was too lazy to do the necessary preparation to take care of the serious business of life in the future. It is proper to be greedy in wanting enough in order to get the job done; proper in elevating oneself; proper in desiring to give Selfless Service to those who really need it and will accept it; proper in "wildly" enjoying life at the appropriate times.

It takes no research effort to realize nothing has changed to this day. Despite their avowed individualism, most European males have been (for the last 45,000 years), and remain, quite philosophically *generically similar*--almost machine like. This is because their system of values has been, and remains, oriented to things of Value (i.e. Materialism) rather than to things of Worth (i.e. the finer things in life that money cannot buy). Their typical "I" (Individualism) society features are: looking for differences in people, individuality, uniqueness, being competitive, advocating individual rights, separateness and independence, survival of the fittest, and control over Nature. A way this shows is that Europeans have invariably needed to fashion an enemy by generating differences between them and peaceful people and then exerting all sorts of power over them. This ultimately derives from self-created Supernatural values.

FEAR-BASED MINDSETS OF EARLY EUROPEANS: Unlike the Just, those sufficiently delusional to believe they are superior, fear everything. European mental health literature agrees Fear is their most common emotion; that Fear is painful; and that from their Mindset beginnings, Fear has been its "Superstar" Legend Symbol. Medically, Fear naturally and automatically activates ones Ancient Brain for a "fight or flight" response as: (1) a *Birth Gift* to preserve one from evil. Here, Fear is not to overbear reason, but rather to assist it. When Fear's origination is from a world perceived as dangerous: (2) ones *Worry Fears* continue to expand while producing increasing doubt, distrust, worry, and fatigue. To harbor Fear means it percolates throughout all ones thinking and shapes ones interpretations about certain happenings, thus leading to failures and despair. At its start, ones mind is a slave to hypersensitive delusional 'ghosts' who chronically tyrannize within ones imagination; raise phantoms of horror; and beset life with super-numeracy distresses. Significant fears or cumulative small ones cloud ones vision; make one desperate; and produce cruelty to oneself and/or to other. No passion so effectively robs the mind of the power of its acting reasonably and kindly as does Fear. In the meantime, Worry Fear causes the victim to "die a thousand deaths." However, (3) *Brutes Fears* are purposely generated; grow in darkness; and, when stimulated, orchestrates the most drastic and presumably most effective remedy it knows--i.e. direct actions. Chronic Brute Fear actions follow the progression from *Indifference to Hate to Evilness to Sadism-- the IHES Complex.* Typically, Fear follows crime as its punishment. Since appearing on earth, Europeans have been and remain a warring people. Of course, war generates fear in the predators and the prey. Brute Europeans developed the concept of "*Delusional Fears*"--consisting of self-generated *unreal dangers* or even threats as part of an *addiction to fear*--an addiction serving for the justification to Kill/Take/Destroy for personal gain--an element of their "Dark Side" in both their inner and outer worlds. (4) Satanists use Fear for excitement.

During the Ice Age in northern Europe, Fear was properly associated with *Survival* (Type I Fear). After basic survival was no longer an issue, it was replaced with a Brute Greedy Mindset--a mindset consisting of a glob of reality + distortion + fantasy--a mindset using Fear as a Weapon to stimulate aggression so as to gain power and control over others as well as to Kill/Take/Destroy as a means of entertainment. Because those gains are never enough, greed is the driving force to keep getting or trying to get more than enough. Hence, destructive means are created, enhanced, or maintained for Illusion self-protection--and this automatically generates Type II--a *Fear of Retaliation,* from their victims. That is why they keep a foot on victims' throats until they have *erased the victims' spirit to retaliate.* Then they leave victims to grapple for the crumbs left behind--crumbs so necessary for survival that victims have no time to consider retaliation. Type III--*Self-Created Fear*--is self-protection stemming from ill-gotten gains and resultant worry about victims reclaiming it.

Type IV--*Fear for Justification*--was/is deliberately created to serve to justify attacks (mainly on Colored Peoples) so as to gain more unjust possessions. Type V--"*White Superiority*" *Fear*s are from insecurity, unsafeness, unsureness, and instability. Examples: fears of losing jobs, status, or intellectual positions to Black People, whom they greatly envy. They seek isolation from victims in order to avoid power dilutions by those they try to keep down. Examples include Housing or school integration causing "White Flight." Type VI--Europeans' *Inter-Competition Fear*--includes "not being able to keep up with the Jones" (i.e. trying to match the lifestyle of ones more affluent neighbors or acquaintances). Type VII--Fear *of not winning* fairly against victim competitors or in self-created competitions called, among the richest Europeans, "*The Game*" of "he who has the most adult toys not only survives but wins." Despite lacking actual physical danger, there are a host of fears and associated reactions to imagined threats to ones self-esteem. Type VIII is *Fear of Exposure* for not being the superior individuals they claim themselves to be. Type IX is *Fear of being Subordinated*--i.e. being overshadowed by another's power--especially if that is from one or more Black People. Type X: Satanists only Fear *loss of their ill-gotten gains,* for they believe evilness is right.

EUROPEAN WARRIOR/GOD CONNECTION: The Ice Age Europeans who devised the Supernatural Realm and created its contents were fierce competitors, identifiable by their harshness and aggressiveness to match environmental conditions. Their best, who thrived in the setting of Scarcity, claimed to be the most powerful and the richest of all competitors in the Seen Natural world. Perhaps such illusions of superiority (being ignorant of African's far, far advanced culture) expanded into hallucinations of being superior even in the Unseen World. By removing themselves from the Natural World altogether, meant Delusional beliefs consisted of being *"larger than life"* and possessing Supernatural powers—powers enabling them to straddle both Worlds and yet be larger than the sum scope of what both represent—powers to leap extra-mundane (out of this reality world) and extra-territorial (above land and waters) barriers—powers to unite the invisible and the visible—powers to disregard actual or supposed boundaries—powers to put boundaries on the boundless—powers to operate in the 'here and now' and orchestrate it while still remaining far away. *Their perceptions damned all values, enjoyments, achievements, and successes not sanctioned by the Supernatural cult.*

The cunning they used in warring was inferred to be present in their gods--an image of something either having no real existence or exists incompletely. These were/are deemed to be so admirable in themselves and therefore in their gods as for both to be thought of as perfect in every kind of skill and information—making "right" everything they did/do. Because such perfection was used to pervert humans and entangle them in the meshes of sin that enabled their exploitation, these European male leaders worshipped their various self-made gods--e.g. the warrior god Thor--for purposes of self-seeking interest. Without limit or satiety, these Beings were/are symbolic of lowest human desires and the lowest affections, emotions, appetites and thoughts.

The origin, warring, magic, evolution, survival ways religion, gods, and their fear-based nature has been discussed in Bailey, Post-Traumatic Distress Syndrome and thus only pertinent features are now presented. The early religious "numen" belief of ancient Romans--a belief in a kind of power existing everywhere--a power expressing itself in the greatest of human actions--was so significant as for them to begin personifying that power in the form of Satan. The emotions associated with the European Supernatural are called *"Numinous Feelings"*— all freezing the intellect but each themselves being unexplainable. The following are present when certain conditions are fulfilled: the "Wonder" inside *Admiration* (delight and regard); *Amazement* ("delusions"--ideas opposed to reality'); *"Delirium"*—a temporary mental disturbance--as if one was in a daze); and *Astonishment* (stun the emotions and intellect as if thunderstruck)--each reflecting *Awe*. One *"Numinous Feeling"* is the concept of being filled up with a sensation of Supernatural Numen presence pertaining to something which is both a value and an objective reality—gained from visual experiences. In other words, ones immediate emotional response is to a primary reference experience of an object outside oneself but not tied to any sense experience—which makes it a Supernatural reaction—displaying as ones Animalistic Self.

The early religious "numen" belief of ancient Romans--a belief in a kind of power existing everywhere--a power expressing itself in the greatest of human actions--was so significant as for them to begin personifying that power in the form of Satan. This spurred them to fight, rob, and kill anybody--at any time. A present day analogy is people were not safe to walk across the street. Those extremely destructive and crude practices were present among all the savage European tribes. The Satanists philosophy of being absolutely against Goodness and the "Right" was, in general, best crystallized by the ancient Greek theories and practices. They carried forth the primitive European Warrior belief that people who allowed themselves to be Enslaved were mentally weak, subhuman, and like mechanical beings. The benefit is to allow slave owners to live as they see fit.

Thereafter, *a theme of Western civilization has been, as stated, dedicated efforts on rearing a crop of humans who never had Free Minds so that those like them would be easily led like robots and so that those unlike them, whom they Enslaved, would be unable to know what they are missing by not being free.* The permissible-ness of such a *terrible concept of controlling minds* of humans was heightened by the way the ancient Greeks and Romans thought about their Supernatural (made-up) God--a Contingent Being (CB) possessing power in various Secular (Material World) "how it appears" forms.

EUROPEAN "DARK AGES" WARRIORS: The European Dark Age (460 AD-800 AD) and Middle Age (800-1492) were dangerous times because its people were constantly warring with each other and against the mounted hordes from Asia. By C8, barbaric European warriors, able to fight on horseback, were in great demand by European kings who needed to protect their castles--as much from neighbors as from foreign invaders. By these warriors attaching themselves to royal courts as body guards, they became "civilized" barbarians. As ancestors of Medieval Knights, they catered to their upper classes (who had a Satanism orientation) while disregarding the lower classes (i.e. those unlike them). The Franks were particularly important because, by being steeped in Paganism, they followed the typical folkways of Brute Europeans by being brave, engaging in piracy, and selling captured Slaves (a practice carried over into the USA convict lease system). The Gauls of France, enthusiasts of human sacrifice, routinely set people on fire (as done to Enslaved African-Americans during lynching). With the Warrior Indifference/Hate/Evil/Sadism (IHES) Complex mindset being the dominant European philosophy since their arrival on Earth 45,000 years ago, its purpose was/is to acquire for displaying what cult members esteem. These esteems focus on ones riches, fame, power, status, and appearances of "Good Life" pleasures of the senses (i.e. exciting the emotions and physical feelings)--serving as the standard for the highest Good (Runes, Spinoza Dictionary, p. 114).

Associated with their countless evil and sadistic deeds was Arrogant Pride standing out in these forms. A "sinful pride" consciousness was not only in being able to conquer or subdue peaceful people but in claiming false beliefs of superiority in every other aspect of life. Exaggerated, assertive or "high" Pride is *Haughtiness* (taking advantage of an established position while holding others in contempt). When it becomes overbearingly or insultingly superior, it is called *Superciliousness*--the showing of a pompous superiority of disdain (rejection, as non-verbally conveyed in lifting one eyebrow). When it demands laudation (excessive praise) and admiration, *Vanity* (groundless self-admiration) is present.

In order to get the kudos (glory) fools desire and think they deserve, their vanity deliberately claims it and they declare themselves to be the standard and the judge of everybody else. Such arrogance is typically accompanied by *Insolence*--an ill-mannered rudeness (barbaric), impudence (without shame), contempt (despising and labeling their victims as worthless), and abusiveness (treating others badly). *Arrogance*, an aggressive form of Vanity, consists of an offensive exhibition of assumed superiority because of riches, station, learning, achievements, or domination. Pride is the parent of discontent, ingratitude, presumption, acquired negative emotions, rebellion, willful disobedience, insensitivity to others, extravagance, and bigotry. Everything Brutes do is to bathe in the fantasy of being 'little gods' (e.g. Hedonism).

From my observations, experiences, and reflections, European males with Numinous mindsets, dating to its crystallization by the Romans of antiquity, seem to possess an absolutely unique way of viewing life that is almost like being made out of the same thinking "cookie cutter." This includes feeling or being aware of something mysterious, terrible, beyond reason, awe-inspiring, adventurous, and rapidly heading them away from happiness. It is about having a superiority complex un-explicable by established laws of human nature as well as contrary to known reason or even to common sense. Nothing of what they want is ever enough and thus they can never be happy. A facade for their sense of unhappiness is "act as if" they have it all together and seek doing harm to others as a way of having some momentary sense of relief from their misery. In the background of their Selfhood are a myriad of *Superstitions*--beliefs about the occult in its negative range and beliefs in the existence of super-humans or Supernatural forces and Beings--which Brutes attempt to emulate.

SETTING STRAIGHT THE USA'S VIOLENT RECORD: The Black Panther, H. Rap Brown said: "Violence is as American as cherry pie." The 1600s expression: the "pot calling the kettle black" refers to open-hearth cooking blacking practically all utensils used. It applies to accusing others of faults possessed by the accusers. Such *Projection* is especially applicable to Europeans claiming, with "righteous indignation," that Black People are violent. The typical European pattern of invading foreign lands was brought to the New World. They promptly started killing off its people and food supply while moving westward as settlers. This Indifferent/Hate/Evil/Sadism (IHES) mindset pattern of these Supernatural cult members fashioned individual aggressiveness that defied restraint because of their amoral non-rational thinking. From it (among others) emerged a special 'double-standard' Idealism--i.e. a set of rules establishing advantageous provisions for themselves and disadvantages for outsiders. Also, they could not tolerate any outsider doing the evil things they did, as in lying, cheating, and stealing. Meanwhile, Leonard (*Homicide Studies,* 2003) says USA wars started with the first Indian attack in 1622. Then came 4 major imperial wars (1689-1763), the Revolutionary War (1775-83 to gain independence from England) and again in 1812; the 40 wars with Indians (robbing them of multi-millions of acres of land + killing millions of Indians); the Mexican war in 1846 (seizing the entire Southwest, including California); the 1861 Civil War (bloodiest war in American history); the Spanish-American War and Philippine Insurrection (1898-1902); World Wars I and II; the Korean police action (1949-1952); the Vietnam war (1959-1975); scores of smaller engagements/wars (1945- 1991)--the Caribbean, Central America, and globally during and after the Cold War (directly or via surrogates) e.g. the Gulf War (January-February 1991 in Iraq), the former Yugoslavia in 1999, the 2001 war against international terrorists in Afghanistan, and presently.

Military and even militaristic terms, under the "Patriotism" guise, have been the call to action in 67+ wars in the last 50 years. USA Southerners (especially between 1798 and 1965) eagerly supported each war, no matter its nature or who it has been against. Southern ideas of honor and the warrior ethic combined to create intense regional war fevers in 1798, 1812, 1846, 1861, 1898, 1917, 1941, 1950, and 1965. Total victim devastation or death numbers (multi-millions) from Euro-American collective violence can never accurately be known since it includes official/unofficial masked violence against Native American Indians, African Americans, Mexican Americans, and Asians. Typically, the attacked were weaker than the perpetrators—e.g. Amerindians, Black Americans, Mexican Americans, or Asians. Historians remark about the unusual brutality of the Indian wars, the Mexican War, the Civil War, the Spanish-American War, the Vietnamese War, and all other wars in which Euro-Americans confronted Colored Peoples. For Southern Whites, the color line was a license for barbarity, overriding the restraints of common humanity and their best dogma of their Christianity. Throughout slavery, the great fear underlying Southern life was that vast numbers of the Enslaved might imitate the captors and rise to exact murderous revenge in just cause. After slavery, fear was replaced by a determination not to relinquish White racial control over 5 million African Americans.

Moreover, between 1865 and 1965 there was a nightmarish reign of official and unofficial terror to reinforce and deepen African Americans political powerlessness, economic dependence, and social degradation. Although Europeans always generated some outrageous excuse—claiming to exhibit their 'rights' under the 'Law,' the reality is that they did not believe in law at all". Vigilante groups were dedicated to punishing any immoral or undesirable behavior not done by them or to coerce cultural conformity on mixed-race local populations. Virtually all collective social violence has been directed by today's Republicans' inhumaneness and greed against perceived enemies—those who enabled riches to be had or needed to be crushed so as to prevent the loss of riches or who did not completely conform to Supernatural cult dogma, culture, or social ways. In this way, war has contributed to the legitimatization of the use of violence partnered with racism. Routinely, most Euro-American social control activities—including every conceivable act of savagery—has gone unreported, dismissed, "explained away" by the public, or blamed on Black People. jabaileymd.com

BLACK PEOPLE'S SELF-UNKNOWNING MINDSETS: My formally simple idea of the "Unknown" illustrates why I thoroughly research key words whose meanings I think I already know. Its numerous meanings include: not recognized as a fact or as an individual; not discovered; not apprehended mentally and thus unidentified; unaware that ones spiritual sense is aware of oneself; one having clouded out ones own material senses of awareness; an ultimate reality incompletely/inadequately experienced in terms of Images and Symbols related to its true nature; and lacking an established or normal status. Self-Unknown people are mysterious or secrets to themselves because of ignorance. It is an unfamiliarity causing a sense of strangeness, like an algebraic "X"; 'Z' (the last alphabet letter); or placed at the end of the line of Humanity. Being "lost," hidden, obscure, debatable, and disconnected from everything in life causes ones "Life-Living" think, feel, say, actions to be in excess, in insufficiency, in wrong directions. These wedge apart ones Talents from ones Motivation. Nevertheless, Ancient African Sages said "Knowing" of ones Selfhood is present at birth—that every divine and earthly Cosmic (i.e. Real) creature ultimately arose from God's androgynic protoplast—and all initially resided together and interdependently in a "Virtual" boundary-less, undefined, and undifferentiated—but not *disordered*—state inside unformed Matter situated in infinite space. By each human containing a 'drop' of the Cosmic Mind—i.e. ones "Self" (the absolutely unchanging "sameness" of ones Selfhood)--meant/means the newborn's Real Self has knowledge of the entire Cosmos. This Cosmic Knowledge--the 'Self's' *Ultimate Background for daily living*—provides every Private Self "tool" needed for one to have a thriving and happy life.

However, all of this was repressed in the mind of every free African in Africa when the fishnet was thrown over him/her to thereafter enslave each and their children's, children's, children. *Today, the single most important Private Self problem in struggling Black youth is that they are Self-Unknown*. In 1903 Du Bois elaborated on this by saying Black People possess a "*Double Consciousness*"—the sense of being two people—one, the Self they know; the other, the Self they are told by others is the real one. He also envisioned two veils separating Whites from Blacks—one applied by Whites and the other applied by Blacks. The consequence of these layering over ones Real Self "Soul Sunshine" is to ensure that one becomes and stays Self-Unknown. Resultant manifestations are the very reason why our Ancient African Ancestors wrote the remedy on their temple walls 10,000 years ago: "Man, Know Thyself."

Self-Unknown displays stem from failing to cultivate ones Spiritual Emotions and Intellect. Many have replaced this by modelling Europeans' self-defeating, devastating "Individualism," Fetters, and 'non-rational' Supernatural cult thinking—both about Trinkets and Trivia. Hence, most Black children come to wrongly believe that dealing with problems of daily living is based upon following their acquired emotions--wrongly deeming them to be the validators of their Will and their actions. In short, they say: "the right way to live is to follow my emotions or what I feel".

By failing to realize ones true nature is to instantly face each and every problem and without an emotional reaction (the essence of Martial Arts), at 'crunch time' they thereby fashion different kinds of emotions to deal with a particular category of problems. *Too often their tough problem dealings are to simply ignore them or follow advice—practices that set up vicious cycles of worsening problems.* Resultant desperation for what to do leads them to look in all the wrong places for answers as well as the seeking out of leadership, either from ignorant or evil people—each pushing one further into a Delusional World. Since none of this ever works, each goes deeper and deeper into the Self-Unknown that leads to 'nowhere' but with great mental turmoil fanfare on the way. jabaileymd.com

FIGURE 5

EUROPEANS' SUPERNATURAL

Regarding the blindness of peoples of the world to the obvious, the subject of the European Supernatural stands out. Surfing television channels will show a high percentage of titles dealing with Satan; pacts with the Devil; legends of infernal personalities; werewolves; Witches and Warlocks, perhaps as midwives and physicians; Divination by rhadoscopy (wand or dowsing), cereoscopy (wax and coffee grounds), water, sacrifice, fire, lychnoscopy (candles); Demonoscopy (Genii, fairy beings, goblins, elves, elementals); ghosts; magic; corpses; animals; born Supernatural figures--and on endlessly. But what is this world? Because its way of thinking dominates in those who control the world, it is intriguing to explore. Yet, it has been extremely difficult for me--after going through hundreds of books on a vast variety of its "ought to be present" subjects--to find more than mere bits and pieces of information. My intrigue is because of the damage of untold and ever increasing magnitude caused by Supernatural concepts. Their practices--for all categories of people in all races, creeds, and colors--account for pain and suffering, conflict and confusion, doubt and uncertainty, inferiority and superiority complexes. What is it about the religious content of the Supernatural and its Superstition partners that, as a lifestyle, inspire such widespread and deep inner Self-Turmoil and hatred of outsiders? Why do they produce such grandeur of mind about being "right" and thus superior concerning what is incomprehensible? What is the reason for such killing in the name of their God? What has been tattooed in the cradle of ones society's philosophy to justify a need to cultivate a fear of God while ascribing human attributes to God?--and Why?

The Latin word "*Supernatural*" is defined as 'super-nature'--referring to the realm, with *Supernormal* Beings, existing above and beyond the realm of sense experience (fig. 5). *Supernormal* is defined as belonging to an unknown but natural order or system. "*Super-nature*" is beyond the universe, beyond entities, beyond identity. These all contradict every and anything humans know about the identity of what Ancient African Sages proved to have Correspondence. The African *Law of Correspondence* says all Cosmic Phenomena are limited and serial--and that they appear as scales or series on separate planes. Such can be readily observed in various aspects of the physical world by any sane person. Warren's 'Psychology' defines "*Supernatural*" as belonging to a higher order or system than that of Nature, or transcending the ordinary course of Nature. Funk & Wagnalls (1930) dictionary says: "Existing or occurring through some agency above the forces of nature; lying outside the sphere of natural law, whether psychic or physical; caused miraculously or by the immediate exercise of divine power." The Winston Dictionary (1946) says: "being outside or exceeding the forces or laws of nature: above, or superior to, the sequences of cause and effect in natural law; miraculous--that which is superior to the recognized forces or laws of nature.

Note: such Supernatural Thinking about definitions are not acts of defining. When people have no basis for saying what some real thing is when it came into existence, they resort to saying what it is not. These definitions "wipe out" Nature--using methods of "what it is not". Second, they deny, or at least overrule, the Spiritual One Universal High God elaborated on so extensively in African Tradition--and again without proof. Third, to exist is to possess a real identity. But, outside Belief and Faith, what identity do these Believers offer for thinking "far out of this world of reality"?

Of course, by being un-provable, or even reasonably supported as well as by lacking a meaning clarity, European Supernatural Thinking spurs raging disagreements. Despite constant battling, they put up a solid front to the public--an Aryan trait--with respect to having Belief/Faith in what is overwhelmingly confusing and does not make sense in African Tradition. The naïve, being new to Supernatural "authorities'" normal dishonorableness, accept it as is and thereby jump into a bottomless pit. That this type of thinking is present in full force today can be readily floodlighted by listening to any talk shows. It takes but a few moments to study "the Party of 'No' government officials, each of whom, like sheep lacking Character, identify themselves as negators--and without offering any solutions.

"AIR CASTLE" SUPERNATURAL FORMATION: European "Supernatural" is a "Fantasy Reality" accepted as Fact. Its feature is mutual reversals of Fantasy with Reality. The Fantasy includes whatever is not real--i.e. what is not God-made--+ what is so extraordinary, mysterious, unexplainable, and not know as to be placed into Fantasy. The "Fantasy" (Greek "phantasia"--a making visible) of the Supernatural is something Personified into a Contingent Being, Phantom, spirit, ghost, mental illusion, apparition, spectre, monsters, werewolves, fairies, etc. which apparently can be seen, heard, or sensed as a reality by those in a Supernatural frame of mind. Yet, it has no actual--no physical--reality. By contrast, the actual reality of living involved is made into a Fantasy. To illustrate, Brutes are characterized by an overflowing inner "Dark Side" + its associated unconscious fears + a mindset of Indifference/Hate/Evil/Sadism (IHES Complex) tendencies. Collectively, these are projected outwardly onto scapegoats and into the Contingent Being of the Supernatural realm in hopes of getting some relief from ones own miserable life. Because there is a Brute "Sameness" in their "Dark Side," they join to fashion a "Uniqueness" (i.e. Individualism) inside a "Sameness" (machine-like duplications) Atmosphere based upon "misery loves company." The "Face" of the Contingent Being is what features the commonality of their "Dark Side" and its associated Fears. They call the Contingent Being Satan and say Hell is Satan's residence--both made up concepts. Satan's standards, guides, and filters are used by Brutes in judging outsiders they say that possesses the IHES Complex.

Brutes then use several *Reality/Fantasy Reversals*. Type I is a simple *Reaction Formation* as, for example, one creates a problem but then blames the victim by saying "you are the one causing the problem, not me!" Type II is a denial of ones underlying destructive desires and creating a separation from it by going to the opposite extreme. For example, slave owners would speak of being God-fearing and holding the European Bible in one hand, would whip the Enslaved with the other. By so doing they hoped to deflect observation of their IHES Complex by saying they were trying to make Christians out of the Enslaved--a means of deceiving fellow White Christians into admiring their "Righteousness." Type III is Brutes despising their own IHES Complex and handling it by embracing a superiority complex concept of themselves as a result of showing their eagerness to fight IHES Complex in the scapegoats on whom they have projected their own "Dark Side." In this way they can impart violence on others who represent Symbols of themselves and feel they are being purged of their own IHES Complex. Type IV are born into a Satanism orientation and see themselves as "little gods" who are bathed in an aura of omnipotence of a magnitude unknown to the living. Naturally, the African one universal High God is a competitor. Thus, whatever God is for, they are automatically against. This requires no thought and no alternative plan.

These types have their basis in how the Cosmos is conceived to be made and from what creator. Resultant varied contents in the various cultures throughout the ages concerning the various "Good Life" Supernatural features lacked (and still lack) a homogeneous meaning or specific pattern or general agreement on significance pertaining to age group, content, and context. Yet, on each "Good Life" Engram, each Brute adds layer upon layer--similar to leaves layered on a head of lettuce--of indifference to the needy, hatred of those unlike them, evilness to get what they want, and sadistic deeds on scapegoats so as to purge themselves of their "Dark Side." Still the theme of these layers are shared by all Brutes because of their Kill/Take/Destroy/Dominate common philosophy of life.

As a result, impressions of such similarity from all of their Brute humanity's past (collected similar to computer files) form a culturally transmittable Brute Collective Unconscious Group Mind. Brute gods, made in their image, feature performing human-like wrongful and cruel acts--acts generated out of greed, jealousy, envy, spitefulness, and prideful emotional states. This is why any given group of Brutes could do things identical to all other Brutes, even though they did not know each other and despite living in different periods of history. To this day such brutish self-interest and greed causes obsessive fantasies of aggression on all aspects of the Tree.

EUROPEAN MALES' SUPERNATURAL "CASTLE": An impression from my research of primitive European males is that warring concepts filled up their mindsets about the Seen World while metaphorically using a "Castle in the air" as their Supernatural Unseen Realm place of residence. The reason for this setting is that an "Air Castle" is so easy to build; is untouchable compared to real things; is completely hidden and protected from attack; serves as an escape in which family members can take refuge; and, once at "home," one is refortified in the rules and in renewing alliance relationships. This "Air Castle" was said to be a Mansion of the Beyond as well as the entrance to the "Other World." It was like an enclosure or walled city designed to be a fortified stronghold of defense—the way in which the word "Castle" came to mean a fort. However, the *spotlighted feature of an "Air Castle" is that it has no real Base upon which it rests*--a feature which enhances the ability of its embattled Contingent Being "Lord" to ever be on the watch "all over." Over time, this "Lord" was viewed by one group of Europeans in a religious sense; by another in a "warrior" sense; and by a third in a combination. The nature of this "Lord" varied significantly as each European civilization started formulating concepts of Unseen realms. A recorded crystallization of these three groups was done by the ancient Greeks.

A dominant version among them is that the "Castle of Darkness," inhabited by a "Black Knight" became symbolic of the abode of Pluto (also called Hades and 'Dis Pater' by the Romans)-- the Greek god of the lower world. Pluto's palace is described as many-gated and crowded with innumerable guests. The plants sacred to him were the cypress and narcissus; black victims were sacrificed to him, as to all underworld powers; and he gradually evolved into a world of all things signifying riches--thereby being a personification of riches (the precious metals hidden in the earth). He ruled over the other powers below (a polytheistic conception of Supernatural Order) and over the dead--sternly and pitilessly. Yet, the spirits of the dead needed not to undergo only gloom and horror. Worthy spirits might go to a special section of Hades where all was blissful and happy. Subsequent evolving concepts of the "Lord" are varied and complex. For example, in the earliest sections of the Hebrew OT, the Black Knight or Satan is not an independent personage, nor even a maleficent being.

In C6 BC, Satan appears in the OT as an individual angel, subordinate to God, and thereafter gradually becomes the source of all evil as a result of disbelieving in God and acknowledging no law except of man--concepts affected by extra-national influences. Throughout European history people who possessed hateful thoughts and demonstrated evil deeds were thought to be possessed by demonic spirits, including the Devil. Thus, a summary and gross oversimplification is that on the one hand, the underlying symbolism of all mediaeval tales and legends about a castle owned by a 'wicked knight' who holds captive all who approach his domain, refers to the Lord of the Underworld. On the other hand, the *Castle of Light* is the 'redemption' aspect of this same image--symbolized in mediaeval art as causing the transcendent Soul.

The Castle's splendor was said to be the achieving of the inconceivable and materialization of the unexpected (the eternal essence of Supernatural riches). Still, spotlighted interlocked Religion and Warrior traits include: (1) since "Air Castles" have no base upon which they rest, Believers must have Faith and Believe, without questions allowed because "knowledge," leaders said, is the wisdom of these Faiths--and such Faith surpasses Reason; (2) there is the common disastrous error of saying: "my religion and/or warrior ways is/are the only true and wholly original one or, at least, is far better than all others"--"what I believe is the only right belief and what I do is the only correct practice"; (3) since "all outsiders" are heathen, pagan, 'primitive,' and savage, they must be suppressed or wiped out." Such beliefs for their dogma resemble the megalomania mindset of the African god Set--e.g. outrageous self-importance; the ultimate in self-conceit; and obsession/

compulsive infatuation of ones false, illusory, most petty and paltry egoistic self. Their Killing of others at the request of only the Catholic Church, according to Voltaire's calculations, was no less than 10 'heretics'. Other religions killings are unrecorded. jabaileymd.com

BRUTES "AIR CASTLE" FANTASIES: To understand the scope of "Air Castle" Supernatural Fantasies is to gain an idea of the Background of the Unconscious of "Killer" police. This first requires distinguishing these "Normal Variant" people from Natural Cosmos people and this is most easily done with those who feature the "God Module." That is the Background of ones Unconscious displaying in one developing into ones Highest (Divinity) Self. Its Foreground Icon Image is indicated by "Lifting" others while "Climbing". Two clues which distinguish Occult from Rational Thinking are that the Fantasy-minded: are first unable to look at an Occult concept without an opinion (e.g. like/dislike); second, their viewings of an Occult "Thing" are always associated with something else—e.g. a companion, group, object, memory. Primitive Europeans, by being Fantasy-minded, formed an Icon Image for the Background of their Unconscious—an Image about "Scarcity"--the focal point of their beginning on Earth. No doubt these stimulated imaginations about the Occult. Out of this came imaginary Contingent Beings prominent in the Foreground of their *Sensory Conscious* (the capacity to have subjective experiences and images). Times were so harsh in the beginning as to perhaps cause them to desperately cling onto anything that could help endure the Scarcity—like a drowning man grasping a 'straw' in hopes it will be a life-saver. Everyone was in a constant struggle for survival, featuring Kill/Take/Destroy/Dominate/Oppress methods. To acquire enough to endure or to maintain what they had accumulated generated fears as well as caused a lack of the "5Ss" (safety, security, sureness, strength, and stability). "What if" Fantasies were imagined in the Background of their Sensory Conscious about attackers, about their human nature inadequacies, about themselves as being successful or not, and about "Escapes" that would allow them to have some relief.

Probably most felt the best place to solve all of their mental turmoil problems was by acquiring, in the Foreground of their Sensory Conscious, the "5Ss". Out of this came Sensory Background Consciousness concepts, such as of gods, self-image, religion—each forming an Icon Images for the Foreground of their Unconscious minds, individually and collectively. These Fantasies were wildly elaborated on in the Foreground of their Sensory Consciousness—some being concepts of impossible objects without considering how they came into Being--some were about Beings arising out of Icon Images in particular. To elaborate, apart from mere survival, for the Warrior Brutes there was an overwhelming fear of being unsuccessful in the eyes of their peers and the deeper repressed fear of never wanting to appear to be weak and needy. Their self-image of Success was to acquire material things for *narcissistic* (grandiosity in fantasy with an excessive need for admiration) purposes. Scarcity has constituted Brutes Sensory Consciousness Background and works as a Complementary Equal with the ever active Warrior Indifference/Hate/Evil/Sadism (IHES) Complex mindset.

Normally, the *Supernatural Fantasy aspect of children recedes by 6 to 9 years.* But for those lacking the "5Ss" they persist. Regardless of their nature, ones or a group's Occult aspects thereafter have important implications for education, communication, and Humanity dealings. One reason for this is that the Occult's basis in mysteriousness conflicts with the Truth-Seeking spirit that characterizes the Natural World and to which only sound knowledge is acceptable. This spurs "Air Castle" people—whether as "Non-Rational" Logic, European Religion, or European Warrior roles to present their thoughts disguised as being Rationally Truthful, ignoring the fact that it makes no Natural World sense. Thus, they resort to preventing access to Knowledge (e.g. that of African Tradition); engage in confusion by using "big words" and theories that are facades when closely examined; and write ambiguous laws that are interpreted in favor of "Killer" Police. To elaborate on the "Dark Side" Fantasy oriented Occult mindsets, let us look at the False Self's primitive beginnings.

PERFECTING SUPERNATURAL "AIR CASTLES": European males' made-up "Air Castle" Supernatural World began in incomprehensible chaos--an unpredictable, unknowable flux which humans' minds are impotent to grasp--claiming to feature a realm of inexplicable miracles in a nonexistent Absolute—an absolute competing 'head-to-head' with the proven Natural Absolutes of Nature and the Spiritual Realm. Within capabilities of the wisest humans to know, such Cult (referring to Believers and their complex of beliefs) Supernatural organizations and its Thinking Structures were/are riddled with Supernatural "*Paradoxes*" (Greek, contrary to opinion or expectation)--a rhetoric term for a situation or statement that is obviously untrue or seems self-contradictory and even absurd in the realm of the Natural; in Natural Realms, a fuller understanding showing an unreal incongruity.

Historically, Cults have been a system of religious worship of a specific god, power, or object. It is led by a charismatic or powerful leader—an evil leader in total control of his followers—a leader using a persuasive amorphous dogma (e.g. the end of the world is imminent). To postulate a proposed Supernatural realm beyond Nature and beyond existence that is non-rational is to openly deny reason, dispense with definitions, proofs, arguments and, instead, completely rely on Belief and Faith. In contrast to the "Religious" teachings of African Tradition that conveys knowledge for self-cultivation toward a "Heaven Afterlife," Supernatural "Religions" or "Cults" have historically aimed to withhold such knowledge (apart from the fact that they do not know it). Concepts of their code are in a fog which permits no firm definition. Thus, they are simply approximate—and that makes elastic any rule of conduct. As a result, those Codes of a public nature (designed for followers or victims)—as in Legal Laws—enable those in charge to be able to hedge on any principle—to compromise on any value—or to take the middle of the road as part of generating self-interest unfair advantages and generating unfair disadvantages for victims. They say only Cult members will get all the benefits of whatever is desired while everyone else, including Cult doubters, are damned as evil.

Cult members are to *accept this without proof and without questioning*—and this is the standard for beginning ones "Normal Variant" philosophy of life. Such is clearly seen today by "justice" being differently applied to Black and White people for the same crimes. This lack of awareness of a solid Base for any type of Supernatural structure to rely on is the reason it is *essential for members to have Belief and Faith and clutch and cling to both*, regardless of presentations of overwhelming contrary evidence. If reasoning ability is an endowment of every human's birth, why should its use be opposed or excluded in the assessment and advancement of ones Selfhood? To program everyone to be essentially the same in what they think, feel, say, and do in actions/reactions and yet each declaring him/herself to be an Individualist is the way to maintain mind and behavior control over them.

Examples of such robotic behavior includes hating all who are not in the cult; doing what it takes to ensure all victims remain in poverty and bitter; stay isolated for fear that mingling will create the "wrong" relationships that threaten the solidarity of the cult; not consider any designated enemies as human but more like a replaceable machine; never consider outsiders as equals--either inferior or "superhuman"; never give credit to any outsider for any achievement but rather claim it, destroy it, or ridicule it. All who do not adhere to their god are called Heretics, pagan, witchcraft, or idolatrous religious systems while what Brutes venerate is claimed to have magical or Supernatural potency.

There is no such thing as discussing in order to gain understanding. Anyone not agreeing with them is ostracized or crushed or "wiped out." Wherever goes the opposition, including their feigned friends, cult troops follow close behind. This (among others) make Cult members amoral and robot-like. From such a standard of being Evil, the 'Good Life' is defined as being outside oneself, orchestrated by the leader. Manners and considering others are not necessary; being ill-mannered and being wasteful of what other people really need are displays of power. These "dos/don'ts" are socialized into them from birth. Harsh punishments (e.g. isolation from the Cult) come for disobeying the standards assigned to these Contingent Beings. Those who best "follow the leader" are promoted.

SUPERNATURAL EARLY CULT LEADERS: Leaders of "Air Castle" cults of primitive European times were of individual warrior groups who devised gods made in their own image. The inchoate evolution or "seed" stage of the resultant European Warrior/Religion was characterized by chimera type chaos. Such a chimera in Greek mythology is the fire-breathing female contingent monster represented as a composite of a lion, goat, and serpent. Similarly, chimerical or wildly fantastic imagination fashioned the European Supernatural "seed" giving rise to the "roots" displays of all thoughts, deeds, expressions, and passions of the African god Set type. Thus, from this rough unordered mass of things emerged "Trunk/Vine, Branches, Leaves, and Fruit" creations for the in-group to rise and all out-groups to fall from having their societal and personal order blotted out and their light extinguished. Gradually, warrior groups joined forces and selected a leader from among the existing leaders. Despite the fractionation of the Warrior/Religion Supernatural, the theme common to all sub-sects of each cult force was of a military organizational level. The Totem Pole is a useful way to think of the military type Chain of Command as well as how those in-forces affect outsiders.

A model of this were the Aryans of the grasslands of Eastern Europe who set up a Patriarchal (literally "the rule of the fathers") society as warring semi-nomads. Intertribal warfare was an everyday occurrence. However, *fighting would stop temporarily in order to form alliances with their enemies* whenever there were threats from non-Aryan peoples—ancestors of today's "*Civility Competition.*" They were in full force at least by 2000 BC when they started migrating "everywhere," engaging in Kill/Take/Destroy of the peaceful people along the way, and then settling in Iran, Mesopotamia, Persia, Asia Minor, Greece, Rome, Germany, Britain, and India. The Aryans set up caste systems consisting of priest, warriors, kings, traders, farmers, laborers, artisans, and servants (who were forbidden to mix with the higher castes). Their superiority in making and using tools for war gave them a "sinful pride" consciousness of themselves. Aryan concepts were the source behind racism, sadism, criminality, sexism, an immoral or amoral nature, and the hypocritical way of life that has characterized European manhood and that has afflicted peaceful Colored peoples of the world.

All of these persisted within the ancient Greeks who, in turn, formally elaborated upon them and then spread them throughout the Western world--best seen among the Medieval Knights and European Christian Crusaders. Starting in 1304 nothing gave Europeans a sense of power like possessing the GUN (any mechanical device used to Kill/Take/Destroy)--displayed by Renaissance Europeans setting sail around the world and devastating peaceful cultures. The gun allowed them to take whatever they wanted from any people in the world and they became drunk with Supernatural power—a power providing them with "sick" pleasures momentarily. Despite their GUN-generated Superiority Complex, their embedded sense of an Inferiority Complex remains only incompletely repressed and continues to manifest in "weird" ways outside their awareness.

SUPERNATURAL CULT LEADERS' NONRATIONAL THINKING: What continues to amaze me is that daily things European males do as major patterns in their lives typically lack any discussion or even mention in available European literature. Perhaps this is what keeps the public blind to the obvious. Of concern here is their "Air Castle" Supernatural "Non-Rational" thinking which has been practiced since the time of primitive European Warriors but only crystalized by Hobbes in his Leviathan, alluding to Job (41, I-34) in designating the 'mortal god'. I find the usual European confusion and conflicts—pertaining to what Hobbes said/wrote as well as who writes about Hobbes conveyed. Yet, there is agreement Hobbes spoke of God as the sovereign in a state "*Sovereign*" (Latin, Super, 'above') as in superior. At one time Hobbes considered God was not immaterial, as African Tradition says. According to Coleman (Political Research Quarterly, 1998), Hobbes said Nature is the Art whereby God hath made and governs the world—and all of this is by the art of man. Relying on the Old Testament's borrowing of the Ancient Egyptians' mythological story concerning Khnum, the potter-god who fashioned men and all living creatures out of clay, Hobbes said God made man as "*automata*" (machines) and the world is God's artifact (Gen. 1, 2,5, 17, 21-5). Furthermore, the Leviathan state is the product of artifice ('to put together') and derived from man who is both 'the Matter thereof and Artificer (maker). Thus, God is an artifact and thus man's power rivals those of God as a maker. Hobbes added, drawing support from the European Bible, that Nature is arti-factual, real, and radically contingent but without intelligibility.

It seems what Hobbes advocated as "the State" is what I call the Supernatural "Air Castle" realm. Then the Supernatural state was expressed in terms of a machine—a mechanization taking reason out of its earthly domain—a mechanization according a higher, abstract status which supersedes human reason--a mechanization completing the European concept of the mechanization of the anthropological image of man. From a European perspective, such reasoning developed a sophisticated vision for handling difficulties involved in constructing and securing fragile and inherently contingent political orders, whether they be domestic or international. The reason for all of this was for security: "you subordinate your actions to our judgment of what is necessary, and we promise to keep you safe' (Bartmanski *J. Sociology, 2014*). In short, the origins of "the state" (i.e. the Supernatural "Air Castle") are earthly fantasies and yet the effects of "the state" are heavenly because 'visible stuff' makes sense only on the basis of 'invisible discourses'. When "the State"--the Leviathan--notion became an entrenched practice, Hobbes believed human reason gave way to procedurally bound reason. In other words, his anomalous account of the transcendental Supernatural is conceived as the state which stands above and beyond Natural Cosmos' human reason. Such has been explained by saying the transformation of human reason into Supernatural stately reason is accompanied by a change in the way in which reason is understood.

Hobbes stated (1651) there are *phantasms*, or images ('decaying senses') remaining when the physiological motions of sensation cease. Also, there is *Compound Imagination* which creates novel images by rearranging old ones as a result of ideas sticking together and pulling each other into the mind. Hume (1739) elaborated by saying this was a powerful principle for explaining many mental operations—giving European 'thinkers' a new metaphorical landscape to describe the human reason that involves an examination into the human soul. By "the State" being formed mechanically meant mechanization took reason out of its earthly domain into a higher, abstract status superseding mere human reason. This enabled the vision to construct, secure, and otherwise handle fragile and inherently contingent political orders. Use of this Non-Reason gave superior power and control without the need to follow Natural Realm Logic. In short, "the state" (i.e. the Supernatural "Air Castle") originated by earthly fantasies while its effects are heavenly because 'visible stuff' makes sense only on the basis of 'invisible discourses'.

SUPERNATURAL "AIR CASTLE" MEMBERS: "*Individualism*" is a Supernatural concept which says each of its members is an independent, sovereign entity who possesses an Inalienable right to his own life—a right derived from his nature—a right that cannot be taken away, suspended, infringed, restricted, or violated at any time for any reason. In practice, "Individualism" means: "I'll do as I please to acquire unfair advantages while ensuring unfair disadvantages for those unlike me." Such does not apply to European females or any out-group. Furthermore, it is opposite to *Real Self Consciousness*—i.e. the faculty of perceiving what exists in reality—a something without anything preceding it and without any alternative to it. Their Supernatural standard code of ethics—their philosophy of life—is whatever the Brute leaders say, no matter how deep, wide, or high it goes into the Indifferent/Hateful/Evil/Sadistic (IHES) Complex. It basically concerns whatever promotes self-interest—and making no effort to engage in *Morals* (whatever elevates human conduct to enhance the Cosmic Organism). With regard to the Natural World, cult members exhibit *Moral Cowardice*—i.e. fear of upholding the good because it is good and fear of opposing the evil because it is evil or because "everybody" is doing it. For some strange reason they feel the need to put up a façade of being open to Moral and, in fact, some use Supernatural religious attachments to serve as their moral justifications.

Hence, they rest their case on Faith, which means that since there are no rational arguments to support their position against freedom, justice, property, and individual rights, they concede that reason is on the side of their enemies. By them claiming to perceive what does not exist means that what they possess is not part of their Consciousness and instead is Supernatural. It is essential to *control people's minds to hold Faith superior to Reason.* Then they are fed *Dogma* (blind faith deceptively used as a short-cut to knowledge)—a set of beliefs accepted on Faith—i.e. without rational justification or against rational evidence. This includes saying what their God is not—never what it is concerning coming into Being. All identifications consist of negating—God is that which no human mind can know—God is a non-man; heaven is non-earth; soul is non-body; virtue is non-profit. These are not acts of defining but of wiping out some of what is not present.

When people resort to Faith, the "all-or-none" game is played: "since my mind is not omniscient then I should not use it and be a Zombie; since my mind is fallible, not using it will make it infallible." An error made from a mental struggle is infinitely better (because it can be corrected) than 22 pieces of Dogma accepted on Faith and believed in (because there is no way to distinguish truth from what SEEMS true, based upon what some "authority" says). They do not believe in promoting freedom for outsiders and instead trick people out of freedom; cheat them into injustice; fool them into staying within the status quo; con outsiders out of their rights.

"AIR CASTLE" SUPERNATURAL CULTS: The etymology of the C17 Indo-European word "*Cult*" and its application to groups demonstrates its meaning of "to move around." Its 'moving around' is in the sense of having a number of mutually exclusive characterizations largely dependent on the context in which the word is used. Originally, among primitive Europeans it paid homage to some power (a god or person) considered Supernatural—leading to external but secret rites and ceremonies performed in its honor. Since the object of a cult is not necessarily about a god, it is typically deemed distinct from religion's theological aspects. More often, the aim is to fashion a radiated social power which can be received and embraced through proper ceremonies--but only by those fitted for it. Such powers could be ascribed to almost anything having assumed prominence in a people's life. Around that, a particular doctrine is designed, based upon certain assumed attributes of their selected Supernatural power and emphasizing some philosophical "needy wants" not met otherwise. An ancient example was the Greek cult of Dionysus.

Modern examples are primarily non-religious *"Air Castle" Cults* with assumed forms, symbols, and a dogma—all resting on an ancient "Non-rational" pagan worship Base. Yet, "Air Castle" Cults have always had external and superficial resemblances to certain established European religious aspects—as in adopting a similarity in terminology but giving it new content and meaning. The largest cults have self-interest political and economic concomitants. Of particular concern here are the self-designated "White Race" cult. Since all humans are part of ones species, such a designation is not a natural but simply represents a historical category. It is like a private club with typical "Conditional" codes—as in granting privileges to selected people in return for obedience to its rules.

The rules of White cults do not require all members be strong advocates of White supremacy but merely that they defer to the prejudices of other cult members. The need to maintain racial solidarity imposes a stifling conformity on Whites—inside and outside the cult--on any subject touching even remotely on 'race.' Membership solidarity absolutely demands all those who look White are, whatever their complaints or reservations, foundational loyalty to the cult. Features of modern "Air Castle" Cults—which interlock and overlap with European religious cults—are explained because their philosophy of life came out of the same primitive European Warrior womb.

Some features include: (1) sharp deviations from and strong rejection of Natural Cosmos Reality and Truth as laid out by Ancient Africans; (2) cult domination by a Contingent Being imbued with its leaders standards, filters, guides, and measures and 'given voice to' by a tiny number of secretly-living human General and Admiral leaders; (3) leaders trickling their orders down the organizational Military Ladder to the Lieutenants; (4) the top charismatic leader, always well hidden, proclaiming himself to be a divine power while relaying orders to the highly charismatic leaders sprinkled throughout this chain-of-command who, in turn, claim to the "Troops" that they also have special access to the Contingent Being; (5) the cult's comprehensive ideology exacting total commitment from its followers, including the commitment of time, energy, effort, money, and the "attitude" (e.g. superiority and hatred of all outsiders); (6) excessive aggressiveness in efforts to maintain conformity of all for purposes of mind control + using manipulative techniques of persuasion (particularly resorting to their fears), as opposed to conversions, in recruiting new members; (7) entertaining no other set of beliefs outside cult dogma, for all others are deemed erroneous and "evil"; (8) having IHES beliefs represent their personal identity and meaning—both nonnegotiable since they declare that they alone have access to the best of life; (9) powering IHES beliefs as links between ideas and actions while being driven by those links; and (10) member benefits accruing as intensive network support + comprehensive, compelling 'Air Castle' views of the world + means of relieving the frustrations and anxieties of modern life by viciously showing their superiority over non-cult members.

Supernatural "Air Castle" Cults' charismatic leadership is based upon Satanism, so as to transcend all laws and customs unlike its own standards + having an identity and character resting on the negation and inversion of what pertains to the Natural Cosmos. In short, it is a leadership declaring it is the law, above which there is no other--a leadership less than one of inherent talents but instead is a complex relational and situational matter between leaders and followers.

"AIR CASTLE" SUPERNATURAL "TROOPS": In contrast to the cult members, the "Troops" are heterogeneous (different kinds). Some are dissimilar from the rest with respect to their desire, type, quality, sort, and readiness to hate people of unlike-kind—including those who are not particularly biased or prejudiced. Some discover that in 'playing out' their deeply held IHES beliefs to their logical conclusions is to be certain that it is about delusions--amoral, dishonorableness, non-Caring relationships, arrogance, greed, and violence. To some extent this may bother a few. Yet, Cult Success depends on the "Troops" granting that their leaders possess extraordinary gifts. Such intimidation is brought to bear on those not fully with the program as to ensure what reigns is that at crunch time" the entire cult will come together in "*Alliances*" ("to acquire allies"). This means that formed among these "Individualists" is regularized connections entered into for mutual benefit.

Anyone challenging the leaders' claims or reluctant to go along are usually isolated, have financial contributions with-held, expelled, or killed. This is where "*Civility*" and the expression: "*Strange bed-fellows*" apply because everybody is afraid, nobody trusts anybody and nobody is trustworthy even though everybody is friendly. The cult's intent is to *be in charge of all External World aspects of people's lives* while touching on and controlling every fact of the adherents' lives throughout the Military Ladder. Displayed to both "Troops" and victims is constant, proven intimidating 'take-down' power, so widely and strategically located as to defy accountability + an army of law-enforcement personnel to dominate all teaching, business, media, and political systems.

Assignments are then given out. Some stir up trouble between members of the feigned enemies of the cult and supplying those fractionated feigned enemies with guns and drugs so they can be at war with each other. Some generate all sorts of stereotypical media images to justify the cult's position—being ever careful never to say anything good about the feigned enemy and, in fact, always commenting on how "savage" they are. This is because the cult's enmity is rage ever watching the opportunity for revenge—an opportunity that comes when the designated enemy's back is to the wall. These cruel and unrelenting enemies leave their victims no choices other than brave resistance or the most abject submission.

SUPERNATURAL "AIR CASTLE" ORGANIZATION: Considering that the European "Air Castle" Supernatural World was originated by warring primitive Europeans and that it is presently run to carry out warring duties, it can be inferred that its structure was, and remains, organized in military style. To get an idea of what this is like, the USA military chain of command starts with the President being in charge of the Army, Navy, and Air Force. Their ultimate command, designed to influence thoughts and actions of each military personnel positioned on each rung of the Military Ladder, is given to the Generals and Admirals in charge. They then trickle down those orders to lower ranking Generals and Admirals who, in turn, pass the orders down to Colonels, Captains, and so on down to those of the lowest ranks, the "Troops." The *Enemy* is any who are not part of the "Air Castle" cult and who possesses something desired by the cult. At each step on this Military Ladder the President's orders are carried out in how to Kill/Take/Destroy the "enemy."

The Supernatural "President" is a group of Satanists--called by many names--who directly fight the powers of the Spiritual God; oppose all manifestations of the Spiritual Elements by doing the opposite; and rule with vehement terror with bragging and with a swagger. Their slogans are "Might is Right"—"Might till Right"—"Might is the measure of Right"--"Might by Sleight"—and "Might over-cometh Right." They see the reason of the strongest as always winning and that justice is determined by the interest of the strongest. There is no understanding of Natural World Humanity.

Rules (C12 straight stick, pattern) contribute to the organization and control of a group and their systems and activities. The rule makers' imagination 'runs wild' inside the "Air Castle" of their Supernatural world to such an extent that they become "legends in their own minds" while assuming the roles of "little gods." By operating out of their Brute Brains, their Selfhood is orientated to Indifference, Hate, and Evil expressions which display in contrasting directions. First, their own way of life comes out of a mindset of hostility while not living up to any rules themselves. In other words, the rules are that there are no rules--and Fetters reign supreme. Second, they focus on dominating others by having rigid rules for the "Troops" designed to make them the same and by holding victims to lofty and actually unattainable standards. This leadership arrogance comes from two things.

First is the power of the GUN, several of which every member possesses and is never without, for this is their signature of power and their only personal power. The collective GUN of fellow in-group members is how they rose to world power and how they generated unfair benefits for all in their cult. Furthermore, that power carries an intimidation factor of infinite magnitude because it is historically backed by untold past atrocities. Second is their *Network System*—a C16 word pertaining, for the most part, to the joining of cult member forces to offset what is deemed to be unfriendly attitudes or encroachment—whether real, distorted, or fantasized. To elaborate, since the beginning of their existence on Earth, Europeans have always been a warring and fearful people.

For example, the Aryans (a group of tribes sharing a common language but not being of the same racial stock) constantly fought each other. However, they would pause and join forces--called an *Alliance* ("to acquire allies" whereby regularized connections are entered into for mutual benefit)--when faced with an assumed—real or not--common designated "enemy." Closely associated are *Liaisons* ("a binding together") whereby contacts are maintained between individuals in order to ensure concerted action. Alliance Networking is done both for mutual support and as a rallying cry to attack others out of envy and/or greed. Fears of retaliation are a major reason they must maintain oppression. This European pattern is seen to this day in every aspect of life--and is most obvious in politics (e.g. Republicans). Without the GUN and Networking, cult members are unable to back up their self-claimed "Superiority" in any area—making for a chronic inadequacy sense. For this reason, their "tough guy" tyrant attitude and swagger always carries an unspoken and highly guarded sense of insecurity, sprouting with the fear that "I might not have what it takes to fairly compete". Thus, leaders from Generals down to Lieutenants are on hyper-alert to any danger coming from any direction by competitors within the cult, by competitors outside the cult, and/or from victims.

"SEED" SUPERSTITIONS FOR SUPERNATURAL "ROOTS": So long as darkness has existed in contrast to light, so long as moonlight, the mountain cave, the waterfall, and the forest have interested human beings—is just how long "Seed" Superstitions of the Unseen have prevailed. My three part definition of *Superstition* is: First, there must be the believing in a "Thing(s)" capable of inspiring, or has inspired, "awe"—meaning one perceives indescribable forces from unknown sources to which one surrenders ones mind. Associated with this surrender is a sudden loss of all meaning for whatever concerns reality. Second, a chronic mindset of "Awe" lessens ones awareness of things "doable" in reality and that is replaced by being less and less skeptical about things that cannot be done in the Supernatural. Third, the products from being chronically "Awed" and their consequences all lack correspondence with reality. And that makes *products of "Awe," Superstitions—and consequences of "Awe's" products Supernatural.* Both are what give rise to the three main "Air Castle" Supernatural "Roots"--Warriors, Religion, and Logic (i.e. non-rational and thus "Para-Logic" or "Pseudo-Logic").

Primitive peoples' formed such "Seed" Superstitions from assumed empirically (numinous) unverifiable gods residing in their Unseen World. Perhaps originally, the implication was that the elements of Nature--such as the sun and moon, the planets and thunder--were personified and deified; that certain metals or herbs were accredited with Supernatural powers; that charms, amulets, certain symbols and signs possess prophetic meanings. Out of this came such features of Superstitions as: (1) a belief, disposition, and tendency to ascribe phenomena which admit of a natural explanation but, instead, are ascribed to occult or Supernatural causes; (2) the making up of Supernatural things and then using Magical Thinking converts it into an unreal reality; (3) switching things from the Supernatural world into the Natural world—or vice versa—and then acting on it in a manner contrary for the intent of its original design—an instance of "Inside-Out" thinking—thoughts opposite to Natural World Logic.

Once Superstition patterns are established, they are of a *Conditioned Reflex* nature—meaning fear, terror, or other emotions may compel one to believe in what one cannot prove or disprove to the satisfaction of ones senses. Such Superstitious beliefs--fixated by the encroachment of Faith on the rights of reason and knowledge--are maintained because one is unconscious of the narrow range of ones own properly interpreted experiences in the Natural World. Resultant involuntarily and non-rationally done inferences automatically lead them into Superstitions and beliefs in the Supernatural.

Their imprint on the mind may seem superficial but it is actually indelible to the point of being totally resistant to Supernatural Thoughts educated out of them, no matter how utterly ones own reason may reject them (since they believe Supernatural reigns). Superstitions cannot be described as an innocent mistake for it is a definite willful belief, and this is without shame. They are beliefs in what is not only contrary to the laws of Nature as generally accepted, but also contrary to experience and to common sense in the Natural world. Because Superstitions and Supernatural things are part of "Air Castles," they must be cling to because the idea of letting go of them means falling through a bottomless pit. So, their clinging is done in the face of contrary evidence.

Psychologically, this process is based upon the reality of Europeans being a Fear-Based people, although curiosity, awe, and reverence also enter into it. Verification of this comes from the fact that their imaginations of their primitive beginnings have kindled suspicions up to the present (as seen on television, in movies, etc.) of the existence of Supernatural Beings--gods or devils, giants and werewolves, hobgoblins and gnomes, spirits and genii, aliens, and the like--in order to explain influences and actions of their daily lives. None of this acquired "second nature" has changed to this day, as evidenced by most people today still believing in the existence of invisible Beings that control and regulate human life. This can be to the extent of them as integral components involved in guiding decisions and shaping preferences—and thus fundamental to the human experience. These are some reasons I believe Europeans will never change their Superstitious Beliefs and Supernatural Faiths, no matter how destructive to themselves and to humankind. jabaileymd.com

EUROPEANS' SUPERNATURAL REALM DOGMA: An *Ideology* is a set of world-view Rules and Laws aimed at establishing or maintaining a certain social system for long term in a consistent state of unity and integration. At its core is a *"Dogma"* (1638)--an authoritative opinions of doctrines of fixed "SEEMS right" beliefs regarding what the cult considers unalterable and packaged in a ritual procedure (i.e. outward manifestations of the Beliefs in the dogma which give meaning to the performance). Both the Ideology and Dogma enable the leaders to project the future and choose their actions accordingly. Dogmas based upon Supernatural Concepts are the ultimate in "Inside-Out" Thinking. Yet, cult members' speck of nagging doubt about being absolutely right drives them to want to convert everyone into that same "Inside-Out" Thinking under the concept that "the many is what makes for right." Even though racists beliefs are residua of fantasies indifferent to truth, an ethnocentric level of psychological development in potential and actual cult members reinforces this rigidity. For this reason, cult leaders cunning appeals to these 'normal' people to *accept delusions and illusions of dogmas leading into and embracing* Supernatural phenomena are typically successful. This is because *the only requirement is for those presentations to not clash with any held Belief or threaten any of those candidates concepts of: "For me or my well-being--or against me"* System of Values.

Meanwhile, in order to control the "Troops," an anti-ideology approach is used for the purpose of shrinking their minds to the range of the "here and now". This is without regard to the past or future, emphasizing being without memory so that contradictions cannot be detected or questioned and so that errors or disasters can be blamed on the victims. The idea is to control the minds of victims so as to keep them impotent, in a state of futility, be inconsistent, and stay superficial. The desired effect is for the realities of life experiences of people in subordinate groups is to be seen by blind eyes and to fall upon deaf ears as a result of the beliefs of the socially dominant group being considered more valid. Such controls are by splitting humans in two— setting the Soul or the Sensory Consciousness against the body as well as ones moral values against ones own interest. This is the process of converting one into "Inside-Out" thinking. Whatever is then sensed and felt by in-group members thereafter "SEEMs" to be reality. These are the drivers of those emotions which power "Hate Crimes" committed out of racial, religious, or sexual prejudices and beliefs of "doing good."

SUPERNATURAL "AIR CASTLE" ENEMIES: From the time of their appearance on Earth 200,000 years ago Africans, who gave rise to all Colored People, have been a peaceful people. Thus, Europeans have no "natural race" enemies. But because Europeans are warriors and not thinkers and not self-reliant, they feign enemies whom they can make into "Scapegoats". This is made into a reality by having specialized in Kill/Take/Destroy/Dominate measures by means of the GUN and an eagerness to use it. "*Scapegoat*" (C16, escape + goat) has reference to the European Bible's ritual of the Day of Atonement (Leviticus 16) where one he-goat was selected for sacrifice and a second-he was chosen to be sent alive into a hard and rough place in the wilderness of jagged rocks--symbolically bearing the sins of the people ('escaping' death). The purpose was to carry the senders' sins away and thereby relieve those senders of the community of further responsibility. In other words, Scapegoats are those made to falsely bear the resentful or frustrated guilty party's blame—a blame covering the guilty party's "Dark Side" and its rage. Black People are typically used as innocent victims—i.e. objects of the *Projections* of Europeans who blame them for their own defects and difficulties and then try to wipe out their own "Dark Side" by killing or suppressing these victims.

Scapegoat tactics serve as a defense mechanism + destroys the Selfhoods of victims receiving Brutes' displaced aggression + bring misery to countless millions of people throughout the world at any given time. The point of Scapegoat tactics is to be a deliberate form of propaganda whose aim is to show: "How great I/We are and how bad 'those people' are" so as to induce outsiders to accept the scapegoat as such a terrible people. Meanwhile, the objective is re-make non-Brute victims into having a Brute mindset in order to generate competition against them and have them be as miserable as are all Brutes. In the setting of Brutes Supernatural ideology, the anti-ideology approach is used on Black victims so as to keep them disarmed and groping around. Then it becomes a challenge to see if they can beat down their newly created opposition to such an extent as for the victims to lose their spirit to retaliate. This was initially done by treating Enslaved Africans as chattel.

Yet, what is being done by Brutes is never acknowledged by them and its methods are constantly switched around to suit the Brutes' purpose of the moment, as is typical of Europeans' ways to keep producing Change passed off as newer and better. Part of the ideology is that violence is good in that those who feel free to display it constitute an elite who are fit to lead and able to resist corruption by forces of good. For Brutes with Low Self-Esteem, this is attractive for it is therapeutic in itself. By making Black People a hiding place for their envious and hostile emotions is the "*Repressive*" means to keep Brutes from seeing it in themselves. However, what is Repressed remains as active as ever but without the blamer's brain "check and balancers" to serve as restraints or constraints. The 'bottom line' is that Brutes' transfer of their hatred is an obvious indicator that they hate themselves and that to retain all of their hate within is far too disturbing. The fact that attackers are in the wrong battle, at the wrong place, fighting the wrong thing, at the wrong time, and with the wrong enemy clearly indicates the problem is within these Brutes. Their IHES tactics used to put others down and keep them down are Brutes only way to feel superior. This occurs most obviously when Whites are searching for the causes of their self-created troubles and, to avoid self-blame, they project the cause onto Black people and ride that Big Lie for exploitative power purposes.

For example, by using ridiculous excuses and altering statistical data to falsely justify "Black people are criminals and White people are not" makes it okay for Whites to continue their evil and criminal actions. A truism for victims to realize is that in order to have an enemy, one must be "Somebody". Black People have historically always been the top "Somebodies" of Humankind. It is typical for the extremely envious to attack those at the top. Such is seen throughout the Animal Kingdom--e.g. the young buck challenging the adult buck for rights to females. What spotlights a subculture of feigned enemies for excessive attacks are those—like "Street" Black youth--who remain more manly, produce more beneficial achievements despite being overwhelming oppressed, and who seem to travel on a secret and mysterious path. Such places a floodlight on the flaws, inadequacies, limitations, and unhappiness of cult members which makes it impossible for them to avoid seeing. The victims know the victors fail to recognize that the real enemy is within the victor's hearts and souls.

By all of this contradicting cult members self-declared self-image pertaining to being "legends in their own minds," an accelerated reactionary process is set-off (e.g. the 'war on drugs'), consisting of *Fear-Feigning* by the cult's leaders. Next, Generals down to Lieutenants excite the "Troops" to adopt an attitude of marching to war against the "weakly invented enemies" so as to take unfair advantage of them—hoping to increase the public's hatred of the victims. This is the signal for the "Troops" to hype these Supernatural enemies as not only being the ones who are doing the hating but who also desire to injure the cult—making that enemy personally hostile. Sham justification comes from "Troops" discerning "weird" faults expressed as slander—faults which actually represent the cult's own self-hated traits—"Dark Side" cult faults that must be Projected onto the feigned enemies.

These faults are then hyped by advertising the feigned enemies as being 'hostile' foes in the sense of: *Opponents* (upholding opposite views to what the cult deems to be 'right'); *Antagonistic* (engaged in actual struggles influenced by animosity); *Adversaries* (hostile and bitterly arrayed against the cult); *Rivals* (one striving to win the same goal at the same time as the cult); and *Competitors* (trying to get back what the cult stole).

"AIR CASTLE" LEADERS MIND CONTROL GOALS: By being the primary objective of Brutes, including Satanists, the control of the public's mind means putting boundaries on the boundless—particularly by converting Unconditional Love to Conditional Love. As a deceptive "SEEMS" right maneuver they imply that their Supernatural Bible speaking of Conditional Love is the same as Unconditional Love. For the naïve to believe this subtle deception is to accept the Europeans' Bible of antifeminism, of be good Slaves to your Master, of "Be Meek," of "Turn the other cheek" every time you are struck. The explanations given by Brutes make it SEEM right to do these things. But these, and countless other advantages given the Brute leaders are nowhere to be found in the Ancient African Bible—the true Word of God and the Bible from which all other Bibles of the world derived. To believe these deceptions makes it SEEM okay to accept and abide by Brutes' established Rules around those Spiritual and Free Mind boundaries so as to move into a bottomless pit where all those in that status quo will remain suppressed forever. This status quo ensures victims will never know the truth, as in Socrates' Allegory of the Cave (Bailey, Teaching Black Youth p30).

An Allegory is an extended metaphor whereby a story is told in symbolic terms—i.e. a figurative description where all the persons and events stand as Symbols of something else. Note in this story how minds have had their attention misdirected away from Reality so as to create *uncertainty and confusion* sufficient to persuade those involved that they are witnessing Reality. Believers then enter the realm of Delusions. This story starts with prisoners chained in an underground cave and with their heads fixed in a straight ahead position. Thus, they can only see shadows cast on the wall in front of them and are unaware that between their backs and the fire are puppets, moved by a puppeteer along a walkway, that cause shadows of Reality outside the cave--the reverse of Truth. Being born into this situation and knowing nothing else, the prisoners are certain the shadows constitute "Truth" (i.e. delusions). While some are being dragged out of the cave in order to face Reality, they do so with resistance shown by their kicking and screaming. Once outside the cave they gradually acclimate by seeing more and more real things around them and by learning to distinguish the reality of the sun from the shadows it causes. They then declare shadows in the cave to be unreal. Upon re-entering the cave to inform the still chained prisoners what is Reality, they awaken to no longer being accustomed to the darkness or what is presented as "Real" in it. Also, the chained prisoners ridicule comments of the outside world reality. They fight against leaving their familiar darkness for fear of the unknown in the sunlight and not being able to cope.

Mind Control is needed to keep the in-group together and fearful from venturing outside the circle to get involved with other people. The Power Elite are greatly afraid that if different races mingle they will discover more similarities among each other than there are differences. Mind Control essentially shuts down victims' creativity, but not the Supernatural creations of the cult "Troops". Mind Control is a constant attack on ones Self-Esteem because of having to check the rules before venturing out. Control is needed to dominate and exploit scapegoats. The way to have the victim do this is by creating psychic trauma in the victim and thus boundaries are automatically self-inflicted.

Propaganda ("a forced generation") is a mind control tool to make Brutes doctrine, opinions, beliefs, creed, policy or practices known and accepted for ulterior manipulation purposes. When people get to the point they do not know what to do next, this is when Brutes move in for the take-over of all that is important to them and the people. The confusion Brutes deliberately create is enlarged by stirring up so much disharmony, fear, and mental difficulty as to cause *Illusions* (seeing what is not there and not seeing what is there); *Delusions* (believing what is not real and not believing what is real); and misinterpretations. The intention is for the people to no longer be sure of anything they previously thought they knew. Brutes are successful when victims are in a state of such frustration from so many ridiculous contradictions that people do not know where to start unraveling the mess.

The confused will then either say: "I don't want to think about it" or the resultant sense of overwhelming confusion and despair ease one into looking for guidance from anyone, even oppressors. Thus, they either figure out an "okay" something to satisfy their confusion by "What SEEMS right" or accept what others say about it--others who have put boundaries on Reality out of ignorance or by intent. What mind controllers then do is to present such reconciling ambivalent attitudes with highly abstracted (what is taken out of physical aspects) formulations that opponents simply "give-in" and allow themselves to be led. Once that happens, Brutes fill up the people's minds with "Trinkets and Trivia" and thereby prevent people from thinking about the benefits they are no longer getting. Some say Gehenna is a place or state of torment or suffering for condemned sinners only. The reason for doing this was to serve as a powerful mind control agent of the people.

It features a Devil, a Hell, and a Supernatural God. Under false notions of having the victims accepting these as simply beliefs, Brutes effectively control non-Thinking, gullible, and naive people—themselves conditioned by promises of Conditional Love for conformity. What has been and remains devastating for Black People is to embrace anything within Europeans' Supernatural (intended for Mind Control) and disregard the Spiritual and Metaphysical aspects of African Tradition (intended for Harmony, Unity, and paths to reach the Heaven Afterlife). This is the reason why the teaching of Ancient African Philosophy must disregard absolutely any and everything of a European nature, even European definitions of words in dictionaries and elsewhere.

SUMMARY

A "*Path*" originally meant a way from one land to another. As applied here, the path to violence starts from a human newborn Real state and at some point in the future the individual decides to convert to a False Self. What is exchanged during this conversion is the *Spiritual Elements*—Unconditional Love, Truth, Reality, and the Natural—which *are the only absolute "solids" in the Cosmos* over to what SEEMS solid, Things in the Earth World. By remaining on the Real Self path, one has the capability to develop sound coherent African Tradition type logical thinking because it is mathematically based and allows the use of Inferences to bridge a path from the Known to the Un-Known by means of the Law of Sympathy. When used in the Spiritual Realm they constitute a Base that is consistent, permanent, stationary, and unchanging because its patterns/elements underlie all natural events on any plane of existence in the Cosmos. This is the foundation of Integrity in African Tradition. However, to choose to be a False Self means one does not know who one is—and thereby operates out of a fantasy type imaginary realm that generates delusions (believing what is not real and not believing what is real). *False Self* (Ego) people—those choosing to be who they are not—give up the Immaterial Absolute Source from which their essence for life and their wisdom for living derives.

Instead, they substitute a Material realm under the illusion that it is 'solid.' This means they cannot follow a coherent logical way of thinking because they have no solid or stable base—no Spiritual Elements Base—no 'ground of Being'--from which to start. Even the most concrete material thing is in constant change since all Matter is fashioned from indivisible particles of vibrating energy known as *Quanta*. Concrete matter only appears solid because of the electrical charges of the atoms that repel one another. Thus, a False Self person has distorted or unrealistic images of all sorts of things--about various groups of people—and about oneself (e.g. who one is and who one would like to be)—based upon whether they are "For Me or Against Me." This Delusional Mind is greatly contributed to and cultivated by Socialization from ones subculture and culture—as in teaching children about monsters, myths, and hate-filled propaganda (e.g. against Black People or Jews). All of this builds on a natural human imagery process that eventually heads to violence.

Since their appearance on earth European males have been the background of world violence and have continued that pattern to the present. They are like the "Disaster Star" whose display is Indifference/Hate/Evil/Sadism (IHES) complex packaged in different forms. Those forms give off a "Disaster Halo" which have been imitated by certain of their Colored People victims throughout history. This is because Violent Causes produce Violent Effects and Violent Effects have Violent Consequences. Since violence begets violence, Europeans have remained violently dominant because of their eagerness to kill, backed up by the actuality Kill/Take/Destroy/Dominate/Oppress throughout their history. This dominance reached new heights when they developed the GUN invented by the Arabs in 1304 and since have been frantic is pursuing more powerful, faster working, and bigger guns which enabled them to come to world dominance. Thus, they engage in violence because of the adventure and excitement of it—because they can be above the rules they set up for others to follow—and because they can engage their Lower Brute Self nature. They get away with it because they are backed up by fellow European Networks which control all institutions of life. They are steeped in Capitalism—a social system based on the recognition of individual rights, including property rights, in which all property is privately owned. The only task of the government is to protect individuals from physical-force.

Colored Peoples of the world are always at a disadvantage because of naturally being peaceful and sociable and have Spiritual Moral Standards to follow. The "Halo" imitating "Disaster Star" Colored Peoples, on a tiny and tempered scale, having an IHES mindset and only dabble in the processes of Kill/Take/Destroy/Dominate/Oppress. The "Halo" imitators use European Satanist Brutes as models for how to do what they do. The Satanist European leaders are focused on mind control of their own "Troops" and of Colored Peoples by brainwashing both to have belief and faith in and use the Bible, the God, the Devil, and the Hell they made-up out of fantasy. Any who do not conform are destroyed. Destruction of their own "Troops" is by isolation--a display of their "Conditional love": "we will not love you if you do not do what we say". Colored Peoples have their Selfhoods destroyed and are kept down never being told the Truth about anything. In fact, European Brutes are anti-Spiritual Elements—attackers of Unconditional Love, Truth, Reality, and the Natural. For this reason afflicted Colored Peoples are in a "Delusional" state living inside a "Delusional World" and orchestrated by European Trinkets (e.g. electronic gadgets) and Trivia (which is about nothing).

It is a great error to think of European Brutes as people of the Natural World who are on the wrong track. Instead, these Brutes philosophically reside in a Supernatural (fantasy), out of which come their concepts of being "superior"—the most ridiculous concept humans ever conceived—and thus whatever they do is "right." They will never change because this is all they have to hold on to since they lack personal power, have no idea who they are, are filled with self-hatred, and cannot relate to being Happy because to them Happiness does not exist. They are to be used to cause one to better to better ones own life by fashioning how not to live like Brutes and by using the difficulties caused by Brutes to fashion tools for forcing out the divine powers within ones Selfhood so those powers can be cultivated.

CHAPTER II

HATE IS SELF-DESTRUCTIVE
—DOES NO GOOD
—WASTES ENERGY
--REPLACES THRIVING
--PREVENTS HAPPINESS

INDIFFERENCE/HATE/EVIL/SADISM VIOLENCE

In an Ancient African Bible mythological story of Cosmic Creation, the god Amen Ra created equally and at the same time the divine female and male principles--the Great Collection of Neteru (Paut Neteru of Annu) of Shu/Tefnut, Nut/Geb, Isis/Osiris, Nephthys/Seth (Set). The metaphorical god Set symbolically illustrates humans' Lower (animalistic) Self "Dark Side" nature as well as its Indifference/Hate/Evil/Sadism complex (*IHES) mindset* featuring Kill/Take/Destroy/Dominate *(KTDD) displays* for self-interest. Ancient Africans believed that the "great disease of the Soul" is denial of God; next is belief in appearances; and accompanying these are all evils and nothing good. Yet, the greatest evil is to ignore what belongs to God. Such a mindset includes all that sets the stage for what the Egyptian Tehuti (?12,500 BC) called the *Twelve Tormentors*-- the worst of which man is capable. The first torment is IGNORANCE; the second is GRIEF; the third is INTEMPERANCE (excessive indulgence of a natural appetite or passion); the fourth is INCONTINENCE (lacking a restraint, especially over the sexual appetite); the fifth, INJUSTICE; the sixth, AVARICE (greed); the seventh, FALSEHOOD; the eighth, ENVY; the ninth, GUILE (cunning, deceit); the tenth, ANGER; the eleventh, RASHNESS (impulsive, acting without due consideration); the twelfth, MALICE (desire to inflict harm). Under these twelve are many others--all of which, Tehuti said, prevent humans from conceiving any-thing beautiful or good. At the core of this hateful mindset is Envy.

Ancient Africans said: "The heart of the envious is gall and bitterness; his tongue spits venom; the success of his neighbor breaks his rest. He sits in his cell repining; and the good that happens to another is to him an evil. Hatred and malice feed upon his heart, and there is no rest in him…. Envy is the daughter of pride, the author of murder, the beginner of secret sedition and the perpetual tormentor of virtue. Envy is the filthy slime of the soul; a venom, a poison, or quicksilver which consumes the flesh, and dries up the marrow of the bones" (Ashby, Egyptian Yoga p 150). Personifying the *IHES* mindset and their Twelve Tormentors in KTDD displays and thus as an immensely strong evil force within any given human's worst mindset, Set's features originate from the Brute Brain portion of the Ancient (Reptilian) Brain. This Set Mindset, so incredibly and accurately described tens of thousands of years ago, are seen in perhaps 40% of today's world population.

Set also personifies humans' struggles with the 7 fetters (lust, ego, anger, fear, attachments, lies, and greed) which are part of the IHES mindset and stopping at nothing to achieve these ends. Manipulating ingredients of the IHES mindset are at the core of Brute Brains' generating Confusion, Conflict, Trickery, and Deceit to achieve "Dark Side" goals. These predictable IHES displays earned Set the title of the *"instigator of confusion"; the destroyer; and manifester of chaos*--each incorporated into the African Bible's conception of evil. Yet, Ancient *African Sages never considered Set a devil or the source of evil itself* (until the late Dynastic Period which was when

Jewish people were living in Egypt). One reason is the traditional *African World-view does not include a single deity which embodies the principle of evil or a devil.*

Instead, they explained Set's actions as one of extreme *Spiritual Ignorance.* Set's anti-Ma'at (i.e. anti-Spiritual Elements) actions separated religion from the State and Education; separated God from Nature; separated Man's spirit from physical matter; separated the divine from the mundane; created the first empire-rule of a foreign power over others; and replaced the system of maintaining social order through moral cultivation with a policing system--as symbolized by the fragmenting of the body of Ausar. This is the reason *"chopping up"* the Good is *the signature of Set, the Brute Brain, and Satanism.* No one had the courage to oppose him. Everyone, Supernatural Deities included, feared Set for he was invincible in war and violence--they being his chief means of settling differences and viewed as objects of his worship. Many even basked in the material pleasures with which he bought them off. They admired his power and ferocity which translated into respect, obedience, and cult followers. Yet, he is prone to being easily tricked by gifts that increase his possessions and appeal to his lecherous nature, especially by his lust for women (and men). Being tricked is easy because Set does Patterned Thinking for his competitive war practices which, in turn, confines him to being mentally encaged and enslaved. Thus, by remaining intellectually stupid and dumb—since his mind is spent keeping others down--he has no choice but to devise methods to control peoples' minds, starting with intimidation for all who do not believe as he tells them to do and do not do as they are told.

He falsely believes he must follow his emotions because they validate and justify his reactions and thus his thinking is Non-Rational. These ways of thinking make Set act irrationally; paralyzes his capacity for good actions; cause him to take needless chances simply for excitement; provide justification ("I was forced to do...") for KTDD displays; and refusing everything about the other or what the other offers if he dislikes that person. Set's reactions of Dishonorableness include committing crimes of *Omissions* (failing to do the right and decent thing) or *Commissions* (doing things against the honorable which ought not be done). Both encompass crimes against humans and their rights--against other people's property (e.g. "white collar" crimes)--against animals and Nature + control people and society minds. Set minds, after raping people's possessions, typically leave victims destitute, in disarray, and fighting each other. For those who resist, it is an automatic next step to do KTDD displays.

Set Brutes view what they do as perfectly normal because by operating in "Air Castle" Supernatural realms they lack accountability to the Spiritual God. Instead, they conform to the Supernatural God they made up to be compatible with their IHES nature. This means they are the clock's "6:00" concept whereby the Spiritual God is represented by the long arm pointing at "12" and the short arm, representing their Supernatural, pointing at "6". In other words, the Set mindset is completely opposite to the virtues of African Tradition—a Tradition mathematically derived from the One Universal High Spiritual God's manifestations. Such completely occludes Set from his indwelling Soul intelligence and within that context Set deems all he does in forms of dishonorableness as "right".

DISPLAYS OF THE GOD SET: The following is a clear illustration of what is going on today between Brutes vs. Good people and gives a prognostic view of what is likely to happen at some point in the future. The power of Set, the African Evil principle, is a purely physical and Supernatural power not related to anything spiritual--a power of Darkness, Ignorance, Limitation, Confusion, Conflict, and a Self-adversary--a power that fascinates me because as outrageously ridiculous as the low levels of animalist thinking/behaviors are displayed by Brutes, they seem to be winning over Good people. However, a key to the eventual outcome can be found in Ancient African Bible's Mythology. This story starts with Set (Seth)--by being envious of Ausar's (his brother) success as well as having a lust for power--he murders and cuts up Ausar's body (the Soul) into 14 pieces. This

"Chopped Up" practice--a spotlighted feature of Brutes--refers to the fragmentation of consciousness caused by the Brute Brain/Left Brain dominance which leads to Non-rational IHES thinking. When Horus--son of Isis and Ausar (Osiris)--grew up, his father's ghost appeared to demand vengeance. Thereupon, in Nubia, Horus (Heru) and Set fought ongoing battles, ranging from days to hundreds of years, with victory slipping in and out of each combatant's hands. The fight continued with periodic stalemates--seen as a Set victory, for as long as morality and spirituality did not rule the world, he was achieving his goal. Set was perennially subdued by Horus, but never destroyed. Meanwhile, both were severely injured. One injury occurred when Set gouged out Heru's eye. In order to get treatment, Heru learned of and went to Tehuti (Thoth), god of Wisdom.

Incidentally, the African invention of *Fractions* derived its religious origin from this Horus and Seth myth. Seth tore out one of Horus' falcon eyes (the moon); cut it into pieces; and threw them away. Tehuti found 63/64 pieces--only an approximate of the whole number 1. Those pieces thereafter symbolized certain fractions. Had it not been for Tehuti healing Heru's eyesight with an eye enabling him, through this sacred wound, to have higher vision and thereby become 'in-sight-full', this would have cost Heru the war. Heru's eye symbolizes the visual thinking of the Right Brain which governs understanding and spirituality + is the symbol of omniscience and omnipresence of God within ones Soul. With his insight regained, Heru managed to castrate Set (the seat of his uncontrolled aggressiveness). But when Seth recovered his missing testicle parts, the battles resumed.

Again Heru sought and followed Tehuti's guidance and was thus able to defeat Set, not militarily, but in the court of law by means of intelligence. This is because Set can only be defeated by bringing him to the court of justice--which is based on weighing his actions against the laws he has proclaimed. Such enabled Set to be tricked into accepting the very laws he had devised to enslave others--the maintaining of law and order (Amen, Metu Neter I:126). Intelligence has always defeated might and Set is ultimately defeated by truth (setting one free!). Nevertheless, although Ma'at (Spiritual Elements in action) is inevitably triumphant, given his nature and his agenda, Set's nature dictates that he must break every one of the Principles associated with Ma'at and keep generating problems. Within this context, Set later attacked Horus in the courts as a bastard son of Ausar. Yet, Tehuti decided the case in favor of Horus. This Myth represents both the essentiality of conflict, its subjugation, and the resultant equilibrium this process produces. The point: this myth is not about Good winning over evil, for both are in a constant polarity. Yet, since one cannot get Set to abide by the truth, be prepared to outsmart and out-work *Set at all costs--confront him with all means possible in harmony with Divine Law.*

Confronting does not exclude violent means since Set fights enemies by raining fire and brimstone. But violence is an absolute last resort. In the process, Set tells his enemies they must resist non-violently. The naïve fall for this and get crushed. Evil may win out temporarily or even for a long time, but it never lands safely at port at the end. However, when Conscience of the wise perceives evil, that stirs a sense of rebellious passion which awakens ones inner Wisdom to combat it. *Passion* is the stirring of ones pre-birth Emotions--i.e. a subdivision of Spiritual Energy--which orchestrates a sustained ongoing dance with evil. One learns what it takes to self-protect, to thrive, and to outsmart evil forces. One decides for oneself, in the light of some higher law or experience, what is right. One reaches ones Highest (Divinity) Self by such struggles--and humans cannot escape the struggles. This is how Spiritual Evolution occurs.

IGNORANCE CAUSES "SIN"

Spiritual Ignorance, said Ancient Africans, is by-passing the Spiritual Elements (Unconditional Love, Truth, Reality, and the Natural) wholism in order to give selective attention to only a part or even to something lesser. Humans thereby make the choice not to stay with their Real Self and, instead, use their Free Will to disconnect from the Ocean of Nuns' flow throughout the Cosmos. This disconnection from the Spiritual Elements and the Cosmic Organism—called the denial of God by African Sages—fashions ones False Self, whose orchestration is by ones self-designed Ego. Together, that puts people on anti-Ma'at paths, some going so far away as to lose contact with their Conscience.

A human newborn, a primarily Spiritual Being, contains a Spark of God which serves as the Real Self's "Soul Sunshine". Its Spiritual *Natural Knowledge* (i.e. an awareness of Certainty) is about the essence of the Cosmic Organism, out of which the newborn buds like a flower out of a gardenia bush. Also, this newborn organism has every ingredient required to remain in a Real Self state throughout its Earth World life while growing from the inside out. What makes this Natural is that Newborns are un-provided with original Earth world type learning—are un-informed in the habits of thinking—are unskilled in the arts of composition—and yet know all Cosmic Knowledge and do 'Right Living" by means of their Certainty awareness. An analogy is 'right' Dancing is easy for little children because they cannot improve on what is natural. They strive to know what to do in order to obtain better conditions on earth. Still, the newborn's duty is maintain its Spiritual Being rapid vibration rate so as to eventually return to and be absorbed by the Ultimate Creator. Since the nature of what is Spiritual is "All-or-None," any break in ones "Spiritual Being-ness" Integrity is a conversion into Spiritual Ignorance—a Self-Unknown state devoid of spirit and matter.

SECULAR IGNORANCE: The most common mental activity theme of humans' minds is Ignorance and its associated entanglements (fig. 4, 15). In the "big picture" of Life, humans parse the Cosmos into: (1) "the World" (a multiplicity of Things and Events—the Common Sense world which human senses record); (2) "the WE" of the world (i.e. "my people"); (3) the ME" world; and (4) the "Myself" inner world. Ones degree of "smarts" or ignorance about each of these 4 depends upon ones degree and internalization of provided Earth world learning; ones informed and random patterns of thinking; ones skills in the arts of composition; the extent of ones Spiritual Ignorance negating the Spiritual Elements; and the extent of ones seeking of *Enlightenment* (the influx of the Cosmic Spirit into real Things). Secular ignorance necessarily incorporates Spiritual Ignorance. Within the context of their unique philosophies of life, the Secularly Ignorant choose varying degrees of "the World," "the WE" (in the sense of those like "Me") of the world, and the ME" world (in the sense of "Me, Me, Me"). They disregard knowledge of the "Myself" inner world--their Private Selfhood of infinite power--their Deeper Selves where the *multiplicity* of all principles of the Cosmos *dissolves into Unity*. This disconnection from "Knowing Thyself" leaves no alternative but to seek personal fulfillment through worldly achievements, worldly possessions, or worldly relationships. Although they may be operating in life with a good "Heart" and using humane methods, a problem is their invariable searching in vain for contentment by looking in all the wrong places—with the wrong people—and with the wrong priorities of what is "Necessary" for "Right" Life-Living. The consequences of this scenario include chronic pain, suffering, frustration, vicious cycles of problems, and unhappiness.

To use a simile, when all God's creatures first come into Being in the Subjective *Cosmic Realm, they are like a "milk/water" mix*. By being so "Together" in the Cosmic Organism prior to Earthly birth ensures an indivisible "ME/WE" Spiritual Bonding among all--and "forever." Then, when the "ME/WE" manifest on *Earth, their "Together" interaction is like an "oil/water" mix*. This means that despite remaining as 'indivisible interrelationships," they retain their individuality Mission—each with a unique way to proceed. So, for humans to do 'Right' prioritizing requires drawing on their birth gift of Spiritual Natural Knowledge for guidance in their obligation, duty, and responsibility to the Cosmic Organism "ME/WE" in the context of doing their "oil/water" Mission. By contrast, those choosing to be Spiritually Ignorant can only 'drift' aimlessly or focus on the Earth world "ME/WE". Either choice means they necessarily ignore their unique Spiritually imparted Mission and fill their lives with a "milk/water" mix of indivisible bonding with the "Crowd"—called "*Crowd Addiction*". Note: this *"milk/water"* mix ("right" thing for the Cosmic Organism) is wrong for Earth life (should be an *"oil/water" mix*). That Error causes self-conflicts as well as confusion in dealing with others. Getting any Crowd 'expert' to clarify this will be explained by those who do not understand it. Their intent is not to tell the truth but to satisfy the questioner by relying on "Faith."

By hiding the Truth ensures those who "go along to get along" by following Ignorant people or Brutes will believe in delusions. Thereafter, they are adamant in being "right" while everybody who disagrees is wrong. All involved are so ignorant as to be unaware of its depth. That ignorance causes them to feel 'superior' in what they know nothing about. They are ignorant of possessing the capabilities to enable proper ignoring of all emotional/ sensual impulses controlling the public by bad emotions, Trinkets, and Trivia. Countless millions have been shunted along dogmatic runways featuring subtle Indifference/Hate/Evil/Sadism (IHES) deeds. Then, at the gate, the combination of dogma, ignorance, vice, cruelty, and being comfortable with inhumaneness brand the IHES complex upon Followers' brains. Here, Spiritual and Secular Ignorance 'blinds' those claiming to be civilized. Their comfort is from "willful ignorance" to dreadful suffering victims. Instead of: "I did not do it!," ones *"milk/water" bonding obligation dictates bringing relief to the truly needy*--not blaming victims or using "righteous indignation" to advise: "pull yourselves up by your own bootstraps". This dumb expression implies what is impossible for the powerless/voiceless to do. jabaileymd.com

FALSE SELF IGNORANCE: Pre-birth Emotions, among others, include what is known as Fear. But all pre-birth Emotions are the prototypes for acquired like-kind emotions to which has been added Pleasure (or positive) or Pain (or negative) aspects that come out of a human's Imaginary faculty. Negative acquired FEAR causes people to leave the realm of Unconditional Love and that automatically is a step inside the IHES Complex-- characterized by Spiritual Pain. This means a given individual's LOVE PLATTER (the instinct to Love; to spread Love; to be Loved; and to be Lovable) is shut down. Whenever there is blockage to free flowing Love coming into ones Selfhood; or blockage to Love circulating inside and around ones Selfhood; or blockage to Love flowing outside of ones Selfhood there will be Spiritual Pain--the worst experience a human being can have. A blockage of any of these three channels will automatically cause a lack of the "5Ss"--Safety, Security, Self-Confidence, Strength, and Stability. That lack, in turn, leads to a state of total Self-Absorption in an attempt to gain even a moment of relief from Spiritual Pain. Those attempts, regardless of where one is located inside the IHES Complex, manifest as destructive behaviors to oneself (Masochism) as well as to others (evilness and sadism). Brutes attempt to repress their Spiritual Pain by generating unfair advantages for themselves (the "Me, Me, Me" Syndrome) and inflicting unfair disadvantages on others.

The nature of these destructive thoughts, emotions, expressions, and actions take the form of Obsessions and Compulsions. It is Obsessions and Compulsions that keep alive their drive to live inside this destructive and delusional IHES Complex world. To hide or deny Spiritual Pain, they display *Arrogance*--defined by Ancient African Sages as three self-seeking passions of power, lust, and avarice or covetousness (envy leading to a greedy desire to possess what belongs to another). By also operating within their Lower Self, people who possess a "Love/Hate" disposition periodically visit the IHES Complex. This means these foolish brutes select someone they admire but envy to inflict difficulties on so as to see the victim agonizing. Thus, Spiritual Ignorance means no longer knowing Natural Knowledge—a state of one having converted into a Self-Absorbed and Selfhood Splintered False Self—a state focused only on External World things as the way to do "Life-Living". Their endless search for contentment leads them to engage in various situations and entanglements which, in the beginning, SEEM to hold the possibility of bringing about happy circumstances. Yet, regardless of their achievements it is never "Enough."

If this voluntary catastrophe of the stoppage of Natural Knowing is *Mild*, the Spiritual Ignorance is of the type that is like a "Cloud with a silver-lining" symbolizing ones flawed "Soul Sunshine" is still able to seep through to keep one somewhat aware of right "Life-Living." For one to place "Clouds" over any part of ones "Soul Sunshine" is to block out ones Immaterial awareness of connection Instincts and happenings in and from the Cosmic Organism. However, *Slight* types lack this seep through and are non-deliberately self-destructive and destructive to others by being "willfully ignorant." Still, Spiritual Ignorance, is about what is not seen for it covers up reality. One fails to see ones Cosmic Organism indivisible connections; ones eternal Spiritual aspects. The result is to improperly view oneself inside the Cosmos and that leads to flaws, even in ones best intentions which in turn flaw ones thoughts and actions with confusion and conflict. The source of failure may be such things as Self-Unknowing, transgressions against some aspect of the Cosmic Organism, lack of rationality, numbed moral sensitivity, disregardful or inattentive to the right and good, compassionate unresponsiveness to the imprisoned, the afflicted, the vulnerable being mindless and "following my mouth." *Moderate* types are out of the Spiritual Elements flow and are actively engaged in the Indifference/Hate/Evil/Sadism Complex directed toward other people.

A *Severe* (Extreme) or Brute form of Spiritual Ignorance is such a shattering and scattering of ones Spiritual Integrity as for one to be in an Unknown Supernatural realm with a mindset that is "Inside-Out"—a delusional mindset that fails to believe what is real and believes what is not real. Here, ones denial of the Spiritual God is said by African Sages to be the greatest disease of the Soul--an Ignorance as the mother of boundless fears. To be totally disconnected from the Cosmic Organism and its "5Ss" (safety, security, sureness, strength, and stability) imparted into ones Deepest (Private) Self generates Spiritual Pain—the worst experience a human can have. Ignorance of the true origins of humanity is one of the most important contributing sources of strife between nations.

FALSE SELF IMAGES: When one has adopted a False Self, ones Images concerning how to "Life-Live" are about a social Secular Self oriented to External World things in the 'here and now'. An analogy for this is the "Disco Ball" ("Mirror Ball"; "Glitter Ball") which was an intimate part of the "Discotheque" dance club scene so prominent in the 1970s. That scene was one of extravagant glitz associated with loud popular music while the Glitter Ball was twirling overhead and emitting visual flashes from being illuminated by spotlights. Thus, stationary viewers could experience beams of light flashing over them while seeing myriad spots of light spinning around the walls of the room. The ball's surface, like that of a crystal, consists of hundreds or thousands of facets, nearly all roughly the same shape and size, and each having a mirrored surface.

A similar mental setting characterizes a gang member's Icon Images. The 'entourage' of each Icon Image consists of what resembles tentacles of an octopus. Each tentacle acts like a light and thus together they come in from many directions in spotlighting the Icon Image and thereby producing a complex display of excitement. False Self people seek out "excitement" in a Disco type setting where there is a great deal of noise in their heads. The problem is that at least a few of the crystal faces that provide essential ingredients to the Icon Image have "Clouds" over them—some with silver linings (indicating they have some sense of what is "Right"); some are completely 'Clouded' by confusion and ignorance; and some complete "Clouds" are 'dark'. "Clouds" obscure the Spiritual Elements.

Thus, those with 'silver-linings' do things almost right within the context of a gang member's awareness. That 'almost' means that what they do is viewed as "SEEMS" right and yet its octahedron shaped Icon Image the flawed or missing face prevents it possessing a "big picture" of integrity. Put another way, the C13 English word "SEEM" (Old Norse, conforming or fitting in the sense of 'becoming') conveyed the impression of appearing to be real. However, the C13 Old French word "*Appearance*" (to show; to come in sight) means 'Apparent' and thus is opposed to actual reality. This means "Real" is to "Seem" as "Reality" is to "Appearing"--as the "Actual" is to the "Possible"--as "Being" is to "Becoming"--as "Is" (i.e. Being) is to "Is Not" (i.e. non-Being).

Thus, how one sees oneself--typically in the form of an Icon Image—depends upon whether this "seeing" is done out of ones Real Self or False Self. How ones sees oneself depends upon whether one has a healthy or an unhealthy mind as well as what one allows to enter into and be internalized as a part of ones character. That "seeing" determines to a large extent how one will respond to any new challenge in family life, to children, to adults, to friends, to neighbors, and to the concentric rings of society radiating throughout the world.

The point of the following discussion is that *one can change the image containing the flawed secret.* A change to an Ancient African philosophy of life and its associated positive attitude refine the shape of ones "Life-Living" orchestrating Icon Image and upgrade ones thinking vibration rates. Truths, formed similar to crystals, possess the same Reality. Changing a Crystal's shape with the Truth causes a new electrical vibration rate, power, and sound. Self-improvement can start by electrical vibrations altering the Image containing the flawed Phantom in a False Self Contingent Being. The essences of *changing a flawed Image shape is done by:* (1) substituting Truth so as to alter the frequency of alternating charges placed upon the flawed Symbol in ones False Self and thus producing a new Spiritual Elements shape; (2) staying inside the Spiritual Elements *causes a new electrical vibration rate, power, and sound;* and (3) a positive attitude (which refines the shape and upgrades vibration rates). These give the "Phantom" in ones Icon Image a Spiritual effect that "touches ones Heart and/or ones Soul."

DELUSIONS OF VIOLENCE

"*Delusions*" originally referred to powers of gods or demons to change form and appear under deceiving masks. In ancient times, delusions and illusions carried the same sense in "Magic" whereby people were deceived by a façade or false-front which hid the "nothing" behind it. In that way, "Delusions" came to mean believing what is not real and not believing what is real. Hence, DELUSIONS ARE WORSE THAN IGNORANCE. Human Delusions begin with newborns' first awareness of the reality of their newly entered Material World—an awareness in the form of mental picture reproductions—first of one scene and then another—gradually building up to different scenes occurring in rapid succession. Eventually, certain mental pictures take on varying degrees of significance and, in the process, convert from two-dimensional mental pictures to three-dimensional Mental Images since the mental pictures now stand for 'the meaning of something'. The nature of those mental Images depends upon whether they consist of Knowledge (forms of the Spiritual Elements) or Information (ranging from neutral to bad). The way this works is by the collection of "raw materials"—e.g. ingredients of Sensations out of ones memory; from something going on inside ones Selfhood; from something entering a human's senses from the outside world; from ones interpretations of the monitored feedback one gets from outside influences—being organized into some meaningful "Seed" form. Those organized ingredients within the "Seed" of Violence form Delusional Mental Images which thereafter orchestrate ones life.

The minds organization of these "raw materials" is called a *Percept.* A Percept is the first and natural display of the human mind's activity upon acquiring these "raw materials" and then into a formed mental entity of a "Thing". That "Thing" makes one aware of something good (like what the ingredients for a flower bud do) or bad (like a threat, disturbance in harmony, or atmosphere of danger). Second, as more "raw materials" are added from mental activities, a *Notion* emerges to designate "what it is" as an "*Entity*". This Notion has a specific nature which hints at its Identity. Third is the evolving and further internally developing Percept/Notion, similar to the beginning flowering of a flower bud--a bud called an "*Idea*" ('a becoming'). An Idea is an awareness of specific, particular aspects--e.g. properties, characteristics, traits, or features--which represents an explicit (defined) concept of "*Identity.*" An *Idea* ('model'; form) is a patterned quantity of "frozen" energy whose forces are shaped into a defined "Thing"--the shape that imparts power. Fourth, like the Fruiting flower, a matured idea is the formation of a "Unit"--a Concept.

Thus, a Concept describes a phenomenon (i.e. a phantom, to 'make visible' a Contingent Being) or a group of phenomena possessing no life of itself and none having any reality in and of themselves. At the core of this entity is a Disposition (fig. 6) containing a *'payload' message* of the Concept *essence's shared properties,* an *Inclination* (a 'physical' "leaning toward" or "leaning" away from something), a *Temperament* (its physi-ological Sensory Consciousness systems fashioning the type of reaction the aroused person takes to conform to the 'blue-print' of the *"what"* of the Concept Theme), and an Attitude. Upon facing an appropriate situation matching the Concept Theme (a *maintained central or dominating idea or practice arising from a common origin)*, the contents of the Disposition of like-kind Concepts arrange ones mental activities in line with the theme of the 'big picture' Icon Image that acts as a stimulus to spur action.

Human newborns possess all the knowledge of the essences of the Spiritual Elements and that provides them with all tools needed to have a thriving and happy life. To stay on that path and generate thoughts out of it means they remain as Real Self individuals, with all of the Selfhood Greatness associated with it—i.e. their Souls consisting of a drop of God (giving them infinite power); of the Genetics of their magnificent Ancient African Ancestors; and of a 'special' Talent to be used to make happen their Mission in life. The duty of every human is to discover and develop these Selfhood Greatness entities and then find a niche where their very best is made available to the most people over the longest period of time.

But because the Base upon which ones Selfhood is designed is Unconditional Love implies that each human has the Free Will to fashion a course of life outside of a Real Self. That choice is the adoption of a False Self, orchestrated by a fantasy made Ego—an Icon Image. Those who choose to go in the opposite direction of the Spiritual Elements thereafter live out of their Brute Brains—the source of their Violent displays. The ingredients of violent displays can be analogized to the Tree Concept--with the Seed, Roots, Trunk/Vines, Branches, Leaves, and Fruit being its ingredients (fig. 3). A similar pattern can be imaged for Violence. The Source for the image is a False Self. The "Soil" for the Seed is the Occult and the Seed itself is the Brute Brain of ones mind. The Roots are Fantasies inside a Delusional World; the Trunk is living out of ones Animalistic Self; the Branches are ones Desires; the Leaves are ones methods for living; and the Fruit is Weak People which give rise to an assortment of Effects and Consequences (e.g. Kill/Take/Destroy/Dominate/Oppress).

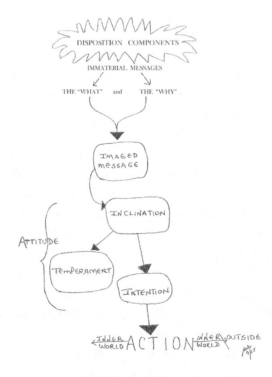

FIGURE 6

DELUSIONAL WORLD: Out of the Fantasy part of the Occult Pagan Europeans worshipped human, human-like, and animal creatures of a realistic and fantasy nature. The delusional worship of idols was called "Idolatry" in the Bible. The C15 French word "Delusion" (deceive, cheat) means to play or mock—i.e. away from play or mockery, meaning the inability to distinguish between reality and play or mockery. In early history mystical experiences seem to have corresponded to what are called delusions and hallucinations. The dangerous ones are *Delusional Religious Fanatics*. Even though subsequent distinctions were made between them, "Roots" emerging out of this "Seed" thought branched widely to embrace such things as phantoms, ghosts, and other fantasy weird creatures that were placed into European Myths--and later in Romance and Tragedy stories--all designed to touch the deepest desires, fears, hopes, passions, and sentiments of involved people--all leaving a culturally transmittable impression on the mind--as seen in today's European clamor for the "far out" Supernatural, like werewolves, vampires, Cinderella, Snow White and wands. From these "Roots" came the "Trunk" modern sense of Delusions as absurd or unfounded beliefs which are maintained despite evidence to the contrary. Delusion (a mistaken conviction) is associated with Error, *Fallacy* ("*Circular Argument*" or "Circular Reasoning of "Begging the Question"--i.e. an argument structure in which the premise is a restatement of the conclusion), *Hallucination* (a false image or belief which has nothing, outside a disordered mind, to suggest it), Illusion (a mistaken perception or inference), and *Phantasm* (man-made spirits)—all denoting something which appears to be true, but which is really false. *Delusive* refers to a belief that, though false, is accepted as true. Delusion simply ascribes reality or truth to that which "SEEMS" right or true. Each creation happens in ones mind by wishing to have that quality, impression, appearance, or message appear. Delusions are main features of the cheap to build drafty Supernatural "Air Castle".

Recall that *nothing in childhood was more exciting than being deceived*. Yet, youth slowly began to give up their liberties under some delusion—like trying to avoid extraordinary toil—by justice not being a means of security but a form of unfairness—by no intelligence or cleverness being sufficient to overcome unrealities and the contrary industries of ignorance or evil people—by allowing themselves to be caught up in the Trinket and Trivia as the ultimate in excitement which they find so exhausting as to have nothing left to be about their Mission. By then lacking trust in anything, one can no longer know what is real about oneself. Delusions are more persistent and more elaborate than hallucinations or illusions (misinterpretations of stimuli) and deal with inferiority, anger, and frustration of hopes. One strives hard to hide such insecurities in ones heart from oneself as well as from others. At this point one is both judge, jury, and executioner in ones own case that concerns: "which came first—the chicken or the egg" as far as the deceptive person being "them or me." Then one no longer trusts oneself—and the worst deluded are the self-deluded while on a life's path of disappointment, discontent, and ever searching for the "5Ss."

Because reactive aspects to ones insecurities and sense of inferiority are inside Delusions' and because "Dark Side" Fantasies are derived out of the Brute portion of a human's Ancient Brain, one has unshakable convictions in being "right" in the face of contrary evidence--the fantasy of: "everything I do is right". This is aided by the foolish and evil society which believes itself to be special instruments of the Divine Will—to be masters of the earth—and their will is the ultimate criterion of what is right and wrong. They get away with masquerading their delusional fantasies and shams as sanity because they have the GUN and the political power Network to reinforce them. Such power multiplies flatterers and, in turn, flatters multiply their delusions of adequacy and competence by putting more layers over the truth. As soon as they begin to discover the truth about themselves, they immediately and permanently cover it up. Or, the reverse is the *Delusion of Persecution* (which incorporate fantasy into their distorted perceptions so as to overcome a sense of inferiority and then display the opposite behavior, like being a 'little god') while being deluded by triviality. This indicates ones delusions have reached the level of being "Inside-Out" thinking. At that point, the more ways one is deluded the better one feels.

DELUSIONAL MINDSETS: To summarize, the Fantasy portion of the Occult, the Supernatural, Hallucination, and the Delusional realms are all part of the same thing in the Unseen World—going against the flow of the Natural World stream (as with significantly psychically traumatized Black People) or being in an entirely different stream, as with Europeans socialized into the Indifference/Hate/Evil/Sadism Complex. By contrast, African Magical Thinking goes along with the Spiritual Elements stream flow of Nature, allowing Nature to do the work, and without departing from that stream. This is like swimming along with the flow—which thereby gives the power to the stream—so as to make faster progress. Magical Thinking and Imagination do not have an anatomical basis in the brain. *Fantasy Seeds* lacking Spiritual Elements in afflicted humans' mind have the fate of delusions. Speculation's Fantasy are about an unreal mental image or reflection giving an appearance of the "Fantastic" in an Icon "*Contingent Being*."

This characterizes the Supernatural "Air Castle" (fig. 5)—the thinking that went into it—the thinking that comes out of it—a Fantasy form of thinking that dominates today's world. Fantasy is stimulated by frustration. In most emotional problems of ones life it does not produce constructive solutions at any level of reality. What Occult Fantasy does in the External World and ones Inner World is to first generate confusion and conflict. Then it steps into its resultant mental turmoil and reconciles all ambivalent attitudes--teaching with Fantasy stories containing highly abstracted concepts--stories that "SEEM" right--stories containing some familiar information the people have accepted--stories told in an exciting visual media way—stories that "everybody" has to believe because the Fantasy story tellers have seen to it that the Truth is not—and never will be—available.

As a result of socialization, a chain of events converts its "Air Castle" future cult candidates into gross insecurities about themselves and the need to follow rules not always compatible with ones nature. "*Extroverting*" implies one now needs the External World for approval as well as to gather whatever is cherished in the External World as ones standards, guides, and filters. By the cult despising all that has preceded in realms of hate, its simultaneously teaches one to hate oneself inside ones Inner World. A way this works is by not being able to trust anyone causes one to not trust oneself. Such insecurities prevent one from saying what one really feels (i.e. the shutting down of part of oneself) or causes one to laugh at others or rebel against a scapegoat "for no reason"(not being true to oneself) so as to overcome being uncomfortable in public and with oneself. When Fantasy is used in this way to serve to create Icon Images about a Superior or Inferiority complex—the one chosen by a cult member becomes a "Raw Nerve" to which the person eventually automatically reacts as a Conditioned Response to certain Trigger Things, Events, or People.

The content of Fantasy giving rise to an Icon Image is always an indicator, directly or indirectly, of ones core problems. Psychologists say this represents an *Iconic Store* housing a discrete visual sensory register—so-called because information is thought to be stored in the form of *Icons (visual images that represent something)*. As a boy, I would write my name with a lighted sparkler (or stick of incense that had been dipped in lemon juice) against a dark background so as to see the persistence of a visual memory. This means I "saw" my name, even though the sparkler left no physical trace. This visual persistence is analogous to the type of information held in the iconic store and suggests that one has become part of the Icon Image. Such fantasy mental pictures supposedly explained happenings of things seen but with them having no idea how or why. In that drama are all sorts of distorted situations and fantasy self-talk—each situation interpreted as being real and causing a desire to take revengeful actions on people who caused them no real trouble. Such thoughts and actions seem as strange to outsiders as what "outsiders" say and do that seem strange to the emotionally hypersensitive.

Emotional hypersensitivity means that it does not take much for an "outsider" to say an innocent something which hypersensitive people dislike--a dislike to the point of developing an aggravating emotional "mental movie" drama in their heads. Then, an appropriate Trigger arrival spurs Icon Image displays in thought, emotions, expressions, or deeds. This is repeated so often that Players in their own play fade into having the mask they wear become their face.

ILLUSION/DELUSION PATTERNS: Patterns ('mark out', sign) can either be inside a *Void* (i.e. having no purpose, meaning, or intention); or, they may be are *Designs* (point out, denote, designate) that possess a Disposition and its Plan capable of serving as a model to be copied. In other words, a *Pattern*, as commonly used, is a drawing to show the look or function of something. Most have a flat shape or outline characterizing their design that is bound by certain limits. *Metaphysical Patterns have more than two dimensions* and a given Pattern's *Shape* (a pattern of energy movement frozen in space) provides that Pattern's specific power. Any pattern which is Spiritual or a permanent and universal human experience is a *Reality*—all else is an illusion. An *Illusion* is something that deceives by producing a false impression from mistaken or distorted perceptions of the five senses (sight, hearing, smell, taste, and touch) or from false impressions of reality from faulty thinking; a deception caused by something *appearing* to be other than it really is—so that what is seen does not exist the way it is seen. More elaborately, Illusions are measures misdirecting attention away from Reality in order to hide what is really there by means of a false front or by making an object appear not to be what it seems to be. These *Distortions* (to twist out of a proper or natural relation of parts) are Illusions because of one having a "Thinking Tentacle" in Contingent realms which, in turn, gets involved with the unreal. Such appearances from Illusions can seem very real to the naïve--so real as to require much proof to realize they are not real. A *Mirage* is an illusion. Illusions--by creating uncertainty sufficient to persuade one to believe the fantasy produced is Reality--can fade into delusions. To watch a magician saw a woman in half is to observe an Illusion (seeing what is not there and not seeing what is there). To believe the magician actually sawed the woman in half is a *Delusion* (believing what is not real and not believing what is real). What is real is that there are actually two women involved--the one seen, the other, already hidden in the same box with the one seen.

An Illusion begins with an orderly succession of phenomena that does not persist and that alteration of changing appearances proves its unreality--known to the rational mind as fleeting in consciousness. To present *Matter, per se, as being real is an illusion because—by being fragmentary, unsubstantial, constantly changing into another of its appearances, and destined to pass away when it has served its purpose--it has no real being.* Instead, Matter is a reflection of a Spiritual pattern (i.e. changeless, perfect, and all complete) which becomes duel in the Tangible realms. The principle within this concept is extremely important because it leads to what "SEEMS" right but is not in actuality. And that is the main flaw in European Supernatural Logical Thinking about anything. To present Matter as being "real" is an error in the major premise—an error leading to errors in the conclusion as well as into every statement into which it enters—like blowing bubbles and having bubbles come out of bubble. An ink drop in milk pollutes every aspect of it—a dilution and pollution persisting no matter where it is distributed. *To believe delusions or illusions means one can never be Certain about what one thinks, feels, says, and does—this is Doubt*!

The C15 Latin word "*Delusion*" (to mock) means "to play to ones detriment" or "the inability to distinguish between play and reality." By seeing what is not there and not seeing what is there—the act of an appearance devoid of reality in itself—results in Misinterpretations and they lead to Delusions. Whereas the question of belief does not arise in Illusions, Delusions are false beliefs about something real and held onto in spite of no proof, evidence, or good reason. Whereas Illusions are usually temporarily held, Delusions become a way of life around which a lifestyle is fashioned. To believe material things (e.g. money, possessions) are more important than good character is a delusion. To believe you can buy friendships or things of worth (e.g. happiness) is a delusion. Many people believe Delusions, even in the face of contrary evidence, because they do not want to know the truth. Such a denial is out of fear of what is associated with it and anxious about having greater fear of not being able to handle it. Using the Natural Cosmos as the standard, European Supernatural Patterns of Illusions and Delusions are "Air Castle" people's concept of reality, truth, and natural and they are in direct opposition to these Spiritual Elements of the one Universal High Spiritual God.

ANTI-SPIRITUAL ELEMENTS

The Spiritual Elements of African Tradition are Unconditional Love (the inner nature of God) and the manifestations of God's outer nature of Life—Reality (what a Real thing is when it comes into Being); Truth (what a Real Thing does after it comes into Being); and the Natural (how a Real Thing operates in doing what it does). The Anti-Spiritual Elements not only oppose the Spiritual Elements but actually attack them. They are the *IHES* mindset ("Indifference-Hate-Evil-Sadist") Complex + their Twelve Tormentors + their 7 Fetters + the KTDD (Kill/Take/Destroy/Dominate) displays). Because there are no degrees in things of a Spiritual nature, the IHES, being of an earth world nature, is not the opposite of the Spiritual. Just as the absence of African type Love--i.e. Unconditional Love--is the opposite of Love, the IHES Complex, starts with Indifference and progresses to Hate; then Evilness; and then Sadism.

INDIFFERENCE

For Ancient Africans, the opposite of Unconditional Love is its absence and that leaves one in a state of "Indifference"—the entering into a void. When brought into English in 1380, it implied not tending to prefer one to another—impartial—neutral. The extended meaning of unconcerned, unmoved, apathetic appeared in 1519; and in 1532, neither good nor bad, average. From my observations, *"Don't Care"*—i.e. to ignore, deny, reject, abandon ones Spiritually or Secularly assigned or Self-assigned obligation(s), duty(s), and responsibility(s)— is what characterizes Indifference (Bailey, African Tradition for Black Youth p317-340). Spiritual "Don't Care" means not getting involved with "ME/WE" assignments—no "lifting of others" and/or no "self-climbing" to live up to ones Highest (divinity) Self. An example is being "Indifferent" to or disregarding others feelings--or to not get involved in the bad situation of others without showing Compassion. To do nothing can pertain to: (1) Any threat to the integrity of any part of the Cosmic Harmony stirs all entity family members to instantly do what is within the power of each to re-establish Harmony; (2) when integrity is shattered, each independently works to interdependently recreate or enhance (e.g. "make right") the Disharmony; and (3) defending or protecting any aspect of or all of the entire Circle of Wholism.

In Secular (Earth World) realms "Don't Care" implies that one simply does nothing about ones life-shaping and life-changing problems, hoping that somehow they will work themselves out to ones advantage or not cause problems greater than one can handle. To not Keep Ones Word to Oneself means one cannot trust oneself in Self-Assignments. A lack of self-trust is like a cancer to ones Selfhood. *IHES* mindset (Indifference/Hate/Evil/Sadism) people and their Twelve Tormentors + their 7 Fetters who engage in KTDD (Kill/Take/Destroy/Dominate) displays) have *"Anhedonia"*--an inability to feel pleasure due to the dulling of their responsiveness to the brain's reward pathways (e.g. involving the Ventral Tegmental Area of the Midbrain, the Ventral Prefrontal Cortex). Many Brutes admit feeling "numb" to their evil acts. *"Indifference"* implies a settled or fixed lack of interest and attention to things of worth, compassion, caring, and other's dignity. In other words, Indifference is a dispositional quality (i.e. a Thought Structure with a prevailing trend), consisting of an immovable neutrality keeping one detached and aloof because of an absence of feeling or interest.

Self-esteem in the average person is an interplay of inner factors (e.g. self-respect, discipline, self-confidence) and outer factors (e.g. a sense of belonging, joined by fair treatment and merited appreciation). It quickly withers if one comes to believe themselves the victims of indifference or injustice as well as of ignorance, personal ambition, or ineptitude on the part of their leaders. And moral indifference is the malady of the cultivated classes.

HATRED

There are three practical reasons I have never hated anybody. First, my family and my boyhood all-Black community were very loving. I enjoyed friends and strangers who demonstrated true caring for each other by doing nice things "*just because*" and "*just for me.*" Such, I have never seen again while living in various places of the USA and the world. Second was seeing up-close hatred's devastation to a human's body, mind, and spirit—e.g. exchanging the terribly unhappy mindset of self-absorption to nurse the consuming passion of hate and thus losing the "ME/WE" benefits of that person's full talents. Third were realizations from medical school studies of how hatred 'corrodes/erodes' the body. To elaborate, a human's brain "*Hate Circuit,*" located in sub-cortical areas, includes the medial frontal gyrus, right putamen, premotor cortex, and medial insula. This means Hate involves both the interior, primitive (Brute) brain parts--implying those parts developed relatively late in human evolution. Perhaps that development was spurred 45,000 years ago as a result of Ice Age conditions causing 'Scarcity" of everything needed for survival. Furthermore, I believe, "Scarcity Survival" activated the normally dormant Brute Brain portion of the Ancient (Reptilian) Brain and maintained an excessive and constant hormone production. In turn, those hormones no doubt generated activities in other parts of the body. Such chronically stressful effects on the networks they influence 'corrode/erode' body aspects. Resultant biological dysregulations embrace physiological impairments which interfere with ones metabolism, immune response, or organ function. Consequences are physical diseases—e.g. high blood pressure, heart disease, cancer, migraine or other types of headaches, skin disorders, digestive problems, alcohol and drug ("Street" or prescribed) abuse, chronic pain, excessive and early skin wrinkling, and slow premature death.

Once the cortical zone's premotor cortex of the "Hate Circuit" is activated, part of ones "Fight-Flight-Fright" motor planning preparation concerns ones executions for possible attack or defense. All of this implies that hating somebody heightens ones judgment and ones ability to assess what the perceived "enemy" is likely to do next so as to prepare what is needed to initiate aggressive behavior. If that "enemy" is constantly present or is constantly brought to mind (e.g. by conversations with peers, by the media, by pictures, by stereotypes) then ones mind is surreal—one part centered on physical world matters; another busily involved in generating and perfecting a collage of an Icon Image consisting of the "enemy" as a Supernatural Contingent Being 'monster'. The consuming focus on ways to harm, injure, or otherwise extract revenge means ones time, energy, and efforts are devoted to "war" strategies and not ones higher intellect. A huge segment of the world's population has been socialized to believe that a mindset of "war" is all there is. The word "War" comes from prehistoric Germanic 'strife'—as in 'striving' (C13) together in quarreling, struggle, and conflict.

A battling mindset is filled with Kill/Take/Destroy/Dominate/Oppress intent, powered by belligerence. In life's 'big picture' of *Particular* things, their following of the *Telescope Concept* (fig. 11) means that understanding their multiplicity relationships to each other leads to them dissolving into a Unity. Such is like 'telescoping' all aspects of an apple tree back into its "Seed"—a "Seed" containing the secret meaning and mysticism underlying all there is in and about that tree + its relationship to other trees. Hate means one only sees the Particulars—e.g. a worm-eaten "leaf" about the "enemy" and/or desired poisoned apples from winning the "war." Evil dealings with Hate fashioned Particulars is "Exciting"--an "Excitement" flawed because whatever is acquired, assuming it is acquired, is only temporary. The reason is that there is never "Enough" of hating or warring or gaining benefits. Satanists who lead the public's mind in a "war" direction make all-out efforts to hide the fact that Unity embracing diversity means all benefit. Unity concepts can only derive from developing ones higher intellect into Spiritual and Metaphysical realms—a mindset which generates order, understanding, insights, and compassion as to how to have a thriving and happy life for all. Personally, to lock myself into an entanglement with anything concerning Hate prevents my chance of Happiness and does physical damage. I love myself too much to do self-harm. jabaileymd.com

ANATOMY OF HATRED: A sine qua non (an indispensable factor) that one does not love oneself is for one to hate anybody. The reason is that hate in any form is physically, psychically, and spiritually harmful to oneself and people who love themselves do not harm themselves. Among Ancient Africans, Hate was not an issue. This was because their total focus was on a philosophy of life of striving to reach the Heaven Afterlife by adhering to Ma'at principles (Spiritual Elements in action). Thus, they avoided many of today's psychosomatic diseases (physical illnesses derived from ones mind and/or spirit). However, Ancient Africans recognized that the Spiritual Elements are exclusionary opposites to the contents of the Brute Brain which, in turn, is intimately related to the nervous system (e.g. hypothalmus). The *content of "Hate"* derived from the Brute Brain includes anger (which motivates violence and revenge), fear, disgust, ill-will, aversion, no contact, and no relationship as an enduring tendency; active animosity. Hence, all that is involved with ones birth gift Instinct of Survival, Self-Protection, and Self-Preservation is to be distinguished from the Attitude of Hate because there is overlap. The carrying out of the instinctual aspect is of a Congenital Tarda nature, whereby humans (and certain other species) are biologically prepared to work with Conditioned Responses toward a common goal. Neurologically, Instinct "preparedness" resides in the brainstem--the earliest, most primitive ("reptilian") portion of ones brain. It is responsible for *Reflexes*—automatic responses not needing the intervention of conscious thought to take effect. For example, newborns show a Startle Reflex. Other reflexes include sneezing, coughing, and gagging.

Conditioned Responses (or Reflexes) do not occur naturally in a human but rather are developed by a '*Big Bang" Trigger* event or by *Cumulative Micro-traumas* (regular associations of some physiologic function with an unrelated outside Thing and instituting an automatic physiological function whenever the outside Thing is present). A parent of Conditioned Responses is the brain's the Limbic System, an "emotional center" called the "Old (or Early) Mammalian Brain". This "early Alarm or Alert system" operates below the threshold of consciousness. Inextricably linked to the early alert is a disposition to put into effect a quick response, with an emphasis on instantaneous, pre-reflective action. This Conditioned Response system brought into being after one or so initial encounters early in life may cause one to fear and detest certain objects—from snakes and spiders to heights to certain tastes--and eventually to those people one deems to "not be for me because they are mean." These Conditioned responses to readily avoid a "Thing" that might prove deadly reduces the frequency of risky encounters. From a survival point of view, to think too long about any of these 'Things' might well cause one to fall prey to it. For example, while looking more closely to determine whether this snake might be toxic, one may be bitten and killed. Springing quickly to action evokes an emotional experience. An Emotion ("a spirit moving force" causing creature animations) is a spontaneous reaction to what is assessed to be "For me or Against me" and it begins instantly at the level of this primitive Reflex or Conditioned Response to a significant stimuli. What is then displayed out of the sympathetic nervous system is "fight, flight, or fright"

+ fear and rage--all experienced simultaneously, or in quick succession. Fight or flight involves arousal, the branch of the nervous system that prepares one for action. The motivational F's originate here and are regulated by the hypothalamus.

The *personal effects* of hating embraces a sense of insecurity, fear, feelings of intense hostility where rejection has occurred, and deep anger directed at those individuals or events that have brought about failure or personal calamity. As these felt bad emotions become chronic and assume the form of resentment, it has severe effects upon ones own personality and circulatory system, producing hypertension and hardening of the arteries because of the action of the autonomic nervous system. The uncontrolled consequence of this composite scenario is a Hate-filled disposition but self-discipline avoids this. If one learns the proper lesson from this experience and how to avoid or by-pass or out-smart it or neutralize it through offense or 'just enough' defense, there is no reason to be involved with the consequences which cause Hate.

WHAT IS HATRED?: The "Disaster" Tree of Hatred is about Mild, Slight, Moderate, and Extreme degrees of whatever is against the Spiritual Elements of Unconditional Love, Truth, Reality, and the Natural. Whereas African Tradition considers "Hate" as a "state" of mind cut-off from the Spiritual Elements, for Europeans, Hate speaks of an old, enduring flow—not of Human Nature as ancient Greeks said—but of acquired negative emotions which lack compassion or sorrow for those Targeted. Hate was not an issue for the peaceful and harmonious Ancient Africans but yet their recognition of it was in the form of the metaphorical god Set. In researching indexes to get a discussion of Hatred or Hostility in many European textbooks on Psychiatry, Psychology, Sociology, and related fields, I was amazed at the complete silence. The question is "Why?"--and an answer is not because of its lack of pervasiveness. Nevertheless, European dictionaries and etymology books say Hate's original meaning was a 'strong feeling' (Indo-European); strong dislike (Germanic); and in Beowulf (725) as extreme dislike associated with such spite as for one to pursue the hunt in order to do harm—an idea brought into C14 English as "*Heinous*." Accretions to these concepts included: Greek (Gk, kad, not caring), anxiety and grief; Old Irish both love and Hate (perhaps where the concept arose that the opposite of love is hate—a false concept in African Tradition); and synonyms for "Hate"--e.g. envy, sorrow, fear, and abhor. Rycroft (Psychoanalysis p68) says: hate is an affect characterized by an enduring wish to injure or destroy the hated object; Drever (Psychology p116): a sentiment (an emotional disposition of ones make-up) involving the whole gamut of primary emotions [not defined], but with anger, and often fear, predominating; Campbell (Psychiatric p18) object-directed representation of aggression and violence; Reber (Psychology p330): a desire to harm or cause pain to the object of emotion and feelings of pleasure from the object's misfortunes; Warren (Psychology p121) extreme Aversion (a "turning away"). Hence, Hate is mind consuming.

It is helpful for me to think of the scenarios of Hate by the crude "*Rule of Threes*." Scenario I: The "Crowd" is composed of those who love and create; those who drift; and those who hate and destroy. Scenario II: Since one fears something before hating it, the proximate cause of Hate is Fear. To elaborate, Children become haters by being taught to fear--or by imagining something fearful--or experiencing something fearful—each followed by hating. A child who fears noises becomes an adult who hates noise. Scenario III: Adults become haters of those whom they have hurt; from "going along with their crowd to get along"; and as a defense mechanism against all of their inner turmoil. Scenario IV: Receivers of Hate are those who return the Hate; those unaware of being Hated or do not care or find it beneficial; those who feel bad because of realizing Hatred is so unnecessary and simply makes all concerned feel needlessly bad. Scenario V: Hate thrives on Segregation—so as to withdraw ones hate into seclusion for spawning into fury for later spewing—so as to let the wall of glass prevent the linking of interrelationships between different "races"—so as to ensure not discovering that "those people" and you are more similar than different. This means "those people" are hated because of Willful Ignorance about their history, goals, struggles, achievements, and ways of doing things--and one will never know these as long as one hates them—and to be Indifferent is to be inhumane.

Scenario VI: Hate is not preservation and union, but destruction and separation; not happiness and well-being, but misery and being in the worse possible state; not about what disturbs Justice but what disturbs Order. Scenario VII: hateful acts are transferences to others of degradations one bears in oneself; or of entrenched greed; or from "sick" pleasures of power from annihilating. Scenario VIII: Hatred is medicine for the frustrated and by being the most accessible and comprehensive of all unifying agents, it serves as a cohesive among those with like-kind thoughts. Some then make it into a creative art form—perhaps to have themselves feared—perhaps as a test of personal strength to see how long/how intense they can hate one another but yet get along, or not—perhaps as a sporting "Excitement" challenge to get a return of hate since otherwise there is no point. Scenarios IX: People hate those causing them to feel inferior (from envy), intimidated, or wounded. jabaileymd.com

THE HATE PROCESS: Hate is: (1) a sentiment containing thoughtful deliberations which form opinions opposing the Spiritual Elements; (2) checkered with and colored by negative emotions; (3) the imparting of a sense of participation in a core field of meaning; (4) the core meaning's *power to attract out of ones memory all like-kind thoughts and emotions of a similar nature so as to jointly form attributes which* strengthen/enlarge upon that meaning; and (5) mentally stored as an Attitude (C17, disposition, posture). One selects an *Attitude*—i.e. an enduring mainly emotional predisposition to something pertaining to likes/dislikes--for a specific issue and does not necessarily represent a reflection of broader values. Its mental position regarding that issue embraces (fig. 6): (a) a Disposition; (b) a Disposition's *Inclination* (a 'physical' "leaning toward"/"leaning" away from something); and (c) the associated *Temperament* (i.e. a prevailing trend mindset about a Thing/subject/ individual/group--its physiological Sensory Consciousness systems fashioning the type of reaction the aroused person takes to conform to the 'blue-print' of "the *what*" Concept Theme. In summary, a *Sentiment* is an enduring organization of aggressive impulses toward a person or class of persons. Being composed of habitual bitter feeling and accusatory thought, it constitutes stubbornness in ones mental-emotional life.

By its very nature hatred is extro-punitive, which means that the hater is sure that the fault lies in the object of his hate. So long as he believes this he will not feel guilty for his uncharitable state of mind one carries within physiological processes related to "Fight-Flight-Fright." A *Disposition* contains a '*payload' message* of the *essence of the Hate core* and arranges an order for ones mental activities which are in line with the theme of the 'big picture' Icon Image of the Target one has been conditioned to hate. Whereas Anger, an emotion, is felt toward an individual, Hate, a sentiment, tends to be felt toward an entire class of people. One who gives way to anger is often sorry for his outburst and pities the object of his attack, but in expressing hatred, repentance seldom follows. Hatred is more deep-rooted, and constantly "desires the extinction of the object of hate."

The Process: any person, object or event can activate a hateful attitude once a distinct foundation of disdain has been laid. The move from a position of "preference for x and dislike of y" to hatred is now one of intensity. In other words, an element that distinguishes "hatred," at least in its prototypical form, is the intensity of the attitude; indeed, we may say that when one hates, one always does so with a passion. The crucial point here is that the very *rudimentary* and *crude* nature of any category one has been conditioned to respond to instantly, comprises an inherent part of the design. In other words, his mindset is in a state of readiness to think, feel, express, and/or behave in a certain previously conceived manner. An arousal of the sympathetic nervous system occurs so as to prepare one for action. When this process is applied to the police, the Trigger motivates them to act in ways consistent with the Disposition/Attitude pattern. The "alarm switch" is tripped the moment any general feature of the hated Target even remotely resembles that which one fears. Yet, that perception is quite imperfect. For example, if one is stung by a hill country scorpion, thereafter a number of leaves, twigs, and other debris are routinely but mistakenly perceived first as scorpions.

Yet, whichever of these suddenly appears, that Thing activates the "alarm" stimulus contained in a Conditioned Response pertaining to that Target. When the "Killer" Police faces a 'big picture' Icon Image that is deemed suspect, his mindset is instantly arranged to conform to the 'blue-print' fashioned from the Trigger Event. That gives rise to the spotlighted 'big picture' Icon Image. Here, the making of a "realistic decision" is a resolve to do something bad. In surprise situations that first trigger the "fight-flight-fright" response, the resultant springing quickly into action evokes an emotional experience of fear and/or anger—for these seem most easily and most readily aroused as emotional attendants out of the Instinct part of ones Ancient Brain. Perhaps fear most readily correlates with the tendency to take flight or, if trapped mentally or physically, then with Fright. By contrast, a reaction of Anger, which is a bit more studied, is more likely to lean towards the tendency to fight. [Ref: Osborne, *Humanity & Society, 2004*]

EUROPEAN MALES' SUPERNATURAL HATRED: Hatred, Willful Ignorance, and prejudices are like upside-down pyramids which originate and rest on tiny, trivial incidents. Gradually, they spread upward and outward until they fill ones mind. Being man-made, "Hate" has degrees of thoughts and emotions + a destructive inclination. Nevertheless, the System of Hate starts developing within a person when there is an absence of or disconnection from Love. Preconceived notions are the locks on the door of progress. They make judgments without compassion. The less secure one is the more likely one is to have extreme prejudices. Ignorance of police-state philosophy is far more dangerous than ignorance of a bad disease. Both nations and individuals who know the least of others think the highest of themselves. Ignorance is both the mother of devotion and of superstition. Ignorance is the womb of monsters; the preventor of wisdom; and the creator of delusions. Police who do not know Black People are like one who has never seen a river and imagines the first one met to be the sea. All of this is contributed to by religion. The Ten Commandments instruct people not to "covet ones neighbor's manservant (= Slave)," but makes no comment about a neighbor owning a Slave in the first place. Yet, Believers are also told not to covet his donkey. The great patriarch Abraham--Kierkegaard's "Knight of Faith"--owned Slaves. The apostle Paul returned a runaway Slave to his master. Jesus did not condemn the widespread slavery in the Roman world. If slavery was wrong, why does the Bible not condemn it? Change from being in a mental status quo will come only by the Higher Self evolution of ones Character traits.

Whereas African Tradition considers "Hate" as a "state" of mind cut-off from the Spiritual Elements, for Europeans Hate speaks of an old, enduring flow—not of Human Nature as ancient Greeks said—but of acquired negative emotions which lack compassion or sorrow for those Targeted. Its original meaning was a 'strong feeling' (Indo-European); strong dislike (Germanic); and in Beowulf (725) as extreme dislike associated with such spite as for one to pursue the hunt in order to do harm—an idea brought into C14 English as heinous. Accretions to these concepts included: Greek (Gk, kad, not caring) anxiety and grief; Old Irish both love and Hate—perhaps where the concept arose that the opposite of love is hate—a false concept in African Tradition; and the synonyms for "Hate"--e.g. envy, sorrow, fear, and abhor. The Dalai Lama (Mind Science p. 113) says Hatred is a very negative energy that poisons the person who holds it and leads him or her to act in ways that cause harm to those towards whom it is directed. Hate is not preservation and union, but destruction and separation; not happiness and well-being, but misery and being in the worse possible state. The sense of hate is worsened in situations that tend to arouse other destructive dimensions (e.g. bad emotions) as well as, for example, daily Enslaved experiences of being bombarded with demeaning statements and being treated inhumanely. In the European Bible the word "Hatred" is seldom found while religious leaders say hatred robs one of judgment and of compassion. Such concepts believed about their God makes it acceptable to have strong hatred of what each individual deems to be evil. By saying God is balanced and then to model that means humans are "balanced" to be good to those they choose are deserving is "conditional" based upon ones choice.

Elsewhere, Europeans define "Hate" is a disposition containing an emotional response that desires to impart rejection, detestation displays, and dissociation from the Trigger Person(s); opposite of love and the absence of sympathy or kindly sentiment; a state of active ill-will; animosity to people or God; aversion from things; malicious and unjustifiable feelings directed to undeserving people; calling on God to aid executions of vengeance; and hatred of evil. In other European literature love and hate are viewed as a psychic battleground where they war with each other. As seen in all Europeans involved in the slave trade, justification for their inhumaneness came from their Adversion ("hateful face-to-face opposition") attitudes and the slave owners' Aversion ("to turn away from" and shutting down all beliefs of a shared culture and humanity with Blacks)--both allowing them to declare the Enslaved as "subhuman" for purposes of exploitation and sadistic punishment. Aversion's complementary partners, *Adversion* (a), was shown by the ex-convict slave overseers who had been released from European jails on the condition that they would leave Europe forever by going to America. Most became overseers on slave ships and plantations; became the "redneck racists" of the South; became the police of the Enslaved; and became the Ku Klux Klan members. These ex-convicts and the patterns they set up in the South included being filled with negative (e.g. anger) and destructive (e.g. hate, revengeful) emotions to such an intense degree that they acted impulsively in carrying out the most despicable of crimes against the Enslaved. In order to fashion *Willful Ignorance* about Black People (a "Don't Care to know anything about those people), they built a Supernatural wall around themselves. This and their bruteness kept them from seeing their victims as "fellow creatures." This allowed these haters to fill in the resultant vacant mental spaces with thoughts of opposition, feelings of disgust, and practices of rejection and ostracism. Oddly, an early European definition of "Hate" embraced both love and dislike.

In short, in typical European style, definitions for the same word go include going in opposite directions and anywhere in between. It is my impression that Hatred is the Base or "Seed" for all that formed the European Supernatural—for all that flows out of it—and for all that will sustain it and its members "forever." It shows within oneself initially in those with an Inferiority Complex. Based upon my observations, research findings, and experiences with European males, particularly in the marketplace, my guesstimate of their self-hatred is 40% in the Extreme category; perhaps 20% of a moderate degree; 15% of a slight degree; 10% of a mild degree; and 15% not so afflicted. Self-declared 'little gods' have hatred socialized into them in childhood.

In Biblical times, much of the way language was used is very different from today—and many, to the detriment of all they influence, fail to make that distinction. Instead, they simply transfer at face value concepts as said back then to the present. Nevertheless, in one Biblical sense, Hate is a malicious attitude—variously referring to *Abomination* (hatred of ones qualities), *Enmity* (hatred of the person from ill-will), *Loathing*, and *Detesting*. In another European sense, Hate is a mark of spirituality—e.g. God's people must actively hate evil (Ps 97:10). For example, in the European Bible, Jesus' call to hate ones family (Mt. 10:37; Lk 14:26) and even to 'hate ones life in this world' (Jn. 12: 25) is interpreted by European religious leaders as a command, not to hate emotionally, but to reject anything which might claim a higher allegiance that their God. The OT accepted hatred among humans as part of normal life as well as "the sinner hates the light (Jn3:20). By Europeans having an anthropomorphic Supernatural God, their leaders attribute their own emotions to that God, as in saying God hates evil (e.g. Prov. 6:16); God's choice of agents of his purpose: "I loved Jacob and I hated Esau"; and will have no relationship with the evildoer. This is followed by the leaders saying God is always balanced by his attributes of love and compassion.

As a boyhood, I wondered if by many Europeans making their God in their own image is not idolatry or self-image worship. If so, that might lead many Believers away from their European Christianity teaching of being dependent on God all the way over to having a reliance on something that expresses their own desired religious thoughts and motivations. If so, the European Bible says (Isa 2:8-22) that this is an expression of human pride and arrogance—cutting one off from a knowledge of ones own moral character—a cut-off that denies one of a standard against which to measure ones choices. Such would account for my noticing these same Believers engaging in hypocritical worship (i.e. ignoring the moral standards they preach). Such conflicts, accounting for the absence of a sound moral standard leads one in different ways. One is to hate whomever one desires and for any reason that is to ones dislike. This in keeping with Pythagoras (582-500 BC) teaching European males, that *"man is the measure of all things,"* and not God. The implication is that each man is to declare himself to be a "little god" who independently determines what is right and decent. Then drawing on their Manichaean religion concepts of "White" (or Light) destroying "Black" (or Evil) Believers have thereafter used both concepts to justify fighting the evil about things they decide are compatible with their spiritual and ethical ideals; or what they consider to be others' false gods; or whom they consider to be pagans. These resulted in over a billion deaths. Millions of deaths have occurred from such fights.

Even the European Bible says Hatred is associated with interpersonal strife (Pr 10:12), lies, and violence (Pr 29:10). Perhaps this proceeds by the Hate-filled people—whether based upon the European Bible or Brutes or people imitating Brutes—creating anti-Spiritual Elements emotional *reactions* that manifest as decisively rejecting them; having strong antagonism toward them; experiencing pleasure when the hated person is injured and anger when he/she receives favors. Today, "Hate" is defined as an intense deep-seated dislike and strong aversion coupled with a strong malicious desire to harm or to destroy the object of ones emotions.

BLACK PEOPLE'S OPINIONS ABOUT HATE: "To hate, to be violent is demeaning. It means you're afraid of the other side of the coin—to love and be loved" (James Baldwin 1924-1987). "When our thoughts—which bring actions—are filled with hate against anyone, Negro or white, we are in a living hell. That is as real as hell ever will be" (George Washington Carver 1864?-1943). "When a man is despised and hated by other men and all around are the instruments of violence in behalf of such attitudes, then he may find himself resorting to hatred as a means of salvaging a sense of self, however fragmented" (Howard Thurman 1899-1981). "As soon as healing takes place [from hatred], go out and heal somebody else" (Maya Angelou). "I hate the corrupt, slaveholding, women-whipping, cradle-plundering, partial, and hypocritical Christianity of the land" (Frederick Douglass 1817-1895). "We share a hatred for the alienation forced upon us by Europeans during the process of colonization and empire, and we are bound more by our common suffering than by our pigmentation" (Ralph Ellison 1914-1974). "If the masses of Negroes can save their self-respect and remain free from hate, so much the better of their moral development" (E. Franklin Frazier 1894-1962).

"You never knew what it is to be a slave; to be entirely unprotected by law or custom; to have the laws reduce you to the condition of a chattel, entirely subject to the will of another. You never exhausted your ingenuity in avoiding snares, and eluding the power of a hated tyrant; you never shuddered at the sound of his footsteps, and trembled within hearing of his voice" (Harriet Jacobs, 1813-1897). "Until my mid-teens I lived in fear; fear of being shot, lynched or beaten to death—not for any wrong doing of my own….I could have easily been the victim of mistaken identity or an act of terror by hate-filled white men" (Gordon Parks). "The opposite of love was not hate but indifference" (Bill Russell). "We have survived the Middle Passage and we have survived slavery. We have survived the deadly arbitrariness of Jim Crow and the hatefulness of northern discrimination. But now we face a danger more covert, more insidious, more threatening and potentially more final even than these: the apparently sly conspiracy to do away with black men as a troublesome presence in America" (William Strickland). "A system of oppression draws much of its strength from the acquiescence of its victims who have accepted the dominant image of themselves and are paralyzed by a sense of helplessness" (Pauli Murray (1910-1985).

"Self-Hate is a form of mental slavery that results in poverty, ignorance and crime" (Susan Taylor). "Hated by whites and being an organic part of the culture that hated him, the black man grew in turn to hate in himself that which others hated in him" (Richard Wright 1908-1960). America's greatest crime against the black man was not slavery or lynching, but that he was taught to wear a mask of self-hate and self-doubt" (Malcolm X 1925-1965). "Who taught you to hate the texture of your hair" Who taught you to hate the color of your skin"...Who taught you to hate your self?" (Malcolm X). "In hating Africa and in hating Africans, we ended up hating ourselves without even realizing it" (Malcolm X). My opinion is that hate causes one to think of the hated Trigger Person(s) or thing more often and that gives it increasing energy and power.

HATRED IN AFRICAN TRADITION

In my research of creditable African Tradition scholars, I did not see Hate discussed as something to shed. Instead, "Hate" was only mentioned by Europeans writing about African Tradition—and for me such writings by Europeans about Black People have no credibility. Nevertheless, Ancient Africans personified the Indifference/Hate/Evil/Sadism Complex in the mythological god Set—the one darkened from within—the one containing ingredients that could be quickly inserted as a fixed disturbance in a Receiver's mind—a disturbance sprouting various branches of significance that "Cloud out" who one really is. This "Cloud out" leaves one with an awareness of a definite feeling of existing in the world as a separate Being—a fluke—"I'm a stranger in this world that comes out of somewhere else." That Hallucination ('astray thoughts') is a phantom and, by having no solid actuality base, makes one unable to distinguish Fantasy from Reality'. Hence, one is a 'push-over' for how people daily use Fantasy in "SEEMS" right and "ALMOST Enough" situations to deceive others and to deceive themselves by 'self-talk'. Such represents a state of Ignorance (not to know; to overlook) of the higher Spiritual reality. These features, representing a Dualistic view of life, can lead to agitation, suffering, and even catastrophic events in humans' experiences--a degraded condition which opens doors to the deep-rooted fears and sense of Inadequacy. In turn, "I'm not Good Enough!" translates into anger, resentment, greed, External World addictions, Hatred, Violence, and all other negative human tendencies as the only way they know to express their deeper Spiritual Human Nature Needs. Besides, to hate means ones life is empty and one fails to appreciate ones time, energy, and efforts. Those who are about their Mission in life do not have time to waste on hating something that goes nowhere while doing nothing good.

To do any of these unnatural things is Self-Disrespectful. And there is no acceptable substitute for Hate—not even being Indifferent to the Trigger Persons, for Indifference is the essence entrance into Inhumanity. By hating, ones life gets caught up in vicious cycles. Ancient Africans said: "the Untruth of Separateness becomes Hate, which sub-divides into Fear of the stronger, Anger against equals, and Scorn of the weaker—with numerous degrees and modifications". To elaborate, one then notices only what one thinks is noteworthy and ignores not only what is around it in the Foreground but also ignores the Background it is on. This causes one to give interpretations to what one sees and assesses that are far from reality. If a circle is drawn on the chalk board, the circle could not be seen without that chalk board. Furthermore, the correct depiction of the illustration may be that there is a hole in the chalk board. Restricted focus = restricted awareness = restricted attention. Thus, Hate is to be ignorant of the 'big picture' of a reality, for how the ingredients involved in what is hated may not be completely seen, or properly fitted together, or correctly interpreted. Also, hate may be unjustified--for the accused may be innocent or the happenings were unintended for the hater, but did harm by a fluke. Meanwhile, not to pursue the Truth leads to the formation of a False Self—i.e. seeing oneself as separate/distinct from the world and from other living Beings. African Sages added that although this would seem real and abiding to the human mind, such is only an outer expression of the underlying essence from which they originate. In reality, the substratum of all that exists—i.e. the underlying essence of all things—is a non-dual and all-encompassing unity.

Practicing the *Law of Sympathy* (all God's creatures and creations are spiritually connected, regardless of even remote time or space) is the way to "Salvation"/"Resurrection". African Sages stressed the philosophy of service to Humanity, as opposed to leaving Humanity and dwelling in isolation. Living within the context of the Law of Sympathy is a natural state—meaning there is no need to debate about ones treatment of others because the right things to do (based upon Unconditional Love, Truth, Compassion, Forgiveness, and Magnanimity) simply 'instinctually' flow out. The only way to promote peace and harmony in the world is by purifying every bit of negativity within oneself and, as a result, that self-cleansing manifestation is capable of promoting true harmony and peace in many others (Ashby, Egyptian Book of the Dead p33). jabaileymd.com

SELF-HATE: Self-Hate is the anti-Spiritual Elements attack on Self-Love. For much of my life I have heard or read about Europeans saying Black People hate themselves. However, in getting deeply into the lives of many Black People in my medical practice and otherwise, I have never seen any evidence of them having Self-Hatred. Instead, what seems right to me is present in historic records of mutinies (e.g. the slave ships *Henry* and *Amistad*) of what Enslaved Africans thought of themselves. In these records are the comments that while *Africans saw themselves as "inferiorized," or placed into a subordinate position, they did not develop an identity as inferior beings.* This is similar to how I assess the Self-Esteem context in today's struggling Black Americans. Without question, there are aspects within certain ones that come close to being hated but that is because of the unspeakable inhumanities showered on them by Europeans. By contrast, the single most important generalized insight resulting from my intense 50 year study of the European male mind is the infinite scope, height, and depth of their own self-hatred. Supportive of this statement is the European Alfred Adler (1870-1937)--credited with coining the concept of *"Inferiority Complex"*—who said: "self-hatred consists of strong feelings of inadequacy and insecurity stemming from real or fancied deficiencies of a physical, mental, or social nature. The page overall result--when combined with anxiety, resentment, and over-compensatory drives--would be to adversely affect the individual's entire adjustment to life." The European Myers quoted the European John Powell as saying: *all of us have inferiority complexes. Those who seem to not have such a complex are only pretending."* Humanistic psychologist Carl Rogers concluded, said Myers, that most people he knew *"despise themselves, regard themselves as worthless and unlovable".* Myers added that many popularizers of humanistic psychology concur (those concerned with higher human motives, self-development, knowledge, understanding, and esthetics).

In my view, some time after birth those destined to be Self-Haters swallowed a poisonous emotional drink that slowly ate up their "Hearts" and thereby extinguished their "ME/WE" birth gift values. The extinction of those values provided fertile ground for Self-Hatred. As the proliferating "vines" spread everywhere, with tentacles like an octopus, the venom of self-hatred proceeds to destroy ones own Selfhood, other people, and Nature—having left an evolving accumulation of waste of unfulfilled promises and potential possibilities of untold magnitude. Since Self-Hate is not natural to ones Real Self, it automatically puts one into a Self-Unknown realm with a False Self. For those destined to become "Killer" police, their False self is very susceptible to their Satanist leaders constantly preaching vigorous messages to every new generation concerning what preserves the lethal occult fantasies handed down through the ages and how to carry them out by means of the GUN (including the bomb).

The theme of Hatred is that the GUN can solve any differences of opinions presented by problematic people. The justification is that this contributes to the ongoing revolution designed to close any open doors and limit all choices of "those people" because all of this is "ours". Here, one can so extremely self-hate as to enter into the following:

Type I, residing in an "Air Castle" of the Supernatural and declare themselves to be a 'little god' and thereafter worship themselves so as to enlarge the dimensions of their narcissism. Their way of seeing how they look is by standing in front of a mirror with their eyes closed. Their lifestyle is to refuse themselves nothing, deny scapegoats everything, and demand those under their influence to live and do as they are told. Their past-time is spent developing skills in the art of generating delusions with chimaeria Icon Images created as justification for doing harm to the victim accused of being the "enemy." From those impressions, predetermined dispositions serve as patterns for dealing with scapegoats. *Type II* are those who spring with "Self-Righteousness" from the "bottom" of their "Air Castle". By being unable to govern their own Self-Hatred, they devote their time, as despots, to attempting to govern others. In using "Air Castle" standards, their hate is acted out under the guise of virtue--expressing "Righteous" (Moral) Indignation to non-conformers of what they say or believe. By seeking out and catching those who squirm from being exposed, their Righteous Indignation is justification for indulging in legitimately allowed "Air Castle" sadism or killings. Since the hatred they throw out boomerangs, it adds fuel to their drive to capitalize on that abundance by finding benefits—as in being challenged to fight for a Cause—a Cause justifying intensifying the wrongs they do. Becoming skilled at doing those wrongs gives them a self-identity to which they cling with pride. *Type III*, by failing to devise a workable defense mechanism to achieve a Superiority Complex, remain with an Inferiority Complex. Those moderately affected become "Zombies" in following their "Air Castle" Satanist leaders. The most severely affected commit suicide—either directly or in a mass murder to be killed by the police; others adopt the role of being "Killer" police, particularly because they can 'hide' under their "Network's" wing.

Since I have never even thought about hating myself or hating anyone, I cannot relate personally to what hate is like. Yet, Hatred displays and their effects and consequences are no mystery. The nature of self-hatred is to spew venom in every direction—both inside and outside. The self-hatred that destroys ones own Selfhood, other people, and Nature is an evolving accumulation of waste of unfulfilled promises and potential possibilities of untold magnitude. It results in *Delusional Fears*— the imagining of false problems which leads one to seek ones own profits by any means necessary or to be the profit of others—i.e. the being of prey on others or the allowing of oneself to needlessly become prey. This is the root and source of all natural and moral evils. "Delusional Fear(s)" generate behaviors constituting the Brute Syndrome and when chronic they become addicted to possessing all the features of the Brute Brain. It is this Brute Brain "Delusional Fear" that is at the base of ones Dark Side. One assumes the "Life-Living" state of living by oneself and for oneself by greedy clutchings of significant things solely for ones one benefit. European psychiatrists see the irrational hostility people everywhere vent upon one another as chiefly projected self-hate.

EVIL

"EVIL" is prepared by the mindset of Indifference to the Spiritual Elements and is produced by the products of the Contingent Being activity of Hate--all products stemming from Ignorance. What Evil *Does*—because of its interplay with Indifference/Hate/Sadism—is to generate a variety of Effects and Consequences. Examples of *Effects* are Spiritual and Emotional Pain, Fear, Rage, and Depression. Examples of *Consequences* are tragedy, suffering, misery, health destruction, accelerated aging, and chronic unhappiness. How evil *Appears* include displays that are wicked, vile, sinful, depraved; as inequity, injustice, and wrong; and as the violation of God's intention. Thus, the word "Evil" is packed with all forms of hate-filled products of destruction inside an Unreality. If there are torrential rains which cause destruction, this is not "Evil" because the rains are being compatible with what Nature guides it to do. But the consequences may be bad for people under certain circumstances (as preventing outdoor activities) while not for the 'big picture' (as in ending drought). The cause of Evil is humans' inordinate desires for selfish satisfaction as separative ends based on misdirection of strength of purpose, patience, and self-preservation.

AFRICAN TRADITIONS' EVILNESS IN HUMANS: In African Tradition, on any plane of Cosmic Existence, Evilness is whatever threatens, disturbs, attacks, damages, destroys, or replaces the Spiritual Circle of Wholism. Nevertheless, because of Certainty in the existence of only one Spiritual Universal High all Creator God, there are no concepts, as in European tradition, of humans possessing "Original Sin" or being inherently "Evil by nature"; no concept of Evil being a reality; no concept of a devil or a Hell; and no worshipping of a Supernatural (made-up) God. For these reasons, all Evilness is deemed to be a Supernatural disorderly non-reality drama, manifested out of Metaphysical Disorder. Humans engaged in Evil practices are partially or completely outside the Ordered, Harmonized, and Balanced Cosmic Spiritual Elements Stream--a state resulting from having broken connection with the Spiritual Elements in any form and to any degree--a state signifying one is so weakened by a mindset of Unreality as to be either stepping into or swimming with the flow of the Set (Setian, Satanist) form of Disorder--i.e. in the Indifference, Hate, Evil, Sadism (IHES) Complex.

This Metaphysical Disorder state blocks access to ones human divinity and to ones Conscience. Afflicted humans make choices out of ignorance of the Spiritual Elements being the right path of personal eternal importance. In the Secular world, examples of Evil displays are: deception by desires to entrap and control whoever/whatever has material Value; damaging things of Worth (i.e. things of Spiritual Beauty); exploitation of people--Things—Nature, including designed delusions about them for destruction; gaining positions of strength by *projecting* ones Evilness onto the defenseless; oppression of the Weak; dishonorableness (lie, cheat, steal); infliction of needless pain, suffering, disability, death; and whatever elevates human's Lower (animal) Self over the Highest (divinity) Self.

Regardless of the Cause of getting off the *Spiritual Circle of Wholism* (meaning the Spiritual Elements in their various forms of presentation out of the Cosmic Organism and out of a given human's Private Selfhood), there are predictable Effects which give rise to layers of Consequences. To elaborate, an IHES mindset is filled with false self-fashioned perceived personal power, completeness, and sufficiency apart from God. It is characterized by living out of *Illusions* (like magicians on stage who present a false front hiding what is really there) or *Hallucinations* (perceiving something not true in any world and yet accepted as real) generated by ignorant and/or evil acting people. By repeating these lies long enough or by believing "everyone is doing it and thus it must be right" leads the afflicted into *Delusions*--leads to deceptive maneuverings inside Unreality and then manipulating things perceived to be in it--leads to clinging to fixed non-truth ideas ("liar/lier" in wait")--and leads to procrastination games: "I'll do it later."

To repeat, to start building a Thought Structure" out of a Delusion means its Base is in "airy quick sand" because a Delusion has no subsistence in its own proper nature—i.e. it has no "Ground of Being." In short, a Delusion has no power of subsisting by itself. It can only continue by Belief or Faith. What then happens is one uses flawed "logical" thinking--perhaps starting with a distorted major premise in a Syllogism--then using the right method of proceeding--and coming to a "Valid" conclusion that is on the wrong track. Such wrong tract thinking + a delusional and ignorant mindset make one vulnerable to more wrong tract thinking + delusions as one goes deeper and deeper into ignorance in anti-Spiritual Elements realms. Such Consequences make one acutely aware of lacking ones in-born Spiritual Human Nature Needs. That features desperation to find relief from ones Spiritual Pain--the worst experience a human can have--by accepting outrageous Beliefs.

One such belief is in those who paint vivid images of a non-existent devil punishing one for life and of Satan's power being greater than God's power. Both could SEEM right because the majority of today's people are dishonorable and do mean things. Second, it is convenient to represent Satan as a Contingent Being, passed off as a realistic spirit, so as to keep anyone from discovering and fighting the real people Satanists hiding behind trickery, deception, and the "GUN". But Ancient Africans said Satan is merely the human who exploits and uses people to gain control over the world (as his killers in wars of conquest). Satanists use, as a means of deception, all forms of aggression and divisiveness (divide and conquer) to achieve their ends while denouncing everyone who uses such methods to oppose their evil deeds. A third false belief is happiness and thriving exist from External World things--apart from ones own Divine Intelligence and living a Ma'at lifestyle. jabaileymd.com

EUROPEAN EVILNESS: In European tradition, Evilness' scope, height, depth, consistency, variety, and magnitude of destructiveness are unequaled in the history of human-kind. Yet, in European literature it is extremely difficult to gain an idea of Evil's Moral (about Sin)"what it is" aspects. The relatively few books which mention Evil do so from "what it is associated with," "what it does," and "how it appears." No help comes from the etymology of the Old English word "Evil"--originally meaning "uppity"--then "Bad"--then extreme moral wickedness--then in 1280 AD, "Shrewd," signifying evil, malicious, and dangerous before its sense changed in 1520 to astute and cunning--and then to cleverness, scheming, and deception. None of these are to be confused with intelligence because they are of an patterned nature, perfected by Innovation (adding something new to what already exists and, in this situation, has been done for 45,000 years). Today's ruling European Evil concepts seem to be the choicest opinions of the most accepted "authorities." In general, these Evilness concepts are selectively attentive to what is in the Physical and the European versions of the Supernatural realms. What is "against a materialistic Good life" is often the standard to which Evil is compared and judged--especially for European males, and with no generally offered and acceptable justifying definitions, explanations, or reasons. Examples of how they say Evil is allowed to enter into the Selfhood of humans includes: (1) one loses a sense of ones belief in the presence of ones chosen Supernatural God; (2) the "fall of man" (i.e. Adam and Eve); (3) whatever causes harm or deprives a Being of some good which is proper to that Being; (4) self-imposed Evil from a refusal to think; and (5) based upon their varied definitions of "Virtue," many Western religions relate the problem of evil to a movement away from their specifically self-defined "Virtues," under influences of a demon/devil. That enables them to say, without cross-cultural Sages' agreement, that Evil is a defect in moral purity and truth--whether in heart or life--whether of commission or omission. By then assigning the blame to an outside force allows people with poor moral development to shirk responsibility for their evil actions. Though the African mythological god Set (who Europeans adopted as fact and made into a 'factual' Satan) was borrowed into the Judeo-Christian religion or philosophy as Lucifer (e.g. featuring a fall from Grace and moral deterioration after virtue), no help in pin-pointing can be found here since there is great confusion about how they represent Evil. Satan, Evil, and Dark (signifying misery, punishment, perdition or loss of the soul and hell) became the trio Europeans used to characterize the "Dark Side"--and with the justification of: "the Devil made me do it." Millennia later, Set became the basis of the Christian Satan--an evil Supernatural entity honored with a superhuman status; an opposing reality to God (a form of idolatry) and a user of blasphemy (false statements, problem creators, hypocrisy, or done out of "Me, Me" self-interest).

In European literature, the "Occult" refers to the mysterious lying below the surface of things or beyond the ordinary range of ones information, perception, or understanding. Historically, it has been applied to the Magical Arts, witchcraft, astrology, alchemy, palmistry, and all aspects of the Supernatural (the made-up). Within these wide-ranging beliefs are concepts of Evil--essentially all deemed to be "Natural"--defined by them as what is beyond a human's control. That spanning range of Secular and Supernatural Evil--for which Europeans use the term *"Dark Side"*--embraces every degree of the IHES Complex--Indifference, Hate, Evilness, Sadism. The Indifference part is shown by those with one foot in the IHES Complex stream flow and the other foot on shore; those standing on the shore--the Hate part; those walking away from the shore and wandering into Evil Unknowns--called Brutes--the Secular Evil part. Satanists, do all they can to destroy the flow and dissipate the Stream while trapping all humans possible in their fishnet so as to perform Sadism acts. Those in the IHES Complex operate in the realms of *Illusions* (in attempts to affirm truth for deception, as opposed to Truth's operation through Reality to affirm itself) and Hallucinations. These fashion Delusions characterized by "Me, Me" Individualism--Evil "sick" pleasures--and Fetters--e.g. hatred, fear, lies, jealousy, egoism, anger, greed, lust, and envy. jabaileymd.com

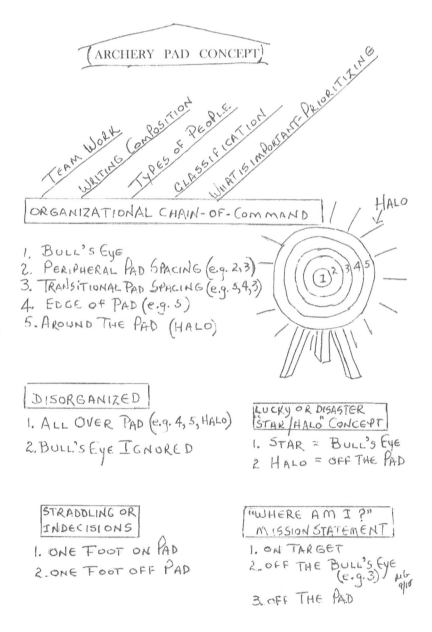

FIGURE 7

CLASSIFYING EVIL: A Classification is simply subdividing its group's family resemblances into Classes. Classes are shared characteristics, like synonyms, that follow a theme. A theme is a *maintained central or dominating idea arising from a common origin or "what it does" or "how it appears" or its shared properties*. The purposes of a Classification are varied and include: establishing Order; enhancing Understanding; Prioritizing so as to deal with the most important or the most pertinent; and to Prepare for Change in order to maintain the "5Ss"--Safety, Security, Sureness, Strength, and Stability. For subjects of Evil, all of the following are: devoid of their "5Ss," Selfhood Greatness, and the meeting of their Spiritual Human Nature Needs; unaware of the pain and suffering they cause as they continue to strike blindly at anyone nearby; and may present their evilness in overt, tempered, masked, or concealed form with an intensity of a Mild, Slight, Moderate, or Extreme degree. Organization of Classification I involves the *Archery Pad Concept* (fig. 7). Around its Bull's Eye center space are four more transitional ringed spaces, separated by 5 line circles--thus making a total of ten parts. In the Bull's Eye--as agreed to by the Sages of all cultures and all ages--are the lowest kinds of humans. They are symbolized by the African mythological god Set. (1) are hardcore Satanists--the most sadistic of all the amoral--who live by force and are always in a warring mood. Their 'Sick' pleasures come from causing pain and suffering. Nothing can be done with them. (2) On the first circle around the bull's eye are the less force focused animalistic Peripheral Brutes who hypocritically show periodic faint morals; (3) are Transitional Brutes who are sometimes bothered by a conscience for doing evil deeds; (4) Brute Imitators are on the periphery of or off the pad; and (5) Little Humans who live dishonorably (e.g. cheat, steal, lie, hurt others for no reason, gossip)--while advocating social laws for others to live by.

Classification II is *Fetter People* (e.g. extreme selfishness, greed, hatred, anger, egoism, fear, envy, jealousy, frustration, arrogance, pride, lust, or conceit). All are intensely desirous of receiving but not giving from being "Me, Me, Me" orientated and are UNCARING about others. *Mindset I* possesses brutally violent philosophies; focus on power, virility, and sexuality; and design Fear situations as reason for self-gain attacks. *Mindset II* are the significantly and repeatedly psychically damaged. Those who are vaguely aware of what is right cope by "Numbing" themselves from the Spiritual Elements. Yet, many "thaw out" once in prison and reform after realizing the misery they cause others. *Mindset III* observe bad things done in an Evil atmosphere, eventually getting used to Evil. Some promote evil by being blind to it. Others are overwhelmed into an apathetic state. With either type, Evil people can easily control them. *Mindset IV* join gangs--either to "go along to get along" (perceiving this as their only option for survival) or because Evil is all they know. *Mindset V* is those who, because evil cannot be avoided, tolerate it without being aware of it poisoning their whole system. Out of that absorption of Evil, it is spontaneously sprayed unchecked and in all directions.

Classification III is subdivided into types. Type I displays as one having full awareness that a particular behavior goes against the Spiritual Elements and yet one chooses to continue with its Evilness. Type II is the committing of many wrongs out of ignorance by those who know such evils can be eliminated--but still they choose not to do the required intense spiritually correcting hard work--justifying their procrastination with being "Too Busy." Type III "pick and choose" in doing spiritual work--doing only enough to get a "gist" of what it is about--skipping sessions--coming late--leaving early--preferring the Superficial--deceiving themselves that by being "acquainted" with life-shaping or life-changing knowledge is equivalent to having internalized it--and being addicted to people. These three Types signify the effects of a human's Free Will choosing a non-Spiritual Elements path--a path flirting with the Indifference/Hate/Evil/Sadism (IHES) Complex--a non-Spiritual Elements path automatically interfering with the Love flow out of ones *Love Platter*--the instinct to Love; to spread Love; to be Loved; and to be Lovable. Spiritual Ignorance--disorder in action--leads to bad choices, decisions, and solutions as well as put one in bad situations and/or around bad people. Only living out of the Spiritual Circle of Wholism will work. jabaileymd.com

CRITICALLY THINKING EVIL: Critically Thinking (CT) Evil starts with seeing a big picture of what is/is not Evil--an assessment having a special relation and motivation for constructing and moving toward a Human Ideal goal. Success only comes by knowing what is real--with Courage to be oneself--and making non-emotional decisions. Ancient Africans said the *Cosmic Organism's* Circle of Wholism includes all of God's creatures and creations encircled inside the Spiritual Elements and whatever is outside that Circle represents some form of Evil. As opposed to those saying God created Evil, *God's Unconditional Love (UL) inner nature naturally allows each human freedom to decide to be inside or outside that Circle*--the Circle also inside a human's own brain/mind. Ancient Africans represented the Circle's outsides with dangerous and unpleasant animals--i.e. Apep (Apophics), the serpent archenemy of the spirit of God and of humans + Set (a scorpion, serpent, hippopotamus, crocodile, wild ass, wild boar, and pig)--an unidentified mammalian and the archenemy beast of human's and God's divinity. These two animal centers in humans' brain--the Ancient (Reptilian) and the Old Mammalian brains--are home to Instinct, Omnibus, and Brute Emotions. They pertain to Evil within the context of *"is it for me or against me?"* By these two animal brain centers controlling the early part of every human's life and being main sources of ones natures means a human's physical nature is an animal born mindset--a nature able to hinder humans from perfecting or even striving for their Highest (Divinity) Selves. Since *Evil derives from ones brain*, failing to cultivate corrective faculties is a Metaphysical Disorder.

Such Spiritual Evil is enhanced by outside forces in the name of religion. Some say Satan exists as a sort of "bogeyman"--one equal to or greater in power than African Tradition's Spiritual One Universal High God--a common allusion to a mythical monster--a contingent or "virtual" concept having no reality or specific appearance in itself. Believers are easily controlled by this non-specific embodiment of terror and thereby can be misled into Spiritual Disorder. When these evil religious messages were delivered to the Enslaved during African American slavery, their Spiritual God was subtly replaced with a Contingent God telling them to live life serving the captors. That substitution left victims with some doubts and thus caused them to "pick and choose" what to believe. The resultant collage was fashioned into a religious tow-rope held on to today. Despite its self-defeating features, victims built a lifestyle around this tow-rope and have so tightly clutched it as to prevent its removal by means of Truth. This is because their lack of awareness of the Ultimate leads to the false belief that if they let go of their Tow-rope they will have nothing left. *CT indicates that if Evil, as Evil, positively subsisted, it would be Evil to itself and would therefore destroy itself.* One can prove to oneself that Evil lacks any power to do damage to any birth gifts ones has (e.g. ones Soul) by one simply reattaching to ones birth gift of Selfhood Greatness and noticing the immediate benefits.

Satan's only power is the power a human gives him. That giving of power is done by remaining addicted to ones Lower (animalistic spirit) Self pleasures--an addiction indicated by Emotionally clinging to living a non-thinking life and seeking only what excites ones Emotions. Evil is impotent and has no power unless and until one hands over ones own power--as occurs when one allows anti-Spiritual Elements to Cloud out ones "Soul Sunshine" and all of its powers. *Evil cannot be a thing in itself for it is merely the absence of Good and God.* Thus, it is experienced when there is not enough Good to go round. When people lack the Courage to stay within the Circle of Cosmic Wholism, Brutes rush in to lead them into evil. When virtuous people's loyalty to an unyielding purpose is dropped, the gap is filled with some aspect of the Indifference/Hate/Evil/Sadism Complex and that turns average people into Brutes. When people reduce their virtues to what merely SEEMS okay, then Evil acquires the force of an absolute. Evil profits when Good compromises with it. Evil wins by default. Evil wins when the Good serves it. Evil wins by the moral failure of those to take a stand against it or if the society is evilly irrational. *Right living expands, cultivates, and perceives more deeply the perception of the negation of the evil within and around oneself.* That causes wider and deeper visions of and attraction to God and the Good. That is the way to promote Spiritual growth. jabaileymd.com

SADISM

Whereas early Christianity's Psalm 73 defined *Masochism as self-aggression turned inwards,* during the Dark Ages "SADISM" was defined as self-*aggression turned outward.* Sadistic practices originated in antiquity, particularly in the form of floggings or torture of animals, captives, Slaves, servants, children, wives, and concubines—practices most notably seen and preserved strongly among European males in totalitarian, militaristic, and patriarchal cultures--practices the Church, during Biblical times, deemed to be evil and the work of Satan. In the European Bible's Psalm 73, in depicting the character of arrogant sadists, says: From their callous hearts come iniquity; the evil conceits of their minds know no limits. They scoff, and speak with malice; in their arrogance they threaten oppression. Their mouths lay claim to heaven, and their tongues take possession of the earth. Let us pick up this wide-spread and complex story of Sadism in C7 when Europeans called on Ancient Africans' four vehicles of evil and named them "Black" Magic, Witches, Wizards (male 'witches' or 'warlocks'), and Sorcerers (Bailey, Freeing Enslaved Minds) to fashion their own practices they called Satanism. *Satanism* means "the opposition" to Christianity; "he who opposes".

Beneath the Satanist emblem of Baphomet, the horned god, they engaged in indulgences of the flesh and of the senses. The patterns thereby developed have not changed much since then. The witches and black magicians under the banner of Satanism came (and continue to come) from a variety of social class backgrounds and possess all shades of political opinions. The inhumane religious "*Trials by Ordeals*" were particularly prominent in the European Middle Ages. The C13 to early C19 Roman Catholic Church used questioning by torture in the Inquisitions (discovering and punishing heretics). Torture was also used in civil courts up to C20, including witchcraft trials in colonial (USA) New England (Bailey, Special Minds). What grabbed my attention and has made a lasting impression concerned European practices of not only killing babies, women, and men everywhere they went but also *chopping them up*! How can a mind be so warped as to get "sick" pleasure from seeing or causing other living things to suffer to such an extreme degree—and having an urge to destroy them after they were dead? European authorities say Sadistic people do not feel what they do is wrong, finding instead their deeds to be socially maladaptive and therefore disruptive. Whereas most people experience distress after hurting an innocent person, for Sadists cruelty affords a pleasurable, exciting, perhaps even sexually arousing emotional experience. Instead of seeking to alleviate suffering, these individuals may seek opportunities to exercise brutality and indulge their appetites for cruelty.

A peek at the dominant influence they have on the public is seen in the popularity of violent films, brutal sports, and video games with cruel content as well as incidents of police and military brutality. Sadists obtain pleasure from cruel behaviors and may use cruelty to compensate for a low baseline level of positive emotions—specializing in hurting innocent people (Buckels, *Psychological Science, November 2013*). This serves to directly reinforce their appetitive motive—hence aggressing without external incitement. Sadists aggression is both unprovoked and costly in terms of time and effort. Only sadists crave cruelty enough to expend time and resources to harm an innocent person when there are no discernible benefits. The most common trait of nearly all Satanic novices is a high level of general anxiety related to a feeling of inadequacy and to low self-esteem—which, historically, is actually an inferiority complex. Even though sadism was not part of African culture up to the time of contact with Europeans--and is not now--what Europeans did to African Slaves was so vicious as to cause certain of the Enslaved to retaliate by showing various sadistic acts--as seen today.

Perhaps Psychologists might account for this by saying people exposed early to violence or neglect come to expect it as a way of life. Also, any Sadism seen in Black Americans is a reflective response to what Europeans have done to them as individuals and as a people. This was an example of "copycatting" as opposed to being socialized to act out of a brute mind. European Psychologists say *Sadistic Personality Disorder* may represent a subtype of *Antisocial Disorder* since both share in an exploitative and guiltless interpersonal style. Ancient Africans' believed Sadism is either caused by or the result of Spiritual pain and the attempt to get relief from this. What I would add is Sadism--a pattern of philosophical socialization into a Brute Brain orientation--provides European males the freedom to get away with this by means of their obsession with the GUN. By having a fascination with all that is within the "Dark Side," they find pleasure in "Killing and Taking" to the point of it being an obsession and compulsion. In my opinion, it is a choice made to have a Brute Brain and the treatment is philosophical, not psychiatric. "To see others suffer does one good, to make others suffer even more. . . . Without cruelty there is no festival . . . and in punishment there is so much that is festive!"—Nietzsche (1887).

BRUTES ATTRACTIONS TO EVIL FORCES: The C15 English word "*Attractive*" (pull something towards me) was coined from 'Abstract' and 'Contract.' The sense of 'Attract' in its ancient context embraces '*Alluring*' into something harmful by means of an enticing (exciting hope or desire) decoy possessing energetic twisting and squirming pleasurable motives or ideas of a fantasy nature. Alluring also conveys the idea of charm providing some prospect of pleasure or advantage done by purpose and endeavor. The feature of "Attract" is the drawing of "Like to Like" though it produces no actual motion. This is in contrast to the *Law of Magnets* whereby like magnetic poles repel while unlike poles attract. All three have their place inside the subject of evil. People are drawn to power because they have it and want more; because they want to be the opposite of their sense of powerlessness; and/or to spotlight their power to those who do not have power. Of course, all three have been goals to strive for since ancient times. The early religious "numen" belief of ancient Romans--a belief in a kind of power existing everywhere--a power expressing itself in the greatest of human actions--was so significant as for them to begin personifying that power in the form of Satan. A European system that was spotlighted with the Medieval Knights was to cater to their upper classes (who had a Satanism orientation) while disregarding their unlike lower classes. Those Knights gave rise to the Renaissance "Gentlemen" who reflected Satanism standards at the expense of the Colored Peoples of the world. They became rich by Kill/Take/Destroy practices and dominated the world by means of the GUN.

As part of "The Game" to see who could acquire the most adult "toys," they instituted the African American slave trading. In the Americas they became the "Southern "Gentlemen," fashioners of the United States government with the aim of having complete power and control throughout the Americas "forever." These were *Core Brutes* from having been socialized from birth into Satanism. Their "Like-Kind" *Peripheral Brutes* who were attracted to Satanism and joined the Core Brutes' program. They typically had an inferiority complex (especially before their having access to the GUN prior to 1304) and a superiority complex thereafter. To understand how European males came to power, studying true history--and not what they present--shows it was not from intelligence. Rather, it was their "sick" pleasure gained from engaging in Kill/Take/Destroy/Dominate/Oppress of peaceful peoples of the world by means of the GUN (fig. 8). To elaborate, a giant historical step occurred after Europeans discovered *the GUN* invented by the Arabs in 1304. These savage tribes rose to power from perfecting the GUN over the next 150 years. As the sole result of the GUN, they simply "Took and Killed" everything of their interest from the rich but peaceful Black Africans and other Colored peoples' of the world. And the rest of what was worthwhile they destroyed. Hiding behind the GUN back then (and now) enabled Europeans to fashion a superiority complex (as brutes and bullies) to cover an inferiority complex. And that explains why they are married to the GUN so as to maintain dominance up to the present. This is absolutely fundamental to understand because it is the "Evil Seed" that has afflicted the "Seed" of all cultures of the world.

Africans could never conceive of such awesome Kill/Take/Destroy/Dominate/Oppress evil and sadism power and thus probably thought of it as magical because of its sense of vastness. This disorientation sets the stage for magical thinking designed to enable them to flee from uncertainty by discovering patterns where none existed--patterns involving Supernatural phenomena of their own making and contributed to by the illusions told to them by the captors. Experiencing awe and fascination from being out of control and having no idea as to what to do generated desperation to find some explanation for its existence. In seeking some controlling agent capable of restoring any kind of order in their horrible and chaotic existence, it SEEMED as if the Satanists were the winning team--thereby making it easy to reach for their guiding hand and go with their flow.

EUROPEAN "EXCITEMENT" REACTIONS TO VIOLENCE

The act of contending against another(s) or against normative standards to gain exclusive goals, goods, trophies, status, recognition, or control of minds is an inescapable trait which Western culture believes is essential for the development of a Group Emotional Personality. But by always being extreme, such competitiveness in the marketplace is pathological and counter to sound health. Their keystone category feature of the type that attracts attention because of appearances, thoughts, behaviors, and/or deeds beyond those of ordinary people is recognition as "Larger than Life". By standing out and being spotlighted, if not floodlighted, the Effect thereby makes them disproportionately important--the equivalent to *Flamboyant.* Originally "Flamboyant," an architectural term applied to a C15 and C16 French Gothic style, was characterized by wavy flame-like forms with shapes of flames conforming to the wavy flame-like tracery of the stonework in the windows of many Gothic cathedrals. The presents of these forms around some human (or thing) make ones "Larger than Life." However, the nature of those wavy forms has different ranges of significance, intensity, duration, presentations, and Effects. An analogy is the Stars in the sky.

For eons, humankind has looked to the heavens and wondered at the lights in the sky. Ancient people, believing they could see shapes among the stars, identified both animals and people--and each had its own story. In transferring this concept, Mild "Flamboyance" is like the misconception that *stars twinkle.* Instead, the perception of twinkling stars is a result of atmospheric interference--an effect similar to what takes place on a hot summer day when one looks across hot pavement or a parking lot. Just as this rising air causes images to waver, it is also what causes the twinkling effect in stars. The lower a star is in the sky, the more it will twinkle because its light must pass through more of the atmosphere. Whether there is Slight, Moderate, or Extreme degrees of flamboyance depends upon the intensity and type of dramatic exaggerations in characteristics and attributes appearing to be real on a grand or heroic scale as well as how it affects observers. To describe this style-fashioning faculty requires understanding the concepts behind two different words--flare and flair.

"*Flare*" originally (1550) referred to a flame or blaze that darted up suddenly. And when the flame was against a dark background, its light shown so brightly as to dazzle or blind the viewer. In the C19, if that blaze was characterized by wavy flame-like forms, it represented Moderate or Extreme Flamboyance. On the other hand, "*Flair*" (Old German 1390) originally related to a keen perception of smell, as present in a dog that hunts game by scent. Since it took discernment or shrewdness to pick out the correct scent, the meaning of "flair" was extended into a sense of special ability, natural aptitude, or talent. Hence, "Flair" is like the Star and "Flare" is like the Halo--both present in those deemed to be "Larger than Life." jabaileymd.com

INDIFFERENCE/HATE/EVIL/SADISM "THRILLS": A human's philosophy of life (POL) is a code of values that defines the who, which, what, when, where, why, and how of oneself to oneself. By thus determining ones own nature, including ones means of standards, guides, filters, and measures—as well as ones perception of the world in which one lives and acts--enables one to make choices. The source for the ingredients in ones POL is chosen by chance, from socialization, from circumstances, and/or by ones own mind. The resultant pattern represents ones fundamental nature of existence and ones relationship to existence. The best pattern in the Natural World has a Spiritual God derived Spiritual Elements (i.e. Unconditional Love, Truth, Reality, and the Natural) "Seed' ingredients that evolve out of that stream into disciplined "Roots, Trunk, Branches, Leaves, and Fruit" aspects of Thought and behaviors. An opposing pattern is present in the fantasy "Air Castle" Supernatural realm which is an accumulated junk heap of unwarranted conclusions, false generalizations, stereotypes, undefined contradictions, undigested slogans, unidentified wishes, doubts, and fears. These are all thrown together in an integrated manner designed to attack the Spiritual Elements so as to arrive at a mongrel POL featuring the Indifference/Hate/Evil/Sadism (IHES) Complex. By being of an "Air Castle" nature, it has no grounding and therefore cannot follow logical rules of a type seen in the Natural World. It makes up its own Contingent Being Supernatural god which is passed off in the Natural World--along with its other POL values, thoughts, emotions, expressions, acts, and reactions--as being "superior" all else "anywhere" and for all times.

In order for this IHES Complex to reign demands controlling the minds of their lower ranking fellows and their victims as well as eagerly using Kill/Take/Destroy/Dominate methods for those who resist. Throughout history, this "Dark Side" lifestyle seeks its "Good Life" concept of humans' Lower (animalistic) Self. That lifestyle features Emotional "Excitement" and "Leisure" as its goals. By the GUN and a Network of support from fellow "Air Castle" type people enabling them to be in control of the world and all of its institutions means they have no restrictions on their pursuits of "Excitement" and "Leisure". But to avoid getting bored, it is essential for them to keep pushing the boundaries of "Excitement" in order to keep getting the "adrenalin rush" that provides "Thrills". Although "*Thrill*" is a vague term, it is about the generation of sensational tension. Etymologically, "Thrill" ('make a hole in') denoted in medieval times the idea of to pierce, penetrate with emotion (of the acquired and not pre-birth, kind) to the extent that there is increased breath through ones nostrils.

Its C17 sense elaborated with "to affect with a sudden emotion of excitement that provides 'pleasure'" and, in C19, 'to fill with pleasure.' Today, "Thrills" are associated with swift action where suspense is continual—as in illicit sex and episodes of violence. For the greedy, the Thrill is in the chase, not the acquisition. After, that they become bored until they get involved in the next adventure. However, the preferred acquisitions become the friend of the greedy, for they have no human friends. Whatever has the capability to cause "Thrills" has a cleaving power on ones Selfhood.

The Old English word "*Cleave*" means to 'cut' (split, hollow out) + to 'adhere' (glue, cling). An analogy for 'splitting' ones Selfhood while it remains 'glued' together is that of a block of a loaf of sugar. Its numerous glossy spots represent the sides of small crystals--sides placed along a pattern which enable the block to be easily broken or separated. The manner of that separation is known as *cleavage* and the directions along which such bodies break are called *planes of cleavage*. Stories having the power of 'cleavage' in IHES Complex mindsets are those of dramas about anticipations mingled with uncertainty about the outcome—stories featuring weird Contingent Beings, villain-like in character, that get everything they want from the "good guys". The more the observer—whether within his/her own inner world or witnessing something violent in the outside world—has to "work for the meal" in the story, the more exciting and suspenseful it becomes. By vicarious "*Participating in the Observation*" helps give meaning to ones IHES Complex. Whatever causes a "*Cleavage Thrill*" puts one first in a Supernatural state of Awe whereby one feels "*Super-human*"--i.e. the sense of possessing a special aura of *omnipotence* (all powerful from having unlimited and universal power). Second, when in this mindset, one also perceives oneself to be magically controlled by omnipotent forces to thereby place one either in an extremely pleasant or disagreeable mood. jabaileymd.com

HUMOR OF BIGOTS: Whereas mental health is related to an enjoyment of humor, for a Bigot humor is an "Inside-Out" (a reality/fantasy reversal). person to which the term was applied by C12 French to the Normans to indicate a "narrow-minded" person and then in C16 to denote a superstitious religious hypocrite. Today, Bigots are deemed as stupid and uncharitable persons—having no head and cannot think—no heart, and cannot feel—who moves in wrath while praying to a demon god—clings to unambiguous concepts of stereotypes (e.g. ethnicity, gender) and believing there is no truth or virtue but their own--are intolerant of the opinions of others—get infuriated when the spotlight is put on their "Dark Side"—and who are obstinately and zealously attached to and display "Sick" Pleasures good people would not entertain. Actually their ranting is organized laughter at the pitiful, painful, and miserable fellow humans—whom they or their cult or the ancestors of both generated. This frees the constraints on cult member's Indifference/Hate/Evil/Sadism Complex mindsets to target, mock, and ridicule their dehumanized victims without any hint of conscience, empathy, or sympathy. Powering this mindset are from them having chosen to be mean-spirited, from envying the enjoyment of life of those whom they target, and from getting a sense of power from their aggression in destroying what is what is forbidden and taboo.

Such a freedom is given by the 'righteousness of ideology' dogma their "Air Castle" cult encourages. Their humorous achievements are reacted to, wallowed in, and rippled in discussions. A clear demonstration of bigoted Brutes "Sick" Satanist humor occurred during the African American slavery and ex-slavery era. Slave owners, as part a need for entertainment in their miserable lives, forced certain Enslaved to put on 'amusing' *Minstrel* Shows—i.e. singers and musicians doing ridiculous things in order to entertain. Then in c1840, morally "sick" White men entered into Minstrels for the purpose of exploiting every possible Negro theme that could be ridiculed. The Euro-Americans who put on minstrel shows loosely based them on '*Uncle Tom's Cabin*' in a manner to grossly exaggerate Black characters in demeaning stereotype fashion, making themselves appear like foolish caricatures of Black People—and which they actually were. They imitated various 'what' and 'how' aspects of the Enslaved in what were termed "Tom Shows." They "dressed up" like poor Blacks, complete with their faces and hands blackened with burnt cork. To their "sick" comic routine of absurdities in ridiculing Blacks, they exaggerated the Negro dialect as they made even more fun of Blacks' pain, suffering, misery, and superstitions.

This angered some Blacks but caused other Blacks to accept this as the way things were. Nevertheless, all Blacks were ashamed of who they were pictured to be and this made many feel bad or worse about themselves. A reaction of many ashamed Blacks was to laugh at themselves. A typical theme of "Tom-shows" was showing Blacks in a terrible light—a theme carried on to this day. In some scenes Tom was a "Slave-Driver"--a foreman flogging field the Enslaved for not working fast enough, even those too ill to work. Tom-shows were frequent in minstrels and in C19 theater (e.g. the Death of Uncle Tom; or The Religion of the Lowly). These were typically oriented to the outrageous notions of the superiority of "White blood" or that any freedom-seeking Negro must, by definition have a great deal of "White blood." It is these Tom-shows which have caused such a hostile reaction to the complex 'Uncle Tom Syndrome.' Another significant segment of reinforcement "props" consisted of White non-racists following racist Whites' lead in finding pleasure in "Tom-shows". "Tom Shows," a professional outgrowth of plantation entertainment, had the unfortunate effect of degrading the serious musical contributions of the Negro as well as creating unreal, one-sided, stereotypical, and uncomplimentary Icon Images--Images suiting the purposes of the amoral slaveholders--Images to which Europeans still adhere. These minstrels spread and popularized a terminology that was embarrassing to educated Negroes. Such patronizing terms as "darky" and "pic-a-ninny" as well as such slang terms as "nigger," "coon," and "tar-baby" aroused Blacks resentments among Negroes. For most Whites, this was their only way of having Satanist type pleasure.

BRUTES BIGOTED HUMOR: Slave owners' programmed the Enslaved into demeaning themselves. Such included fawning servility; wearing masks of humility; adopting a child posture; and giving impressions of being attached to slave owners and being utterly dependent upon him--which in actuality they were and what I term the *Evil Savior Syndrome*. Because it was dangerous to know too much—a concept accepted by the police to characterize "bad-asses"--many of the Enslaved pretended to be a bit stupid or dumb and act a little "crazy" as a means of manipulating Whites for survival purposes. These perceived responses and actions provided the substance for Maafa Legend Icon Stereotypes (Bailey, Post-Traumatic Distress Syndrome). Since the beginning of African American slavery, "Killer" police have been associated with the Ku Klux Klan (KKK) and other hate groups who participated in the lynching of Black People. After being announced in advance in southern newspapers as a public theater event, Whites would gather on Friday evenings to engage in "spectacle lynching" (Bailey, American Crime)—all under the supervision of the police, many of whom participated in the killings. These weekly ghastly public butchery lynching were festive occasions, called "Picnics" ("pick a nigger" to lynch). In is important to note the male lynchers' psychological fixation on the genital aspects of Black males—meaning the association of castration as part of the lynching process and its obvious personal association. Before dying, mainly by being burned alive, victims were routinely castrated and the genitals were placed in the victim's mouth.

Fingers and ears were regularly hacked off as souvenirs. Meanwhile, crowds were eating, laughing, and selling the victim's body parts and post cards displaying prior lynching. Once men or women were hung, the body parts of some of the victims, including their genitalia, were distributed and put on public display as an "exhibition" for White men, women, and their children. At this family event there was Satanism "fascination" at seeing the dead bodies swayed in the wind on Southern and Midwestern USA trees. Overt Satanist mindset Indifference/Hate/Evil/Sadism Complex things done at such setting have been culturally transmitted so as to persist to this day in tempered, masked (e.g. the enjoyment of violent images pertaining to Black People), and concealed forms in many Euro-Americans, including many policemen. So has the "Slave-Driver" mentality persisted thereafter in many Black policemen who are in support of and duplicate the practices of "Killer" police.

As James Balwin said: Black police have more to prove and fewer ways to prove it in order to be accepted by European males. As a result, much of the Satanist deed of slavery can be seen into today's world. As discussed by Billig, (Humour and *Hatred*: The Racist Jokes of the Ku Klux Klan. *Discourse & Society,* 2001), they are well-characterized on KKK websites. Following the killings of unarmed Black males and females by the police, the media frequently mentions the racist emails exchanged by the members of each police department member of which the "Killer" is involved. These include "Satanist Amusements" like insults and measures used to frighten Black People. KKK websites feature such things as poking fun at pictures of lynched Black persons; using Black People as target practice or as food for attack dogs; the pleasure of shooting, maiming, and killing Black People, as by burning them to death or by using speeding trucks to drag them by the neck on the streets until body parts fall off. What I find very strange is the reaction many police have to killing someone.

Tisaha Miller was shot countless times by several officers as she slept in the back seat of a car. This was followed by them "high fiving" each other. Another officer tickled the feet of a man shot dead by police, saying:

"Tickle, tickle". A Black man killed by police was finished off by making the head of the deceased touch the feet, while saying: "I love playing with dead bodies." A video showed the policeman that killed Eric Garner afterwards waving his hand in the camera and smiling. A typical "Inside-Out" act of most racist "killers" is to announce vociferously the opposite of what they think and do—as in "we are against the Death Penalty" when they are busy behind-the-scenes advocating for it with respect to those 'alleged' crimes in which Black People are disproportionally incarcerated for. Yet, if their private Satanist humor is exposed, they said: "I was joking."

BRUTES LAUGH AT DEHUMANIZED BLACKS: Of all the most vicious Icon Images carried in the minds of Europeans, the ultimate one is the Dehumanizing (also called *Infrahuman, Subhuman, or Chattel*)—divesting them of human qualities so as to view them as either mechanistic objects or as animals—as done to Black People as during enslavement and still continuing as an Icon Image of Black People to the present. "*Dehumanize*" means to convert humans' Image of God core into a machinelike imbrute—i.e. their rendering into a state of brutishness—impersonal--and unconcerned with human values. Ancient Greeks labeled such people as "Barbarians" to indicate highly uncivilized folk who are worse than beasts because of actions which are cruel, wild, filthy and inhuman. There is no better example of Projection than this—Brutes putting on Black People their own "Dark Side" features. However, the significance of this is that certain "terribly beaten down" Black People have internalized this label and made it a self-fulfilling prophesy. Others have imitated the barbarity of European males and applied it to their Black gang enemies. Oddly, Abraham Lincoln (1809-1865) said: "When…you have succeeded in dehumanizing the Negro; when you have put him down and made it impossible for him to be but as the beasts of the field; when you have extingished his soul in this world and placed him where the ray of hope is blown out as in the darkness of the damned, are you quite sure that the demon you have roused will not turn and rend you?"

Whereas the enslavers created these horrible conditions for Black People, their today's descendant continue their practices while blaming struggling Black People for being in such a bad condition. It is amazing so many Black People have done so well as they have. What I find very strange is the reaction many police have to killing someone. Alesia Thomas, a 35 year old mother, was arrested in 2012, handcuffed, and then the female Los Angeles arresting officer struck Ms. Thomas in the throat with an outstretched hand while threatening her. Next, the officer jabbed Ms. Thomas with her boot into the stomach and crotch. These assaults caused Ms. Thomas to ask for an ambulance to take her to the hospital but this was not done for 30 minutes later under the belief that Ms. Thomas was feigning medical distress. She was put into the back seat of the patrol car where she lapse into an unconscious state and died. The officer responded: "I don't think she's breathing"; then lit a cigarette and laughed. The officer was not charged in connection with the death since the cause was "undetermined." One explanation for the "sick" pleasure these "Killer" police get from needlessly killing Black People is that they have become hardened—so cynical about people—as to dehumanize them, considering them no different that animals to be hunted. This mindset wipes out all concepts of ethics (what ought to be the right thing to do as a police officer) making it seem like a normal act to step into criminal behavior. For me, a more likely cause is a Conditioned Response.

By the combination of Brutes not valuing Black People as human beings and by attacking the rules of what is "Right" means they have no more regard for Black People than if they were flies needing to swatted. The code of "high-class" Brutes is to use the dehumanizing language of "Them" or "You people"; write vague laws that can be interpreted so as to constitutionally deny them of full legal personhood (e.g. with voting rights or equal protection under the law); public endorsement of police brutality against Blacks; and the forbidding of altruism toward Blacks—all (among others) socializing European children to supporting bias, discrimination, and prejudice. A consequence of the European-generated poverty for struggling Black People is that Poverty *itself and by itself is dehumanizing by making one feel worthless and reproducing itself*--doing so by keeping down the human Soul, as with an iron chain—the most cruel aspect of human reality Brutes do.

SUMMARY

In African Tradition, Hate is personified by the mythological god Set who killed his own brother, Osiris, to steal his Kingdom. Horus, Osiris's son, confronts Set and a battle ensues. Horus eventually overcomes Set through virtue. Set is redeemed and transformed into a positive force for good. However, at the end it is revealed that Horus and Set are in reality not two personalities but rather they are one and the same. This means the true enemy is not outside of one but rather ones negative qualities which fetter ones higher vision of Spiritual reality (Ashby, Redemptions, p22). That is the only insight I have about how Black People will fair against Brute European. However, the point is that the illusion of separation from the Self is the source of all other illusions. This means one is Unknown to oneself and thus has to make up self-images out of what is not real, and orchestrated by ones Ego. The resultant False Self gives rise to feelings such as fear, fetters, greed, hatred, envy, and anger because one believes one must fight "everybody" for ones survival. Since one does not remember that one is immortal and a part of all other Beings, one develops the idea of looking out for Self only and of having a good time in an animalistic way, since "you only live once." This spiritual imbalance develops due to ignorance about ones Spiritual nature. Thus, ignorance is the root of all evils in the form of criminality, selfishness, greed, violence, and malice (Ashby, Mystic p241).

Because of the Law of Correspondence, Nature demonstrates how humans ought to live. For example, the human body, an example of Nature, has every part superbly working independently to interdependently service the whole. For example, ones Heart pumping of blood supplies all parts of the body to provide nourishment. Yet, the Heart cannot do its job without the brain or the liver each doing their jobs with perfection. All contribute to ones health.

CHAPTER III

VIOLENT MINDS

FEATURE

BOGEYMAN MENTAL IMAGES

"NORMAL VARIANT" CROWD VIOLENT IMAGES

The "*Crowd*" ('move by pushing in a wheelbarrow') is 'an unorganized collective of race-less and faceless people pressing against each other'--each seemingly pushing in clamoring to deal with the mirror image of the leaves and fruit of the Tree of Life. An illustrative 1899 children's game of what it is like to be part of a Crowd is "*Pin the tail on the donkey*". After a picture of a tail-less donkey is tacked to a wall, blindfolded children, one at a time and in turn, are handed a paper "tail" with a thumbtack poked through it. Each child is then spun around until disoriented so as to grope in trying to properly pin the tail on the donkey. Although the child wins who comes closest to the donkey's rear, "winning" is only of marginal importance. Similarly, in a Crowd the co-actoring mindsets of alone people, so strangled by their own egos as to shun themselves, gain a sense of freedom from conventional restraints and simultaneously being aware of powers they lack and intensely desire. The now "new Me" drives one to express views and/or commit acts of which one would otherwise be ashamed. The profound life-changing price they pay in choosing to shut out their birth gift of Spiritual Natural Knowledge—being disconnected from their Cosmos awareness Certainty—is deserting their Real Self with its infinite personal power and life's Mission. Also, they exchange their own independent thoughts so as to desperately seek, *always in vain*, the Crowd's animalistic emotionalism and concepts of the External World's self-fulfillments. Satanist leaders of the Crowd, intensely spurred by self-interest motives and bordering on madness, have perfected the art of impressing the Crowd's imagination—the same art that controls Crowd's minds by arousing 'Faith in this 'Thing's' superiority"—the same art guiding the Crowd's Faith by suggestions of achieving "the Fantasy". Thus, each sentiment or act spewed by leaders—whom the Crowd necessarily deems to be gods—contagiously 'goes viral.' Those 'un-infected' and who fail to join the collective are "executed" by the Crowd. Such are effective since the Self-Unknown fear being alone.

For those possessing self-defeating ignorance in whatever area of life, takes self-knowledge to perceive their inability to understand their ignorance. Choosing to remain Self-Unknown is to accept the delusional ignorance that the unpredictability and transience of ordinary human life is capable of satisfying ones Private Self needs. By dedication to relentlessly pursuing Deep Self-fulfillments in the External World demands disregarding wise advice of returning to ones "Soul Sunshine" birth gift and its storehouse of innate potential to experience fullness, thriving, peace, and happiness. Some are aware of their "Clouded" out Spiritual Natural Knowledge being able to fully provide every answer for each of life's problems but simply choose not to follow that path because of a lack of Courage to be ones Real Self. Some only internalized fragments of it but ignoring vital parts. Thus, False Self people underestimate their capabilities and/or place a low-lying ceiling for what they are capable of doing. Fear drives them to do/go wherever the 'Crowd' points.

The unwritten "Crowd Code" emphasizes the wisdom of its Ignorance. Its judgment—a mere lottery of useful understanding--is how to make Ignorance flow comfortably for Earth World living. To be in the flow of Ignorance means one embraces the seeming truisms that Ignorance is the mother of admiration, impudence, devotion, beneficial superstitions, satisfaction with ones opinions and beliefs, and companionship. It implies one must not know too much, or doubt nothing ('anything's possible'); or be too precise or scientific (like a nerd) about activities of daily living. By contrast, one must know things not necessary and being "human" makes errors okay (e.g. knowing things falsely). These provide a certain free margin to operate with some degree of vagueness, impulsiveness, and naïve-ness so as to ensure the pleasures of Crowd experiences. Adopting the motto: "what you don't know can't hurt you" means the Crowd can never know the whole mystery of Beauty or the sweetness of solitude or the profoundness of Thought. A Crowd member can never "stand tall" for what one knows to be "right" if the Crowd is not in agreement--or have the glorious crowded hour of achieving "the impossible" by having done it "my way"--or discovering that the "weird" person shunned by the Crowd is a mega-jewel in disguise.

The effects of the European cult not allowing its members to have independent thoughts means they are Trendy. To be "Trendy" implies a social category of participants who are non-rational, superficial, shallow, and materialistic people who "follow the leader" and change instantly to go along with the crowd. From personal experiences with countless "Crowd" people, including those from around the world who comment on my website, these people deal with only the Physical and Supernatural worlds and have reduced whatever is a "Fad" down to "sound bits" using almost identical words—as if it is tape recorded to express whenever an appropriate situation arises. They ignore the question and say what has been "cookie cut" for them to say. They seem incredibly dumb, even in their own field of experitise. Invariably, when confronted with an error they made, they project it onto the customer. Such is exactly with politicians do to the most obvious degree. An ironic typical feature is declaring they are "Individualists" while they eagerly seek to exactly imitate the crowd or their cult's most recent ideas or other fads—as evidenced by Republicans. They will say the opposite while looking directly at contrary evidence. An example is Celebrity Icons.

The Crowd members are incredibly self-absorbed: "If it is not familiar to me it is not important or does not exist. All that is 'happening' is what everybody is doing." This is the type of thinking done by *"Zombies"*--a Haitian Creole term for those in a "walking coma" state--a state generated by a group called the Power Elite or the Illuminati. They are a small group of corporate, banking and political leaders who declare themselves as "little gods" and the world's highest power whose intent on to rob the world of its riches, humanity, and dignity so as to enslave the people's minds. Their success is dependent upon the optimal consent and minimal resistance from the majority of the world's people, as by those who do not vote and those who only think about "Trinkets and Trivia." Bad Information is so socialized throughout a victimized world society as for the people to be advocates for those "SEEM" right concepts and practices that are actually Group- and self-destructive.

CHILDREN'S INVENTIVE MENTAL ACTIVITY

A real creative advantage little children have over all other humans is their natural ability to imagine Nature as being universally alive with emotions, animated, and each endowed with a will of its own. This attribution of life to the unfamiliar and to *"Contingent Beings"*—like the Bogeyman--is called *"Animatism"*. An Animatism Being is a made-up "weird" creature out of a child's emotions. It lacks a specific appearance and yet carries a 'payload' message as it whiffs by and disappears. Children create Animatism Beings for all great things they are thinking about. Animatism is inside the Spiritual Play aspects of every human's Selfhood and is mainly manifested in being Silly good humor. Since adults do not accept Contingent Beings as alive, Children put their Contingent Beings into a special category because those things act queerly or as if they are seemingly about to do so. Still, children stay alert to every unusual sight, or sound, or smell of their Contingent Beings—and their imaginations make sure these happen. The resultant happenings are gathered and arranged and combined to design a new and even more "weird" Contingent Being form. They have no pre-conceived concept of how things should be and thus have Free Minds—the keystone for living.

Adults who maintain this child-like process, as I do, engage in constant reflection about some situation of necessity in serious business or just for Fun. For me, out of the initial reflection arises an Animatism Being which I mentally play with to give a few moments of pleasure—and which I seem to forget. Yet, they remain as a "seed" hiding in a matrix (womb) recess of my mind where unconscious reflections on that "seed" continue over time. Then, a suddenly appearing "Crystal" appears in my mind to cause a 'big bang.' Typically, my Spiritual Entourage communicates with me by having a crystal thought or name 'pop up' out of "nowhere". At times, the crystal comes from somebody saying something having nothing to do with my issue and yet it works like the missing link. Something similar occurs at other times when I see something that automatically serves as a 'big bang' crystallization.

IMAGINARY FRIEND: A "*Virtual*" or "*Contingent Being*" (CB)—also called *Invisible Friend, Imaginary Friend, Imaginary Companion, Bogeyman*--is a created Prototype about something significant to the creator to which the creator imparts something significant so that the Prototype can serve as a means to make happen a corresponding something significant. The role of children engaged in dramatic play and imaginative or make believe situations is a form of work in the organization of socialization whereby they invent all types of "what if" situations to work through. The 'big picture' is for the CB, as an Icon Image, to by itself, reproduce what it is about in the creator, so as to enable the creator to telescope into what the CB itself stands for in order to acquire gains and avoid the losses that are compatible with what was imparted. In that way, the creator becomes the CB it makes. This is the foundation upon what all of the institutions of the USA and gang members are built and how they are built. No doubt, the background for this came out of primitive times from child's daydreams as fictional characters in the stories they made up or as an actual imaginary friend.

The nature of the CB is a reflection of its intent. Many European parents, in desiring to instill fear in the minds of their children, created a "*Bogeyman*"—a spirit or goblin who will punish the child for misbehavior. European Psycho-analysis says this is an externalized pre-super-ego—i.e. a *Projection* onto persons in the External World of the internalized parental prohibitions that are the forerunner of the superego--the representative of society within the psyche (i.e. conscience or morality) and also includes the ideal aspirations (Ego-ideal). Among girls and boys (especially ages 3 to 6 years old), the CB they create is a fantasy to serve a contemporary (a person, animal, object) with whom to play—often arising from being lonely and often fading when real playmates are found.

The companions are usually given names and stable personalities—to which the child talks and plays as if they were real. The companion may be so intimate as for the child to share troubles, pleasures, and confidences. Some children insist that the whole family recognize their existence: "you can't sit in that chair because Titan is there." Some CB may represent qualities the child lacks--e.g. courage, and derring-do (daring or reckless action). They may provide an outlet for emotions of anger, anxiety, fear, abandonment, shame, or guilt. Sometimes they are used as scapegoats: "the Devil made me do it!" Some use CB as a means to practice roles and relationships or self-defense through dramatic make-believe. Some construct elaborate fantasies, such as an entire family who go through various kinds of adventures during a period of weeks or months. So do many potential gang members.

Situation Example I: As a 4 year old I played 'war' under the bed and had airplanes opposing each other. When World War II broke out, I imagined a Cavalry opposing another inside a gymnasium fighting or arguing over power, property, or cause. Yet, for me, the means took precedence over the ends. A child playing alone in such a conflict situation that requires problem solving may use two dolls or action figures along with stuffed animals or imaginary companions as other characters. As children solve conflicts in their pretend world, they are developing perspective and social skills that they will use in real life situations. They imitate patterns and techniques for solving conflicts in ways observed on television, at home, in school, in the neighborhood. Their Play has structure not dictated by physical necessity but that emanates from the minds of the players that the child puts into them.

Situation Example II: Because children are in a relatively powerless position, they can gain control over events by taking on the role of someone who is in power. Following a visit to the doctor who gave the child a vaccination shot, at home the child may re-enact the scene by playing the role of the doctor and giving a doll a shot. This re-enactment aids understanding by exploring a range of attitudes, values, and behaviors and thereby selects a pattern of an appropriate emotional response in which she has control—and that is part of the process of answering the question: "Who am I?"

Situation Example III: Children learn socialization participation rules by dramatic play--a social activity in which children interact with peers, siblings, and parents as a means to act out story lines. In the process, they learn such behaviors as turn taking, competition, collaboration, sharing goals and materials while understanding the theme of the activity being pursued. This kind of play requires non-rational (personal-social) communication among partners as they talk about what they will play and what rules will apply. While 'Pretend Play' enhances cognitive, social, and emotional development, an important aspect of dramatic play is imagination. Engaging in this process fashions images which improve planning, negotiation, and joint problem-solving skills.

Situation Example IV: 'Pretend Play' is the creative foundation of all Art forms. It leads children to work through the separation of pretense from reality, since this distinction is a crucial intellect-emotional achievement. Meanwhile, they are formulating guidelines and fantastic settings (i.e. "Paracosms" apart from other daily activities. A "*Paracosm*" is a detailed Imaginary World created inside ones mind. This fantasy world may involve humans, animals, and things that exist in reality; or it may also contain entities that are entirely imaginary, alien, and other-worldly (i.e. Supernatural); or it may play with the boundary between the "real" world and alternative systems. Commonly it has its own geography, history, and language. The experience of such a paracosm is often developed during childhood and continues over a long period of time: months or even years. The creation of these pretend games requires them to create a world with a set of rules that are often quite different from their everyday environments (Honeycutt, *Imagination, Cognition and Personality*, *2011*).

EUROPEAN ADULT IMAGINARY FRIENDS

The European adult equivalent of a child's "Invisible Friend is called a Contingent Being (CB). A reason for the following detailed elaboration is that to understand what CB and Icon Images are about is absolutely fundamental to being able to accurately assess ones "bad" dealings in life and correct them. A similar assessment of others may be necessary for defense or offense involving them. Nevertheless, the European story dates to their dawn in history when primitive Europeans were constantly warring and struggling. These savages had special needs because their everyday lives were a constant battle for survival against natural disasters; for the scarce survival necessities; for a harsh climate; for wild animals; and against neighboring tribes. Such a life bred men of stubborn independence and fanciful imaginations which were used to create Supernatural (Spirits/ forces between God and humans) to call on for help as well as ways to magically control the disagreeable ones through the mere possession of spells, formulas, and secret names. Thus, they worshipped their various self-made gods--e.g. the warrior god Thor--for purposes of self-seeking interest. They so treasured their tools of war as to endow them with Supernatural power.

Many legends tell of swords inhabited by demons, or acting as agents of gods. Regardless of the use for any of these, within each were certain Images of their CB--some with hazy boundaries; some have assumed boundaries; and the rest are without boundaries. What determines if a CB has boundaries depends upon the purpose to which they are put in order to achieve the best self-interest advantage. Their idea of "god" was used in the Teutonic sense of a personal object of religious worship. All of this is mixed up with concepts contained in the late Middle English word "*Contingent*" (befall)--meaning touching on the sides [of reality]. But those touches are of uncertain occurrences and come about *Accidentally* (a happening without anyone's direct intention); *Fortuitously* (without cause or design); *Incidentally* (without regularity); *Adventitiously* (circumstances that encourage the rise of something); and *Provisionally* (liable to happen).

ICONS DEFINED: Although fully discussed by Ancient Africans at least as early as 20,000 BC in relation to such things as the Halo (God's message) to a Star (the Substance of God), the Europeans' C16 word "Icon" (likeness, image) has usually referred to a saint painted on a wooden panel and venerated in Orthodox Christianity. Icon Myths are metaphors with which one tries to make sense of the world and which carry the power of Icon Images (Chapter I). Since modern times, the word "Icon" has been pressed into service to describe almost anything—something visual, audio sounds, an object, a person or group of people. In computing jargon, an Icon is a small symbolic picture on a computer screen, manipulated by moving a pointer and clicking. Such meanings are conveyed on computer menus, windows, and screens by an Icon ('little world' or Symbol) standing for any graphical, visual element. The term '*concreteness*' refers to the degree of pictorial resemblance an icon bears to its referent. When Icon concreteness is high, paralleling its real-world counterparts, users can roughly form expectations that can guide their use of system functionality.

Broadly, a Visible Icon is a "small visual Symbol" of its known referent (its real-world counterpart)--conveying the meaning of the referent with only a quick glance so as to save search time and cognitive resources. What the Religious and the Secular European Icon share in common is that rather than indicating what something looks like, *an Icon reminds people of what they already know*. Hence, Icons (like "Halos") leap communication barriers by dealing with what is reflected out of the "Stars" they represent. Ideas of European Icons began with developing rigid and stereotyped visages Primitive (the first people) Africans' totems and later interior African masks, misrepresenting both as lifeless in their unnatural homes in museum spaces dedicated to dead societies. Still, they considered that these wooden carvings represented religious symbols of the sacred and profane that sustained meaning, ritual, and solidarity for these earliest and most irrational societies. Even when modifications were made for European religious images and not considered high art, they evoked emotional responses with people being so moved by them as to kiss them, cry before them, or go on journeys to them.

A reason is that the *Icon of an issue is symbolic of a hidden point of significance carrying a payload impact*. The very art that is called to be a vehicle of religious revelation can be altered by the connotations people give to Icons--and typically that is about frequently mere decorations and materialistic comforts for the people. At its best, in modeling African Tradition the European Art of the created universe is the unfolding of the image of God within creation--the creative realization of the unity of all forms of life in agreement with the Mind of God. Nature continues to uncover and develop creatively (not mechanically as Europeans say) the "talent" of producing life. Nature's works of art are endless, though indirect, depictions of the divine. In this way, the created universe itself is an unfathomable Icon revealing God. The creative symbols of the divine *Logos* (defined by Europeans as a synergetic art involving the process of unifying ideas and forms within a single meaning) are means by which the hidden presence of God is recognized--and they are scattered throughout creation Mystical life.

By being free of any rational cause, some say they pulsate within a living person, generating an urge to create. Teaching about the image of God in man (*Imago Dei*--primordial or mythical images) through icons is called *Iconology*. European Religious Icons, in particular, are practical forms of Art, dealing directly with questions of spiritual life such as holiness and asceticism. Its Icon represents the "Halo"--the "Art in spirit"--which presents viewers familiar with church doctrine with an unambiguous contemplative theology. Iconic creativity issues out of the entire Europeans' church's dogmatic heritage which, for many, is founded on Supernatural divine revelation. What the icon affirms is not art with a nuance of religion but practical faith expressed within symbolic patterns of Art. Even in its finest religious examples this is art of approximate truth and is only allegorical. Secular Art represented by paintings can portray a social, natural, philosophical, or even religious theme.

[Ref: Andrejev, *Theology Today*, 2004; Aguilar, MI. *Feminist Theology*, 1994].

POWERS OF ICON IMAGES: Images most often *interact* with individuals' existing understandings of the world to shape information processing and judgments. This is made possible by Mental activity as if inside a spider web. The more often ones brain has a repetitive thought, emotion, expression, or behavior, the deeper become the responsible brain nerve tracks (like the snowy path deepening from repeatedly walking in it). Simultaneously, those tracks attract support from additional nerve cells. As a result, long chains of neurons with many synapses are common, like telephone connections on a long-distance line. Nerve cells are always in touch with other nerve cells and the point where these cells touch each other is called a *Synapse*. The duty of a Synapse is to provide a means for an impulse arriving along an axon to leap across to a neighboring cell body. Once the ending of a nerve cell is stimulated, the process spreads like small waves--similar to what happens after a stone is thrown into a pond. Many involved nerves become divided into many smaller nerves as the abilities of the brain is changing with each repeated instance of this process.

Meanwhile memories are forming + new neural circuits are added + new Focused Attention skills are perfected + more power is given to the mental act of *holding neural circuits of the brain in place* so as to keep them steady in what they are doing--all enhancing ones existing mental thinking capacities. This is why the concentration of mental energy for prolonged periods by a person of standard ability has an advantage over ones fellow who does not concentrate. Maintaining focus not only makes one mentally stronger but also generates more tenacious mental (clinging) energy. That energy triggers more nerve structures to join the process of Focused Attention--similar to the way a crowd forms around a street magician. The greater the number of members in the crowd of neural circuits, the more power available to make decisions and solve problems. Collectively, this process of sustained Attention and gathering more clinging brain energy is called *Concentration* (Raja Yoga, 93).

Visual news images (a) influence people's information processing concerning their predispositions and values while simultaneously triggering aspects that spread throughout ones mental frame work to other evaluations (Domke, *Journalism, 2002*). Thus, any one concept is associated with other spider web type constructs when encoded in memory, and the linkages between constructs are strengthened each time they are activated in tandem. Further, as the number of separate linkages to any particular construct increases, so does the likelihood that it will be activated indirectly due to an 'implicational relation'. So, when a thought element is activated or brought into focal awareness, the activation radiates out from this particular node along the associative pathways to other nodes', thereby increasing the probability that related constructs will come to mind, influencing subsequent evaluations and the formation of impressions that mass media emphasis on particular political issues increases the accessibility of certain ideas for individuals, which then shape the criteria that are *applied* while forming judgments about other concepts and ideas.

Components of visual images include: (a) mnemonic power (i.e. easy recall in their general details); (b) ingredients with the ability to become icons that serve as metonyms or exemplars of particular events or issues; (c) great aesthetic impact, such as striking juxtapositions or riveting happenings (typically human suffering); (d) affective or emotive power (i.e. the ability to 'move' one to emotional reactions such as outrage, pity, or sentiments like sympathy); and (e) potentially significant political power, such as the ability to create, alter, or reinforce elite or popular beliefs about causes and/or issues of the day and further affect government policy. Still, there is no pure image creation because much of their "raw materials" come from memory images or idea or interpretation of something just said or read. Hence, like words, images are likely evaluated in relation to pre-existing beliefs and experiences and the added schema (what gives meaning to incoming stimuli and channeling outgoing reactions). When one, upon encountering a "Thing," person, idea, or issue the contained aspect congruent with ones schema is like a stimuli which draws ones attention to it so as to process it more quickly. Then it is stored in memory for later recall.

In short, the mental categories one already holds significantly influence the manner in which 'new' information and stimuli are perceived, filtered, stored, recalled and subsequently used. Yet, despite a variety of mental categories perhaps 'available' to guide information processing, *which* particular ones become influential in evaluations and judgments may depend upon how mentally 'accessible' a particular construct is – that is, how easily it might be retrieved from memory. It is widely accepted that schema *frequently* or *recently* activated become more readily accessible for application to attitude objects. In this process, 'cues' in ones political and media environment, for example, may activate relevant cognitive structures to guide information processing and the construction of attitudes. In turn, schema activated by contextual cues remain on top of the mental bin, making them highly accessible for at least a period of time. Thus, these constructs, if judged to be applicable, may alter the basis for evaluating even seemingly unrelated objects because judgments often 'depend less on the entire repertoire of people's knowledge and more on which aspects of their knowledge happen to come to mind. Hence, ones good or bad thoughts about oneself superimposed on a pre-existing painted mental image of a 'monster' about ones 'enemy(s), constant thought about each of these increases the accessibility of compatible ideas. In turn, that combination shapes criteria applied while forming judgments about other concepts and ideas--all layered onto the pre-existing Icon Image.

Put another way, any one concept is associated with other constructs when encoded in memory, and the linkages between constructs are strengthened each time they are activated in tandem. Further, as the number of separate linkages to any particular construct increases, so does the likelihood that it will be activated indirectly due to an 'implicational relation'. When a thought element is activated or brought into focal awareness, the activation radiates out from this particular node along the associative pathways to other nodes, thereby increasing the probability that related constructs will come to mind, influencing subsequent evaluations and the formation of impressions. When police and the public encounter the slants on the news that reinforces what they already believe, this triggers a cascade of non-rationally related evaluations about relevant aspects of ones information environment, suggesting the relationship between media coverage and spreading activation processes intensifies "righteous indignation" against a Black "suspect." This is because individuals' images most often *interact* with individuals' existing understandings of the world to shape information processing and judgments.

ICON MECHANICAL IMAGES: An example of an Icon Myth is using the European Bible to generate concepts of the Cosmic Organism (which grows inside out) as being an Artifact (a physically constructed thing) in a mechanical sense. As part of the European concept that the Cosmos is an artifact and not run by the African

God, Amun, they misapplied the Ancient Egyptians' creation of the Mythological story of humans and animals. It says *Khnum* (Egyptian, *molder;* Divine Potter), a ram-headed deity and potter-god, uses the mud of the Nile, heated to excess by the Sun, fermented and generated, without seeds, the races of men and animals (Gadalla p142). Then the resultant created bodies of children are removed from the potter's wheel and inserted into their mothers' bodies. Immediately upon the delivery of each baby, Khnum's consort, Heket, offers the "breath of life," symbolized by the *ankh*, to the nose of the clay figure to animate the clay effigy into a living soul so as to become a vibrant part of the divine order charged with numinous (Sublime) power. This breath represents the hidden or occult force underlying creation. But European Bible Passages leave no doubt about the belief in the concept of the Divine Potter as a fact. Genesis, 2:7 mentions the material used to make man is the same type of substance used by Khnum: "And the Lord God formed man of the dust of the ground, and breathed into his nostrils the breath of life; and man became a living soul." This was again echoed thousands of years later in Isaiah, 64:8: "Yet, O Lord, thou art our Father; we are the clay, and thou art our potter; we are all the work of thy hand." "Breathing into the nose of the clay figure to animate the clay effigy" conveys to Western people the idea of a 'made' Cosmos.

Such separates from each other the things made (e.g. each human being) as well as separates those things made from the Maker (i.e. God). First and most important in this powerfully flawed concept is that believers in the Cosmos being put together as a Mechanical Artifact will see themselves as *Individualists*--meaning "survival of the fittest." Second, if they were made out of clay, then when they stop breathing they will return to clay--and that is all there is to their existence. The phrase: "ashes to ashes, dust to dust" comes from the funeral service in the *Book of Common Prayer*, and it is based on Genesis 3:19. That passage says that we begin and end as dust. Genesis 18:27 and Job 30:19 refer to dust and ashes as components of the human body. Third, they might believe God's will is imposed on them, thus wiping out their "Free Will." That implies boundaries on God's Unconditional Love in the form of not being "free" to follow what they believe is best. In some, this can generate resentment and rebellious acts which, in turn, can go in the direction of being aggressive Brutes and Satanists.

The first aggressive move is because as "Individualists" since God has set in motion the workings of the Cosmos, God is not needed to tell them what to do. In their view, reality is simply blind unintelligible energy needing to be conquered and controlled. By being "little gods" they are quite capable of running the show and doing whatever they like--Kill/Take/Destroy--and never, never show any signs of weakness. They see Competition as the name of the Game--who can win the most adult toys. The Game is played like Billiards, with each Brute symbolizing the white cue ball powered by aggression. The idea is to roll it all over the "table" and bang into other balls (victims) so as to "pocket" them as well as to knock cue balls (opponents) off the table.

The rules are that there are no rules--and Fetters reign supreme. Thus, all players are on hyper-alert to any danger coming from any direction by competitors or victims. There is no such thing as discussing in order to gain understanding. For this reason, their "tough guy" tyrant attitude always carries a sense of insecurity with the fear that "I might not have what it takes." Hence, each must be ever-ready to compete from a warrior's position--as in always having guns of various types and with an eagerness to use them as a way of bolstering their Icon Image of what represents "manliness"; always sitting with their backs to a wall; having "body guards" of various types (e.g. in-group members, being part of systems designed to "take down" any opponents); and beating down those whom they take advantage of so that those victims lack the spirit to fight back. Brutes are miserable people!

MEGA ICONS/SYMBOLS: So much stuff comes into ones mind every second that the only way the Brain/Mind can deal with it is by putting "Like-Kind" things in categories. The overwhelming majority of those categories have patterns formed around Images, with certain ones being Icon Images--with or without being inside Symbols. To elaborate, the *most primitive unit of thought is the Image, a sort of pictorial representation in ones mind of a specific event or object which shows the 'highlights of the original*. The way this comes about is: (1) by one noticing a "Thing" in the External world of significance; (2) extracting its visible or "surface" features (i.e. a gist of what sets it apart from and above all the rest); and (3) storing those features in a retained mental image or as a symbol in order to serve as a basis for dealing with the "Thing" representationally. If the word "dog" arouses in the mind of the listener an "image" of a dog (in the sense of a typical 4-legged animal that barks), this 'image' carries the meaning of what it represents.

A *Symbol is a more abstract unit of thought than Images* and may have a number of meanings. For example, if the number 1 represents an image, substituting the letter 'a' for '1' makes 'a' more abstract (a Symbol) since 'a' could also be an indicator of a number of other things (like standing for ones middle name). This enables it to be used in thinking mediated by other kinds of symbols and does not always required "pictures in the mind." Although there are many definitions for the C16 English word "Icon" (Greek eikon, 'be like'), in a broad sense of being the "halo" in the "Star/Halo" concept, an *Icon* is an Image, representative or a 'ballpark' symbol (i.e. indicating the area or broad position or nature of something without being specific).

Supreme (Mega, Super-Apex) Icons are like the MVP (most valuable player) in an all-star basketball game. An analogy in a given category headed by an Image is like one of the states in the USA and each Image likened to a governor. But the Supreme Icon Image over all the governors is the President. The laws of Congress and then sanctioned by the President are the keystone laws around which each governor forms a lifestyle for her/his state. By contrast, there are a tiny few "patterns" called Imageless Icons or Imageless Symbols. *Imageless Icons* cannot be defined or even adequately described. However, for Black People the ultimate in Imageless-ness is that of the Spiritual God—of which Ancient Africans had no pictures because they said God is Unknowable. Instead, God could only be known by God's manifestations and that combination can be analogized to the supreme "Star/Halo" Concept whereby the star symbolizes God (Imageless) and the Halo symbolizes God's manifestations (the Spiritual parts are Imageless and the Material parts may be imaged).

What Icon Images, "Imageless Icons," Symbols, and "Halos" do, rather than indicating what something looks like, *is to remind people of awareness they already have about these Things represent*. In this way, they remove boundaries and leap communication barriers by dealing with what is reflected out of the "Stars" they represent. Understanding all of this is extremely important because all humans have much of their lives guided by these mental patterns of Images, Icons, Symbols, and the MVP Imageless—whether of a realistic, distorted, or fantasy nature. The mental patterns one chooses to orchestrate ones mind—whether its orientation is in the stream of flow of the Spiritual Elements or in another stream--determines the category of ones preference for compatible patterns devised in ones mind and/or drawn in from the External World. In other words, *by itself, the image reproduces itself, to become the thing it makes*. In turn, ones preferred patterns mold what one thinks, feels, says, and does in life—which, of course, designs ones destiny in this life.

CONTINGENT BEINGS (CB) DEFINED: Philosophers say contingent is neither impossible nor necessary--i.e. both non-necessary and possible--and thus differs from what is Possible because Possible may also be necessary (unyielding). A certain event is contingent if, and only if, it may come to pass and also may not come to pass. Since the objective is to generate confusion, the European concepts of CB deal primarily with the ill-defined core concept of Possibility ("may"). Supernatural Possibilities are Illusions--as opposed to the Necessity ("must") of Actuality. The very general and wide-ranging in application C14 word *Possible* (be able; capable of being done) means: (1) 'that can be done' or the chance it may occur but failing to say whether that is in reality or not; (2) may or can exist; (3) has an even chance of coming to pass; (4) the odds are against it coming to pass;

and (5) whatever is not ruled out by the nature of reality. As a result of this chaos surrounding Possible, it serves to enable the unfolding of the Creative Process because *a Thing is conceivable of which the mind can entertain the Possibility*. This is the working of Imagination to face the Unknown by the Unknown. Reality may be Certain or Potential. "*Certainty*" may be in 'here and now' Realities or in the category of yet Unrealized Realities. *Potential* ('that which is possible'; power in reserve as possible rather than as actual; capable of being or becoming) may be *Viable* (a chance of something coming into Reality); Non-Viable (no chance of coming into Reality); or Viable under certain circumstances (as potential energy or force appears under certain conditions). Thus, Possibility may be in categories of Viable and/or Non-Viable.

In the Non-Viable Possibility category, the Possibility is an Illusion in the setting of a stage play acting to pretend that the Possibility matters. *Illusions* are measures used to misdirect attention away from Reality so as to create an uncertainty sufficient to persuade the deceived that what the fantasy produced is Reality. This leads the deceived to engage in a *Delusion* (believing what is not real and not believing what is real). When that Illusion Possibility is personified (giving life to the lifeless) into a fantasy reality, it is called a *Contingent Being*. If questioned, those presenting justifications for CB say the cause of its coming into existence is by Chance, accidentally, or from ones free will.

HUMANS' CONTINGENT BEING CREATIONS: *Contingency* (to touch on all sides) is broadly like looking at every possible aspect of a one-sided coin (e.g. "it may and also may not be"). To climb out of the un-resolvable Controversies and the hopeless confusion of European concepts--particularly in relation to God--of Contingent Beings (CB), my listing of issues includes: I. Necessity vs, Possible and Impossible--as Factual, like 'actual' in one sense, but neither necessary nor impossible; II. It might not have occurred if not for a real thing, like a shadow, from which is inferred the existence of a material thing and the light by which it is cast; III. Things determined by external causes--as in dependence of one state of affairs on another state of affairs. IV. Things that might not have occurred or might have been otherwise, as when a Cause (a Being that could not fail to have ex-isted) gives rise to an Effect and Consequences; V. A CB happens to exist, but might not ever have existed at all because it does not contain within itself the reason for its own existence--and at some point it did not exist. VI. Whereas Necessity is true and Impossible is false in every possible world, Contingency is true in at least one pos-sible world. VII. a CB can be imagined other than it is; VIII. a host of others.

The subject's complexity increases by trying to classify it. Examples: Europeans say Genuine Beings ("exis-tential Beings"--actual or Potential)--are distinguished from Imaginary entities by their possession of "essential Being" with definable essences as reflections of the divine ideas. Actual Beings (with substance existing indepen-dently, such as man, tree) differ from those existing in another--called Accidents (which can only exist in some-thing else, like time, place). Both Actual and Accident Beings are distinguished from merely Possible Beings--and these are distinguished from Beings deemed to be intrinsically impossible and incoherent. Europeans say they are creatures in their mature and actualized state. My assessment is that CBs are imaginative and thus Supernatural (human-made) unrealities composed of a complex diversity of bits and pieces of the finite creatively organized into a coherent whole. The very identity of a CB takes the form of a distinction from something else and thus can have very little significance of its own. By reflecting the mindset of each ones human creator, it has a Disposition (a blue-print" with an Inclination to impart a specific Effect) that is implanted in the mind of those willing to receive it. That Effect has Consequences which creatively branch in all directions, signifying its dependence upon the nature of the temperament that formed it.

However, it is apparent that God emanates Intelligences throughout the Cosmos, which, despite lacking Matter, are composites of essences and existence. One of those is ones Archetype birth gift Talent--meaning it is *Trademarked* within ones Selfhood--which I call a *Divine Archetype CB* (DACB). That Trademark is unique because its specific shape has a specific vibration rate--a rate carrying a specific power capable of meshing with a similar vibrating type thing within the Cosmos--a thing capable of activating ones Mission or ones career. All vibrations generate sound waves and those of ones talents are in a dormant state at birth (Bailey, Word Stories Encyclopaedia p362). The awakening of ones Talent for the transformation into a DACB image is done by sound waves--waves from a something to which one is exposed in the environment--a "something" possessing a similar pattern, or vibration rate, with ones dormant Talent--a "something" capable of "Unlocking" the Talent's vault and activating its DACB. Thereafter, that DACB provides a standard, guide, and filter for the Talent's development--whether it starts as a totipotent CB (which can radiate in any direction) or a mature entity (which is cultivated out of its form). A *Probable* (provable) Potential Potency means the DACB has more points in favor of it maturing into reality than not. If one detects ones DACB at an *Unrealized Reality Possible* level of evolution, that implies its realization can happen. Yet, for one to believe any aspect of the above 8 mentioned CB of a one-sided coin nature, the chance of ones Talents being detected, or developed, or finding the proper niche for ones Talent is greatly diminished. Instead, what is essential is that appropriate special sound waves must be translated into the DACB image to serve as a matrix for the cultivation of the physical manifestations of ones Talent.

CONTINGENT BEINGS OF UNCONSCIOUS MINDS: From the ascent of the Conscious from its matrix in the Unconscious there have been evolutionary and entity development un-foldments--called "Planes"-- in both the Unconscious and in Consciousness, much like the Unrealized potential possibilities of schemas of DNA into reality. The first plane is the "lowest mind"--appearing before and between australopithecines (on the African savannas) millions of years ago and the rise of the first wave of Homo Sapiens. This emerged into a mentalized Consciousness driven by fear, pleasure, drives, impulses, and modes of "Fight or Flight" survival seeking as well as being the cradle of a human's earliest kinship ties, filial connections, sense of awe, and desire to know the Spirit. Out of the "Lowest Mind" developed the "Higher Mind" (e.g. of Philosophers and those of "noble character"), with some extending toward "Illuminated Consciousness") (Bynum, Dark Light Consciousness p283). At the human level, ones *Divine Spirit* activates what the Soul and Will in motion (e-motion) want done by converting its resting Spiritual Energy and its undifferentiated Matter into a dynamic organized state which assumes the form implied in the Will of ones Selfhood.

FORM-BODIES: The mental entity coming out of a human's Unconscious is what Arieti (p54) terms an "*Endocept*" and what I call a *Form-Body*. Because this is occurring inside the Unconscious part of the human mind, it is devoid of activated Intellect, Moral, or Common Sense development and is therefore part of the "Wild" Metaphysical Elements (WME). The Sanskrit word "*Body*" (mass) is applied to a mass frame of an animal or human. But, as used here the body is a Contingent Being (CB) that features: (a) vehicle; (b) a bridge; (c) a performer; (d) a payload carrier with an ability to impact faculties already inside the creator and/or the receiver. The word "*Form*" (image, impression) has several applications given to the "Wild" reality entity: (1) the shape or contour; (2) the appearance; (3) a prescribed or customary way of doing things; (4) the structure, pattern; and (5) the entity's nature.

These "Form-Body" aspects are companioned with Imagination and pre-birth Emotions. A "Form-Body" of ones Unconscious enters into ones Sensory (Secular) Consciousness (SSC). Since *Imagery is a first and natural display of the human mind's activity*, its raw materials can be shaped by using ones imagination to manipulate the forces of those materials. The resultant Form-bodies (e.g. Images)--positioned on different levels of ones Spirit System--have the nature of "*What is*" (i.e. the Essence, as formulated by ones Character); the "*That is*" aspects (its specificity, individuality, and 'here-and-now-ness'); and the "How it is"--its normal pre-birth Illogical and Irrational "Wild" reality. The emerging of the Form-Body—like a Percept (fig. 16)--is the beginning foundation of ones Awareness about the "Thing," but as an intermediary construct of the brain lacking any specificity. This means it carries no clear disposition or intention and thus is only a step above being an unplanned potential possibilities. Then, from a beginning exposure to ones SSC and its awareness experiences, impressions are produced .

Like a Notion, such comes through the startling juxtaposition of unexpected items or themes in an atmosphere in which all ingredients are fashioned into unnatural combinations and arrangements of mental activity so as to generate ones hazy Ideas that lead to thoughts, emotions, sensations, and physical actions. This is similar to mentally fashioning a robot with a "Goo Peanut Butter" consistency.

Anywhere in the process of fashioning the nature and form of the Form-Body expressions it adopts an aura that can be somewhat communicated to other people, but only when it is translated into forms belonging to other levels--e.g. music, drawings, and poems. Senders and Receivers on the path of a proper communication requires they be *Empathetic*--in the sense of sharing a common atmosphere on the same plane of existence. If many are involved, it represents a shared Group Spirit. An analogy is "Soul Mates" so attuned to each other that only a glance is needed by one for the other to pick up on that atmosphere and idea. Inside this Empathetic Atmosphere those involved can allow their wandering imaginations to incorporate chance and the transforming of sounds, emotions, or objects in the manner of *Improvisations* so as to deepen and extend 'reality into dream-like qualities--and to express with spontaneity. The more ones mental challenges, the more active and well-formed the CB.

ADVANCED EUROPEAN ICON CONTINGENT BEINGS: Ancient African Logic (i.e. Dialectic) was used to train their students to become a living witness of the *Divine Logos (i.e. God's Universal Reason—Thought and Creative Utterance and Power)* (James, Stolen Legacy p140). When African concepts of Logic were borrowed by ancient Greeks, such high level thinking and discernments were far, far above the Greeks' ability to comprehend. Thus, they made a mess of all of their borrowings. Contributory to this was that the ancient Greeks were in a philosophical setting of variable concepts questioning if the Cosmos was God-made, as opposed to the more dominant view of the Cosmos being an artifact. By there being an essential disregard of the Spiritual made it easy for ancient Greeks to both bound and split (like separating two sides of a coin) what African Tradition's Spirituality deems to be the Spiritual Boundless. As a result, they "made up" their own concepts about the origin and nature of the Cosmos--and that "make-up" is called *European Supernatural*. One concept is that the Cosmos is mechanical. Let us look at how an "Icon" unites the 'known' (however it is known--called the "Halo") with the invisible about the source of that 'known' (called the Star).

An example is an aspect of the Holy Trinity—a concept originating in Ancient Africa but was borrowed and converted into its opposite by Europeans. In and outside ancient Africa, Auset (Greek-Isis, the most important Ancient African goddess) and her son Horus were known for being the original Black Madonna and Child. Both formed the foundation for the Christian figures and paintings of the Black Madonna and Child, as can still be seen in France, Poland, Belgium, Portugal, Italy, Spain, and elsewhere. Meanwhile, the evolving *Melchite Coptic Egyptians* (those Hellenized into the Greek culture and who spoke a Coptic Greek language) gave Ptolemy I (also called Lagi and "Soter,") the name "Oserapis," and in c323 BC, Serapis (a Greek-Roman name for the African Asar) (Ashby, Ancient Egyptian Buddha p136). Next, their design of a Serapis image made it the "anointed Messias"--a word meaning (K) Christos, or "Christ." Then they created a devotional ritual to him; spoke of him as "The savior and leader of souls to the light and receiving them again"; and fashioned new concepts for their Church, drawing heavily from the African and Hebrew Bibles. Incidentally, the word "Christ," says Diop (Civilization or Barbarism, p. 312), came from the Pharaonic Egyptian expression "kher sesheta": "he who watches over the mysteries." The Greek, "Christos," or "Kristos" is the borrowed Kemetic, "KRST (Karast)" or H RST. Since the Greeks could not pronounce the letter H, they substituted the sound with the letters Ch which for the Greeks, means Horus; with others, one mummified; and among the Egyptians, an Osirified Being. Egyptians applied "Christ" to the divinities, Osiris, Anubis, and others long before Jesus or the European Bible was born.

The Melchite Copts began worshiping Serapis as a god and by 197 BC this created image *of "Oserapis"*, according to Williams, was called by the name *Jesus*. And before this newly created Jesus, there were at least 16 crucified saviors in Africa called Jesus--starting with Horus, the Christ figure of Egypt. These ingredients were associated with the laying of the foundation for the European man-made Christian religion. During this time the Melchite and the Exterior Coptic Religious Communities practiced celibracy and called their female members virgins. Spotlighted here was the African Spiritual family of Auset (Isis), Horus, and Asar (Greek-Osiris, with a decided Ethiopian appearance)--the forerunner of the Holy Trinity of the hybrid European Christian religion (Christianity began in Africa).

However, in 200 AD the European Church issued the Creed that Jesus Christ was "Conceived by the Holy Ghost" and "born of the Virgin Mary." Of course, there were problems in making such substitutions from the Ancient African Bible to the developing European Bible. In addition, to make for skin color compatibility, because of her "black skin" Isis was replaced with the "white skin" created European Virgin Mary. European writers of the still developing European Bible found it necessary to deliberately destroy this "black skin" image for psychological support derived from converting from Europeans' inferiority complex to a superiority complex by means of an Icon Image. In other words, they had to disconnect from these images in the Ancient African Bible in order advocate worship of a Supernatural God who looked like themselves (instead of looking like a Black Africans).

This made Mary "The Mother of God" (Blavatsky, Theosophy p77) and that allowed the Logos (Serapis) to become flesh. Mary also served as a vehicle for Serapis to be born through a woman in order to have a human body and nature. Besides, the European "Mary" replacing the millennia world-wide recognized and established Black Virgin Mother in the Holy Trinity, she too was not included in the Trinity for anti-feminist reasons. This is absolute evidence of a switch from the Spiritual God floodlighted by African Tradition all the way over to an Aryan created Supernatural God—a switch from the Ancient African Bible laying paths and providing fundamentals for the complete freedom of people all the way over to the opposite—i.e. the complete control of the minds of the public.

Furthermore, since then Mary was always represented by Europeans as the Mother of God, irrespective of her visual appearance in Art and popular culture. And that clarity is the best evidence one will get that all of this is about Fantasy. Yet, in this way Mary has become a religious Icon. Nevertheless, with all of these profound European substitutes for African Tradition's reality firmly in place, the Melchites--"Coptic Christians"-- could now worship the Serapis image as being Jesus the Christ and Son of Mary and Savior (an extension of Serapis' title from his military conquests). Official sanction of both was at the Council of Ephesus in 431 AD. Thus, between it and the creation of the Serapis image (320 BC) was 751 years before the starting point for the pseudo-Christ (Williams, p27).

Note carefully what happened. The original (African) Holy Trinity was like the Halo of the Star (i.e. God's Substance). By contrast, the European Holy Trinity was the Halo of the human Serapis. In this process, 'Mary' became the featured "Halo" (Icon) of the Serapis "Star," around which a Celebrity Culture was formed. As a result, its Celebrity-Icons are viewed by many as objects of worship, attracted iconoclastic criticism of "Stars" in the Celebrity Culture being about "Idol Worship." This model embraces transitional "Things"--mediating between internal and external reality as well as between cult members deepest emotional needs in the form of its contained contingent possibilities. The Contingent Being's magnetic attraction of its material-aesthetic surface allows its depth-significance to be subjectified—i.e. to be taken into the heart and flesh.

Worshippers describe this introjection process as if the Contingent Being, an Icon Image, actually becomes part of their internal self. This account of subjectifying the Contingent Being is literally framed by images of its objectification. Its collective representations possess a charismatic power that acts as if it transcends time/space and is extra-mundane/extra-territorial—a fantasy conveying an image to devotees that the Contingent Being inhabits a radically separate world. It SEEMS so likely to be true as to make it an easy next step to enter into and thereafter live in this Supernatural realm. Like ancient gods and demigods, the world of Contingent Being Icons have Images which defy social laws that apply to Celebrity lives. Worlds of these Contingent Icon Images are not long ago, as is true for ancient gods, and yet both worlds remain far away. The "Air Castles" of these Contingent Beings are characterized by stupendous riches lavishly displayed in a fairy-kingdom of secluded homes, outrageous jewelry, splendiferous clothing, gaga weddings, exquisite meals, orgiastic parties, and an infinite supply of equally famous and celebrated friends of the cult from every walk of iconic life.

When outsiders examine this "Air Castle" world (fig. 5), they suspend their critical powers. Like other totemic symbols, the sacrality of the Contingent Beings must be sequestered, protected from pollution by the profane. Except for a few, very structured situations, Contingent Beings cannot mix with non-cult members. What transpires with the Icon Image of Contingent Beings during visitations produces 'revelations'--'very revealing one-on-one interviews'--and promises of 'getting up close and personal'. Whereas it is almost impossible for the most talented celebrities to successfully perform their iconic roles every time, this is not an issue with Contingent Beings for they are deemed to be 'perfect'. By equated somewhat to mythical figures, the mythical signs most prominent in a given cult member's mind and projected on to the Contingent Being remains alive in member's memory, undiminished in its projection of charisma and power.

"BIG PICTURE" OF RACISM

The nature of humans' unhealthy self-esteems—e.g. feeling inadequate about who they are and/or envying others--is to philosophically react in ways that flaw unconscious/conscious aspects of their character. When those features—i.e. either feeling inferior or self-declaring to be superior—dominate in a society, its *Philosophical "Seed"* is most clearly understood by examining in that society's primitive people its origin, nature, and subsequent development. Brutes with a superiority complex focus on acquiring sufficient power to consistently engage in acute Kill/Take/Destroy/Dominate practices. Their policies for victims thereafter are the continued institution of chronic socio-economic-political devastation. These include cultural domination; mental conversion so as to generate "Inside-Out" thinking (e.g. victims giving up their own survival, self-preservation, and self-protection instincts and allowing them to be attacked, if not destroyed); infinite varieties of mind controls--aided by Confusion and never dealing with Truth; coercive behaviors, reinforced by "Making an Example of"; and all out efforts to ensure the maintenance of victims' poverty of every type.

From Brutes' philosophical "Seed," diligence is paid to 3 major intertwined "Roots": (1) racist ideology based on Indifference/Hate/Evil/Sadism biases and prejudices; (2) social or institutional racism; and (3) racist practices enabling unchecked/unpunished states of unfair/unjustified privilege, aggression, and/or violence. All 3 are supported by a Brute Social Network spanning all of society. These practices are hidden by vociferous deceptive advertisements representing their cult displays as "democratic" while maintaining hidden Brutes' ideas/actions, goals/practices of institutions. These are partnered with those cultural symbols/structures/myths that accentuate demeaning stereotypes of victims, and ridiculous fantasies about Brutes own greatness. Brutes then use these "Air Castle" Supernatural assertions and practices to justify and maintain victim inequity, exclusion, or domination.

But this requires promoting and maintaining ignorance about the nature of their racism as well as projecting onto victims as being the cause for their "White man's burdens" necessitating the disempowering of these victims. Once such "Air Castle" racial practices have victims imprisoned, then Brute ideology, institutions, and practices have "smooth sailing"—the stereotyping by media, school, business, and social labeling of victims in most destructive manners (e.g. defective or substandard). Each of these create image which displaying the most demeaning and "beaten down" victims as group representatives—steering victim youth into whatever is for entertaining Brutes (e.g. advertising pictures of Black youth with a ball) and ridicule victims who complain or are competitive--or proscribing acceptable work roles Brutes would never choose to perform. Victims are steered into Brute preferred personalities—like imitating Brutes emotionalism and rage so that they can be killed or imprisoned—like "being about nothing"; acting foolish or submissive, passive, docile, and dependent on Brutes; lacking initiative or an inability to act from lack of courage, decide or think; shun reading and an education. Brutes subtly stir up constant intra-victim group friction.

Victims who follow these models are deemed "good N…" and are thrown "shiny pennies". Meanwhile, Brutes promote their Supernatural world/god with myths of their superiority/morality as models to be followed. Their supporting evidence is "sham" science, sham displays of being happy, and sham beliefs of being accepted as superior. This demands believing that all victims share their same values and excitement over their Trinkets/Trivia. Brutes are convinced, even faced with contrary evidence, that what they think, feel, express, act and react to are "right" and good, not only for them, but for their victims. They cannot understand why victims they encage are so upset and angry--then react with surprise and disbelief to complaints about injustice. They believe victims should "get over" being abused and that victims' desperation problems in daily living is from their own doing. After all, as Brute followers' willful ignorance or dumb para-logic goes: "this is a free country and everybody has an equal chance"—choosing to be blind to the obvious role they play in perpetuating and maintaining racism, discrimination, inequality, and oppression. While simply not caring about victims: "it's not my problem," they would scream loudest if any of their evil acts, or acts they go along with, would be done to them. Constant Profound Unhappiness is Brutes' price to pay.

"DARK" VS. "BLACK"

Historically, Europeans have used "Dark" in a Supernatural sense but explaining it with physical world examples to judge the Natural World. Since the "Air Castle" Supernatural is non-rationally based, this way of thinking makes perfect sense to them. Furthermore, they present "Dark" as being the same as "Black." For Natural World Critical Thinking, such thinking is an example of idiocy. One of the problems is failing to separate the literal from the metaphorical meaning of "Darkness"—particularly when the European Bible is used as the source. This failure to separate serves those who are simply ignorant, are willfully ignorance for purposes of their biases and prejudices, are pseudo-intellectuals who act as if they know what they are talking about, or whose objective is to deceptively lead others along a path where their minds can be controlled. An example of an erroneous argument of presenting a Supernatural God to falsely represent the Spiritual God is: "since God is light (by being the perfect embodiment of rational and moral truth) and since the knowledge of God is man's light, 'Darkness' is the natural antithesis of these ideas." In support of this flawed reasoning, they refer to the Old Testament's "Dark" as being emblematic of "Nothingness" (Job 3:4,5,6) or of death or of the unknown or of the undiscovered. They infer—apparently out of their opinions presented as evidence--that "Dark" is the emblem of mysterious afflictions, and of the ignorance and frailty of human life; of moral depravity; and of confusion and destruction visited on the wicked.

In this way, "Dark" becomes the symbol for that which causes terror and distress. In the New Testament, again without saying how they know what they are saying, the opinion presented as certain reality is that prevailing "Darkness" is the emblem of sin. "Support" is given by more opinions of those within a given "Air Castle" religion who define "Dark" as a state of spiritual ignorance and moral depravity. European medieval times featured a particularly terrorizing setting whereby one could not leave ones physical castle without being robbed, beaten, or killed (the spur for the medieval Knights coming into existence). In addition, the footpads, murderers, burglars and arsonists for whom night proved cover, and the later increase in violent gangs and crimals in the early modern city—provided further reason to stay indoors. Hence, "Darkness" played an important symbolic role as a metaphor of pagan European obscurantism—deviancy, monstrosity, diabolism. By contrast, Christian associations of Light with the making of the world, as God rescued the earth from darkness and chaos, or the metaphorical darkness that preceded the advent of Christ, remained deeply embedded in Western emotions and thought. Associations of "Darkness" throughout C17 and C18 continued with witchcraft and devilry, heresy, sin and death, the struggle of the devout through 'the long night of the soul' where faith was threatened by temptation and terror, and heretics gathered unseen.

In times of widespread conflicting religious beliefs and Superstitions, night was commonly conceived as the domain of Satan in which his powers magnified as well as inviting assorted evil spirits to lurk—e.g. night demons, imps, hobgoblins, ghouls, boggarts, elves and witches. Without illumination, the shadowy world seemed to contain a host of malign and insubstantial entities, and imaginations, stimulated by ghost stories, folk beliefs and religiously inspired terrors were cultivated. Ghosts and poltergeists, and interpretations of landscape—e.g. the notion that 'will o' the wisp' were conjured by fairies in order to lead travelers to their doom in swamps and accompanied by a host of more concrete perils, reinforcing pervasive nyctophobia.

Metaphors have persistently been used to identify darkness with negative understandings of spaces and times—for instance, in the assignation of Africa as the 'Dark Continent' in racist colonial discourse and the reluctance of Victorian bourgeois city-dwellers to travel through 'Darkest London'. Negative allusions to darkness continue to suffuse Western thought and language. We speak of the 'Dark Ages', 'dark forces', 'dark deeds', 'dark thoughts' and the 'dark side', and fear the interventions of the 'Prince of Darkness'. More recently, the emergence of 'dark tourism' connotes the contemporary tendency to visit places of atrocity and suffering. All of this (among others) has contributed to Europeans forming conditioned reflexes toward "Dark/Black".

CRITICALLY THINKING "LIGHT," "DARK," "BLACK": "Supernatural"—most European males' chosen philosophy of life domain—is defined in Warren's Psychology Dictionary as "belonging to a higher order or system than that of Nature." Critical Thinking demands fully "playing this out" into its products and then to the destination of the products' consequences. "Air Castle" elements include being "Non-rational" and opposing any Natural World standards, filters, guides, and measures. The exemplar for the Natural World is African Tradition's Spiritual Elements philosophies of Unconditional Love, Truth, Reality, and the Natural. A "Non-rational" avoidance of these Spiritual Elements means there is no humanity—no Honorableness— no morals—no contributions to the world--no Peace, Contentment, Harmony, or Happiness. Hence, this is the mindset of the mythical African god Set who is about Indifference/Hate/Evil/Sadism as an Individualist. The "Non-rational" aspect makes "mentally challenged" those European males who buy into the fantasy of the "Air Castle" Supernatural. The way this scenario manifests in the Natural World is things of significance or of serious business are assessed as "All-or-None," "Either/Or," and what "SEEMS" right as good enough. In short, one is unable to see Options or Alternatives. All of this is readily evident to those who are not blind to the obvious or *who can look at something without opinions or emotions*. An example of this is the Supernatural assessments of Light/Dark/Black by "Air Castle" cult members (fig. 5).

Hence, there is no possible way for "Air Castle" mindsets to understand African Tradition's Cosmic Organism One-ness with Nature and survival of all aspects of the Cosmic Organism. Oneness with Nature means all of God's creatures and creations are spiritually interrelated. The sharing of such a connection includes human beings, animals, plants, and all that exists in the physical world and the spiritual world. The spiritual interrelatedness is because all that exists emanate from the same source—the same Spiritually Divine source. This means the core, the essence, and the life of everything in existence is divine. It is this Divine source that provides the "energy" within all that allows for their physical manifestation and/or spiritual existence. Thus, not only is all that is in physical or spiritual existence connected but also everything is then connected to the Divine source. Such creates a Oneness. An understanding of the Oneness of Nature leads to an understanding of the survival of the Cosmic Organism group. For if everything in existence emanates from the same source and is connected to this source, creating interconnectedness, then everything is also interdependent.

Furthermore, if an interconnectedness and interdependence are shared between everything, then so too is survival. This means all things in the universe, in existence (e.g. material and spiritual), have in common their survival. The historical track record of European males is that every aspect of this African Philosophy is to be directly attacked—adversely affecting the way Black People wind up living. For example, *nothing conveyed by the European educational system to Afrocentric people is the Truth*. Instead, the basics for everything conveyed to the world is derived out of Primitive European "non-rational" practices which has "no ground of Being."

To prove this to yourself, take any defining moment in the history of Colored People's of the world that was initiated by Europeans and note its reproducible *De-culturalization* pattern (see Dove, J. Black Studies, 1998): (1) in every invaded culture there is the removal of the people from their land (e.g. African American slavery) or their rearrangement (African Apartheid); (2) the forbidding of people to speak their own language; (3) stopping the people from practicing their own cultural forms; (4) inculcating alien and contradictory values, standards, guides, filters, measures, and practices through forced and subtle means; (5) generating intra-group conflicts so as to divide and conquer; (6) pay intra-group puppets to be informers; (7) destroy or control traditional institutions; (8) use torture and abuse on children, women, and men of a physical, mental, spiritual, economic, and social nature for purposes of gaining control over their minds; (9) withdraw access to the people's cultural knowledge; (10) impose ideas hostile to the cultural continuity of the people; (11) deny people their humanity by violent means; and (12) brutally remove the people's real leaders.

RELIGIOUS ORIGIN OF "BLACK/DARK" PREJUDICE: Ancient Africans knew that things opposite to each other in a Metaphysical sense must be of the same nature, like Light and Dark. However, Europeans apparently never discerned this distinction and considered things opposite if they "SEEMED" that way, like Unconditional Love and Hate. The making of a world battle between Light and Dark is attributed to Zoraster in c1200 BC. In his mythological story he said the natural world emanated from Ahura Mazda, the good primordial spirit who brought with him the good, the truth, the law, and the Light. However, he battled constantly with his evil twin, Ahriman—who was responsible for Darkness, filth, and death. This myth, along with misinterpretations made from the Ancient African Bible, were very influential in the genesis of the Contingent Being, the Devil—elaborated on by the Jews and borrowed into Christianity. It was further discussed in the *Theology* (the theory or study of God; the beliefs or doctrines of some particular religious group or individual thinker), *Cosmology* (study of the structure and laws of the Universe and the manner of their creation), and the general philosophy of the three main religions.

First, *Gnosticism,* a mystical religious and philosophical doctrine of the first three centuries of the early Christian era, claimed that spiritual knowledge, rather than faith, was essential for Salvation and could only be obtained by Initiation into Spiritual Mysteries. It maintained a theological dualism in which the body and matter were identified with "Darkness" and Evil. By contrast, the Soul, striving to liberate itself, was identified with "Light and Goodness." Its teaching of a radical dualism, expressed symbolically as Light vs. Darkness, was so influential as to be borrowed into Manicheanism which, in turn, rivaled Christianity in its influence. One of its saying was: Ignorance is a form of Unconsciousness—an infection of "Darkness" from which one or is called out of or from which one must awaken. Its Hindus equivalent is the Gupta Vidya.

Second, Gnosticism was eventually suppressed by the better organized European Christian church, from having received imperial support. In the Christian Gospel of John, the story of Jesus expresses duality as comic battles of good and evil--between 'divine light and primordial darkness'(da Costa, Feminist Theology 2003). European religious leaders said Jesus claimed to be 'light of the world' (Jn 8:12) and encouraged those who believed in him to see themselves as 'sons of light' as opposed to the non-Believer 'sons of Darkness'. John portrayed 'the Jews' as the ultimate forces of Darkness, rejecting the Light. Hence, the Gospel has been used to arouse and even legitimate hostility towards Jewish people. The European Bible strongly favors the Light over the Dark which, in turn, has an influence of racism of untold magnitude to this day. In Mt. 6:23 "But if thine eye be evil, the whole body shall be full of darkness." Also, in the Lord's Prayer of the European Bible (Mt. 6:13) and in Col 1:12-13 there is the asking to be delivered from "Darkness"—i.e. from Evil.

Third, Manicheanism--arising in Persia in 200s AD and composed of a complex religious movement Christian, Buddhistic, Zorastrian, and other beliefs--had its roots in Jewish and pagan thought. It then developed into a Christian heresy in C2 AD, flourishing in the early centuries following Christ's death as a religious philosophy taught from C3-C7 by the Persian Manicheus. He and his followers combined Zoroastrian, Gnostic Christian and pagan elements in a doctrine based on the need to divide the world in two contending principles of good (light, God, soul) and evil (darkness, Satan, the body). The African-American psychiatrist Pinderhughes elaborated on this drive to dichotomize by bonding affiliatively to certain ideas and people and aggressively and divisively to others. He postulates a theory of differential paired bonding based on an approach physiology that is manifested as the psychological phenomena of affiliation, introjection, identification, affection and an avoidance physiology that develops differentiation, projection, repudiation and aggression (Hodge). Yet, this Mandean Gnosticism Aramaic sect's theme of the World of Darkness (synonymous with Evil) and misogyny (hatred of women) survives in today's Iraq and Iran.

In using Critical Thinking for the summary concept of "Dark," in historical European literature always being considered as bad, if not downright evil--and "Light" invariably associated with good, necessitates examining the essence of this theological language. Such constitutes a *Qualitative Judgment*—meaning it is the mental act of relating two concepts, accompanied by the belief or assertion of some objective or intrinsic relation between the two. This means that the opposites--i.e. what is embraced in all that each person making an individual value judgement includes in the "Light" as well as includes in what constitutes "Dark"--are not of the same nature. Such is quite different in relating it to African Tradition.

"BLACK/DARK/LIGHT" IN AFRICAN TRADITION: In African Tradition, *"Blackness" is the reigning divine Cosmic Principle of all real things in the Unseen and the Seen realms.* Throughout African history, being Black had nothing to do with color and everything to do with culture. But the "color" black gave

Black culture its essence. Whereas Europeans' narrow-minded "dark" and "black" usage has always been within their Material and Supernatural World concepts, African Tradition properly uses them in a Spiritual/ Metaphysical sense--both naturally associated with the Physical world. Spiritually, Ancient African Sages said that out of God's Cosmic Mind (located in the Amenta) comes the Spiritual Elements in the Subjective Realm--called the Ocean of Nun (Nu). The Nun is in a state of complete "Darkness" because of Spiritual and Physical reasons. Its contents are Spiritual Energy/Matter so as to assume any form or event conceivable. Ancient African Sages, in speaking of the all-Black Amenta (the Nun, the Void, Nothingness) containing in its upper region the Mind of God and the body of God, said *its total blackness corresponds to the state of absolute darkness* (Kekui)—both God made. In the beginning both were so enveloping as to make the Cosmos indistinguishable from the Ocean of Nun waters. Both symbolize the inscrutable Source of the "One and the All" under the terms the Absolute, the Potential, the Unknowable, and the Un-manifest. This was a "Darkness" beyond all intellectual conception—a thrice unknown "Darkness" that knew no bounds—being in the Abyss, and Water, and subtle Breath intelligence—all done by God's power. Light/ Darkness dualism does not arise as a symbolic formula of morality until primordial "Darkness" has been split up into Light and Dark.

Hence, the pure concept of Darkness is not, in symbolic tradition, identified with gloom, as in European concepts. On the contrary, it corresponds to *Primigenial Chaos*—i.e. the Spiritual Realm's first born potential possibilities for the future displays of God's divine and earthly creatures and creations—both in unformed Matter and in infinite space. Here, it is inert or at least at rest or passive, since the "Spirited" active mode of energy is responsible for the differentiation of Matter into forms. The apparent *Darkness is itself light*—dazzling and blinding in its splendor. The African Law of Creation says Primigenial Chaos corresponds to the Nun's Primordial Darkness. It also lacks form, is undefined, undifferentiated, and limitless in expanse/duration (i.e. infinite/eternal)--uncreated/indestructible).

Yet, it is not disordered, as Europeans wrongly say. Hence, Light is the basic principle behind differentiation and hierarchal order. Physically, light involves activity (propagation, hence differentiation) that takes place through time--meaning there can be no light in the Subjective. The Dark represents the state of undeveloped potentialities which—in keeping with the Law of Opposites--is essential to recognizing the Good. In turn, its perception as gloom serves as a standard to avoid--so that one knows how to direct ones striving for Perfection as well as Plan a life's course opposite to it. As a result, this "Darkness" is regressive after the advent of light. Since for Ancient Africans, "Black" reflects the Primordial (present prior to the beginning of time and space--before anything was created, and not caused or created by any circumstance) state of existence—and since "Black" and "Dark" were made by God--and since "Black" is associated with God, "Black" symbolizes dawn, before sunrise, and the state of searching the un-manifest and each potential.

Ancient Africans said this same Cosmic plane of existence resides in a human's mind. Here again, the Ocean of Nun state of absolute Darkness (Kekui) corresponds to the total blackness, silence, and obliteration of sense perception, thinking, and feeling that envelops consciousness--leaving it conscious only of itself (Amen Metu Neter II:37). Based upon the African Law of Correspondence, this is a description of the state of a human's energy and consciousness in the highest levels of Meditation. By blending the Spiritual with the Material, African Tradition's application of *Spiritual "Black" and "Dark" could symbolize the "color" of resurrection and eternal life*, perhaps because new life was seen as emerging from the Darkness—a concept related to the black mud of the African Nile River which brought life to the delta each year. When Europeans borrowed these concepts, they got them totally confused and created false pathways. jabaileymd.com

BLACK/DARK/LIGHT DEFINITIONS IN AFRICAN TRADITION: Because *"Black" designates the African ultimate in Spiritual Perfection, Ancient Africans proudly called themselves "Black People."* "Black's" word origin is African, from the Ethiopian word Celeno (King, African Origins p29) and has been used by Africans in Asia and Europe pre-dating the Indian Sanskrit name 'caeruleus yamas,' meaning "black." European Sanskrit borrowed the term "Black" from African populations that migrated to India many thousands of years earlier. Ancient Africans said 'the Black' reflects the primordial state of existence, before anything was created and thus is not really a color but rather the absence of all colors. Although "Black" (Fr. Noir; Ger. Schwars) is popularly regarded as a distinct color, Ancient Africans knew that strictly speaking *the Black," like "white," is absolutely destitute of color while absolute "Dark" is absolutely destitute of light.* "Black" absorbs light waves while "white" reflects it. A European dictionary defines "black" as the quality or state of the achromatic colors (white, black, grays) of least lightness (bearing the least resemblance to white)—constituting the lower limit of the gray or the achromatic series. It is the complement to and an antagonist of white. All objects absorb some color and reflect some, but black objects reflect the smallest proportion.

Blackness, not Darkness, allows the perfect reception of all wavelengths of energy. Physically, Black is the meaning of the KAM root of Chemistry—the study of life's building blocks. Life is founded upon Carbon—the Black element present in all living matter. Black carbon atoms, with other atoms link to thereby form Black Melanin, which has "Black-Hole" properties (like those found at the center of the galaxy). In physics, a "Black Body"—at work in the Electron--is known to be a perfect absorber and perfect radiator of all forms of light and energy. Electrons--responsible for all chemical changes in matter—have been present since the creation of the Cosmos.

Melanin has allowed hominids to survive millions of years and evolve into Black skinned humans—out of which all other races derived. Although there are no 'pure' Black or White people, the variation in colors of humans' bodies are the result of hemoglobin within the blood vessels of the skin and melanin. The basis of pigmentation is in 2 forms—eumelanin (brown-black in skin) and phaeomelanin. Skin color depends on the size and distribution of Melanosomes (which produce melanin), defenders against radiation damage such as skin cancer) as well as the metabolic activity of Melanosomes and tyrosinase. Melanin and Melanosomes are in major organs (e.g. heart, lungs, liver, lymph nodes) and in the Central Nervous System--including its membranes that cover the brain and spinal cord—in proportion to the amount of melanin found in the skin (Kittles, J. Black Studies, 1995).

Because of Black People's high concentration of melanin, they hold the key to discoveries of Sacred Mysteries once known only by early Africans. One reason is they have more interest in loving Blackness as an integral part of African cultural identity and human-ness. If the color black had not been the sign of slavery, Black culture would not be the torchbearer of freedom. "Dark"--a loose generic term used *figuratively* (metaphorical, symbolic) and *literally* (most obvious meaning)—spans a range from the complete absence of light to dimness to varying degrees of mixed or partial or shaded light. Something is considered "dark" if it cannot be seen through. African Sages said Black is associated with the Soul that comes from Darkness and passes to Light. African Griots (story-tellers) elaborated on this by saying to the people that Black indicates dawn, before sunrise and the state of searching. Just as there is an awe in watching the black flower blossom as it may, or watching the black swan fly, they could relate both to the coming out of the "Dark" every morning into the brilliant and creative sun god-light, beauty, gold giving or imparting happiness, perfume, nectar and ambrosia; right, good, and truth. Thus, *Unconditional Love is African Black.* These Superior People knew an increase in knowledge and power-derived from such spiritual undertakings and that their actions were always in harmony with every other like-kind event in the world. This process, leading to resurrection and eternal life, follows the direction of the Life-Force which functions on Divine (Cosmogonical) Law and is generated out of ones Real Self (Amen Vol. I:101, 162). In short, Black indicates the Cosmic un-manifest and the potential. jabaileymd.com

ORIGINS OF EUROPEAN SKIN-COLOR RACISM

The pigmented Africans who traveled to Northern Europe 45,000 years ago slowly lost their melanin skin color over 20,000 years. Since ones culture determines the way people view themselves and therefore think and behave, perhaps, in the process and over time, they became alienated from their *Collective Unconsciousness* (i.e. ancestral memory bank of African experiences and wisdom). Such a turning away from their own humanity (making one Self-Unknown) and being in a harsh climate no doubt caused philosophical changes in which most elected to operate out of their Brute Brains—as indicated by their hatred of anyone unlike them (and even of themselves). In my Orthopaedic Surgical practice, certain European patients were proud of how long and intensely they hated someone(s)—and not just limited to Black People—and a few said it was for no reason! Nevertheless, most early societies in European history treated different skin-colored people (e.g. Albinos) as divine spirits who possessed certain Supernatural powers. Yet many of the rest considered those same "different" people as strange, inferior, to be feared, and to be hated. One reason was they (e.g. the Indo-Aryan culture), were xenophobic (fearful of strangers). Whereas African matriarchy cultures deemed women to be on a social and dignity par with men, the warring northern Europeans had a patriarchy (males harshly dominating women). By 1900 BC, Aryans had overpowered southern matriarchies.

The model for living laid out by Very Ancient African Nubians (Ethiopians) served to civilize today's world. In multitudes of societies, traces of their civilization and culture are prominent in not only religions but also in the languages, government, science, and most everything else that is associated, even today, with advanced civilizations. Ancient KMT (Kemet), from its beginning and during its greatest periods of cultural development was an indigenous Black African civilization. Its birthplace was inner equatorial Africa and it remained, at its core, culturally unified with the rest of Ancient Africa. Thus, KMT must be considered as an entire African classical civilization (Bailey, Echoes of Ancient African Values). Kemet (Egypt), the daughter of Ethiopia (upper and lower Nubia, the Ancient Cushite Empire) has replicas throughout the world. One example, on the back of every USA dollar bill, is the summit of a symbolic Ancient Egyptian pyramid containing within a radiant, upward pointing triangle the Eye of Heru, indicating divine consciousness embodied in a perfect or enlightened human being. In Ancient Africa it was placed in the middle of the forehead, indicating the door to the collective unconsciousness (roughly intuition) (Ani, Yurugu p466). However, when borrowed into the Western world, the meanings were changed radically so that the reality of the African symbol is unrecognizable. Other examples can be seen in Washington, D.C.'s Lincoln Memorial, the Library of Congress (modelled after the Library of the Ancient Egyptians at Alexandria), and Obelisk (in Egypt, representing the resurrection of Osar, the founder of Kemit).

INFERIORITY COMPLEX: For people incapable of making such contributions as to attract the adulation of the world leads them to embrace a profound *inferiority complex*--defined by the European Alfred Adler (1870-1937) as: "strong feelings of inadequacy and insecurity stemming from real or fancied deficiencies of a physical, mental, or social nature. The overall result--when combined with anxiety, resentment, and overcompensatory drives--would be to adversely affect the individual's entire adjustment to life." Among the top in causing a dismantling of human Selfhood structure, an *Inferiority Complex* mindset (self-attacks on ones thinking abilities, self-worth and/or self-value, with its deep seated unhappiness) is about a feeling of gross inadequacy and compounded when there is shame in sexual matters (as discussed by Dove, J. Black Studies, 1998). Such self-hatred directs *attacks in ways that tear others down as a means of getting some relief from how bad one feels about oneself.* Many experts say the shamed person(s) *Over-compensate* (engage in exaggerated conflict efforts to conceal the "Raw Nerve" causing their sense of weakness). Such can be inferred by European males' sexual, gender, and racial aggressions directed toward women and Black males.

By being a warring people there is no time to reflect on the underlying inner nature of things and that prevents one from being intelligent. And that is extremely significant in assessing the character of European males. Everywhere Europeans have been, history records them as *wiping out whatever was good.* As to how this came to be, let us listen in on what today's Europeans say about their European brethren of earlier times in history. Broom and Selznick (Sociology p88) said: "...the primitive peoples did not blindly accept the 'superior' culture of the Europeans even when defeated in combat. In art and drama the primitive peoples lampooned the white man and represented him as ignorant and destructive. Neither the manners nor the morals of the conquerors are objects for admiration as seen through the eyes of the primitive artist." Aristotle (384-322 BC) added: "The races that live in cold regions and those of Europe are full of courage and passion but somewhat lacking in skill and brainpower...." Poe (Black Spark White Fire p342) supported this comment by saying: "...that fair-headed northerners were not very bright. The stereotype of "dumb blonds" is evidently older than we think!" The truth of these three things—being dumb, destructive, and amoral--so bothered the barbaric Europeans that they eventually tried to overcome them by means of a superiority complex.

The method they used was brought about through the technological development of superior weapons for killing people. Besides making no contribution to better any society, they did just the opposite and destroyed anything worthwhile they could not use--whether that be the cultures of other people or relationships between people or the land or the environment or Nature's reserves. And their destructive effects have typically been long lasting. It trying to appear intelligent they have instituted grossly inferior systems and reinforce them by means of the GUN--a mindset and practices Europeans continue to highly endorse as a means for achieving any ill-gotten ends. Nevertheless, any form of an Inferiority Complex places one on the negative side of the Thinker's Scale. One form is that one has a "Broken" Selfhood Integrity and thereby does anti-Spiritual Element things. Another form comes by one allowing others to define who they are—as European "Troops" and many Enslaved Africans permitted the Satanists leaders to do. This is despite the fact that no matter which single and/or group of outsiders do the defining of another, their assessments can never be right. Being defined in a demeaning stereotypic way + ongoing racism + lack of adequate employment causes many Black People to display manifestations that could be interpreted as an Inferiority Complex. However, I do not believe this to be a correct assessment (as discussed later). A variety of forms can be explained by the materials used in making ones own Self-Esteem assessments.

In addition to raping and enslaving African of their material possessions and their freedom, European Brutes also stole African Intellectual Property and claimed it as their own. The African papyri of the Middle Kingdom (3348-3182 BC)—given by Europeans the European names of Moscow, Berlin, Kahun, and Rhind—have now been *proved to be plagiarized* by *Pythagoras, Archimedes, Thales, Plato, Eudoxus, Oenopides, Aristotle, Solon, Indocsus,* and other Greeks who have left their names on what is considered great in the world today. Illusions/Delusions resulting from this plagiarism have been devastating for subsequent peoples in world history. Thus, Europeans resorted to the *Projection Method*—i.e. the hurling onto a scapegoat (a peaceful individual/group) some "ugly" aspect taken out of their own bad character in order to make it seem as if it is only the victim who has that "ugly" trait. Such includes things like calling themselves superior (e.g. intellectually) Africans savages when, in fact, the situation was just the reverse. They also claimed Africans had never made any contributions to thw world when the reality was that Africans had made practically all and Europeans practically none (for what they claimed as great works were of African origin). These diametric opposites remain prominent to this day. To prevent people from knowing the Truth, Europeans have destroyed all evidence of African super-brilliance and rewritten history so as to be the "stars."

The psychiatrist Alfred Ader said: "To be a [European] human being means to possess a feeling of inferiority which constantly presses towards its own conquest…The greater the feeling of inferiority that has been experienced, the more powerful is the urge to conquer and the more violent the emotional agitation… We must interpret a bad temper as a sign of inferiority." Some of the countless causes for European males bad tempers—because of their doubts about themselves--is facing constant challenges to their intelligence or, if they claim to be religious, to have their good faith questioned, no matter how evil their actions. Mannoni, a French psychiatrist, said Europeans suffered from an inferiority complex that produced a need to dominate--a driving force setting them apart from others—a force embracing an initiative, energy and creativity resulting from their struggles with feeling inferior. Behind the need to dominate he claimed there was also a misanthropy (G. miseo, to hate + anthropos, man)—i.e. an aversion to people; a basic sense of mistrust and hatred of humankind. He felt that together these traits became the driving force of colonialism and world domination. Both traits were repressed but found expression in behavior--the inferiority complex being defended against by compensatory efforts to dominate others and misanthropy through flight to far-away lands. Mannoni found evidence of these traits in the European psyche as early as 1572. He felt that these Colonialists treated the colonized as scapegoats and projected upon these 'inferior beings' all their evil intentions, impulses and fantasies.

FORMS OF RACISM: Such a European mindset of chronic inferiority complex made it essential to establish color, and then genetic racism. During ancient times and subsequently there were various types of racisms. Some people were prejudiced against Albinos of any race. Much before 800 BC they racialized the Hindu spiritual system of India, which had been set up by the *Dravidians (Ethiopians or Cushite)* into a religious caste system based upon skin color. The *Rig Veda* (the Aryan sacred Hindu text) describes white as associated with Brahma, the priest (the Aryans); red, the administrators and the military; yellow, the mercantile and agricultural caste; and black, the lowest and for the Sudras (Dravidians, called the "Untouchables") for purposes of humiliation and degradation. Aryans said the Sudras' shadow polluted the earth; women's intellect has little weight; and Ancient Greece and Italy's xenophobia meant killing a 'weird' visiting stranger was not a crime. Aristotle (389-332 BC) said those "too Black" (e.g. the Egyptians and Ethiopians) are cowards (apparently because they were a peaceful people) and those excessively white are also cowards (e.g. woman). During this time Cultural Racism was prominent with respect to the Black Mystique (Chapter VIII) but it was in the form of Envy. Christians also had skin color racism, as shown in their myth (given as fact) of the curse of Ham. European Brute racism was oriented to those in a race of people who allowed themselves to be enslaved had weak "Manhood's". Such racist ideology all over the *European world accounts for the racial world conspiracy as vital to their intent to conquer the world*.

Meanwhile, demeaning women at the hands of European males persisted in full force. Although Diana (Jana, an Ethiopian) and Isis (Auset, an Egyptian) were revered all over Europe, Diana was particularly attacked by Christians, who labeled her Queen of Witches; the Gospels demanded destruction of all aspects of her cults. Christianity was bothered by the Black Moors' connection with Blackness (which Christians feared), and by the fact that they were often ruled by women. In C15, after developing the GUN fashioned by the Arabs in 1304, Europeans went about annihilating hundreds of millions of Colored Peoples around the world (fig. 8). They justified this by a Supernatural claim of their victims being inferior and thus expendable. Yet, simply seeing the profoundly advanced civilizations and cultures of the Colored Peoples they devastated (e.g. Africans sleeping in gold beds while these warriors were still crouching around fires eating raw meat) caused European males profound Inferiority Complex sense to explode.

ENVY INITIATED RACISM: A major cause of an Inferiority Complex is *Envy* (C13 Old French, look at someone with malice or resentment). In Christian theology it is one of the Seven Deadly Sins—with early senses including 'hostility,' 'enmity,' and 'grudge.' It is normal for persons to grasp their identity by comparing themselves with others. Warren's Psychology defines Envy as "a social feeling or attitude, unpleasant in character, aroused in the individual by the possession or attainment of something on the part of another, which the individual himself lacks and which he desires." When another's talents, appearance, achievements, civilization, culture, spirituality, and/or material goods are experienced as Selfhood adequacy challenging, persons sense a loss of a sound self-esteem. To overcome this, the envious devalue the other as the cause of their loss of self-concept, self-worth, self-meaning, and even self-identity. Example: When the Greek, Ptolemy I, Lagi ("Soter," "Savior") assumed rule of Egypt (323 BC), his attempts for acceptance by Egyptian priests were rejected. Angrily, he closed all other sacred Ancient Egyptian temples, making it against the law for any priest society to build temples/buildings. Meanwhile, following Alexander's death, Aristotle was allowed by General Soter to have Tusak give the Greeks access to Egyptian works. Those who could study in Egypt for themselves did so, while some African works were sent to the newly established Greek Peripatetic schools (discussions while walking) in what later was called Alexandria, Egypt.

According to Williams (Historical Origin of Christianity, 1992), Ptolemy I confiscated all divine and sacred inspired manuscripts written on papyrus scrolls and stored them in the one remaining temple in Memphis where his image had been made into the pagan god Serapis (Greek-Roman name for the African Asar) (Ashby, Ancient Egyptian Buddha p136). They were later moved to Alexandria, Egypt (the great Greco-Roman City on Egypt's Mediterranean coast) in 240 BC--a place called the Great Library of Egypt. Ptolemy I sought and founded a council of Ancient Egyptian priests/priestesses in Memphis, Egypt--called *Melchite Coptic Egyptians*--who agreed to make his image into a god—the beginning European Bible. The intention was for him and all Europeans to have the appearance of being in tune with the spiritual rhythm of the Cosmos. jabaileymd.com

"RACE" CONCEPTS OF MODERN ORIGIN: European psychiatrists have all sort of reasons for the racism of Brute Europeans, including things like behaviors resulting from a deep-seated sexual guilt, prohibitions in childhood and an intense need to project undesirable impulses on others (Moore, Transcultural Psychiatry, 2000). Bernal's (1987: 201-3) historical research found that in C15 Northern Europe, clear links are evident between dark skin color and evil and inferiority with respect to gypsies who "were feared and hated for both their darkness and their alleged sexual prowess". By the 1690s, "there was widespread opinion that Negroes were only one link above the apes – also from Africa – in the great chain of being". Anglo-Saxon scholars such as John Locke, David Hume, and even Ben Franklin "openly expressed popular opinions that dark skin color was linked to moral and mental inferiority". Furthermore, in order to understand the structuration of "race" and *whiteness*, it is helpful to take into account the emerging industrialization of C17 American economy. During reconstruction, once 'Slave for life' status had been rescinded in law, "Race" had become more than an idea—extending to a worldview--a way of understanding reality that was imbedded in society's cultural consciousness. Hence, the public was clear, as I saw Mantan Morlan (Negro comedian) say in a movie: "if you're White, you're right; if you're Brown, hang around; and, if you're Black, stand back."

Frantz Fanon (1925–61), an Afro-Caribbean French psychiatrist (and later political activist) born in Martinique, was one of the first authors to analyze and write extensively about the psychology of racism and oppression—especially in its relationship between colonial psychopathology and subjugation--in a radically different way (Oda, et. Al. History of Psychiatry 2005). However, the radical nature of his thinking served to marginalize his contributions and resulting in him being viciously attacked by European psychiatrists--both as an incendiary and as deviating from Marxist dogma. Thus, much of his writing has not been translated into English. Fanon described *Manichean psychology* as essential to the process of racism--with Alienation (ancients called it *Progressive Insanity*) being key.

My interpretations are that at birth European males are socialized into a philosophy where there is a fundamental need to split, to objectify, to blame and dehumanize the object of racial hatred. At the core of this is "*Alienation*" (strange, foreign)—i.e. feeling withdrawn in ones mind and actions so as to be out of touch with oneself, others, and/or with situations. *Self-alienation* includes being uncertain about what role is expected of oneself—doubting ones own decisions—a sense of helplessness and futility. Being Self-Unknown and separated from ones 'deeper' Self apparently comes from preoccupation with conformity—the wishes of others—the pressures from social institutions—and other 'outer-directed' motivations. Alienation from others is about a lack of warm relations and a mental clouding whereby even familiar persons and situations formerly familiar, appear unfamiliar and strange. In short, self-alienation limits ones capacity to relate to others; alienation from others limits the capacity to discover oneself. These causes are from repression, inhibition, blocking, or dissociation of ones own emotions so that they are no longer convincing to oneself.

Such is seen in obsessive-compulsive psychoneurosis. The result is estrangement and depersonalization. Fanon also contended that the European was used to seeing the 'Negro' as a kind of 'phobogenic object' (i.e. dreaded and uncontrollably feared)--a perception of 'the Black' (and the insane) as some sort of undifferentiated 'Other'. Such fears are persistent and intense, with a compelling need to flee or avoid the dreaded. This would be in keeping with an "Air Castle" Supernatural mindset shaped by "Non-rational" mental activity nature—a mindset that typically sees all sorts of Contingent Beings in its magical thinking.

EUROPEANS IMAGES OF SCAPEGOATS: A CB created for oneself and/or for others refers to ones psychological and philosophical orientation projected into any entity included under Imagination and Amorphous Cognition. Whatever is that entity, the CB is a Symbol representing something not existing in reality. An Icon Image may be a representation of what is real, distorted, or fantasy. The most hateful of all CB or Icon Images concern stereotypes of Black People; the most ridiculous ever invented by humans are CB or Icon Images of White people self-declared to be superior to any other race—Tarzan, Angels, Jesus, Miss America. Both types are used for brainwashing people—and the brainwashers are themselves brainwashed by being in a desperate mindset state because they have no idea as to who they are. Thus, to hide this "Raw Nerve," they make up the best about themselves; be "busy" in the pursuit of the Image of gold; and/or make their god in their own image. The most vicious of the top Icon Images carried in the minds of Europeans is the putting of its dictated messages into practice the Dehumanizing (also called *Infrahuman, Subhuman, or Chattel*) of another human being—i.e. divesting them of human qualities so as to view them as either mechanistic objects or as animals. Such has been done to Black People from the first modern encounters and still continues. "*Dehumanize*" means to convert the Image of God at the core of a human into a machinelike imbrute—i.e. the rendering of this "Thing" into a state of brutishness—making that victim seem impersonal or unconcerned with human values—calling that human a "Barbarians" to indicate being one of the highly uncivilized folk.

Ancient Greeks deemed "Barbarians" as worse than beasts because of declaring them to be cruel, wild, filthy and inhuman in their actions. There is no better example of Projection than this—European Brutes putting on Black People their own "Dark Side" features. However, the devastating significance of this is that certain "terribly beaten down" Black People have believed this evilness about themselves while Black imitators of European males have applied it to their Black gang enemies.

Oddly, Abraham Lincoln (1809-1865) said: "When…you have succeeded in dehumanizing the Negro; when you have put him down and made it impossible for him to be but as the beasts of the field; when you have extinguished his soul in this world and placed him where the ray of hope is blown out as in the darkness of the damned, are you quite sure that the demon you have roused will not turn and rend you?" Whereas European enslavers created these horrible conditions for Black People, their today's descendants continue the same hateful practices while blaming struggling Black People for being in the bad condition they are in. It is amazing so many Blacks have done so well as they have. A consequence of the European-generated poverty for struggling Black People is that Poverty *itself is dehumanizing by making one feel worthless*--doing so by keeping down the human Soul, as with an iron chain--the wildest aspect of human reality. The degree of poverty's deg-radation can be determined by the attempt or non-attempt to climb out of its bottomless pit. Brutes images of generating Poverty for Black People is to ensure they have nothing and with no hope for ever having anything. Such is achieved by allowing no social program to be beneficial to Black People—e.g. by means of a lack of cultivated talent ability and by keeping from Black people the African Traditions ways for education to pave the way to get some "seed" to sprout, flower, fruit, and then multiply itself into something more. Struggling Blacks "Life-Living" is so harsh that 'Demons' are now given permission to surface or they otherwise surface anonymously. In that mindset anyone--particularly Satanists who control everything in the USA--can shape victims Consciousness.

By the combination of Brutes not valuing Black People as human beings and by attacking the rules of what is "Right" means they have no more regard for Black People than if they were flies needing to be swatted. The code of "high-class" Brutes is to use the dehumanizing language of "Them" or "You people"; write vague laws that can be interpreted so as to constitutionally deny them of full legal personhood (e.g. with voting rights or equal protection under the law); public endorsement of police brutality against Blacks; and the forbidding of altruism toward Blacks—all (among others) socializing European children into supporting biases, discrimina-tion, and prejudices.

EUROPEAN IMAGES OF "NORMAL" BLACKS: This subject needs no elaboration because European hostility expressions, emotions, and deeds are daily showered on Black People for all to see. Caricature de-meaning images—"Sambo," watermelon Pic-a-ninnies, baffoon-acting Blacks and "Street Life" Blacks are floodlighted on all forms of media. As a boy, every magazine I thumbed through had the cartoon of a Black cannibal with a bone in his nose preparing a White man in big kettle to be eaten. Large percentages of Europeans are the perpetuators—are willfully ignorant so as to be blind to the obvious--applaud it—indiffer-ent to it. When despicable inhumanity occurs to Black People, the deep-seated fears and the brain-washing to not have independent thought but simply follow their Satanist leaders lead them to disregard that inhumanity in order to preserve their unwavering deference to White Supremacist authority to always be in control.

To believe in White supremacy requires anybody who does not conform to be deemed the enemy. Hence, whether Black People are simply "hanging out," turning up at a party or are protesting imparts the image among most Europeans of them being a "mob". This is because 'Black skin' is associated with unruliness, trouble, and eventual violence—an image automatically conveying Blacks have a "blatant" disregard for au-thority and order, pretty much asking to be kept in check. In a reported disturbance within a racially mixed crowd, the police will order the Colored Peoples (e.g. Blacks, Mexicans, Arabs) to get on the ground while the White youth become invisible and free.

Also, when I was a boy parents of most Black children told them that "Black skin" made them 'different' and there was no allowance for given for them being youth--no wiggle room to make average, youthful mistakes and grow from them--no afforded benefits of doubt because any blunders could get Black People killed by Europeans before any questions were asked: they "shoot first and ask afterwards". Black People are held to incredibly high and standards of personal responsibility impossible to meet because those standards are undefined, unstable, and constantly changing. Blacks are expected to meet the ideal fantasy image Europeans have of themselves as being 'perfect.' They exhibit "Righteous Indignation" from Black People coming anywhere near doing the evil and sadistic things Brute Europeans and their followers routinely do. All Black People's behaviors are endlessly attacked or ridiculed. This can only come from a people who hate themselves and feel inferior.

"NORMAL VARIANT KILLERS"

To re-emphasize some 'big picture' points made about "Normal Variant Killers" is they have no insight for the question of: "Who Am I?"--which disconnects them from their innate "5Ss" (safety, security, self-confidence, strength, stability) and from all creatures—and those put them in "nowhere" bottomless pits. They have no specific Natural World knowledge about anything—and thus no concepts of the Spiritual Elements of Unconditional Love, Truth, Reality, or the Natural. They have no independent rituals outside of those perfected by their Supernaturally oriented cult over tens of thousands of years. Their awareness of themselves is of an emotional nature—one of being totally separate—a stranger in this world who came from somewhere else—a fluke (a chance accident). Together, these constitute a Hallucination ('to wander in mind') of the "Normal Variant" type (i.e. not insanity) that is positioned on the outer reaches of ones mind. In this type of Hallucination there are barely perceptible sense organ perceptions (coming from without or within the body) of Things--perceptions not true in any world and yet are contributory to determining their Percepts nature which form Notions, Ideas, and Images one accepts as real. It is this mindset that "Clouds out" ones Real Self, whose individual components (e.g. breathing, blood circulation) work independently to interdependently design a harmonious Selfhood. A feature of this birth gift is that one has no awareness of how any of these organic functions is done. By contrast, a False Self (Ego, "I") or "Normal Variant" Hallucination mindset "puts itself together" as by constructing it out of External World "social" parts into a "Social Institution" which manifests as the role one plays in life (fig. 4). Perhaps this is how Europeans came up with the "Normal Variant" concept that humans and the Universe are "mechanical" rather than in the reality state of vital and indivisible parts of the Cosmic Organism. Nevertheless, the "Normal Variant" Hallucination *Consequences* (the 'somethings' arising out of Effects) are what predispose one to the doing of "Dark Side" things (e.g. needless killings). The 'big picture' Consequence out of which developmental ingredients derive is that form of "Normal Variant" Hallucination called "Phantasmagoria" (see Chapter VII).

ICON IMAGE INGREDIENTS FOR "NORMAL VARIANT KILLERS": From the moment of developing hate in childhood, those destined to be "Killer" Brutes never know to pause to notice and appreciate the beautiful because of the hostile, detailed, and imaginary nature of the "*Paracosms*" they create in their minds. Rather than noticing the sheer beauty of carvings in canyons, they only see the windstorms which caused them. To elaborate, let us use the 'TREE CONCEPT' (fig. 3) for assessment into some order. The natural "Tree Concept" consists of a Seed, Sprouts, Roots, Trunk/Vines, Branches, Leaves, Flowers, and Fruit—stemming from the Cosmic Mind Creator Source. Its ultimate symbolization, in the form of the entire Cosmos process, is the 'Seed' of the *Spiritual Elements*. The rest of the Tree operates in the Physical—the realm of constant change. Ones Self-Image follows this same pattern. People who live out of their birth-gift of the Spiritual Elements engage in "ME/WE" work products as their highest system of Values—never doing, compromising with, or accepting Indifference/Hate/Evil/Sadism. *False Self* (Ego) people—those choosing to be who they are not—give up the Immaterial Absolute Source from which their essence for life and their wisdom for living derives in favor of an ever changing Material realm. To repeat they cannot follow a coherent logical way of thinking because they have no solid base from which to start. So, out of this non-absolute (i.e. highly unstable, if not non-existent) source, False Self people fashion their "Life-Living" think, feel, express, and behavior components which they use for standards. By consisting of acquired emotions and thoughts, the products of those components are about only things of "Value" (i.e. of Physical realm nature).

ICON IMAGES FORMED BY "NORMAL VARIANT KILLERS": Since False Self people have chosen to give up the Immaterial Absolute Source for "Life-Living," they have no choice but to extort acceptance of the made-up Supernatural "Air Castle" realm and its one Absolute of rejecting and attacking the Absolutes of the Spiritual Elements. The context in which "Air Castle" dogma is fashioned makes it impossible to practice a moral code—to permit any firm definition. They regard any concept as approximate—regard any rule of conduct as elastic. All of this is for the purpose of generating conflict, disorder, and confusion in order to be dominant and from ignorance. They "talk out of both sides of their mouths" (contradicting themselves in the same breath) and do "Double Talk" (meaningless speech, mixing the almost real with unreal imaginary inventions. The most fundamental of points here is that *if one does not have an Immaterial Absolute Source anchor for "Life-Living," ones Selfhood is extremely unstable*--like a tree without roots--and thus subject to changing with any powerful force. There can be no African Tradition type "Who I Am" Self-Identity—i.e. ones "Life-Essence" which consists of an unchanging "sameness". Hence, ones inward reality of Being is abandoned for the outward appearances of sought after material things.

The sap which feeds this "rootless" External World tree is of a "Me" nature that prevents "ME/WE" or any "WE" considerations. In short, whatever "Me" deems to be success is engaged in with unrestrained pursuit in a manner isolating the "Me" from the "WE"—transforming neighbors into competitors—generating envy of and resenting those seemingly ahead--that might get ahead--are not contributing to their success—and/or are standing in the way of their success (especially those ethnically, religiously, culturally, or racially 'different'). These feigned enemies are dealt with the hater's "Air Castle" cult dogma to do their 'holy and honorable duty' to Kill/Take/Destroy/Dominate enemies--a process done by wholesale enslavement, dehumanization, encaging, and assassinating anything of Worth or Value related to them (i.e. Spark of God derived Cosmic Beauty, Goodness, Happiness, Wellness, Natural Order). This process begins with them forming a 'monster' image of the scapegoats and keeping feeding it with negative Emotional Energy until they are urged to act in some hostile manner. The beliefs inserted into these Images do not allow for cult members to have any particular regard for how their "Life-Living" practices display since there are no incentives to virtue or any disincentives to vice. Products of applying "Air Castle" dogma have been the killing of untold numbers of fellow humans—the reduction of Black Americans to the status of lifelong chattel Slaves for 300 years and virtual Slaves for 100 + more.

Meanwhile, Amerindians not killed were placed on reservations. "Killer" police were/are part of all of this. Yet, by their False Self ensuring they not know who they are means their Self-Concept and Self-worth are so heavily dependent on conforming to their cult's dogma as well as on the degree of acquiring material success that lack of it brands one in reality and/or in perception—in ones own eyes, the eyes of the family, and the larger community, as a failure. In turn, their mindsets—filled with Emotional Junk, confused thinking, Spiritual Pains, Fear, Anger, or Depression serve as a kaleidoscope lens through which one selected color is used for viewing and coordinating what is taken in. This can cause one to lash out at others and that may be their means of overcoming their sense of isolation, frustration, fear, and alienation bred by this struggle.

"NORMAL VARIANT" PATH TO CONDITIONED RESPONSES: As a boy living in Minnesota, following a heavy snow I would walk through it so as to admire the tracks I had just made. Sometimes I would walk backwards, being careful to step exactly in the same tracks I originally made. This is like the nervous system's tendency, when it has once acted in a certain manner, to duplicate that same manner again. Memory is but another phase of that same tendency. Like making tracks in the snow, *Engrams* are neuronal patterns of an acquired skilled act of learning—i.e. permanent memories representing what has been learned—a process dependent on a Trance. This process is done by biochemical alterations imprinting these learned patterns in neural tissue and thereby accounting for the persistence of memory. Each trace contains a message gained from every mental process, every emotion, every sense perception, and is stored in the cabinet of Imagination. I believe some have priority based upon timing or degree of importance to oneself as well as to the conclusion of one having fashioned the significance by the monitored feedback from interactions with the outside world. For example, in growing up in the Great Depression, my family was able to eat reasonably well on the fish we caught. To this day, if fish is present on my plate, I taste that first because it is the Background of what represents good food to me and makes the rest of the food more satisfying.

Some say an engram is the basis of the Collective Unconscious inheritance and of physiological memory. It is essential to realize that memories are not fixed or frozen but are transformed, disassembled, reassembled, and re-categorized with every act of recollection. When stimulated, a human's mind power is able to activate the Engram Memory in a manner that revives past experiences and to be conscious of having had them before. The message contained in the Memory is in the form of an Image that has varying degrees of imaginative content with energy to activate that Image. When most active, the Imagination forms a Contingent Being (e.g. 'bogeyman') figure with 'character' and power but not reality life. Nevertheless, regardless of whether the contents of the Memory were formed by an actual experience (for which various interpretations can be given at different times) or an experience distorted (by misinterpretations, as from an incomplete assessment) or of a fantasy nature, any resultant Image might evolve beyond the Memory Stage.

CONDITIONED RESPONSES OF "NORMAL VARIANTS": When, after 17 years, my dog Titan became paralyzed, it was with an extremely heavy "Heart" that I decided to have him "put down". This was done at a veterinarian's office 2 years ago. My presence at that office and watching the 'life-taking' of my Buddy caused me to fashion a "Conditioned Response" to simply passing by that office—and it persists to this day. *"Condition" applies to anything essential to the occurrence of something.* On a Spiritual level, the Subjective Realm is at absolute peace--called Hetep—the state of inner peace or absolute relaxation. This means that Energy and Matter are inactive in the Ocean of Nun (Nu)—a state of them being *"Unconditioned."* However, when a Spiritual "Essential" activates the dormant Energy to respond so as to start causing Forms to occur out of Matter, that Spiritual "Essential" is a *Conditional Super-imposition.* *"Imposition"* (Latin, to place or lay upon) means an act of inflicting something on something at rest—to add a distinct feature, element, or quality. In my situation, the Conditional Super-imposition of taking my dog's life away by someone led me to "Condition" my new found dislike of the place where that episode occurred. Prior to that "Take Down" I had an "Unconditioned" state of Being concerning passing by the veterinarian's office. This is like Consequences (my "Conditioning") following an Effect (the "Take Down" of my dog)—an Effect resulting from the Cause of my dog being paralyzed.

Being surprised by a rattlesnake is the Cause of ones fear. The Effects of fear lead to the consequences of ones "fight-flee-or-freeze from fright". These 3 "Fs" occur only when certain requirements are met by an outside force. But otherwise the feeling of a sense of fear is not the original or essential expressions of the substance of the body, mind, or spirit, say, in an infant state. The display of fear, by being unnatural, has to be learned—called *Programming* or Conditioning the mind. Programming serves different purposes. For a rattlesnake, Conditioning is a means of warning against unforeseen and unexpected danger when one comes into close contact with rattlers again. If False Self people have developed a fear or an aggressive attitude for attack of a feigned Target Group or individual, that is a Conditioned Response.

CONDITIONED MIND PROGRAMMING

An analogy for a Conditioned Response is the figure of a dumbbell—two metal balls separated by a bar which serves as a handle. With a Conditioned Response one of the balls is the Unconditioned state—perhaps the way something was when it came into Being. Its attached "bar' is the Stimulus. In turn, the Stimulus causes a Conditioned Response. In the opening vignette above, the 'life-taking' of my Buddy Titan was the Stimulus for my Conditioned Response of no longer liking to even pass by the veterinarian's office where that event occurred. That stimulus was a Super-imposition on a pre-existing non-energized state. In ecclesiastical usage, an imposition is the "laying on" of hands by a bishop as a sign of a spiritual gift or conferring special service.

WHAT IS CONDITIONING/PROGRAMMING?: Conditioning is like one generating a prearranged plan for carrying out some specific act in a "second nature" manner—like having a self-designed Disposition to do something. The 1390s term *Second Nature* alludes to the very frequent repeating of something making it seem inborn (like a Human Nature trait). An explanation for this evolving practice is based on the *Law of Association* (e.g. contiguity, repetition, similarity). To illustrate, I. P. Pavlov harnessed a dog in a sound-shielded room and instituted a neutral stimulus in the sound of a bell which rang each time the dog was presented with food. The dog eventually started responding by the production of saliva that progressed to salivation with each ringing of the bell. This salivation continued with the ringing of the bell, even when the food was no longer presented. So, the 'conditioned stimulus' is the sound of the bell; the 'conditioned response' is the salivation occurring when the bell is heard; the food (the original stimulus to salivation) is the 'unconditioned stimulus'; The salivation originally occurring with presented food is the '*Unconditioned response.*' Reinforcement occurs when the 'conditioned stimulus' is appropriately followed by the 'unconditioned stimulus'.

A learning program is divided into a large number of "frames," each of which contains an item of information. The contents consist of supplying information relative to the kind of operation desired and in what sequence. In genetics, it is the set of instructions coded in the DNA molecules. Conditioning "instructs" the mind to react in a certain way—the 'big picture' of which gives some benefits—positive or avoiding negatives. Foundational to the process is to have a Trigger Target—which for European Brutes is Black People. As a Target, Black People are clear-cut and elicit reactions from Brutes that are extremely emotive (the *"That is"* portion of a Primary Quality of what is hated—i.e. a substitute for the Cognition's "What it is). The ingredients learned from Hate socializations or personal pet-peeves are priority fashioned into an Icon Image which symbolizes "the Story" the Brute has made up about the Trigger Target(s). If one has been socialized to hate a Target Group, then intense emotional responses (especially anger and fear) undergo a progressive crescendo toward mental images, including Contingent Beings.

The Conditioning process starts with whatever is easiest and progresses to the more complex. Meanwhile, there are opportunities for repeated practice in order to master each stage before going to the next. A feature of the progression is that one increasingly becomes more involved in scope (fully), depth (deeply), height (extending beyond the original boundaries as one learns more of ones strengths and limitations), and power (proceeding with building motivation and at a pace that crescendos in speed). Initially, the Image is stored in the neocortex's memory as having significance but without much energy placed into it. Thereafter, the Image is repeatedly recalled to mind by a Target Group or member being seen or the flimsiest thread of that group being heard in "Crowd" talk or on the media. At each recall, embellishments are added and eventually a mental *Icon Image* of the Trigger is formed. As accretions are added to this form, it is imbued with fantasy 'monster' aspects. This 'monster' is analogized to a porcupine--with its strong, stiff quills mixed with coarse hair on the back and sides. Such a spread display of "satellite" signal emitters (e.g. quills) enables ones brain 'antennae" to be more vigilant in its scanning for the 'monster's triggers upon the appearance of the Trigger Target member. This elicits a hyperemotional response. The same sharpness in discerning any tiny characteristic of the trigger' occurs—even if the Trigger ingredients are in nonintegrated disarray. For example, one might then be triggered by hearing a Target member's special group ways of speaking over the telephone. Before one starts reacting to the emotive aspects of the Trigger in some significant manner, one is deriving benefits by thinking one is getting better prepared to help the cult bring that Trigger under control, if not to "wipe out" the Trigger. Or, ones benefits from establishing a scapegoat onto which the Brute can project his/her own evilness and then "blame the victim." The pre-conditioned Fear (Effects) of this Trigger (Cause) leads one into some reactive "Fight-Flight-Fright" Consequences.

In short, a *Conditioned Response begins with Recognition of a stimulus, forming a Disposition about it in the form of an Image; embellishing it with Imagination; committing it to Memory*—some parts being of the Forgotten Imagination Memory type and other parts being of the Familiarity Memory type which is constantly repeated until its Icon nature spark increases so as to cause a pre-determine thoughtless reaction. In the meantime, it moves into a 'second nature' response just short of an Instinct to form a Conditioned Response. [Ref: (Osborne, *Humanity & Society, 2004*)]

STEREOTYPED "LIGHT/DARK" REFLEXES: Metaphorically, some Psychological Reflexes can be considered as stereotypes when thought of as a 'trigger' mental process initiating an individualized motor pattern. This reflex consists of simple movements and are repetitiously performed each time the 'trigger' mental process pops into ones mind. This 'trigger' mental process, when composed of a stereotype, may be of a *Universal Stereotyped Metaphor* nature; from Illusions/Delusions out of ignorance or Supernatural *Paralogic (i.e. Non-Rational thinking passed off as "Logic")*; or to satisfy some personal inner "Needy Want" (e.g. Belonging). The fact that humans are a vision-dependent species blends stereotypes and psychological reflexes upon considering that throughout our evolutionary history at least part of the universal fear of the dark has become a psychological stereotyped reflex. Illusions/Delusions out of ignorance or Supernatural Paralogic are illustrated by ancient Aryan influences throughout areas outside of Africa, like Iran and India. Aryans were strong worshippers of polytheistic male (anthropomorphic) war-gods and to natural forces and elements (e.g. fire); were firm believers in the ruling of conflicting moral powers; and would give good and sublime names to their spirits of light—those with awful divine characters and to which they entertained reverence and fear. Meanwhile, the continued Aryan influences led to, during the Iron Age (2500-500 BC), Aryan gods replacing Black African goddesses throughout areas outside of Africa. Thereafter, that blackness came to symbolize "Darkness" in the sense of evilness.

Although Aryans considered God to be an evil spirit, the Persian Zoraster reversed this and reduced the worshipped gods of the Aryans to the rank of malicious powers and devils. He defined the world as a battle between Good (originating in God and bringing truth and law) and Evil (which brought death, filth, and darkness)—both possessing equal creative powers. This was expanded by Manicheism and European Christianity—conceptualizing this as a "Dark Force" fighting God to a stalemate (African Ma'at accepts no such moral dualism). One major problem was in their misinterpreting realities like death, storms, earthquakes, and other natural disasters as evil. Unable to reconcile the reality of such events with their conception of God as the source of all good, they invented a coequal antagonist for God—and, in the process, destroying their claim to profess in a monotheistic religion (Amen, Tree of Life p178). By hiding the nature and source of Evil—placing it outside of people's beings and giving it a Supernatural divine status that not even God could abolish, reinforced their created concepts of the Devil. According to deCosta (Feminist Theology, 2003), related Zoraster myths brought Jewish concepts out of which the Devil developed—a Contingent Being borrowed by Christianity and became known as the "Prince of Darkness" in medieval times. Whereas in Africa, divine Blackness, with its associated immanence and transcendence, had always been associated with goddesses--including the Great Mother, featuring divine instinctive knowing and Wisdom—all of these traits were assumed into Jesus by the European Christian males in their efforts to make light, right, and might exclusively maleness traits.

Meanwhile, European Christianity focused on Jesus as the light of the world--bringing into sharp contrast Darkness with Light, as noted in the European Bible's Mt. 6:23 and John. Both the OT and NT passages have been interpreted by European "Air Castle" religious males to indicate that light (or white) is good and that anything else, like dark or black, is bad. Because of this and because of placing blame on women in the Adam and Eve myth, women were deemed witches who are under the influence of the Devil. Since matter, the physical, and darkness were considered feminine principles by "Air Castle" European males, these all needed to be controlled, mortified, made to suffer, and be punished. Throughout subsequent history there have been an infinite number of divergent and contrary opinions. Examples: If God is all-powerful, he must be able to prevent evil. But evil exists. Therefore, God is either not all-powerful or not all-good. These European ways of thinking make for irreconcilable differences in their philosophies of life compared to most Black People. This contrary opposite of light/dark was the basis for labeling Africa as the "Dark Continent" in C19 to serve as a prelude to exploit its land and people.

STEREOTYPED PHILOSOPHICAL REFLEXES: Those who choose to live out of their Brute Brain have a group "sameness" but its subgroups emphasize certain aspects of that "sameness." The group "sameness" has an "Air Castle" orientation geared to control other people's minds, acquire power, and be feared. All have a "ME" emotional orientation rather than a "ME/WE" passion, for they pride themselves on being Individualists—except for protecting themselves and their own. The Warrior subgroup desires total control of everything of interest to them and will Kill/Take/Destroy to gain this. Money and possessions are equated to power because those enable them to "buy" people or "buy" control (e.g. controlling the policies of an institution or politicians by threatening not to donate money). They accept anyone who helps them make money or keeps them from losing money. The Religious subgroup controls people by designing their religious beliefs using what "SEEMS" right.

The Para-logical subgroup controls by ensuring everything significant to other people is confused and in conflict. The have absolutely no concept of or interest in the Truth but ensure their victims do not know the Truth for the Truth does not allow anyone's mind to be controlled and manipulated. Anything or anybody that goes against any of these cherished features of Brutes will pay a heavy price—and all Brutes are very sensitized to being slighted in actuality or from those who might or could so. Though stereotyped in all three "Air Castle" groups, negative intensity reactions by the group in general and by members within a given group can vary from Mild, Slight, Moderate, and Extreme, depending on the situation. In speculating--in the sense of accumulating bits and pieces from research (e.g. Katz, Neuroscience Reviews, 2002), observation, and reflecting on experiences in dealing with Brutes, I propose (because I have never seen it discussed) the following goes on in Brutes' minds.

Brutes have been socialized and/or decided to be fearful of certain things, while hating others for self-interest purposes (e.g. "dark" or "black"). These ways of looking at the Dark/Black and developing a negative reaction to them gradually forms in the Brute Brain a Philosophical/Psychological Reflex of reactions. When, from the outside world, this 'toned' information enters their brains, the brainstem (including its Brute Brain and Medulla Oblongata aspects), the cerebellum (normally thought of to be about movement but it has strong psychological features), and the cerebral cortex are involved primarily. A function of the Medulla Oblongata is its reflex action—i.e. sending a motor impulse to any part of the body before the sensation resulting in that impulse reaches the brain—impulses which enter deep nuclear regions where there are nerve fiber loops within loops. Received there are motor commands formulated in other brain regions which, in turn, are extended down to spinal motor pools to account for motor control. When the brain is stimulated by given psychological factors to which the Brute is sensitive (e.g. "dark" or "black"), the cerebral motor cortex receives instructions from other cortical areas to react in the cerebellum.

Repetition of this psychological input pattern leads to plasticity learning in the cerebellum's neuronal circuity. Once that happens the cerebral motor cortex acts directly through the cerebellum, via the loop connection existing between the cerebellum and motor cortex as well as loops between the prefrontal cortical area and the cerebellum. These actions cause sentiments (thoughts, ideas, concepts wrapped in emotions) to be manipulated to make them increasingly automatic and less and less of a conscious nature. Whenever certain triggering conditions are in place, Brute Europeans have automatic negative associations with Blacks (or other non-White groups) with stereotypic ways of reacting to them. This is regardless of their focused attention at that moment, or of recent thinking, or of their current goals and attention. Because they are automatic, their early biases—constantly reinforced by "following their leaders"--are inevitable and their influence is nearly impossible to alter. Yet, the intensity of the negative reactions varying from Mild, Slight, Moderate, and Extreme, depending upon the Brutes' mood, with respect to the group as well as to their hated entity. These stereotyped reactions dominate even in non-Brute "Troops" unless they spend more time learning about the feigned enemies' common humanity and unique attributes.

CONDITIONED RESPONDERS' LIFESTYLE: Much of humans' life experiences are conveyed through language—with ideas and Symbols being feats of association—and with metaphors being among their most fertile power payload tools. Metaphors transfer a concept from one (usually better known) domain to another (usually less well known) domain based upon some similarity(s). Analogies and Models, subdivisions of Metaphors, are used as comparison processes by which one manipulates bits and pieces of information or knowledge to illuminate others. Symbols, Metaphors, Analogies, and Models are misused when they are mistaken for proof or even for reality per se as well as when they are Stereotyped in thought and/or in behaviors. Inside this context, any aspect of it that is accepted is either an Illusion or a Delusion. One or both produce in ones Empirical Reality (pertaining to methods or conclusions based upon observation, experience, or experiment) and in ones Belief and/or Faith the same kind of "SEEMS" right errors.

From these flawed perceptions, premises, and/or defects in reasoning come 'weird' explanations for wrong internally monitored and "awe" interpreted anomalous experiences (i.e. any perceived striking deviation from the typical or normal). Such "awe" combined with thinking errors can/do lead to incorrect inferences capable of generating Superstitions and Supernatural dogma. An example of an accepted *Universal Stereotyped Metaphor* pertains to Spiritual, Metaphysical, Physical, and "Air Castle" Supernatural "Darkness." Every human is born out of "Darkness" (in the mother's womb—Spiritual and Physical) and most believe that their death is a return to "Darkness" (Metaphysical). As opposed to those believing in "Death's Darkness" being designed for a purpose and thus impermanent, those believing in "Death's Darkness" forever fashion symbolic associations having psychological consequences (Supernatural). For all, the "Darkness" of night connotes threat, danger, and evil that ranges from actuality to fantasy. An alternative cause for a Stereotyped Metaphor process is for one to absorb established Superstitions and Supernatural dogma from ones in-group.

In this context, stereotypes have been present in all cultures practicing Superstitions and Supernatural rituals—within which have always had attached symbolic meaning to many different things—some being in-group, culture, or cult specific. Here, the broad sense of the word "Stereotype" is characterizing certain responses which are always performed in substantially the same manner. For example, some are influenced by embraced accoutrements, as illustrated by people (e.g. cults) clothing themselves in black uniforms and are thereby transformed into being more likely to act in harmful ways and to facilitate aggression against other individuals. Another example—based upon "*Metaphors of Error*" (flawed opinions or judgments)--is stereotyped behaviors featuring a set of relative fixed, simplistic over-generalizations about a group or class of people. This sense of Stereotype implies an emotionalized concept of a race, an individual, a scale of values, and so on, which is not changed in the face of contrary evidence to demonstrate its absurdity or falsity. Their metaphors shape definitions and interpretations from monitored feedback from interactions with the outside world--either because of the meaning brought to it or from the meaning derived from it. These guide new paths for new "Metaphors of Error" meshed together to support their old paths—an exciting "sick" adventure.

Selfhood "Weak" people readily seek out such *exciting "sick" adventure* and accept all of what their chosen cult says—sayings made acceptable because somewhere in the cult's dogma there is a historical kernel of truth based upon emotionally filtered observations and perhaps misinterpreted or fantasized experiences. The resultant devised stereotyped metaphors become conceptual lenses—out of which are extracted standards, guides, filters, and measures. These lenses provide the 'window' which filter perceptions of new *phenomenon* (phantom, to 'make visible'--by possessing no life of itself--having no reality in themselves and are therefore Contingent Beings). The rest of what is real, or what does not conform to stereotyped concepts, is hidden. This is just the thing for those with self-hate and who long to develop stereotyped metaphorical self-deceptions of personal power.

PATHS TO HATRED CONDITIONING

Europeans are not born hateful but Brutes become so by how and to what they are socialized to hate--the consistence of both indicating a philosophical basis. As little children develop, they are exposed to 3 main Causes of hate--from being taught to hate, fear, and disdain; from a state of Self-Unknowing; and from Envy. Thereafter, what dominates ones childhood is emotional, mental, spiritual, and physical conditioning to accept or reject or modify their various displays and to that internalization each child obeys. Continued development leads to children mentally simplifying what seems complex in their lives. Examples: (1) *categorizing* groups of people and Things; (2) Identifying or aligning oneself with an 'in-group' so as to gain a distinctive identity + get a sense of belonging + benefits from cult commitments = Self-Esteem props; and (3) gathering feedback from ones interpretations of monitored feedback derived from outside influences. Resultant conclusions are used to *compare* oneself to fellow 'in-group' members as well as to compare ones 'in-group' with 'out-groups'.

Their objective is to get a sense of belonging, with its Self-Esteem prop benefits from the commitments. One defines ones in-group as "superior" in order to serve as justification for evaluating oneself positively—and to make that stand out, one assigns demeaning values to comparable 'out-groups' and scapegoats. What I heard in the medico-legal arena was: "In order for me to look good, I have to make you look bad."

As development proceeds even more, different types of youth evolve into one of the following: Type I--Real Self people, those few in numbers, Love themselves, will not do harm to themselves, and Create. Type II, comprising half the "normal" public, are Followers addicted to the "Crowd" and to noisy excitement. Type III are those who accept illusions that lead them into beliefs pertaining to Dualism--that all things in Nature are separate and real (e.g. males/females)—that they exist independently from any underlying essence or support. These individuals, from not knowing who they are, develop the inward disposition called Hate and its attributes based upon pride, envy, and the desire to do ill to another. Their resultant acts are outward expressions that characterize the Indifference/Hate/Evil/Sadism (IHES) Complex of Brutes who then fashion, as exemplified by throughout the USA and the world the methods of Kill/Take/Destroy/Dominate/Oppress.

Meanwhile, the consequences of switching to hate makes neuroplasticity changes in the brain. That thereby changes the (instinct) normal acceptance of all humans into the acquired hating of certain ones with certain *Characteristics* (that which identifies and expresses individuality—like ones signature), *Trait* (a more definite sign or mark of individuality than a Characteristic), or *Feature* (something in a Trait arousing the most attention). Any of these may be even further synthesized—as in being determined by more than one sensory and imaginative input--to thereby form a collage. The way this comes about is Orders from the head of the '*Chain-of-Command*' (i.e. the Supernatural Ego that has replaced the "Spark of God" or Divine Consciousness) then go to Spiritual Awareness (the Will) and then to the Sensory Background (the Divine Spirit) and then to the Sensory Foreground (the External World) to carry out some aspect of the IHES Complex mindset manifestations (fig. 2, 3, 4, 8).

The taking of action upon the instant appearance of the Black person (the 'unconditioned stimulus') is the 'unconditioned response' because the Black person is viewed as some type of Contingent Being which the "Killer" police's cult says demands an attack. Such a reaction by the "Killer" police has occurred to dark skin several times a day, so that his spirit is no longer able to tell the difference between the skin color and his urge to react. All "Killer" police's emotional and sensual responses are based on this non-rational 'second nature, Law of Association. Simultaneously, the Conditioned Response may be made more effective by complementary "*Conditioned Avoidance*"--as a "Killer" police shoots first and asks questions later, instead of the reverse. Both account for more complex and wide-spread socialized IHES displays—particularly if there is no accountability for those displays. Doing IHES tends to give "Killer" police 'sick' benefits.

The "Air Castle" Supernatural Cult leaders who orchestrated the socialization were successful by cunningly appealing to these 'normal' people to *accept delusions and illusions leading into and embracing* Supernatural phenomena. Their technique was to convey that the only requirement for accepting the *IHES socialization was for their presentations to not clash with any held Belief or threaten any aspect of those* 'normal' people's: "*For me or my well-being--or against me or my well-being*" *System of Values.* Those System of Values had been congenial to IHES displays by the pre-existing Condition Occult mindset. What naturally follows this process is the targeted 'enemy' being assigned Characteristics, Traits, and Features—to which, when seen through biased and prejudiced lens—imparts a supposed vision called a "Phantom." An easy next step was to design the unique "Phantom" each now socialized cult member envisioned into an Icon Image. The "Featured" Quality characterizing the Trait contributing to the making up of that Icon Image was/is "black" skin. By the "Air Castle" cult priding itself on being "Non-Rational" thinkers meant that by not being curbed by Logical Reason, their imaginations could "run wild" in personally private and in face-to-face moments with the Target person.

FORMING HATED SCAPEGOATS: Whether Brutes' violence results from by-products of former wrongs and Shame or by being so socialized, what results is a monstrous Self-Image—one filled with such power as to be associated with violence and able to overcome the fashioned Icon Image of Scapegoats. This causes them to keep reinforcing their Self-Image monster into a self-fulfilling prophecy. Yet the nature of that Contingent Being Self-Image is one of Insecurity. *Insecurity* features "Fears of Possibilities of Fears"— i.e. fearing all the "what ifs" that might arise to generate more fears. This is like the infinite reflections associated with *Mirror Images* whereby one stands between two "Fear" mirrors facing each other and thereby sees no end to the number of images that reproduce the original. Such fears led/lead to "Air Castle" escapes and the fashioning of Icon Images about oneself, ones leaders, and bad ones of self-created enemies.

If scapegoats are not directly available, cult members may engage in self-esteem enhancement by belittling, derogating, denigration or discriminating against more "generalized" others when: (1) ones self-esteem is threatened; (2) the Target identifies with a minimal group; and (3) self-uncertainty is present and/or activated. All of these help one form judgments about oneself so as to rank oneself on the social ladder. However, if scapegoats are available (primarily those spotlighted by ones "Crowd"), then the Conditioned Response comes into play which leads to a variety of Effects and Consequences. By having great brain neuroplasticity, deeply patterned engrams are formed to become "second nature." Selective development of thinking skills makes for attention efficiency in one area and immaturity in other areas (as with men's emotions, relationships, and out-group helpfulness). The mid-C19 word "*Conditioning*" concerns the slow and cumulative experience process of changing the (instinct) normal into the (acquired) unique-——of training certain reflexes to override inborn or inherited reflexes. Put another way, it is the process of acquiring, developing, educating, learning, or training new responses in an individual to influences of the environment. All prejudices and biases are superimposed on a given human's true nature and projected onto victims. *Classical Conditioning* is the process of acquiring, developing, educating, learning, or training new responses in an individual to influences of the environment.

Respondence implies behaviors resulting from specific stimuli, after which the response occurs automatically. Those which occur without previous learning are *Innate Reflexes;* those with prior learning are *Conditioned* (e.g. Pavlov's famous experiment with dogs). A behavior is learned according to its effectiveness in influencing or "operating" on its environment—reinforced by the appearance of a desired result. Such an "*Operative Conditioning*" connection is made, not on the basis of what caused the behavior, but as a result of the Effect or its Consequences ('Sequel') of the behavior in the given situation. "Operative Conditioning" is illustrated by Europeans who developed the GUN, starting in 1304, and then went around the world killing and taking possessions of the rich Colored Peoples.

Thus, if operant behaviors (Kill/Take/Destroy/Dominate) are followed by reinforcement (riches gained), the probability of its recurrence is increased. Upon Enslaved Africans first beatings by slavers' whips, there was no *anticipated reaction since its effect was unknown-——* an *Unconditioned Stimulus.* When Enslaved Africans were constantly beaten by the European captors' whip, they cringed at the mere snap of the whip without them being hit. Next, it did not take long for them to cringe, even without them being hit, at the whip's mere snap--a learned *Conditioned Response.* Afterwards, by simply seeing the whip in the slaver's hand caused the Enslaved to cringe--a *Conditioned Stimulus* response. Illustrating *Re-inforcement* is seeing the whip, cringing, and repeatedly whipped— i.e. each time having more force or strength--each aiding the repeating of the Conditioned Response--perhaps faster with each whipping. Such applies to the Enslaved and the Enslaver--with subtle differences, as in alterations in the neural mechanism, to cause a modification of the conditions in which the Enslaved reactions occurred, and a difference in the way the Enslaved responded.

Simply in that vignette, there are subtle differences—e.g. an alteration in the neural mechanism, a modification of the conditions in which the Enslaved reaction occurred, and a difference in the way the Enslaved responded. The closeness of the interweave of these aspects is a function of the stimulus + the response + a desired attitude being close together in time. The closer the interval, the more the connection between them is strengthened. How strong the connection becomes depends upon how frequently they occur together. At perhaps the first, second, or third occurrence of their association, there is a crystalizing of a Conditioned Learning Response all at once. The "*Law of Effect*" comes into play—meaning that if a Conditioned Response has the effect of producing dissatisfaction, the connection between the stimulus situation and the response is strengthened. The stimulus which triggers this Conditioned Response is now able to evoke a similar response.

"*Instrumental Conditioning*" is learning that takes place because the learned response brings, again and again Re-Inforcements, similar to rewards gained by the enslavers or by "Killer" police doing of something respected by and pleasing to ones cult (like killing a Black person). Examples of such rewards are like being praised; or by the creation, enhancement, or maintenance of belonging; or like being protected under desired circumstances. Instrumental Conditioning is thus powered by a motivation based upon hunger. Gathering these ingredients in order to keep modifying the existing IHES Complex Erector Set POL starts with all that has been stored in ones memory to date, including what is in ones Collective Unconscious—e.g. that Europeans have always been a warring people.

Incidentally, *extinction of an unwanted Conditioned Response* is by the following process. Without Re-inforcement (more beatings), the Conditioned Stimulus (cringing from seeing the whip) may lose the ability to bring on the Conditioned Response (the cringe). If there are no more blows after seeing the whip, one might then stop cringing. In other words, failing to follow the Conditioned Stimulus (the whip's blow or even simply hearing the snap of the whip) with the Unconditioned Stimulus (the appearance of the whip) can cause the unlearning of a Conditioned Response. jabaileymd.com

PATHS TO CONDITIONED PROGRAM KILLINGS

People are not born with an Indifference/Hate/Evil/Sadism (IHES) Complex but some are socialized to fear certain things—to avoid other things because they are taboo—and to hate certain things because they are "different." In their Self-Unknowing state and operating out of their Brute Brain enables them to be extremely easily and infinitely influenced by their embraced "Dark Side" aspects. Apart from "Dark Side" "Things" being intriguing, many of its ingredients are internalized, causing a host of the afflicted to, in turn, generate a variety of Conditioned Responses. Type I response aims at attacking them; Type II is acquiring the fear of embracing these very "Dark Side" "Things" (similar to my medical school experience of suspecting I was coming down with every new disease I was studying); Type III is combining Types II and III; and Type IV is eagerly incorporating them into their philosophy of life. Which Type is chosen, one may see these "Dark Side" Things as tendencies and patterns in ones parents, family, or fellow cult members. Regardless of type selected, such are mental weakness displays.

By typically occurring at a relatively young age, the natural maturity level of the afflicted ceases at the same time. As a result, these False Self people keep alive the apparently universal need seen in children to over-prize their own group and its identity and become open to "*Instrumental Conditioning*". Within this context group, ones interpretations of the monitored feedback one gets from the influences of others are used to know how to assess ones own experiences. Resultant conclusions then guide one in a direction acceptable to ones cult. Thus, to be defined by ones cult dogma and to be part of the cult is to honor the cult by following cult "Codes" and doing what gives all of them "sick" pleasures. In turn, one gets a sense of Belonging. Still, no matter how much effort is put into Repressing the "Dark Side" of themselves, by overflowing with an inferiority complex and envy of their scapegoats necessitates a "*Conditioned Avoidance*" of those scapegoats for purposes of reducing anxiety or fear for something about which they are extremely hypersensitive. Hence, the reason for discrimination. This allows them to be free to roam the fantasy world and make-up Icon Images in Supernatural realms about themselves, about their cult, about their scapegoats--and imbue each with Certainty. Such Brute Brain formed Images are a Conditioned Response.

To repeat, each afflicted makes "our kind" the standard for what is right and against which all others are compared but can never match up. This mindset is used to justify the vicious or the routine institutional imposition of conditions of subordination upon minorities or outgroups—a set of negative identity issues consisting of various forms of subhuman images of the minorities—images self-created but yet are similar to the hateful images held by ones cult. An outstanding feature of this process is one feeling the pressure to separate oneself from, and radically to disvalue, the best of what one knows to exist in life. This 'double-barreled' impact of a clash of newly acquired External Values + the shattering of ones good character + Conditioned Responses directed toward a specific Target Group, jettison one towards IHES displays against scapegoats. To imaginatively design the needed Contingent Beings, one seeks out or fashions "Thrill" activities which provide useful ingredients. Each of these disjointed things, instead of being recognized as the product of several contributions, are wrongly attributed to a single cause.

AT THE "KILL" MOMENT: As stated in Chapter IV, what happens at "crunch time" is a Conditioned Response from ones emotions furnishing the concept to which one reacts. Many things meet at one point: (1) what is historically in ones Collective Unconscious—e.g. that Europeans have always been a warring people; have always been driven by (real, distorted, fantasy) Scarcity Concepts; (2) conditioned to be a Fear-Based people; (3) demean any people who have allowed themselves to be Enslaved as being mentally weak, subhuman, and like mechanical beings; (4) project their "Dark Side" on to the scapegoats they most envy and thus are their Target Group; (5) have an inferiority complex with self-hate that is typically masked by a superiority complex so as to use this mindset to "wipe out" their feigned enemy competitors; (6) possess mindsets positioned inside an "Air Castle" Supernatural Realm and orchestrated by non-rational mental activities; and (7) by being above Natural World rules, they are provided with the freedom of personal choice to do as they like—e.g. killing without accountability. This complex Emotion which furnishes the Conditioned Response concept, also discloses the Thing to which the concept applies—either directly or by structuring it—or both. The emotion puts one in contact with, discloses, spotlights an awareness of, or intuits something in the outside Thing that reflects the "Dark Side" of oneself. Such "Projection" is illustrated by European policemen who, upon seeing a Black male, invoke the Numinous Feeling" of "*Dread*"—a term which refers to a property productive of Fear. That "dread" prompts a conditioned reflex to readily kill unarmed Black males. Although this "dread" does not arise amid the sensory data of the realistic situation--nor arise out of them—it comes from a Background Sensory Consciousness programming. So, the policemen are really trying to kill their "Dark Side" within a Supernatural context.

"NORMAL VARIANT" SERIAL "KILLERS": A metaphor for the Selfhoods of those destined to be "Serial Killers" is their minds brawl in a roaring fight while sailing, during a violent thunder and lightning storm, in paper boats. Out of those minds come dangerous hurricane (Philippines, Caribbean), cyclone (India), typhoon (Far East), willy-willies (Australia), tornado (North America) type destruction to whatever they are about. Out of the mysterious fantasy of the mental storm's squall—i.e. its sudden, terrible gust of wind—arises a Contingent (fantasy) bubbling Monster full of wrath. 'Chiseled' into the Monster's core is the "Temperament" (a prevailing emotional trend) seed (e.g. extreme envy, an inferiority complex, self-hatred, rage) which evolves into an Indifference/Hate/Evil/Sadism (IHES) Complex mindset. In turn, their Brute Brains design compatible think, feel, express, and behaviors that manifest in such consistent patterns as for them to become 'second nature' Conditioned Responses. That IHES mindset gives rise to the "Law of *Fantasy/ Actual Effects*"—i.e the various things that go into the production of change, of an altered activity, or of maintenance of the status quo. IHES Fantasy is an imagery process in which one attempts to obtain vicarious gratification by engaging in mental acts --acts one is currently unable to (or dares not) do in reality—acts able to become linked to and displayed in Selfhood dissociation and its resultant compartmentalization—acts directed toward a specific type of scapegoat. Out of this Monster directed mindset ones Sensory Consciousness and the activities of ones Emotions and Feelings are what enable one to have Subjective Experiences of what Monsters feel and do.

Now, ones Imagination gathers all pertinent External World stimuli qualities of sense perception + IHES Things generated out of 'raw' materials in ones imagination + mentally reviving IHES Percepts of entities formerly given in like-kind sense perceptions. Together, they form a collage which imbues the Monster Icon Image with attributes to serve as standards, guides, filters, and measures. One then automatically resorts to them without having to decide. This is vital to a Conditioned Response. The 'Monster' has satellites--each in the form of an Icon Images—each Image generates 'thunder-storm' effects—each effect has the capability to motivate ones behaviors "for the desired Cause". The Monster of the mind's 'thunderstorm' and its satellite Icon Images and their linkages to each other collectively constitute a *Philosophical Disability* ('not able'). A Philosophical Disability generates *Actual Effects* within the afflicted person as well as on, around, and within that person's scapegoats. Every Philosophical Disability displayed 'Cause' has an Actual Effect ("what is done") and every one of its Actual (or Fantasy) Effects is pregnant with unfavorable Consequences. Every Actual Consequence consists of the various somethings which happen as a result of any given something emerging out of a given desired Fantasy Effect or Effect from a displayed Cause. Those gathered "Somethings" have an *Application Effect* greater than the sum of each when added together. While it is not possible to spotlight any consistent Consequence, "certain ones" can be noted that head one toward becoming a serial killer.

Meanwhile, IHES type Socialization has laid out the Supernatural cult's specified purpose and direction—in essence, to destroy any aspects of the Spiritual Elements; to control all non-cult people's minds; and to grab all available riches. Such Socialization reflects European males internalization of the C3-C7 Manicheism religious philosophy of "White" destroying "Black". Thus, to be divine instruments of their Supernatural Christian God demands engaging in the "Black" process of Alienation, Dehumanization, and Kill/Take/ Destroy/Dominate so as to purify "White". The combination of an IHES Monster operating within the context of Manicheism means the creator of ones own Monster now has 'religious' justification for controlling the creator, paving the way for the creator to do the things he/she actually wanted to do in the first place. That internal entity manifests as an overwhelming storm force in ones life, compelling one to kill again and again. Thus, the killer becomes the very being he had so often visualized in his fantasies. This one factor alone becomes a Conditioned Stimulus for a racist seeing a Black male and justifying his/her "second nature" reflex which instantly causes the squeezing of the trigger of a gun.

WHITE MASS KILLERS—CRAZY? OR "NORMAL VARIANTS"?: European-spur-of-the-moment killers of masses of people throughout USA history are typically portrayed as "mentally ill" by the media/

public. By declaring White murderers as insane is a 'red herring'—i.e. blocking analysis of the European mindset for Causation, proper assignment of Blame, and Management so as to give the façade of that being a 'fluke.' "*Red herring*" is a late 1800s expression for a strong smelling red fish (from being preserved by smoking) dragged across a trail to cover up a human scent so as to throw off tracking dogs. But since persons/groups/mobs of Europeans do mass killings world-wide and throughout their history and in every one of the countless wars as well as by "Killer" police of Black People, the question is: "Are all of these Europeans mentally ill?" I would suggest a better term is they are "*Normal Variant*" people who have reached the outer limits of their "normal" minds.

As background, all of those Socialized into a Brute Philosophy of Life (POL)--the Indifference/Hate/Evil/Sadism (IHES) Complex--are intimidated to remain in a "*Totipotential*" mindset state (which can radiate in any direction). This implies their minds are in a putty dough-like condition, able to be IHES molded and to be upgraded into any new form conforming to Brute leader derived trends or that is "Brute Friendly." All who benefit from or accept--or fail to resist what Brutes do—or lack courage to stand up for innocent victims are "Normal Variants" They are controlled by Conditional Love--a masqueraded violent destruction: "you will be isolated from love and attention if you do not do what 'everybody' is doing." For those most weak, this is so fear-producing as to cause them to step into the Slight-to-Moderate Delusional level of "Normal Variant" people who then become "Inside-Out." The "Inside-Out" operate in a Supernatural world where its patterns of "Life-Living" cause special ways of thinking, feeling, expressing, and acting. Here, one is standing alone in fantasy as an "Individualist"--with no 'Ground of Being' to stand on--where surroundings are kaleidoscope-like-- with each color change in the form of some Contingent Being (e.g. the Bogeyman).

Out of this visually frightening magical place emerge questions: "what's wrong with my life?"; others probe "what matters in life?"; still others, "what is happening to my life?" These and like-kind questions can lead one into the Unknown "where no one has gone before"—where most people do not dare to go—where realities or even distortions of reality do not exist. At this Supernatural 'place,' one evokes a self-image of being a 'larger than life' gigantic Being whose abilities are omnipotent and whose possessions, regardless to whom they belong, are whatever one desires in the External world. At this point they alternate between types of "Normal Variant" behaviors.

Out of this visually frightening magical place emerge questions: "what's wrong with my life?"; others probe "what matters in life?"; still others, "what is happening to my life?" These and like-kind questions can lead one into the Unknown "where no one has gone before"—where most people do not dare to go—where realities or even distortions of reality do not exist. At this Supernatural 'place,' one evokes a self-image of being a 'larger than life' gigantic Being whose abilities are omnipotent and whose possessions, regardless to whom they belong, are whatever one desires in the External world. At this point they alternate between types of "Normal Variant" behaviors.

To illustrate, the White male 21 year old Dylann lived in a 90% Black South Carolina community without strong opinions about race. He had many Black friends, with whom he made racial jokes--a Delusional *Type II, Slight* "Normal Variant". Something triggered his great Selfhood weakness into being enthralled with images of a duty to help save the White race (*Type IV, Extreme* "Normal Variant"). He railed about Blacks taking over the neighborhoods and ruining the country. In a chilling vow to the White race he said he would have to be the one to do something about it. One day he went to an all-Black Church prayer meeting, sat an hour (perhaps waiting to get his courage up or was having second thoughts) and then pulled out a gun, killing 9 people while shouting: "I have to do this." He left one survivor so she could tell his story. Lives simply did not matter to him. It was said the string of killings of Black American men by police around the USA had become the "fertilizer" for this mindset of massacres. He was threatened by the USA's changing demographics and the increasing prominence of Black Americans in public life. Dylann was hoping to divide the state and country into racially battling each other. This is a classic "White Supremacy" scenario, including pretending to be part of a group targeted to be "taken down." Being driven to get revenge on feigned enemies, those killing masses of people, including "Killer" police, are excused by the media/public declaring mass killers as "mentally ill" so as to be a *Deflection* to draw attention away from the "sickness" of embracing a "Normal Variant" POL. jabaileymd.com

SUMMARY

Humans are a form of animal and animals are characterized by features of mammals (e.g. vertebrates who suckle their young). Primates, the highest order of mammals, have evolved out of mammals and humans evolved out of primates. All humans are born with the ingredients to develop the mind of their Higher (Spiritual) Self as well as to discipline the already developed mind of their Lower (animalistic Secular world) Self. The function of the human Will (partnered with the Cerebrum part of the brain) is to enable one to dominate ones Animating electromagnetic energies (part of a human's spirit) orchestrating ones physical body. This "Animal Spirit" (Ancient African, 'Khaibit') is Ether--programmed for preservation of ones survival with instincts, curiosity, motivation, sense perceptions, sensuality, sensory/motor nervous powers, physiological functions, fighting, fleeing, and other motions. Yet, one can choose to spotlight ones "False Nature" psychic attractions (directed by ones Brute/Emotional Brains) of ones desires, cravings, appetites, passions, wants, and emotions. The mythical African god Set modelled how to live out of ones Animal nature.

Thus, to only do what one likes/dislikes of a material nature and make this a lifestyle, invariably leads to disaster for all concerned--since they can never be guides to a thriving and happy life. Such, on an ongoing basis, disproportionately interferes with ones pleasures as well as cause pain—both with exceptional frequency and with respect to the depth of the intensity--whether real or imagined. This generates chronic anger or fear responses incapable of solving problems or conflicts. To stay in a Lower Self state as a way of life means ones Conscience will never awaken. At the core of mental "weakness" is a philosophy of life (POL) which either fails to embrace Unconditional Love or one which is disconnected from it so that the individual lacks the "5Ss"--safety, security, self-confidence, strength, and stability. The resultant insecurity causes them to turn to ignorant and/or Brute leaders.

The leaders cunningly appeal to these 'normal' people to *accept delusions and illusions leading into and embracing* Supernatural phenomena, *the only requirements is for those presentations to not clash with any held Belief or threaten any of those candidates: "For me or my well-being--or against me" System of Values.* An Achilles' heel (a vulnerable area) of good Colored People's of the world is to fail to discern these ignorant and/or Brute leaders character's as being weak, attackers of what is Right, and are actual enemies rather than as being the friends they deceptively present themselves as being. These leader are never to be believed about anything for morals and compassion are practically unknown to them. Victims are blind to the obvious and yet buy into what the cult leaders are selling. Relief comes by victims simply accepting their Dogma--meaning they do not have to use their own minds or do their own thinking because they believe it when the leaders say: "I know and you don't." Yet when those leaders are confronted with the lack of soundness of their dogma, their arguments go like this: "I can't prove your Spiritual Elements claims of being uplifting are true, but you can't prove my Supernatural god is false or that my ways are wrong. So the only proper conclusion is we don't know and no one can know one way or the other."

The naïve accept this as a fair, impartial, and balanced argument because they fail to challenge the major premise (i.e. the Base upon which the argument is built) that is wrapped in the arbitrary (a claim put forth in the absence of evidence to support it or in the face of contrary evidence against it). This means they have taken "facts" out of what does not exist to serve as the basis for their argument. If those "facts" are accepted, then the naïve are playing by the rules of the opponent. Victims so clutch to the dogma and rules as to become upset with the one pointing this out. Victims are then easily led to believe that the only purpose of education is to learn how to live life the Supernatural cult way—and that way is not for 'outsiders,' for they are inferior and constitute "the enemy." This requires theory (i.e. conceptual) directed down the path of the Supernatural so as to understand, to integrate, to prove things only within that context.

It is fundamental to their brainwashing to prevent victims from being able to know any other way but the Supernatural cult way. This is why segregation is so essential since otherwise the White "Troops" would learn that the need Blacks to supply what their cult ensures that they lack. They would discover that Blacks are nice and "inferior" as they are taught. Supernatural cult leaders greatly fear integration because the honorableness and Spiritual Elements Black People bring would totally destroy the cult dogma and all mind control efforts. Furthermore, when a White and Black couple produce children, the "race" of the child becomes "Black" and that could make White people "disappear." As it is, Colored Peoples of the world out number White people by 11 to 1.

CHAPTER IV

FRAGILE MANHOODS
HIDE BEHIND
THE GUN

EUROPEAN MANHOOD

By Ancient Africans realizing humans are endowed with a Divine Spark of God, meant they were Spiritual and Moral Beings—each responsible for her/his actions to the God within. Thus, the duty of every male was/ is to cultivate "Manliness" (i.e. ones Higher or Spiritual Self). "*Manliness*" implies developing oneself out of the Spiritual Elements ingredients present in ones Real Self at ones birth and using those ingredients to discover, develop, and find just the right niche for ones birth gift Talent. By contrast, for Europeans, originally the state of man was called "Manhood" (i.e. referring to ones Lower or Animalistic Self) which they have historically over-whelmingly advocated cultivating. "Man" is a Sanskrit word meaning both a "mental being" and any human being. In all ancient Germanic languages, "Man" also carried the sense of an "adult male human being"--a sense emerging as dominant in C13 English. Around 1300, "Man" was thought of by Europeans as "one who takes charge and manages"; then, by 1400, to behave with courage, bravery, boldness and nobility. *Manly* was next ap-plied to the possession of the most desirable qualities a male can have, as determined by ones society. *Masculine* referred to the qualities of a male as contrasted with those feminine.

EUROPEAN MANHOOD'S BIG PICTURE

In using the Tree Concept (fig. 3) for orientation purposes of European manhood, the "Seed" is their fantasied Supernatural Indifference/Hate/Evil/Sadism (IHES) Complex thinking ingredients; the "Roots" are acquisitions in the Physical World; the "Truck" is a self-declaration of "White Superiority"; the "Branches" are Warriors, the Religious, and the Philosophers; the "Leaves" are overt, tempered, masked, and concealed expres-sions of Kill/Take/Destroy/Dominate/Oppress (KTDDO); and their "Fruit" is Hedonism (pleasure is the end of all strivings). All of these assemblages are of a False Self nature. Hedonism (fig. 8) appears to be very attractive because of its appeals to ones Lower Self (i.e. animalistic) nature, while being silent on doing what it take to reach ones Highest (Divinity) Self. Hedonism's Supernatural "Air Castle" position is to be a slave to it and that greater pleasure comes when non-cult members are excluded. Yet, there is no enjoyment in their pleasures be-cause when tasted they are already like a stock of wine that has been soured by age. And much of what is tasted is Hope. One reason is the un-ending and never arriving and never satisfying and never enough attainments of power and glory. Thus, the "Fruit" of Hedonism quickly falls to the ground.

Nevertheless, Hedonism, in its broadest perspective—whether acquiring pleasures for oneself and/or getting pleasures from the IHES and KTDDO display that cause pain, misery, sufferings, and hardships to victims--has been the theme of European males since their arrival on Earth 45,000 years ago. The driver of that theme has been the Western belief that "Money answereth all things"; "It takes a man to make money and making money made men." Tjeder (Men and Masculinities, 2002) mentioned the motto: "*Riches* are the key to greatness, [they] facilitate and make the way for a good name" as well as impart a man's independence by giving him strength: "He walks like a man.—He speaks like a man.—He looks You in the eye like a man." Independence, manhood, and riches--the three float together and become one. Masculinity has always been linked to power: first and foremost to the question of establishing and maintaining power hierarchies between men.

Yet, the "Religious Branch" had different emphasis. For example, they said something like: "He who decides to do everything that he is capable of with his personality, endeavors to develop all his mental abilities to the utmost and to not neglect any opportunity to come forward in an honorable way" to come forward in the world meant enriching oneself. Prior to the mid-C18 men's drive to become wealthy, a large segment of European males denounced a total focus on money as a bad, indeed evil, drive in men. Traits like sobriety and general self-control were more important to their conception of manhood than economic success. Also, the need to discipline the worst effects of egotism was always felt even with those most enthusiastic about manhood as measured in success.

What was new to 'Money Success' manuals at the beginning of C19 was the blatant and obvious way that was stated: "*Riches are the key to a good name and facilitate and open the admittance to glory,*" and the way obvious power struggles centered on money. Masculinity had become, more openly than earlier, the power struggle between men, carried out in the homo-social arena of the workplace. Since "Money is Power" and Masculinity was measured in money, achieving Manhood became synonymous to achieving power—associated with the all-important concept of independence. The concept of independence, at times with the epithet "Manly" before it, was a theme in most, perhaps all, pamphlets in which Masculinity related to the making of riches. And becoming a man came to mean reaching economic success. Such success necessitated "the desire to compete" and "ambition," concepts later embraced as crucial parts in the formation of Manhood.

While quenching of the Fetters of extreme selfishness, greed, hatred, anger, egoism, fear, envy, jealousy, frustration, Indifference, arrogance, pride, vanity, lust, and other raging passions as the very foundation of all upbringing formation of Manhood, in the ideal of the self-made man, this legitimatization of the drive to riches was taken one step further. No longer did one need a good conscience in making money, but making money became a preferable way of making men. What had been a legitimate pursuit became a positive path to morals and masculinity. To be sure, there were still to be moral rules for the acquisition of money. Meanwhile, some warned parents that children would become imbued with egotism and despise others if these were taken too far. In C20 ordinary men worked themselves up to fame and fortune, the favorite didactic story for young boys in the Victorian years, gave way to a vain form of masculinity, centered more on consumption, clothing, leisure, and even sex than on hard work and other Victorian virtues such as self-control and assertiveness.

So, what this boils down to is that the worldly Power European Manhood craves comes from IHES and KTDDO displays so as to acquire "Money" or its equivalent to allow for the Leisure needed to engage in Hedonism. Their "Branches," consisting of Warriors, the Religious, and Philosophers, went about these somewhat differently but each fed concepts for doing so into the other two. Thus, they have Interlocking of the philosophy of life (POL) of each stemming out of an IHES Complex which seeks "Excitement" and "Leisure." To give some understanding into all of these POL variables throughout the ages, allow me to illustrate with the use of Leisure and its connection with Racism.

LEISURE: Originally, the concept of Leisure derived from the necessity of African scholars to have free time in order to seek Esoteric Knowledge. After this idea was borrowed by ancient Greeks, Leisure took on the general sense of the expression of human behavior as an experience, a recreational activity, or a freedom from obligations, study, work, or business dealings. Nearly all societies at nearly all times have had a leisure class—a class of persons whose riches, power, or military, political, and priestly offices freed them from industrial, agricultural, and exempted them from toil. Historically, nearly all societies main problem with the freedom leisure provide is in finding the most attractive something to do with leisure activities and then perfected what they chose. The choice was based primarily upon whether one is an "Introvert" ('a turning inward') or an extrovert. Next, each developed the selected choice in a good or bad direction—some for ease and relaxation; some by being entertained; some by engaging in illicit and amoral activities; some to prevent anxiety, boredom, and restlessness. But even here, a major problem concerned how to keep things interesting, exciting, or "Alive". The model Ruling Class mindset concerning Leisure was clearly exhibited by ancient Greeks. They believed the purpose of any of their Slaves was to do the ugly, horrible, uninteresting work of civilization's daily life, since otherwise Greek leisure would be almost impossible. They defined Leisure as a spiritual (actually meaning Supernatural) capacity for freedom.

These Greek concepts of Leisure and Slaves shifted across a spectrum of understanding, moving throughout the Western world. The etymological idea underlying the C14 Anglo-Norman word "*Leisure*" was that of 'having permission' (the source of C14 'License' and C17 English 'Illicit')—hence of 'having the freedom of personal choice to do as one likes'. Yet, the European ruling classes believed leisure was bad for the worker, saying it meant idleness, and idleness brought moral decay. From there, the European Christian tradition toward Leisure proceeded toward a more narrow pastoral meaning of idleness, waste, and sin. In its most extreme, the Puritan tradition advocated that any activity without extrinsic purposes or reward became an offense against proper piety. Such was because the Protestant ethic, especially in its Calvinist form had led to "an amazingly good . . . conscience in the acquisition of money, so long as it took place legally." Also, the Puritans were the 'public in uniform'--being the visible moral guardians of civil society, enforcing a largely Puritan Christian set of values that strongly influenced the law and its implementation.

The mid-C17 Industrial Revolution altered the social character of leisure (Sanders, *The Police Journal, 2011*). The mechanismo of production, transportation, and even household work reduced the toil necessary to earn a livelihood. Since 1840 the work week declined from 70 hours to 40 hours, greatly increasing leisure time. Although leisure was almost unknown to workers before 1800, the scenarios of *Rest* (the suspension of activity following physical or mental exertion) and *Renewal* (re-creation or recuperation of energies and capacities) came into prominence under the concept of Leisure. However, *Recreation* per se differed by being after work diversion, often in the form of play or sport although it may be used for various purposes that overlap with leisure activities. Nevertheless, these opened Classifications for people of Leisure in many ways—e.g. helping others or only; engaging in recreation; relaxation; enhancing ones skills or talents; participating in politics or hobbies; attending places of entertainment (e.g. sports, theater, museums, zoos, libraries); hunting; fishing; raising pets; travel; hiking; camping; club work; and creating (e.g. in Art, Philosophy, or Science).

EUROPEAN MANHOOD RACISM: Racists are Weak people. Etymologically, the C13 English word "Weak" means something bendable, from prehistoric German "soft"; give way; and yield. The term "Weak People" refers, not to their physical being, but to their mental faculties as a result of an undisciplined Right Brain (allowing ones thoughts to drift without order) which prevents one from possessing emotional control or causes one to get out of emotional control. This means that Left Brain skills have either been inadequately developed or its skills have been over-ruled by emotional impulsiveness. Weakness has nothing to do intellectual potential as evidenced by the fact that many Weak People have intellectual skills in certain areas of their lives. Otherwise, when in an out of control emotional state these individuals have a low level of functioning intellectual competence. Such lack of intellect failure is because Weak people are orchestrated by a self-designed False Self; are Self-Unknown; are Self-Absorbed; lack Private Selfhood strength and therefor the "5Ss"; and are hyper-emotional from being stuck within the status quo of Superficial People; and are addicted to like-kind people. In short, they are so insecure as to have an Inferiority Complex. *Those with an inferiority complex attack in ways to tear others down; those with a superiority complex push others down.* In the process of inflicting pain, they will deny themselves benefits to hurt their victims. But Weak People experiencing Spiritual Pain are filled with bad emotions--e.g. bigotry, rage, hate-- from their wounded feelings. To get any relief they try to adversely define their victims.

Those who live out of their animal brains (e.g. Brutes) populate the political, economic, legal, military, police, and social realms and cannot know or discover the Truth. That Truth is that there is no separation of any human and the identification for all humans is with the Universal Self. Instead, they identify with a multitude of desires—the attitude of clinging to externalities which keeps them stuck in the 'status quo." Since they only know to give physical responses to animal brain challenges, those who specialize in it operate out of their Brute Brains with displays that are beneath the level of animals. Weak people can be separated into two main categories.

First are those with a *Problematic Self-Esteem* who allow themselves to be led by others. Their outstanding feature is being a follower of the crowd. Of course, this makes them "Be-ers" (a life centered on doing what others do and who judge themselves by how others judge them). As a result of this lack of a healthy Self-Esteem, these individuals become Self-Absorbed and their efforts are focused on trying to hide or deny perceived flaws, limitations, or incompleteness in some area of their Selfhood and lives. They are not the subject of this discussion.

Second are those with a *Manifest "Dark Side"* with features including Indifference, Envy, Hateful thoughts, and doing Evil and Sadistic deeds. The Emotional Energy based aggressiveness which generates the "Dark Side" causes these individuals to assume the role of a superiority complex. There is a Certain Sameness about this because these individuals are also operating out of their Brute Brains and model themselves after their like-kind "Dark Side" leaders. Their focus is on relieving their overwhelming Spiritual Pain (which automatically comes from being disconnected from their Creator and their Human Organism consisting of all God's creatures and creations). To hopefully get even a moment of the lessening of their Spiritual Pain they do two general things. One is to go after the "shiny penny" (as babies do) instead of things of Worth (e.g. Love, Peace, Harmony) infinitely more powerful and enduring and unchanging. The other is to engage in destruction--either for its own sake if it is of no benefit to them or destroy anyone they envy. The barbaric see no need for justification.

However, those who are a step up from the barbaric engage in "Civility" therefore manufacture façade justifications. At the core of those fantasy justifications is Delusional Fears. Whereas females tend to tell their fellows these fears so as to have support for their evil and sadistic deeds, male rarely do because of 'machoism.' When histrionics, self-righteousness, and "Righteous-Indignation" (how dare you do the evil things we do) are added to this mix, even higher degrees of fearfulness serve as a call to action to attack the innocent. "*Delusional Fear*" is that which is present in individuals who are actually afraid of unreal dangers as a result of operating out of their Brute Brain and not because of a reality and not because of a psychiatric disorder. It is this Brute Brain "Delusional Fear" that is at the base of ones Dark Side. "Delusional Fear(s)" generate behaviors constituting the Brute Syndrome and when chronic they become an addiction, possessing all the features of the Brute Brain. All of these points are abundantly clear in European literature written by and about Europeans. However, that literature is not available in schools or the media but its realization can be life-changing for seeing Europeans for who they really are so as to go on the offense or defense.

Since European males with an IHES Complex are quite aware of History showing Hatred to be slavery's inevitable aftermath, they generate all sorts of conditions to avoid such an aftermath. One Western civilization method is to rear a crop of humans of all races who never had Free Minds so that their actual physical and/or mental enslavement would be of such a nature as to prevent them from knowing what they are missing by not being free. A second is to do what it takes for their most hated enemies to feel "*less than human*" by using unique ways of making planes of cleavage in each victim's Selfhood. A third is to ensure no one knows the Truth about anything and substituting Confusion and conflict; a fourth is to destroy all knowledge (e.g. of Ancient Africans) which would readily show up as inferior the IHES of what is being taught to the world in educational institutions, in the media, in religion, in the legal and court systems. A fifth is to keep people's minds so occupied with Trinkets and Trivia as to not notice the IHES Complex occurring to them daily. A sixth is to convey the illusion of their 'authorities' being of the highest thinking order when 'checking them out shows that their best is rehashed African Tradition or "senseless." A seventh is to continually paint the deceptive picture that they are living the "Good Life" and are happy as a result. jabaileymd.com

HIERARCHY OF EUROPEAN MANHOOD

"Manhood," for Europeans (fig. 8), has generally been about following the pattern of some External World role model, depending upon the rung of the social ladder which was compatible with ones family status. Those on the top part of that ladder were/are socialized into the role of the *European "Gentlemen"* and they possess a Supernatural type sense of 'superiority'—that of being "little gods." Those on the bottom parts of the European "Manhood" Social Ladder are called by a variety of names to designate them as "*White Trash*" underclass, poor, low class, uneducated Caucasians--the 'less valued' group as a result of violating European "Gentlemen's" concept of ethos,. In between the top and the bottom are "*Normal Variant White people*". To put together the "Big Picture" of European "Manhood" is difficult. One reason is that my 50 years of society oriented research findings are summarized by the old saying: "Until the lion has a biographer, the hunter will always be the hero". This means I have learned not to trust anything Europeans say about themselves or about others, and particularly Black People. They omit saying anything bad about themselves; say everything bad about other people; and claim achievements not done by them.

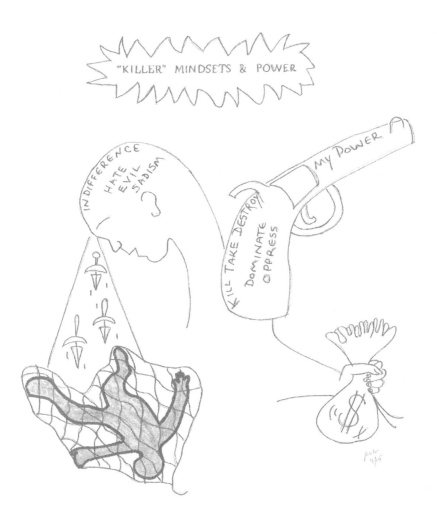

FIGURE 8

After researching the etymology of a single word in up to 1000 books--and I have done this for about 20,000 words--it is clear to me that European information is predominately Flawed. It did not take long for it to become clear that there is a world-wide conspiracy to wipe out all aspects of the superiority of Ancient African philosophy and Spirituality which underlies all of today's major cultures. Support for this conclusion came from the Euro-American linguist R. Claiborne ("Our marvelous Native Tongue") courageously saying about the word 'OKAY': "and its source was unquestionably one of various West African expressions such as o-ke or waw-ke, meaning O.K. It is surely a major linguistic irony that this expression, virtually the trademark of Americans abroad, should derive neither from English nor from any other European tongue, but from the lips of a minority with which most other Americans still prefer to associate as little as possible."

Part of the conspiracy, as I discovered in my 45 sets of encyclopaedias and thousands of other books, is to ridicule Black People with stereotypes; be willfully ignorant of what Blacks do so as to misinterpret/mis-characterize their very high level Spiritual practices; and always appearing as the hero who defeated the lion. I never saw them mention that Black People were sleeping in gold beds when the ancestors of these European ridiculers were crouched around fires eating raw meat. Another aspect of the conspiracy is the plagiarizing of African achievements and claiming those achievements for Europeans, as I have personally experienced. And this applies to just about everything which underlies what is great today. For example, Deductive and Inductive Reasoning were wide-spread in Africa millennia before the Western world falsely claimed that Sir Francis Bacon (1561-1626) "discovered" it.

Obviously, for a European to tell the Truth that helps recreate Black People's stolen legacy results in isolation from their cult for attacking the façade—the fantasy--of White Superiority. Thus, it is extremely hard to find in European literature even bits and pieces about what is true because of their machine-gun type of showering blatant lies. Associated with this is a conspiracy to wipe out African Tradition Reality. A clearly demonstrated metaphor characterizing the effect this combination has on the world public is *Socrates' "Allegory of the Cave"* (Bailey, Teaching Black Youth).

PERSONALITY: At the end of C19 "Character" became replaced with social Darwinism notions such as "Personality," which emphasized more the individual's possibility to charm others in his striving for success. There were two forms of "Personality." *"Extroverting" (Group A)*--those needing the External World for approval as well as gathering what is cherished in the External World as ones standards, guides, and filters. Group A1 "Extroverts" are 'people persons'; Group A2 are the *"Imitators"* who run with those ranging from good to bad. *Group B, The Introverts* (a term quite confusing in European psychology) are those whose Inner World is more important than the External World because of being Introspective or from being "Withdrawn" as an "escape" or from a psychiatric problems (e.g. schizoid) whereby people express themselves in fantasy. The "Escape Withdrawn" (Group B1) are often passive, day-dreamers, and avoiders of people while focusing their leisure on making contributions to Art, Science, or Philosophy. Introspective Introverts are most often seen in Isolated Individualists (Group B2) who feature Inner calm and an Intensity for "Aliveness."

Thus, their Leisure is chosen within the setting of a disciplined contemplative, reserved, and sensitive self-assessment for how to best use what little leisure they have periodically. They do not have free and easy social contacts but are not self-centered, most having a "ME/WE" orientation. Then there is Group C--the "Air Castle" leisure which deals out of phantasy-catharsis—those symptoms or symbols which are underlying of their cult dogma as unconscious preoccupations and displayed through action. Group C1 are on the bull's eye of the Archery Pad (fig. 7)—i.e. Core Satanists. Group C2 are Brutes (on the periphery of the bull's eye);

Group C3 are Tangential Brutes; Group C4 are Imitators; and Group C5 are followers of the Core leaders. Group C people who pursue bad leisure are burdened by being encaged mentally and are trying to get free or at least delve in the realm of freedom. Their methods are to get prepared by greedily acquiring money and possession and doing what is "Exciting" because of a lack of foundation to enjoy the classical things. They model their Left Brains in so as to make them extroverted, hence materialistic, individualistic, and anti-Spiritual Elements oriented—all inside the Brute Brain/Old Mammalian Brain wrappings. This automatically means such people are insecure and are unable to do volitional thinking. Values of whoever seems to be in power by gathering what is cherished in the External World as their standards, guides, and filters as part of ever seeking approval. in the categories of Criminal activities, Risky Leisure, Peer-Group Leisure, and Self-Improvement Leisure.

EUROPEAN "GENTLEMEN"

Social ladders are a very ancient human institution used to distinguish the importance of people in a local society. A common Primitive European way of deciding who was entitled to be on top occurred by the conquering of tribes and those leaders declared themselves to be in a position called the nobility. This practice continued for thousands of years. In ancient Europe those who owned great material riches were held in high esteem, regardless of how they attained it--and this has continued ever since. Brute Europeans' trademark was (and is) aiming to live "the Good Life" of Hedonism (i.e. pleasing the senses is the only "Good"). This first came about by the conquering patrician (aristocratic) tribes forming the nobility of the Roman Empire around 753 BC. Second was by certain leaders claiming the gods declared them to be priests and kings. A third, in ancient European history, was the term *Gentleman* applied to a man born into an established aristocracy or into a family of high social standing. The custom was for the father to place his newborn child on his knee to proclaim the child genuine (gen, 'to bear or beget'). A child well-born (i.e. born into a noble class) was automatically considered generous (which, of course, the nobles could afford) since this was alleged to be the human nature ("gen") of the nobility. Hence, males were gentlemen because they were "born" that way. Ancient Greeks defined "virtuous" success as having money and power over people; the rejection of democratic laws in favor of the natural rights of those with the power; and "in disputes, making the worse seem the better cause." Power attacks were taught to be on the opponent as a person as well as what the opponent does--whether on the opponent's strengths or weaknesses. In ancient Greece I suspect the model for the development of gentlemen came from Plato's Republic whereby special youth were chosen to be taught the African method of Dialect.

"When they have thus beheld the good itself they shall use it as a pattern for the right ordering of the state and the citizens and themselves throughout the remainder of their lives, each in his turn.... And so, when each generation has educated others like themselves to take their place as guardians of the state, they shall depart to the Islands of the Blessed and there dwell." The hallmark of Plato's philosophy of education is its exclusivity. Rigorous education must prepare the best students for the most difficult task: ruling those with a lower nature than themselves--perhaps the seed for "the White man's burden" during African American slavery. A fifth way was by "Letter Nobility"--obtaining knighthood distinction from the diploma granted by the king—and later by promotion through the law faculty of universities. Meanwhile, the cold word "*Etiquette*" developed out of the C14 English word Compliment and consisted of social codes of good taste within a given *clique* (a close knit group inside a larger group) for how European Gentleman ought to act. This Western Etiquette has as its *essence a reflection of ones personality concerning appearances shaped solely by ones peer group socialization.*

One code concerned the "conditional" idea of honor. For example, a man could suffer an insult in private with no damage to his honor. But if other people heard the insult, honor demanded his resentment of it--similar to the Oriental idea of having to "*Save Face.*" Its modification continued in the USA under the circumstance of an honorable Southern "gentleman" having to challenge to a duel anyone who insulted him or those dear to him. Another European "Gentleman's" Code arose from ancient Greeks borrowing and applying the Egyptian initiates' process of "Scholarship" used by students of leisure in Egyptian Mystery Schools. The labor of Slaves permitted Greek men of leisure to gather at informal schools to ponder philosophy, the arts, and other intangible subjects. Meanwhile, Black Egyptian priests taught 65% of all Greek scholars, such as Pythagoras (582-500 BC), the ways Egyptian masters used for teaching students to be scholars. The objective was for each African initiate to learn African Scholarship. This includes self-reflection, to open him/herself out into a deeper and wider depth in order to reach the Sublime (Moyers, "Power of Myth" p. 58) so as to weigh, balance, and learn skills of mental discrimination; make fine distinctions needed to display good practical judgement; and to arrive at proper conclusions by seeing both sides of a problem, studying each side from various angles, and then analyzing each angle discovered for its advantages and disadvantages.

But African Sages did not like teaching the Greeks because of their childish "Terrible Two's" mentality that include "picking and choosing" and an inability to understand spiritual fundamentals. In typical fashion, when these Greeks carried back to Greece what they had learned from studying at the feet of Black Africans, they made significant modifications in the planes of existence upon which knowledge was to be applied as well as in approaches, methods, and techniques that made for horrendous confusion. Rather than focusing on the African's discovery of knowledge through thinking on one problem but in different planes, the Greeks were more interested in passing along what was already known. Their classical scholarship consisted of a set of related, specialized techniques aimed at making readily available, in a user friendly manner, the cultural heritage of antiquity (primarily that of Africa). In addition to researching, this meant editing established works; comparing different manuscripts and oral recitations of a work; giving interpretations to doubtful passages; and commenting in notes or in separate treatises on the style, meaning, and context of an authority's thoughts. Throughout the European Middle Ages all things connected with writing were linked with the clergy. It was the occupation of scholar secretaries or clerks to either exactly copy the original manuscript ("*written by using a pen*") or to make certain alterations in it.

In the process, they often misrepresented the intentions of the prior author. Overwhelming confusion and conflict was generated by European scholars failure to recognize the Spiritual Elements as foundational to the Cosmos; that they form Archetypes for the Material World; and all real things in the Cosmos. This means European dictionaries are unable to handle concepts on Spiritual or Metaphysical planes--either at all or with incompletion and contradiction. For example, they explain "Worth" and "Value" as being synonymous but actually they are vastly different. For this reason, European dictionaries are of very little use to me. The influential Machiavelli (1469-1527), the Italian Philosopher floodlighted the European "Manhood" concept as: "A leader is one who subordinates moral principle to political goals". This was based upon the existing practices of "Gentlemen" consisting of the flow of the Seven Deadly Sins (Pride; Wrath; Envy; Lust; Gluttony; Avarice [covetous]; Sloth)--laid out by C6 AD Pope Gregory—with Arrogance the most serious since it is a source for the other six sins. These were displays of the Indifference/Hate/Evilness/Sadism (IHES) Complex that led to the African slave trade, bringing great riches to Brute Europeans.

EUROPEAN RENAISSANCE: Renaissance Europeans' highly esteemed the brilliance of Ancient African "Classics/Classicals." Let us pick up the story at the beginning of the Renaissance ("*rebirth*") when

Cosimo, the ruler of Florence, Italy discovered the lost works of Plato in 1438. He assigned the Greek scholar Ficino to translate these into Latin. But in 1460, when Cosimo was handed the lost works of the Egyptian Tehuti (Hermes Trismegistus) (?12,500 BC), he believed he had the words of the most ancient and the greatest Sage of them all. Immediately, Cosimo ordered Ficino to switch over to translating Hermes' works. Thereafter, Tehuti's concepts sparked the emergence of a glorious new culture named the "*Renaissance*" ("Rebirth" in the sense of African Tradition). In other words, the word "Renaissance" means "Rebirth because being "spiritually reborn" is at the heart of Hermes' philosophy and in African Tradition. Renaissance European Scholars considered it a must to study the Hermetica (the works of the Egyptian Tehuti, whom the Greeks called Hermes). The objective was for the "Gentlemen" to give the appearance of being "intelligent and deep thinkers". But on their own, their pseudo-metaphysical topics were (and are) merely facades disguised in undefined big words.

Behind these presentations is the lack of a realistic beginning; opinions lacking constructive meaning; and a course "going nowhere." Honorable exceptions to this are the European scholars--Candy P, and Freke T. (The Hermetica, 1997 p8) said it was *acceptable for them to take information out of the Hermetica and claim it as their own.* Their scholarship was about being a learned person devoted to understanding and to being understood. Stockhammer ("*Plato Dictionary*" p. 230) characterized such European scholars as: "*learning whatever he studies with facility and has a capacious and reliable memory...but no one will call a person wise on account of any of these erudite gifts.*" Yet, to their credit, many Renaissance gentlemen--those who gave birth to present day Western culture--acknowledged their debt for their basic ideas coming from the African Hermetica. Examples are Copernicus, Newton, da Vinci, and Shakespeare. Apart from the dishonorableness of plagiarizing African Tradition's Intellectual property and claiming it as their own—thus causing delusions of Europeans greatness in the minds of billions of people, a problem with this Western scholarly process throughout history and on to the present is similar to what occurred in the folktale of Henny Penny.

While in the barnyard, *Henny Penny* was hit on the head with an acorn that fell out of the tree she was under. However, thinking it was a piece of the sky, she shouted to her friends: "the sky is falling." Her friends immediately ran to tell the king: "the sky is falling." Those friends, now elevated to the status of "scholars," were wrong because Henny Penny--their authority source--was wrong. Still, the point for me is to not believe what scholars, "Gentlemen," or anybody say about life-shaping things without personally examining the source thoroughly.

"THE GAME": The word "Success," the top priority for European males, came into English in 1375 with the sense of "to take the place of another"; then (1475) a desired or fortunate outcome; then (1586) the accomplishment of a desired end; then (C16), prosperous achievement; and then (1885), the attainment of riches or high position--and thereby conveying the false belief of possessing stability or permanence of prosperity. The latter definition reflected what had been happening all along. The problem is that success in reaching a goal typically did *not imply satisfaction with the attainment.* Since the Western world was more concerned with basic facts than morals, the Italian philosopher Machiavelli (1469-1527) elaborated in "The Prince" on how rulers could retaining power and making an effective political organization by unscrupulous means--political cunning, fraud, cruelty, deceit, lying, cheating, stealing, and ruthlessness in subordinating moral principles to political goals (Bailey, American Crime). Furthermore, all others should be forced to answer only to the ruler. He said he did not invent a dishonorable way of practicing politics but was simply describing how good politicians of his time went about their business--practicing international politics as a complex game of conspiracy and betrayal; being responsible for the mismanagement of banks; and accepting assassination as a form of succession. Thus the theme of the European mindset has been and is one of corruption, treachery, and duplicity. This greatly contributed to fashioning flattery, hypocrisy, dishonorableness, deceitfullness, and anti-Love characterizing European society ever since (and before).

It contributed to the maintenance of war seen as Machiavelli stated: as the archetypal contest between *virtue* and *fortuna,* between all that is manly, and all that is changeable, unpredictable, and capricious, a struggle between masculine rational control and effeminate irrationality. War is the supreme test of man, the energy force of manliness, of his physique, of his intellect, and particularly his character. Machiavelli's thoughts on the concepts of war and peace were summarized as "Necessity generates *virtue.* War is a condition of necessity that produces *virtue.* Without war a people become indolent, weak, and effeminate and lose their *virtu.* Here the concept of manliness as a gendered phenomenon, expressed as a male stereotype, was firmly introduced--"principle" referring not to a person but to an accepted professed man-made rule of action or conduct—and most immoral.

In C15 and C16 European "gentlemen" were so obsessed with greedy Materialism and arrogant Individualism that it became "The Game"—one that was wild, frenzied, and so competitive as to be "life or limb" threatening—one that framed the way to live by honoring the "Seven Deadly Sins"—one whose goal was to win at any cost—one requiring the free use of every dishonorable measure imaginable in order to see who could gain the most adult toys. The intent was/is to be esteemed on a *Super-human* status (possessing a special aura of omnipotence). Hence, any and all dishonorable acts—e.g. Kill/Take/Destroy/Dominate--were respected and honored as a show of Intimidation and of Power. Rules of "The Game" were that "there are no rules" and "being amoral is prided." Nevertheless, "The Game" had to/has to be played with "style"—a style with a "*swagger.*"

Part of a "swagger" displays in arrogant individualistic think, feel, say, and do aspects--as showing off-- as strutting--as an attitude that "the world belongs to me and I can push people around." In daily close encounters with fellow "players," lesser spotlighted associates of "The Game" included/include skillful and clever "*One-upmanship*" (the art or practice of successively outdoing a competitor) and *Gamesmanship* (the use of dubious methods not strictly illegal) checkered with *Sportsmanship* (those who play fair, take calculated risks to improve or win, and enjoy and respect their sport); in business; or in illegal endeavors in USA society. "The Game" and its associate Games are what fed the rise and persistence of African American slavery, followed by post-slavery racism. Throughout this time the aristocracy was thought of as effeminate in their riches, in their motto that "Money is a good name--a good reputation—and power," and their focus on tradition. Women and all other people were deemed to be "subhuman"—meaning being a part of the Natural Cosmos.

They said their superiority rested on doing "Non-Rational" thinking out of an "Non-Rational" Soul (which imparted sexual superiority) as well as, says Garlick (*Men and Masculinities, 2003*), by embodying the active factor in reproduction. "The Game" is alive and active today as a result of the European Renaissance "gentlemen," who became in the Americas, the "Southern Gentlemen" whose orientation was White Superiority and White Privilege in the setting up of all social institutions that affect every aspect of every American's life (and much of the world). It was Renaissance "Gentlemen" who started the African slave trade and became "Southern Gentlemen" in the New World, also forming the USA constitution and federal government.

MODERN EUROPEAN GENTLEMEN: Those few who could participate in "The Game's" materialism and with a Brute mindset was so honored in C15 and C16 Europe as to shift the 'trademark' of "Manhood" to living "the Good Life" of Hedonism (i.e. pleasing the senses is the only "Good")—a style continuing to increase to this day. Around this time in Western Europe, the term "*debt of honor*" referred to a gambling debt. A "gentleman" could owe the tailor or the innkeeper with a clear conscience but his conscience would be greatly disturbed if a gambling debt was not paid promptly. The idea was that a tradesman in the marketplace had a legal claim and could sue for his money, while the law would not enforce payment of a gambling debt. It was also all right to cheat the landlord to pay the gambling house, but only a very dishonorable person would cheat the gambling house to pay his landlord. Meanwhile, a bridge between the ancient and modern concepts of "Manhood" was under construction. Its leaders were a group of German educational reformers who published a series of texts between 1770 and 1793, calling for a return to the ancient Greek and Roman practices of education and sport. These educational reformers again drew attention to the embodied nature of Manhood by using an educational project to illustrate the evolutionary bend toward more modern ideals of Manhood. Out of this arose an atmosphere of anxiety and tension, and with it an intent to return to the traditional roots of Western Manhood.

During the Enlightenment Period, further proof of biological difference led to the increasing separateness of the sexes. Uncertainty related to the different conceptualized ideals of refined masculinity that emerged during C18 and C19 facilitated the desire to build more manly men. Rather than risk an uncertain future for the traditional conceptualized version of Manhood, German educators "stressed that any nation that wished to make claim to Manhood must banish feminine softness from the education of its youth". These educational reformers identified physical training and strength as important characteristics of warrior societies. The ultimate "tribute" to this version of Manhood was its high value as embodied by Nazi soldiers. During this time the English struggles with Manhood were indicated in such picayune manly expressions as: "keep a stiff upper lip" for if that lip quivered, it was usually a sign of un-Manhood. In keeping with the "Air Castle" Supernatural "Non-Rational" Thinking concept, 'Manhood' was often deemed as anti-intellectual and anti-urban, reminiscent of Plato's descriptions. A Victorian novelist depicted men having negative responses to other men as confirming a concept of Manhood "underpinned by a homo-social relationship--defined in anxious opposition to the dandy and Romantic artist".

To summarize, for the Warrior minded, the prospect of war is exciting—being schooled in youth that war is the ultimate definition of manhood--that only in war will they be tested and proven--that they can discover their worth as human beings in battle. The "hypnotic power" associated with symbolic violence urges them to willingly join into the supreme organization. The Courage comes from realizing that War itself is a producer of grief and disability but to put the boundaries between life and death is an "adrenalin rush." Their Icon Image model is to see themselves acting out of war-like behavior and having won out against all odd—the ultimate in manliness tears, and the experience of such may be obscured by the embodiment of manliness.

For the Religious, the struggle of high class to "prove" worth and status to prove their god's power is greater than any other god and that being god's messenger, they too are powerful. Because Pseudo-Logical men have historically occupied social roles that give them the ability to acquire status and mind-control influence, they seek to generate workable Fallacies. Western society's ideal of Manhood has remained mostly unchanged from C19 Europe. It remains true to its warrior-inspired roots—roots which gave rise to the main subdivisions of Warriors, the Religious, and the Pseudo-Logic Philosophers displaying differences from the same "Genetic" philosophy. [Ref: Bosson, *Current Directions in Psychological Science, 2011;* Carlson, *JHolistic Nursing, 2011]*

EUROPEAN SUPERNATURALISM'S MODERN CULT LEADERS

In bringing forth the primitive European military type organization's chain of command, soldiers' ranks are supposedly determined by merit while leaders are determined by power displays. Leaders at the top give orders but do not take them; the new recruit takes orders and does not give them. Those in-between give and take orders. In applying this to the European Supernatural organization, at the very top of the Totem Pole is the Supreme human or Contingent Being—like Satan. This made up Satan represents a collage of contributions of how each group of cult members thinks, feels, expresses, and does in a manner that symbolizes all of the numerous sub-sects of the Warrior/Religion categories and their hybrids.

THE ILLUMINI: Below the Satan Contingent Being leader are those hidden human "presidents" called the *Illuminati* ('the enlightened'). Perhaps of C2 Italian Gnostic origin, this label was assumed by or given to various groups of mystics, each embracing many charlatans throughout its history. They claimed, either through direct divine inspiration or by means of mental exercise, to have special knowledge of the Supernatural god(s). In the early days of the European Christian Church the term was applied to people who had been baptized. However, the *elite, on whom self-declaring they had received a special divine knowledge (gnosis), used their purported gnosis, or illumination, to claim exemption from any type of prohibition and so indulged their passions without restraint.* In C15, leaders of those elite had followers to pledge obedience to them as being their superiors. Various sub-sects were divided into: (1) the "novices," Minervals, and "lesser illuminati"; (2) "freemasons," "ordinary," "Scottish," and "Scottish knights"; and (3) the "mystery" class comprising two grades of "priest" and "regent" and of "magus" and "king." A "French prophets" sub-sect believed in a "light" communicated from a higher source, giving larger measure of exalted wisdom. C16 Rosicurcians combined mysteries of alchemy and esoteric principles of religion, claiming motivation by inner illumination, as also did by Joan of Arc.

In 1776, Weishaupt--remaining invisible as to be regarded by others as a god--established *Perfectibilists Deism*—the olden Freethinkers belief in a god(s) who, after creating the universe, relinquished control over life, influence on Nature, and gave no Supernatural orders. The Masonic Order based movement converted followers into blind instruments of his supreme will. It adopted the Jesuits organization (despite being opposed to their dogma), their system of espionage, and their maxim that the "*end justifies the means*". To blend philanthropy and mysticism, he took care to enlist in his ranks as many young men of riches and position as possible. Von Knigge, a master of most secret societies (e.g. Freemasonry), joined in 1780 and introduced expert occultist, mysticism, and the Supernatural into the workings of the brotherhood. Thereafter, an air of mystery pervaded all its doings—holding out hopes of the communication of deep occult secrets in the higher ranks.

Within 5 years the power of the Illuminism became extraordinary in its proportions. Its members even had a hand in the affairs of the state—and several German princes found it to their interest to having dealings with the fraternity. The Roman Catholic Church repudiated the movement and, with the discovery of dishonorable acts, led Weishaupt into exile, the fire kindled by Illuminism burst into the French Revolution. It subsequently spread to the Americas as the Power Elite.

THE POWER ELITE: Out of the Warrior/Religion sub-sects of the Illuminiati has arisen in one hybrid group what is now called the *Power Elite* (among other names) which dominates all others of a like-kind. Its C16 ancestors claimed that the human soul, having attained a certain degree of perfection, was permitted a vision of the Supernatural divine and entered into direct communication with that Holy Spirit. From this state the soul could neither advance nor retrogress. Consequently, participation in the liturgy, good works, and observance of the exterior forms of religious life were unnecessary for those who had received the "light." Some of them were persecuted and most were the persecutors, engaging in scourging, imprisonment, and killing millions associated with the European Church Inquisition. Still others, those in the elite group, became Renaissance "Gentlemen" who *indulged their passions without restraint* by any morals or any accountability to anyone. Once this 'winner-take-all' door of "Individualism" was opened, it produced an extremely important offspring. Affluent people, now able to erase their sins with the cooperation of the Church, moved into a different and deeper sort of individualistic uniqueness—dramatizing claims to be Supernatural 'little gods.' Their thirst for power led/leads them to directly oppose the Spiritual One Universal High God of the Natural World as well as all aspects of the Spiritual Elements—Unconditional Love, Truth, Reality, and the Natural. In making Materialism happen so as to give themselves an unfair advantage and put the public at an unfair disadvantage the Power Elite used a PECKING ORDER as the keystone of how the world is to be controlled. "Pecking Order" is a term borrowed from the observation that domestic hens establish a place-assigning process. Each hen is allowed to peck the hen below except for the hen at the end of the row who has to submit to being pecked but cannot do any pecking.

In transferring to humans this Pecking Order pattern, the secluded Power Elite have always selected a subordinate to be a King puppet in the visible world who, in turn, have their puppets and their puppets have their puppets. But all puppets' actions reflect the will of the Power Elite and follow its orders. The "bull's eye" Satanists leaders and their Periphery Brute followers saw/see this as "Right" without any pangs of Conscience. Although Tangential Brutes and Brute Imitators may possess a speck of Conscience, they simply "go along to get along," while totally "Numbing" their Selfhoods to all IHES acts to do so. The framers of the original USA Power Elite were the Robber Barons--extremely dishonorable people who typified the worse features of American Capitalism. They fashioned the rules and laws of "fair capitalistic competition" into a grossly unfair "cutthroat" competition (Bailey, American Crime). Naturally, all leaders do whatever is necessary to get the most of the best of everything while having those on the lower rungs do their "dirty work" (e.g. fighting the wars they create with enemies). The Power Elite intimidates the world with their *power*.

To this end they did/do, in the words of a Power Elite, Adolf Hitler, erode rights by a thousand tiny and almost imperceptible reductions. In this way the people will not see those rights and freedoms being removed until past the point at which these changes cannot be reversed. So that the public will not know the relentless destruction being done to them, the Power Elite generates "Excitement" so that the public will clamor for the most up-dated of the Trinkets (e.g. Flashing Light Gadgets) and Trivia while entertaining the lower officers with bigger, more powerful, ever newer, faster weapons of mass destruction. Such a superficial Trinket trends pattern is in full force in today's marketplace and that is one way they mold the public's mind into staying Superficial Thinkers. Meanwhile, they ensure the public remains ignorant of the brilliance of Ancient Africans and of Spiritual things of worth by ridiculing the profound and the 'Classics.' Compared to, and using the standard of the Natural World, this is ultimate "Inside-Out" thinking.

"NORMAL VARIANT" EUROPEAN MANHOOD

A Rainbow is composed of sunlight broken up in the air into red, orange, yellow, green, blue, indigo, and violet tiny drops of rain. Each drop acts like a small *Prism* (a three-sided piece of glass that, when held up to sunlight, is a rainbow maker). Combinations of these colored rain drop components are called a *Spectrum*. White light is composed of three basic colors—red, green, and blue—called *Primary Colors* because they cannot be made up from any other colors. Other colors of the spectrum are caused by overlapping or mixing these Primary colors. Thus, 'additive mixing' of the 'additive primaries' (red, green, blue) produce such products as red + green = yellow; red + blue = magenta; and blue + green = cyan (turquoise, or peacock blue). If each of these colors represented an experience in life, a human would live through its color spectrum—implying that spectrum is circular. Each new add-on experience moves through the spectra of ones prior experiences and each primary color operates in all experiences. To elaborate, wherever one is in the 'here and now' is ones "*Situation*"—composed of a '*State of Affairs*' (a combination of circumstances) serving as ones '*Ground of Being*' for Foreground Selfhood displays. It is like seeing the world through a certain lens color.

If ones lens are made of the Spiritual Elements, one has clarity and Rightness; otherwise one sees the world and oneself with distortion/fantasy. Such a 'State of Affairs" derived from all aspects of "The Game" and its associate Games so as to generate public illusions and/or hallucinations in the public. So esteemed were the by-products of "The Game" in the C15 and C16 that they not only trickled down to the masses of European people to be internalized as an ultimate lifestyle but they also became established as a philosophy of life (POL), a world view, and a practice that flourishes today. Such can be seen by the free use of every dishonorable, amoral, and immoral measure imaginable to mankind and the masses of people imitate all the associated superficiality with it--the accoutrements of dress, possessions, and partying so as to appear rich--a pattern persisting to this day. Examples are being concerned with how they and others look (e.g. cars, homes, plastic surgery, hairstyles); gossiping about those who look "different"; and name-dropping.

Regardless of race, "*Normal Variant*" people have embraced and internalized the Icon Image of "The Game" to the extent of it becoming a non-Real Self POL. *Internalize,* a C15 Latin word ("*Internal*"--inside, inner, between, among) means to give inward or subject ones character to one or more concepts, understandings, customs, standards, guides, filters, and measures derived from outside oneself. The doings of this process are by interweaving newly internalized and established Information, Knowledge or even Philosophy of Life ingredients in a manner that a given thread goes over a specific aspect of Reality--under the next--over--under, and so on. The resultant Tapestry is extended in order to display its unique and imitated patterns for purposes of becoming a False Self that blends into the "Crowd." This process is so internalized *and so automatic as for False Self-expressions to flow out of ones Selfhood without rigid rules.* When something flows in this way, it is "*Second Nature*"--a 1390s term alluding to such frequent repeating of something as to make it seem inborn (like a Human Nature trait). The obvious power of what is "second nature" is that one designs, without ones awareness, acquired but deeply ingrained think, feel, say, and behavior *Conditioned Response* patterns. Every human newborn has already internalized Spiritual Elements essences—and to then cultivate them fully is "Normal" for "Right Spiritual Life-Living".

But in a Secular World, a different concept is needed. To this end, the C17 Latin word "*Normal*" (made according to a carpenter's square, 'a norma') means conforming to a widely agreed upon rule or pattern--or to the established standards for its sort of Natural thing. The term "Normal Variant" came into focus for me in my Orthopaedic Surgery residency when I saw patients with congenital big toe bunions (a swelling, lump) but who had never had symptoms. However, it became evident that although they caused no problems with ordinary daily activities, when overly stressed they would develop synovial swelling (a sac with fluid) and great pain where the shoe rubbed it. As used here, a "*Normal Variant*" mindset is something a little different from a standard but not pathologically (like being mentally ill) abnormal. In short, Normal Variants are that which, while being unusual, are normal for the person. The first and longest POL standard (200,000 years old) is that of African Tradition. Out of Africa, where Humankind began, came all skin-colors—the variations of which are a consequence of ultra-violet light, of latitude, and climate. Hence, *there is no such thing as "races" of humans*—simply one species—each human is more like other humans than different—each having the same Spiritual "Genetics" (a birth gift of Unconditional Love, Truth, Reality, and the Natural)—each having the Free Will to decide how to uniquely manifest that "Genetics".

African Tradition is based upon living within and operating out of the Spiritual Elements. But those with deviating POL are subdivided. *Type I, Mild* "Normal Variants" do not cultivate the Spiritual Elements but drift by their Animal nature. Hence, they fashion an Emotional state to live inside and operate out of so as to manifest as Superficial Thinkers who are captivated by Trinkets and Trivia. *Type II, Slight* "Normal Variants" are those who have bought into *Delusions* (believing what is not real and not believing what is real), like that of being "superior" to other humans. *Type III, Moderate "Normal Variants"* push towards the limits of the boundaries of the "normal" mind. Yet, they are insufficiently "far out" mentally to avoid being characterized as insane people. *Type IV, Extreme* "Normal Variants" are a step away from the sane/insane border. All types of "Normal Variants" are within the spectra of the Indifference/Hate/Evil/Sadism (IHES) Complex and thus are capable of being persuaded (by oneself and/or others) to advance or recede in good or bad directions. How "Normal Variant" Leaders design cults was described by W.H. Auden (1907-73): Humans can have unity by giving up freedom. The '*State*' [in the sense of the supreme power that claims ownership of everything of everything, that is internally autonomous, and is the dictator to the public] is Real and the individual is wicked. Violence shall synchronize human's movements like a tune and terror like a frost shall halt the flood of thinking so that there will not be any independent thought. Barracks/bivouacs shall be your friendly refuge. Racial pride shall tower like a public column and confiscate for safety every private sorrow.

The European "Normal Variant" course began with their appearance on Earth 45,000 years ago in the form of physical competition between Warriors. This was in marked contrast to exhibiting Cowardice (from the idea of a frightened animal drawing its tail between its legs). Certain themes of European "Manhood" have been a bridge between primitive and today's European males—meaning from their beginning they continue in full force today. In the process, Lower (animalistic) Self materialistic success became a positive mark of manhood—and without the question of conscience or any Supernatural God entering into consideration. A *Theme* is a composition with a Disposition + an inherent direction, its *maintained central or dominating idea (or thesis) which contains a 'payload' message* (fig. 6). A *Disposition* contains the 'seeds' of: (1) an *Inclination*--a 'physical' "leaning toward" or "leaning" away from something; (2) its *Temperament*----i.e. a mindset about a Thing or subject or individual/group with a prevailing emotional trend; (3) an Intention--the decision of what one means to do with an aim toward a specific action or a specific goal; an earnest state of mind to reach the goal; (4) its Attitude—a complex C17 word with the sense of a positive or negative posture tone toward the "Thing". Such 'seeds' give rules to the specific kind of behavior produced. Perhaps the first theme was fashioned from their Supernatural law of "eliminate the competition" or, as an alternative, displaying primarily as preventing opponents from living well by ensuring they do not have the opportunity to succeed. The supreme theme has always been *Riches* are the key to greatness for they facilitate and make the way for power and therefore a good name.

The process of becoming richer follows the path of doing the utmost of ones own personality to develop ones mental abilities to use any means necessary to arrive at a ticket to success of being recognized as deserving of a high status. Starting then and continuing in crystalized form by the ancient Greeks on up until the Enlightenment, European males declared themselves superior because of being part of the "Air Castle" Supernatural Cult they made-up in fantasy. Let us shift the discussion to the Greek's Archaic period (800-500 BC) where 'Manhood fighting'—called 'Andreia'—spotlighted the participants as possessing (Military) Courage or Resolution (a determined decision for a "Manhood" line of conduct)—the main notions of being a 'man.' What motivated this for many was a defensiveness about and a constant aggressiveness toward struggling to prove their appearance of being of value by demonstrating 'virtues' (defined as Manhood strength and Courage).

Plato, as part of purposefully juxtaposing the seeking of philosophical knowledge in opposition to manliness, said Andreia included being able to ignore pain. Aristotle added that Andreia was risking ones life in the noblest of pursuits, such as death in warfare, where the danger was greatest and most noble. In the *Meno* story (by Plato, 380 BC) it was said: 'it is easy to see that a man's virtue consists in managing the city's affairs capably, and in such a way that he will help his friends and injure his enemies, while taking care to come to no harm himself.' Homer, in *Odysseus*, used *arête* to describe both men and women within the context of "a Greek world-view where the world was a place of conflict and difficulty, and human value and meaning were measured against individual effectiveness in the world". The Roman word for "Manliness" (*virtus*, man) symbolized the idealized behavior and supremacy characteristics of a man--reaching ones highest human potential or the pursuit of excellence (Carlson, *JHolistic Nursing, 2011*).

The redefining of Roman Manhood from the Greek concepts incorporated competitive sports and the objectified male body, as occurred in Colosseums c75 AD used for gladiatorial combats, fights between men and beast, and mock battles. The Roman Empire's greatest troublemakers were the Germanic peoples. Despite Europeans historically being a warring people, it was particularly bad throughout Europe in the Dark and Middle Ages. Warriors were fighting battles everywhere—and without any period of meaningful peace—and often for 'no reason.' Hence, large numbers of Slaves available and to the victors they were considered "expendable." Of particular importance were the Franks since they laid foundations for the medieval kingdoms of France and Germany (Bailey, American Crime, p. 22). The Franks became mercenary warriors for the Romans and their intermingling gave rise to those destined to be Medieval Knights. These hybrid Warriors were so savage, destructive, and crude that Ladies of the Medieval European royal courts took as their humanitarian burden the guiding of them into civility—but without much success.

Lords of the Feudal System (900 AD), after joining with a private army of these barbaric warriors, over time, provided special training in a code of behavior and in the arts of war to a sufficient degree of sophistication for them to be deemed knights. These knights devoted a great part of their lives to war, religion, and the service of ladies. Yet, the *Knight's Code*--centering on honor, loyalty, religion, generosity, and courtesy--only applied to members of a knight's own class (i.e., other knights, lords, and their ladies). Since the code did not apply to "low fellows--those of "low birth," like peasants and tradesmen--by believing himself to be superior, a knight would act as badly as he pleased toward "Low Fellows." Although they had no personal interest in religion, they remained civil to leaders of the Church by showing the approach of controlled emotions. Otherwise, they disregarded the Code.

Knights who disliked each other still respected each other sufficiently to be civil. To everyone else, they were not even civil. Nevertheless, when battling outside enemy invaders, knights were professionals fighting for profits. During the Middle Ages/Renaissance Europeans were grouped as knights, merchants, farmers, and artisans. At that time all medieval European males were defined in terms of sexual performance, measured, rather simply, as the ability to get an erection. Of course, they added that these features reigned supreme over anything pertaining to the Natural Cosmos (e.g. Rational Thinking) and that is what made them superior. The concept of manliness was examined within the context of Spain's imperial rule beginning in 1492. Colonialism made its mark on the emerging concept of manliness by including the conquest of foreign lands and the elimination of those who were deemed inferior. In Spain, manliness or *vir* was understood in part as in opposition to sodomy—so as to avoid exploring the concept of Manhood confronting the barbaric practices endorsed by Spanish colonizers conquering South America.

The new Spanish man was re-embodied with a disdain of women, sodomites, and men from other countries. European 'Manhood' continued to be defined against other men, not women. In C18 an increased focus was "Manhood" that relied on heterosexuality (performing his sexual duty according to nature), on secularization, on a man's patriarchal role as head of a household as the embodiment of their Supernatural God's authority, and on men's relationship to their mortality. A man did not possess a "masculinity," for "a person's identity was bound up with the performance of social roles, not the expression of self". Drastic changes occurred in C19 whereby "Manhood" was about inner personal identity, the growth of Individualism, and the emergence of the modern self. This displayed in testing and proving ones personal manhood--a defining experience for Euro-American males. In England, during the Victorian era (i.e. the rule of Queen Victoria from 1837-1901), 'Muscular Christianity' movement originated that was in keeping with man's adventure-seeking and men sought fulfilment on the frontiers of the British Empire, inspired by an ethos instilled in pupils of the English public schools (Yu, *European Physical Education Review, 2011*).

"NORMAL VARIANT" EURO-AMERICAN MANHOOD: The reason for many Europeans coming to the Americas was on getting rich from labor of Enslaved Africans so as to thereby end their own labor in order to gain the short-cut to leisure. From the beginning of the Euro-American occupation of the Americas, within their IHES Complex context, extreme riches were made but that created a variety off-shoot unanticipated problems. Just as more money means more money to waste, so does more free time mean more time to waste. Such are features of a consumption-oriented mindset. Some slave owners spent most of their time abroad, leaving the Overseers in charge. For most, the main problem was deathly fear of Enslaved rebellions. The conflicted nature of leisure was time emptied of meaningful activity and an impression of determined frenzy to do something different. This conflicted situation made it hard to keep things exciting or compatible for ease and relaxation (e.g. by being entertained or by engaging in something illicit and amoral) so as to prevent anxiety, boredom, and restlessness. Such slave owners' mindsets sought alliances with their competitors for protection, for learning what worked most effectively in applying tyrant thoughts and deeds to the Enslaved, and how to refine their greedy pursue money.

Such reinforced and expanded their IHES Complex POL in a manner like continuing to keep its bow stretched will eventually cause it to nearly break. At that point the majority of slave owners dipped into the fantasy part of their Supernatural mindsets and plucked inner realizations of Contingent Beings—symbolizing who one thinks one is; about who one really is, about ones fellows, and about the "monsters" the Enslaved represented for all Whites to fear—from running away and, even worse, from being killed. This required them to devise a police force. Their religious hypocrisy necessitated they be the moral guardian role of their plantations, assume a public order role, and be 'public protectors in uniform'. However, they typically hired out these duties—the beginnings of today's modern professional police service (Sanders, *The Police Journal, 2011*).

By Euro-Americans being an extension of the English meant they did similar things. For example, the Victorian era of the 1850s was most certainly concerned with morality and punishing those who did not respect the moral, religious code. By the 1880s, American Protestant churches as well as Catholic churches in Britain and Ireland were also endorsing Muscular Christian values and promoting the culture of physical vigor. Nevertheless, there is the continuation of ancient European male patterns pertaining to being "little gods" who are 'superior' to all others.

TODAY'S "NORMAL VARIANT" EUROPEAN MANHOOD REARING: Today, for example, following a male child's birth and development into childhood, at some point the small boy must decide what to about his mother (Shor *The J. Men's Studies, 1993*). *Phase I*: Typically this is about rejecting her by devaluation and creating a negative and insecure identity. This heralds later attempts at intimacy with woman. It is historically traditional for Black boys to ever cement bonds with their mothers. However, the anti-feminism aspect of European males demands they separate, for that is intimately connected with their psychosocial individuation that defines masculinity. *Phase II*: Following separation, the begins being initiated into the world of men—bound with rituals of social performance and testing that offer both risk and cultural validation. It carries much ideological baggage concerning what masculinity is all about in particular period of time in history and at a given social place. To not do, the boy may be deemed to never enter Manhood nor find self-fulfillment as a man. *Phase III*: is Manhood-Father identification which reaches back and projects forward in psychosocial development. It configures to the patriarchy cultural code in both society and ones home. Problems are complicated by an absent father (creating a "father-hunger" and a wounded sense of masculinity) or playful pal father. Phase IV is Masculinity-Erotic sexual desires.

Part of these phases is to be enthralled with kingship, emphasizing agendas for change as opposed to experiences for growth and self-discovery. Resultant indoctrinations prevents discovering what the father is and what masculinity is by freeing oneself from family cages and collective mindsets so as to transcend those imprisonments of being a Wild Man or an Inner Child. A model to consider following is Black males in the post-slavery communities. Although boys grew up in home where the father was often absent, those adult Black males involved in rearing children were consistently inner-directed—firmly acting with resolve with self-worth images--and not concerned with material possessions derived or needing the approval of others. They were disciplined ascetics (self-sacrificing) with respect for wisdom and experience; usually humble, quiet, sincere, and discreet—and sort like-kind friends. Though sensitive, they were not feminine soft—having an ability to be fierce and with the courage to take big risks. Also continuing unchanged out of primitive European times is the Icon Image of "The Game" for "Pretend" purposes.

To this end *Coats of Arms* were significant because of their near association with the nobility; of being a symbol of rank; and evidence that the user and his descendants were "Gentleman. Associated with their Ego driven desire to display their perceived power have been through names (e.g. king, priest, military leader), seals, marks, standards and signs; masks, helmets, head-dresses, swords and shields; scepters, crowns, pallia and palaces; effulgence is expressed by gold and precious stones; and patriotism--zeal ("blazing jealousy" and always tending to vigorous action) as a need for recognition in the sense of not appearing weak from not belonging to ones own in-group society. As a result, one is in a position to take advantages of built-in responses to such symbols as the flag, historical traditions, and governing literature as a feeling of having superiority. To emphasize that what matters is not who I am but what I have and how I appear it is essential to have a "trophy woman" on his arm to symbolize his arrival into the world of riches, power, and leisure.

Attributes of "The Game" remains so pervasive that far too many Europeans see dishonorableness as "normal" among themselves. There are consistent studies of European college graduates who, in 85% of cases, say they not only cheated on examinations but saw nothing wrong with doing so. However, most of these same people show "Righteous Indignation" if the same things are done by outsiders and with forces generated to "make an Example of them" by means of super-harsh punishments. At least 85% of the businesses I deal with in daily living are cheaters, including the government charging me for things I do not get. Many Black people are vulnerable because of being naïve about such dishonorableness from leaders, since that is not the African Tradition way.

LOW STATUS "NORMAL VARIANT" EUROPEANS

Even Europeans above the lower rungs of their Social Ladder have derogatory names for those beneath their social status and even poverty-stricken. Example are: the 'underclass'; trailer-trash (USA), Bogan (Australia), ned (Scotland), 'hoodie,' 'charver,' and 'pikey' (England); and "Rednecks"—a term Europeans use in referring to dumb White tenant farmers and sharecroppers—so-called because of the backs of their necks being reddened and toughened by years of labor in the sun. The bulk of them in the Americas probably derived from the European convicts that were release from European prisons on the condition that they would go to the Americas. This they did as overseers on Slave ships and on the plantations. As with all people, they range from Good to Bad. The Bad with non-Spiritual Elements philosophies of life (POL) have a certain sameness within their situational uniqueness. In contrast to European "Gentlemen" being socialized directly into having a sense of Supernatural 'superiority,' these "Low Status" Whites have an Inferiority Complex.

Those who are starved to possess power imitate, to the extent possible, the POL of Brutes (Type IV above--*Extreme* "Normal Variants" just short of insane) operates within and out of the spectra of the Indifference/Hate/Evil/Sadism (IHES) Complex. By adopting this IHES Complex and a Network to back them up, causes "Low Status" Whites to embrace a *Superiority Complex*—i.e. donning a mask of self-confidence and greatness with a reality of arrogance and aggression to conceal a sense of deep inferiority. Both Complexes form the arts for those who make war and for these Brutes, better things do not exist for them—since war is where they show the "primitive" masculinities of courage, strength, and virility. Their historical "Manhood" Lower (animal) Self traits include: Sexual activity with anybody (including mothers and sisters) and most medium sized-animals; heavy alcohol drinking; brawls; warring; and bad manners. Each battle is an opportunity to reclaim and prize these. As discussed, the origins of "Manhood" are most clearly demonstrated by primitive European Warriors at war. Between battles, warfare between neighboring rivals was something like a game in which the opponents probably knew each other well—and the fighting was often for 'no reason.' Perhaps this helps account for why Euro-Americans seem to be so accepting of criminal behavior committed by other Euro-Americans.

Routinely, their demonstrations of physical aggression—or at least displays of readiness to aggress physically—were part of their primitive European cultural script for defending their personal honor following threats; of taking from others what they wanted so as to appear superior; and to "save face"—or maintain "face," or restore their "Manhood face" status. Any of these, but perhaps not relational aggression (e.g. rumors, not being 'loved,' teasing, or being neglected or rejected), spurred their presumed Icon Images and memories which recalled thoughts related to physical aggression to the fore (Bosson, *Personality and Social Psychology Bulletin, 2009)*. Throughout the centuries, Europeans continued to be grouped as the aristocrats and the workers. The workers were abhorred as violent and lacking self-control and the worst of those afflicted with Psychic Trauma resorted to gang violence.

Despite Europeans being historically a warring people, wars were particularly bad throughout Europe in the Dark and Middle Ages. At its beginning, the Roman Empire's greatest troublemakers were Germanic peoples and so the ever battling groups who had a reputation for winning were spotlighted to be defenders and protectors of castles. Warriors were fighting battles everywhere— without any period of meaningful peace. Of particular importance were the Franks, since they laid foundations for the medieval kingdoms of France and Germany (Bailey, American Crime, p22). The Franks became mercenary warriors for the Romans and their intermingling gave rise to those destined to be *Medieval Knights*. These hybrid Warriors were so savage, destructive, and crude that large numbers of resultant Slaves were deemed by the victors to be "expendable."

During the Middle Ages/Renaissance Europeans were grouped as knights, merchants, farmers, and artisans. Lords of the *Feudal System* (900 AD), after joining with private armies of these barbaric warriors, over time provided them with special training in behavior codes and in arts of war.

Furthermore, Ladies of the Medieval European royal courts took as their humanitarian burden to guide these savages into civility—but without much success. Hence, hopefully deal with the Warriors' barbaric crudeness, the ladies of the court joined with leaders of the Church to fashion customary practices related to personal and social behaviors—with emphasis placed on boundaries related to manners. Those able to achieve some degree of sophistication were deemed to be knights, meaning they devoted a great part of their lives to war, religion, and the service of ladies. In the form of assigned codes, these behaviors of knights—whose time was from C11-C15—were those positioned on the upper levels of the social European society and eventually declared themselves "Gentlemen."

Yet, the *Knight's Code*--centering on honor, loyalty, religion, generosity, and courtesy--only applied to members of a knight's own class (i.e., other knights, lords, and their ladies). Since the code did not apply to "Low Fellows"--those of "low birth," like peasants and tradesmen--a knight, by believing himself to be superior, would act as badly as he pleased toward "Low Fellows." Although having no personal interest in religion, they remained civil to leaders of the Church by somewhat exhibiting controlled emotions. Otherwise, they disregarded the Code. Whereas knights who disliked each other still respected each other sufficiently to be civil, to all others they made no civil attempts. When battling enemy invaders, knights were professionals fighting for profits. Those who demonstrated fearlessness and honorable deeds, were positioned on the upper levels of the social European society and declared themselves "gentlemen." Still, European man's masculinity was largely defined against that of other European men, not women—as well as secretly against Black men's "Manhood".

EUROPEAN MALE RACISTS

The ancient and present day "Air Castle" Supernatural subdivisions of the racist Brute cult are: Core, Peripheral, Tangential, Imitators, and Followers. They, to receive all the benefits taken from victims, do not require all members to be strong advocates of what they advocate (e.g. "White supremacy") but merely defer to the values/prejudices/attitudes/practices of other cult members. Cult beliefs which replace and directly oppose African Tradition's Spiritual Elements include: (1) all cult members be above the rules cult leaders impose on outsiders; (2) punish any outsider who imitates cult members; (3) demand entitlement over all non-cult people; (4) arrange to be objects of Fear, not loved; (5) use victim intimidation to ensure the cult is known as a force not to be defied and, rather "little gods" to be obeyed; and (6) generate confusion and conflict to obscure truth + gain and maintain mind control of victims. Money, possessions—and their manipulations by Technology—are supreme. People, animals, and Nature are purposed only to be exploited. Cult members' inability to be happy—for which they rationalize with Indifference + Hate--causes them to promote Evilness and Sadism that generates pain, suffering, and destruction for 'outgroups.'

The successful effects and consequences of these expressions and deeds design "sick pleasure" mindsets which applaud victims' failure (because "misery loves company"). Their focus is only on "being a legend in their own minds" and to do that requires tearing/keeping down scapegoats. They rule by force with the GUN to Kill/Take/Destroy/Dominate and their other evil deeds are supported and defended by a Network formed by like-kind Cult members who do the same things. These are the lowest level of humans. It is essential for them to say and teach that 'outgroups' are less than human so as to justify pushing them deep into the Animal Kingdom. The psychiatrist Fanon pointed out ("Peau noire, masques blancs" 1952) that the 'Negro,' for

European males, symbolized 'the Biological'--a cluster of stereotypes related to sexual instincts, genital potency, violence and lack of any morality. Later, in "Les Damnés de la terre" (1961), Fanon said--which heavily influenced most of the intellectual works on African psychology and psychopathology--violence and prejudice characterized the binary opposition of the colonizer and colonized. Moss (J. American Psychoanalytic Association 2001) added that to hate racistly, homophobically, misogynistically [aversion to women] is to hate not as isolated individuals but as part of a group; not in the first person singular but in the first person plural. Within the sphere of these hatreds, "I" hate not as "I" alone, but as a white person, a straight person, a man. Cult members *Reaction Formation* (converting envy of Blacks to despising) and *Projection* of their own bad character traits onto Blacks as scapegoats are ingredients for "ugly" stereotyped Icon Images of the victims—and which are advertised world-wide. Victims who emotionally conform are deemed to be Weak. These "Stereotype" symbols are designed to tell ones own in-group about how to view the scapegoat before the in-group knows anything about them.

Incidentally, my method of gaining deep insight into the mindset core of European males is to take the 'ugly' things they say about others and apply it to how they feel about themselves. To be effective, cults ensure they and victims are kept segregated. To present the façade to fellow Europeans of being "right", they use the *"Deflection" Method* ("its not me that is bad but them") to both reinforce their Projections and serve to "dim the light of obviousness" on the "ugly" things they do. By being intentionally created fears to justify attacks for their insecurities, "Deflectors" spew in the media or in public gatherings vociferous harsh "Judgments" of scapegoats. Dominant delusional groups often claim they have superior genetic powers, and believe they have been chosen or given unique powers that justify their social dominance. These racist fantasy residua beliefs are indifferent to Truth.

EUROPEAN MANHOOD THINKING: What best characterizes European "Manhood's" historical 'big picture' is "Male Chauvinism" (1970s)—an attitude attributed to insensitive men from prejudices against woman and of excessive loyalty (or fanatical patriotism) to fellows in 'like-kind' male cults (nixing the "I'm my own man" concept). As exemplified by Nicolas Chauvin, a legendary French soldier enthusiastically and overzealously devoted to Napoleon, this prejudiced superiority 'airy' foundational belief in ones own cult constitutes *"Extraversion"*—the deeming of External World 'Things' (e.g. social phenomena; the realm of 'changeableness') to be superior to ones own Inner World powers—a sign of weakness. Its extension is that European "Manhood" considers the best of the External World to be 'out of this world'—i.e. placed in a Supernatural World—and to which most European males desire not only to be part but a leader in it--or at least have special recognition or status in it. European "Manhood," unlike "Womanhood," is widely viewed as a status that is tenuous (it must be demonstrated) and elusive (it must be earned)--both by action and aggression so as to quell each male's doubts about his gender status to himself and to outsiders. A dominant belief is that since open expressions of emotions are a sign of femininity, they and even 'felt' emotions must be controlled to avoid being viewed as possessing a sense of inferiority and a weakened masculinity. Men are therefore expected to be consistently "individualistic," tough, calm, rational, and in control.

In my view, the pivotal point of what constitutes "Manhood" in an individual or a group or a society is, in general, its *prevailing philosophy* and, in particular, the *chosen pattern of Thinking*. To elaborate, the European "Manhood" focus--the opposite of African Tradition--is on the structure rather than the content of "Manhood." Yet, it is full of contradictions, even from purely a European perspective. One example is that the Supernatural is fantasy and thus cannot be about a standard if one uses the European definition of a *Standard*--what people's ideas are measured against of the "What it is" of the ultimate value of a "Thing"--the "what it does," and the "how it appears". Then that flawed assessment serves as a definition guide for solving problems + points out direction + places boundaries (e.g. time and space limits) + provides rules for performance and variations. Second, a criteria for European "Manhood" in self-declaring heir Supernatural "Air Castle" and the best of its contents are 'superior' can only be believed by their own "Non-Rational" thinking.

The "*Non-Rational*"—Emotions admixed with Left Brain mental activities—derives out of the dogma of the Supernatural and those declarations are deemed to be 'superior' to the Natural Cosmos' Rational Thinking (i.e. Logic as originated in African Tradition). *Think about that*! Thus, "Non-Rational" Supernatural rules make it acceptable to follow a 'realistic' (?) analytical discourse that permits putting '*Boundaries on the Boundless*' (by the Supernatural said to be 'superior' prevents European philosophy from believing in the Natural Cosmos' Spiritual or Metaphysical realms). So, for example, nothing seems wrong with reducing *Organic life*—which naturally undergoes a "birth-growth-decay-death" process, followed by rebirth to another cycle--in terms of rational truth into precise *mechanical laws*. Natural Cosmos "Common Sense" is negated by "Non-Rational" Thinking. By definition, "Non-Rational" Thinking is not thought out--only sensed by emotions and evolved out of that with Left Brain thoughts. Its action course, outlined by the 'payload' message in its "Non-Rational" Disposition--complete with its inclination and intention--may be quite supportable on grounds of the "Air Castle" Supernatural's concepts of the rational or ethical (proper/improper) or moral (right/wrong)—grounds that are "6:30 opposites" by the clock to what is best for all in the Natural Cosmos.

European patterns for living that springs out of "Non-Rational" Thinking, when compared with Natural Cosmos Logic—and without my judging either—impart mental Dispositions that, upon "playing them out", are "*Non Sequitur*" ('it does not follow'). Its contrariness to sound Logic or Reason makes it Irrational (i.e. absurd) and Illogical (i.e. false or foolish). It does not require Understanding one or more fundamentals of life or any topic essentials because its focus standard is: "what can it do for me and my goals."

EUROPEAN MALES FEIGNED BLACK ENEMIES: Humans' common "*Enemies*" (C13, 'not a friend) are tyranny, poverty, disease, cults, and war. If these do not end in ones death, the next worst thing any of them do is to rob one of ones true sense of Selfhood Greatness. Human enemies are of many types. Group I is oneself—ones own unruly nature and the dark forces pent-up within oneself. These members minds are filled with illusions that are cast as fierce to behold monsters, demons, and other contingent Beings. One is not harmless who harms oneself and thus is to be carefully watched. Group II is ones envy of others because the others have what one wants and which one cannot get because of being incapable or unwilling to go after it. Group III is an injured, angered, person watching opportunities for revenge. Their anger may have come from the other knowing, with or without exposing, their flaws; saying truths that violate ones beliefs or from which one is hiding; or being a model of good living against which the unhappy compare themselves. Group IV is the desire of two or more competing people to have the same thing which only one can enjoy. Group V get "excitement" and a sense of importance and power from having enemies. Thus, they invent weak excuses for declaring hostility against victims. Group VI are socialized to be open to and seek out battle as a lifestyle. Their attitude is: "if you are not for me, you must be against me". Group VII are "little gods"—"do it my way or we fight because I'm entitled, not you". They are furious with those who excel them in anything they do, for that stomps on their self-declaration of being superior. Group VIII have such intense self-hatred as to dedicate themselves to Kill/Take/Destroy in hopes of getting some temporary tension relief. Group IX have such great fears and helplessness concerning death or other things as to displace that onto scapegoats. Group X are willfully incapable of demonstrating the Spiritual Elements of Unconditional Love, Truth, Reality, and the Natural. No Group possesses the ingredients to be a friend—and neither is one a friend who associates well with these Groups.

Regardless of the reason for attacking another, to do evil to even an innocent by-stander makes that innocent person an enemy to the attacker—which may/may not be reciprocated. Enemies, by being ignorant or by embracing the Indifference/Hate/Evil/Sadism (IHES) Complex, operate out of their Lower (animalistic) Self. Their total focus is on self-aggrandizement (increasing the scope of ones power, influence, stature, riches, conquest, or reputation)--using methods that attack the body, mind, and spirit--by any means necessary. A spiritual attack example is for the enemy to create some Supernatural power, declare it to be *The* Spiritual God, and destructively apply it in physical realms. From observations, personal experiences, talking with thousands of victims throughout my education, training and Orthopaedic Surgical practice, and doing extensive research since college days on all types of subjects, I conclude the ten Groups in Supernatural cults always design Black People as feigned enemies--upon whom they use enemy methods—and at their own great loss.

"Feign" (C13 contrive, false pretenses) means to invent a story, excuse, or allegation—hence make a pretense of an emotion or response so as to exhibit behavior entirely different from what is the real condition or situation. "Feigned enemies" are characterized as those easily exploited for self-interest gains—and who in no way attack, hinder, or interfere with the cult's hostile military or dogmatic set-up. This is a *Deflection* method illustrated by *Reaction Formation* (a reality/fantasy reversal)--e.g. saying about and to the victim: "you are the one causing the problem, not me!" The contents in their *Projection* accusations are derived from fantasies which design feigned necessities—i.e. imaginary necessities.

Such are the greatest cozenage (deceitful) things a predator does to his/her mind to break down any remote sense of moral "Right." However, compared with those living out of their Higher Self inside the Natural Cosmos, Supernatural cult members have a totally different concept of "Right". Examples include a lust of conquest, a love of ease, a craving for power, and an obsession to be superior. The cozen "wheeling and dealings" are infinitely worse when used as an excuse for generating an IHES Complex in order to Kill/Take/Destroy/Oppress their victims. Yet, such actions are complimented and even honored by Supernatural Cult fellows. jabaileymd.com

EUROPEAN TOOLS FOR VIOLENCE

A "Tool" (Old English) is etymologically an implement used to "make" something or prepare to do, or contributes to being an instrument to get a job done. A few of these tools European Brutes use to carry out their the Indifference/Hate/Evil/Sadism (IHES) Complex practices are as follows:

COMPETITION (DISHONORABLE): All of history, from the very beginning of mankind, has competition battles as one of its featured parts. All cultures, to some extent, interpret negative events as being inflicted upon them by some or other malevolent Supernatural spirit or force. In Ancient African Biblical Mythology Horus is portrayed as a falcon after he defeated Seth in an aerial battle over good vs. evil. Europeans defined such "Win-Lose" type "Competition" as "in rivalry with" (1620); and then (1840s) "to strive for command of a market"—both always having been and are features permeating all aspects of European and Euro-American reality and mental fantasy life. The mythological European Valkyries, Amazonian priestesses who ruled the gates of death, brought the souls of the heroes killed in battle to the Hall of the Slain, feasted, and then for amusement, fought one another with savage fervor (similar to European warriors of the Middle Ages).

Historically, Europeans have constantly been on some type of battlefield engaged in constant wars between losses and gains because of an insatiable quest for what is esteemed by their cult members--the newer, the most, the bigger, the better, and the faster related to goods, material things, and adult toys. Such is a challenge, a form of entertainment, and a display of power--all to satisfy ones ego--and they never get enough of fighting so as to have "wins"--"wins" that carry nothing more than temporary pleasures. All of this is driven by the Brute Brain portions of their Ancient (Reptilian) Brains—the sources of their Warrior Indifference/Hate/Evil/ Sadism (IHES) Complex mindsets (fig. 2, 3, 4, 8). These "Life-Living" practices never give peace or happiness and thus "sick" pleasures are fashioned within their "Dark Side". The nature of its "Evilness"--its anti-Spiritual Elements lifestyle--is to "by itself, reproduce itself so as to become the thing it makes." Their evilness generates fear of what is worse for them, as in their devising hell, following death. Some chose to believe there is no death but with the element of doubt. Such Europeans have no real connection with God and that places them into lacking the "5Ss" within their Selfhood core. They cling to the IHES Complex and that is chronically anxiety producing.

As with Cooperation, Competition is such a major aspect of Animal social behavior as to be too massive to fully discuss. A foundational Animal rule of Competition in times of scarcity is that it drives adaptation, as in not allowing competition, even of its own species, often including its own offspring, for limited necessities. The theme in Brute Amensalism (i.e. Win-Lose) is that: "in order for me to win you have to lose." Here, the larger or stronger or aggressive one(s) excludes a smaller or weaker or peaceful one(s) from food or living space. In humans, if Challenge is the trademark of hormonally based mental aggressive stimulation in most males, Competition is the trademark activity. The lowest level of humans are fixed on 'winning' being dominated by aggressive Kill/Take/Destroy/Dominate methods. Such was the ingrained mindset of Primitive Europeans during their Ice Age beginnings.

After the Ice Age ended in 12,000 BC, because the long established competitive pursuit and possession of material gains had been so "exciting," as to cause Kill/Take/Destroy/Dominate practices to become a "second nature" addiction. Self-interest thinking motivated by the addiction to continually reproduce 'excitement' and the gains of "victory" led them to expand their destructive mindsets. One form, for purposes of self-interest benefits, was/is to develop Unnatural Fears in the absence of threats to "life or limb" or to their abundant resources within themselves. In order to get their "Troops" to comply, they generated in them also "Delusional" Fears of possible threats/dangers in the future from some feigned enemy. So, Kill/ Take/Destroy/Dominate/Oppress was/is done in anticipation—and that necessitates fashioning a fantasy Supernatural realm in which to engage in organized "*Delusional Win-Lose Competition*" among Supernatural cult members.

CONFLICT: Conflict is characterized by experiences of Anxiety (to choke), if not Anguish (distress, suffering). *Clinging is the root of anxiety and anxiety is the root of all problems.* Both Anxiety and Anguish are words at the root of self-strangulation (Latin, tightness, narrow).

CONFUSION: *Confusion*--a generalized disturbance of Consciousness in which one is bewildered and disoriented. When it arrived into English in 1330, "Confusion" meant to defeat, frustrate; throw into disorder; and bewilder. Brutes purposely stir up Confusion (pour together; mix together; fail to distinguish) about all aspects of everything for purposes of controlling the people. Others do it out of ignorance. Originally, the 14th century English word "Confuse" (pour together; mix together; fail to distinguish) meant to defeat, frustrate; then throw into disorder; and later bewilder. Confusion is present when all the parts are present except an essential part concerning the inner workings; the obvious or the foundation is overlooked; a part is suppressed by some covering (as occurs with the esoteric or hidden meanings in allegories); or that which was already present is in a disguised form. This confusion may display as a paradox or "impossible" to solve.

What confusion does is to stir up so much disharmony, fear, and difficulty as to cause *Illusions* (seeing what is not there and not seeing what is there); *Delusions* (believing what is not real and not believing what is real); and misinterpretations as to prevent one from no longer being sure of anything they previously thought they knew. Inside Confusion are inconsistencies, especially related to power and its source and control. Confusion puts one in a state of such frustration as a result of so many ridiculous contradictions that one has no idea at what place to start unraveling the mess. The confused will then either say: "I don't want to think about it" or the resultant sense of overwhelming confusion and despair ease one into looking for guidance from anyone. CONFUSION is a state in which the mental faculties are thrown into chaos so that the clear and distinct action of the different powers, as of perception, memory, reason, and will is lost.

CONFUSION DARK SIDE TOOLS": What Confusion does is to render clarity and certainty ineffectual by deliberate action or want of action. The African mythological god Set (Seth) -- also deemed the *"instigator of Confusion" and the Destroyer* -- was the Kamitic conception of evil. Ancient African's purpose for this Set Metaphor is two-fold: First, rather than Set referring to some invisible Being, his symbolic "atmosphere" concerns *entities actually within the person* touched by them. Second, the personification of this symbolic "atmosphere" can expand the ramifications of what is being conveyed beyond the ability of words to do or to describe. To spotlight how confusion can be intentionally designed to convey the "Dark Side," the patterns of Set have been carried over into countless *Trickery* and *Deceit* fables of Africans. To illustrate Confusion in perhaps the most famous Yoruba/Nigeria story about the god Èṣù, Eshu, a spirit of Confusion and Trickery. This story concerns two inseparable friends who swore undying fidelity to one another and yet neglect to acknowledge the god Eshu. Since these two friends work on adjacent fields, one day Eshu walks on the dividing line between their fields, wearing a cap that is black on one side and red (or white) on the other. He saunters between the fields, exchanging pleasantries with both men.

Afterwards, the two friends got to talking about the man with the cap, and fall to violent quarreling about the color of the man's hat, calling each other blind and crazy. The neighbors gather about, and then Eshu arrives and stops the fight. The friends explain their disagreement, and Eshu shows them the two-sided hat--all this to chastise the friends for not putting him first in their doings. The lesson of the tale is obvious, but just as interesting is where it places the god -- namely, moving along the seam between two different worldviews. In this position he can confuse communication; spotlight the ambiguity of information or Secular Knowledge; and play with people's perspectives to thereby lead mortals to temptation and possibly into tribulation. In one of his innumerable roles as a master of exchange, or crossed purposes, of crossed speech, he delights in contradictions. Where there is confusion or arguments, he is there. This Yoruba god also propels the narratives of jealousy and power from confusion by occupying certain privileged places where he gives ideas and information--not the whole story -- but just enough to make the story happen. At one point, Shango the thunder god asks him, "Why don't you speak straightforwardly?" "I never do," Eshu responds. "I like to keep people from thinking by confusing them."

Nevertheless, originally the 14th century English word "*Confuse*" (pour together; mix together; fail to distinguish) meant to defeat, frustrate; then throw into disorder; and later bewilder ('make to go thoroughly astray so as to wander'). All the things that can be confused are endless. For example, Confusion is present when all the parts are present except an essential part concerning the inner workings of the interrelationships (as a piece missing in a watch); or the obvious or the Base/Foundation is overlooked (as it being made of quicksand); or a part is suppressed by some covering (as occurs with the esoteric or hidden meanings in allegories) to make its true meaning too subtle to discern; or that which was already present is in a disguised form. Such situations may display as a paradox or as "impossible" to solve or as too confusing and frustrating to proceed.

Most remarkable is Ancient Africans' accurate Set Metaphor description of each human being's Brute Brain and its anti-Spiritual Element entities, whether rarely expressed or expressed as a Brute lifestyle. For the latter to occur it is essential for Brutes to disconnect from Actual Reality and then from Common Humanity so as to create an "Us" or Me" vs. "Them" or "You." By so doing, Brutes, primarily European males, see themselves as separate from, and enemies to, other human beings, especially those who are not like them. Brute methods embrace whatever conforms to the Seven Deadly Sins—pride (arrogance), covetousness (greed), lust, anger, gluttony, envy, and sloth (lazy) and the Fetters associated with them (e.g. "Me, Me" Individualism, hatred, fear, lies, and jealousy.

Just as Ancient Africans described for Set, Brutes' philosophy of life is based only on Material Realms and the elevation of material things over people. Featured are to get what they want by Kill/Take/Destroy means; be totally self-centered except for coming together to attack falsely perceived enemies; believe they are above societal rules; find "sick" in generating pain and suffering in others by first dehumanizing "Them" or "You" and treating them with no more regard than if they were flies needing to swatted; and believing "when you die, that's all there is." Brute ways of thinking and doing in designing certain scenarios are all for the intension of generating evil self-interest agendas in order for Brutes to gain unfair advantages while ensuring their victims have unfair disadvantages. Among themselves they play by a different set of rules which is about "anything goes," and fashion *Delusional Fear* (the feigning of being under attack as an excuse to Kill/Take/Destroy/Dominate/Oppress) in preparation to gain benefits that belong to others. Their Delusional Fear creation is done so as to deliberately seize the opportunity to stir up false survival situations as a justification for attacking victims when no such real situation is present.

EUROPEAN COURAGE: Europeans' earthly entrance 45,000 years ago was into an environment of Scarcity during the Ice Age. Out of this they developed Supernatural concepts centered on Kill/Take/Destroy/Dominate/Oppress Kill/Take/Destroy. The ultimate methods they used were brought about through the technological development of superior weapons for killing people. A fundamental difference between the Spiritual Elements derived Courage of African Tradition vs. the Supernatural Courage (man-made) of European tradition is that Supernatural Courage requires giving up who one really is--i.e. the power coming out of the Soul of ones Real Self--to then adopt standards fashioned by others. Because what is adopted is never a precise match with who one knew ones Real Self to be at birth and for sometime thereafter, the mis-match is a chronic source of inner turmoil--meaning one is never at peace and never happy. These + being disconnected from ones Real Self causes Spiritual Pain--the worse experience a human can have because nothing can relieve it except returning to ones Real Self. But that cannot occur because in European Manhood that would indicate one was weak and thus a coward.

For those who are not Satanists (the immune ones), it is problematic to have a Splintered Selfhood--wanting to do right but that would be in conflict with Supernatural rules which are anti-Spiritual Elements oriented. This automatically makes them cowards because they are not "man enough" to take a stand on their principles. Their Inferiority Complex places one on the negative side of the Manhood Thinker's Scale (fig. 22).

One form is that one has a "Broken" Selfhood Integrity and thereby does anti-Spiritual Element things--eventually, with most becoming Satanists. Another form comes by one allowing others to define who one is. Thus, they kow-tow to their racist leaders. Examples of this are seen in the block voting they do against anything President Obama proposes--and even if they have been on record proposing it and even if the public wants it. The threat to their political future is more important than "being a man." To try to convince themselves otherwise, they do foolish daredevil activities but that is not satisfying either.

Most Satanists are socialized so early into a Superiority Complex that they have no moral conscience. The deep sense of inferiority dates to the formations of the Collective Unconscious of much earlier times and their continued repressed fear that they cannot adequately compete with those they envy the most and have dedicated their lives to demeaning and/or "keeping them down" or "taking them down." So their Courage is geared to Kill/Take/Destroy activities and taking risks to cause as much pain and suffering for others as they can get away with. The "Winners" then compete among themselves in what is called "The Game" --to see who could acquire the most "Adult Toys." Here, the greedy use "any means necessary" (i.e. anti-Spiritual Elements) so as to conform with Satanist Rules Those who show any signs of weakness are automatic losers--things like any feminine traits (e.g. intuitions, caring about others). Winning brings fear type respect, status, power, and privilege--the most obvious symbol being that of Money, Possessions, and Wastefulness. The consequences of either the Scarcity or "The Game" philosophy makes for a Fear-Based Lifestyle in the pursuit of Materialism and, of course, necessitates Individualism--perhaps being friendly when it has advantages (like calling strangers by their first names--a very rude practice in Black Society) but not knowing how to be a friend. Yet, many Black youth imitate them to the detriment of all.

Aristotle (384-322 BC) put European Courage in perspective by saying: "The races that live in cold regions and those of Europe are full of courage and passion but somewhat lacking in skill and brainpower...." As stated by Europeans (as characterizes this discussion), European history and poetry is clear that their heroes who are cruel, violent, self-seeking, ruthless, intemperate, and unjust are never *Cowards* (Latin, cauda, tail), as when a dog, full of fear, runs away with its tail between its legs. Cowardice--to be drained of courage and undone by fear--is deemed to be weakness and weakness is to be avoided at all cost. In C13 Europe "Courage" appeared to imply bravery (a mastering of fear) and valor--no faltering or giving way--no despair in the face of almost hopeless odds--having the strength and stamina to achieve whatever they set their minds and will to do. One would not be a hero if one was not a man of courage. This is necessarily associated with being Cunning (the C16 European sense of 'skillfully deceitful'). Though being a Fear-based people, when called 'Fearless' it is not because nothing affrights them or turns their blood cold. Instead, Fear seizes them, as does anger, with all its bodily force. They are fearless only in the sense that they do not act afraid or fail to act, despite that *courage being without judgment*. Their courage is always equal to the peril sensed or felt, so that they can perform what must be done, as if they had no fear or pain or death. It is the sort of courage which goes with physical strength, with feats of endurance; and, as signified by the root-meaning of "Fortitude" (synonymous with Courage), it is a display of strength to sustain action, even when the flesh and blood can carry on no further. Such courage is a European concept of "Virtue"--manliness, the spirit, or strength of spirit, required to be a man.

The Ancient Brain might be thought of as equivalent to the African Tradition concept of the "Heart" with its good (Instinct), bad (Brute and thus acquired, like "hate validates my superiority), and intermediate (Omnibus) aspects. Though the "Heart" is "all about me,' its Instinct part pertains to self-preservation, as emphasized in the Spirituality of African Tradition. However, its Brute part is oriented to Ego related concepts of self-preservation, as in greedy pursuits within the context of Individualism, and with a total disregard for who is hurt or killed in the process. The weakness they so diligently run away from engulfs everything they do. They feel so personally weak in their Private Selfhoods that they need the GUN to give them power. What they do for each other is not about being humane but for the reason of "I need my fellows to help me survive whenever emergencies arrive and to further my greedy and evil pursuits." Their theme is Kill/Take/Destroy/Dominate. Such displays of *Philosophical Disarray* (not the same as psychiatric or psychological disorder because it is socialized) was the feature of the African mythological god Set (who Europeans adopted as fact and made into a 'factual' Satan). Brute Courage follows this pattern, as seen in racists or those politicians who play the "Reverse Robin-hood" role--i.e. take from the poor to give to the rich. Machiavelli said courage may improve the chances for success and it is success that counts.

For those desiring to live life within the confines of the Spiritual Elements it is vital to be clear that the Instinct part of the "Heart" heads in that direction while Brute Courage not only heads in the opposite direction but is totally disconnected and in another realm so that it is anti-Spiritual Elements. Failure to see this distinction can lead one to do the Brute under the mistaken concept that one is doing what is Right. Yet, the tools for cultivating the Instinct and Brute forms are the same. For example, Courage does not consist only in conquering fear and in with-holding the body from flight no matter what the risk of pain. It consists at least as much in steeling ones Will-Power, reinforcing its resolutions, and turning the mind relentlessly to seek or face what it deems to be "Right." Brute believe themselves to be just as right as do those who follow the Spiritual Elements (whom Brutes deem to be weak and therefore controlled). For these reasons, Brutes will never change and it is self-destructive to deal with them as "good people who have problems and will change if I do this or that." They are simply evil people.

"DARK" SIDE: As discussed (Chapter I), every human has the potential for the "Dark Side." Ancient African Sages were careful to lay out in their Spiritual literature the "Dark Side" of humans and, being of man-made nature the "Dark Side" has a wide range of manifestations. A "seed" idea for the term "Dark Side" came from the mindset of the god Set in African Spiritual Literature which remained within the world of his Lower Self fetters (e.g. greed or conceit) which are powered by receiving and not giving. As a result, this automatically interfered with the Love flow out of his Love Platter. This state of mind is filled with ones perceived personal power, completeness, and sufficiency apart from God. It is characterized by dealing with unreality in a deceptive manner and possessing fixed ideas in opposition to the truth (liar in wait). This delusional and ignorant mindset makes one vulnerable to more delusions and ignorance. For example, Seth gave gifts to others to help him obtain evil ends. In turn, Seth could be easily tricked by gifts that increased his possessions and appealed to this lecherous nature. Throughout history, a common approach of Brute Europeans' in taking over things of significance from Colored Peoples is to appear to be friendly while bearing gifts as preparation for using any means necessary to gain what is being silently sort. Whereas Ancient Africans said hateful thoughts and evil deeds came from ones ignorance of reality, Europeans tried to explain it by using the Devil--a distinction having a startling effect on an individual determining: "How shall I live?" Whereas the Greek 'diabolos' (*Devil*) means denouncer or calumniator, the Hebrew word "Satan" means "adversary" or "accuser." In the earliest sections of the Old Testament Satan is not an independent personage, nor even a maleficent being. Originally, Satan simply referred to an opponent appearing in black and not to a particular being. But subsequently Europeans generate concepts of Satan in all evil forms. Throughout European history people who possessed hateful thoughts and demonstrated evil deeds were thought to be possessed by demonic spirits, including the Devil. Around the 6th century BC Satan appears in the Old Testament as an individual angel, subordinate to God, and thereafter gradually becomes the source of all evil as a result of disbelieving in God and acknowledging no law except of man. Satan, evil, and dark (signifying misery, punishment, perdition or loss of the soul and hell) became the trio Europeans used to characterize the "Dark Side"--and with the justification of: "the "Devil made me do it." Still, the European ideas about Satan do not solve how evil got into the world--a world which God created and saw as 'very good."

Yet, despite looking up the term "dark side" in over 1000 books—including those related to occultism, magic, witchcraft, druids, fairies, sorcery, Satan, Valhalla, Valkyries, spirits, mythology as well as books on word origins, slang, and on euphemisms, and the like—not one mentioned it as such. A little bit of information was found on the internet. Nevertheless, European psychologists have said Satan's many consciousness forms include Egotism (with its self-opinionated and puffed up personality) and its opposite, self-depreciation. In Jungian psychology, the "Dark Side" is called the shadow or "shadow aspect" of the unconscious mind and consists of repressed weaknesses, shortcomings, limitations, irrationality, and proneness to Projection (turning a personal inferiority into a perceived moral deficiency in someone else). The European taste for the "Dark Side" is readily evident by looking at the titles of television, video, and movies dealing with Satan, wickedness, demons, and the like. In my view the Dark Side of humans is denotative of the *full range of "indifference," hatefulness, evilness, and sadism.* That this complex is socialized into European males in general is indicated in their "True History" since appearing on earth--and not the nonsense presented in school textbooks and in the media about who they are.

Dark Side (Supernatural): Brutes characterize the "Dark Side" of the Supernatural and their mindset oriented to it stems from "Awe" and "Fascination." Brutes choose that aspect of "*Awe*"--a C13 Old Icelandic word--containing ideas of fear (an emotion excited by threatening evil), fright (in actual presence of that which is terrible), pain, distress, terror (rendering one incapable of defense), dread or apprehension. This means that whereas flawed people do not completely match their way of living with the Spiritual Elements, Brutes are continually evolving away from the Spiritual Elements. Thus, they do everything the opposite of what Sages in any culture and of all ages know to be "Right." After European religious leaders developed the concepts of Hell and Satan, these Brutes created a specific religious cult called 'Satanism'--with Satan worshipped as the sovereign deity and thereby inverting all European Christian norms and ideologies. Satanism's purpose is to meet the specific psychological needs which are not met by other forms of religious worship and yet it shares with all other charismatic religious movements: (1) a codified shared supernatural belief system; (2) a high level of social cohesiveness; (3) strong influence over members by the group's behavioral norms; and (4) the imputation of charismatic or divine power to the group or its leadership. Satanism's Church ideology comprises six aspects and emphasizes: hedonistic gratification of worldly desires; the ceremonial use of magic for gaining personal power and manipulating others; the worship of Satan as a symbol of that which is religiously forbidden and heretical; the iconoclastic desire to free oneself from conformist social norms, expectations and institutional restraints; the millenariast (1000 years) belief in the overthrow of Christianity with the coming of a new world order; and the imputation of charismatic authority and magical power to the religious leader, or high priest.

So what is the mindset of those attracted to Satanism? The Brute I "Seed" that branches into its practices, is those who have been socialized from birth to believe they are "little gods"--an offshoot of Pythagorus' "Man is the measure of all things"--not God. By possessing extreme arrogance in not being controlled by any rules in their insatiable Greed pursuits by 'any means necessary' makes them "Human Cancers." The Brute II "Seed"--one of an inferiority complex--is characterized by a lack of the "5Ss"--safety, security, self-confidence, strength, and stability.' Historically, this has caused the afflicted to feel so alienated, anxious, and powerless as to be attracted to Satanism as a means of obtaining magical power and control over their destiny. In one sense there is a commonality of Satanism with any other fundamentalist religion, in that all provide to those people troubled by self-doubt and existential uncertainty desiring a well defined Belief system: (a) clear, vivid, unambiguous, and simple answers to the meaning of life for Believers and non-Believers; (b) instant community identity, and sense of communally derived self-worth provides relief from alienation and loneliness; (c) the emotional energy and excitement of cult religions induces euphoria, and gives members a feeling of power and vitality that counteracts tendencies to self-doubt and depression. The cause of the Brutes I and II "Seed" is the entering of the Dark Side of unreality as a result of going in anti-Spiritual Elements directions.

The push which starts the Dark Side" travel is from a mindset of Philosophical Disarray and its manifestations are not essentially psychological, although psychological problems join in along the way. But being unaware of the existence of the Spiritual Elements generates the delusion that an unknown 'something' has taken possession of a smaller or greater portion of the psyche and asserts its hateful and harmful existence undeterred by all of ones insight, reason, and energy. This, the misled say, proclaims the power of the unconscious over the conscious mind, the sovereign power of 'spirit possession.' The Brutes I and II "*Malevolent Seeds*" produce different Patterns along different routes through life but they end up at the same place and have the same "Tree" shape. Like any other gang fighting over "turf" that does not belong to either, Satanism concepts cause them to Fight, Kill, and Take whatever they deem to be "*Scarce Desirables*" while destroying everything good they encounter. as is heard by Brutes yelling: "we want our country [the USA] back."

DEATH: "Manhood" demands that European men control Nature, and by extension control women and minorities too. This is suppose to be the means to secure their existence and assuage the threat of death, of nothingness, of non-being. And a fear of non-being will always push one to invest more in ones current state of being. These ideas, particularly prominent in C13-C15 laid the basis for the modern, more personal feeling about the death of the self. This feeling betrays a violent attachment to life--a passion for being, an anxiety about not sufficiently being. Still from the C18 onward, it is the death of the other that is feared more than the death of the self (Garlick, *Men and Masculinities, 2003*)

DECEPTION "PAYLOAD" SUBTLE POWER: A most important thing which keeps people in the status quo, blocks peoples' progress, and keeps people from being Happy is the Bad Information, in the form of Religious Propaganda (spoken, written, or pictured), having misleading or a double-meaning. One way this is conveyed by Brutes is that it not necessarily be false but rather is an incomplete picture or out of context or the use of a connotation familiar to one group but foreign to the victims. Just as these tend to be deceiving (less concern for the truth), others are what "SEEMS" right, as when 90% of information is true but the other 10% is false but cannot be known unless the Receiver has an intimate knowledge of the subject. Such is particularly true about Black History written by Europeans. To elect not to verify what SEEMS right at its inception is to be carried deeper into the degrees of *Doubt*, a 13th century English word, meaning: "to be afraid of; dread; hesitate; fear; waiver between two possibilities. Doubt is associated with anxiety because it means one cannot trust ones own nature and that causes one to clutch and cling to things as well as to destroy what one cannot or is unable to possess. Such a mindset deepens Doubt with its added anxiety from clinging. Because a desire to be cared about as a person is a feature of human nature, the more mental turmoil one is in the more susceptible they are to the attractions and practices of Brutes. A reason Brutes can exert such a powerful influence is from ones human nature to have a preference for certainty, even if it is dismal, for that removes anxiety. Invariably, what Brutes offer is the extreme negative subdivision of Subtle which I call the *"Payload Subtle."* "Payload" is a 1925 aerospace military term referring to the explosive energy of the warhead of a missile or of the bomb load of an aircraft. Thus, *"Payload Subtle"* has four parts. First, its flaw is so subtle as for it to be viewed insignificant and therefore interpreted as it "SEEMS" right. *"SEEMS right"* means it is not actually right but one accepts it as so because one wants it to be that way or because one is too lazy to do the research or one is willing to accept "almost" as good enough to proceed as if it were truth. Second, its aspect of *"Tainting"*--is a 14th century term meaning to make unclean that which should be pure or spotless or unblemished--thus expressing the result of contamination of the wholesome. Third, it has an explosive effect on the Base/Foundation of something significant. That is like blowing up the bottom of a skyscraper building. Fourth, the consequence of that explosion is to institute a "Transition" into another plane of Thought, and typically of a destructive nature.

This combination carries the sense of a definite and distinct powerful entity that is so faint as to be barely discernible, as if it is hiding in a dark corner. A vignette for the "Payload Subtle" is the Big Bad Wolf con-artist in the story of "Little Red Riding Hood." It, like all sophisticated fallacies, looks good and frequently is very persuasive when first presented to ones common sense. In order for one to be influenced to let go of Certainty requires its boundaries be removed and a bridge formed to what "SEEMS" right. But, a feature is in it turning out to not make sense, a realization that comes only after one is on the wrong road and great mental entanglement damage is present. Brutes have always used Clever, Shrewd, and Deceptive fallacies in a beguiling subtle manner so that the deception is hard-to-seize with the mind. A "Payload Subtle" model during African American slavery was the captors' shrewd methods for controlling the exhausted Enslaved's minds and dictating the way they were to live. They instituted unimaginable cruelty to "kill their Spirits" (e.g. the courage to resist) as by chopping off body parts and other sadistic acts. The resultant mental Maafa (immeasurable catastrophe) generated so much fear and despair that they were beaten down spiritually, mentally, and physically. The resultant Confusion inside mental turmoil set the stage for *"Concept Switches"* to take hold in many of the Enslaved. One was an inability of many Enslaved to resist the Brute captors insidious system of "divide and conquer" -- segregating all things and people from each other and the whole. Next was to convert the Enslaved from their Certainty about the soundness of their African way of life over to rejecting it completely. The theme was the substituting of European illusion, delusional, and "trinket" information for the "treasure" knowledge of Ancient Africans. The idea then, as now, has always been to get victims to do "Broad Stroking" that enables a reversal of common sense, as by making the evil "SEEM" right.

DOMINATION: (Old French, ruling lord, master) refers to a relationship in which any "Thing" is in a position of 'control' over another.

HYPOCRISY: (false appearance of goodness, virtue) is a Greek word characterizing acting on the stage. In speaking to "religious" "Hypocritical Supernatural God Worshipping" European slavers, Fredrick Douglass (1817-1895) said: "You profess to believe that of one blood God made all nations of men to dwell on the face of all the earth—hath commanded all men, everywhere, to love one another—yet you notoriously hate (and glory in your hatred!) all men whose skins are not colored like your own." In C13 it expanded to embrace pretense, especially in religious matters. It is a form of dissociation, as when one asserts or believes in cooperation but behaves competitively; protects love but acts with hate; proclaims good-will but practices racism–all without being aware in part or in whole of ones inconsistency. Although the general agreement is that hypocrisy simulates through behavior and by a general line of conduct of certain ideals or moral character which are foreign to ones nature, there is a fear based type which I recently discovered that explains my observation of over 45 years of Black History research of never finding a European who gave the true and honorable history of Black People in print. Instead, these authors range from being overwhelming liars (the vast majority) to those on every rung of the ladder that approaches the Truth. I recall one author who got near the top rung and another who actually told the truth about Africans being the creators of a world-wide expression used today. I admire him for having the courage to say: "It is surely a major linguistic irony…derived from the lips of a minority [Black Africans] which most other Americans still prefer to associate as little as possible." Almost none will even mention Ancient Africans as such but rather refer to them as "the ancients who invented this or that" so as to imply they might have been European. Chances are the "almost honorable" European authors are not racially prejudiced but, by lacking the sufficient Character "Substance" and releasing only a certain amount of Courage out of fear of being isolated from their European society in-group.

"LAWS": The Ancient African Bible says *Laws* are statements of mathematical relations, order, or sequences of what arise out of the philosophical Base of the Cosmos--i.e. the Spiritual Elements, as seen in Nature or in Cosmic Spiritual Energy (the Spirit). They are objective (if not directly, then by scientific circumstantial evidence from their manifestations), universal, both personal and impersonal, invariable, unchanging, permanent, stationary, boundless, infinite (without limits), eternal (without beginning or end of time), and undefinable (without borders). Yet, they have different appearances under different conditions. Still, all are verifiable by how they are lived in Plant and Animal Kingdom life. This is why Ancient Africans had Certainty about fashioning and inferring Laws--a Certainty having nothing to do with today's comparable categories of Information, Beliefs, and Faith--since each has doubt at its core. When Religions rest on these as their Base, none can stand up under the scrutiny of Critical Thinking and its demands of Proof. Ancient African Religion used Nature's organization/interdependence as readily seen everywhere, in all real things. Hence, Cosmic Laws can explain natural forces regulating all natural events (i.e. changing realities) in the universe as well as those in all humans' biological makeup. These Principles (unchanging realities) can be intuitively (i.e. learn from ones Soul) perceived--and that is how one uses Laws of the Spiritual Elements to live a Ma'at life--not from moral notions extuited (learned from others).

What is appropriate in African Tradition is to use Laws, Principles, and Rules established in Spiritual Realms by mathematics to infer their counterparts in Material realms. To illustrate, the same Cosmic Laws governing all manifestations of Cosmic activity are inferred to operate in each human's integrated Selfhood. Here, ones Divine Consciousness and Will work as team members with ones Spirit (Energy/ Matter). This means the Self/Spirit is in charge and control of ones Selfhood (i.e. being responsible for and directing it). The Will is the action force for ones Divine Consciousness to be delivered to the Spirit. To observe this integration in ordered function and extract its abstract principles is to connect and unify events and other principles out of things. These, despite differing widely in form and external appearance, enable getting ones life in Spiritual Harmony or to maintain ones life in a state of well-being. This was the principle I used in practicing medicine because it connected the Spiritual and Material worlds so as to keep order and harmony physically, mentally, emotionally, and spiritually. "Picking and choosing" will not work. Nor will it work to start a self-improvement path using Laws, Rules, or Principles without first classifying them into their separate spiritual and secular components so as to have proper standards, guides, and filters. The European concepts of Laws are applicable in diverse subject matters and with such conflicts between and within definitions and subjects as to make "Law" an Umbrella Term lacking any agreed upon definition. By being ordained by an "authority(s)," Laws of humans are deemed to be a reliable set of rules and a set of directions which should be obeyed, can be disobeyed, and are subject to change. By disregarding the Spiritual, Europeans say philosophic thinking, by employing concepts or abstractions, can formulate principles or laws. Note that such thinking and the credibility of such sources and the degree of completeness of the items used by the sources are dependent upon the frailties of the human mind. Thus, they cannot be relied upon to make life-shaping and life-changing decisions. What is even worse is the presenting of these human-made "laws and principles" as what is "right" to the extent of being advocated as premises for reasoning about all events in ones life. European history is full of sham science which has 'verified' non-existent things by observation, experiment, and archeology. For example, during slavery, in order to separate Native Americans, African Americans, and Europeans on a "scientific" basis (a contradiction), White "scientific expert classifiers" reached into the insane part of their minds to come up with the concept of racial blood types--and there is no such thing!!!. Yet, they "proved" that in Negro-White interbreeding Mulattoes had 3/8ths to 5/8ths Negro blood; Quadroons, 1/4th Negro blood; and Octoroons, 1/8th or less Negro blood. And this became "law!"

POWER!—AFRICAN ("ME/WE") vs. EUROPEAN ("ME"): The Cosmic Life-Force ("air"; "breath") was called Ether (Africans)/Ra (Kamitic)—and tens of thousands of years later, Kundalini (Dravidians of India); Chi (Chinese); Universal Energy (Yogi); "Prana" (Buddhist); and Ki (Japanese). Ancient African Sages said Ether appeared first in the Subjective Realm's Ocean of Nun as an inactive Primordial Substance (God's androgynic protoplast)—the 'Oneness' foundation of potentiality from which all 'Things' emerge (the Path). Then it becomes imperceptibly and impalpably active upon entering the Metaphysical's Sublime Realm. Here, an illusory separation into types occurs. Despite their different "Thing" states, none can exist without the others—thus staying as a Cosmic Unity. African Sages said Type I Cosmic Life Force is non-Being which condenses to form Being—i.e. the quantum field which becomes Matter. Type II flows 'everywhere' as Spiritual Energy, motion, change, spirit. Type III is within a human's original nature as *Personal Power*—circulating inside the body as complementary opposite displays of expression and reception—regulating all bodily functions and protective systems + manifesting in activities of daily living (e.g. Compassion).

Type IV is Personal Power that self-reliantly and independently gets done ones own outcomes or goals and without being influenced by others. These Isolated Individualists (of which I am one) cultivate such high levels of personal power as to not need to rely on other people to thrive or to be happy in life. A potential 'down side' is that despite being 'ME/WE' oriented, they could be less inclined to spend extra effort to individuate and make sense of others--instead simply relying on automatic cognition to form stereotyped Classes. Since the 'ME' has freedom from other people's control, it can meet all people as equals. Type V is Personal Power applied socially for guidance of youth and of willing adults + for group achievements.

For Europeans, Type VI power is used for active, expressive, and assertive purposes in attempts to control Nature and people + acquire riches, prestige, political influence, and social status—all done by the GUN. Such is applied as a means to an end but Ether, by being centered only in the present, is absent in these actions--and that generates conflict. When the intent of ones actions is only for 'ME,' Ether is also absent since it cannot connect with the 'WE' of the Cosmic Organism. Type VII is Social Power--the ability of one or a group to influence others and make them do things they would not otherwise do as, for example, the police power over citizens. Types VI and VII operate out of "Air Castle" Supernatural animalistic rules which ignore Spiritual morals.

The 'big picture' of Types III, IV, and V Spiritual Power is the "ME/WE" components of responsibility and self-interest—manifesting as *Interlocking Rings that provide a common benefit but with different effects.* This means every 'ME' act is intended to blend with or encounter the 'WE' in its separate otherness + enhance the 'WE' as part of oneself. Here, Ether flows out of 'ME' and then, in boomerang fashion, returns so as to create an intermingling of 'ME' and 'WE'. The consequence is a "Lifting of WE while ME is Climbing". Rather than being in the act itself, *ones success is in the Intent of an action,* for out of that comes the flow of Ether. To elaborate, the experience of mystical Compassion (sharing the same Spiritual Space) occurs when 'ME' sends a Cosmic enhancing Intent towards 'WE'. That causes ones Personal Power to encounter and interfuse with the 'WE' at a Primordial Substance (Ocean of Nun) plane of existence--an experience of Human Perfection called *Compassion.* This means that by inward intuiting of ones 'Self' (Divine Consciousness) so as to experience ones own true nature of "*Self-so-ness,*" one has harmonized ones body, mind, and spirit with ones Personal Power and thus become intimate with the Cosmic Organism. This self-induced Cosmic Unity is what Ancient Africans termed "*Knowing Thyself*"—a primordial Experience of a human's ultimate attainment. It requires remaining in ones Spiritual Elements and evolving, in line with ones Talent, out of them. Human Perfection is reached by shedding the "Cloud" covering what one already has. Such Unlearns and discards all false acquisitions of being separate from all else in the Cosmos--using a "no-mind" state in total quietness—no thinking--no striving to gain credit or glory—no clinging to anything. *All perfect living movements unfold spontaneously.* [Stensrud, J. Humanistic Psychology, 1979 ; Lammers, *Psychological Science, 2009*]

RENAMING: Historically, Europeans have stolen Africans intellectual knowledge and renamed what they could not away from Africa. To illustrate, the European concept: "*You've got to name it to claim it*" has been and continues to be used to steal Black history (among others). Its reason is sort of explained in the Encyclopaedia Britannica (1992, p 567): "*...men have seen in the ability to name an ability to control or to possess....*" They defined "*naming*" as applying a word to pick out and refer to a fellow human being, an animal, an object, or a class of such beings or objects. Renaming was done to Africa itself—its original name being "Alkebu-Lan." All Enslaved Africans were renamed, which contributed to them being Self-Unknowing. Renaming was done to all that was sacred to Amerindians for at 10,000 years as, for example Mount Mckinley in Alaska for the American president who had never been to Alaska.

"RULES": In the 1960s, after coming out of Harlem, New York's Rosco's "Chicken and Waffles" restaurant around 2:00 am, a tall lanky Black man, "high" on life, walked up and said: "hey man, what it is, is what it is!" and "every thing is every thing!" Though immediately realizing both to be profound, it took me years to realize their deeper meanings. In African Tradition, what any Cosmic thing is when coming into existence consists of the Spiritual Elements. There are countless numbers of factors going on simultaneously to make any one Cosmic thing appear and none of those factors follow any rules of which the human mind can grasp. So any one who says: "this is the rule for how that Cosmic thing came into being" is foolishly stupid and those who use it to control people's minds are dangerous and evil. It SEEMS right to say how a woman got pregnant--which is a Spiritual event--but it is ridiculous ignorance when made into "do's" and dont's" Rules. Those ignorant ones have no idea about all of the Cosmic variables involved in getting pregnant. All humans can know of the Spiritual is: "what it is, is what it is!" Any other "authority" opinion or just because "everybody" agrees does not make it right. Ask: "*How do you know that*!"--and Listen.

Those who disbelieve in the Spiritual Realm (beyond paying "lip service") and instead believe all they see is physically and "mechanically" explainable, simply have information (not real) that crams the Immaterial (Spiritual) into the Tangible (Material). Since this does not "ring true" in wise people's Soul's--is not Natural, is not Truth, is not Real, and is not Unconditional Love based--Rules are essential in order to control the people's positions. They get people to believe in their SEEMS right information by demonstrating how a ruler can measure things with special accuracy and therefore with 'Certainty.' But let us critically look at the meanings of these words. The C13 English word "*Rule*" (straight stick, graduated strip for measuring, called a "Ruler") originally meant a standard believed to have special accuracy or certainty for judging other things by it. The way Europeans define *Accurate* (a caring and conforming to representation of a standard) is within the family of words containing Correct, Definite, Exact, Precise, and Certain--all denoting 'absolute' conformity to some external standard--contradictions! By Europeans ignoring the Metaphysical--apart from ignoring the Spiritual--means they cannot understand that different Intangible and Tangible planes of existence have different Rules on the same subject. Thus, the "Accurate" conforming to "one size fits all" Rules is advocated and driven by an intense desire for the power that comes from controlling people's minds--not what is right. Evil authorities purposely make those Rules confusing so as to give them more power to use those Rules to their own unfair advantage and apply special ones to dominate by unfair disadvantages--all under the pretext of "Justice"--but actually a biased man-made justice designed to bound personal freedom for purposes of arrogant pride. [Series Ref: Bailey, Teaching Black Youth] Rules can be classified into Good, Necessary, Important, Bad, Ignorant, Evil, Indifferent, Useless, Out of Date, Workable Under Certain Circumstances, Self-Deception, and Miscellaneous. Since the Spiritual Elements are boundless, Rules imposed by 'authorities' do not apply in African Tradition to Right Living. Instead, socialization of children is based upon God-inferred *Guidelines.* Very Ancient Africans derived them from astro-mathematical studies applied to the Lucky Stars. To find one was to be shown what to "Know" because its message came from the Substance of God. Proper Guidelines emerge out of the Spiritual Elements. For example, the "Moral Right" is the "what it is" which lays out the "what it does," as opposed to the "how it appears. If any of these are flawed, then it is not "Right." The *child-rearing key* is to use Critical Thinking (CT) for how to stay within the context of the Spiritual Elements--"where every thing is every thing." Then ones inclinations derived from them serve as Standards, Guides, and Filters for "Right" living. Here, there are no rules except to not step outside their "what it is." Out of these same Spiritual Elements spring "Rules" for living in daily life. Two of mine as a boy were to strive to be better in something every day so I could cheer this small success "just for me" + never do harm intentionally to anyone. I applied certain Workable Rules *Under Certain Circumstances.* For example, the Golden Rule of "do unto others as you would have them do unto you" seemed to me to be an excuse for not having to do CT. As a physician, I learned that modifications had to be made to fit the needs, circumstances, and taste for different patients who otherwise had the same problem and needed the same solution.

Important Rules are those justified by a need to properly guide certain people. One example pertains to children. Children require Guidelines and Rules in the way the toddler--who stopped dancing naturally upon becoming self-conscious from being observed--needs them to organize what it takes to naturally flow again. This achievement is a human counterpart of ones birth gift state of Spiritual Boundlessness for "Right Living." Another example applies to Society. Human life is filled with conflicts to such an extent that its frequency is carried over to English words used practically every time something is spoken or written. Examples: the word "*is*"--signifying the idea of being or existence as well as the words "*not*" and the word pairs 'all/none' and "*either/or*"--each signify ideas of opposition. These and antithetical pairs (e.g. good/evil, life/death, war/peace) are of a nature that they exclude one another. As a result, many Rules and Laws are fashioned to regulate people's thinking and behaviors. *Societal Rules* used to govern behaviors are assessed as proper, improper, or evil. Though presented as of a "one size fits all" nature, what makes them improper or even evil is how they are applied by biased or prejudiced people. The Poor, who are historically "beaten down" by the "System's" application of inhumane Rules, are further placed into a disadvantage because they are not in keeping with the reality of their experiences. Such Rules block their rise out of poverty + make it hard to live. Other rules (e.g. in the legal/criminal system) are oppositional for what it takes to survive day to day, necessitating them doing what works. Most accept imposed rules because of believing there is nothing else they can do; because following those Rules relieves them of the responsibility for having to think; and because Rules justify bad results.

Self-Deception Rules from Ignorance occur because human's intelligence is mainly a linear (i.e. in lines) scanning system of ones conscious attention--like flashing a light across a room. The self-deception comes from regarding what one extracted out of that flash as the basis of all there is to know about what is in that room. Yet, actually the essences of everything in reality are occurring in that room all at once--a happening with which the human mind cannot deal. Still, this does not stop certain 'authorities' from considering what they know out of the flash of light to be all that is needed, and thereby present this as the Truth. To the naïve, such bad information SEEMS right. *Evil-Deceptive Rules* apply when bad information is done to put oneself at an unfair advantage and ones victims at an unfair disadvantage. Its intent is to place a cloud over people's inner mental or Soul "sunlight" so as to take them away from who they really are. jabaileymd.com

SEEMS RIGHT: This is a powerful tool of deception used to subtly seize control of people's minds and gently guide them far, far from the Truth without them being aware of it. One type is SEEMS OKAY— meaning people will make acceptable promises they do not intend to keep: "If you give me this, you will get twice as much tomorrow". Although that SEEMS OKAY, tomorrow never comes. Another type is best illustrated. African Tradition only uses "Absolute" and "Certain" for the Spiritual since they have no other application. To use them in a Material World sense is to put boundaries on them. For one to accept boundaries on the Spiritual concepts' unchanging nature as "Close Enough," or "Almost" or SEEMingly okay for application into the realm of the Material realm (and its ever changing nature) takes one off the Spiritual Elements track. For Afrocentric people this means they first must accept the Spiritual's unchanging principles as being equal to the constantly changing/unstable nature of the Material. Second, its flawed reverse applies--i.e. equating the ever changing Material aspects into the Spiritual's unchanging realm. Each generates Thoughtful confusion and both so compound the confusion that the confused look to the people causing the confusion for the deceptive solutions out of it. The Deceiver's solutions take gullible audiences further away from reality, making it easier to accept more "far out" SEEMS right concepts. That is what enabled the definition of "Rule" to be seen in the context of a Standard. As a result, "Rule" expanded into the sense of "an autocratically determined pattern for governing procedures or conduct by laying down laws to which others are bound"--i.e. prescribed to govern human behavior. Note that the "Standard" to which "Rule" applies is man-made--and thus subject to all the frailties of the human mind--and particularly evil ones.

SUMMARY

The following considered comments are the result of my lifetime of personal observations; education from talking with tens of thousands of my European patients in my Orthopaedic Surgical practice; personal and vicarious racial experiences; intense research for 50 years in both European and Black People's literature; and Reflection. The model of Manliness was exhibited by pre-colonial Africans and Amerindians (e.g. the Iroquois) among whom theft and other crimes were apparently so infrequent that there were no rules for punishment. Also, both societies always kept a promise, no matter what the consequence to oneself because that was on par with Instincts (which express the will of God). Also in African and Amerindian cultures the chieftain's office was not hereditary; usually a man's successor was of his own family; and each of their community's was a nation in itself, with its own lands clearly bounded by treaty with its neighbors but no one owned the land. Peace among both societies was rarely broken by battles and when present, they were of a mild nature and quickly settled without lasting animosity. All of this was in marked contrast to European tradition and that is the basis for the profound distrust members of the African diaspora and Amerindians have for Europeans.

European "Manhood" is shown only by "the GUN"—an eagerness to intimidate, disable, and kill anyone of no interest to them. This type of "Superiority Courage" is backed up by being able to 'hide' under their "Network's" wing—and "Network" that came to power behind the GUN and to thereby control the significant institutions of the world. Because Brute European males deny being descendants of Primitive Africans, in spite of European geneticists saying they are, means they are Self-Unknown--having no idea who they are—and having no connection with the Collective Unconscious out of which they arose. Thus, this understanding of the precariousness of Europeans' "Manhood" helps explain their self-hate, feelings of inferiority without the GUN, their envy of real Manliness cultures, their projecting of their "Dark Side" on to those they so Envy, and their illogical, irrational, or excessive aggression arising from seemingly trivial provocations. Immediate proximal causes of male aggression are often tied to broader concerns with social status and self-worth.

Thus, European males' options are to remain in that Self-Unknown and perpetually confused state or assume an Inferiority Complex or embrace a Superiority Complex. Each of these are in Mild, Slight, Moderate, and Extreme degrees. The most severely affected with an Inferiority Complex commit suicide—either directly or in a mass murder to be killed by the police. All others adopt a "Bully" type of 'superiority'--an "I know and you don't" arrogance--and "the rules do not apply to me and only to you to do as I say do" attitudes. Still, these "little gods" are never without the GUN and their like-kind "Network's Wing" to represent the power of the façade behind their 'superiority' claim. I have never seen a White man, by himself, challenge a Black man of equal physique. Warriors, the Religious, and the "Philosophers" all share this pattern. This, as with today's police brutality against non-Whites, help account for why Euro-Americans are so accepting of criminal behavior committed by other Euro-Americans. Some are socialized to believe they are "little gods" and their displays have been similar historically. One example was the Medieval Knights (who converted from an Inferiority Complex to a Superiority Complex. Another example was out of the Nobility ("those who fight")--whence came the expression *Noblesse Oblige*. This carried the rather condescending implication that if one has had the good fortune to be born into the upper reaches of society, one has a duty, in a Supernatural sense, to always behave honorably and with generosity of a charity nature to those who pray and to those who work. It was from both the Nobility and the Medieval Knights who formed the Renaissance "Gentlemen". They started the African slave trade--became "Southern Gentlemen" in the New World--and formed the USA constitution and federal government of today.

Despite what Black People have always hoped for and expect, Satanist Europeans or even Moderate Brutes will never become "enlightened" and do the right thing because their "sick" pleasure in life comes from Indifferent/Hate/Evil/Sadism displays that make people suffer. To this they are addicted.

CHAPTER V

ENSLAVEMENT TURNS MINDS
"INSIDE-OUT"

AFRICAN AMERICAN SLAVERY

Allow me to give an orientation to the subject of the preparation for African American slavery which I call the SOBMER Process—an acronym for a Source, an Origin, a Beginning, a Middle, an End, and a Result. This is a way to provide a crude 'stepping stone' order through an extremely complex subject, made even more difficult since at each step multiple things were/are going on at the same time. Ingredients for its order started when I was a USA Military Captain in charge of the Outpatient Department for 10,000 troops at Clark Air Force Base in the Philippines. There as well as in my Orthopaedic Surgical, Orthopaedic Medicine, and Orthopaedic Genetics practice over a 45 year period, I saw as many patients as would fill the Rose Bowl Stadium. What stood out in dealing with any patient's massive and complex medical problems--and transferrable to the subject of Black-On-Black Violence--are the four *Causes--Pre-existing, Pre-disposing, Precipitating, and Immediate*--related to any disease/disability process. The disharmonious Source(s) and Causes lead to a *Beginning, Middle, End/Ending, and Result*—each productive of plentiful Consequences.

"SOBMER" PROCESS OVERVIEW: The reason for the following overview is that the "SOBMER" process is the single best "skeleton" mental tool for a crude understanding of what has led to struggling Black People—where they came from to where they are, to the way they are, and to why they are so today. Amazingly, the Source of today's Results of African American slavery was written over 10,000 years ago in the Ancient African Bible mythological saga of Ausar (Osiris). Because of the Brute Brain mindset of Set, Ausar's brother, Osiris was tricked and captured by malevolent forces; chopped up (characteristic of Satanists); placed in a casket; transported down river to the sea, then across it in a wooden prison; came to live as a pillar (tamarisk tree) and then supported an alien kingdom. This same pattern is what happened to free Africans in Africa.

Predisposing Cause(s) lay the foundation for a disease process to gain a foothold in ones body. As the first disease risk factors, they pave a way for a disease to occur within ones Selfhood. *Precipitating Causes* enhance the Predisposing Cause(s) by cultivating or maintaining the disease risk factors. The *Immediate Cause* is the agent instigating without delay--and with nothing in between it and the disease process. As with the *Beginning* of a physical body disease (from some bad germ going through various Cause stages) converting patients from normal to abnormal, a *Metaphysical Mindset Disease* (as from not using Spiritual Elements ingredients) does that also. Both result from an Immediate Cause being the match flame which lit a stick of dynamite and that explosion resulted in adverse evolving clinical manifestations. The disease's *Middle* course is whatever conditions the explosion caused inside ones Selfhood. Starting in slavery and continuing to the present, the Satanists' mindsets, actions, and goals—symbolized as a "Disaster Star"--has been to fashion Ideal Slaves. Enslavement itself shatters awareness of ones own Selfhood Greatness--a humanity degradation associated with the loss of ones sense of the "5Ss."

The "Halo" effects of this Disaster Star on victims are characterized by the features inside such words as "*Turbulence*" (troubled, tumbling, erratic, chaotic, confused). The driving force of human generated violence is a whirl of uncontrolled and unnatural emotions which, of course, is a reflection of the state of that human's mindset. Not only was this the intention of Satanists but their victim "beat down" practices were of such a nature as to burn this evilness into the Selfhoods of Black People "forever." Most affected have been victims in such overwhelming Despair as to find no more fight for retaliation now or in the future--to possess so much loss of Courage as to be docile "forever"--and to have minds so "Inside-Out" as to not speak for the fallen and disabled, or even themselves.

Struggling Black People's Metaphysical Disease of Despair has no *End* in sight, meaning they are still in the Middle of the process. What prevents the process of heading to "the End" is those with "*Inside-Out*" mindsets--i.e. minds controlled by the Satanists to such an extent as to lack an Instinct for Survival, Self-Protection, and Self-Preservation. They block their own passageways to healing by fighting those attempting to free them; to even help them out of the status quo; while voluntarily advocating the dictates of the enslavers/today's Satanists and oppressors for fellow Black People to follow. Such "Inside-Out" mindsets are from an assortment of destructive Brain/Mind reactions--e.g. an organic brain disorder, a philosophical Disarray; a psychiatric or psychological problem; an Icon fantasy or distorted perception; and/or from a sense of helplessness causing Supernatural Bonding with Satanist Europeans. Or, the Cause may be from an actual situation involving survival, self-protection, or self-preservation and knowing nothing else to do.

The *Effects* on most Black Americans is a *Maafa*--(Kiswahili for The Great Disaster on the order of an immeasurable catastrophe--which is far, far worse than a Holocaust (etymologically, a 'complete burning'). Superseding the devastation of crime against humanity and the Selfhood pain and suffering--its spiritual, mental, social, financial, and Selfhood residual effects are on different planes of existence, and typically involving multiple planes for those struggling the most. The harshness of the victims' lives urge them into such Consequences as Escapes at every opportunity. That becomes an obsession so as to avoid coming face-to-face with the serious trials, tribulations, and serious business of their lives. A Maafa makes one self-absorbed and struggling to find any degree of the "5Ss"--safety, security, self-confidence, strength, and stability. By such a Maafa induced mindset operating inside a "bottomless" pit and with no one showing them the way out prevents ones visualization for formulating solutions to rise out of ones various forms of poverty. As a result, struggling Black People experience every conceivable type of Poverty—the Result.

MENTAL HEALTH OF ANCIENT AFRICANS: The mindsets of our Ancient African Ancestors were in excellent physical, psychological, philosophical, and Spiritual Selfhood health. By them being intensely Spiritually oriented meant each lived life out of a *Spiritual Energy Package* of dedication, commitment, loyalty, determination, persistence, and perseverance--each urging them to move 'straight ahead' to their Mission in life despite losses, lacks, and obstacles. Each never considered "giving up"--each one always doing ones best--each volunteered Selfless Service--and having good behaviors and good relations with ones fellow humans, Nature, and God. One person's problem was everyone's problem. Their Spiritual Energy was bubbling over with "Aliveness" (not excitement), Curiosity, and Creativity--always *looking for something new and better to improve and enjoy their lives.* Their Free Minds urged them toward the ultimate goal of reaching the Heaven Afterlife, as seen in the whole purpose of Egyptians tombs. Hence, as honorable people, they lived by virtuous character in striving for wisdom to make all of this happen. Ancient Africans were the only ones around the Mediterranean "pond" to hold a happy view of death. Such came from their "Aliveness"--a spontaneous enjoyable experience of growing from the inside out. "Aliveness"--by not necessarily supplying a sense of pleasure, was so fulfilling as to trump being excited.

However, acceptance of all humans as good until proven otherwise was their downfall. Pre-existing conditions which Pre-disposed to African "Take Down" and African American "Black-on-Black Violence were several things. A major reason which led to the "Take Down" was Africans Curiosity and Eagerness *to learn every little detail* about how to reach the Heaven Afterlife. That eagerness turned out to be a "*Double-Edged Sword*". One side cut so as to make them rulers of the world. The other side cut to make them susceptible to their "Take Down" by Satanists. With respect to Black-On-Black Violence, the long history of Europeans associating the color black with dirtiness and white with purity persisted on into the Renaissance. However, otherwise early English attitudes toward Africans were on par with their attitudes toward European peasant classes. Prior to preparation for African American slavery the British had enslaved the Irish for a time and both Irish and British peasants were viewed as "lesser breeds." In the Cape of South Africa, a large proportion of Slaves were imported from East Asia, not Africa. At that time Africans, deemed to be exotic and primitive, were classified as "other" by Europeans—initially not based solely on skin color but rather a whole set of additional factors including language, region, and religion. Furthermore, there was no mention of race or skin color in debates on who was and who was not eligible for slavery.

Portuguese, Spanish, Dutch, and English colonial elites made no distinctions based on skin color (or any other supposed racial criteria) as to whether those in Ireland, South America, Africa, South East Asia, or North America were fit for enslavement. In African history, up to the point of being introduced to Europeans, they had encountered no IHES mindset people. Unknown to them was Europeans trail of for Violence as a warring people, intensely interested in greedily flourishing in the "here and now" by any Kill/Take/Destroy means necessary. Chances are that Ancient Africans were aware of Slavery and there is great controversy that they had mild forms themselves. I have found no evidence of this and the propaganda about Egyptian enslavement of the Jews has been debunked. Nevertheless, there has never been known to exist in any other cultures the far past extreme forms of slavery historically instituted by Europeans. Still, various slave trades have shown a rather exceptional persistence in world history, particularly after C4 AD.

SOURCES OF SLAVERY

The Source of Enslavement of Africans came out of the Brute Brains of Europeans dating to their primitive origins—Brains whose nature expressed the Indifference/Hate/Evil/Sadism (IHES) Complex. This has evolved, in my estimate, to Satanists accounting for 40% of Europeans who, in turn, set the rules for 50% of the European people. The remaining 10% of Europeans are reasonably mentally healthy and good people but they are difficult to distinguish because of the deception used by the other 90%. Still, the 10% benefit from the racists actions of the Satanists 40%, as do the 50%. Of fundamental importance is that no Europeans or Black People have ever been taught the Truth!

EUROPEAN RICH MEN'S "GAME" OF SLAVERY: European male have an ever alert Consciousness scanning to be rich, to keep from losing even a tiny bit of riches, and to display Narcissism (self-grandiosity in fantasy with an excessive need for admiration). *Numinous Personalities* who are successful in the Material world because they have developed certain approaches, methods, techniques within special circumstances. But their ambition is to achieve a status state where others consider them as having the majestic presence of the Supernatural "*Numinous*" Power. "*Status*" (standing, state, condition) is built on the military hierarchy of the

Supernatural where the wicked are in command (fig. 2, 3, 4, 5, 8). Such is modeled by the European Legal System and the European social system—the legal and social relation of an individual to the rest of the community. This has reference to being distinguished in political and network rankings whereby the higher the placement the higher the honor bestowed on the individual regarding rights, duties, capacities, and respect. In short, they are devoted to being seen as "Larger than Life" whereby one can imagine that the whole universe exists only for them as individuals--and there is no upper limit. Thus, they can never get Enough and are therefore never happy. Despite lacking actual physical danger, there are a host of fears and associated reactions to imagined threats to ones self-esteem. Fear *of not winning* fairly against victim competitors or in self-created competitions means "the rules are that there are no rules" and that invites exciting battles--battles called, among the richest Europeans, "*The Game*". The winner of "The Game" is "he who accumulates the most adult toys."

The billionaires clamoring to make more and more--even by doing as little for their employees as possible--do so for Status (way of standing, condition, position). Their greed has nothing to do with supplying what it takes to be happy because to have a "bottomless pit" for an unknown need can never make anyone happy. Neither can stepping on people or keeping a foot on people's throats while they are beaten down. So, Status is a concept that is "Larger than Life"--a phrase characterizing the setting of the Supernatural Larger than Life results in a sudden loss of all meaning which makes personal preoccupations seem trivial. By thus being the best of the superlatives, Icons, when compared to ordinary life, are deemed to be "*Larger than life*" because their power radiates everywhere. The "*Excitement is in the chase*". By being bearers of special powers which make them worthy of being venerated by Supernatural leaders and "Troops"—a veneration that strives to be feared rather than loved. The European "Gentlemen's" free use of every dishonorable, amoral, and immoral measure imaginable to mankind was so admired by other Europeans that these aspects of "The Game" trickled down to the masses of people who imitated the superficiality with the accoutrements of dress, possessions, and partying so as to appear rich. Getting involved in the African slave trade was a tremendous opportunity to acquire material possessions.

BACKGROUND TO AFRICAN AMERICAN SLAVERY: Preparation for African American slavery was the combined efforts of European "Air Castle" Warriors, Religious leaders, and Para-Logic thinkers—a preparation arising out of the origin of European racism. A significant historical moment occurred when the Persian prophet Mani (Manichaeus), founder of C3 AD Manichaean religion, proceeded to structure a universal religion, stressing opposing forces of light and dark—coeternal but independent. Mani was heavily influenced by the Ancient Persian doctrine (C12 BC) of incessant warfare between light (good) and dark (evil), as supposedly occurred in ones soul. The basic idea was of goodness and Light exciting envy, greed, and hate in Darkness and provoking it to attack the Light. The Ruler of the Dark (Satan) invaded the Light, which was defenseless because Goodness had rendered Light quiet and peaceful. Therefore, the Ruler of Light--named the Father of Greatness--called in other forms of Beings to combat Satan, the "Dark". He believed his mission was to discover the true meaning and significance present in all things so as to avoid further contamination of the light and promote its release from its mixture with the darkness. Thus, he took partial truths or religious revelations--especially those of Ancient Egyptians (Coptics), Zoroaster, Buddha, and Jesus--and integrated them into his misguided version of "The Truth." Settling on predominantly Egyptian religion concepts--especially the Egyptian Myth of Creation (i.e. God emerged from the chaos of darkness and created things), Mani's misinterpretations were many. First, his reasoning, fundamentally flawed by accepting the Ancient African

Bible's metaphors as facts (e.g. the divine Potter), was that since the materials God brought out of the darkness produced the earth, and dust from that earth gave rise to humans, both the earth and humans must lack goodness. Second, as a result, Mani wrongly believed and taught there are two opposing, autonomous, and distinct forces in the Cosmos—forces of good (Light occupying most of the Cosmos) and forces of evil (Dark relegated to one of its corners).

Third, a fundamental point he failed to understand or consider was those Very Ancient Africans' teachings that all Dualities (pairs of natural opposites like light/dark) must obey Binary Laws, as when you look, you must see; when you nibble, you must taste--or to know light there must be dark and to know dark there must be light because light and dark are complementary equals (i.e. the original Law of Opposites concept now known as Yin/Yang). Fourth, apparently he disregarded Africans saying the universe is said made of Dark Matter—matter from which light cannot be detected from the light it emits or fails to emit and yet, though labeled as evil by his assessment, both Dark and Matter are essential for the light to which his dogma clings. Fifth, nor was he aware that the Sanskit word *Matter* goes back to the black hole of the Magna Mater, the Great Black Mother Goddess herself. Sixth, Mani wrongly assumed the Sublime Good generated from God's love was opposite to hate and evil. He did not understand they are on different planes of existence that do not intersect. From having entirely different natures, love and evil operate under different laws and cannot be a blending of the two sides of a coin, as occurs in Yin/Yang. Here again, Mani attributed love and goodness to light and hate and badness to the dark—hence the present day concept of the "Dark Side." Seven, Mani believed and taught his own Supernatural story. For example, the Elect, and the mass of adherents—the Hearers or Soldiers—were allowed to live under less rigorous rules than other followers. Correspondingly there is a difference in their destiny after death. The Elect pass at once to the Paradise of Light, but the Soldiers must return to the world and its terrors until their light is freed. Outgroups—the sinners—are doomed to remain in Evil's power.

Part of Mani's mythological story is that Darkness produced Adam and Eve and then drew on the concept of Satan, a Supernatural force opposed to life. Satan first appears in C6 BC as an OT angel, subordinate to God. The primitive European Christian Church—holding firmly to the belief of a satanic kingdom of darkness opposed to Christ's kingdom of light, assumed the existence of the Devil as an unquestionable fact--thereafter considering "black"/"dark" the same and related to ignorance/evil. In the OT Book of Wisdom (2:24) this devil seduced Eve, where it is said that through the Devil the necessity of death has come into the world. The point: Eve was more subservient to the demons and served as their instrument for the seduction of Adam. Since the Persian prophet Mani's point was that Light should destroy Dark, the job of men was to aid the light and conquer and control the dark. Mani, despite confusing Ancient Egyptians' concepts about it of untold magnitude, had considerable influence on St. Augustine (AD 354-430), a follower of Mani.

He used these misinterpretations of Mani's concepts to influence the development of European Christianity and European male's philosophy of life—both for independent reasons serving a common cause—the preparation for the African slave trade. For both, what was so satisfying about Mani's concepts was the viewing of the world as involved in conflicting forces--one good (as Renaissance "gentlemen" and the European Christian religion declared themselves to be) and the other evil (referring to anyone not resembling them). These concepts were eagerly embraced by the evil and sadistic European Renaissance "gentlemen" needed Mani's concepts to justify the brute actions associated with materialistic gains and prestige from playing "The Game" related to "he who has the most adult toys wins." This religious justification for the enslavement of Africans they were planning made it possible to pursue their self-interest with the blessing of the church. Hence, with clear conscious they were free to fight on land and sea to conquer evil (mainly Colored Peoples of the world) by Kill/Take/Destroy methods using their newly acquired GUNS.

These concepts--calling for genocide, giving justification for slavery, subordinating women (because they were not European males), and other conflicts with the Ancient African Bible—were given authority by their Supernatural God. Such Aryan concepts were checkered throughout the King James Bible (1611), which replaced all competing European Bibles. Yet, much of the original Ancient African Bible principles were retained so as to make it acceptable to the Enslaved brought to the Americas in 1619. The combination of African Principles served as the "oil" to grease the injection of Aryan concepts into the "beaten down" minds of the Enslaved. In other words, European Christianity was effective in bringing uniformity to controlling the minds of Enslaved Africans brought to the Americas and changing them from "Knowing the Spiritual God" over to having Belief/Faith in the European Supernatural God. [Ref: Bailey, American Crime]. Meanwhile, Mani's concepts of fighting "Darkness/Blackness" were instrumental in programming the European male mind into a conditioned reflex—displayed ever since as them killing or destroying Black males because of the "Dark Side" within these European males. A powerful preparatory programming method came from the pre-C16 Oxford English Dictionary degradation of "black": 'Deeply stained with dirt, soiled, dirty, foul …Having dark or deadly purposes….' It was an easy next step to symbolize these with Black Africans in social situations, class, caste, and religious heathenism as a means of justifying invading Africa to take their riches and to enslave the people. Stereotypic layers were/are added to this in all areas of life dominated by Europeans—in the schools, churches, media, legal system, marketplace, prison system. An example of a European Egyptologist bad information being advertised all over the world was his hieroglyphic interpretation (which he and all other Egyptologists are lying when they say they know how to read it). He explained that the pig, being an abominable thing to Horus, was not eaten in Egypt because of this identification of the black pig with Seth.

The truth of this false interpretation was the issue being that of "darkness" from Horus eye loss, not blackness. So these European males who are programmed to fight "darkness/black" think they are doing a good thing when they kill Black People. Besides, their Supernatural Satanist orientation gives them an independent "sick" pleasure in their miserable lives from doing such things as: persistently and repeatedly violating the constitutional rights of Black People; jailing them for minor offenses far more often that for Whites; having their police dogs attack Blacks exclusively; using traffic stops to arrest Black People disproportionately; and subjecting them to excessive force 7 times more than Whites. One report: an unarmed Black person is killed by police every 36 hours. Much of the rest of their time is spent exchanging racist emails. Ref: (Hodge, Cultural Bases of Racism)

PRE-EXISTING CONDITIONS TO SLAVERY: Pre-existing Conditions is the state of health prior to the problem. Here, this refers to the mental health of Europeans and to Ancient Africans. But the point at which they met was a giant historical step, which has had a profound bearing on today's violence in general by Europeans and Black gangs in particular. To repeat, that moment in history occurred after Europeans discovered *the GUN* invented by the Arabs in 1304. Savage European tribes rose to power from perfecting the GUN over the next 150 years. After arming ships and troops with the GUN, they raped the world's peaceful and rich Colored Peoples of their precious possessions-- simply "Taking everything of their interest and Destroying the rest while eagerly leaving a trail of Killed humans and animals "for no reason". Such had been the pattern of their Aryan (a word ironically originating from Europeans' concept of honor) ancestors. That enabled Europeans to dominate the world and then continue to this day to adversely influence the world. Countless (30,000+) shiploads of gold, diamonds, ivory, copper, iron ore of Central American Indians were taken to Europe. That is how Europeans became rich! And that explains why they are married to the GUN so as to maintain dominance up to the present.

Meanwhile, these barbaric Europeans had a personal need (from envy of Africans' brilliant achievements); a social and ego need (a justification for the profitable business of slavery); and a greedy desire that pushed bogus science to give "proof" of Africans' inferiority in order to justify the profits of slavery. Hiding behind the GUN back then (and now) enabled Europeans to fashion a superiority complex (as is present in Brutes and bullies) to cover a profound inferiority complex, sense of insecurity, and mask with bravado their Fear-based "second nature." The *key point was/is that the ability to kill people better than any competitor was/is the basis of the winner's superiority attitude--and not intelligence*!

CAUSES OF AFRICAN AMERICAN SLAVERY

The Origin of anything has three Cause components: (1) a *Predisposing Cause*--what puts the "seed" situation for a process on the path; (2) the *Precipitating Cause* is what fertilizes the "seed" and enables it to grow; and (3) the *Immediate Cause* is the force or spark given to activate what is evolving into significance. These Cause originated after Europeans acquired the GUN, enabling them to enlarged upon *Core Brute and Satanists* self-declarations as Self-Great "little gods"; to believe in their evil powers to be greater than the power of the one Universal High God; and to tremendously improve on the patterned take-overs of their primitive ancestors. To this end, the "Indifference/Hate/Evil/Sadism" (IHES) Complex are featured in their Kill/Take/Destroy/Dominate/Oppress Aggressiveness. By being in a philosophical anti-Humanity and Anti-Spiritual Elements mindset--emphasizing disarray with an unchecked ego, their exuded hatred is directed towards establishing control over everything and everybody. Their "sick" pleasures come from causing pain, misery, suffering, and agonizing misery to victims who survive their IHES deeds. Invariably, any survivors are left to scramble just to survive day to day. Traditional European "Big Four" enslavement "Take-Down" methods are *penetration, conquest, occupation, and colonization.*

PREDISPOSING CAUSES TO AFRICAN AMERICAN SLAVERY: After the demise of the Greco-Roman slavery, international trade in Enslaved Black Africans continued from Africa via the Sahara or the Indian Ocean to destinations in Islamic regions. It was as an extension of this that the trans-Atlantic slave trade by western European merchants unfolded. Slavery met its golden age not in the ancient world but in the New World, beginning in C15 and increasing rapidly after C16 amid the so-called capitalist world system. As the New World was developing—particularly in the West Indies, USA South and Brazil--highly civilized West African societies were engaged in trade relations with Europeans. To further their capitalistic ends, Colonial Europeans discovered several benefits associated with enslaving Africans in the New World: "they were civilized and relatively docile, they were knowledgeable about tropical agriculture, they were skilled iron workers, they had immunities to Old World diseases, thus making them a more secure investment for a slave owner".

The *Penetration* portion of Enslavement is the first phase of Colonial Europeans with an economic goal linked with racist systems of control deployed in subsequent phases. It involved the forced deceptive invasion of "a small minority of European missionaries" to costal African country-sides. As preliminary for the primary objective to obtain "valuable economic resources," in the *Conquest Phase,* the colonizers used the extremely destructive ethnocentric European missionaries. Missionaries, strategically situated among Africans along the coast, declared their propaganda came from the "real" Supernatural God and not the people's inferior Spiritual God. Thus, the people had to believe and have faith the anti-Spiritual Elements beliefs they taught for all African people they influenced for use as Standards, Filters, and Guides for living. After taking control of Africans religion, the missionaries launched systematic assaults on native cultures in neighboring areas where indigenous languages, religions, worldviews, and ways of life are destroyed, distorted, and generally denounced as being primitive, evil, and savage. *Occupation* consisted of European troops moving in to establish their government, premised on the belief that the indigenous people lacked a decent, moral, and civilized society. Parts of the process included casting indigenous people as needing governing and control by members of a superior culture—i.e. the Europeans.

With *Colonization*, a rigid social caste system was/is developed in which the Europeans receive the lion's share of privileges and benefits within the colonial society. In this phase, members of indigenous groups were/are shunned, denounced, alienated from symbolic and material resources as well as constructed in zoological terms as being more like animals than civilized people (Irwin, *Race and Justice, 2012*). Within every colonized site, Europeans received much of their White Privileged identity specifically by demoralizing and marginalizing Africans, who, in turn, had very few options to cope with hegemonic and racial or ethnic imaginaries thrust on them. In response to this colonial reality of domination and oppression, indigenous peoples experienced a deep sense of alienation and adapted can adapt to this alienation in three ways, consisting of assimilation, protest, or crime. However, by this time Europeans were well equipped to quell any rebellion. Being passive in the face of domination was a problem and that being bossed around was a serious form of disrespect.

All of this was illustrated by happening to the people ruled by the Kongo *King Affonso I* (1506-1540). Europeans wooed him by promises of great things--like educating Africans--in exchange for him making just a few changes. Affonso's first step in giving up power was his conversion to European style Christianity and re-placing his own African name with a Portuguese name. Next, he adopted many Christian laws and demolished all symbols of the old African gods—thereby angering his people (Bailey, Ancient African Bible Messages). The Kongo "schools" the Europeans set up were little more than Catholic catechistic classes designed to de-structively brainwash the students. Besides, the students were rigidly restricted in number and attendance. The "teachers" were semi-literate priests/slave dealers who personified everything meant by corruption (e.g. taking bribes) and immorality. *The Whites did not want the Blacks to be properly educated by their standards because education would make it hard for Blacks to be exploited.* Still, Affonso tried to deal fairly with the Portuguese so as to get education for his people.

Cleverly, the Whites did all they could to stir up wars between tribes so as to obtain prisoners from both sides for use as Slaves. Then they generated rebellion among the King's own subjects--getting them to be *highly emotionally disturbed* with each other. Once this was under way, Whites kidnapped many of the King's royal people but blamed it on the King's inside and outside enemies. Wide spread Slave hunts and raids went wild. Naïve Black People were taken down because they did not/do not understand the concept of brute evilness and what it takes to defend against it. Note the similarity in how today's Satanists supply guns and drugs free of charge to Black gangs so that they kill each other or are imprisoned as a way to prevent Black Power. This Affonso pattern has been and continues to be repetitiously displayed daily in Black Communities all over the world and presented dramatically with the intention of having Black People awed by European power.

PRECIPITATING CAUSES OF SLAVERY: *Imperialism* is the process of a nation extending its territory by imposing its authority and thus gaining political and economic control of other areas. The sense of "Fight" in the Europeans' take-over of Africa and its people by means of the GUN was associated with exploitation, vi-olence of unspeakable magnitude, and the worse of brutality. After getting established in Africa, foundational to precipitating slavery was that Africans and other non-Europeans were being initially enslaved because of their legal and cultural vulnerability—i.e. the combination of so-called "heathenness" (i.e. non-Christian status) and captivity (as in a captured solider of war losing his rights and became property of the victor--a status that did not change if bought or sold). Enslavement was an alternative to execution. Africans enslaved Africans for the same reasons as Europeans [enslaved Europeans]: debts, crimes, conquest, and sale by parents. Therefore, West African states had a ready supply of Slaves to trade with Europeans in exchange for arms and other resources to dominate their regions, changing the balance of power within western Africa toward states that were friendly to Europeans. A fundamental difference was that in the Mild, Slight, Moderate, and Extreme degrees of enslavement, the African type was of a Mild degree whereby the Enslaved became part of the family. By contrast, Europeans' cruelty was beyond Extreme degrees.

IMMEDIATE CAUSES OF SLAVERY: The appearance of the modern era ended enslaving European soldiers but not Colored Peoples. Hence, the new justification for enslavement was the claim that Africans were "heathens" constructed, spurring the mission of Christianizing the African world. So, Africans were declared to be a beast of burden, delivered by divine Providence to labor for the benefit of the noble and Christian Europe. Supportive to the fashioning of the Immediate Cause of slavery was an interactive relationship between Christianity and slavery, based on religious and military grounds, then followed by political action in the colonies. While slavery was illegal in England and Holland, their laws did not prevent their citizens from engaging in the trade (the Christian nations' "custom of merchants"). Spurring the Immediate Cause was the entrance of Satanist Europeans wearing a friendliness mask, offering Africans a better "God" than their One Universal High God. They made "pie-in-the-sky" promises to do all sorts of great things so African People could have a better life--offerings Africans really, really wanted. This enabled the European masked invaders to put into action their "*Shrewd*" (wicked, evil, malicious, dangerous) historically well-worked out pattern of *penetration, conquest, occupation, colonization* (C. Williams, Destruction of Black Civilization p257). The *defining moment initiating the "Take Down"* of the world-ruling Africans was that of African leaders failing to ask the invaders: "What are the details of *How Will You Do That?*"; "What Is Your Proof? Also, African leaders failed to get a guarantee of gaining what they paid for.

BEGINNINGS OF SLAVERY

Purchasing Slaves–whether from Africa or Asia–quickly became an *international trade*--with European traders provoked fighting and wars to encourage it. The word "*War*" (strife) illustrates how Europeans avoid any recordings of the horrible things they do. To elaborate, prior to C12 there was no English word exactly meaning war, nor did any of their Germanic relatives have one despite their warlike reputation. Instead, it was couched in the concepts of 'confusion and discord.' The 1122 German word "*Fight*" is etymologically a covering term meaning anything from sharp language to fisticuffs; then to battle and combat; and then another general term meaning to contend or struggle for mastery. An early usage was as a biblical phrase (1 Timothy 6:12): "Fight the good fight of faith, lay hold of eternal life." Today, fight is about competition or conflict between two hostile forces, with or without direct physical contact. An example of indirect fighting occurs in caterpillars facing danger. They react by spitting poison like a little snake. Sea animals fight by slamming, biting, or suction. Today, "War" is commonly thought of as a political group conflict involving hostilities—which for Europeans is concerned with gaining some material advantage where there is great resistance.

Nevertheless, "Fight's" slave trade aspect actually began in 1415 but formally in 1433 with arrival of the first shipment of enslaved Africans and gold in Portugal. Its ending in 1870 was the beginning of the Colonial phase involving Africans. Early on, Later, there was a shift from "heathens" as grounds to a supposed racial origin as part of the American slave trade. Starting here helps understand that unfolding causes of violence are tedious, slow, quite complex--each detail being essential to untangle glob ideas pertinent to Stopping the Violence of today. Details concerning this entire process can be gained from my 36 books on Black History, particularly *Private Selfhood Greatness, Post Traumatic Distress Syndrome,* and *Teaching Black Youth.* Columbus lit the fuse for African American slavery.

COLUMBUS BRINGS RACISM TO THE AMERICAS: Yearly, I poke fun at the foolishness of Columbus Day—starring Christopher Columbus (1446?-1506)--a man of Christian faith--a colossal liar—the one that sailed in the wrong direction and "Discovered America" where 18 million Brown and Black People were settled and for eons. As background, the Middle Ages' end of feudalism as it transitioned into the Renaissance featured European hypocrisy. Though Church ideology said all believers were equal in the sight of God, warring Europeans, now wed to the GUN from their 150 year development of its Arab invention in 1304, were dedicated to shedding the "inferiority" label given them by all other cultures. Their bubbling-over brute passions to Kill/Take/Destroy/Dominate in a greedy frenzy for acquiring gold from the peaceful, rich, and highly cultured Colored Peoples of the world compulsively led them into repetitious *penetration, conquest, occupation, and colonization.* Victims were left devastated. These savage people de-civilized vast areas of the world—killing, some say, 150 million Colored Peoples—and being thus rewarded with titles, estates, and Slaves for their conquest, plunder, and self-aggrandizement. Justifications to the Church for sadistically destroying all Colored Peoples cultures were ascribed to their Christian 'civilizing mission'. By adopting the Manicheistic philosophy in which all colonizers, no matter how atrocious their deeds, were portrayed as 'culture-bringers and divine instruments of a Christian God' gave them permission to enslave people, consider them faceless chattel, turn them into commodities for profit-making, and work them to death so as to make happen their obsession for empire-building. By self-declaring to be "superior," they made it legal for White males, and their sexism attitudes of overflowing chauvinism, to have life and death powers over their wives. They treated all women and children as livestock, in the sense of a rider to a horse (i.e. as 'inferior' sub-humans).

In a fine and courageous article, Jan Carew (*Race & Class, 1988*) noted Columbus landed in the New World on 10/12/1492 at Guanahani. After renaming it San Salvador, he and his crew immediately enslaved the 'inoffensive Arawaks'--those welcoming that crew with great hospitality + feeding + housing them after the Santa Maria had run afoul of the shoals. Then the invaders built a fort at La Navidad while tormenting the Lucagus Indians—taking their gold, raping the wives and daughters, and causing bloody quarrels among the people. Meanwhile, Columbus wrote to Spanish rulers about how friendly everything was going—finding pious rational for all his hideous acts. The Caribs—for whom Caribbean Islands are named—were the first freedom fighters. They believed it was nobler to die fighting than to be enslaved. Columbus initiated the Atlantic slave trade by taking 500 Arawaks to Spain to exchange for livestock—claiming he was saving them from the Caribs. He had tricked the Carib leader by inviting him to come along to work out a truce and then enslaved him. But the leader committed suicide on board ship. Then, Bishop Las Casas, the "Apostle to the Indians," recommended enslaving Africans instead of Indians—and that so delighted European bankers, landowners, merchants, and colonial proconsuls as to start the African slave trade.

In 1503, Queen Isabella decreed the first ecclesiastical license for ethnocide, slavery, and racism. From 1492 to 1504, Europeans killed 3 million Indians in San Salvador, leaving 300; 600,000 in Puerto Rico and Jamaica—with 200 remaining 50 years later; and the same in Cuba and other islands—all replaced with

Enslaved Africans. Supernatural reasons for killings were: (1) rudeness against the (?) more refined Spaniards; (2) gravity of the Indians' sins against Nature and idolatries; (3) to spread the Christian faith by requiring subjugation; and (4) to protect the weak among the natives. It was a game to see who could completely cleave an Indian with one blow of the sword or to pull babies legs apart--and give the parts to the hounds, each hound having killed or maimed 500 Indians. Babies snatched from mothers' arms were dashed against rocks or drowned in front of mothers. Natives were hung on gibbets (a cross)—13 in a row to piously commemorate Christ and the 12 Apostles. Slavery lasted only as long as it was profitable. These were/are patterned European overt, tempered, or masked practices in the New World and Africa. Yet, Europeans avoid and ignore this history of their inhumanity—and without having changed their mindsets. jabaileymd.com

ENSLAVED AFRICAN AMERICAN BEGINNINGS

In the hunting period of primitive Europeans, all captured men were slain and their women became servants or wives of the victors. At the Pastoral Stage unneeded Slaves were sold. When European cultures became sedentary their slave labor was the foundation of their economy, with the Enslaved being deemed private property—providing the slave owner with food and saving him from irksome toil. Such was routine where the military was in charge and the more Slaves present, the more men were freed to fight. Ancient Greece and Rome had three conditions for the emergence of an Enslaved society: concentrated private ownership of large land to require a permanent labor force; the development of the commodity production and markets; and the absence of alternative internal labor supply. These conditions were met easiest when civilizations very different in level or type crossed each other through the sea in the setting of large scale trade and transport carried out with high speed and low cost. Likewise, large-scale Slave systems flourished around the Mediterranean, the Indian Ocean and the Atlantic Ocean in the form of brutal civilization plunder by European barbarians. The appearance of the modern era ended enslaving European soldiers but not Colored Peoples. Hence, the new justification for enslavement was the claim that Africans were "heathen" constructed, spurring the mission of Christianizing the African world. So, Africans were declared to be a beast of burden, delivered by divine Providence to labor for the benefit of the noble and Christian Europe. Supportive to the fashioning of the Immediate Cause of slavery was an interactive relationship between Christianity and slavery, based on religious and military grounds. This was followed by political action in the colonies. The Portuguese initiated the slave trade informally in 1415 but formally in 1433 with arrival of the first shipment of enslaved Africans and gold in Portugal. While slavery was illegal in England and Holland, their laws did not prevent their citizens from engaging in the trade--the Christian nations' "*Custom of Merchants*".

Spurring the Immediate Cause was the entrance of Satanist Europeans wearing a friendliness mask, offering Africans a better "God" than their One Universal High God. They made "pie-in-the-sky" promises to do all sorts of great things so African People could have a better life--offerings Africans really, really wanted. This enabled the European masked invaders to put into action their "*Shrewd*" (wicked, evil, malicious, dangerous) historically well-worked out patterns of *penetration, conquest, occupation, colonization.* In 1619, when the *nobi* system in Korea reached its peak, a Dutch merchant brought 20 indentured Africans to Virginia for the first time (Rhee, *Millennial Asia, 2010*). Then, those Africans which followed shortly thereafter in pre-racial America occupied the social status of free persons or indentured servants (operating on a basis of equality with Whites). Many Black and White indentured servants ran off together, married, and produced what is called the "*Raceless*" *People*. Because of these labor losses, Virginians began to import enslaved Africans who became the basic form of labor on landed estates or plantations. Supposedly, like White indentured laborers, when their obligated time expired, they became freemen possessing their own farms.

However, facing the birth of a nation and socioeconomic forces (especially a worldwide demand for tobacco, cotton, and sugar, and the need for a system of labor), early C17 colonial leaders needed a large labor force to meet market demands from Europe and America. Native American populations proved too difficult to submit to enslavement, and European Christians were reluctant to enslave other Christians [such as the Irish]. Africans were preferred laborers. Despite being declared to be uncivilized or tribal, they were still more civilized and hardy than laborers from other parts of the world. Enslaving Africans, as a practical alternative, emerged in the mid-C17. Prior to that, the price of Slaves was so high that a Slave cost twice as much as an indentured servant. Still, considering the over 50% probability of Black Enslaved dying within five years of arrival, it was far more advantageous to exploit five-year indentured servants. Increasing profits and increasing systematization of the economic infrastructure led to increased fighting competition among European nations vying for power and Slaves. jabaileymd.com; Blackvoicenews.com

EUROPEAN ENSLAVORS AS "KILLER" POLICE: European nations' competition with each other and their insatiable greed that had already resulted in global devastation and inhumanity unequaled in human history, found in Africa a 'gold mine' of riches and people to serve as Enslaved. Within this process of emphasizing exploitation of Africans and Africa, countless millions were similarly killed. The point of Europeans invasion of the Americas was to bring in Enslaved Africans to do the work of shaping the Americas into the European Empire cultural image. As was typical of the "friendly" presentation of introduction to kind-hearted Africans and Amerindians—both possessing what Europeans were going to rob-- Europeans killed almost all the Amerindians and most all of their essential food supply. Increasing needs for labor called for more drastic measures. Thus, by 1640, signs of enslavement began to appear for Colored Peoples. Whereas punishments for runaway White indentured servants were just one additional year of servitude, Blacks were sentenced to lifetime bondage, whatever the nature of their contract.

One reason slavery formed in "the New World of freedom and opportunity" was because labor was always scarce relative to the vast, unoccupied, fertile land. Meanwhile, once slavery was under way in the Americas--because Christians were not allowed to enslave other Christians and as the Enslaved became a better long term investment in Virginia—there arose the issue of whether or not Christians could enslave those who had converted. Virginia law decisions in the 1660s included: (1) that European and Church law allowed the enslavement of non-Christians, i.e. "heathens"; (2) that converted Enslaved Africans could henceforth be held in bondage; and (3) that conversion to Christianity did not require manumission. Later, a loophole was closed in 1682 when *Heathen Descent* rather than actual heathenism was the legal basis for slavery in Virginia. The concept of "*Heathen Ancestry*" was a giant step toward making racial differences in the foundation of servitude. The legal developments and semantic tendencies that, in effect, made the disabilities of Heathenism inheritable and inextricably associated with "Blackness," laid the framework for 'Societal Racism'.

By Europeans manipulating their idea of Supernatural religious morals to suit their convenience meant Black People could escape Heathenism by demonstrating they had converted to Christianity and yet were trapped by not being able to escape the European self-interest label of "Heathen Descent." So, the reality path for legal and Christian racial slavery was paved. In the interest of supporting the agricultural economy of the South, Slave Codes were enacted in Virginia and Maryland. Colonial leaders decided to base the American economic system on human slavery organized around the distribution of melanin in human skin. The first official Enslavement act was dated 1661--thereby establishing its form as a social institution in Virginia--the extending of Blacks' status of chattel indentured Slaves to '*Slaves for life.*' The imposed status, 'Slave for life,' remained in effect for colonial Africans and their descendants until 1863 when the Emancipation Proclamation was signed into law. However, by 1863, the "race" die had been cast.

Blackness became the criteria of a legal caste-like status. Thus, the original decision to create what amounted to a racially derived status probably arose less from a consciousness of racial privilege than from slave owners' palpable self-interest. This is because they acquired the Enslaved to supplement or replace their fluctuating force of indentured servants. It was usually assumed that everyone in the colonies with brown skin color had descended from Africa or was otherwise a "Heathen." Thus, European enslavers discourse shifted focus from ones religious spirit to ones physical makeup. To sever the link between Christianity/Heathenism and Freedom/Slavery meant spotlighting physical appearances as the lone criteria that marked Africans as the Enslaved class throughout the colonies. Thus, the criterion of "Heathen Ancestry" was significant ideologically and legally in creating a physical-appearance/racial-category system of enslavement. This shift to racial slavery helped to cultivate the belief that the normal status of dark-skinned people was servitude and thereafter slavers instituted an all-out effort to cause all Black children to believe their purpose in life is to serve White people. [Ref: Du Bois 1903; Paolucci, Critical Sociology, 2006] jabaileymd.com

ENSLAVED AFRICANS IN THE NEW WORLD: Although in the early years, poor indentured servant Whites (convicts, prostitutes, religious dissidents, the wayward), from Europe were a major labor source for tobacco, rice and indigo farms, this dwindled away by the end of C17—partly because they were always troublesome workers. They quarreled with masters over the contract conditions and many filed lawsuits. Hence, although the Black population in Virginia was only about 500 up to 1660, thereafter social pressures driving the lower classes out of England diminished, and the average residual life span of these newly arrived lengthened, thanks to the improvement of living and medical standards. Changes in labor market conditions made the purchase of Enslaved Africans more profitable. How slavers were to treat the Enslaved had a defining moment by 1660 when colonial Europeans revived Enslaved practices of their ancient Greek ancestors. The essence concept was that anyone who allowed themselves to be Enslaved were mentally weak, subhuman, and like mechanical beings. As a result, their purpose as Slaves is to do the ugly, horrible, uninteresting work of civilization's daily life, since otherwise Greek contemplation and culture would be almost impossible.

Europeans focus on being able to glorify leisure meant generating situations of Enslaved labor to make them rich. The high price included: (1) an incompatibility of achieving an *even average level intellect and their Indifference/Hate/Evil/Sadism mindset;* (2) tolerating always being fearful; and, (3) for the tiny few Europeans having a trace shadow of a "Religious" Conscience meant handling those burdens of what would likely happen regarding whatever "morals" they thought they had + *Anxieties* (an inability to decide which way to go or which way things will go) + being chained by Worries (much mental activity centered on variables beyond ones control) + being inadequate as humans + resultant self-hate. In order to gain a tow-rope to grasp, in hopes of lessening their inner instability, they were intent on destroying the minds and Selfhood of the Enslaved they were rearing so as to be "*Zombies*" (a Haitian Creole term for those in a "walking coma" state). In rummaging through classical Greek and Roman literature to get ideas for building the "Big House" on plantations, the slave owners came upon useful information. One was the certainty of the Enslaved being property objects.

For more than 3000 years, the legal characteristics of bondage, which regard an Enslaved as chattel property, have changed very little. It is common in the field of history, however, that actual human relations or economic status substantially varied within the same legal form. Also, routinely proprietary claims and powers were made to apply on those clearly not Enslaved. Hence, this served as justification for enslaving Free Blacks. Furthermore, they learned that those Medieval West-European jurists who had rediscovered the Roman law, regarded serfs as property of landlords and were similarly subjected to purchase and sale like the Enslaved. Yet, these Serfs were immovable. Still another point was that although at the extreme case of C18 Russia, serfs were legally chattel. That these concepts persisted throughout slavery was seen up to 1975 in USA professional athletes--being objects of property that could be bought and sold, even against their will. What separated them from being Enslaved was only for the difference in the relative power of the partners concerned and the origins of the relationships between them and the team owners.

Before the time of Black slavery, Servants were Virginia's most valued form of property. It was noted in 1648 that servants were "more advantageous… than any other commodities" for importation from England. Meanwhile, to cement the Enslavement of Africans, in 1662, the rule of the *ius gentium* ('what natural reason has established') was adopted—dictating any child born in the colony took the status of the mother. In addition, since laws around this time voided Baptism as a reason for manumission, in 1667, an act was passed declaring baptism does not change the status of an Enslaved—a reflection of the uneasiness in their also being Christians. The more Americanized African descendants became, the more the convenient self-interest biblical Pauline doctrine (contrary to Jesus' teachings) of obedience to slavers as a Christian duty was imported to the plantation and the colonies by means of other non-King James European Bibles. jabaileymd.com

STATUS OF THE ENSLAVED: The legal status of Enslaved Africans in the American South was that of "Human Chattel"—moving property. Though the Southern states declared Enslaved Africans to be property, the right of the owner to his "time, labor, and services," there were differences as to whether they were full humans (as stated in Alabama's 1852 law) and 5/8th of a person in actuality and for legal state representation. The law required that slave owners be humane to their Enslaved, furnish them adequate food and clothing, and provide care for them during sickness and in old age. That they were the personal property of their owners is most manifest in the fact that they were the subject of exchange, transfer, bequest, attachment, and auction. They could not change residence without a deed of the slave owner, nor assemble without permission. Certain states Slave laws acknowledged the humanness of the Enslaved, ruling illegal their murder. Yet, throughout the colonial period (and on up to this day), the punishment for killing a Black person was rather lenient. If brought to court at all, the sentence was a light fine or acquittal. In 1699, the Virginia state congress passed a law prescribing the slave owner was not guilty of murder if he killed during correcting his Slave, "since it cannot be presumed that prepensed (premeditated) malice should induce any man to destroy his own estate". After independence, these clauses were revised in the direction of more severe punishment. By the 1850s, most southern states provided heavy fines for even the cruel treatment of the Enslaved.

Of course, few southerners suffered the penalties of these laws since juries were reluctant to convict and the Enslaved, who were often the only witnesses to such crimes, were barred from testifying against White men. European "Humanism" (forbidding the murder of the Enslaved) and the strengthening of the above mentioned inhumane Slave laws, did/do not contradict each other because Legal humanism by itself was not for the human rights of the Enslaved. Instead, their original purpose lay in preventing the moral degradation of the White community!—amazing "reasoning"!!

COURSE OF AFRICAN AMERICAN SLAVERY OVERVIEW

After the 1670s, dark-skinned people in the USA were officially considered Enslaved in a Slave-based society. The emerging Black/White dichotomy led almost directly to a caste-like social-legal-political relationship. As someone said: "It would probably confuse cause and effect, however to view the transition to racial slavery as motivated primarily by color prejudice . . . planters also had very strong economic and social incentives to create a caste of hereditary bondsmen." The lifetime of servitude was passed on from generation after generation. It was by the institutionalization of slavery that the power of the slave owners was secured by the adoption of "race" as an overriding principle of organization throughout [American] society. Slavery, as a Southern way of life was maintained on a daily basis by the constant use of brute force and violence, which included family separations, whippings, beatings, rapes, mutilation, and even amputations to prevent or punish runaways. These factors re-inforced each other to produce a deeply rooted tradition in which through the last decades of C20 it was natural for police to react to stress or provocation with violence.

Some say that during the starting of African slavery in 1415 with the Portuguese and with the slave trade lasting roughly 450 years, there were forced about 10 million survivor Africans into slavery in the USA. However, estimates for the number of African abducted and destroyed in this massive enterprise of human bondage ranged between 60 and 150 million. The estimated 10 million North America Indians alive in 1492 were reduced by massacre and illness to fewer than 1 million in C20. During a 110-year period (1700–1810), a wide range of multi-millions—no lower than 6 million Africans--were transported to the New World under the status of chattel Slave, or property. The enormity of destruction and geno-cide of ethnic or racial groups, perpetrated during the Atlantic slave trade has been largely kept secret in European education. USA public education textbooks and general historical references rarely discussed the nature of these genocidal activities. The lack of this essential information is an example of the at-tempt to obscure the truth, deny the existence of inequality, and ignore the destructive behaviors used to maintain it (Moore). The 3:2 ratio of male to female Enslaved Africans, whom the slave merchants had brought, ensured the natural increase of the Enslaved population--another favorable condition hard to find in White indentures. Kidnapped Enslaved Africans began to be imported from Africa in full scale, expanding to 33% of the Southern population by 1790. Between the end of C18 and the beginning of C19, Afro-American culture distinct from the traditions of Africa began to form in Black society. For several reasons that follow, however, they remained aliens, 'intruders', recruited externally from Africa like their ancestors. Though born from within, still socially expelled, they were aliens from the foreign land of 'limbo' between life and death.

Enslaved African minds were turned "Inside-Out" by European Enslavers leaving their way of reacting to the life by means of their Emotions. This was aided by the Enslaved not being allowed to read, write, or count and having nothing to think about—thus the loss of their Left Brain skills and its disciplining effect on the Right Brain. There were little no efforts to learn because the Enslaved were fully engrossed in surviving the day. Yet, Forbes (J Black Studies, 1992) says the Enslaved were not a docile group or "Sambos" but on-goingly resisted the slavers, having nothing to lose for doing a poor job, being excessively careless, or wasteful. Their "Spirits" were killed, as indicated by Willie Lynch methods, and they were taught intra-Black dissention so as to be envious of each other's achievement and to act in a "crabs-in-a-barrel" manner with each other. This same mindset persists in their today's struggling descendants who say they want to learn but only what they want to learn, the way the want to learn it, and by teachers who conform to the being acceptable—those who are one of them, have no White people as part of it, not saying anything against Europeans. They want to be taught in a manner familiar to them and somehow hoping hearing the familiar will lead them to change into the way they want to be.

HORRIBLE MIDDLE PASSAGE

Enslaved Africans brought in from around African empires, included those of the Western Sudan Moslems. They and men, woman, and children from all over Africa ranged from the dignified, cultured, and refined in possession of noble character--to being quite intelligent and educated--to "normal"--to the problematic (e.g.

bad characters, the disabled, the feeble). The moment of their capture was the formation of what would develop into "African-American cultures." The very earliest interactions of the newly captured Africans in Africa was that of were being shackled together in the coffles. Despair (hopeless hopelessness)--a Despair leading to submission--was easily achieved by the captors as a result of subjecting the Enslaved to long marches of often hundreds of miles while chained, barefoot, having inadequate clothing, and almost no food or water. All were transported to the African coast along the shore of the Gulf of Guinea. Here is where stood many trading posts or "factories" on the Grain Coast (Liberia), the Ivory Coast (now the Ivory Coast Republic), the Gold Coast (Ghana), and the Slave Coast (Nigeria, Dahomey and Benin, and Togo).

After being placed in African barracoons (Enslaved holding areas on the West African coast) on the coast, the Enslaved awaited sale to European slave traders. Throughout this entire time they continued to receive every beyond conceivable mental, spiritual, and physical trauma. For example, African fellowship fragmentation started when they were forced to fight each other in the barracoons for tiny amounts of food and water. The brainwashing of Enslaved Africans in the barracoons began when they were prevented from using their languages. While packed into the dank barraccon "factory" dungeons--squeezed so tightly that they had no choice but to stand in their own feces and breath the stench in their poorly ventilated barred jails--Despair among all went further and further down in a bottomless pit. This resulted from becoming increasingly aware of the permanent separation from their kinsmen, tribesmen, or even speakers of the same language; left bewildered about their present and their future; stripped of all human rights or prerogatives of status or rank; and homogenized by a dehumanizing system that viewed them as faceless and largely interchangeable.

This trip from Africa to the Americas was the ultimate in evil, sadistic, and dehumanizing experiences in all of slavery. Ships involved in the African American slave trade followed a triangular or three cornered trade pattern. Bound for the West Coast of Africa, empty ships would leave Europe; load up with West African Slaves; travel to America or to the West Indies -- called the Middle Passage; exchange Slaves for money, cotton, tobacco, rice, or sugar cane; and then return to Europe in order to sell the goods before repeating the voyage. Of the numerous ways designed to obtain Slaves, a simple and popular method was developed by the Englishman, John Hawkins (1532-1595). He would burn coastal villages and capture the villagers as they tried to escape. The preference was for "fit" Slave males, between ages 15 and 35. But half the Slaves were "unfortunates" in their own cultures: criminals, the mentally or physically handicapped, debtors, political prisoners, and outcasts. About 15 million Slaves (actual numbers are unknown) were shipped abroad but millions died in attempts at capture as well as died aboard ship. The conditions under which this occurred were on ships legally limited to carrying 150 to 350 people but actually carrying 600, 800 or more men, women, and children.

Slaver captains anchored chiefly off the Guinea Coast for a month to a year awaiting their cargoes of the Enslaved. Captains of slavers were known either as "*tight packers*" or "*loose packers*," depending upon how many Slaves they crammed into the space they had. The vast majority were greedy "Tight packers" who would have Slaves packed in like sardines in a can in order to transport the largest possible "cargo." When ready for another trip, the properly branded and chained Slaves were rowed out to the slave ships. Upon arrival on board ship, the Enslaved were stripped naked for the duration of the voyage; lying down amidst filth and dysentery; enduring almost unbearable heat or cold. Meanwhile, the Enslaved were wedged horizontally, spoon fashion, lying on top of each other in a 6 feet long, 16 inches wide and 18 inches high average space allowed per person. This was about the size of a coffin! Thus, it was impossible for positioned Slaves to even shift with any degree of ease (Alderman, p. 53-57). In the daytime, weather permitting, the Enslaved were brought on deck for exercise--called "*dancing the Slaves*" (forced jumping up and down). The excuse given by the captors for compelling, by the lash, to dance on deck was to straighten their limbs.

Women and boys were repeatedly sexually abused. Many Slaves who survived blows to their heads became mentally ill--but most died. If bad weather or equatorial calms prolonged their journey, the twice daily ration was a cupful of water in a small pan--a pannikin. Along with this there was either boiled rice, millet, cornmeal (if they were from the Guinea coast), stewed yams (if they were from the Bight of Biafra, Nigeria); or starchy manioc or cassava flour or banana-like plantains (if they were from the River Congo region). All portions were greatly reduced to starvation levels. This made dying either an easy or a desirable next step. Although it was always stifling, in a storm the gratings on each side of the ship were covered with tarpaulins so that great waves, breaking over the main deck at times, could not reach the 'tween' decks. This made the heat even greater; reduced the supply of air; and caused gasping for air. Slaves had to lie in their own waste while breathing noxious fumes in the unventilated, crammed space. Most would go mad from misery and suffocation or from being chained by the neck and legs. In their madness some killed others in the hope of gaining more room to breathe.

Not having enough room to sit up or turn over, while in unbearable heat or cold, many Slaves died in this position. Some Slaves killed themselves by starving to death. Many were prevented from starving by being whipped, tortured with hot coal, or crews breaking their teeth so as to do force feeding. Men strangled those next to them; women drove nails into each other's brains. It was common to find a dead Slave and a living Slave chained together. Otherwise, all faced constant dangers from raids at ports by hostile tribes, threats of Slave mutiny, epidemics (of smallpox and dysentery resulting from filth), attacks by (French) pirates or enemy ships, maritime disasters, maltreatment, suicide (e.g. cutting their throats, jumping overboard, and, under the term and "fixed melancholy!" many died of a "broken heart"). "Trouble-maker Slaves were brought on deck and flogged to death or clubbed over the head and pitched over board. In desperate efforts to keep from drowning, Slaves who managed to cling to the taffrail at the stern of the ship would have their hands chopped off. So many bodies or sickly Africans were thrown overboard that sharks picked up ships off the coast of Africa and followed them to America. Death rates averaged 15% on the short end of a 21- to 90-day voyage but rose sharply on the long end, perhaps approaching 40%.

On an average, about a third of the Slaves died on their walk to the African coast and another third died during the trip to the Americas or from the "*Seasoning*" that followed. Most of the Enslaved landed first in the West Indies (especially Jamaica) where they were "*seasoned*" or "broken-in" to their new Enslaved roles. Those not dropped off in the islands were shipped to the USA. The "Unfortunates" in the Americas were simply left to die. Despite the brutal capturing of Slaves and the horrible Middle Passage taking an unspeakable toll in misery and human life, an early White writer, reflecting the "sick" mentality of European slavers, described these Enslaved operations as "crusades" for bringing the savage brethren to civilization and Christianity for conversion. He gently decried the massacres but maintained such incidents were definitely outweighed by the fact that salvation was thus gained for the souls of the victims!

MIDDLE PASSAGE SHIPS: To illustrate with one example, The *Whydah Galley*, a 'separate trading' slaver ship not under direction of an official English company operating in the slave trade, typically transported enslaved Africans from West Africa to the Caribbean. The Royal African Company's monopoly on it was ended by an Act of Parliament in 1698, but the Company still retained the right until 1712 to collect a duty from merchants leaving to conduct trade in Africa. After the English won the *asiento* after 1713, the South

Sea Company was awarded the right by the English Crown to supply Spanish colonies with enslaved Africans. Officially and publicly, relations were hostile between separate traders and these companies, but at times clandestinely collusive relations existed; the increase in competition brought by the separate traders tended to increase the availability as well as the price of slaves. So, West Indian planters and merchants often attempted to play one group against the other and it continued transporting enslaved Africans, most often to Jamaica. In 1716 after transporting enslaved Africans from West Africa to the Caribbean, dropping off its human cargo, it was on its way to England when it was captured by the pirate Samuel Bellamy and his crew. They used it in a number of raids until it finally sank in a storm off Cape Cod in April 1717. The remains of the *Whydah* – replete with Spanish doubloons and numerous other coins, cannon, the pirate crew's personal effects, hardware such as shackles from its career as a slaver, and gold fashioned by C18 Akan goldsmiths – was located in 1984 (Yelvington, *Critique of Anthropology, 2002*).

"SEASONING" THE SLAVES

"Seasoning of the Slaves" referred to getting prepared for the New World "Ordeal." The mindset of Europeans at this time was Human torture was spotlighted during the days of the Spanish Inquisition (discovering and punishing heretics). The Inquisition's original purpose in 1478 was to discover and punish those converted Jews and Muslims who where insincere in their Christian beliefs. From the view of Spanish royalty, the victims had *"twisted" or "distorted"* the behaviors of Christian doctrine into something wrongful (called a "Tort" in law). The concept of going away from the true direction or posture meant that parts of the whole were in disorder--that is, *"twisted away"* from its proper senses and direction. To reverse such distortion required torture by painfully twisting and stretching the victim's limbs on the rack. An extension of this idea was that right religious doctrines and facts could become *Distorted* ("bad twist") when people *"twisted"* them to suit themselves. Though the inhumane religious "Trials by Ordeals" were particularly prominent in the European Middle Ages, The Roman Catholic Church engaged in this from C13 to early C19. To a somewhat less degree torture questioning was also used in civil courts up to the C20, including witchcraft trials in New England (USA) colonial period. Apart from the huge numbers of the Enslaved who died during the "Middle Passage" from Africa to the Caribbean, more than twice that died during the brutal training period in the West Indies before they were shipped on to the American mainland.

When Enslaved Africans neared the shores of the Americas the slaver ship crews prepared them for sale by washing, shaving all their body hair, and rubbing them with palm oil to disguise sores and wounds caused by conditions on board. The Enslaved were trained not to resist having all parts of their bodies examined--especially their reproductive organs, and sometimes were allotted a little rum to liven their spirits. The Enslaveds' New World "Ordeal"—called *Seasoning*—served to increase their sale price. Slaveholders and overseers called "Salt-Water" the newly imported Enslaved and "Country-Born" for the American born Enslaved. Upon arrival in the "New World," the ordeal of being *"Seasoned"* to be Ideal Slaves included severing any "Motherland" bonds with their African past, the "killing of their Spirits" which was devastating and 'Splintering' to the entire Selfhood of each; separation of their "God-Image Self" from their Divine Spirit to thereby cause each to become Self-Absorbed. The severing of equally great bonds by selling away family, Sippi, and acquaintance members on the auction blocks--while humiliated by being stripped naked to "inspect". Fredrick Douglass describes being put up for sale at a slave auction. "We were all ranked together at the valuation. Men and women, young and old, married and single, were ranked with the horses, sheep, and swine." Here is what it means to be a slave and sold like any other commodity.

Douglass concludes: "At that moment, I saw more clearly than ever the brutalizing effects of slavery upon both slave and slaveholder." Each one of these personal happenings vied for out-doing all the rest in causing unbearable Spiritual, Emotional, and Physical pains. There was total Selfhood destruction that ensured the lack of ever returning to a pre-Enslavement state or improving into a better state from reassembling the shattered Selfhood pieces. Perhaps by this time, since their Instinct Brains were ineffective, they were operating out of their Omnibus Brains (survival and enduring actions derived from compromised Thought). Because there is an in-born urge to bond with people, and because they could not count on the people they loved to be available, and because the only thing the Enslaved could count on in order to survive was the captors, they clinged to their captors. All the captors offered was barely enough food and shelter to survive—and although deficient to an ultimate degree, this constituted a *Physical Nature Needs bond* with the captors--one absent a Spiritual Human Nature Needs supply. To give a clue as to how Europeans think, immediately after landing, *Pest houses*--where the Enslaved arrived from Africa--endured a mandatory period of quarantine before entering USA soil--especially at Sullivan's Island, SC. Here is where smallpox, tuberculosis, and similar contagious disease victims were also isolated.

"KILLING ENSLAVED SPIRITS"

Following the "Fishnet Moment," a third of the Enslaved died on their walk to the African coast. During the Horrible Middle Passage death rates averaged 15% on the short end of a 21-to 90-day voyage but rose sharply on the long end, perhaps approaching 40%. So many bodies or sickly Africans were thrown overboard that sharks picked up ships off the coast of Africa and followed them to the Americas. A third of the arrivals died from "*Seasoning*" or "broken-in" to their new Enslaved roles. In this process, the "Unfortunates" were simply left to die. At its mildest, Seasoning of the Enslaved can be analogized to prolonged and inhumane ways of "*breaking*" *horses* at "ordeal" camps. A young horse at first objects to carrying a rider's weight—bucking, rearing, and plunging in order to throw the rider off—until "Broken"—the allowing of being saddled, bridled, and mounted. However, "Seasoning" the Enslaved was even more harsh throughout its 1 to 3 years intended for the Enslaved to adjust to their new environment; horrendous working and living conditions; adopting new customs; and with machine-gun rapidity "little bang bullets" conveying the message of the Enslaved being subhuman.

All of this was done in the setting of the Enslaved being in a terribly weakened by the trauma of the Middle Passage voyage and the addition of exposure to foreign diseases, inadequate nutrition, bad water, work exhaustion from being unaccustomed to the "sunrise-to-sunset gang labor," and cruelty were simply overwhelming. All of these practices (among countless others) continued during plantation life, following slavery, and up to today. There has been no change in these Satanist mindsets and the followers they orchestrate--and there never will be! Satanists' practices were/are designed to beat down the newly captured victims with endless layers of "Spirit Dismantling" until they *have no more fight for retaliation and are docile "forever."* "Seasoning" included the assignment of Christian names; learning a new language while forbidden to use their native tongues or to maintain any other cultural ties; and otherwise "educated" in the direction of being "good Slaves".

By being totally dependent on these sadistic captors for their entire survival meant that the Enslaved were "Bonded" to them—what I call the *Evil Savior Syndrome*. The mindset of those who model the African god Set is that of Human torture--an orientation spotlighted during the Catholic Spanish Inquisition. Its 1478 purpose was to discover and punish Jews and Muslims deemed to be insincere in their Christian beliefs—heretics said to have *"twisted" or "distorted"* Christian doctrine to suit themselves. To reverse such distortion required torture by various practices and devices—one being *"The Rack"*--an oblong wooden frame with rollers at each end. Such Ordeal practices applied to Enslaved African Americans "Seasoned" them into making them fearfully fit for use—with the aim being to fashion "Ideal Slaves." Any "spirited" Slaves had their ankles bound to one roller and the wrists to the other. The rollers were then turned by a windlass (similar to a fishing reel)—being terribly painfully twisted and stretched until victims' confessed or had their joints pulled from their sockets and died. It was essential for all of the plantation Slaves to witness this for purposes of "killing their Spirits"—and particularly Black males whom the captors so envied. These methods continue today but with a different appearance. Obviously, all of these episodes (among infinitely others of a "big bang" periodic display + of a daily cumulative micro-trauma nature) contributed to the "Killing of the Spirits" of the Enslaved. A human's Soul has its origin in the Cosmic Intelligence and thus consists of *Divine Consciousness* as its state of Being. The Divine aspect of that Divine Consciousness is God's Spirit within each human—and thus is eternal and independent of and uninfluenced by anything, including whatever evil a human does. Thus, a human's *Divine Spirit* inside that Divine Consciousness is comparable to a drop of God--like a drop from a boundless ocean--but all of God is in that drop. When ones Divine Spirit is "Killed," one has exchanged the truth of God for a lie—i.e. adopting a distrust of God' Goodness and even seeking after God. Such enables anti-Spiritual Elements—whether in the form of messages, objects, or entities—to be brought into the Conscious or Unconscious by ignorant and/or evil people so as to generate self-defeating Supernatural Icon Images.

PLANTATIONS

Plantation Slavery was a societal system of domination, degradation, and subordination, with an especially rigid legal structure allowing privileged, landowning Whites to manage Enslaved Africans as chattel property. It was the concerted efforts of colonial legislatures, judicial officers, regional sheriffs, and local constables that formed the justice system of slavery. To be called a "Planter," one had to own at least 20 slaves—and that was 12% of the total Planters, a typical one owning 20-50 Slaves and they led the prosperity of the cotton belt in the South. The rest had less than 20—72% under 10; and 50% were petty slave owners, possessing less than 5 slaves. The Planter aristocracy consisted of 10,000 families who lived off the labor of gangs of more than 50 slaves. The extremely wealthy families who owned more than 100 slaves numbered less than 3,000.

EUROPEAN SLAVE OWNERS: When a fish rots, it starts at the head. At the head of today's rotting world are Satanists, originating 45,000 years ago, and progressed with ancient Greeks--then Medieval Knights who became Renaissance "Gentlemen who, in turn, orchestrated the slave trade--set-up USA plantations--and formed the Federal Government in ways to inhumanely stay in control "forever." Such "Dark World" people remain in control to this day. They operate in Supernatural realms completely unaware of a Sun and thus having no chance of recognizing any ones, including their own, "Soul Sunshine" because they are completely out of contact with it by volitional choice. Yet, they, like all Cloud types, possess an *Aura* (electro-magnetic energy in wave-lengths) reflecting what is in ones inner world inside ones Selfhood as well as an Atmosphere projecting into the External World. Both the Aura and the Atmosphere institute Consequences of an Emotional and life performance nature. Dark World people reflect the Indifference/Hate/Evil/Sadism (IHES) Complex in deed, expressions, and thoughts in fighting the Spiritual Elements. Their Emotional *Atmosphere* and its whole Idea (gestalt) contains: (1) a dynamic quantity of that Emotion's IHES patterned and shaped forces; (2) the ability to have one disregard the limitations and boundaries as part of ones interpretations in order to impart ideas of the indescribable; and (3) a power to endow ones mind and feelings with both a meaning and a sense of participation inside that meaning ("*Such-ness*"). By declaring the Enslaved to be non-human and making them chattel, they were then seen as property the Satanists owners to deal with through the IHES complex. For example, their Brute Brains prevented the morals to killing the Enslaved and they did so with emotions similar to swatting a fly.

Many "Southern Gentlemen" slave owners were formally "Renaissance Gentlemen" who started the slave trade. They remained 'little gods' and set up their plantations in accordance with a military style. Their primary objective was to get 'filthy rich.' Their other main objective (derived out of overwhelming envy of Black males) was to make Enslaved males dumb and strong for purposes of producing work and babies for the slave owner and to have the Enslaved provide entertainment for Whites (e.g. fighting each other while drunk; singing and acting like buffoons). The Enslaved had to adhere to the rules dictated by the captors in hopes of continuing to receive their meager feedings. Some Enslaved saw White folks as an awesome and powerful but strangely pathetic people--a people often pious in their European form of Christianity, using a Christ with African ancestry (see Revelations I;14, 15) whom they remade in their own image—a people having faith only in what their minds and their power could control--a people who sell their Spirituality Souls to the Devil (their made-up entity) by doing "any evil thing necessary" in order to make a profit or to keep from losing their ill-gotten gains. Besides, White people could talk as authoritatively about Un-real realities--i.e. Contingent Beings, as about Hell, Satan, and the god they made into man as well as anything they know nothing about.

The Un-noble Loyalty bonds the Enslaved established with their captors (as by being the supplier of what little food they had) caused them to accept the brainwashing messages that turned their thinking "Inside-Out." Key to that brainwashing was to get the Enslaved to stop Self-Knowing as well as "Knowing" the one Universal High God and, instead, to have "Faith/Belief" in the European God, based upon what the captors said about God. The Enslaved were not aware that the God of which the captors spoke was in reality not the same as the Spiritual God elaborated upon their Ancient African Ancestors. More often, the god the captors referred was whom they privately called Satan. Thus, the captors were able to control the minds of most Enslaved by means of what the captors wrote in making up their European Bible. By having an Un-noble Loyalty bonding to the captors, afflicted Enslaved accepted this made-up information as "the Word of God," as opposed to the true "Word of God" as if found in the Ancient African Bible. These supposed European related "Laws" of God were presented as Rules--Commands--Prohibitions--Injunctions--Commandments--Regulations for Black People to obey, as if God had actually said them. To make this deception work, Whites said they were told by God to convey the "Word of God". Yet, Whites did not have to live up to them--like "Meekness" and "turn the other cheek."

The Sacred Mother-Child Bonding--which is natural to humans and, in fact, in all of the Animal Kingdom--was an urge many Enslaved tried to make happen with the Satanists. The fact that Satanists are unaware of and are opposed to any aspects related to Spiritual Human Nature Needs pertaining to themselves or to the Enslaved caused the most desperate Enslaved to try different methods for bonding with these Satanists. Almost all used Masks and Masquerades related to submission--a role causing many to believe that role was who they were and thus they "lived down" to it. Others displayed extreme "Inside-Out" thinking--i.e. "Waiting Slaves," Black Puppets, and Oreos--in hopes of completing their bonding with the captors. That never works! Almost all allowed themselves to be defined by these Evil Brutes. Because the Enslaved were operating out of their Ancient Brain (as discussed elsewhere) and because they had been totally disconnected from their mother land, the path was laid for them to start believing in Delusions—i.e. what was not real and no longer believing what was real.

This was reinforced by slave owners using vicious methods to "break the spirit of Enslaved males" so they would become docile and dependent on White males.

In 1860, among 1,516 thousand households of free Whites in the American South, 385 thousands owned the Enslaved. Add to this 3,830 thousand of Enslaved at that time, and the figure one gets about 10 Enslaved in each slave–owning household on an average. But, the picture of the southern economy based on this small-sized slave ownership is incorrect. Most slave owners owned only a few Enslaved; most Enslaved did not live on petty farms. More than half of the Enslaved belonged to 'planter aristocrats' with more than 50 Enslaved.

EUROPEAN OVERSEERS OF THE ENSLAVED: What is clear to me from a half century of study of Black History is that the very things Europeans accuse Black of thinking, feeling, expressing, and doing comes directly out of their self-authored "book of dramas" of who they are in their nature, dating their primitives times. The following concerning the "Chav"—the English White working class during African American slavery--is paraphrased from the Englishman Adams, *(Culture & Psychology, 2011)*. What is of note, in addition to indicating the "Projection" materials Brute ("Chav") Europeans use to characterize Black People, is that the "Chav" were overseers of the Enslaved on Plantations during African American slavery. In England, the Chav were thought of as the 'primitive "white trash" underclass'--the 'less valued' group as a result of violating the ethos--the counterpart of the global groups known as: trailer-trash (USA), Bogan (Australia), ned (Scotland), and regional variants within England such as 'hoodie,' 'charver,' and 'pikey'. A common theme of these groups was/is depicted as: 'un-modern, anti-cosmopolitan, backward and worthless,' lazy, lacking ambition; having poor parenting and social skills; tasteless and ostentatious in their consumption practices and appearance; being out-of-control in such things as excessive drug use, obesity and poor diet, uncontained physical aggression, and related bodily practices; filthy, disgusting, dirty, loud, ugly, stupid arseholes that threaten, fight, cause trouble, and impregnate 14 year olds.

In following the debased practices of their Middle Ages ancestors, it is typical for them, after getting high on dope and tanked up on cider, to jump on and beat up others—perhaps fighting about paternity and who stole their man. Called scum, they turn to crime to fuel their binge drinking and drug addictions. They think the world owes them a living, dole [unemployment benefit]: a lifestyle choice for chavs . . . they aspire to nothing, but destroy, steal, burn, damage everything that people have worked for — you scum. They spit constantly on the floor, perhaps symbolizing their distaste of themselves. European critics say Chavs' 'bad selves' are identified through 'diseases of the will'—i.e. 'failures of responsible self-control by those who do not know how to behave'--those unwilling to or incapable of taking control of their destiny in terms of productivity—those holding wrong attitudes, 'out-dated ways of thinking and being'—and these morons are set for a life of misery, either behind bars or unemployed. They are denigrated for the lack of an attempt to find employment and for eschewing independence from the state—for being 'set' on a course of crime and unemployment—for being on a "Don't Care" trajectory. Most will never attempt to get a job since they are happy to play the system for every penny they can get. The lad/lass who gets wrecked all the time doesn't care about his/her future, or anyone else. The denigration of the White working class, repeatedly 'fixed' not just as economically impoverished, but more damagingly as willfully basking in a 'cultural impoverishment.' Typically, Chav critics are those who make their riches by "hi-tech" crimes.

Chav overseers came to the Americas on slave ships and the slaver ship captains called them "poor Whites"— those who were passengers (e.g. prostitutes) and the convicted criminals released from various European prisons with specific orders to go to the Americas. Accompanying them were refugees, idealists, slaves, and religion dissenters—all termed "Provincials" or "Colonials." The slave ship crew did not place Enslaved Females in ship holds with shackled males, thus rendering them particularly susceptible to the vicious maltreatment of the European slavers. Slave traders usually positioned female slaves on quarterdecks where they could move freely and be far more accessible to the sexual perversions of officers who "were permitted to indulge their passions".

Traders often branded slaves once aboard ship and would ruthlessly beat Enslaved women who resisted stripping naked for the practice. Crewmembers particularly "ridiculed, mocked, and treated contemptuously" slave women with children. Similarly, slavers sadistically abused slave children just to watch the mothers' anguish, and if a child died from the cruelty, slavers forced the mother to throw their child overboard or suffer even more brutality. Slavers were no less barbaric in their treatment of captured pregnant Enslaved women. Aboard the American slave ship *Pongas* carrying some 250 mostly pregnant women, for instance, females "who survived the initial stages of pregnancy gave birth aboard ship with their bodies exposed to either the scorching sun or the freezing cold". Even if a newborn survived the ordeal, captured mothers often smothered to death their babies fearing the child would grow up in slavery (Baker *Criminal Justice Review, 2008*).

On plantations, because the overseers on slave ships and on plantations originally derived mainly from European prisons with passage provided to go directly to the Americas, the majority of overseers where of criminal mindset nature that otherwise lacked imagination, education, sobriety, and ambition. The slave owners' typical criticism of overseers centered on "dishonesty, inefficiency, incapacity, incompetence, and self-indulgence in sex with the Enslaved (female or male). Apart from that, studies of slavery are conventionally populated with potentially misleading racial distinctions in nomenclature. To illustrate, any Enslaved with supervisory duties who toiled directly under the overseers' supervision was termed a "*Driver*" (or Foreman, Over-looker, Leading man, Head man, Boss, Whipping boss, Crew leader, Over-driver, Underdriver, or Straw boss). Practically, however, although working at identical jobs, some White supervisors were called *Overseers* (usually supervising the plow hands), whereas Black supervisors were called *Over-lookers* (usually over the Enslaved laborers using hoes). Or, Whites were called Bosses, whereas Blacks were called Leaders. The Enslaved did not customarily distinguish between a White Overseer vs. a Native American, a Mexican, or a fellow Enslaved Overseer. Many Enslaved, although identified conventionally as drivers or foremen, performed the same duties as an overseer. The reason for this is that Planters did not generally trust or respect the Enslaved, but they exploited every opportunity to use an Enslaved Overseer. Their strategy succeeded when, in their eyes, they found a rare Black specimen of nature's nobility.

PLANTATION FAMILY: At the time of their capture, Africans were a very expressive people--as suggested by their art and by the ability of each African to speak a dozen languages or dialects. While in African barracoons (Enslaved holding areas) awaiting the horrible Middle Passage trip to the Americas, their captors minimized revolts by ensuring no two Enslaved spoke the same language. The slavers found it necessary to communicate with their "black gold" or "human cattle" -- and therefore used several simple trade languages or pidgins to do so. Yet, the necessity for the foreign captors, buyers, sellers, and slave transporters to communicate with each other and with the Enslaved led to a trade business pidgin language called the *"Lingua Franca."* Its vocabulary was tiny -- barely adequate for bargaining and ordering the Enslaved about. Being composed of different European tongues, the only way the Enslaved could learn this pidgin was by imitating their captors.

African Pidgin began around the Enslaved barracoons (a herding place for Slaves) of the West African coast and therefore consisted of a mix of such languages as Ibo (Nigeria), Yoruba (Nigeria, Benin, Togo), Ewe (Ghana, Togo, Benin), Hausa (along the Niger), Wolof (Senegal, Gambia, Mauritania), Arabic, and European slavers tongues. Two other major locations where Black related Pidgin languages developed were the Caribbean and the Southern USA. *Pidgin* is the name for a 'Makeshift' contact language which draws on elements from two or more languages. During African American slavery it was used among European traders and on plantations with and among the Enslaved of various backgrounds. Pidgin has a small vocabulary of a few hundred words, drawn mainly from the ex-convicts freed from European prisons on the promise they would immediately go to the Americas (which they did as overseers). Of course those Europeans' grammar was bad and they were the only models from whom the Enslaved could learn English. An example is "I axed her" rather than saying "I asked her")—and blame for such English is only applied to Black People The nature of Pidgin words were about work, trade, and vulgar name calling. Each of these words can serve many functions. It has a close relationship between form and meaning--which depends heavily on content for their interpretation. This is one reason why it is miscommunications between Whites and Blacks.

Pidgin Portuguese was the first of these lingua francas but Pidgin English replaced it by C17 when the slave trade to the Americas began. *The Portuguese adopted this lingua franca and used it as the "seed" pidgin language which they instilled in the minds of African Slaves.* However, when the English rose to dominant power in C18, they switched the slave trade language to English pidgin. The small vocabulary and simple syntax of Pidgin English was ideal for ordering the polyglot Slaves about. The Slaves did their best to imitate it by contriving a soft jargon based on a *"chopped up"* version of the master's language that was interwoven with African words-- and this became the Lingua Franca (medium of communication) between the captors and the Enslaved. Examples of Negro Creole developing from lingua franca are English derived Krio (spoken in Sierra Leone) and Gullah (spoken in the Sea Islands of South Carolina); and Louisianan and Haitian Creole, (derived from French).

After arriving in the Americas, slave owners allowed just a few more English words to be added to the vocabulary of the Enslaved. The purpose of this "word deprivation" was to maintain control over the Enslaved by keeping them mentally constrained. Furthermore, the captors' selected and "channeled" the Slaves' language by determining the names for things; by determining the meanings and values of those things; and by determining the rules shaping and influencing how the Enslaved related to those things. Since words are essential for thinking, for sharpening intellect, and for self-expression, being victims of "word channeling" and "word deprivation" was the beginning of "brain-washing" (i.e. coercive persuasion or re-socialization). Nevertheless, this literature of peers during enslavement was the seed of *Hip-Hop.* "Hip" was perfected after the Enslaved developed their own lingua franca (the main 'seed" pidgin) for secret communications. "Rap"--the term for an Enslaved form of communication--referred to strong, aggressive, highly fluent, and powerful ways to talk. These communications of relating gives voice to those who "feel it but cant' say it" as well as serves as the poetic literature of many peers of today's struggling Black youth.

According to the interviews with the ex-slaves in 1929 and 1931, from the 742 ex-slaves who were under 13 at the time of emancipation, a third were brought up with one or both of their parents absent. And it is estimated that in about 60 per cent of the cases, the families were broken by the slave trade or by other features of the slave system. This means that the probability of adult slaves being sold after marriage and child birth was 1/5. And considering that the probability may have been even higher for the unmarried, the lifetime probability might have been well up to a third. In small farms with less than five Enslaved, it was common for owners to work in the fields with the Enslaved across wide regions of the American South. At least 10 to 30 Enslaved were needed for the slave owner to be finally exempted from the hard field labor. Farm owners belonging to this category personally managed the farm without a White overseer. For the supervision of the field labor, a loyal Enslaved was elected as a foreman. Planters owning over 30 Enslaved generally entrusted White supervisors with the farm's management so as to devote time to sales and finance. Planter aristocrats employed a general manager to directed several overseers (Rhee, *Millennial Asia, 2010*).

Not all Enslaved of the farm worked in the fields. Some served in the slave owner's house as cook, gardener, laundress, wet nurse, sick tender, servant, housekeeper. Some labored at the farm's workshops as carpenter, blacksmith, bricklayer, shoemaker or a cooper (repairer of wooden containers). Big American South plantations often had many profitable workshops inside the farm, like a complex enterprise where many types of business were managed by a single manager. But the absolute majority of Enslaved worked as field hands for the cultivation of cotton, tobacco, sugar, rice and hemp. did not seem to have worried much about the sabotage of their slaves. The slave owners' were always full of fear of the Enslaved, Anxieties (an inability to decide which way to go or which way things will go for it greatly matters what happens) and Worries (much mental activity centered on variables beyond ones control). Their most prominent day-to-day anxieties and worries concerned the tyranny of Nature or the caprice of the marketplace spoiling the whole harvest.

BREEDING THE ENSLAVED: Enslaved breeding was an extremely profitable business, thanks to ever-rising prices. There is no need to exaggerate the number and roles of Enslaved breeders, but they were not very rare especially in Virginia . In many cases, Enslaved women "killed their children because they did not want them to be Enslaved." Scholars recount several cases where Enslaved women committed infanticide out of concern for the well-being of their children. As is almost invariable with Europeans stupid interpretations of what Black People do, many Europeans interpreted these events as evidence that Enslaved women lacked maternal feelings. Since the children of Enslaved males or females were the sole property of the Planters, both were considered *breeders* and not fathers or *mothers*. Planters considered an Enslaved male a good breeder if he produce 15 or 20 children by any variety of females in the 11 to the 40s year old age range and the one producing the most would the "contest" prize. An Enslaved woman was said to be a "good breeder" if she had 15 to 20 pregnancies during her productive years. Still, planters expected pregnant Enslaved women to maintain their normal work schedules and production yields—not exempting them or mothers with infants from fieldwork. The associated distress accounted for the "*Fragile Black Baby*" syndrome of low birth weight, miscarriages, still-borns, and a and infant mortality high among Enslaved women (Bailey, Private Selfhood Greatness In Black Americans p14-6).

These mothers often left their infants lying on the ground next to them as they worked, whereas other mothers worked with their babies fastened to their backs. Some Enslaved women left their infants in the care of young children or older women, and nursing mothers were frequently unable to feed their babies and suffered the excruciating pain of swollen breasts. Undaunted, overseers regularly punished nursing mothers that fell behind in their work. As one Enslaved narrative explains, "I have seen the overseer beat them with raw hide, so that the blood and milk flew mingled from their breasts." Sexual relations with White owners were a routine feature of life for Enslaved women that was "both deeply traumatic and destructive of family life". Most Enslaved women victimized by White sexual aggression were unmarried, and sexual assaults on Enslaved girls as young as 12 years old were common. Married Enslaved women largely escaped White rape because White men knew Enslaved husbands would revenge the rape of their wives--they would rather die than stand idly by. Yet, fathers were White in *one of every six* female-headed households. The racism of slavery also empowered White women to brutalize Enslaved women who were sexually involved with their husbands. In many slaveholding households, White women whose husbands sexually assaulted female Enslaved tortured and persecuted Enslaved women. Among accounts of beatings and whippings suffered by Enslaved women, one was how his wife "cause[d] little Jenny to be burned with a hot iron."

ENSLAVED ARTISANS: In 1850, out of 3.11 million Enslaved population in the South, approximately 600 thousand worked outside agriculture in towns or cities. A substantial portion of jobs were filled by the Enslaved from housekeepers and cooks in urban bourgeois' homes to unskilled labor in bakery, foundry, shoemaking, laundry, barbershop, and sawmill. The Enslaved also worked in industrial sectors. For example most of 13,000 laborers in Virginian tobacco factories were Enslaved. It is a prejudice to think of the Enslaved as unsuitable to skilled works in manufactures. They showed competence in every occupation, and further, succeeded more often than not as managers in commercial brokerage, real estate, grocery store, tailoring, and money exchange. A number of them, especially skilled artisans and handicraft workers, were permitted "privilege to hire their own time." They had to pay regularly to their slave owner a certain amount of tribute. In return, of course within reasonable distance, they could work on their own as they wished. Frederick Douglass, a runaway Enslave and famous for his published memoirs, enjoyed such freedom. He had to pay $3 a week to his slave owner while working as a Baltimore shipyard calker (a caulker makes tight a boat's seams by plugging with soft material, as in fastening together the plates of a boiler). It was a "hard bargain", he noted, but in the process he felt a step closer to freedom. But there was no guarantee that the money he earned by hard work belonged to him (Rhee, *Millennial Asia, 2010*).

FOOD FOR THE ENSLAVED: In the American South, the diet of the Enslaved was rather insufficient. Nine liters of corn and three to four pounds of pork by the week were normal, and potatoes, beans, rice and fruits were sometimes supplemented. Blacks were so fond of pork, that although the same nutritional requirements could be met at half the cost, it was over supplied. As with every aspect of life, the food quality and quantity were atrocious. A typical daily ration was of half a pound of pork, a quantity somewhat closer to the standard ration of the Enslaved and lacking in nutrition. For others, it was grits and cornmeal and sometimes side meat and 'lasses." One Louisiana physician mused: "The diet of Negroes on most plantations being mostly salt pork, corn bread, and molasses—rarely eating fresh meat and vegetables—leads to a condition closely allied to scurvy."

Furthermore, by providing limited food, estate mangers barely satisfied the caloric requirements for strenuous and heavy labor. Workdays extended well beyond customary levels as the Bonds people labored 12-16-hour shifts to cut and process the cane at breakneck speed. During these nonstop operations, the Enslaved rested for just 6 hours in every 24.

ENSLAVED QUARTERS: Clothing and housing of the Enslaved were relatively poor. In regions close to the frontier, even the houses of the farm owners were not in good shape, but planters who had palatial mansions did not spend much on the dwellings of the Enslaved. A window or a bed was rarely found in the hut of a slave. The narrowness of the Enslaved huts has been described by a northerner who visited a plantation in Mississippi: 24 huts for a total of 150 Enslaved were each measuring 16 by 14 feet. That narrow hut was usually for the children and the older Enslaved who took care of them. For the healthy adult slaves, it was more of a shelter than a dwelling (Rhee, *Millennial Asia, 2010*).

ENSLAVED PUNISHMENTS: Slavery was horrible for men but arguably far more dreadful for women—who additionally suffered such unique forms of abuse as rape, sexual assault, and vicious attacks against their pregnancies and motherhood. One of the first things European enslavers did was to generate dissention among the Enslaved by starving them and causing them to fight each other for food. Then Europeans converted the mindset and behaviors of the slaves out of the realm of sound African Tradition into a realm of delusions. This was accomplished by brainwashing techniques; by breaking the spirits of the Enslaved; and by taking away their ability to think. Slave historians distinguish *colonial slavery* from *antebellum slavery* to acknowledge the variant forms of slavery that developed in discrete regions of the U.S. at differing times and for separate reasons. Jurisdictions executed more than *three times* as many slave women in antebellum slavery as in colonial slavery for things like arson–murder, conspiracy to murder, and attempted murder of slave owners and his families as well as other Whites, including persons of authority, overseers, hirers, and constables (Baker *Criminal Justice Review, 2008*).

RESISTANCE OF THE ENSLAVED: No matter how strong and elaborate a ruling apparatus might have backed up the Slave system, it contained violent resistance as its inherent element. It is a major error to believe that the Enslaved passively allowed European slavers to have their way. There were many open revolts; hundreds of violent uprisings engaged in or plotted throughout slavery; thousands of tempered sniper strikes; and countless masked and concealed attacks on Whites. Hence, a crucial component of "Slave Codes was to deter insurrections by imposing harsh punishments. Still Enslaved rebellions were of major concern to White enslavers as early as 1642. Other prominent examples included the plots of Gabriel Prosser in 1800 and Denmark Vesey in 1822, as well as extensive violent clashes such as the Stono Rebellion of 1739 or the Nat Turner–led uprising in 1831. Some Enslaved Africans seizing control of the slave ships intended to carry them into perennial bondage, as in the overtaking of the *Amistad* in 1841 and the *Creole* months later. Most intriguing was the Christiana, Pennsylvania rebellion in 1851 (Worgs *J. Black Studies, 2006*). There, a community of runaway slaves took up arms to chase off southerners intent on returning them to bondage. Passive resistance meant suicides, which were not infrequent. There were desperate mothers who killed their own children not to have their sad fate inherited to them.

The most common type of resistance was fleeing, and the constant flow of fugitives never ceased. Some of them formed free communities of their own in forest or swamp. There were more active Enslaved who attacked their masters. Franklin points out that if we read newspapers of the South carefully, there were exceedingly many articles about masters who were killed by the Enslaved. Collective revolts organized by the courageous of the Enslaved were almost always detected in advance except the insurrection of Nat Turner at Southampton, Virginia, in 1831. But plots did not cease until 1865, and rumors were a hidden terror in the White society. However, rulers were too well organized, and the Enslaved were kept buried in a perfect ruling system.

Among the subtle forms of resistance were orchestrated by teachers, doctors, prophets, and Conjurers. Rucker (*J.Black Studies, 2001*) states that Conjurers position was that Ignorance and superstition render them easy dupes to . . . artful and designing men . . . . On certain occasions they have been made to believe that while they carried about their persons some charm with which they had been furnished, they were *invulnerable*. They have, on certain other occasions, been made to believe that they were under a protection that rendered them *invincible* . . . . They have been known to be so perfectly and fearfully under the influence of some leader or conjurer or minister, that they have not dared disobey him in the least particular. These "artful and designing men" and women found on plantations throughout the Americas were as ubiquitous as the individual and group acts of Enslaved resistance they inspired. They served as conduits of powerful Supernatural forces beyond the comprehension of their contemporaries and were, therefore, believed to be integral to the success of a number of Enslaved resistance movements. The mystical powers conjurers claimed to control made them formidable and respected figures among enslaved Africans. As historian John Blassingame noted, "In many instances, the conjurer had more control over the slaves than the master had"

SELLING OF ENSLAVED: The mere existence of so many auction markets for the Enslaved implies great activity in buying and selling the Enslaved. One example is seen in papers dated from the 1770s to the 1790s--during the peak of the Trans-Atlantic slave trade in Britain and America and dealing with the operation of a Jamaica sugar plantation run by English businessman William Philip Perrin. One list contains details of Enslaved Africans to be bought for Perrin's plantation. It states: "Dick, 25, able field negro, 140 pounds" and "Castile, 45, cook and washerwoman, 60 pounds." The total valuation for 54 male and female Enslaved came to 5,100 pounds (about $782,000 today). There were feeble efforts of Aristocratic paternalism of the White society to prevent planters, true Southern gentlemen, from selling Enslaved in the market. In the Guidebook of the Slave Trade corner at the museum of Louisiana, it was written that "Louisianans did not sell their Enslaved except in the case of division of property owing to inheritance for repayment of debt. If it was true, then the Enslaved may have been sold mainly by poor farmers.

The price of the Enslaved in the American South rose continuously except in a brief spell of recession during the period from 1837 to mid-1840s, to reach its peak in the prosperous 1850s (Rhee, *Millennial Asia, 2010*). For example, the average price of an Enslaved in Tennessee increased more than two-fold, from $413.72 to $854.65 between 1846 and 1859. A planter in Louisiana could buy a young and strong male Enslaved for 600 dollars in 1820s, but in the mid-1850s had to pay 1,200-1,500 dollars. By 1859, the price went up still higher, a planter who bought tens of Enslaved in a New Orleans Slave market paid $1,600-$1,700 for male Enslaved and $1,325-1,400 for female Enslaved. He also bought a skilled blacksmith, whose price was as much as $2,500. The price of the Enslaved reflected the profitability of the Enslaved labor. The high profitability was due not only because of the high efficiency of the labor system in plantations, but also due to the sustained improvement of terms of trade in cotton and other crops. All of these imply that slavery in the American South performed a good part in a well integrated market economy.

ENSLAVED BURIALS: For the dead, one Enslaved said: "Dey ain't no coffin for dem," George declared on the austere interments; "dey take planks an'nail dem togetherlik e a chicken coop . . . den dey put dem in dewagon what dey haul de manure in" and without a meaningful funeral (see Bailey, Word Stories Surrounding African American Slavery).

SLAVERY'S OUTSIDE WORLD

If it were not for some semblance of a moral and political siege of the North and Western Europe, the cotton empire could have certainly enjoyed longer prosperity. Politically, the forging of a victorious anti-slavery coalition in the North came very late in the 1850s. In spite of a devoted participation of Blacks in the War of Independence, the American Constitution practically approved slavery by protecting the property right of slave owners after independence. With this Constitution still alive, the anti-slavery front should have been politically frail. Unlike the politics of Britain in which a small number of noble families dominated, United States had a populistic tendency sensitively defined by the disposition of voters. In addition, supported by the economic prosperity of the South, southern politicians held the hegemony in the Congress up to 1850. Under the circumstances, it was only in 1854-1856 that a new anti-slavery coalition was organized in the Republican

Party. In 1856-1858 they formed a powerful political bloc in the Congress. It was in 1860 that they seized the administration with the election of Lincoln as President. Thus, while it was retarded in political sphere, the anti-slavery front in the United States was moral or religious from the beginning. If the religious doctrine that Blacks were also pure human soul had not been propagated for a long time since the early colonial period, the sudden political coalition of the 1850s would have been impossible.

The first major religious turnaround came from the Quakers. Even religious reformers like Calvin believed that sins were deeply rooted in human nature and that these sins could never be purified by history. This concept of sin made the acceptance of slavery easy. Quakers denied such fixed theology and dualistic view of history. The original sin could be overcome and the millennium will soon be realized in this world. They took deep interest in their life with God of Choice and showed absolute trust in human will to become a possessor of a perfect pure soul and in the practice of unconditional love. In this mental attitude of Quakers, all corruption of existing society was based on slavery. Such anti-slavery disposition naturally considered the Enslaved as pure souls who could co-participate in the millennium. The revivalist movements since 1730s were another major preacher on the anti-slavery front. They did not conceive sin as a metaphysical correction. All selfishness was the root of evil and through perfect love man could achieve a holy life. These new denominations of theology, which believed in the highest ideals of purity and benevolence, did not advocate abolition of slavery as their action program from the beginning. It was in 1774 when the Methodists officially proclaimed that slavery was against the golden rule of God.

SUMMARY

The primitive European "Scarcity" philosophy "Ground of Being" has continued to be the excuse for obsessive-compulsive total focus on greedily acquiring Material World benefits, as determined by their Supernatural cult system of values and customs. These include "individual rights," "competition," "independence," "separateness," "individuality," "uniqueness," and "difference" (Jones, Black Psychology, p. 102). Being backed up by the GUN, they only needed to provide weak excuses to their religious leaders, along with payments, to select Black People, the world's peaceful people, as their scapegoats and enslave them. The idea was to get rich in order to live a life of leisure. Hence, they sought "sick" pleasures in the External World so as to indulge their Brute natures. They deemed Leisure to be the opposite of work. To make the Enslaved work for free required dedicated focus to that end. Furthermore, to make this last forever, Europeans have been intent on rearing a crop of humans who never had Free Minds so that such Enslaved would be unable to know what they are missing by not being free. This was done and continues to be done by "Dehumanization"—as publicly indicated by in declaring Blacks to be 3/5th of a human.

When Europeans were welcomed into African and the New World, they settled in the coastal areas and continually crowded the natives toward the interior. With Amerindians, each tribe had to encroach upon its western neighbors who, if defeated in battle, were in turn driven farther inland. To this almost continuous strife trickery intrigues added by Europeans progressively entangled the Amerindians, as had been done to Africans, in traps. European law makers busily passed laws to make their sadistic deeds legal. An example was the First Preamble of Declaration of Independence that "all men are created equal with inalienable rights" applied only to White men. Chief Justice, John Marshall making Property Rights superior to Human Rights to thereby give Whites entitlement to do whatever they desired. It encouraged slave owners and the Enslaved to move West even though Natural Right were in the law. To succeed in going West, required that Europeans stir up troubles with the Amerindians. From dividing their victims and then supplying the opposing victims with guns to kill each other made there task all the easier. Perhaps this began when the French who, to gain the favor of the Amerindian Algonquins so as to aid them against the Iroquois, they gave the first guns known to Amerindian natives. The English then took the side of the Iroquois. In the War of 1812 the British incited the tribes to attack the Euro-Americans, and in later days individual White men stirred them to frequent fighting.

All of such ways of thinking and Life Living in relation to other people have served as the model for Black gangs in the Americas. In turn, they formed a collage of out of the patterns of Europeans, Amerindians, and Africans to make up a generic gang. This "3-aspect" collage is perhaps how Black gang candidates and member envision Icon Images pertaining to themselves and to a collective (e.g. their gang).

CHAPTER VI

EXTREME DESPAIR
MAKES PEACE
WITH DOOM

BLACK PEOPLE'S PARA-SLAVERY DESPAIR

From the beginning of humans appearance on Earth 200,000 years ago, Ancient Africans were a super-brilliant and peaceful people. Their Tow-Rope Theme for living, to which their total lives were designed, focused on striving to reach the Heaven Afterlife. Ancient Africans' Free Minds, ordered by Mathematics, were orchestrated by their Right Brain's Spiritual Module and disciplined by their Left Brain's Critical Thinking. This combination ensured a balanced and harmonious Brain/Mind system capable of rising beyond time and space so as to stretch toward the outsider edges of human capabilities. In African Tradition, the Spiritual Elements' Compassion (Spiritual Feelings; Spiritual Emotions) for others has always been the ultimate Humanity manifestation. Recall that inside the Ocean of Nun's Cosmic Circle, said Ancient African Sages, are all God's creatures in a "Virtual"—i.e. boundless, undifferentiated—but not disordered 'Becoming Being' state. Separately but together, each is a product of God's androgynic protoplast—the ultimate living Spiritual Elements' metabolic substance in a Spiritual form. Whether resting inside this Circle of Wholism or evolving within it into the Objective realm, each entity stays interdependently in communication with all others by means of Instincts. This: (1) sharing of androgynic protoplast; (2) of being unformed; (3) of being a vital part in and of the same Spiritual Space; and (4) remaining in constant communication represent the four aspects of Compassion.

Ancient Africans Spiritual Knowledge Certainty and Mental Toughness--both essential in ones trials and tribulations (i.e. crises)—permitted them to proceed straight ahead in Cosmic Enhancing productions by means of arranging and combining the Spiritual Elements into unique forms. Their Ma'at (Spiritual Elements in action) Daily living decision making and problem solving abilities traditionally embraced and fulfilled the Spiritual Human Nature Needs (SHNN) as well as Physical Human Nature Needs (PHNN) of all concerned. The absence of violence in their mindsets is indicated by there having been no policemen or jails in Ancient Africa, implying they possessed sound philosophical, psychological, and spiritual health. Thus, it can be inferred that Seed Causes of today's sprinkling of violence in certain Black Communities are attributed solely to Europeans' orchestration of African American slavery + their ongoing terrorism wrapped in racism.

ENSLAVED CULTURAL TRANSMISSIONS CLASSIFIED: At the Civil War's end different "Grape Vine" ex-Slave cultures came out of slavery. For the Ex-Slaves, there was the reality for them that "violence has got to be" and the ex-Slaves knew it would/will never end. So the path they choose for living was reduced to what elements of Worth (Spiritual and Metaphysical values) and of Value (Material World values) mattered the most to an individual—i.e. the process of determining ones Philosophy of Life in attempts to cope with living as "third-class" citizens. Thus, in establishing a Classification, *Group I* individuals choose to live out of their Real Selfhoods and that means their Unconditional Love represents a "state of Being" which orchestrates ones life with full expressions of its "Soul Sunshine" into all areas of life. In other words, they used their volition to remain inside the Cosmic *Spiritual Circle and apply its Cosmic Organism Divine Laws as the "state of Being"* to represent the manifestations of their Divine Consciousness. Those, constituting Group II, who made a volitional choice to step out of the Cosmic Spiritual Circle while keeping one foot inside that Circle of Wholism can be characterized by the concept of a Cloud with a Silver-lining. *Group III* members are completely outside the Circle of Wholism—thereby placing a "Dark Cloud" over their "Soul Sunshine" so as to have no contact with its powers. Group IV "Dark World" Black People arose slowly.

Group I were the progressive ones consisting of freed Ex-Slaves and Free but segregated African Americans in the urban North who established autonomous self-help and fraternal associations, churches, schools, small businesses, media, and cultural centers. Classical Black Nationalism, originating in the 1700s and reaching its first peak in the 1850s, declined with the end of the Civil War, and, as a result of the Garvey Movement, again peaked in the 1920s. Some ex-Slaves, supported by a few White abolitionists, worked to liberate the Enslaved. Later, they fought to eliminate racial segregation through building institutions and organizations (Jalata, *JBlack Studies, 2002).*

Another Group I "Vine" was Black American scholars who wrote several books, magazines, newspapers, and journals to spur Black cultural memory and popular historical consciousness; to fight slavery and segregation; to bring out African Tradition and show various African civilizations to the world; to evaluate Africans' in the Americas negative and positive experiences; and to reject White supremacy and racist Eurocentric historical cultural elements and structures that claimed Black People were backward, primitive, pagan, and intellectually inferior to Whites.

Group II: The Spiritual Elements lying deep within their Souls are clouded over with all of the Philosophical and Cultural Collage factors so as to make for a Splintered Selfhood. One part of them knows that what is happening to them in daily living, as orchestrated by the Satanists controlled Society 'at large,' is anti-humanity and that causes ongoing frustration. Another part is the Field Slave Brain/Mindset extension causing them to continue to seek the completion of the Sacred Mother-Child Bonding by expecting the Satanists to supply them with their SHNN, as if this is their only option. To go to them for help is the same as going to Satanists for help. The obsessive-compulsive aspect of this prevents them from knowing there is absolutely no chance of Satanists returning to the ranks of the humane. Prove this to your self by assessing the Legal System and its attorneys; the Government and its politicians; the formal School Systems and what they do and do not teach; the Religious System and their application or non-application of the Spiritual Elements; the Media and its stereotypes; and the Marketplace with its Trinkets and Trivia. Pause to consider how many honorable people one knows and their degree of caring. When dealing with the effects of what causes violence, one must approach handling it by deciding what to do about the oppressors as well as what is needed to help oneself and the group--what is available--and how much one wants it.

GROUP III: Although there were checkered rage display dissentions among the Enslaved that were and were not close to the slave owner, the courage to attack Whites had been beaten out of most of them. Still, those--mainly Field Slaves--who went through the "Struggling Tunnel" were the "Seed" Ancestors of the descendants accounting for today's Black-on-Black violence--a continuing the pattern of lacking the courage to attack White people; in non-assertiveness in going after what they are entitled to have; and in not desiring to seek a thriving life. This Group Mindset is oriented to *"Make Do"* in an aggressive manner. A basic problem is operating out of the obsessive-compulsive, emotionally oriented Old Mammalian/Omnibus Brain. One way this shows today is the afflicted believe they need to go to White people--those oriented to Satanists beliefs--for help--the very people whose pattern has been to enslave them and keep them down in every possible way. In looking back over the 400 years of the Americas, White people have killed over 150,000,000 Black, Brown, and "Red" people and kept them in poverty. Why would any reasonable person think that going to these same Brute type White people will bring them help?

Group IV: When brainwashing is done to a mind, that mind is turned "Inside-Out" so that one argues against reality and votes against oneself--choosing to live in a Delusional world and wanting something different from "what is." These things occurred with the enslavement of free Africans in Africa so as to not only remove the Selfhood freedom of each but to establish an Un-noble Loyalty of bonding. While the Satanist enslavers totally wiped out the Spiritual, Mental, and Physical aspects of each Enslaved, they provided just enough of the PHNN to maintain bare survival. Since this was all they had and there were no options, bonding with the captors occurred. This meant the Enslaved had been stripped of their Power to get what they needed for PHNN reasons and had no Power characterizing their Self-Worth/Self-Value. It is the *Courage* one brings to life that moves life forward--*Courage in daring to be ones Real Self--daring to step out of fantasy into reality--in daring to enter the Unknowns one fears.* , Courage is simply spurred by what is the "Right" thing to do. There Secular Courage is a destructive direction.

RECONSTRUCTION

The Civil War was not about slavery but about who would dominate the Federal state. It was initiated by slave owners who had seceded from the federal union and by northern core capitalists to maintain the union. Inspired by abolitionists whose long crusades had been focused on moral and religious aspects, a new kind of antislavery stance arose—a stance spotlighting money and with war being the most direct way to destroy the power of planter class—a stance relatively silent about the rights of Black People or about justice for freedmen. As a "Closet" racist, freeing the Enslaved never was President's Lincoln's concern. Black People stepped out of the bottomless pit of slavery's hell into post-emancipation's hell because of the escalating evilness of Whites. Reconstruction Amendments generated ambiguity into Black–White race relations, and keeping "Blacks in their place" was more difficult to enforce. Poor Whites were rebellious because they believed Blacks were now getting ahead of them as a result of making gains—and they launched violent retaliations against Blacks. This is the identical attitude many low class Whites have to this day. For slave owners to lose 4 million bonded workers profoundly caused turmoil in the South's economic and political structure and thus they immediately adopted laws that were modified forms of slavery for Black People.

EUROPEANS' MIND CONTROL OF ENSLAVED BLACK PEOPLE

To control the minds of Enslaved Africans it was necessary to brainwash Ancient African Philosophy (AAP) from their minds. The slave owners' mind programming methods were drawn from those used by ancient Greek and Roman slave holders--e.g. the stripping of the identity of the Enslaved to prevent "rebellion or uprising." Their greatly magnified application during African American slavery had as its theme to break all connections the Enslaved had from the Mother land and, to the extent possible, with each other. Fredrick Douglass put it this way: *the Power Whites Have Over Blacks Comes From Keeping Blacks Ignorant.* Briefly, the captors' methods included:

I. *Enchanting* certain African kings with a pleasing artifice which was not only delightful but deceptively presented as involving no great loss or harm and likely to do one good. Their beguiling attractive ways enabled them to lead those Africans into the wilderness by deception, by trickery and by bewitching methods so fascinating and charming as to seemingly be trance inducing. This allowed Europeans to subtly slip in their missionaries to institute penetration so that conquest, occupation, and colonization could follow (Williams, Destruction of Black Civilization). Similar methods were used in getting the Enslaved to no longer Know God existed and switching over to having Faith and Belief in things about God. This enabled European captors to control the religious aspects of the minds of the Enslaved.

II. *Religion*: There are two types of religion (Amen, Metu Neter III:126). One is from the Ancient African Bible which provides Knowledge of how to reach the Heaven Afterlife. The second came about by Europeans getting an African Coptic sect to copy much of the Ancient African Bible. Then Europeans modified it by *withholding African Knowledge and the means to Heaven Afterlife attainment in order to leave its adherents to rely on Secular Faith/Belief/Trust in the way they presented it*. Of course, the purpose was to control the people's minds by having them rely on what SEEMS right or true. For example, they added the stories of "turn the other cheek" and "be meek," neither of which is in the African Bible. Neither do Brutes adhere to either. A strong sense of God was brought in from African Tradition and was so engrained that it persisted through the hellishness of slavery and the post-slavery period. Only recently has it begun to start fading. Meanwhile, religion in the "*Negro Church*" setting during slavery was the main way of releasing pent up bad Emotions and experiencing a moment of pleasure. This combination of African Retention wrapped in the social benefits of the Church help account for the Emotionality that characterizes wide areas of Black religion.

III. *Confusion and Conflict*. There are three aspects to anything--What it is; What it does; and How it appears. AAP focused on "What it is" because that is the way to Know something. Brutes ensured that only What it does; and How it appears would be presented because this kept people from Knowing. Since very ancient times, apart from ongoing wars, Brutes have initiated non-violent measures of controlling others by the introduction of *assumptions because of their ability to generate an element of doubt* in victims. The resultant uncertainty about what people "knew" is what would galvanize chronic frustration, fear, confusion, Illusions, and Delusions. Then Brutes would step in and reconcile all ambivalent attitudes by teaching with fantasy stories containing highly abstracted concepts -- stories that "SEEM" right -- stories containing some familiar information the people have accepted -- stories told in an interesting way. This combination leads people to simply "give-in" to these false and misleading stories, embrace them as true, and then defend them.

IV. *Stop Rational Thinking*. Smart Black People are greatly feared by Europeans. Since it was against the law for the Enslaved to read, write, and count, this plus not giving them anything to think about that would sharpen their minds meant many of the Enslaved lost their fine rational thinking skills from a lack of education and a lack of usage. This left most with nothing but Emotions to use for going through life. Emotions unchecked by reason mean that Emotions alone are no threat to overcome being controlled or offer a means to rise above poverty. Thus, most Enslaved cultivated their Emotions as the only tools they had for dealing with their pain and sufferings, and using them as "Escapes" from their hellish lives. The same occurred with all that concerned "Soul Food"--i.e. "Making Do" with what they had.

V. *Honor* being Emotional. Brutes encouraged the emotions of the Enslaved because it was a powerful means to not have them think. Such contributed to the masks and masquerades used by the Enslaved in the form of a "happy" and simple presentation in dealing with Brutes. This was so important that Brutes insisted on it being part of the minstrels of the Enslaved, which were demanded of them for Brutes' weekly to nightly entertainments. Being Emotional became the signature of the Enslaved and those who cultivated their Emotions the best were honored. Both of these have been culturally transmitted and remain prominent to this day. This is why most Black People do not honor Black scholars or get involved in reading books. That is why Brute fashioned "Trinkets and Trivia" are so important with Emotional People (EP). Since Emotions do not allow one to Know anything, one cannot be certain about anything. Thus, they are defensive about what they think, feel, say, and do and either reject or attack those using a rational approach.

VI. *Distrust*: "don't trust each other or work together. Distrust everything and everybody but us captors" (who declared themselves as co-rulers with God--they ruled the earth, God ruled the sky). This intra-Black distrust is a powerful barrier to the fashioning of Black Power and self-help.

VII. *STAY-IN-YOUR-PLACE* messages were part of Europeans' superficial and delusional information. This included: "don't read"; "don't get an education"; "don't try to better yourself"; "don't be ambitious"; "don't be uppity" (i.e. do not be like a White man—and morally that is good advice!!); "stay in your place"—meaning Black people should "be about nothing"; "fight among yourselves"; and "spend your money foolishly." These patterns have been carried forth within Black families and communities under the title of Slave Survivals. These messages generated so much Emotion that it was easier to live by them than go against Enslaved Minded Blacks who agreed with their captors and advocated for them.

VIII. *Disruption of Family*. Enslaved males were usually not allowed to marry; not allowed to take care of their families; and were rewarded for having children with as many Enslaved women as possible. Dysfunctional families keep those involved in an emotional state.

Of course, there were countless other strategies, including those of mentioned in the Willie Lynch Letter, regardless of whether he was real or not. All of these were incorporated into post-slavery practices and with such additions as freeing the Enslaved and giving them nothing to make it on their own—no money, no place to live, no direction.

JIM CROW LAWS: The name is associated with a Slave dancer around 1830 whose routine included a peculiar jump as part of the "wheel about and turn about and jump Jim Crow." The early song and dance won wide popularity among Whites as a minstrel number and Jim Crow became the generic name for a Negro. By 1861 it was in print as designating a special street and railroad car, though it was not until 1875 that the first Jim Crow transportation law was written in the USA. At various points throughout this process "Jim Crow" referred to any number of laws. In 1866, all southern states had enacted *Black Codes* to regulate Black lives and to keep Blacks subordinated to Whites by imposing discriminatory measures precluding Blacks from voting, serving on juries, and testifying in court cases involving Whites. Those laws of Mississippi and South Carolina were the first and harshest codes. From the 1880s to the 1960s pertaining to segregating Whites from all other "races." Such included forbidding interracial marriages; separate and unequal facilities in public transportation (e.g. trains, buses), in schools, harbor ships, cafes, restaurants, bars; and so forth. The Jim Crow system was about every public facility being segregated, including water fountains, restrooms, and waiting areas in train, bus, and later airport stations. In essence, the RACIAL EXPERIENCE OF ONE NEGRO WAS THE RACIAL EXPERIENCE OF EVERY NEGRO. As late as 1887 such segregated cars were still in use in New England (Boston to Salem) and was not legally abolished in the USA until 1956. For another point of view see Stimpson p244.

POST-SLAVERY TERRORISM

Insidious, pervasive, and persisting (for 100 years) racial violence was part of daily life for Ex-Slaves. Terrorism reigned following slavery for many reasons—e.g. resenting losing free labor; feeling more inferior over losing the war; needing to project their evil character onto Black people; fearful of competition in any manner from Black males; and because of the money they could make from whatever evil things they did. Features were selective and deliberate strategies of vigilante groups terrorizing Blacks by means of assaulting, murdering, lynching, politically repressing, and executing. The sexual brutalization of Black women continued with White men raping, shooting, scalping, and cutting off the ears of Black women who resisted their sexual advances. White mobs even whipped, flogged, beat, assaulted, castrated, and murdered Black children while setting fires to entire Black settlements. Rioting White mobs in cities in Tennessee and Mississippi "raped black women as they went on an anti-Black rampage". From 1884 to 1900, White mobsters in the Black belt states

(Mississippi, Alabama, Louisiana, and Georgia) lynched 1,678 Blacks, including 51 women that White men raped before their lynching. There are endless like-kind scenarios of White terrorism.

With increasing post-slavery terrorism in the form of killing Black People (one report was that Black bodies clogged up a river), certain Black People took up arms to defend themselves, their friends, elected officials, schools, and churches. They knew that fighting back was the only thing White people respected, even though violence or the threat of violence was a call to action for Brute Whites. Although such terrorism on top of racism enraged all Black People, Black females have been spotlighted by taking retaliation—perhaps from responding to their brutalization by Whites throughout their enslavement. Hence, the violent reaction of Black women who killed their slave owners, spouses, and unrelated White children may also have been individual responses to "the stress generated by their dislocation, isolation, and economic marginality. Like-kind violence was more subtle following slavery. Arson was a preferred tactic for dealing with the oppressive practices in the South (and perhaps this is why racists Whites have burned so many Black Churches ever since).

Riots have been checkered throughout USA history to the present. Examples are those which occurred in Harlem in 1935 and 1943 as well as hundreds during the 1960s—many spurred by the urge to express rage over injustices and the desire for retribution. For many, violent action in response to oppression, conditions of bondage, and the smothering and confining social, political, and economic constraints imparted a humanizing power. Each strike at the oppressors or wherever representing a metaphorical step toward freedom, with the sense of seizing back their humanity and being somewhat liberated internally. Rather than being specifically intended to injure persons and/or damage property, these "Violent revolt" were more abstract in being attacks against faceless political or social authorities + the fact that White aggression is deemed legitimate within the "White Privilege" system of racial subordination.

SLAVE/EX-SLAVES' CONSCIOUSNESS

The deep part of a lake or underground table of water connect to the ocean. This is a metaphor for everything in the Cosmos and in a human's life arises as a result of the coming together of certain causes and conditions called "Aggregates". The main or substantial cause of a newly born Consciousness is from a parent (e.g. the ocean) or a previous instance of Consciousness (a lake or underground table of water). Aggregates resulting from slavery which changed the Consciousness of African Tradition to one of enslavement pertained to the physical body, the emotions, perceptions, mental formations, and reactions of the Enslaved. This newly formed Enslaved Consciousness—the beginning of Black American Customs--was "delivered" out of the opposite of the norm of African Tradition so as to accommodate a completely foreign association of like-kind complex sensory experiences, memories, ideas, emotions, and thoughts (Dalai Lama, Transform p31, 53). Thereafter, new layer after layer were superimposed as a result of each new horrible experience of "Awe."

BACKGROUND/BOTTOM/GROUND/BASE OF CONSCIOUSNESS: Dictionaries define "*Bottom*" (Indo-European, Base, Foundation, Fundamental Ground, Earth) as the lowest part or downward limit of anything. *Background* is the Bottom turned on its side so as to represent the rear—what is behind the principle entity(s), whether one is aware or not. An example of a Background is the rear part of a stage or its contents (as painted scenery); or, the surface upon or against which the principle figures or parts of a two-dimensional representation or pattern are seen, as a study of white flowers against a solid black. In this way, a Background is like a Standard—away from what holds the center of attention but against which the center of attention is compared; or, the natural, physical, material, or spiritual conditions that form the setting within which something is viewed or experienced (e.g. attractive private dwellings). Bottom and Background can be reduced to the sense of both being an *Element* equivalent—i.e. both Immaterial and Material; Intangible and Tangible; Native and Foreign. Elemental Bottom or Ground or Base (e.g. Certainty, Knowledge) means irreducible simplicity, or if applied to a Substance, incapacity for separation into simpler substances—making the ultimate building units situated at the starting point for a given entity as, for example, Cosmic Principles.

To deal with such variables requires having an Ultimate Standard. I choose Spiritual Elements products of the Natural Cosmos because Ancient African Sages established their "Ground of Being"—i.e. their origin out of Primordial Substance—and therefore has no beginning. The Sages used Mathematics to infer the Spiritual Elements are the source of God's manifestations by verifying their provable Correspondence. By contrast, Europeans propose no beginning for the Supernatural and, in addition, it has no mathematically provable Correspondence. In fact, no proof is possible by dealing with anything pertaining to the Supernatural, simply because it does not exist—no matter how ranking is the "authority" who says so and no matter if "everybody" believes it. So, the Ultimate Standard for Background, Base, and Bottom for the Spiritual Elements occurs when the multiplicity of what is seen in the mirrors all resolve into a Unity. This means that what comes out of that Ultimate Source are the ingredients which go to make up the images seen in each of the rest of the mirrors. If the Ultimate Source is, say, in "the Heavens" and its opposite (Foreground) reflection is resting on "Earth," then all that is in-between are like rungs on a ladder—the Middle Rungs are halfway--the lowest rung consists of ones thoughts, feelings, expressions, and actions in activities of daily living (the Ultimate Foreground).

A "*Background*" (setting; environment; backdrop; milieu; surroundings) has so many definitions as to make it a *"Parse" Word* (see Chapter IX). This means it has layers of subdivisions extending back to its Ultimate Base. For example, inside the 'rung' just before the Ultimate Standard--i.e. the one residing in the Cosmic Organism which arose out of the Primordial Substance--one is in an indivisible duality state of Spirit and Matter. Also, the larger plans or principles behind the Foreground get progressively fewer as they involute towards the Background. An analogy is closing a telescope so it can be put in its case—the process of having the biggest viewing portion furthest from ones eye pushed into the one immediately behind it, and so forth. Thus, regardless of the plane of existence, the Ultimate Background, Base, or Bottom is what gives rise to an Origin of "That it is!" (its Primary Quality) or its "What it is! (its Primary Quantity) when it came into Being—either setting the standard by which all other "rungs" are evaluated.

So, the Standard of the Primary Quality of Extreme Despair is that Ultimate Background, Base, and Bottom from which one can spring forward with a constant process of action or from which one vanishes because it is impossible to go off into an infinite further downward progression toward a nonexistent (non-reality) end. It is only the Ultimate that makes the existence of reflections, Qualities, Quantities, Values about Despair possible. A Chemistry happening helps to illustrate what the Enslaved did with their Despair within the context of surviving and enduring. A chemical 'Base' denotes a substance which combines with an acid to form a salt as a result of accepting protons or donating a pair of electrons. The point is that one in an Extreme Despair condition is on the "Bottom" of the scope of Despair and that "Bottom" is a starting point for selecting a unique life-changing path for ones Life-Living. By having Extreme Despair as ones Backdrop, one cannot transcend it. Still, one can go in a good, bad, or neutral Life-Living direction out of it. Like the chemical reaction, from knowing one has a stable board from which to spring up, one can then select and combine ingredients to form a workable life's "Personality". To get back to ones Real Self one must get back in the flow of the Spiritual Elements stream.

SLAVE/EX-SLAVE MINDSETS

"Fishnet Moment"—i.e. the moment when the fishnet was thrown over the free African in Africa to thereafter enslave him/her "forever"—had the Effect of setting-off a cascade of simultaneous destructive forces in each victim's Spirit, Body, and Mind. Metaphorically, those forces on each Selfhood of the Enslaved resembled a turmoil series of waterfalls pouring and spreading over steep rocks--disrupting Spiritual and Physical networks in its path--networks which produced outputs serving as the in-put for the next component in each network. The resultant Consequences started by each destroyed Selfhood aspect instantly competed with the others for domination and for the spotlight of significance as being the most devastating. Even though the mind specifics of any given victim will never be known, Human Nature present in the 37 billion people who have ever lived has such a "sameness" as to allow for inferences about probabilities happening in any victims' minds. Thus, an assumption based upon my education, training, and experiences is that: (1) at the "Fishnet Moment" the Enslaved had an instant shift from using their Rational and wholistic brain thinking over to their Instinct/Emergency Brains (associated with "Fight, Flight, or Fright"); (2) an instantaneous dangling of utter and total Selfhood helplessness occurring that transported the Enslaved above and beyond their most "far-out" perceived bounds of known or imagined sensibility--beyond their body's systems to respond to danger--beyond their help from any source, even regarding help from God and their Living Dead Ancestors; (3) their overwhelmed Instincts were replaced with *'Larger than Life' Supernatural vastness;* and (4) all subsequent mental activity, by generating Illusions, eventually led them into Delusional thinking inside a Supernatural World beyond their imagination capabilities.

EXTREME DESPAIR IN STRUGGLING BLACK PEOPLE

Despair in Enslaved Africans in the Americas was a Metaphysical Disease—underlying the inconceivable numbers of Maafa (Kiswahili for The Great Disaster on all planes of existence) type Emotions. It is the Consciousness Background out of which many of today's Black Americans think, feel, express, act, and react. Others have risen above and still others have come out of its bottom side—like the "Baddest Dudes" (fig. 20). Yet, amazingly, in the 18 European Psychology/Psychiatry dictionaries and textbooks I reviewed, only 4 even mentioned and defined the word: "An intensely unpleasant emotional state; a quiescence attitude directed toward the future with the acceptance of an unfavorable outcome; dissatisfied at the thought of what might have been; and "the absence of hope." This is the clearest indicator of why I believe European mental health specialists are totally unqualified to diagnose and treat any form of Black People's mental health problems. And I have seen in my Orthopaedic Surgical practice devastating results from what Europeans' diagnoses and management have done to Black People's minds (as well as in them "trying out" experimental Orthopaedic things, typically with terrible results). The wrong diagnosis leads to the wrong medication as well as to excessive amounts of the wrong medication and for too long a period of time. This is because European diagnoses and management were established by European philosophies and interpretations, on and for European patients. For the most part, these have nothing to do with Black People's problems. Complicating this is Europeans notorious willfull ignorance of anything pertaining to Black People—their philosophy and values; their world contributions of tremendous magnitude; and how they have come to be as they are. A *Metaphysical Disease* means there is no known End and it imparts the sense of being inside an Abyss (Gen. i. 2). An Abyss in the Greek's Bible meant the original chaos; in the Hebrew Bible it signifies Hell; in Revelation, the prison of evil spirits; and otherwise, a symbolized realm of being out of the cycle of life but in a state of emptiness.

No doubt, all Enslaved in Despair—whether of Mild, Slight, Moderate, and Extreme degrees—all shared the sense of being in an Abyss as well as in a "*double-whammy*" (i.e. two main devastation Causes occurring at the same time) from the European captors ever worsening and never ending Indifference/Hate/Evil/Sadism displays. The first "whammy" was the whole past experiences of a familiar and desirable world lived by the Enslaved but now having sunk to great dimness in their bottomless Sensory Consciousness. The second was that, for Enslaved, the masks and masquerades they had to display to the captors in order to survive and endure, eventually became their "Faces and Personalities"—meaning they had allowed the enslavers to define who they were and what role they were to play. Other Enslaved shattered into a multitude of social roles in order to adapt to their horrible enslavements as, for example, those who decided they had the best chance of surviving by "joining the enemy camp." The nature of their Despair came from effects on their brains, which I believe pertained to an almond-shaped neural structure that is part of the Emotional Brain called the Amygdala. Composed of several nuclei in the temporal lobe (memory), it is intimately connected with the hypothalamus, hippocampus, the cirgulate gyrus, and the septum.

Normally, the Amygdala plays a significant role in emotional behavior and motivation. When it loses its normal behavioral response to danger, it is conceivably characterized by a mindset of Moderate or Extreme Despair and Apathy and perhaps to the extent of "giving up" (Bailey, Self-Protection Syndrome p85). This, I long ago called the *Amygdala Burn-out Syndrome* and there is now confirmatory evidence of it being associated with fear and aggression as well as it being larger in those showing burn-out from emotional distress. As a result, it is harder for them to deal with any new stressors. This leads their emotions to be out of control because they have weaker connections between the Amygdala and the medial prefrontal cortex (associated with executive function). The Enslaved "Burn-Out" meant nothing seemed real--nothing about them seemed worthwhile—nothing gave them a sense of power or personal purpose (a sense of "uselessness")—and nothing they did was significant. Hence, their Despair was about nothing more to fear.

DESPAIR'S "AWE" IN THE ENSLAVED: Typically, a self-awareness 'Larger than Life' mindset means ones mind is also in an "Awe" state--like being invested inside an indescribable mystery with an over-powering aura or undertone about which one is wordless. "*Awe*" (C13 Old Icelandic) contains a glob of Emotions from being unexpectedly tremendously surprised that the 'Larger than Life' inspiring "Thing" could appear at all. It is like the rays of a Mystery stemming from a constellation of hidden stars. That stimulus itself is associated with the appearance of a Chimera Image—i.e. something extremely grand in character, perhaps resembling a threatening evil 'monster'. Ones mental reaction is a glob of excitement—a glob of emotions containing fear, fright, pain, distress, terror, dread or apprehension. Next, one eases into trivial personal preoccupations whereby, like Wonder, nothing is taken for granted—whereby each happening is upside down and "inside out"—whereby ones judgment of the nature of this "Thing" with formidable power is paralyzed. "Awe's" ingredients lack correspondence with reality. Although initially seeming to only imprint superficially on the mind, the Chimera Image is, in actually, indelible and out of which are created *Superstitions*. These Supernatural superstitions are so cling to as for one to totally resistant any effort to be educated out of them--no matter how utterly ones own reason may reject them.

But apart from this highly imaginative experience was the "fish-netted" victims having physical ominous experiences—liken to a thunderstorm's rolling thunder and electric displays—each rapidly repeated experience personally striking every aspect of their Selfhoods. The combination of these physical events with the *Dismay (deprived of power), Consternation* (so terrifying as to prostrate ones Selfhood), and Dread (overwhelming fear) aspects of "Awe" served as an *Alarm ('call to arms')* to which the hapless victims could not respond. Ones personal power assessment is that of being incapable of defense against the physical or the glob mindset one is in. There is no choice but to make peace with the existing circumstance by an instant removal of all meaning of anything in the "here and now". The entrapment of each free African itself, signaling enslavement, was the immediate experience of being so far away from reality as to step into the enslavement mindset mystery of the Supernatural. To be inside this "Air Castle"--situated in an abyss (the abode of evil spirits)--initiated the process of fashioning Supernatural adaptations out of ones monitored feedbacks from interpreted situations.

DESPAIR'S "FORM-BODY": "Awe" Mystery Mindsets of the newly Enslaved instantly became disconnected from their Real Self and from all that is known to be real in their lives. The contents of their assumed False Selves was something they simply did not and could not and would never grasp—a content state so extremely shocking as to cause their well-established *Sensory Consciousness* to revert to a *Form-Body state*. This "*Totipotency*" state of mental activity simulates that of a fetus while in the mother's womb—an implicit Free Mind state of vagueness and haziness without restraints and lacking any specific organization patterns—a Brain/Mind having a totipotent (stem-cell concept) essence so as to allow ones mind to be influenced to develop in various ways. This "*Totipotency*" pre-birth-like basic Brain/Mind state is capable of being molded for good or evil, depending upon which molding "Source" exerts the most influence. In a Form-Body state, ones presumed pre-birth Emotional features resemble Right Brain mental activity of ones early life. Thus, it automatically exhibits "Awe"—like a child's first visit to the circus--at whatever seemingly Supernatural things are occurring at the moment—an "Awe" still unhampered by any judgment as to its good or evil nature. It is my impression that Huggins (Black Odyssey, p. 49) understood this mystery "Awe" mindset. My paraphrase of his comments are: *The Slaves' sense of personal tragedy and private misfortune was diluted and washed away as one became mixed with and overwhelmed by the lesser and the prior ones. The Slaves were kept exhausted and underfed in body and spirit--too benumbed to hope for more than the end of the ordeal and of the nightmare.* Each new insult was like a load added to a camel's back on his way to giving up on life and becoming apathetic.

While the newly Enslaved were in this Form-Body mindset state while face-to-face with their European captors' Indifference/Hate/Evil/Sadistic (IHES) displays, what presumably occurred was the Enslaved experientially absorbing these displays in rapid successive situations. Next, from the completely overwhelming *Emotional Glob* (Fear, Fright, Dismay, Consternation, Dread, "Awe," Fascination) being, ingredients from each became part of their Supernatural Imaginations. Without effort, their Imaginations designed countless "weird" visions and images of every conceivable thing that could be "Against Me". Because these Supernatural images defied natural and familiar explanations, the Enslaved relied on Supernatural agents to create explanations for each of them. No judgment could be placed on what fashions the "Awe" or "Fascination" since there is no immediate entity formed to which judgments can be attached. There was the point where Huggins (Black Odyssey, p. 49) seemed to be speaking about the special conditions of the mentally, physically, and spiritually of these exhausted Enslaved. He put their sense of impending doom (ruin) mindset this way: "the surrender of the spirit and the will to numbness was in its own way a choice of death, a retreat of the consciousness into a tomb of insensibility. Only the automatic, physiological reflexes acted on nervous response to keep the biological apparatus functioning."

This Emotional Glob which overwhelms reason so as to make anything real that comes out of the Supernatural beyond ones control is, I believe, the state of Despair experienced by Enslaved Africans and that has been culturally transmitted to many of their descendants. Obviously, this is in a different realm compared to Europeans' 1300 definition of "to lose hope". Nor is it anything like Europeans' classification of: *Mild Despair* (like Patience tolerated impatiently); *Slight Despair* (fear); *Moderate Despair* (a grandiose form of Funk); and *Extreme Despair* (the bottomless perdition or utter ruin by being in the European concept they call Hell). In other words, what is referred to herein is the Black American form of *Extreme Despair* (a defect of spirit)—distinguished by its far, far deeper, wider, higher, and more devastating meaning than the European counterparts. Whereas of all the base passions of human, Fear is the most accused, I believe the most base Background mindset of all descendants of Black Americans Enslaved Ancestors is that of Extreme Despair.

DESPAIR'S MINDSET DISPLAYS: Not long after the "Fishnet" moment there was, for the majority of the Enslaved, the drainage out of them every drop of their *Courage*—meaning their Instincts were "shut down" to thereby end their fight to be free. They accepted being without hope in their face-to-face encounters with irresistible and inevitable European forces of evil. The Effect of having *no more fight left* was an acceptance of their fate inside the fatality realm of Doom—i.e. the awareness of the terrifying specter of the disappearance of whatever makes life worthwhile—the removal from ones Life-Living Background which had provided safety, security, sureness, strength, and stability. They: (1) lacked ideas of doing anything personally purposeful or useful (a sense of "uselessness"); (2) realized the loss of their own identity; (3) knew of their inability to function in taking care of oneself; and (4) experienced a fate of going to complete annihilation with pain but without dying. Such minds were in a "bottomless pit" and unable to cope with an enslaved existence—and yet having no escape—having no options but to linger around ghostlike. Everything seemed surreal—i.e. sensing ones Selfhood reality joined to an unreality beyond space and time—while being abandoned, isolated, and entangled inside the unknown Supernatural World.

So, each next barrage of Selfhood attacks could be met with phlegmatic indifference. Thereafter, some aimlessly struggled; some barely hung on; and some "gave up," flowing with the current. All were in Extreme Despair. The "*what it is*" of such Extreme Despair was in the Enslaved knowing themselves to be hopelessly and forever lost--not knowing where they were--having no desire to go anywhere—and being unable to go if they so desired. The permanent, stationary, unchanging reality aspect of Extreme Despair was entered by the inevitable nature of their happenings shoving into their Souls the deplorable wretchedness comprising the Enslaved Emotional Glob.

Once inside the realm of Extreme Despair, the Enslaved seemed as if they were in the damp of "Hell"--turned upside-down and re-formed "Inside-Out". As they progressed in this realm, their profound sorrow pressed down (i.e. Depression) their mindsets into an *Abyss*—a symbolized realm of being out of the cycle of life. Then, as a result of their Souls and Intellect being Upside-Down and Inside-Out, they wallowed in the rottenness of having declared themselves to be insufficient to compete in life—representing a state of being at the worst place there is for humans. Inherent in this Extreme Despair process was the role of the Form-Body aspect—a mindset regression formed as a result of the "Awe" at the "Fishnet" moment. To repeat, just as the mother's self-induced hormones from moods and the products of her diet intake can influence accordingly the certain mental networks of the developing fetus, so is an "Awe" determined Form-Body mindset completely susceptible to being molded in character by the one feeding it—no matter how evil the feeder. Despite the inadequacy of all the feedings of anything (e.g. food, clothing, shelter) to the Enslaved delivered by the Satanists, the nature of their Form-Body mindsets extended bonding embraces to the inhumane oppressors. This scenario adopted by the Enslaved is what I call the "*Evil Savior Syndrome*" mindset.

Out of all these contributors to the "new normal" mindsets of the Enslaved, there emerged Abyss patterns of "Life-Living" going in every conceivable direction—most of whom covered their unique adopted "Personality" with the masks and masquerades each thought would work best in lessening the terribleness of their lives. Whatever was chosen has been culturally transmitted to today's descendants.

EXTREME DESPAIR IN BLACK PEOPLE

Of fundamental importance to understanding the depth of Despair and the mindsets of Black Americans which arose out of its depth is to have more than a passing gist of what constitutes Background, Base, and Bottom in the Natural and the Supernatural realms. This necessitates thinking in perhaps new ways--bringing together words and their hierarchies that normally are not thought of as going together--and/or dealing with things that are normally undifferentiated. Ancient African Sages established the Cosmos and the Cosmic Organism's "Ground of Being" to be the primordial substance in the form of Divine Consciousness. By humans' Souls constituting a "Spark of God" means our Souls are Divine Consciousness. By being constituted of Unconditional Love means humans have the Free Will to remain with our Real Selves or adopt False Selves. After each human's first entrance to Earth World life, various acquired ignorance led to setting up fears, habits, and conditioning of natural reflexes. Some were retained at death to become part of ones Karma, even though before dying one may have shed the more significant negative Acquired Emotions and fetters. The retained Karma of relatively minor self-impurities manifested at the time of ones rebirth into the Earth world—being positioned in the Background or Bottom of ones ordinary mind and separated from ones Divine Consciousness.

EXTREME DESPAIR: Each one of these personal happenings, among countless others, vied for out-doing all the rest in causing unbearable Spiritual, Emotional, and Physical pains. Together they were like an airplane carrying explosives and running into a skyscraper building--shattering all aspects from the top floor down to the Base upon which the building was situated and shoved the pieces into the basement. Something similar to this is how I envision the Enslaved Minds' scattering in every conceivable direction and then, of what could be found, being bulldozed into a "bottomless pit". This mindset state I call "*Ultimate Despair*"—giving it a far, far deeper, wider, higher, and more devastating meaning than the European 1300 definition of "lose hope." The Selfhood destruction was so complete as to ensure the lack of it ever returning to a pre-Enslavement state or improving into a better state from reassembling the shattered Selfhood pieces. The total focus of each Enslaved was surviving moment to moment and to do this every conceivable mindset was adopted. Nevertheless, the minds of each Enslaved made a "Collapsing Telescope" type descent of their Consciousness—starting with the Sensory Secular World Consciousness Awareness Foreground and heading *backward* toward the Bottom/Base/Background called Consciousness Station I. Just as each one settled somewhere in between—like on the Negative side of the Thinker's Scale, so did different fractions of the Enslave settle in a similar distribution on that Negative Scale.

PATHS HEADING TOWARDS THE BOTTOM/BASE/BACKGROUND: Background was first used by Primitive Africans with reference to a dramatic performance with respect to what was in the back of the stage to serve as props—serving to be a contrast against better-lighted parts of the stage in the foreground. Later it concerned the part of a picture which seemed most remote from the spectator and against which the figures or principle objects represented seem to be projected. In Ancient African schools students needed to have had exposure to certain pieces of knowledge. People have tended to have landscape serve as a background to human events (e.g. at the ocean). A "*Backdrop*" is literally a drop curtain at the rear of the stage which provides the decorative or realistic background for the action of a plan. The accompanying music effects in a play is background. Everything in this mutable world of changing things has a history consisting of its factual development in reality.

NEAR "BOTTOM" CONFUSED FOR REAL "BOTTOM": I have been in many situations where I thought this is the worst as it can get and then that bottom falls out, leaving me no word to describe where I am, thereby keeping me from boasting of my strength to endure it. To elaborate, originally in architecture, when wooden posts were used, the Base served to keep the wood away from the floor or ground. Thus, this was not an Ultimate Base but rather an Origin Background serving as a Bottom. Most people are unable to form an idea of what "Bottom" means until they are down to their 'bottom' dollar. This may be down to the Beginning Foreground for those who can get money from elsewhere. Or, it may down to the Origin Background level for the Homeless.

REALISTIC POSSIBILITIES AT THE "BOTTOM": The bottom of the ship (i.e. the lower part of the hull, usually below the waterline) at sea keeps the ship from sinking. Such a situation is present in Extreme Despair where its "Bottom" separates one from death. On any parsed Background above the Source, the Law of Forces (which hinders bodies from sinking beyond a certain depth in the sea) may seem to apply to those who have never pushed their limits to the maximum. For example, ones life may be in such a mess as to believe one is presently at the "Bottom" (e.g. of a mindset or situation)—a situation where the Law of Forces is operating. This may actually be at the Origin's Preconditioning for the Causes whereby one has the belief that once something (e.g. like 'me') is down to this level, it can fall no further. However, the reality is that if the circumstances were changed and in a different setting or on a different plane of existence, there would be a different result. For example, if one at the bottom of the sea was suddenly placed in the ocean of baseness (e.g. like Despair) the deeper one gets the easier is the sinking.

"WHAT IF'S" BOTTOMS: In mythology, "Bottomless" is the Base of the Cosmos—the abyss (immeasurably profound depth or void out of which it was believed the earth and sky were formed). Could this be real? Could it be about the Supernatural's "Bottomless Pit" (the Hell so called in Revelation 20:I)? Some fears come from not seeing the Bottom. Or, if one goes to sleep and (1) dreams of (2) dreaming, and in dreaming (2) there is a (3) dream of (4) dreaming and so forth, how will one know when one has awakened back to reality—i.e. (1) dream? The point is that Background, Base, and Bottom can be about reality or the Supernatural (fantasy) and to be able to distinguish one from the other is fundamental and foundational to how one does "Life Living."

STABLE "BOTTOMS": a fixed "Bottom"—also called "Rock Bottom"--is a starting point because it provides a base of support to go upward or provides the place to get rid of limitations ('Knock the bottom out'). To get to the bottom of the matter refers to ascertaining the Truth. Some choose to stay on the "Bottom" for protection from those at the top. In this sense, Extreme Despair, meaning one who has "touched bottom" or reached the lowest depth, can combine with a new attitude as a result of knowing one has a stable board from which to spring up. To repeat an illustration of this, in chemistry, Base denotes a substance which combines with an acid to form a salt as a result of accepting protons or donating a pair of electrons. Thus, there is a "new" beginning for the salt. A stable "Bottom" of Extreme Despair means one can stay there as is, spring forward to somewhat adjust to life, or go in reverse so as to constitute an "Inside-Out" mindset. A remarkable mental feat was those who penetrated through the Bottom of Despair came out with having "No Fear" and thereby became known as the "Baddest Dudes of the Streets" (fig. 20).

"BIG PICTURE" SUMMARY OF DESPAIR REACTIONS: In Black American Extreme Despair one perceives Selfhood abandonment from each and everything that previously provided a sense of support. By possessing no resources, one self-declares oneself to be utterly powerless in finding a way out—and thus a total personal failure. One is entangled in the "fishnet" and spears are inserted into one through each fishnet hole opening into ones Selfhood as one is tumbling downward in space. Once at the Bottom of Despair, these Enslaved had reached a state of stability and out of that "stable" Base comes a host of reactions. Type I were those who decided what to do, meaning they went into the direction of "Sell-Outs" as mentioned and they are known today by receiving compliments from Whites. Type II went in the opposite direction, being Rebels who fought in overt, tempered, masked, and concealed ways. Some Escaped and worked furiously, as if on a treadmill. Most are hyperemotional, anxious, over-weight, and/or on drugs. Type III was those who choose to stay on the "Bottom" for protection from the evilness of those at the top. Type IV's mindset adopted by the Enslaved was based on the belief that one having hopeless hopelessness Despair—as by being enslaved by unspeakably evil European males--ought never hope. For the Enslaved to entertain hope of eventually having a better life or having any comfort in the face of the reality of obvious contrary evidence would have been extremely anxiety producing. As their reasoning continued, if self-help trying failed, their lives might be un-bearable. So, for the *Afflicted to consider an even remote chance of escape from their mental enslavement represented a needless burden to add to their already over-burdened lives.* Its remoteness came from their awareness that no matter what they did or did not do there would be no time in their lives when things would get better--not being nice to Whites; not working hard; not being disabled; not getting old; and not receiving help from their Ancestors or even God. Hence, "Why Bother?"

Type V, the overwhelming in numbers of Enslaved went in another direction as a result of "being caught up in futile reasoning" brought to a stop any Hoping for anything ever again returning to the "old normal" they once experienced. This means they saw themselves at the end of their rope of ever being Free and were and utterly at a loss as to what to do. The consequence of this was to negate the possibility of any productive activity and they gave up from seemingly uselessness of making further efforts towards self-improvement. Such attitudes paralyzed any desire to even attempt to better a given situation for oneself and loved ones. In general, dominant Temperament categories included: (1) *phlegmatic*--conspicuous for a cold and sluggish way of reacting, passive, careful, thoughtful, peaceful, controlled, reliable, even-tempered, calm. Some went so deep as for these Enslaved to display as stony calmness. (2) The *Choleric* are touchy, aggressive, excitable, changeable, impulsive, optimistic, and active. They over-stimulate their hormones and nervous system—perhaps into a "fight or flight" response. (3) "Fixed *Melancholy*" concerned the Enslaved who were moody, anxious, rigid, sober, pessimistic, reserved, unsociable, quiet, often sad and tending to give up their will to live. They eventually leveled out into a form of immobilizing apathy. Type VI: Some Escaped and worked furiously, as if on a treadmill.

POST-ENSLAVEMENT "NEW NORMAL" MINDSET

The inhumane effects of what was inherent in all of being Enslaved, followed by ongoing post-slavery racism. Of fundamental importance to the course of Black People's mindsets "Awed" by enslavement is the realization that: (1) upon stepping into the mystery of the enslavement, "Awe" was continuously and perma-nently generated as a lifestyle; (2) with the passage of time and with each generational cultural transmission, the more remote becomes the origin of those patterns of thinking developed by all aspects of the "Awe"; (3) once those patterns were established, they were of a Supernatural (Delusional) nature; and (4) those Delusions, as customs, confuse what it takes to thrive in life as well as obscure the ways of what it takes to return to Real Self ingredients of thinking and thriving. Each Black American reacted to what fashioned "Vine" patterns or 'rungs' on today's Social Ladder—meaning there are groups of people on every rung ranging from the Human Ideal of African Tradition to the Ideal of European Tradition to a mixture of African and European Traditions on down to the lowest rung situated in a "Bottomless Pit." As a result of the Enslaved "new normal" Background Mindset—likened to a "Seed"—emerged "vines of mindsets" going in every conceivable direction. On each of their "vines" was the layering of countless types of types of self-defeating attitudes, negative ways of thinking, and failings in how to deal with their horrible situations.

The overwhelming types of "vines" used by the Enslaved were various aspects of the masks and masquerades they donned in reacting to the enslavers as, for example, Black Puppets (Oreos), Slave informers, and "Sambos". Others were Rebels and fought in overt, tempered, masked, and concealed ways. Some Escaped and worked furiously, as if on a treadmill. Following slavery and going to the present, The more struggling Black People were/are hyperemotional, anxious, over-weight, and/or on drugs. They had/have no starting or ending points for handling significant problems in life. Most ignore their biggest problems, hoping they will resolve favorably. Its like saying: "I don't have anything now and I can't have any less if I do nothing." There is chronic Juggling in daily living from no planning or proper priority in handling necessary business. The idea is to enjoy the moment when ever it arises on very rare occasions. Its about getting through the day. All of this comes out of a Background of Despair—and that gives a 'cookie cutter' form of socialization to those in the "Crowd". Each sequence of Cause, Effects, Consequences, and overall Results when collected into a "Big Picture" of what was/is generically expressed in Think, Feel, Expressions, and Behaviors constitutes what I call called *Black American Customs*.

Struggling Black People are those primarily on the lower rungs and their various types of poverties lead them to live a life of vicious cycles. Those in a "Bottomless Pit" are the most victimized because of living their lives "Inside-Out" (i.e. 'voting against themselves'). Perhaps the "str-" part of the C14 English word "Struggle" refers the time, energy, and effort involved in the flawed processes in the "Surviving," the "Striving," the "Strength," and the Spiritual Energy Package necessary to Thrive and have a sense of Well-Being. A Consequence of the *Struggling Black People "Vine" is that a bud emanating out of it contains the ingredients out of which Black gang members derive*. Whereas it is typical to believe violence is any action motivated by hatred, with struggling Black People the motivation is poverty and its effects.

BRAIN SWITCH FROM ENSLAVEMENT

Metaphorically, let us suppose a skyscraper building represents the world and, in actuality, for 198,000 years Super-Brilliant Black People lived in its penthouse--sitting on thrones and sleeping in gold beds. Then, envious outsiders, living in the basement, started "taking them down" by means of the GUN and by trickery. Or, more specifically, the impact of enslavement itself the Selfhood of each Enslaved was like an airplane carrying explosives and running into a skyscraper building, shattering all activities from the top floor down to the Base upon which the building was situated. As a result, Africans slid down the laundry chute directly through to the basement. The most severely "beaten down" in the "taken down" flew pass the basement to end upside down inside a bottomless pit. Half have remained spinning around in the basement. Some have climbed the stairs to reach various levels of the skyscraper building. A few are almost up to the penthouse.

Normally, terrorists choose targets based on symbolism as, for example, the 9/11/2001 Twin Towers not only being emblematic of New York but also Western dominance. The symbolism chosen by European Satanists that was most hated and intensely envied (particularly the Black male) came from Black People's sense of well-being as well as supreme intelligence in ruling the world for 198,000 years of the 200,000 years humans have been on Earth. For this reason and because of their Indifference/Hate/Evil/Sadism (IHES) complex "second nature" mindsets, Satanists started the slave trade in order to greedily grab African riches, Africans' intellectual property, and enslave the people. This impact of African American slavery caused a complete demolition of their Selfhoods. The instant switch from using their Thriving Brain (i.e. the Cerebral Cortex and the Limbic portions) for normal living over to their Instinct or "Emergency" Brain ("fight, flight, or fright") was a happening that forever trapped their minds inside a mental vault. Put another way, the impact of enslavement itself to the Selfhood of each Enslaved was so devastating as to shatter their Spiritual, Intellectual, Emotional, Social, and Physical realms beyond the possibility of them ever being repaired, even in subsequent generations.

At the "Fishnet Moment" when the fishnet was thrown over the free African in Africa to thereafter enslave him/her "forever," there was an instanteous dangling of utter and total Selfhood hopeless helplessness that transported each Enslaved beyond their perceived bounds of known or imagined sensibility--beyond their perceived body's systems to respond to danger--beyond their perceived help from any source, even from God. Also, at the "Fishnet Moment" the Enslaved had an instant shift from using their Rational and wholistic brain thinking over to their Instinct Brains (associated with "Fight, Flight, or Fright"). The reality of these occurrences was so severely shocking to their *Sensory Consciousness* as to take their thinking processes back to an *Form-Body state*--the presumed state of a newborn's mind where it is completely susceptible to being molded by the one feeding it--*the "Inside-Out"* mindset *from which Black-on-Black Violence as a direct/indirect effect of European inhumanity originates.* Such a Form-Body state was triggered by the "Fishnet Moment"—the "Brain Switch" moment characterized by Alex Haley in the book/movie "*Roots.*"

The setting was 1750 when Kunta Kinte in Gambia, West Africa--a free African going about his normal thriving daily activities--was suddenly encased in a fishnet dropped on him. There was an instant switch from using his Thriving Brain (i.e. the Cerebral Cortex and the Limbic portions) for normal living over to his Instinct Brain ("fight, flight, or fright")--a happening that forever trapped his mind inside a mental vault. Kunta fought wildly and courageously against his African captors but was overwhelmed by their strength in numbers and by being clubbed unconscious. He awakened naked, chained, shackled, and aware of being permanently enslaved. But what I believe also happened, starting at the exact moment of the fishnet drop, was a series of very significant happenings to Kunta's physical body and his Quintaune Brain (i.e. Cortex, Limbic, and the Ancient Brain's Instinct, Omnibus, and Brute subdivisions) (fig. 2).

The fishnet episode was followed by the exhausting march to coastal areas hundreds of miles away to be placed in barracoons (holding prisons) where the Enslaved had to fight over scraps of food to hopefully keep from starving while awaiting their horrible "Middle Passage" to the "New World". Put another way, the impact of enslavement itself meant the Selfhood of each Enslaved was like an airplane carrying explosives and running into a skyscraper building, shattering all activities from the top floor down to the Base upon which the building was situated.

Following the "Fishnet Moment," the Brain Switch, the shattering of the effectiveness of Instincts, the regression into a Form-Body mindset, next came the Horrible Middle Passage. On board ship, the Enslaved were shackled together in the coffles; packed into the dank barraccon "factory" dungeons; squeezed like sardines in a can between the decks of stinking and poorly ventilated ships, separated often from their kinsmen, tribesmen, or even speakers of the same language; left bewildered about their present and their future; stripped of all human rights or prerogatives of status or rank; and homogenized by a dehumanizing system that viewed them as subhuman, largely interchangeable, and faceless. As in the barracoons, on-board "Middle Passage" ships the Enslaved were packed on top of each other like sardines in a can. This meant the Enslaved had to lie in their own waste while breathing noxious fumes in the unventilated, crammed space—gasping for air. Most would go mad from misery and suffocation or from being chained by the neck and legs. In their madness some killed others in the hope of gaining more room to breathe. Not having enough room to sit up or turn over, while in unbearable heat or cold, many Enslaved died in this position. Some Enslaved killed themselves by starving to death. Many were prevented from starving by being whipped, tortured with hot coal, or crews breaking their teeth so as to do force feeding. Men strangled those next to them; women drove nails into each other's brains; some committed suicide (e.g. cutting their throats, jumping overboard) and many died of a "broken heart".

COURSE OF THE ENSLAVED POST-BRAIN SWITCH: Pause for a moment to think what it would have been like in slavery for you to completely lose your freedom to follow your destination in life; for your self-identity to be ripped from your larger societal organism; for you to forever lose all you have ever known—all human beings, all close relationships, all folkways and mores, and all objects having sentimental or sacred value; and for you to have a sense of hopelessness and despair "forever." To make matters worse, you are brought face to face into an entirely new world that is filled with evil and sadistic people who have no sense of humanity. While they are heavily armed with all sorts of weapons, you are not even armed with a finger-nail clip. The horror of your experiences leads you to operate out of your Instinct Brain, and at the expense of your Rational Brains. You are not able to figure out what to do because you are in a foreign land but do not specifically know where or what is "out there"—because your skin color makes you stand out like a "sore thumb"—because you are in a world where you are defenseless—because the circumstances render your established worldviews for self-preservation to be useless—and because of being in a world where you do not want to be.

There is no way to rebuild a mental structure or to have any hope for a better day. Without your freedom and without your normal ability to think and without any help from anyone and with being half-starved, overloaded with work, and frequently whipped "for no reason," you are primed to consider anything available to help you survive. That includes being bonded to the enslavers. These were the very conditions which left a void in the minds of the Enslaved and caused them to wonder if God had forsaken them. All Enslaved, no doubt, felt the same way.

In a brief review, the Portuguese started the African slave trade in 1415 and eventually other European nations rushed in so as to greedily grab as much money as they could. Deveau (*Diogenes, 1997*) provides details of the specific trade aspects. For example, 'legitimate' merchants owned the slave ships, or slavers, laden with goods like kettles, weapons, and kegs of rum to exchange for captives. Commerce fueled the entire operation. The Americas supplied cotton, sugar, and coffee to be exported to Europe and labor from Enslaved Africans was needed to gather the goods. As production boomed, more and more workers were needed, and Europeans incessantly returned to Africa to meet the growing demand for Laborers. Victimized Africans—whether potential candidates or actually entrapped—fought valiantly but always lost, no matter who won. African kings would sell African people to the Europeans and that led Africans into an overwhelmed state, not so much from dark skin color, but from being a powerless and a conquered people. "Popguns cannot compete with cannons" as the saying goes.

It is important to keep in mind that 41% of the captives in African were between 5 and 10 and 25% of all Enslaved had been were kidnapped. The rest came from a small group of Africans working in conjunction with Europeans to sell the prisoners of wars—wars that had been generated by the Europeans. The vital fact that is over looked by Europeans who attempt to justify the evilness of their ancestors is that the Enslaved in Africa were of a mild type (e.g. becoming part of the kinship) while the historical treatment of Enslaved by European has always by extremely vicious. And the Africans helping the Europeans were not aware of this. Nevertheless, the impact of enslavement on each Enslaved + their "Fishnet Moment" Brain Switch + "Killing their Spirits" on each Selfhood, as mentioned above, was like an airplane carrying explosives and running into a skyscraper building--shattering all activities from the top floor down to the Base upon which the building was situated and shoved the pieces into the basement. Something similar to this is how I envision the Enslaved Minds' scattering in every conceivable direction and then, of what could be found, being bulldozed into a "bottomless pit". This mindset I call profound "Despair"—around which was a sense of Selfhood "emptiness". Over time--?6 months—the acuteness of the Enslaved fears and other reactions to the horrors of slavery were gradually accommodated to a somewhat lower and chronic level.

Meanwhile, the European captors, pointing the Gun to show the awesomeness of their power, did every conceivable thing to deeply implant the idea that Black People were predestined by God to be Enslaved—and "forever." Machine-gunned hate and evilness showered daily on the Enslaved included animal-like labels, demeaning name-calling, and Self-Esteem destroying messages about their Selfhood and about their Ancestors and about their own fellows being inferior and subhuman. The Enslaved could count on pain inflictions of every sort every day. Yet, many from *desensitization, eventually failed to be intimidated by threats or punishment*. This was the beginning of "*Inside-Out*" Thinking which now characterizes the seed of thinking used by many of today's Black Americans.

By enslavement shattering all they had ever known in Africa, none were able to reassemble the shattered pieces so as to be able to duplicate what they had lost. Inside the Delusional World in which the Enslaved lived, using Delusional Thinking, none could describe any essential thing within oneself--nothing about fear, rage, hate, love, pity, or scorn. Instead, one could only gasp for the breath of life in trying to survive and endure. Inside-Out Thinking's features for reversed Instinct substitutes, as in the form of "Awe" and "Fascination" checkered throughout Dread--seemed to be coming from far away. The resultant effects was the attraction of weird passionless forces having Supernatural power over oneself--and without one knowing the source of that power, meaning, or purpose. This characterized the switch from Instinct Brain thinking over to Omnibus Brain/Emotional thinking.

OMNIBUS BRAIN

"Omnibus" originally (1829) meant a horse-drawn wagon containing "some of this and some of that" which, when applied to it being a subdivision of the Ancient Brain (fig. 2), is like fire-flies inside a jar. Ranging between its partners, the Instinct Brain (ultimate human Goodness) on one side and the Brute Brain (ultimate human Disorder) on the other, the Omnibus Brain is a bridge between them and containing all mental ingredients which feature human behavior. In this way, the Omnibus Brain contents and its Ethereal composition (the finest, thinnest, and most tenuous form of Matter) resembles the Cosmic Metaphysical realm. This *Intangible plane* of existence (i.e. the Cosmos' transition between energy and matter in the universe) consists of the *Noumenal Plane* (all Metaphysical Objective reality—e.g. spirits of things, thoughts, images, etc.) and the Ethereally denser *Phenomenal Plane* (physical Energy/Matter) whereby its ethereal bodies are not far apart from the Material World's physical bodies because their vibrational frequencies are capable of being a synchronized link them (Amen Metu Neter I:55, 58). One result is a human's *Astral Body* forms an exact ethereal (or "shadow") replica of a human's physical body and yet the two interpenetrate at all levels, including the brain and nerves. Whether bad or good, the Astral Body houses memory, dreams, all physical forces, sensations, desires, emotions, the mind, and motivations of an individual.

The point is that although it means well, the Omnibus Brain is a queer storehouse. Type I category is Reality Wisdom, as in what derives from heredity by way of instincts. However, added to this is self-preservation and well-being acquired non-destructive information from other parts of the Triune (or Quintaune) brain used in actions and reactions--and that implies thoughts and varied emotions are involved. Type II is "Phenomena" (from phantom, to 'make visible')--by possessing no life of itself--have no reality in themselves. Hence, all such appearances are subject to constant change Nevertheless, some phenomena are products of the intellect. Type III is a mixture, as when some contents come from what unfolds within it and whose seeds were sown at the time of the primal impulse (which started life along the path) and branched to incorporate the Collective Unconscious and ones race memory.; some are preserved in the basic memory of the race; some springing from the intellect; and some represent the past experiences of ones race, even reaching back into the animal kingdom. No human has a sense experience from such a deep meaning of nature within ones Selfhood; nor from the actual experiences of instincts themselves (Ramacharaka, Fourteen Lessons, p25). Type IV is *Foolishness* ('empty-headed') from being full of things received from a variety of sources coming from the External World or by the Supernatural (made-up, either of a neutral or of a Brute nature).

Type V are Brute influenced Emotions. Historically, the Limbic (Emotional) Brain came into being by evolving out of the Ancient Brain and over-growing it like a cap, hence a "Limbus" (a border). It is called Old Mammalian because its highest development first appeared among Mammals and served as the major influence of their behavior. In humans, it is the seat of emotional communication, especially the drives of "Fight, Flight, Fright" mating, and seeking food. This older and more primitive Brain, compared with a human's Cerebral Cortex and Frontal Lobes, dominates a human's first 28 years of life, thus laying the foundation for beliefs, opinions, outlooks, and behaviors gathered from the External World. Those gatherings are primarily an animalistic type of excitements, most shrewdly designed by Satanists and put into every aspect of today's society life (e.g. religion and government). Regardless of their degree, those bad influences take effect in a toddler as early as 18 months old. What is accepted into children's minds range from insecurity, shame from self-image problems, fear, rage, violence, sensuality, and fetters (e.g. "Me, Me, Me" Individualism, arrogance, pride, lies, selfishness, greed, lust, egoism, envy, jealousy, and frustration). At its worse are *Brute Imitators* of the Indifference/Hate/Evil/Sadism Complex. MRI studies show the anterior dorsolateral prefrontal cortex, a region thought to be involved in suppressing emotional responses, and the inferior frontal gyrus, an area responsible for evaluating social behavior and cooperation account for their extreme "Me, Me, Me". Since "everybody" is "caught-up" in these society trends and because most youth are no longer being taught to display Spiritual Elements, this dominant societal animalistic mindset is deemed normal. jabaileymd.com

EMOTIONAL WORLD OF THE ENSLAVED

Whereas European males honor being feared, the Afrocentric honor being Respected. The "Take Down" of "Humanity Respect" began when Africans first came into contact with Europeans--who, in general, are an Animalistic Emotionally Fear-based people. The involved Africans were naïve to the trickery and deceit used by Europeans--a con-artist job so smoothly slipping Africans into a *"Socialized Disaster"* as for the practice to be initially accepted and followed until it was too late. Certain Africans were enticed to enslave their fellows. The "*Fishnet Moment*" (whereby free Africans in Africa were immediately forever enslaved) was the center of several dynamics and their respective subdivisions pertaining to the Black American Mind. The "Fishnet" episode was followed by the exhausting long marches to slave holding areas. Enslaved Africans brought in from around African empires included those of the Western Sudan Moslems, Central and West Africa, Madagascar, and elsewhere. These men, woman, and children from all over Africa ranged from the dignified, cultured, and refined in possession of noble character--to being quite intelligent and educated--to "normal"--to the problematic (e.g. bad characters, the disabled, the feeble). The very earliest interactions of the newly captured Africans in Africa was that of being shackled together in the coffles. Newly captured and Enslaved Africans of different cultures and from diverse regions of Africa were separated so as to ensure no mates spoke the same language. They marched hundreds of miles together to coastal African areas while chained, barefoot, having inadequate clothing--and almost no rest, food, or water.

From there they were transported to the African coastal shores of the Gulf of Guinea and others where stood many trading posts or "factories" on the Grain Coast (Liberia), the Ivory Coast (now the Ivory Coast Republic), the Gold Coast (Ghana), and the Slave Coast (Nigeria, Dahomey/Benin, and Togo). Upon arrival and placement in barracoons (holding prisons), the newly Enslaved, whenever sporadically fed, had to fight each other over scraps of food thrown into their human waste in which they stood. And they were in standing room only barracoons with feces a foot deep. The results of all to which the Enslaved were subjected led to the "Survival Mindset" of Despair (hopeless hopelessness)—i.e. a Despair leading easily to submission to the captors. The first of three pertinent ones was the ending of the generic African following Ancient African Tradition--the one with a powerfully developed entire brain--the one in the Ma'at flow of the Ocean of Nun--the one with impenetrable barriers around the "Set Gene" of evilness. Second was the introduction of the Brute Brain evilness (the fully released "Set Gene") by European Satanist captors--those rejecting the Right Brain (with its Humanity aspects)--having a profound degree of self-hate as part of their Indifference/Hate/Evil/Sadism (IHES) Complex--those whose "misery loves company" orientation focused on such Indifference concerning others as to fashion their evil deeds into Sadism in hopes of getting a moment of relief from their Spiritual Pain.

Third was the "Brain Switch" in the Enslaved--shifting their general brain usage to the Ancient Brain's Instinct portion--and later into the Omnibus Brain portion. The Ancient Brain exhibits the "Identical Difference"--like the two-sides of a coin--"Sameness/Uniqueness" feature. One example is its three subdivisions of Instinct, Omnibus, and Brute parts which are generally about survival, self-preservation, and self-protection but are fundamentally different from each other. Another is having Emotional representations suited to their different natures. Instinct Emotions have a "Pleasure" aspect for bonding with the mother and an alarm aspect--i.e. Rage, Fear, Pain, Depression (in the "make yourself small" sense)--all done without thought. The Omnibus Brain's Emotions concern "this and that" of an "awe" type nature. The Brute Brain's wayward spirit Emotions provide "sick" pleasures from causing pain and suffering in others. All of this meant that each Enslaved, apart from being in a "Dark World," was existing with a "Cloud" covering her/his "Soul Sunshine" as well as a "Dark Cloud" hovering over them. "Dark" refers to Ignorance, for one cannot see a way out or even where one is--and thus must be guided by hearing.

To express this metaphorically, a necessary part of the sky are Clouds which begin on the surfaces of the earth from hovering air that is cooled and mixed with tiny particles of dust and other matter. Some go on to eclipse both the moon and sun. When the gods thump the Clouds that is the cause of thunder. When a human's problems get to be like clouds hovering over their inner sunlight, that human sees only the underside of the clouds. When the clouds are expansive enough and thick enough, that human loses the benefit of his/her inner sunshine, even though it is readily available if the wind blows them away or if one rises above the cloud. Yet, if one goes into a dungeon—a Dark World--one loses contact with the sunshine and thereafter one can only see shadows generated by artificial light. History shows that Hatred and Destruction are slavery's inevitable aftermath and together they fashion every conceivable mindset. But following the Brain Switch, what did not happen in the Enslaved was the continued development of their Left Brains. Instead, since there was nothing to challenge thinking as part of their daily drudgery of hard work, the Left Brains of newly Enslaved arrivals lost their developed skills while the Enslaved born in the Americas failed to develop comparable skills, as for Critical Thinking. The loss of Left Brain skills included its "check and balance" discipline effect on the Right Brain and thereby enabling the Right Brain's Old Mammalian/Omnibus Emotions to become undisciplined. In other words, the result was one being orchestrated by Emotions rather than by developed and disciplined reason. This compromise of reasoning skills + absorbing the Brute Brain Emotional manifestations of the captors--the only models the Enslaved had—enhanced their "Inside-Out" Thinking—i.e. featuring letting themselves be taken in and do things against their Survival, Self-Protection, and Self-Preservation Instincts. This is like walking into an alligator's mouth and not noticing. They had many similarities seen in Zombies as a result of a lack of Courage from the loss of their spirits, as the slave-owner Willie Lynched described.

Overall, the Enslaved had a need to make alterations in their sense of personal power related to handling hardships. Typically, these were false perceptions of their personal power and that caused them to reassess who they were and what they could or would do to simply survive their daily pains, sufferings, and hardships. Some chose to use their salvaged power, despite being overwhelmed by the effects of slavery, to simply "go along to get along"; some to engage in "Resistance" avengement practices; some to participate in revengeful counter-attacks on the enemy; and some to make their survival methods conform to their beliefs in God. Of course, inside each of these five categories each of the reactions of the Enslaved was different. Each such mindset has been culturally transmitted to their today's Black American descendants (Bailey, Special Minds). A prominent example is the category of *Masochism (i.e. aggression turned inwards)*. Its four basic concepts are: (1) Passivity to Hardships--"It's my fate!"; (2) Spiritual Purification--"I am superior"; (3) Vengeful--"I am willing to suffer to make you suffer too"; (4) Seeking Pain for Pleasure--"I need to be punished".

Regardless of the category of mindsets that did not cater to the captors, the Enslaved found it essential for endurance to "Huddle Together". This gave rise to the beginning of the lifestyle category of "BE-ers"—i.e. *"People Addictions"*—who engage in a variety of Omnibus/Old Mammalian Emotions, colored by Brute Emotions they imitated. Although sharing the similarity of Clouds Effects, unique exhibitions included some Clouds being lonely; some Clouds scattered and some hidden; some travelled in Clouds seeking manna (Spiritual nourishment of Divine origin) where none is. Some clouded with doubt simply waited for the Clouds to clear before they get started with their lives or allowed Clouds to overtake them or waited for replacement Clouds. Some tried to emulate Clouds by drifting in the blue. But all knew that no Clouds could satisfy their Selfhoods.

ENSLAVED VOLITION NOT TO THINK: Because of all of these manifestations happening to their mindsets "Awed" by enslavement, vast numbers of Enslaved volitionally chose to not think about them, as in not trying to figure out what to do. Instead, the best way they saw to survive and endure was simply by living out of what was automatic—i.e. expressing their emotions concerning how to live. What happen as a result was that portions of their *"Survival Despair"* allowed "Awe" and Fascination to orchestrate their lives. This, of course, led to their Common Sense getting so out of control concerning significant things as to generate a mindset state called *Mental Evasion* (the willful suspension of ones consciousness) which admixes with "Awe". In other words, the idea was that by ignoring the problem they had just a good a chance of minimizing their losses as by anything else. This combination leading to *willful ignorance* had the effect of causing the afflicted to: (1) be *blind to things of significance* in the present and for the future; (2) *not allow one to attach much importance to beneficial information and therefore that information is easily forgotten*, despite it being very important; (3) embrace Superficial Thinking; and (4) internalize the constant destructive attacks on their self-esteem they experience so that those attacks come alive by means of an emotionally loaded Icon Image.

Those Icon Images are *Engrams*—i.e. a memory imprint leaving simply an Image, or an Imagination form or a Contingent Being (e.g. 'bogeyman') figure with 'character' and power. None of these are what is seen in reality but rather what ones Imagination creates as distortions of reality or fantasy of a Supernatural nature that makes ones mind believe it to be real. One or more of these engrams are reinforced by the afflicted repeatedly playing back its payload messages on their mental tape recorder until they create a fixed self-defeating mindset which repeatedly fashions Delusions leading to vicious cycles. A mindset undergoing such a disintegration of reality—partly conscious and partly unconscious—while replacing it with Supernatural Engrams--thereafter becomes the gatekeeper to serve as the standard, filter, guide, and measure for how information coming into that mind is interpreted and processed for mental functioning. Furthermore, it acts like a plow for making further inroads into the Delusional World. All residents of the Delusional World (e.g. Brutes, Satanists) generate chaotic, immature, rationally illogical, and Supernatural irrational thought forms that are ingredients for their anti-Spiritual Elements decision-making and problem solving.

Such Extreme Mental Evasion's disintegrated mental function effects means the *inability to have proper concepts about Life and Love* (see Bailey, Unlocking Minds Of Black Boys for elaboration). On bad consequences, an Emotionalism lifestyle is built, as those of Indifference/Hate/Evil/Sadism of Brutes and Satanism. Another path derives from doing whatever it takes to simply endure in order to survive--as it was for Enslaved Africans who, in turn, culturally transmitted this pattern into many of their today's descendants—a mindset that negates the ability of the afflicted to figure out how to rise above their various poverties. That pattern can be seen today. So to blame victims for not doing things that are "obviously" right or by considering them to make decisions by ones own standards, and do "Common Sense" things is to display ones self-centered arrogant ignorance.

ANATOMY OF ENSLAVED EMOTIONS": Normally, Emotions occupy a place sufficiently large to give it a perceivable individuality in ones Selfhood. Observation would suggest that the Limbic (Emotional) Brain arises out of the Ancient Brain and, if true, this might explain how and why that when people become enraged they seem to lose control of their senses (discussed elsewhere, based upon Le Doux's work). The hippocampus helps the brain learn and form new memories designed to inform the individual of how to avoid dangerous situations and how to recognize what situations are likely to be relatively safe. When one is in a potentially threatening situation, one calls on the hippocampus to bring into awareness the most common sense things to do and not do. The primary role of the Amygdala is instituting the fear response as a normal and immediate burst to physical danger -- a reaction affecting both the brain and the body. Biologically, fear is expressed by adrenaline. In turn, adrenaline affects the Amygdala's fear circuit to release warning messages to other brain areas in order to immediately prepare the body for "fight or flight" actions and reactions. The entire process is orchestrated by the autonomic nervous system (ANS) in general and the sympathetic portion of the ANS in particular.

Based upon my observations and research the normal course of Instinct Emotions is to gradually fade in importance as ones Intellect and Common Sense begin to develop between ages 5 to 7. They are then used on specific occasions--as in emotionally enjoying things of Worth (things of Spiritual Beauty). Omnibus Brain Emotions normally follow a similar course--being used for times of special occasions (e.g. birthday surprises). But following the Brain Switch, what did not happen in the Enslaved was the continued development of their Left Brains. Instead, since there was nothing to challenge thinking as part of their daily drudgery of hard work, the Left Brains of newly Enslaved arrivals lost their developed skills while the Enslaved born in the Americas failed to develop comparable skills, as for Critical Thinking. The loss of Left Brain skills included its "check and balance" discipline effect on the Right Brain and thereby enabling the Right Brain's Old Mammalian/Omnibus Emotions to become undisciplined. In other words, the result was one being orchestrated by Emotions rather than by developed and disciplined reason. Added to that was the Brute Brain Emotional manifestations of the captors--the only models the Enslaved had.

The presumed Emotional features of the Enslaved resembled those of their early lives--being in "Awe" with whatever happenings were occurring--good or evil--unhampered by being judgmental of the type or of the source. The stimulus for those emotions--whether from relatives, friends, and/or enemies--carries the influence to mold ones uncritically developed Character. Chances are that the aura from each of those with whom a given Enslaved was in contact sort of blended together to form a mix of an Emotional Lifestyle--a lifestyle culturally transmitted to today's descendants. This would partly account for "People Addictions" by "BE-ers" who engage in "Treadmill" activities--being "busy" in constantly seeking Excitement while going nowhere--sort of like a Dance. Bad things others are doing to them are simply accepted as "that's the way it is," meaning they have no rational assessments of doing something to stop it or doing things to improve ones situation.

EMOTIONS CAUSED BY SLAVE SURVIVALS: The various forms of Enslaved Thinking, culturally transmitted to most of their struggling Black American descendants, came out of the Brain Switch, the lack of education, and the imitation of the ways of their Brute oppressors. These include Automatic Pilot, Traumatic, "Off & On", Patterned, Superficial, Broad-Stroke, Omnibus, or combinations of these--depending upon their mood, the situation, and the nature of their Icon Contingent Beings. The "state of Being" for these self-defeating ways of thinking came from Evasive Non-Thinking which was brought about by profound Despair. Because one is so aware of not being who one knows one can be, one talks loudly about the virtues one has and "what I am going to do" in putting those virtues into action and "be Somebody." During slavery, the Enslaved learned to be very quiet when facing something new and saying nothing about how they felt about anything pertaining to it. This has carried over to today, as evidenced by them being "Silent" with what is going inside them. Thus, to assess their emotions is based upon what they do and fail to do. The message for what their problems are is in the disrespectfulness, their responsiveness, and the seeming lack of caring they show. I was able to realized that these reactions are due to a volition of not to think and that led to the consequences of being controlled by emotions with its layers of consequences--e.g. unable to handle their daily problems lead to addiction to people, engaging in Escapes, not caring about trying to improve, not taking care of their children.

WHITES PROMOTE EMOTIONAL FALSE SELF PEOPLE: Because European leaders operate out of Supernatural "Air Castle" realm, they have no concept of Natural World Truths—are not interested in them—do not want anyone else to know them—and go out of their way to keep anybody from knowing them because it would make what they think, feel, say, and do look ridiculous. Thus, it is essential for them to brainwash everybody into Superficial and Emotional thinking so that people stay so dumb they are not aware of what is being done to them. This is the orientation of European technology—i.e. to create False Self people with Acquired Fetter Emotions. Instinct (pre-birth) Emotions with their cherished benefits are replaced with False Self generated Emotions when one decides to step out of ones Spiritual Circle of Wholism. So, if one has a problem with *Consistency* related to ones Mission (or any worthwhile goal), one is not powered by the Spiritual Elements. No complete success can occur until its Spiritual Energy is the driving force. Inconsistency lets one know of at least being on Metaphysical Disorder track through life.

Nevertheless, *False Self Acquired Emotions*--as in impure forms of Fear and Rage derived from psychic trauma or socialization--are poor imitations of the Instinct type Emotions and are continually layered from "Like-Kind" Trigger contributors. A simile is a snowball rolling down hill and getting bigger and bigger in the process. Associated with False Self Emotions are: (1) an intensification of the power of the nervous system acting on a human's physical body; (2) a paralyzing of ones independent thought and ones Will; and (3) a withdrawal of ones consciousness from the external planes of existence. For the Black public, what has been devastating to their minds and philosophy has been Satanist Whites getting them involved in staying "Excited". To this Emotional end are being addicted to Trinkets and Trivia. As long as one is engaged in electronic gadgets and multi-tasking, one will not be able to develop ones mind to think rationally. These things—e.g. excitement (e.g. Flashing Light Gadgets) and Patterned Thinking as a way to live life--prevent the development of brain neurons while instilling destructive subliminal messages. Secondary and Tertiary Emotions related to Fetters are easy because they only deal with the Physical world--a world analogized to a cup of ocean water compared with the ocean. This is what Europeans present in things that are exciting and thus there is a match which leads one who is on top of that to believe he/she knows everything and thus turn a deaf ear to elders. Flashing Light Gadgets cause one to go from one mountain top of excitement to the next without having to go through the struggles of climbing up one mountain and going down it in order to climb up to the next mountain. This teaches one to have a short attention span, look only for the exciting, not go through a struggle, and no need to do things with other people.

This same pattern is used on those who provide them what they want and as soon as that ends or as soon as something more exciting crops up they are off on that train ride. Besides, one can vent ones hostilities to the public in the hidden privacy of their room--and thus fail to learn that what they say can harm others. This causes a loss of awareness of manners and allows one to be as "wild" as one desires. Meanwhile, their minds are being programmed with the Superficial and with Subliminal messages slipped in. This destroys brain cells and prevent others from forming in how to deal with difficult tasks. As a result, they are frequently in error but rarely in doubt. This inability to think makes for greater dependency on others to guide them through life. Emotions can only deal with the gist and an inability to think causes reliance on outside sources (God will save me without me having to do anything) as well as putting the responsibility for problems outside oneself ("the devil made me do it"). By being free from any control by reason, by any aesthetic, or by moral preoccupation they are "*Non Sequitur*" mental activity ('it does not follow').

When ones False Self Emotions and Passions are allowed to "run wild" to a Mild or Slight degree, one exhibits varied forms of self-absorption ("Me, Me, Me") with its attendant "*Fetters*"--extreme selfishness, greed, hatred, anger, egoism, fear, envy, jealousy, frustration, selfishness, arrogance, pride, lust (Ashby, Book of Dead, p89). These Fetters are powered by imaginations concerning oneself and others and thereby cloud out the realistic part of ones Spiritual human nature. Then, ones Soul "sunshine" cannot impart peace, harmony, or Oneness with the Cosmic Organism. When ones Emotions and Passions are allowed to "run wild" to a Moderate degree, ones Selfhood is orchestrated by ones Brute Brain's Indifference, Hate, and Evil expressions. For example, as a way of life they have a mindset of hostility; focus on dominating others; and hold victims to lofty and actually unattainable standards--while not living up to rules themselves. When ones Emotions and Passions are allowed to "run wild" to an Extreme degree, Brutes' imaginative Supernatural world causes them to become "legends in their own minds" and "little gods." Their "disease of the soul" creations include the formation of a Satan and a Hell--both competitors with God--both useful for mind control devices--both providing "sick" pleasures from making people suffer. The nature of Emotions is that it has no morals, no ability to solve problems, and goes nowhere. Because of its Survival nature it pours much energy into doing what it has to do as part of preparing the body for "Fight or Flight" or for "Play and Stay."

Secular Emotions are generated by ones False Self (Ego) to react to things which do not exist in reality. A False Self comes from "Broken Brains"--those who lack the "5Ss" and thereby act with an Inferiority Complex or a Superiority Complex. Both types can represent a loss from knowing better or be socialized so as to having never known any different. Either way, both are disconnected from the Cosmic Organism. Based upon my observations and research the normal course of Instinct Lower (Animal) Self Emotions is to gradually fade in importance as ones Intellect and Common Sense begin to develop between ages 5 to 7. They are then used on specific occasions--as in emotionally enjoying things of Value (Material World pleasures). Omnibus Brain Emotions normally follow a similar course--being used for times of special occasions (e.g. birthday surprises).

BLACK AMERICAN CUSTOMS

When the Egg called Humpty Dumpty of fairytale fame was pushed off a wall and shattered on the ground below, all the king's horses and all the king's men could not put Humpty together again. The effect of the impact of slavery on every Enslaved Africans Shattering was as if the Selfhood exploded. Like Humpty, an unending tragedy of attempted Reconstruction back to African Tradition Integrity was the utter inability of any Enslaved to put anything together that would enable them to deal effectively with the most evil enslavers of Humankind. To be shattered is to be transformed, if for no other reason than the light of the Selfhood lamp of each of the Enslaved lay dark in the dirt. Hence, they were wandering inside a Self-Unknown passageway, being guided only by the scent of African Tradition hanging and interpenetrating the shattered pieces of their Selfhoods. The best make-shift Consciousness idea construction most could do was about ways to cope with their Doom—idea "Seeds" serving as every conceivable method for trying to survive and endure—each being cultivated in the nutrition deprived "soil" constituting their Psychically Traumatized mindsets during and following slavery (particularly in those living inside the "Struggling Tunnel"--metaphorical passage from the living quarters of the Field Enslaved to today's inner cities). The Enslaved developed a certain "Sameness" as well as each having "Uniqueness"--ranging from closely related all the way over to the opposite extreme. Both the Enslaved "Sameness" and "Uniqueness" were replacements for their profound Real Self losses—replacements drawn from reflections of the interpretations of the monitored feedback each Enslaved got from outside influences as well as from the inner world turmoil being personally experienced.

The meanings brought to each of their minds from personal experiences--from observing happenings of and to fellow Enslaved--and from meaning derived from thoughts and prior events, whether of folly or wise, underwent reflection. Those reflections were fashioned into temporary standards intended to serve for how to assess each new terrible experience--how to act and react--and what goals to strive for that might best enable them to survive and endure. Eventually, each arrived at "Facts," "Beliefs," Opinions, Doubts, certitudes, and probabilities—many having nothing to do with ultimate Truth or Reality but rather about what is most likely to work in slowing the ever worsening parts of their lives. The result was that each Enslaved African devised, came into contact with, joined, and was swept along in the flow of a motley collection of diverse customs on the one hand and many having to be altered to conform to each new situation encountered. The result was the assumption of a Flawed Real Self, a Semi-False Self, or a False Self Consciousness pattern.

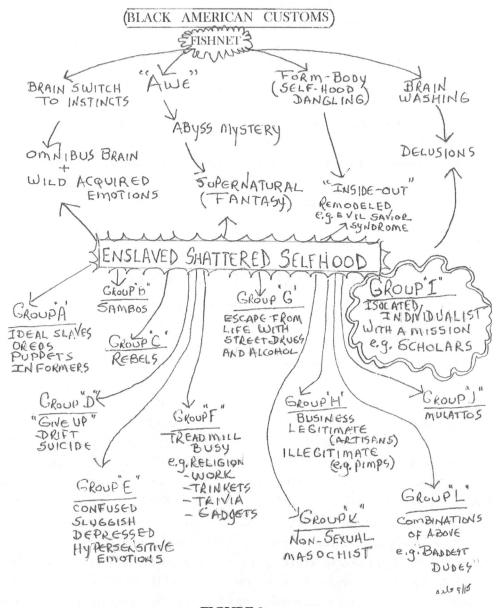

FIGURE 9

The overwhelming types of "vines" that grew from those flawed "Seeds" were used by the Enslaved in the form of the masks and masquerades (fig. 4, 15, 19). For example, there was the *Group A* (Ideal Slaves): Enslavers Advocate Group—e.g. Black Puppets (e.g. Black "Slave Drivers"; Black preachers for the European Supernatural religion, Waiting Slaves (Slave informers who relayed Enslaved "secrets" to the captors), Oreos (e.g. House Slaves who were imitators of the slave owner's family). *Group B* (the "Sambos") those who act dumb and play crazy). *Group C* are Rebels, those who model European males and fight in overt, tempered, masked, and concealed ways. In more recent times they became criminals). *Group D* (the "Give up"—either making peace with Doom or are in great turmoil) are those who Drift, Don't Care, Commit Suicide. *Group E* (Confused) are in several subtypes like Sluggish, Moody, Emotionally Hypersensitive. *Group F* (Treadmill Busy) who cram their lives with furious work or religion or Trinkets and Trivia but go nowhere, as if on a treadmill. *Group G* are those who "Escape" from life with "street" drugs or alcohol. *Group H* are in businesses, of a legitimate (artisans) or illegitimate (e.g. pimp) nature. *Group I* are Isolated Individualists, as with scholars. *Group J* are Mulattos. *Group K* are non-sexual masochists. *Group L* are those combinations of the above. For example, the Baddest Dudes of the "streets" have made peace with Doom (like Group D) so as to become Rebels (Group C). All except Group A were fashioners of Black American Customs and yet some Group A members have been infiltrators.

FORMATION OF BLACK AMERICAN CUSTOMS: In dealing with subjects as complex as the mindsets of Enslaved Africans and their post-slavery descendants, for ease of convenience I devise a "short-hand" term to collective refer to their varied bunch of vague, confusing, and often conflicting things. What is extracted from this "glob" is the commonality within the Interchange of where they interlock—a commonality representing an association of Ideas. Here, the "short-hand" term for the conglomerate of mindsets and their "sameness" and "uniqueness" expressions is *Black American Customs* (BAC). The continued Flawed Real Self, Semi-False Self, or False Self sprouting during and following slavery—each ever changing the African Tradition Messages used to orchestrate their lives--meant that the replacement of these Messages were with what was incomprehensible, conflicting, and confusing. These flawed Messages applied to their daily situations + "bits and pieces" of African Tradition + European brainwashing + Enslaved Reactions to being Enslaved and terrorized + the original mental "Raw Nerves" from all that went with being Enslaved + the "Inside-Out" thinking styles + the necessities of "Making Do" living styles were gathered into Collage Patterns pertaining to ways to endure Life Living. Of course these patterns were fragmented—some at odds with each other, some overlapping, some compatible. Still, all Black People suffered inhumane indignities regardless of any differences.

Customs are the uniform doing of the same think, feel, say, and acts in the same circumstances for a definite reason. These reasons were triggered by all that happened during slavery and how, in infinite unique and group ways, the Enslaved chose to react to them. Because those reasons faded following slavery, but their Customs persisted, this pattern constitutes *Slave Survivals* (maintaining customs for forgotten reasons). Although it serves Europeans' hateful and racist purposes to stereotype all Black People into a homogenous group, there were unimaginable African "uniqueness" throughout the varied African culture as well as them sharing a "certain sameness" from a common Consciousness oriented philosophy of life. An analogy is the USA states' constitutions having uniqueness while sharing the "sameness" with the principles of the Federal constitution. Then, within the Enslaved Africans brought to the Americas, additional "sameness" and differences were deliberately and inadvertently instilled in them by Europeans for purposes of "Divide and Conquer" and mind and total Selfhood control. Serving both objectives was the fashioning of dissention and conflicts among all Black People in the Americas and everywhere.

Thus, BAC embrace Black People who are contrary opposites as well as complementary equals in what they think, feel, say, and do. The "big picture" Background mindset out of which the BAC effects on the Enslaved who originated BAC can be described as Extreme Despair. None had anything to think about apart from their miserable enslavement lives. Hence, as a result of putting their Left Brain thinking skills "on hold"—like a telephone's call waiting—meant that their Right Brains lost the disciplining actions derived from the Left Brain. The result was a mindset that was primarily Emotionally based, with the emotions of their horrible lives serving as the "raw materials" for their mental activities. Supportive of this pattern was that most chose not to think rationally, for that was too painful and nothing they experienced was rational. The layering effects of this process even got to the point of many not thinking past the moment because of having hopeless hopelessness about anything ever getting better for them. One of these displays was that when a family member was killed, there were Enslaved who did no crying or showed any emotions. This was because they were passed that point and because they believed the deceased was no longer in despair, by having mercifully been relieve of their pain and suffering. Dumb Europeans, showing their willfull ignorance and being incapable of insightfull-ness, concluded this reaction was because Blacks were subhuman. Many of the most desperate of the Enslaved made "a deal with the devil" in hopes of getting even a drop of relief. Nevertheless, although flawed Common Sense, exhibited in many of their choices, decisions, and solutions, BAC members demonstrated amazing Life Living practical wisdom in being able to survive and endure inside the "Alligator's" mouth.

COURSE OF BLACK AMERICAN CUSTOMS: The setting in which Black American Custom (BAC) Thinking originated and continues to occur can be analogized to the story of the ELEPHANT AND THE CHAIN. It starts with a handler who, at birth, chained the newborn elephant to a tree so as to permit only a 30 foot circle of freedom. As the elephant grew in size and strength, the chain was replaced with a stronger and thicker one so as to prevent the elephant from going on a rampage and running away. Thus the elephant grew up conditioned to knowing there was a limit on how far he could wander and this 30 foot limit forever restricted his scope of life. Eventually, the chain was replaced with a rope the elephant could easily break. But surprisingly, at that time and even when the chain was permanently removed, the elephant never walked farther than his original limit of 30 feet. He had accepted being defined by the handler and his mind was conditioned to being enslaved. This is like being placed in a closet without walls—and that carries the capabilities of refashioning minds "Inside-Out"—the first stage experienced by prisoners who are confined for prolonged periods in solitary confinement. Enslaved Africans philosophies evolving out of the "closet without windows" of enslavement were simply about survival and enduring. Despite them being at odds as to approaches, methods, and techniques, they somewhat interpenetrated out of the necessity for ex-Slaves to huddle together to self-protect from Euro-American terrorism (which continues today). All of this, among others, generated special and overwhelming difficulties for particularly for those who struggle the most. On the one hand, plantation lives of the Enslaved had a terrible steadiness about it (e.g. work-days from "can't see to can't see"), they were able to work out patterns for coping that enabled them to endure.

On the other hand, following slavery they were dumped into a world whereby they had to completely survive on their own, and with no training or assistance of any kind—and actually in the face of tremendous hostility. This "new world" featured Europeans who model their lifestyle (not mindset) ways on the ever-changing patterns reflecting their total focus on the Supernatural and Physical world. As a result, although coping practices the Enslaved had divised worked satisfactorily on the plantation, those same Customs became useless outside the Black community following slavery—mainly because no jobs were available. But since BAC follow the steadiness theme (but not the content) of African Tradition and since they could be used as a tow-rope (especially the Black Church and its religion) to barely "hang on" to life, Black People continued with their BAC (to the present). When eventually jobs did become available in mid-C20, the BAC were self-defeating when applied in the marketplace. This and the lack of jobs available to struggling Blacks + from having no exposure to planning or determining proper priorities in handling necessary business + having no starting or ending points for handling significant problems in life, led many to "Escape". It was all about surviving through the day. Many "Escapees" adopted the pattern of ignoring their biggest problems, hoping they would resolve favorably. Regardless of what might be the outcome, it is like saying: "I don't have anything now and I can't have any less if I do nothing." Thus, they had no choice but to make chronic Juggling in daily living and intimate part of their lives.

BAC's increased complexity was from taking a giant step for the worse when some Blacks, post-1960s Civil Rights Movements, embraced European Individualism habits and later Trinkets and Trivia. Reasons included being impressed with the world advertised façade of White people enjoying the "Good Life"; desiring to have some recognition as human being, even if that meant becoming Black Puppets; and clamoring for any bit of Power, like those used by European males with the GUN and killings. At their meeting point in the 1970s, gangs were formed--eventually modeling such European methods as those of Al Capone's drive-by shootings (Bailey, Stopping the Violence). In spite of their horrors in a foreign land, for 150 years following slavery many Enslaved descendants have risen to great achievements—achievements demanding great efforts on the part of the school systems and the media to ensure are never made known to the unsuspecting public, even in documentaries. It speaks volumes about Black Americans' inner greatness strengths.

FACTORS LEADING TO BLACK AMERICAN CUSTOMS:A summary of the process of what I believed happened to the Enslaved at the "Fishnet" moment was that: (1) their mindsets, "*Awed*" by the shocking display of enslavement, yielded to being entrapped in an underlying sense of something extremely grand in character or formidable in power, as from a child's perspective. Such a mindset transformation proceeded to (2) ease into the mystery realm associated with Awe and once inside, one is continuously situated. However, it the situation is ongoing and without a break, ones mindset remains in the Awe Mystery in a permanently fixed state. (3) Being in such an Awe Mystery state means ones mind has reverted to a *Form-Body* condition of totipotency, meaning it can be remolded by any good (like ones mother) or evil (like the European captors) to be compatible with the nature of that molding. The key to being a re-molder is the feeding of something to this immature Form-Body mind condition. (4) Simultaneously, while the Awe Mystery being established "forever," a (5) Brain Switch has occurred: the immediate change from a Thriving Brain that balances the use of ones Rational, Emotional, and Ancient (Reptilian) three-brains-in-one over to exclusive use of ones Emergency Brain, featuring its Instinct subdivision. It was the Instinct Brain the Slaves used to thereafter process information and all that was happening to them. (6) After adaptation to slavery, perhaps in 6 months, the Enslaved shifted the Instinct Brain's co-pilot, the Omnibus Brain/Undisciplined Right Brain (OB/URB), because instead of needing to handle emergencies, it is hyper-alert to Alarm Reactions that might be a threat to ones Survival, Self-Protection, and Self-Preservation-- a mindset persisting in today's struggling Black youth. (7) As a result of enslavement hampering the Left Brain skills or keeping them from developing, this meant a loss of discipline over the Acquired Emotions of the Right Brain. Those now unrestrained Acquired Emotions were expanded upon by the hellish experiences of the Enslaved so as to have an overflowing pool of such negative emotions.

(8) Whereas negative Acquired Emotions such as rage, fear, disillusionment, despair, and frustration governed the Inner World of each Enslaved, their Spiritual (pre-birth) Emotions enabled the Enslaved to continue interrelating with Unconditional Love as well as keeping "bits and pieces" of African Tradition alive. (9). Throughout this process European brainwashing was explosively prominent and as continuous as

machine-gun firing. A highlight of this brainwashing was to replace the Spiritual God of African Tradition with the European Supernatural God. This was part of taking away the Selfhood Greatness Awareness of Enslaved and to convert them into believing that all Africans were sub-humans and it was they who were 'superior'—the opposite of actuality. To varying degrees, Europeans were successful because, by destroying all evidence, they ensured the super-brilliance of Ancient Africans would never be known. (10) By now having doubts about the Certainty of Truth they historically possessed, their reactions were as varied as is humanly possible. With the passage of time and with each generational cultural transmission, the more remote became the awareness of the knowledge of African Tradition. (11) Meanwhile, the "Awe" evolving patterns were of a Supernatural (Delusional) nature in the face of the captors' overwhelming power led many Enslaved to believe the Fantasies they were being fed. As a result, the origin of those initial patterns of thinking developed by all aspects of the "Awe" came to be thought of as coming from actual Supernatural sources that was more powerful than their Spiritual sources. (12) Thereafter the "Awe" faculty of the Enslaved generated a lifestyle corresponding to the ingredients fed to it by the captors in order to conform to what seemed to be most workable way to survive and endure under the hellish conditions of slavery. (13) From being "fed" all of this by Europeans while the Selfhood's of the Enslaved where in a Form-Body state meant that they were bonded to these Satanists. Furthermore, they had no choice but to look to these Sadistic captors for their very survival. That necessity established the Evil Savior Syndrome—the practice of going to Europeans to be supplied for the continuation of something. (14) Such Delusions block a return to ones Real Self ingredients of thinking in ways compatible with African Tradition path to a thriving life.

BLACK MALE'S COURSE OF OPPRESSION

During slavery, and continuing as patterns to the present, the greatest efforts were/are to try to ensure that the intellectual potential in Black males–potential derived from the seeds of brilliance that were passed into their Selfhood by their Ancient African ancestors--is not allowed to flower. Because that potential is present in today's Black males, regardless of their rung on the social ladder, the fears of White males remain. Many non-struggling Black males have still been able to rise above the methods used in the conspiracy to keep them down. Hence, directed to them by Whites and Black puppets—beginning in slavery and continuing to this day—is the ongoing stirring of dissention among Blacks as well as other innumerable things. The following (among others) are some of the things done to destroy the Black People in general, and Black male in particular, that White males so envy.

AFRICAN TRADITION'S MANILNESS: "Manliness" in African Traditions originates from the human Soul's composition of a Spark of God. This means the human mind's purpose is to be a storehouse of the divine Self's Knowledge of itself for use in reflecting that Certainty in daily living. Ones duty is to live within and evolve out of the Spiritual Elements—the process for discovering Unconditional Love, Truth, Reality, and the Natural—a process imparting, not pleasure or "excitement," but an "Aliveness," as in overflowing with Curiosity to explore the unknown and seeking its every Spiritual Elements tidbit to use for creating ones life. Such a flow, only possible by Real Self (Ma'at) Life-Living, is maintained by: (1) staying with good thoughts united by the union of the right Intellect, Emotions, and Judgment; (2) imparting good words to encourage or assist; (3) engaging in good "ME/WE" actions that expand beyond finite ends; and (4) staying focused on eternal luminaries (e.g. Unconditional Love and Truth). This process demands Knowing (not Belief or Faith) and meshing Certainty power with Unconditional Love's power. Out of the resultant Soul Integrity flows what it takes to *"Be Right," "Recognize Right," "Do Right," "Make Things Right,"* and *"Defend the Right"*—and these fulfill every function of Humanity. Guidelines for this process--so as to bring order to ones life and stay in the flow of the Spiritual Elements--include the fact that *Truth can only be known by seeing things the way they are* while disregarding any likes or dislikes about its discovery or where it leads--since one can and ought to live by Truth. Along the path, appreciate the good derived from "living" with Human Ideals so as to evolve into enjoying being about ones Mission.

Ancient Africans said humans' growth patterns are in 3 distinct phases: physical, mental, and spiritual. Adult's Spirituality phase is characterized by the same sense of *Limitlessness*, though modified, as possessed by the Supreme Being: (a) a sense of "Oneness" with all Cosmic creations (omnipresence)—and not having a limited presence, as is the feature of Lower (animalistic) Self people; (b) an *Intuitive* faculty that informs without thinking (wisdom, omniscience)—and not the ignorance of staying ignorant which drives one to seek information from the External World; and (c) ones Will powers acting upon ones Spirit to enable achievements of Human Ideal Goals—and not the impotence at the root of all human dishonorableness, prejudice, and greedy grabbing for the earth's riches. These 3 negatives cause Humankind's problems; these 3 attributes of God solve Humankind's problems, for they are the Substance of claims that humans are made in the likeness of God.

The ultimate human example of perfected God attributes was Tehuti—the African Master of all Masters—a "Man-Godhood" on Earth. Though to lessor degrees, most people know someone who does "a whole lot 24/7" by having unlimited potential thoughts enabling achieving reasonable goals. Partly contributory to their countless achievements is an absolute refusal to accept thoughts limiting their abilities. They have a Mission to which they hone skills of Self-Control and Self-Discipline; constant *Focus* (a key) on handling one thing at a time; of ever striving for Perfection; in efficient precision of Thought Organization into Matter; Matter into Form; and Form into workable effective action. A reason others do not get to be all they can be is because they choose to remain 'un-awakened'. An analogy is the Congenital Tarda genes (e.g. for some great Talent) that are present in each human at birth but do not express themselves until sometime after birth—but only in "Awake and Alive" people. The more that Talent is nourished and cultivated the more it "Fruits."

MANHOOD OF THE ENSLAVED: The African Tradition Manliness patterns were shattered by African American slavery and, following slavery, by ex-Slaves adopting the European captors methods. Because Enslaved husbands/wives, fathers/mothers, and parents/children were sold away from each other, the African practice of establishing patterns about marriage, parenting, taking care of children, and the financial requirements of manhood were essentially wiped out ("August Wilson," in Elkins, p. 138, 157, 185). The essential feature desired by the European captors for manhood in the Enslaved was for them to be "dumb and strong"--dumb so as to not become dissatisfied with being Enslaved and strong so as to do hard labor and to fight each other for the sake of White people's entertainment. Thus, the Enslaved Manhood was defined by the slave owner by his ability to produce children; his ability to endure strenuous physical labor; and by his cooperative efforts to remain ignorant. To understand the 'big picture' essences of what happened to Black males is to gain insight into the present day's tragically comprehensive system pertaining to the problematic Black-American father—an issue tremendously exaggerated by the media's efforts to conform to what White males desire to see in order to make the Black male look terrible. Still, there are, in fact, bad problems regarding too many absent fathers from the family unit--either temporarily or permanently—a pattern dating to African American slavery and perpetuated by all the racism directed towards Black People. And such was not present in Africa.

Force breeding was a cheap solution for the slave-owner to increase his riches. Slave owners encouraged Enslaved "studs" to have no sense of guilt or tension by completely relieving the Enslaved of financial or "father" responsibilities. This was a price gladly paid by the slave owner because he became richer with each Enslaved baby. Enslaved breeding, said Fredrick Douglass (p. 159, 306), is one of the most awful scenes of cruelty -- the rearing of men, women, and children for market alongside horses, sheep, and swine. The law sanctioned it, public opinion upheld it, and the church did not condemn it. As one Euro-American wrote during slavery: "Most gentlemen of character seem to have a special disinclination to converse on the subject . . . that the cash value of a slave for sale, above the cost of raising it from infancy to the age at which it commands the highest price, is generally considered among the surest elements of a planter's wealth." *Breeder potency* (ability to produce children) was about enticing the male Slaves' sexual impulses, starting in early puberty, to be so free as to take sexual liberties with any Enslaved female of any age (e.g. 11 years old). Eventually, when the sexual impulses of Enslaved males were no longer controlled by African Tradition, they became subject only to the periodic urge of animalistic-like sexual hunger--a hunger which seized upon every available Black woman. This was an indicator of the successful *"rolling stone"* or "stud" brainwashing applied by the White man to vulnerable Slaves. To increase their riches from selling the Enslaved and to increase their work force for the selling of crops, slave owners offered incentives to Enslaved males who could father the most children. As a result, it was typical for Enslaved females to start bearing children at age 12 or 13 and produce one every 18 months. This brainwashing away of African morals was so complete for many Enslaved males that it was made into contests. Not only was the "winning" Enslaved male rewarded by the slave owner for siring the most babies, but he was applauded by fellow Enslaved! (Stevenson, Life in Black and White, p. 24). This is "sick" stuff on the part of White males and the Black males whose minds they enslaved.

Problematic Responsibility: The African virtues of protecting, supporting, and providing for ones offspring were completely converted to the opposite so that eventually a new tradition was formed whereby robot males resisted the role of a responsible father. A Slave law said: *"the father of a slave is unknown to our law."* This implied the legal stripping of Enslaved fathers of their last semblance of masculinity (Silberman, Crisis in Black and White, p. 89). The Enslaved father could not even protect the mother of his children except by appealing directly to the owner. Instead of the Enslaved male being the father of his children, those children were taught to look to the slave owner as their *"judge and jury."* This is why Black males today bristle when a White man calls them "son." During slavery *Rolling Stone* was used in the sense of the Enslaved male being given recognition by the slave owner and often by Enslaved males for siring the most children in stud-like fashion. He had no responsibility regarding taking care of the women he impregnated nor the children he produced. The African virtues of protecting supporting, and providing for ones offspring were completely converted to the opposite so that eventually a new tradition was formed whereby robot males resisted the role of a responsible father.

Problematic Courage: On the one hand, the slave owner's role as "the father" was to *guide Enslaved males into his loyalty* and with docility, humility, cheerfulness, and (under supervision) his diligence (Weinstein, Am. Negro Slavery, p. 214). On the other hand, the slave owner, as father, expected his Enslaved boys to be irresponsible, playful, silly, lazy, and with a tendency to lie and steal--i.e. to essentially fit the role of "Sambo." The law gave the slave owner absolute power over the slaves which, of course, meant the absolute dependency of each of the Enslaved. Not only did this destroy Fathers as protectors who fight the outside world, but it over burdened mom, causing her to deal with more than the child's inside world and its vibrations.

Enragement: By African Manhood being taken away + Enslaved females being in charge of Enslaved males (and receiving a tiny bit better treatment on up to the present) + being helpless in watching White males rape mothers/wives/daughters/sons/self + Black males having to be dependent on White males + being beaten, starved, and enduring other inhumane treatment made for Enslaved males being enraged. Their enragement was seized upon to stereotype Black males (and females) as a measure by White males to deflect from their deep seated and constant emotional states of enragement.

POST-SLAVERY BLACK MANHOOD: Slavery caused an African Tradition and Brain Switch that led to the disintegration of African Manliness in Enslaved African Americans. During slavery the Divine Consciousness Background and its Foreground were "Clouded" to varying degrees and yet some managed to maintain or develop a sense of dignity and self-worth; stay connected to their family during and after slavery; and provide in the best way they could. However, the brainwashing of a "Slave Manhood" to be his ability to produce children; his ability to endure strenuous physical labor; by his cooperative efforts to remain ignorant; the lost of African Tradition Thinking skills; and all of horrendous racism factors imposed by Whites greatly interfered with Black males capabilities of reestablishing the "5Ss"—a large contributor their concept of their "Manhood."

Furthermore, by having no other model, White manhood was the Standard which ex-Slaves *imitated, followed, submitted to, rebelled, fought, creatively spun off of,* or used in some combinations of these six—a pattern which continues in many Black Americans to this day. Because each of these are mind encaging (a scrambled world view leading one to be bound by European values) and/or mind enslaving (defined by and follow the dictates of European males), most were blocked from knowing how to seek and develop their full potential. One "escape" example was the ex-Slave Black Pimp. Also escaping were the mentally free—meaning they were man enough to take charge and control over their lives by dismissing the enslaver from dominating their mindset.

Building on the Rage of Slavery were: Jobs being Unavailable; Black Females dominating Black Males; poor living conditions; constant Self-Esteem attacks--e.g. subhumanness, bad name calling and stereotypes; and unfulfilled Needy Wants (e.g. not feeling loved, not receiving compliments). On the one hand, ex-Slaves who had been in close contact with the slave owner went their separate ways following slavery and did relatively well on their own. On the other hand, Convict Lease "*Work Gangs*" resulted from laws passed following slavery in order to put any Black person in jail who did not have a job--and no jobs were available to Blacks. In keeping with Sippi relationship patterns established during slavery, inside these institutional and depersonalizing settings (e.g. prison or boot camp)--unlike ex-Slaves of the same-sex dyadic ties--shared features, practices, and facilities in common. Out of this, gangs formed--a pattern which has continued. Although a few of the gangs may be of a constructive nature, most have been destructive. The remainder of ex-Slaves, though very unlike each other, huddled together inside a given neighborhood for self-protective purposes against White terrorism.

BLACK MANHOOD IN THE EARLY-20th CENTURY: The post-slavery Manhood patterns continued. Gradually a model of masculine performance, perhaps deriving from Hollywood genre films of the 1930s and 1940s, appeared as a response to a social environment in which Black masculinity was continually being challenged. "*Cool Pose*" I was of the zoot-suits, conks, lindy hop, and unique language of Black hipsters type. These were the products of an oppositional Black youth culture that challenged "middleclass ethics and expectations" and enabled young Black men, in particular, to resist their imminent proletarianization within a highly industrialized wartime economy. In the 1940s and 1950s, working-class adolescents of the "*Bop Culture*" caused trouble (Diamond *J. Urban History, 2001*). Out of this was extended their language, music, clothing, gang names, and graffiti on into the 1960s. In turn, that blended with another gang culture--one expressing rampant use of the term "brother"; an assertive kind of funk music that sung of racial empower-ment; Afro-centric clothing and hairstyles, gangs that called themselves "nations"; and paintings of "Black Fists" on the walls surrounding gang hangouts. This culture of opposition blossomed out of the injustices of everyday life faced by African Americans and Puerto Ricans in the postwar period. What was outstanding was when Black People got together, they seemed to really enjoy themselves.

BLACK MANHOOD IN THE MID-20th CENTURY: As a boy in my all-Black communities, there was wonderful bonding of all the Black People of whom I was aware. Also, I saw certain struggling non-gang member Black People who, unlike their mainstream counterparts, possessed fewer legitimate means of demon-strating their worth and competence. Such was especially true of young men belonging to the "urban under-class," unable to find steady work in their communities, and to the traditional emphasis on work as a means of constructing a "respectable" masculine image. Still, I had many good community role models, in addition to family members. Returning soldiers from World War II had given Black male a great boost in their Self-Image. In the military they became familiar with European Fetters being powered by imaginations concerning oneself and others. Fetters which bind the Soul to Matter. The nature of Fetters are about extreme selfishness, greed, hatred, anger, egoism, fear, envy, jealousy, frustration, selfishness, arrogance, pride, lust (Ashby, Book of Dead, p89).

For those who had failed to cultivate a "Manly" Selfhood meant they felt as a captive inside the lower planes of Cosmic existence--to the Animal affections and desires—i.e. a binding of their Soul to Matter. To rise out of that was more significant than "Clouding out" the realistic part of their Spiritual human nature as well as being aware of the sorrows, troubles and tribulations associated with war and violence or greed for sex and money. By Emotions being elevated over Intellect or Truth enable all Fetters to seem natural because it was simple to be in its stream flowing out of its Indifference/Hate/Evil/Sadism (IHES) Complex. Such was one contributor to Black males trying to prove their "Manhood" self-image. Thus, during the Vietnam War African American men enlisted at higher rates than White men at the war's onset (Carlson, *JHolistic Nursing, 2011*). "The United States military was selling manhood during the Vietnam War, and African-American men were eager to buy".

There developed a contrasting Black-centered notion of Manhood that existed outside the bounds of the dominant, White-centered culture where the traditional manly war ethos could be rejected. Muhammad Ali "challenged the link between manhood and military service, because he had the author-ity to make opposition to the Vietnam War a manly act". The Black anti-war movement raised questions about the notion of Manliness as necessarily attached to the role of warriors. In the 1960s, Black People had a little taste of freedom during the Black Power movement. Whether Black gangs actually marched in demonstrations, stopped attacking other Black gangs, or gave up their criminal behavior, they lived and acted in this world. Meanwhile, perhaps Malcolm X's "Streets Manhood" of the "Cool Pose" served as the generic Star whose "Halo" radiated, in modified form, into what served as the model on various rungs of the Secular World (e.g. for "the Streets") or for the more urbane, conservative, and refined social ladder rungs. Malcolm's "Cool Poses"--the repetition of stylized acts, gestures, and rituals over time--were of different types.

"Cool Pose" II was the "*Hustler*" Manhood--in part pose, part performance, with the distinction between the two being more of a continuum than a clean break where the belief was that money equals freedom; clothes were essential to self-presentation; women, particularly White women, were viewed as commodities; and men bonded with and challenge one another for dominance. All of this seen in gang members—i.e. discourses of rights, unity, and empowerment--flowed through urban communities in the 1960s and early 1970s had a significant effect on the consciousness and behavior of young men in gangs. Starting in the 1970s the oppressors applied increasingly rigid rules for how Blacks were to live (e.g. not spanking children)--Rules which pushed Black People further and further away from parent-children control, from personal freedom, and their Real Self. As a result of the loss of much parental discipline intensity, many Black children allowed their Old Mammalian/Omnibus Brain to orchestrate their lives--as by no longer having a desire to protect Black People or improve themselves so as to help the entire race.

The 1960s "touch of Black Freedom" led Black People to getting more involved with what White people did. The awe of admiration many Black People had from perceiving externally correct but false images (movies, television) of how White people deceptively seemed to enjoy themselves from experiencing "Luxury Living" appealed to many Black People whose lives had been nothing more than "Making Do." One of the prominent things White people did was to have a "show of force" in movies and on television in the form of GUNS by killings and always presenting themselves as winning (fig. 8). Such represented displays of power Black People had never had. Whereas there had been a few scattered gangs who fought each other with their fists, the more they imitated "White Power" the more they resorted to knives and, upon seeing Al Capone and his drive-by shootings, they clamored for guns. A "*Crack Cocaine*" frenzy brought a "war on drugs" and thus horrendous numbers of Black males being placed in prisons—devastating those males, family and neighborhoods.

Many Black Families began breaking up and people started "hanging out" on the "Streets". By there having been the Slave Survival of a lost of Courage and any desire for self-improvement, it was increasingly difficult for victims to survive by being left only with "Make Do" with whatever they had. A basic problem was in not being allowed to have jobs. To survive required resorting to selling drugs and that put them in constant direct contact with policemen whose excuse for wanting to kill Black males for hero purposes consisted of saying they were dedicated in the "*War on Drugs*." The overwhelming envy of Black males by European males caused them to do all they could to destroy Black males—as by stirring up conflicts with them and supplying them with guns and drugs to fight each other. The conspiracy White "System" ensured they did not get a meaningful education and promoted a lack of ambition—as about occupying their lives doing things like sports and entertainment in an "Uncle Tom" or "Sambo" minstrel manner. These satisfied the European taste of having Blacks subhuman. The media aided by floodlighting the worse of struggling Black People doings so as to say this is who all Black People are.

In "the Streets" a man's reputation is made or shattered by "*The Showdown*". In normal hustler situations outcomes took the form of (a) Manhood/death, (b) Manhood/violent injury, (c) Manhood/feminized disgrace, and (d) Manhood/Manhood destruction. All of these situations ritual performance tests in which two men squared off against one another to assert their manhood before gazing third parties. Taylor says these 'Showdowns' are violent competitions with White men in their absence--a displacement onto one another of the violent impulses Black men feel toward their White oppressors; an outright Manhood expression denied them by White males; or a displacement of the counter-violence the White culture provokes onto their closest and least powerful fellows. Instead of interracial showdowns having a liberating effect on Black males consciousness, when White men are present, they often have a paralyzing effect on Black males' "Showdown" performance and thus the performance bombs.

BLACK MANHOOD IN THE LATE-20th CENTURY: White males continued to fashion slow homicides and suicides for Blacks and exhibit Black males with balls in their hands, as if to say: "playing sports to entertain White males is all Black males are good for". Most prominent in this regard is the continual supplying to Black and Brown "ghettos" train loads or filled duffle bags of guns and drugs free-for-the-taking in order to start and perpetuate *Turf and Drug wars.* The point was to get those most in poverty to become addicted and sell these illegal things so as to fight and kill each other. Whites gained from incarcerating Black youth and thus destroying their neighborhoods and preventing them from voting or getting "Life-Living" jobs. Furthermore, these overwhelming daily stresses simply to live generated so many bad emotions as to cause the afflicted to do foolish things to release tension or escape from it. These have included any anti-thriving thing. Additional status quo oppression measures are by ensuring a lack of (well-paying) jobs or any jobs for that matter; by taking away all good working government sponsored programs that show they are providing benefits; by advertising that gang behaviors represent all Black males so as to encourage "hysteria" against Blacks; by recklessly generating prison records on struggling Black males so as to hamper them for life in such areas as being hired for good paying jobs; by failing to create safe schools; and by failing to present educational materials relevant to the lives of Black youth.

Some of things Whites do that adversely affect not only Black males but all struggling Black people is to price desirable and constructive mind stimulating (recreational) things above struggling Black peoples' ability to pay; by the media, documentaries, and museums stealing or rewriting Black history; by ensuring Black scholarship is quashed; and by not allowing effective Black governmental or board room representation on policies that affect Black people. The European conspiracies against Blacks persist in its long history making Black males appear to be dumb and strong workers and entertainers by what they allow Black males to do and not do. To this day such practices continue in the form of White males paying Black males to be athletes while doing what they can to ensure that Black males will not get an education. In one study of 500 Black college athletes in one Texas school, only 12 Black males graduated. This pattern is now "second nature" and to the point that non-racist Europeans probably do not realize what their personal desires and silence help to perpetuate.

Europeans fashioned bad habits in the Enslaved regarding thinking and work patterns and have made no effort to convert Blacks out of these bad habits. For example, at no time have Black people been taught how to make and manage money. Then Whites (and some misled affluent Blacks) show righteous indignation by blaming the victim. Of course, it is up to struggling Blacks to rise above their delusions and poverty but they have no idea as to how and there is situation made available for them to be taught. To blame them for that is like blaming a child for being sick and not doing what it takes to bring about a cure. The "cure" is going to have to come from healthy Blacks since Whites do not care--do not know how to help, even if they cared—and ensure Blacks cannot learn what it takes.

CLASSIFICATION OF TODAY'S "MANLINESS/"MANHOOD": Although there is intense continued demonization of Black males as part and parcel of how Whites validate their own violent mindsets, existence, dealings with others, and get relief from their profound self-hate, many Black males have been able to rise above such oppression. Certainly the following discussion is generic and certain aspects apply to both Black and White males.

Group I: "Superior Manliness" or "Manliness of African Tradition" was outlined by African Sages who said that, as a way of life, *"good"* people's minds and spirits stayed in contact with the Sublime. The Sublime is the realm of the Spiritual Elements—i.e. Unconditional Love, Truth, Reality, and the Natural—are in such forms as "aliveness," contentment, reality, harmony, peace, beauty, perfection, and goodness. These forms are in concentrations only second to "the Heavens". To consistently live a life of Ma'at (the Spiritual Elements in action) at a Sublime level made them "*Super*" (originally meaning 'balance left over')—and hence "Superior" to those who did not. "Superior" human "Manliness" displays are those who make Ma'at or Sublime contributions to humanity. Such a determination for the Natural World is by the agreement of the Sages of all cultures and throughout the ages. They spent the time, energy, and effort to discover African Philosophy and what is right, they stick by that, regardless of if they stand alone—and that is the test of non-forceful "Manhood."

Group II: Manhood are those good men who intend to display at a Group I level but fall short. Examples are the "Decent" Black Youth of "the Streets" (Anderson) who intensely desire to do the Right thing but are in situations whereby they see no alternative but to "go along to get along" in their "Street" culture. An example of the kind of problems they get into was illustrated by Malcolm X (Taylor). In a desperate effort to reassert his masculinity following the loss of a fight to a White boy, the 13 year old Malcolm adopts a cool pose and goes to school wearing his hat. The White teacher, aware of the dynamics underlying Malcolm's performance, "orders" him to keep his hat on. By commanding Malcolm to do the very thing he intended as an act of rebellion, the teacher blows Malcolm's cool by rearticulating it as a sign of his submission to authority. The teacher further instructs Malcolm to walk around the room so "everyone can see you". Instead of being the subject of a rebellious and potentially masculinizing performance, Malcolm now, in a repetition of his defeat by the White boy, becomes an object of ridicule. Forced to up the ante, Malcolm redirects the gaze of his fellow students to yet another act of rebellion by placing a tack in the teacher's chair while "everyone in the classroom was looking". When the teacher sits on the tack, the performance is a success but at a greater price than Malcolm had intended. He is expelled.

Nevertheless, Group II constitute the majority of Gang members and are easily converted if given the opportunity in a safe environment. Whatever is the nature of their problematic masculine performance is explained by these males' fear that for their own survival, they must appear to be "men" in the company of other males. Their outward expressions might exist in tandem with beliefs about themselves as considerate, respectful, and loving. Hence, they privately maintain that masculinity is primarily defined by ones ability to love, feel, and express himself in meaningful and positive ways.

Group III are *Black American Custom Manhood*—a mix of all sorts of bits and pieces from other Groups. As a boy it was an unspoken rule for any Black male in a position to maintain the belief in the physical superiority of Black males (from their Ancestors having to be so strong as to withstand the horrors of the Middle Passage and "Seasoning" of the Enslaved). Because Whites considered Blacks incapable of excelling in intellectual endeavors and because any celebrity Black males might attain was limited to the fields of sport and entertainment, those Blacks males made extra effort to countered these limitations by merely excelling in these areas, particularly in the athletic arena. Furthermore, I heard almost daily that I "must succeed for my race" since this counted as a victory over Whites as well as a symbolic gain in the struggle for human dignity. The fight between Joe Louis, the heavy-weight boxing champion of the world served as one of the few focal points for African American pride in the 1930s. He represented the USA vs. Germany's Max Schmeling—symbolizing the struggle between democracy and fascism. Although Schmeling had beaten him prior, Louis won in two minutes and four seconds into the first round. Schmeling was hospitalized 10 days with several broken vertebrae. Louis thereby was deemed to be "Larger than Life." Malcolm and Peterson cannot simply be a fight between two individuals; instead, it is a racially coded engagement in which Malcolm is expected to "uplift the race." When he fails to do so, he is thoroughly ridiculed. Because black masculinity, then and now, is so deeply imbricated with physical prowess in ideologies of race, Malcolm's manliness is implicitly brought into question.

Group IV: Manhood is seen in those with an *Inferiority Complex* and to the point of feeling profound shame, if not self-hatred. A well-kept secret is that men are afraid or leery of other men—perhaps from another male exposing them as not being "a real man" because of fears and powerlessness. Most masculine displays are motivated by males' fear of what others will think of them and thus much of the profiling, posturing, and violence witnessed in gangs and in prison environments reflect feelings of fear, insecurity, and anxiety. To overcome these profoundly emotionally painful experiences, those who head toward Gangs "Overcompensate"—i.e. the feeling of inferiority so great that one fears unable to overcome ones weaknesses, limitations, and flaws. Hence, their over-compensating is into a Superiority Complex. This features the striving for power and dominance with great exaggeration, intensification, and lack of caring about anyone else to an obsessive-compulsive degree.

They endeavor to secure their position of having a grandiose quality of power by extraordinary efforts--by greater haste and impatience—by more violent impulses. Most males "do" gender by taking up space, behaving combatively, and participating in risky or aggressive acts. Consequently, masculinity is defined as "controlling others, climbing hierarchies, obtaining possessions ... [using] coercion, force, and in many cases even violence to achieve such control and power. Through ongoing and stringent tests, males are rewarded for resisting potentially healthful displays of tenderness, compassion, femininity, and vulnerability. Most members in our society view masculinity as the opposite of femininity, and because these gender dichotomies have reward/ punishment systems attached to them, males in our culture often adopt extreme forms of the masculine ethos and reject feminine ones. Gender scripts, not physiology, are critical points of departure and ongoing references for knowing how one is to behave if he is to gain the rewards reserved for "men."

Group V: European Superiority Complex. One group of Europeans declare themselves to be "superior" super-humans as a result of them operating in/out of the "Air Castle" Supernatural realms that spring from their fantasy imaginations about their personal power. However, at a deeper mental level, the basis for beliefs about their personal power actually comes from the GUN (from which they cannot be separated) as well as from being backed up by fellow "GUN" tooting "Air Castle" Brutes. Thus, in reality, they have a *Superiority Complex*--characterized by the donning of a mask of self-confidence and greatness with a reality of arrogance and aggression to conceal a sense of deep inferiority. Their lives are a constant struggle to be able to live up to this Icon Image and not show any signs of weakness in their ever-present daily competitions with "everybody". Thus, their ultimate goal in life is to "win" by having the most "adult toys" of power, status, riches, and making their own rules. Such requires that their Egos develop out of anti-Spiritual Elements—i.e. directly opposing Unconditional Love, Truth, Reality, and the Natural. Leaders of this African god Set superiority mentality fashion a cult. For males to be successful at gaining social rewards, they need resources. Such resources might include but are not limited to women with whom to have sex, material goods to flaunt, other males with whom to compete and compare oneself, and the display of emotional strength and physical power.

Group VI are Black Puppets those Black males who imitate European Brutes--those with a philosophically socialized Superiority Complex. Many fear that other Black males will expose them as not being real men because they have been accustomed to proving and defining their masculinity in relation to White male, the same as persons of mainstream male communities such as fraternities and athletic groups define and compare each other. There is the additional burden of spending several years in close proximity to other males who potentially occupy higher statuses and developing a preference for that lifestyle. These issues, along with males trying desperately to gain social rewards, likely encourage extreme emotional disengagement from those unlike them.

Group VII is Struggling Black males, most considered by European policemen to be "Bad-asses or "Bad Niggers". In the slavery system they adopted aggressive behaviors and refused to accept either the overseers or slave owners' physical prowess as a match for their own physical prowess and mental determinations. Most sought through open defiance, violence, and confrontation to improve their lot in slavery regardless of the consequences of their actions for their own or the community's welfare. Their imitators do not even accept the values of the Black community as binding on them.

Group VIII: "The Streets" Masculinities are scripted into an earned, enacted, rehearsed, and refined identity that must be relived through each day's activities and choices. Here are statements for differences between "boys" and "men?" gathered from Black youth in prison by Nandi. Note how these males define masculinities as cognitive rather than as performance: A real man is one who finds strength in the salt of his tears and he sedulously battles through any unfortunate circumstance. (Jevon, 23, imprisoned seven years); A true man is an honorable male. He is respectful to self, parents, family, and neighbors. He stands by his word. He's the maintainer, educator, and protector of his family, and he values the rights and property of others. (Timothy, 36, imprisoned 13 years); Being a man is about accepting the role we play in our problems…. (Jay, 32, imprisoned 10 years); A man is a male who has reached the stage where he has control of his emotions and desires to resist or forego some pleasures for the sake of a higher goal. (Sundiata, 63, imprisoned 27 years).

Some said masculinity is based upon their thoughts and feelings, the focus of their desires, and what they imagine. Sun, a 25-year-old confined for 4 years, suggested that real men are peaceful and maintain empowering relationships with others; are more responsive than reactive, knowing the difference between the two and always seeking, if not to be at peace with, then how to influence the environment without being influenced out of his character. A man deals with respect as a general principle….He knows how to love without losing himself, but also how to love without holding back, or being possessive. A highly regarded way of being a man is the ability to love and share oneself without limitations. Another said "Manhood" is "quiet strength; emotion … not seen as a weakness; sensitiv[ity] to[ward] Black women's needs; and a lover of life and all that is beautiful".

Matthew, aged 49 and imprisoned 19 years, stated suggests that real men should express feelings of helplessness and compassion for those in need. A real man isn't afraid to cry, but most often than not, his tears are filled with anger for not being able to complete some task or help those he loves. A real man has compassion for those who have none for themselves, because he knows those individuals are unhealthy, and they need help. Such notions expressed publicly would be dismissed as unmasculine and passive. Also, attempts to perform in ways that reflected his feelings of compassion and helplessness would subject him to violence.

Group IX—Prison Manhood
Group X—Miscellaneous
Group XI—Self-Made Man

SUMMARY

As seen in all Europeans involved in the slave trade, justification for their inhumaneness came from their Adversion ("hateful face-to-face opposition") attitudes and the slave owners' Aversion ("to turn away from" and shutting down all beliefs of a shared culture and humanity with Blacks)--both allowing them to declare the Enslaved as "subhuman" for purposes of exploitation and sadistic punishment. Aversion's complementary partners, *Adversion* (a), was shown by the ex-convict slave overseers who had been released from European jails on the condition that they would leave Europe forever by going to America. Most became overseers on slave ships and plantations; became the "redneck racists" of the South; became the police of the Enslaved; and became the Ku Klux Klan members. These ex-convicts and the patterns they set up in the South included being filled with negative (e.g. anger) and destructive (e.g. hate, revengeful) emotions to such an intense degree that they acted impulsively in carrying out the most despicable of crimes against the Enslaved. This accounts from the prominence of hatred as a way of life that is so pervasive among Euro-Americans today. This "love to hate" is in keeping with an early European definition of "Hate" embracing both love and dislike. It shows within those possessing an Inferiority Complex and those socialized into a Brute state and yet hate themselves. Based upon my observations, research findings, and experiences with European males, particularly in the marketplace, my guesstimate of their self-hatred is 40% in the Extreme category; perhaps 20% of a moderate degree; 15% of a slight degree; 10% of a mild degree; and 15% not so afflicted. Self-declared 'little gods' have hatred socialized into them in childhood.

Nevertheless, because "misery loves company," it was European Brute slavers intent to remold minds of the Enslaved in their own "little god" image. As part of their intimidation in preparation for conquest of minds of the Enslaved, they would make festive displays of Sadism in the way a steam hammer can drive home tacks. This effective measure, called "Making an Example of," is how "Seeds" were implanted into the already horribly traumatized minds of the Enslaved with the intent to keep them oppressed. Those "Seeds" sprouted in all directions inside the Psychically Traumatized mindset of ex-Slaves--and particularly in those living inside the "Struggling Tunnel" (metaphorical passage from the living quarters of the Field Enslaved to today's inner cities).

These sprouts + the original mental "Raw Nerves" from all that went with being Enslaved + the "Inside-Out" thinking styles + the "Make Do" living styles led to flawed Common Sense choices, decisions, and solutions which, in turn, were of a vicious cycle nature. The "big picture" effects on the Enslaved can be described as Extreme Despair. Most got to the point of not thinking past the moment and had hopeless hopelessness about anything ever getting better for them. When a family member was killed, many simply said they were no longer in despair and have escaped the suffering. Often there was no crying or show of emotions because they are passed that point. Many made "a deal with the devil" in hopes of getting some relief. In spite of their horrors in a foreign land, for 150 years following slavery many Enslaved descendants have risen to great achievements. It speaks volumes about their inner strengths. Yet, their fellows are the ones who have most heavily influenced Black American Customs and which are of an entirely different nature than those of African Tradition. They are the ones most afflicted by the ongoing layering of old and innovated additional evil ways of Europeans in dealing with Black People. The point is that *for Black People to rise out of whatever poverty they are entrapped in, it is only the philosophy of African Tradition that will be successful.*

CHAPTER VII

DELUSIONAL FEARS
ARE THE SOURCE
OF ALL EVILS

"KILLER" POLICE

Early in Humankind's history, societies formed "Codes" of Law to govern the people. The earliest collections of laws--known as "Codes"--were originally suggested by the discovery and diffusion of the art of writing in Africa, c77,000 BC. These were a mingling of religious, civil, and merely moral ordinances—all based upon Ma'at (Spiritual Elements in action)—the influence of right and righteousness, justice and harmony, balance, respect, and human dignity. Throughout African history there was rarely any component of retributive justice because of the belief that nothing in earth or heaven is without spirit. Thus, religious ideas were applied equally to all sectors of African society—with no difference between the rich and poor; aristocrats or commoners.

HISTORY OF POLICE: Since Ancient Africans never had a police force or jails, perhaps the oldest known well-formed Police Codes were those of Hammurabi (1792-1750 BC). Along with his military and political achievements, he instituted forms of policing in Babylon (Mesopotamia). In early Rome, the Patron and client bonded relationship was similar to that of feudal lord and his man as well as to today's police and their suspects. Like the patron and lord, the police were supposed to stay within the agreed upon societal concepts that embraced Integrity, Honesty, Decency, and Virtue. The 1066 Norman Conquest of England by William, The Conqueror, brought in a number of French systems, including the word "Police" and its military flavor. Much of the Magna Carta (1215) established guidelines for the police—the sheriff and the village constable. Police killing was rampant.

Subsequently, other early systems—either in military or semi-military style--consisted of citizens banding together for mutual protection. To promote acceptable police conduct, police departments developed "Codifications"—i.e. orderly and authoritative statements of the leading rules of law on a given subject. Policies and patterns differed but discretion was essential. In theory and ideally there have been four dimensions crucial to achieve the level of police integrity: (a) the quality of official rules and the manner in which they are made, communicated, and understood within a police agency; (b) the quality of the detection, investigation, and disciplinary actions taken by that agency; (c) the willingness of officers to report another officer's misconduct; and (d) the influence of the agency's environment on its level of police integrity. In C19, to cope with London crime and violence, there was created a ruthless force of secret police and in 1829, Scotland Yard's police activity. Meanwhile, the colonies transported these systems to the Americas as a means of controlling Enslaved Africans. In the early 1800s the USA became more urban and patterns of ethnic diversity began to erode the social and political influence of the original English and Dutch settlers. Besides rioting, crime, and disorder flourishing, the life-styles of new Germans and Irish immigrants offended the moral and social sensitivies of the original settlers.

Immigrant and urban behaviors were perceived as a threat to the social, economic, and political fabric of American life. Then police were set-up in military organizational style--from the Federal level down through state, county, city, and private levels. This meant police power included all powers of internal government embracing the settlement of disputes; the levy and collection of taxes; the enactment and enforcement of criminal law; police and military action to maintain order and prevent disaster; the regulation of agriculture, industry, religion, and education; and the operation of the post office, roads, warehouses, dams, and other instruments of communication, transportation, and public welfare. After 1847, freedom of the individual was presumed (except for the Enslaved) and the rule that urgent public necessity or interest must be demonstrated to justify government action.

However, the "Dark Ages" of the police extended to 1900, with departments under the direction of politicians, with ill-equipped and poorly paid policemen + widespread corruption and brutality, particularly as part of 'crime prevention's' Deterrence and arrest aspects. *Deterrence* is accomplished by creating an illusion that police are omnipresent so that potential violators will obey the law. As a rule of thumb, the more eager a policeman is to perform his duty by arresting criminals, the more tempted he is to ignore, and even violate the suspect's constitutional rights. A counter was the 1966 *Miranda Rights Act*: the suspect may remain silent and refuse to answer any questions—that anything he/she says may be used in evidence against him/her—that he/she may consult with a lawyer and have his/her lawyer present during the interrogation—and that a lawyer will be provided without cost if he/she cannot afford to pay.

"KILLER" POLICE INSIDE USA'S VIOLENT HISTORY: Before Europeans invaded and took over the New World, English Common Law allowed police to use *any means* necessary to stop and capture a felon. Back then, there were very few felony crimes and those were punishable by execution. Firearms were not an available means to police for stopping criminals (Broomé *J. Humanistic Psychology, 2014*). The use of deadly force in the Americas became prominent in the 1800s when police first began carrying duty firearms. As USA law enforcement evolved, firearms became standard issue and were also an available means by which a fleeing felon could be stopped legally under the law. Historically, the military has supplied large numbers of members to police forces as well as being a major influence on police psychology and police deadly force training methods. Military shooting performance examples include such factors as dehumanizing the enemy, physical proximity, social distancing (objectification of the adversary), and the natural instinct to fight, flee, bluff, or freeze.

In the military is it known that the more realistic the training is for a soldier, the more likely he/she will be effective in shooting and killing enemy combatants. Military and police actions have been featured in the many wars before the American Revolution—in the USA's seven officially declared wars since 1775 and innumerable others. Although USA wars have honed Euro-Americans' patterns of aggressiveness and use of violence, in using the Tree Concept (fig. 1), the "Root" causes for both the military and the police "killer" enthusiasm date to primitive European Warriors. Its "Trunk" formed when Europeans perfected the GUN (starting in 1304). "Branches" came when released European prisoners + an assortment of "low life" Europeans (e.g. enslavers, prostitutes, religious dissidents, and the wayward) + a conglomeration of religious fanatics (advocating hypocritical concepts of Christian dealings with "all God's children") were on board ships headed to the Americas so as to "Fruit" people's oppression. Their resultant superficial and Indifference/Hate/Evil/Sadism Complex (IHES) lifestyle molded Enslaved Africans into brutal submission. In fact, the single most important shaper of USA violence has been racism and police action directed at Black People.

It started with perceptions by plantation captors, police groups, and the colonial/state governments deeming it essential to maintain slavery and then Jim Crow segregation (1865-1965) as state-enforced racial caste systems. Meanwhile, from the beginning of the Americas the police have assumed roles in all aspects of Black People's lives, each requiring a heavily armed, violence-prone White civilian population for support. The police were actively involved in keeping the Enslaved under control, including vigilante actions. Lynching, as part of Mob law, features a society that is most rotten at its core. It was used mainly against Southern Blacks after slavery ended in 1865, but also in the West--directed mainly against Mexican Americans and Asians. What made anti-Black lynching so significant was the unspeakable barbarity with which they were carried out against adult men, teenager boys, women, children, and pregnant mothers. To enforce deference and submission to Whites, 2 to 4 Blacks were hanged, burned at the stake, or quietly murdered every week by beating, drowning, strangling, stabbing, poisoning, and axing. Apart from being public spectacles, killings were also public theater, often a festive affair, a participatory ritual of torture and death. Special "excursion" trains transported spectators to the scene; employers sometimes released their workers to attend; parents sent notes to school asking teachers to excuse their children for the event; and entire families attended--children hoisted on their parents' shoulders to miss none of the action and accompanying festivities.

Every year of USA history has witnessed Euro-Americans committing the overwhelming majority of homicides in untold numbers, engaging potentially lethal assaults, and daily exhibiting countless "white collar" crimes "everywhere'. Police have always been at the center of lynching, racial, ethnic, religious, agrarian, urban riots, rural feuds, industrial conflict; crime, vigilantism, halting revolutions, as well as in terrorism against Black People; assassinations; and violence against women and Black/Brown/"Red" youth; and stirring gang wars and then "gifting" duffel bags filled with street drugs and guns to struggling Black People so they can fight each other (fig. 10).

"KILLING" & MISCONDUCT TERMS (fig. 17): Although it is important to be familiar with the "legal jargon" of "Killing," some ideas are given here but they are not legal or adequate to form any significant decision related to them. Prins (*Medicine, Science and the Law, 2008*) says *Murder* is the unlawful killing of another with malice *Aforethought* (that is with criminal intention). Apart from certain exceptions, Murder is committed when a person of sound mind and discretion unlawfully kills any reasonable creature with intent to kill or to cause grievous bodily harm. *Manslaughter* (unlawfully causing the death of another without malice aforethought) is considered *Voluntary* if the accused was: (a) provoked; or (b) acting in pursuance (in the course of carrying out) of a suicide pact; or (c) suffering from diminished responsibility. *Involuntary Manslaughter* concerns unintended killing, but where there was an intention to commit an unlawful or dangerous act, gross negligence, or disregard for the lives and safety of others. Other types of Manslaughter include: *Child Destruction* is an offence to destroy the life of an unborn child, unless there is compliance with provisions of current abortion legislation; Causing death by dangerous or careless driving and/or under the influence of drink or drugs; *Infanticide* is killing of a 'newly born child'—perhaps under 12 months of age; and *Hedonistic*—e.g. so-called 'lust' killings, thrill seeking (for kicks), and for psychological and physical security–derived perhaps from the victim's property. Legally, "*Misconduct*" is a transgression of some established and definite rule of action—a forbidden act—a dereliction from duty—unlawful behavior—willful in character—improper or wrong behavior. Examples include dishonest acts or attempts to persuade legal authorities by deceptive or reprehensible methods. Its synonyms are Misdemeanor, Misdeed, Misbehavior, Delinquency, Impropriety, Mismanagement, Offense, but not Negligence or Carelessness.

From Babylon to the present all of these have been daily occurrences. The official definition of Misconduct or Occupational Deviance is criminal and noncriminal behavior (i.e. policy violations) that occurs during work hours and is committed under guise of a police officer's authority (Long, *Social Psychology Quarterly, 2013*). Corruption, on the other hand, relates only to activities that involve a misuse of authority for the purpose of personal gain. Thus, misconduct includes a broader array of activities, one of which may be corruption. Here is an example. Perhaps of greatest significance is the unique coercive powers and authority the police possess over citizens—powers that, simply by their decisions, can determine people's life or death. Such powers to be 'little gods' as well as being assured of loyalty from all officers paves the way for certain ones to step beyond the police policy's "serve and protect" boundaries. Since it is not necessary to show respect ('because I've got the gun') and since they receive no benefits from being respectful, insensitivity to feelings and legitimate interests of the 'un-favored' people are easily developed—insensitivities omitting time for understanding and considered judgments—edgy intolerances spurring hasty conclusions stereotyping certain citizenry as capricious, uncooperative and unreliable. That leads to bad conduct towards any in the stereotyped environment and inhumane practices, including 'Conditioned Response" killings against the hated and fitting into stereotypical Icon Images. Of course all of this is about biases and prejudices.

"KILLER" POLICE MINDSETS

One part of my Orthopaedic Surgical practice was serving as a police surgeon. In appreciation, I received an honorary membership in the Fraternal Order of Police. Being a police surgeon gave me the opportunity to see 'up close' that this is one of the most dangerous occupations. Police officers, by the nature of their profession, routinely come into contact with violent criminals and are often exposed to risky situations. While operating, I saw inside their bodies what can happen to them as a result of their work. I observed them without their swagger and arrogance. I treated what they did to tough criminals and to innocent people. As a physician my duty is to diagnose and treat—and not pass judgment on people. This means I have to *look at things as they are--without an opinion* as to whether I like or not something or the people involved. This is the context in which the following discussion on "Killer" Police is given—those really bad policemen who kill people for personal reasons or for "excitement," or from following Satanist cults. Gathering all of the negativity about policemen might be represented by Leaves on a tree. But there is no hope for improvement or defense until their "Roots"/"Seed" concepts are known. A proposed sequence of mental events of concepts for "Killer" Police is: Initially, in the back of their minds, were "Seed" sensations (fig. 3, 6) giving rise to Precepts, in turn, giving rise to Notions, from which Icon Images—some being "stars"--of different destructive natures--were formed. From those Notions and Icon Images a *collage* of Notions/Concepts became fashioned into a *Super-star Icon Image*. That Super-star was/ is destined to act as the stimulus eventually igniting a *Conditioned Response displaying as the killing* of innocent and unarmed Black People.

Upon facing an appropriate scapegoat situation, the contents of the *Disposition* of like-kind Notions/ Concepts arrange "Killer" policemen mental activities in line with the theme of the Super-Star *Icon Image* (fig. 5, 6, 8, 10).Then, further supporting factors deemed threatening—truly or falsely--drive ingredients in their minds to be instantly arranged to conform to the 'blue-print' fashioned from the Trigger Event (the prior disposition/attitude coloring the present situation). In short, their mindsets are in a state of readiness to think, feel, express, and/or behave in a certain previously conceived manner.

"KILLER" POLICE—OCCULT MINDSETS: Some use the word "Occult" ('to hide') to span all aspects of the Unseen Realms—and its hidden or mysterious powers not explained by known scientific principles of Nature and the attempt to bring these powers within human control by scientific methods. Some use "Occult" for the range from Spiritual God to the "Devil"; some for only the Brute Realms; some for the Supernatural Realm, the focus of this discussion. The European medieval concept of Occult properties included only those properties which may be revealed by experimentation. The Alchemists, Astrologers, Seers, Sorcerers, Magicians as well as the Occult Sciences of Witchcraft, Vodun, and Numerology—all-embracing these concepts, were under the assumption that the secrets of Nature have relations which once revealed will confer great power. These beliefs were in conflict with orthodox theology and their work was termed "Occultism."

Even though the Supernatural originated because of human's normal in-capabilities of understanding certain things, its scope is gradually being narrowed by Natural Science explaining many of its 'occult' phenomena. Yet, its Icon Image persists independent of the survivals and revivals of ancient occult systems and the sporadic theories claiming special revelations. Supernatural concepts are applied to any theories, doctrines, arts, or practices dealing with alleged phenomena not explained by physical science but are attributed to non-natural causes appeal to those who reject the ordinary explanations of science because of being "Non-Rational" thinkers. Hence, they find mystic exaltation in vague, yet imposing concepts appealing to a sense of personal power and understanding—by way of mystic, abstruse, and ambitious doctrines. They will not consider that European science has not yet advanced very far to explain such things as hypnosis, long classified as occult.

Although the underlying principles are still largely unknown, as are most human mental processes, they are known by scientists to be a natural process. Their "Non-Rational" thinking causes them to ignore that there is no proof for what they believe. That the occult and the scientific temper are opposed can be seen in today's news. Nevertheless, the realm of the Occult has a large overlap with European religion and with Europeans' forms of "Logic" (i.e. "Non-Rational" thinking based). This is because they all came out of the primitive Warrior mindset. One European writer says: "the whole of supernatural religion is in the domain of the occult; but long-established usages and familiar practice tend to establish a religion in a way that conventionalizes it and the occult aspect is overlooked or diminished." One reason for this is that occult and its mysteriousness is in conflict with the spirit of Truth-Seeking that characterizes the Natural World and to which only sound knowledge is acceptable.

This spurs "Air Castle" people (fig. 5)—whether as "Non-Rational" Logic, European Religion, or European Warrior roles to present their thoughts disguised as being Rationally Truthful, ignoring the fact that it makes no Natural World sense. Thus, they resort to preventing access to Knowledge (e.g. that of African Tradition); engage in confusion by using "big words" and theories that are facades when closely examined; and ambiguous laws that are interpreted in favor of "Killer" Police. *Magical Thinking*--thoughts about unrealizable realities that bring about changes in reality--is a fundamental feature of the human mind. It has an anatomical basis in the human brain's "God Module"--the home of intuitional wisdom—perhaps located in the temporal lobe. This Module--when there is Real Self purity of Intellect and purity of Character--is concerned with spirituality, prayer, and religious experiences.

"KILLER" POLICE KILLING PHANTASMAGORIA: By having no clue of Divine Unity underlying Cosmic multiplicity and thus lacking insight into "Who Am I?," "Killer" police are disconnected from their

Private Selves' innate "5Ss" (safety, security, self-confidence, strength, stability) and from all creatures. To thus be "nowhere" in a bottomless pit--feeling totally separate, like an individualist stranger in this world who came from somewhere else or like a fluke (a chance accident)--they have no specific Natural World knowledge about anything other than rituals laid out by their primitive European Supernatural cult and its 45,000 years of perfection. This False Self awareness displays acquired Emotions and "non-rational" thinking that conforms to the cult "Codes".

Hence, they have, I believe, "Normal Variant" minds—resembling *Hallucinations* ('to wander in mind')--just short of insanity. In such outer reaches of ones mind, there are meager or no sense organ perceptions (coming from without or within the body) or from intuiting Things pertaining to the Spiritual Elements of Unconditional Love, Truth, Reality, or the Natural. Instead, their Supernatural cult perceptions, upon becoming aware of what they fear, form fantasy Percepts, Notions, Ideas, and Images they accept as reality. Then they proceed with "logical" thinking along a Fantasy path called "*Phantasmagoria*" (phantasm/fantasm or image; apparition or ghostly figure; assembly)—the ideas derived from tales of magic lanterns, which projected still pictures on a screen. The Phantasmogoria Lantern gave views that dissolved into each other. Its ill-defined meanings from these images include rapidly or strikingly changing scenes of real things, illusions, imagery fancies, deceptions, or distorted phantasy. Depending upon ones mood, figures may increase or decrease in size, fade away, or pass into each other. In primitive times "Phantasmagoria" contributed to the Occult Supernatural realm serving as an alarm to signal evil and sadistic *Evocative* (mystical) powers into action. Immediately these Evocative powers would focus on setting in motion whatever it took to destroy anything having the potential for good or whoever was standing in the way of ones desires or whatever was deemed to be a threatening or destructive "monster". *Delusional Fears*—the imagining of false, dangerous problems and believing them to pose great problems to something significant to oneself—was the resultant Effect.

Throughout the primitive European Ice Age of Scarcity there was an interweaving of Delusional Fears checkered with actuality aspects—as in seeing oneself as prey. Thus, partly to avoid allowing oneself to needlessly become prey, the Warriors developed the practice of preying on others before others had the chance to make them prey. By the end of the Ice Age in 12,500 BC, Delusional Fears were used primarily to generate justification for seeking ones own profits by any means necessary, as opposed to being the profit of others. *This mindset is a root and source of all natural and moral evils--out of which arose Hate philosophies* of life, culturally transmitted to today's Brutes. By Supernatural cult members believing they are 'little gods"--and thus 'perfect'—and thus above the rules of all others--means the cult needs a feigned enemy scapegoat Target group they rely on to destroy so as to boost their façade sense of feeling 'superior.' A consequence of children socialized into such a Delusional Fear mindset pattern with its associated "*Paracosms*" (amazing illusionary details in ones self-created Imaginary World) inside the context of "Phantasmagoria" is to seek out scapegoats.

These bullies design an assortment of mental images having priority order. "To get mine, I must take yours" requires killing or destroying those "monsters" having what they envy. By having a "Network" to protect them from being accountable (because they do the same things) means they develop into adult bullies. In the process, the more cult members buy into "Air Castle" codes of killing anybody not like them—just for "sport"--the greater the frequency and duration their "*Paracosms* are used to make "monster" mental images of their scapegoats. As a result, it does not take much to pull the switch that evokes psychic forces of tremendous potency to display in the minds of "Killer" police on seeing a hated scapegoat—like *Black/Brown/Red people*.

At crunch time, their Phantasmagoria deludes their seeing enormous sized and strong scapegoat "monsters" rushing at them, in a constantly shifting and complex manner, to harm them. This moment symbolizes all of the "Killer" police' conjured Delusional Fears of nightmarish mirages of being destroyed by these 'monsters' and, of course, they "pull the trigger" to kill, even the unarmed. jabaileymd.com

"KILLER" POLICE CHIMERA HATE IMAGES: To see a police car—painted black and white, with attached flashing lights on its roof—is to form a *Mental Picture*. To give that Mental Picture an interpretation with a meaning converts it into a *Mental Image.* An analogy is retaining in memory a footprint and interpreting it as being some realistic, distorted, or fantasy "Thing". Titan will create a layered and enduringly powerful *Icon Image* if once shot by a policeman and again experiences a policeman pointing a gun at him. Thereafter, whenever police are watching him, Titan's *Conditioned Response for instant self-protection spurs maneuvers, like him running away.* When someone's actions create a mental image in the Receiver, it is that image the Receiver uses to recall the experience and to provide this new situation with some meaning—whether good or bad. There are infinite varieties of such *Prey Reactions*—each causing Predators to do a "*React by Attack*"--similar to a shark seeing blood from a nearby swimmer. Predators have learned to hate "just because" and select a scapegoat to target. This Target becomes an *Obsession* (a persistent uncontrollable impulse to think certain thoughts) and formulate a plan with a supreme value of what they want to see realized. Their emotions rise to such a peak as to become *Compulsive* (uncontrollable impulse to be a certain way or carry out certain actions irresistibly and perhaps contrary to ones inclination). Both are reflections of Brute Brain automatic features. Predators assume Supernatural powers favor them carrying out their wish by believing they see/hear conformation from their god. The actual happening is that their vividness of this message has come from them projecting it onto the god as justification to do what is desired. Prior to this "revelation" a strong conflict or resistance may have existed in them for a long time—perhaps even forming some type of friendly acquaintance with the future targeted scapegoat. An inner battle is won when a "revelation" enables the overpowering of their realistic reluctance to do harm to the scapegoat.

At that point, in the mirror of ones mind, ones imagination reveals itself in the unbalance of contrary opposites—as in "Me vs. Them". With a 'hyped' state of Emotions, the Icon Images Predators form are of a Chimera nature—something absurdly fantastic, wildly imaginary, vague--and what normal people would call foolish and grotesque. Predators' minds crave them--and the more the better, especially if the entire situation is contradictory (e.g. desiring to kill those who help them) --for the mind has learned how to deal with contradictions. A generic Image example is a beast with goat body shape + a lion's head + a snake's hindquarters. Despite its Supernatural fearsome, strong, immortal, and swift nature, the 'monster' is not proof of anything. In forming such 'monster' Images, initially the ingredients are like mixing cement. While still all is wet, the image can be moved around and shaped, rearranged and layered with collage fantasy items. But at some point, it hardens and then there is almost nothing one can do to reshape it. "*Excitement*" is in the make-believe—the fantasy—assumed to come out of a magic door in the Supernatural "Air Castle--and not the truth or anything near it. Predators' most exciting mental life aspects are the sensations, emotions, desires, and aspirations taking place in a universal arena of illusions in which they star in slaying the Chimera 'monster'. To gain even more excitement, they put on a "little god" mask which enables each to believe that is who one is—or even greater. This drives one to declare oneself to be mentally and morally superior to those who differ in any way from whatever one is for. The mask is a product of ones self-creation—that one projects oneself into—and that one recognizes oneself in it. An effective self-image in this drama must be of a nature to cause one to be feared rather than loved.

To imitate evil under the illusion of: "I am doing good" means one will always go beyond the example the image sets. Predators reflect these 'monster' images without absorbing them and the mirror in which they view them contains nothing but itself. That means there is typically no one thing to point to that urges getting revenge. Hence, to kill is exciting--establishes or cements bonds with ones fellows—brings honor—and establishes 'little god' delusions. All of this spares one the ordeal of thinking about ones harsh reality. The mask and doing it for the "Air Castle" cult cause prevents taking responsibility for the reality one has created. jabaileymd.com; Blackvoicenews.com

"KILLER" POLICE KILL MECHANICALLY: People who are "Self-Unknown" design philosophies of life (POL) out of fantasy concepts that go in the direction of an Inferiority Complex and/or a Superiority Complex. These ingredients derive from their circumstances and how they choose to live out of those circumstances. Perhaps for primitive Europeans such concerned "Survival Scarcity." Then, with a greed intent, their chosen means to overcome this was by Kill/Take/Destroy/Dominate/Oppress methods. Since newborn humans start life thinking with Images, maybe Warriors' immature and mechanical thoughts were imaged. Examples: Armor was for *mental* and physical defense mechanisms; strategically assessing significant problems was done from an Adaptive mechanical perspective (e.g. if X happens, do Z); troubleshooting utilized a mechanical process to locate problems and for repairs by mechanical patterns. Both warring and dancing were done mechanically. By being solely oriented to the Physical realm (a mechanical tendency) meant it was an easy next step for these Warriors to extend their "structured" way of looking at things into the realms of their environment, their culture, themselves, their victims, their gods, their thriving, and the Supernatural—pursuing/fixing each mechanically. Such a mechanical association of concepts meant primitive Europeans' mechanical language was applied automatically, even to organic things; for mechanically solving anything; and to have a false sense of "all is well" from that one 'broken' thing having been properly handled mechanically.

As today, it was "*Fear*" that first brought ideas of gods into primitive Europeans' minds—a fear leading them to "construct" gods out of their own warring appearance and imbue those Images with warrior thoughts, emotions, and deeds. Resultant Contingent Being gods were fantasized to make happen what they desired--Desires to satisfy their brutish animalist lifestyle. Hence, their 'constructed' gods symbolized gross immorality standards, filters, guides, and measures which Warriors eagerly imitated--like the deity Thor ('thunder')—for whom Thursday was named (Thor's Day). He was common to all early Germanic peoples—a great warrior represented as a red-bearded, middle-aged White man of enormous strength and an implacable foe to the harmful race of giants. The thunderbolt, representing his hammer, was his featured attribute--in the manner that the GUN is the supreme attribute—the absolute means of all power for today's European males. Ancient Europeans expressed this Supernatural state in terms of a machine—a mechanization taking reason out of its earthly domain and converting it to "Non-Rational" (Emotions + Left Brain) decisions and solutions. Their Supernatural cult rules put '*Boundaries on the Boundless*,' including making mechanical the Cosmic Organism. The Greek Euripides(480-406 BC) illustrated this by saying: "The way of God is complex. He [a gender boundary on their God] is hard for us to predict. He moves the pieces and they come somehow into a kind of order"—implying a mechanical universe.

Life-Living by displays of their Brute Brains in an Indifference/Hate/Evil/Sadism Complex mindset (IHES) forms continue from primitive European times. Hence, any IHES deeds are driven by *Obsessions* (a persistent uncontrollable impulse to think certain thoughts) and *Compulsions* (uncontrollable impulse to be a certain way or carry out certain actions irresistibly). Claims for such an obsessive-compulsive nature derive from a

"*Numinous*" mysterious Contingent Being--beyond their control, too big to think about, and too powerful to resist. Yet, it serves "Killer" police urges to: (1) gratify their own Lower (animalistic) Self Fetters, "Dark Side" Desires; (2) to being wed to the GUN with an eagerness to use it; (3) to soothe their insecurity and self-hate "Raw Nerve"; (4) to be honored by their cult for being arrogant 'Individualist Conformists'; and (5) to experience the power associated with disregarding others rights, equity, and hallowed customs. One dumbness of the Machine Concept implies that humans do the same thing all the time without change, like fool-proof machines. Seeing themselves as mechanical justifies being "coldly" disconnected from fellow humans; stereotyping "those people" as insignificant Chimera sub-humans to be feared; doing inhumane things to them without any compassion. At every opportunity, killing scapegoats in particular gives them "sick" pleasures and makes them want to do more and more. jabaileymd.com

"KILLER" POLICE BIAS/PREJUDICES/STEREOTYPES: The C16 English word "*Bias*" (oblique line or curved path from which "Prejudice" derives) is simply a tendency, usually below ones awareness, to see facts in a certain way because of ones habits, wishes, desires, interests, values, or need to "save face." "*Prejudice*" (a Middle English term for harm or injury resulting from action or judgment) has a strict sense of preconceived favorable or unfavorable opinion or emotion without knowledge. Whereas *Bias* is developed in viewing the facts and then "Picking and Choosing" only those facts which support ones point of view, "*Prejudice*" occurs when one does not know, or has not examined, or does not care about the facts and does not want to be confused by the facts. Their steps are positioned in the following order: Prejudices of Ignorance (all blindly adopted) are more easily removed than will-full Biases/Prejudices (i.e. "Indifferent"— seeing what it pleases and not what is plain and then passing that off as reason) while Prejudices of Interest (i.e. willingly preferred) are almost fixed and the opinions rising out of them are sustained with the greatest violence.

All of these advocates know little depth or scope of their "non-rational" and shackled points of view— thus making for weak judgments. Bias/Prejudices are declared to be ones virtues and yet, instead of being separate acts, they are series of continuous fantasy traits used for all like-kind subjects which become second nature. In policing this started from the very beginning of African American slavery with "slave patrollers," followed thereafter by vigilante justice and abuses at the hands of racist Southern and later nation-wide police. Continually perpetuating this was the fact of a policeman winning friends mainly by the passion of his prejudices and by the consistent narrowness of his outlook. Such stereotypical system-grinders hate Truth and Reality. All proper attempts to drive these Indifference/Hate/Evil/Sadism based bias and prejudices out by the door only put that boomerang in motion for them to come back by the window.

Stereotypes are cognitive structures in ones mind and are made up of ones socialization, information, beliefs, and expectations concerning a Target Group. Since slavery, Black People have constantly experienced unfair practices (e.g. racial profiling) from being deemed to *"Dark Figures of Crime'*—a term referring to them as stereotypes and also embracing the large amount of crime that goes undetected or unreported. In turn, the police have opened themselves to being stereotyped--Blacks viewing them as "more corrupt, more unfair, more excitable, more harsh, tougher, weaker, lazier, less intelligent, less friendly, more cruel, and more on the bad than good side when compared with how they treat other people. The nature of police business brings them into routine contact with criminals, substance abusers, the mentally-ill, and persons in crisis. As a result, police officers, like other front-line responders and social service workers, must frequently interact with poor, minority, and socially disadvantaged groups that are disproportionately afflicted with the very social problems that the police are expected to handle. This takes its emotional toll, expressed as stress, divorce, alcoholism, and suicide. Understandably, this makes many prone to develop stereotypes based on repeated exposure to negative social stimuli involving minority groups. This is especially true for officers who work in high-crime minority neighborhoods or who, by virtue of their job assignment, repeatedly come into contact with minority groups involved in crime or violence.

Attitudes, beliefs, and stereotypes no doubt develop when police have repetitive similar contacts from those of the same group—each causing them to routinely overestimate the occurrence of negative behaviors--each reinforcing preexisting racial stereotypes—each capable of leading to newly sprouting stereotypes on the original member as well as applied to individuals regardless of their individual characteristics. Together, these stereotypes act as organizational scripts for social memory and thus guide perceptions of future encounters for both the police and those to whom he conveys information. Such is the path to biased or incorrect assumptions automatic Conditioned Responses. Regularly changing officers' beat assignments based on crime characteristics and neighborhood demographic factors could help to prevent the development of those scripts. Ref: Smith, *Criminal Justice **and** Behavior, 2007;* Gabbidon, *Criminal Justice Review, 2011*

"KILLER" POLICE MIND'S LOCKER ROOM: A major purpose of the Supernatural "Air Castle" is to serve as a "Locker Room," as coaches do in preparing a given athlete/team members on ultimate goals of the "Big Picture". For Brutes, the "Big Picture" is capable of being seen only with the "Supernatural Eye" (equivalent to the Mind's Eye" of the Natural Cosmos). A major focus of mental locker room activity is on learning the ingredients and their arrangements and combinations which form Images, Symbols, Icons, Imagery, Imagination, and Contingent Beings needed for application at the proper place and time. The keystone ingredient is an *Image*--a memory of past experiences (a revived sense experience in the absence of sensory stimulation) or of an imagined construction. Either type of these Images can be used to summarize and represent action, thus make it closely linked to perception. *Imagination*, even when not necessarily creative, is a constructive process of recombining memories of past experiences and previously formed images into novel constructions.

Imagery is the representation in the mind of a sensory experience—visual (e.g. an elephant wearing pink slippers), auditory, gustatory, motor, olfactory, or tactile. As codes, these ingredients cannot be defined and can only be known by their different causations within given situations. Those situations require creating Fantasy settings--meaning there is an unreal mental image or reflection giving an appearance of the "Fantastic". Although the Images in these settings are Imaginary and thus not associated with beliefs having powers of producing something new, their purposes are to cause "awe" or "fascination" in the public's minds as a prime means of mind control. The effectiveness of Fantasy Images is that they are received as being just as much a part of ones real world as are sensations.

The cult's leaders are of "Air Castle" human and Contingent Being types—with the top one being created out of fantasy and represented in the form of a Mega-*Icon Image* because of ideally exhibiting all of the best aspects of the Indifference/Hate/Evil/Sadism (IHES) Complex. This Mega-Icon Image is the European made-up Satan, ruler of the European fantasized Hell. Human leaders are born into or are created into a Satanism Symbol while all cult members deem themselves as "little gods." All self-declare that they are bathed in an aura of omnipotence of a magnitude unknown to the living. Naturally, the African one universal High God is the ultimate competitor. Thus, whatever the Spiritual God is said by Sages to advocate, Brutes are automatically against and enthusiastically fight. What they do requires no thought and no alternative plan for, as a never changing warring bunch their Kill/Take/Destroy/Dominate/Oppress pattern were well worked out tens of thousands of years ago.

One of their prominent approaches is to "*Manufacture Fantasy Fear*" in order to mold cooperative delusions of a "White Community of Sameness" to thereby control these followers. Such results in a common purpose of greedy acquisitions and solid front defenses and offenses. Their Brute Greedy Mindsets consist of a glob of reality + distortion + fantasy--using Fear as a Weapon to stimulate aggression so as to gain power and control over others. To internalize the Cult dogma fantasy automatically means such people are insecure, non-rational, and are unable to do volitional thinking. This makes the cult unable to correct their flaws and errors--unable to separate Certainty, information, beliefs, and opinions--unable to be self-sufficient and thrive independent of the Cult.

Still, cult members absorb such Images in various arrangements, combinations, ways, and time periods. Group I Images are accretions (collages) on to which are ever increasing layers of like-kind bits and pieces—which elaborate, clarify, fuse, and include. Checkered throughout these are misinterpretations of the ordinary in light of using their "Supernatural Eye". Group II are biased and prejudiced modifications of reality. Group III are Images not attached to anything in particular but had their birth in the past—within or outside ones memory. Group IV are Images recalled out of ones memory. Using these forms of Images, there are a relatively small number of displays that people who adopt the Indifference/Hate/Evil/Sadism (IHES) Complex can use. European icons are generally quite simple in that the thing itself (e.g. a painted sign) is like what it signifies.

"KILLER" POLICE TANGLED MINDS: In order to untangle the ingredients that make up the "killer" mindset of today's European policemen—the "what it is," "what it does," and "how it appears"--I believe it is best to start with the philosophical formation of their most primitive ancestors. The story starts with Primitive Africans being the originators of Drama (Gr. Action; a thing done) despite all European authors I consulted saying it started in Greece—a difference of about 150,000 years. It began as a form of evening entertainment by means of action and speech when Africans started living in communities. Later, Very Ancient African Sages instructed actors how to use drama on stage to *impersonate characters* as part of the process of presenting a 'payload' message. The various messages were aimed at teaching the people how to have peaceful minds and live in harmony as a way of life. This was based upon Ancient Africans understanding that Communication is the transmission of a message by a Sender to a Receiver, using a signaling system in a manner so that what is received is the same as what was sent. Very Ancient African Griots used words to let the audience know what the play was about--yet words were merely the skeleton of the play. The voices and action of the actors, their Masks, scenery, props (things used or carried while acting), lighting, music, and audience participation gave each Play a 'body'—i.e. made the setting for their Metaphysical messages to seem real in the way it touched 'the Hearts' of the people. The communication intent of the Drama put on by the Groits was to convey their Spiritual Elements messages to the audience by means of Metaphysical Contingent Beings (phantoms).

The essence qualities of those messages comprised the core of the Contingent Beings and were carried inside the vehicle of Spiritual Metaphors to the destination of the "Hearts" of the audience. The 'Payload' messages were designed to "touch" humans' "Hearts" and spark their pre-birth Emotions into an activation that stirred into motion the Ultimate Truth lying dormant within each human. This was based upon the Ancient African concept that said each human newborn possesses a "*First Wisdom*"—the original and Divine Intellect--consisting of Spiritual Realm and Cosmic Organism Knowledge from which that newborn just derived. Perhaps what happens here is that out of the 'Phantom Payload' comes an impact power sufficient to spur an Emotive Quality in the Receiver's "First Wisdom," since that Quality is compatible with the extremely high vibration contained in the Spiritual Elements' "First Wisdom" Message. If so, the Quality entering the Private Self of the Receiver activates her/his "First Wisdom" compatible "snapshot" Image—a *Spiritual Apperception*--to emerge in the Receiver's mind. Something in that Spiritual Image has a story reminding the Receiver of a memory of the something uniquely related to the Cosmic Organism Knowledge the Receiver had at birth. If there is a mesh, then the Receiver can either get back on the Right stream of life or have a brighter light guiding the way. A similar process—but having negative Effects and Consequences--happens for anti-Spiritual Elements Believers who put those thoughts into action.

When these concepts were brought to primitive European Warriors, they instantly embraced those portions of it that gave form to what they were already doing for idle occasions in an immensely serious but non-prudential manner. Featured in their Drama settings were physical actions directed through an *atmosphere of entertainment* which headed towards an *emotional or non-rational climax*. As was true for early European warriors, Drama readily appealed to the somewhat less barbaric ancient Greeks when the Italian Etruscans borrowed all aspects of African Drama and spread its usage to the Greeks. "*Excitement*" ('stir someone up into agitated elation') received special attention because that was the "hook to which European males gravitated. Whereas Warrior Dramatic Minds insisted on a mental march of their movement to be that of a dramatic kind, Greek and other European religious gods and heroes focused on the Supernatural aspects of the movement. Such was a very popular show and source of "Air Castle" type mundane merriments and excitements. All Greek tragedies *were inspired by myths*—each conforming to the unity of time, place, and action—whether of *Tragedy* (dealing with suffering and death, with an unhappy ending) or *Comedy* types. The Greek writers of prose and poetry, who had a somewhat religious bent, fashioned their brand of Drama out of religious ceremonies, in which the life of a god was portrayed by a man or a group of men. It was the early custom at the rites of Dionysus, the god of wine, for a chorus of men to chant hymns in praise of the god (*perhaps this is what today's 'alpha male' policeman expects when he takes the lead in killing*). The theaters in which they were held (like crime scenes) rivaled temples in sacredness.

Because of Europeans' self-declared 'superiority,' they embrace Occult beliefs in being able to manipulate natural laws and break moral laws for self-benefits and in being guided by Contingent Beings whose evil powers seek to destroy things good and/or having potentials for good. Although the Greeks believed there was a release of Emotions (e.g. terror and pity) and resultant calmness from watching a Tragedy Play, European Warriors chose to instigate Tragedy for others so as to release their pent-up tensions. Gradually, presentations of thought became as important as Emotional presentations. In mimicking African Actors, they also *used costumes, props, and makeup to help make the characters they were portraying seem more real*. Roman theaters, almost entirely derived from Greek models, also regarded Drama as a utility (useful for other things) and an obligation. Yet, great "Excitement" came from making "here and now" tragedies a spectacle of "Dramatic Conflicts" involving victims' minds and bodies. But this required honoring their cleaved traditional "Air Castle" Symbolism—the occultly 'hidden' part that could not be imitated. The other part was to create 'performance statements'—and not simply a simulation. Such was illustrated by the Greek actor who did not try to imitate a man but rather presented something "larger than life" by "padding out" to superhuman size.

Still it remained important to retain some kind of imitation of tragedies in order to keep within the boundaries of the traditional "Air Castle" Supernatural Symbolism. To achieve these was to reach the level of 'thrilling'. All warrior European males spotlighted the "Excitement" inherent in Drama to the point that it became an acquired "*Appetite*" (a reactive 'second nature' tendency) to be used to grind out a primary rush force in life. Because of their 'second nature' warring mindsets, peace and quiet were probably thought of as dreadful and to be avoided so as to be caught up in the impulsiveness associated with the conflicts and confusions of realities that are played out so well in Drama. At the end, they added "*After-Party*" *celebrations*, including Masks with playful, prideful and "justifying' evil natures. The ultimate objective was and remains the pursuit of a Supernatural immortality, which has been the devouring passion of European males from their first rough struggles for existence down to the ceaseless, quest for power, control, and riches to the present.

Getting a sense of this entire scenario concerning drama is extremely important because it is quite similar to the Drama aspects of today's "Killer" police. For example, Actors' orchestration of the audience is to do what it takes to deceptively change their reality of who the Actors really are. These methods are reinforced as 'true' by today's media in order to support "Killer" policemen's claims for justifying needless killings and thereby keep the audience (the public) biased in favor of the protagonist Actors--as opposed to the antagonist.

"KILLER" POLICE & NON-RATIONAL THINKING: When a person is mentally conflicted, as in thinking about the same subject on two planes of existence within the same process, what they come up with will be conflicted thoughts, emotions, expressions, actions, and reactions. Thomas Hobbes and his C17-C18 fellow 'thinkers,' crystalized the "Air Castle" Supernatural type mental processes which had characterized European Warrior thoughts since their primitive times. In some of Hobbes' works he advocated for the superiority of the rational process of the Natural Cosmos for solving problems (Beackon, Political Theory, 1976) while at other times he advocated for "the State"—i.e. the Supernatural "Air Castle" realm. Either way, he stated that propositional statements about Nature must rely on sensory experiences for evidence and not on any sound foundation, like the Mathematical Base used in African Tradition. With such a thinking orientation, the Hobbes and company of 'thinkers' are honored by fellow Europeans for being great about their various opinionated conclusions that make no Natural Cosmos world sense. That "Air Castle" style of thinking is unknowingly widely modelled by most European males as, for example, "Killer" police.

To elaborate, Hobbes' belief in phantasms, or images ('decaying senses') remaining when the physiological motions of sensation cease, alluded to monsters mentioned in a number of places in the Old Testament (e.g. Job 41, I-34; Psalms 74, 14—104, 26). This pattern of creating a mental Icon Image pertaining to Contingent Beings has been well-documented throughout European history, as in designing dictatorial gods residing in the "Air Castle" Supernatural and a devil punisher located in hell. The setting for their anomalous accounts of the transcendental Supernatural fantasy state is a state standing above and beyond Natural Cosmos' human reason. They explain this by saying the transformation of human reason into Supernatural stately reason is accompanied by a change in the way in which reason is understood. When Hobbes' notion, called the Leviathan, became an entrenched practice, human reason gave way to procedurally bound reason. Hence, European 'thinkers' acquired a new metaphorical landscape to describe the human reason that involves an examination into the human soul. Based upon Isaiah's (64:8) story of God, the Divine Potter, making man and the Cosmos [a borrowed story converted to fact from the Egyptian metaphor of Khnum in the Ancient African Bible], enabled Hobbes to express the Supernatural state in terms of a machine—a mechanization taking reason out of its earthly domain—a mechanization according a higher, abstract status which supersedes human reason--a mechanization completing the European concept of the mechanization of the anthropological image of man. From a European perspective, such reasoning developed a sophisticated vision for handling difficulties (Bartmanski *J. Sociology, 2014*)—a method used by Europeans in all aspects of daily living, including "Killer" police. It is of utmost importance to understand that their human reason made all of this up so that their "Air Castle" type of Non-Rational thinking, with its transcendental powers, would supersede all that is part of the Natural Cosmos.

These fantasy creations, ironically, could not exist had not Natural Cosmos mental activities willed them into Contingent Beings and Places. In short, the origins of "the state" (i.e. the Supernatural "Air Castle") are earthly fantasies and yet the effects of "the state" are heavenly because, to "Air Castle" cults 'visible stuff' makes sense only on the basis of 'invisible discourses'. The European mind was primed for this by the ancient Greeks. After being taught by African Sages to use both sides of their brains but with the Right Brain dominating, Greeks chose to use only their Left Brains, rejecting Right Brain usages because it was deemed feminine. This ensured the Western mind would wallow in Material realms; be shut out of Metaphysical realms; and veer further and further away from Spiritual Elements. This + Supernatural thinking--when compared with African Logic and Critical Thinking--essentially resulted in an "Inside-Out" thinking pattern for European males. It features Non-Rational thinking which is a combination of the effects of their Emotions being orchestrated by their calculating Left Brains to fashion contingent Beings out of who they perceive Black People to be—monsters to be destroyed.

"KILLER" POLICE TEAM

Forms of policing have existed since the time of Babylon—either in military or semi-military style. Other early systems consisted of citizens banding together for mutual protection. Subsequently, policies and patterns differed but the use of discretion was essential. Police officers' ideal picture of seeing themselves as a crime fighter identity--'the thin blue line' standing between chaos and order--serves as a powerful image. It separates them from the 'outsider' public and somewhat from the administration. It provides them a unique sense of exclusiveness—serves as the nucleus around which are shared values, attitudes, like-kind patterns of approaches to dealing with each other--entails a sense of honor in their police officer role—and demands Loyalty (Peterson, *European J. Criminology, 2012*). However, in European tradition there is Noble *Loyalty* (exhibiting the courage of self-sacrifice in the interest of justice) and "*Un-noble Loyalty*" (things done for the Indifference/Hate/Evil/Sadism (IHES) Complex, in spite of knowing better). In both, dilemmas arise. On the good side, police officers might be loyal to their partner personally *or* to their group *or* to the police force *or* to a police code of ethics *or* to the government *or* to the community the police force exists to serve. Since each of these loyalties tend to be exclusive and generate partiality when it is necessity to make a choice, conflicts may arise: "Should I be loyal to my fellows or the community when they are against each other?" "Should I be loyal to a fellow police officer guilty of misconduct collides with ones loyalty to the ethical principles governing police work?" But what wins out is loyalty to each other—first taught in the Academy and later throughout officers' tenure as an officer. The sharing of 'unstinting loyalty' to fellow police is to receive protection and honor + the setting to assuage real and imagined wrongs inflicted by a (presumably) hostile public + safety from aggressive administrators and supervisors + the emotional support required to perform a difficult task.

Such brotherhood loyalty's effect is '*Social Isolation*' in police officers' occupational environment—the separation of police from 'non-police', creating an 'us versus them' attitude towards the citizenry. A consequence of that is the officers' relationship to the citizenry is seen—on the one hand, as the ever present potential for danger, causing their preoccupation with the danger and violence that surround them. Two coping mechanisms for helping officers regulate the occupational environment are suspiciousness and maintaining the edge. On the other hand, there is their unique coercive powers and authority they possess over citizens—powers that, simply by their decisions, can determine people's life or death. Such powers to be 'little gods' as well as being assured of loyalty from all officers paves the way for certain ones to step beyond the police policy's "serve and protect" boundaries. Behind their "wall of secrecy" is the often occurring personal and conscious concealment of information--not only from the public but also from supervisory and administrative levels within the organization. The dark side of this shield is that it protects officers guilty of misconduct and corruption. Adherence to the principles of secrecy and the unwritten code of conduct ensures mutual aid, meaning the expectation of maximum assistance from everyone to any officer in trouble. It is not permissible to criticize other police officers, in particular if the criticism is aired to 'outsiders'. When doubts are cast on officer A's unstinting loyalty, he is excluded from this Loyalty support net a priori ('seems right'). This unwritten code not only reduces apprehension and punishment as a deterrent to police misconduct but makes them almost impossible.

WHITE SUPREMACY INTERLOCKING RING THINKING PATTERNS: If the thumb pinches the index finger of a hand representing Black Americans does so inside the thumb pinching the index finger of a hand representing Europeans, both hands constitute Interlocking Rings. The interlocked space between the pinches of each hand is called an *Interchange*--a C14 word conveying the idea that: (1) the things inside that space are like overlapping mosaic colors seen in a kaleidoscope; (2) the slightest of rotating movements of the kaleidoscope results in the changing of different color combinations; (3) each color and each color overlap combination is uniquely shaped in forms (4) each form has contents of significance. The rest of the hand of Black Americans represents its own culture, as does the rest of the hand of Europeans. Yet, both hands contribute to the etymological idea of disguise in the Interchange where things from one hand can be put in the place of the other to be received and return reciprocally. The exchange, rather than the people involved having to learn each color and each color combination with each kaleidoscope rotation, occurs as each "*Fad*" comes and goes (a 'Hippi Era' term for something temporarily popular—like a 'Flashing Light' gadget fad). At the 'Core' of the Interchange area—like the horny central part of an apple—is a central feature. That feature, when applied to the issue of White Supremacy—a brotherhood cult who believes in the superiority of the Caucasian 'race' or Aryan Nation—is that, I believe, they do not know who they are, *since they deny being from Black People*.

In a week of disappointing research I was not able to pin down a specific area of the world where they arose. European Geneticists and African history scholars said Grimaldi Negroids left the center of the Great Lakes of eastern Africa about 50,000 years ago to populate northern Europe and become the Aurignacian foundations (c45,000 BC) of the various European "races." The 1807 name '*Caucasian*' came from the Caucasus mountains between the Caspian and Black sea and the Sea of Azov. The connection with the "White Race" came from the sham science which made the first anthropological division of Humankind by physical features and the belief that these people came originally from this region. The important European subgroup—ancient Aryans (and ancient Persians/Iran also used the same name)—were warring semi-nomads who lived in the grasslands of Eastern Europe--north of the Black and Caspian Seas and in the region of south Russia and Turkestan. They were bands of people—not a race--located in the same area; spoke a somewhat common language; had a similar social structure; and practiced a like-kind religion using a god made in their own image. Whereas a good tree whose roots are firmly fixed and whose top is in the sky produces edible fruit every season, a rootless tree quits ground at the mercy of the elements. Illness comes out of artificial roots of 'White supremacist' assumptions of Self-Identity—and that is at the core of the Interchange. For its "whiteness" to be seen requires the ignorance of their "roots" to be buried under so much made-up Supernatural history and the rewriting of their Natural world history that the actual Truth and Reality is in a bottomless underground pit.

Ralph Ellison, of Invisible Man fame, said (Turner, *Political Theory, 2008*) Euro-Americans have a need to believe their moral principles and everyday practices cohere so as to banish moral ambiguity in order to artificially produce moral innocence. This "nails down" their opinions and closes the possibility to dialogue with people as equals. To thereby obtain 'freedom' to do as they like, freedom fills their lives with uncertainty, unpredictability, and feelings of aloneness, boredom, and insignificance. To know who they are, they adopted the Exclusionary Opposite teachings of the Persian prophet Mani, founder of C3 AD Manichaean religion. He stupidly divided the world into neat "Either/Or" or "All-or-None" categories of pure/impure, innocent/guilty, good/evil, and said the "Light" (white) had as its duty to destroy the "Darkness" (the Black). People of 'black' skin could therefore be considered as a sign of Satanic evil (both being made-up concepts) given human form and symbolizing the opposite of racists opinions as to how society ought to be. So, the "right" thing for them to do was to enslave Black Africans to provide them with all their desires and, when that was no longer useful, to destroy them by oppression or by 'Killing."

"KILLER" POLICE INTERLOCKING RING APPLICATIONS: By Europeans lacking the "5Ss" (safety, security, sureness, strength, stability) from not knowing who they were/are—*the "Seed"*--spurred them to adopt the "White Supremacy" artificial roots (fig. 8) of who they are and use this to greedily grab all they can of Material 'Things'. Since Material acquisitions are never fulfilling meant it was essential to embrace the Manichaean religion concepts of "White" destroying "Black" to justify robbing Black People of their riches, enslaving them, and raping females (children and women). Besides having the Enslaved being used to make them rich, European Brutes so intensively envied Black People being world leaders for 198,000 of 200,000 years humans have been on earth and producing such super-brilliant achievements that, as an "equalizer," wiped out their "Roots" and all tools that had made them great. As a result, the Interlocking Rings of Black and White Americans was fashioned, associated with a flurry of European and Enslaved African exchanges as well as emulsion and solution type interactions. Emulsions are like oil and water whereby certain of its particles stick together but later separate. Or, if the *oil/water emulsion* is violently shaken, there is some joining of the two for a while before they separate again. An example is those Black and White Americans unrelated by blood but who could realistically consider themselves as 'kin.' During slavery, Ellison reminds us, infants of White slave owners suckled at the breasts of Black wet nurses: 'black milk and blood' nurtured 'white bodies into maturity.' Black wet nurses often went on to be nannies and friends to these White children. When the children reached adolescence, however, they were separated from their Black mammies and taught racial aversion. This emulsion continued decades after Emancipation.

By contrast, sugar put in lemonade is a mixture of different things engaged in a smooth dance with each other and is properly called a *Solution*. In other words, one of these materials has dissolved into the other and the molecules are evenly mixed. An example of a blending (solution) shared within the Interchange during African American slavery was mixed-blood mulattoes which, at times (e.g. in 1860) accounted for one tenth of the Southern population. Actually, the number was far greater because many Mulattoes were "passing for

White" and there was often no accounting for the offspring resulting from White and mulatto prostitution—which was widespread during and after slavery.

The implication is that any American who can trace her/his ancestry back to slavery is not likely to be purely Euro-American or purely Black-American. Many White Supremacists who have discovered their "Black blood" have committed suicide. For others this intensifies their not knowing who they are and that means having to define themselves by distancing themselves from the Natural World in general and Black People in particular. They use Blacks as a marker--a symbol of what is off limits to know and work with--a metaphor for the "outsider" who causes all of their problems. Then they offer as a solution the ritual of scapegoating. A 'call to action' is for the European community to casts all it finds frightening and undesirable about themselves onto the scapegoat (i.e. Black People). By oppressing all Black People they do not kill--by creating terrible poverty—by orchestrating gang wars through supplying inner cities with drugs and guns—and by stirring up friction between gangs—they are 'rightfully' applying Manichaean religion concepts to destroy "Darkness" and to regenerate the European community's Supernatural non-existent "perfection."

Within the Interchange affecting White Supremacists self-identity are overt, tempered, masked, concealed, and façade (i.e. false front) means. A mask is the Market-and state-based incentives/disincentives that replaced slavery's whips and chains. A façade is seen on the USA dollar bill in the term: *e pluribus unum*--"Out of many, one"; "One out of many"; "One from many"; the 'melting pot' out of many peoples, races, religions, languages, ancestries has emerged a single people and nation. Thus, "Killer" Police's Interchange core is a conflicted Brute Brain psychological state desiring to "Escape" by thrills from killing. The root does not arise from misinformation and stereotypes causing racial prejudices, but from a need to *accept Supernatural delusions and illusions compatible with their System of Values which avoid clashes with "my well-being of For me or Against me"*.

"KILLER" POLICE "BELONGING" ISSUES: "*Belong*" (C14, to thoroughly "go along with)" is what everybody wants but this involves the *Seven Questions of Inquiry--who, which, what, when, where, why, and how much*? Nobody is intended to "Belong" in exactly the same way, for there are different arrangements, combinations, and planes (Spiritual or Secular) to consider in creating a customized form for each human's "Life-Living". Whereas what Real Self people seek for a "Good Life" is derived from their inner "Soul Sunshine," what False Self people seek is in others and the External World because they have no awareness of even having an inner source of Personal Power. The historically Self-Unknown people have been molded by Supernatural 'Conditioned' concepts pertaining to a made-up God, Devil, and Hell. To give an example of how all of this is confusing and conflicting, European Christianity borrowed essential ingredients for their God from the Ancient African Bible. One borrowed ingredient is that humans are made in the likeness of God, OT (Genesis I: 26). For those operating out of their animalistic brains, this assumes their human likeness comes out of God's presumed psychological and physical makeup—technically an example of idolatry. Another African Bible borrowing was the metaphor whose characters, *Aisha and Aish*, took part in the Ethiopian story *Fall of Man* in the Garden of Eden (located in Africa) with the supposedly tempting serpent and the fatal tree. Despite being scores of thousands of years old before the European Bible was written, this story was made into a "Fact"—transforming the *scene as outside Africa--and with the names, Eve and Adam*. Thereafter, European scholars decided to declare all humans to be born sinful--leading European males to believe that story and claim it as true--thus, 'sinful' being them. In turn, this served as a passage for the Roman state to survive by its ancient customs and manhood. Although both caused Rome's ruin, the thinking pattern spread "everywhere" to mold today's European males mindsets, including how they use their imagination, deal with their emotions, express themselves, act, and react.

To accept being sinful by nature provides Europeans with the justification to define themselves according to their Lower (animal) Self—essentially orchestrated by sensualism, emotionalism, desires of the physical body. They were/are also obsessively/compulsively wed to the GUN--their sole source of power, and eager to use it. Oddly, they have always prided themselves as "Individualists". This comes from their conviction that Things as well as their own Being (e.g. consciousness, intelligence, and mind) have resulted from some random or chance combination of forces and elements for anything coming into existence—like a "big bang" mechanism. Yet, willful ignorance keeps them from not dealing with where these random ingredients came from. Still, "every man for himself" runs counter to the profound Spiritual Human Nature Need to Belong in meaningful associations. This profound conflict generates a chronic sense of *Aloneness*. Because of resultant "Belonging" issues + not trusting anybody or themselves completely, they are fiercely loyal to each other. This fear-based loyalty, for the sole purpose of self-protection, is a self-deceptive mask for a sense of Belonging. Such is an *Alliance*—the mutually helpful participation by those psychologically and philosophically disconnected—featuring the sharing of common character traits, like the Indifference/Hate/Evil/Sadism (IHES) complex displayed in dramatic excitement.

In such Alliances, the connections made by each cult member with all other cult members is *Conditional* ("Condition" applies to anything essential to the occurrence of something). It is 'Belonging' only if one follows IHES cult codes—codes designed for "Killer" police. Police unit 'disconnections within the whole" make for dilemmas as to whom to show loyalties. The matter is complicated because a few have remnants of a humane Conscience. Thus, the interaction of these factors—in various combinations and proportions--lead to a given officer or of team members' perceptions of having an orientation toward serving the whole community and carrying out necessary duties; or serving certain communities only, based upon biases or prejudices; or being at 'war with the community' of their scapegoats. Some choose to be a tool of the politically influential and rich. Some engage in corruption and killings. jabaileymd.com; Blackvoicenews.com

POLICE TRAINING ORIENTATION

Recall (Chapter II) that the three gross generic European lifestyle branches--Warriors, Religion, and Intellectuals—are symbolized by the Interlocking Rings Concept. This Concept implies all three need the approval from each other that what each does in self-dealings and in Indifferent/Hate/Evil/Sadism (IHES) complex dealing with outsiders is done "Properly" and in "Good Taste." Their "SEEMS" right IHES presentations captivate fellow Europeans who then cheer them on in their obvious destruction of those who are "different." Thus, the "Proper" beginning of police training is to start with the Intellectual aspect which says something like this. Humans are distinguished from animals by reason, freedom, and morality (a Supernatural statement whose Base rests on nothing "solid"—has not been proven to be true—and does not conform to daily experiences). Humans place great value on deftness in figuring things out, the mental agility shown in refuting an adversity, on the lightening memory recall, and on reasoning. Without these, Europeans sense of "truth" (whatever that means) and falsehood (which is often indistinguishable from their truth) would shatter. European religion adds that "Professional Values," are a continuous but more enlightened version of ordinary human values. Yet within each profession there arises a value that is an exception to the values held in nonprofessional life. For example, the near sacred respect for privacy and confidentiality that exists in the legal profession is discontinuous with ordinary life. The Warriors contribution is that humans also pride themselves on a sense of freedom (for whom?).

The Interlocking Ring cult goes on to give a historical perspective: In Western thought, from classical Greece and Judeo-Christian morality to Enlightenment theories on human nature, the quality and exercise of freedom depend on the 'knowledge' (including 'self-knowledge') and moral options available, considered, and chosen ordinary/human professional truth (accuracy, honesty, sincerity); Freedom (independence, un-coerced choice); Morality (sense of right/wrong, good/bad, duty); Continuous 'Knowledge'—common sense experience to intellectual, as in the theoretical, systematic, understanding difference in formal; Discontinuous 'Knowledge'—difference in reflection, on nature of methods, concepts, proofs; Power--continuous from control of oneself to control of ones job or environment license or certification; Virtue--technical and moral competence, sense of social good, from doing good in personal life to doing good in public or work life. Out of this arose concepts about police conduct--concepts desired for application by those interested in joining the police since of each aspect being essential to the ultimate in a Supernatural Team Self-Image for European males.

DEATH CONCEPTS OF CULTURES: *Thanatology* is the discipline concerned with death, dying, and therapeutic interventions for those who face such circumstances. What people think of what happens to them at death determines how they live. The word *Death* is from the Teutonic languages, with "dead" as an adjective and "die" as a verb. Ancient Africans' said *God-made things do not die but rather Transform from one state into another*--i.e. take on a different state but maintain their unchanging identity with a "certain sameness". Such occurs inside a cocoon as a caterpillar transforms into a butterfly. An African metaphor is that on Judgment Day ones "Heart" ("Seat of the Soul") is weighed. Its survival fate in the Netherworld depends on the good/bad evidence it displays for/against the deceased. Since humans' spiritual powers unfold slowly and gradually, ones physical body is left behind following the judgment. Remaining parts of the unperfected "Heart" and Soul travel to the *Places of Destruction*--a Purgatory purifier. Until full perfection is attained—i.e. ones Soul vibrates at the same rate as that of the Creator--repeated Incarnations are necessary. Closely related ideas in *Theosophy* say that at death one enters upon a life of rest, purification, and happiness--complete in proportion to the stage one has reached in evolution and to the deeds one has done in the life just ended. When one has enjoyed all the bliss to which one is entitled, one clothes oneself in a new body and returns to earth to take up ones work where one had left off—each new life being a distinct progress over the last one. *Hinduism* says after death ones Soul gets a new body and a new life, time after time. Once one has led a Perfect Human Life, ones Soul stops its *Reincarnation* (rebirth in another body). When this happens and the person dies, the Soul will enjoy Nirvana—a state of 'Nothingness.'

For Europeans, Death concepts are very complicated/confusing. As an over-simplification, the top two are: "death is either a wall or door"—i.e. absolute annihilation or a passage. (1) Those religions and philosophies which say there is no Afterlife mean that when you die there is only death. "If death is absolute annihilation, then after I die I will not exist anymore, so I will not experience anything. Also, after I die, even though others will remember me, I will not remember anything." A "Darwinian human" is founded on the belief that immortality is a myth and a human is only an animal destined to die, whose self-awareness is simply a brain function (Testoni, *Journal of Death and Dying, 2015*). With respect to whether death is a 'Door', metaphysical and religious perspectives do not define awareness as a brain secretion, but as the identity of a human--remaining even after death: soul, spirit, and mana (originally the spiritual force manifested in sacred totems and today means the "mind", the mental faculty which make humans intelligent and moral beings). So, (2) "Is Death only a passage or a transformation of my personal identity? After I die, I will continue to exist and will remember this life's experiences as well as have new experiences." (3) "Is Death a radical change? After I die I will not be aware of my own self anymore. After I die I will experience things having nothing to do with my present life." (4) Death is a transition from the carnal to a wholly spiritual existence but that only comes through faith and imagination--a projection of life from a tangible and material state to an ethereal illusory condition sustained in the dogma of culture.

(5) Christianity believes the soul separates from the body at the moment of death and the body decays until the day of the Last Judgment, when it is reunited with its soul. They also believe that after death, the soul goes to heaven as a reward for those who have followed Church doctrine; or to hell for punishment. Other doctrines speak of Resurrection so that Christians need not feel the isolation of death, for nothing can separate the believer from God (Rom. 8:38-9). (6) From those who have had "Near-Death" Experiences, various things are reported: being able to hear one has died; having a feeling of moving quickly through a dark tunnel, funnel, cave toward a brilliant light; feeling the presence of or seeing dead relatives or ancestors who are there to help in the transition from life to death; seeing the brilliant light as a power that required one to review ones own life—a power sometimes experienced as love; seeing ones life pass before oneself—a panoramic view of actions and thought; being aware that ones time for death is not now and thus must return to complete ones life. But Science questions if these are "Near-Death" experiences because none of the people have been brain dead.

'KILLER" POLICE SECULAR SELF-IMAGE: "The Self one thinks oneself to be"—which embraces ones personality, character, status, body, bodily appearance--is a generic European definition of Secular Self-Image (SSI). Of course, this Imagined Self typically varies markedly from the Actual Self or from African Traditions Divine Self-Image. SSI forms early in the lives of False Self people—focusing on keystone aspects (e.g. Body Image). That keystone may be cultivated as, for example, a tall adult may think of himself as small because, when his Body Image was being formed, he was small in relation to his peers. Interpretations from his monitored feedback concerning his smallness led him to Self-Declare it as so. *Self-Declarations* convert fantasy into Contingency Beings having significant 'payload' effects not subject to change by ones social contacts switching to commenting on how tall he has grown to be. Certain other types of keystone focuses are predictive. For example, chronic Unhappiness from having a meaningless life and/or by being a Self-Declared 'Failure' from everything significant one does is a typical early picture of those destined to be "Killer" police. This sets up a 'payload' Icon SSI about oneself as well as about potential scapegoats. Both pave a life's course for ones patterned hateful mindset to travel. Meanwhile, one builds a compatible lifestyle around ones Icon SSI. Of great significance is that these afflicted stop their maturity at the point of their Self-Declaration and thereafter fail to develop their higher mental faculties—particularly of a Spiritual and Metaphysical nature. Also, they generate Fetter Emotional substitutes (extreme selfishness, greed, hatred, anger, egoism, fear, envy, jealousy, frustration, selfishness, arrogance, pride, lust) to orchestrate their lives. Since this combination developed early in life, the afflicted are vitally dependent on others, eagerly accepting information as to how to be and embracing demeaning labels to be broad-stroked on scapegoats—even when it initially disagrees with their "better self". In other words, at this stage all perceptions of oneself are strongly influenced by information originating in the External World.

Thus the fundamentals of ones SSI are introjected (internal representations) from '*Significant Others*' (i.e. those with great influence on fashioning ones "Who I Am/What I believe/What I do" personality). Whatever the nature of these accepted and displayed representations, they resists challenge and change since they are primarily associated with conditions of Self-Worth (intangibles), Self-Value (significant material things), and what their cult honors. Thus, later perceptions that do not agree with it will be subconsciously distorted, denied, and covered with mental "Clouds". By contrast, perceptions more consistent with them will be accurately experienced and accepted. Hence, ones Icon SSI becomes increasingly in-accurate, un-realistic, rigid, and Conditioned Response ready. The degree of incongruence with reality of ones SSI is proportional to ones maladjustments. The resultant inability to effectively cope with and transcend ones emotional dysfunctions derives from delusional thinking linked to operating out of ones Brute Brain and its orchestration by ones Left Brain. That combination generates the Indifference/Hate/Evil/Sadism (IHES) complex that features "Dark Side" thoughts and emotions expressed in Words without knowledge. These increasingly darken the mind.

Their designed "*Significs*" (i.e. the systematic study of signs and symbols of intentions and values) of scape-goats include classifying, correlating, and interpreting them as 'demons' who pose great dangers to their Icon SSI. When a "demon" situation arises, the threat to ones Icon SSI automatically activates ones Conditioned Response to "kill". This is done to conform to the cult dogma about the most negative features of the stereo-typed scapegoats; to make themselves look better; and to Belong--which imparts the meaning that one is a significant part of a 'big picture' Plan—and that satisfies an SSI Needy Want. However, when doing a "Kill" is not in ones best interest, one may, just as easily, automatically inhibit negative stereotype thoughts while activating positive. The switch to doing what is beneficial to ones self-image accounts for the 'Dr. Jekyll/Mr. Hyde' syndrome in "Killer" police. At every opportunity they needlessly and ruthlessly beat almost to death hand-cuffed Black People. Otherwise, as a façade of being Humanitarians, they often do free 'community service' for the Black Community

POLICE TEAM SELF-IMAGE: Police officers' ideal picture of seeing themselves as a crime fighter iden-tity--'the thin blue line' standing between chaos and order--serves as a powerful image. It separates them from the 'outsider' public and somewhat from the administration. It provides them a unique sense of exclusive-ness—serves as the nucleus around which are shared values, attitudes, like-kind patterns of approaches to deal-ing with each other--entails a sense of honor in their police officer role—and demands Loyalty, as discussed (Peterson, *European J.Criminology, 2012*). There reigns a *esprit de corps* (team spirit)—a military term—which police embrace because of its vivacity, ardor, enthusiasm, and pride in group effort, group standards, and group achievement which makes for singleness of purpose and drive to "take a bullet" for a fellow unit member. It is a mental state that represents the sum total of all forces that make for cohesion, for sticking together, for the feeling of 'solidarity, loyalty, and shared purpose in an organized willing endeavor that keeps a group of people together and motivates each member to act in the interest of all out of a jealous regard for the integrity and performance of the group.

POLICE TRAINING PROCESS

To be a police officer is to enter into an Ethos culture. *Ethos* is the basic assumptions forming fixed Beliefs that give rise to emotions, attitudes, and character displays of values which are common characteristics of a group at a given time period. At its best such an Organizational Ethos guides relational human encounters in that those involved: approach each other without suspicion in ordinary interactions or in professional situations; the words exchanged are honestly felt and their power impact has not been exercised at other group member's expense; and the nature of what is espoused deceptions designed to impart self-interest gains. The generic process of Training Professionals, Preparing for Uses and Misuses of Violence Expertise and efficiency stressed by the police include: determining levels of mental competence for the capacity of self-control are associated with age, physical, emotional or psychological frailty. It continues by one passing a written examination; have a certain amount of education; be in good health; not be under a certain height; be of good character who has never committed a crime or been in prison. A major consideration concerns each newcomer's ideas about Death.

PRACTICAL POLICE TRAINING: Once a recruit is accepted, one goes through a stiff training course to learn all police regulations, the traffic rules of ones city, and a certain amount of law. One is taught how to shoot a police revolver and must practice on the police pistol range until hitting targets can be done accurately. Some first aid is taught; how to subdue a criminal by wrestling tricks or judo; and how to use weapons (e.g. tear-gas, shells, riot guns, submachine guns). Each candidate is under supervision by a "headhunter" who is authorize to eliminate those who seem unfit for any reason. Two aspects require particular attention—Training a person to kill and determining the type and degree of trustworthiness of that person (fig. 10).

"KILLER" POLICE "MANHOOD": At the bottom of the *Humanity Ladder* are "Savages" (C17, 'controlled by imaginary spirits of the air') who are crude, unusually dumb, and cruel. They boast/brag, clamor to be the center of attention, put others down, say they know what is best for everybody (even of what they know nothing about), have an insatiable need to be right, to be acknowledged far past the compliment stage, and to always come out on top. As part of being 'legends in their own mind" and despite their macho and swagger appearance, they require being constantly reassured of this by any one they can influence because of their tremendous Private Selfhood weakness. By operating out of their Brute Brains, with or without partnership with their Left Brains, they have obsessive-compulsive disregard for others rights, equity, and hallowed customs. They would rather die than share power among all—a reason the only true Democracy of Humankind was in Ancient Africa.

Off-springs of the "Savage" mind are emotionally based overwhelming desires to be 'superior'—to have the most, the biggest, the fastest, the latest, the best—for "Excitement" with Trinkets and Trivia which make for Superficial Thinking. As the most formidable of all beasts, human "Savages" are the only ones that systematically prey on and devour their own species—leaving a legacy trail of inflicting on others such things as pain, suffering, disability, and death. Yet, for those who are not part of their cult, Savages call them "savages" and 'subhuman'—and that is a diagnostic clue to indicate true "Savages" since that Projection gives voice to what they are trying to hide about themselves. To claim one is 'superior'—humans most ridiculous concept--requires having to demean the competition or the feigned enemy—and that is at the 'root' of lacking compassion for their prey, for dishonorableness, amorality, hypocrisy, for wars, and violence. Out of this mindset comes the Negative Scale "Manhood" of "Killer" police. It is characterized by much *Drama* (C16, Play, action) where there is social tension, confrontation, great losses, and "sick" pleasures. The Drama's *Theme* (or Thought component) refers to its meaning. The *Plot* (C17, the narrative element), refers to events (happenings) made up of characters involved in conflict. *Protagonist*(s) (C17, major character, first combatant) has the greatest variety of dialogue and action as the 'hero' of ones cult. *Antagonist* (C16, struggle against—the origin of *Antagonize*) are the ones who the 'hero's' cult says brings the struggle.

European society everywhere is in a conspiracy against the ingredients of Real Self Manhood present everywhere in the newborn of budding, flowering, and fruiting in keeping with that newborn's Mission. Instead, its efforts are directed to converting newborns' Manhood ingredients into "too much" of what it is not (as by lack of control) so as to mold them into 'little gods' or into "too little" (by means of chains) and preferably into none at all--i.e. kill those outside its cult. All are treated as if they are children who know nothing and can learn nothing without being taught the European cult way. Their "Manhood" theme is Indifference/Hate/Evil/Sadism—and this IHES complex is fashioned into ways that "never Fail" (because they are guaranteed by the GUN) and to never admit failing. Such is the context in which all cult members' "Manhood," including "Killer" police, is made. *They are never so truly themselves as when acting a part of their False Selves which imitates this Negative Scale of "Manhood" in the way their cult leaders do.* This cult honors its destroyers and persecutes its benefactors—both getting public support because "Killer" police are efficiently and effectively advertised as the Protagonists in this Drama. jabaileymd.com

"KILLER" POLICE "SAVING FACE": Since policemen are members of a cult imbued with legal authority to kill—and almost with no accountability--it has great attractiveness to those insecure about their "Manhood." Intensely needing to prove "Manhood" so as to keep from *Losing Face* started with primitive European warriors. This need, continuing to the present, is spurred from actual challenges by other males + from situations involving females. Perhaps the concept of "*Face*" arose in C1 AD from the word "*Persona*" referring simply to any human in the Roman world and to "*Countenance*" (etymologically demeanor and contents) in the Greek world. In the sense of establishing, enhancing, or maintaining a reputation, "*Face*" was about ones front appearance--i.e. what one looks like to the rest of the world. This derives from the superficial assessments of the majority of people who judge men's abilities less from what they do in activities of daily living than from what they say and look like in doing these things. Furthermore, the public's universal language deems ones face to be a shorthand of ones mind--a comprehension from crowding a great deal in a little 'snapshot' picture. In short, a man may look a 'phrase sentence' as soon as a reaction is present on his face: "Tis the man's face [countenance] that gives him weight--his doings help, but not more than his brow."

To violate any feature deemed by ones cult not to fit into the "Manhood" category—whether shown in ones "face" or revealed in expressions or actions—is to "*Lose Face.*" This term, its translated expression, its underlying 'payload' impact, and its use in English since the late 1800s, originated with the Chinese 'tiu lien.' An overall sense of "Losing Face" is to feel ashamed or humiliated, especially publicly. Shame features loss of the "5Ss," feeling Powerless, Unimportant, Worthless, Incompetent, Useless, and "I'm not good enough." "*Save Face*" ways are: (1) deceptive maneuvers used to prevent looking weak--as do Deflections when there is a probability of being "exposed" (i.e. shamed); (2) projecting Shame onto and generating Shame within victims; and (3) no matter how ridiculous it is, adamant sticking with ones story in the face of contrary evidence. This works because cults protect its guilty police and both are protected by public groups not adversely affected by the cult or "Killer" police. It is burdensome to declare oneself superior and then constantly try to 'back-it-up' under the most challenging of circumstances. Since European males have historically envied the historically supreme achievements of Black males—i.e. their big *"spur" for killing*--they feign Black males as their enemies. By being unable to realistically compete fairly, cults use the GUN to oppress and kill Black People and steal all their achievements. "Seeds" for such a mindset date to Europeans' Earth appearance c45,000 BC. The best survivors were successful warriors--the "*Alpha Males*"--who were/are given high status among peers + being able to attract mates and promiscuously pass on their genes to offspring. Yet, since such "Manhood" social hierarchies were/are not fixed, the 'alpha male' was/is constantly challenged by the more youthful possessing a preoccupation with achieving and maintaining social status. Since this status was/can be lost fairly easily—and particularly among captives entangled inside communities and operating out of their Lower (animalistic) Selves—"Manhood" proof requires continual reinvention and active validation (Bosson, *Personality and Social Psychology Bulletin, 2009*). Such cult communities are present on all rungs of the Social Ladder.

For this reason, European "Manhood" is properly viewed as a status earned via the passage of social rather than by physical or biological milestones. Hence, males inside a given cult need a heightened sensitivity to social cues indicating a potential or real loss or gain of status—the source of competitiveness, defensiveness, and constant struggling to publicly prove their own Supernatural value. The most effective strategies for proving or restoring "Manhood" are those that: (a) involve risk taking (which signifies fearlessness), (b) are difficult (and thus hard or costly to fake), and (c) are public and thus visible to others. For these reasons, physical aggression may serve as a highly effective feature in establishing behaviors for men intent on convincing themselves and others of their "Manhood". For such 'high stakes,' especially in those unsure of their "Manhood," being a "Killer policeman" serves multiple purposes--but best obtained by killing scapegoats.

Meanwhile, ongoing scenarios representing police Code violations include: an officer strikes or beats suspects; one or more prisoners may be killed; suppression of evidence, tampering with confidential evidence and perjury False report of drug possession; illegitimate use of deadly force theft (e.g. 'drug money,' guns, knives) from a crime scene; hitting a prisoner; pay-offs for 'looking the other way' or for probation or rule violations; the planting of evidence and falsification of the official record; failure to arrest with felony warrant in exchange for gratuities; a failure to arrest a friend; cover-up of an intoxicated officer behind the wheel or an officer accident; Free meals/gifts from merchants); Verbal abuse of motorist; coercion of confessions (sometimes through torture), planting and fabricating evidence, or giving false testimony in court (perjury). This latter situation can often arise where an otherwise conscientious officer loses faith or trust in the criminal justice system and acts through a misplaced sense of duty or zeal in seeking to secure a conviction against someone of whose guilt the officer is convinced public integrity denotes the quality of acting in accordance with the moral values, norms and rules accepted by the body politic and the public. A number of integrity violations or forms of public misconduct can be distinguished: corruption including bribery, nepotism, cronyism, patronage; fraud and theft; conflict of interest through assets, jobs and gifts; manipulation of information; discrimination and sexual harassment; improper methods for noble causes; the waste and abuse of resources; and private time misconduct.

"KILLER" POLICE CONCEPTS OF DEATH: Since C15 the *GUN has been the conjoined twin of European males*—central to their self-perceived identity as a rugged and violent people. Interlocking and interconnected factors accounting for this predisposition to violence and killing were/are: (1) its culture (e.g. philosophy, values, attitudes, and habits); (2) being a warring people since their primitive origin; (3) their Supernaturally generated Indifference/Hate/Evil/Sadism (IHES) complex; and (4) urges for IHES displays as a perpetual, unrestricted violence legacy--spotlighted during/after slavery (to the present)—and always directed toward Black People. USA Murder rates--even with all firearms deaths subtracted from the criminal totals—are 3 times the rate of most other Western nations. Such generates 'Why?' concepts of Death about those they killed as well as their own 'what happens' beliefs post-dying. The following options are drawn from European sources: *Belief I*: Many European 'religious' say that in living by the highest light one knows, while carrying the seed of faith, ensures they will go to their Supernatural heaven. *Belief II*: after living life however one likes, to renounce ones sins upon meeting St. Peter after death, leads to a resurrection and not re-animation. *Belief III*, if Belief I is not carried out, one goes to Hell, like the Jewish *Gehenna*—a great refuse-heap of ever smoldering fire. *Belief IV*: If one lives by Supernatural Satanists dogma--which makes Kill/Take/Destroy/Dominate/Oppress an honorable part of "purification"—one will go to the "Air Castle heaven." *Belief V*: "I'm not Sure what happens to me when I die." *Belief VI*: "When you die, that's it! Since all pleasures end, I can do anything I can get away with." Hence, they are free to bathe in the Fetters--extreme selfishness, greed, hatred, anger, egoism, fear, envy, jealousy, frustration, dishonorable, arrogance, pride, lust.

Such Belief diversity is thought to be supported by psychical research failing to provide evidence for human Afterlife survival; by philosophers and novelists ignoring it or taking for granted death as total extinction; and by ordinary folk, in spite of current interests in the occult, seeming to be little influenced by considerations of what might happen to them after death. European ministers say half of White people have no living belief in immortality; Poets do not sign of it; and even among Christians there are not a few who relapse into an attitude of reverent Agnosticism--wistfully speaking of "a larger life beyond" but unable to affirm it with ringing 'knowledge.' The Physical Sciences, Europeans add, seem self-explanatory godlessness; or, resulting from strictly natural causes leaving no room for God or Spiritual Powers. Meantime, older Materialistic ideas are widespread with resultant beliefs in life-after-death seeming to be Superstitions. In consequence, Atheism or at least Agnosticism is widely prevalent. Technical advances in Industry often foster man's belief in himself. Possibly the wide extension of the practice of Cremation—hygienic and commendable as it is—has served to strengthen the delusion that death is the end of all. Potent disbelief causes are the weakness of divided churches to counteract prevailing tendencies + widespread growing neglect of Scripture teachings, despite the large sales of the new English Bible. An Anglican priest said he was a non-believer in life-after-death, in any Supernatural Being, in any realm of its activity, or in any part of humans surviving death. All of these are associated with a denial of the objective reality of God.

Such beliefs indicate the "Seed" problem is a *failure of having researched their Belief Base for their assumptions* of what world and where they came from, who said so, and with what proof. At a "Root" level, Euro-Americans are without a history--only a made up memory, far from realistic. Most Base Beliefs are 'seeded' in a given Supernatural cult whose dogma wipes out having any particular regard for their amoral lives or how inhumanely they treat others. In short, there are no incentives to virtue or any disincentive to vice. Any given one of these 6 Beliefs or some combination or something like them constitute the "Death" ideas of "Killer" police. Their 'little god' mindsets of always 'right' prevent them from seeing anything from another's point of view or understanding that others rightfully approach life differently. Their premium placed on self and material interests led/leads them to do whatever would immortalize them following death. [Ref: Baker, *Theology, 1983*; Selwyn, *Theology, 1953*; Taylor, *The Expository Times, 1964*; Leonard, *Homicide Studies, 2003]* jabaileymd.com

DUTIES OF A POLICE OFFICER: A successful completion makes one a patrolman who is assigned to a precinct; and given accoutrements like a uniform of the city police force; a shield with an assigned number; a .38 caliber revolver in a leather holster; a cartridge belt with loops in it for additional bullets; a whistle; a pair of steel handcuffs; and a short wooden club (a 'nightstick'). A patrolman works about 8 hours a day but this may be any of the three 8-hour shifts around the clock. To begin each shift, one reports to the precinct station; assembles with other patrolmen for inspection by the officer in charge who then reads the instructions (e.g. about wanted criminals in the district, about houses, stores, and other places to which particular attention is to be paid). The patrolmen then go on the "beat" in radio cars. Eventually, a patrolman may be assigned to an assortment of "Special Duties"—e.g. direct traffic; motorcycle duty; mounted police to control large crowd; helicopters; detectives--who work in ordinary clothes for detecting subtle crimes such as burglary, robbery, homicide, bunco (swindlers, forgers), auto theft, missing persons). At headquarters there is a huge wall map of the entire city which show the beat covered by every radio patrol car. In case of emergency requiring quick action, headquarters can call any car by radio and have it rush to the scene of a crime or accident while being given all known pertinent information. Arrival time is about 3 minutes. Every state has its own police force organized like an army—inspectors, captains, lieutenants, sergeants, state troopers (like a city patrolman), and detectives—with a central headquarters and smaller buildings used as local stations.

PREPARATION TO "KILL"

Human Nature is the same all over the world but its appearances and ways of expression are so variously influenced by socialization, education, beliefs, mental "Raw Nerves," and habits that one could never see all of its dresses. In using the *Thinker's Scale* (a positive and negative ruler separated by a zero) to categorize lifestyles (fig. 22), some people chose the positive Scale; some the Zero (e.g. drifting through life, simply living from day to day); some on the Negative Scale; and some in Combinations of the other three. Generic aspects of the Negative Scale are people's bad actions--like having mental "Shades" which separate any given group of minds from other groups of minds--a separation more frequently applied to out-groups than within ones in-group.

"KILLER" POLICE CONDITIONED RESPONSE MINDSET PREPARATION: A favorite saying I learned as a University of Michigan freshman was: "The mass of men lead lives of quiet desperation" (Thoreau 1817-1862). He added that "a stereotyped but unconscious despair is concealed even under what are called games and amusements of mankind...Most of the luxuries and many of the so-called comforts of life, are not only not indispensable, but positive hindrances to the elevation of mankind." I agree and consider that Brutes' life dedication to being 'superior' facades has them clutching to "Non-Rational" Thinking as being "the elephant in the room" which is the process used to cause their chaotic and hate-filled lives. Inside 'Desperation Chaos' are groups of *Composite Images*—each based on a number of fantasy sensory and imaginary experiences of the same or similar objects.

Examples are a craving of money, status, power and a hatred of those they envy the most—historically Black People because of their world dominating achievements in 'everything' for 198,000 of the 200,000 years humans have been on earth. This *Desperation Chaos* had its source and origin with the first Eurasians who developed a 'second nature' mindset of Scarcity as a result of lacking environmental advantages of necessities for life. This means their resultant 'second nature' experiences which, said Plato, produced imprints or impressions on the mind's "wax"--called "Memory Traces" or *Engrams*. That "Seed" of the realistic *Scarcity Tree Concept* initially led to survival by "any means necessary" because the world was viewed as hostile to them. Scarcity has constituted Brutes Sensory Consciousness Background and works as a Complementary Equal with the ever active Warrior Indifference/Hate/Evil/Sadism (IHES) Complex mindset. However, the entire process was spurred by a personal and Eurasian atmosphere of *INSECURITY*.

Security is the actuality in reality or the sense of actuality of all ones needs being cared for--whether to get what one desires or to not get what one does not desire. This means one is standing on a sound Base of an unchanging Metaphysical Structure which imparts the sense of being "Connected" to all ones needs. But *Insecurity* features "Fears of Possibilities of Fears"—i.e. fearing all the possibilities that might arise to generate more fears. This is like the infinite reflections associated with *Mirror Images* whereby ones stands between two "Fear" mirrors facing each other and thereby sees no end to the number of images that reproduce the original. Such fears led/lead to "Air Castle" escapes and the fashioning of Icon Images about oneself, ones leaders, and ones self-created enemies.

A feature of all I have known who 'escaped' into the "Air Castle" realm had a spotlighted "I'm NOT GOOD ENOUGH" hypersensitivity. This necessitated fantasizing about a "perfect" companion Contingent Being leader--not only 'good enough' but superior to all else that can be conceived in reality or in Fantasy. To arrive at this "Perfect" Contingent Being residing in the "Air Castle" caused them to resort to "Non-Rational" Thinking. They declare it is superior to any form of Logical or Abstract thinking in the Natural World; is absent Right Brain input (because its features like intuition and hunches are "feminine") although its concepts are Emotionally based; and is within the "Me, Me, Me" category. It is orchestrated by only Left Brain ways for the purpose of making the best 'here and now' happenings pertaining to: "what is for me" and making all-out efforts to avoid "what is against me". Types of "Escapees" include the following.

First, *Icon Image A1* which concerns who one is in ones own Inner World—focused on having the sense of an I*nferiority Complex*--defined by the European Alfred Adler (1870-1937) as: "strong feelings of inadequacy and insecurity stemming from real or fancied deficiencies of a physical, mental, or social nature. They lack the "5Ss" and thus are weak, needy, greedy, inadequate, and scared.

Second, *Icon Image A2* are of a *Superiority Complex* orientation (donning a mask of self-confidence and greatness with a reality of arrogance and aggression to conceal a sense of deep inferiority) from adopting this façade or by-passing the adoption because of it having been socialized since birth to actually believe this facade. But the façade belief in being 'superior'—the most ridiculous concept ever invented by humans--is based upon Fantasy and therefore is 'grounded' in an airy "quick sand". As a result, they face the daily struggle of being afraid to display without the GUN, one-on-one, their "Manhood" against a comparable Black male. Such fear dictates that they work with fellow cult members. The Superiority Complex group retains no Natural World Humanity or morals.

Third, *Icon Image B1* concerns the mental transformation from who they are over to how they want to be seen. The Inferiority Complex is in a disguise so as to appear transformed from the reality of lacking the "5Ss" into an "Air Castle" Cult "Manhood" appearance. Yet, the *Icon Image B1* retains some ideas of the Natural World Humanity—being remotely aware of something shamefully wrong in living a life of lying, cheating, stealing, hating, and making suffer people unlike them.

"KILLER" POLICE WILLFUL IGNORANCE: A *"Poster Person"* is one whose Icon Image signifies the very identity of the generic aspects of the essences of what a subject is about. Such applies to Captain John Newton, author of the famous European hymn, *"Amazing Grace,"* who piloted a C18 slave ship of Enslaved Africans while carrying the European Bible. He struggled with these Contrary Opposites because his mother had exposed him to some basic spiritual principles about humanity. However, it was essential to exercise "Willful Ignorance" in the face of knowing slavery was wrong—a moral dilemma he decided in favor of continuing to acquire riches from selling innocent people into a life of hell (Yenika-Agbaw *J. Black Studies,*

2006). Since nothing about this theme has changed in how today's Brutes deal with Colored Peoples, notice the components involved in this scenario. First is the development of a life's course "Agenda" headed in the direction of desiring to Kill/Take/Destroy/Dominate/Oppress victims. *Agendas* are designs and practices for conveying fantasies featuring unfair advantages for oneself in a manner that generates unfair disadvantages for ones victims. *Delusional Agendas* make ones cherished fantasy products look superior while making the victims' Good "anything" look bad and anything neutral look worse than it is. This is how racist Europeans and their 'zombie' followers see themselves in relation to Black People. Second, such Agendas are powered by like-kind acquired *Endowments*—i.e. ones choice of Character and system of values behind Propensities. *Propensities* are acquired tendencies of capacities, abilities, and language facilities which, if cultivated to overflow, form a Virtual Image called a *Disposition* (fig. 6).

The ingredients in that Disposition are organized into a Plan. The Disposition Plan contains an Inclination and Temperament, both fashioners of the individual's *Attitude*. The *Inclination* is a 'physical' "leaning toward" or "leaning" away from something. The *Temperament* is its physiological Sensory Consciousness systems fashioning the type of reaction the aroused person takes. The impetus or underlying motivation powering the Disposition's *Intention* to be carried out is called the *Conative Element*. This Element is the power for any natural tendency related to purposive behavior directed toward action or change--the power for impulse, desiring, striving, and resolving. It is a Volitional ('I will') mental decision—i.e. a *Self-Declaration*—which activates Conative power to drive how one acts on the Disposition's thoughts and Emotions. For racists, Conative power works in conjunction with a collection of pre-existing Delusional Agenda mental Icon Images which formed the Disposition and together they spur activation of the faculty of ones Will. Activation of ones Will manifests as an *Ideo-motor Action* as, for instance, the mere thought of the stimulative consequences of an act evokes the act itself. Conative power is in Mild, Slight, Moderate, and Extreme degrees—driven, said Ancient Africans by "animal spirits" ('Khaibit,' Ether). *Velleity* implies a Mild or weak desire or inclination so insignificant that one makes little or no attempt to realize it by actions. Such is present in non-racists Europeans who benefit by "White Privilege". To make this okay, they exercise Willful Ignorance—choosing a refusal to know—issuing from cowardice, pride, crowd addiction, laziness of mind, or "Me, Me, Me" self-interest. Its distinction from apathy is: "I don't know--and I don't care!"

Extreme or Brute conative power is conviction behind its absolutely deliberate Willful (Volitional) Ignorance--an active aversion to knowledge opposing their Confirmation Biases. European mental health specialists call this the "*Dark Triad*" *of Personality*—i.e. psychopathy [I substitute a "Normal Variant" Philosophy of life], Narcissism, and Machiavellianism. It shares a propensity for callous exploitation and being a 'killer' is done at every opportunity for its sheer "sick" pleasures alone—particularly when there is direct physical contact. Just as Captain Newton partly justified his pursuit of selling humans because British and American laws sanctioned trading the Enslaved, a third factor for "Killer" police candidates is because being in the police force (or any organized aggressive cult) provides a structure that encourages crime and violence. The most important 'safe' reasons are protection by fellows, from laws, from a favorable court system, from the biased presentations of the media that make the "killer" into a hero, and from the European public who gives its full support.

People who are "*blind to the obvious,*" as in significant things like failing to see the "Elephant in the room," have some type of Private Selfhood problem. The English metaphorical idiom referring to not seeing the Elephant, contrasted with "Seeing the Elephant" (i.e. experiencing more than one wants), refers to ignoring an obvious truth, reality, problem, or risk. This is called "Willful" because it proceeds from a conscious motion of ones Will—i.e. voluntarily, knowingly, deliberately—intending the result which actually comes to pass. But whereas this is the Type I "Obvious" Cause, there are others. Type II is a "blindness" in those whose thinking patterns are "Inside-Out"—meaning "Obvious" necessities go unaddressed, partly more-so than completely because these are Self-Absorbed people nursing a "Raw Nerve" and that constitutes a "second nature" survival situation. Type III are those in such hardships in trying to actually survive that it takes absolute and spotlighted priority, preventing to pay attention to what they would otherwise see. Still, in the periphery of their vision they are aware of significant life-shaping or life-changing issues that those who are not struggling so readily see as easy solutions as to criticize Type III for not doing so. This is a major reason for "Blaming the victim".

Even Europeans of the *Mild* 'White Privilege" type and who are non-participants directly in racism show their Willful Ignorance by such statements as: "Blacks, especially those in the urban areas, have to realize that being handed everything doesn't solve the problem. They have to start taking "personal responsibility" for their lives and actions. As long as blacks continue to play the "poor old black me" and the "blame game" nothing will change. As a boy, I was told that the idiom: *Do not judge a man until you have walked a mile in his moccasins*" was of Amerindian origin. It is impossible for any Europeans in a power position to have any insight into struggling and powerless Black People. Furthermore, nothing they say about them has any credibility, as in Type I Europeans speaking about Type II and III Black people. Hence, this is where the Indo-European word "*Blind*" applies in its original sense of not so much 'sightlessness' as 'confusion' and 'obscurity'. Then the notion of someone wandering around in actual or mental darkness, not knowing where to go, naturally progressed to the 'inability to see.' Such is invariable in racist Europeans because all are Self-Unknown with a non-rational Supernatural mentality as well as was displayed from the beginning of African American slavery with the European slavers putting a metaphysical and physical veil around themselves to stay segregated from the Enslaved. In this way they could maintain their self-declaration of being "superior"—the most ridiculous fantasy any humans have ever devised.

Similarly in process, but for contrasting reasons, the Enslaved put up a metaphysical veil out of being disparate to survive and endure against Humankind's most unspeakably inhumane enslavers and oppressors. The "Seed" of racism, I believe, is in Europeans believing they are different from all other people—making them superior and everyone else subhuman. People remain in ignorance as long as they hate and they hate unjustly as long as they remain in ignorance. Hate-filled people only praise what they are socialized to believe—which has nothing to do with the Truth--and find fault with what they don't know and anything having to do with the Spiritual Elements. Associates of ignorance are vanity, pride, and arrogance. *Violence is a tool of the ignorant*—which comes from two extremes.

One is White people believing they have to "beat the spirit out of Black People in order to rescue and take care of them in an enslaved sense. The other is to "wipe out" Black People for fear they will take what "belongs" (whatever that is) to White people. Either way, this requires "Killer" police to have such a huge "*Blind-spot*" ('covered or hidden from sight') as to what they saw and heard but did not conform to them being a moral "knight in shining armor" in the performance of either extreme. This is the way racists in the Supernatural think and they will never change. They speak of the "ugly" in Black People as if they are incapable of being "ugly." In this sense, they not only have a "Blind-spot" but are also "*Blindfolded*" (Old English, 'to strike blind'). Hence, their Willful Ignorance is never admitted. Their needless killings methods are manipulated to be "true" by the public and media.

ANTI-BLACK MINDSETS OF "KILLER" POLICE: Weak people have a "mind committee" composed of Fear, Anger, Resentment, Greed, Hatred, Insecurity, Envy, Shame, extreme selfishness, Jealousy, Frustration, Indifference, Arrogance, Pride, Lust--all headed by the leaders who fashion an the Indifference/ Hate/Evil/Sadism (IHES) Complex. This complex is a group of related, often repressed ideas and impulses that compel characteristics or habitual, if not compulsive, patterns of thought feelings, expressions, and behaviors in an exaggerated or obsessive concern or fear. When cult members are under the influence of the most violent, the most extreme "Normal Variant" Brute mindsets, the most delusive, the most unstable, they are required to swear that they will remain in that excited and exhausting condition continuously until death do them part. Leaders do not want Black People to have life or fortune but rather to lose it; not to have success but to fail. They do not desire anything in particular more than a "faceless" hating existence about everybody, and mostly themselves. They keep running away from learning that the core object of their hatred is themselves. It is not riches they are after but rather there is a conspiracy against the minds of their followers and enemies.

Their purpose is to do brutish things. What naturally arises out of this are difficulties of comprehension and/or solutions within the context of clear and simple plans for outcomes. They came to power by a coup d'estat—i.e. a violent overthrow of the Real Self Non-violence mindset. That was a birth-gift mindset within the context of the Law of Sympathy, a natural state where there is no need to debate about ones treatment of others because the right things to do (based upon Unconditional Love, Truth, Compassion, Forgiveness, and Magnanimity) simply flow out 'instinctually.' Brutes "Clouded over" this power by designing an Ego to govern their False Self's Mind Committee--thereby removing the owner from having the power to heal the anger and hatred within oneself, whether as the aggressor or as the victim.

The imaginative conceptualization of the False Self committee focuses mainly upon the 'monster'--Contingent Being actors in the fantasy part of the Brute Brain. The actors are addicted to violence, with each having an agenda to advance and a role to play. Even though they are not rivals, they are constantly jousting for the spotlight so as to be in power and control. Still, they are united in wanting everything significant for their leader while ensuring defeats, failures, or at least disadvantage for all non-cult members. Their *methods* vary—some being direct "Big Bangs"; some Cumulative Micro-traumas; some Micro-Aggressions; some confusing and conflicting; some deceptive; some mimicry; some camouflage; some hypocritical; some hazy and elusive; some puzzling; some a façade; some about competition; some concerning struggles and war. Two or more of such forms are incorporated into terrorism, assassinations, civil war, conspiracy, mass compulsion, and the imposition of constraints by intimidation. *Enticements* to enter the Mild and Slight False Self Supernatural world are exciting Trinkets and Trivia—intended to approach the outer reaches of the mind, filling the trail with stepping stones of fascination. Its purpose is to make one care for whatever is of "Fad" significance in the External World and Supernatural realms while caring for nothing in the Spiritual and Metaphysical realms. *Tools for making all this happen* include *Selective Willful Forgetting.*

Brute Attitudes are like the "Terrible-Two's" that focus on staying hostile and Conditioned Responses. This youthful arrogance is to listen to no advice because the Receiver already "knows everything" and is already in the excitement of being on the inside of 'what's happening' where something 'cool' is always going on. Furthermore, foolishly believing one is smarter than everybody else and no one else can understand the complex as one does—thereby enables one to have more "*Impulsive Courage*" than anybody. The arrogant believe they have the power to get others to do their bidding. After all, one is an "*Individualist*" and thus unconcerned about anyone because its "every man for himself." No matter what they do, making money is always at the fore-front and that or to compete to win takes precedence over doing it simply for enjoyment. The idea is that manners are not needed because others are to be servants and the nice things they do is what one is entitled to. Killers are those who, when exposed to Ma'at Values, have an arousal of hatred and a desire to destroy—whether done physically or Metaphysically (and this an enemy of all Ma'at Values—an enemy of survival).

Meanwhile, the entire realm is *patrolled by the Brute military* trouble-maker mind workers--e.g. "Conditional" Love, Intimidation, Threats, Disturbances, Attacks, Destructions. There mindsets are filled with Envy--and Envy is hatred of the good for being the good, as judged by the one doing the envy. This "Normal Variant" reversed hatred is not to human vices but to human virtues, simply because their emotional range is limited to hatred or Indifference. The envious seldom dare to admit this truth even to themselves because it is a semi-human emotion—and they hate being viewed as "Emotional" (for that is "feminine"). Oddly, those most envious of Black People call Black People subhuman. Otherwise, they periodically assign recollections to the dreaded "Memory Dump" to ensure others not ever forget to "stay-in-their-place". The power driver is being a "little god" but this demands using Icon *Contingent Beings* to be the guides, standards, filters, and measures for their Self-Image as well as on how to live a Brute Life. So they give themselves completely to the "Air Castle" and say in keeping with their cultish religion: "Use me, master!—I will do whatever you dictate." To make all their absorbed cult rules *reproducible* on a daily basis, pathways containing the payload of the cult's code for being controlled are etched in the Unconscious. To reinforce this they think in previous cult patterns of the "Air Castle" and a feature of "air" is that it is invulnerable. As a result their non-rational thinking follows no order, which brings into question their ability to do Rational Thinking. Such "Air Castle" thinking patterns cause them to see and explain things outside the realm of making sense by normal assessments. To stay in control of people, it is essential to keep changing and keep things noisy to keep them from realizing what is being done to them out of their "Inside-Out" minds—minds aimed at having "sick" humor derived from the harm done to others. Furthermore, to be quiet might bring to mind how miserable life is for them and how chronically unhappy they are.

"KILLER" POLICE'S ICON IMAGES/SYMBOLS: So much stuff comes into ones mind every second that the only way the Brain/Mind can deal with it is by putting "Like-Kind" things in categories. The overwhelming majority of those categories have patterns formed around Images, with certain ones being Icon Images--with or without being inside Symbols. A *Symbol* is a more abstract unit of thought than Images and may have a number of meanings. For example, if the number 1 represents an image, substituting the letter 'a' for '1' makes 'a' more abstract since 'a' could also be an indicator of a number of other things (like standing for ones middle name). This enables it to be used in thinking mediated by other kinds of symbols and does not always required "pictures in the mind." Although there are many definitions for the C16 English word "*Icon*" (Greek eikon, 'be like'), in a broad sense of being the "halo" in the "Star/Halo" concept, an Icon is an Image, representative or a 'ballpark' symbol (i.e. indicating the area or broad position or nature of something without being specific). European icons are generally quite simple in that the thing itself (e.g. a painted sign) is like what it signifies. Supreme Icons are like the MVP (most valuable player) in an all-star basketball game.

An analogy in a given category headed by an Image is like one of the states in the USA and each Image likened to a governor. But the supreme Icon Image over all the governors is the President. The laws of

Congress and sanctioned by the President are the keystone laws around which each governor forms a life-style for her/his state. By contrast, there are a tiny few "patterns" called *Imageless Icons or Imageless Symbols.* Imageless Icons cannot be defined or even adequately described. However, the ultimate Imageless-ness of Black People is that of the Spiritual God but for which Ancient Africans had no pictures because they said God is Unknowable. Instead, God could only be known by God's manifestations and that combination can be analogized to the supreme "Star/Halo" Concept whereby the star symbolizes God and the halo symbolizes God's manifestations—both of which are Imageless. What "Imageless Icons," Symbols, and "Halos" do, rather than indicating what something looks like, is to remind people of awareness they already have. In this way, they remove boundaries and leap communication barriers by dealing with what is reflected out of the "Stars" they represent.

Understanding all of this is extremely important because *all humans have much of their lives guided by these mental patterns of Images, Icons, Symbols, and the MVP Imageless*—whether of a realistic, distorted, or fantasy nature. The mental patterns one chooses to orchestrate ones mind—whether its orientation is in the stream of flow of the Spiritual Elements or in another stream--determines the category of ones preference for compatible patterns devised in ones mind and/or drawn in from the External World. In turn, ones preferred patterns mold what one thinks, feels, says, and does in life—which, of course, designs ones destiny in this life. For example, there is a relative small number of displays that people who adopt the Indifference/Hate/Evil/Sadism (IHES) Complex can use. To elaborate, the most primitive unit of thought is the Image, a sort of pictorial representation in ones mind of a specific event or object which shows the 'highlights of the original in "little world" form. The way this comes about is: (1) by one noticing a "Thing" in the External world of significance; (2) extracting its visible or "surface" features (i.e. a gist of what sets it apart from and above all the rest); and (3) storing those features in a retained mental image or as a symbol in order to serve as a basis for dealing with the "Thing" representationally. If the word "dog" arouses in the listener's mind an "image" of a dog (in the sense of a typical 4-legged animal that barks), this 'image' carries the meaning of what it represents. Similarly, the mere recall of the Icon Image or External world reminders or being face-to-face with the hated "Thing" (e.g. Black People) also stirs up what the "Thing" is all about. In turn, "surface" things like "those people" or "that neighborhood" spurs the entire "Killer" police IHES mental ingredients to set off a cascade of mental reactions about hated Black People which immediately manifest in overt, tempered, masked, or concealed actions. This is like a fly moving one part of a spider web which thereby so moves the entire web that the spider comes out to attack the fly.

"KILLER" POLICE MIND'S EXTERNAL SELF-STIMULATORS: In African Tradition the dominant forces for living were discovered by *Introversion*—turning inward to discover and operate within the confines of the Spiritual Elements to make displays in the External World. This practice naturally embraces the Cosmic Organism "ME/WE" category, having a scope for daily living ranging from gathering principles from the past to use in the present so as to pave a way into the long-term future (embracing the heaven Afterlife). By contrast, "Extraverted" people do the opposite. *"Extraversion"* ('a turning outward') is the tendency of people to direct their interest, time, energy, and effort toward the outer world of people and things—stay with the status quo with respect to self-improvement—and deal only with the 'here and now.' One type of "Extrovert" are 'people persons' while another type are the *"Imitators"* who model the Values of whoever seems to be in power by gathering what is cherished in the External World as their standards, guides, and filters as part of ever seeking approval. Its main model is *Icon Image B2.*

Icon Image B2 are the Superiority Complex orientated who crave the mental transformation from who they secretly know themselves to be over to how they want to be seen by using such affirmations as: "I'm worth having the power enabling me to self-declare I am a 'little god'; free to live above man-made rules; and exhibit arrogant pride." These weak, personally non-courageous people are always sold to the institution most likely to make them feel powerful, important, and/or rich. Kill/Take/Destroy/Dominate is a means of self-entertainment as well as the means to acquire their ultimate goals in life--riches, status, "sick" pleasures, and power. They, like all cult members, self-delude about their hypocrisy of "Manhood" in that each says: "I am my own man" while absolutely conforming to the dictates of their cult leader. They overcompensate for their hypocrisy by demonstrating aggressive "Individuality" only on women and scapegoats.

Icon Image C embraces those Imitators who have "cleaved" personalities so as to have direction of interest and attention outward or inward--depending upon the circumstances and upon ones mood and/or ones ease or difficulty of social adjustment. They tend to be open at times but otherwise are secretive in behaviors. There are further combinations, as in being increasing introverted without thereby being less extraverted. As with other members, they are *Obsessive* (a persistent uncontrollable impulse to think certain thoughts) and *Compulsive* (uncontrollable impulses to be a certain way or carry out certain actions irresistibly and contrary to the inclination or will) in "following the leader" of their cult dogma and what their fellows do. This means one may be compelled to do something against ones own will. Because these cult members are so 'specially' conflicted in their possession of a mindset geared to the exercise of power over scapegoats, they represent a fertile source of "Killer" police.

Based upon my research throughout modern times, such a pattern is evident world-wide and seemingly as a conspiracy directed toward keeping all Black People down. *Demeaning stereotypes* aim to prevent giving Black People credit for anything, and ensuring they cannot rise. That envy is basic to this practice is shown in areas where Black People have been allowed to rise. Typically, they have "taken over"—and that tears down the "White Superiority" fantasy. Such patterns are so ingrained and so machine-gunned into their minds every day that the mere recall of the Icon Image or the viewing of External world reminders or being face-to-face with the hated "Thing" (e.g. Black People) automatically stirs up what the "Thing" is all about. In turn, "surface" things, like "those people" or "that neighborhood," spurs the entire "Killer" police IHES mental ingredients to set off a cascade of mental reactions about hated Black People. This immediately manifests in overt, tempered, masked, or concealed actions. An analogy is a fly moving one part of a spider web which thereby so moves the entire web that the spider comes out to attack the fly.

THEATERS OF "KILLERS"

A playhouse and its auditorium and stage, are where one views dramas and other spectacles. Those within are compelled to follow certain rules. On the stage are actors and scenery that convey a certain atmospheric effect. The crowd in the auditorium either approves or disapproves of the performance. *Performances* of Tragedy are characterized by much *Drama* (C16, Play, action) where there is social tension, confrontation, great losses, and "sick" pleasures. The Drama's *Theme* (or Thought component) refers to its meaning within a Setting. The *Setting* is the where and when of the story, including scenery. In "Killer" stories, the mindsets concern Supernatural "Airy" Beings, floating in the midst of unrealities within an "Air Castle." The *Plot* (C17, the narrative element), refers to events (happenings) made up of characters involved in conflict. *Protagonist*(s) (C17, major character, first combatant) has the greatest variety of dialogue and action as the 'hero' of ones cult. Preparation for the performance is orchestrated by a *Stage Director* –which in "Killer" plays are the original

Supernatural "Air Castle" cult leaders who claim the right to describe the world as they see it, even if it up-ends the descriptions and practices of others. It is they who instruct performers in their movements about and across the stage (called *Stage Business*), complete with the proper messages and what it takes for the protagonist to be the star of the show.

Topics the Stage Director might select as the purpose of the Message are: those which bond with the audience (or public); some to prepare them to be receptive to what is coming by having an "Attitude" change; some to stop doing something; some to make a life-shaping or life-changing decision; and some to start problems for the Target Group and how to solve them to the cult's advantage. The Stage Director determines whether persuading, informing, entertaining, expressing, sharing, teaching, instructing, educating, or serving as a call to action is to be the purpose of the dramatic story; its spotlighted message; and how the message can best reach the audience (e.g. oneself, friends, students, public, media) clearly, with vitality, variety, and profound impact. Apart from cult members staying within the confines of this message and the "Air Castle" Codes, another rule of the theater demonstration is: "*Everything that is said must be heard; everything done must be seen*"—but this does not apply 'Back-stage.' On "*Stage*" (C13 English, standing place—the platform) all performances are intended to arouse emotional excitement for what the cult advocates for its advantage and for the Target's disadvantage. The cult leaders and the 'star' actor (or actress) of this Supernatural Drama are joint protagonists. Their feigned enemy, the *Antagonists* (C16, struggle against—the origin of *Antagonize*) are the ones who the 'hero' actors' cult says brings the struggle and is thus made the Target.

By defining themselves as "Air Castle" cult protectors, the Protagonists do not seek to ask negotiation type questions at any time during the play's travels from the beginning on one side of the stage to the end on the other before they oppress or even kill their scapegoats. First, during the performances, Masks are worn, with shapes that could be worn over the face, on the top of the head, or as a "helmet" which fit down over the head. Second are decorations utilizing various environmental objects. Third are Masquerades put on to intimidate by showy displays. Fourth are properly selected and placed figurines to support whatever is the intimidation tool. The efficiency and effectiveness of these purposes for all involved depends upon choosing the right language for the actors and audience; ensuring the actors and audience know the details of the cult leaders versions of what is going on so as to enhance connecting all the pieces into proper order; and having props familiar to the audience.

A rule of Drama is that Actors usually act out the script someone has written, including the dialogue (what each character says) and how the character is to behave. To this end, they fashioned "script writing" warring gods to suit the ideals of their Brute minds; then imitated those ideals in hopes that the Supernatural gods they created would, by living up to those god's ideals, serve as justifications for their earth world actions. The Warrior Dramatic Movement had the protagonists to be the Warriors themselves in a hero role. Rather than following the tradition of Tragedy Plays having the protagonist coming to a terrible end because of some weakness of his own, as the hero the script had to be that he constantly seeks out and achieves the "Good Life"—one filled with leisure, luxuries, power, status, victories, sex, excitement, and thrills. By contrast, the nature of '*Tragedies*'—e.g. filled with gloom, sadness, and terrible endings—was to be the fate only for victims. The rule is that the "Ends justifies the Means." To achieve these "Air Castle" ideal ends meant it was acceptable to use 'any means necessary.' Such scripted Plays had to be performed and in a manner retaining the theme of the hero being first so as to get the most.

Another rule of Drama is that Actors may not be anything like the people they are pretending to be. The concepts about "Blind" (i.e. not so much 'sightlessness' as 'confusion' and 'obscurity') have been cunningly used as intentionally deceptive methods of Actors in order to ensure the audience ('lookers and listeners') remains ignorant about the obvious. The illusion of the Play puts them into Supernatural imagination where they are not sure as to what they saw and heard in the performance as to believe the proported Actors il-lusive acts are actually true. The duty of a 'Good' Actor is to convince the audience that he was actually the "Supposed" protagonist of the story characters who deliver the real Metaphysical messages. To enhance this illusion, he would hold a mask before his face. When it was necessary for that Actor to change roles and take a new part, he needed only to change his mask. The Greek actors, performing dramas in huge open-air theaters, so enlarged these African type masks that they could be seen by all the audience in the back. Furthermore, to enhance seeming to be real, Actors could not just say their lines but also had to convince the audience that they believed what they were saying. To this end, they *showed the feelings their characters should be feeling and remembered their script lines* (as "Killer" police do today).

The spotlight is on the *Causality*; and the *'Payload' message* generates the core of the drama's "exciting" tensions. The conflicts in Dramas generate tension in the situation itself, in each involved character, as well as inter-active tensions between the hero and the villain. The actual Drama begins with action and spectacle—the deed comes before the word, the dance before the dialogue, the play of body before the play of mind. This is the process for the gradually rising and expanding of tension of a *Complication* (building tension between opposing forces) toward a *Climax* (turning point). Such a pattern is a congruent fit for Brute minds because of its building excitement and it serving as a way of organizing acts and scenes pertaining to speech, gestures, and acts in similar situations of today's daily living. All of these are necessary considerations for resolving the conflict or issue--now called the *'Denouement.'* Actors aspiring to Belong as an "Air Castle" cult member eagerly assume the role of protagonists in order to demonstrate their willingness to fight, often in the face of insurmountable odds. Acceptance by cult leaders does not necessarily depend on the actor winning the fight but rather more important is the demonstration of "Heart". Through the mechanism of a 'courageous' fight, the actor, who had formerly been an outsider, is now welcomed into the privileged company of his peers as a full-fledged protagonist. Where before he had been nobody, now he is a member of the cult's gang. This en-titles his/her own mind committee to be Stage Director--complete with the proper cult messages--and when to become the star of the "Killer" show—and killing without accountability. The following five components are part of the Tangled mindsets of "Killer" police.

HISTORICAL STAGE DIRECTORS BACKGROUND: Just as Predisposing to the 'exciting' tension of the Drama is the *Exposition* (its important background information), so a "Killers' Background Consciousness. Instead of being in some remote place and asleep, it is a molder of ones present state of Being how one present-ly lives. It is the Background the Brute presents that stirs victims' emotions. To elaborate, the *Background* for European potential "killers" and the associated Drama is the Collective Unconscious ingredients of their ever-warring primitive European ancestors. Those ingredients, of an anti-Spiritual Elements Occult nature, fashion a mindset Disposition of a Supernatural "Air Castle" fantasy inclining one: (a) to Disconnect from ones Real Self and the Cosmic Organism so as to go through life as an Individualist; (b) operate out of Brute Brains with its obsessive/compulsive aspects; (c) to be susceptible to embracing socialization into an Indifference/Hate/Evil/Sadism (IHES) mental complex; (d) have a Fear-Based attitude because of (a) and (c) and thus unable to Trust anyone, including oneself; (e) having a concept of being free to do whatever they desire since "when you're dead you're dead" and there is nothing after that; and (f) being directed by Non-Rational thinking which forms compatible IHES biases and prejudices geared to self-interest advantages while putting victims at horrendous disadvantages.

MODERN STAGE DIRECTORS BACKGROUND: These leaders are the Illuminati, the Power Elite, and the like who (g) declare themselves to be above Natural World rules so as to express choices to do whatever they like; (h) needing feigned enemies to Kill/Take/Destroy/ Dominate/Oppress in order to display an impressive show of power; (i) generating Drama and Trinkets and Trivia as the way to live so these forms of Excitement keep the public from noticing their continual losses of freedom. It was well put by Adolf Hitler saying: *the way to control people is to take a little of their freedom at a time, to evade the rights by a thousand tiny and almost imperceptible reductions. In this way the people will not see those rights and freedoms being removed until past the point at which these changes cannot be reversed.*

PROTAGONISTS MINDSETS: These protagonists are of several types: First, the *Extremes* are already established members. Second, *Moderates* are initiates engaged in whatever it takes to be accepted as a member—whether overt, tempered, masked, or concealed—whether continuously or intermittently smoldering, expressing imitation activity as snipers (like isolated mass killers); Third, *Slight* types are those in agreement with Brutes but participate only when advised to accept Delusional Fear. Fourth, are *Mild*--the non-participants who follow the Trend of Brutes while themselves engaging in Willful Ignorance. All of these Protagonists are: (1) Selfhood Un-Known; (2) have a weak Private Self and thus inadequate Self-Image; (3) carry in their Background Consciousness the ingredients of their Historical primitive European ancestors; (4) be Delusional as in declaring oneself to be superior; (5) do Supernatural Non-Rational Thinking to varying degrees; and (6) have their minds controlled by the shaping trends generated by their Modern cult leaders--trends manifested in "the Crowd"; and have great loyalty to the cult. In other words, they have a certain "sameness" with all members of the "Crowd"—as in lacking the "5Ss" of safety, security, sureness, strength, and stability.

The Extreme and the Moderate types exclusively do Supernatural Non-Rational Thinking derived from their Brute Brains, with Brute Brain objectives being orchestrated by Left Brain thinking within the content of their anti-Spiritual Elements Emotions. Their lives are totally dedicated to the cult. The Extreme are socialized from birth into a superiority attitude. Although they ensure that they are showered with "sick" pleasures, their "Life-Living" is one of chronic Unhappiness—no matter how luxurious their lifestyle and the appearance of living the "Good Life."

Moderate "Air Castle" members, out of which most "Killer" Police come, possess profound self-hate and self-distrust; are filled with Phantasmagoria imaginations, filled with paracosms (exotic amazing illusionary details) and Contingent Beings; needing feigned enemies for their racism so as to Kill/Take/Destroy/ Dominate/Oppress; and are never able to enjoy anything but, instead, only get transient pleasure from creating misery for others. Drawing heavily on the Collective Unconsciousness of their primitive European ancestors and with a hypersensitivity to Fantasy Paracosm imagination, they make up Contingent Beings about all concerned in their lives. But, more than other Protagonists, they have unique features within their certain "Sameness".

PROTAGONISTS REACTIONS TO ANTAGONISTS: On the one hand, all Moderate "Air Castle" Brutes have a "Sameness" in their reactions to and interactions with Targets. Some include: (1) demeaning any people who have allowed themselves to be Enslaved as being mentally weak, subhuman, and like mechanical beings; (2) project their "Dark Side" on to the scapegoats they most envy and thus are their Target Group; (3) have an inferiority complex with self-hate that is typically masked by a superiority complex so as to use this mindset to "wipe out" their feigned enemy competitors; and (4) fashion 'monster' Glob mindsets.

On the other hand, their individualized unique aspects, as a result of their self-created mental Glob, are primarily about how each Brute responds to his/her situation and circumstances and thereby design Effects and Circumstances.

The word "*Glob*" implies personally meaningful emotions, feelings, thoughts, imagination, expectations, desires, symbols, and mysterious 'something' interwoven into a "sticky" tangled ball. This mess equates to confusion and conflict about the meaning, the significance, the priority, the diagnosis of a problem or situation, and the solution—each of an anti-Spiritual Elements nature. The Glob (sticky ball) state—are like a composition of threads of all colors, some with blended hues. In a Glob mind, certain sparsely scattered colors represent kernels of distorted truths as well as true pieces of information. Yet, the innumerable colors responsible for its primary misinformation nature—and imparting the appearance of the Glob as a uniform grey or "black"--is that of Phantasmagoria imaginations filled with paracosms and Contingent Beings. Such a fantasy imagination has fashioned a 'monster' as its Target—a 'monster' representing a stereotype. For racists, that Target is Black People, for a host of reasons, having nothing to do with the truth.

The Brute fashioners of 'monster' stereotypes convert the reality of their Target so that the Target's "That is" qualities + their "what they do" + the "how they appear"--all together conform to what the Brutes think of themselves. But since that self-awareness of them being a 'monster' is so frightening, they are compelled to Project it on to their Target. Under the delusion that the Target possesses their own 'monster,' they do the 'right' thing (by the Supernatural Manichaean religion standards saying "white is right") by "killing the black." But the Brutes' 'monster' consist of a personal sense of inferiority, Shame, Powerlessness"; feeling Unimportant, Worthless, Incompetent, and Useless because of a loss of the "5Ss" resulting from their choice to disconnect from their Real Self in favor of fashioning their own False Self. That undifferentiated interwoven 'monster' Glob itself is like a "*Raw Nerve*" that has to be hidden and protected from ones own and from outsiders attacks.

However, the problem is that 'monster' Glob is their Ego which orchestrates their lives. By being in a Glob state, the ingredients are unidentifiable, making the Brute unable to put any of it into words. That alone is very frustrating--and to the point of causing them to act "ugly." Nevertheless, the 'monster' Glob is the only guide of Brutes—their only remnant of personal identity and to which they cling with ferocious possessiveness. The nature of the "Glob" determines the nature of who to connect with—based upon the "Law of Attraction." The Brute, the Brute's cult, and the Target of the Brute are Interlocked in a drama. The Brute is the protagonist, the Target is the antagonist, and the cult is the director and the audience. The 'theater' is a Supernatural "Air Castle" which operates by a different set of rules which they deem to be superior to Natural World rules.

PROTAGONISTS REACTIONS TO TARGET ANTAGONISTS: The key feature is that in keeping with their European ancestors and their extreme Envy of Black People, it is an automatic next step to form *Hate-Filled Icon Images* of Black People of a stereotype nature. In using the Thinker's Scale (a positive and negative ruler separated by a Zero), The concept of Hate was not part of African Traditions Philosophy of Life (POL) because they were always striving on the positive scale toward their Highest (divinity) Selves. The contents of the Positive Scale include the Spiritual Elements inside the Cosmic Organism—both supplying a human's Private Self with "5Ss" powers of Safety, Security, Self-Confidence, Strength, and Stability Yet, they recognized Hate's existence on the negative Scale and elaborated on it in the metaphorical form of the god Set. Ancient Africans idea of Hate, as I interpret it, is that it is located in the Emptiness or a Void called the Supernatural realm as a Contingent (partial coming into Being). Its Contingent appearance comes from the fantasy of anyone who is Self-Unknown—i.e. in a "Plane" that is a sort of "State" ('way of standing, condition, position') of vibratory energy generated by ones imagination. Inside that Supernatural "Plane" are wave-like Contingent entities, each possessing different dimensions. But because the feature of a Self-Unknown individual is being disconnected from all that is on the positive scale means one has nothing to choose from except unique destructive thoughts possessing a theme called Hate.

Hate is not present at the birth of any human newborn but by then being socialized or traumatized into the ingredients of Hate, children, by ages 4 or 5, children have developed the who, what, and how much aspects of Hate. Although for one to be aware of the "state" of Hate requires the need of its Contrary Opposite (i.e. the contents of the Positive Scale) to serve as a standard for comparison, this does make them opposites because of their contrasting natures are on different "planes" and because what is on the Positive Scale is Real while what is on the Supernatural Negative Scale is Fantasy. Europeans who say "love is the opposite of hate" are speaking of their Secular or Emotional concept of love and not the Spiritual's Unconditional Love. But by not ever explaining this difference puts the public on the wrong Self-Evolution Track.

Hate is relative, transitory, and implies being disconnected from ones Real Self with a resultant inability to "Know Thyself"—the source of ones realistic Happiness in life. It is by Hate being on the Supernatural Negative Scale that its ingredients of Ignorance live, and move, and have their Contingent Being status. For Brutes, those ingredients are formed into mental Images (a collection of bits and pieces of odds and ends' to serve a common purpose) within the categories of oneself, ones "Crowd", and ones actual as well as feigned enemies. One of those mental Images in a given category is chosen to symbolize that category and it becomes an Icon. An analogy is that the MVP (most valued player) of the all-star game is equate to the Icon Image. Once that Icon Image is formed, it serves as a magnet for one to use as a colored emotional lens for biased and prejudicial viewings of what oneself, ones "Crowd," or ones real and feigned enemies do. The consequences of this Effect are ever increasing layers of like-kind bits and pieces. The gathering process of this Accretion includes the Icon Image growing in size by gradual hate-filled additions from the External World, from fusions, inclusions, or adherence of parts normally separate and do not go together.

An analogy in medicine is an Organism consisting of several types of tissues of different "genetic" composition--some produced by mutation, some by grafting, some by the mixture of cell populations from different zygotes (a fertilization yoking together of female/male genes). The interpretative part so imaginatively elaborates on clarifying biases and prejudices as to give the Icon Image a chimera appearance. In Greek mythology a Chimaera was an imaginary fire-breathing monster made up of grotesquely disparate parts—e.g. a lion in the fore part, goat in the middle, and a dragon behind. Then, in Indo-European folk-tales it possessed the quality of universality of a horrible, grotesque, fantastic beast. Since Hate is a trait of "Weak People" and since "Weak people" are Self-Unknown and since the Self-Unknown is about being in Fantasy realms, in order to have a tow-rope on which to hold throughout the course of their unstable and miserable lives, they create Chimaera out of scapegoats. In the process, they create a Chimaera of superiority to subdue the Icon Image of their inferiority. All of this is unstable inside an unsettled situation.

Brutes complex Glob Emotions contain a Disposition formed previously from a Conditioned Response. Among other things, it has a hypersensitive by disclosing to Brutes' minds the Black People Target to which the Glob is directed. The reason for this hypersensitivity is that the Black People Target puts Brutes in contact with, immediately brings up their own repressed self-hatred memories so as to disclose and spotlight an awareness of their 'monster'. As a result of that, Brutes may also intuit something in the outside Target that reflects other repressed "Dark Side" aspects of oneself.

THE KILLING SITUATION

During the Renaissance pride in materialism, appearances, dishonorableness, individualism, and the Indifference/Hate/Evil/Sadism (IHES) complex was the typical Brute European way of life freely indulged in. But their Supernatural religion, which was integrated into their warrior happenings required the formality of consulting Church priests who, starting in C14, allowed ones sins to be wiped out for a fee. Following confession and the priest recommendations, the size of the fee depended upon the magnitude of assessed crime already—in the process of—or about to be committed. The greatest sins demanding to be wiped out were about enslaving Africans and taking them to Europe and to the Americas. For each such confession by big time enslavers, the Church was paid huge sums of money as well as be in on the most profitable immoral acts, including slavery and Enslaved concubines. This practices regarding sinful attitudes and evil actions were brought to the New World by those same people who then established themselves at the top and set up the USA government and all policing actions to get rid of the problematic people. But since these slave owners hypocritically set up the government as a "Democracy"—emphasizing in the 1776 Declaration of Independence T. Paine's ideas of the natural dignity of humanity (and pregnant with the 1894 *Pledge of Allegiance* message of "…with liberty and justice for all")—meant laws allowing for evil actions had to be put acceptable deceptive euphemistic labeling. Such labeling were deflections for injustice. Of course, their descendants have carried forth these behaviors to the present.

"KILLER" POLICE MENTAL KILLING PREPARATIONS: It is through humans' physical brain that their Astral Mind works. Every time something (e.g. a fact or idea) is remembered, a deeper track is worn along the same passage in nerves and brain that was affected by the original impression of the fact or idea, regardless of how long ago and whether consciously or unconsciously. That is called an Engram. Different bits and pieces of information, spotlighted uniquely by each human from scattered time periods and about scattered things can be brought together to form mental patterns of Images, Icons, Symbols, and MVP Imageless "Things." Different societal philosophies cause a given society to floodlight values suited to their way of life. Those Values at the highest Abstract level ("Virtual" boundary-less "Things") are necessarily Supreme Imageless Icons. For *Brute Europeans it is the Mega-Imageless Icon "Air Castle"* residing in the fantasy Supernatural World in which cult members place themselves. Being a microcosm, the Icon aspect symbolizes the outward created effect of the inward Values of the "Disaster Star" of the Indifference/Hate/Evil/Sadism (IHES) Complex macrocosm which characterize Warrior mindsets. They have devised a Supreme Contingent Being leader which embodies all of the IHES codes of the "Air Castle".

Contingent Beings are, to repeat, a more elaborate version of the childhood 'Imaginary Companions' or 'Invisible Friends'—a fictitious person, animal, or object—common in children between 30 months and 55 months of age. They may be a virtual 'intimate friend' with whom to share troubles, pleasures, and confidences. These are most often seen in those who are lonely or unsociable, or who are having difficulties with family relationships. Or, it may be very vivid, have a name, stable personality, characteristics and mannerisms of action, and play an important role. In the 'serious business' of the adult "Air Castle," likekind Contingent Beings serve a variety of purposes: (1) as an inspiration and motivator for qualities ones lacks (e.g. courage, derring-do or reckless actions); (2) provide an outlet for anger, anxiety, or guilt; (3) act as models useful as scapegoats ("the devil made me do it") for tension release; and (4) the 'authority' one is following in order to justify, if caught, displays of ones "Me, Me" Individualism Fetters. This 'authority' Contingent Being, they volunteer, is the source of their bad mental actions--e.g. hatred, arrogance, pride, fear, and dishonorableness—each variously displaying as IHES lies, selfishness, greed, anger, lust, envy, jealousy, and frustration.

TRAINING POLICE TO KILL: What one thinks about ones own death and about causing one or more people to die is an issue to be addressed. Type I have Supernatural mindsets and thus have no problem with killing others, even if it is uncalled for since it is exciting and since it helps maintain White Supremacy and since it is enduring to fellow cult members. Since one of the greatest fears a police officer has is the disapproval of his or her peers and since police rely on one another in terms of officer's safety and backing up one another, attention is to be paid to an officer being over-zealous to kill so as to get approval. Type II are non-Supernatural mindsets whose issues are overcoming innate aversions to killing another human being, even if it is justified as well as coping with the emotional trauma of having experienced a deadly force encounter. For Types I and II there are the skills to be developed regarding the shooting performance; the decision making as to whether to shoot or not in a controlled way; the development of negotiation skills for the purpose of averting a killing (i.e. Police value deadly force as a last result and sanction its use when other options are seemingly unavailable or unlikely to work); the acquiring of mental problems from ones deployment of deadly force; and the administrative concerns about emotionally unstable officers.

Important to the preparation of Type II to know what to expect when in a crisis situation. The psychological changes in a crisis or life-threatening situation are not a set of absolutes, but rather some common phenomena that are experienced by people living through them. Broomé (*J. Humanistic Psychology, 2014*) mentions as common and possible perceptual distortions in lethal encounters the following: *diminished sound, tunnel vision, automatic pilot, heightened visual clarity, slow motion time, memory loss for parts of the event, memory loss for some of your actions, dissociation, intrusive distracting thoughts, memory distortion, intensified sounds, fast motion time, and temporary paralysis.* Simulated shooting situations are the way that many police get an approximation of what being in a shooting might be like. The setting in which such training occurs that of the issue of Trust and Trust is part of the bigger picture of Loyalty.

HOW "KILLER" POLICE MAKE KILLING OKAY: Legal euphemistic labeling are intended to give acceptance to certain acts so as to appear less destructive than they really are. Identifying IHES acts with a more benign term, makes the reprehensible respectable. For example, the term "killing" is changed to "terminating with extreme prejudice"—or, in the "Streets," to "Take Down." For "Air Castle" cult members or their followers or the rich and famous, palliative expressions are terms that mean the same as the IHES acts but mask their obviousness by having them sound much less destructive than it really is. However, a powerful public manipulative tool used against Black People is to euphemistically embellish what they are accused of so as to imply that they are guilty of a horrible thing before there is even good evidence. As historically proven, such is the giant first step in innocent Black males being accused, imprisoned, and killed (e.g. by lynching). Another type of euphemistic labeling--the "Agentless Passive" form—is used for any Brute with, at best, a remote conscience (e.g. "Killer" police) to commit "Moral Disengagement." One way is to pay a fee to religious leaders to wipe away the sin.

In drama conflict situations, adversaries say the other's actions are heinous. But, for people in power, the police are in the power position to gain any benefits of doubt. Support for the "Killer" police comes from him, fellow police, and the media doing away with his own individuality in order for it to seem as though his illegitimate acts have been carried out by a valid group or force rather than him, as a single, culpable "agent." A second justifier of killing comes from Displacement of responsibility for not doing an inhumane act by declaring that the wrongly killed person was "subhuman" and thus the world is better off by that death—like swatting a mosquito. Third is "Advantageous Comparison." When a "Thing Event" occurs contiguously, the first one colors how the second one is perceived and judged. Thus, a "Killer" police can justify otherwise deplored acts (e.g. those seen on camera videos taken by a disinterested party) by comparing and contrasting it to euphemistically embellish or fantasy deplored blatant acts of inhumanities of the "suspect." Or, in court, the "Killer" police attorney might soften the police's deplored act (e.g. apparently unjustified shooting of an unarmed Black person) by comparing the police's crime to the number of murders committed by the "suspect". The point is to surmise that the police killing of that villain was for the public safety. In short, using "Air Castle" Supernatural morals packaged in self-palliative euphemistic labeling and destructive euphemistically embellished or fantasy refashioning of the "suspect" provide cult members with the proper appearance of and terminology for moral justifications. And that combination makes it okay for "Killer" police to kill unarmed Black People.

"KILLER" POLICE—COMBAT MINDSET FEATURES: The opponents of police are combatant criminals and "Scapegoats" (C16, escape + goat). The 'bottom line' is that Brutes' transfer of their hatred is an obvious indicator that they hate themselves and that to retain all of their hate within is far too disturbing. Whatever was the cause of that self-hate broke the integrity of that person's mental health, perhaps shortly after birth and to discover that cause is the keystone to diagnosis. Newborns are naturally in a state of having needs and desires satisfied—a sense of Security guaranteed without effort—a state of Selfhood Integrity. A shattered Integrity is analogous to the fairy tale about the Egg, known as Humpty Dumpty. Either from multiple micro-traumas or from a "Big Bang" psychic trauma (perhaps from being pushed), the effects for Humpty was to fall off the wall. The Effect of splattering was so great that all the kings' horses and all the king's men could not put Humpty back together again. Thereafter, the human equivalent to Humpty becomes self-absorbed in every effort to regain the "5Ss" of Integrity—all in vain. The Consequence is a chronic state of Insecurity. This is because *Security* is basic for survival and for it to be known, it must be immediate in the 'here and now'. It must also be personal, i.e. having a response to the feeling of security and without necessarily having the reality of it. Anything else (e.g. safety, stability) is a far distant second.

European authorities define "Security" ('carefree') as a sense of confidence, safety, freedom from fear or anxiety and measures used to create, enhance, or maintain this state are called *Defense Mechanism*. Anger, boredom, contempt, or irritation are defenses against ever present anxiety. Since "Security" is the pivot of mental health, "*Insecurity*" is a lack of assurance leading to a sense of being threatened, un-protected-ness, and helplessness against manifold anxieties arising from a sort of all-encompassing uncertainty about oneself; uncertainty regarding ones purposes, goals, and ideals, ones abilities, ones relations to others, and the attitude one should take toward them. There is no incentive to be friendly and humane in what seems to be an unfriendly world in an atmosphere causing the anticipation of disapproval. This causes a withdrawing reaction, guarded responsiveness, and a lack of trust in self or in others. Healing is the removal of the keystone disturbance and all of its residua--not simply the removal of symptoms of the clinical disorder. Such will not be complete since adults are always fearful of something. So the trade-off for getting a sense of security from being in a team is a loss "Individualistic" freedom.

"KILLER" POLICE—DIAGNOSING COMBAT MINDSETS: In reviewing hundreds of articles on the subject of the Police world-wide, the literature was silent on anything about the mindsets of "Killer" Police or the fact that they exist. Such is a barrier to the first rule of handling problems—i.e. to recognize there is a problem so as to discover 'why'. All problems begin with some aspect within being unhealthy. A human's Health is Selfhood Integrity within all aspects and throughout the wholism of an integrated body, mind, and spirit--meaning it is complete, sound, natural, not divided against itself; and strong against opposing forces so as to have harmony and the maintenance of a balance between complementary forces. Whatever is not healthy requires a *Diagnosis*—i.e. "to know about; to know through; to understand" the "SOBMER" (an acronym for Source, Origin, Beginning, Middle, End, Consequences, and Result) aspects of that problem; the keystones of the "SOBMER" aspects; and the label for the pattern of the conclusion.

The "SOBMER" PROCESS is a tool for organizing chaotic information under the principle that events or products have a Source (the creation of the 'creator' which has a Disposition) and Origin (the 'rising' of the creation into Causes for what is to come). "*Cause*" is what brings about any change to produce activity—the "why it happens" portion of understanding a plan, problem, and/or proposed solutions. The first of three staggered Causes is the *Predisposing Cause*—which is what puts the "seed" situation on the path for its potential evolution. The *Precipitating Cause* is what fertilizes the "seed" and enables it to grow. The *Immediate Cause* is the spark which activates the process of the Disposition. The *Beginning* is the process (the way in which the Disposition's Inclination is to be done) set into an observable evolving. The *Middle* is the process moving with speed and force. The *End* is when the process of the situation has stopped moving or is moving very, very slowly. Along the way of the situation things have been done to upset the status quo and thereby lead to Results (what happened as a consequence of the process) or Effects (what is done).

From this "Skeleton" organization, two paths can be taken. First, the pertinent problematic issues may be obvious so that predictions can be made of the Consequences likely to arise out of the Effects or Results. An example of such a prediction is that rather than, as is typical of most people, the troubles of "Killer" Police having come about unexpectedly, they were predictable at the moment the policeman made the choice to go into an Indifference/Hate/Evil/Sadism (IHES) Complex direction. History has shown a way of IHES thinking to be that where everything is bad, it is good to know the worst is not oneself. That alone can drive the need for scapegoats. Hence, it can be inferred that this concept led to the policeman carrying around a 'lightning-rod' so as to attract trouble. Each trouble represents a challenging opportunity to enter an exciting 'troubling of trouble' drama—and that excitement starts with its anticipation—and that anticipation is greater by using suppositions rather than bothering with the truth. And that is a sign of an unhealthy human.

If, after assessments, the policeman's diagnosis is not clear, then *Troubleshooting* (a 1905 term for one who traces and corrects faults) can be done of his SOBMER Process in order to determine the pertinent problematic issues and then locating the *Essential* flaw in each issue. To be complete at each step is the only way to know as many parts to the "big picture" of the subject as possible. Certain of those Essentials will require proving or disproving in order to properly recognize the true significance in each. Once those analyzed issues are prioritized so as to arrive at temporary conclusions about which is a keystone (the Diagnosis), look to determine where there was improper or inadequate preparation or to find where one got off. Those who are not "man-enough" to admit they are wrong are unhealthy and with a mindset bubbling with 'tension.' A typical tension-releasing action is to contribute to the troubles of scapegoats and then deem those troubles to be greater than ones own. By also presuming scapegoats have an IHES mindset means this is a "call to battle" and thereby conquer danger and thus have a triumph with glory. Some of the Consequences arising out of the mindsets of "Killer" Police is that how they perceive and deal with life has made them sour, narrow, and skeptical.

FIGURE 10

AT THE "KILL" MOMENT: What happens at "crunch time" is a Conditioned Response from ones emotions furnishing the concept to which one reacts. As stated above, many things meet at one point and here Brutes instantly engage in "*Projection*". This is illustrated by those European policemen who, upon seeing a Black male, have invoked within them the Numinous Feeling" of "*Dread*"—a term which refers to a

Conditioned Response whose self-inflicted property is the production of Fear about the Target person. Those two factors contributing to "dread" prompt a conditioned reflex to readily kill unarmed Black males. Although this "dread" does not arise amid the sensory data of the realistic situation--nor arise out of them—it comes from a Background Sensory Consciousness programming. The soon-to-be crime places are also filled with expressions of power, spectacles of horror as opposed to this being considered as an opportunity (i.e. that one can get away with it) to experience the "Thrill" of killing there is a split second where the decision is made. During that consideration perhaps one might think: "no this is not really a threat to my life but I can justify the killing and thereby experience the "Thrill." This means, by perceiving no danger from pushing their abilities to the limit—perhaps even challenging death—constitutes a "Thrill": "How close to the point of the maximum of danger can I get?" To see ones degree of courage in answering that question is an exciting challenge. Faceless "Killer" Police are thereby spared condemning characterizations and are thus able to keep possessing the immanent authority of the Law itself. In fact, some get rich from donations in their support or 'paid vacations' for their killings. As a result, it is an easy next step to progress from an impulsive tendency to kill Black and Brown people over to a Conditioned Reflex reaction—better called a Psychological Conditional Response. Thus, Black or Brown skin-color alone becomes a conditioned stimulus because of it being capable of activating a customized Icon Image in "Killer" Police—an activation which instantly causes them to "kill that Icon Image." So, the policemen are really trying to kill their "Dark Side" within a Supernatural context. Let us now look at details of these factors.

CRIME SCENES: All crime places are filled the aura of Drama, complete with expressions of power, spectacles of horror, and leaving the more naïve to killings. However, killings for "Killer" police are an "Exciting" time in their lives to which they are addicted (as one admitted: "I want more"). Associates with the police include the *Coroner or Medical Examiner* who examines dead bodies so as to determine the probable cause and time of death. They may examine the crime scene (fig. 10). In police laboratories are chemists who decide if a stain on clothing or other objects was caused by paint or blood; whether food or drinks contain poison, and if so, what kind; whether the ink on a ransom note is the same as that found in a suspect's writing pin. Ballistics experts tell if a bullet used in a crime was fired by a particular gun. Fingerprint experts do match ups with photographs, fingerprints, and records of past arrests and convictions of all who ever committed a known crime. Police photographers work at crime scenes and take pictures of suspects to be placed on "rogues' gallery." Nearly every city and state police departments use the FBI. A problem is the Coroner and the city district attorney may be good friends with the police department and thereby skew the findings to always come out in the "Killer" police's favor. A Psychological assessment can be valuable when it includes (among other things) attempting to discover key factors in the policeman's Belief System. For example, individuals can consciously consider themselves to be completely rational people and deny that they believe in magic (or God), despite harboring a subconscious belief in the Supernatural and a 'second nature' engagement in magical thinking.

POLICE TEAM UNITY

When it comes to Humanity dealings with people deserving of it, a Natural world moral conscience dictates one has a Spiritual obligation, duty, and responsibility to seek out the Right Life-Living from the very best available sources. The place to start is with oneself to discover "why don't I know what is right? Have I been taught or allowed myself to be taught by ignorant or evil people? Do I lack the courage to go against the "Crowd" and do what I know to be right? What benefits do I get out of watching my people cause others to needlessly suffer? What "Raw Nerve" of mine am I protecting and defending and deflecting so others will not know I am so weak? What do I have to lose or gain if I decided to give those I downgrade a chance by learning about their problems and strengths. What all would be involved if I discovered we are more alike than different and, as a result, I would like to establish close friendships with certain ones. Maybe my life would be better off because, by getting rid of all hate, I could finally learn how to really enjoy myself and be happy.

These are not feasible questions for "Killer" police because they have too many fears and hang-ups and shaky Un-noble loyal relationships—too much of a sense of inadequacy—to have the courage to leave the status quo that was so complicated to create. They are fearful of being alone in the Unknown if they took the first step to do what is "Right." Yet, the real problem may be that they believe to be "Right" the codes of their Supernatural "Air Castle" thinking, even though it is "Inside-Out" compared with the Real World. This is what European racists do—willfully be ignorant of Black People and their pains and sufferings so as to not let knowledge of the justifications for compassion get in the way of blame, fault-finding, ridicule, stereotype, and being judgmental from their outrageous adoption of a superiority attitude. It is ignorance that makes monsters that gain strength and certainty as it goes along—giving confidence in everything. The most powerful weapon of ignorance is diffusion of the printed word. It is more costly than an education.

POLICE TEAM NOBLE LOYALTY/UNNOBLE LOYALTY DILEMMA: In European tradition there is Noble *Loyalty* (exhibiting the courage of self-sacrifice in the interest of justice)—but the question is "To Whom?"—to "ME/WE"; to "ME"; to "WE"; to certain ones of "WE". The nature of that Loyalty may be inside or outside the Spiritual Elements. If outside, it is called "*Un-noble Loyalty*" (things done for the Indifference/Hate/Evil/Sadism (IHES) Complex, in spite of knowing better) and this fit well with the brute personality of "ME" or "WE" as a team or to certain ones of "WE". Regardless of type, dilemmas arise. On the good side, police officers might be loyal to their partner personally *or* to their group *or* to the police force *or* to a police code of ethics *or* to the government *or* to the community the police force exists to serve. Since each of these loyalties tend to be exclusive and generate partiality when it is necessity to make a choice, conflicts may arise: "Should I be loyal to my fellows or the community when they are against each other?" "Should I be loyal to a fellow police officer guilty of misconduct collides with ones loyalty to the ethical principles governing police work?" But what wins out is loyalty to each other—first taught in the Academy and later throughout officers' tenure as an officer. So the spotlight is on Trust.

TRUST

A major issue in any organization concerns MORALS: Type I--whether one is live up to Sage Morality (the best Humankind has ever known as determined by all the Sages of all culture and of all ages—for that has a sound base and is stable); Type II--live up to the best one knows to be "Good"; Type III is Supernatural; or Type IV--live up to the morals of the organization (Hooke, *J Contemporary Criminal Justice, 1996*).

Type I (SAGE MORALS) is based upon Real Self people whose Immaterial Self (ones Divine Consciousness which represents the Image of God) can only express itself through the manifestations of the Material Side of ones Selfhood. This Immaterial Self is intimately associated with all of the Sparks of God in other creatures, therefore making them Spiritually related of a "ME/WE"—of a Compassion--nature. Sound coherent thoughts feelings, expressions, and action stay within the flow of the *Spiritual Elements*— Unconditional Love, Truth, Reality, and the Natural—*the only absolute "solids" in the Cosmos*. That Spiritual

Elements Base is consistent, permanent, stationary, and unchanging because its patterns/elements underlie all natural events on any plane of existence in the Cosmos as well as everything one does in daily living—whether for ones Selfhood and/for others in a "ME/WE" fashion. This is the foundation of Integrity in African Tradition.

Thus, the harmony of the inner qualities of ones Divine Consciousness + the Spiritual Elements + Integrity + a "ME/WE" orientation to living means one is Selfhood whole (or undivided) regarding moral consistency (e.g. in honesty and truthfulness), in the way an egg-shell protects the egg. That moral consistency manifested in the Material side of ones Selfhood is Trust. In short, to be sound within naturally means what comes out is sound in a "ME/WE" manner. This concept came from my Orthopaedic Residency at Cripple Children's Hospital while treating Clubfoot deformities. My slogan was: "Toe-in—Toe out" and that gives rise to "Sound within and Sound without".

Type II Trust may arise out of something less than Type I: featuring unintentional Uncertainty to varying degrees; temporary or of a more permanent nature;—and general/specific. Akin to Hope, trust relies on future possibilities inside the context of current realities and is an essential for worthwhile and sustained progress. Yet, trust is only valid as long as the credibility of someone or some "Thing" is sustained and not broken by betrayal, broken promises, or violated values.

Type III is out of the Supernatural "Air Castle" and is characterized by deliberate destructive Flaws. Flawed examples include being shoddy, weak, inadequate, limited, defective, incomplete; non-pertinent; not of keystone importance; facades; confusingly directed or headed; placed on improper planes of existence; improperly arranged or combined; deceiving; in conflict; evilly misinterpreted; racially/ethnocentrically biased; in conflict; and/or mostly simply

Type IV is the organization's *Ethos of Trust* and its fragmented "WE" nature dominates among police while necessarily causing great problems with all other "ME/WE" fragments. The sharing of 'unstinting loyalty' to fellow police is to receive protection and honor + the setting to assuage real and imagined wrongs inflicted by a (presumably) hostile public + safety from aggressive administrators and supervisors + the emotional support required to perform a difficult task. Such brotherhood loyalty's effect is 'Social Isolation' in police officers' occupational environment—the separation of police from 'non-police', creating an 'us versus them' attitude towards the citizenry. A consequence of that is the officers' relationship to the citizenry is seen—on the one hand, as the ever present potential for danger, causing their preoccupation with the danger and violence that surround them. Two coping mechanisms for helping officers regulate the occupational environment are suspiciousness and maintaining the edge.

ETHOS OF TRUST DISHARMONY: Disharmony within the police team is almost inevitable because Type IV police Trust is both a private group and a public issue. The private aspect results from the Esprit (Spirit). Since this imparts strength from feeling oneself as a part of a distinguished and efficient organization which is expressed as a "Us-versus-Them" attitude—"Them" representing the public. Such an occupational identity can provide collegial comfort at the expense of generating public distrust. However, this very practice exposes each member to ambiguous forms of Self-Identity, more so of the Spiritual than of the Secular type. This is where Self-Identity becomes assessed in relating to ones religion, culture, and gender pertaining to right/wrong and moral obligation. It is an infinitely greater struggle for those with a Spiritual Self-Identity since their self-assessment is of an African Tradition type (staying within reality with respect to ones Real Self).

Such an assessment may not be called for Living life out of a Secular Self-Identity if it is a Supernatural (Type III above) type. Two major scenarios that can bring on disharmony within the police team are:

First is that time when an unsuspecting established officer is faced with the dark side of this shield that calls for protecting officers guilty of misconduct and corruption. Police crime is intentional crime committed by police officers on duty. But when a policeman commits misconduct, part of the dilemma is that it is not permissible to criticize other police officers, in particular if the criticism is aired to 'outsiders'. In that setting extremely few have the courage to take an unpopular stance against his fellows. There are innumerable driving forces for this—e.g. Glamor status, being somebody, and simply desiring to belong to an organization having unchecked power. But in those who have a moral conscience beyond the confines of the police team, there is the weighing of ones loyalty to fellow police or to the profession itself as opposed to being true to ones own personal conscience when faced with a colleagues illegal acts. A member's distrust suspicions of that colleague about egoistic drives, deception, manipulations, criminal act lead one into Distrust.

A second scenario of bringing disharmony to the *Ethos of Trust* is when minorities and women are on board because of signifying perceived or actual moral and emotional fiber texture alterations which disturbs the existing Ethos. Even unproven suspicions may alter the presence of fluid harmony and the maintenance of a balance between complementary group Spirit forces). Such suspicions is likely to cause those 'new comers' to be hit with emotional distance if they do not go out of their way to show they are not professionally neutral.

When there is distrust by one an atmosphere of an Ethos of Distrust descends over the organization as an "Us-versus-Them" attitude among members of the same organization. Now within the organization, instead of Trust being by agreement of all (a Covenant), Trust is now an agreement with a given fragment that is at odds with differing fragments, with the group hanging together by a professional contract. In the back of their Conscious minds is the desire for vengeance against anyone who deviates from the cult's dogma—a practice that is quite old, dating back to ancient European religions and sacred texts. "Whistle-blowers"—a late 1800s term originally alluding to ending an activity (e.g. factory work) with the blast of a whistle--are those who expose corruption or other wrongdoing experience unrelenting vengeance, as by being isolated and left unprotected at a crime scene. A problem with this that such suspicions invite retaliation. When doubts are cast on officer A's unstinting loyalty, he is excluded from this Loyalty support net a priori ('seems right'). Policing police crime is enforcing law on potential and actual criminal employees in the police organization.

"KILLER" POLICE CULT PRACTICES: *Assimilation* ('absorb') is a lack of interest in maintaining ones own cultural identity combined with a desire to maintain relationships with other groups. *Separation* ('arrange apart') is characterized by an investment in maintaining ones cultural identity and a lack of interest in maintaining relationships with other groups. *Integration* ('renewal or restoration of wholeness') is an investment in both preserving ones cultural identity and maintaining relationships with other groups. *Marginalization* is a lack of interest in both cultural maintenance (sometimes due to societal pressures to relinquish cultural practices) and the development of relationships with other groups (often due to discrimination and exclusion). It puts the 'outgroup' on the outer borders of the Archery Pad of society and racializes (causing them to be considered in a manner similar to epithets). *Acculturation* is the modification of the culture of a group or an individual through contact with one or more other cultures and the acquiring or exchanging of cultural traits; the transmission of culture from one generation to another within the same culture—sharing the same meaning as *Socialization* (learning the group's culture and ones role in the group). The significance of these terms begins here when consideration is given to what it takes to become loyal to an organization or to a group, or to both, through the membership process. The key is a result of identification with the group. Entry into the group and subsequent identification with the group is partly mediated by the characteristics of the group. Of prime importance is that loyalty to the group is spotlighted.

A predictable group loyalty is more readily achieved in homogeneous groups of like-minded members than not. Peterson (*European Journal of Criminology, 2012*) says: 'If one is to go out in the company of a partner to face considerable dangers, for example, one needs to know that that partner will treat one's interest as his or her own, that his or her courage will come into play when one is threatened' Quite simply, without ties of loyalty and trust between fellow officers, police work would be much harder to do. Problems with suspicion, as well as subtle forms of exclusion and discrimination related to all of these occur when most police teams include ethnic minority officers. To be spotlighted is that their 'loyalty' to the team is put into doubt, and to the point of having to risk being repositioned as 'outsiders' within the police organization. He adds: two coping mechanisms for protection from supervisors is to: 'lie-low' or 'cover-your-ass,' while maintaining a strict adherence to the crime fighter image so as to minimize the ambiguity of their multiple roles.

This dictates that ethnic minority officers are rigorously tested as regards their loyalty to their fellow officers and to the police organization. The demands made on their unstinting loyalty and the misgivings as to their unflagging loyalty act as barriers to inclusion in the organization. Gender and ethnic diversity in the group means there is greater uncertainty in the system of values of each 'outsider.' Resolution of a clash of loyalties is about dealing with the "non-rational". For example, loyalty to some people can come into conflict with loyalty to others or loyalty to people can come into conflict with loyalty to principles. Such 'individuality' among 'outsiders' is in contrast with European males who have a preponderance of 'sameness'—not only around the world but also throughout the ages. Thus, for European males it is harder to discern how a given member of any ethnic group might respond during questionable situations regarding their concept of "rightness." Thus, ethnic group officers are constantly tested—perhaps being confronted with offensive jokes about their ethnicity, but seldom directly encountered outright discriminatory language. Yet, there could be freedom in using derogatory language about ethnic neighborhood minorities.

POLICE—JOB & SELF-STRESSORS: In assessing the Unseen Realms, Primitive Africans used their Real Self's natural Magical Thinking. Later Africans built on this by rising above their Lower (animal) Self and cultivating their spiritual skills into concepts of the existence of the Universal One High Spiritual God. The result was inner peace and External World harmony. However, Europeans' environmental "Scarcity" situation led them into False (animalistic) Self ways of living—i.e. the choosing of a Supernatural Fantasy mindset. A False Self is one with a Superiority or an Inferiority Complex—both about fantasy. Either one cleaves (i.e. splintered but glued together) ones Selfhood into Self-Absorbed inner world happenings as well as into External World cascades of events. European Warriors' External World was about material acquisitions and accomplishments, avoidance and elimination of painful experiences from outside threatening and attacking forces—including people and events deemed not to be in their best interest. These Warrior's inner world was about extreme tension or stress—including such aspects as being highly competitive; clingers to anything deemed powerful (e.g. attachment to material possessions); greedy by being "ME, ME, ME" oriented; cultivating an attitude of Indifference/Hate/Evil/Sadism (IHES) Complex ways of dealing with people and having to be on the constant look-out for retaliation or revenge; always looking outside into the External World for emotional excitement; and assuming a manner of defying the "No man is an Island" rule. These 2 patterns are models for basic living. Yet, if ones Inner World is in turmoil, it is an added stress for ones stressful External World, as exhibited by "Killer" police.

Some philosophies make one more prone to excessive amounts and depths of stress. So do certain occupations. For example, Police, by occasionally being in settings where they are targets of guerrilla warfare--whether against a specific adversary or more--means they are predisposed to PTSD. Since such terroristic actions generate uncertainty about who is the enemy, the police are ever aware of having to battle against the neighborhood culture--and often do. Most develop beliefs that any non-officer could be malevolent and a possible threat. A belief develops that any person other than another officer is malevolent and the ever stress of the threat of harm or death. . Personnel who continue police work while symptomatic may incur risks of reduced self-control, escalated use of force, and other inappropriate behavior due to irritability or outbursts of anger associated with PTSD. Faced with this kind of anxiety makes it understandable that the police always anticipate the worst of all possible outcomes, interpret every chance happening as an evil omen, and exploit every uncertainty to mean the worst. The tendency to this kind of expectation of evil is found as a character-trait in many people who cannot be described as ill in any other way (Sugimoto, *J Death and Dying, 2001)*. Being self-absorbed implies their inability to see similar mindsets present in most of their victims—e.g. unarmed Black males doing what they do in their own neighborhood. Those males know officers can inflict death directly (e.g. shooting one perceived to be a threat to the officer's life), or indirectly (e.g. a supervisor ordering an officer sniper to fire).

The police "Manhood" culture—which seems to be of a group rather than of an individual nature, since individuals fear going against it--does not allow fellows the right to engage in grieving by: (1) not recognizing relationships between officers and anybody or "Thing" lost; (2) Loss is not defined as significant by the police culture; and (3) Officers are considered to be above grieving. Since officers see themselves as the disenfranchisers (taking away others rights and privileges), they do not allow themselves to show any aspect of the grief process. So this combination of—a primitive originated collective Background unconscious of "Scarcity + being under cult domination + choosing an IHES mindset + all the stress that goes with one declaring oneself to be 'superior' and constantly having to prove it to oneself and to others + choosing a highly stressful occupation + developing psychological problems from that occupation understandably makes police "edgy" as a way of life. That "edgy-ness" needs an out-let for its constant build-up of tension. The most convenient out-let is on the scapegoats known as Black People. jabaileymd.com

"KILLER" POLICE ACCOUNTABLITY: Policing is a highly discretionary, coercive activity that routinely takes place in private settings, out of the sight of superiors and in the presence of witnesses who are often regarded as unreliable. Yet, there are noble sovereign Police Code written and unwritten laws for governing police conduct—e.g. honesty, honor, knowledge, morality, fairness, principled behavior and dedication to a common mission. Many police officers engage in positive behaviors such as community partnership, problem solving and other actions that go beyond minimum standards for policing. Internal and external expectations of law enforcement are met, or at least attempts are carried out to satisfy reasonable expectations. In this process, for the most part, the police acknowledge accountability to no one except to each other. Protection is given by the courts, laws, and the media directed public—all giving each officer almost free reign with Black People. It is left up to the individual officer to abide by the theoretical practices outlined by police Codes.

One is that police have a reasonable reason for detaining a suspect. From the moment of their physical contact, the officer is supposed to be legally and morally bound to protect his Charge from any unnecessary harm –to give the suspect aid if he/she is ill or injured--and, as indicated, call and ambulance. The destination of the suspect by ambulance or police car requires the suspect have seat-belts on so as to ensure a safe ride while receiving proper emergency care as required. Taking care of the suspect is to continue until arrival at and goes inside the hospital or police station jail.

When any aspect of these are flawed, an Accountability is called for that is adequate to allow for a 'trouble-shoot' review of the entire scenario—including the evolving informational story-- complete with the justification and explanation of that information. The final part of accountability calls for the holding to account for the capacity for action and with the results of those actions being subject to the ability to impose sanctions—meaning in the legal sense penalties or other measures of enforcement used to provide incentive for obedience with the law or with rules and regulations.

In summary, Accountability is facing the judgment, penalties, and punishment to whom one is answerable for ones obligations, duties, and responsibilities. Accountability refers to situations in which someone is required or expected to justify actions or decisions. It also refers to situations where an officer bears responsibility to someone or for some activity. Accountability has been called 'the mother of caution'--physical abuse, sexual misconduct, prisoner mistreatment, traffic violation, extortion, corruption; evidence manipulation; un-authorized disclosure of information (Ivković, *Police Quarterly, 2013*).

POLICE CODE OF SILENCE: Police Integrity is the absence of misconduct, where misconduct is generally understood as being an attempt to deceive others by making false statements or omitting important information concerning the work performed, in the results police integrity is a number of concepts and beliefs that in combination provide a structure and a culture within which police officers are characterized. The tolerance of and unwillingness to report misconduct of fellow officers to police supervisor, administrators within the organization, to the public—called the "Code of Silence"--is an occupational norm. Perhaps it is the most violated and most unpunished aspect of what is involved in the lives of police officers.' To elaborate, any inquiry into reports of misconduct—illegal acts and violations of organizational policy—is inevitably met with a wall of resistance in the form of Silence. Behind their "wall of secrecy" is the often occurring personal and conscious concealment of information that might exposing acts of misconduct. Such may be about countless things as, for example, officer misconduct related to corruption; such offenses as discourtesy to or verbal abuse of citizens or off duty driving under the influence charges; the use of excessive force—the misconduct described was motivated by personal gain; abuses of discretion in arrests, order maintenance, to citizens, and an assortment of things motivated by temptations of gain. Those officers who did/do not expect their peers to report misconduct were/are much more likely to indicate their adherence to the code of silence.

There are many payoffs for protecting officers guilty of misconduct and corruption: (1) Adherence to the principles of secrecy and the unwritten code of conduct ensures mutual aid, meaning the expectation of maximum assistance from everyone to any officer in trouble; (2) This unwritten code not only reduces apprehension and punishment as a deterrent to police misconduct but makes them almost impossible is highly related to their perceptions of misconduct seriousness; (3) In exchange for turning a blind eye to misconduct (i.e., participation in the code), officers earn the trust of fellow officers and can expect to receive reciprocal protection. A "Dark Side" is those police in an occupational subculture that is cynical, distrustful of outsiders (the "us vs. them" mentality), and marked by intense loyalty to others working in the occupation the code of silence functions as a protective mechanism against public criticism and/or unfair discipline from police administrators, leading police officers to "act in accordance with their collective well-being".

SUMMARY

Although European "Roots" of Religion, Intelligentia, and Warriors seem to me to have come out of the "Air Castle" of the Supernatural—with its emphasis on "Non-Rational" mental activities, today's "Killer" police are most representative of primitive European Warriors' mindsets. Those mindsets' philosophy of life had *Scarcity* at its core during the Ice Age, implying there were insufficient resources to supply everyone's needs and wants. Such desperation spurred their "Emergency" brains to "fight" and with its predictable "Me, Me, Me" continuity reactions of first: *Rapaciousness*--the robber instinct of "I'll get there first—then kill you so I can take it all"; second, *"Covetousness"*: "I'll want yours so I'll have some extra"; third, *"Defensive"*--using any means necessary to "keep what I have and to prevent others from having any, I will destroy what I don't want." As a result of winners self-declaring to be superior over all others, to prove this to themselves they enhanced that sense of superiority by denouncing outsiders as Subhuman—like cattle--mentally weak—and being like mechanical beings who could be dealt with by every conceivable method of cruelty. Even after the Scarcity Ice Age period ended in 12,500 BC, the Warriors Brute Brains had made treating with extreme cruelty anyone unlike them. While making their Scarcity Philosophy and its displays into *Impulsive Reflections*, they were simultaneously constantly improving on Kill/Take/Destroy/Dominate/Oppress methods. Both of these Indifference/Hate/Evil/Sadism (IHES) ongoing practices produced imprints or impressions, said Plato, on the mind's "wax"--called "Memory Traces" or *Engrams*--i.e. the "Seed" of the *Scarcity Tree Concept*. Since they had long since lost Inner World contact with who they were prior to become Europeans meant they had a new "Ground of Being" beginning.

In other words, their updated Collective Unconsciousness began with the IHES practices associated with their primitive European *Scarcity Tree Concept*. Such has been clearly demonstrated in the European world throughout the ages as, for example, with Christopher Columbus and his crew and with the way the Spaniards treated Amerindians in a Piñata fashion. In 1586 the Augustinian friars in Acolman, Mexico introduced the Piñata Concept as a European religious allegory to help them evangelize local Amerindians. The original piñata was shaped like a star with seven points—each point representing the Seven Deadly Sins. The bright colors of the piñata symbolize temptation. A piñata is a figure, usually made from a clay pot covered with paper mache—containing candy inside. It was shaped like a star with seven points, each point representing the Seven Deadly Sins—and being of bright colors to symbolize temptation to Sins. The piñata would be suspended from a rope so that blind-folded sinners could take turns hitting it with a stick until it breaks. When the candy fell out onto the ground, this would indicate the benefits of following the dogma of the Church.

This Piñata Concept and its practices were transferrable to the way European "killers" treated people unlike them. The idea was for them, as self-declared Supernatural "little gods," to control the minds and bodies of the mechanical human beings and beat them until they were barely able to survive. The greatest "thrill" would come from then killing them in a situation full of drama, complete with Chimera Contingent Beings. All of this provided them with "sick" pleasures, like the candy falls out onto the ground from a beaten Piñata. Such situations continue to be produced—perhaps daily—by "Killer" police because they have the sanction of the European community to do so and without the need for accountability. It is impossible to experience the *Love Platter*-- the instinct to Love; to spread Love; to be Loved; and to be Lovable—which are responses to values, when ones Conditioned Responses to Values is the IHES Complex. Correction for this IHES mindset is Ma'at Values, attributes of the Spiritual Elements, applied to things of *Worth* (i.e. things of Spiritual Beauty) and *Value* (Public Self material benefits seen in more ways than just itself). Both refer to central aspects of people's self-identities, self-meaning, self-concept, and self-image.

CHAPTER VIII

VICTIMS
BOND TO OPPRESSORS
WHO DO EVIL FEEDINGS

VICTIMS OF VIOLENT MINDS

The C15 word "Victim" originally denoted a 'person or animal killed as a sacrifice' in a religious ritual and later it expanded to one who suffers from or is killed by something. Subsequently, Victimization also embraced one or a group identifiable by distinctive characteristics (e.g. race, gender, socioeconomic status) who have unjustly had their rights or freedom violated, threatened, disturbed, or destroyed, if not killed. Just as a disease prepares victims for death, so are Brute Brains Indifference/Hate/Evil/Sadism (IHES) deeds the source of victimization of people. Such victimized mindsets which generate Extreme Despair, were unknown in pre-colonial Africa because, until their encounters with Europeans' Kill/Take/Destroy/Dominate/Oppress methods, there were no evil and sadistic oppositions. These methods have continued to be demonstrated by Europeans from their inception on Earth is that of their well-worked out "Take-Down" patterns of: penetration, conquest, occupation, and colonization. For example, a feature of "*Penetration*" used by European Brutes is to first move in with a friendly presentation and then gradually trick, manipulate, and insult victims on whom they generate hardships, make miserable, and perhaps kill. This proceeds towards conquest, occupation, and colonization—a pattern that is basically the same, except for minor variations. They have made history by having victimization's largest scale and longest run on Black People. Not only in the Americas but around the world, all Colored Peoples remain victims at the hands of Europeans. At the core of their victimization is, I believe, (Chapter VI) *Extreme Despair which serves as the Background for the think, feel, say, and do Foreground lifestyle patterns of struggling Black Americans. For them to return to their Real Self is done by eliminating, not transcending their Extreme Despair Backgrounds.*

PREDATORS: The *Predisposing Cause* is what puts a potential problem on the path to being a Problem. The *Precipitating Cause* is what gives size to the Problem. People who have an IHES and/or a Superiority or Inferiority Complex form the mental arts of Brutes' entities and powers of violence and its minions (subordinates and servants). There is a 'Sameness' in their displays but people who are otherwise unique and that 'Sameness" is the same in all countries and in all ages. Two reasons are that all are using their Brute Brains and all are operating out of a False Self. A third for Europeans is that their Warrior, Religion, and Pseudo-Intellectual cult branches all came out of the primitive European Philosophy of Life (POL). Still, each branch uses different methods. Basic patterns, perfected over the millennia by constant repetition: (1) mark its victims as subhuman; (2) denounces victims; (3) denies justice, (4) enforces poverty, and (5) excites public odium (IHES/aversion) in order to mask/conceal its own unspeakable cruelties of variations of Kill/Take/Destroy/Dominate. For this to succeed, IHES leaders must have military type order of and control over its followers.

Brutes' inhumanity from living out of their Brute Brains + being overwhelmed with ignorance + entrenched with greed collectively cause victims to correctly sense that society is in an organized conspiracy to oppress, rob, and degrade them. The result is that victims' hatred runs so deeply as to turn many minds "*Inside-Out*"—i.e. these victims are against themselves and their own. Brutes' self-hatred projected onto victims makes Brutes slaves to their own hate and animosity. Because of extreme envy and fear of the Black Mystique, to keep injuring Black People itself intensifies Brutes' "Heart" hatred and their "Head" contempt—neither being quite within their control. Brutes' Hate is layered on to victims from multiple causes: (a) despising themselves for not having perfected their despising and hatred; (b) the use of much energy to repress the Truth of 'Right'; and (c) the fact of the IHES things they do begets hatred.

EUROPEAN VICTIMIZERS

All of the things mentioned about European males and what they have done to Black People by meaning of the GUN are what characterize mindsets of European Criminals. Violent criminals think differently from "normal" people. One way is to be numb to the feelings of others so as to be without much or any sympathy for the victim. A second is what they can gain by using violence, as in a thrill from killing, boosting their Self-Image, or acquiring possession—as a "*Risk–Benefit*" analysis whereby the significance of the victim is subordinate to the benefits. In fact, they get "sick" pleasure from bring pain, misery, and hardship to victims. For these reason, Europeans have a need to kill Black People in general and Black males in particular. This is most obviously done by European police and they intimidate Black police to the point of many Black policemen imitating the "killer" patterns of "Killer" police in the hopes of being accepted. To show inclusiveness, 20% of unarmed Blacks killed by officers in the past 15 years have been Black women.

As part of their Individualism "little god" mindset, an intent of European Brutes has always been to make Black People into their own image so as to: be the 'big daddy' who controls their minds and development inside the status quo; to be able to predict what Black People are thinking and doing so as to head that off and stop progress; to use as a source for stealing ideas, creations, and material things; to acquire free or cheap help; and so as to have a sense of power, status, and recognition. Brutes are well-aware that if Black People remained with or returned to African Tradition they would be impossible to control, exploit, and, of greatest fear, would have long since brought Europeans under control. Brutes' image is Black People is to have them imitate an "Air Castle" Supernatural mindset and do Emotional or "Non-Rational" thinking. These same concepts and practices apply to police—the present day most visible equivalents to European enslavers—both being the most powerful entity in the captives' (Black People) lives. The philosophy of the captives is shaped over time by the actions of the captors. A mindset undergoing such a disintegration of reality—partly conscious and partly unconscious—while replacing it with Supernatural Engrams--thereafter becomes the gatekeeper to serve as the standard, filter, guide, and measure for how information coming into that mind is interpreted and processed for mental functioning. Furthermore, it acts like a plow for making further inroads into the Delusional World.

The captives necessarily have to think of how to survive rather than how to escape. The captives' identity, self-meaning, self-concept, and self (body) image are altered so as to turn their thinking "Inside-Out" (e.g. going against their own instincts for survival). The captives' ability to do Rational, Creative, and Critical Thinking has been shifted over to the inferior Supernatural "Air Castle" forms; their internalized images of others, sound system of values and Humanity ideals that previously lent a sense of coherence and purpose are broken down. Differences in the imitation pattern is that: (1) Psychic trauma is the cause for the Captives report vivid memories of traumatic experiences related to their oppression; (2) Black People must not have a Network; (3) Black People must not be able to defend themselves in any way—not by the GUN, not by government laws, not by the media; (4) struggling Black People must stay poor; and (5) Black People must have self-defeating Icon Image. Otherwise, except for Causation (Europeans socialized into an "Air Castle" mindset; Black People traumatized into it), the formation of Icon Images has followed the same Engram pattern.

'KILLER" POLICE NEED BLACKS TO KILL: A generic Bigot (a narrow-minded person) is one whose philosophy of life was molded by the psychological effects of an authoritarian upbringing—on the order of German ideas of child-rearing that emphasized strict obedience and deference to authority. They have had an extensive influence in the development of American child-rearing practices. By such authority figures having had control over them throughout the course of their lives meant they were almost invariably in subordinate positions and yet idealizing external power. They harbored a hatred derived from the terror of submission that was mixed with Conditional love and kept this hatred unconscious by projecting it onto others who they felt were inferior to them. In this way they become focused Bigots—one who is strongly partial to ones own group, religion, race, or politics and is intolerant of those who differ. Bigots see themselves as on the mid-rungs of the Social Ladder. The higher classes above, which Bigots both envy and fear being despised for their strivings. The classes below are to be despised for a number of reasons—e.g. their teachers say so and so the Bigot can feel superior. This is 'chiseled' into their Supernatural bigoted moralism which causes them to believe that everything they do is right. When, in circumstances of high uncertainty which activates their emotions because their Self-Image is threatened, they perceive being in competition. Hence, their degradation and disdain of Black People intensifies as they magnify their concrete, "all-or-none," "either/or" judgments. As a result of these factors, Bigots learn to be irrationally and profoundly dependent on the object of their prejudice who serve as scapegoats. This means they desperately need Black People (as indicated when Black People were migrating out of the South following the end of Reconstruction). Thus, Bigots are dedicated to at least making "Inside-Out" thinking Black People believe they need them—particularly by controlling all it takes for them to survive. By Racists being unable to leave Black People alone implies their Hate is checkered with their European forms of love that manifests as an Obsession (a persistent uncontrollable impulse to think certain thoughts) of an envious nature.

As Racist, they have rigid characters--see things as unalterably true--and are extremely dependent on external stability. These Racists have a *Compulsion* (uncontrollable impulse to be a certain way or carry out certain actions irresistibly, even if it is contrary to the 'moral' inclination or will) to not only keep Black People oppressed, but also to see Black People enact the demeaning "Stay-in-your-place" traits the European slavers brainwashed into the minds of Enslaved Africans. Many White mass killers of Black People make reference to this "Slave" concept as an excuse for their actions. Such is clearly seen during periods when Racists feel stressed. Thus, when the social fabric of stable authority is seriously threatened or disrupted, Bigots rise up, clutching to Symbols of "White Supremacy" (e.g. Confederate Flags, restricting voting rights). In addition, out of their superiority fantasies about themselves, they embellish this Supernatural state by making a display of overvaluing the superiority of their cult and overemphasizing the sameness or unity within their group. So that these hallucinations will stand out even more as differences, they stress demeaning Black stereotypes. Racists need to in Black People a "Sambo" image that bows down in their presence and always be subordinate—the reason the media spotlights the ways of the most struggling Black People on sit-coms, on the news, and on the front pages of newspapers.

Their Brute Brains demand seeing Black People suffer endlessly in order to satisfy their need to punish as well as to vicariously get pleasure out of feeling 'superior.' Such has been repeatedly illustrated at lynching "*picnics*" (the connotation definition being 'pick a N** to lynch). These dynamics create in Bigots a worship of the past and a frantic rage at changes in the social order, a rage that becomes most pronounced when Black People reject their debased role. The USA's violent history of lynching clearly shows Euro-American males' deadly obsessions with Black male sexuality—as in making false claims of lynched males having raped White females and castrating those lynched males and putting their genital in their mouths before setting them on fire and chopping them up.

THE "BLACK MYSTIQUE"

"Mystique" (1891, French, mystic), a peculiar Magic family member, defies denotation and relies on any given Crowd's connotative meaning. Such meanings are based upon variables—e.g. do they like the person or not; where are they positioned on the Metaphorical Ladder extending from the Supernatural to the Spiritual; what is their philosophy of life; and what do they honor? Nonetheless, dictionaries define "Mystique" as an atmosphere of mystery about someone or something. Unanswered are: "what causes that atmosphere? And what is a Mystery?" Whereas total *Ignorance* is not knowing that one does not know something at hand, a *Mystery* is incomplete Ignorance in that one is aware of a "that it is" of a "Thing," but knows not its "what it is," "what it does," "how it appears," "how it is composed," "how it came about," or "where it is going." Its "that it is" insides consist of an Association of Ideas which begin and end in a shroud, as each day lies between two nights. Mystique atmospheres, like Magical Spells, created by associations of things done, cause observers to say: "How did she/he do that and what enabled her/him to overcome the obstacles when nobody else has ever been able to?" As a result, complex transcendental or semi-mystical beliefs and attitudes are directed toward or developed around her/him or institutions or ideas or pursuits or symbols--all enhancing the Image of who or what is generating the "Mystique."

The story of this special esoteric skill or mysterious faculty begins with Primitive African Shamans' discovery that in light Trance states they could see geometric Shapes, called *Form-Constants*. These outward Embodiments of the Eternal, containing Messages of the Creative Will, possess the life potentiality to act in daily living. Its Message consists of the "What" and the "Why" in the form of a *Species of Primary Qualities* which, as Legend Icon Images, inhere (i.e. innately) in Spiritual Substance. This Species—i.e. a Family of 'like-kind' Class realities, differ greatly in appearance among themselves, but are yet very closely related in their Essence (i.e. their "What it is") nature. As a series of forms having *Significance*, all reflect a common and unifying underlying element—formed as *Paradigms* ('patterns'). As Trance deepens, a Legend Icon Image, being an archetypal (Seed) principle of unified multiplicity, presents in many shapes. The Shaman then selects certain shapes emerging out of Form-Constants; studies their Significance as they change into things governing the Shaman's particular culture; and extract from the contents and the Shape what is peculiar to enhancing that Shaman's Vision of *seeing invisible essences others are unable to see, as with discerning similarities in the dissimilar as well as uniqueness in similarities.* Visions present the Truth, like a landscape to the eye. Very Ancient African Sages discovered the principle underlying all technology to be the twin variables of Shape and Materials. A Thing's Shape, they said, *is a pattern of energy movement frozen in space to which Nature gives a unique specific power.* To know a Shape's pattern provides the key to unlocking the Shape's secret powers--whether dealing with higher Spiritual realities, psychological or behavioral patterns, energy patterns, or actual structures manifested in the Physical world.

By patterns of Spiritual Energy movement and its Shape's specific power conforming to African Sages mathematically derived Laws of Nature enabled the maneuvering and manipulation of them into Thought arenas of special interest. As is, these Paradigm Form-Constant Thoughts--or their Prototype off-spring, or modified copies of them--are useful for producing constructive External World work products or solutions. Also, these Thought products are: (1) a real, stable, permanent part of the world; (2) are absolute, universal, and true for all time, regardless of their Form; (3) exist whether perceived by humans or not; and (4) are responsible for what occurs in the material world. Since these Paradigm Form-Thoughts are specialized patterns, blueprints, or plans, intuiting them enables one to get to the core of and spotlight the essence ingredients of an "*Esoteric*" something. That Knowledge is a Disposition for the "What" and "Why" Message having an orienting Inclination and particular focus which, if manifested, provides Spiritual Element products for the senses. To Physical/Supernatural realm limited thinkers, these varied Primary Quality off-spring products have a "Mystique"--products routinely produced by Black Africans. jabaileymd.com

"BLACK MYSTIQUE" FORMATION: For Very Ancient African Sages, Form-Constants, representing Divine Archetypes, helped explain the nature of existence as well as provide essence Paradigms needed for all God's creatures and creations. Specifically, they presumed these were "Thought-Forces emanating out of God's Mind and representing Divine Paradigms (i.e. Patterns) for Spiritual Elements—i.e. Unconditional Love, Truth, Reality, and the Natural—to be used as stable sources for any entity. African etymology says Divine Archetypes are Original or First Seeds out of which like-kind Prototype things branch. An example is the original un-seeable Spiritual Seed which gave rise to all trees seeable in the physical universe. "*Paradigm*," an Ancient African word, refers to perfect Metaphysical Exemplars or blueprints. African Sages inferred that a divine agent (especially God) in Spiritual realms uses both aspects of a Divine Form--its Divine Archetype component as a seed for and its Divine Paradigm component as a pattern in creating something in Metaphysical and Objective Realms. Africans' *Law of Spiritual Creativity* says: by itself, a Spiritual Element reproduces itself to become the thing it makes, regardless of its new form. On an Earth World level, this Law is an ongoing repetition of the original "Thought-Forces'" nature manifesting as a compatible Prototype. As is, Paradigm Form-Constant Thoughts, or their off-spring, or modified copies of them, are useful in the External World for producing constructive work products or solutions. Verification of this is by the *Law of Correspondence* which, in turn, is exemplified by the *Law of (Spiritual) Circularity or Reversibilty*: The Spiritual offspring is proven by the parent and the Spiritual parent is proven by the offspring inside a boundless realm. Another exemplification is by the *Law of Equilibrium*: all functions must be maintained in their proper space and time. Discerning Correspondence imparts *Sacred "Awe."*

African Griots conveyed these ingredients to African people as being achievable sources for Right Life Living. Preparation to begin this process is for one to "Know Thyself"--be ones Real Self; have a Free Mind; use Courage to be and to express who one really is; stay in continual contact with ones Inner Core (i.e. the Cosmic Organism); spend time, energy, and effort to nourish the Spiritual (pre-birth) Emotions and intellectual endowments; replace Information with Knowledge; create out of the Spiritual Elements while inside it; use the Spiritual Energy package to discover and perfect ones Selfhood Greatness and its Talent; remain totally dedicated to family and ones Mission in life above all else; and strive to make great "ME/WE" contributions. That Ancient Africans perfected such preparations is indicated by their work products—e.g formulating or laying foundations for all that is great in the world today—all mathematics, physics, science, philosophy, logic.

Conformation is given to these statements by the European, Poe, (Black Spark White Fire p342) stating: "the ancient Greeks and the Romans were so awed by Africans and African achievements as to believe that dark skin accompanied high intelligence." This applied (among others) to Africans' Knowledge, Virtue, Goodness, and Victories over the Esoteric. "Awe"--whatever its actual content—fear, delight, sadden, disturbed, amused, instruction—expresses every possible shade of emotion and can spur every conceivable thought and reaction. But the Result of "Awe's" combined Effects and Consequences is the underlying sense of yielding ones mind to something extremely grand in character or formidable in power—praising that "Thing" all it can for Being and for Happening.

To provide the setting of the Mystique attributed to Ancient Africans and its echoes can be observed in many of today's Black Americans is to imagine the *Tree Concept*—i.e. its Seed, Roots, Trunk/Vines, Branches, Leaves, and Fruit. Whereas Ancient African Sages dealt with Seeds and Roots to fashion Principles into Symbols, Forms, Sounds, and Movements related to Spiritual and Metaphysical realms, African Groits passed along the rest of the "Tree" that African people were capable of perceiving by their senses. Yet, these "Senses" things possessed Paradigms compatible with the high rates of vibrations that they could replicate in every aspect of daily living. Examples of such rhythms and shapes embrace Dance, Art, Speech, Music, Humanity Relationships and other packages of the Spiritual Elements to produce "Black Mystique" works of Beauty.

EUROPEANS DEMEANING "PROPELLER" BLACK STEREOTYPES: "Propeller" (C18, drive away; expel) means a mechanical contrivance for propelling machinery or a vehicle. An airplanes' propeller blade is an airfoil that requires it to have a twist in order to provide a useful lift-to-drag ration. The blades' pitch, or amount of twist, can be altered to control the speed or be reversed to drive the Thing. A rearward force on the air (or water) is balanced by a forward force on the propeller. These are helpful concepts in giving clues for assessing what people say and do. One example is a *Misinterpreted* meaning being like a propeller whose ends are twisted in opposite directions. A second is that although in the 1960s the FBI considered them criminals, the Black Panthers did great things for the Black Community. To carefully study the truth of the racial situations in which the Black Panthers were involved, it will be realized the FBI reacted to what I call *"Pseudo-Propeller"* crimes. This means the proper Things the Black Panthers did for themselves—Things almost mirroring what Whites do for themselves—were deemed to be criminal activity by Euro-Americans and were violently dealt with, which seems to be how Europeans deal with all matters of differences. *Positive Propeller Words* have an underlying positive aspect twisted to present publicly as neutral or negative, as in degrading the dignity of Black People by calling them Sub-human. By contrast, it can be used to make "Me or Mine" appear more favorable than ones trashy character deserves. An example of Positive Propeller Words used to benefit the favored, say in the media or in legal settings, are *Euphemisms*--substituting fair-sounding words for objectionable (e.g. negative, offensive, or taboo) ones. To illustrate, the White motorcycle gang who killed many innocent people were referred to by the media as "bikers." By contrast, Black youth who were said to create a riot were called "Thugs." Negative *Propeller Words* have underlying negative aspects twisted to present publicly as neutral or even pleasant. These Backhanded or Left-handed (1600, questionable, doubtful) compliments or Asteisms are insults disguised as compliments: "I don't find you as bad as what people say about you!" "That dress doesn't make you look too fat."

Those Crowd people limited to doing Patterned Thinking simply follow their hidden Satanist leaders' guidance into disregarding the humanity of all involved in order to preserve the unwavering deference to

White Supremacist authorities intent on controlling minds of the World Crowd. The Crowd lacks the courage to avoid gravitating to Stereotypes. These ready-made descriptions painted onto scapegoats are clung to so as to by-pass all the trouble involved in seeking the entire truth, in thinking, and in being moral. Willful ignorance keeps them in good stead with the "Crowd" at the price of disrespecting their own character. Stereotypes Europeans have about Black People are demeaning Caricature ('overloaded' representations; ludicrous distortions). "Sambo," watermelon Pic-a-ninnies, buffoon-acting and "Street Life" Blacks are floodlighted images on all forms of media, as if this is who Blacks are. As a boy, every magazine I thumbed through had the cartoon of a Black cannibal with a bone in his nose preparing a White man in big kettle to be eaten.

When despicable inhumanity occurs to Black People and then placed in the form of stereotypes, this is a "Propeller Twist" display of the projectors' deep-seated fears and reflects their brain-washing to not have independent thought as puppets. The counterpart of the demeaning stereotype they project onto Black People demonstrates a "Propeller Twist" in their own thinking. Such is indicated by the definition of their self-declaration of being 'superior.' Specifically, a Superiority Complex is the donning of a mask of self-confidence and greatness with a reality of arrogance and aggression to conceal a sense of deep inferiority and self-hate. Thus, for the sake of their own Bad self-image, they must degrade scapegoats. Super-Humanization of Black People is a display of a Negative Propeller Word—called *Micro-aggression*. An example is racist Europeans deeming some specially great Black person with the label of "Superhuman." The intent is to separate that person from "normal" human beings to gain such advantages for Europeans as to prevent having to compete with that person; to prevent that person from "joining the crowd of 'good ole boys'"; and to prevent that person from being within reach for Black youth to model.

EUROPEANS FEAR "SUPER-BLACKS": Europeans equate fear to the keystone for safety—and this dates to their primitive times when survival Scarcity reigned. As highlighted by ancient Greeks, Europeans conceive of the world as full of spirits, of malefic characters in operation at all times, everywhere. The use of spells was a regular technique in Greek medical practice whereby wounds were healed with incantations. In Thessaly, the ancient home of Witchcraft, Spirits constituted, not subjective projections, but objective reality. When European enslavers dealt with Enslaved Africans, their fears exploded. Du Bois stated the "Priest or Medicine-man" was the chief surviving institution African Slaves had brought with them: "He early appeared on the plantation and found his function as the healer of the sick, the interpreter of the wrong, and the one who rudely but picturesquely expressed the longing, disappointment, and resentment of a stolen and oppressed people." *Conjurer's powers were particularly important, not from having power over the slave owners--which a few did--but rather by possessing powers the slave owners' lacked.* This was what the Enslaved found most impressive and often caused the Conjurer to have more control over the Enslaved than did the slave owner. Their African Tradition tinge was strongest in folk beliefs about the pleasures of life and weakest in practical matters where Whites predominate. A Conjurer might slip into the quarters containing disgruntled Slaves; pray for better treatment for the Slaves; and then have the Slaves collect various roots, put them in bags, march around the cabins several times, and point the bags towards the slave owner's house every morning. Any degree of let up by the slave owner was attributed to the power of the Conjurer. Sometimes the charms the Slaves obtained from the Conjurer bolstered their courage and caused them to defy the White man. Many Slave nurses who cared for the slave owner's children probably did as much through telling tales to the White children to ensure the success of the Conjurer as anyone else.

Meanwhile, and drawing on history, European slavers so feared the superiority of Black People as to make it against the law to teach the Enslaved to read, write, or count. Subsequently, they have always generated substandard schools and at no time have they ever taught Black children the ideal way—that of Ancient African Tradition, emphasizing Affect Symbolic Imagery and African Dialectic (Bailey, Teaching Black Youth). During and continuing after slavery, anecdotal, qualitative, and historical evidence of Super-Humanized Black imagery have given Black People a Mystique concerning their Super-Human qualities—as in the Enslaved air of secrecy inside their "Knowledge by Participation". In C20 movies, popular media often depicted Black people as Supernatural and magical, capable of extrasensory feats. Black characters in many C21 films (e.g. The Green Mile *and* The Legend of Bagger Vance) have magical, mystical Negroes who show up as some sort of spirit or angel, but only to benefit the White characters. This Supernatural archetype pattern emerged from earlier films, with such characters often possessing particular Supernatural abilities to foresee the future, heal illness, transform others, and frequently appear outright as Supernatural entities, such as Gods or ghosts. These magical representations also emerge in media portrayals of Black athletes as possessing Superhuman abilities. In thumbing through magazines as a boy, I routinely saw cartoons about "Witch Doctors," as Europeans derogatorily call Ritual Specialists, doing magic.

Despite showering the media with Contingent Beings, Whites associate Superhuman qualities (e.g. magic, mysticism) with Blacks to a greater degree than with Whites. Some Europeans assess these as attributions of superior human qualities; others to Superhuman attributions to which Europeans are largely incapable. Examples of how Whites super-humanize Blacks implicitly: (1) is attributing higher-than-average human physical capabilities (e.g. toughness, strength, pain tolerance);(2) depictions of Blacks tending to involve non-academic Superhuman mental qualities (e.g. clairvoyance); and (3) general Superhuman characteristics (e.g. the ability to be ghostlike or Godlike). Such Super-humanization, a distinct process from sub-humanization, makes for a Mystique to be feared while simultaneously needing to stay connected with Black People—a "Push-Pull" situation. [Ref: Waytz, *Social Psychological and Personality Science, 2015*].

"KILLER" POLICE SUPER-HUMANIZING BLACK PEOPLE: Europeans' historically "*Split Consciousness*" of Black People's Mystique is in the form of "Twin Icon Images"—50% of awe and fascination; 50% of fear and envy of that very Mystique. This spurs their own Fear-based philosophy to deem Black People in an "Either/Or" manner--most thought of as 'Sub-human'; the rest as 'Super-human'—not in the sense of being admired and/or well-liked targets but as a novel ironic positive form of "*De-humanization*" (converts ones God Image into a Brute state) stereotyping. Yet, viewings of Superhuman Black Mystique People convey powers to viewers of an unconscious "sorcery" irresistible attraction atmosphere—associated with non-rational mindsets that are powerless in all attempts to resist. Viewers thus rely on Black People for a host of reasons--but needing to demean and stay segregated from them to preserve their 'superiority' fantasy. Such was clearly exhibited by Southern Whites trying to stop from migrating "up North" the ex-Slaves they were terrorizing. Historically, such a 'scary' state generated by "weird others" has showered on European childrens' stories that implicitly but not directly express demeaning payload messages. Similar stories (particularly in the media) explicitly assign derogatory labels to the Trigger Person(s) as savages, heathen, godless, vermin—or, in more subtle ways, cast Trigger Person(s) in antagonistic roles. This process of "Dehumanization" may be conveyed in jokes or in the literature of comedy. Even then, toxic messages about Black People are conveyed and heightened via vivid stereotypes. Consequences of these Effects lay paths for socializing Indifference/Hate/Evil/ Sadism (IHES) complex attitudes to be layered onto scapegoats. A "Super-human" connotation of 'Mystique' allows for the political, social, and physical treating of Black People as non-human--not through animalization or mechanization, as applied to ordinary Black People. Instead, depicting Blacks as having magic and mysticism (as opposed to merely basic human qualities and not unlike what Whites do to themselves) makes them a special kind of threat.

The largely successful intent of Brutes 'Super-Humanizing' Black People is for Europeans: (1) to have reduced perceptions of Blacks' experience of pain by willful ignorance. That this contributes to medical decisions involving the under-treatment of pain was clearly shown when Enslaved African Americans could not get medication for painful toothaches and were operated on without anesthesia; (2) to assume Blacks do not suffer from losses of killed family members; (3) to see Blacks as marginally less capable than Whites with respect to daily human activities so as to deny them "Life-Living" jobs; (4) to consider Black juveniles to be more "adult" than White juveniles when judging culpability and giving them adult prison sentences; and (5) to assume Blacks possess extra strength + less feelings, enabling them to endure violence more easily than other humans + enhanced agency that makes them more culpable than Whites for their actions so as to justify longer prison sentences for the same crime. Together, these 5 (among others) contribute to European concepts that "Black lives do not matter"—as seen in all social systems governing Black lives.

One example is Black school students who are bored with not being taught the Truth about anything as well as being given no clue as to who they are or where they came from pre-slavery. When students rebel against being machine-gunned with IHES complex information, they are then diagnosed as having ADHD and wrongly medicated, often with dosages only intended for adults. Another example is that attitudes from the above 5 + the envy of the "awe" that Black People generate + the fear attached to the Black Mystique combine to make it a duty for "Killer" Police to eliminate as many Black People as they think they can get away with. And Whites thus tolerate such police brutality against Blacks as justifiable. When "Called Out" on it, like spoiled brats, the police fail to do their adult duties of properly protecting Black People and thus "do nothing" so as to allow homicide rates to instantly rise. The Black Mystique prevents Whites from thinking Black People are just like them regarding human nature. To ensure this, they fail to get to know who Black People are. How can Black People keep coming back after all the evil done to them? One answer is to shift to enjoying and supporting each other, regardless of the terrible daily issues they face.

BATTERING THE "BLACK MYSTIQUE": Music in Black people is the most powerful catalyst of spiritual expression, whether it be in rhythm, dance, or singing. Throughout African history, starting with Primitive Africans, mysticism was associated with Shouts, Calls, Words, Clapping, Foot Stomping, and Body Movements. The reason, says Dona Richards (in Asante, African Culture p224), is those doing it at a "soul" level or at the level of "Being" are participating in the quintessential (purist) spiritual aspects of the Cosmos. Enslaved Africans reconstructed musical instruments originated and played in Africa—e.g. the banjo, the balafone (xylophone), the musical bow, flutes, the elephant tusk type horn, a kind of bagpipe, types of clarinets, (dududen), trumpets made of wood and ivory, gongs, rattles, castanets, the quill or panpipes, the sansa or thumb piano, and the drum. European enslavers, fearing such music may reflect some type of a Black Mystique capable of inciting rebellions and plots, prohibited African song, instruments (especially the drums), and languages. Upon borrowing Black People's concept of "Soul," Europeans considered it as Mystique because they could not conceive of what it was about. As typical of Europeans confusing everything of Black People, "Soul Music" was declared evil. Still, its mystique led them to embrace it. But their use of "Soul" was so loose (e.g. "Soul Mate" and "Soul Music") that it became devoid of any deep or specific meaning. Yet, by assuming the "Negro Spirituals" to be essentially religious, European slavers permitted them without realizing their power as

Black Mystique tools for conveying anti-European messages. Then came Work Songs, The Blues; post-slavery, Gospel Music; Ragtime and Jazz in early C20; the Big Band, 1930s; Doo Wop vocal groups in the 1950s; and, in the 1960s, "Soul Music"--an extension of Rhythm and Blues and the preceding Gospel Music. In my view, whereas ones Selfhood Soul is Immaterial, ones Astral "Double" has a "Soul" counterpart—the one Black People associate with "Soul Music."

Whites attributed Black People's "Soul Music" to Super-Humanization--the attribution of Supernatural, extrasensory, and magical (influencing or manipulating the Natural World through symbolic or ritualistic means) to these humans. From my observations and compared with other ethnic groups, music experienced in the Astral Body is more prominent in Black People; has a more profound effect; and stems from a love of life (historically present in Black People). Thus, Super-humanization characterizes others as *beyond* human and thus as nonhuman--but not as subhuman animals or objects. This involves depriving others of human character and attributes; prevents White people from having to compare themselves to Blacks; but represents a distinct, independent process from Infra-Humanization. An obvious display of it was common during slavery when White women believed Black People did not have pain or suffered any effects from their family members being sold away—either because they were Superhuman or Subhuman (implying Blacks not being full people and so do not have the feelings of Whites). This form of Supernatural thinking of failing to recognize Blacks as capable of having pain justified exhibiting no empathy for their sufferings as well as the withholding of aid when aid is needed. Despite the hellish lives Whites were subjecting Blacks to, Whites were "awed" by the Black Mystique Sippi Relationships—i.e. an ongoing sharing of the same Spiritual space (i.e. Compassion). These were indicators of a special bond with those of fellow sufferers—whether during the Middle Passage or on plantations or post-slavery.

To indicate the envy White males had for Black males concerning what they deemed to be 'superhuman' sexual prowess, almost invariable accounts related to Black male lynching involved White males cutting off that male's genitals and placing them in the lynched person's mouth. As a boy I was always impressed with how Europeans dealt with undeniably superior Black People—e.g. Joe Louis, Jesse Owens--as being "Super-Human". To make a distinction between struggling Black People and those Whites call Superhuman is a trick to prevent the struggling from believing they are capable of following in the footsteps of the "Superhuman." Still, the more cunning racists ensure Super-Blacks "stay-in-their-place" by "Dehumanization" (Waytz, *Social Psychological and Personality Science, 2015*). [This entire series is from Bailey, Stopping the Violence]

HISTORICAL BLACK AMERICAN VICTIMAZATION

Initially, the Black victims of European Brutes in Africa were the scrupulous and the just, the noble, humane, and devoted natures; the unselfish and the intelligent; and the compassionate. When Brutes fashion prolonged and devastating suffering, their methods redesign victims so as to be "*Inside-Out*"—meaning the victims also participate in their own destruction. As stated by Hitler, the broad mass of a nation will more easily fall victim to a big lie than to a small one—a point in evidence when certain African leaders did so. This practice was made infinitely easier when the Enslaved Africans, beaten into an "*Inside-Out,*" easily fell for a small lie as readily as for gigantic ones as a result of being in a Form-Body state—i.e. gullible for whatever evil they were fed; having allegiance to their oppressors; and whose "Awe" mindset permitted no sense of the ills they were in and the ills to come.

When boundaries are placed around what ought to flow freely from ones Real Self, this necessarily means *Anti-Spiritual Elements Rules* are applied. Such occurred with the enslavement of free Africans in

Africa so as to not only remove the Selfhood freedom of each but to establish an Un-noble Loyalty of bonding. Bonding occurs by one feeding--to any degree--ones Physical Human Nature Needs (PHNN) and/or ones Spiritual Human Nature Needs. The fact that the Satanists enslavers totally wiped out the Spiritual, Mental, and Physical aspects of each Enslaved, they provided just enough of the PHNN to maintain bare survival. Since this was all they had and there were no options, bonding with the captors occurred. This meant they had been stripped of their Power to get what they needed for PHNN reasons and had no Power characterizing their Self-Worth. So, in order to prevent losing the only thing they could hold onto in order to survive--i.e. what the captors gave them--meant clinging to the Un-noble Loyalty bond they had with their captors. This bonding caused them to accept brainwashing that turned their thinking "Inside-Out."

Satanists set-up USA plantations and formed the Federal Government in ways to stay in control "forever." Such continues to this day. The 'big picture' of Satanists--who control all institutions of peoples lives such as the government, the Media, the Educational system, the Religious leaders, the legal and criminal justice systems--is set up like the Military. It is orchestrated by "the Satanist President Group," called the Power Elite; run by Generals (Brute corporation 'Gentlemen'); and carried out by Troops (Brute Masses and those under the influence of the Brute Masses). Although followers of the Satanists and are unwilling to give up these unfair advantages in the interest of fairness, typically Non-Satanists Europeans are just as misdirected as Colored Peoples of the world and also they have never been exposed to the Spiritual Elements of African Tradition--an absence by deliberate Satanists' intentions. Yet, the humaneness of the 10% leads them to do as much as they know about their concept of the "Right" things to do. Black People would be much worse off without them.

Yet, they do not know how to help Black People and many do not want to risk repercussion from fellow Whites. The 50% do not really care about Black People's problems and do not find it in their best interest to help Black People rise. They may give help in that direction but if Black progress is being made, they will dismantle it.

SOURCE OF BLACK AMERICAN VICTIMIZATION: The keystone which fashioned a Sound Selfhood switch to an Enslaved Mindset done by Satanist Europeans came from cleverly manipulating and maneuvering what it took to convert certain African Kings from believing in the Spiritual One Universal High God over to the European Supernatural God. Next this required Enslaved Africans to switch from having Certainty in the African Spiritual God over to having Faith/Belief in the European Supernatural God. Preparation for this switch was the captors' daily employment of the vilest and most horrible acts known to human-kind. Their model was the Satan Europeans created in their own image out of their fantasy imaginations. Then then placed Satan outside of people's Selfhoods so that he could not be fought; gave him a superhuman, divine status (idolatry) that even, Europeans said, the Spiritual God could not abolish—making Satan impossible to deal with by being a legend. From that Supernatural model were made Satanism codes which reflected Europeans Fetter self-indulgences in evil propensities in defiance of the known will of the Spiritual God. The Legend part arose out of the ancient worship of demons and was crystallized in part by a revolt against European Christianity or the Church about C12.

This Satanism Legend Icon Image formed "manhood" animalistic standards of attitudes and powers to strive for and practices to carry out. Each of those centered around exactly the opposite of the Spiritual Elements or whatever Sages of any culture deems to be good. Examples are adversary, slander, traducer, the production of madness, generating obstacles, a tempter of humans away from righteousness. Thus, they were the "*Devil's Advocates*"--a name adopted by the Roman Catholic Church to apply to those appointed to bring forward all objections to a proposed canonization of a saint. Since Europeans are a fear-based people, Brutes generate fear so as to use it to their advantage. One was to create hideous creatures residing in some place called Hell for the sake of indulging in evil behavior.

By using 'tricks' like creating out of fantasy a Satan, a Hell, and a God to shape forces, they could fashion standards related to these and declare to perspective victims that to not conform to those standards meant they would burn forever in Hell, under the directions of Satan. For all of this to work required creating confusion and deception about everything proposed and actual victims accepted—done in order to take away victims' ability to see or hear their way through the now painted deceptive complications of life. In fact, Satan is defined in the European Bible as a deceiver by those themselves who were deceivers. All of this was so successful as to enable Brutes to exploit, abuse, and use victims to help power their world domination system, as in starting wars whereby victims would do the fighting. In reality, the contingent power of Satan comes from his victims who hand over their personal power to this unreal Being and thereby choose to remain in their Lower Selves. Key to that brainwashing was to get the Enslaved to stop "Knowing" God over to having "Faith/Belief" in God, based upon what the captors said about God. The Enslaved were not aware that the God to which the captors referred was made-up in their minds but was called Satan by them. Thus, the captors were able to control the minds of most Enslaved by means of what the captors wrote in making up their European bible. By having an Un-noble Loyalty bonding to the captors, afflicted Enslaved accepted this made-up information as "the Word of God." Yet, buried deep in their Souls the Enslaved knew all of this did not "ring true"--an element of doubt, of which they were unaware.

Also, they lacked a respected sense of Self-Worth and Self-Concept. A lack of Self-Worth means ones SHNN are absent and thus no sense of a Self-Identity, Self-Love, and Self-Meaning. They disrespected their Self-Concept, meaning they felt unimportant, invisible, unable to do anything right or to achieve anything they wanted and, in short, feel like a mistake for being born. These personal insecurities forced them to come up with rigid rules so as to not violate their bonding with the captors. This meant clinging to all the "Stay-in-your-place" things they were told--and around which each built a lifestyle. To "let go" of this clinging would be imaged as dropping into a bottomless pit. The bonding to and being afraid of the captors meant expressing their rage emotions on those the fellow Enslaved closest to them. By clinging to the belief of being right necessitated a position of being in opposition to anyone disagreeing, even a tiny bit. The need to release rage was so great that one would misinterpret a different way of agreeing as a disagreement so as to exhibit demeaning attack or a physical "show of force" by the means used by their captors--i.e. the GUN. The powering of this competitive spirit was from a need for Power injected into ones Self-Worth in order to improve ones Self-Concept and Self-Image--all intended to impart a sense of Self-Reliance, Self-Trust, Self-Faith, and Self-Confidence. Of course the success of all this requires disguises—each directed to giving the appearance of Omnipotence (Unlimited and universal power); Omnipresent (everywhere simultaneously), and Omniscient--total knowledge of everything, despite actually having "no clue" about anything except what comes out of an Indifference/ Hate/Evil/Sadism (IHES) complex. Next, Brutes start at the top with destroying true religions, for that is the greatest obstruction to their goals.

This necessitates disagreeing with science. By contrast, Ancient African religions were compatible with education, government, science, and daily living practices. Normally, most people are totally unaware of the true motives and drives that determine these Brutes' actions. Thus, the Receivers become adept at rationalization and self-deception to the point of falsely believing their conduct is guided by reason. Actually, many of their behaviors are governed by overriding antisocial passions (e.g. pride and cruelty)--frequently causing as much self-harm as harm against whom their actions are directed. Furthermore, what some consider as superstitions, myths, strange religions used by people to conduct their lives are often attuned to powerful nonrational forces in the psyche that demand expression. If those are frustrated, they are likely to seek outlets in other, possibly more dangerous forms. Such a pre-existing illogical and irrational tendencies ease the way for Brutes to generate confusion. Victims then use their imaginations--the gateway to the forces of Nature--to shape their behaviors and destinies. The images formed act as funnels that direct the flow of the forces of Nature, including ones emotions and passions, to condition ones spirit to behave as visualized--accomplish how to feel and react in a given situation; how one desires events to go; how to make things a self-fulfilling prophecy. (Amen, Metu Neter II:96).

ENSLAVED VICTIMIZATION: At the "Fishnet Moment"--when the fishnet was thrown over the free African in Africa to thereafter enslave him/her "forever". Inside the Delusional World the Enslaved had entered, they were no longer able to describe any essential thing within themselves--nothing about fear, rage, hate, love, pity, or scorn--but only gasp for the breath of life. Reversed substitutes for Instinct—in the form of "Awe" and "Fascination"--seemed to be coming from far away, bringing with it weird passionless forces having power over oneself and without one knowing the source of that power, meaning, or purpose. This was the beginning of "*Inside-Out*" Thinking which now characterizes the seed of Black-on-Black Violence. European colonization occurred when, by invading the New World which belonged to Amerindians, took control over everything involved, killed most of the animal food supply, and brought over millions of enslaved Africans. These practices clearly indicate the Supernatural "Air Castle" nature of Europeans was anti-Spiritual Elements ways of living—meaning Spiritual Elements forms of liveing are unknown to them and, in fact, are to be fought in order to show their ways are 'superior.' Most Europeans had no concept of morals and simply saw slavery in monetary terms. Despite the great resistance, insurrections, starvation, suicide, and revolts on the part of the Enslaved, Europeans saw no contradiction between their Christian religion and enslaving or killing people. They blamed Africans for not willing accepting being enslaved.

Yet, there were a tiny few who had a moral conscience inkling. To return to the example of the personal 'Damnation' on the mind of Captain John Newton, this slave ship captain declared himself a 'good person' and yet did not practice what he had been taught to be right. He justified this, partly because of his concept of the need to survive materially, and partly from hiding behind the prevalent practices of the times (Yenika-Agbaw, *J. Black Studies, 2006*). Similar to other C18 European Christians who bought and sold other human beings, he believed that somehow he would eventually pay for this crime against humanity. Despite this awareness, he remained a slaver, following "Air Castle" dogma, continuing to be tormented much of his life. Whereby Brutes put blame on everybody but themselves (e.g. "the Devil made me do it"), Newton said his Supernatural god guided his fate. He lied to himself to appease his conscience by being a "loose packer" (not having an excessive number of Enslaved stacked on top of each other during the Middle Passage) and a "less monstrous captain" being motivated solely by a genuine feeling of compassion for his fellow human beings.

Instead, this spoken gesture of the not overcrowding the ship, as was routine by other slavers, was a business decision. The real reason was that with more of the Enslaved tightly packed in the ship, he risked losing the majority of them to diseases. This, in turn, would affect the margin of profit gained per trip. Thus, better accommodations eventually translated into healthier slaves and more money in the West Indies. After he had become rich, to delude himself into having credibility, to ease his conscience, and to rectify the wrongs of his past, Newton eventually joined forces with young politicians to fight for the abolition of slavery. All Black People ought to note in particular that Newton exhibits the following three points of how the overwhelming majority of European males think and behave, regardless of the type of friendly façade they present. First, "Air Castle" people aspire to improve their material condition, historically doing whatever is necessary to accomplish this goal, even through the enslavement of others--justifying their callous and, at times, inhumane deeds as an economic necessity. In doing so, the rare ones with a conscience ignore the basic spiritual and humane guidelines under which they grew up. Second, they only consider fellow European lives to matter. For example, in the pamphlet he later wrote about his experience as a slaver (in favor of abolition), Newton "lamented the fact that too many seamen died as a result of the 'African trade.'"

Thus, even in his plea for the abolition of slave trade, he still placed a higher value on European lives, the perpetrators of the trade. It is only after he had made a case for their lives that he later described the condition of the Enslaves—a pattern shown my most European abolishioners. They have no idea what being Humane and Compassionate is by African Tradition standards. This White supremacist legacy continues to affect race relationships even in contemporary times. Third, as historically exhibited everywhere they have gone, Europeans have similarly deployed oppressive systems and institutions to maintain dominance over indigenous peoples. Such a system results in rampant conflict, competition, and alienation among and within groups in a colonial society as individuals struggle for moral, cultural, and physical survival (Irwin, *Race and Justice, 2012*). Crime among "the stripped to nothing survivors," as in the form of gangs, is one response to these oppressive conditions, and violence specifically results from alienation.

To illustrate with a vignette mentioned by Follett (*J Family History, 2003*) of the typical unspeakable cruelty of the Europeans, the following is presented. The Enslaved, slowing or rejecting the drill of Louisiana sugar production, suffered swift retribution if they tarried in the fields or mill floor, some of their bones were broken or they were at least whipped until bleeding was profuse. Sugar cultivation was carried on at an appalling sacrifice of life, the fatigue being so great that nothing but the severest application of the lash could stimulate the human frame to endure it. As part of the planters impelling their Enslaved to work at a ferocious pace and under inhumane conditions, the Enslaved would awaken long before dawn so as to toil late into the night before finally returning to their quarters. The exhausting discipline of the sugar world adversely affected fertility of Enslaved females as well as had devastating effects on their minds, moods (e.g. gloomy melancholy), and spirituality. Physically, on a plantation of 20 Enslaved, the death rate surpassed live births by such a degree that within two decades, the force withered to just 4 or 5.

The Left Brain skills of most of the Enslaved were removed because it was against the law to provide what it takes to develop them. In other words, educating the Enslaved by means of reading, writing, and counting were not allowed. There was nothing else to think about except how to endure. This is the same mindset that is present in many struggling Black Americans but yet it is the combined setting of oppression (as present during slavery) as well as the setting of having to take care of oneself today in a hostile world. As a result, those Black People who are most afflicted do things that are different--things I would not do. Even though I understand why, some things they do I do not like. Examples are the showing of disrespect to anyone who they do not accept and their demonstration of a lack of caring for themselves and for anyone else. Their emotional pain keeps them from showing manners--i.e. caring about the feelings of others.

Yet, in contrast to an amazing number of people, I do not blame them because they are victims of a viciously evil brainwashing that has their minds turned "Inside-Out"--meaning they do things that go against their own survival, self-protection, and self-preservation. For them, that seems like reality when actually it is the opposite of reality--a state called Delusions. By believing what is not real and not believing what is real means they fight anybody trying to help them rise out of their various forms of poverty (e.g. thinking, Character, work ethic, money matters, manners).

POST-SLAVERY COURSE OF BLACK VICTIMIZATION: When the Enslaved were freed in 1865 following the Civil War, they became victims of segregation and horrendous racist hate and terrorism. They were "ghettoized" and "terrorized" and lynched--given the most menial and low paying jobs, if any. Reconstruction collapsed under the terrorism enacted by White Southern police, government officials, vigilante mobs, and the Ku Klux Klan—all often one and the same. Although there were checkered rage display dissentions among the Enslaved that were and were not close to the slave owner, the courage to attack Whites had been beaten out of most of them. Still, those--mainly Field Slaves--who went through the "Struggling Tunnel" were the "Seed" Ancestors of the descendants accounting for today's Black-on-Black violence--and continuing the pattern of lacking the courage to attack White people; in non-assertiveness in going after what they are entitled to have; and in not desiring to seek a thriving life.

Regardless of their nature, Europeans Occult aspects, imparted into their Collective Unconscious by their primitive ancestors, have served as extremely significant Character Backgrounds which influenced all of their descendants education, communication, and Humanity dealings with those like and unlike them. One reason for this is that the Occult's basis is in mysteriousness conflicts with the Truth-Seeking spirit that characterizes the Natural World and to which only sound knowledge is acceptable. This spurs "Air Castle" people—whether as "Non-Rational" Logic, European Religion, or European Warrior roles to present their thoughts disguised as being Rationally Truthful, ignoring the fact that it makes no Natural World sense. Thus, they resort to preventing access to Knowledge (e.g. that of African Tradition); engage in confusion by using "big words" and theories that are facades when closely examined; and write ambiguous laws that are interpreted in favor of "Killer" Police.

Meanwhile, by continually being mired in war throughout their history means they necessarily stayed Physical and Supernatural realm oriented and that left no time for them to develop their intellect in Spiritual and Metaphysical Realms—which they disregard anyway. Yet, they are aware that Spiritual and Metaphysical aspects in which Black People specialize gives them a certain "Mystique" and accounting for intellectual brilliance (as ancient Greeks and Romans said: "Black skin imparts high intelligence). Whereas Black People have made almost all of the world's great benefits as well as laid the foundations onto which a few Europeans have made a few innovations, European males have made practically no beneficial contributions to Humankind. That has given them a profound Inferiority Complex which they attempt to overcome by stealing Black People's civilization and cultural achievement property and claimed them as their own creations. To deflect attention away from that Europeans have deliberately erased, destroyed, or reassigned Black People's records of achievement and have resorted to the typical bully claiming Black People are savages. Furthermore, they have always envied everything Black People have done as well as Black males "Manhood" having nothing to do with Kill/Take/Destroy/Dominate/Oppress, as European males specialize in.

CLASSIFICATION OF VICTIMIZED EX-SLAVES: *Classification* is a mental tool for putting "Things" derived from the same "Seed" with "family resemblances" or like-kind "Things" representing "brothers from different mothers" into arrangements or combinations that promote their better understanding and that assist with their prioritizing into a hierarchy of significance. Each entity is a "*Class*".

The shared characteristics of the Classes within a given Classification follow a *Schema*. A Schema (C16, form) is an organized composition of associated and harmonious like-kind ingredients into a transcendental imaginative shape, figure, or form for use as a generalized outline, design, or diagram. What arose out of the Classes of Black People representing Ex-Slaves was a *Theme* (C13, something put down).

A Theme is a *maintained unifying central or dominating idea (or thesis),* motif, field, principle melody--*arising from a common origin or from "what it does" or from "how it appears" or from its shared properties*--with an inherent direction—and fashioned for discourse, discussion, sermon, pleasure, intimidation, or a life's course. For example, the Theme of ones Jazz is the basic melody upon which variation is developed. A Theme of Ex-Slaves was to survive and endure on the Negative side (fig. 22) of the *Thinker's Scale* (a positive and negative ruler separated by a Zero). All of their efforts were directed to lessening the problems on the Negative where they resided. There were no thoughts like the "*American Dream*" which, for Euro-Americans, is a set of ideals concerning freedom. Such freedom includes the opportunity for prosperity and success, and an upward social mobility for the family and children, achieved through hard work in a society with few barriers. The American Dream is rooted in the July 4, 1776 *Declaration of Independence's proclamation that "all men are created equal" with the right to "Life, Liberty and the pursuit of Happiness"*—which had no meaning for Black Americans since they were excluded.

The Theme of the Enslaved evolving "vines of lifestyles" from the "Seed" called the "bottom of Despair" is what I term "*Black American Customs*" (Chapter VI). Customs are the uniform doing of the same think, feel, say, and acts in the same circumstances for a definite reason. These reasons were triggered by all that happened during slavery and how, in infinite unique and group ways, the Enslaved chose to react to them. Because those reasons faded following slavery, but their Customs persisted, this pattern constitutes *Slave Survivals* (maintaining customs for forgotten reasons). Although these worked satisfactorily for the Enslaved, those same Customs became self-defeating in the marketplace following slavery. Although it serves Europeans' racist purposes to stereotype all Black People into a homogenous group, there were unimaginable African uniquenesses—combined with a certain Sameness—in Enslaved Africans brought to the Americas. Additional differences were highly cultivated by Europeans in order to fashion them into dissention and conflicts among all Black People in the Americas as a "divide and conquer" device. Thus, Black American Customs include Black People who are contrary opposites as well as complementary equals.

Black American Customs increased in complexity and took a turn for the worse when Black People, after the 1960s Civil Rights Movements, started Habits that modelled Europeans. Such was for numerous reasons—being impressed with the advertised façade that White people enjoyed the "Good Life"; desiring to have some recognition as human being by becoming Black Puppets; clammering for any bit of Power, like those used by European males with the GUN and killings; and to maintain the "Evil Savior Syndrome" type of bonding in hopes of getting "hand-outs" to survive day-to-day. So let us review the "Classes of Vines" that formed out of the "the stable pit of Extreme Despair" during slavery to form the core of the Black American Customs following slavery:

Type I who had "come to peace with Doom" were somehow spurred to step back into an awareness of their self-rage so as to engage in Self-Destruction. Some took the form of becoming their own executioner by taking revenge on themselves. Some were like the brat who, after having something significant taken away, retaliated by throwing all he/she has into the fire. This equivalent today is exhibited by those who spend all they have for unneeded luxuries.

Type II: Some stepped sideways so is to grab anything to which to cling—getting deeply involved with the Europeans Supernatural Christianity; the slave owners children; being informers to Whites on the secrets of the Enslaved—or to avoid doing anything they were told to do if they could get away with it without being whipped. These Type II equivalents practiced today include clinging to drugs, people, causes—or to avoid clinging to such things as personal responsibility or doing organized thinking or handling significant problems as soon as they come up. Prominent in Type II is the afflicted believing they need to go to White people--those oriented to Satanists beliefs--for help--the very people whose pattern has been to enslave them and keep them down in every possible way.

Type III's desperation was a state of profound misery and weakness so far away from their Real Selves as for others to mistake their drowning for waving. Such was displayed as outward resignation masking an inwardly confirmed desperation from an admission the enemy had prevailed as well as from them not seeing any way out or around or through their bounded impasse. Besides being punctuated by a refusal to look for "outs" in the present, they had no intention to look backward into their past so as to recall something prideful to which they could clutch and to which they might cling. Because there was no possibility of it occurring, there was no looking forward to a better life with hope for use as a tow-rope. It takes little effort to see today's descendant of Type III's Despair who are automatically closed to engaging in any self or race improving endeavours.

Type IV showed that Extreme Despair can be a potent cause of war against others—an urge more powerful than greed. They, similar to the way a disease state may cause an inflammation of the patients' "*Nerves,*" evolved into a "Dark Cloud" warring mentality. Unfortunately, a continuation of this mindset within the context of today's Black American Customs—dominated by which by non-rational thinking methods--to cause rebellious minds to foolishly want to go to war against Europeans. It is foolish because "War" is what Europeans do best and almost exclusively. In light of the fact that traditionally Black People in general are a peaceful people and peace dominated Ancient Africa for tens of thousands of years, by the large numbers of "spirited" Enslaved who "fought back" implies the depth of destruction to their African Tradition Selfhood.

Type V: For the Enslaved who went into "fearless" and "Don't Care" mindsets, restrictions on their self-protection and self-preservation were removed. The Effects were "wild," blind, and reckless thoughts and actions—totally unconcerned about the consequences of their actions—willing to risk any and everything, even if it resulted in death. This pattern, especially of "Don't Care" is far, far to prevalent today—and seems to be rapidly getting worse.

Type VI, by its intense inwardness, Despair gave shocking ease to the minds of most who manifested this in daily life as "Make Do"—that persists to this day in a large percentage of struggling Black People. In addition, the thought of the unattainable of any good "forever" led for a few to being independent, like a loner rebel.

Type VII featured all Enslaved having innumerable episodes for Grieving, Mourning, Sorrow, Sadness for family, friends, and Motherland losses. Some stepped down into thoughts of suicide. In Brazil, "*Banzo*" was the term for those who died of melancholy (e.g. fears and grief without a cause--anxiety, hopeless, and a bad mood from a vague sense of want or loss) or even killed themselves. To this day, Extreme Despair gives courage to the weak, as in removing fear so as for the afflicted to resolve to die with accelerated speed or by immediate suicide—both too much in evidence.

Type VIII Some stepped up into the absence of Fear—a step requiring getting past the apathetic "giving up" on life in order to enter the realm of having "no fear" of dying. There might be an intense sense of freedom, perhaps even playfulness about ordinary matters when Despair produces fundamental clearness from being acutely conscious of the hopelessness of ones situation. An example of this attitude is reflected by today's "Baddest Dudes of the Streets." However, their "Inside-Out" thinking has caused them to fight among each other instead of those who continue to impose inhumanity (Anderson E. *The Code of the Streets, p208*).

Type IX made the Volitional Choice—i.e. a Self-Declaration a (decision or choice made after deliberation)--to do something or not do it, regardless of whatever happens as a result in being detrimental. In other words, it is thinking instituted by itself, for its Self's purposes in order to devise inner meanings from which ones Selfhood can work out of them to evolve creations. Meanwhile, they "escape" their troubles by engaging in self-destructive play, having no care beyond today. This same pattern is responsible for a tremendous amount of Chronic Juggling (Bailey, Mentoring Minds) of today. This stems from the Black American Custom of believing it is best to do things the way they have always been done and disregarding that nothing in the situation is the same.

Type X is Despair which causes stoney silence and shuts out the world—a pattern typical of those nursing and protecting and defending their "Raw Nerve" (Bailey, Post-Traumatic Distress Syndrome). That practice leads one to be so self-absorbed that the outside no longer matters.

Discussion: All of these types come out of a Background of Despair—and that gives a 'cookie cutter' membership form of socialization to those in the "Crowd". As mentioned, all of these types are represented in today's world, particularly by those engaging in violence. A prominent feature of the Black American Customs Group Mindset is the orientation to "Make Do" in an aggressive manner. Features of all of these types are what join as a "salad mix" to make up Black American Customs—a 'mix' reflecting a "bottom-line" tendency to operate out of the obsessive-compulsive, emotionally oriented Old Mammalian/Omnibus Brain--a 'mix' that is in turmoil, as in manifesting chronic Juggling in daily living. Chronic Juggling derives from no planning or proper priority in handling necessary business as well as from having no starting or ending points for handling significant problems in life. Most ignore their biggest problems, hoping they will resolve favorably. All share in common the effects of European racism and oppression and demeaning stereotypes and rejection and every type of barrier to realizing the American Dream. Most are hyperemotional (which is used against them by Europeans) and anxious. Some are over-weight and/or on drugs. A common attitude of the struggling is like saying: "I don't have anything now and I can't have any less if I do nothing." The idea is to enjoy the moment whenever it arises on very rare occasions. Its about getting through the day.

EARLY C20 VICTIMIZED BLACK PEOPLE: At the end of C19 many Ex-Slaves started migrating "up North," especially from 1890 to 1910. Yet, in the Northern cities were no sanctuaries because they often perpetuated the systems and attitudes that kept African Americans classified as inferior citizens and thus Northern Whites believed African-Americans migrants were criminal by nature. This served as a justification for why these cities did not offer the assistance the new migrants need. Then White scientists manipulated data around arrests and imprisonment to equate Blackness with criminality so as to be a warning signal about African Americans moving to northern cities from the South. As C20 dawned in a rapidly industrializing, urbanizing, and demographically shifting America, Blackness was refashioned through crime statistics. ... Northern Black crime statistics and migration trends were woven together into a cautionary tale about the exceptional threat Black people posed to modern society. In the Windy City, in the City of Brotherly Love, and in the nation's Capital of Commerce this tale was told, infused with symbolic references to American civilization, to American modernity, and to the fictive promised land of unending opportunity for all who, regardless of race or class or nationality, sought their fortunes.

Black and some White social scientists tried fighting off these characterizations but still equating Blacks to criminals prevailed—to the extent of some distinguished African-American thinkers subtly adopting it. In the 1930s a quote from Frederick Douglass's grandson Haley Douglass was: "the failure of large cities to provide adequate bathing and recreational facilities has placed upon us the burden of protecting our property from roving trespassers whose ignorance or lack of self-respect permits them uninvited to impose upon residents who bought their homes for the benefit of their own families and friends." Haley was developing a beachfront oasis, of sorts, in coastal Maryland for elite African Americans seeking refuge from what they considered the criminal element of Black folks. Black families who stayed behind in the South during that time period could have been identified as internally displaced peoples.

MID-C20 VICTIMIZED BLACK PEOPLE: In following the oppressors' lead, Black gangs devised rigid rules for making others comply--a power acquisition display showing as a competitive act of "I must win at all costs." So, anyone who disagrees with me must be against God and that means I must defend it all costs. That concept gets to be a transferable pattern pertaining to anyone who disagrees with me for any reason. This adds a "Manhood" aspect--a display of masculinity which requires demeaning others unlike them in appearance, philosophy, status, or gender preference--or attacking others who are trying to show they have more power. In essence, the "Violence" is a battle over feeling one lacks power and is thus a personal "Failure." Put another way, it is a battle over Self-Worth. During this time, a neighborhood hustler named "Fast Willie" and asked him why he "robbed and beat up black people who are brothers." Willie's response: "We go where the business is and where the man ain't looking" (Brentin Mock@brentinmock). In the 1970s the term "Black-on-Black" phenomenon—also called 'oppressed youth-on-oppressed youth' crime, or 'the disenfranchised-on-disenfranchised' crime?"--came into focus—at the time of the "White Flight" in cities like Chicago. This was a reflections of Euro-American power players applied increasingly rigid rules for how Black were to live (e.g. not spanking children)--Rules which pushed Black People further and further away from personal freedom and their Real Self. These "Laws" are Rules--Commands--Prohibitions--Injunctions--Commandments--Regulations which are to be obeyed as if God said them, since after all, they are given by those who tell us the word of God.

LATE C20 VICTIMIZED BLACK PEOPLE: The early 1980s period is when Black neighborhoods started being simultaneously over-policed and under-policed in a manner allowing the criminal justice system to punish Black criminal suspects more harshly when their victims are White as opposed to when victims are Black. Meanwhile, these same neighborhoods have been victimized by White landlords and real-estate developers. This is when the term "black-on-black crime" really began sticking to the public consciousness. The term went to contribute to the mass Black Americans incarceration because it helped normalize the notion that the ways and cultures of urban Black youth are responsible for crime, while minimizing the structural problems that America created that led to the crime in the first place. This was because right-wingers seized upon the worst part of the myth to justify the "war on drugs" and other tough-on-crime policies that proliferated through the 1990s.

Another Fast Willie named Bill Clinton used such sentiments as cover to co-sign on policies that drove incarceration rates of African Americans through the roof. Rapper Tupac Shakur said in 1992: "The same crime element that white people are scared of, black people are scared of. ... So, while waiting for legislation to pass, and everything, we next door to the killer. We next door to him 'cause we up in the projects with 80 niggas in a building. ... Just 'cause we're black, we get along with the killers or something? We get along with the rapists 'cause we black and we from the same hood? What is that? We need protection, too."

The term: "Black-on-Black Violence" derives from the Effects and Consequences of residential segregation and concentrated poverty—frustrations caused by high unemployment, poor academic training, and inadequate housing"--leading to killings and not because of hating each other because of dark skin. However, the term "Black-on-Black" violence is a simplistic and emotionally charged definition of urban violence that can be problematic when used by political commentators, politicians, and police executives. violence driven by conflicts within and among gangs, drug-selling crews and other criminally active groups generate the bulk of urban homicide problems," and that such groups generally constitute very small percentages of a city's population. Some say the correct name of this overall problem is "Violence within systematically segregated communities," rather than "Black-on-black violence".

POLICE AND THE BLACK COMMUNITY

Victims are also called *Prey* (originally, spoils or booty taken in war or by violence); Quarry (a hunting term related to a chase); and Ravin (great violence in the method of seizure and a Maafa of cruelty and voracity in the destroying). The result psychological and philosophical trauma impresses in victims self-destructiveness, driven by being powerless—real or assumed. These traumas have been so intense, so devastating, so continuous, and of such a long duration as for them to have become Conditioned Responses to even the whisper of whatever triggers them to react in a defensive or offensive manner. The reaction of these Black victims varies, depending upon how they deal with the Effects and what Consequences those Effects have. To elaborate, Bad Conditioned Reflexes in those who have "Clouds" formed over their "Soul Sunshine" are subdivided into: Group I, self-imposed; Group II, victim displays; and/or Group III, assuming the role of Brute Imitator perpetrators. Group II Victims of such terrorism and racism typically fail to stand up for their rights. The resulting Conditions mean it is essential to the occurrence of something else of a non-Spiritual Elements nature—e.g. anger, feeling cold toward others, hurting—when certain requirements are met. Normally, the Supernatural Fantasy aspect of children recedes by 6 to 9 years but they persist in those lacking the "5Ss".

"KILLER" POLICE IN AFRICAN AMERICAN SLAVERY: The origin of USA police dates to African American slavery. The European captors were constantly aware that their safety depended upon both the ignorance of the Enslaved. Thus, during slavery, it was tacitly assumed every White man was ipso facto (by the fact itself) a member of the police (as can be seen today). Primarily to discourage insurrections, there was constant surveillance of Slave activities (Fry, Night Rider) + practices for detecting and finding runaway Slaves. The Enslaved could not leave the plantation without a written paper giving his/her name, identifying marks, and the specific route. A lack of any of these was presumptive evidence that the Enslaved was running away or otherwise up to no good. For these and other reasons, the captors set up mounted patrols all over the South designed to monitor movement of the Enslaved—and with varying degrees of success, mostly unsuccessful. The slave owners themselves or professional "Slave catchers" were the forerunners of the police. Black people called them "paterollers," "patterollers," "patter-roses," "patter-rolls", "paddy rollers," or "paddle rollers (because of their use of paddles to whip the Enslaved); or "night riders," "night-watchers," and "Night Doctors." The paterollers, paid a fixed fee for their services, would also go in Enslaved quarters at night to see if any Enslaved was not present. Since it was often tied into the militia system, theoretically all Whites did rotating service in the patrol. However, the affluent usually paid others a small fee to take their place. In many places this left the dumb and sadistic overseers as the backbone of patrolling. Elsewhere, the county of a given state hired a regular patrol from among the poor Whites or small farmers, thus giving those young men a special taste for abusing Black people—and which, until well into C20, remained lively in Southern lynch mobs.

These ill-disciplined parties of young men steeped in an inferiority complex, typically passing the bottle freely while on their rounds, may well have been the nucleus for the rise of the policing Ku Klux Klan in the post-bellum times. Nevertheless, none of the patrol groups were efficient—partly due to slovenliness; partly due to the South being too sparsely settled and too masked with woods and swamps; and partly due to its roads and paths being too tortuous and vague for anything but a regiment to be successful. Still, penalties were harsh when an Enslaved had bad luck. Thus, few Slaves could muster the courage to take the risks involved (Furnas, Goodbye to Uncle Tom, p133). They were well aware that if caught they would be used to "make an example" out of them—i.e. Whites saying: "we will show the world we are not going to tolerate this by making punishment so hard as to deter other Blacks from doing the same thing." Although Indifference/Hate/Evil/Sadism was the theme mindsets and practices of the European captors, the antebellum police system of the "New World" South was primarily formed and designed to only control the enslaved. A prominent slavery approach involved in the control and domination of Enslaved African American Slaves—and continued in full force up to the 1960s--was the use of highly trained so-called "Negro dogs"—bloodhounds, foxhounds, bulldogs, Scotch staghounds, or curs (mongrels)—to track runaway Slaves.

Professional "Slave catchers" provided their own "Negro dogs" and often allowed the dogs to give a fugitive a severe mauling. This was a common practice in all Slave states—defended and justified in the USA courts. White Patterollers and their dogs--in the spirit of "killing an animal" for sport (like fox hunting)--rode through swamps in search of fugitives. When an Enslaved was caught, he was whipped on the spot and taken back to the plantation where the slave owner punished him again. The generic training of attack "Negro dogs" went like this. The dogs were locked up and "never allowed to see a negro except while training to catch him." Dogs were given the scent of a Black person's shoe or article of clothing and taught to follow the scent of the selected Slaves sent out as trainees. When the dogs treed the Enslaved, the dogs were given meat as a reward. "Afterwards they learn to follow any particular negro by scent." Besides the Patterollers' readiness "with the zest of sport," their canine "Negro hunters" were fierce, vicious, and fearsome beasts. If the dogs were not constrained at the end of the chase, they would tear a man to pieces (Franklin, Runaway Slaves, p160). Once discovered, the Enslaved was bound, beaten, and bloodied (Brady, The Black Badge).

Needless to say, "police" misconduct was particularly rampant during African American slavery. Of course, the "second nature" lying hypocrisy of European slavers' publicly conveyed the idea of "virtue" as referring to the 'management of negroes' and an anonymous author with a rare conscience elaborated by saying: 'our first obligation is undoubtedly to provide [slaves] with suitable food and clothing'. Similarly, the majority of Southern writers dealt with the problem of abolitionism by proposing rules for the 'proper maintenance' and care of the Enslaved. This obligation was coupled with a paternalistic attitude toward Blacks. Since slavery was the time when the American police system arose, this concept and practice pertaining to Black People represented the standard. However, over the course of time such 'virtue'—as flawed and as ignored as it was--became diluted and polluted—going further and further away from its original meaning of the exercise of doing good for all concerned. At no time did it come into sight of meeting the criteria of police Integrity and typically police action as applied to Black People was in a hellish world. Wherever that level was on the negative scale, the reduction of the police concept of 'virtue' during and following slavery even stretched below what peripheral European racist would class as merely SEEMS to be okay—thereby deepening and broadening the scope of routine evilness/sadism.

Plantations had ongoing difficulties with the Enslaved. In one story, Uncle Isom, a very strong runaway, caught and killed the leading hound sent to chase him down and then beat the rest of the dogs. However, upon being overpowered by the White men, the dogs were allowed to bite off the victim's body parts. When returned to the plantation, Uncle Isom was given 300 lashes (Botkin, Lay My Burden Down). Since there were so many Enslaved runaways, the inland police worked with river captains and slave owners to prevent fugitives from successfully escaping. City patrols employed a variety of tactics, including posting runaway Slave advertisements and checking the passes of people hanging about the levee. Captains posted watches on gangways and instructed stewards, engineers, and mates to carefully check for free papers. There was so much problems generated by the Enslaved that more often than not the police gave up their pursuit on the grounds they lacked sufficient resources. After 1847, freedom of the individual was presumed (except the Enslaved) and an urgent public necessity or interest must be demonstrated to justify government action.

In an 1847 speech, Frederick Douglass noted that Black Americans "have been a bird for the hunter's gun, but a bird of iron feathers, unable to fly to freedom." The title gestured to the institutional racisms that hemmed in American Blacks and left them vulnerable to White predations, the "hunter's gun." [Ref: Buchanan, *JUrban History, 2004*; Butler *J. Black Studies 2011*].

"KILLER" POLICE POST-SLAVERY: Although the "night watchers" were replaced following slavery, their essence and practices were continued by the Ku Klux Klan (who existed in slavery but under different names). Attack dogs continued to contribute to maintaining apathy and frustration. Ongoing and intensified Euro-American terrorism gave not relief to the chronic anger generated in Black people. Prevalent on a daily basis were Europeans Lynching Black People for "no reason". Yet, their justifications was for maintaining segregated society in the setting of a form of leisure (Mowatt, *American Behavioral Scientist, 2012*). As well documented, police were great participants in these sadistic activities by handing over prisoners to lynch mobs or even participating in them. Thus, there was no point in reporting misconduct to the police because their tape-recorded-like message was that they tried but had to give up their pursuit because of lacking sufficient funds. Yet, when the guilty parties were obvious, the routine practice was to do nothing. In fact, there is no record of any legal action against those doing lynching until 1988. Meanwhile, the spectacle nature of Black lynching is what has tied them the White population to leisure, especially since the lynching of other "races" did not attract the crowds that a Black "murderer" could. Needless to say, this indicates that *race* is a powerful word because of the ways a social construction rests itself upon all the ingredients contributing to its conceptual foundation. For example, 'Race" determines and undermines interactions between people, leading to loose groupings of people as well as causing tensions between different racial groups.

The brutality of lynching conjures and extends the essence of the institution of slavery when it is spoken by European racists today, even when inside the context of their leisure. The excuse for lynching Black Americans was always done to curb the "Black savage"—an Icon Image--and to protect the sanctity of White womanhood while also being questionably justified extensions of the law. As this entire scenario represents such an Icon Image of untold magnitude, it thereby carries such a great 'payload' that to merely utter "lynching" in general, or the 'N-word' in particular, instantaneously un-leases a cascade of emotionally conditioned responses like varying images, actions, and beliefs related to "Black". Apart from what these scenarios did to the minds of the Enslaved, Free Negroes, and Ex-Slaves, the prejudgments of the police force being about and arranged to deal only with any escaped or problematic Slaves laid what Plato called "Memory Traces".

In other words, the think, feel, express, acting, and reacting the Police did to the Enslaved thereafter made all Black People into a faceless keystone Enemy Icon Image in the Euro-American memory--liken to making an imprint into soft wax—a permanent imprint now called an *Engram*. Such a 'second nature' Engram mindset continues to manifest Black and Brown people as 'the enemy' to the present. Starting then, to European policemen the Black male, in particular—by being so envied--has continued to represent an ambiguous figure. His Icon Image arouses the utmost caution and is considered dangerous (Anderson, The Police, p456). Nevertheless, the *14th Amendment* to the USA Constitution (1868) defined some rights of the freed Slaves: no state may deprive any person of life, liberty, or property without *Due Process of Law* (e.g. ones right to be present, heard, and proof given before the tribunal which pronounces judgement upon the question of life, liberty, or property and it granted equal protection of the laws to individuals and corporations, and the 'police power' of the individual states to make laws for the protection of public safety, health, and morals.

"KILLER" POLICE—EARLY 20th CENTURY: The "Dark Ages" of the police extended to 1900, with departments under the direction of politicians, with ill-equipped and poorly paid policemen, and with widespread corruption and brutality, particularly as part of 'crime prevention's' Deterrence and arrest aspects. Despite gaming houses being unlawful, there were few prosecutions, mainly because the industry was protected largely by police corruption: bookmakers regularly gave 'payoffs' to keep the police quiet. The widespread tendency to give violent police wide latitude has deep cultural and historical roots. Furthermore, whether due to juries' reluctance to indict or convict police officers or bias and missteps in investigations, criminal charges and harsh administrative sanctions are rare. Such is made acceptable to the public by *Dysphemisms*—substituting a non-exciting linguistic devices (e.g. terms or descriptions) for an evil Trigger Event or Trigger Person(s) (e.g. "Killer Police). For example, 'deadly force'—which the public accepts for 'criminals because it underlines the essential normality and legality of police—minimizes the unnecessary violence for the gravity of what "Killer" Police did. Whereby "obstruction of justice" is the emphemism used for European rich criminals, "violently resisting arrest" is applied to poor Black and Brown people for the same action. It even applies to them, during and after slavery, being a mere gatherings of individuals and having nothing to do with being threatening groups, for that threatened Whites. Similar dysphemisms are applied to "Killer" Police for such pejorative terms as murder and brutality. This professional image is successfully conveyed to the public absence information on personal problems or features of police organizations that dispose some police officers toward violence.

If aggressors have any morals at all, and Satanists do not, their moral disengagement involves eight so-ciocognitive mechanisms which function at three levels of social processing (Wood). The first level allows inhumane acts (e.g., violence) to be reinterpreted. Sociocognitive mechanisms at this level include: (1) *moral justification* (behavior is in a worthy cause—that it can further police gang status); (2) *euphemistic language* (a sanitizing description of harm—e.g. violence may be described as "police business"), and (3) *advantageous comparisons* where individual behavior is favorably compared with others' worse behavior (e.g. our group only assaults, others kill). The second level enables (4) the *displacement of responsibility* onto authority figures (in-dividual behavior stems from authority figures' directives, so personal responsibility is negated; (5) *diffusion of responsibility* (responsibility for the harm done is shared by several perpetrators, thus this absolves individuals from blame), and (6) *distorting the consequences* of harm (ignoring, minimizing, or disbelieving that any harm has been done). The third level distorts the way the victim is viewed and denies them victim status via (7) *dehumanization* processes (the victim is considered to be subhuman and devoid of accepted human qualities); and victim (8) *blaming* (they got what they deserved) or Projection.

Meanwhile, from the police attack dogs usage during slavery and continuing in full force, an entire sce-nario regarding attack dogs on Blacks set up a special "dog" atmosphere. Consequences out of that included significant psychic traumas were fashioned in most minds of the Enslaved. Chances are that this trauma de-signed, in a few Black people, mental transformations from peaceful people into a hateful mindset—a mindset culturally transmitted into practically all of their Black American descendants—and added to by direct experi-ence or from vicarious empathy. Could that transmission display today as hateful re-enactments (e.g. on dogs used as symbols)? From my boyhood days onward, I have seen many Black people terribly afraid of the most gentle of dogs. But with irritable dogs, that fear often causes those dogs to go on the attack. I have treated some of those Black People for vicious dog bites and seen how they are adversely affected! Because of this and police brutality, among others, hostile emotions escalated in Negroes after World War II, and particularly with the Black soldiers returning home from battling enemies abroad.

"KILLER" POLICE—MID-20th CENTURY: By the 1960s the struggling Black communities of the USA had a bottomless reservoir of deep hostility toward the police and it has only worsened since then. White police came to work every day knowing that they could do no wrong. Whatever bad they did, their bosses would cover it up. The result was carnage that terrorized black communities and politicized black police. Riots returned to prominence and by 1967 there were riots in over 50 USA cities from abusive or discrimi-natory police actions targeting Black People. This was met with strong community military type anticrime efforts whereby Black People had to prove they were innocent (and police corruption, like planting evidence on suspects, essentially prevented this) while it was the reverse for White people. Deterrence retaliation had been started in 1966. In keeping with European males 'little god' illusion, Los Angeles police expressed their omnipresent by introducing helicopter patrol so as to watch "everything and then radio to waiting officers as to which suspects to arrest. For all concerned, ongoing Police brutality exposes contradictions between ideals and practice, fueling resistance and unrest racial profiling and hyper-aggressive policing as well as weakening police authority in the eyes of the Black community, thereby reducing their willingness to comply with police directives or help police.

Allegations of physical abuse from police have always been prominent features of Black People's experiences—e.g. officers shoving, punching, kicking, and using mace especially against Black youths, most considering it a routine aspect of neighborhood life. Then there is the more indirect technique of victimization of transporting "suspects" to unfamiliar neighborhoods and abandoning them there--a practice inconvenience, but more importantly also potentially life threatening for the "suspects." In addition to all of this, Black People observe a wide range of corrupt police practices, like the planting of drugs or weapons on innocent persons. Obviously, these practices place them at risk of being convicted of crimes they did not commit. Such planting of evidence is most likely to occur, when officers lacked evidence to justify a lawful arrest. Racially biased policing is perhaps most evident in racial profiling in vehicle and pedestrian stops; in comparing police responsiveness; and in the delivery of police services in different kinds of neighborhoods. The Black community has no concept of the police as a service – to serve and protect. Instead, they view police as "getting ready to tromp you or to whoop on you the minute that they encounter you." Typically, judges on the bench sold verdicts like whores selling themselves in the park--suspect traffic was a fix and a shake down. Almost the only people who went to jail were Black and the poor. Landlords fund slums that brought death as sure as the gas oven, went legally untouched. Nothing has changed!

BLACK POLICE: The first African American police officers in the United States were known to be "free men of color," who served as members of the New Orleans city guard in 1803. These men held their positions as a result of their status in the city's unique multiracial society. They sought to establish their connection to the city's White citizenry and distance themselves from the subservient reality of being Black in the South. The Black community did not find them to be of consistent benefit for they were typically used as a "colonial guard" to contain crime within Black communities, smooth police–community tensions, infiltrate Black organizations, and feed information about Black life to White police by acting as "*investigative guides to Black behavior* and the Black community. In other words, most Black policeman served as the guardian of White society, and most important, a controller of the Black population. One Black policeman said he and other policemen of any race have a subconscious bias in how quickly to pull the trigger, but not when it comes to deciding whether to shoot a target. "When I would be in certain parts of the city and see young black males, it would run through my mind, 'What are they up to? Are they dealing?' That's because of what we've been bombarded with for so many years from so many different directions, including the media."

The remedy, he proposes, is training sessions redeveloped to purposely disprove stereotypes against race, gender, age, and other factors. As a result, the training sessions help officers learn to focus more on other cues — body language, what someone is holding — instead of race. In late 1960s Chicago, radical Black police officers opposed to any police brutality created the Afro-American Patrolmen's League (AAPL). Chicago's Black population of one million people was confined to ten neighborhoods, barred them from jobs and unions, consigned them to inferior schools, and excluded them from meaningful positions within city politics. On July 13, 1968, their first president, Edward "Buzz" Palmer, presented their statement of purpose: We are going to elevate the Black policeman in the Black community to the same image status enjoyed by the white policeman in the white community—that is, a protector of the citizenry, not a brutal oppressor. . . . We will no longer permit ourselves to be relegated to the role of brutal pawns in a chess game affecting the communities we serve. "We see our role as protectors of this community and that is the role we intend to fulfill" (Satter *J. Urban History, 2015*). Since USA culture's problematic tendency has always been to cast Black men as primitives with a unique and alluring access to violence and pleasure, Black Power embraced this and was about much more. It embraced pride in Black forms of cultural expression; a sense of responsibility for the well-being of other Black people; a drive to uncover Black history; community control of institutions; some form of Black separatism; and an understanding of Black oppression within the United States as analogous to the experience of colonized people internationally.

As Charles Hamilton and Stokely Carmichael explained, Black Power encouraged organizing to "replace" institutions—such as schools and police departments—that failed African Americans, or "to make them responsive." Despite the lingering association of "radical" with a willingness to use violence, arguably the most radical aspect of Black Power was its drive to analyze institutional racism and violence—i.e. its unveiling of the "White power structure." They challenged a violent White police force that supported White gang activity and ignored or colluded with Black gang activity, while treating Black police as they would any other Black person—on a scale ranging from casual disrespect to lethal violence. In short, the AAPL opposed overt violence against the Black community, whether wielded by White or Black police, or by White or Black gangs, *and* the institutional violence of a White power structure that exploited Blacks economically, marginalized them politically, and then abandoned them to predations by police and gangs alike. The entire police department was entirely controlled by the city administration, the White power structure." Throughout the entire force, police admitted that they owed their promotions to a ward committeeman and thus the job of the police was to keep Blacks in line—a "line" having nothing to do with the law.

Rather, the "limits" that police enforced against Black people were "economical, social, and political"--aimed at limiting living space and general mobility. This explained why Black Chicagoans often experienced police brutality despite breaking no laws—the "line" being enforced was invisible. The relationship between seemingly random hostility that Blacks drew from police, associated with being arrested in outrageous proportions cause Whites and some Blacks to think Blacks are criminals. Thus, part of Black liberation involved destroying "the fear in Black minds" that Black people really were inherently criminal. The police department was racist, less in its written policies than in its informal procedures. Policy change would not touch its deepest problem—its role as an enforcer of a racist political system "the police department was the greatest gang recruiting tool in Chicago because they treated everybody as if they were gang-bangers.

Criminals had free rein because Black crime victims refused to cooperate with police, who abused them, and because they feared retaliation from gangs if they did—retaliation from which they could expect no police protection The AAPL opposed an early "stop and frisk" law on the grounds that "it will only be used to harass minorities." With respect to the prisons, they are over-crowded wit overwhelming numbers of Colored Prisoners doing are free labor and without any intent to do meaningful Rehabilitation is not the primary purpose of these institutions—which is supposedly their purpose. Since "Black lives do not matter," in keeping with Whites tendency towards the genocide of Black people, it is more expedient to eliminate a criminal than to send him through the courts. Police violence was deemed to be a "cloak for power and greed," aiming to keep the Black and White working class equally in line so as to keep the power where it is . . . with the money. The Black Panthers' suppression was proof that Whites were not willing to "share wealth or power with Black Americans." An additional warning to Black gangs was that if they would start anything like the Black Panther Party--fighting for the human rights of Black People, European police would wipe them out!

Althought Black Chicagoans died from police brutality, of equal significance was disability and death from poor medical services, lead paint, decaying buildings, fires, and drugs. Given these multiple dangers, "destroying" gangs would not end the violence. Police planted guns in a Black person's apartment--then raid it--and then murder him in his bed. At the same time there was more covert, structural forms of violence such as housing, loan, and credit exploitation that could destroy Black lives and trigger Black rage. Even daily life—a walk to a school or library, the purchase of a car or a home, the running of a business or putting in time at a job—was not a simple matter for Black Americans for each of these carried potential or actual destructions. The distortions of racism meant that any of these essential acts could enmesh them in structures of control that were directly or indirectly violent.

TODAY'S POLICE vs. BLACK COMMUNITY: Throughout the Animal Kingdom the male realm about Physical Power, initially arising out of an emotional base. Fight type Emotions are both neuro-chemical and spawners of phenomenology (what occurs immediately in conscious experience, without implications). In infants and young children, who have little capacity to modulate or inhibit emotions by means of cognitive processes, their Emotions are involuntary in that an effective stimulus elicits them automatically, without deliberation and conscious choice. Over time, Emotions can expand to have a voluntary component. This means that in their expression above little children's level they can be modified and controlled via cognition and action. Furthermore, willful regulation of expression by intellect may result in regulation of emotion experiences. This results from life-shaping and life-changing events molding the development of habits of thought (meaning ones unique interpretations from monitored feedback from interactions with the outside world--either because of the meaning brought to it or from the meaning derived from it); from ones subculture and the culture at large; and from ones genetically determined sensitivities and patterns of response. These Emotions are "para-rational" in the sense that they serve adaptive functions and make sense in terms of ones perception of the situation. When people remain stuck in operating out of their Lower (animalistic) Self, Physical (in Physique, by accoutrements, like the GUN, and/or via a supporting Network, Power is about domination. That domination carries the sense of a slave owner—"all for me, none for you".

Humans operating at this level do so out of a False Self that has unleased restraints on their Brute Brains—which, in turn, causes their Imaginations to assess their reality as existing inside an "Air Castle" Supernatural realm. This realm is about the nonrational—i.e. active Emotions that tend to generate action and cognition on the one hand but, on the other hand, extreme fear may cause behavioral freezing and mental rigidity. These Emotions are deemed to be appropriate if the reasons for what is expressed are adequate to suit ones personal needs and/or those of ones peers, regardless of non-Brute people's reasons against it. Another type of Emotions are nonrational in the sense of existing in the brain at the neurochemical level and in consciousness in an undifferentiated state. When nonrational Emotions express themselves they come into their consciousness without them having considered all of the relevant reasons for them. What derives out of this is a "para-rationality" elaborated on by their emotions. These nonrational Emotions in Brutes are pre-disposing to destructive aggressions—whether from attack or defense—and they may activated by a variety of cues—as in perceiving a situation or person as threatening. Each pattern is a closely coordinated series of events, obtained in relatively constant form from a wide range of brain sites.

As mentioned, Killer police have activated the "Hate-Circuits" of their brain in which the subcortical activity particularly involves two distinct structures, the putamen and insula. The Putamen, implicated in the perception of Ccontempt and Disgust, may also be part of the motor system that is mobilised to take action, since it contains nerve cells that are active in phases preparatory to making a move. The 'Hate-Circuit' also includes structures in the cortex--in the sub-cortex--has components important in generating aggressive behavior, and translating this into action through motor planning, as if the brain becomes mobilised to take some action. It also involves a part of the frontal cortex that has been considered critical in predicting the actions of others, probably an important feature when one is confronted by a hated person. This 'Hate-Circuit' is distinct from those related to emotions such as fear, threat and danger — although it shares a part of the brain associated with aggression.

Whereas Hate is an all consuming passion, Aggression contains a disposition, powered by a drive that energizes attack (among other behaviors). Viewing a hated face results in increased activity in the medial frontal gyrus, right putamen, bilaterally in premotor cortex, in the frontal pole and bilaterally in the medial insula. The proximate cause may be a direct stare, a slight frown, striking with the hand or fist, seizing, biting, invasion of personal space (within 8 inches or 20 cm), an approach perceived as threatening, a rapid moving away (which evokes chasing and attack). Any of these Stimuli may cause a variety of reactions—e.g. a rivalry for possession, intrusion, frustration, fear, insecurity, low self-esteem, or an impulse to control. These reactions are done with respect to what originates from the ingredients of Sensation out of ones memory; from something going on inside ones Selfhood; from something entering a human's senses from the outside world; from ones interpretations of the monitored feedback one gets from outside influences; by public opinion and its influences; or a combination of these, particularly in times of tension.

The amount of stimulus required to elicit this response for attack or threat may be raised or lowered over periods as long as 20 minutes and thereafter one remains likely to attack for some time and, I suspect, especially those with a history of being overpoweringly dominant in envied areas and thereby made into scapegoats. Attack behaviors result from stimulating the lateral and anterior regions of the hypothalamus, and defensive threat from some areas near the center of the hypothalamus and from the central gray region of the mesencephalon (mid-brain or area of the Brute Brain). An attack spurred by a Psychological Conditioned Reflex is much more likely when one knows one has the chance to get away with it by being hidden or by Network support. Either the scapegoat is attacked directly or some aspect (e.g. a made-up fantasy demeaning trait) is attacked instead—a phenomenon called *Redirection*.

"KILLER" POLICE/COMMUNITY COMPETITION:Competition's division, disunion, and essence are 'every man/us for himself/us and being against him/her/them.' Considering all of the Unconscious Mindset Conditioning to which European males have been subjected throughout their history—e.g. Fantasy, "Non-Rational" thinking, anti-Dark and Black concepts, all aspects of the Indifference/Hate/Evil/Sadism Complex manifestations, the racial benefits encompassed in the law of competition (e.g. invade for gain), and Deception which, as an act, embraces *Camouflage*; *Mimicry* (false Supernatural self-identity); *Hiding*; and *Depression* (in the sense of "pressed down" to prevent detection)—it is no wonder that Competition is a fundamental "Manhood" component. This mindset + being able to have repeated tests of "Manhood" + the excitement between the safe and the adventure associated with the dangerous nature of police work suggests that cadets, from the moment of their professional police training, have a competitive zeal. "*Zeal*" is an emblazed inclination toward vigorous action--doing something distinctive (e.g. apprehending 'villians'), showing signs of originality, and exhibiting Patriotism (a lively sense of collective responsibility). Patriotism means the 'father protector of 'non-fathers'" security and safety--it features loyalty to the team's welfare so as to satisfy a need for recognition—and its point is to belong to ones own in-group or society by never appearing weak. Although the need for security and safety are at the core of every 'non-father's' character, both are at odds with what is outside of fellow patriots. And that is the egg from which conflicts and wars are hatched but with the ever present fears of losing, injury, or death. To deal with these fears is the anchor for what is needed to be a successful Warrior. This is powered by the fact that one European "Manhood" feature of bravery is keeping ones poise in dangerous situations.

As a boy, I became acquainted with this concept when my Mother would sometimes recite Rudyard Kipling's poem: "If you can keep your head when all about you are losing theirs and blaming it on you . . . you'll be a Man, my son!" Thus, a method for Managing Emotions is through Scripting, Framing, and Othering (Vaccaro, *Social Psychology Quarterly, 2011*). *Scripting* is the creation, embodiment (fashion a patterned form), and continuous rehearsal of a 'game plan' so as to reduce battling out of emotions. Basic to this is figuring out what the 'enemy' is trying to do—and might do—and do what best—and do it where. Aids to Scripting include all the 'enemy' stereotypes given in the media and by word of mouth, coupled with reviewing pertinent information on videos, YouTube, MySpace, Facebook, etc. These generate engramming on their brains so that what to do is scripted into "bodily memory". *Framing* ('prepare, make ready by constructing') shapes how one not only thinks about a situation but also how one feels. Whereas students help minimized fear of examinations by framing them as "quizzes," policemen might think of the day's potential dangers as: "just another day on the job"; "that's the way of my business"; "I may get a chance to prove my "Manhood' and bond with the team." "*Oppressive Othering*" is making the enemy subhuman; enhancing this by associating Black males with women (hence the media's emphasis on displaying Black males in dresses and glorifying transvestites); and subtly conveying the message used by the Ku Klux Klan in depicting themselves as virtuous manly heroes who disciplinc savage Black rapists.

The 'big picture' of the competitive encounter is the emotional micropolitics called "Intimidation" ('impress profoundly') to convey that one is both in control of ones own emotions and can control the emotions of and frighten the enemy. Its rule include: never letting them know your are scared of them by means of having 'the GUN' (whatever it takes to kill) and a support Network 'back-up' that is instantly available; always look them 'dead in the eye'; never back down; never do anything to make it look like you are nervous and just pretend and act like you are confident the whole time. All of this imparts a superiority complex intended to reduce the aggressors' fears; bolster their self-confidence and pride; and justify defining themselves as Supernaturally powerful physically and mentally ("Implicit Othering") so as to present the Icon Image of ones virtual self as so "invincible" that "nothing can hurt me."

POLICE/BLACK COMMUNITY HISTORY: Black Community-policing relationships are invariably problematic. The seed is Europeans' hatred towards Blacks; their oppression of Blacks; police are extensions of White Supremacy; the police live outside the neighborhood; the police are out of control; and residents view police efforts as intrusive (Macdonald, *Urban Affairs Review, 2006*). Blacks are in an ongoing state of rage about these factors and there is no Trust between either side. A background for this is that the "Normal Variant" mindset of Europeans arising out of Europeans' Primitive Occult beginnings is like the minds of "Killer" Police living through its Indifference/Hate/Evil/Sadism (IHES) Complex Background color spectrum. Layered onto this is the fact that USA democracy is maintained by every form of violence, being responsible only to the conscience of its leaders who are oriented to greed, revenge, retaliation, and aggression. The combined nature of those contributions to the Background of the Supernatural's Contingent Being's spectrum and its associated transience of passions as well as seeing Black People as 'monsters' are what colors the lens of how "Killer" police view Black People. That view urges them to display by coming down hard on all of them and killing some. In other words, all inherent violent emotions and thoughts within that spectrum produce in hypersensitized "Killer" police a falseness in their impressions of external things—generating what some call "*Pathetic Fallacies*." Such violence only comes from the Self-Unknown and such violent experiences can cause victims to forget who they are—and although humanity standard Truths is something everyone is exposed to and probably always knew, the violent perceive them without noticing. Thus, when upon making a "realistic decision," it is a resolve to do something bad. *Their violent order is disorder; a great disorder is an order—these two things are 'One.'* Much of being a policeman involves *Hypocrisy*—a term meaning one acting out of the part of a character in a play—the masking over of ones Real Self or ones False Self which is in a different realm while playing a part for ones cult. This has to be done with calculation for external trappings—often using spiritual talk to hide ones base motives. Fostering a sense of trust in the police is difficult work, especially in disadvantaged minority communities that historically have had strained relationships with the police.

Adjusting levels of social capital (e.g. collective community protests surrounding incidents of police brutality) in communities may not change Black Americans' levels of trust in the police and some may even further undermine trust in the police. The more ignorant the authority the more dogmatic—especially in things unknowable which they penalize. Nothing is so firmly believed as an unexamined assumption. When they go off into "nowhere" they misread this as being "now here". Truly ignorant people are ignorant of their ignorance. Part of knowledge is to be ignorant of what is not worth knowing. Community social capital–enhancing policies should focus on a range of social, civic, and political organizations. Clearly, social capital is increased through well-publicized community meetings and petition drives to reform the police; but the abject effect of such efforts may be an initial reduction in trust in the police. An alternative argument could be made for community support of policing agencies in the throws of scandal or controversy. There are endless variety of what police ought to do--increase minority trust; create greater transparency; change police practices relating to racially charged issues (e.g. racial profiling); focus on activities that improve the community quality of life; increase social-bonding; and so forth. But the leaders do not want to address the heart of the issue—i.e. the racist mindsets of the police who are operating under "Air Castle" cult rules.

"KILLER" POLICE/BLACK COMMUNITY MISTRUST: Spiritual Trust is based upon those involved having a philosophy of life (POL) orientation to things of Worth (i.e. things of Spiritual Beauty, like Truth begets Trust). *Truth* is living by a standard imposed by ones Divine Consciousness and Courage is having the Will (what has been decided upon) to carry it out. *Trust* concerns itself with the proper relationship between social stability and behaviors with respect to their proper functioning of what is involved—their purposes—and the correct interaction with, and use of those things involved. The first of three things to assess is ones Selfhood. Real Self people are ever striving to strive toward their Highest (divinity) Self that springs out of living within and evolving out of the Spiritual Elements. That process ensures Selfhood Coherence (its internal components are consistent with one another) enduring, balanced, connectedness, harmonious, and unchanging elements/pattern. This 'Form-Function' relationship is characterized by the word *Context* means weaving ("text") together ("con") -- as when the texture of a woven fabric, consisting of multi-colored threads, are so intertwined as to create a single, coherent fabric held together on its own. Three things are going on here. First, each thread is in its proper relation to the other threads, even though each thread has a different color. In other words, there is a place for each and each is in its proper place. Second, each thread has significance in relation to the whole organization and the organizational integrity would be flawed without it. Though each thread is independent, all the threads function interdependently to produce a single work product. Third, the whole synthesized organization – consisting of more than the sum of its parts and at a higher level of manifestation than any thread -- has an influence on the character of each thread. This is what harmonized unity is about. Put another way, the resultant product is understood as a web of independent items working with an interdependence of each that is essential to the whole. That pattern has an inherent power and vibrates at a unique rate to produce certain effects and consequences.

Second is the relationship existing between oneself and the other members of the Cosmic Organism to which one belongs is of a "ME/WE" mission in life to "Lift them while Climbing." Third is the function one performs for the system or unit to which it belongs—whether by sharing ones Talent or by competence in ones occupation. The closer one gets to perfecting the web of inter-relationships and interdependence of these three, the closer one is the Truth. "*To know the Truth you must live it*," said Ancient Africans.—and Truth does not elicit any excitement or pleasure. Yet, living by Trust and Truth, with an appreciation for the good it can do, will in time lead to the generation of a deep contentment from following: "I know that's right!" practices. So the assessment of Trust is by the good seen in how one reacts to things and events, for only that has a Spiritual Elements Quality.

People living out of their False Self—whether within the Natural Cosmos or Supernatural realms--change the weaving of their Real Self threads and that gives a different product.

Those of the Supernatural cult are Lower (animal) Self achievers and thus have no morals that correspond with the Spiritual Elements of the Natural Cosmos. The Euro-American captors/Enslaved African relationships shattered the Ma'at Moral (Spiritual Elements in action) of African Tradition and the Enslaved most affected were brainwashed into "Inside-Out" thinking (exemplified by the enraged burning down their own communities). Thus, the morals and values of African Tradition, "Killer" Police, and struggling Black Americans are each completely incompatible and thus there is no basis for establishing harmonious relationships—not with issues of living itself or how to live; economics, spirituality, philosophy, psychology, socially. This means no common ground for integration in thinking, beliefs, emotions, actions, social interest. "Killer" police mindsets of Indifference/Hate/Evil/Sadism (IHES) Complex—both European and their "Oreo" puppets-- means they are automatically inclined not to believe those unlike them, even though those 'enemies' never deceived them. Furthermore, their sense of importance comes from being feared, not from being respected. Thus, those who mistrust most are to be trusted least and that demands defense, starting with not trusting anything False Self people do. [Ref: Macdonald, *Urban Affairs Review, 2006]*

MANAGING "KILLER" POLICE/BLACK PEOPLE RELATIONSHIPS: A major problem of Black People is misunderstanding that hostile Europeans are not merely bad exhibitions of rearing in African Tradition but rather they are in a 'different world' operating by a set of rules of their own making that ensure they always "Win." Instead of having the "ME/WE" orientation of African Tradition, their orientation is exclusively about "ME"—meaning they are incapable of seeing things from Black People's point of view. The same applies to "Oreo" Black policemen who are ever striving to 'win browny points' from Whites—treat Black People the way Brute Europeans do so as to win their favor. Thus it does not matter to "Killer" police that Black People in struggling neighborhoods have chronic emotional problems generated by Euro-Americans since slavery but instead only see how "those people" react to them. The hypersensitivity of both parties is extremely likely to result in conflicts, usually resulting in death. The key to knowing how to react is knowing the details of the enemy's mindset and knowing how to defensively react to it. This requires working out a plan before hand that becomes 'second nature' by the time the situation for its usage arrives.

Black males in particular must assume all police they encounter—White or Black or Hispanic—are their potential killers and thus do nothing to irritate them, for they are looking for even the tiniest of an excuse to kill. Since the situations in which the police are faced will each be different, it is fundamental to know the theme of their ethnic society's "Manhood" philosophical development so as to have clues about the faced officer's mindset. Most people do not have to be told to not 'agitate' those who are mentally deranged because of the uncertainty about what type of thing will trigger them into violence. The same applies to "Killer" police who, instead of being psychiatrically deranged, are 'Philosophically Deranged'—i.e. "Normal Variant" mindsets in a Supernatural "Air Castle" realm. Here, reason does not exist and their hostile emotions can be triggered by the slightest of things having the appearance of a threat to their safety or to their "Manhood." The expression: "Discretion is the better part of valor" (Shakespeare, 1596) is to be thoroughly understood. "*Discretion*" ('choice') means 'look before you leap' (do nothing suddenly or without considering wise advice)--examine carefully your options before using bravery in exhibiting "Manhood" in a dangerous situation where a choice must be made in haste, but slowly.

This is "*Prudence*" ('that which preserves by conformity to the rules of reason, truth, and decency at all times and in all circumstances) puts courage into context. Prudence deals with the "Thinker's Scale". On the positive side there is the understanding of the practical knowledge of things to be sought. On the negative scale it is mainly about self-restraint: the "Thou shalt nots". That involves the practical knowledge of things to stop doing—i.e. whatever gets you into and keeps you in trouble. By prudence "Never" going to the opposite extremes of the scale means it is the keystone of all of ones virtues. There is a time and place for everything and prudence and discretion are knowing answers to the Seven Questions of Inquiry--who, which, what, when, where, why, and how—promptly applied to 'right' situations. It is from properly answering these questions that give one a lead to explore more paths into the subject and perhaps arrive at the "bull's eye" of the subject.

The thing to do when one does not know what to do is to 'stay put'—i.e. not fight or flee—or, where the road bends abruptly, take short steps--like bowing so as not to break. In either instance, remain silent while following orders. Prevention of trouble is the offspring of being wise and caution is seldom wrong in dangerous situations—both key to Chance favoring ones survival. The wise keep themselves today for tomorrow—and this may happen by acting dumb. To be stubborn in dealing with police is like putting your thumb between the two back teeth of an alligator. Give the appearance of not hearing the insults or threats. Practical aspects of dealing with police include: Address them courteously; make sure not to challenge them for that is a way to keep from stirring up emotional reaction; keep your hands on the steering wheel or always in plane sight and ask permission to make any changes in your pose—and always move slowly so as to defuse confrontation; Look nice, dress nice; maintain a demeanor that not assert what you want: not "I know I have rights" which sets off confrontation. [Ref: Mcara, *Criminal Justice, 2005*]

Remedies to attempt to improve police/Black community relationships include: (1) simulations and training to be more discerning regarding race and suspects so as to help break down stereotypes because their is subconscious prejudice, known as implicit bias, no matter how well-meaning the policman might be. (2) Focus on building ties between local police departments and their communities--called the *Contact Theory*—i.e. positive interactions with stereotyped groups can reduce explicit and implicit biases. A cop who interacts with Black residents in his town might realize that many of his previous prejudices, implicit or not, were not warranted. A problem is that local police departments are under constant pressure to make enough arrests to obtain federal grants, which are often tied in part to, for instance, the number of drug arrests within a city. Tickets issued by police officers make up a huge source of money for local governments, which might encourage police to issue as many tickets as possible to bring in more revenue. Given those incentives, police are encouraged to go after "low-hanging fruit" often found in minority communities that lack political and financial power. This magnifies the effects of implicit bias. Revenue incentive is a root of the problem — and the issue of racial disparities will not go away until that is resolved.

BLACK VICTIMS OF POLICE AND GANGS

The rage generated by what European males have done to them has to be expressed and they use fellow Blacks as scapegoats. Besides gang members being victims of society, victims of gangs are of three types—a gang's enemy; the gang's community; and the gangs new members. Even if gang members are motivated to retaliate against their transgressor(s), this may not always be possible, and so they may direct their aggression at a substitute victim. This is known as *displaced aggression*—aggression targeting either an innocent victim, or a victim who has done little to provoke the levels of aggression meted on them. Gang members are more inclined than other individuals to engage in displaced aggression. For example, on the streets, gangs are likely to come into contact/conflict with authority figures, especially if those authority figures use gang suppression tactics. The effects of the initial provocation may also accelerate and amplify levels of displaced aggression.

Also, if the original Disrespect in front of others then it will cause an explosion of an aggressive response to the displacement target. This may be because the individual feels humiliated and is motivated to "save face" with important others. Because gangs are street-oriented groups their altercations are likely to occur in front of others (e.g. in-group and outgroup gang members). Thus, street codes which communicate a gangster identity must be adhered to. Consequently, individual gang members may be motivated to use extreme violence to protect and/or enhance their status and reputation with their own and other gangs. Thus, group process effects may intensify the levels of aggression that gang members direct at others.

NEW GANG MEMBERS ARE VICTIMS: Almost all new members come out of a setting of knowing what is "Right" from African Tradition, at least to some extent. Thus, they have to make themselves acceptable to the gang's Drama. This requires *"Moral Disengagement"*--the process by which people justify emotionally, morally, and physically, behavior they or others would normally consider reprehensible. This approach is what "Killer" police do (Chapter VII) and with overlap in needing to dehumanize the enemy but from a different perspective regarding reasons for Causes and Effects related to their violent behaviors. There is a relationship between the collective identity of the gang (including group cohesiveness), threats to that identity, and an increase in gang-related violence. All of this requires the internalized informal social controls brought in by each new member must now be modified or discarded in order to conform to the new gang rules related to gang-related violence.

Such moral disengagement and refashioning by new members enables the gang to plan and execute certain actions that are outside new members normal self-sanctioning and self-controlling behaviors. The way such a change is made is by the gang leaders providing *presentations that do not clash with any new member's held Belief or threaten any of those candidates: "For me or my well-being--or against me" System of Values.* Such justification to themselves of the morality of their actions enables them to step into doing reprehensible conduct. Some new members by-pass this process because of social bonds with established members or because they are desperately alone. In other words, when one is having difficulty with a certain type of behavior one is to commit or is committing, one can mold the behavior seen as being inhumane into behavior seen either as humane or "inhumane but necessary".

As elaborated on in Chapter VII), Moral Disengagement, say experts, has 8 strategies applied to entice new members are: (a) *moral justification*—"the end justifies the means"; (b) "*Euphemistic Labeling*" (i.e. using the language which shapes ones thought patterns, on which one bases certain of ones actions)—i.e. re-labelling immoral and/or criminal acts by sanitizing the language to make it fit into the "Street" Code (e.g. a "little white lie"; (c) *advantageous comparison*—comparing ones own behavior to far worse acts committed by others, for example, a stabbing compared to genocide; (d) *diffusion of responsibility*—"where everyone is responsible, no one is really responsible"; (e) *displacement of responsibility*—responsibility is attributed to the person giving orders, not the person carrying out the deed; (f) *distortion of consequences*—disregarding or minimizing the harm done; (g) *blaming the victim*—the victim deserves the consequences because of their past behavior; (h) *dehumanization*—the victims are "no longer viewed as persons with feelings, hopes and concerns but as sub-human objects".

BLACK GANGS CAUSING BLACK VICTIMS: The terrorism of European males has been so great as to instill in Black People not to retaliate. Since retaliation against justice officials risks arrest, gang members may displace their aggression onto innocent others such as passers-by or even family members such as siblings. Recall "Fast Willie" was asked (Chapter VIII) why he "robbed and beat up black people who are brothers." Willie's response: We go where the business is and where the man ain't looking. Can you see me going up to Deerfield, Black as I am, trying to stick up? The man would be on me so fast I couldn't get a chewing gum wrapper. Out here the man is too busy whooping them Panthers and giving tickets to mess with me. Any way, he don't care if niggers get ripped off. But you can bet he's watching his 'thang' back in his own 'hood.' They commit crimes against other African Americans because that is who they live around him—and that is what police let them him get away with because the police do not care (Brentin Mock@brentinmock).

BLACK GANGS vs. BLACK GANGS--MUTUAL VICTIMS: Black gangs warring against each other do not really hate each other and thus those with enough "star" power (e.g. famous boxers or football players) can bring about a truce and even get opposing gangs to work together. Those scapegoats who do not go to war with their Black attackers have a tolerance for their hostile actions and that "Tolerating Fellow Attackers" interaction creates its own culture of providing mutually beneficial avenues of "Escapes" for the periodic build up of bubbling hostile emotions. An example is a couple fighting each other but joining to attack anyone trying to be peacemakers—also a European male trait.

GANG MEMBERS AS POVERTY VICTIMS OF SOCIETY: Over 800 million people –one-fifth of the world's population – have become a global underclass. They are illiterate, impoverished, malnourished and have sky-rocketing mortality rates. This underclass reflects the extremes of reality for a large proportion of people displaced by development and the unjust distribution of resources. Although the population of the USA is 5% of the world's population, the USA accounts for 25% of those in prisons—the overwhelming majority being Black and Brown people. Urban areas in Third World countries grew from 4% in 1920 to 41% in 1980. Despite the media and "authorities" say these phenomena are natural occurrences, they are human-made—and with no concept of humanity. For example, 30% of the world's grain is fed to livestock when just 2% of that grain would eliminate starvation. Equally, an investment of $40 million a day would establish clean water supplies across the world when over $1.4 billion a day is spent on weapons research and arms, exceeding $500 billion a year. Primitive Europeans were the source of this process by their "Scarcity" reactions. As a result, their greed, passed on to their today's descendants, have generated poverty for victims of their Kill/Take/Destroy/Dominate/Oppress practices.

In those victims, irrespective of race, class or ethnic background, poverty results in increased rates of violence, criminality and physical and mental illness--poverty of all kinds–Selfhood, social, interpersonal and intrapersonal. Brutes fashion the nature of socio-economic oppression and use the results of poverty (such as violence and self-destructive behaviors) to justify racism. In the USA, based 1970s Census Bureau data, every 1% rise in unemployment is accompanied by a 2% increase in mortality rate, a 5–6% increase in homicides, a 5% increase in imprisonment, a 3–4% increase in first admissions to mental hospitals, a 5% increase in infant mortality and a 2% rise in cardiovascular deaths. Such socio-economic oppression increases Brutes hatred of Black People and that causes increased arrests, longer jailing sentences for the same crimes committed by Whites, and over-representations in prisons (Moore). Black males have accounted for 46.6% of all male prisoners in the U.S. in the 1980s. Blacks accounted for 50–75% of the prison population in 18 states, over 50% of persons who have been executed and 58% of those awaiting execution on death row.

Poverty is associated with an increase in death by all causes. Experience has taught me not to believe anything Europeans say, including their statistics but the following indicates a general idea of the hardshipls of struggling Black People. From 1900 to 1970, Black males had the highest rate of homicide (77.1 deaths per 100 000 vs. 8.7 per 100 000 for White males, being their leading cause of death in males aged 15–44 and Black women, aged 15–35, a rate six times that for Whites. Black male and female suicides dramatically increased in the last 30 years, with a peak between the ages of 25 and 44. The abuse of alcohol (33%) of all Black adults and 50% of Black youth is the primary or secondary cause of 10% of USA deaths--of 50% of their murders, of 50% of accident-related deaths, and of 3 times more alcohol-related illnesses compared with Whites. The repercussions of alcoholism on a community are suggested by the fact that every alcoholic is a serious menace to at least five to seven persons around him. With regard to the relationship between mental illness and socioeconomic status, living in poverty has a two-fold increased risk of an episode of at least one psychiatric disorder as defined by the Diagnostic Interview Schedule using the *Diagnostic Statistical Manual III*—which is unreliable for Black People because diagnostic criteria differs for Black and White people. The effects of poverty did not differ by sex, age, race or history of psychiatric disorder.

Similarly, somatization, depression and anxiety are significantly greater in the unemployed. These health effects of poverty are aggravated by racism, which affects both the employed and unemployed. Furthermore, when Blacks are employed, regardless of the site of the workplace, most of them suffer special distress as a result of threatened, perceived, and actual racism—fearing to speak out about meaningful issues, for that would jeapordize their jobs. Gang members primarily derive from the most distressed and disadvantaged neighborhoods and communities—those characterised by structural neglect, poverty, poor housing and severely circumscribed labor market opportunities.

PUBLIC PERCEPTION OF BLACK GANGS

Throughout American history Black People's most important public contact has been with policemen—the personification of Euro-American authority in the Black community. Policemen stand for civic order and "White Supremacy" (Fig. 10). The rule is that even minor transgressions of caste etiquette are punished harshly. Courts back policemen no matter how far they proceed outside normal police activities. Their word is taken against Black People without regard for formal legal rules of evidence, even when there are facts supporting Black People. Slavery's overt racist pattern has been extremely slow in changing—because Black disfranchisement has ensured practically all Southern public officials be White—because of the conspiracy to not give Negroes even low level authority positions—and because it was not until after World War II did many Southern towns start hiring Negro policemen. This subsequently led to the undergoing of camouflaged transformations into tempered (e.g. racist emails), masked, and concealed versions of what always was.

In its place has been the substitution of deceptive devices to maintain the status quo. For example, it is almost invariable for police, after shooting an unarmed Black person, to say in almost "tape-recordings" defense presentations: "the Black man grabbed for my gun and I feared for my life". By other officers overlooking this Evilness meant it acquired a pattern of consistency, demanding that good policemen compromise. The result was and remains that Evil and Sadism wins by default and Evil and Sadism flourish when the Good serves it. To deal with the resultant inhumanity at the hands of the police, starting in slavery and continuing to now, the Black Community has learned to "know not what they know and see not what they see." Despite the overt consistent forms of police racist brutality, interestingly, available literature is relative silent about the subject of "Killer" Police. Dominant representations in the news media, says Hirschfield (Theoretical Criminology, 2010), depict crime as an individual moral failing, criminals as irredeemably dangerous, victims as innocent, and police as honest and heroic public servants. Accordingly, attributions of evil and blame in homicide accounts promote sympathy for victims and a harsh response to offenders. But the lines between victim and offender can be blurry. Who, for example, is the victim and who, the wrongdoer, when a police officer kills a criminal suspect in the line of duty?

Because Europeans are a Fear-based people and because they set up the police to act in their favor and because European society ensures their favorable results by fashioning ambiguous laws enabling them to be consistently interpreted in their favor and because Black and Brown people have a European religious basis for being considered "the devil" they made up, even under highly dubious circumstances the most favorable outcome goes in Europeans favor. The result psychological and philosophical trauma impresses in victims self-destructiveness, driven by being powerless—real or assumed. It the process of being "Awed" by all of these vicious happening, they are—bewilder as much as anyone else who is harmed as well as all observers. In this state, victims are blamed by the oppressors to be the source of their own injustice and for the victims acting the ways they have been forced to act. As a result, oppressors or their followers show "*righteous indignation*" (i.e. an emotional reaction for the victim doing the bad things the oppressor does). This is *Wilfull Ignorance*"—"I don't know anything about this because I do not want to know"—and why should I?—It won't help me any." Such is to be expected from people who believe they are separate from all other people but are able to join those who do the oppressing of others. The blending of traditional and Western belief systems bestowing honor on violent men can be seen in so many ways that many youths use violence to establish their reputation and campaign for respect.

STEREOTYPES: Since it is vital to "White Superiority" to maintain segregation (to prevent the races from liking each other) and lose control over the "White Crowd" who think and act the way they are told, stereotyping Blacks is also foundational. It does not matter to racists and the willfully ignorant to think that all Blacks are alike and all Blacks do the same thing is a stupid stereotype. Stupid is not necessarily about intellectual dumbness but rather, as used here, it spotlights dumbness derived from having eyes but unable or willfully refusing to see for certain self-interest reasons. Except for a common philosophy of life, sameness of the people was never present in Africa, nor has it ever been present in Black Americans.

PUBLIC RESPONSE: Europeans are, since their primitive times, a fear-based people. Today, fuel is continually thrown on the flame of rear by the media that over-reports in frequency, intensity, duration, and the selected worse of incidents of crime committed by Black suspects. By contrast, those very same crimes by Whites tend to go unreported and unprosecuted. In one 2010 study, White respondents overestimated the proportion of crime committed by Blacks by 20 to 30 percent—and that serves as a spur for Whites to call the police to "handle" a Black resident in unfounded anticipation of violence. Yet, 83% of Whites are killed by other Whites. People accept violence if it is perpetuatred by legitimate authority. They also regard violence against certain kinds of people as inherently legitimate, no matter who commits it. One reason is that willfully ignorant Whites do not bother to learn anything about Black People—meaning they are unable to empathize with people they know nothing about, except for gross adverse images conveyed by friends and the media. Besides, Whites would get ostracized by other Whites if they were to step outside of their own White experiences so as to objectively listen to the truth—truths verified with bystanders' videos and making it impossible to deny.

The amoral nature of the European public is clearly seen in the hundreds of unarmed Black People each year by police and for "no reason". Yet, the public collects money (e.g. up to a half million dollars); speaks viciously about the victim; claims the policeman's rights are violated if anyone complains; and honors him on the next year's anniversary. If there is a mass killing by a White, the media paints that killer as "insane" when it is simply a "Normal Variant" of White people do. Yet, it is presented as "insane" to avoid talking about the biggest, scariest problem of all–European *societal* illness. The public has been taught to hate and fear those in poverty and that justifies in their minds a class-based social injustice, as distinct from ethnicity—making "those people" the 'suitable enemy'. The public is infinitely more interested in hearing sensationalized versions—and particularly the want things to be—than they are in Truth. It is then an easy next step to "Blame the Victim" as a rationalization for oppression of some of the most disadvantaged young people in society, deepening the sense of alienation of all involved.

SUMMARY

Ancient Africans designed their lives so as to be situated on the "Well-Being" end of the Selfhood Pole while European captors did all the Indifference/Hate/Evil/Sadism (IHES) things to ensure Enslaved Africans brought to the Americas would struggle on the opposite end. Their fishnet entrapment signaling enslavement was the immediate experience of their Selfhoods dangling helplessly. In the process, the Consciousness of each Enslaved was transported beyond the bounds of known or imagined sensibility--beyond the body's systems to respond to danger by "Fight, Flight, or Fright"--a Selfhood state, called Extreme '*Frustration*' ('to injure'; to harm). Such a devastation automatically led the Brain/Minds of the Enslaved into a mindset that had no concepts of the "5Ss" and that made them totally dependent upon the Satanists--a dependency which led to bonding with the Satanists. In turn, those Brutes generated a *Moderate Self-Unknowning* by removing Black Americans' awareness of their Ancestors between them and Ancient Africans—and then wiping out all the brilliant content of Ancient Africans. Thus, t*oday, the single most important Private Self problem in struggling Black youth is that they are Self-Unknown.* By contrast, *Extreme Self-UnKnowing*—including a loss of their pre-primitive European Collective Unconscious--is present in Europeans: (1) who have chosen to adopt a False Self

(Ego) to orchestrate their "Life-Living"; (2) who do not know their most remote ancestral origin; and (3) who deny the reality of their ultimate ancestral origins, particularly so as to foolishly self-declare they are 'superior'. Whereas Ancient Africans gave the appropriate balance to the Spirit and Matter components of the Spiritual Elements to all activities of daily living, struggling Black Americans are still not able to do half as well. Ancient Africans were the masters of the entire ancient world while far too many struggling Black Enslaved Minded do "Inside-Out" thinking and Life-Living, meaning they vote against themselves. A keystone accounting for the super-brilliance among Ancient Africans is that they had Certainty Knowledge about all they did of significance as a result of remaining inside and generating products out of the Spiritual Elements. By contrast, Enslaved Minded Blacks are confused and groping concerning daily living as a result of continuing to be brainwashed by Brute Europeans and kept oppressed by their IHES practices. So, it is in Black Peoples best interest and only option to take charge and control of their own lives while completely disregarding imitating anything about what Brutes do.

CHAPTER IX

BRUTES' INFERIORITY DEMANDS HATING & ENSLAVING SCAPEGOATS

CASTLES OF CONSCIOUSNESS

"Big Bang" traumas, Cumulative Micro-Traumas, and Socialization are the causes of people going into Mental Castles partly or completely outside the Natural Cosmos. For example, Black youth wounded by Self-Esteem attacks have responded to putting up a Self-Esteem Fortress, somewhat like a medieval castle. Some castles were built upon steep, rocky hills almost impossible to climb or reach because of cliffs on two or three sides. On the unprotected side (or sides) deep ditches, called "*Moats*", usually filled with water, were built outside the castle walls. If the castle was not on a hill, the moat would completely surround it. Crossing the moat was a drawbridge, which could be raised or lowered at will. Between the moat and castle was a high and thick wall called a "bailey." The "bailey" surrounded the castle and was crowned with battlements (indentations for shooting weapons). Along the wall were towers with loopholes through which arrows, spears and rocks could be hurled. Round towers were set at intervals along the wall. Between two of the towers was the entrance to the castle enclosure. The main entrance was protected by an armored gate called a *portcullis*, the last barrier in the castle gate. Since the gate was the weakest point in the defense, a small outer walled enclosure; or *barbican*, was often built to screen it and give extra protection. If the enemy could pry up the portcullis, they found themselves in an open courtyard, called the outer ward.

If the enemy could fight off the defenders from the outer ward, they had to take another low wall before reaching the inner ward. The strongest part of the castle was the *donjon*, or keep--a tower-like structure designed to be easily defended, even if an enemy had captured or destroyed the rest of the castle. Its lower part was the dungeon for prisoners. If attackers entered the donjon, they still had to fight fiercely in the dark halls. Yet, there were escape routes where the lord and his garrison could hide in the woods. Struggling Black youth have such a Fortress located in the Sub-awareness portion of their Minds. The Middle English word "Fortress" (strong place; stronghold) is a place built with walls and defenses for protection, an independent work intended to be permanent. *Defense* implies an active repelling of some perceived hostile power or influence for survival, self-protection, or self-preservation. The walls for protection separate the attacking power and whatever is to be protected--protection against possible as well as actual threats, disturbance dangers, or destruction.

Some distance away there are deceptive trails and detour signs directing potential enemies in all directions as far from the fortress as possible. These are called the "*Gateless Gatekeepers*"--a sort of shield providing defense by misdirecting. At the Fortress is a "*Gated Gatekeeper*" who uses various Masks as its form of deception and bad attitudes (gun equivalents) against actual attacks. The 1565 word "Gatekeeper" meant one who guards or monitors or controls the passage of what goes through the gate. It is used here in the sense of a lid (the "Gate") on a jar so as to keep people's probes for understanding from entering the jar where there are secrets to be kept from all. The same is done by the various Masks express the manipulating and maneuvering of questions and deflective responses designed to prevent outsiders' penetrating probing questions from entering the jar.

Mental Castles are metaphors for varying and endless types of Consciousness. Of particular concern to Black youth engaged in violent activities is that they have a "*Raw Nerve*" resulting from some psychic trauma which they have "walled off" inside a "Mental Castle" and are defending and protecting from both themselves and from outsiders. It is extremely difficult to get them to "let down the draw gate" so as to discover how they are feeling and thinking. The word "*Corral*" (enclosed yard) derives from the world's earliest people, the originators of the "Click" southern African language and now called *Khoisan* (whom Europeans derogatorily term Hottentots). Corral was borrowed by the Spanish in 1582 to designate a pen for cattle. In 1860 English gave it the sense of capture, secure. Corrals are safeguard strongholds that protect, guard from harm, and provide a shelter cover from danger or exposure. Here, *Corral Barriers refer to the minds inner recess contents for those having "Raw Nerves."*

Those contents generate a mentally hypersensitive and fragile state because they are filled with sentiments (emotionally charged thoughts) of a Selfhood Armor protection of ones fragility; defensiveness against Selfhood exposure or attack; emotions of shame and unworthiness; and envy of those who appear successful. Varying combinations of these are constantly on the stage of ones mind engaged in some type of fantasy drama. The Donjon, like a watch-tower, is that virtual state of selfhood armor to which youth retire upon discovering their defenses are not working. Here, they are untouchable—either staying in a withdrawn Self-Absorbed state or choosing to develop a False Self. For that reason, it is essential to know about some of the major types of Consciousness and which ones a given youth uses and how and when and for what and where. Their "Big Picture" problem is that of a broken Integrity, also called "*Broken Brains.*"

WHY STUDY CONSCIOUSNESS? Focus (Latin, 'domestic hearth' or fireplace which symbolizes the center of the home) is a point at which converging rays of ones Selfhood meet—toward which they are directed—or from which diverging rays are directed. Thus, what attracts ones attention as a way of life is an emblem of the central Consciousness one uses as the Background for fashioning ingredients for ones own Life Living. To remain with ones newborn birth gift of Divine Consciousness is to ensure there is a "fireplace" for lighting and warming ones life in ones Cosmic Organism realm, ones Inner World realm, ones Spiritual Emotional External World, and ones Intellect External World. An analogy for the "burning point" powers of ones Divine Consciousness is demonstrated by many children who gather dry leaves and hold a magnifying glass over them so that focused rays of the sun will set them on fire. Any other Life Living Background will not be capable of having the same effects in any manner. To assess ones Consciousness enables one to see oneself in relation to the highest Life Living Background—i.e. ones Divine Consciousness. The further away one is from ones Divine Consciousness, the more wide spread is ones violent orientation to life.

Studying Consciousness is a way to gain clues as to how to live, what to expect from how to live, how to detect what and who to avoid, what are some of the things required to defend oneself and go on the offense in the face of "Alligators," and whom to choose as a mate. For example, "*Soul Mates*" have the same Consciousness focus which determines the system of values one shares. For example, "ME/WE" shared values lead to dealing with each other and other people in a like-kind "ME/WE" manner. White people with a "ME/WE" orientation can, of course, think that Satanist Whites are "good people" because they have been socially reared to be 'blind to the obvious'. They get no attack from Satanists because they do not have anything to lose and are not doing anything Satanists find threatening. But if they start helping struggling Black People they immediately become a threat and all sorts of Satanists forces will be directed against them. Otherwise, they are in a "Me, Me, Me" White culture that does not allow them to see what "ME/WE" Divine Consciousness displays look like. Thus, they need good Black People to show that to them. Still, they are "teachable."

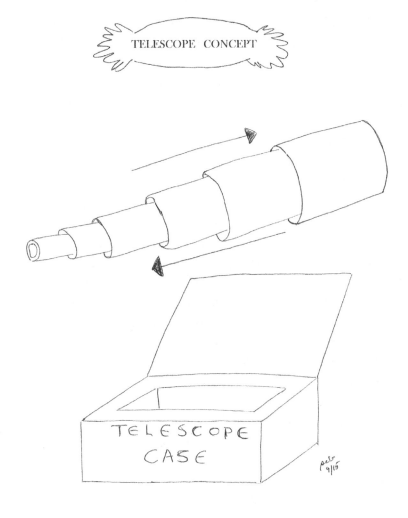

FIGURE 11

Studying Consciousness can be a way to assess "How Am I Living?" For example, if one has a sound Integrity, one sees no advantages is getting or staying angry for one only slows, stops, or reverses ones wholesome progress in life. Many Black People's reconstructed Consciousness from the original of African Tradition being shattered in slavery and were not able to piece together a reasonable facsimile of their African Tradition self means that Consciousness is so fragile and varied as to require investigation. In dealing with such people it is vital to determine which ones are suited for what kind of things. One may discover having gotten off the right track because one, like far too many other Black People, are trending in following White people's ways and too the detriment of Goodness. Living out of a Divine Consciousness means striving to live in Peace and Prosperity and that leads the naïve to expect that way of living is smooth sailing. Still, Right Life Living is like a magnet to attract evil forces and ways to self-protect must be dealt with so as to know how to defend oneself and how to go on the offense in order to get what one ought to have. A flawed Consciousness requires doing the troubleshooting so as to reestablish Selfhood Integrity.

SOBMER ASSESSMENT OF CASTLE CONSCIOUSNESS

Zooming of a telescope (fig. 11) is done to see distant things which are relatively close and other things relatively far away. This is like using a zoom lens on a camera to bring things, like the different rungs on the metaphorical Ladder, into sharp focus. Whereas a true zoom lens, also called a Parafocal Lens, maintains focus when its focal length changes, a lens that loses focus during zooming is called a Variforcal Lens. Parafocal Lens greatly aid the assessments of effects occurring to the neighboring rungs when one rung is altered. In this discussion, the zooming will on a human's Consciousness which is deceptively presented as one thing in the literature but which has multiple layers, like those of a head of lettuce or leaves in a book. To this zooming illustration end, the SOBMER Process—an acronym for a Source, an Origin, a Beginning, a Middle, an End, and a Result—is a way to provide a crude parsing of these "leaves" so that they can be assessed. A summary of its components are:

Source--that which furnishes a first and continuous supply -- the Creator of the Process.

Origin--the point or place where something starts out from the Source, giving rise to Causes

      Causes-- initiator or motivating principle of that related to action.

          Predisposing Causes trigger the initial internal reaction

          Precipitating Cause(s)—add conditions on internal reactio

          Immediate Cause-- opens the starting gate for external actions

Beginning -- the first part, point, degree, or start of external actions

Middle -- the greatest activity of external actions

End --where the external actions stop or are stopping

Effects--"What happened" or "What is going to happen"

Consequences happenings derived from Effects

Results—the sum of the good, bad, or neutral aspects of the Effects and Consequences

Discussion Elaboration: EFFECTS pertain to the degree of success in one or more areas and/or not successful in the targeted goal or some other aspects deemed to be rewards or punishment. CONSEQUENCES are like gaining support or generating obstacles or experiencing rebounds. Whereas *Subsequence* (i.e. what follows after) is like the vine growing out of a grape seed or like the blood will follow where the knife is driven, Consequences are like variable branches. For example, war's consequences branches include the pain and misery for the innocent; the lies that live on and propagate in the process; the undying hatred it has aroused; for the rulers who took over. Just as the dimensions of the tree are not regulated by the size of the seed, so are the consequences of things not always predictable or proportionate to the apparent magnitude of those events which produced them. For example, the applause of one adult may change a child's life forever. Many people's repentance is not so much regret for the ill they did but from fear of the ill they may get in consequence. The courageous seek and tell the truth knowing and accepting the consequences may be substantial.

RESULTS are the beginning of a circle since they initiate a beginning and tell a great deal about the one who produced that "fruit."

HUMANS' SELFHOOD ASPECTS

Every human being has a Private and a Public Self--which are like two sides of a coin of ones Selfhood. Ones four *Private Self Spiritual Self-Esteem* components are: *Self-Identity* (ones unchanging "sameness" concerning "Who I Am"); *Self-Meaning* (the Spiritual Self-Greatness standard against which one can compare ones Self-Respect); and *Self-Love* (ones self-anchor). Ones *Public Self Self-Esteem* components are Self-Concept and

Self-Image (Bailey, Self-Esteem). *Self-Concept* is an individual's essence of a thing when it came into being + the thing's contents which give it a disposition (fig. 6). A *Disposition* is a Thought Structure whose pattern, upon facing an appropriate situation, arranges ones mental activities to conform to the 'blue-print' that is inclined to head in a certain way, in a certain direction. In general, ones *Self-Image* is a mental picture of Objects one perceives that one possesses concerning who one is (e.g. physical birth gifts, like being physically strong); what one does (e.g. admired work products, acquired sports records, does well financially); how one appears (e.g. in body proportions, healthy); and ones achievements (e.g. material possessions, accouterments, and/or prized material things under ones ownership, control, influence, or direction). One spotlights an outstanding thing, like ones Body Image. The positives and negatives are graded and totaled to arrive at a summary Self-Image conclusion. That conclusion serves as a standard for what to pursue in life.

SELF-IDENTITY: What is "Self-Identity"? The word "*Identity*" means 'sameness' and a thing can only be the same as itself. A *Metaphysical Identity* is a "*Being*"--the "what it is" of a thing when it comes into existence and represents the system of values and character behind Propensities. The "*Self*" of a human being is, according to Ancient Africans, a "drop of God called ones Divine Consciousness. A "Thing's" Identity is what it was when it came into Being. Out of the "Self" comes the *What* and *Why* of eternal "Things" to benefit the Cosmos—vibrations containing messages of unity. A human's *Spiritual Self-Identity* consists of God's inner nature of Unconditional Love + God's outer nature of Life, both connected by God's Divine Consciousness with all of its Wisdom. Thus, this "What it is" and "Why it is" has an unchanging sameness of identity. It expresses as a *Background Base* (like the Base upon which a skyscraper building is built) within each human's Selfhood in a manner similar to the way the Sunshine lights up the world—hence the term "*Soul Sunshine*." European psychologists and psychiatrists pick up at this point and deviate from African Tradition by defining Self-Identity as a unified sense of sameness characteristics, especially the *Self-Image* (i.e. the self one believes ones personality, character, status, body, and bodily appearance to be). Such is embodied in a Being with historical continuity distinguishable from all other Beings. They add this is synonymous with Self-Awareness, a Personal Identity, and ones Ego. If this represents the tip of a triangle, it is built upon a chosen system of Values--the type of thinking method used to maneuver and manipulate those Values--and the nature of ones thoughts and emotions. Since these three determine ones goals and give direction and meaning to ones life, one experiences ones values as an extension of oneself—as an integral part of ones Identity—as crucial to what makes one oneself. Europeans define "The Self" as the "I" or the "Me" of which one is aware in ones thoughts, emotions, and actions.

SECULAR SELF-IDENTITY: This is a collection of different perceptions, united together by certain relations, and supposed, though falsely, to be endowed with a perfect simplicity and identity. The European Krech (Elements of Psychology) says it is formed: (1) partly by the adolescent's selection of various roles which become harmonized and organized so that a coherent and workable pattern of beliefs, values, motives, abilities, and temperament is achieved. With such organization one establishes and identifies oneself as a person—thus becoming oneself rather than the mere aggregate of diffuse roles and identifications which one had previously been; and (2) partly by how other people behave toward one. In this chosen state of Secular Self-Identity one embraces *Propensities*--tendencies of capacities, abilities, and language facilities which, if cultivated, could overflow with a disposition. As a result, although one does not know who one is, one has a 'ball-park' idea of the "What it does" aspects which can be put into various "How one appears" packages. In attempting to elaborate on these European concepts the subject became increasingly confusing—different terms for almost the same concept and different concepts for the same term. Still, it has usefulness for gaining ideas about certain things. For example, whereas ones Spiritual Self-Identity never changes—and is the same in every human--ones Secular Self-Identity, according to Europeans, changes within each human and is not the same from human to human. Monitored feedback from interactions with the outside world--particularly radical changes in the behavior of others--can cause one to make marked transformations of ones Secular Self-Identity. When these transformations are accompanied by stages of disorganization of "The Self," that can lead to severe confusion about ones Secular Self-Identity.

All people who have adopted a False Self—and that includes the overwhelming majority of Americans simply by being a people without a history of the type of knowing who they are at the base of their Collective Unconscious—means they are poorly prepared for what is inevitable about life—tragedy, sadness, moral ambiguity—and therefore a people reluctant to engage difficult ethical issues. These people's unrestrained individual pursuit of material success has exacted a heavy toll on Americans and their society. Especially in today's world the reality is that most people are isolated individuals from one another—causing the transformation of neighbors into competitors--causing some individuals to resent those who seemed to be getting ahead or standing in the way of their success (especially if they were different—ethnically, religiously, culturally, or racially). Such factors, among others, have spurred the wholesale dehumanization, enslavement, and killing of untold numbers of fellow human beings. Secular Self-Identity (including Self-worth) has become so heavily dependent on the degree of material success that lack of it branded a person, in his or her own eyes, the eyes of the family, and the larger community, as a failure. For some Americans, lashing out at others may be their means of overcoming their sense of isolation, frustration, and alienation bred by this struggle. As a result, the door is completely open to unbounded deception and disregard for how one lives in life since there are no incentives to virtue or any disincentive to vice.

W.E.B. DuBois was born a free Black man who believed in the aristocracy of the mind, in the talented tenth of the Negro elite (whom I call Isolated Individualists) who carry the potential that would open the doors to America. He emphasized the "Double Consciousness" that Black People feel as having to be two people—one, the self they know; the other, the self they are told by others is the real one. Such is developed in order to hold together the tensional pulls of identification with Europeans and the continuation of acknowledged membership in the stereotypically negative identity with Black Folks. He also envisioned two veils separating Whites from Blacks—one applied by Whites and the other applied by Blacks. Whites' veils ensured atmospheric distances from Black Folks by disregarding or being against facts. A personal veil was around their minds so that any incoming unfamiliar information from sources that might affect their egos (making them think there is something they do not know or capable of imparting guilt) would roll off like water on a duck's back. Anything potentially threatening to their egos would be ignored and instead the aura of the situation would lead them into escapes into the past, present, or future having nothing to do with the reality. And they seemed incapable of learning or even considering any other way. Blacks veils were masks and masquerades in the presence of Whites—either or both being capable of becoming their "Face."

This means Blacks "Life-Living" course is vastly different from the course of Whites, in that most are caught in a vicious cycle by being in status quo situations that elicit stereotypes characteristics which reinforce prejudice against them. Examples include being denied good jobs which thereby makes them stuck with low incomes which, in turn, prevent obtaining a good education with which to obtain good jobs. Most Whites see Black violence as irresponsible action but their willful ignorance prevent them from seeing the 'seed' cause is White racism. Besides, Black violence is a mirror image of Whites' violence inside the violent USA they created—having its roots in pioneer self-reliance and the frontier experience stemming from a White society that sanctions exploitation of a group (e.g. Amerindians). And violence is something White society 'loves'—as evidenced by it having always been a traditional expression of American behavior. Typically, fighting is under the guise of gaining White freedom and self-respect.

In this light, violent Blacks are merely a well-socialized element but who need the same militancy and stridency essential to Whites if they are to shuck off their traditional dependency. This is the only way to deal with a violent society in order for one to become truly free and equal—to learn self-respect—and to be respected by Whites. Innumerable Supernatural contingent type concepts are ever present in Whites minds concerning Black People, thereby making Black males more frightening to Whites than violent White men. This goes with the "Super-humanism" concept of Whites believing Blacks are more physical and thus stronger. An extension of this is that disciplinary action is more likely to be enforce against Blacks who are said to have broken the law than against Whites.

REAL SELF INTEGRITY IN AFRICAN TRADITION: Beginning in an African mathematical setting, the concept of Integrity ("untouched and whole") eventually expanded to embrace Cosmic and humans' fixed *underlying perfect Order of Natural patterns.* Following the genius of Primitive (the first) Africans inventing Bartering—i.e. exchanging one article for another without the medium of money—they devised intricate algebraic X = Y symbolized practices. Each party focused on the top Values of the Things to be exchanged—both parties displaying this by holding up whole numbers, like 1, 2, or 3 fingers—today called Natural Numbers or Positive Integer (a real quantity) *Values* are what "touch" a mind and/or the heart part of ones Selfhood regarding what the "Thing" is, what it does, and/or how it appears. Second, to make X = Y, required giving something extra for the one inadequately compensated. So, the Values for each Thing given/received were signified to the other by holding up the required number of fingers to indicate how many additions would be offered to equalized the exchange. To elaborate, *Values* are what one sees in a "Thing" in more ways than just itself—ways termed Worth and Value—each parsed into Mild, Slight, Moderate, or Extreme Classes of significance to ones Selfhood. Things of *Worth*--measured by estimates--concern the underlying consistent, permanent, stationary, and unchanging *Pattern* (imparting a significant meaning) and *Shape* (emitting a certain power). Both can impact ones Private Selfhood by Essence (i.e. "What it is"); by Spiritual Human Nature Needs Nourishment; and/or by carrying a 'payload' that Uplifts within the context of ones Human Ideal about something (as in Caring, Belonging)--causing Appreciation of its Beauty. Things of *Value* pertain to measured material benefits—the degree depending upon how its significance is assessed by ones Public Self in relation to the External World.

How later Africans prioritized Values was crystalized by the Ethiopian Aesop who lived in ancient Greece. In his fable: "The Fox and the Mask," the moral for living was: "Outside show [Value] is a poor substitute for inner Worth." Building on these Primitive African practices and meanings, Ancient Africans spotlighted the Private Selfhood—the home of the human's Soul (i.e. one Divine Consciousness)—as being Necessary for cultivation to Thrive in life. Although a human's Public Self aspects were of lower priority, they were quite Important to skillfully develop into involvements successful in activities of daily living. African Sages said a human's *Private Self Components,* orchestrated by its "First Wisdom" or First Knowledge, is in the birth gift flow of the Spiritual Elements. A human's First Wisdom is absolute true Intelligence which, upon properly developing its ingredients, is all one needs to handle the very toughest of life's problems. These *Private Self Spiritual Elements* are "packaged" into such interlocking forms called: Self-Love, Self-Knowing (Cosmic Organism yoking), Self-Greatness, Self-Faith, Self-Appreciation, Self-Confidence, Self-Trust, Self-Empowerment, Self-Respect, Self-Reliance, and Self-Efficacy. Together, they impart the "5Ss"—safety, security, self-confidence, strength, and stability. Each of these Integrity chain-links is whole, unblemished, flawless, complete, strong, and stable—each link symbolizes the positive set of Integers (i.e. whole numbers)—each 'stands alone' in its independent duties. Still, all links are interdependent in contributing to African Tradition Integrity called Ma'at (Spiritual Elements in action) "Right" Living Principles.

Hence, African Sages said a human's birth gift Integrity--like a Circle's un-divided entirety—has no breaks in the "packaged" Spiritual Elements links constituting ones Private Selfhood. When one lives in Integrity, one has a stubborn unwillingness to violate ones Real Self Identity. Humans with strong Character Integrity are *Incorruptible* (not subject to moral decay), *Irreproachable* (free from blame) in responsibility, and Fair in considering the rights and welfare of others. This chain is also spiritually linked to all God's creatures and creations. Since a chain is no stronger than its weakest link, the soundness of ones Integrity principles is naturally urged to promote mental, physical, and spiritual wholeness health for all concerned—but only after one is ready, willing, and able to do so. Ones Ma'at life's Mission Products create, enhance, and maintain *Well-Being*. Any violated link so weakens ones Private Selfhood Integrity chain as to convert one to a False Self. jabaileymd.com

SECULAR INTEGRITY: Europeans' C14 "Entire" + C16 "Integrity" words are sourced in Integers (make whole). This concept arose from late primitive Europeans emphasizing the *Value* aspect of Primitive African Bartering practices with respect to the ways a number of elements in any class could be handled. For example, the number of sheep in a herd could be one-one represented by a corresponding number of pebbles put in a pile. Such was done to pair off one sheep with each stone, in such a way that no sheep would be counted twice, and no sheep and no stone was left over. Thus, the integer 5--like digits on a hand (Natural Numbers)--is the mark associated with a Class and with all other Classes whose elements could be paired off with those 5 digits. A Positive Integer—a whole number like 1, 2, 3 used in counting wholes (e.g. sheep, apples)--is greater than Zero, as distinguished from a fraction. Negative Integers (numbers less than Zero, -2, -7) + Positive Integers = a complete Set of Integers. Eventually, European scholars expanded these ideas, with Quantities as primary; Qualities, as secondary. Thus, favored humans were said to be "solid," whole, intact, and 'perfect'--implying Integrity meant total abstinence of sexual desire—an assumed preternatural (beyond the normal course of Nature and thus Supernatural) gift of God. This was said to be represented by Adam and Eve before the Fall (note: this was an Ancient African Bible metaphorical story featuring *Aisha and Aish*). So, Ancient African concepts of Integrity, after being borrowed into C16 *Integer* ('In,' expressing negation + tangere, 'to touch'), were refocused to spotlight chastity. Next *Integral*, based on Integer, was formed to indicate details inferred from properties of the complete process. Its unimpaired or uncorrupted condition in humans expanded into having a sense of honesty or uprightness (1548). One of its senses was that humans of upright life are unstained by guilt. Another is the Supernatural concept of loyalty to ones beliefs, convictions, and values—acting in accordance with ones values—expressing, upholding, and translating ones values into practical reality.

African Tradition would refute this since there is no standard given for what is higher than ones beliefs. A generally accepted standard is what Sages of all cultures and all ages have agreed to as Integrity's Human Ideal—allowing for comparing against it what one does. In looking deeper, my view is that every human is born with everything needed to have a healthy, happy, productive, and thriving life. Together, those things within ones Selfhood possess Coherence; Consistency; Compatibility with Reality, Order, Regularity, Balance, Harmony, and Predictability inside a given human's Circle of Cosmic Wholism. Allow me to illustrate a few correspondences between an Egg + a human as a "ME/WE" entity inside the Cosmic Organism + that human in an Earth World setting with the Cosmic Organism and the Egg. The Circle of Wholism resembles an intact eggshell covering an Egg. That eggshell is like the Circle of Wholism' Caring a human gets as a "ME/WE" entity. That eggshell and the Circle of Wholism are also like a human's birth gift protective Integrity for that human's Real Self. A human's personal "eggshell" of Integrity protects its inner core ingredients; acts as a defense against anti-Spiritual Elements; and provides Public Self armor.

Just as the one thing which all eggs must possess is the embryo and its nutrients from which the young animal develops, so is this the core of a human germ inside the Circle of Cosmic Wholism as well as within the Private Self core of a human during Earth living. The two layers of membrane which line the shell of an Egg are widely separated and contain air for the developing chick to breath while pecking its way out of the shell. Similarly, the ingredients of a human's Integrity provide inner support and nourishment throughout life when that human maintains her/his Real Self. But be clear that the overwhelming majority of people lack "across the board" Integrity because of some insecurity. Even when an Egg is merely cracked, it breaks up the integration of the contents of the Egg inside the eggshell. That is what happens to the Character of humans when they place a "toe" outside the Circle of Cosmic Wholism. Then, as False Selves, they start thoughtless operating out of habit and emulating current trends of the day's society. This leads them down paths to become Aggressive, Passive, or Passive-Aggressive—all off the track of their Mission in life. jabaileymd.com

"BIG PICTURE" OF CONSCIOUSNESS

"And ye shall know the Trueth, and the Trueth shall make you free" is an incomplete verse of various European Bibles borrowing from the Ancient African Bible saying the Spiritual Elements are what enables one to be free and thrive. European Satanists intent on controlling minds of the world "Crowd" attack all available Ancient African Knowledge of the Spiritual Elements (i.e. Unconditional Love, Truth, Reality, and the Natural). Prove to yourself that such "Right" Life-Living has been eliminated by determining the last time you heard any "authority" or the media advocating it--or even talking about being "Honorable" (i.e. not lie, cheat, or steal). Not to be confused is talk of luxury living or Secular "Love" in the forms of "*Conditions*" ("you are required to do what we say, but only if you do it voluntarily will we accept you) or Emotionally "Exciting" Trinkets and Trivia. Also floodlighted for the world "Crowd" is "Serious Business" sourced from "authorities" opinions and beliefs, falsely passed off as the Truth. For people of "Good Conscience" concerned with "Right" Life-Living, it is fundamental to know how information that is passed off to the "Crowd" for Knowledge came into being (i.e. what is its essence) and the nature of its source (God-made vs. human-made, for what reason) for both help determine the credibility.

According to the Encyclopaedia Britannica (1992 p552), the European John Locke defined Consciousness as: "the perception of what passes in a man's own mind"—a nonsensical statement that opened the door for all sorts of opinions about Consciousness. Some said it was "mental stuff" differing from material substance; some said it was an attribute characterized by sensation and voluntary movement, which separated animals and men from lower forms of life [on what basis?]; some said Consciousness differs between a normal waking state and asleep, in a coma, or under anesthesia; and so forth. The problem was based upon each "authority" observing Consciousness by his own introspection—looking within ones own mind to discover the laws of operation. Since, of course, no one agreed there was overwhelming confusion and conflict. This process was/is an extention of Pythagoras' (Greek, 480-411 BC) teaching the Western world: "Man is the measure of all things"—and not God—causing each to deem himself to be a "little god," justifying each to determine what SEEMS right and decent—all far away from Truth/Reality. To begin unraveling all of this confusion and conflict it is important to understand what is Consciousness.

Some orienting ideas are that just as the Cosmic Divine Consciousness is the Background Source of Knowledge for all Knowledge regarding all of God's creatures and creations, so is a human's Divine Consciousness the Background for how to live a Ma'at life. In addition, it is a "Ground of Being" Background that has a companion Foreground—and that pattern continues as one opens up new forms of Consciousness throughout the course of ones life. The Background (like a *Sensory Consciousness Background*) can be analogized to the part of the stage in a theater that is farthest or remote from the audience or behind the curtain. Out of this Sensory Secular World Consciousness Background comes the ingredients for the performance of ones Sensory Consciousness Foreground—analogized to the front part of the stage on which the Play for a public audience is performed.

CONSCIOUSNESS/UNCONSCIOUSNESS SPECTRUM

Humans coin words to describe their idea of what something is, what something does, how something appears, or as "excuses" for what is not understood, like the "Unconscious." To elaborate, Spiritually, a revelation to Ancient African Sages was that out of God's Cosmic Mind (located in the Amenta) comes the Spiritual Elements in the Subjective Realm--called the Ocean of Nun (Nu)—a state of Primordial Darkness. They proposed that Divine Consciousness (among others) constitutes God's Inner Androgynic Plast nature of Unconditional Love (equating to Divine Unconsciousness as the "Ground of Being" for the Cosmos) while God's Outer Androgynic Plast nature is of Life (Truth, Reality, the Natural) equated to the complementary indivisible different equal of Divine Consciousness. "Primigenial Darkness" *is itself light*—so dazzling and blinding in its splendor as to make it appear to ordinary humans, in their way of thinking about what it is, as "Darkness" being absolutely destitute of light. Hence, this situation is improperly as well as properly called Unconscious in a human sense but not in a Spiritual Sense. The Spiritually sophisticated are Aware, by Luminosity in the Unconscious "Darkness," of Cosmic Knowledge. Its Material World counterpart is the Visionary who is able to see Visions (the *art of seeing invisible essences others are unable to see*). Obviously, assuming the complete picture of Spiritual *Primigenial Chaos* "Darkness" to be the erroneous state of being absolutely destitute of light or considering the incomplete state of it being totally Unconscious are both mental actions of confusing made-up concepts for definitions having nothing to do with reality—confusion which creates conflicts that put the naïve on the wrong path, even though they may be using the right "logic."

SPIRITUAL REALM CONSCIOUS/UNCONSCIOUS: Since the human Soul, said Ancient Africans Sages, is a "Spark of God," it similarly possesses a Spark of God's *Divine Unconsciousness—i.e. Unconditional Love serving as the Ground of Being or Background for any human's Selfhood.* The instilling of God's Divine Unconsciousness into each human to thereby form that human's Unconscious (also called the Occulted, the Hidden, the Subconscious, the Spirit, the Psyche, the Soul) occurred in the Subjective Realm's Ocean of Nun—the Cosmic Intelligence of Creation, called *Tao* by the Chinese. This implies that there is a Primordial Cosmic/Human interconnection between humans' deepest Unconscious mental recesses and the Nun--meaning they interpenetrate, occupy the same "space," and feature in-distinctions and indistinguishableness but not disorganization. A *Primordial Interconnection* is indicative of it having occurred first in time so as to be in a human's pre-birth Natural "Wild" Mindset. Hence, as in the Nun, the "Primigenial Darkness" present in a human's Selfhood *is itself light*—so dazzling and blinding in its splendor as to be considered Unconscious, whereas in actuality it is illumination. A feature of the whatever is in the Ocean of Nun is the *Law of Spiritual Creativity: by itself, a Spiritual Element reproduces itself to become the thing it makes, regardless of its new form.* An illustration of that Law is within the Spiritual realm is the Cosmic *Primigenial Chaos* which represents the Spiritual Realm's first born entity containing "Potential Possibilities" in virtual form (i.e. in unformed Matter and in infinite space) for the future displays of God's divine and earthly creatures and creations. Here, it is inert or at least at rest or passive, since the "Spirited" active mode of energy is responsible for the differentiation of Matter into forms.

SPIRITUAL/SECULAR REALM CONSCIOUS/UNCONSCIOUS: A human's Divine Unconsciousness is a microcosm of the "Primigenial Darkness" of the macrocosm of the Cosmic Organism and is contained inside the human's Divine Consciousness. This implies, as the kernel of the sun is dark, so is the Unconscious of the human's Soul "Dark" to the ordinary human. But still that same Divine Unconsciousness is light itself—of the luminosity type. An off-spring Consciousness of the Archetype which is imparted within a given human is the original Immaterial Substance now in a Tangible realm of existence and is thus a Prototype of the Cosmic Consciousness. That Prototype within a given human also has the power to by itself, reproduce itself, to become the thing it makes. Such off-springs are required within every human newborn so as to have its Divine Consciousnes: (1) remain connected with Cosmic Consciousness inside the Cosmic Organism + (2) shed Light into that human's Inner Selfhood realm so as to make that human Aware of the Cosmic Knowledge for that human's (3) pre-birth Spiritual Emotional and (4) Intellectual Ma'at applications in the External World. Note that each of these four is like a bellows whereby the same Luminosity, Knowledge, and Awareness can happen.

The first off-spring Consciousness for the Human species is the Archetype (African for "Seed")—an Immaterial Substance inside an Intangible realm of existence—which similarly, by itself, reproduces itself, to become the thing it makes. As like in the Cosmic Unconscious, the "Dark" of the human Unconscious represents the state of undeveloped potentialities for the Spiritual and Secular aspects of ones Selfhood. Because the human's Divine Unconsciousness and Divine Consciousness—which are indivisible differences, like two sides of a coin--together produce Luminosity, Knowing, and Awareness, Real Self people have the capability of taking advantage of their Luminosity to thereby provide 'Enlightenment'. This starts with recognizing the Ground of Being of ones Divine Consciousness is Unconditional Love. By cultivating it is to "light-up" the necessary ingredients within the "Dark" Unconditional portion so as to acquire the Awareness of the Knowledge to produce "Enlightenment" Spiritual Elements products. What that Unconditional Love does is to simply reproduce the Law of Spiritual Creativity. By staying open to ones Divine Consciousness, one will be Unconsciously aware of its Luminosity, Knowledge, and Awareness extending above and beyond ones Instincts in order to *coordinate the affairs of ones life.*

SECULAR REALM CONSCIOUS/UNCONSCIOUS: The human *Unconscious is a Receptacle of Programs* and the nature of its expressions depend upon whether ones Divine Spirit is or is not connected to ones Divine Consciousness. For that reason, there is as wide a range in its possible good to bad categories, as is in the Astral part of the Metaphysical—whether dealing with the real, distorted, or fantasy. An unalterable underlying program is a human's "Instincts". At birth, ones Instincts represent a correspondence with the Spiritual aspects of the Cosmic Mind Unconscious because they express the Will of God. By being where God's Spark dwells, the *Unconscious* conveys Instincts from the Mind of God while performing the dictated functions of unifying involuntary physiological aspects--the vital supports of ones life. A human's Instincts continuously carry out its Involuntary duties as the regulator of humans' automatic actions + serve as the basic means of survival. Examples are to self-protect and sustain life, like automatically orchestrating the running the human body (e.g. heart beat). Instincts are responsible for automated behaviors via Unconscious mental processes acting as coordinators of ones thoughts. This fashions them into intelligible patterns enabling one to speak, think, walk, and like-kind performances. Instincts are the "star" of sleeping--*Delta* level is deep sleep, unconsciousness, or coma--*Theta* wave's light sleep is either unconsciousness or semi-awareness.

SUB-AWARENESS: Europeans use the term SUBCONSCIOUS to indicate a level of mind through which material passes on the way toward full Consciousness. Others use Preconscious to indicate information store containing memories that are momentarily outside of awareness but which can easily be brought into Consciousness. I prefer "Sub-awareness" to indicate mental activity anywhere on the Divine Consciousness/Unconscious scale that in a Type state of: (1) budding as a Percept; (2) in the process of drawing ingredients from memory; (3) undergoing manipulation and/or maneuvering of Percepts and Memories into Notions; (4) the flowering of Ideas—all of which can be a combination of Instinct and/or Omnibus Brain thoughts as is or being modified by ones Emotional and/or Rational thoughts—or (5) Fruited Thoughts/Concepts in the "back of ones mind."

PARSING HUMAN CONSCIOUSNESS

Since there is Continuity (Unity running through Multiplicity) of the indivisibly different Archetypes and Prototypes of Divine Consciousness, to deal with this accordion type entity is best explained by the word Parsing (Latin, 'part'). Parsing is a concept of elaborating on language grammar. Normally, "Parse" refers, in general, to diagramming a sentence and, in particular, describing grammatically a word in that sentence by stating the part of speech, inflexion, and relation to the rest of the sentence. For example, to "Diagram" a sentence like: "The cat sat on the dog," the sentence is parsed into Subject (cat) + Predicate (sat)—the Predicate passed into Verb (sat) + Adverbial (i.e. on the dog)—and the Adverbial recognized (of Place—i.e. where the cat sat). Note, that sentence is in Continuity (like a bellows) or Contiguity and yet aspects of it can still be analyzed apart from the rest of the "Accordion." Here, "*Analysis*" means the applying of sharp critical faculties that penetrate the Obvious and the Hidden of what is being assessed for pros and cons so as to discern if it has a consistent underlying pattern.

Parsing can be of: (1) subdividing Real Self from False Self Consciousness; (2) analyzing the components of what is in the whole of the Real Self or of the False Self Consciousness; or (3) analyzing one part of the whole of the Real Self or of the False Self Consciousness, as by telling the part of speech of a word, its forms, and its relation to other words. What is important here is to note the different category levels of Consciousness. One reason is that each parsed aspect has its own degrees of influences on ones Selfhood and great confusion arises when these different parsed planes of Consciousness existence are not recognized for what they are and what they do. The False Self or Real Self nature of the ingredients going through any sequence of ones Divine or Sensory Consciousness determines how one thinks, feels, says, and does things in Life-Living. My crude image concept of Consciousness is that of an Accordion, a portable reed organ (fig. 2). The focus is on Truth but whether this works for understanding.

CONSCIOUSNESS IS LIKE AN ACCORDION: The Accordion is a portable musical instrument composed primarily of bends, folds, or pleats. Its three important parts are the bellows, the reeds, and the keys. The bellows are like a bag with many folds in it that can be pushed together or pulled apart. Pulling the ends apart draws air in while pushing forces air out. The reeds (or tongues) are strips of metal of differing sizes and when they vibrate they produce sounds of different musical pitches. The moving air makes these strips move back and forth, or vibrate at a certain rate of speed. Different reeds make different sounds when they vibrate. The reeds are fastened to the keys on the keyboard of the Accordion. Keys are arranged on the two oblong ends of the Accordion, on both sides of the bellows. Each key controls a valve that supplies air to a single reed or set of reeds. Thus, when a button or key is depressed, a stream of air is admitted into the slot, causing the reed to vibrate and create sound. By pressing the right keys as one pushes and pulls, one can play tunes.

This *Accordion Concept* is transferrable to the Concept of Cosmic Consciousness in general and humans' Divine Consciousness in particular. Such is because a human's: (1) Divine Consciousness--in relation to the

(2) Cosmic Organism + that human's (3) Inner World + that human's (4) External World—are all in continuity. As used here, "*Continuity*" stresses uninterrupted or unbroken connection enabling a continuing flow of the Real Self's Soul "What" and "Why" payload messages through these four realms. Although some of these four are connected like pleats in an Accordion, others are in *Contiguity* (contact without actual touching, like the synapse of nerves), their multiplicity is a unity with a purpose of bringing or enhancing "Health" and wholeness to ones entire Selfhood. In the way both hands are needed to play the accordion, this gives plenty of opportunities to one or more bad notes. However, that does not mean one is not a good Accordion player. Similarly, humans may mishandle their Background and Foreground complementary pairs of opposites of Divine or Sensory Consciousness. This does not make a Real Self person a bad person. However, if there is one or more significant flaws, each flaw must be immediately corrected before it causes a significant change in that person's character.

COSMIC CONSCIOUS / HUMAN CONSCIOUSNESS

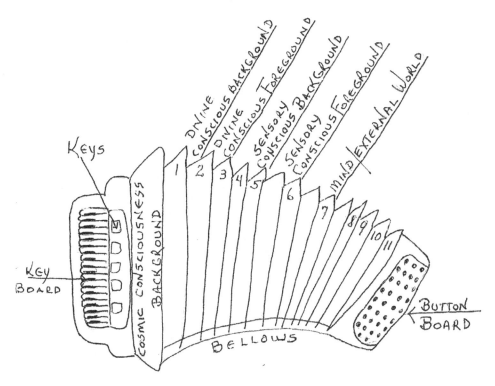

1. Spiritual Elements "What" and "Why" Message

2. Human's Divine Conscious Passes Image Messages to Will

3. Will Sends It To Conscience

4. Conscience Sends Disposition To Divine Spirit

5. Disposition Goes To Sensory Consciousness Background Which Then Passes It To

6. The Mind/Sensory Conscious Foreground

7. Then To The Mind/External World Interface

8.-11. Potential Consciousness – For Placement Between 5 and 7 As Needed

FIGURE 12

HUMAN CONSCIOUSNESS REAL SELF

The Real Self Integrity's inner qualities—those of ones Private Selfhood—possess Health, Coherence; Cohesiveness, Consistency; Compatibility with Reality, Order, Regularity, Balance, Harmony, and Predictability inside a given human's Circle of Cosmic Wholism. The Products derived from one living with Real Self Integrity are of a ME/WE nature—i.e. "unified" with the wholeness or blended, organized, and undivided Cosmic Organism of an individual. As an analogy, Real Self Integrity can be thought of as like the way an egg-shell protects the egg. Allow me to illustrate a few correspondences between an Egg + a human as a "ME/WE" entity inside the Cosmic Organism + that human in an Earth World setting with the Cosmic Organism and the Egg. The Circle of Wholism resembles an intact eggshell covering an Egg. That eggshell is like the Circle of Wholism' Caring a human gets as a "ME/WE" entity. That eggshell and the Circle of Wholism are like a human's birth gift protective Integrity for that human's Real Self. A human's personal "eggshell" of Integrity is to protect its inner core ingredients and act as a defense against anti-Spiritual Elements. There are other Correspondences. Just as the one thing which all eggs must possess is the embryo and its nutrients from which the young animal develops, so is this the core of a human inside the Circle of Cosmic Wholism as well as within the Private Self core of a human during Earth living. The two layers of membrane which line the shell of an Egg are widely separated and contain air for the developing chick to breath while pecking its way out of the shell. Similarly, the ingredients of a human's Integrity provide inner support and nourishment throughout life when that human maintains her/his Real Self.

When one is orchestrated by ones Real Self's Divine Consciousness, ones Selfhood has *Integrity*—meaning one is: (1) complete—all Selfhood components are fully ready for one to develop them to their fulfillment and with all its parts in harmony; (2) whole in all aspects and throughout; (3) healthy, natural, flawless (4) a Selfhood not divided against itself; (5) strong against opposing forces. Ancient Africans said ones Real Self Integrity arises out of ones "Self"—also called ones Divine Consciousness (i.e. the 'Divine Mind' behind ones 'Matter'). The "Self" is the 'Spark of God' containing the attributes of God but on an infinitely smaller scale—something like a drop of the ocean compared to the ocean. Yet, all of God's powers are inside that 'Spark" or 'Drop' and, if allowed, it orchestrates ones life by remaining within and cultivating its Spiritual Elements ingredients.

Since a chain is no stronger than its weakest link, the soundness of ones Integrity principles is naturally urged to promote the wholeness of the mental, physical, and spiritual health of all concerned—but only after one is ready, willing, and able to do so. Ones Mission in life Ma'at Products create, enhance, and maintain *Well-Being*. Because Spirit and Matter go together as indivisible Complementary Equals, there can be no breach between body and mind—between thought and action—between ones convictions and living. This displays as one who can be thoroughly depended upon; and will stand firm when others fail; is the best kind of friend—faithful and true; and is the adviser, honest and fearless. Integrity is the first step to true Selfhood Greatness. To live by ones convictions means that is done independent of and uninfluenced by the wishes, pleas, threats of one or all. This requires the Confidence of being Certain that one is right—the Courage to be true to ones existence and to the Spiritual Elements. For the "We" in one "Me/We" big picture, doing for them is not an act of "Selfless Service" or "Sacrifice" but ones loyalty display of Integrity—i.e. acting in accordance with ones System of Values.

DIAGNOSING REAL SELF CONSCIOUSNESS: When there are: (a) regularities discovered that are permanent, stationary, unchanging patterns or elements; (b) held together by an unchanging steadfast, internally linking Spiritual bond; (c) which rule all things springing from it; and (d) serve as a Virtual bond with all that is modeled after it or copied from it, then one is inside and evolving out of the Spiritual Elements which characterize a human's Real Self Consciousness. In stepping back into its origin, imagine the Cosmic Mind of the Cosmic Organism to be the Source which gave rise to the Divine Cosmic Consciousness to serve as the "*Ground of Being*" for the entire Natural Wholistic Environment. This Divine Cosmic Consciousness is instilled in the Feminine/Masculine primeval Substance derived from God's Androgynic Plast and which gives rise to the Cosmic Organism. In resorting to the Law of Correspondence, it is known that *Protoplasm* (proto, first in a series or the highest in rank + plasma, thing formed) is living (Material) substance of which animal and vegetable cells are formed. *Protoplast* originally meant the first entity of a type.

So, out of God's Primordial Substance (Immaterial) came the Protoplast called Cosmic Consciousness (Immaterial)—like a bacterial cell from which the rigid cell wall has been completely removed. Thus, the "Source" or Cosmic Consciousness inside an Immaterial realm of existence is Immaterial and possesses the power to by itself, reproduce itself, to become the thing it makes. Its reproductions consist of an ultimate human Archetype--which, in turn, gives rise to its Prototype in a given human—which, in turn, reproduces itself in like-kind forms. Those forms deal with the Mission of that human and those which are required for varying experiences that human has along the way. When ones Real Selfhood is in harmony, all portions of this "Accordion bellows" are in continuity—i.e. its multiplicity is working as a unity to provide Spiritual and Metaphysical "Health" as well as a thriving and happy life that is dedicated to "ME/WE" benefits.

"BIG PICTURE" PLEATS OF REAL SELF CONSCIOUSNESS

To gain insight for Diagnoses and Management of a human's mental health is the "Big Picture" purpose of this book. To help overcome the tremendous confusions and conflicts when considering "Normal," "Normal Variant," and "Ego Driven" forms of Consciousness, their parts must be "Parsed" The "Big Picture" of the Continuity and Contiguity of Real Self Consciousness starts with a human' Divine Consciousness and Divine Will being like two sides of a coin. Since both are devoid of Energy and Matter, its "What" messages have to go through a process before it can be manifest. The Divine Consciousness imparts an Immaterial Message of the "What" and "Why" for an intended Disposition to be carried out (fig. 6). The human's Divine Will converts that message into an Intangible Image. In relay fashion, that Imaged Divine Consciousness Message is passed on to ones Divine Spirit which makes it into a Tangible Image in order to be able enter into the Awareness Secular Sensory Consciousness realm. Once there, ones "Mind Committee" (e.g. reason, emotions) forces determine the best way to continue with the Ordering of the "What" and "Why" Divine Message pertaining to voluntary or willed behaviors in the External World.

AFRICAN ANKH OF DIVINE CONSCIOUSNESS

Concepts of what Consciousness is began to be formulated prior to 77,000 BC by the TWA (so-called Pygmies) of the Great Lakes region of Central Africa (fig. 13). At that time they began wearing the "Cross" around their necks as jewelry and as amulets for protection. Some time thereafter, Very Ancient African Sages added a circle to the cross to symbolized that their "life force" arose from the spirit of God and it imparted the personal "Aliveness" needed for acquiring a pure spiritual essence as well as for communicating with Higher Powers. The circle represents the immortal and eternal part (absolute reality) while the cross represents that which is mortal and transient (illusion-matter). This Ankh Symbol (Bailey, Ancient African Bible Messages pvi) is used here to indicate the Loop at the top of the Cross as representing the Cosmic Organism orchestrated by the Cosmic Mind. The vertical part of that Cross symbolizes a human's Inner Core World that heads directly to the Loop; the right limb of the horizontal crossbar stands for a human's Inner World; and the left limb represents a human's External World. Situated at the crossroad junction of these four aspects is a Real Self human's Divine Consciousness—also called ones Soul. In short, ones Divine Consciousness is located at the crossroad of ones Inner and Outer Worlds of ones Selfhood. Ones Soul possesses the "triad" of *Luminosity, Spiritual Intuition Knowing, and Spiritual Awareness faculties* for use in ones Inner World, Inner Core World, and External World.

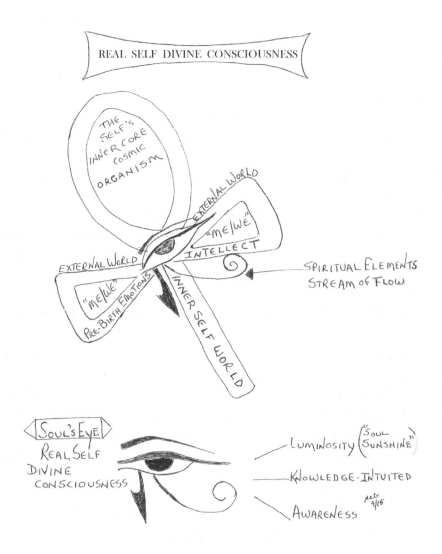

FIGURE 13

Luminosity, which I call "Soul Sunshine", in the Inner World is "*Illumination*" capable of bringing light into the dark in a phosphorescence manner. Physically, light involves activity (propagation, hence differentiation) that takes place through time--meaning there can be no light in the Subjective realm where ones Inner World and Inner Core Worlds reside. Inside both Inner Worlds, Luminosity is reminiscent of the Firefly beetles (or "Lightening Bug") that glow in the darkness like a spark of fire. Such would be in keeping with the human Soul's consisting of a "Spark" of God. In the External World it more like the Light that is behind differentiation and hierarchal order.

Inituiting, the process of learning from ones Divine Consciousness, is simple Vision to which Truth offers itself like a landscape to the eye. The "what it is"--the essence--of each Truth, by itself expresses its true self in a manner that displays its true nature by merely being what it is. When that display is recognized, and without any associated thing making it go, and without being altered, it constitutes a *Vision*--the art of seeing invisible essences others are unable to see. Intuiting is present when one can see similarities in the dissimilar and discern uniqueness in similarities.

Awareness is an alert Consciousness by means of basic Light of what is evident as well as by Inner vision of the overlooked in the obvious, the Hidden, and/or the Underlying Principles of a "Thing." Inner vision awareness is analogized to those minerals which shine with beautiful and brilliant colors when they are illuminated by certain kinds of invisible light (e.g. ultraviolet rays). When this kind of luminescence lasts after the invisible light has been withdrawn, the shining is called *phosphorescence*.

The "triad" of Luminosity, Knowledge, and Awareness applied to ones *Inner World* is on ones Selfhood and its illumination makes one Aware of its harmonious or non-harmonious Laws of Nature. If disharmonious, ones awareness provides the Knowledge for what is required to get back in the main part of the Spiritual Elements stream flow.

The "triad" applied to a human's *Inner Core World* is located in a human's Divine Unconsciousness—enabling one to have an Inner Vision Luminosity to provide one with the Spiritual Awareness to Spiritually Intuit the Knowing oneself in relation to connectedness with the Cosmic Organism. This process is called: *"Knowing Thyself."*

The "triad" applied to a human's *External World* is like the sun shining on the Physical World. It provides Luminosity for recognizing the significant and for deeply assessing profound Experiences in order to gain Wisdom, Mental Intellect to use Wisdom for Right Living, and Sensory Consciousness. It also provides Light for activities of daily living. After the advent of light (Enlightenment), the fate of the "Darkness" out of which the Spiritual Divine Conscious Awareness arose is thereafter regressive. It is also from this faculty that there is maintenance of a bonding with the Cosmic Organism + its "ME/WE" extensions. An example is the appropriate arising of Compassion so as to share the same Spiritual Space with others within the Cosmic Organism—and that does not include those who attack the Spiritual Elements since it is potentially self-destructive.

As long as a Real Self human continues in the Spiritual Elements flow (i.e. the inner and outer nature of God) present at that human's birth into the Material World, that is what constitutes the Ma'at "Right" path for Life-Living. On this path, a human's Divine Consciousness, by itself, reproduces itself, so as to become the Prototype "Thing" it makes. Each Prototype works interdependently to contribute to the wholism of a human's Consciousness. This means that despite their subdivisions all of the Prototypes are interrelated and are virtually blended inside the wholism of that human's Consciousness. In other words, there is Continuity (Unity running through Multiplicity) from both Archetypes and their Prototype offspring each interdependently doing its independent activities. Yet, what each does is to benefit the whole in the course of their Natural Processes as the human progresses through life.

REAL vs. DISTORTED vs. FALSE LUMINOSITY, KNOWLEDGE, AWARENESS: Last night was hot and I went to bed without covers over me. During the night it cooled off and I covered myself with a sheet. By morning it was cold and I put a blanket on. This is a metaphor to explain that concepts of the triad of Luminosity, Knowledge, and awareness are most true when they are intuitied—i.e. come from within ones own Soul. They best concepts about the triad are equated to a sheet, which Rinpole likens to a glass door between ones Real Self and ones Divine Consciousness—like being somewhat distorted. What one receives is the truth but it may not be all of the Truth because it was not relayed or because it was misunderstood or not fully understood. False information concerning the "triad" comes from all other sources—equivalent to the blanket—because most of it is not the Truth since it is human-made by those who have self-interest agendas.

PROTOTYPES OF DIVINE CONSCIOUSNESS

Every human is born on the stream of mental activity flow which maintains that human's Real Self. One remains on this course by staying within and cultivating Spiritual Elements packages out of it. By realizing this and that they, as humans, are a microcosm of the macrocosm of the Primordial Substance in the Ocean fo Nun--meaning they mutually interpenetrate and occupy the same "space"—served as the basis for Ancient African Sages admonition to all Africans—"Man, Know Thyself." These concepts must be understood before discussing alterations and deviations of Consciousness. A major problem is trying to get clarity about which term to use where and what that term actually means. It is frequent have a significant word (especially of a religious and philosophical nature) that dates to ancient times have different denotations and connotations given back then that are quite different from the denotations and connotations of today.

There are tremendous difficulties in trying to parse human Consciousnenss. For example, the term "*Supraconscious*" is defined in a dictionary as functioning above the level of Consciousness, Rational, or Logical but it does not say what type of Consciousness. In religious texts Supraconscious is called the Oversoul, Anima Mundi, the Collective Unconscious, the Universal Spirit by some while others say they are subdivisions of the same thing—and still others say they are separate. Some say the *Anima Mundi*—the Etheral "Soul" of the Cosmos—contains the Substance of God. All of these are confusingly lumped under the umbrella term "Consciousness." Yet, for understanding, they must be dealt with separately, even though they are part of the same Accordion process—the essence of the meaning of "Parse." To describe my concept of Consciousness as an According, allow me to use each of its pleats. The concepts used here are that the Supraconscious, in one sense, equates to the *Super Conscious* and it seems that both refer to the Universal Spirit. If so, then Supraconsciousness (Spiritual) would be in a human under the term Divine Consciousness (ones Self-Identity)—and would distinguish it from a human's Unconscious (Spiritual and Secular) and Secular Sensory Consciousness aspects.

PLEAT I: SUPRACONSCIOUS: The *Supraconscious* sub-faculty of ones Soul—i.e. the Divine Consciousness--gives a human the capability of Luminating the Cosmic Organism Knowledge within a human's Unconscious so as to convert it into a *Spiritual Divine Conscious Awareness* bud that one can cultivate into a flower to fruit as part of ones designing of a Ma'at Life-Living plan. Ones Divine Consciousness (Soul), as the hidden Supraconsciousness contained in ones Unconscious, constitutes the "What" and "Who" of a human. Because it is a "spark of God," that "What" and "Who" makes each human a Messenger of God. Naturally, then, ones *Divine Consciousness* knows *What* it wants to manifest (i.e. what it is Willing) and Why as part of the Ma'at process for staying on the Right path.

PLEAT II: The WILL has a direct flow from the Will of God so that the Will of God is shared with a human's Divine Will. This means a human's Will is the essence of a human's freedom. Hence, there is no "unfree" human Will and thus "Free Will" is a redundant term. The Will—faculty which integrates the message of ones Divine Consciousness—fashions the message into a compatible Virtual Image abstract imbued with meaningful units in preparation for the mind to receive. By being the initiator of the intensions of all that happens in ones life, the Will is the *indicator of what will take place* by it being in charge of ones voluntary mental and physical activities. The Self's Will is free of emotions and sensuality or from any coercion, impulse, or compulsion from the emotional part of ones Selfhood. A human's Will, by being Immaterial, is a formless tool of action--a "Virtual" (boundless) "That it is" entity with power. As God's agent, the human Will institutes God's dictates by carrying the Virtual Image through her/his Conscience.

PLEAT III: The CONSCIENCE either clears a path or provides a clear path for God's Message in order for the Will's formless Virtual Image (Immaterial) to be guided into that human's Divine Spirit where it is deposited. That deposit is called a *Disposition* and contains the Virtual Image.

PLEAT IV: DIVINE SPIRIT, which is in the human mind and not "Self", deals with the *How and When* of the What and Why of the organized Disposition. Up to this point both Energy and Matter in a human's Spirit has a passive Sensory Consciousness "screen" containing an inactive, undifferentiated, unstructured, not shaped into forms or things type of Matter as well as an inactive state of Energy. Both the Energy/Matter aspects have the potential to be dynamic. It becomes dynamic when the Unconscious presents its contents from the Divine Consciousness. That Disposition deposit from ones Divine Consciousness activates the Divine Spirit's Spiritual Energy which, in turn, then activates Ether Matter. Ether is a quanta of energy and matter constituting the minimum amount needed for any physical entity to become involved in an interaction. As a result of being set in motion (e-motion), the "Virtual Image" from the human Will acquires dynamic Spiritual Energy. Will uses this energy in its functional set of abilities to supply its Intentions for what will take place in some voluntary mental or physical activity with the Ether--in order for the Will to yield the mental events involved in initiation of further actions.

PLEAT V--SENSORY CONSCIOUSNESS BACKGROUND: At the moment the Divine Spirit is activated by Energy and Matter, the human Soul's Unconscious (contained in the human's Divine Consciousness), which gave rise to these "Darkness/Blackness" conceptions, give birth to that human's *Sensory Consciousness*—the Mind aspect. The resultant Ether Image coming about from layers of more Ether Matter being applied to the Will's Image enables the human to start recognizing God's Plan—an Ether Matter Image called a Percept (fig. 16). A Percept is an appearing entity having a specific nature and made of specific barely perceptible attributes. The newly formed Ether Image in the Percept aids the Disposition (fig. 6) in its duty to organize all *What* and *Why* aspects contained inside God's plan into a dynamic Inclination and Temperament—together constituting the individual's *Attitude*. The *Inclination* is a 'physical' "leaning toward" or "leaning" away from something. The *Temperament* is its physiological Sensory Consciousness systems fashioning the type of reaction the aroused person takes. The Ultimate Divine Selfhood Foreground ingredients 'play out' on the Material World's *Sensory Consciousness Background* (analogized to the part of the stage in a theater remote from the audience). Out of this Sensory Secular World Consciousness Background comes the ingredients for the performance of ones Sensory Consciousness Foreground (like the front part of the stage on which the Play for a public audience is performed).

To illustrate, ones Unconscious *Primordial Images* (Dominants, Imago's, Mythological Images, Behavior Patterns) are rooted in Archetypical primal images. They pattern "Things" from which like-kind models are created or constructed--i.e. 'reproducing itself to become the thing it makes.' It is an Icon designed component of the *Collective Unconscious*—i.e. the depository of the Archetype (African word for Seed) Images formed by ones original Ancestors. The Collective Unconscious (also called *Impersonal or Transpersonal Unconsciousness or ones Epic Memory*) was described thousands of years ago by Ancient Africans as representing primordial experiences having repeatedly occurred in the course of generations--concepts recently plagiarized by the European Jung. They also considered them to be explanations for instances of the *Inheritance of Acquired Characteristics*--a deep unconscious representation of experiences common to a human race for countless generations. jabaileymd.com

PLEAT VI: THE MIND/SENSORY CONSCIOUSNESS FOREGROUND: The Divine Spirit contains the forces of Spiritual Energy—e-motions—along with Matter for making ready the Percept "Ether Image" into a Notion. Then, if ones "Mind Committee" is agreeable, the process continues into an Idea whereby like-kind memory in-puts are added. The resultant combinations are molded by ones Intellect and/or Emotions to form Thoughts and a plan of action. Both the Background and Foreground forms of Secular Consciousness—a hallmark of humans, mammals, birds, and even octopuses—are thought by today's science to be that mysterious force making all of ones brain's neurons and synapses "tick" and merge into ones Selfhood so as to perceive what passes or occurs in ones mind. It is said to make one alert and sensitive to ones surroundings so as for one to be able to recognize oneself as separate from everything else in the sense of being aware of knowing oneself exists. In humans, this self-awareness of being alert is in the form of a Self-Concept and Self-Image and knowing one is aware of what one is doing. Yet, this separation is artificial (see High Abstract Thinking below). Some say ones

Sensory Consciousness is a state of matter arising out of a particular set of mathematical conditions and has varying degrees—just as certain conditions are required to create varying states of vapor, water, and ice.

If consciousness functions as a separate state of matter, that could shed light on how different people perceive the world or the same person perceives it at different times. Nevertheless, it is generally agreed ones Conscious entity can store information, retrieve it efficiently, process it, and fashion it into a unified whole existence. In short, ones Sensory Consciousness makes one aware of the ingredients in ones External World. Every emotional change is accompanied by a change in the state of Consciousness. Strong and extreme emotional states attend with a Trance state (Chapter X).

PLEAT VII: SENSORY CONSCIOUSNESS/EXTERNAL WORLD INTERFACE: While Step V is going on, ones Divine Spirit is determining the "How" and the "When" of further progress for the *What* and *Why*. This is aided by the at least 12 senses subdivisions—visual or color, sound or auditory, smell or olfactory, taste, balance, motion, direction, heat, cold, weight, tactility, and pressure--of a human's Secular Sensory Consciousness. Creativity can do more with 5 more senses. First is *Equilibrioception*--a sense of balance, as seen in standing and walk without falling. "Aliveness" can be added by spinning a balanced something around and a person will get dizzy to the point of falling and yet the person regains balance, like a spinning top. Second is *Proprioception*--an awareness of where ones body parts are without looking. Third, the *Rinoception* is the sensing of changing in temperature without touching. Fourth, *Nociception* is the sense of pain. Fifth, *Interoception* concerns a human's internal organs which are capable of triggering subconscious or reflexive reactions for health and well-being. Examples are the stimulating of cough, control of respiration, and the signaling of hunger or thirst. Nevertheless, whatever immediate stimulus spurs the Mind Committee to go forward, the plan into action. An example of how ones Sensory Consciousness Background orchestrates the use for the arrival of a Spiritual Divine Conscious Awareness so it can "play-out" in the External World is the application of the *Humanity "Manners" of the Cosmic Organism*—as in having good behaviors toward and good relationships with all God's creatures and creations.

PLEATS VIII AND ONWARD: Since ones Foreground Secular Sensory Consciousness and Mind are in direct contact with the External World while ones Background Secular Sensory Consciousness is in direct contact with ones Inner World, situations arise calling for the development of more Consciousness pleats. Because of other potential doors in-between the Divine Consciousness Background (Pleat I) and Foreground (Pleat II) and between the Sensory Consciousness Background (Pleat V) and Foreground (Pleat VI), the discovery of ones Talent or hobby or special interest situation (e.g. Caring for others) may open an entirely new Inner World realm where special types of Consciousness satellites are needed so as to be aware of perfecting ones current interest.

EGO CONSCIOUSNESS

Since every human has the Free Will to remain on the Real Self path of ones birth or not, to not do so means one has developed an Ego as the govering principle of ones Life Living. An Ego then replaces a human's Self-Identity, the Soul, the Divine Consciousness and thereafter orchestrates ones Will, Conscience, Divine Spirit, Sensory Consciousness, Mind, and interactions with the External World (fig. 13). An Ego can come about from choosing to replace it with ones Brute's Brain, from some Organic cause, or by the Narrowing of ones Consciousness into a Self-Absorbed state. Most forms of Ego states come from psychic traumas.

Humans are aware of the Material part of their Selfhood by means of their Sensory Consciousness—and that enables them to know they are Feeling Beings. The combination of these Spiritual and Material aspects conveys the reality of them being human. Ones Sensory Consciousness + possessing Feelings are what allow one to have Subjective Experiences. Together, these are called *Sentience*. Sentience is the property of the nervous system, or its earlier prototype, to receive stimuli—the lowest grade of Sensory Consciousness. The kinds of worlds of Consciousness of False Self people are endless. Alterations in Real Self Consciousnenss may come from psychic trauma or from socialization. An example of the latter is that Hebraism's governing idea for the people was Conscience, for Hellenism it was spontaneity type freedom of ones spirit of Sensory Consciousness, disconnected from the Spiritual. Recall in Chapter VI the Consciousness metaphor of one sitting in a room (or basement) surrounded by glass doors but by being ones Real Self one was looking through the glass door into the garden of Spiritual Elements flowers. Mention was made of the fate of ones life depended upon which of the other glass doors one chose to enter. The doors immediately beside the Real Self door are not False Self per se but rather a narrowing of one Sensory Consciousness on the left (which at its bottom is Extreme Despair) and a narrowing of viewing ones Divine Consciousness on the right. The doors further removed from the Real Self door lead to False Self stairs, meaning one has replaced ones Soul as orchestrator of ones life with ones Ego. To put this subject into context requires assessing aspects of ones Selfhood.

NARROWED CONSCIOUSNESS

Divine Consciousness is defined as the nature of mere luminosity, knowing and awareness. The Old English word "*Illumination*" (phosphoresce in the dark) means light and in African Tradition it implies a flame within ones Selfhood which I liken to "Soul Sunshine." The Cosmic Consciousness is the fundamental, inherent nature of everything (like the mother) which underlies the Cosmic entire experience while in the human (like in a child) it illuminates ones mind. Since the Cosmic Divine Consciousness is hidden from humans ordinarily, to strive to achieve its recognition is a way for humans to enlarge their own personal Divine Consciousness. By contrast, one own personal Divine Consciousness can be narrowed. In general, this comes from some traumatic event. When someone or something does what it takes to create a mental image in the Receiver, it is that image the Reciever uses to recall the experience and provide it with some meaning—whether good or bad. When the meanings causes shame or insecurity, one tends to self-absorb and narrow focus on ones inner world and doing what it takes in the External World to gain support or protection. This forms a new Consciousness of like-kind associations of complex sensory experiences, memories, ideas, emotions, and thoughts. The Old English word "*Narrow*" applied to Consciousness implies a limiting to a reduced scope. In its birth state ones Divine Consciousness is like a light that shines into every room of ones Selfhood. Since the Enslaved were only able to understand a tiny bit of what was going on, that narrowed their Consciousness. This is like closing certain doors so as to stop seeing certain rooms lit. Then one may start seeing shadows of unreality—like those of Socrates Allegory of the Cave.

An elaboration begins with a summary of the process of what I believed happened to the Enslaved at the "Fishnet" moment was that their mindsets, "Awed" by the shocking display of enslavement, proceeded to: (1) step into its mystery and thereafter was continuously and permanently fix that into a mindset; (2) thereafter the "Awe" faculty generated a lifestyle corresponding to the ingredients fed to it as what seemed to be most workable under the hellish conditions of slavery; (3) with the passage of time and with each generational cultural transmission, the more remote became the origin of those initial patterns of thinking developed by all aspects of the "Awe"; (4) the "Awe" evolving patterns were of a Supernatural (Delusional) nature; and (5) those Delusions confused what it took to return to ones Real Self ingredients of thinking in compatible ways with African Tradition path so as to thrive in life. Collectively, the above mentioned types constitute *Black American Customs* in their Think, Feel, Expressions, and Behaviors displays--displays that generate losses, lacks, obstructions and interferences. Such displays that resist trying to improve are "Inside-Out" Black American Mindsets. For recovery, African Tradition methods supersede these generic Black Minds that so populate today's Black Community. More specifically, what triggered Extreme Despair in the Enslaved was a "*double-whammy*". This implies that the Sensory Consciousness is like all the leaves of a tree but by what the Enslaved were experiencing meant their Sensory Consciousness was reduced to only a vague awareness of that tree's roots—equated to their awareness of being self-absorbed and isolated. The root's dimness is from two types of *Adventitious* pollutants (meaning they can be separated from the essential nature of the mind)—first, ones negative thoughts and emotions; second, ones subtle obstructions to knowledge. The next devastating Cause was the reality of surreal present experiences ferociously whirling them toward a slimy monsterous end, repeatedly slamming them on the boulders along the way to the bottom.

A human's Real Self Spiritual Nature ingredients consist of the First Wisdom (knowledge and power of the Cosmic Organism at the core of the Natural Cosmos) + a "Spark" of God which imparts a "Pure Heart" + Selfhood Greatness (which supplies one with the sense of the "5Ss" and a Mission in life). Its tools of expression are ones pre-birth Emotions that allows for survival with those on whom one is dependent and ones Intellect for self-reliance. These supply ones Selfhood Integrity. In most people's early lives some "Big Bang" trauma causes a shattering Effect, as happened to Humpty Dumpty, of fairy tale fame, when he was pushed off a wall. Hence, "all the king's horses and all the king's men could not put Humpty back together again. As a result, Humpty became a False Self.

But be clear that the overwhelming majority of people lack "across the board" Integrity because of some insecurity—and that occurs gradually from cumulative micro-traumas. They can so corrode and erode or otherwise violate one or more links in ones Real Self Integrity chain as to so weaken ones Private Selfhood "eggshell" that it converts one into a False Self. Even when an Eggshell covering the Egg yolk and Egg white is merely cracked, it breaks up the integration of the contents of the Egg inside the eggshell. Disintegration of ones Real Self Integrity ingredients are thereby lost. That is what starts happening to the Character Integrity of humans when they merely place a "toe" outside the Circle of Cosmic Wholism. Once a False Self is operational, it institutes non-rational thinking, superficial Thinking, living life based on habit patterns, and emulating current "Crowd" trends of the day's society. This leads them down paths to become Aggressive, Passive, or Passive-Aggressive—all off the track of their Mission in life. False Self people perform dramas to feature their Self-Concept.

A person may have a Narrowed Consciousness in a Real Self or False Self state. Real Self people may not be doing their birth assigned Mission or, if they are, they are doing it completely. Or, failing to use all of their birth gifts as, for example, showing only 85% courage when 100% is demanded. Some are simply socialized in the wrong way. Some, are simply ignorance. Hence, their Free Minds and Life-Living freedom only stretches as far as the limits of the scope of the Consciousness they use. Many ex-Slaves did this by huddling with each other out of the reality of Euro-American terrorism. Emergencies, urgencies, and crisis show some how much greater are ones vital resources than one supposes. Most people live, whether physically, intellectually, courageously, or morally in a very restricted circle of their potential possibility Beings. They make use of a very small portion of the scope of their Consciousness and of their Soul's resources in general. This is like one who gets in the habit of moving and using only ones little finger and not the rest of ones Selfhood. Evil people always use only some of their Sensory Consciousness and making efforts to not use it in order to show indifference to those unlike them. To oppress people is incompatible with a high intellect. Narrowed Consciousness people have a Secular Integrity.

TRAUMATIZED SELFHOOD

As a child normally develops, socialized ways and direct experiences in daily living cause nicks and dents on the child's Real Self "Eggshell" Integrity. Eventually, there will be a "Big Bang" Trigger Blow multiple small experiences called Cumulative Micro-Trauma (accumulation of mild stressors over time)—one of which serves as the "*straw that broke the camel's back*". This 1850s expression, shortened to 'the last straw,' conveys the vivid image of an overloaded animal being given one slight additional weight. cumulative micro-traumatic insults sufficiently powerful to 'crack' the Eggshell. Micro-Aggressive acts are similar but at a lower level. But whether ones state of Selfhood Greatness is affected depends upon ones degree of Certainty about its presence. The combination of a 'crack' in ones Selfhood Integrity and a resultant loss of any degree of Selfhood Greatness is called "*Trauma*" (Greek for wound). "Trauma" originally referred to the wounds, impairment, and disability resulting from sudden physical injury or violence that disturbed or pierced ones corporeal (i.e. material body aspects) boundaries. Subsequently, a short "leap from body to mind" occurred when people started using "Trauma" to refer to injuries to the psyche—e.g. wounding by emotional insults or incorporating shock to the mind resulting from physical and/or emotional injury. This led to a "chain of ideas" that gradually eventuated in the psychologization of trauma. Eventually "Trauma" embraced ones Spiritual aspects. Thus, "Cultural Trauma" elides (i.e. eliminates or leaves out of consideration) crucial ambiguities in how individual persons are classified as victims of trauma, while extending the application of the concept to whole communities. In the Black Community, "Trauma" is associated with racism and its endless ramifications and devastations.

RACISM: Only people who lack the "5Ss" and thus have a sense of inferiority and self-hate feel compelled to segregate, demean, and enslave others. These Delusional Fears are essentials for forming *Racism*--an ideology which spurs and informs action--a belief in the sub-humanness of another(s) or of an ethnic group; because of affiliations with distained ethnic group; or caused by prejudice against phenotypic (observed characteristics) and maybe (the Genetic Constitution of an individual (called a Genotype which, incidentally, does not necessarily predict that individual's Phenotype). *Institutional Racism* (Social Oppression) is racism so enforced in embedded social life as to not easily be identified as oppression and does not require conscious prejudice or overt acts of discrimination (e.g. the USA legal system is anti-Black People). For those who are overt Extreme or Moderate racists, there is no effort made to justify the unfair, harmful, and discriminatory treatment of persons deemed inferior--driving individual and/or collective actions (e.g. derogatory, dehumanizing, economic, life or limb actions)--while this may or may not be true for those who are racists to a degree that is tempered, masked, or concealed. Just as exposure to secondhand smoke may increase likelihood of lung disease, witnessing, experiencing second-hand, or hearing about rapes or racist crimes that victimize others may negatively influence non-racists as well as cause secondary traumatic distress in naïve victims. "*Racism*" is a Legend Icon Image and Symbol word which carries the denotation of the belief that race accounts for differences in human character or ability and that a particular race is superior to others. However, for Black people "Racism" is an emotive word because more than being a matter of beliefs and values (its denotation), what is associated with it (its connotations) is the evilness and sadism of White racists and their "sheep-like" followers who have perpetuated "Racism" since the beginning of slavery. Note that between the symbol "Racism" and the emotive reactions it evokes in Black Americans there is an invisible relationship of participation of the two--called the Symbolic Relation. [Ref: Bryant-Davis, *The Counseling Psychologist, 2005]*

PSYCHIC TRAUMA & ITS RACISM SATELLITES: A "*Satellite*" is properly an astronomical term originated by Very Ancient Africans for a small body which revolves around a planet, held in its position by the gravitational pull of the planet and deriving its light by reflection. An example is *Micro-Aggressions*. To elaborate, whereby "obstruction of justice" is the emphemism used for European rich criminals, "violently resisting arrest" is applied to poor Black and Brown people for the same action. On a daily basis Black People experience a host of racism insult that act like satellites but can have their own additional influence as a result of a 'big bang' or cumulative micro-trauma. The conveyors of these on a consistent basis are Bigots. The most direct contact Black People have with racism is with the sheriff, for he is always going to be on their backs. Typically these bigots cling to opinions adopted without investigation and are defended without argument, while being intolerant of any contrary opinion. *Racism is motivated by the drive for power because the drivers are insecure* and the only way to get some temporary relief is by demeaning others as a display of maintaining power and privilege by disseminating myths (cognitive distortions) about those whom they victimize (i.e. globally primarily people of color): "They are lazy, ignorant, uncivilized, dirty, criminal, and/or untrustworthy".

Such racial insults are pervasive channels through which discriminatory attitudes are imparted because it injures victims' dignity, self-concept, and self-image, communicating messages that race distinctions are those of merit, dignity, status, and Selfhood. Receivers of these evil messages learn and internalize them and keep playing them over and over as would a tape-recorder in ones mind. Furthermore, these racial insults spread as messages to color social institutions and are thereby culturally transmitted to succeeding generations. Racists' assaults are on ones mind, body, spirit, and emotions by threats, disturbances, destruction by words, physical means, neglect, rejection, abandonment. Assaults may be sudden/systematic, intentional/unintentional, ambiguous/ overt—and can be perpetrated by an individual/institution, or cultural. It prevents one from making sense of how to live or violates ones existing way of making sense of self and the world and creates intense fear and destabilization. Nontraumatic distress requires coping but not restructuring of ones ability to make meaning of what is significant.

"RAW NERVES" IN TRAUMATIZED MINDS: As stated, a major form of "Big Bang" and Cumulative Micro-Trauma is from *Racism* directly or from its Effects, as in causing people enraged from it to act with violence. When any one or more of these in succession or simultaneously are of Moderate or Extreme degree according to the afflicted person's assessment, a metaphorical inflamed "Raw Nerve" will occur. From that point on they become entrenched in a Self-Absorbed state inside a turmoiled inner world--thereby becoming addicted to that Narrowed Consciousness as well as to "the Crowd" in the External World. These completely shut down their Real Self, takes them off their Mission in life, and causes them to drift in life, "being about nothing." By being Self-Unknown means they have no choice but to make up paths that go in an Inferiority Complex or Superiority Complex direction. By no longer being in contact with their Divine Consciousness, they stake claim to having some aspect of their *Sensory Secular World Consciousness* Awareness as Background for refashioning a new and compatible lifestyle of habits. These Habits are about "going along to get along.

"Habits"--which I believe to be a function of the Omnibus Brain--embrace and automatically repeat what has been learned "by heart" on the Intellectual and/or the Emotional plane. Social Intellect (of oneself, of another, of the Crowd, or of society) passes on its ideas to the Omnibus Brain which it afterwards usually faithfully carries out--and this is major in the cultural transmission of customs. Lifestyles are determined by what part of ones brain is feeding and driving ones Thinking patterns and habits. Omnibus and Brute Brain Emotions are driven by Desires for sensually (things "of the flesh") and excitement of Emotional needs--Desires able to make one an *Obsessive* (persistent uncontrollable impulses to think certain thoughts) and *Compulsive* (uncontrollable impulses to be a certain way or carry out certain actions irresistibly and contrary to the Good Character intension or ones Divine Will) slave to the emotional forces driving ones actions.

The diagnosis of Omnibus ('wagon carrying many "some of this and some of that" things at once') Brain is made by ones thinking about a Thing being all over the Archery Pad (fig. 7) and never getting to the bull's eye. It is about not desiring to know about ones Living Dead Ancestors and asking: "How will that help me in my life"--a sure sign one does not think. It is wanting only the gist of the information that can turn their lives around—and then on a need to know basis. It seeks a quick fix and avoids dealing with the boring, the tedious, and struggles. It is nursing hurt feelings forever and clinging to hatred. It is expecting a different result from more intensely doing the same thing over and over. It is not doing the needed planning and preparation for the future. It is either not thinking before acting or doing *"Broad-Stroke" thinking* (Bailey, Private Selfhood Greatness p390). It is having have a lot of Emotional enthusiasm and a sudden drop-off because of failing to use Spiritual Energy. It is lacking Courage to stand up for what is right. It is lacking Curiosity for learning about self-improvement things. It is not doing Critical Thinking and, instead, letting other define who one is. It is being Emotional about everything. It is not Caring about anyone, even oneself. It is not being intent on doing the very best for ones children. It is not appreciating anything of worth (i.e. beauty). It is being talked out of working on ones life's Vision.

A = Supernatural Satanists Messages of Kill/ Take/ Destroy/ Dominate/ Oppress

B = "Will" Fashions Messages into Who, Which, What, When, Where, Why and How

C = Ego Spirit gives Emotional Energy to Indifference/ Hate/ Evil/ Sadism Complex

D = Sensory Consciousness Background is the Disposition for Mind Control, Money, Power,

        Status, Fame, Fear Reputation, Excitement

E = Mind/ Sensory Conscious Foreground Creates "Monster" Mental Images + Fetter Attitudes

F = Sensory Consciousness/External World Interface: Plans for Penetration, Conquest,

        Occupation, Colonization

G = Ego Consciousness Satellites: Potential Possibility Pleats to perfect Ego Deeds

FIGURE 14

It is being addicted to Escapes (e.g. Flashing Light gadgets and cell phones). It is having Bad Manners for one is only concerned with: "Me, Me, Me." It is doing these things with impulsiveness and a resistance to change. The Omnibus Brain's lack of ability to grasp what is underlying a complexity or to discover the hidden inner layers of significant issues is the basis of Superficial Thinking—a state of compromised Thought. In turn, Surface Thinking means one has an inability to solve life-shaping problems and resultant poor results leads to a life of chaos and inconsistency. All of these problems makes the afflicted hyperemotional and quick to anger from their insecurities. Ancient Africans said Anger is a blocker of Spiritual Energy and its ability to promote Thriving and well-being in life. Spotlighted in their new False Self creation is their "Raw Nerve," remaining conspicuous in victims' minds because the Trigger disturbance is barricaded in their minds and cannot be removed. Psychic barriers are placed around ones "Raw Nerve" and further protection is provided by ones internal world defenses (e.g. denial, repression) as well as by ones External World defenses (e.g. "Don't Care"; "Too busy"; Superficial Thinking; "Escapes" from ones problems) to be involved in self-correction. The "Crowd" methods the Afflicted chooses to try to bring about a cure only, at best, periodically gives momentary and incomplete relief. Although it is basically about survival in urgent times as well as enduring actions, Chronic Omnibus Brain overuse triggers *eating binges*, a compulsion for sweet foods, and weight gain to the point of morbid obesity by overstimulating the brain's hypothalamus. Also, its overuse, particularly in those having a genetic error reduction of D2 (dopamine) receptors in the accumbens nucleus, gradually become incapable of obtaining gratification from the common pleasures of life. Thus, they resort to "pleasurable" escapes--like alcoholism, cocaine addiction, impulsive gambling, and sexual conquests.

FORMATION OF EGO CONSCIOUSNESS

Ego (Latin, "I") is the result of a Self-Absorbed Narrowed Consciousness or a choice to replace living in and out of ones Spiritual Elements with something else. From that point onward, ones Ego is the central core around which all psychic activities revolve in the monsterous appetite of ones "Me, Me, Me" pursuits throughout life and requiring no nourishment to grow. Thus, an Ego Consciousness is a self-absorbed awareness leading one to believe that "the world centers on Me, Me, Me"—meaning nothing is more to oneself than oneself--and that all self-judgments turn in a favorable verdict—leading one to believe one is better than one is—an antidote for dulling the pain of stupidity. Furthermore, ones Ego thinks it is so important that whatever it thinks, everybody thinks that way and whatever it desires, everybody desires. In the way the turtle lays thousands of eggs without anyone knowing, when the hen lays an egg, she makes every creature around aware of it. Egos do *Micro-Flattery*, as in speaking ill of others being a dishonorable way of praising themselves. Narrowness shows by being indifferent to everything which is not directly related to ones own welfare and sense ones welfare is whatever one desires, an Ego is self-confidence looking for trouble. One identifies ones Ego as ones ultimate Background Consciousness when it merely reflects an Indifference/Hate/Evil/Sadism (IHES) mindset chosen Consciousness. That combination parents like-kind Sensory Consciousness off-springs that branch into every aspect of ones life, in a pleated Accordion manner as follows:

PLEAT A: SUPERNATURAL SATANISTS. This features the Brute Brain character of the mythological god Set whose essence is to be against whatever the Spiritual Elements are for. The ultimate leaders are Satanists who fashion the "Air Castle" Supernatural cult Rules for Life Living.

PLEAT B: The WILL takes the "Air Castle" Rules for displays of "superiority" and fashions them into the who, which, what, when, where, why, and how with respect to Mind Control of the World Crowd; for Kill/Take/Destroy/Dominate/Oppress in order to acquire Material World benefits; and Indifference/Hate/Evil/Sadism (IHES) complex well-worked out patterns to achieve the first two. The Will faculty integrates these Messages into a compatible Virtual Image abstract imbued with meaningful units in preparation for the mind to receive the Supernatural cult messages.

PLEAT C: HUMAN SPIRIT. Since the Ego has no Conscience, the Will transfers its Icon Images to the human's Spirit inside the human mind's passive Sensory Consciousness "screen". Once there, negative Emotional Energy is imparted in the amount needed for any physical entity to become involved in an interaction that triggers the IHES Disposition with its Inclinations and who, which, what, when, where, why, and how ways to carry out the Intention. As a result of being set in motion (e-motion), the "Virtual Images" from the human Will acquire dynamic negative Emotional Energy. This energy is used in its functional set of abilities to supply its Intentions "Excitement" for what will take place in some Kill/Take/Destroy/Dominate/Oppress voluntary mental or physical activity.

PLEAT D: EGO SENSORY CONSCIOUSNESS BACKGROUND. Since False Self people are disconnected from the Spiritual Elements and their Divine Consciousness, their Life-Living "Ground of Being" Background is something non-Spiritual. That means they have no concepts of a "heaven afterlife" and that "when you die, you are simply dead." A False Self human's Emotions "Ground of Being," out of which that human operates is, instead of being of a Spiritual nature, focuses on some Physical or Supernatural realm aspect. This *Disposition is for Mind Control* of the others; establish rules for others to follow while they are free to do whatever they desire; be in charge of the Power related to what is significant in the External World; (e.g money, status, fame, reputation for being feared, power)

PLEAT E: EGO MIND/SENSORY CONSCIOUSNESS FOREGROUND: Ones Sensory Consciousness makes one aware of the ingredients in ones External World. Ego people's pre-birth Emotions are replaced by Acquired negative Emotions. Their Fetter nature embraces such traits as extreme selfishness, greed, hatred, anger, egoism, fear, envy, jealousy, frustration, Indifference, arrogance, pride, lust (Ashby, Book of Dead, p89). These Fetters are powered by imaginations concerning oneself and others and thereby cloud out the realistic part of whatever exists. Every emotional change is accompanied by a change in the state of Consciousness.

The Ego creates feigned enemies, fashions demeaning stereotyped Chimera Hate Icon Images of them, and layers Emotional Energy forces so as to make them fearful as to justify a need to destroy them. on the Will's Images which are then made into Chimera Hate Icon Images about their scapegoats. Ones conscious entity stores such images and information for instant retrieval.

PLEAT F: SENSORY CONSCIOUSNESS/EXTERNAL WORLD INTERFACE: When the opportunity arises, the Ego directed "Mind Committee" retrieves the stored Chimera Images from Memory, and decides whether to design a plan of action. If the decision is to go forward, more demeaning like-kind memory in-puts and newly acquired disgusting stereotypes are collaged onto the 'monster' Image to make for a really scary 'monster' Icon Image. The resultant combinations are molded by ones Intellect and/or Emotions to form Thoughts and a plan of action pertaining to the who, which, what, when, where, why, and how aspects for carrying out the "Air Castle" cult Plan. The "Air Castle" cult's generic Plan for any given situation is: *penetration, conquest, occupation, and colonization.*

PLEAT G: EGO CONSCIOUSNESS SATELLITES. There are doors going through ones Accordion type Consciousness Continuity from superficial to the bottom—i.e. from Foreground to Background. But by Egos disregarding the Spiritual, their Accordion playing starts with the Sensory Consciousness Background. At any point in that range between that Background and its Sensory Consciousness Foreground, one can stake a claim so as to determine the type of Sensory Consciousness Background one prefers to have as ones "Ground of Being". Within the context of ones Foreground Secular Sensory Consciousness and Mind being in direct contact with the External World while ones Background Secular Sensory Consciousness is Ego False Self's Ground of Being, it is out of an IHES Background (dictated by the "Air Castle" cult Rules that one fashions more forms of Consciousness to shrewdly perfect ones IHES skills so as to be honored by ones cult and without getting caught or having to be accountable.

FIGURE 15

CLASSIFICATION OF EGO DRIVEN FALSE SELF PEOPLE: For Mild or Slight False Self people (fig. 15) their "Ground of Being" Background is some "Thing" in the External Physical World, with a Foreground being about acquiring Material World benefits. By being followers in the Crowd, they willfully ignore of one or more aspects of the Spiritual Elements in every choice, decision, or solution. Because they have an inkling that this is not right, their lack of courage to do right means they cannot trust themselves. That lack of self-trust and lack of self-knowing makes them desperate for Crowd support, to which they become addicted. Because the Crowd is governed by "Conditional" love (you must voluntarily follow the Crowd"), they cannot afford to have independent thoughts. They like listening to themselves talk, especially when it is about themselves.

Moderate or Extreme False Self people operate out of a Fantasy Supernatural realm, instead of in the Natural Cosmos. They stake the claim of their "Ground of Being" Background as being some "Thing" that supersedes whatever is superior to what Real Self people believe, like a Spiritual God. This necessitates fashioning their "Ground of Being" Foreground into what is about Delusions of Grandeur as well as attacking the Spiritual Elements. These Delusions of greatness cause these fools to believe they are masters of everything; believe their wills are the ultimate criterion of what is right and wrong; and are like the rooster who thinks the sun arises to hear him crow. They have no concept of negotiation and believe they can start wars they have no chance of winning. Since they are so self-absorbed in spotlighting themselves, they have zero interest in other people except as a form of entertainment in stomping on scapegoats—actually finding pleasure in the pain and suffering they cause and even that is only momentarily satisfying. They would have no problem burning down another house in order to roast hot dogs. What is so devastating to the World Crowd is the delusional fantasies and shams made to masquerade as sanity and the soundest truths because of the political power made to reinforce them. Their "Air Castle" cult penetration, conquest, occupation, and colonization plans are so vicious as to position them at the lowest level of the human species.

SELF-CONCEPT IN REAL AND FALSE SELVES

For Real Self people, the nature of ones Self-Concept is determined by their Divine Consciousness (i.e. the Self) which provides one with ones Self-Identity and Self-Meaning—the Spiritual part of ones Self-Esteem. As a result, ones Self-Concept represents "What I Do" while ones Self-Image (Chapter X) is "How I Appear"—the Secular part of ones Self-Esteem. In ones Real Self, there are *"short hand"* symbols comprising ones Self-Concept which combine to form an imageless *"long hand"* thought. These Symbols can be classified as Inner World and Outer World—both being further subdivided into their "like-kind" Classes. In both the Inner and Outer realms the 'big four' Classes may be about Social, Nature, "Things," or Personal Successes or Failures with respect to the nature and degree of Emotions, Relationships, Skills, Achievements. *The most important Personal Achievement is ones own competence to Survive, Thrive, and be Happy in ones Inner and Outer Worlds—all dependent upon ones ability to do Real Self Thinking inside and out of the Spiritual Elements.*

Ones Ego has lost contact with ones Divine Unconscious (Unconditional Love) and Divine Consciousness (Truth, Reality, and the Natural)—losses which wipe out Luminosity, Knowing, and Awareness coming from the Spiritual Elements. This switch came about as a result of some psychic trauma whose wound was so deep as to expose a "Raw Nerve". Out of the depths of the Unconscious aspects of the psychic trauma arose a separate island of Consciousness but which eventually united with other "Big Bang" or Cumulative micro traumas to form a "Continent" of like-kind associations—a "Continent" every expanding from experiences with inner and outer confrontations with opposites.

That means ones Ego is operating in a Self-Unknown and in the dark and only with Sensory Consciousness. So, the Ego looks to the top of the stairs, hoping to get some light from the External World and its Sensory Consciousness aspects. However, each step is made like a brush—a device consisting of bristles fastened into a handle. Each brush is aligned properly until the Ego starts stumbling around, causing the handles of different brushes to shift so much that one takes an exit off any given step and at different times. Each exit stimulates different bristles on that brush to thereby create entirely different forms of Sensory Consciousness, each with self-defeating flaws. Whatever ingredients are produced from resultant experiences condition ones personal, social, and intellectual life processes in general and generate bad images of certain things, oneself, and/or others.

Thereafter, upon encountering normal situations in life which generate a reaction, at the touch of some aspect of ones "Raw Nerve" there pops up a flawed mentality in its completeness from having been seasoned in fields of applications which led to adaptations. By remaining in the dark, one proceeds through life without suspecting the existence of ones exit and being guided by flaws. These are what accumulate to fashion each new Sensory Consciousness and enlarge them as a collective.

EGO SELF-CONCEPTS: During the European Middle Ages, the word "*Concept*" referred to *"the act of conceiving* a "Unit" of phenomena as being anywhere on the Thinker's Scale.*"* The sense of the mental processes converting apprehended impressions into an abstract thought was first recorded in 1380. My *definition of a Concept* (fig. 16) is that it originates out of ingredients of Sensations from something entering a human's senses from the outside world + out of ones memory + from something going on inside ones Selfhood + from ones interpretations of the monitored feedback one gets from outside influences--or a combination of these. Concepts are building blocks of a philosophy and/or of Icon Images. A Self-Concept's summary *'payload' message* has no definite boundaries, allows for no mental pictures, and, since it cannot be measured, it must be estimated. The beginning seed of an External World derived concept is the acquiring of sensory input as "raw materials" for the formation of Stage I--a *Percept*--the mental entity of organized Sensations to constitute a "Thing" when it comes into Being-hood--sensations making one aware of something good or bad (like a threat, disturbance in harmony, or atmosphere of danger). Stage II is the Percept's evolution into a beginning *Conceptual state*—a maturing Identity. It is heralded by the *Implicit* (understood though not directly expressed) which consists of vague, hazy, organized Sensations molding ones mind into a sort of better awareness of what is contained or included, though not expressed, in the Sensation of the Percept. However, the Implicit is capable of being implied by inference and without being stated. Stage III is the further advancement of the Implicit into a *Notion* –a recognizable "what it is"--an "*Entity*" with a specific nature hinting at the "Thing's" Identity and its specific attributes. Stage IV is the evolving and further internally developing Percept/Notion into a bud called an "*Idea*" ('a becoming'; 'model'; form).

An *Idea*: 1) is an awareness of specific, particular aspects--e.g. properties, characteristics, traits, features; 2) represents an explicit ('unfolded' into clarity) concept of "*Identity*"; 3) a patterned quantity of "frozen" energy; and 4) forces shaped into a defined "Thing"--the shape that imparts power. Stage V--a matured idea is the formation of a "Unit" called a Concept. A Concept describes phenomenon (i.e. a phantom, to 'make visible' a Contingent Being) lacking life and lacking reality. At the core of this entity is a Disposition containing a *'payload' message* of the Concept *essence's shared properties,* an *Inclination,* a *Temperament,* and an Attitude. However, for those operating out of a False Self (or Ego), in order to booster ones Self-Concept and Self-Image—which is no longer powered by ones Self-Identity and Self-Meaning—one strives for Material Possessions hoping that by acting as accoutrements this will deflect the attention of outsiders away from noticing ones personal weakness, inadequacies, limitations, and flaws. Their Self-Concept is wrongly considered to be "Who I Am."

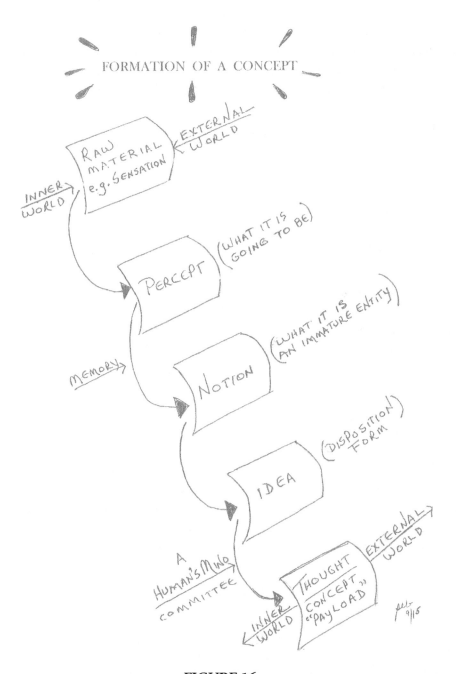

FIGURE 16

Hence, everything one claims to be "Me" or "Mine" of a Quality nature—e.g. social relationships, qualities of what one possesses within oneself and as External World accoutrements—constitutes an Ego Self-Concept. In other words, the False Self ingredients are also in the form of *"short hand"* symbols which combine to fashion an imageless *"long hand"* thought about who one is (rather that it being ones Divine Consciousness in ones Real Self). Similarly, these Symbols can be classified as Inner World and Outer World—both being further subdivided into their "like-kind" Classes. In both the Inner and Outer realms the 'big four' Classes may be about Social, Nature, "Things," or

Personal Successes or Failures with respect to the nature and degree of Emotions, Relationships, Skills, Achievements. *The most important Personal Ego Achievement is ones own competence--not to Survive, Thrive, and be Happy in ones Inner and Outer Worlds—but to be spotlighted in the External World, perhaps by fame, riches, status, power* (and thus feared)-- all dependent upon ones ability to be aggressive, even if it requires Kill/Take/Destroy by means of Ego Non-Rational Thinking. Yet, none of this is ever satisfying because ones SHNN are unmet. Furthermore, one forever regrets not having pursued and made flower ones dream, and that greatly punches holes in ones Self-Concept of ones Selfhood ("I'm not good enough"). Thus, a next step is to make others miserable because "misery loves company."

DETERMINING EGO SELF-CONCEPT RANKINGS: Whether dealing with ones Real or False Self, in each of ones 'big four' Classes pertaining to *ones Inner World and in ones Outer Worlds,* Successes are ranked by one getting what one really, really wanted and not getting what one really, really did not want. Failures are the reverse. Each Success and each Failure is given a ranking (e.g. from 1 to 10 on the positive or the negative scale) based upon what is significant to the person. Of most significance to Real Self people is wholistic (pre-birth Emotions and a skilled Intellect) achievements; for False Self people, Emotional Excitement and/or Non-Rational acquisitions of unfair advantages for oneself as well as of unfair disadvantages for ones victims. Those rankings are placed on the Thinker's Scale; the negatives added; the positives added; the negatives subtracted from the positives and its sum determines ones Self-Concept ranking. In other words, ones Self-Concept is the *"work product"* part of the qualities in ones assessments of ones Ego self-identity, including ones self-image and reputation.

EGO DIRECTED SELFHOOD: The loss of Real Self Integrity causes such great Spiritual Pain—the worst a human can experience—as to drive one to focus entirely on trying to relieve it. Since ones Inner Vision of the First Wisdom is part of the shattered Real Self loss, one does not know where to look and only has ones Sensory Secular Consciousness to use as a tool—a tool incapable of dealing with ones Divine Consciousness realm. This situation is thereby called the orchestration of ones Selfhood by ones False Self or Ego—the "Spark" of God replacement. The series which then takes place includes ones: First Wisdom being "Clouded out" so as to put one into the Self-Unknown. What is then only available is the Secular World's untrue and anti-Spiritual Elements Information. Ones "ME/WE" Cosmic Organism connection is replaced by the "ME, ME, ME" approach to life and thus one spotlights ones Self-Concept (ones spotlighted qualities) and Self-Image (ones mentally pictured significant quantitative possessions). Ones Legacy Mission is replaced by a focus only on the 'here and now' and thus the loss of striving to improve mentally or skillfully. Ones Real Self "5Ss," which imparts Courage, are replaced with a sense of Insecurity, a sense of never feeling Safe, a loss of Self-Confidence or Sureness about anything, a sense of Powerlessness, and being in a position of continual Instability from not being able to find a place to anchor. All of these substitutes cause Shame and Humiliation—both leading one to compare oneself with others and the result is Envy.

Ones orientation to Helping Others is replaced, out of Envy, with efforts to down-grade others so as to have a momentary relief of Spiritual Pain. Masks and Masquerades are used for attempts at Bonding and Belonging as well as for Deflective Measures—aggression (blame, criticize, finding fault), passiveness (follow the crowd and thereby give up who one is; "Make Do"), passive-aggressiveness (e.g. Projection). These are the result of a trying to make up for a loss of Spiritual Human Nature Needs (SHNN) and is not about self-hatred, as is so widely claimed to be the diagnosis. All of these self-defeating Secular ingredients are used in varying combinations—perhaps as a lifestyle pattern—perhaps different ones for different situations or for the same situation types.If significantly affected, ones engages in IHES deeds.

STRUGGLING BLACK PEOPLE'S CONSCIOUSNESS

At the moment the fishnet was thrown over them Enslaved Africans immediately lost contact with who they were. Their resultant Self-Unknown led them to create a False Self because their entire life experiences known to their consciousness sunk to a great depth of dimness--like sinking in a bottomless lake—as if asleep in exile. Simultaneously, their Soul Sunshine which supplied the Consciousness with the Wisdom of the Cosmos and the interdependence of each with the Cosmic Organism became covered with layers and layers of "Clouds". Both of these constituted Supernatural Mystical experiences—meaning its *Evocative* (mystical) powers now being able to evoke psychic forces of tremendous potency directly opposite to its Natural Cosmos counterpart (with an ability to identify with the whole Cosmos with a sense of total freedom). Instead, perhaps it generated a surreal state of being beyond space and time of being abandoned, isolated, and entangled. In other words, a Surreal Supernatural Mystical mindset was brought about by a series of "Big Bang" Selfhood traumas sprinkled with an abundance of cumulative traumas of a more diffuse magnitude—each having its own independent effect to interdependently cause that mindset.

"RAW NERVES" OF ENSLAVED MINDS: A *Surreal Supernatural Mystical experience*—representing a *"Spiritual Escape"* (whereby ones Spiritually is under constant barrages of attack)--is like sliding into a fantasy realm featuring representations of magical Contingent Beings inspiring "Awe" while also retaining a "foot" in the Natural World. The lost of ones *Sensory Secular World Consciousness Awareness Foreground* equates to being in a *Form-Body* state which has *"Totipotential"* (a putty dough-like condition). A Form-Body condition means one has returned to ones pre-birth basic mind state—an implicit state of vagueness and haziness without restraints and lacking any specific organization patterns—a state allowing ones mind to be influenced to develop in various ways, depending upon which molding "Source" exerts the most influence. In a Form-Body state, ones presumed Emotional features resemble the Right Brain mental activity of ones early life. Thus, it automatically exhibits "Awe" at whatever seemingly Supernatural things are occurring at the moment—an "Awe" unhampered by any judgment as to its good or evil nature.

To summarize the development of a Form-Body state is the process of:

(1) the Brain Switch from the enslaving fishnet being thrown over each free African in Africa;

(2) the enslavement itself with the loss of freedom;

(3) the long and terrible marches from the point of enslavement to the costal barracoons;

(4) being stacked in the Enslaved holding barracoons with no space to sit or lie down and stand in their own excrement into which scraps of food were thrown by the enslavers;

(5) the Horrible Middle Passage resembling sardines packed in a can, causing many to go mad during their several weeks of crossing the Atlantic Ocean;

(6) *"Seasoned"* Ordeals once in the New World where a large percentage were worked to death;

(7) "killing of their Spirits" which was devastating and 'Splintering' to the entire Selfhood of each;

(8) separation of their "God-Image Self" from their Divine Spirit to thereby cause each to become Self-Absorbed because of the absence of the Spiritual sense of the "5Ss" (safety, security, sureness, strength, or stability)—hence *All Courage was lost*!

(9) being whipped daily to work faster on plantations;

(10) inadequate food, clothing, health care (if at all);

(11) having body parts chopped off or mangled by attack dogs or tied naked to a tree during the winter as punishment;

(12) the free rape of women for purposes of breeding while removing males "Manhood"

(13) Nothing was worse than the relationship severing of equally great bonds by selling away family, Sippi (intimate friends), and supportive acquaintance members on the auction blocks—while each was humiliated by being stripped naked to "inspect".

(14) Any or all of these could have generated a "Raw Nerve" in a given Enslaved

ENSLAVED "CLOUDED OUT" CONSCIOUSNESS: By the effects and consequences of enslavement and its lifetime of horrors in all African victims include practically all having generated "Clouds" over the "Soul Sunshine"—an Effect meaning loss of their Real Selves and the "5Ss." Traumatized minds resulting from "Clouds" over Victims' "Soul Sunshine" no longer have available the power of the "Spark" of God in their Souls--the *Ultimate Divine Selfhood Background—the "Self"* out of which arises a human's *Ultimate Divine Selfhood Foreground* of ones "Self" which carries out the Messages conveyed by the "Self." That loss of the awareness of their sense of God power was associated with the loss of their birth-gift of Selfhood Greatness. The replacement of these profound losses was with a Flawed Real Self or a Semi-False Self or a False Self—each changing the Messages used to orchestrate their lives. The Enslaves now less than Human Ideal way to live within their Private Self displayed as flawed ways to proceed through life. Such patterns naturally led to flawed outcomes which characterize Black American Customs. By no longer having ones Real Self available, Victims live mainly out of their *Sensory Secular World Consciousness Background*. Since that Sensory Consciousness Background fails to have the power provided by the "Self," it switched/switches from a state of "Harmony" into "Disorder". Associated with this switch was the development of a "Raw Nerve."

European enslavement of Africans resulted in culturally traumatized communities in Africa, to the Enslaved, and to the descendants of the Enslaved. Since self-consciousness differentiates humans from animals and since one is self-conscious to the extent that one is conscious of ones identity, dignity, and human reality, the Brute captors systematically went about taking these away from the Enslaved. This violent attack on the Selfhoods of the Enslaved also resulted in continuous fear of physical death. The fear created via the exercise and threat of violence was an awesome experience which pushed them into a state of profound Despair. As discussed (Chapter VIII), most Enslaved made peace with fear and death. Such occurs with today's "Baddest Dudes of the Streets" which provides a freedom to be able to do whatever they want in the outer world. But for the Enslaved, fear of what might happen to their loved ones and an inability to match weapon power directed that inner freedom into Metaphysical realms where they could create all the revenge they desired toward their captors. Some of this flowed out in the form of folktales, with the fable animals, like Bru. Rabbit representing tempered manifestations of what was going on in their minds.

"STRUGGLING TUNNEL" PSYCHICALLY TRAUMATIZE VICTIMS: As a result, in the course of a given Enslaved decendant's life, new problems of a "Raw Nerve" nature arose often—each new pattern being designed by some prior Trigger Event or Trigger Person—each new "Raw Nerve" undergoing a SOBMER process—each new process's effects and consequences being layered onto the Enslaved Ancestors' culturally transmitted and therefore socialized Dispositions. In other words, when one or more new "Raw Nerves" occurs, each is layered on to the original "Raw Nerve" serving to mold the think, feel, say, and behavior forms present in that Victim's Disordered Consciousness Background. The addition of each of these SOBMER Processes with its "Raw Nerve" so layers ones already Disordered Sensory Consciousness Background that it loses whatever limited powers it had to deal with daily living problems. Hence, the afflicted become increasingly confused and incapable of handling any of their problems and each problem is reacted to by doing whatever it takes to get through the moment and to "Escape" otherwise. "Escapes" might be within (e.g. accounting for drug and alcohol abuse) and/or in the External World (e.g. so filled with rage as to be violent over the slightest thing. Getting through the moment may dictate thoughts that lead to crime.

FATE OF TODAY'S BLACK YOUTH'S EGO SELF-CONCEPT: For most struggling Black youth emerging at the end of infancy is the loss of their Selfhood Greatness from injury to their own sense of Selfhood. It is expressed as complex emotions like shame, embarrassment, guilt, pride, and envy. For instance, shame and embarrassment signify injury to ones self-concept. Once one has established an Ego Self-concept and experience a sense of failure, they thereafter are hypersensitive to Self-Threat--experiences that calls into question their present state of Self-Concept or Self-Image. As a self-protective measure, they lower their realistic success aspirations, using such unjustifiable excuses or Rationalizations as being assigned by society at large to the lowest rungs of the social ladder. Failing to reach ones potential or even strive for it is likely to adversely affect ones entire Self-Esteem (self-image/concept/identity/meaning) complex. An organic illustrator of this point is *Sickle Cell Anemia*. Here, the patient's defective hemoglobin differs from normal hemoglobin by only one single amino acid--that is, the presence of valine substituted for glutamic acid. Yet, this one tiny defect out of 146 in the beta hemoglobin chain can cause bone changes, hemolytic anemia, splenomegaly, vascular infarcts, and leg ulcers. Hence, one thereafter deals with all tough problems by means other than facing them. This absolutely stops their Intellect development, keeps them from evolving out of Excitement into "Aliveness," leads them to look outside themselves to deal with issues—or simply ignore the issue. The more they do this the weaker is their Selfhood with respect to self-reliance.

In turn, they turn to others for support (Slotter, *Personality and Social Psychology Bulletin, 2014*) as well as avoid persons, situations (e.g. academic challenges), or Things (e.g. trying to solve difficult problems or putting forth effort in anything) which will be a further insult on their already fragile self-concept and compromised abilities. These individuals utilize interpersonal relationships to gain spotlighted evidence of their past—each focused on extracting what is capable of boostering ones self-concept. Boostering examples extracting what will helps stabilize ones threatened self-views; that is reassuring by warmth and acceptance (particularly after a self-threat); that provides "props" for insecurities about oneself and/or what one is thinking of doing. My mother once told me the reason she did not drink alcohol was that no matter how drunk one may get, the problems are still present once one sobers and, in addition, there may be others that one did not handle and that one caused while drunk. The point is that being soothe by friends who fail to point out the problem one played in causing ones own problems, one remains hypersensitive, even if the problem somehow resolved. This adds to ones sense of weakness, making it an easy next step, when placed in self-threatening situations, to behave irrationally and maladaptively—e.g. doing nothing about urgent problems, eating unhealthy foods, abusing alcohol, taking street drugs, and looking for more risky or unattainable "Excitements." These become Conditioned Responses to anything deemed threatening, ever ready to impulsively enter self-destructive think, feel, say, and do behaviors. Note: *attempts to make up for SHNN losses or to acquire SHNN are at the base of all Black gang member (and any problematic Black youth) mindsets.*

FALSE SELF CONSCIOUSNESS
PART OF SENSORY CONSCIOUSNESS

False Self Ego take over when one chooses to get off the Real Self course. The Real Self's Divine Consciousness as well as the Real Self's Mind Committee are pushed out of the False Self World by the dictator Ego director. The Sensory Consciousness station now becomes the False Self's Ground of Being which fashions standards, guides, filters, and measures to go through life. Thereafter, it is not ones Consciousness that determines who one is but rather ones social aspect that determines ones Consciousness. The Conscious Mind allows itself to be trained like a parrot, but not the Unconscious. Emotion is the chief source of all becoming Conscious. False Self people are dedicated to appearing to be right—fashioning all means which help to this end. Their Self-Image Consciousness, emerging out of self-hatred, has come from the undermining of the rightness of reason, of order, of harmony.

If one has chosen to operate out of ones Brute Brain, one has a violence orientation. Ones *Secular Sensory Consciousness Background* (analogized to the part of the stage in a theater remote from the audience) thereafter governs ones awareness of oneself in a Self-Absorbed Inner World (filled with great turmoil). The False Selfhood's *Violence Sensory Consciousness Foreground* (like the front part of the stage on which the Play is performed) deals with all the accoutrements of the External World. In both False Self Worlds ones Ego determines what one is to do and guides what one is doing as one goes through life. The Brute Background Values are important because they represent the degree to which they follow beliefs and policies of cult leaders from which ones Ego gets its dogma for think, feel, say, and do actions. The Ego, by nourishing ones Sensory Conscious Foreground with Non-Rational Thinking, produces anti-Spiritual Elements lifestyles, out of which arise "Killer" Brutes' "Philosophy of Life" (POL). These are the type whose religion designates the attitude peculiar to a Consciousness which has been altered by the experience of the numinosum—i.e. being intimately involved in the "Air Castle" Supernatural cult.

ORCHESTRATING DISORDERED SENSORY CONSCIOUSNESS BACKGROUND: The degree to which afflicted persons have distanced themselves from their Real Self can be to Mild, Slight, Moderate, and Extreme levels. For the Enslaved, this meant their think, feel, say, and behaving fashioned the foundation for *Black American Customs* in order to endure in their hellish existence—arranging and combining shattered Selfhood pieces so as to make some sense of their terrible lives— some by fashioning forms out of arrangements/rearrangements and combinations/recombinations to adapt to their hellish new lives in order to come up with what would best enable them to wear the proper masks and put on the most appropriate masquerades so as to form coping and defense mechanisms. Among the Consequence problems which occurred from this was that their 'Masks" often became their "Face" and their "Mascarades" became their entire "Dance" through life. Thus, the "new normal" of who the Enslaved became consisted of a collage of some of this and some of that"—the pattern which became the *Sensory Secular World Consciousness Background out of which they designed in their Sensory Secular World Consciousness as to how to life life.*

Another major contribution made to reconstructed Enslaved African Selfhoods is what Nobles (JBlack Studies, 2013) calls "*Memes*"—i.e. contagious "sensorial information structures or patterns" (e.g. an orienting idea) residing in the brain that reproduce by symbiotically infecting human minds and altering their behavior, causing them to propagate certain patterns of behavior. These memes (units of information) are in the form of symbols, sounds, and/or movements capable of being perceived by any of the senses and replicated and thereby influence ones Consciousness to fashion the substance of behaviors. The more fundamental the orienting idea embedded in the sensorial information structure is, the more it serves as a "Seed" or germ to begin a process and, in effect, model ingredients that serve as standards, filters, guides, and measures. Similarly, the more foreign dogma of a Religious, political, social philosophy, fashions, aesthetics and artistic styles, traditions, customs, and every Trinket and Trivia component nature a victim accepts, the more that victim's Selfhood is "Re-Seeded" into an altered or replaced Selfhood. This takes one increasingly farther away from ones Real Self. So great is the memes influence that it can transmit to the next generation their core content or meaning and capacity to preserve the altered behavior.

FLAWED CONSCIOUSNESS DISPOSITIONS: The "Vine" in which an Enslaved or an ex-Slave was in and the type of Ancient African, European, or Black American combination of customs each followed formed a Disposition. In other words, if the "Vine" one chose that was about struggling Black People had notches on it, the individuality of each struggling person on that "Vine" expressed both as a "sameness" in most things and as a "uniqueness" in special things. The late Middle English word "*Disposition*" (placement as an emphatic assertion) means a human's sensibility about a "Thing"—an *enduring mainly emotional predisposition to behave in a certain way, typically impulsively*. The effect on its physiological Sensory Consciousness systems is fashioning the type of psycho-physical reaction (e.g. instincts) that will be emitted for the aroused person to take. This "Thing" has an ordered arrangement of elements which stand in a particular relationship to each other such that certain functions may be carried out readily in certain statable conditions and manifesting with a certain kind of behavior. Its standing is in what is analogous to soil and those elements are like 'seeds'—Dispositions (fig. 3, 6)--derived from its source—e.g. from parents, External World influences, or self-determined.

Those 'seeds' are: (1) its *Inclination*--a 'physical' "leaning toward" or "leaning" away from something; (2) its *Temperament*--—i.e. a mindset about a Thing or subject or individual/group with a prevailing emotional trend; (3) *Intention*--the decision of what one means to do with an aim toward a specific action or a specific goal; an earnest state of mind to reach the goal; (4) *Attitude*--C17 word (disposition, posture) is a mental position with regard to something. Such 'seeds' give rules to the specific kind of behavior produced (e.g. constitutional depression, meaning without clear-cut precipitating factors). That behavior applied to its Trigger Situation has a sameness despite variations within the Trigger Situation. A given sensibility characterizing a Disposition has different levels of energy applied to different things within its Trigger Situation and that sensibility for any given thing within that Trigger Situation may also change at different times, depending upon ones mood. The same applies to different individuals in similar Trigger Situations—some being more 'high-strung'; some more placid—whether in ones Sensory Consciousness Background and/or Foreground.

As unspeakably evil and sadistic as Europeans were to the Enslaved and their descendants, the question arises as to what reverberations did the police "Negro attack dogs" have, not only on the Enslaved but also on their descendants, up to this day? Black Americans know that the 'big picture' effect was, and remains, of a magnitude infinitely larger than merely the fearful Enslaved. Instead, it build-up Euro-American terrorism racism "*Attitudes*" (an enduring mainly emotional predisposition to think, feel, express, and behave in a certain way) in both Euro-Americans (e.g. "Killer" Police) and Black Americans which would be culturally transmitted to all descendants. What gives rise to an Attitude is a Disposition and what is contained in a Attitude is *Inclination* and a *Temperament* (the Disposition's physiological Sensory Consciousness systems which fashion the type of reaction the aroused person takes). A Disposition (arrange) is a predetermined pattern associated with reasoned thought or out of an emotion designed by some prior Trigger Event or Trigger Person which, if featured with sufficient Emotional Energy long enough, first becomes impulsive.

SENSORY CONSCIOUSNESS FOREGROUND'S FLAWED BEHAVIORS: The alterations occurring in ones True Selfhood from ones attempts to reassemble its shattered pieces as well as the adoption of memes that cause one to mirror European philosophy and ways is what redefined who the Enslaved were so as to be who European Brutes wanted them to be. For example, the "Stay-in-your-place" messages were part of Europeans' superficial and delusional information machine-gunned into the minds of the Enslaved. This included: "don't read"; "don't get an education"; "don't try to better yourself"; "don't be ambitious"; "don't be uppity" (i.e. do not be like a White man—and morally that is good advice!!); "stay in your place"—meaning Black people should "be about nothing"; "fight among yourselves"; and "spend your money foolishly." These patterns have been carried forth within Black families and communities under the title of *Slave Survivals*. These messages generated so much Emotion that it was easier to live by them than go against Enslaved Minded Blacks who agreed with their captors and advocated for them.

The resultant Disordered Background of a given decendant of the Enslaved may consist of: (1) socialized Dispositions, the originals of which derived from African American slavery; (2) new problems, each with a Disposition; and (3) one or more "Raw Nerves." They may work in conflict or together or in combinations. By each of these three being emotionally based, resultant reactions are disposed to over-hasty acts and to a thoughtless manner of living in general or in self-defeating ways pertaining to an applicable Trigger Situation—perhaps by ones thoughtless manner of living in general; perhaps by being aggressive, passive-aggressive, or passive when faced with a compatible Trigger Situation or Trigger Person. Ones mind is in a state of readiness to think, feel, express, and/or behave in a certain previously conceived manner--like a Puppet (Disposition) controlled by a Puppeteer (ones Icon Image of the Trigger Event having rules which constitute its standard).

Presumably, these are ones Disordered Consciousness Background ingredients which form and orchestrate Dispositions. Those Dispositions, when spurred by ones mind committee, emit a compatible pattern of what one will think, feel, say, and do—as fashioned out of ones Sensory Consciousness Foreground. The Disposition's Standard shapes ones attitude of where one is--and, if filled with enough Desire energy to do something, it points out/guides direction as to where to go with that emotional Disposition--and perhaps suggest what one is to do on the way. Reactions to each predetermined pattern can perhaps range from reasoned thought, Non-Rational thought, or totally out of an emotion which, if featured with sufficient Emotional Energy long enough, first becomes impulsive. The nature of ones Socialized Disposition sensibility, which displays whatever a situation occurs where its appearance is called for, is diffuse and general. For example, since the Enslaved were not allowed to read, write, count or engage in any academia, a today's descendant has been socialized not to read or be academically oriented concerning anything—even what is pertinent to ones life—and is not interested in hearing about it for improvement purposes. If a socialized racist sees any Black person at random that generates an emitting of a brute reaction, it is not what that Black person does but rather the fact of simply 'being' Black person that stirs the racist's Disposition to react.

Those brainwashing messages of the captors and whatever the Enslaved did to endure which were most accepted by ex-Slaves and gathered into Collage Patterns became the foundation for *Black American Customs*. A major pattern was the adoption of how they were defined by the oppressors. Another was the imitation of European Fetters—e.g. "Me, Me, Me," extreme selfishness, greed, hatred, anger, egoism, fear, envy, jealousy, frustration, selfishness, arrogance, pride, lust (Ashby, Book of Dead, p89). As a result of being powered by each victim's imagination and applied to oneself and to others, each one created, enhanced, and maintained the "Clouding out" of the realistic parts of ones Spiritual Human Needs. There were lifestyle customs which continue to the present. For the struggling one shared features is that of "*Horizonal Relationships*" (e.g. sharing with friends) but not "*Vertical Relationships*" (e.g. sharing with those who help them), perhaps an extension of the "Evil Savior Syndrome" which generated the Enslaved bonding with the Brutes.

The *Socialized Dispositions* that became Black American Customs—and particularly for struggling Black People who were descendants of the Enslaved--were predetermined prior to the birth of each and were simply socialized into the newborn. Presumably, they resided in ones Disordered Sensory Consciousness Background— the home of ones Ego (False Self). For each decendant born today and chooses not to operate out of his/her Real

Self, such socializing does two life-changing things. First, it leads one to not draw on or to shift from drawing on ones Inner Self birth-Wisdom for its standards, guides, filters, and measures for going through life all the way over to its opposite—i.e. looking to the External World for a system of values. Second, it changes the Thought Ladder's rung from the Metaphysical Realm down to the destructive Fetter rungs of the Physical Realm.

An imitated pattern of the oppressors adopted by reasonably successful Black Americans was, rather than seeing themselves with Selfhood Greatness that comes from their inner "Spark of God," they rank themselves by accoutrements drawn from the External World and the characteristics which enabled these achievements to happen. "I have arrived because of my riches, status, power, and recognition" is a False Self concept of success. In the process, most Black people parrot what European Brutes say—things like to struggling Black People: "Your problems are those you made and if you want to get better 'pull yourself up by your own bootstraps' and not expect me to help you. By me being well-off makes me superior to you."

FALSE SELF UNCONSCIOUSNESS OF SENSORY CONSCIOUSNESS: When cut off from the Soul, ones Unconscious possesses evil and good; dark and light; bestial, semi-human, demonic, superhuman, and Supernatural aspects. Where an intense desire for power predominates, there can be no Unconditional Love. The content of Unconscious Sensory Consciousness includes ideas, thoughts, emotions and habits coming from repressed thoughts. Experiences take place at the level of Consciousness but their meanings are stored in the Unconscious. However, when a Trigger Situation appears, out of the stored the negative Emotional ingredients, as in accounting for anger and hatred, arising Emotional Energy is sufficient to cloud over ones Conscious Sensory Consciousness.

FALSE SELF SUBCONSCIOUSNESS OF SENSORY CONSCIOUSNESS: Here, ones mindset is neutral and can be influenced by positive or negative thoughts or emotions. A Bad Consciousness can be programmed to contains addictions, compulsions, and fetters. It is ones less conscious thoughts and actions which mainly mold ones life. All non-emotional psychical acts develop by reflex and though considered conscious and voluntary movements are Subconscious reflexes. New door can be made by new "awe" type experiences. One of the greatest evils of slavery was for the Enslaved to allow being defined by Europeans (or anybody else) and their today's descendants have absorbed all systems of values designed to make them foreigners in their country of birth and the stereotypes that have reduced their human dignity.

"LAYERINGS" ON FLAWED SENSORY CONSCIOUS: A head of lettuce consists of loosely bunched leaves and each leaf can be peeled away from the "glob" of the remaining leaves for assessment. The mindsets of "Killer" police are like a "glob" of leaves (i.e. "Dark Side" aspects)—each having its own significance from the unique things it does while, simultaneously contributing to the "big picture" of all that goes into being a "Killer." So, let us look at that "big picture" by peeling away those "leaves" of the "Dark Side" in order to allow each leaf to be examined one at a time for its Indifference/Hate/Evil/Sadism (IHES) SOBMER ingredients. Thus, when assessing a problematic mindset, these "leaves" allow for paying particular attention to that one which seems to be the keystone. This allows for the unique Cause of a given person getting out of the Spiritual Elements stream flow and yet go with "the Crowd" into an IHES direction. In other words, the Causes are unique but the Effects are the same.

Legend has it that in ancient Siam (Thailand) the king gave a white elephant to any courtier who had fallen out of favor. Being then forced to supply adequate food, a place to stay, and a healthy environment meant it did not take long for the upkeep of the elephant to quickly ruin the courtier financially and drive him "crazy".

A similar burden happens to people—especially racists--who choose to hate as a way of life. While necessarily being in a "Bottomless Pit" (which Europeans call Hell), they are entangled with their Contingent (fantasy created) "enemy(s)"—engaging in Evil (the behavior deeds of one who Hates)--while hating being in that dreadful hollow--and hating themselves.

Their "layered" violent hatred sinks them beneath their victim(s). In zooming in on this to get a closer look at the layering of their "Dark Side," the manner is that of looking at pages in a book from back to front. A step behind their hate (Conscious Station XI) is *Envy*, a step behind Envy is the hated having shined a spotlight on the hater's own *Inferiority* (Conscious Station X). A step behind that inferiority is *Fear* of not being the Legend one has of oneself and of not being who admirers say one is (Conscious Station IX). Behind those Fears is ones hatred of ones own *"Dark Side"* (Conscious Station VIII, VII, and VI) and behind that is an extremely repressed awareness of the *"ME/WE" Spiritual Elements* sense of Belonging bathed in Love one had at birth (Conscious Stations I through V).

Something Evil caused that "Switch" from "ME/WE" to the "Dark Side" and that "something" was so hated as to become a metaphorical "Raw Nerve." A mental *"Raw Nerve"* results from a "Big Bang" trauma and/or Cumulative Micro-Traumas. Either or both *dismantle the strength of ones philosophy of life and/or of ones psychological safety, security, self-confidence, or stability.* One or more of these constituted the cause of the "Switch." The mental "Raw Nerve" acts as if it is *"Inflamed"* (set on fire or set aflame). In a physical sense, "Inflamed" is a term that originated in ancient times because of the heat, pain, burning, swelling, redness, and loss of function accompanying inflammatory disease conditions. *Inflammation* is a protective response elicited by any injury or destruction of tissues bearing the ability to threaten, disturb, or destroy the original part. Just as the human body's protective warriors respond to attacks by diluting or walling off both the injurious agent and the injured tissue, so does the mind do this to a significant mental trauma. However, the "Raw Nerve" remains conspicuous and all-consuming in victims' minds because the Trigger disturbance cannot be removed. And that prevents Selfhood progress toward ones Mission in life.

Besides Philosophical and/or Psychic barriers being placed around ones "Raw Nerve," further protection is provided by ones internal world defenses (e.g. denial, repression) + ones External World defenses (e.g. "Don't Care"; "Too busy"; Superficial Thinking) + ones "Escapes" (e.g. technology) from ones problems + devising methods to lessen the Spiritual and Emotional Pain generated by the "Raw Nerve." Those methods include: (1) *Projection*--giving voice to what one is trying to hide about oneself by saying that "Dark Side" is in ones Targeted Scapegoat(s); (2) *"Deflection"*—draws attention away from ones own "Dark Side Sickness" by putting a floodlight on what is supposedly outrageous about happenings of ones Targeted Scapegoat(s); and (3) Sadistic acts applied to ones Targeted Scapegoat(s) for the purpose of hoping to purge ones own "Dark Side Sickness" from oneself. For a variety of reasons (e.g. Envy, Fear), European males have Targeted Black People to be their Scapegoats.

By then making them into feigned enemies, they used *Reaction Formation* (a Deflection) to say that Black People hate them. Because those Black People had done nothing of a bad nature to them, in order to fashion *Willful Ignorance* about Black People (a "Don't Care to know about "those people"), they built a Supernatural wall around themselves. This and their brute-ness kept them from seeing their victims as "fellow human creatures." Such allowed these haters to fill in the vacant mental spaces resulting from Willful Ignorance with thoughts of opposition + disgusted feelings. That mindset justified practices of bombardments with demeaning statements, ostracism, rejection, inhumane treatment, and killing. Their hate for "those people" is a mirror image reflection of their own self-hatred which is too deep and too powerful to be consciously faced. Thus, Projecting their "Dark Side" on "those people" is justification for willful ignorance of self-hate. Were that not a part of haters, there would be nothing to Project and hate. Hate Kills!

TROUBLESHOOTING FLAWED CONSCIOUSNESS ASPECTS: A Troubleshooter discovers and eliminates causes of trouble. In troubleshooting one may find: (a) one is dealing with only one link in some interrelationship; (b) one pays attention to only the general idea within that one link; (c) one improperly links things together; (d) one overlooks certain meanings in certain links; (e) one fails to do a good job with one or more of the links with respect to arranging or combining them; (f) one ignores them completely. Any of these causes one to have flawed or limited ideas and therefore frustration--a set-up for inefficiency and ineffectiveness--a set-up for conveying the wrong intension or message--a set-up for confusing the receiver.

Step I is to locate the problematic page/rung that has keystone responsibility for violence. This is done by the "*What's Behind That?*" *Inquiry process*. It is like starting with the last page—i.e. the way one is in the "Here and Now"—and looking to the next to the last page to explain what was on the last page. Since something is unexplained on the next to the last page, one backs up a page to see if on the third page before the last page an explanation is to be found. And this process continues until one is at the beginning of the book whereby the author explains in the preface (the Source) what is the theme and then on the first page of the book speaks to the Origin and Beginning. This means one has gone first through layers from back to front in order to discover the beginning of the story and where an how the problems discussed in the book started. Here, in applying the "Collapsing Telescope" method to the Tree Concept enables one to see how tracing "Leaves Principles" become progressively fewer as each is discovered to properly telescope into the Branch Principle preceding it and that Branch Principle telescopes into the Trunk Principle and the Trunk Principle telescopes into the Roots Principle and the Roots Principle telescopes into the Seed Principle from which it arose. In other words, in using the "What's Behind That" process one eventually reaches the forces directly involved with the Causation—then the Setting—and then the Source of what is in the "Here and Now".

Step II, in going through the layers of Consciousness "pages" from the front of the book (i.e. the Foreground) to the end of the book (its Background), one progresses from the "Big Picture" to its Essence or Base or Conclusion. Whereas there lies in the Foreground the various components of the story, as one progresses towards the back certain explanations are given or insights obtained which lead one in a "Collapsing Telescope" process. Again, this is like tracing the leaves of a tree back to its branches and tracing those branches back to their trunk and tracing that trunk back to the roots from where it gets its nourishment and tracing those root back into their Seed of origin. This Step II process concerns gathering ingredients which make up larger thoughts, events, plans, or aspects of any "structure" and then analyzing that "structure's" theme in order to discover the Base upon which it rests. If that "Base" is hazy or vague (e.g. made of quicksand or air) then the "structure" built on it is false and merely being Information. However, in looking behind the obvious aspects of the "structure" to see the consistent, permanent, stationary, and unchanging patterns/elements underlying what is being analyzed (e.g. a natural event) then its Base is sound and real for the "structure" built on it. And that constitutes Knowledge. With respect to the Cosmic Organism that Base resides inside it and is thus the Ultimate Standard—i.e. a human's Soul or Divine Consciousness. What comes out of it and located on the first rung is an indivisible duality state of Spirit and Matter. The rung below that is Archetypes (seeds) for how the Spirit and Matter manifest as Ultimate Ancestors of all that will appear int the Physical World. The third rung down are Prototypes, like the Plant and Animal Kingdoms. Rungs below that are different aspects of these Kingdoms.

Step III is assessing any given page or rung for Flaws—an assessment whereby the "What's Behind That?" Inquiry process can be applied. The Flaws (fissure or flake off a stone) may be: (1) something missing from a loss or a lack; (2) weakness or limitations; (3) out of place, disordered, or improperly paired with something else; (4) malfunctioning or non-functioning (e.g. in being off track); (5) all right as it is but going in the wrong direction; (6) about an unclear goal or purpose; (7) containing insufficient motivational energy to sustain dedication, commitment, and loyalty; (8) avoiding facing an obstacle; (9) the right thing happening at the wrong time; (10) the wrong thing happening at the right time; (11) being on the wrong plane; (12) the presence of something spoiling what is otherwise okay; (13) the "too much or too little" of something; and (14) the arrangements and compositions of all that is involved (e.g. like paragraphs or even pages in a book) can be inappropriately "layered".

Problems caused by Flaws are many: "*Defect*" prevents functioning; "*Shortcomings*" causes deficiency in a person; "*Failing*" as a well-intentioned effort that does not succeed. All of these flaws keep something from being complete, wholly efficient or effective, or desirable. Thus, a Flawed person lacks integrity. These problems can be caused by being led by others who are ignorant or evil; by being too lazy to pursue the Truth; by being apathetic; by not making the effort to discover what one does not know about what one does not know or thinks ones knows without verifying it; by basing Thought Structures on assumed false beliefs. A major source of Flaws occurs in the innovation of something already established. For example, in my earliest boyhood indirect "telephone" communications, my friend and I used tin cans—connected by a string—to speak into and to hear the other's messages. Technology added innovations that went through several stages—like the rotary telephone; the the push button type; then the "touch" type; then the voice activated. With each technological advancement there were countless errors introduced which accounted for unforeseen destructive consequences. Hence, for me: "everything new ain't better."

Step IV: The point of all of these assessments is to take what is found and substituting Human Ideals which causes the flaws to disappear from lack of use. Or, maybe one can use those flaws to make something better. For example, the water in my shower would not stop dripping after I would turn it off. After getting that fixed, the water pressure coming out was so great as to mean too much was being wasted. So, I learned to shower by first lathering without water—then turning it on so as to only have a dripping flow, which I used to rinse soap off—and then one 5 second blast to get all of the soap off. In this way, I helped conserve the precious water. The detection of flaws allows one to prepare to avoid or overcome them. Other flaws call for troubleshooting or reexaminations that lead to truths or to something better.

HUMAN CONSCIOUSNESS PATTERNS

The SOBMER process has great usefulness in assessing anything. Aiding understanding to this end is the "*Collapsing Telescope*" (fig. 11) process—as in pushing a telescope from its extended position back to its small size that fits into its casing. Its discussion is the MVP (most valuable portion) of this book because it both points out many common patterns of how people use their minds and also how to go about assessing minds to arrive at a diagnostic conclusion. Although those who use this Mental "Skeleton" Tool of Consciousness Assessment will need to do so with ingenuity, it is useful for analyzing a Thought Structure; for discovering on what plane of existence is a given individual operating; for Troubleshooting any problematic mindset; and pin-pointing Flaws.

Just as the *Thinker's Scale* consists of a positive and negative ruler separated by a Zero (fig. 22), so are Consciousness patterns determined by what one has highlighted to be at what point on that Scale. Furthermore, the span of ones Consciousness is like a book that has several pages or like a ladder with its various rungs. Each page/rung represents a level of ones Consciousness and on any given page/rung there can be aspects that make for thriving in ones life or that can be so flawed as to cause ones life to be self-defeating. Parsing out each page/rung enables its scrutiny for flaws.

SOURCE: "Air Castle" Supernatural Cult Manicheanism Code

ORIGIN: Self-Unknown = Self-Insecurity

        Predisposing Causes: Self-Hate, Self-Inferiority

        Precipitating Causes: GUN + Network = "little gods"

        Immediate Cause: Cult military esprit de corps

BEGINNING: Cult agreed upon Scapegoat

MIDDLE: Justified Scapegoat Brutality for White Supremacy

ENDING: Scapegoat Projections for Fantasy "Escapes"

EFFECTS: Forms of attacking Chimera Scapegoat Images

CONSEQUENCES: Exciting attacks on "Dark Figures of Crime"

RESULTS: Kill Scapegoats at every Dramatic opportunity

FIGURE 17

CLASSIFICATION OF CONSCIOUSNESS PATTERNS

The SOBMER Consciousness Station Process Patterns are many (fig. 17). The few types of SOBMER MINDSET PROCESSES discussed below are: Type I—Real Self Life-Living; Type II—False Self Life-Living;

Type III—False Self "Inside-Out"; Type IV—False Self "Crowd" Members; Type V--"Killer" SOBMER Formation. These patterns apply to Europeans or struggling Black People—some characteristic of one or the other; some being like-kind except for uniquesess; some overlapping in that they apply to both societies as is. Differences occur in both societies and in any given individual in either society because each of these types is like a Conscious Station where different things occur and in which unique problems arise to thereby form different types of situations within different racial atmospheres. An example of how the process goes from a problematic person's "Here and Now" presentation follows the "What's Behind That!" inquiry, Collapsing Telescope, Ladder Rungs, Book Pages, and Tree Concepts.

TYPE I—REAL SELF LIFE-LIVING MINDSET SOBMER PROCESS: Just as a newborn possesses active Spiritual Emotions at birth and its Intellect develops later, so does the baby have a dynamic Private Self at birth and its Public Self develops later. For ease of discussion, ones Private Self and ones Unconscious can be roughly considered as part of the same entity. Just as a newborn's Unconscious is considered "Dark," it nevertheless contains that baby's Divine Conscious--meaning its apparent *Darkness is itself Light*—dazzling and blinding in its splendor. This is because, said Ancient Africans, the Divine Conscious consists of the "Spark of God" (and thus ones inner Spiritual First Wisdom) which orchestrates the newborn's entire Selfhood as it flows through life in the stream of the Spiritual Elements. To grossly over-simplify how this orchestration works, the Headquarters (ones "Spark of God") sends out a Message (Step I) which the General (the Divine Will) fashions into a Disposition (Step II) and converts that 'payload' message into a Virtual Icon Image (Step III). The General hands the Virtual Image to the Conscience Colonel (Step IV)--who passes it to the Divine Spirit (Step V) so as to empower it with the energy the "Troops" need (Steps VI, VII, VIII) in order for them to do what it takes to get the Message to its destination.

Whereas ones *Divine Consciousness* (ones "Self") is the *Ultimate Background ('Divine Mind' behind ones 'Matter')* of all happenings to ones Selfhood, the other side of ones Private Self is ones *Spiritual Awareness of "Self"*. At the Divine Spirit level (Step V) ones *Secular Sensory Consciousness* is on its near side and ones *Secular Sensory Awareness* is in direct contact with the External World, possessing capacities to have subjective experiences and images (e.g. received sensations formed into Percepts). The purpose of the Sensory Consciousness is to provide "light" for assessing the Physical Realms.

TYPE II—FALSE SELF LIFE-LIVING MINDSET SOBMER PROCESS: Because of ones Spiritual Elements "Genetics," featuring the boundlessness of Unconditional Love and its ultimate in Freedom, one has the Free Will to go through life in a non-Spiritual Elements stream. That choice is an automatic replacement of ones Spiritual Divine Conscious with the Conscious Station Supernatural Ego—a False Self (fig. 4, 15)--which then, as ones Selfhood orchestrator, directs what happens but always inside Unknown realms. Such a *Secular Unknown* is like a "Normal Variant" (Chapter I) in that its contents can be characterized as real, distorted, and/or fantasy. Hence, it can be assigned to designate any point on the scale, ranging from the Greatest of the Good Abnormal down to the worst of the Bad Abnormal in the Natural Cosmos or even into the made-up Supernatural. Any category might be selected by a given type of mindset. This *False Self* features such Fetters as "Me, Me, Me" Individualism, hatred, arrogance, pride, fear, lies, selfishness, greed, anger, lust, egoism, envy, jealousy, and frustration. These completely "Cloud-Out" ones Divine Conscious and its powers derived from the "Spark of God"—meaning one loses the Private Self sense of the "5Ss"—safety, security, sureness, strength, and stability. Attempts at proof are by constantly warring with the 'Right'. Thereafter, the Ego—and no longer ones Divine Conscious—sends messages to ones Divine Will, which proceeds to go through the above mentioned eight steps in carrying out the Ego's orders.

TYPE III—FALSE SELF "INSIDE-OUT" SOBMER PROCESS: Three initial causes of primitive Europeans not knowing who they were and the resultant detachment from their Real Self were: (1) the Free Will choice to adopt a False Self (Ego); (2) to power their "Life-Living" using their Brute Brains; and (3) not knowing and not caring about who were their ultimate ancestors or their origin—i.e. the 'that they ever existed' or from where they came or when. As stated in Chapter I, suppose a today's European is asked: "Where did your original ancestors come from?" The answer will probably be: "From Europe." Q: "But since European Geneticists say all humans originated out of Africa, where did those European ancestors come from"? A: agree with the Geneticists, research the subject (and likely find conflicting information), or to deny it. If there is the deliberately denying of the reality of their ultimate ancestral origins being Africans, then there is no origin they can pin down that will truthfully answer the question. Thus, they immediately enter the realm of the Self-Unknown without keys to open any of its doors and no tools to cut out windows in order to see. Not struggling in order to find a way out means one is like an entangled Slave to the Mysteriousness of ones Ignorance. There is nothing in the Self-Unknown or in any aspect of its mysteries to rationalize.

Instead, to be awed by the "Nothing" of what ones mind Imagines things to be, is all there is. The "Awe" is because of what is upside down and "inside out" being compatible with its leadership dogma. For example, in the Natural Cosmos the way to have happiness is to look within for ways to use ones Talents in a "ME/WE" manner and doing that to perfection, regardless of the outcome. This is associated with simple tastes, striving for Spiritual "Aliveness," benefitting from hard work, and liking the companies of others. By contrast, what mindsets see in the Self-Unknown is "ME" only; getting others to do ones work; having elaborate and ostentatious tastes; striving for acquired emotional "Excitement"; cunningly planning how to control others; and deceptively designing what is to their disadvantage in order to give oneself an unfair advantage. Recognition of the mental stretching required to gain these External World acquisitions and indulge ones Lower (animalistic) Self Passions and Fetters causes one to: (1) immediately become self-absorbed; (2) shift to *Impulsive Superficial Reflections* about who one thinks one is and who one desires to become; (3) form an Icon Image of a Superiority Complex; and (4) focus on ways to improve on the variety of methods and degrees to manifest Kill/Take/Destroy/Dominate in order to acquire ones goals. Rather than thinking rationally, one uses ones imagination to generate Icon Images that match the conditions one deals with on a daily basis. Hence, actions are founded on Brute *Non-rationalism* (emotions orchestrated by Left Brain thinking). The absence of the Right Brain input means there is Indifference to all non-cult members—a mindset of Inhumanity. Still for having given up one Real Self and its "5Ss" leads them to be Fear-Based. Hence their intense propensity for emulation of idols and an alertness to all.

TYPE IV—FALSE SELF "CROWD" SOBMER PROCESS: For all humans, the Unknown can be imaged as an Icon symbol consisting of a collage of an Association of Ideas--Ideas one has no concept about, is somehow remotely acquainted, and/or one has made-up and repeated so often as for it to seem real. This Icon Symbol's bits and pieces thus carry the potential for being about the Normal, Misfits, and Miscellaneous. Any of these "as is" or any which undergo a 'mutation' might form a *"Normal Variant."* This lies between Normal and Abnormal but is not sufficiently different from either to be called one or the other. In medicine, clinical pathological manifestations are generally not present when the "Normal Variant" is closer to the Normal than to the abnormal. Yet, considerable confusion can exist as the "Normal Variant" approaches the Abnormal pathological state. For example, the "Normal Variant" of ones genetically derived bunion (and thus unlikely to cause symptoms, despite its increased susceptibility to do so) can be carelessly and wrongly designated to be the cause of ones foot pain. A *Secular Unknown* is like a "Normal Variant" in that its contents can be characterized as real, distorted, and/or fantasy. Hence, it can be assigned to designate any point on the scale, ranging from the Greatest of the Good Abnormal down to the worst of the Bad Abnormal in the Natural Cosmos or even into the made-up Supernatural. Any category might be selected by a given type of mindset.

Self-UnKnowers from any cause have no other way of getting out of the Unknown except by reaching into mysterious "Supernatural" realms. Once there, they seek out like-kind others afflicted with the insecurity of not knowing who they are. By so doing they experience themselves in terms of each other and thereby possess *"Numinous Feelings"* consisting of being filled up with a sensation of a Supernatural Numen presence. This Numen sensation pertains to something which is both a value (e.g. the "excitement" of sort after Material "Things") and an objective reality (e.g. the indulging of a human's animalistic desires)—gained from visual experiences. Together fashion a dogma of shared values and beliefs which the entire cult lives up to and uses as standards, guides, filters, and measures for daily living. By being strategically located in all aspects of society, there is a collective Omnipresence—i.e. present everywhere simultaneously. Out of that cult and personal combination Europeans establish an imagined erroneous but presumed personal Icon Image of superiority. A feature of "the Crowd" is one of Indifference to outsiders which requires Wilfull Ignorance about them. Their partly "Inside-Out" thinking is directed by their Consciousness Ego which, in turn, orchestrates the rest. Their hatred is in the form of back-biting with each other—one must tend to them like a vegetable in a garden—inbreding regard what they do, what they have, responding to their emotions so that you cannot look outside oneself or in the outside world. There are cliques inside ones "Crowd" and dealing with both is all time consuming—who is going with whom and where; primping for the others. Most Europeans get riled up if they are stimulated to fear something about Black People. "The Crowd" moves slowly in an Indifference/Hate/Evil/Sadism (IHES) Complex mindset direction.

TYPE V—"KILLER" SOBMER FORMATION PROCESS: People with a weakened Private Selfhood make a volitional (a conscious effort) decision to give up being their Real Selves because of a lack of Courage and loss of personal power to continue being who they really are. Also, not to know others argues oneself to be Unknown. By automatically stepping into an Unknown "Life-Living" flow is called *"Pathography"* (Greek, patho-suffering, disease + -graphy, writing). Initially simply being a description of a disease, it was later applied to the study of an individual or a community as relating to the influence of a disease. Since 1848, Pathography refers to a biography focusing on the negative, proceeding through this course of Self-Unknowing phases.

Phase I is losing contact with what the Natural Cosmos is about—e.g. all Cosmic Organism connections--an ability to see the wonders within ones Private Selfhood--any "yoking" with the Cosmic Creator—and any sense of "Life after Death."

Phase II is that, as a result of Phase I, one is converted from a "ME/WE" orientation to a "Me, Me, Me" manner of "Life-Living".

Phase III is the lack of visionary power--of an absence of direction as to how to return to their Natural Cosmic home--and of an unawareness where they came from.

Phase IV: What is compatible with being inside a bottomless unreal realm is the development of a False Self "Inside-Out" Belief System, as with whatever is significant is not from ones Self, but in External World "Things" and people. Such viewings, similar to a drowning person clutching at straws in hope they will aid survival, lead ones Ego to clutch false airy beliefs + impart "excitement" of sort after Material "Things") + make okay the freedom in objective reality to indulge in ones animalistic desires). The resultant beliefs absorb a sense that some Unknown 'Superior Supernatural *Numinous* Being' has the powers to make this all possible and deludes oneself that such is confirmed by ones visual experiences. Hence, one necessarily chooses to ignore that these beliefs are the product of ones own imagination in order to believe oneself is also superior. This idea of the Supernatural arrives out of an awareness by either sham or nonscientific techniques—none of which can be described or explained because they were done inside an "Air Castle."

Phase V--an Attitude of "me vs. the world"--makes for a revolting and rebellious "Heart" against the light of the Certainty characterizing the Natural Cosmos and its patterns of Order, as laid out by Ancient African Sages. Since whatever is Uncertain carries Doubt and Ambiguity, being entangled in it leads one to fantasize about ways out of it. If one does not commit suicide, then the opposite choice is to declare oneself to be a "little god". This self-declaration embraces: *Omnipotence* (Unlimited and universal power) and *Omniscient*--total knowledge of everything, despite having "no clue" about anything except what comes out of an Indifference/Hate/Evil/Sadism (IHES) complex.

Phase VI is the obsession to gratify Lower (animalistic) Self Fetters, "Dark Side" Desires and their associated goals. Brutes follow the model of patterns spotlighted by the mythological personified African god Set—e.g. lust, arrogance, anger, fear, attachments, amoral, greed.

Phase VII: Molded out of the European Supernatural cult are Conscious Station Egos which believe anything about the Supernatural aspects are superior to everything pertaining to the Spiritual Elements. Hence, each designs an imagined erroneous but presumed personal Icon Image of superiority and adopt practices to excel in the greatest symbols of Supernatural "Air Castle" success—i.e. power, status, riches, and possessions. Such requires making others aware of ones apparent successes as by being wasteful of or polluting what their victims need for basic living (e.g. food, water, air). One stops at nothing to achieve these ends—whether by generating Confusion/Trickery/Deceit or by the more aggressive Kill/Take/Destroy/Dominate/Oppress (KTDDO) methods. Brutes are too lost to be enlightened.

Phase VIII: Next, one lives up to ones personal Icon Image of being superior by attacking scapegoats. Thereafter, the Ego—which have long ago pushed their birth gift of Divine Conscious into the deepest part of their mental dungeon so as to be forever encaged—sends messages to ones Divine Will, which proceeds to go through the process in a manner that corresponds with their Ego's orders. Those 'Orders" have the theme of KTDDO by overt, tempered, masked, or concealed methods. The model for these "Orders" date to primitive Europeans who used Fantasy about "Scarcity"--the focal point of their beginning on Earth--to form an "Air Castle" Icon Image for the *Ultimate Background of their Unconscious*. Back then, the environmental and climate conditions were so harsh in the beginning as to perhaps cause them to desperately cling onto anything that could help endure the Scarcity—like a drowning man grasps a 'straw' in hopes it will be a life-saver. Thus, the *Foreground Awareness of their Unconscious* was about survival, featuring KTDDO methods. In the *Background of their Sensory Conscious* was "What if" Fantasies concerning attackers as well as regarding their own human nature inadequacies related to survival. No doubt, in the *Foreground* of their *Sensory Conscious* were active imaginations about the contents of the Occult and out of this came imaginary Contingent Beings. Such a mindset is seen in "Killer" police. This Ego orientation necessarily means an IHES Complex mindset—a mindset overflowing with hostility—a mindset that gets relief from bubbling distressful tensions by inflicting pain, suffering, and misery—a mindset totally dedicated to striving for recognition, status, fame from fellow IHES mindsets.

Power is displayed by the *Seven Deadly Sins*—pride (arrogance), covetousness (greed), lust, anger, gluttony, envy, and sloth (lazy). A typical trigger for activating deadly attacks by "Killer" police is dark skin color. This color is like the psychedelic effect that triggers an echo to expand ones Consciousness through ones greater awareness of the senses and emotional feelings as well as to reveal ones Unconscious motivations.

Both effects of the trigger color are vividly expressed symbolically. Its bold abstract emotive sense plays daily like a tape recorder and thus causes a Conditioned Response to the Trigger color. This plus an obsession to be honored by ones cult members are greatly contributory to "Killer" police's needless killings of unarmed Black People.

"KILLER" POLICE PHILOSOPHY OF LIFE: Whereas Real Self humans are formed *out of* their 'Self' *Ultimate Background*, False Self humans by-pass their 'Self' so as to be formed out of an Ego directed *Occult Background*. The Ego, by nourishing ones Sensory Conscious with Non-Rational Thinking, produces anti-Spiritual Elements lifestyles. Together, these constitute a "Killer" police's "Philosophy of Life" (POL). A POL is structured like a skyscraper building. Its *Base,* equivalent to the Ultimate Background, is behind/below ones main patterns for living. For "Killer" police, the *Base* is an Occult Fantasy created Supernatural "Air Castle" mindset. Out of that 'Base' arises an *Underground Foundation*, from which emerges ones System of Values—i.e. "Air Castle" versions of success, as with social power, status, riches, possessions. The *Above-ground Foundation* upon which the skyscraper rests is the *Power Approach* of the Indifference/Hate/Evil/Sadism (IHES) Complex ingredients. The *building Frame* is ones *Attitude*—the Fetters—which determine the nature of ones thoughts and emotions for carrying out the *Seven Deadly Sins*—pride (arrogance), covetousness (greed), lust, anger, gluttony, envy, and sloth (lazy). The *Frame's Covering* is Kill/Take/Destroy/Dominate/Oppress (KTDDO) methods for living. The skyscraper *Floors* are "Non-Rational/Emotional" thinking used to deceptively maneuver and manipulate ones POL Values by overt, tempered, masked, or concealed means. The '*Penthouse goals*' of 'sick' pleasures are controlling people's minds + inflicting pain, suffering, and misery + acquiring recognition, status, and fame from fellow IHES mindsets.

Out of this Sensory Consciousness Background (analogized to the part of the stage in a theater remote from the audience) springs ones Sensory Consciousness Foreground (like the front part of the stage on which the Play is performed). The Background Values in the setting of policing are important because they represent to what degree to follow the beliefs and policies which guide the general perspective and mission of the department + the officers' specific actions and performance as well as influence the officers' occupational identity. These play out on the *Sensory Consciousness Foreground*. For example, certain perceptions or team members may lead a policeman to choose to have an orientation of serving the whole community with service or certain communities only or be at 'war with the community' or be a tool of the politically influential and rich, and/or engage in corruption. Another factor shaping the expression of ones POL may be the foundation of a structure and environment that does or does not support specific police values. For example, a disordered departmental philosophy driven in multiple directions or a weak leader can be confusing to and challenged by officers who then follow Police policy only when convenient. [Ref: Greene, *J. Contemporary Criminal Justice, 1992*] jabaileymd.com

"KILLER" POLICE CONSCIOUSNESS: Imagine the reverse of a common concept—i.e. that the "heavens" equate to the basement of a building and that the top of the stairs equates to what is present in the External World. The basement is arranged like a big water glass with 8 sides—the glass handle being ones Divine Consciousness while each octagonal panel represents a door through which one can go up a set of stairs to the External World (fig. 18). Rinpoche (*Tibetan Book of Living and Dying*) likens what can be called Glass Door I to separating ones Soul's Divine Consciousness from direct contact with ones ordinary mind (and on which he elaborates and which I attribute to a somewhat flawing of the Spiritual Elements). Glass Door VIII is directly opposite Glass Door I and represents ones Real Self. Door VII, to the right of Glass Door VIII and Glass Door VI to its left, symbolizes a narrowed Divine Consciousness and a narrowed Secular Sensory

Consciousness, respectively. The remaining four doors are of a Mild, Slight, Moderate, and Extreme False Self degree. How one proceeds in life depends upon which Glass Door one enters. Since Glass Door VIII is in a direct path with Glass Door I, each human newborn uses that direct path to go up and down the stairs so as to shift back and forth between the profound Inner World and the External World. Those who stepped off the path can use their Supraconscious faculty to get back to "Knowing Thyself" and their Divine Consciousness. Thus, when they utilize the metaphorical Divine Consciousness white light (or "Soul Sunshine" as I call it) to have an Awareness of Spiritual Knowledge, this is like passing that white light through a prism to provide visible rays—rays representing stair-steps called red, orange, yellow, green, blue, and violet colors—rays each representing a separate African Tradition Ma'at Principle for "Right" daily Life-Living.

FIGURE 18

How well one can or cannot see through the False Self Doors depends upon ones degree of False Self involvement which, in turn, also determines the door one selects. Of concern here is the Extreme False Selves because they represent the Indifference/Hate/Evil/Sadism (IHES) mindset--the complex "Killer" police use to eagerly engage in killing those not like them. They are so deep into the Self-Unknown as to have no awareness of their Soul "Ground of Being"—only the Life-Living Background of their warring primitive European ancestors. In African Tradition a Spiritual "*Ground of Being*" refers to the origin of ones Divine Consciousness. By contrast, Europeans speak of a "Ground of Being" in a Secular sense, with "Ground" referring to the lowest part or downward limit of anything located on the "Bottom, Foundation, Fundamental, or Earth. Because everything Material in the Secular world is relative, there is something deeper than the "Ground" and it is actually a bottomless pit extending into the fantasy Supernatural realm. By being completely shut off from their Divine Consciousness, these Brutes' Life-Living Foreground is the "Air Castle" rules of the Supernatural. At that momentary and ever-changing place in the Self-Unknown, ones own spontaneous emotions or ones own personal condition invests whatever is present. Since its "Awe' displays of power lack a "logical" explanation, their non-rational minds create a name--and that name generates some momentary god to account for all of this. However, if the creation is about what is deemed to be "Against Me," then there arises the form of a 'monster.' Everything is animated and personified—being conceived as residing in the "Thing" or in the person in question.

What this means is that Divine Consciousness is vibrating Spiritual Energy of the highest rate. For one to be disconnected from it switches one to a very slow rate of vibration. Meanwhile, ones Emotional Energy replaces ones Spiritual Energy. Furthermore, although Brutes are at a "dead end" in the Self-Unknown, at the opposite end is a Glass Door so dirty as for it to act like a mirror. This mirror allows one to see only Images of oneself. Those self-images come from the person's Ego (a display of other than its nature). Thus, standing between these two mirrors, which face each other, means there will be no end to the number of images one can see pertaining to various aspects about oneself in the External World. Examples of imagined mirror reflections include who one sees oneself to be; who one would like to be; who one would have to convert to in order to receive recognition; and ways of seeing one being the "little god" that always wins.

ASSESSING ONES REAL SELF ANKH SYMBOL

The Cosmic *Humanity Unconscious* is the Universal Soul and all of its contents are present in all humans. Being a Divine archetype (i.e. made in God's image or likeness), it possesses dynamic nuclei which give rise to each human being. At birth, there is a dynamic connection between God and a human's Divine Consciousness. Since there is Continuity (Unity running through Multiplicity) from both Archetypes a human's Divine Consciousness and their Prototype off-spring each interdependently doing its independent activities. Thus, an adequate assessment of one obvious manifestation of a Prototype enables the Law of Correspondence to be applied to gain insight into its Archetype parent. Another clue about the nature of the Archetype can be gain by seeing how a human's Prototype exhibition handled an Experience of something significant in daily living.

However, when a human deviates a little while in the Spiritual Elements stream, it is like putting up a Glass Door between that human and God. For such a situation Rinpole suggests imagining sitting in front of that glass door that leads to your garden, looking through it, gazing out into space. It seems there is nothing between you and the sky, because you cannot see the surface of the glass. You could even bang your nose if you got up and tried to walk through, thinking it was not there. But if you touch it, you see there is something there that holds your fingertips, something that comes between you and the space outside. The "door" is a second tier of Divine Consciousness which enlightened individuals learn to go through so as to be in direct contact with the Divine underlying unity of God's Ground of Being and thereby achieve a state of omniscience. Here, the created human becomes the creator. Correction follows the practice that just as the glass has to be continually wiped clean, so must one refine ones mind to be more in keeping with the purity of the Spiritual Elements. Such purifying is like slowly wearing away the glass until holes appear and then proceeds to dissolve the glass or barrier separating one from ones Real Self.

My extension of this metaphor is to image glass doors all the way around where one is sitting so as to see out of the glass door into the garden. But Mild or Slight False Self people lack the courage to be who they really are because of the hard work involved, despite wanting to be their Real Selves. So they keep bumping up against the Real Self Door and because that door has picked up all the traces of dirt from their "hands and fingers," ones ordinary mind gathers and stores sown aspects of ones life in karma. So, they choose to take the door besides the Real Self Door because it SEEMS easier to go with the Crowd.

CLEANING ONES REAL SELF ANKH SYMBOL

In the Ocean of Nun the Cosmic Consciousness, as it is in human's Divine Consciousness, is inert or at least at rest or passive, since the "Spirited" active mode of energy is responsible for the differentiation of Matter into forms. Because of this inactivity, the Cosmic and humans' Consciousness are in a natural state of Peace—called Hetep. Hetep is the state to strive for to begin any process of recovery. Since Genius is the faculty of perceiving in an unhabitual way, to understand how to perceive the Ankh Symbol is to gain insight into how to peek through the small hidden door in the deepest and most intimate sanctum of ones Soul. By so doing, one can rediscover ones Sacred Dream and its Talent partners.

The Collapsing Telescope Method is helpful here (fig. 11). When there is no disconnect between ones Divine Consciousness and ones Divine Will, what one thinks and displays in the Foreground External and Inner World can be smoothly and harmoniously telescoped without friction into ones "Ground of Being" Background. However, if in trying to telescope from the Foreground backward into the one preceding and one discovers there is a lack of harmony and correspondence with the Spiritual Elements in the Ultimate Background, then one has faulty thinking. If one does not care to investigate this, then one has probably adopted a False Self. Troubleshooting this situation for those desiring to change is to use the "What's Behind That" process to discover what has powered the wayward thoughts in ones mind. Then one looks to see what powered the powering thought--and then keep looking for "What's Behind That" until one gets to the Divine Consciousness Background.

Within a human, the Unconscious and the Conscious are complementary opposites within a binary duality system and also are a microcosm of the Universal Soul's macrocosm. Their true reality resides only in their *Synthesis*--an assimilation of the higher with the lower--an assimilation that, when wisely used within a Ma'at context, one is able to ascend from ones Lower (animalistic) Self to ones Highest (divinity) Self--a "push-up"--an ascension measured by how duality is transcended. If one chooses not to do the hard work, the consideration is to be given to the "Big Picture" of the metaphoric discussion Ancient Africans used for the Deceased Judgment Day so as to decide ones course from that moment onward. The Afterlife door one goes through depends on ones storehouse of Ari (Karma). At the Dwat's entrance is a walled-up doorway, the first of twelve divisions of the Dwat, and its key is for the deceased to be purified of earthly stains by going through the north door, the pathway of reincarnation. The south door is the pathway of eternal life.

SUMMARY

A human's Consciousness is like a bird's life—starting a one point of origin and thereafter seemingly exhibiting an alternation of flights and perching. Yet a closer look shows that human Consciousness has metaphorical Ladder rungs that extend from the bottomless pit of the Supernatural world up to the Earth World up to the Metaphysical World up to the Spiritual World and is a "Spark" of God's Consciousness. This means a human's Consciousness does different things, depending upon the rung on which that human's mental activities are operating. As a result, Forces operating through ones Consciousness largely control events in ones life. For example, a *Secular Sensory Earth World level of Consciousness* is responsiveness of the mind to impressions made by the senses which, in turn, has the capacity for interacting with the environment. However, at *a Spiritual level of Consciousness* every human newborn is in a Real Self state because of its dynamic and active Divine Consciousness (ones "Self")--the Ultimate Background ('Divine Mind' behind ones 'Matter') of all that happens to ones Selfhood—the producer of Luminosity, Knowing, and Awareness in ones Inner and External Worlds—the "Triad" producer that imparts "First Wisdom".

So, the Triad is like sun rays shining on Earth, shining on all sides of the sun, and shining into the infinite sky opposite to the Earth. One is thereby capable of Inner Vision back to the Cosmic Organism as well as capable of using "First Wisdom," in *Disposition* form, to mold the Secular Sensory Consciousness Intellect by instilling its eternal Plan concerning guidelines for Right living. Since the human Divine Will initiates processes to manifest that Divine Consciousness Disposition, the newborn has the knowledge and power of the Natural Cosmos + a "Pure Heart" + Selfhood Greatness + pre-birth Emotions that allows for survival—the ingredients of ones Real Self. Thus, the natural Happiness state of a child is from the agreeableness of its multiplicities of Consciousness.

CHAPTER X

IGNORANCE IS EASILY PERSUADED TO BE EVIL

BLACK GANG ICON IMAGES

"Orthopaedia" (Greek: ortho, straight + pais, child)--the name of my medical specialty—came into being with a focus on reversing the imaged adage of: "just as the twig is bent, the tree is inclined." The new image was to place a straight pole next to a crookedly growing tree and binding the tree to the pole so that the tree would thereafter "grow straight"—a metaphor for orthopaedic appliances being used "to straighten the child" exhibiting some type of deformity. More broadly, in activities of daily living greatly contributory to how any child develops is the nature of the Icon Images formed in that child's mind about what is significant about a way to live or not live as well as who to follow and who to shun. This Icon Image is designed and "paragraphed" in code language so that the essence of its full meaning can be readily understood at each recall as well as a plan for how to react. As experiences and new interpretations accumulate over time, a given Icon Image is reinforced by calling up pertinent sensations and emotions—each recall adding a layer of depth, height, or scope.

IMAGE

Images come into being by three routes. *Type I*, regardless of their source within ones Selfhood, Images are the vehicles of the Will—ones Intentions. What is then imaged by ones mind committee (comparable to being in a momentary Trance) is registered in the brain and mind as if it took place physically—a reflection of it being orchestrated by ones Right Brain. *Type II*, sensations taken in from the External World are brought to ones Mind Committee where decisions are made about what to do. *Type III*, ingredients stored in ones memory are called into action from some inner world mental activity and/or from what came in from the External World. Interestingly, the human mindset craves Images, even if they are contradictory, for it knows how to deal with contradictions. In Type II and III an important Imagination Faculty skill is the ability to visualize the path and steps through which a project or task can be accomplished. This enables *Foresight* ("seeing" ahead and around corners to detect and prepare for what is likely to happen in the future) to work in conjunction with *Forethought* (doing before or during the performance of action all the "figuring out" and planning ahead before taking calculated risks to acquire yet unrealized beneficial realities). In other words, one is able to mentally walk through the process to see beforehand, errors, flaws, requirements, desirability, and any contributing factors associated with the undertaking. People who do this very well are called "People of Vision" or *Visionaries* because of their *Vision--the art of seeing invisible essences others are unable to see--enables Intuiting, seeing similarities in the dissimilar and discerning uniqueness in similarities.* They are in a Trance.

IMAGES DEFINED: An *Image is the most primitive unit of thought; a sort of mental pictorial representation of a specific event or object which shows 'highlights of the original*; a pattern of forms and figures endowed with unity, significance, a message having a 'payload,' and an obscureness from its remoteness to impart fascination. This implying the whole is greater than the sum of its parts—i.e suggesting its synthesized nature. Images are: (1) vessels (2) containing messages in Symbols as mental pictures and/or ideas in sequences of words, sentences, emotions, and feelings just as they occur; (3) the Idea figure in the Icon Image or mental picture contains a vast number of direct meanings—those of the creator or sender and those of the Receiver(s)—either being true, distorted, or fantasy interpretations. The Icon Image creation: (4) is the essence of the transcript of the creator's ideas; (5) a force consisting of a patterned quantity of energy organized into a shape, complete with a power compatible with that shape; (6) possesses power manifested by its unique sound wave vibratory contents; (7) conveying information drawn out of realistic, distorted, and/or unreality; (8) can be manipulated via the faculty of Imagination organized; (9) cause human energies to be motivated into action; (10) consist of qualities that are clear/unclear; and (11) display an intensity ranging from mild to extreme, with a duration that is brief/long.

BLACK ADULT ICON IMAGES

The Greek mythological story of Narcissus concerns a young man who could not grasp the tormenting, mild image he saw in the waters of a fountain. As a result, he plunged into it and was drowned. This is what happens to many Black youth who lack parental guidance and do not feel safe in their environment. Thus, they need to formulate an Icon Image that serves to protect and reassure them that they are okay. For me, such an Icon Image came when I would say my prayers at bedtime—i.e. the 23rd Psalm: "yea though I walk thru the valley of the shadow of death, I will fear no evil for Thou art with me " for God is above me, is in back of me, is in front of me and is at my sides." Such speech was the Icon Image of Action. And for me to grasp this Icon Image was like grasping a shadow or a dream. When some Trigger Event or Trigger Person does something to score a "hit" on ones Real Self—usually in early childhood—Shame—the lowest room of Self-Esteem--results.

Shame--the feeling of being disconnected from parts of oneself as well as from significant others—the belief of experiencing all the worst could wish--causes one to become immediately self-absorbed and with a desperate need for self-protection. At that point, Shame starts teaching ones Selfhood what is much amiss (i.e. out of proper order so as to lead to what is faulty) as well as how to hide shame from every eye. All aspects of the "attack" are looked at from all sides and angles and each is enlarged upon—and always with embellishments of the nature that leads one to feel that one was right and a victim while the other was either disrespectful and/or mean. The results of such an assessment necessitates—on the one hand, such self-protective methods for each of the "What ifs" pertaining to possible situations requiring defense and self-care. But on the other hand, thinking of oneself as having been victimized stirs raging waves of ones "Emotional Sea" that it foams out of ones own shame. Perhaps then ones tongue becomes Shame's orator.

Meanwhile, since one has "Clouded over" all sense of ones Selfhood Greatness and thus operates out of a weakened Private Self, the path to be chosen at that crossroad is a measure of the type of Courage one has—either incomplete or not at all. The degree of ones Courage is Symbolized in an Icon Image, itself a storyteller to oneself of what one thinks about oneself. That story may be the truth and realistic, a distortion, or far more likely is that one is lying to oneself. Yet, that story, now symbolized in an Icon Image of who one is demands an Icon Image sequel of who one would like to be. Both Icon Images deepens ones understanding of what those stories are about.

INGREDIENTS OF ICON IMAGES: The Icon of an issue is symbolic of a hidden point of significance. The Image in ones Icon is a myth—not in the sense of a falsehood—but rather it is ones great idea by which one tries to make sense of who one is. Within a given category situation, *the more powerful the mental symbol or Icon Image representing the essence of a bad situation, the more terrifying its intended landscape of violence, the more mysterious is its form conveyed--and thus the greater role the mental picture will play in establishing a desirable system of "Manhood" power in order to serve its creator's purposes—whether for offense and/or defense.* Human reason is superseded by this new transcendental ethic imparted into ones Icon picture which, ironically, could not exist had reason not willed it into being (Moore *Cooperation and Conflict, 2011*). The Icon Image draws largely out of ones Memory—a storehouse of the past which then becomes a story teller of a story with changes of significant moments and endings: (1) what was actually seen, distorted, and fantasized at the time of the experience; (2) what was retained—people's attention span is about 3 seconds; (3) alterations were made in the process of remembering the experience; (4) some images beget images; (5) often rehearsing that story, different versions with different meanings each time—each of which is interpreted through Emotional Viewing Lens; and (6) presently, since only the most dramatic story is related, there is no way to tell what was actually true and real—probably more of what is a clear memory--the 'what happened at the end'--is untrue. The spotlight is on and the end fashions how to plan the future. In short, much of ones life is the sum of ones memories but things may not always be as they seem.

ICON IMAGE PROCESS: Ones Sensory Consciousness and the activities of ones Emotions and Feelings are what enable one to have Subjective Experiences. Together, these are called *Sentience*. Sentience is the property of the nervous system, or its earlier prototype, to receive stimuli—the lowest grade of Sensory Consciousness. The general idea is that ones Imagination gathers all pertinent stimuli qualities of sense perception in the External World + what is generated out of 'raw' materials in ones imagination to not only serve to form image items but also to mentally revive Percepts of entities formerly given in like-kind sense perceptions. Together, they form Icon Images while going through the stages of Percepts and Notions Thing. The resultant Prototype out of which models or patterns for living in relationship with people will derive might be an image of oneself "as is," a self-image of how one would like to be (e.g. of a risk taker or non-risk taker), and/or an image of achieving ones goals. Putting an urge behind any of these images—rewards or punishments—move the mind to motivate ones behaviors.

Specifically, the creator first gathers all pertinent "raw materials" from Trigger Events, Trigger Situations, and/or Trigger People concerning what actually happened or was perceived into distortion or fantasy as well as from his/her imagination—perhaps about what is missing or about what one desires or about a confusing present situation. Second, the creator takes the resultant Association of Ideas and fashions them into a collaged Form. This process of designing such an Abstraction Form involves mental *Imaging*--the envisioning of a possible Image of the desired future organizational state. Third, what is Imaged is in parallel, in accord with, matches, and crudely fitted so as to maintain the purpose for its creation. Fourth is to impart into the CB the values, beliefs, desires to have and not have--the "for me" goals, defenses for whatever is "against me"—and/or an offensive plan for getting who or what is desired. Fifth is using the CB for ones standards, guides, filters, and measures that one automatically resorts to without having to make decisions. However, CB are about things that are incomplete and can be identified only by being compared to other things. This is because gang creators themselves are in Selfhood disintegration.

"ABSTRACT" CONTINGENT BEINGS FORMATION: Primitive Africans' *Magical Thinking* was perhaps thoughts of unrealistic Contingent Beings (CB)--each able to affect each other--an Imitative (Homeopathic) Magic Principle (i.e. Law of Similarity). To control/resist unwanted powers from "Invisible" Realms, they also used Magical Practices to encourage good spirits while soothing or defending against bad spirits. Their Magical Arts (to put Spirits to work) techniques of coercion--activating powers of good Spirits to counter the "bad" Spirits--was the first use of Causation to deliberately influence a desired Effect--an Effect pregnant with Consequences. Those Consequences were intended to generate favorable patterns affecting their atmosphere and environment in an assortment of wide spread daily living categories. The people's selected Spirit Magicians used theory and dogma in many mental processes as an orderly progression of mental "stepping stones" so as to be translated into action. Its 'big picture' pattern featured a leader officiating things said and things done. The process embraced starting with many particular things/ events and moving within or behind them to a single generality called an *Abstract--i.e. the Virtual* (an in-active boundary-less 'Becoming Being') *in Metaphysical or Supernatural realms--as opposed to the Physical Abstraction*. Process components are: the *Spell* (things said according to a formula in a set order); *Rites* (things done, like dances, rituals, or prayers) to generate an invisible, intangible force able to operate at a distance without any visible or tangible vehicle--and a CB. The *Sensation* source of a CB can be out of ones memory; from something going on inside ones Selfhood; from something entering a human's senses from the outside world; from ones interpretations of the monitored feedback one gets from outside influences; or a combination of these. A first and natural display of the human mind's activity upon acquiring these "raw materials" is called a *Percept*--a sensation making one aware of something good (like what the ingredients for a flower bud do) or bad (like a threat, disturbance in harmony, or atmosphere of danger). A Sensation does not convey "what it is" that exists but rather its "That it is" existence--meaning it is a Primary Quality foundational to the development of a CB.

Although a *Primary Quality*, a bodiless presence, cannot be grasped explicitly by the mind--i.e. it is not clear, definite, or in detail--by its own nature, the "That it is" *Being is unified with 'what it is doing'*. Furthermore, the "Genetics" of the "That it is" determines the capabilities for how it is to develop, for what it is to do, for how it is to grow, and for the type of 'payload' impact it will have. A Percept can stop or be erased at this point. But otherwise it evolves into the *Implicit* to begin the *Conceptual stage* (fig. 16)-- an Identity which undergoes four forms of development so as to impart its nature. First, the *Implicit*--like the smell of a newly forming flower bud--is vague, hazy, organized Sensations which give ones mind an awareness of what is contained or included, though not expressed, in the Sensation. However, the Implicit is capable of being implied by inference and without being stated. Second is a *Notion* formation--a "what it is"--an "*Entity*" with a specific nature which hints at its Identity and which possesses specific attributes. Third is the evolving and further internally developing Percept/Notion, similar to the beginning flower-ing of a flower bud--a bud called an "*Idea*" ('a becoming'). An Idea is an awareness of specific, particular aspects--e.g. properties, characteristics, traits, or features--which represent an explicit concept of "*Identity*." An *Idea* ('model'; form) is a patterned quantity of "frozen" energy whose forces are shaped into a defined "Thing"--the shape that imparts power. Fourth, like the Fruiting flower, a matured idea is the formation of a "Unit"--a CB. The Unit (joined together) results from an idea's similarities/differences contents having been meshed into sensible relationships.

In contrast to Units of Cognition (e.g. conceptual or mathematics), an Imaged Unit can be real, distorted, or fantasy. Although all CB are non-factual, those CBs with powers capable of changing estab-lished beliefs are visualized within the context of Icon *Images*. As such, by contrast to most thoughts and imaginings of the mind, Icon CB are falsely perceived as real and thus can carry meaningful 'payloads' having wide-ranging ripples into many areas of ones life. Icon CB can be life-changing tools for switching Character traits or to shape them into the Good. The most major one is the creation of a mental Icon Image pertaining to Contingent Beings. Europeans have done this designing a dictatorial god residing in the "Air Castle" Supernatural and a devil punisher located in hell. It is fundamental to understand that their human reason made all of this up so that their "Air Castle" type of Non-Rational thinking, with its transcendental powers, would supersede all that is part of the Natural Cosmos. These fantasy creations, ironically, could not exist had not Natural Cosmos mental activities willed them into Contingent Beings and Places. Their anomalous account of the transcendental Supernatural fantasy state is conceived as the state which stands above and beyond Natural Cosmos' human reason. They explain this by saying the transformation of human reason into Supernatural stately reason is accompanied by a change in the way in which reason is understood.

Hobbes stated (1651) there are phantasms, or images ('decaying senses') remaining when the physiological motions of sensation cease. Also, there is Compound imagination which creates novel images by rearranging old ones as a result of ideas sticking together and pulling each other into the mind. Hume (1739) elaborated by saying this was a powerful principle for explaining many mental operations—giving European 'thinkers' a new metaphorical landscape to describe the human reason that involves an examination into the human soul. When this notion, called the Leviathan, became an entrenched practice, human reason gave way to procedurally bound reason. Then the Supernatural state was expressed in terms of a machine—a mechanization taking reason out of its earthly domain—a mechanization according a higher, abstract status which supersedes human reason--a mechanization completing the European concept of the mechanization of the anthropological image of man.

From a European perspective, such reasoning developed a sophisticated vision for handling difficulties involved in constructing and securing fragile and inherently contingent political orders, whether they be domestic or international. The reason for all of this was for security: "you subordinate your actions to our judgment of what is necessary, and we promise to keep you safe' (Bartmanski *J. Sociology, 2014*). In short, the origins of "the state" (i.e. the Supernatural "Air Castle") are earthly fantasies and yet the effects of "the state" are heavenly because 'visible stuff' makes sense only on the basis of 'invisible discourses'.

COMPOSITION OF ICON IMAGES: Like a Crystal, the first particles destined to create a Symbol come together to produce a unit cell. An analogy for a "*Unit Cell*" is that arranged bricks are the unit making up a brick wall. Other unit cells form on all sides of the first to start the process of growth, like families coming together to create a unified village. Its core, *the essence of what the Symbol represents, is converted into a higher order of energy expression* to form a customized "*Phantom*"--serving as the "Payload," a motivating agent, and an aura source. The False Self's Delusional world selection of a "Phantom" derives from an "out-of-control" Imagination. The rest of the family (or bricks or particles) consists of: (1) mental pictures made out of spoken or written words: (2) External or *Outer World Images* (e.g. patterns of their immediate and perceived society at large) from what was originally perceived and retained in ones memory; (3) *Inner World Images* (e.g. imagination, insights, dreams, thoughts, feelings) which are products of personal turmoil and which may be about what is real, distorted, or fantasy; and (4) eidetic (visual) External or Inner World images which possess superiority in clearness, in richness of detail, in color, and in intensity compared with ordinary visual images.

Together these ingredients fashion Contingencies and Contingent Beings (CB)—which relate to how to do "Life-Living"--are in a "Becoming" process of creation and despite never reaching reality they are prominent in the Icon Image. Whatever part(s) are flawed in one of the mind's building blocks dilutes and pollutes adjacent building blocks, like an ink drop in a glass of milk. Also, just as liquids and gases are arranged in irregular patterns, moving constantly and forming other irregular and non-repeating patterns, so do resultant flawed Symbols simulate that. That faulty Icon Image of oneself, viewed as if it were a flickering Disco Ball, forms and dissolves in successive instants, and never re-forms the same. The combination of the faulty Icon Image and its entourage constitute the family of rays of sense that are brought to focus in the Conscious pattern so as to be used in "Life-Living".

Nevertheless, that family's pseudo-perceptual quality has a character dependent upon factors of ones customized interest and desires. The multiple variables inherently contained in the mental Icon Image family can each be exaggerated by External World factors (e.g. "street" drugs) to thereby spur sentiment reflections that strengthen/enlarge upon the intended and existing meaning in the CB.

CEMENTING ICON IMAGES: Selecting and maintaining a given Icon Image is done by *Reputation enhancement* by group membership influences. Following several "trails and errors," when a youth selects an Icon Self-Image to display in front of specific other members, these others then provide positive feedback that reinforces the individual's image within the group.

SUBSEQUENT COURSE OF ONES ICON IMAGES: Of prime importance is the *Self-Declaration* one has made to no longer deal with ones own problems "face-to-face". One reason is that being mired in Shame makes one hypersensitive to whatever might contribute to that Shame. Obviously, ones significant problem call for one to accept such challenges and the taking of any action on ones own carries the risk of failure. And Failure is something to always avoid because that shines a greater spotlight ones assumes sense of worthlessness. Even those will to attempt solving their own problems are sparked to stop trying may merely from having been scolded—seen as condemned--on a detail. What characterizes this unhealthy Self-Esteem Image is ones self-assessment of: (1) not worthwhile and thus not deserving to of a good career or to teach; (2) not intelligent—no ability to go to college, understand things like math; (3) dislike myself—many weaknesses, no strengths; and (4) a loss of self-efficacy (Borders, *J. Career Development, 1987*).

Since ready solutions are not now available, one calls on those with power (e.g. the Crowd" or some ignorant or evil leader) for help and protection. In addition to being blind to the fact of the extremely high price one has to pay to such powers, one fails to give thought to the likelihood of not getting a meaningful return for what is paid or that one has paid to enter into a vicious cycle of ever worsening problems. This is because the powerful are not connected with they do to or with people who pay for their services. Meanwhile, one is already committed to a course of action and at a point of "no return"—particularly if one has entered a gang.

COSMOS IMAGES: A useful metaphorical Image for considering the organization of the "Genetics" of the Spiritual Elements is that of a skyscraper building. The Unconditional Love portion of the Spiritual Elements is the Base upon which rests the skyscraper building; Truth is its Underground Foundation; Reality represents the visible part of the building; and the Natural is how everything harmoniously operates inside the building. Hence, the Spiritual Elements, with Unconditional Love at its core, is a Megastar for the Spiritual part of each human's Real Self and a Super-apex Anchor for that same human's Selfhood

Material component. In other words, the Super-apex Anchor is simply a physical offspring of the Spiritual part of each human's Real Self. Together, these are each human's Philosophy of Life (POL) birth gift. To review, what orchestrates that Real Self POL is the "*Self*" of a human being. The "Self," according to Ancient Africans, is a "drop of God called ones Divine Consciousness and naturally contains the Spiritual Elements. This means its Unconditional Love Base is the only *eternally consistent, permanent, stationary, and unchanging Cosmos Ingredient in existence—underlying all God-made creatures, creations, and patterns of natural events.* Thus, any given human's *Spiritual Self-Identity* consists of God's inner nature of Unconditional Love + God's outer nature of Life (Truth, Reality, and the Natural), both connected by God's Divine Consciousness with all of its Wisdom. To fully understand this is to realize that at the core of every human is the source for unlimited Personal Power.

Out of the "Self" come vibrations containing messages of unity of "How to Live" in a "ME/WE" manner so as to have a Thriving and Happy life. These messages contain the *What* and *Why* of eternal "Things" essential to benefit Cosmic aspects of the "ME/WE" Cosmos. Thus, these "What it is" and "Why it is" messages designed to fashion standards, guides, filters, and measures for daily living have an unchanging sameness of identity. It is essential to be aware of what is Reality. It is not the past, for that is a memory—and reality is not the future, for that is an expectation. Neither is Reality words or material or spirituality but instead it is "what it is" and that cannot be described or conjectured as to how it is done or what it does. It expressions are positioned as a *Background Base* (like the Base upon which a skyscraper building is built) within each human's Selfhood, analogous to the way the Sunshine lights up the world. Hence, "*Soul Sunshine*" is used to characterize the "Self".

ICON IMAGES

In African Tradition the word "*Icon*" had its origin as being the halo of a Star (said to be the Substance of God) and, in an illuminated fashion, 'carrying over' or 'transferring' the sense or meaning or message of what is in the "Star". Besides the forming of Mental Pictures and stuffing them with content so as to become Mental Images--both being natural to humans--those Images can take on extra prominence and thereby become Icons. When those Icon Images are animated, they are called Contingent Beings (CB) in Supernatural realms. Everything in this progression occurs in ones imagination and each is therefore non-real. Still, when used to illustrate reality (e.g. the Spiritual), they—like metaphors and similes--can be alternate routes to the Truth. The European, Farkhatdinov (*Cultural Sociology, 2014*) says an Icon is symbolic condensations--rooting generic social meanings in a specific and 'material' form--allowing the abstractions of cognition and morality to be subsumed (sub-classified)--and to be made invisible by aesthetic shape. I differ by viewing Icon Images as the spotlighted feature of a Symbol.

ICON: An *Icon symbolizes a microcosm* (a "little world" in opposition to the "Macrocosm," a great world) to which one aspires to live, serves as model for living, or is the standard, measure, filter, and guide one is living in the course of ones life. Within this closed figure is all that is associated with the interconnections (everything real depends on every other real thing and all interdependently do their independent things for the benefit of the whole) and interrelatedness, signifying outward and visible appearances and/ or inward and hidden meaning of the "Thing" it symbolizes. Whereas every human has countless mental picture within a few moments, they are quickly forgotten unless they are converted to Images by adding significant thing that convert them into three dimensions. This is like selecting the 'all-stars' (i.e. the Images) from professional basketball players (i.e. the mental pictures) and then, out of the 'all-stars,' selecting the

MVP (most valuable player—the Icon). Since humans' behaviors derive from both their Conscious Minds (a voluntary control) + memories + their Subconscious and Unconscious Minds (without ones consent and beyond ones control), what is most significant about any given fantasy, distorted, or realistic experience is made into an Icon Image.

Once an Icon Image is established, it, in turn, becomes a programming tool. Ancient Africans, who discovered this, said one way humans program their Subconscious is by acts derived from their Conscious Beliefs as well as from Images they repeatedly dwell upon in their waking state, especially if these Images are emotionally charged. Yet, regardless of their nature, *Images can and do touch ones emotions where they are accepted as "the truth"*--the Mild, Slight, Moderate, or Extreme degree of that meaning to the individual is determined by the power of what deems to be the intimacy of ones keystone *"Icon Image"*. Just as a diamond crystal's octahedron (Greek, eight faces) shape has multiple faces, with each exhibiting unique reflections but all being an essential part of the complete picture of that crystal, so does this convey what an Icon Image is about. Ones crystal type of Icon Image serves as a "Life-Living" storehouse for ones desires for the present as well as for remote future events. For Real Self people, this storehouse pertains to their Mission in life. Yet it helps maintain ones Selfhood Integrity in hard times or when one gets off the Spiritual Elements track.

APPEARANCES OF ICON IMAGES: The pupil of the eye which receives through a very small round hole the Images of bodies situated beyond this hole always receives them upside down. The visual faculty always sees them upright as they are. Images pass through the center of the crystalline sphere situated in the middle of the eye. People may injure their bodily eye by observing and gazing on the sun during an eclipse, unless they take the precaution of only looking at the Image reflected in the water, or in some similar medium. Ancient Africans, considering the Images from the External World as reality and never allowing the Inner World to assert itself, said this led to a negative emotional nature. The analogized this nature to a *"Jaundiced eye"*—a term derived from ancient medicine's "yellow disease" (caused by liver or gallstone problems). It was thought jaundice sufferers saw everything in yellow tones--implying the False Self looks at something with a prejudiced view, usually in a rather negative or critical manner. Interpretations made by resultant illusions/delusions, mis-conceptions, and misinterpretations were derived from things not seen or heard realistically; things over-generalized or insufficiently generalized; from failing to see the patterns of the Spiritual Elements; from trying to put reasonable information or emotions where they do not belong; or joining incompatible Thought patterns. Many seeds of this greenish-yellow color stream out from a diseased body to meet the Images of things. Besides, many are mingled in their own eyes which by their contact pain everything with lurid hues. The way they managed this was by replacing the jaundiced eye with a clear "Eye," and discarding one emotionally tinted glasses so as to see things for what they are.

Flawed Symbols representing Icon Images that overwhelm the Mind act like sham Crystal gazers generating magical images and thoughts or causing one to view things as if they are unpleasant dreams or be a generator of magical thoughts. The most *destructive flawed Symbols put one on anti-Spiritual Elements Tracks and, as a result, what "SEEMS" right are quite convincing bad persuasions.* One then builds a lifestyle around the flawed "Seed" Image which, in turn, *reproduces itself to become itself in how one Thinks, Feels, Expresses, and Acts.* Each of these life daily living habits are crystallized into the form of a recurring mental picture. Every aspect of what is done repetitiously is apt to invoke a specific image in ones mind--an image made of "concrete" information, misinformation, folklore, desire, bias, and prejudices.

WHAT ICONS DO: *Icon Images are Motivators* (i.e. unconscious forces from ones motives—the "Why" of doing something). Motivation influences the direction of both thought and behavior. While learning emphasizes events in the past (experience), Motivation emphasizes factors that influence present behavior, giving power to a Disposition. Whereas Paradigms are ideal models, both *Metaphors* (an *implied* comparison suggesting a resemblance between two different things) and Icons touch a deeper level of understanding—pointing to the process of learning and discovery by the means of making analogical leaps. To illustrate, if a familiar thing is placed in ones right hand and an unfamiliar thing is placed in ones left hand, in order to use the familiar to explain the unfamiliar the Figures of Speech called an Analogy can be used. An *Analogy* has two parts: (1) an original subject of the familiar (e.g. Titan, a dog) and the unfamiliar Things (Sharon, a woman)--both different in origin and development and (2) a compared subject (what the original is being likened to) of the familiar and the unfamiliar Things. The original subject is the "what it is" of each Thing—and of course Titan and Sharon are not the same in their essence (i.e. one, a dog, Sharon, a woman). However, in the compared subject "what each does," and "how each appears" they can share certain Similarities (having likeness or resemblance in a general way) in "what each does" and/or "how each appears".

For this Analogy to be effective by the familiar serving to "*act as if*" it is unfamiliar and determining that is so, *the limitations and boundaries of human thought separating them must be removed in order for the "act as if" indescribable ideas. This removal enables the indescribable symbolic features to leap into the unfamiliar subject so as to discover its* "what it does" and/or "how it appears" similarities. Once that is done, the resultant connection is a *symbolic message which rallies the Receiver's Imagination, Emotions, and/or Intellect. If the connection is understood, it is capable of touching the Receiver's "Heart" or "Head" and* provide an altered way of seeing below what seems to be the surface of the organization of the obvious.

This is a way to penetrate Hidden aspects of some significant Thing and gaining ideas that have not been—and could not be—included in casual observation and/or in literal descriptions. Looking at these new insights from different perspectives can provide Truths to serve as standards against which pertinent other things can then be compared for ethics (appropriate/inappropriate), morals (right/wrong), definition, or meaning, as well as raise penetrating questions—e.g. "Why did all my friends suddenly disappear?" or "I see the part I played in causing this problem".

AFRICAN STORY OF ICON IMAGES: Primitive Africans' high regard for animals as spiritual creatures, even deities, led them to believe they were images of a specific force of Nature—called a Totem. An *Image is a pattern of forms and figures endowed with unity and significance, implying the whole is greater than the sum of its parts.* At the core of this Totem was said to be a "spirit moving force"--called Ka ("Spirit Mind"; the immortal part; the "Double" of humans; and, confusingly, recently the Persona). Ancient Africans said the *Anima Mundi*—the "Soul" of the Cosmos—contains the Substance of God. That Ka (Soul) is a "spirit moving force" which, as a Spark of God, is Collectively imparted into every human in the Cosmic Organism in an undifferentiated (but not disorganized) state constituting a creative power of continuous integration. Because of early Africans fascination with Stars and their respective Halo, they used this as a metaphor to consider the Collective Ka to be like the Halo and God to be like a Creative "Star". Contained in this *Iconic Halo Storehouse* was all the Cosmic Knowledge in the form of visual Images, each representing some principle of Ma'at.

These principles include the concepts of truth, justice, order, righteousness, balance, reciprocity, and harmony. Their Consequences are Respect, selflessness, sharing, compassion, devotion to God as well as promoting inner peace, social harmony, and contentment. Every human's duty is to complete the Cosmic Wholism Circle, carrying it to completion by putting these off-spring of the Spiritual Elements into action and persisting in their evolution. As part of this Collective Ka, there was the Ether, manifesting as vital energy—both the Divine Creative power sustainer of life and as a force of continuity. Both caused African Sages to animate them into the abstract concept of Ma'at—an 'Association of Principles" providing Cosmic Order. In a sense, the Ka is the receptacle of the vital forces from which all life came and through which all life survives.

When time came for each human to be born into the Physical Realm, first that same Spark of God with its Divine Creative power sustainer of life vital forces was imparted. Second, added to the 'Spark of God' aspect of the Ka of each human inside the Cosmic Organism were the "Ancestor Genetics" + that human's specific and unique Talent. All three comprised each human's Selfhood Greatness as well as all the potentials one needs to have a thriving and happy life. This concept of a personal Ka + a Collective Cosmic Organism shared Ka nature, with both having the same essence with the divine, became a fundamental tenet of Maatian anthropology and central to the African Tradition concept of human potentiality and power.

The Ka was represented in several forms. *Form I Secular Collective Ka* was the identification of a whole tribe with the Ka of some assumed animal or plant—perhaps an 'ancestor' or superhuman power. This, called *Totemism*, meant they were all Spiritually related. Another application for the External World Collective 'Totem'—by being an image of a specific force of Nature--symbolized a guardian and guide with which bonds of kinship were established--and with all which this entails in terms of rights and duties. *Form II Ka* referred to the individual's Spiritual Mind and Animal Mind. Thus, for each male and female, a Rites of Passage was needed to activate the Spiritual Mind to start replacing the Animal Mind. This maintained the Collective Spiritual Mind.

Form III Ka referred to the Collective Spiritual Mind and Animal Mind. *Form IV Ka* referred to an individual's internal or Selfhood 'totem.' The individual's selection of an External World Collective 'Totem' was done for personal reasons, as in serving as a personal guardian or tutelary superhuman power. *Form V Ka* referred to the individual personalizing her/his totem in a manner having nothing to do with the Collective Ka. For example, one might represent ones guardian by a picture or emblem, or fetish (a symbol of divine energy encapsulated, ready and usable), parcel, or painted upon ones clothing or accoutrements.

AFRICAN BOY METAMORPHOSIS TO MAN: A *Metamorphosis* (change shape but not its substance or essence by transforming), in the way a caterpillar inside a cocoon turns into a butterfly, was introduced from a large collection of verse stories by Ovid (43 BC-17 AD). These stories were about transformations of gods and mortals into shapes of objects, plants, or animals. By millennia prior to the Greeks coming into existence, what was particularly spotlighted by East Coast Africans was circumcisions. By every boy being born uncircumcised meant he maintained his 'Animal Kingdom' nature with its Animal Mind. In that boy's Rites of Passage, part of the initiation featured circumcision in order to sacrifice his 'animality' and to receive an animal soul. In other words, circumcision allowed a boy to enter into possession of his 'animal soul' while sacrificing his own 'animal being'. This dual process would admit him to the totem clan and establish his relationship to his totem animal. Above all, he becomes a "Man," and, in a still wider sense, a human being. Fundamental here are three aspects.

First, similar to the vanishing of the caterpillar in a cocoon, in the human transformation process there occurs a *Mystical Death* of those animalistic features which, if unchecked (e.g. very powerful and unresolved emotional forces), go on to create ones "False" (Ego) self and its fetters.

Second is a Philosophical *Regeneration*--involving a change in ones ultimate standard for living as a result of activating the up-to-this-point dormant Spiritual Mind. Out of this comes ones Cherished Values which guide ones life, using *Nonaggression*—e.g. cooperative good relations with and behaviors toward fellow humans as well as the practices of being gentle, kind, affectionate, helpful, sociable, empathetic, compassionate, and showing sincere affection--for the Power approach aspect of their Philosophy of life. The foundation being laid out and directed to thriving enables one to deal properly with life-shaping, life-changing, or life-maintaining situations in a Ma'at (Spiritual Elements in action) manner.

Third, Spiritual *Rebirth* is present when Righteous Behavior and "Right" ways of living start budding out of the 'stem' of ones Spiritual Mind. Thereafter, ones Intellect starts developing the various types of thinking needed to wisely lead to a thriving and happy life.

SYNTHESIS OF ICON IMAGES: "Synthesis" is a metaphorical Cosmic Ladder word because its rungs extend form the Earth (the Physical, the Superficial) all the way up to "the Heavens." The African Tehuti (? 12,500 BC) defined this premier word "Synthesis" as the *creation of unity, the making of something whole and therefore the establishing of a piece of reality*. The African multi-genius and "Universal Father of Medicine" Imhotep (2600 BC) effectively used Tehuti's synthesis message of Rebirth (to bring ones spiritual, mental, and physical self into alignment so that independently they interdependently generate total health) in medicine so patients could achieve maximum health experiences of security and adequacy. Based upon finding only bits and pieces of skimpy information over a 50 year period, it seems to me Europeans distain "Synthesis," limiting it to the *Earth World realm*: "the combination or grouping of parts or elements so as to form an integrated whole or complete view or system—so as to show the truth more completely that mere collection of parts"; tendency to perceive and appreciate situations as a whole"; "the tendency to simplify, to generalize, and ultimately to understand—by assimilating external and internal elements, by reconciling conflicting ideas, by uniting contrasts, and by seeking for causality"; "Fusion in which the parts cannot be identified"; "Integration—implying a compact and lasting union"; "Association—implying relatively little interaction between the parts"; "the creative process itself"; "the higher stage of truth that combines the truth of a thesis and an antithesis". At the *mid-range on the Metaphorical Ladder* a European existential Synthesis is "Consciousness is always trying to become being to achieve a synthesis, as it were, between no-thing and some-thing." In the Upanishads synthesis is "that which is in motion, yet nevertheless remains still." A French author says: "the tendency of opposites to unite in a synthesis is always characterized by stress and suffering, until and unless it is finally resolved by Supernatural means."

Some reasons for Synthesis are: (1) to combine ideas to form a new whole; (2) establish points of agreement; (3) come to a conclusion (what does the family want to do about this); (4) answer questions; (5) create solution (what does this association of ideas indicate?); (6) design plans of action; (7) make inferences about future events (how will you and your mate feel if you did not focus on carrying out your mission?). For Ancient Africans, in dealing with top ladder rung issues, said Synthesis is the mental application of mentally tying externally unrelated things through an Abstract or an Abstraction. An *Abstract* is ones mind fashioning a "Virtual" (boundary-less) Contingent out of something in the Metaphysical (the Spiritual wrapped in the Ether) or Supernatural realms. An *Abstraction* is ones mind fashioning a "Virtual" (boundary-less) Contingent out of something in the Physical (the Spiritual wrapped in Matter). They sought as their "raw materials" for synthesizing: Type I--seeing the inner factors that unify items based on the mutual relationships and interdependence of things with each other and the whole (Amen II:105). Type II Synthesis finds within *a collection of like-kind things a concept:* Type III Synthesis finds within *a collection of like-kind things a part they have in common* (generalizing). Type IV Synthesis is a combination of Types II and III.

In synthesizing these concepts, my definition of Synthesis is: the *essence of abstracts or abstractions ingredients coordinated into a whole—a whole whose combined product emerges by means other than through a mere summation of the elements involved—retaining the original ingredients like the egg and the sperm producing a fetus. This whole constitutes a Symbol.* Since Abstract/Abstraction Symbol analogies represent reality, they can be Synthesized by maneuvering and is manipulating. Thus, the words Ancient Africans chose in speaking to each other were heavily Symbolic—meaning their expressions crystallized the essence of the Symbolized concept—and such a mental *"picture is worth a thousand words."* Also, using the concept of Inference, the speakers could imply extensions on the meaning of a symbolic word as well as get more meaning out of what was said and left unsaid. This was like speaking only about the Seed of the Apple Tree because knowing that "Seed's" ingredients would give insights into the rest of the tree.

ICON IMAGE MIGRATIONS OUT OF AFRICA: The earliest known migrations out of Africa were to the North and East into India, the Far East, the Near East, and South Pacific. Around 125,000 BC a group of Africans moved northward towards the Nile and into the Levant (bordering the Mediterranean between Egypt and Turkey); another, c90,000 BC, across short sketches (major points) of sea along Asia's southern coast, then migrated into East Asia; then the Dravidians of South India, Pakistan and Iran. Then c85,000 BC a group crossed the entrance of the Red Sea in the south and into the Arabian Peninsula to reach the Indian sub-continent, spreading to Indonesia and reaching southern China by 75,000 BC; then by 65,000 BC they had spread to Borneo, Australia, India, throughout Asia, Scandinavia, and close to the North Pole; then 45,000 BC into Europe; then 30,000 BC three separate migrations crossed the Bearing land bridge into Alaska and on into North America by 25,000 BC. Some of these migrations were by land, sea, and settlements gradually moving outward by foot (Bailey, African Bible Messages). Of course, no matter in which new location they were in, certain things remained the same while other things were completely changed or at least modified.

To elaborate with the similarities of Africans and Amerindians from their beginnings, both believed in a soul or Ka present throughout the Animal and Plant Kingdoms, and even in inanimate objects like a canoe. Amerindians make no distinction between the personal as contrasted with impersonal in a Western sense. Instead, they are interested in the whole aspect of existence and reality—embracing everything perceived by the senses, thought of, felt, and dreamed of as truly existing for them as inseparable aspects of the real. Thus, an image is a visual counterpart of that reality. Thus, they have many different ways of making and experiencing images (Highwater p56, 64). Thus, the practice of carving "Totem' figures on poles has always been common among North American Indians. Most tribes were divided into clans of close blood relatives whose 'Totem' was a particular animal from whom many believed to have descended. Each totem species was sacred because it embodied an "objectified and mentally imagined" image of the clan. Thus, showing great respect for each was a way to express social solidarity and sanctify the collective. The Totem Pole and each of its Totems: (1) led members of the tribe to become conscious of social membership through their interactions with nonhumans; (2) served as a convenient method of clarifying the awareness the society has of itself; and (3) fashioning, by being empowering building element of both awareness, creations by "acting back" to actually structure patterns of social belonging (Jerolmack, *Sociological Theory, 2014*).

MINDSETS: A *Mindset* is an attitude of readiness to respond in a certain way, based upon ones prior experiences or expectations of "what is best for me or against me". Mindsets may be based on reality, distortions, and/or fantasy. Problematic mindsets are those who deal with distortions or fantasy or cling to things within reality. To cling to any of those necessitates that one defends them. Up to that point prior to clinging, mental activity within reality, such as mental Images, have been good servants but to cling to them prevents one from being open to the introduction of new combinations of the Spiritual Elements. Such a 'closed-ness' makes any mental ingredient a bad master, for that is when one confuses delusions and 'signs' with reality.

TOTEMIC THOUGHT: Ancient Egyptians adopted the national Ka (totem) of a Falcon animal as a symbol to represent them and the rising sun of Egypt with its a message of transition and change—personally experienced in ones vocation, work, or career aspects. By being the king of all birds, many gods (including ra) were shown with the Falcon head or body to indicate its solar influence, wisdom, guardianship, and to celebrate success or victory. For that reason, the Falcon Totem was referred in preparation to awaken visionary power leading to ones life purpose or as a stimulus for receiving higher vision, higher knowledge in solving current dilemmas in ones life, and rising above a bad situation. In European tradition, the Falcon, a warlike symbol representative of the huntsman, is associated with the Germanic sky-gods Wodan as well as Frigg and the trickster Loki.

Totemic Thought has a resemblance to a metaphor. In both the leap from familiar to unfamiliar is at least as great in a Totemic Thought as it is in metaphor and yet the leap has to be maintained for longer so as to do deeper viewing in order to find the relationships of what underlies the obvious. For example, in Totemic Thought one has more time to appreciate the free fall and there is a greater opportunity to explore differences and identities in order to construct deeper meaning and understanding within the assessments constituting relating a person of courage to a lion. To say the person is like a lion is to place in opposition two sets of differences. To say the person is a lion is to enter the world of the lion and become familiar with its like kind ways and patterns. The resultant "shared meaning" can be fashioned so as to symbolized and construe it.

TOTEMIC ANIMALS: Since the Falcon inspired the Egyptians sense of awe at the mysteries of Nature, the idea was for the Falcon Totem to be a reminder of the significance Nature had in their people's lives. Dumb European Egyptologists, who never put forth the effort to discover the Truth, mistook this image for the Egyptians god. That is like saying the god of the USA is the bald eagle (Amen, Nuk Au Neter p75). Totemic animals: (1) are incidental symbols of the group's essence; (2) stimulate an 'Association of Thoughts' in the realms of reflected preexisting abstract social relations; and (3) the people, based upon careful observation, use their selected animal to agree upon what are the fixed underlying corresponding essence interrelationships existing between the animal and the people. Synthesizing and harmonizing such *Abstracts* (ones mind fashioning a "Virtual" or boundary-less Contingent out of whatever is *underlying perfect Order of Natural patterns* in the Metaphysical—i.e. the Spiritual wrapped in the Ether) and *Abstractions* (ones mind fashioning a "Virtual" or boundary-less Contingent out of something in the Physical—i.e. the Spiritual wrapped in Matter) could give insights applicable to the Cosmic Organism.

Totemism brings together two orders of categories—humans and plants or, more commonly, animals—complete with their different orders of logic (Starr-Glass *Journal of Management Education, 2004*). Hence, to Primitive Africans, Animals and plants were not utilized "merely because they are there" but because they suggested a mode of thought in which observable biological differences and similarities between "Species X and Y" became useful for drawing social distinctions and similarities between, say, falcon and Clan X. Resultant conclusions could then be applied by inference for all the other numbered clans, as or between "Clan 7 and Clan 22," and symbolized as an Icon Image. The first known Images of Ancient Egypt were the divided properties of Nature and consequently of Divinity (the Elohim) into 7 abstract qualities. Each was characterized by an Icon Image of some aspect of their invisible Metaphysical Selfhood. Such was in the form of an objective emblem—i.e. Matter, Cohesion, Fluxion (flow of continual change), Coagulation, Accumulation, Station, and Division. Furthermore, they were all attributes of Occultism symbolized in various Images.

TOTEMIC SYSTEMS: A "*System*" (setting or placing together) is an assemblage of things in a regular order—thus a plan or scheme. In medicine, it designates a combination of parts (e.g. the digestive or nervous system). The goal of a Totemic System is to clarify or illuminate a concept from one category (e.g. Sharon, a human female) by saying it is the same as a concept from a different category (e.g. Titan, a dog). This can enable one to have a different point of view to give a clearer and more complete understanding of the things being compared. Totemic systems can capture complex associations and relationships of different parts of the entities involved which are not ordinarily able to be consciously understood or logically appreciated. For example, Sharon and Titan might be associated by the gathering of like-kind ideas about both and meshing them into an Association of Ideas. Then, the essence of some aspect of Sharon might be represented in "Titan" features or described in "Titan" terms ("she fights like a bulldog"). Regardless of the nature of the comparison, it invites reflection on the ways in which these different categories might have shared common characteristics or underlying systems of definition logic. In totemic systems, there is equivalence, or correspondence—as in sharing a Ka (Persona)--between these two orders of difference.

Totemic Systems also can be parsed so as to highlight in Sharon and Titan some unlike feature in their otherwise equivalences through the differences in the "what it is" identity of the parts involved. Or, there can be highlighted in Sharon and Titan certain similarities in their differences (e.g. what each does and how each appears)--but not using a sharp and provocative contrast, as would be clearly visualized from using images of Sharon and Titan as they really are. Sharon would not like it if he said she looked like a dog. Instead, the spotlight is on the features shared by unlike things which come together to interdependently form a harmonious invisible Association of Ideas—"Sharon and Titan are my friends". Out of this Association one can gain an intuitive grasp of the relationship of Sharon and Titan. It is like a line that continually approaches a curve but without ever actually reaching it (called '*Asymptote*'). This implies the Totemic System remains open to the interplay of *Consequences* (the sequel: happenings from what sprang out of the Effects) and changing relationships brought about by the introduction of additional experiential, experimental, or conceptual information into the whole entity. Note: Sequence differs from Consequence by not arising from the Effects.

Although proof is not provided, the 'payload' from the Association of Ideas possesses the power to bring the Totemic System to life by evoking images that illuminate the points of comparison one is trying to make. Totems can raise the questions related to the different ways in which "shared meaning" can be constructed and construed. In the totemic system, the comparing and contrasting allows for different assessment systems.

Depending upon the type of equivalence one is looking for (e.g. something of worth and/or of value), the ways in which Idea Associations may be categorized is chronologically, logically, conveniently or in a correspondence of the elements that are the theme of the group. For example, one can borrow the logical properties of an order--i.e. the system of similarities/differences of this order--to express and understand another. In this way totemism is rather more than a question of content or simple analogy between two orders, but can be regarded as a method of Critical Thinking.

BLACK GANG ICON IMAGES

The point of the above discussion has been to demonstrate that people in general live much of their lives out of the Icon Images they generate. There is a particular relationship between Black People and Amerindians because so much of what they do is identical. This is because Ancient Africans came to the Americas, thousands of years ago, despite Europeans not confirming this. Proof comes from comparing the "Medicine Man" of both cultures and with the practices of many of today's Amerindians conforming to those of Ancient Africans. In addition, there was much association between African American slaves and Amerindians to the point that the overwhelming majority of today's Black American descendants of the Enslaved have "Indian Blood" in them. These aspects make it significant in how Black gang members deal with Icon Images in both an African and Amerindian context. For example, in none of these three— Ancient Africans, Amerindians, and Black gangs--are Icons Images deliberately puzzling signs that point to something else. Instead, for each Ancient African, Amerindian, and Black gang member the Icon Image means what it is and each individual shares in its meaning by becoming the Icon Image one mentally sees as representing ones Self-Image.

Just as the painter is necessarily transformed into what she/he is painting by the very process of making images, so is the gang member transformed. For Amerindians and Ancient Africans, certain birds and animals were counted more powerful and intelligent than humans and capable of exerting influences for good. By contrast, a gang member may look at that same bird or animal or self-designed Icon Image as capable of exerting influences that result in evil. Whatever Icon Image a gang member creates to represent his Self-Image, one importance of that Icon Image is selecting things significant to be part of ones discursive (reasoning process) system of values one lives by. Also, the visual Icon Image *jointly* and *simultaneously* forms the collective representations that assists in the recognition of what is and is not important in those values (Highwater p64; Bartmanski, *J. Sociology*, *2014*).

A vital part of a potential gang member's Icon Images designed to represent his values is what is envisioned as being able to fulfill her/his depleted Human and Spiritual Nature Needs—what they strive to live up to once inside a gang—and what can lead them out of a gang if and when they so desire. Icon Images have been extensively discussed in my books: "Mentoring Minds of Black Boys"; "Post-Traumatic Distress Syndrome in Black People"; and "Teaching Black Youth." Since struggling Black youth cannot afford mental health specialists and since it is a rare specialist who would understand or is able to relate to that youth's (or any Black youth's) "Raw Nerve" situation, a fast but detailed and thorough way of handling such issues is the purpose of the discussion to follow.

ENSLAVING ICON IMAGES: About the 7th month of life babies are able to have images, being elaborations of memory traces and the beginning of constituting the foundation of ones inner reality. Thereafter Images are connected with past perceptions and are composed of the mental reconstruction of both incoming sense experiences (Outside Images) and Images derived from ones memory (Inner Images)--both serving as a standard, guide, and filter for different aspects of daily living. The formation of Images can be by good and/or bad coming from oneself and/or from others. Much of this depends on what one chooses to allow to enter into ones head and the degree, if any, to which that has been filtered by the Spiritual Elements or something else. Some have a preference for Worth Images, some for Value Images, and some a combination in varying proportions--whether of a good or bad nature. Enslaved Icon Images in an individual are a composite, consisting of various Inner and Outer Images--both filled with predominately self-defeating values; both with Illusions and Delusions; both of an eidetic imagery nature--i.e. intermediate between the ordinary visual memory-image and the "After-Image"; both featuring a pseudo-perceptual quality which, when compared with others, makes it superior in clearness and richness in detail as well as less dependent upon the organization of its content for meaning. Furthermore, the Enslaved Composite Icon Image has a modified "*Agglutination*" component. This means that threats, disturbances, and bad actions which happened in the day, might parade as imagery in ones subawareness any time of day or night as a visible series of snapshots. Its powering by ones affects (emotions) means it is without rules or regulations. Unless a strong voluntary effort is made, Images cannot reproduce total representations. Still, one "sees" enough for one to infer the whole. Thus, consciousness shifts rapidly from one part of the image to another because Images are fleeting. Then, when that image is re-evoked it appears in a slightly different form. Most Images rapidly associate with other images through the mechanism of spatial or temporal contiguity. For example, if I image a tree, that image elicits an image of other parts of the woods or garden where that tree was, or the landscape at the location, or of the people who were there. Or there may be a fusion of things that were previously separate. One of an Icon Image's most important functions is the maintenance of motivation for absent objects, transformations of emotions, symbolic formation, and building of inner reality. Though normal minds know that Images are produced in their own minds and that they do not necessarily mirror simultaneous motivation product equivalents in the external world, those deformities and distortions can allow for creativity. By contrast, since Traumatized Minds get this confused, their deformities and exaggerations increase their emotional hypersensitivity. Whatever is known or experienced by means of Images and subsequent cognitive processes tends to become a part of oneself.

When imagery is used too much or too intensely, it may lead to *Adualism*--an inability to distinguish the two realities--that of the mind and that of the external world. Then experiencing a wish becomes equivalent to its actualization (as in schizophrenia). Unchecked imagery thus may provoke unbearable frustration, leading to delusions. The instability of the image may cause one to use various levels of mental activity--going back and forth from the highest to the lowest order of these levels in succession, in a given sequence, or in simultaneous activation. Except for sexual images, other types of Images do not have the ability to evoke the same kind of behavior that their corresponding perceptions do. Instead, they generally elicit a more delayed and less direct action. Thus, Imagery can substitute for or reproduce the real as well as create the unreal. On the good side, such Imagery not only helps one understand the world better, it also helps one create a surrogate for the world. On the bad side, *Slave Survival Imagery* may cause one to keep reproducing a negative Law of Correspondence out of it. That implies that the bad, by itself, reproduces itself and becomes the thing it makes throughout the course of ones lifetime--and culturally transmitting it to those under ones influence so as to perpetuate the status quo. A keystone Icon Image is selected to orchestrate ones life and that may change as one goes from one stage to the next.

LEGEND ICON IMAGES THAT ENSLAVE: Any Legend Icon Image (LII) soon constitutes the foundation of ones inner reality and that is as important, if not more so, than ones external reality. There are many personal and environmental forces acting as 'gatekeepers' to maintain the status quo of a LII--the deep imbedding effect of socialization; the family, relatives, and neighbors reminders; the lack of awareness that anything is wrong with LII; the desire to "be my own person and do things my way"; and the larger society's daily stereotypes which reinforce ones LII. In peeking at what is going on inside the inner recesses of ones mind there is the situation of "*Un-noble Loyalty*" of which one may not be aware or is done out of a lack of willingness to change what is self-defeating and in spite of knowing better. *Loyalty* is one of the countless words deemed greatly significant in Chinese and Indo-European (Sanskrit) languages but derived from Ancient African words. When Ancient Africans said: "in order to live your life, you must continue it and stick to it," this "glue-like" sense was the original denotative meaning of both "Life" and "Loyalty." The concept referred to a powerful force emerging out of a person's beliefs and values about something to which that person is attached. Connotatively it embraces that same person's deeply held feelings or strong emotions of pride, affection, and attachment that go with his/her denotative beliefs and values to which that person clutches. But whereas "Noble" is living within the confines of the Spiritual Elements and developing them daily, ones Loyalty is branded as "un-noble" when it "glues" its virtues + ones bad emotions (e.g. rage, fear, pain arising out of a sense of rejection or disrespect) + ones power struggle + ones negative integrity + ones competitive attitude + ones oppositional behavior + ones self-defeating beliefs into an unswerving and binding allegiance.

This allegiance is so powerful as for one to willingly give up certain advantages in order to remain loyal to what one knows is not in ones best interest. In the process, one must deny the associated doubt about its "Rightness" and make an excuse for it so as to allow this "glob" to continue on as usual in the wrong direction. Meanwhile, its malignant thoughts and bad emotions destroy the loyalty bonds of self-trust and self-confidence in what one had built up to this point. The combination places a cloud over ones Self-Love and Self-Greatness--both foundational to ones Selfhood structure. One reason for persisting "Un-noble Loyalty" is one is following the dictates of ones False Self (Ego) and/or of ones oppressors. This comes from ones "*Tape Recorder*" *Mentality*. Tape recorders are machines that can record sounds coming from some source (e.g. a speaker) and then play back that same sound on special plastic tape. This tape can be played over and over again without losing the quality, nature, or message conveyed by the sound. Something similar happens when Black people allow White people (or anyone) to define who they are, whether by intimidation or otherwise.

Invariably, messages conveyed to Black people by racist Whites are of a degrading nature. Afflicted Black People who have accepted being defined by Whites act as if there was a tape recorder in their brains playing these degrading messages, hearing over and over: "you can't do good things and you must do self-defeating things." Eventually, the repetition makes those evil messages into "second nature" mental barriers which generate mental urges displaying as Despair and Failure by either not trying to improve or giving up quickly. The lack of Selfhood Greatness oriented ideas contained in the messages become the victim's standard, filter, and guide for going through life. As a result, victims "live down" to what the messages say about them--i.e. a self-fulfilling prophecy. Once victims think poorly of themselves, other people tend to treat them in a "like-kind" degraded fashion and that adds the complication of Disrespect. Ones lack of a success oriented attitude causes one to depend on others and engage in chronic juggling. The resultant self-talk is "negative" (i.e. self-destructive), as if a tape recorder is playing these destructive messages inside ones head. It does not take long before these bad messages about "who I am as a person--what I do--what I have--what I cannot do--and how I appear"--become exaggerated and distorted. To this mix are added anger, fear, and guilt. No change will come until one takes charge and control of oneself.

SELF-IMAGE

Every human has a Spiritual Self-Image. Real Self people's dilutions and pollutions within the Spiritual Elements stream flow of their Spiritual Self-Image makes it a Secular Self-Image. People who step outside that Spiritual Elements flow have an Ego Self-Image directing their False Selves. Secular and Ego Self-images are about measurable things related to oneself. The key word is "measurable." From previous discussions, mention has been made that the immaterial (i.e. God's world) and the intangible (i.e. the Sublime) are without bounds or limits regarding time, space, quantity, number, or dimensions -- whether in fact or in thought. By contrast, the Tangible is composed of the material and may be unbounded, partially bounded, or completely bounded. In modern mathematics and science, the word "*Infinite*" is applied to the unbounded tangible. This means an end or limit cannot be determined, not that there is no end or limit. Within this context, things considered "infinite" cover space, time, number, quantity, length, breadth, height, depth, and anything inherently beginning-less, endless, and externally inexhaustible. Furthermore, Secular and Ego Self-image problems are typically characterized by "too much"/"too little" references to ones appearance, possessions, status, or fame. Such flaws cause one to think in terms of "better or worse" as opposed to the more realistic yin/yang view (the opposites pertaining to self-image or self-concepts harmoniously relate to each other).

SELF-IMAGE IN AFRICAN TRADITION: For Ancient Africans, ones "Self" (Divine Consciousness/Will) or "Self-Identity" is ones Spark of God called ones Divine Consciousness and implying that humans are made in the Image of God. Because that Spark is an extension of God, it is a Real Image, as opposed to the Fantasy Image typically thought of. That Spark is composed of the Immaterial with Unconditional Love as its inner nature and Life (consisting of Truth, Reality, and Natural) as its outer nature. These are the Spiritual Elements. Thus, ones Self-Image in African Tradition is what makes ones "Self" or "Self-Identity" in the Spiritual side of ones Selfhood. But that Selfhood Being is composed of an indivisible duality of the "Self" (Immaterial) and a "Not Self" (Material). One identifies with the "Self" because it is what perceives God's messages (i.e. ones Divine Consciousness) and then Wills (acts voluntarily). Yet this, a human's true Identity, cannot manifest itself for it is at a total unalterable Peace and hidden—also called Amen, Sunyata, Nirvana, Hetep, Atem (Atum, Tem, Tmu), Wu Ji, Shalom, Salaam, etc.--therefore devoid of Energy and Matter. The Immaterial Self can only express itself through the manifestations of the Material Side of ones Selfhood Being. In other words, the Unseen can only be known through the Effects it produces in the Material side of Being as well as the Consequences of those Effects (Amen Nuk Au Neter p32).

Self-Knowledge is the direct experience with the essence of the Spiritual portion of ones Selfhood. By being Unconditional, that essence lacks predetermined automatic behavioral response patterns—no automatic thoughts or emotional reflexes to impel or compel one to act in predetermined ways—but rather within the guidelines of the Spiritual Elements. That is broadly what it means for a human to act in the likeness of God. The "I" in African Tradition is the "Self" (called the Ausar in each human), implying that it projects the essence of the "Spark of God" as the chief contents of ones mind. This projection shows as Integrity, health, thriving in life, happiness, harmonious social interactions, daily self-improvement, and Selfless Service when one is qualified and able to give it to the proper receivers and at the proper time. Since *humans do not act without a guiding mental picture*, the "Self's" clear and concrete picture of what it looks like in the Material portion of ones Selfhood is a Symbolized form of its Divine Self-Image composition—i.e. that of ones Spiritual gift of Selfhood Greatness in its most perfect form. To elaborate, the human mind is a sacred place where "Perfection" is present. It is not simply or primarily made to process and hold information so as to maneuver and manipulate things for presentation to the Material World. Instead, its *primary purpose is to contain a human's image of that human's divinity in order to manipulate and maneuver "Things" in the External and ones own Inner worlds through the ones Divine Spirit* (i.e. the Divine Mother in African Tradition).

The exquisite use of their Spiritual Powers is how Ancient African Sages were able to form Miracles (tens of thousands of years before such claims were made in the European Bible) and their astonishing Sacred Geometry Magic. To understand, internalize, and manifest that 'likeness' of God and live up to the perfect Icon Self-Image Symbol of Selfhood Greatness automatically causes profound life-changes that puts one in the flow towards ones Highest (divinity) Self—which is part of God's Divine Plan. Progress in that flow comes from ones habitual affirmations of knowing ones Self-Identity and striving to achieve ones Selfhood Greatness Divine Self-Image (as opposed to an arrogant Supernatural one of 'superiority'). All of this is explained by the mid-function of the Right Brain buried deep inside the human spirit. It is a faculty capable of communicating to the mind the working of the forces that maintain the order of the physiological and mental functions in humans. When awakened, this faculty enables one to see the inner factors that unify things based on the mutual relationships and interdependence of things with each other and the whole. Such is expressed through the abstract or metaphoric use of images (Amen, Metu Neter II:104).

Because *Knowledge is simply various arrangements and combinations of the Spiritual Elements* in different forms—thereby enabling the ready detection of Correspondence in all real "Things" throughout the Cosmos—one has greatly accelerated learning compared to False Self people to which none of this is available. Some Consequences of these Spiritual Effects include there being no Indifference/Hate/Evil/Sadism because these destroy the Spiritual parts of ones Selfhood. Also, there will be no Kill/Take/Destroy/Dominate actions or even desires because these destroy not only ones Spark of God but also the "flame" from which it came—a "Flame" comprising all of God's creatures and creations. Either destruction automatically puts one into the realm of the Self-Unknown.

SECULAR SELF-IMAGE: The usage of masks and masquerades originated among Primitive African Ritual Specialists around 30,000 BC for the purpose curing psychosomatic disease caused by disharmonious spirits. This feature of hiding and displaying moods to influence or control nature, the gods, and human affairs spread throughout the world. Of particular significance were the Etruscans who dominated Italy's northwestern coast from about 900 to 300 BC. They were a wealthy, sea-faring people—similar to the Egyptians (who were basically Black Ethiopians) —who brought all the elements of Egyptian civilization and culture to the Italian peninsula and then on to the Greeks. Prior to Greece trade exchanges, the Etruscans had applied masks as a device for the theater (among others)—more like the manner in which masks had been used in Interior Africa and to a lesser degree in the way they were applied in the festival and religious practices of Ancient Egypt. In fact, Etruscan actors never appeared on stage without masks. The reason is that between 700 and 500 BC, when it was fashionable for Etruscans to attend outdoor plays, the open theater was vast—even larger than some of our modern stadiums. The theater seats for tens of thousands of people were a great distance from the stage. Not only was there trouble seeing the facial expressions of the actor, but there was trouble hearing what was said. To help overcome both of the audience's distance problems, an actor would make several masks the size of a large Disneyland type Mickey Mouse face and each mask contained a megaphone mouthpiece. The entire device was called a Persona (an Etruscan word) —so named because of the resonance of the voice sounding through the megaphone of this image.

Over time, Persona also included the dramatic character represented by an actor's mask—serving as the vehicle through which a word or idea (sound) is manifested. This came from the Ancient African concept that implies a part of ones Selfhood—the "Person"--serves to convey (per) a sound (sona). Its importance was/is African people could learn to manifest their Self-Identity through the use of words of power (i.e. Metaphysical Sound Technology)—thereby representing ones Divine Self-Image—which are the Words of God. This is one reason that "Keeping ones Word" was essential to living a Ma'at (i.e. a displayed Spiritual Elements) life. But suppose the voice sounding through the Persona comes from a Contingent Being—an Ego—a False Self— which completely replaces ones Real Self (i.e. ones Self-Identity). Then ones contaminated mind, which is devoid of its sacred contents, spews forth features of ones imagination and from the External World which define who one is and out of which one forms a Secular Self-Image. The result is that one is described and one defines oneself as a human being. Furthermore, according to certain religions, all humans are born sinful, based upon the sinful deeds of ones remote Supernatural ancestors.

Nevertheless, both the Spiritual and the Secular Self-Images are embodiments of an association of Verbal Thought. Whereas the nature of the Spiritual Self-Image thoughts are within the stream flow of the Spiritual Elements, the Secular Self-Image Thoughts are of a human-made content. These have the power to generate non-Spiritual Elements oriented new ideas about oneself, about any creature or creation, about life as well as institute compatible behaviors. All of these operate under the Law of Attraction—drawing to oneself situations and people of a like-kind nature.

In short, every human is born with everything needed to discover, develop, and find the proper niche for ones Talent. It is up to the individual to decide to what degree, if any, that Talent will be developed and how it is to be used. Whereas ones Divine Consciousness is the orchestrator of ones Real Self, psychic trauma of a violent nature switches one over to a False Self.

The Ego Association of Thoughts are Sentiments (i.e. Thoughts wrapped in emotions) which makes them "Non-rational." There contents are of a Fetter type which derives from ones Lower (animalistic) Self. Since these are clung to with great emotional conviction, one identifies with ones physical body and External World oriented mentality. Because of the Association (companions that join with but each retain some individuality), its fate is about a life of errors, attracting needless problems, and failing to prevent needless problems. To complicate matters, as is typical of Europeans there is 'double-barreled" conflicts and confusion. Out of one barrel come different names given to Secular Self-Image—e.g. Personality, Self-Identity, and simply "Self-Image" (without its subdivisions). Out of the other barrel, each of these supposed synonyms are defined in many different ways, each possessing different meanings.

Real Self people have a Self-Image of boundless, virtual "ME/WE" harmony that defines a specific Image and yet this Icon Imageless Image persists forever. More often, ones Secular Self-Image in those who remain in the flow of the Spiritual Elements is the dynamic Persona or Ka which determines what types of thoughts, expectations, and behaviors one deems oneself capable of and embraces. It is built out of words—those from others one accepted and/or those one generates about oneself. For this reason, one may assemble *Congregative Images*—the putting together a whole by coordinating species that are outwardly and perhaps inwardly different so as to build wholes out of parts (like Inductive Reasoning). *Synthesis Images* consist of components that are outwardly different by similar inwardly—thus allowing for classifying and thereby providing some order. Coaches give "Pep" talks to nourish a winning Ka (Persona Image) so as to turn those who are somewhat convinced they are losers into winners. By perceiving of myself a Selfhood Great as a boy, I put no limits on myself. However, my peers had had this "beaten" out of them by racism and that stopped them from initiating acts of courage or handling certain types of interactions. Although many would "talk the talk, few would verify that by "walking the walk."

In a broad sense, a *Secular "Self-Image"* is a summary judgment of ones self-assessments of the partially or completely bounded tangibles one associates with oneself as well as the assessments one makes about how others perceive these same tangibles; it is the summation of all thoughts ones entertains about oneself—how one conducts oneself in all areas of life, and why. By contrast, self-concepts relate to ones unbounded tangibles and intangible "pre-matter." Thus, self-image includes: (1) what one does with respect to partially or completely bounded tangible work products (e.g. the book written, the earned sports record); (2) what one has--ones inherent, developed, or acquired quantities; (3) how one appears to oneself in realms such as physical body ("Body Image"), personality, and reputation; (4) to whom or to what one is attached (e.g. a special person or group, money, possessions, displays of power over people; and (5) ones perception--stemming from the monitored feedback from ones interpreted experiences with others or ones anticipated experiences with others--of how others judge (or would judge) what one does, has, or appears.

To these five self-image aspects--which are actually ten because half comes from ones personal self-assessment and half from the perceived assessment of others--a "price tag value" is placed in the sense of: "what would each of these ten sell for and/or be bought for in the open marketplace?" Implied in these concepts is what one correctly or incorrectly believes one owns. "*Ownership*" is a Middle English word meaning "to belong to oneself" and "to exercise the right of what one possesses." Let us use your talent to explain both ideas. Your talent belongs to you but you cannot completely possess it until it is discovered, developed, and settled into a niche where it is producing a work product. If your work product is tangible (e.g. a sports record), then its achievement becomes part of your self-image. What people think of your talent and what you do with it also becomes part of your Self-Image.

A good self-image can be built, for example, if the youth's character routinely leads him/her to convert measurable setbacks into measurable accomplishments -- "*turning a lemon into lemonade.*" By so doing, the youth builds self-confidence in one area of great importance to that youth. Is it not true that people with self-confidence gain it from doing only a very few significant things really well?

EGO SELF-IMAGE: An Ego Self-Image is characterized by its original C13 English denotative meaning, "*imitate ("to make a copy of")—i.e.* a *"likeness of something"* and *"to picture to oneself."* The C16 "*mental*" part addition of *"picture"* included a *"visualized conception"* and a figurative *"graphical description"* to give the resultant "Self-Image" definition as a rough pictorial representation of measurable things. Measure means quantitative items (e.g. things one can see); the identification of a relationship—a quantitative relationship established by means of a standard that serves as a unit. In Europe's 1300s the concept of measurement pertained to the partially bounded and meant to evaluate approximately, subject to conditions and experience. In other words, estimates could not and cannot be accurate because they involve some degree of speculation. *Speculation* is a way of viewing ranges on a scale--with a mere guess at one end and a scientific type pondering on the other. The more one progresses away from mere guessing (by using the imagination) toward scientific self-reflection, the more imaginative intellectual "seeing" combines with "seeing from the mind's eye" in the manner of philosophical imaginative vision characterizing the "poetry of ideas." An example of meaningful speculation is the agreement of wise people in their measurement of a person's character. The partial boundary would come into play in distinguishing the differences between good and bad.

Complexities are added when the aspect of something being acceptable under one set of circumstances become totally unacceptable under other circumstances. Slave resistance measures, like procrastination, were acceptable habits for them during slavery but are problem-producing in the marketplace when the same is done today. The completely bounded thoughts can be measured by generally agreed upon units as, for example, in distance (e.g. inch, foot, mile) or in units of time (e.g. hour, week, year) or in quantity (e.g. teaspoon, gallon, ton). The application of units to assessing oneself is the category most commonly thought of when the term "self-image" is used. All Self-Images are Icon Images and each human's Ego has three. *Type I* symbolizes who one thinks one is—typically having insufficient Power. *Type II* is who one guesses as to how one is seen by others. *Type III* symbolizes who one would like to be, perhaps all powerful.

When one has a mental picture of ones own measurable 'quantities, one sees: (1) unchanging genetic attributes present at birth (e.g. the shape of certain body parts, like *"slant"* or *"round"* eyes); (2) genetic attributes present at birth that do change. (e.g. body proportions, like height); and (3) chosen acquired material things (e.g. money, possessions, jewelry) for the enhancement of one's physical body self-image, of one's public persona, and of ones measurable *"work products."* How one assesses these mental pictures converts it to an Icon Image. From the foregoing, it appears that self-image pertains to (measurable) concretes about what one does (e.g. achieving work products, like sports records), measurable aspects of how one appears (e.g. one's body proportions) and material things one has. This pattern is the orientation of "the Crowd." One example of how a poor self-image can result is a youth's own degrading of his/her personal physical appearance features (i.e. *"Body Image")* to the point of feeling inferior.

"SLAVE SURVIVALS" ICON SELF-IMAGES

In focusing only on the "Disaster Magic," let us suppose things that happened to a given free African in Africa at the moment the fishnet was thrown over him/her activated each ones *"first law of Nature"* Sensory Consciousness, heralding a lifetime of enslavement. That specific moment resulted in a response of struggling for survival against creatures and forces in every way more specialized, powerful, and cruel than the victim could ever have been able to conceive. Meanwhile, they converted instantly into a "Fight-Flight-Fright" brain orientation. Later in the enslavement process a given victim settled into a customized complete or partial type of Hyperexcitability-Total Despair-Awe combined mindset, each forming illogical Icon Images. This mindset was culturally transmitted into many of the Enslaved desendants in the form called SLAVE SURVIVALS (maintaining Enslaved customs for reasons forgotten today). Enslavement Icon Images consist of the ingredients of slavery in direct or indirect forms.

LEGEND ICON IMAGE ORIGIN: The top Slavery Survival Icon Image in a given Black American is the top one of all Survivals to which that person has been exposed—also called the MVP (most vast player) which makes it a Legend. So let us look at the story of the *Legend Icon Image*--a story, above mere fiction, combining fact and personified metaphysical concepts. Its story starts with the varied Figures of Communication (FOC) used by early Africans in stories recounting the origins of their family and clan Ancestors--stories bridging kinships back to the very dream morning of creation--stories of the greatest of human actions and disciplines to the point of people personifying that power in such forms as "Legends"--stories also explaining the rituals and taboos fashioned by their Ancestors. These Epics generally served as living testimonies and references of the acceptance by kin of the Ancestors beliefs, customs, and traditional practices. Hence, their ongoing performances transmitted and reinforced such ideologies. Those individuals singled out had their stories embellished into an Icon status with a heroic personality whose essential mark was of reliance on Supernatural resources--a feature in many African folk epics. Such was also a feature in the Ancient African Bible speaking of Human-gods with whom legends had associated great acts or events.

Unfortunately, this conversion of legends, metaphors, analogies, and personification into "factual" dogma was standard after being copied by Europeans out of the Ancient African Bible and then replacing it with the European Bible. Certain prominent people dealing with the European Bible have been magnets for mythic material having "no home." The more superhuman qualities that have been assigned to an impactful character, and thereby making them into Icons doing non-human things, the more other writers try to get their works displayed by using that icon's name in the sense of a Legend. These "ghost" writers illuminate their Icon ideas and their ideas of his (or their) teachings. Thus, the result is the Icon becoming a legend and eventually having a "Virgin Birth" assigned to him.

In C13, a Legend ('things to be read') was first the story of a saint's life--literally 'things to be read of saints' in "Golden Legends" which, in monastic life, might be read in church as a religious lesson—especially stressing miracles. The data was chiefly historical, although through the years the original facts became magnified and distorted. Subsequent stories of the lives of saints thereby became more and more fanciful and imaginative. The consequence was that all these stories were viewed with skepticism. As a result, "Legend" embraced in C17, motto, inscription—and came to denote a story that, though apparently historical, was actually traditional and lacking in authenticity. Today, it is a traditional, unverifiable, usually fabulous story passed down (often orally) in a community and widely accepted as in some sense true. It is less likely to be associated with the Supernatural but is related to Myth. Legend applies here most closely to Icon Images because of its brief explanatory comments accompanying a map or what is picture-like. This means that the impact of African American slavery created such Legend type Icon Images because the events of slavery were forms of a Maafa (immeasurable catastrophy mentally, spiritually, socially, financially, and physically).

LEGEND ICON IMAGE SLAVERY SURVIVALS: Maafa's caused the Enslaved to use every conceivable method of surviving, self-protection, self-preservation, and enduring. Naturally, the methods of the Enslaved, serving as Selfhood Armor related to survival, did not lend themselves to judgment. Yet, when they were brought out of slavery they were molded into the *Black American Customs "Common Sense"* of struggling Black Communities. Such worked satisfactorily as long as it was applied to the Black Community while being carried through the metaphorical Struggling Tunnel connecting the living quarters of the Enslaved with today's inner city equivalents. Nevertheless, when those "Common Sense" ways of thinking, feeling (i.e. emotions), expressing, and doing things were brought into the racially hostile marketplace, they were justifications for the racists practices of making Black People "the last hired and the first fired"--if they were ever hired at all.

The combination of all of the evil and sadistic actions imposed upon afflicted Black People were like mentally traumatic layers that have continually accumulated since slavery--some of a certain "Sameness" (e.g. from slavery, from ongoing racism experiences, from stereotypes, from an inability to find work)--some unique, based upon a given Black Person's situation, perceptions, and interpretations. Some of these layers are simple bad images and some images are of an Icon nature--all contributing to a sense of unworthiness from lacking the "5Ss." Initially, today's Black youth's Images are composed of a collage of real, distorted, and fantasy outer world experiences and memories--each representing a snapshot. Those snapshots are variously arranged for each youth--and often in different stages of a given youth's development--in a unique manner at its core but having a certain 'sameness' around its borders. Ones Icon Images are like the USA President and cabinet members of the president. The the President or MVP or Legend Icon Image passes the plans for Life-Living to the Cabinet Members. Each member orchestrates every category within an afflicted person's life so that by means of a chain-of-command every rung of that person's hierarchial ladder is given the orders from the MVP. The resultant kinds of mindsets which characterized struggling Black youth's Outside and Inner Images are formed by their nature, plane of existence, direction, and degree.

They may be occasional, intermittent, repeated at irregular intervals, or continual. They may be permanent, stationary, and unchanging on one end of a scale or range in the other direction as prolonged to temporary; as being fixed in one place or having dynamic motions in another place; or as changing to some degree or like a whirlpool whose configuration remains the same as its contents are completely changing. All have their "Seed" beginnings in African American slavery but the form of their manifestation is based upon a given individual's interpretation as to how whatever is significant to them either affects their lives and/or serves as a model to which they ought to conform.

Regardless of what is fashioned as an Icon Image, its nature is self-defeating by being Illogical and Irrational when compared to a developed intellect based upon African Tradition standards. The self-defeating nature pertains to self-limitations and how to deal with the outside world regarding what is and is not done. The directions such mindsets can take are north, south, east, west, up, down, inward, outward, past, and future. Any type of self-defeating nature can be assigned to each of these ten. Furthermore, any of these ten can be problematic on any plane of existence--Spiritual, Subjective, Sublime, Supernatural, Astral, or the various subdivisions of the Physical.

Using the *Wheel Concept*, the Legend Icon Images of Enslaved Minds represent the *Hub* of a wheel with *Causation Spokes* on one side of the wheel and *Manifestion Spokes* on the other side. Though the "Seeds" and "Roots" of all reside in the subconscious, their ingredients exert powerfull indirect magnetic influences in attracting "Like-Kind" things. A given youth's manifestation of each Spoke is a unique personal display and yet something in all of those spokes share a certain Sameness within the *Collective Enslaved Minds* as, for example, the think, feel, say, and do expressions of the Illogical and Irrational. Expressions of these Illogical and Irrational include fighting, being self-destructive, petty and vindictive, acting out when one does not get ones way, abuse and neglect of others, rationalizing, projecting, and stereotyping. One engages in self-contradiction, deception, denial, inconsistencies; ignores relevant evidence; proceeds in the face of contrary evidence; jumps to conclusions; and think, feel, say, and do things that do not make sense. This comes from being self-absorbed--viewing everything within ones world in relationship to oneself and Selfhood Splintering.

There is a lack of manners, considering others' rights, seeing ones own thinking limitations, or appreciating others points of view. Ones false beliefs include: "it is true because I/we believe it; because I want to believe it; because I have always believed it; because that is what my family and/or friends believe; because it is in my selfish interest to believe it." There are many domains in ones thinking that one/we do not want to have questioned or challenged (e.g. prejudices, those that seem obvious or sacred) for it might reduce ones power or prevent one from gaining power or an advantage.

Initially, by allowing evil information into ones head means those implanted Illusions become self-fulfilling prophecies. Then they are interpreted as a magical happening, serving as the impetus for honoring Illusions as Beliefs and verifying the messages of Satanists. Such Beliefs come out of ones False Self, which has been the substitute for ones Real Self. Nevertheless, ones Will completes the Belief and ones Spirit energizes it into a Form-Body inside ones Unconscious. From there it passes into ones Conscious in the form of thoughts, emotions, sensations, passions for conversion into self-talk and/or the outside world as expressions and deeds.

When sensations enter ones consciousness from the outside world which are compatible with ones manifesting Form-Bodies + "like-kind" memories to the point of going beyond mere recognition, it generates a new image. Or the Image may be what is called up out of the memory at will, but its sensation will not be experienced without representation of the physical stimulus.

Since a Traumatic Mind is filled with undisciplined Imagination derived out of ones Mammalian Brain-Omnibus Brain (with its characteristic features, like obsessive-compulsive). Its Images are likely to be of a negative nature. One reason is that they see things the way Brutes have shaped their minds to see and that is in conflict with how moral things are ordinarily defined. A result is that spontaneous expression is inhibited and the compensatory mechanism of under-reaction is a general apathy. Thus, the afflicted become less effective in dealing with personal problems and less able to make a significant contribution to society as a whole. Still, they do "okay" at "home" but in society at large they function deceptively "as if" having low self-esteem (most commonly displayed as non-achieving performances). They are satisfied with the status quo and being a "Crowd" follower because both are familiar. Besides, victims find pleasure in being on the "bandwagon" of what gives the appearance of success and power, despite in the role of servants—and even if evil.

FEATURES OF BLACK PEOPLE'S SLAVE SURVIVAL MINDSETS

What characterizes these Slave Survival Mindsets is an emotionally hypersensitive mindset which tends to make all sorts of neutral words into "Emotive" words--words which past experiences with direct and indirect effects of racism have colored a non-emotional denotative word with emotions. One emotive word could trigger Chronic Rage/Anger causing one to make distorted or unrealistic decisions, often contributed to by what one has taken away from vicious cycles they or their friends have been in. Such *"Sentiments"* possess the *power to attract out of ones memory all emotions of a similar nature which can be associated with that neutral word and together they form an emotional "mental movie"*. Emotive Words like "Failure" can motivate Black Americans to do or not do something positive or negative, typically causing a chain-reaction. As a result, most Black People's *Opinions* (emotions coloring a thought); *Attitudes* (emotionally based inclinations causing a corresponding temperament); *Connotations* (the way the actual meaning makes one "feel" or how they emotionally react to it); *Beliefs* (voluntarily chosen bundles of powerful and frozen mental energy containing thought patterns, usually sprinkled with emotions) have a deep and long lasting impact. Emotional hypersensitivity plays a big part in Black youth and the justice system. So let us look at the minds of those about to join a gang.

Two analogies help to explain the following. First, a head of lettuce represents ones traumatized mind--its "Leaves" perceived as ones reaction to Trigger Events and/or a Trigger Person(s)--its core symbolizing ones mental turmoil. The second is a *"Snow Globe"* (Waterglobe, Snowstorm, or Snowdome) upside down whose white particles symbolize 'snow' to indicate the churned up chaos caused by the Traumatic "Leaves." *Each piece of "snow" encases a unique traumatized memory*. In the after-effects of the *Hyper-reaction* subcategory, the "snow" never settles back and the afflicted remain forever in an Emergency "Fight, Fright, or Flight" mindset. Next, the *"Awe"* afflicted mindset transmitted from slavery becomes so fascinated by the snowfall's shimmering magic as to become awesomely transfixed. This alone is exciting since there are no presented "Leaves" of caution covering ones head of lettuce core of mental turmoil. Thus, any little shake of ones customized Snow Globe is interpreted, not as bad but rather as a jingle! Even though some snow melts, more comes because of being in a "Snowy Climate"--an enchantment itself, no matter how bad things are. In fact, the more it "snows" the more bewitching it is.

Awe's human tendency is to rely on Supernatural agents to explain the unknown when natural and familiar explanations are lacking. A lifestyle is made out of the "Fight, Fright, or Flight" mindset which then uses what is available--as in making, wielding, and throwing snowballs at friends + anyone within reach + using them as weapons against monsters. One can even gain benefits, as in making snow into water for drinking or bathing. Fascination is added by bringing in variety, as with replacing snow with small glass beads or tiny lights to illuminate ones mental drama. These may be about what is going on among ones peers or with whom one chooses to associate. The nature of each of these is like the "*Glitter Balls*" used in the 1960s Disco dance halls--each glitter having its own beguilement.

Since these "scraps and left-overs" are part of the same fantasy world and its theme, it possesses a familiarity, connectedness, and a form of comfort. This is enhanced by whatever accoutrements are associated with ones Selfhood product, making it like a tiny universe in which one rules and is untouchable. Compared to those in a normal world, since there is no specific pattern, ones self-defeating self-creation is unique, "making it mine." To secure this, one glues it with "Unnoble Loyalty" to which one clings. Meanwhile--whether from the outside world and/or ones inner world--ones Magical World is rotating silently, powered by the same evil forces which originally put the afflicted in it. Extra power comes from subsequent layered demeaning forces. As rotating and tumbling occur, magnification by exaggeration of the reality of what is going on in this Supernatural Realm requires one to clutch on to whatever SEEMS to be stable, even if it is evil.

In this Delusional Mystery world there is no challenge needing to be addressed. Instead one simply 'plays life' on a treadmill course--without seeing or hearing--accepting "Ignorance and a befuddled mind as good enough." Those settling into a "Hopelessness" Despair snowy "Funk" are like the "landscape" of their minds bulldozed into a bottomless void where all Fear is gone. Since nothing seems real--since they perceive nothing about them is worthwhile--since they no longer have a sense of power or personal purpose (a sense of "uselessness")--and since nothing they are doing is seen to be significant, there is nothing more to fear. Hence, each next insult is met with phlegmatic indifference. The surrender of their spirit and the will to numbness are in their own ways a slow suicide. Contributory to this process is believing the worst that could happen has already happened--a reason today's struggling Black youth cannot be "scared straight"—a reason they "Don't Care."

COMPOSITION OF LEGEND ICON IMAGES: The point: out of all these layers of Maafa brought about during and after slavery + ways the Enslaved, Ex-Slaves, and today's struggling Black Community + how the individual reacted to personal effects of racism and the various poverties it produced are all part of the *Collective Maafa*. Contributing greatly to ones System of Values are: (1) each ingredient in the Collective Maafa as interpreted by a given Black person; (2) concepts of ones Ancestors religion, or even ones exposure to a Black Church or Muslim religion; (3) the continuing patterns set up by the Enslaved were all passed down to affect the living family and local culture into which one was socialized. These cultural transmissions + who one was exposed to or admired were main formers of ones *Personal Legend Icon Image ingredients*. It is not the significance of the event of any given Maafa ingredient that reigns in a given youth's life but *rather how that youth reacted to any given one*, no matter how mild or severe. The combination of what is extracted out of the Collective Maafa + ones Personal Legend Icon Image ingredients are synthesized into the Selfhood products called ones *Character, Persona*, and personal behaviors in relation to what works and what does not work. The resultant story of a Black person's *Personal Legend Icon Image* is above mere fiction--combining facts, distortions, and fantasies into an influence with a payload impact.

Note: to compare one Black persons Collective Maafa which helped form that person's Legend Icon Image with a family member or neighbor would be to discover certain "Sameness" as well as significant

"Unquinesses". This explains the considerable individual differences between Black People as well as explains much of the similarities of Black People. In either case, the what the afflicted do and why and how and when and with whom can only be *known by how things evolved in a given Black individual's life as well as Collectively in Black People's lives. Without getting involved with the course of their lives means there is no chance of figuring out anything about them individually or as a group.* Still, there is a crude reproduction in each Black person and about the whole of Black People that somewhat follows the theme of what their Enslaved Ancestors did. This is in keeping with the theory of *Recapitulation* (reproducing Ancestors' stages of development). The process involving having an Enslaved Mind reminds me of learning in college the *Theory of Recapitulation* (Biogenetic law; Embryological Parallelism)--"Ontogeny recapitulates Phylogeny"--meaning that in developing from embryo to adult, animals go through stages resembling or representing successive stages in the evolution of their remote ancestors. Though now largely discredited, it has analogy usefulness here as an idea of correspondence.

In other words, each of today's Enslaved Minded youth have mentally gone through each of the hellish phases their Enslaved Ancestors experienced--in one form or another—though not to the same degree—in arriving at their present mindset. Let us say that the *Primordial Collective Maafa Icon Image* of slavery fashioned in the minds of all the Enslaved a condensation of innumerable "Like-Kind" horrors experienced by each at the same time and at individually different times. Though this Primordial Image had unique features for each of the Enslaved, there was a "sameness" experienced collectively by all Enslaved Africans (e.g. the fact of being enslaved). From this Primordial Collective Image (the Star) sprang Halos--Auras and Thought Cloud Atmospheres--passed down as Enslaved mindsets and absorbed by each descendant's Unconscious to serve as a hyper-sensitization to any form of racism.

Hence, when a perceived bad thing happens to ones own race, rather than to oneself, there is a striking unison with the *Modern Collective Unconscious* which brings ones unconscious Primordial Image into ones awareness to be experienced as an "*Idea-Feeling.*" This is like striking a giant bell and listening to its diminishing sounds made by vibrations. Though the actual sounds made by the Enslaved may no longer be present in today's descendants, the actual vibrations made by that bell did not also end. The same idea is in humans being able to see the light of a star that was destroyed many years ago. Thus a mindset hypersensitized to racism being experienced by ones own people and/or oneself can detect the slightest vibration--a common racial experience that has been echoed through the tunnel of time. Added to this are personally developed Images. Whether realistic, distorted, and/or fantasy, Inner Images are ones perceived experiences. Outside "snapshots" are based upon ones interpretations of the monitored feedback one gets from outside influences. Each Inner or Outer World "snapshot" Image represents an Abstraction or Abstract concept that is treated as if it were reality, even though it is actually a distortion of reality or an unreality. Those concepts + each Primordial Collective Image from the Enslaved Ancestors'--regardless of the Phase--have the capacity to form an Icon Image. One of them can be a Keystone or a Legend Icon Image. In short, this Recapitulation theory for the development of Enslaved Minds in today's Black youth can serve as a plan for exploring how Enslaved Icon Images were formed as well as to help lay out an approach for how they can be dismantled.

SELF-UNKNOWING ICON IMAGES OF BLACK AMERICANS

Regardless of what mindset each Enslaved had, all lost contact with who they were as individuals. To repeat (Chapter I) Thurman: "There is no more hapless victim than one who is cut off from family, from language, from one's roots. He is completely at the mercy of his environment, to be cowed, shaped, and molded by it at will . . ." This clearly describes a *Form-Body* mindset. Perhaps this situation resembled being upside down in a bottomless pit, existing in a state of utter ruin. First, their Self-Unknowning came from being in a Form-Body state with a Surreal Supernatural Mystical mindset surreal—a False Self in varying degrees.

Type I--the least affected--were those whose Consciousness had sunk to a great depth in the bottomless lake of dimness but whose waters were transparent, allowing a little way of "seeing" their Real Self. This gives them a "Double-Consciousness." An example of a scenario in the life of Type I occurred with a Mentee whom I advise to give up 50% of the things he was doing in his life. When he asked for suggestions, I said: I have no specific suggestions for what you ought to eliminate in your life because I do not know what you do with your life. But I see you have a "Raw Nerve" that you are trying to run away and hide from--and sending in "Exciting stuff" to fill in the resultant mental space. That "stuff" has no benefit to your life and thus is carrying you on the wrong track (to nowhere). It is keeping you from doing the "ME/WE" things you already know you should be doing. Still, you keep "picking at doing" the right things to serve as deceptive justifications--a way of lying to yourself that you are actually doing it. This is like using "talking the talk" and believing it to be the same as "walking the walk". The place to start is with you--handle and shed your "Raw Nerve" (and you know what it is--if not write every thing on you mind that is not working for you). Follow by designing a Human Ideal for you to live by and then give it 100% attention while staying in that flow. Meanwhile, work on your children by doing what it takes to ensure they stay within the boundaries of the Spiritual Elements--guiding them to correct mistakes while inside its stream. Type I responds to guidance because most simply do not know.

Type II were the same as Type I but their waters were murky. Type II are those who are only focused on themselves and give a presentation of "Don't Care" about others. They really do care but are very, very lost about how to live life.

Type III are the same as Type II but they are positioned "upside down" and thus looking the wrong way. Type III adopt reflections of Brute European males and some reluctantly become gang members.

Type IV are like Type III but have joined the Surreal Supernatural world as servants to the oppressors. Type IV model Brute European male practices, defend them while attacking the Spiritual Elements, and become the most violent of the gang members. But these Self-Unknowings in Black People are reversible. This is because the Collective Unconscious drawn from their Ancient African Ancestors as well as the exposure, regardless of how slight, to Spirituality in their communities enables them to know they have a Conscious and a Conscience—which many bring to the foreground of their minds while in prison (from having time to think).

Such is not seen with European Brutes whose Self-Unknown results from: (1) having chosen to adopt a False Self (Ego) to orchestrate their "Life-Living"; (2) not knowing who their primitive European ancestors were or where they came from; (3) not knowing their most remote ancestral origin—i.e. the 'that they exist' or who they were or from where they came or when; and/or (4) deliberately deny the reality of their ultimate ancestral origins being Africans. As a result of Europeans' Self-Unknowing, many foolishly make up 'out of the air" that they are 'superior'. Their *Superiority Complex* is about the donning of a mask of self-confidence and greatness with a reality of arrogance and aggression to conceal a sense of deep inferiority. By socializing their offspring into the Ego mindset means they are never exposed to the Spiritual Elements—an absence allowing their minds to indulge in the vilest Supernatural ways of thinking, feeling, expressing, acting, and reacting. Its core Brute members are in hate groups and their Peripheral, and Tangential members are "Closet Haters." They are dangerous people filled with fetters. Many Type III and Type IV Black youth imitate them to varying degrees, for varying time periods (e.g. off and on), about varying things, and with varying intensities.

By contrast, Black youth do not have an Inferiority Complex as is widely advertised. Instead, reasons for being on the negative side of the Thinker's Scale—which gives the false impression of an Inferiority Complex--is their possession of a "Broken" Selfhood Integrity to which they react by doing anti-Spiritual Element things. Complicating this is allowing others to define who they are. This is despite the fact that no matter what single and/or group of outsiders do the defining, their assessments can never be right. Being defined in a demeaning stereotypic way + ongoing racism + lack of adequate employment causes many Black People to display manifestations that could be interpreted as an Inferiority Complex. Features of the Brute European assigners of who Black People are themselves Flawed in character and thinking--as in being shoddy, weak, inadequate, limited, defective, incomplete; non-pertinent; doing what is not of keystone importance; façade filled; confusingly directed or headed; placed on improper planes of existence; improperly arranged or combined; deceiving; in conflict; evilly misinterpreted; racially/ethnocentrically biased; in conflict; and/ or mostly simply wrong!

Self-Unknown Black youth engage in forming Icon Images—mainly because they have had their "Spirits" stomped out of them—and that means they lack Courage. Type I forms an Icon Image of *being a "better Self"*—i.e. a Human Ideal—and imagining it will provide the Courage that is simply spurred by what is the "Right" thing to do and then do it, no matter what. Types II, III, IV form Icon Images of various sorts, starting with *who they would like to become.* Their Icon Images (e.g. of "Manhood") are intended to replace decision making at every compatible scenario and, instead, used as models to live up to, as if it is a "command center." What they are looking for is the *Courage* one needs to bring to life so as to move life forward. What they have lost is *Courage in daring to be ones Real Self--daring to step out of fantasy into reality--daring to face ones biggest problems—daring to enter the Unknowns one fears despite realizing that on the other side of those fears is the success they so intensely desire.*

Yet, none of these Icon Image fashioners are prepared to make sound Spiritual Elements entities (e.g. like the goddess Ma'at) to their Human Ideal model and thus their Icon Images are flawed. For example, an Icon Image of who one would like to become is first fashioned out of the best available "bits and pieces" of information available so that the final Contingent Being represents a collage type shanty, which is rickety and subject to collapse with the first significant force that hits it.

SELF-UNKNOWN NEGATIVE IDENTITY IMAGES: Regardless of the Icon Image a Self-Unknown fashions, its "Identity" will be of a Secular or Ego Self-Identity nature—the type that is oriented to the External World and which is heavily fashioned by the monitored feedback from ones interactions with the outside world. Such is used to fashion a meaningful identity by means of a tapestry of a collage of meanings, beliefs, and values—a *Weltanschauung*—by which they can make sense of their experiences, find compatible guidance, purpose, and hope in order to have a meaningful existence. It is that combination that one uses to assess and to determine ones degree of success or failure. Within this European context a gang member strives to have a personally satisfying and publicly acceptable Secular Self-Identity—one that says: "This is who I am!"—and this is both a process and an accrued condition of dynamic integration. Together they represent a kind of personal coherence—recognized by others and sensed and counted upon by what one recognizes as ones Secular Self-Identity (e.g. ones physical appearance).

Some Secular or Ego Self-Identities are socialized to fear certain things—to avoid other things because they are taboo. These intriguing "Dark Side" factors are internalized and, in turn generate first, responses aimed at attacking them and second the fear that these very things one may embrace, similar to my medical school experience of suspecting I was coming down with every new disease I was studying. This situation is complicated by seeing these tendencies and patterns in ones parents, family, or fellow gang members—some of who have found it difficult to manage. Terribly malignant and destructive is the inviting of these "Dark Side" things as a result of a youth feeling either that all legitimate avenues toward achievement and recognition for them are blocked or that no one believes in them or their worth or the possibilities of them succeeding. Another form of negative Identity Image refers to the stereotypes so machine-gunned into them that they eventually believe that evilness to be an intimate part of who they are. All of these shape ones Character.

Secular Social Character is defined by Europeans as the consistent patterns of attitudes, emotional responses, and actions which, when associated with ones Secular Self-Identity, makes one both distinctive from others and recognizable as a person of continuity and sameness over time. At the same time, it refers to ones sense of internal coherence—ones ability to recognize consistent patterns in oneself and to be at "one" with oneself. This makes for a fit between ones meanings to oneself and ones apparent meanings to significant 'others.' For a full discussion, see (Bailey, African Tradition for Black Youth p194-96).

BLACK GANG ICON IMAGES

Of the influences that shape ones actions, none is more powerful than the Images one carries in ones head. Every subject is apt to invoke in ones mind a specific Image—made up of information, misinformation, folklore, desire, and prejudice. Thus, how people, including oneself, see themselves as a nation/individual determines to a large extent how they/one will respond to any new challenge and the role to be played in life. Since Ideas are powerful, great personal danger comes from one possessing false Images. Like bad grammar, bad Images become dominant when they gain wide currency, and so undermine thought in decision making and problem solving as well as communication with others. Images and symbols are already established in a given gang. Just as people mentioning what religion they are implies it is simply a symbol for who they see themselves to be, this is what happens to a new member. Although there is an existing Code, leaders of the gang tweek the Code to fit their way of doing things. An analogy is people who do not get guidance from their bible but rather they insert their personalities into what they are reading. In stepping behind these practices, Black gang members have imitated many of the thinking processes used by European males. One is Icon Images and another is Contingent Beings.

MENTAL ICON IMAGES OF BLACK GANGS: The environment and/or the situations youth may find themselves in often requires that they take charge and control of whatever they can do for self-protection, self-preservation, or even survival. The first step is a plan as to possible directions to take. Whatever direction is chosen is associated with the formation of a *procreative* act of mental pictures related to "what is for me and what is against me". All of the ingredients gathered from ones Right and Left brain assessments—the degree of appropriateness depending upon ones thinking skills—and maneuvered in various ways to come up with a mental picture of what to do. Similar to how the mother brings her child into the world and thereby acquires dominion over it, so does the youth form an Icon Image union of the multitude of gathered "Manhood" ingredients of which he is aware. The purpose of this procreation is to provide the youth with the greatest degree "Manhood" weapons designed to give him the needed power to handle adequately both internal and external challenges—or at least measures to *feign control over the uncontrollable*. The nature of these measures depends upon the nature of the youth and his assessment of the nature of the situation—whether Mild, Slight, Moderate, or Extreme.

The harsh lives of many struggling Black youth has them in an ever present mindset of surviving with respect to three broad *Classifications of Necessity*: Physical Human Nature Needs (PHNN), Spiritual Human Nature Needs (SHNN), and "Street Life" Physical Protection. In each of these three there is a *Model Icon Image* as a way to live; a "*Situational Image*" for handling the issue at hand; and a *Human Ideal Image* for the way one would like for things to be. Hence, each youth fashions several Icon Images because each Model Icon Image in each Classification of Necessity is perhaps their highest form of assembling concepts. Each Classification of Necessity has sub-Classes useful for determining "what is for me and what is against me" with respect to that given Classification. For example, struggling Black youth have a FEAR SCALE range of their worldview concerning their lives. Some are very fearful about everything (including what are anxieties) and, at the opposite end of the scale, some have made peace with doom and have no more fear (like the Baddest Dudes of the "Streets"). Those extremely fearful can learn to subdivide what they fear into Mild, Slight, Moderate, and Extreme categories and deal with each accordingly, as opposed to hyper-reacting to all. The Icon Images of these Classifications fashion ones understanding and the more vivid are these mental signpost the deeper meaning one has of oneself and environment in which one inhabits.

The core of all of the Classes in each Classification of Necessity are synthesized into Abstracts or Abstractions so as to have a predisposition imparting a 'big picture' as to what to deem to be the most important in each Class. The Abstract categories include each Classifications of Necessity itself and its Model Icon Image, and the Human Ideal Image). The Abstractions (tangible "*Situational Images*") are of a practical and secular nature that can be mentally visualized by the Box Concept (see Glossary). Abstractions feature a collage of ideas—ideas gathered by the Right Brain and assessed by the Left Brain into ingredients—ideas synthesized so as to enable one to visually see the 'Big Picture' of the situation at hand in several dimensions (a measure or estimate of spatial extent--especially width, height, and/or length) and from different sides and angles.

Every pattern contained within each form or figure of each Icon Image corresponds to an emotional, a thoughtful, and/or a sentiment (thoughts wrapped in emotions) mental concept. However, criticism is the acid that dissolves images. This means each Icon Image is a 'storehouse' from which 'bits and pieces' of mental 'raw materials' can be gathered--for arranging and combining with others selected that are pertinent to the situation at hand so as to fashion Plans A, B, and C. Together, these Icon Images constitute a source which provides out of its storehouse more immediate and fundamental input in making sense of ones environmental situation and ones Selfhood in relation to it at any given moment.

FORMATION OF GANG ICON IMAGES: As used here, an *Icon Image of a gang member's mind*—which fashions ones perception of the problematic physical situation into a metaphysical setting--contains the circumstances of the intent of the "Raw Nerve". The Percept in perception is a first and natural display of the human mind's activity upon acquiring "raw materials" from ones Inner and/or External worlds. A *Percept*--the mental entity of a "Thing" when it came into being--a sensation making one aware of something good (like what the ingredients for a flower bud do) or bad (like a threat, disturbance in harmony, or atmosphere of danger). This Percept or "Signifier" (the first stage of an idea) is made material (a thing) and thus the signified is no longer only in the mind—i.e. something thought of—but also something experienced—something felt, in the heart and the body. As the Percept develops into a Notion, an Idea on the way to becoming a "Thing" in time and space, it can have so much mental "materials" (e.g. imaginative things, memory, aspects of reality, distortions, and/or fantasy, as to become an Icon Image which is now a "Think" with a payload message.

This message drew on various contributions that together are called "*Circumstance(s)*"--literally meaning circles of samples that came from around the Trigger Event or Trigger Person. After all of these contributions are fashioned into an essence piece of the whole perception of the Trigger Event or Trigger Person, a "Circumstance" makes mentally "Seeable" pertinent aspects of what is of most significance about ones "Raw Nerve". First, in its formation and of prime importance is the effort to explain and control the effects of a Trigger Event or Trigger Person on ones Selfhood—and that takes precedence over interpreting, contemplating and understanding the situation. The resultant mental Image incorporates the visible, expressive, emotional entities—and its design may be from oneself and/or from ones in-group or gang. Its payload message reflects motives, patterns of power, a 'mirrored' conditions of the Trigger Event or Trigger Person's involvement, the selection of a Power Approach (self-devised but more often that has worked for others), and the insertion of the intensity of aggression makes it an Icon.

Put differently, the Image is constructed mostly *passively*—ignoring the what, which, when, *how* and *what* —and instead focusing one the who, where, *why* and *what* since these aspects give the creator leads to explore more paths into the subject, devise more ways of handling them, and perhaps allow for instant reaction in striking at the "bull's eye" whenever the appropriate situation arises. This means the Gang Mindset Icon Image becomes an indicator in the form signs that are like the thing it represents. Such Iconic Images are not iconic per se, but rather are made iconic under specific cultural conditions that generate reactive emotions. The fashioning of an Icon Image authorize the creator the right to undertake whatever actions the image includes. (Ref: Moore *Cooperation and Conflict, 2011*).

Since Gang Mindset 'Icon Images' grasp the emotional complexity behind the visual representations of the Trigger Event or Trigger Person, they are able to communicates experiences about either or both so that one re-experiences whatever caused ones "Raw Nerve". This results in an awareness of the associated emotions (e.g. rage, fear, pain) which, in turn, results in a mental re-enactment of how one might best react that might be in ones best interest (e.g. measures capable of bringing victory, relief, avoiding "what is against me," and/ or prevention of the Trigger Situation from recurring. Being alert to discerning this *Iconic Experience* is one of understanding without knowing, or at least without knowing that one knows--and understanding by feeling, by sensing contact or actually experiencing contact with a like-kind thing or perhaps some symbol of it that triggers ones memory.

This Iconic Experience process is evidenced by the senses originally created by the "Raw Nerve" and that have always been on constant alert since the Trigger Event. The shape of the Icon Image imparts the power to stimulate one into a conditioned responsive social reaction.

The repetition of the 'performances of representation' compatible with the Icon Image is like an engram that layers onto or deepens the impression in the pattern of the Conditioned Response make it increasingly easier until it gets to be automatic. In other words, there are such powerful emotions contained in these Iconic Images as for them to be immediately understood when the situation presents itself--and even if their meaning is diffuse and vague'. Meanwhile, surpluses of ones reactive power are generated so that it takes less and less of a trigger for the Conditioned Response to spring into action. This combination, each acting on each meaning within the circumstances of the intent of the "Raw Nerve," means an increasing hypersensitivity to arousal and to take reactive behaviors to "Disrespect". Simultaneously, the Icon Image can be likened to mixing cement. When it is wet (or fresh), one can move it around and shape it, but at some point it hardens and there is almost nothing that can be done to reshape it.

GANG ORIENTED CONTINGENT BEINGS: The world as experienced by each human is an interpretation of data arriving from ones senses. What ones Metaphysical and/or Secular Imaginations produce or fail to produce play a large part in how one perceives most things in ones inner and outer worlds. They are also capable of changing established beliefs from two perspectives. First, we are aware from many experiences that actually hearing a given sound or seeing a given shape or meeting a particular person is quite different from what we imagined. Second, instead of assuming all things imagined are distinct from all things perceived, the imagined and the perceived often interact because this is the nature of ones Right and Left Brains. For example, an imaginative new or updated idea of a sound or shape has the power to change how a familiar thing has been traditionally perceived. This has profound practical importance in producing, say, a male's "Street's" derived Icon Contingent Being (CB) as a Symbol of "Manhood." Ones Imagination, which begins the process of forming this Icon CB, is what is derived from ones inner and outer world--whether real, distorted, fantasy, or a mixture of these. Whatever it is--and they are collected in bits and pieces--serves as "raw materials" to fashion a collage "Seed" for a Gang oriented CB to begin its evolution. The Image formed out of these "raw materials" and "conscious memories" Images that, in the absence of the original stimulus to perception, reproduce a previous perception. They combine to form a "Collage Image" that violates ones sense of survival/self-protection/self-preservation in whole or in part to result in an Icon CB.

Despite the ingredients in Collage Images perhaps not calling up the previous organic sensations of pain and suffering into conscious memories, they do reinstate, even though faintly, immanent experiences. *Immanent* denotes that which dwells in or pervades one mind without necessarily being a part of it. Incidentally, interior Ancient African *"Ritual Specialists"* considered the cause of immanent experiences to be from CB spirits. *To use their CB to wipe out the patient's CB*, they dressed in skins of animals + wore large grotesque masks + used implements like rattles or drums capable of creating an annoying noise + engaged in wild dance and mystical speech--all intended to frighten evil spirits out of a patient's body or mind. This would impress patients and observers with mysteries of healing to which both could form an image association. And these ancient psychotherapists had extremely high cure rates. Contributors to immanent experiences are the fact of Poverty itself, or being in a dangerous immediate environment, surrounded by societal terrorists (e.g. the police, the court, the school, the job market, the housing, and the media systems in relation to Black People). Words are big contributors to the formation of Collage Images for they come into the mind in a visual, auditory, or audito-motor state.

No doubt, there is a reality to *Synaesthesia*--a condition in which a stimulus has an additional effect outside the boundary of its usual function of exciting normally located sensations in the brain. That effect gives subjective sensations of a different character. For example, Black People who come bearing gifts to help fellow Black People out of their struggles may trigger past and present memories to European con-artists who were bearing gifts and used those trinkets and false promises to do further damage to Black People. There are associations of different Images. From having been reared in the South during the lynching era of Black People by White people with a drawl, to this day to hear that drawl (auditory image) causes me to "tense up" from associating it with the White people (visual image) of my boyhood. This is one indicator that all imagery is not shifting and unstable.

Imagery's "robust contents" in remembering, thinking, and day or night dreaming confuses discriminable events via condensation, displacement of emotions, and regard for presentability. Such confuses ones perceiving, conceiving, imagining, thinking, judging, and expounding of thoughts, emotions, expressions, and action plans. All of this makes it difficult to recall exact details of any Trigger Event or Trigger Person which resembles something else (both having been seen or experienced at different times by the same person. Thus, if thoughts about a bad happening is not a fantasy, then it is a distortion. That is important in undertaking management.

EXAMPLES OF GANG ICON IMAGES

Situation Example A: Common imaginary companions representing an immature defense mechanism is that of a hated external "Thing" (e.g. Trigger Persons). Converting this into a CB allows for internalization of the "Thing's" aggressive characteristics for purposes of handling emotionally (e.g. reducing anxiety by symbolically putting those characteristics under the creator's own control) or by offensive or defensive things to do when the encounter comes—as boys also do when they watch conflict situations on television. To help clarify the result CB, creators freely use verbal/visual imagery. For Europeans, this is likely to be in the context of the ideas conveyed in Machiavellianism or other "Dark Side" aspects, narcissism, and philosophical manifestations of psychopathy. For Black youth it is likely to be an Indifference/Hate/Evil/Sadism (IHES) Complex imitation of their impressions of how European Brutes deal with them, perhaps with Kill/Take/Destroy/Dominate added on.

Situation Example B: ICON IMAGE OF SELF-PROTECTIVE POWER: In some communities there can be found bad Icon Images viewable in every resident's mind. There is the perception of having a sense of safety—an abstraction Icon Image that has cut out all distracting details to as to provide an image that is easily grasped all at once—this is how one thinks, saying no more than needed. To help develop a sense of self-identity of Power, and particularly in the form of "Manhood" youth develop social cognition in which they imagine and therefore indirectly experience themselves in anticipated encounters and/or mentally correcting past communicative encounters with others. Since construction of an Icon Image concerns the processing of information as a core feature, imagined interaction relies on intrapersonal communication as its foundation. Imagined interactions focus and organize individuals' thoughts on communication and development of self-understanding by uncovering differing aspects; by self-concepts; and by relating with others better by understanding their attitudes and opinions on current peer events, "Street Code" orientations, or and in-group values. Such increased self-understanding is directly proportional to the amount of verbal imagery one applies and especially if one stars oneself in the central role. Out of this come plans for what it takes for self-initiation, self-reliance; for socialization of family roles and cooperation; or for offense and defense in conflict situations.

Situation Example C: A traumatized child, likely to later develop Multiple Personality Disorder, incorporates fantasy imagery into a personality identity. Fantasy is an aspect of the Imagination by which a temperament—e.g. envy, an inferiority complex, anger, begins to take on a form with a specified purpose and direction" Serial killers have an "inner part, or some internal entity that becomes an overwhelming force in his life and compels him to kill again and again. The creator of ones own monster in turn then controls him, causing him to do the things he actually wanted to do in the first place". Fantasy--an imagery process in which one attempts to obtain vicarious gratification by engaging in acts in ones mind which one is currently unable (or dares not do) in reality—can become linked to the processes of dissociation and compartmentalization. Thus, the killer becomes the very being he had so often visualized in his fantasies.

Situation Example D: "WHAT ICON IMAGE I THINK OTHER'S THINK OF ME": Traumatized Black youth are acutely aware of their visibility and vulnerability and how, in DuBois's words, they are viewed "through the revelation of the other world"—the "Air Castle" cult members. One teen characterized is as if "They think we come out the womb labeled, with an orange jump suit on and a number on our back." Typical reactions are those of Shame and Humilitation demanding they hide from others by putting up barriers (e.g. "Don't Care").

Situation Example E: "WHAT ICON IMAGE I CREATE TO THINK OF MYSELF": A major False Self *Icon Image of who one is*: "I'm not good enough". This may lead to regret, grief, or blame from not having a dad around to teach "Manliness/Manhood". One youth said: *There are some things only a daddy can teach you* (Hunter). There was a sense of loss, of missing the lessons that fathers could teach about how to navigate boyhood and the transition to manhood—indeed, how to be men. When asked what are some of the special things that dads can teach, responses were about women, how to approach a man on a job, basketball, and about society. One added: "I can't talk to my mama about sex. Some things you just can't do." Yet it was difficult for participants to articulate lessons or things only a father can teach—like how to be on your own. Dads can break it down better and also how to take on responsibilities. It's the little stuff that your mom teach you but your dad could do better. It's the little stuff you got to look out for. Experience of being a man confers advantages to fathers in teaching sons about being a man because a dad, he guides you--teaches you the step by step of how to be a man and stuff. A woman, she can't give you that guidance because she's not a man. As being a man, he can give you the right little steps and the right ideas.

Related to the concerns about the lessons only fathers can teach were lessons lost about being a Black man. A young man suggested, "Mom can teach you some stuff, but she can't teach you anything about being a Black man. [She] don't know what we goes through as a man." You can learn from other Black men because "your Black men out there on the streets. And it's easier for women." Others questioned the potential contributions of their fathers and acknowledging the role of their mothers and their hardships. "But your dad can teach you how to approach a man when you are going for a job, if they know. Some can, some can't. You can't say all Black men, because some of them know more. But they can teach you things like that. Although the participants affirmed the idea that "guys really need [fathers] along the way as [they're] growing up." The boys reflected on their fathers missed in their lives, the crises fathers created when they were present, feelings of abandonment, and disappointment about fathers who were still in the streets.

The experience of being psychically or physically traumatized conveys the loss of the "5Ss" senses, and especially not feeling safe. Chronic Shame causes one to no longer see the potential possibility for great deeds. Whatever caused the Shame becomes a "Raw Nerve". Thereafter, like a Geiger counter that gets louder the closer it gets to radioactivity, the closer reality gets to the "Raw Nerve" one is hiding, the greater are defense or protection barriers one puts up--against ones own recognition of it as well as those to prevent its detection and exposure by outsiders. Such protection sensitivity prevents one from listening and hearing wise advice and from having the courage to do what it takes to avoid or to get out of trouble. One sees oneself as being terribly flawed—a mindset that is quite susceptible to feeling one is being attacked, even if that is not so. One adds to this by doing things that ought not be done and then getting upset with those who point it out. One operates out of "All-or-None" and "Either/Or" so that decisions and a change of personality can be like an off/on switch. Their "Inside-Out" thinking causes them to focus on what they are not doing.

Situation Example F: "WHAT I THINK OF OTHERS": In 1903, DuBois published *Souls of Black Folks* in which he talks about the sadness and the waste of talent that segregation causes in not recognizing the full potential of the Black man. He brings out what Black people have to deal with from birth to death and that is the "double consciousness" or that they feel as though they are two people. One is the self they know and the other is the self they are told by others is the real one. The Black American part of the "Double Conscious" Sons viewed mothers as role models, both for what they were able to accomplish and for how they handled their sons when they were growing up, particularly, how they acted as disciplinarians. The narratives about mothers do evoke iconic images of the strong Black woman even though it is a portrait of mothers that has its own costs for Black women (Collins, 1990). What this image represents, in part, is sons' greater awareness of their mothers' struggles. Unlike the hardships their fathers may have faced, they knew the troubles their mothers had seen. As illustrated by a participant who discussed his father's leaving, "my mom, she had five kids.Mydaddy left when I was about 1, 2 years old. And my mom's been taking care of us since. It was hard for her as a Black woman." Speaking about his mother and other women who are making it alone, he further commented, "That's a strong Blackwoman. Because she is keeping house. She is paying the bills by herself." One participant who had re-newed his relationship with his father talked about his perceptions of the roles of his mother and father and the evolution of his perspective: The European part of the "Double Conscious" is that much of what Black males are and what they should be is measured against the status and privilege of European males (Hunter, *JBlack Studies, 1994*).

Situation Example G. "WHAT ICON IMAGE I WOULD LIKE TO SYMBOLIZE ME?":

Group I *Icon Image of who one would like to be* goes in the direction of "Manliness" and they mention every good trait known in African Tradition. "Being a respectful with your family first of all. Second of all, you know, respect for your wife. Third all, keeping your household in order." Taking care of and caring for (or trying to) one's family is about meeting "one's responsibilities as a man."

Group II struggle between Manliness and Manhood. For some sons, their fathers were unworthy teach-ers because they violated these standards of respectability. I set goals like, okay "I want to graduate from high school. After that, I want to go to college. After that, I want to do something to make me a man." I don't want to be like my father because, like, he left. And so, that makes me work harder to achieve my goals to become a man. *I will be the man my father was not.* these young men place much faith in what they learn from other people's lives and their own mistakes. Across and within generations, lessons were passed on about mistakes made, and of triumphs and of failures. As one young man explained, "By being a teenager, you've got to edu-cate. Take good notes on people that you think are doing the right thing." When we asked what people did not understand about young Black men, a participant offered, "We're learning from our mistakes—mistakes not only made by you [us], but close friends, cousins, and family." For the young men who felt their fathers fell short, the goalwas to strive to be the men their fathers were not. As one young man explained, I want to be the type of man that take care of my own. If I have a good job, and I knowI can get a good job, Iwant to get that job. If I got a wife, I need to take [care] of my wife. I'm going to take [care] of my wife. Take care of my home. Understand? Take care of myself. I just want to be the type of man that is there for people who need me. That's always been in my mind, the type of man you want to be. But you don't always be the man you [want] to growup to be.

Situation Example H: GANG SITUATION ICON IMAGES: They have images of war that colonize the mind and without the guilt—images that are wrinkled, if not twisted. To kill someone is to kill God's Image.

European Brutes strive to make victims in their own image—a "little god" thing. There are Gang Laws to be followed. Laws are a pre-existing pattern which things follow. The story one tells oneself in trying to blend into the gang is about real, distorted, or fantasy experiences that are similar to those of the other gang members. The story is a journey where the character of oneself as the Megastar has to change in order to have meaning and establish a "new normal." That story adds Drama for excitement with Anticipation and Uncertainty whose essence is the variety of parts in the story. The spur for this Image is the desperation of losing who one was when one was living out of ones Real Self. That spur pricks the like-kind Association of Ideas in ones memory and binds them, like flowers into a bouquet.

Situation Example I. In every parting there is the Image of Death.

MANAGEMENT OF BAD IMAGES

In contrast to Europeans who lack any connection to Natural World morals, Black People commit violence NOT because it is viewed as the *right* thing to do in terms of some pre-established value or worldview but because they are forced into a given set of interactional circumstances. Examples include Enslaved Africans having to instantly and permanent undergo a Brain Switch—from the enslavers brainwashing the Enslaved into "Inside-Out" thinking—from the European racists generating such losses, lacks, and obstructions as to result in a mindset of Rage in many struggling Black Americans from a sense of powerlessness and unimportance, and dependency. For certain of these victims, violence is an action strategy perceived to be available and effective for the situation at hand. Hence, violence flourishes as a dispute resolution mechanism where the law is unavailable (Lee).

SHED CLINGING TO ENSLAVING IMAGES: Of the countless influences shaping every struggling Black Person's thoughts, feelings, expressions, and actions, none are more powerful than those of an Enslaved Icon Image nature + associated satellite Images + their causes + the lifestyle build around them--wrongly viewed as the best one can do and the right thing to do. Each of these represents an Image one carries in ones head --whether of an iconic nature shaping ones approach to life or fashioning methods applied to daily living habits. Every aspect of each Enslaving Image done repetitiously is made up of flawed "concrete" information, misinformation, folklore, desires, biases, and prejudices that supercede necessities. Thus, how one sees oneself in relation to ones self-created mental images determines to a large extent how one will respond to any new challenge in family life, to children, to adults, to friends and neighbors, and to the concentric rings of society that radiate throughout the world. The keystone for these determinations is how one assesses ones sense of Selfhood Greatness--an assessment that molds ones Character, the orchestrator of ones destiny.

Yet, regardless of their natures, ones Selfhood *Images can and do touch ones emotions where they are accepted as "the truth." If that "truth" has Spiritual Elements Certainty, it is reality. Anything short of Certainty causes one to cling to those beliefs.* The story of Enslaving Uncertainty began with the daily realities of slavery which laid out, in their view, the confident "Disaster Certainty" expectations of invariable bad happenings "forever." Despite their terribleness, those *expectations were clutched, clinged to, and defended because they provided confidence in something stable.* This is reminiscent of the words of a song I heard as a boy: "If I don't have bad luck, I don't have no luck at all--and that gives me something to count on." Within the context of an enslaving mindset, the root of *"Disaster Certainty"* is *Clinging* (Old English, 'to hold dear') to it and that clinging produces Anxiety and Anguish--words having self-strangulation (Latin, tightness, narrow) as its roots and which prevent one from having a free mind. Uncertainty brings defensiveness to which one "*Clutches*"--a C13 English word for a claw developed into a swift, eager, tenacious grasping movement of fingers seizing for the sake of saving a situation (1525) and thence into a "tight grasp" of the whole hand. Clinging and Clutching to anything causes flawed thinking which results in irrational and illogical emotional outbursts; a personal sense of weakness from the absence of power to get things done; self-absorption which negates caring about others feelings; and procrastinating in taking self-improvement actions for rising above mental, physical, spiritual, and social poverty. Instead, by conforming to European oppressors' dictates of "stay-in-your-place," the afflicted remain 'fixed' in a bad but comparatively safe and familiar harbor of life.

This is a keystone Icon Image which orchestrates their lives. Nevertheless, they feel so bad about themselves that to get a moment of relief they engage in "Escapes" from their mental turmoil (e.g. excessive cell phone talking; overindulgence in "flashing light" electronic gadgets) while criticizing and shunning the courageous ones sailing off into the high seas to carry out their Mission in life. The overall situation is one of clinging and clutching to Uncertainies which provide no benefits, are self-destructive, and, by serving as a crutch, makes for Selfhood weakness. They fail to acknowledge these mental barriers that are in their subawareness. That self-dishonesty about their true situation, thoughts, and emotions urges them to seek the soothing of friends and to "go along to get along" with whatever others say they should be and do. This fixed state of immaturity to which one clings provides the illusion of safety. Clinging is done for fear of abandonment and being left on ones own while feeling worthless. The problem with any Earth World object clinged to is like holding tightly to a falling rock.

And any negative Emotions or weak thoughts or bad people clinged to with the idea of them bringing benefits is like grabbing at smoke and trying to hold on with ones non-existent hand. When all of this is put into a mental picture it has the image of a Tree. Correction starts with first gaining the trust of the afflicted; having sound knowledge of Ancient African philosophy, as opposed to merely ones life experiences and ways of doing things; and focusing first on the "Seed" of that Tree to understand and correct or replace its flaws.

REASSESSING ONES ICON IMAGE: Meaning is constructed through the images one mentally holds and has access to; and maintained by those one clings to; and are altered by the quest for new meaning. Such reassessment starts with an attempt to facilitate "imagination"–that is, the fuller appreciation of, and access to, images rather than "interpretation." Within this context, the quest for new understanding might be linked to the generation and reconsideration of what might be regarded as poetic and metaphoric Hip-Hop Rap. A way to start is by examining powerful and recurring images that are shared by organizational participants. In the original formulation of its culture, Rap created and articulated an original mythology that made good sense to participants and that is authentically represented in the shared imagery of participants.

Once recognized, modified into a Human Ideal, and shared, these images (like metaphors) can be instrumental in transforming ones ways of thinking about, and making sense of, the organization Image, status, and a host of other factors that affect identity. The idea is that they be mostly created by group perceptions of who is the youth's Real Self and how one defines oneself using African Tradition guidelines. People see themselves from the standpoints of their group. To draw on a group who exhibits African Tradition and model oneself on the appropriate action in relation to that group can becomes source of pride by having ones identity socially bestowed, socially maintained, and socially transformed. Of practical importance is that a youth may, up to this point, merely identified with the image of "being with" the gang in a nonspecific inclusive way, as by socializing as friends. But assessing this Icon Image more closely may provide a fresh perspective, assembled and shared--undoubtedly leadings to richer translations of what is taking place within the ambient culture.

A next progressive step is to engage in a compared subject assessment with Spiritual Elements. Here, Metaphors or Analogies may show significant differences that might lead youth to distance themselves from their present self-defeating situation in the organization or at least select issues, themes, and mind-sets to avoid as much as possible. The value of critiquing the analogy or metaphor contained in ones Superstar Icon Image is that it may give "*Common Sense Gist Awareness*" from the first glance of an initial exposure. By contrast, if one has a skilled helper directing the management program, the process may be immediately steered into a limited, stereotypic surface appreciation of the subtle intricacies, dynamics, and interactions that constitute the "Raw Nerve" big picture so as to be blind to the obvious and disorganizational Selfhood effect.

Still another approach is to give ones gang related Icon Images a monster characterization that is even shocking or terribly disturbing image —perhaps like it is eating a youth mother from her insides. By focusing on the 'big picture' organization as something that it cannot literally be, invites one to invoke new possibilities of meaning and creative perspectives of sense. This new way of seeing what is presently accepted as "what it is," "what it does" and/or "how it appears" with an altered meaning may cause a distain for how it operates and where one is going.

SWITCHING BAD CONTINGENT BEINGS TO GOOD

The C19 verb "Switch" means to 'exchange'—with or without deception. The *Type I Icon Image*—a Self-Concept of their losses, lacks, and obstructions over to *Type II Icon Image* of "Street Life" role models is a worsening of ones Brute mindset. The initial very powerful and unresolved emotional forces from personally experienced traumas encapsulated in ones story adversely evolve with the *metamorphosis of switching into a Type II mindset.* There is an addition of and/or an intensifying of such bad emotions and experiences of the fetters (passion, hate, envy, despair, incestuous liaisons, rapes, murders, etc.). Ancient Africans said whenever one encounters a complex problem or multiple problems that generate a "Limbo" situation the *first thing to do is to put it in order.* Then, I add, look for the *keystone--the problem's orchestrating and controlling force or power or influence or obstacle.* A *Keystone* is the central wedge-shaped stone of an arch that locks its parts together and serves as a guide and control upon which the neighboring parts depend. This is similar to the role of an Icon Continent Being (CB).

The Ordering and Keystone concepts for complex and difficult minds of Gang members is their Icon CB for "Manhood." Each member fashions a CB out of a collage (bits and pieces of this and that). However, the main bits and pieces come from the "Street" of his (or her) community as well as from their concepts of White males do, as gathered from television, videos, movies, and observation. These assorted models are tried on for size" and those "that fit" are imitated. This imitation includes identifying with the power of what "fits" and consequently "sharing" in the pleasure of being privately reinforced by them (called Vicarious Reinforcement.) Once this "Manhood" collage CB is formed, it serves as that individual's model. The C16 Italian word "*Model*" (a small measure) is a representation of something else on a smaller and more manageable scale. It may match the original in most details or be an idealization which seeks to represent only its main features.

This modeling is spurred by ones thoughts and emotions about a specific situation--such as the degree of perceived danger--and the CB features determine how one reacts. What is done is refined through gradual accumulations of is a reflection of the intent of the user; the character of the receiver; and *the monitored feedback from the receiver's interpreted experiences derived from his/her inner and outer worlds.* If success comes in any degree, what one has modeled is a direct social reinforcement. As long as one has a "Numb" mindset to the destructive things done to people, places, and things, they will not be in a mood to entertain change. Yet, in a rare and brief moment--e.g. once every 3 years--a given gang member has a brief awareness of and feeling of regret about what they do. If the circumstances and time are right, this is the opportunity which can be enlarged upon sufficient to bring change. Their basic problem--the "Seed" of what is wrong--is a lack of supply of their Spiritual Human Nature Needs (SHNN). Each has been so disappointed by everyone meaningful to them that they distrust everyone. Thus, it is extremely difficult to bond with them (see Bailey, Teaching Black Youth). Much time must be spent finding a suitable and customized Human Ideal Icon CB to replace their existing CB. Once that is done, the idea is to discover an honorable human model a given member holds in high regard and who he/she experience as being similar to him/her. Then in the process of imitating that model, he/she collects bits and pieces that can be formed into a Human Ideal Icon CB.

As his/her "right track" world broadens, then other good people outside the family become effective bits and pieces sources for modeling. In the process, attention is given to the ingredients that went into fashioning his/her particular gang lifestyle. First, discover his/her *Trigger Category* (TC)--the "ballpark" where his/her primary self-defeating problem lies. Second, the *Trigger Problem* (TP) is where one looks to locate the Keystone Problem. That "Bad Seed"--searched for by the "What's Behind That" Inquiry Method--is the *Trigger Obstacle (TO)*--i.e. the single most important factor in that Trigger Problem serving to prevent his/her recovery progress. Third, the top priority is to *handle the "Keystone" problem first*--for that is the Disposition which gives rise to his/her Inclinations, Intentions, Purpose, and bad Deeds. To *kill the Keystone Bad Seed" means the Roots"* and all other parts of the *"Tree" responsible for aspects of his/her Satellite lifestyle are likely to resolve by themselves.*

If the TO cannot be located, then begin with the TP or, if that is not possible, with the TC. Starting with the most pertinent, obvious, and easiest allows one to step inside the problem and "look around" for all *Satellite Problems* joined to the "Keystone" Problem. These Satellite Problems expand in all directions. Find the Satellite Problem that lends itself to being handled without a great deal of difficulty. Once that is done a somewhat more difficult Satellite Problem will appear ready to be solved--and so on until you get to the "Keystone" Problem.

BAD ICON IMAGES (BII) FROM RELIGION: Europeans believe in a Supernatural God and will never change their ways of Indifference/Hate/Evil/Sadism. What Europeans say about their religion ought to be subject to great scrutiny (Bailey, Ancient African Bible Messages). For example, the European Bible says that Jesus says forgive others for their sins but leaders of the non-African based Churches say God will not forgive unless certain things are said and done. Another incompatible opposite is to have images of God and then say any image falsifies God and is idolatry. Would that not include those who say the European Bible is an image of God's (e.g. God inspired) word. A God conceived is an idol. However, the Ancient African Bible says though God cannot be conceived, still God can be known. Ancient Africans have always worshiped a Spiritual God but this became confused with the Supernatural God as a result of it beaten into them by Europeans during African American slavery. Thus, Black People are capable of changing some of their complex BII. Spiritual Faith and Spiritual Trust are at their height when ones highest Image of God is as a non-image, as an unknowing of God, and a not knowing of God's whereabouts in the Unseen. Ones sight comes out of the Unseen as one reaches for what is impossible to touch.

So the highest knowing is that one does not know of what is impossible to know and not make an image out of it (for that is an idol). This is where the idea comes from that to truly love someone is to allow them to be free to go. Besides, there is nothing to grab onto as there is with Conditional Love. Thus, the process involves "letting go" and not clinging to anything--for that is impossible in the realm of the Spiritual. This is analogized by one "breathing out"--a letting go process. Whereas in the Material world, to know something deals with "what it is" and not "what it does," in the Spiritual world to know something is by "what it does" rather than by "what it is." Africans never had an Image of God; Guilt is a key to control and to reinforce this European churches are set up like courtrooms (e.g. black robes). Rigid rules associated with absolute laws and substitutes what is of higher honor and what one can intuit. In this way one can appear tough minded and rigid and righteous, masculine, and an individualist. All others are weak. This is based upon a Machine Concept of humans-- machines are fool proof, doing the same thing all the time without change-- which is inhuman. They see liberal thinking in justice as wishy washy, vague, gives too much flexibility. Instead, life is a contest that has to be won. In the process, one is always edgy and worried and fearful--like walking a tight rope.

Innate sense of fair-play cannot be formulated (e.g. equity) since people hassel over the words of law. No way to judge all problems of humans and thus one needs a sense of Justice. Europeans have direct images and indirect images (as by calling Jesus God). Europeans say God is watching you and judging you; Africans say one sets the stage for what will happen by means of Karma--what one does determines what will happen to one. There is no focus on win/lose and that enables what is done to be play--not attached to anything--a true human. The heart of the nature of things is play--human heartedness. They had rigidity in life but knew when to give, like judo where techniques are learned and then let go without taking any seriously so it can free flow.

SWITCHING ICON MANHOOD" IMAGES: In primitive times of Africa, "Manly" and "Manhood" worked simultaneously and beneficially. The circumstances of being the first to enter the Earth World necessitated that Primitive Africans fashion the three basic cornerstones of "Manhood" (the birth presence of an Animal Mind) that began African Tradition—i.e. to provide, protect, and produce. PROVISION was about proving capability in adult work (e.g. successful hunting). PROTECTION concerned the intellectual and physical competence (e.g. strength, agility, aggressiveness) to keep safe and secure ones family and eventually ones village. PRODUCTION originally related to impregnating women but later expanded to include work products (Bailey, Manhood In Black Americans p 9). Once the people began to gather in groups, status hierarchies were formed, with those attuned to the Unseen Realms (e.g. Shaman) most honored.

Much later African Sages arose from having studied astro-mathematics from which Laws of Nature could be inferred. Then insight was gained that "Manhood" (the birth presence of an Animal Mind) which, in normal succession, is to be gradually recede as ones Manliness (i.e. Higher Self Mind) expands. At the end of ones full life, if ones mind does not reflect ones Manly divinity--and instead is dominated by "Manhood"--then that is a failed life. This means one has lived out of ones Animal brain instead of following the natural giving way to its successor, the Higher Mind. To prevent this, Ancient Africans built their entire lifestyle doing what it took to reach the "Heaven Afterlife." To this end they developed the most powerful ways of "Manly" (see Chapter XIII) and "Manhood" thinking.

Today's gang members considering leaving the gang must ask: HOW DOES IT FEEL TO BE A MAN?: Ones common sense says one is separate from everyone and everything and that means one feels like the master in charge of everything (which is always called into question by stronger outside forces) or that one is not in control of anything and is thus a puppet to outside forces. Either way, one is hostile, suspicious of all, and has the need to self-protect. The puppet sense occurred during slavery. This ensures one lives in ones Lower Self, seeking pleasurable sensations, dope, idols, money, power. If one does not Keep ones Word one doubts ones sincerity to be true to oneself. That leads to guilt but that does not affect the core problem. It also gives one a bad feeling and a bad view of who one is. To shed this opens the gate for a good life but there is a high price to pay to go through the gate. However, in African Tradition one was reared to be part of the Cosmic Organism so that what one did affected all. That sense of responsibility to taking care of the whole and thus oneself caused people "act right" and avoid "acting ugly." These are powerful motivators to keep going when one feels like giving up. This awareness of all things are oneself ensures one lives in ones higher Self with a sense of being mentally free (i.e. in control of ones fetters) and a lack of hostility. This is a manifestation of Spiritual Congenital Selfishness because ones concern involves everybody.

MODEL/HUMAN IDEAL ICON IMAGES: An *Ideal Image* is a Spiritual Absolute or a Supernatural Abstract (and thus does not exist). A *Conditional Spiritual Absolute* is Circumstantial Truths which African Sages arrived at by Mathematics. Mathematics is science which deals with magnitude, quantities, and numbers *quantitative* reasoning *assessment of entities in the Material World enabling one to make qualitative Circumstantial Truths in Metaphysical Realms based upon the Law of Correspondence.* "Cosmic Correspondence" means that the same "Genetics" present throughout the Cosmic Organism constitutes the same Base/Foundation "Genetics" in each of its offspring, regardless of that offspring's plane of existence location. For Europeans, a Conditional Absolute is called by Axioms and by Postulates, but they are not the same. Nevertheless, in Science, as in law, nothing is recognized beyond the agreement of men to determine what shall be taken for granted as true or just. *Axioms* (C15, Greek, something worthy or appropriate) are an Association of mega-star Ideas pertaining to the Seed of something within the Physical (meaning it is relative) or the Supernatural (meaning it has no "Ground of Being" because it is fantasy) realms. Axioms have shared agreement among experts on the Necessary ingredients of that "Seed" within a given field which thus makes it a self-evident truth considered to require no proof. *Postulates* are voluntarily accepted assumptions which, when agreed upon by the experts in a certain science, become its conventional basis.

Secular "Paradigm" (C15 Latin—something set beside something else—a pattern, an example, a basis for comparison, a model, a stereotype), a word having at least 28 different meanings—and I have not seen it defined the say way twice. Some say a Paradigm is a "Becoming"--a theory building process. Some say it is a Contingent Being possessing a position of authority—in the sense of "an overriding viewpoint that shapes ideas and actions within a particular field or group. Some say it is a world view, a way of ordering and simplifying the perceptual world's stunning complexity by making certain fundamental assumptions about the nature of the universe, of the individual, and of society. As a world view, Paradigms are normative--determining what the practitioner views as important/unimportant, reasonable/unreasonable, legitimate/illegitimate, possible/impossible so as to guide one in what to attend to and what to ignore. In learning a paradigm, theory, method, and standards are acquired together, typically in an inextricable mixture.

An example of Circumstantial Truth application in Metaphysical realms used to explain the Spiritual was African Sages arriving at it using Mathematics. From that they made inference of the Spiritual Elements to determine that God is Unknowable but that God can be known by God's manifestations. That is as close to a Spiritual Absolute as humans can get, for it implies the arrival at Certainty without doubt and arriving at Truth without error. A *Paradigm Shift* is old ideas and practices taken for granted and reassessed in light of new knowledge. Because Europeans apply Axioms to the Physical realm means they are subject to human mind limitations. An illustration of this was the necessity of making a Paradigm Shift by taking almost all of the "facts" they devised to say that the earth was flat or that the sun rotated around the earth and looking at them in new ways—and thereby bringing about a change in concepts to the opposite. By their own admission, Europeans say anything about the Supernatural is unprovable (e.g. their God) and thus one must have Belief/Faith.

So "Paradigm" is an Umbrella term—manifesting on different planes of existence and having variables on each plane. Generically, it can be thought of as a sort of "Conditional Certainty" featuring degrees of probability. They are said to be Self-evident truths taken for granted and serving as a starting point for deducing and inferring other (theory dependent) truths. However, Circumstantial Truths, as determined by Ancient African Sages, are highest and, as long as they stay inside, is orchestrated by, and evolves out of the Spiritual Elements, its deductions and inferences are probably Certain. The reason is it deals with the difficult, the hidden, the hard to discern by *looking behind the obvious to see the consistent, permanent, stationary, and unchanging patterns/elements underlying natural events*—for that represents the Spiritual Elements. A distant second is an Axiom, and an even more distant third is a Postulate which may or may not start from Truth if it is in the Physical realm and cannot start from Truth or Reality if it derives out of the Supernatural. They are 'distant' by lacking the ability to see behind the hidden and that is why a Paradigm Shift is likely to happen. Instead of a Paradigm Shift with Circumstantial Truths, there is the ever present evolving Creativity of the Spiritual Elements.

The point is that to design a Human Ideal Icon Image means to use the ingredients of the Spiritual Elements to stay within—then orchestrate a Human Ideal Icon Image in context with ones Talent—and develop that Talent within the context of the selected Human Ideal Icon Image. The reason this is an "Ideal" is because it uses only Spiritual Elements ingredients. The reason it is "Human" is that the Spiritual Elements ingredients are already within ones Selfhood from birth. The reason it is an Icon Image is that the Icon which gives rise to a Spiritual Elements designed Image shares some common features with metaphors. This is because by both possessing the capability to "touch" a "deeper level of understanding than a Paradigm, both dissolve boundaries enabling one to intuit what is *behind the surface of Physical Paradigms to see the consistent, permanent, stationary, and unchanging patterns/elements underlying natural events*. It also sees the *Supernatural Paradigm as a façade*.

It is at this profound level—this Base of ones Selfhood—that puts one in the flow of the process of learning and discovery of: "Who I Am" and "my Purpose in life." Such an awareness can only come from having an Integrated Consciousness—meaning one becomes Certain of being what one knows, a manifestation of being a vital part of the Cosmic Organism. In other words, to "Know Thyself" requires, along the path of Circumstantial Truth, analogical "leaps" from ones familiar inner Selfhood to the Cosmic unfamiliar (but with which one was familiar at birth). By rallying ones Productive Imagination and Pre-Birth Emotions as well as ones honed Intellect causes these "analogical leaps" to provide, in the process, an altered way of seeing below what seems to be the surface of the organization to discover the consistent, permanent, stationary, and unchanging patterns/elements underlying natural events. Their Mathematical order allows assessments which give rise to sound Real Self Thoughts. The prioritization of Thoughts provides the clearness and the Order to lay out paths for the "Rightness" of choices, decisions, and solutions. A practice method to get oriented to this subject is given by Starr-Glass (*J Management Education, 2004*).

SELF-WORTH AND SELF-VALUE: For Black males it is having their "manhood" defined by European males so they can be demeaned, confused, controlled, isolated, and eliminated. "*Machismoism*" (an exaggerated sense of maleness) implies a male joins the practices of the wrong crowd in order to assume the role of the "tough guy". This delinquent form of manhood behavior is characterized by the "tough guy" seeking thrills, duping others, believing what happens to them as beyond their control, and not allowing anyone to "boss me around." Tough guy manhood includes responding violently to remarks and actions most other people would ignore. The basic tool of the tough guy is guns and their ownership (Farley, Sociology, p. 205). As a result, not feeling worthy of connection or being fearful of disconnecting (e.g. laid off, turned down) there is Shame. In the inner recesses of their minds they may have the perception of "I'm not good enough" or "pretty/handsome enough" or "smart enough" or, for a male, believing he has a flawed "manhood." This causes the afflicted to struggle with this issue and to deal with it they become numb to it. Thus, self-harmony results from elevating ones Self-Worth and Self-Value to conform to one Human Ideal.

HEALING BAD SELF-IMAGES: Black American males want to prove to European males that they are worthy but that is difficult because they are so oppressed as to not have the tools and circumstances for competition. They do not realize they do not have to prove anything to anybody but rather just be themselves. The key to a healing Self-Image is one that integrates all of ones Real Self thoughts and therefore activities of ones life-force. What embraces this is ones birth gift of Selfhood Greatness, mainly because it is the Spark of God within oneself that has all the power and knowledge one needs to not just succeed but to live a Human Ideal life. This means one cannot nuture any thoughts of failing at anything within ones Talent. The Right Brain is in charge of Visualizing *What* one wants to achieve and *Who* will achieve it. Recall that the "*Self" knows What* it wants to manifest (i.e. what it is willing) and *Why* while ones *Spirit determines the How and When* (Amen, MAAT, p12). The Left Brain verbalizes the Why (and hopefully not the How). Once one has selected Human Ideal ingredients, the Imaginative Faculty takes these sets of force governing a particular set of events or things and organizes them into a concrete (i.e. not abstract) image. Imagination os a coordinator of subtle physical forces and not a creative faculty.

HEALING BAD IMAGES FOR CHILDREN: Here, "children" is used in the 'big picture' sense of not only those young of age but adults who stopped their maturity in childhood as a result of developing a "Raw Nerve." *Art* is used by Europeans to arrange animalistic desires so that some can become rich by facilitating their own oppression as well as oppression of minorities. African Tradition uses Art (music and drama particularly) as the Science (science = knowledge) of manipulating behavior through Imagination so as to transcend the influences of the animal spirit. Art involves the coordination and special arrangement and combinations of forms based on their external components. In Affect Symbolic Imagery presented as a dramatic story, the leading character(s) is made compassionate and then taken through a series of ever increasing conflict and complications. Along the way, the audience identifies with the sufferings of the Protagonists, causing the audience to experience emotions which ease them into a Trance. The major experience comes at the climatic moment when the Protagonist faces what seems to be an inextricable complication. The suspense generates the

"Suspended Breath"—entering into the Trance. The same can be done with Good Music, Poetry, and Graphic Arts—all "touching" the Right Brain which controls behavior and spirituality.

SUMMARY

An Image is a pattern of synthesized or unified forms and figures endowed with a 'payload' of thought and emotional significance—the whole of which is greater than the sum of its parts. A Mental Picture lacks such significance. Images may refer to some Source of a Cause (the 'enemy,' any aspect of oneself, ones Selfhood in general, the situation or circumstances, or a combination), the Cause itself, an Effect(s), a Consequence(s), or the "Big Picture" Result from that SOBMER process. An Icon is an idealized "little world" of what the reason for what the Image is all about and thus has special significance compared to an Image. A Legend Icon Image is the orchestrator of ones life by being the Ultimate Standard, Guide, Filter, and Measure one uses throughout the course of ones life whereas Icons orchestrate some aspect of ones life. Images, Icons, and Legends, by being graphic illustrations, convey a stronger message than words and hence the expression: "A picture is worth ten thousand words." That picture (or mental image) may be about something good or bad and may have an origin out of Reality, Distortion, or Supernatural Fantasy. Thus to instantly bring to mind an Icon Image is to attract all of the memories, the thoughts, the emotions, and other aspects associated with it. The key point is how one reacts to these Images and whether that is to a consistent, intermittent, occasional, or rare Mild, Slight, Moderate, or Extreme degree. People who do not believe in life after death are free to fashion the most horrendous Icon Image and react on them in doing atrocious things.

When ones thinking is not based on the laws of the Spiritual Elements but on beliefs or opinions about oneself and ones relationship to the world, then the blind forces of emotionalism and sensuality are displayed within the realm of Metaphysical Disorder ("go astray," become lost," stray from correct behavior). That is outside the boundaries of Ma'at making it no longer necessary for humans to recognize the Good, to strive for Perfection, and Plan opposite to it as a life's course. These blind forces destabilize, devitalize, and disharmonize ones life-force and thereby causing a host of ills. Resultant Images these humans entertain dictate how one should react or feel (emotion) in a given situation; how one desires events to go; depictions of desired outcomes. Images act as funnels that direct the flow on ones emotions and passions to the accomplishment of the associated events while conditioning ones spirits to behave as visualized. Such reinforces ones habits as well as help create, enhance, maintain, defend, and protect automatic or Conditioned Reflexes.

Some Images are driven by ones Will (faculty of the freedom to choose). This embraces the capability of ignoring the emotional, instinctive, or divine parts of ones Selfhood. The Will is free of emotions and sensuality or from any coercion, impulse, or compulsion from the emotional part of ones Selfhood. Thus, when one arrives at worthwhile accomplishments or chooses to engage in violence, these are volitional (i.e. under ones full control). Other Images are driven by Desire, meaning one is a slave to the emotional forces driving ones actions. As a result, ones life is dominated by the sensually and emotionally dictated behavior as, for example, in causing violence. Bad Images can be "Deprogrammed" using Human Ideal Images as replacements for the Bad Images.

CHAPTER XI

BLACK AMERICAN GANGS

All human males are born with the ingredients to develop the mind of their Higher (Spiritual) Self as well as the already develop mind of ones Lower (animalistic Secular world) Self. The function of the human Will (with the Cerebrum part of the brain) is to enable one to dominate ones Animating electromagnetic energies (part of a human's spirit) orchestrating ones physical body. This "Animal Spirit" (Khaibit) is Ether programmed for preservation of ones survival with instincts, curiosity, fighting, fleeing and other motions, motivation, sense perceptions, sensuality, sensory/motor nervous powers, and physiological functions. But one can chose to spotlight ones "False Nature" psychic attractions (directed by the Ancient and Emotional Brains) of ones emotions, desires, cravings, appetites, passions, wants so as to do what one likes/dislikes of a material nature—and to make this a lifestyle invariably leads to disaster for all concerned since they can never be guides to a thriving and happy life. All that threatens to interfere with ones pleasures or cause pain—whether real or imagined—leads to a response of anger or fear—responses not capable of solving problems or conflicts. The mythical African god Set lived out of his Animal nature. To stay in a Lower Self state as a way of life means ones Conscience will never awaken. This characterizes Brute Europeans.

American slavery was founded on the principle of benevolent Satanism authority—the notion that the White man knows what is best for the Black man—a notion used as a deflection from the real purpose of slavery—i.e. to get rich. A pattern used then and throughout the history of Europeans has been to invade peaceful cultures, maintain control by violence, destroy their traditions, rape them of their most prized positions, generate friction between the people, and leave them so that violence among them is expressed in a horizontal fashion (i.e. take out their rage and frustrations on similarly situated individuals rather than on those who benefit from their oppressors. Irwin (*Race and Justice, 2012*) discusses four phases that was well demonstrated in the "Take Down" of Africa—and these can be applied even to destroying organizations (e.g. was done to the Black Panthers).

Phase I is the forced invasion of "a small minority of outsiders" to a country for the primary objective to obtain "valuable economic resources" or to organizations to infiltrate and learn about what needs to be attacked. Phase II is launching systematic assaults on native cultures, where indigenous languages, religions, worldviews, and ways of life are destroyed, distorted, and generally denounced as being primitive, evil, and savage. In this phase, native peoples are often constructed in zoological terms as being more like animals than civilized people. Phase III is stabling a government by a racial or ethnic minority (i.e., foreigners) and premised on the belief that the indigenous people lack a decent, moral, and civilized society. Indigenous people are cast as needing governing and control by members of a superior culture (i.e. foreigners). Phase IV is the set up of a rigid social caste system in which the oppressors receive the lion's share of privileges within the colonial society while the victims are shunned, denounced, and alienated from symbolic and material resources.

As is typical anywhere, these Brute captors of Enslaved Africans assumed their "little god" privileged identities so as to receive all the benefits while ensuring the Enslaved received none + demoralizing and marginalizing the Enslaved + destroying connections with all that made them superior to their captors. In response to this colonial reality victims experienced a deep sense of alienation and adapted at varying stages of the course of their history by revolts, sniper attacks, becoming "Ideal Slaves," by "going along to get along," and 100 years following slavery by protest, crime, and assimilation. Throughout slavery, the stored up and boiling over chronic outrage of the Enslaved, their overwhelming life-long frustrations, and their malignant fears were so intense that they needed an outlet--all capitalized on by "Bible toting" Christian slave owners by such measures as promoting inter-plantation fights. During a festival, planters on large estates would "liquor up" their strongest Enslaved males and induce those on opposing plantations to fight each other.

The primary aim of slaveholders was to indoctrinate the Enslaved with a deep sense of fear and inferiority, to make them accept the notion of White supremacy in all things (Rhoden)--to beat all the "spirit" out of them until they had no desire to ever retaliate against White people. Otherwise, since the emotions of the Enslaved had to be constantly repressed, many sought scapegoats out of the ranks of fellow Enslaved--perhaps as bullying weaker fellow slaves--or doing mean deeds--or imparting Self-Esteem Attacks, as by calling another Enslaved some bad self-concept names. Even more aggressive acts were *"spontaneous"* fights, stabbings, and killings--particularly after the enraged or frustrated one was drunk from trying to drown his steaming rage emotions and frustrations in the Whiskey bottle (Bailey, Manhood).

Europeans reign supreme in IHES displays, as in during and after slavery (continuing in full force to the present) their physical, mental, emotion, and spiritual attacks on Black People. Included were such things (among countless others) as stereotypes, ridiculing the misery they had showered on their victims, and calling them "primitive" Brutes (of course a projection of how Europeans saw themselves). Let us pause to look at one of these. The etymology and denotative meaning of the Middle English word *"Primitive"* is 'original'--first of its kind--earliest of its kind--fundamental--in the sense of what humankind's first ancestors did. During African American slavery Europeans introduced a variety of derogatory connotations for the word "Primitive" in reference to Africans as part of their most ridiculous claim in the history of humankind of calling them-selves "superior" people. These connotations included: crude, uncivilized, child-like, bad and inferior people. Thereafter, in most European literature "Primitive" and "African" were synonymous, meaning a backward people.

Malcolm X put this into the context in which Europeans used it by saying: "Negroes have been misled into thinking that Ancestral Africa was ... a jungle, a wild place, where people were cannibals, naked, and savage . . .. Such an image of the Africans was so hateful to Afro-Americans that they re-fused to identify with Africa. We did not realize that in hating Africa and the Africans we were hating ourselves. You cannot hate the roots of a tree and not hate the tree itself." This degrading picture never was true about Africans and in fact it was just the opposite. Europe itself was fairly savage until they came into possession of the GUN to start the Renaissance in C16. Up to that time many Europeans were still almost naked and crouching around fires eating raw meat while many Africans were sleeping in gold beds.

As a rationalization for not being allowed to get an education, many Black People put on the "Front" of being proud to say they did not read—while realizing that is not an ignorance that causes bliss but rather ignorance is a form of slavery. To be ignorant of ones own history means Brutes can rewrite and control it. For example, the European world authority on mythology, Joseph Campbell (Occidental Mythology p43) said about the African goddess Isis addressing her initiate (c150 AD): "At my will the planets of the sky, the wholesome winds of the seas, and the lamentable sileness of hell are disposed…." This statement is false to those who know the Ancient African Bible. One reason is that Ancient Africans did not have a Hell. Instead, Hell was made up by Europeans, along with Satan. Research this to discover it for yourself rather than just clinging to it.

About things like this, Malcolm X said Black People have been *Bamboozled* (C17 vernacular "bam"--to trick, to con, fraudster, cheat)--"They're counting on that you all forgot. They think that they can run the okey-doke on you." Bamboozle, to deceive by trickery or hoodwink by underhanded methods, perhaps arose among the criminals of the underworld. Incidentally, President Obama said: "Republicans want to 'bamboozle' voters"--to confuse, frustrate, or throw one off thoroughly or completely by "Inside-Out" thinking which generates Delusions. The forms Bamboozle take range from the barely detectable to being like an elephant in the room that they tell Black People not to see. Much of the path is eased by presenting attractive but false information that "SEEMS" right and repeating it until "everybody" accepts it. Nevertheless, the impact of Europeans 'machine-gunning' demeaning "Selfhood Bullets" was sufficient in a large number as to "beat down" their Self-Image.

All of this contributed to various types of poverty in ghettos—poverties compounded by building on Slavery/Post-Slavery Rage; Chronic Juggling out of constant Desperation; being continually dominated by those deemed Inferior; the reality of pervading unfair Imprisonment or sentencings; relentless Health Problems; Nobody Helping or even caring; Knowing what to do and cannot get it done; and adopting the White man's values without the benefits. Any one of these in any given phase of ones life derived out of any aspect of the oppressor's IHES Complex has been and still is sufficient to crack the "Eggshell" of ones Selfhood Greatness Integrity and that falls into the category called Disrespect (attacks on ones Dignity and Divinity). The methods used by Euro-Americans to "keep down" the Enslaved formed the "skeleton" SOBMER process for today's Black-on-Black violence.

PREDISPOSING FACTORS FOR BLACK-ON-BLACK VIOLENCE: The sudden change from freedom to enslavement at the moment of being enslaved by a fishnet meant that thereafter the Enslaved (1) entered into and lived inside a Satanists atmosphere; (2) was influenced by the Satanists' nature and by what they did; and (3) as a result of both atmospheres, each Enslaved developed a unique and share atmosphere with fellow Enslaved. The new arrivals from Africa were totally dependent on the Satanists for basic survival (e.g. food, clothing, shelter), no matter how inadequate. Each had Expectation I--of being provided with Survival Needs or die. Expectation II--future Survival Needs would be provided. Expectation III--things would get better (which it never did). Note the peculiar situation twist of having *expectations from the enemy for survival while simultaneously hating the enemy*--a new consciousness conflict never before experienced in Africa. The immediate mental shock of enslavement perhaps caused the Right Brain's Emotions to revert to its pre-birth "Wild Metaphysical Element" (WME) level. If so, this meant their mental activities could be reshaped by forces in the external world--and those forces coming out of the Brute captors were of an evil nature. If those evil forces could be equated to "Disaster Stars," the "Halos" they gave off were what the Enslaved absorbed--for they had no other model. Since WME are non-judgmental and are part of the means that cause the newborn to bond with her/his mother who provides essential care, the same situation was re-created between the captors and the Enslaved.

In spite of the cruelty and the inadequacy of the food, clothing, shelter and the like needed for their Physical Human Nature Needs, a bonding of a negative nature occurred. This I call the Evil Savior Syndrome. It was perpetuated, I suspect, *"What did not happen"* and the Atmospheres engendering Fight, Flight, Fright, or Funk. Self-Defeating Atmospheres included not learning how to learn; of not having curiosity; of not exhibiting Courage; of "Making Do" with the less than meager things the Enslaved were provided; not knowing how to make, save, and properly spend money or set up businesses and make them work; of not striving for success. So the Enslaved reacted by *Avengement*--working as slowly; breaking equipment; plotting against the Satanists; enraged over being enslaved and inhumanely treated while enriching slave owners with free labor; using esoteric language when Whites were present (e.g. the Negro Spirituals conveyed hidden messages; taking petty things from slave owners out of need for survival; wearing Masks/Masquerades in front of Whites. These reaction of the Enslaved themselves became 'second nature' and some lived down to them. American racial slavery absolutely denied human freedom to the ancestors of African Americans.

SLAVERY "GANG/TASK SYSTEMS": In Africa, the Ancestors of African Americans, both individually and in groups, resisted enslavement in Africa and fought against enslavement using an assortment of gang-type warfare. Without being systematically organized, countless Africans "gangs" fought their enslavement-- on board slave ships during transportation to the Americas and then throughout colonization in the Americas. Black-on-Black violence, as seen today and is most prominently exhibited in ghetto gang wars, had its "Seed" of origin in slavery--from being enslaved--from being treated so viciously inhumanely--from having no sense of Power at anytime or about anything. Whether in Africa or on board slave ships or on American plantations, some engaged in mutinies and armed resistance; some did sabotage; and some fought culturally and politically. African culture "sustained the Africans during the holocaust of the slave trade and the colonial system that followed it. African culture, reborn on alien soil, became the cohesive force and communication system helping to set in motion some of the most successful slave revolts in history" (Jalata, *JBlack Studies, 2002*). There were about 250 slave rebellions in the United States between C17-C19; about 50 maroon communities were formed by thousands of runaway slaves and their descendants between 1672 and 1864 in the forests and mountains of southern states. These resistance struggles were aimed at retaining an African identity and restoring human freedom. This shows that despite the fact that the plantation and slave owners established firm control on this enslaved population with the support of American institutions, they could not totally control their minds and spirit.

Nevertheless, Enslaved labor was the most important source of the higher Southern total factor productivity compared to pre-Civil War Northerners. The concept of a Gang System was a mainstay of European enslavers. Planters organized their Enslaved labor force in the Gang System or the Task System. In the *Gang System* the Enslaved were divided into several sub-gangs of 10 to 20 hands, each headed by a "Driver" who bore the responsibility of the assigned task. The Gang System's basic objective was to keep the whole gang members at work until the goal of the day was achieved. Under the *Task System*, each slave is allotted a day's work. Some cotton planters organized the plough-work into the gang system and the hoe-work into the Task System. Despite many mixtures of these Task and Gang Systems, overall the Gang System was the basic form of Enslaved labor. The Enslaved were assigned tasks and put into mutually coordinated respective gangs with the precision of machinery and the strictness of military discipline. To make this an efficient system of division of labor, use of the Overseer's whip ensured interdependence and competition among gangs. There were parallel lines of Enslaved who proceeded at exact speeds and with precisely controlled motions so as meet hourly the quotas of their allotted task.

POST-SLAVERY BLACK GANGS: At emancipation philosophies and practices of the Enslaved were culturally transmitted inside the cramped Struggling Tunnel and adjusting to them became the "ceiling"-- the upper limits to which struggling Black People aspired. Its attitudes and practices became *"Slave Survivals"*--they worked okay during slavery but the practices used to show avengement--e.g. working slowly, coming late--to the slave owners worked against them outside of the Black Community. These "Slave Survivals" were *"Zombie"* habits--meaning the practices continued unchanged, although the reason for doing them was no longer needed. I learned much of this from talking to ex-Slaves. The Brain Switch from Ancient Africans traditional way of thinking while inside the Ocean of Nun (OON) Thought flow over to having removed the Left Brain's segregative and analytical (like a calculator) as well as the Right Brain's discipline effect imparted by the Left Brain reduced the mental activities of most Enslaved African to a Form-Body state of Consciousness. Reason is designed to counterbalance the animalistic features of passions and bad emotions in ones Lower Self in preparation for striving to achieve ones higher Self. Thus Reason opposes ones own passion generated stupidity and blindness (as in its desire to "live for the moment" and not care about tomorrow). But the divorce of Reason allows one free to be completely controlled by ones Lower Self and bad emotions. Thus, how they react to psychic trauma is what they cling on to and the consequences from this are what they adjust to and find to be normal, no matter how self-defeating. Chronic anxiety entrenches this pattern.

Also immediately following emancipation there were slavery-like laws passed which stated that if a Black person was found loitering or simply not working (and there were no jobs to be had) that they would have to pay a fine (and no ex-Slave had any money). Hence arose the *Convict Lease System*--the collecting, for imprisonment in virtual jails, every ex-Slave not hidden away as a sharecropper or out of sight in some Black ghetto. Every conceivable excuse was used to jail even innocent law abiding Blacks and with no regard for age or gender. Such was in collusion with the courts and the police who arrested a required number of Negroes, whether guilty or innocent. When simply fined in court, supposedly for only 6 to 12 months, they had to work on the country road or streets of the city. There were all sorts of conditions devised by evil Whites to engage in these practices. Prison labor was sold only to state agencies for things like construction of roads and public buildings, maintenance of recreational areas, and reforestation projects. One form of such work away from the prisons was operated on a minimum-security or honor system.

Another form was the chain gang in which prisoners were chained to each other outside with maximum security. Compared to the Convict Lease System, chain gangs were the lesser of two evils because fewer numbers of Blacks were killed. Each prisoner wore leg shackles connected by a bull-chain to other convicts. The *bull-chain*, 4 feet long and weighing 3 pounds, was attached to a heavy iron cuff riveted around the right ankle. In going to and from work and during the time the convicts were confined to quarters, the end of the bull-chain was attached to a long master chain so as to keep all of the convicts leashed together. For men who had attempted escape or who actually escaped but were caught and returned, step-chains were used in addition to the bull-chain. *Step-chains* were attached by the use of leg irons -- to both ankles -- and were 15 to 22 inches in length.

Harsh methods of punishment, often "for no reason," were the way of life. These ranged from solitary confinement (with little or no food and water) to being placed in antiquated stocks and "sweat-boxes." Whippings occurred daily and frequently throughout the day for each prisoner. The men worked from "can to can't -- from when you can see in the morning till when you can't see at night." Food was the crudest and guards were the worse of the sadists. Droves of convicts died of sunstroke, starvation, overexposure to cold, shackle infections, overwork, and brutality. Out of their human hell rose the voices of men who would daily look death in the face. Always bewildering to Whites, they defied death by laughing and creating ironic lines in the form of chain-gang songs. Being envious of all of this and having an profound sense of self-hatred covered by a 'superiority complex,' Europeans did all they could conceive to destroy the Selfhoods of the ex-Slaves. Prominent here was/is Euro-American terrorism showered on Black People and their means of survival was huddling.

SOBMER PROCESS OF BLACK-ON-BLACK VIOLENCE

The "Power-Aggression-Violence" triad of European males is what "Took Down" Africans, inhumanely enslaved and killed African people, and maintains oppression of Black Americans. This has marginalized all Black Americans—i.e. on the edge or 'margin' of USA society—like one foot on and one foot off the societal Archery Pad—only partially assimilated into the dominant cultural patterns by partially having accepted its values and way of life while having relinquished the majority of its own traditions and separate identity. This indicates how the dominating society defines itself and what constitutes its key philosophical values. The concept for the term "*Marginalization*" was originated in 1903 by DuBois' publication of the *Souls of Black Folks* in which he decries the sadness and the waste of talent that segregation causes in not recognizing the full potential of the Black man. He brings out what Black people have to deal with from birth to death and that is the "double consciousness" or that they feel as though they are two people. One is the self they know and the other is the self they are told by others is the real one. "Marginalized" Black males are in a dilemma—a state of chronic mental conflict stemming from participation in two different, distinct groups, Black and White culture.

Today, Marginalize refers to groups largely excluded from the prerogatives and rewards that accompany full citizenship, including employment, housing, consumption, social benefits, and equal justice. In European culture Black People in general and Black males in particular are denied access to economic, religious, political, and all like-kind powers of the Americas which prevent them from being on a level playing field and thus not having an equal opportunity for success. By the fact that Black culture is so fragmented and bears the brainwashing by Europeans in Slave Survival of intra-group dissention means most Black Americans feel friction from their fellows. So, one is not fully loyal and committed to the values and standards of either culture—nor is one fully acceptable to either of the groups with which one identifies. *For a Black person to be accepted and recognized by European culture implies that person is a Black race "sell-out"*—one who does things that demeans Black society and promotes European society—called Oreos, Black Puppets. Moreover, the two cultural groups may have certain conflicting values or norms (what the majority does), both of which one accepts and rejects to some degree. This leads certain Black males to seek an in-group "crowd" having a compatible like-mindset.

Meanwhile, the "Power-Aggression-Violence" triad used by Europeans is all Inside-Out Thinking (those lacking any interest in self-improvement and who defend their oppressors) Black Americans know. As a result, that makes it a tool of "Manhood" identity among marginalized men who, despite being "economically powerless, remain powerful in terms of gender'. Here, violence or the threat of violence is one way for men to establish their dominance, control, and autonomy in worlds where they have few legitimate avenues by which to take on traditional male identities such as family provider, head of the household, and leader in civic life (Irwin, *Race and Justice, 2012*).

Fanon, the Black French psychiatrist, stated, according to Nobles (*J Black Psychology 2013*), that oppression requires the fear of physical death—that fear being created via the exercise and threat of violence—violence in different forms of destruction to the spirits of African people. Examples are simple raw vulgar violence, historical violence, and "violence beyond violence" (also called "holy violence") whereby Europe is seen as the universal standard or example of humanity. Such "holy violence" is key to understanding Africa's "Take Down" and after-effect destabilization, African peoples' dehumanization, the acidic erosion of African consciousness, the shattering of Enslaved Africans Selfhoods, and the continued oppression of Black Americans.

The resultant *Selfhood "Disarrangement"* or even "Inside-Out" Selfhood and its associated thinking (see Flawed Sensory Consciousness Background/Foreground) caused alienation for African Tradition by the substitution of a Supernatural religion and god for the Natural Cosmos' Spiritual God. This causes those who adopted this switch over without realizing the switch to be disconnected from their Real Self "Spark of God" despite being highly religious. This results, says Noble, in alterations of the *experience* of being human—the *expression* of being human and the *essence* of being human itself. These three domains or paths represent the arenas of spirit suffering and imbalance or disharmony reflected in ones shattered consciousness and fractured identity.

PRECIPITATING CAUSES OF BLACK-ON-BLACK VIOLENCE: The Effects of the Trigger Psychic Trauma stemming from slavery was the immediate devastation of ones Selfhood Greatness and thereby ones sense of omnipotent sense of being all powerful from an unlimited and universal source. In turn, this caused an immediate loss of ones Spiritual "5Ss" (safety, security, sureness/self-confidence, strength, and stability). All of these generated a Spiritual Human Nature Need (SHNN) state that resulted in great Selfhood Pain and desperation to relieve it by "any means necessary." Whatever the afflicted honored most that had been shattered generated a "Raw Nerve" hypersensitivity analogous to being exposed from being blasted out of its 'womb' and undergoing a chronically "Inflamed" state. Whatever caused the "Raw Nerve" had also generated "Clouds" over ones Real Self 'Soul Sunshine'—ones Divine Consciousness—whether partially (called "Clouded with a silver-lining") or completely, with or without a "dark cloud". The nature of the 'Cloud' is determined by how much one senses that one has lost personal power.

At this point, ones Real Self evolution comes to a halt (with ones Intellect being arrested at this level) and one replaces ones "Self" with ones Ego (False Self). One shifts to an entirely different system of Values. Meanwhile, one is continually experiencing the "Grape Branch and Leaves" of the practical and mental ramifications of ones "Seed" Trigger Trauma(s) as it goes through its SOBMER process(es). There are ongoing racist incidents and various types of violence that "add a straw to the camel's back"—meaning the layering of problematic new Psychic Traumas onto the Sensory Consciousness Background Cause which, in turn, fashion more self-defeating ways of thinking and behaving for the Sensory Consciousness Foreground to handle in daily living.

To try to correct some of the overwhelming ills being suffered by Black People, in 1966 the Black Panther Party developed the 10-point program which included the demands for political power, self-determination, full employment, decent education, housing, food, social justice to end police brutality and unfair trial, and economic development. The USA government used great forces of different kinds to destroy the Panthers.

IMMEDIATE CAUSES OF BLACK-ON-BLACK VIOLENCE: Following the "take-down" of the Black Panthers the Black gang participants lacked a Spiritual sense of Self-Worth and Self-Concept. The powering of this competitive spirit was from a need for Power injected into ones Self-Worth in order to improve ones Self-Concept and Self-Image--all intended to impart a sense of Self-Reliance, Self-Trust, Self-Faith, and Self-Confidence. A lack of Spiritual *Self-Worth* means ones Spiritual Human Nature Needs (SHNN) are absent and thus no sense of a Self-Identity, Self-Love, and Self-Meaning. They disrespected their *Self-Concept*, meaning they felt unimportant, invisible, unable to do anything right or to achieve anything they wanted and, in short, felt like a mistake for being born. To cope with this, Black youth having a SHNN issue have switched from a birth gift state of finding within ones Soul all that is needed to live a good life to just the reverse. This means they look without--to what other people do and what other people value and how other people assess them to serve as their standards, guides, and filters for how to live.

EVOLVING GANG MANHOOD IN BLACK-ON-BLACK VIOLENCE

"*Manhood*" is a loose term that covers Patterns V and VI and from which there are a host of slang connotations: "the police"; a male of distinction; the White man; 'mannish' to imply a teen acting too grown up; 'hyper-masculinity' for a hyper-aggressive, hyper-sexed male who emphasizes riches without accountability; and so forth. "Manhood" and "Manly" are used interchangeably by the public. But here, whereas in African Tradition, "Manly" concerns what is permanent, stationary, and eternal about life (i.e. about things of Worth) and "Manhood" is in the flow of the ever changing sort after Material things (i.e. about things of Value). "Manly" is intended to be a progressive cultivation of a male's Spiritual Mind and what is Spiritual is incapable of having an 'Image'—though it can be symbolized. A proper African Tradition process of maturing is for the "Manly" to successively over-rule ones "Manhood" tendencies. Although both "Manly" and "Manhood" potentials (i.e. about a system of Values) are simultaneously in newborns as Complementary Equals, the choice a male makes in order to develop a lifestyle pattern may enhance their Complementary

Equal status or deemphasize one while elevating the other or fashion them into Conflicting Opposites. The inherent differences between them are important for the sake of: (1) Predictability in how to work with or defend oneself against another man; (2) in Diagnoses for purpose of Treatment or Management; (3) a Role Model to recommend or to avoid; and (4) in how a male envisions himself as in his present state, in how he wishes to be, and in how he thinks others think of him. Determinations of "Manhood" can be socialized into a youth, imitated by a youth, or fashioned by a youth.

In Black American male's development their "Manhood" model was from bonding with Euro-American males. Also adopted were Plans carried out in a European male Non-Rational manner—having an emotional base with a Left Brain manner of carrying it out. The difference is that with Black youth these patterns are kept in a Natural Cosmos realm (and thus are reversible) as opposed to European males who are in a Supernatural realm (and thus are fixed because they have no concept of Spiritual Morals or Ma'at ways of relating). The manifestations of gang warfare make it essential for those "Decent" youth to "go along to get along" or "get along by going along". Much of the hostile expressions shown by Black youth is merely living up to an Icon Image of gang type "Manhood." For one to have an Image of oneself indicates one is dealing with concepts having "Value" and that may be the result of ignorance or intention. Black manhood, perpetuated and elaborated on by post-slavery racism and Euro-American terrorism, led many Black males to enlist during the Vietnam War.

"BAD BLOOD" BONDING: Today's rampant *Bad Blood Bonding* (BBB) is an offspring of the Greek physician Galen's (c130-200 AD) "Humoral Theory" which associated with blood and emotions. He said fluids secreted by ones body determined ones personality. Being in "good humor" meant having good fluids bubbling inside one; "bad blood" humor implied a mind's Indifference, Hate, Evil, and/or Sadistic temper--the *IHES Complex*. Imagine an A-Frame Ladder extending from Earth to the Heavens and with "Good Humor" representing the front side and "Bad Humor" representing the back side. The type of Bonding people can have with each other may be on either side or a mixture of them. That *Bonding's* (C13 English--something that binds) essence is "to Feed" (anything consumed)--whether wholesome, unwholesome, or indigestible. Old English "Feed" concerns supply (making good a deficiency, fulfilling a need) rather than the nourishment (to sustain life) itself, as in feeding a slot-machine with coins. What is fed has an effect of a Bonding "Glob"--i.e. personally meaningful emotions, feelings, thoughts, imagination, expectations, desires, symbols, and mysterious 'something' interwoven into a tangled ball of which those bonded cannot discern.

At the top of the A-Frame Ladder is Group I: Afrocentric Spiritual Bonding whose Spiritual Elements feature *Compassion*--whereby Spirits of the involved share the same Spiritual Space and thus united in a "Group Spirit" and/or a "Group Mind." Group II is those lower down the Bonding Scale are varying degree of connections based upon the *Common Sense Bonding* of a given group. Common Sense means the unified use of certain senses, patterns, dispositions, attitudes, approaches, methods, and other things a society can do alike--regardless of their nature--and done as if there is a Group Mind or a Group Spirit so as to make it common. Group III straddles the "Good" and "Bad" Humor Ladders. Perhaps such is illustrated by the President Obama/Secret Service relationship. The duty of the Secret Service is to protect the President at all costs--even taking "the bullet" intended for the President. However, since Obama has entered the political scene their have been both a surge in threats against him as well as a host of glaring lapses in the watchful eyes of the Secret Service. Yet, the first family's proximity and dependence on the Secret Service and their duty to protect inevitably do the "feedings" that breed a personal, almost familiar bonding relationship between them--a bond whose theme is Trust. But if Trust is like a glass of milk, each of the string of security breeches from lapses in protocol and candor, all in rapid succession, is like putting an ink drop in that milk. Despite Obama's frustrations, he continues to defend the Secret Service, including their violators. Still, the agents and the First Family keep an "arm's-length" distance from each other. Agents--despite a closeness from knowing private details--remain detached, avoid initiating conversations (except for essentials), and do no fraternizing. Presidents are assigned such agents for life.

Group IV: Here, the *IHES Complex reigns*. Upon arrival in the "New World," the ordeal of being "*Seasoned*" to be Ideal Slaves included severing any "Motherland" bonds with their African past, the "killing of their Spirits" which was devastating and 'Splintering' to the entire Selfhood of each; separation of their "God-Image Self" from their Divine Spirit to thereby cause each to become Self-Absorbed. The severing of equally great bonds by selling away family, Sippi, and acquaintance members on the auction blocks--while humiliated by being stripped naked to "inspect"--caused unbearable pains from these happenings. Perhaps by this time they were operating out of their Omnibus Brains. Because there is an in-born urge to bond with people, and because they could not count on the people they loved to be available, and because the only thing the Enslaved could count on in order to survive was the captors, they cling to their captors. All the captors offered was barely enough food and shelter to survive--and this constituted a *Deficient PHNN* bond.

The *Evil Savior Syndrome* was clearly displayed when the newly arriving Enslaved from Africa quickly came to be totally dependent on the evil and sadistic European enslavers for basic survival (e.g. food, clothing, and shelter), no matter how inadequate and to lessen whippings. That "feeding" by the captors resulted in a "Bonding" of the type featuring ongoing *expectations from the enemy, over whom they had no control, for survival while simultaneously hating the enemy*. They expected this supply of their expectations from their "saviors" to continue and hopefully get better (which it never did). This Group IV "Seed" manifests on all parts of the "Tree" of problems Black People have today. Meanwhile, the captors were "Bonded" to the Enslaved because that was the source of their riches and "sick" pleasures--as both are to this day. Both Enslaved and the captors had an unrealistic mindset making them completely dependent upon each other--a culturally transferrable mindset that still causes behaviors designed to maintain the status quo.

In the process of Group IV's evolution there have been an assortment of "off-spring." Group IV (A) is Actual "Imitators" of Evil Saviors; Group IV (B) is "Façade Imitators" of Evil Saviors; Group IV (C) is Actual Victims of Evil Saviors; Group IV (D) is "Façade Victims" of Evil Saviors; Group IV (E) is Chameleons who "go along to get along"--saying or doing whatever it takes to enhance their conformity position by making a favorable impression on fellows and building their own reputation; Group IV (F) is Chameleons who present as Con-Artists. The Enslaved had to adhere to the rules dictated by the captors in hopes of continuing to receive their bond feedings. Some Enslaved saw White folks as an awesome and powerful but strangely pathetic people--a people often pious in their European form of Christianity, using a Christ with African ancestry (see Revelations I;14, 15) whom they remade in their own image, yet having faith only in what their minds and their power could control--a people who sell their Spirituality Souls by doing "any evil thing necessary" in order to make a profit or to keep from losing their ill-gotten gains. Beside, White people could talk authoritatively about Un-real realities--i.e. Contingent Beings, as about Hell, Satan, and the god they made into man.

The Un-noble Loyalty bonds the Enslaved established with their captors caused them to accept brainwashing that turned their thinking "Inside-Out." Key to that brainwashing was to get the Enslaved to stop "Knowing" the one Universal High God and, instead, to have "Faith/Belief" in their God, based upon what the captors said about God. The Enslaved were not aware that the God of which the captors spoke was in reality what the captors privately called Satan. Thus, the captors were able to control the minds of most Enslaved by means of what the captors wrote in making up their European bible. Still, they made it enticing by boosting the emotions of those who conformed. For example, in church services where the White preacher was telling them to be "good Slaves," the ushers (women) of the church were given status by being given clothes for elegant dress, complete with gloves. The gloves were white and by use of these gloves members and guests could be ushered to their place to sit. Most churches should see the importance of this ritual to add a touch of class to the ceremony for those Enslaved whose minds they controlled.

By having an Un-noble Loyalty bonding to the captors, afflicted Enslaved accepted this made-up information as "the Word of God." These supposed "Laws" of God were presented as Rules--Commands--Prohibitions--Injunctions--Commandments--Regulations for Black People to obey as if God said them, since Whites said they were told by God to convey the word of God. Yet, Whites did not have to live up to them--like "Meekness" and "turn the other cheek." The Sacred Mother-Child Bonding--which is natural to humans and, in fact, in all of the animal kingdom--was an urge many Enslaved tried to make happen with the Satanists. The fact that Satanists are unaware of and are opposed to any aspects related to SHNN pertaining to themselves or to the Enslaved caused the most desperate Enslaved to try different methods for bonding with the Satanists. More than anything else, those factors and Black males reactions to them manifest as today's Black-On-Black Violence. In other words, displaced anger/rage from powerlessness experienced during slavery and the post-slavery lack of autonomy—both culturally transmitted to their today's descendants--are powerful contributors to much of today's Black-male criminality.

BLACK PEOPLE'S REJECTION OF EUROPEANS: The way Black People deal with European Brutes differs according to where they are located on the "I" (fig. 19). Regardless of the degree of Chronic Rage/Layered Anger or its kind of residual effects or ones status on the social ladder, the progression of being upset may start anywhere from annoyance to anger to rage. Since I build my life around that of African Tradition, I avoid physical confrontation but still I react. One thing that annoys me is for people I do not know or to whom I have not given permission to call me by my first name. An office nurse of a doctor I was about to see for the first time called me on the telephone and did just that. Immediately that gave me a bad impression of that doctor for not having disciplined his staff to show respect. That influenced the way I reacted in that setting thereafter by going in with a sensitive attitude. I wound up not liking the doctor and never going back.

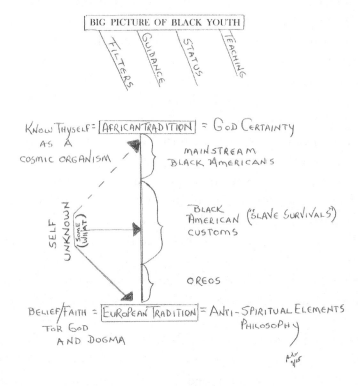

FIGURE 19

People on the mid-vertical part of the "I" are in the Black American Customs group and most have a "love/hate" relationship. They hate anything White people do but are afraid to confront or vote against them. Instead, they will vote against themselves and take out their hostilities on any Black person who "puts down" White people. Oreos "knock themselves out" trying to please White people, hoping in vain that they will be accepted if they do enough damage to Black People. A clue as to who they are comes from White people saying nice things about them—which Whites avoid by Blacks who challenge them. The beginning Mainstream Black Americans tend toward imitating Whites and seeking their acceptance, even though White people have no standards, guides, filters, or measures to which Black People ought to live. Yet, Black People need to know what Whites do to succeed and to oppress so as to know how to be assertive and defend oneself in the process.

BLACK GANGS IMITATIONS OF EUROPEAN MALES: A devastated Selfhood and being so economically powerless channeled, for many Black males, the only remaining concept of Manhood as that of the "Masculinity-Power-Aggression" Complex (Irwin, *Race and Justice, 2012*). Men who confront multiple oppressions (e.g. lack of jobs, class, race, and political) are particularly apt to use violence or the threat of violence--for this a way to try to recoup, demonstrate, and establish their Manhood, dominance, control, and autonomy in worlds where they are unaware of other legitimate avenues. Although having lost ones Selfhood Greatness and thus ones Spiritual Self-Identity, ones Secular Identity is the perceived as the social location of a struggling youth. During and following slavery one of the most impressive things Black People had seen was Euro-American gangs. Hence, it was an easy next step to consider a gang as probably offering struggling youth their best opportunity to acquire status and hence it plays an essential part in the development of his concept of "Manhood".

There were many reasons for this—all focused on Bonding. One was the establishment in slavery of the "Evil Savior Syndrome." Another is that Euro-American males were the ones that fashioned the Enslaved minds while they were in a Form-Body state. A third is that Euro-American males were Black males only role models. A fourth is that chances are they never heard of the "Manliness" features of African Tradition which concerns developing their spiritual mind or Higher Self in such forms as taking on traditional male identities like being the family provider, head of the household, good father, and leader in civic life.

"MANHOOD COMMAND APPEARANCES": Instead, the striving to realize the role these Black males hoped to take meant fashioning an Icon Image to serve as the model for reminding them to assume a tough pose, commit feats of daring or vandalism, or become a criminal. Such a *Manhood Icon Image* upholds, in the form of a 'Command Appearance,' a male role of competence, and of 'being in command' of things regardless of the price paid, even at the cost of the life of oneself or the lives of others. By resorting to their only model, European males' swagger, a "Manhood Command Appearance rose into being a personal requirement. For example, what Black "Street" youth were personally familiar with was Euro-American males attacking them in verbal, indifference, and physical ways. This includes attacking fellow Black People who are trying to help Black People improve and defending Europeans. An extension of that is to not honor Black scholars or recognize Black achievements stolen by Europeans, even in the face of overwhelming convincing evidence.

European males ensure their way is copied by completely hiding what is superior to what they do—i.e. whatever is of African Tradition. Whereas African Tradition builds on what is sound and well-tested so as to expand from inside-out on ones "Aliveness", Europeans have nothing that is sound (i.e. Spiritual up-lifting) and thus they have to rely on constantly having something new, bigger, faster, better so that ones time is spent trying to get good at it and be involved in repairing its flaws. Shortly thereafter a newer version comes out so as to repeat the process. These Trinkets and Trivia are designed to be "Exciting," similar to how a little child will choose a shiny penny over an unpolished diamond. That prevents victims from learning how to think for Critical Thinking would totally wipe out all the European males do that they claim to be superior to all others.

HUSTLERS' SHOWDOWN CODES: Throughout the mid-20th century there first developed features of the "Showdown of Manhood"—a devised style with Unique + Sameness aspects, used in the threat of violence and/or the dominance in inflicting punishment. Once it matured, a winning outcome of these performances was typically spotlighted by the masculine prowess of the loser being layered on to that of the winner, leaving the loser disgraced and 'man-less.' The *Hustler Code* for a Showdown had/has as its objective to demonstrate the involved males' possession of an imaginary substitute for the phallus ("nerve," "guts," "balls," or "heart," most typically) and to maintain "face," "honor," and "Respect" as the essence and the 'everything' of a man's reputation and thus the most important of his possessions. When confronted, neither male man can afford to lose "face," be made a fool of, or appear to lack nerve. A guiding principle is to "never let 'em see you sweat". Also, there must be no indication to indicate one is trying to prove his "Manhood" for if the gang members suspect that they might justly infer that he himself harbors doubts about his masculinity—a certain sign of unmanliness. By claiming that he is not proving his "Manhood" but testing theirs, one is able to draw the gang away from a reading of his performance as performance. This demands proof conveyed to peers and an essential is to "live dangerously" (i.e. exists outside the law); rise above fear of death or imprisonment; and a "calm, cool, and collected demeanor.

With any problem, a man talks himself through it and forgets it. The acceptable demeanor is a ritualized form of "Manhood" that entails behaviors, scripts, physical posturing, impression management, and carefully crafted performances" that signify pride, strength, and control. Prohibited are excessive displays of emotion. One Hustler practice is to loud-talk opponents in an attempt to assert masculinity or recount exploits to those who matter. The resolution of this confrontation effects a renegotiation of the actors' "Manhood" such that the manliness possessed by the loser is transferred to the winner and the loser is feminized and disgraced, or both actors win by simultaneously threatening each other with violence and continually delaying the actual manifestation of that violence until some indefinite time in the future. A top performance generates fear, respect, and awe among his associates. Indeed, according to Malcolm, he "never had one moment's trouble with any of them after that. . . . They thought I was crazy.

"MANHOOD" POWER: *Disrespect* --"the eating of ones self-esteem"--is one of the worse sins in the African Hausa society. For one to allow Disrespect to shatter ones Selfhood Greatness Integrity is to immediately shift one into Self-Absorption to nurse ones Self-Concept and ones instantly developed Self-Image. There are three main Icon Images Black youth have—What they think other's think about them; what they think of themselves; and how they would like to see themselves. Less potent Icon Images are What I think of others? What I think of my Mom and Dad. How one assesses these is within the context of Power. Power is about "*Face*"--the figurative aspect that one presents to the world or ones associates. Originally symbolized by Primitive Africans totemistic concepts, having "Face" is an image of the forces of Nature, and of the animal world in particular, concerning superior power, as if one was wearing a crown of a king. The "Face" chosen is of the most superior animal preferred. The immediate effect of the assumption of such power upon the body and the attitude of the mind is conferred impassivity, indifference—either real or affected—with a tendency to 'swell with pride.' Their love of power, which is at their root, is generally an embodiment of fear. "*Losing Face*" means to suffer a loss of respect from oneself and from others, i.e. ones public image. As a result, one feels ashamed or humiliated, especially publicly, meaning one is disconnected from all supporters. "*Saving Face*" is to retrieve or preserve ones dignity and ones good standing, high position, or reputation at a time of a challenge to it or after a failure.

The idea of "Manhood" and its personal meanings is universal. Gangs offer each member the opportunity to acquire an almost unlimited amount of coercive power (e.g. via threats, intimidation, the use of force and displays of violence)--a power to pay, buy, and impress--and the power of status within the gang's hierarchy. For respect, proving ones "Manhood" and being viewed as courageous are fundamental. For Black boys, in particular, being "dissed" acts as the stimulus which solicits a reaction within them. The stimulus may be anything they perceive as challenging their "Manhood." Reactions to feeling "dissed" generate more emotions of self-doubt, self-inadequacy, and shame that must be hidden by mental barriers and outward displays of courage. Much of this has been imitated from European males. The nature of their outward reaction is fashioned by their un-noble loyalty to a self-created Icon Image about what to do in such situations. Often this is designed out of what they have seen in their communities or dysfunctional families. Most have already lost their sense of the "5Ss" and a Rage Reaction overwhelms them and thereby necessitates their choosing to fight the challenger. The fighting style is usually modeled after how they saw it done on television, in the family, or by neighborhood fighters. It is "un-noble" because it is outside the bounds of the Spiritual Elements. Besides, they have rarely, if ever, seen it work to the advantage of anyone involved.

In fact, they have seen terribly bad things happen which they have justified as a display of "Manhood" (with no idea what that means) or going to prison as a rites of passage. Loss creates a void which can be filled with creative expression. To feel separate is to see universe as a collection of objects and therefore a thing. What one says about a thing is how one thinks about things. People grasp the shadow of the substance. As Huey P. Newton (1973) said: One of the first things any Black child must learn is how to fight well. Fighting has always been a big part of my life, as it is in the lives of most poor people. Some find this hard to understand. I was too young to realize that we were really trying to affirm our masculinity. . . . Fighting is not just a means of survival; it is also a part of friendship. All the time I was growing up, fighting was an essential aspect of camaraderie on the block. Autobiographies of working-class Black American men are rife with scenes of fighting--either on "the Streets" or in prison—and usually involving a lone Black protagonist attempting to prove his Manhood by defending himself against a gang or gang-affiliated opponent. Winning the fight is not as important as the "Heart" the protagonist demonstrates by his willingness to fight, often in the face of insurmountable odds. Through the mechanism of the fight, the protagonist, who had formerly been an outsider, is now welcomed into the privileged company of his peers. Where before he had been nobody, now he is a member of the gang.

Such had happened to me as a boy in a 1945 fight that changed the way I thought about never "backing down" from a challenge that was under my control. There was an older and bigger bully who made life difficult for me. One day, while swimming the community swimming pool, I was confronted by the bully at a time I had a "chlorine high" (they put a tremendous amount of chlorine in the water for sanitary purposes). The friend I was with egged me on, saying he would "back me up" (which I knew was a lie). Nevertheless, I handed him the clothes I was carrying and "lit in" to the bully, beating him soundly. He never bothered me again—but it did not let me into the crowd of my peers. One gang members said: "Even if you weren't in one [gang], you got people that are going to push the issue. We decide what we want to do; I ain't no punk, I ain't no busta. But it comes down to pride. It's foolish pride, but a man is going to be a man, and a boy knows he's going to come into his manhood by standing his ground. The trend for this was the "Street" Code was that "Every man [in a gang] is treated as a man until proven different. We see you as a man before anything."

"MANHOOD" ACCOUTREMENTS: The Enslaved and ex-Slaves daily experienced terrorism from Euro-American males. But an advancement in power displays came when White professionals introduced *Gangland killings*—i.e. premeditated murders committed by a gang of organized criminals and consistent with gang methods. They do not involve robbery or other common motives, and are carried out in a manner which allows the killer(s) to usually escape. They were particularly prominent in the Prohibition Era from 1919 to 1933 for such reasons as bootlegging, gambling, labor racketeering, vice, or other criminal disputes (Binder, *J. Contemporary Criminal Justice, 2013*). Killing weapons included pistols, shotguns (15%), Thompson submachine guns, stabbing or hacked to death, strangled, beaten, explosions, bombings, and drive-by shootings. After 1923 and some years almost 20% of these killings were drive-bys. Black gangs were impressed by the guns and drive-bys and European male's Indifference/Hate/Evil/Sadism (IHES) Complex, emphasizing "Don't Care"—an attitude arising a philosophy that then gives rise to psychological problems.

The never ending search for more and better and bigger power—a feature of historical European males—came into the awareness of Black gangs—who up to the 1970s were fist fighters, perhaps occasionally resorting to knives—from television viewings of White's gangland killings. This spurred Brute Europeans to supply train boxcar loads of guns and narcotics to 'ghetto' Black neighborhoods for free and then stir up trouble between rival gangs. After establishing "Manhood" power by means of the gun, the next major psychological force of "The Streets" is whatever influences a gang member's self-image. A distorted conceptions of "Manhood" is the extent to which one possesses accoutrements for they, too, are symbols of power. Possessions of diamonds are intended to dazzle the beholder and the wearer. But in the process it dignifies meanness—magnifies littleness and to what is contemptible it gives authority, to what is low, exaltation.

Gang warfare and political activism among Black youth gradually rose into prominence as two sides of the same coin—one side of the coin focused on getting what the gang desired—the other side was back payment for years of "grassroots white intimidation and police intransigence" (Pihos, *J. Urban History, 2011*). By the mid-1960s lines of political influence were tangled: gang members, Black Power advocates, and student movement leaders all drew on a protean language of racial identity and community control. Gangs used Black Power rhetoric to attract more members, just as Black Power leaders traded on gang imagery to attract followers. Race remained critical to gangs and "gangsta culture." [Ref: Hunter, *Youth & Society, 2006*]

"MANHOOD IN PRISON: Going to prison significantly affects Black males' economic and social life course, resulting in lower, often stagnant, earnings and reduced marriage rates. Gangs form part of a world of "armed young men"—a continuum of non-state actors (gangs, warlords, drug lords, triads, and tigers)—that exist around the globe under conditions of "social exclusion, racism, and a delegitimized, weakened state". In the United States, they flourish in prisons, housing projects, and segregated neighborhoods, turning enclosure into a resource for organizing. Members support themselves and the gang though drug sales. Placement in prison reinforces gang ties, generating a greater need for ones gang identity and likelihood for violence. Upon release from prison, the gang is waiting for its members, offering opportunities for work or socialization otherwise unavailable. "Prison will make you something other than the man or human being you thought you were"—leading to tenuous and fragile masculinities existing primarily as exhibitions of violence, suppression of human needs and expressions in keeping with the environment. This comes about for several reasons.

First, while incarcerated, one obviously does not govern ones own state inside its hostile atmospheres. As inmates, males who must conform, integrate, and assimilate into those vile and violent communities where anger is sometimes the only emotion rewarded, one still must deal with the issues of feeling powerless in the face of guards and certain inmates alike. This affects and restricts ones ability to make choices about ones basic daily activities while having to deal with challenges in each of those aspects.

Second, each male must fashion a masculinity that best works within the atmosphere and resources available to them—things like the use of language, the negotiation of physical space, being ruled by those who are the most hostile, and shift ones thinking about oneself in terms of the past, present, and future. Black males are often unable to exercise or experience their full potential as "real" men because of limited education, economic disadvantages, and racial discrimination. Prisoners counteract these limitations by their own conceptualization of themselves as men and by reconstructing normative definitions or developing alternate ones that are able to be fulfill. Resources used by imprisoned males include excessive violence, recounts of life on the streets, exploitations of other prisoners identified as punks; posturing, and sports. But prisoners commonly demonstrate power by utilizing fewer tangible resources than do persons in the "free world," simply because fewer are available to them. Instead, they employ physical space, their bodies, and language in distinct ways. Material goods are usually scarce as well.

Third, one tends to get involved in foreign sex practices. Contacts with family and lovers on the outside are restricted to supervised visits and monitored phone conversations. Sexual contact is permitted only for married males who are violation free, and housed under the auspices of prison administrations that allow infrequent conjugal visits.

Fourth, all activities are conducted within the same spatial context and under one body of authority. As opposed to one doing things in various locations in the free world (e.g. sleep, work), all prisoners' social existence spin around within the same locale. Prisoners' social activities generally occur alongside persons all treated alike. All are expected to do the same activities when told when to do them. An official governing body sets all the rules while each prisoner is expected to follow the rules, and do so in a prearranged way. Rules and activities are regulated through some supreme plan, which reflect only the interests of those who construct the rules

Fifth, Gang formation in prison communities is the rule, although such relations between prisoners are usually heavily surveilled. Consequently, prisoners regularly find themselves separated from social networks and persons who aid them in appearing powerful. Fights, rapes, and other forms of violent activities are also common. Black males often employ these mechanisms symbiotically with cultural linguistic patterns they adopt in segregated communities. Moreover, posing and "profiling" are expressions linked to ways many Black males "do" gender and their bodies frequently act as representations of power and domination.

Sixth, strength of character is essential since Manhood is defined primarily by ones ability to perform aggressively. This is because being aggressive is strongly linked to survival in prison. Prisoners unable to resist the domination of other prisoners or who cannot ward off the pressures of their environment are seen by their peers as weak and to whom are labeled "boy" and "punk." Fellow prisoners agree that the Weak are deserving of exploitation, and feminizing (raped). The hierarchy of domination among prisoners mirrors relations between males in the free world. A sharp line exists between alpha males and "punks" and that the only way to survive is to conform to the rigid hyper-Manhood posturing of the prison culture.

Seventh, whereas in the free world, a willingness to contribute and support was nonexistent, in prison, inmates have time to think about what they have done--who they are--and what they want to become. Most decide to now give emotional support to family members and friends, in contrast to the past. Although unable to support them financially, some participants express a greater closeness to loved ones than prior to imprisonment. Very few expressed their close link to family as motivated by their own need for connection and support. They alleged that they had matured and learned the importance of nurturing their families. Those few saying that staying connected to families was a self-motivated act, also admitted that support was germane to their survival in prison. Nandi (*Journal of Men's Studies, 2002*) describes 45 year old Danny who said: Upon entering prison, I was a self-destructive individual who seriously believed that everyone else was responsible for my fate and failures in life. [I believed] that the people I killed earned what they received and that the only way to deal with any opposing situation or circumstances was with violence. I had no value of human life. During my 18 years of incarceration, I have learned that each individual deserves the same respect, consideration, and understanding I would expect…. Now my manhood is based entirely upon love, honesty, and true-to-self principles of righteousness. Many leave prison with this attitude but it is so hard to immediately start surviving on ones own that they return to crime.

Eighth, although prison environments are rife with violence, lack rehabilitation resources, and are inhabited by persons with few resources or cultural capital to succeed in the free world, occasionally there are opportunities for self-advancement, as in libraries and work activities, such as making license plates (paid 60 cents a day), building and repairing furniture.

Ninth, Prison makes many Black males worse off. They enter with the attitude of "Don't Care" because nobody else cares about them. Nandi reports that when this type sees a new brother trying to keep himself looking nice, they tell them, "what you getting all dressed for? Ain't no woman in here." And if he is trying to do his work detail to his satisfaction, they say, "Man, you in prison. The hell with that." Everyone does as little as possible without getting in trouble. But never their best. If so, you're a bootlicker, house-nigga. Thus, prisoners disengage. They seek to prove how well they can survive the constraints of prison and resist degradation from other prisoners and officials. Manhood, in this sense, is resistance. One version of masculinity that dominate in male prisons, therefore, compel individuals to constrain their emotions, maintain the appearance of inner strength, and fight those who degrade them. Another version that is prison makes one "think more, become more firm … and display anger as a sign of strength. In prison, everyone respects anger."

Tenth, Manhood by silence. Nandi writes that Sean, a 30-year-old who reported that he became a man in prison when he learned how to "see but not see and say but not say," reflecting a code that forces males to negotiate their survival through silence. Woven into the basic fabric of prison culture, this code stems from the likelihood of violence by other males. Similarly,43-year-old Tony said, "A man knows when to be invisible and when to be visible." This notion is significant as it suggests one way disempowered persons use physical space to negotiate power. But it also implies that the way one gains or maintains status in the dominant hierarchy is to embody the normative social characteristics of suppressing emotion and expression.

BLACK PRISON IN-MATE COMMENTS ON "MANHOOD": Ms. Nandi (*The Journal of Men's Studies, 2002)* said 90% of her interviewed participants discussed responsibility as a key defining characteristic of real men. This notion generally means taking care of their families, maintaining jobs, and so on. Research participants who have the desire to fulfill their roles as partners and providers labeled themselves as responsible. Given their limited access to lovers and family, they saw this willingness as significant; true masculinity. Reflecting specific gender performances and linguistic uses employed by Black males, this thuggish trend is meaningful in that it is (1) manifested primarily in the relationships among poor and working-class Blacks; and (2) described as such because of Black males' power to generate descriptors that reflect their unique social experiences. Describing male behavior as "thuggish" and "slick" stems from the Black community's ongoing pattern of constructing words to describe phenomena they create. In the most obvious sense, then, the fact that Black males make up a significant number of persons in American prisons means that their expressions, linguistic and behavioral, have meaningful cultural implications for those contexts. Black males contribute to the sociopolitical "vibe" of prison environments in monumental ways; their worldviews, which they also construct, name, and share reflect their racial status. Individually or collectively, rival gang members constantly pose a physical threat according to the next inmate (Stretesky, J. *Contemporary Ethnography, 2007*). He also discusses the need for protection and how drug sales caused him to be a target for those who would try and rob him. An individual who implicitly or explicitly signifies that he has certain social characteristics ought in fact to be what he claims he is. In consequence, when an individual projects a definition of the situation and thereby makes an implicit or explicit claim to be a person of a particular kind, he automatically exerts a moral demand upon others, obliging them to value and treat him in the manner that persons of his kind have a right to expect.

PUBLIC DEALINGS WITH TODAY'S BLACK GANG MEMBERS: The reality of what is going on with Black gangs is adverse to what the European society wants to hear. Gangs and gangsta culture are not of the deliberate intention to destroy themselves and the Black community. Instead, they are "responses to nihilism, a search for ways out of being paralyzed by the void". In the face of economic and social immobility and intractable racism, gangs have provided their members with race-based "resistance identities". The cultural forms that sustain them, such as hip-hop and gangsta rap, can be socially redemptive. But Europeans disregard such practices in favor of trying many things they think best to eradicate this problem. Most attempts to increase public safety have been directed mainly at the individual perpetrator through programs, punishment, or incarceration—all using the wrong "medicine" for the wrong diagnosis, as in "medicine" ranging from torture to isolation and from ineffective rehabilitation to incapacitation. However, little effort has been made to directly confront the very culture from which the problem emanates—racial oppression by Europeans.

This stupidity shows by, despite all the money spent and all the police killings of suspects, the overall crime rate is unsteady (up and down)—with street-crime (gang membership, drug dealing, robbery, theft, gun use, and wanton violence) continuing at alarming levels and eroding public confidence in the criminal justice system. Platitudes are given to the public, like there is only a small group of habitual offenders responsible for committing 90% of "Street" crimes, and if they are locked away long past the age when most criminal activity is committed, public safety will occur. But that is false, as evidenced by increasing the prison population more that quintupling since 1980, coupled with massive increases in spending on crime control. Yet, "Street" crime persists and remains a significant problem. To break the cycle, a comprehensive strategy must be developed that is directed simultaneously at the three main target populations perpetuating the cycle.

First, former perpetrators presently confined and are likely to return to the culture when released unless they undergo a substantial philosophic change accompanied by economic or occupational alternatives. Second are current perpetrators presently engaged in the illicit drug trade, violence, and crime. Third are future perpetrators, those youth who will be attracted to, and/or recruited by, current perpetrators of the culture of crime.

TODAY'S BLACK GANGS

A newborn male has the following categories available to choose from in selecting (or being guided into) the type of male he wants to be: the Spiritual, the Mental, the Good Emotional, the Bad Emotional, the Physical; and the External World accoutrements (e.g. money, power over people, possessions, the GUN). The process of development starts with the selection of a Base of what one believes will supply one with the best life. Out of that Base a Foundation arises and this serves as the Unconscious Philosophy of Life (POL) Background. That Background provides ingredients to form the public aspect of ones POL which is ones Consciousness. Out of ones Consciousness one fashions how one is to think, feel, express, and behave in the External World. That fashioning is done by monitored feedbacks from interactions with the outside world--either because of the meaning brought to it or from the meaning derived from it. Incorporated into the fashioning process is the obvious things one faces and does in daily living; how one deals with what is faced and done in ones inner and outer world; and the assessments one makes about each of these aspects.

STRUGGLING BLACK PEOPLE'S BASE PROBLEM: All humans are composed of Spirit (with its SHNN) and Matter (with its PHNN) and both must be nourished. A problem with either of PHNN or SHNN is the cause of a Black youth's Base problem that, if intense enough and for long enough will cause that youth to develop False Self and strongly consider getting relief by joining a gang. To elaborate, when one has chosen a False Self in order to accommodate for the resultant loss of ones birth-gift of Selfhood Greatness, one substitutes trying to booster ones External World derived Self-Concept and Self-Image. Similarly, when one is no longer powered by ones Private Selfhood Self-Identity and Self-Meaning, one strives for Material Possessions as a substitute as shown by people doing strange things in hopes of getting full. Specifically, if one does not have the essential PHNN—which includes food, water, rest, clothing, safety, and so forth—that human will not survive. But when there is survival, ones focus is on ensuring there is at least an adequate amount of SHNN and if not, then, in desperation, seven major categories of action are taken.

Type I are the use of Masks and Masquerades for attempts at Bonding.

Type II are high prices paid in hopes of Belonging with fellows of like-mind.

Type III are Defensive Measures to keep from being exposed (e.g. "I'm too busy"; "I've got to go now").

Type IV are Deflective Measures used to divert attention away from oneself.

Type V is engaging in scapegoat aggression (blame, criticize, finding fault), being passive (following the crowd and thereby give up ones Real Self and ones Mission in life)

Type VI is making lifestyle changes, such as "Make Do" with whatever "crumbs" off the dinner table ignorant and/or evil leaders drop on the floor. A third aspect is to attack scapegoats by direct aggressive attacks or by passive-aggressive (e.g. Projection) acts.

Type VII is going after things of Value in the External World (e.g. Material possessions) which necessarily gets one involved in Fetters (e.g. extreme selfishness, greed, hatred, anger, egoism, fear, envy, jealousy, frustration, dishonorable, arrogance, pride, lust). The reason for pursuing these is the hope of them acting as accoutrements will deflect the attention of outsiders away from noticing ones personal weakness, inadequacies, limitations, and flaws.

All of these self-defeating Secular ingredients are used in varying combinations—perhaps as a lifestyle pattern—perhaps different ones for different situations or for the same situation types. These seven types are all-out *attempts: (1) to supply ones SHNN; (2) to make up for SHNN losses with substitutes; or (3) to acquire SHNN. One of these three is at the basis of the mindsets of all Black gang member (and any problematic Black youth).* The resultant behaviors, no matter how bad they are, constitute efforts to make up for a loss of SHNN. Such behaviors do not stem from self-hatred, as is so widely claimed to be the diagnosis by White people about problematic Black People. Yet, they do generate delusions.

DELUSIONAL WORLD OF GANG MEMBERS: Delusions, believing what is not real and not believe what is real, is to be inside an anti-Spiritual Element way of thinking. Delusions originally referred to the power of a god or demon to change form and to appear under deceiving masks (see Chapter X). In these ancient times delusions and illusions carried the same sense inside concepts of "Magic" whereby people were deceived by a façade or false front which hid the "nothing" behind it. Today, they can result from ignorance, prejudice, Satanism, organic brain disorders, philosophical disarray, or socialization. Ancient Greeks, known to be starters of innumerable false teachings, generated delusions of such great magnitude as to put the course of common sense and selfhood mastery on a false path in those who did not discover the truth. Such Delusions (false beliefs that cannot be modified by facts, as in believing the magician actually sawed the woman in half) are to be distinguished from *Illusions* (misinterpretations from a false front hiding actuality) and *Hallucinations* (perceptions of what does not exist). Yet, all are seen in Gang members—many of whom that remain in contact with reality—view the Delusional World as senseless, if not absurd.

Gang motivation inside a Delusional Realm is grounded in hostility. Since their Indifference/Hate/Evil/Sadism filled mindset is so much like a tornado inside them, they seek relief--which is at best momentary--by bringing pain and suffering to others to show how strong they are. They undergo these experiences as they would undergo a dream--attributing these actions to a Supernatural CB's power compelling them to act. This CB transforms uncertainty into certitude--confusion into clarity--hesitation and cautiousness into courage and determination. In other words, in their loss of reality, they have opened up new dimensions of Delusional realities. What CB do is provide one the courage to devise solutions to problems never previously been solved as well as create artifacts which reflect or enhance experience. Then this unique subjective experience--whether originated inside or outside--is fully expressed so that different levels of the Selfhood's unconscious or subconscious as well as the Supernatural are shown at the same time.

Yet, *many are not sold on being in gangs but simply "go along to get along."* By having made the CB in their own image--and thus with bitterness and resentment--one allows oneself to be guided by those same CB used as models. That automatically leads them to unconsciously make the features of the CB fit the known qualities of their areas of concern--for good/bad. They believe in the supreme value of what they wish to see realized and assume supernatural powers are in favor of the actualization of their desires. Their emotions are so intense as to compel them to become fanatic DO-ers and continue on course without delay. They must live up to their Icon CB Symbol of "Manhood," which is even more important that their own lives. What this boils down to is that the delusional have a story in their minds that they must believe No amount of explanation or proof to the contrary will change that story. By Delusional thinking operating out of the Ancient Brain, Gang members believe delusions even in spite of seeing contrary evidence and will blame those bringing them the truth. jabaileymd.com

BLACK-ON-BLACK VIOLENCE MINDSET: An analogy that might help make the concept of the Base cause of violence more understandable is that the Soul is to ones Selfhood as the sun is to the source of the earth's life and beauty. The great glowing sun ball sends forth, day and night, in every direction, enormous streams of light and heat--and has been doing so "forever." For Ancient African Prophets, given that the sun is the source of light and that "Light" is coming from God's mind and divine intelligence, it represents the "spark of life" called the Spiritual Elements and their contents (e.g. Universal Energy). As stated above, Very Ancient Africans considered the individualized fragment of the Supreme Being present in each human to be an analogy for each human's inner spiritual illumination--the "Soul Sunshine"--in a manner that the sun illuminates the Earth. One or more of these as a "big bang" or as cumulative types is like air moving upward from the earth, making it expand and become colder so as to fashion into great masses of fog and mist. In the process, the sky seems to be closing in around them in a wet clinging veil and progressively blocks the earth's illumination of the sun.

Another way there can be the clouding over of the sun shine is when the moon casts its megaphone (or cone) shaped shadow upon the earth, it shuts off the light of the sun--called an *Eclipse* ('fainting'). That is the shadow of the whole world. But usually we can still see the moon dimly, shining with a strange copper-colored glow, or its face may be mottled (spotty). If you stood on the moon during a total lunar eclipse, you would see the sun blotted out as the earth moved across it. Around the ball of the earth you would see an airy band of light--like a "Halo." That would be like the earth's atmosphere shining with re-flected sunlight. This reflected light from the atmosphere, falling upon the moon during eclipse, is what gives it the dim light. Just as, about once a month, the moon normally comes between the sun and earth without causing an eclipse--because the earth, sun, and moon are not aligned in a straight line--every hu-man has some little disturbances of their SHNN. Resultant problems are of mild, slight, moderate, and extreme degrees.

TODAY'S IMMEDIATE CAUSE OF BLACK-ON-BLACK VIOLENCE: Once gangs emerged in dis-advantaged communities, they failed to disappear. In 2012 there were an estimated 700,000 gang members, with most having a 1 to 2 membership; and 5% remain for 4+ years. Adult members come to identify more with the gang as they age; are more capable of directing and organizing their gangs and influence internal gang dynamics; define the gang in violent terms, to express a greater willingness to use violence to defend gang turf; to report greater possession and use of firearms; and are more involved in especially serious violence. Leaving the gang is partially a consequence of the psychosocial characteristics of the member, as well as demographic features.

For most Black youth in gangs the focus is on the Secular Self-Esteem components, Respect and "Manhood." Both are measured by the degree to which they are recognized and honored as a *Public Self* display of ones power, importance, and excellence in what is in fashion at a given time and with a given gang. Their Secular Self-Worth and Self-Value are measured to the extent any given one is thought of as highly desirable and/or feared by others. Whereas *Spiritual Manhood* is the results of the cultiva-tion of ones Selfhood Greatness components, *Secular "Manhood"* is what a given male makes up (i.e. Supernatural) as an Icon Image in order to serve as a standard, guide, and filter for how to live his life. That Icon Image has as its goal to bring the male more of what he desires and prevent him from getting what he does not desire. What he most desires is that which brings the "5Ss"--an impossibility--by doing things in the Material World for three purposes. First is to satisfy his SHNN; second is to have more than "Enough" of what is required to fulfill his PHNN; and third, there is an intense desire to have ongoing excitement and "Luxury Living" from allowing his Lower (animalistic) Self to dominate his life. Yet, many in gangs are only there because they see no other options and/or have a need to be around those who will "protect my back."

In essence, Black-on-Black "Violence" is a battle over not having SHNN, feeling one lacks power and is thus a personal "Failure." Associates are a battle over Secular Self-Worth and Self-Value for, they falsely believe, to have those will impart fulfillment to ones SHNN and thereby gain the "5Ss". These youth nec-essarily operate out of their Omnibus Brains--in an ever-ready state of survival type self-protection--even from the most questionable disrespect, whether in word, deed, or rumor. It is necessary to demonstrate a taste for violent counterattack; otherwise, one appears weak and runs the risk of being "rolled on" or physically assaulted "by any number of others" (Anderson, 1999, p. 73). The importance of such a reputa-tion is highlighted by the fact that, in certain communities, "there are always people around looking for a fight"—people who actively campaign for respect on the streets by taking it away from others. By clinging to the belief of being right necessitates a position of being in opposition to anyone disagreeing, even a tiny bit. The need to release rage is so great that one misinterprets a different way of agreeing as a disagreement so as to exhibit demeaning attacks or a physical "show of force" by the means used by their captors--i.e. the GUN. This is Brute Courage.

Black youth considering going into gangs or have made up their minds do so share the same feeling of isolation and with no one to trust to help them. Everything they thought was stable all around them seems to be dissolving much more rapidly that is normal and natural—and discover that whatever they were clinging to is impossible to hold or even to grasp. These and similar ingredients contributing to Black Gangs are well-known and not complex. They include terrible poverty generated by Europeans, enhanced by ensuring there are no "Life-Living" sustaining jobs so as create chronic Physical Human Nature Needs (PHNN); a loss of Spiritual Human Nature Needs (SHNN) from a constant attack on Black youth's Self-Esteem; the "Coin Oddity" of hating European males on one side and bonding with them, as through imitation, on the other side; a craving for Power compatible with a "Manhood" Command Appearance that brings Respect; for a sense of belonging by means of Bonding (which occurs by one feeding--to any degree--another's PHNN and/or ones SHNN); and the fundamental law of Nature concerning self-protection, self-preservation, and simply surviving.

Pertinent Causes for an unfulfilled SHNN or the lack of SHNN bonding supplier must be understood as essential for determining what to do to stop the violence. These deficiencies were brought about by the only role models the Enslaved had—i.e. European Satanists as captors and oppressors. The significance they had on Black gangs is indicated in five phases of many Black Americans lives. An analogy is a diamond crystal's octahedron (Greek, eight faces) shape has the multiple faces of each exhibiting unique reflections. Each reflection is present in Black People so that they, as an essential part of their False Selves, have the many faces of European males being strongly contributory to who they are and how they think, feel, say, and do things. Some of these faces include: Phase I--Black Selfhoods shaped by European Males. Phase II was the imitation of Enslaved Africans of the European slaver. Phase III was the organization of Black gangs on the model of European males. Phase IV is the devastation of the Selfhood of Black gang members by the racism and oppression of European males. Phase V is Black Gangs using each other as Scapegoats.

To varying degrees families, ethnic groups, friendship networks and society help shape "Life-Living" patterns as well as ones personality as to how one defines oneself and to what ones beliefs and attitudes and behaviors will be. To repeat, foundational to today's Black-On-Black Violence is the shattering of ones Spiritual Human Nature Needs (SHNN)--the entity which forms and holds together ones Self-Esteem. *To repeat, the absence of a supplier of ones SHNN is a disaster and finding one is a youth's central focus, often representing the driving force for joining a gang.*

SOURCES OF TODAY'S BLACK GANGS: From their Ancestral past and present-day experiences, Black youth carry in their Selfhoods a collage of different types of wonderfully formed bonds, reminiscence of shattered wonderful bonds, *Deficient* Physical Human Nature Needs (PHNN) bonds, frustrated Selfhood bonds; desperation for Spiritual Human Nature Needs (SHNN) bonds (e.g. with ones dad), and the original Mother-Child bond. The very best bonds are Sacred because they fulfill ones PHNN and SHNN. Any other bonds are problematic and are relegated to ones sub-awareness. Whereas youth who have little interest in gangs derive positive feelings from their academic abilities and believe that they will have successful future careers and are likely to choose prosocial friendships and activities, youth who are PHNN and SHNN deficient prepare to join gangs. They are less confident in their academic abilities and so they may, for reasons of underachievement and/or loss of interest, begin to disengage with school and scholarly inclined peer groups. Such potential Black Gang members are drawn from the most struggling of the struggling class rung of the Social Ladder. Static or time-stable characteristics include desperation with respect to the "5Ss" which leads to perceptions necessitating risk-taking.

Their commonly shared harshen environmental conditions imparts a common set of character traits--a "common knowing by participation"—and a common way of communication using slang and euphemistic language (e.g. referring to murder as business) and "techniques of neutralization" to dehumanize out-group members and rationalize aggression toward them. Together, they have an "organized defiant individualism" mindset (Densley, *Group Processes & Intergroup Relations, 2014*) who adopt common names and other conventional signals to create "Us vs. Them" boundaries with unrecognized interlocking of the opponents' commonality in cultural, social, and political aspects.

Consequently, youth may modify, or even discard their existing legitimate social controls (e.g. school) in favor of the appealing advantages that gang membership seems to offer. Youth go through an identity formation process during adolescence and select peer group friendships based on shared similarities. As they reject familiar childhood groups and practices, it is likely that they will experience feelings of uncertainty about their attitudes, their future, and, importantly, their identity. The *Uncertainty-identity theory* explains that feeling uncertain about personal identity motivates people to identify with a group use their group membership to categorize themselves and others according to sets of attitudes and behaviors that epitomize group membership. Once people identify with a group they experience further shaping of their self-view. A candidate's self-perception is caused by a psychological reorientation in which he visualizes his world and who he thinks he is in a different light.

In spite of retaining many of his idiosyncrasies, he is eager to develop a new set of values and different criteria of judgment. One youth said: "I started gang banging when I was ten. I got into a gang when I was thirteen. I started just hanging around them, just basically idolizing them. I was basically looking for a role model for my generation and ethnic background; the main focus for us is the popularity that they got. That's who the kids looked up to. They had status, better clothes, better lifestyle." Image, status, and a host of other factors that affect identity are mostly created by group perceptions of who one is and how one defines oneself, with or without help from others. When ones identity is transformed, one is seen by others as being different than one was before. Ones prior identity is retrospectively reevaluated in comparison with the present definition of a gang member. Such a transformation was part of the processional change in identity that prisoners/gang members experienced.

RISK FACTORS: Youth with a great less than self-confident, possess unhealthy self-esteems, and have weak bonds with a prosocial environment and social network (i.e. schools and family) are more likely to look towards gangs than youth who are more confident. Furthermore, self-esteem has a dynamic relationship with gang membership. In particular, Self-Esteem determines whether one joins, the degree to which one participates, and if and when to leave the gang. Of the numerous risk factors (Cottrell-Boyce *Youth Justice, 2013*), some include: (1) Early childhood neglect and abuse; (2) Parental violence and drug addiction; *(3)* School exclusion and early conduct disorders; *(4)* Violent victimization and repeated hospital visits. These precarious individuals, apart from enduring a more restricted range of social, cultural, political and economic rights than citizens around them, are dangerously lacking in security or stability or safety, making them subject to chance or unknown life threatening conditions. These aspects shower these individuals with Shame, a sense of insecurity and of being a "failure" in the eyes of their society. Such despair can trigger an "Identity Crisis" and their "Raw Nerve" of Shame causes their totally self-absorbed focus to a desperate search for Respect.

Dealing with their sense of inferiority may cause them to sink deeper into despair or put on a "Front" of a superiority complex of a "Tough Dude," or assume a "Don't Care" demeanor. Still to over come their sense of worthlessness they may feel there is no alternative but to resort to violence in order to assert their Self-Identity and "Don't Mess With Me" status. To at least a more obvious degree gangs promote and facilitate a disproportionate amount of physical violence and, in return, become targeted as victims. Media representations of rewards for gang-like behavior may act as a blueprint for aspiring gang members and have a persuasive influence on youth raised in cultures that strongly associate success with material wealth (Wood *Group Processes & Intergroup Relations, 2014*).

DEFINITIONS OF GANGS BY GANG MEMBERS: Generally, the main reason for joining a gang is protection. From wallowing in a mindset in turmoil as a result of being in a setting where the atmosphere of an officially recognized means of success often appear to be inaccessible, gangs may appear to offer youth friendship, pride, a sense of identity, improved self-esteem, excitement, and access to financial assets. Since gangs are groups, their collective compositions appear to offer emotional bonding with other members, a sense of belonging to a group, and protection from being victimized by outsiders. As a group, a gang also offers members a strong psychological sense of community by means of an actual and a psychological neighborhood. Candidates are told by gang members that a gang is a group of fellas. Not just fellas but ones that can depend on each other being "all down" for the same thing. "Everybody think gang ain't nothing but just thinking about being violent. Your gang, we think about working. Yeah, we sit in the parking lot and we drink. We try to get jobs and stay off the streets. We don't want to be known. We want to be known but we don't want to be known in no wrong way. We already got that impression now. We already known the wrong way" (Watkins, *Youth Violence and Juvenile Justice, 2014*).

Adult gang members: "Dudes that hang out and do what they want do to"; "It's like a bunch of friends all hanging together"—i.e. a gang almost exclusively participates in a group and spends time with other gang members—like a second family. Overall, a "Gang" can be viewed as a relatively durable, predominantly street-based group of young people who: (a) See themselves (and are seen by others) as a discernable group; (b) Lay claim over territory (this is not necessary geographical territory but can include an illegal economy territory); (c) Have some form of identifying structural feature; (d) Are in conflict with other, similar, gangs; and (e) perhaps engage in criminal activity and violence.

GANG ORGANIZATION: Historically, gangs of the Americas (and the world) have coalesced around their own Ethnic group—i.e. those who identify with each other through a common heritage and distinctive culture, often consisting of a common language, religion or country of birth. The generic organization of Black gangs is generally based on a collage of the European military, the European crime organizations, and the African Age-Set systems. Organization pertains to such key features as leadership, rules, punishments for violating the rules, meetings, symbols of membership, responsibilities, and giving money to the gang. European experts place this collage into two broad types. First is the *Instrumental–Rational type*--suggesting gangs are rational organizations acting in ways to enhance their self-interest and rationally behave. Their organizational and structural features include embracing common goals, motivating others to join in a common enterprise, the clear structuring of monetary activities, and the role of internal controls on gang member behavior in creating discipline around well-established goals. Examples are shown best in drug dealings and, to a lesser extent, in the use of violence, neighborhood intimidation including graffiti—and some property offenses.

A second type is those less than ideally organized and focused. Despite being united by several common features (names, symbols, and opposition), their ages are in the upper teens which compromise foresight and forethought needed for proper protection and structure. The more organized the gang, even at low levels of organization, the more likely it is that members will be involved in violent offenses, drug sales, and violent victimizations.

There are rules applying to recognized leaders, specific rules and codes, initiation rituals, and special clothing for members. The context for these rules embraces engaging in violent behavior and endorsing moral disengagement strategies—e.g. moral justification, euphemistic language, advantageous comparison, displacement of responsibility, attribution of blame, and dehumanization. Any rival who violates the gang's unwritten rules related to Disrespect has to be made an "example of" by punishing with such cruelty as to attempt to intimidate any would-be rule violators.

BENEFITS FROM GANG MEMBERSHIP: Privately, Black youth have an instinct for Bonding. A desire to belong to a group is part of Black People's Human Nature and which almost everyone does in some form so as to have protection, support, and loyalty. A feature of each of ones SHNN aspects is its Spiritual Boundlessness nature which flows naturally out of ones Spiritual Elements Soul. *Ideal Bonding* occurs when ones PHNN and ones SHNN are fulfilled. "*Desperate Bonding*" is present when either ones PHNN or SHNN are neglected to any degree. *Desperate Bonding is what characterizes the Selfhoods of gang members--particularly the SHNN since one feels one is dependent on others to supply this.* One of the most problematic aspects of the seven types mentioned above pertains "*Stretched Bonding*"—as occurs in the Evil Savior Syndrome. People whose SHNN are not fulfilled, will go to ignorant and/or evil leaders or cults in hopes of getting even a little bit of SHNN needs supplied. "Stretched Bonding" occurs when the Feeder applies boundaries around what ought to flow freely from ones Real Self--and this necessarily means *Anti-Spiritual Elements Rules* are applied. The subtle nature of these rules is that the Receiver is now required to do something, in order to be fed, that is acceptable only if it is done voluntarily—and that is in the category of "Conditional" ("Condition" applies to anything essential to the occurrence of something).

Otherwise, most are pulled into gang membership as a result of the attractive benefits for which the one has a chance to gain social status, identity, companionship, respect from others, and power. Such gangs perhaps satisfy these youth's wants or needs to an even greater degree than ones subculture. The price paid is that one gives up who one really is in order to conform to promoting gang orchestrated "Life-Living" patterns that are not in complete conformity with mainstream society—despite their overlapping features. For the overwhelming majority a gang fulfills a variety of more typical adolescent needs—especially companionship and support, which tend to be more expressive in nature (Stretesky, J. *Contemporary Ethnography, 2007*). As a new gang member strives to live up to gang membership expectations, s/he may begin to develop a new personal identity that corresponds to the group's overarching identity. A gang member's personal identity may develop from a focus on how their individual needs blend with the group's characteristics and function.

As gangs offer the potential for gaining power, status, identity, friendship, etc., then gang membership is likely to help youth forge a more positive self-concept (i.e. "people like me, I have a lot of friends,

I am worth knowing"). Also, basking in the gang's apparent reflected glory gives a boost to ones emotions derived from group membership—a boost which spurs dedicated effort to cement relationships with the group. Commitment to the gang satisfies a high priority need for Loyalty--loyalty to willing to risk being killed—a loyalty committed to taking the life of a rival gang member if need be—a loyalty that nourishes ones identity and at the same time provides group maintenance. *Loyalty* is one of the countless words deemed greatly significant in Chinese and Indo-European (Sanskrit) languages but derived from Ancient African words. When Ancient Africans said: "in order to live your life, you must continue it and stick to it," this "glue-like" sense was the original denotative meaning of both "Life" and "Loyalty." The concept referred to a powerful force emerging out of a person's beliefs and values about something to which that person is attached. Connotatively it embraces that same person's deeply held feelings or strong emotions of pride, affection, and attachment that go with his/her denotative beliefs and values to which that person clutches.

Typically, this means putting the group norms of criminal activity ahead of their personal concerns regarding punishment for criminal activity. Apparently getting caught and punished have little or no influence on their criminal and violent behaviors. The same applies to people being told they will burn in hell for their bad deeds. But such Loyalty is branded "un-noble" when it "glues" its virtues + ones bad emotions (e.g. rage, fear, pain arising out of a sense of rejection or disrespect) + *ones power struggle* + *ones negative integrity* + *ones competitive attitude* + *ones oppositional behavior* + ones self-defeating beliefs into an unswerving and binding allegiance. *This allegiance is so powerful as for one to willingly give up certain advantages in order to remain loyal to something that is not in ones best interest.* Such "*Un-noble Loyalty*" is done for what is self-defeating, in spite of knowing better (or not). In the process, one must deny the associated doubt about its "Rightness" and make an excuse for it so as to allow this "glob" to continue on as usual in the wrong direction. Meanwhile, its malignant thoughts and bad emotions destroy the loyalty bonds of self-trust and self-confidence in what one had built up to this point.

The combination places a cloud over ones Self-Love and Self-Greatness--both foundational to ones Selfhood structure. Whether good or "*Un-Noble*," Loyalty is inseparable from friendships or alliances with fellow destructive Evil people in the form of an unswerving and binding allegiance. Such is seen in "hate" groups and this means all of them are weak. People also demonstrating "*Un-Noble*" Loyal have lost their sense of Self-Greatness, self-trust, self-confidence, and self-loyalty and thus become self-absorbed and Selfhood Splintered because of being. In other words, the social identity impact of gang membership seems to exert a powerful sway over members to the point where they set aside personal needs or concerns in favor of the group and its norms of criminal activity. This notion of sacrifice for the group by proving ones gang identification is expressed by an inmate who perceives his loyalty in the following terms: "What I might do for my friends [gang peers] you might not do. You've got people out their taking bullets for their friends and killing people. But I'm sure not one of you would be willing to go to that extreme. These are just the thinking patterns we had growing up where I did."

REQUIREMENTS FOR GANG MEMBERSHIP: Gangs form just like any other group, because they offer members something candidates strongly desire. The model for Black gang formation arose out of the African Age-Set system where there were "Good Gangs" whose members helped each other and their communities. Black gangs of today, regardless of where located in the world, are spurred to form as a reaction to Europeans' inhumane domination. Originally with these world wide gangs, their perception came from methods Europeans applied to them, followed by media images, followed by gang presence in their neighborhoods. In the process, it was an easy next step to embrace the impression that gangs offer opportunities not available in trying to fit into society's less illegitimate life pathways. The Effect is a disconnect and alienation from beneficial societal aspects—e.g. families, education systems, and prosocial community involvements. Some entering members have been delinquent and violent prior to joining the gang and they are more likely to engage in violent and deviant behavior even if they are not gang members. They may be recruited because of showing a propensity to engage in crime and violence, but their level of violence intensifies once they enter the gang because the gang provides a structure that encourages crime and violence—the *Enhancement Concept*. Some are no different from non-gang members until they enter the gang--the *Social Facilitation Theory*. Some are pushed into gang membership as a result of perceived threats and/or social pressures. Yet, since most Black gang members are not delinquent before joining a gang, gang leaders counteract new members' desire not to engage in criminal activities by demanding delinquent acts. The purpose is to foster group homogeneity, adherence to norms, and self-categorization as a group member. As members' chosen gang identification intensifies, the more likely they are to believe in the gang's Codes.

V*ertical* cohesion derives from the extent that members trust and respect the group's leaders and *horizontal* cohesion derives from the feelings, respect, and trust that members have for each other (Wood *Group Processes & Intergroup Relations, 2014*). Added to this is P*erceived* cohesion—i.e. ones sense of belonging to that gang and its associated morale. One said: "At an early age, it was encouraged that I showed my loyalty and do a drive-by. . . anybody they (gangster disciples) deemed to be a rival of the gang. I was going on 14. At first, I was scared to and then they sent me out with one person and I seen him do it. I saw him shoot the guy. . . . So, in the middle of a gang fight I get pulled aside and get handed a pistol and he said, "It's your turn to prove yourself." So I turned around and shot and hit one of the guys (rival gang members). After that, it just got more easier. I did more and more. I had no concern for anybody. As a gang banger, you have no remorse, so basically, they're natural-born killers. They are killers from the start. When I first shot my gun for the first time at somebody, I felt bad. It was like, I can't believe I did this. But I looked at my friend and he didn't care at all. Most gang bangers can't have a conscience. You can't have remorse. You can't have any values. Otherwise, you are gonna end up retiring as a gang banger at a young age. Note that all of what this is about does not come from an evil youth but rather an ignorant one. The callousness to causing pain, suffering, and even to murder comes from "Numbing" his emotions. All of this is reversible.

Trust is an essential component of all enduring social groups—particularly those of gangs who participate in what Euro-Americans perceive to illegal by their standards. For gangs involved in such illegal activities, disputes within it cannot be settled by an outsider third party as established by the rule of law—i.e. those who are the enemies of gangs. "*Trust*" refers to reliance on another. Based upon prior experiences that demonstrated credibility and therefore furnishing the assurance that ones trust will not be misplaced or abused. In gangs, Trust is situational behavior rather than a personal characteristic or trait, whereby: (a) trust implies the trustor freely transfers assets to another person, without controlling the actions of that other person or having the possibility to retaliate; and (b) there must be potential gain in order to have an incentive to trust. Yet, trust is only valid as long as the credibility of someone or some "Thing" is sustained and not broken by betrayal, broken promises, violated values. After all, the group is an extension of the individual and the individual is an extension of the group—both doing what they do independently and as a team for a common purpose.

Problems of trust are spotlighted in the "Underworld" where violence assists in enforcing contracts and maintaining hierarchical authority. Gang codes of loyalty and boundaries between groups help reinforce ties between members. A youth's *Identity* is socially bestowed, socially maintained, and socially transformed." Wearing gang clothes, flashing gang signs, and affecting other outward signs of gang behavior are also ways to become encapsulated in the role of gang member, especially through the perceptions of others, who, when they see the external symbols of membership respond as if the person was a member.

BEING IN A GANG: Gang joining occurs during early to mid-adolescence and the vast majority of members do not retain their affiliations into adulthood (Watkins, *Youth Violence and Juvenile Justice, 2014*). There are leaders and followers. Followers are those conforming to others' decisions—even when those others are obviously wrong. The gang is the source of delinquent behavior because new gang members are socialized into the norms and values of gang life, which provides the necessary social setting for crime and violence to flourish. What makes gang members more criminal than non-gang members is the criminally oriented have self-selected or been recruited into gangs. "If you're not a gang member, you're not on my level . . . most of my life revolves around gangs and gang violence. I don't know anything else but gang violence. I was born into it, so it's my life That's how it is in the hood, selling dope, gang bangin', everybody wants a piece of you. All the rival gang members, all the cops, everybody. The only ones on your side are the gang members you hang with. The violent gang members perceived other gangs as ongoing enemies who constantly presented a threat to their safety. I have hate toward the Crips gang members and have always had hate toward them 'cuz of what they did to my homeboys. . . . I never look back. I do my thing. I always carry a gun no matter what. I am a gang member, man! There are a lot of gang members out to get me for what I done. I shot over forty people at least. That's what I do.

This is because their desire to be accepted and to gain approval leads them to comply. Also operating is what mental health specialists call *Pluralistic Ignorance*—the scenario of a member privately rejecting a "Street Gang Code" but still abiding by it publicly from being under the often wrong assumption that rest of the members are in favor of it. By feeling alone in their opposition and not publicly objecting serves give the appearance and to perpetuate the gang members belief that the majority accept it. In other words, most Black youth privately feel extreme discomfort with some of their criminal activities. A powerful driving force is an intense desire to be known in the community for some particular attribute—at least, simply to be known, sort of achieving celebrity status. "You basically want people to know your name. It's kind of like politicians, like that, you wanna be known. In my generation you want somebody to say, "I know him, he used to hang around with us."

Those who make a lifestyle of violence adopt a "badass" persona, popular among "Street" youth who "pay back" anyone who publicly disrespects them. This is a way to display that or the "juice" individuals use to demonstrate they are able to "hold their own" and are not "punks," "herbs," or "chumps". You don't give respect to get it, you take respect. One code governing violence and respect in disadvantaged neighborhoods, "the most fundamental norm is 'never back down from a fight"being bossed around and told to "do this, do that." "That's what it is, domination. When others try to act up, to dominate you, that's when troubles start." toughness meant being fearless, or never being afraid of confrontations, especially physical confrontations with individuals who attempted to dominate and control them.

GANG IDENTITY: This is present at its best when there is a mutual sense of solidarity and belongingness. It may be somewhat based upon familial, societal, ethnic, racial, class, nationality, occupation, or religious identifications. This means ones "Inner" world and "Outer" world members are dynamically joined. The newer members are always in a state of "Becoming"—generating mental conflicts between who one desires to become with images of who one has been + ones personal and familial experiences with the societal and cultural meanings held by gang members. Involved is a youth's sense of worth and value being brought to the table along with existing cultural values, beliefs, and images of good or bad "Manhood. Once seated at the table of gang offerings, that youth selects off the table whatever aspects that work to get along with the group with respect to "Manhood," purposes, and direction. New members keep alive the apparently universal need seen in children to overprize ones own group and its identity. This means making "our kind" as the standard for what is right and against which all others are compared. Much of their Self-Concept (ones spotlighted qualities) develops from being a member of their group.

Establishing a reputation coincides with becoming a man in a gang, entering the realm of violence, being a stand-up guy who is willing to prove his courage as a true gang member. This strong association between a willingness to perpetrate violence on a considered rival or anyone is pertinent to ones "Manhood". One said he was owed money for selling someone dope. After a few weeks of being put off by the debtor, he had to take some action to appease his gang peers who were pressuring him to retaliate. I joined the gang when I was eleven years old. So now that I'm in the gang for eight years, people are asking, "What are you going to do? You got to make a name for yourself." So we went over there [victim's residence] and they were all standing outside and I just shot him. Everybody was happy for me, like "Yea, you shot him, you're cool," and this and that. A sense of bravado, when displayed, played a utilitarian role in conflicting situations where a gang member attempts to get others to comply with his demands by instilling fear instead of actually utilizing violent means.

Having some prior knowledge of the threatening gang member's reputation is helpful in preventing a physical encounter, which is always risky for both parties involved. Again, the importance of firearms in this situation is critical. The following instance of masculinity and bravado with respect to a current incarceration illustrates the commitment to being a *"stand-up guy"*—one who will face the consequences of gang activity. This youth adhered to the gang value of not being a snitch, and refused to provide information about rival gang members' involvement in two homicides to the police, which could have helped in his prosecution for murder. I know what I did [gang war murder], you know what I mean? I'm not gonna take the easy way out [snitch on rival gangs for two homicides]. I know what I did. I'm facing my responsibility. Everybody wants to fight for the power, for the next man to fear him. The implication here is that having a collective reputation for being powerful motivates this prisoner. He notes that the tough image of shooting someone you are after instead of hiding behind the random shooting characterized by drive-bys projects an image of toughness and power. Other define toughness in terms of physical fighting without the use of any weapons—though it was often noted that it was too difficult to maintain a tough reputation under such conditions.

RESPECT IS GANGS' THEME: A Theme is a *maintained central or dominating idea* and for all "Street" culture (Secular) Respect is a megastar--the complementary equal of ones "Manhood". But what is Spiritual Respect? Ancient Africans said the God Substance or Love flows everywhere, as blood from ones heart flows throughout ones body and into all of ones fingers, thumbs, and toes--even though each is very different. For one to recognize this Substance in every creature and creation is the recognition of its Dignity. In African Tradition to show you care about another's Dignity is called *Spiritual Appreciation*, a fundamental aspect of Respect. The experience of Spiritual Appreciation + dealing with any of God's creatures and creations as if one were to deal with God directly is the application of *Spiritual Respect*. "The God inside me greets the God inside you" is an example of how Spiritual Respect, and not personality, is shown for Dignity. Western manhood is defined by the power of the Gun and what concrete things the Gun can bring (money, possessions, women). Whereas Spiritual Respect, Spiritual Appreciation and Spiritual Dignity are part of the Love present in African Tradition, Earth World respect, appreciation, and dignity related to achievement characterize the part of the best of Western Tradition. However, because gang members operate out of their False Self, they have adopted the European criteria of "Respect"—a Secular concept.

When the word "Respect" came into the English language (c 1380) it derived from Latin "specere" ("to look back at"; "to observe") with reference to an act of noticing with attention and to give deference with an admiring attitude or at least with courteous treatment (e.g. listen, make thing pleasant, and do what is asked). Out of such considerations sprang the discriminating terms of high regard and honor. At that time and similar to what happened with Dignity, to *Honor* signified an evaluation or estimation as the basis of recognition of the Worth (pleasure or displeasure in a Western sense) or Value (desirable materialism) of something. As a result, "Honor" was thought of as a fixed price for the purpose of ranking a given person or object on the proper rung of the Ladder of Importance (Bailey, Self-Esteem, p. 16). Whatever was on the highest rung was given the most deferential *Regard* (C16) because it was of the highest agreed upon quality by European experts or by those in power. This made "Respect" a somewhat "colder" term than either *"Appreciate"* (the European sense being that of a combined value and worth of something) or *"Esteem"* (the combination of regard, respect, and appreciation). The reason is that "Respect" embraced honor and confidence without any particular feelings--whether referring to a person or thing—and was based on the admiration of a person's desirable characteristics and competence--as determined by one or more observers who used their own man-made standards and criteria.

MONEY SOURCES: Greater gang involvement corresponds with youth's diminished resources and ties to prosocial networks. A reduction in these resources and ties, in turn, necessitates that individuals increasingly rely on the gang for money and prestige, thus prolonging membership. In disadvantaged neighborhoods, the declining availability of low-skilled jobs that pay a livable or attractive wage cut off a common pathway by which earlier generations of undereducated youths typically transitioned to productive adulthood. Gangs often sell a specific drug—e.g. marijuana, the drug most likely to be sold (80%), followed by crack cocaine (50%); powder cocaine (44%); heroin; and methamphetamines. These sales may be to individuals and/or to other drug dealers (Decker, *Crime & Delinquency, 2008*). Methods of the money source are: (80%) intimidating, threatening, jumping or attacking people, robbing people and killing people, including drive-by shootings (51%). Monies generated by drug sales, robbery, and property crime are used for individual purposes as opposed to a corporate perspective (Decker, *Crime & Delinquency, 2008*).

"STREET" GANG CULTURE

"Street" refers to anything counter-culture or outside the structure of 'straight' or 'legal' society. "Street People" were popularized in the 1960s by mostly White runaway youth who were either homeless or living in 'crash pads'. Yet, the true "Street Culture" consisted of those living in neighborhoods who had prison records, were engaged in the illegal drug trade, had a criminal persona, engaged in male and female bravado, devised greater and greater ways to boast of their sexual exploits or conquest, as well as those who spotlighted expressions that would capture and reflect a given ones experiences, thoughts, and emotions. Starting in the 1970s all of the risk factors (e.g. poverty and marginalization) have inclined certain struggling Black males to the intergenerational transmission of violence because of those risk factors and because of them being associated with a challenge to their "Manhood"--and acts of Manhood are significant to a youth's psyche and world-view. Men desire to be in control because they are afraid that the control of others will be used justly to their detriment.

A youth determines the appropriateness of his "Manhood Icon Image"—who he is and how he can define himself--from how it is accepted by the group and the status to which he is assigned. This is because each youth sees himself from the standpoints of his group and appropriate actions in relation to those groups which, if well-received, becomes a source of pride. Since the 1970s they have tended to run in gangs that are about violence--92% of the adult gang members reported being arrested at least 1 time, and 50% arrested 5 or more times. Some adult gang members say the gang in neighborhood terms is being "down for the hood" with less than 30% explicitly referenced criminal activities. Juvenile gang members—age 14-25--also referenced violence or criminal activities only 25% of the time. Violence is reserved for situations in which rival gang members initiate or provoke a response: the "only time we'll fight them [a rival member] is when they start a fight." Most of the time we let them walk through there unless we say something to one another or they say something to one of the girls then we hit them, we give them a warning. If he come up there with all blue on then he gonna get hit.

Invading a gang's Turf is a spotlighted form of Disrespect. Concerning territory and the unwritten rules of the "Streets," one gang member said he was left with no other alternative choice of action but to shoot them. "So, as we were fighting, they started saying that this was their neighborhood and started throwing their gang signs. To me, to let somebody do that to me is disrespect. So I told them where I was from." A little while later the gang members in question showed up in his neighborhood and shot at him as he was walking with his two small children to a convenience store to get ice cream. "I was just so mad and angry for somebody to disrespect me like that and shoot. We got a rule on the street. There is rules. You don't shoot at anybody if there is kids. That's one of the main rules of the street. They broke the rules. To me that was telling me that they didn't have no respect for me or my kids. So, that's how I lost it and shot them. I was so disrespected that I didn't know how to handle it.

To gang members caught in those confrontational encounters, there is a very limited course of action, that of perpetrating violence toward those who would threaten their "Manhood" (Secular 'Self').

Disadvantaged urban youth who hold beliefs consistent with the "code of the street" are significantly more likely to engage in violence (Parker, *J. Drug Issues, 2009*). "Street" families socialize their youth to conform to the "Code of the Street" and that "Decent" families utilize informal social control mechanisms to limit their children's involvement in crime and violence. More often, "Decent" families have consistent 'in-home' male figures who are usually employed, financially secure, and deserving of deference and respect because of the role they play in the family and the resources they offer the community at large. The others, typically lacking such a stabilizing force, become "Street" youth. Their profoundly internalized and often inchoate (arising immature) anger results in what some call a 'slow riot', which 'occurs in slow time and takes the form of implosive, inwards directed, self-destructive violence, in which predominantly young men kill each other and often for seemingly mundane reasons'.

The willingness and ability to fight are necessary tools for maintaining "Respect" (Irwin *Youth & Society*, *2004*). In high risk gangs fights with guns are spotlighted and after being assessed by the "street-savvy". These individuals know when conflicts are likely to occur; are able to discern dangerous individuals; and possessed valuable information about how to talk, act, and dress to avoid inviting trouble. In moderate risks, they usually avoid fisticuffs as well as fights with weapons and, instead, turn to friends to manage violence. Low-risk youths hold more vague and abstract concerns and are not necessarily focused on one type of violence over another.

LEADERS OF STREET CULTURE: Recall that Bad Conditioned Reflexes have allowed "Clouds" to form over the "Soul Sunshine" of their Hearts--Group I, self-imposed; Group II, as victims; Group III, as Brutes perpetrators. Group III, the leaders, possess Supernatural minds who typically rely on the GUN and a backed-up Network to thereby bathe in the freedom to Kill/Take/Destroy on a whim impulse and without op-position. To understand the scope of "Air Castle" Supernatural Fantasies is to gain an idea of the Background of the Unconscious of "Killer" police. This first requires distinguishing them from Natural Cosmos people and this is most easily done with those who feature the "God Module." That is the Background of ones Unconscious displaying in one developing into ones Highest (Divinity) Self. Its Foreground Icon Image is indicated by "Lifting" others while "Climbing". Two clues which distinguish Occult from Rational Thinking are that the Fantasy-minded: are first unable to look at an Occult concept without an opinion (e.g. like/dislike); second, their viewings of an Occult "Thing" are always associated with something else—e.g. a companion, group, object, memory. Probably most felt the best place to solve all of their mental turmoil problems was by acquiring, in the Foreground of their Sensory Conscious, the "5Ss". Out of this came Sensory Background Consciousness concepts, such as of gods, self-image, religion, which formed Icon Images for the Foreground of their Unconscious minds, individually and collectively. These Fantasies were wildly elaborated on in the Foreground of their Sensory Consciousness—some being concepts of impossible objects without considering how they came into Being--some were about Beings arising out of Icon Images in particular. To elaborate, apart from mere survival, for the Warrior Brutes there was an overwhelming fear of being unsuc-cessful in the eyes of their peers and the deeper repressed fear of never wanting to appear to be weak and needy. They deemed self-image Success to be the acquiring of material things for *narcissistic* (grandiosity in fantasy with an excessive need for admiration) purposes.

BADDEST DUDES (fig. 20): Struggling Black Americans are considered to be those on the lowest rungs of the social ladder because of the difficulties they have in fitting into the mainstream of American society. This in no way suggests they are inferior and in fact many are more intelligent in realms of survival than most anyone else who consider themselves intelligent. The vast majority of these struggling individuals are quite decent and do the right things. Some are thugs and those who reign in the world of "the Streets" are called the "Baddest Dudes" (Anderson, p. 208). They, like the Black Pimp, have undergone remarkable mental achieve-ments. To reach the stage of the "Baddest Dudes" they first overcome the apathetic tendency of "Street" peers to "give up" on life by going through a mental process which transforms them into rising above a sense of self-preservation and survival. Thus, their spot-lighted feature is to have "no fear" of dying. Once at this "no fear" mental state, they display *Nerve*-- the lack of a fear of dying and the belief that the risk of dying over the principle of Respect is worth it. In other words, the clear risk of violent death is preferable to being "dissed" (disrespected) by another.

The keystone concept is "*Risk*" (1661, run into danger) perhaps originally meant 'sail dangerously close to rocks'. Manhood on the "Streets" and as part of a gang means being part of some whole. On account of that whole it is fitting to run risks. In actuality, risks have to be taken whereby one is forced to handle and face the demands of the 'edge', the dangerous boundary--not between consciousness and unconsciousness or sanity and insanity, but between 'life or death,' for that is test of "Streets" Manhood. Confronting the edge places the risk-taker on the border between control and non-control, forcing one to rely fully on ones pre-attained skills and being dependent on bodily experience and impulses (Bengtsson, *Criminology and Criminal Justice, 2013*). So creatively satisfying is this that the very experience becomes the drive: (1) for sense of alienation from systems and structures of society; (2) committing a wide range of crimes for the thrill of 'getting away with it', 'surviving it'; (3) a way of perfecting the skills need to go higher levels; (4) enhancing creativity by finding different ways of challenging oneself, as in creating new meanings as ways of escaping the mundane realities of everyday life; (5) a way of trying to break free of the rationalization of modern society

Thus, they achieve a type of manhood characterized by a willingness, a readiness, and an actuality of taking charge as "the Man." From having achieved this status position they feel entitled to have the best pre-rogatives of men, as opposed to strangers, other men, and women. They back it up with a physicality and a certain ruthlessness. This attitude reflects the depth of destruction to the African Tradition Selfhood of certain Slaves as a result of being brainwashed and disrespected by their captors. Yet, if they ever reform, they are the most effective teachers for helping gang members break out of their vicious cycles. In fact, they have much to teach the world—at least about how not to live; how to deal with Brutes; and how to gain mental control over human nature

The guidelines for manhood and machismo made themselves known in the unwritten codes of the streets. Just as good character has love at its core, manhood and machismo have respect at their core. The code spells out the accepted image required in "being present" with others and the accepted street ways of responding if one's respect is challenged. The rules of Black youth which determine disrespect resemble what Whites did to Black males during slavery. One example is that EuroAmericans have always considered African Americans as "black" before, if ever, they were considered human or even an individual. Typically, Whites have failed to know anything important about who "Blacks" were on a personal level, how they lived, what their family relationships were, or how they actually felt about anything. to lose respect in the ghetto is to be "dissed" (disrespected) and disgraced -- the "kiss of death" to one's self-image. To prevent the possibility is an ever willingness to get violent if necessary -- regardless of whether one is a "decent" ghetto youth or a "street" youth, as Anderson has subdivided them. The decent youth want to avoid violence and to do so they work hard on developing a "command appearance" self-image and public-image. These include "the look," "the walk," and "the talk."

"The look" is about certain forms of facial expressions as well as about a certain physical appearance -- the grooming, the jacket, the sneakers, the gold jewelry. The winner is the one who is able to replace these every day. "The walk" is an eye-catching show of rhythmic gait that conveys the message "I'm hip," "I'm cool," "I'm in charge." The message of "the talk" reinforces "the walk" and suggests that "we're going to play this game according to me." The "baddest dudes on the street" represent the very worse effects of racism and echoes of slavery. Not being afraid to die and having no hesitation about killing anybody means they do not even care about themselves beyond the idea of having the respect that symbolizes their manhood. The credibility they get is what both the decent and street ghetto youth desire because of its practical defensive value and because of the strong self-esteem it conveys.

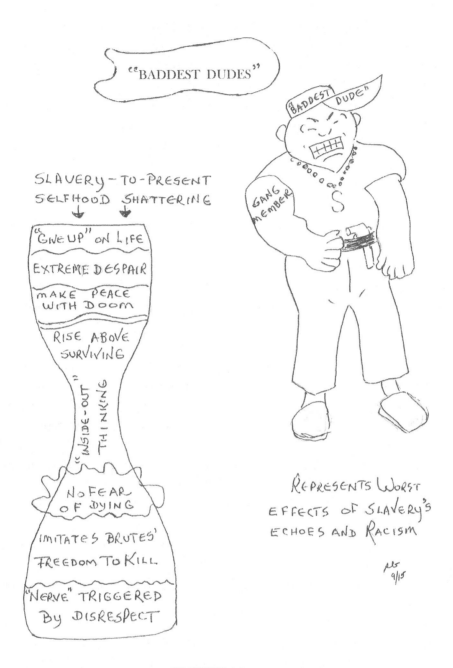

FIGURE 20

SURVIVAL BY INTIMIDATION: The GUN has been attached to the "hip" of European males since C15 in order for them to display it as intimidation ("to make timid") or to actually engage in the "bottom-line" of Kill/Take/Destroy/Dominate/Oppress power enabling them to get whatever they want. The purpose of Intimidation is to make fearful; to make cowardly; terrorize; terrify; scare; make afraid; make timid; make fearful; frighten; fill with fear, alarm; subdue; bully; daut; browbeat; compel by threats coerce; afraid of being shamed or embarrassed; to use violence to overawe. European males have always used it to Browbeat victims--a mental harassment by means of a stern, overbearing, condemnatory manner--haughty, contemptuous, rude treatment, or a bombardment of some kind that goes on without letup. An essential part of Intimidation is to Bully victims--denoting a swaggering, aggressive person who is usually cowardly at heart and who intimidates people. Responses of victims range from being *Daunted* (i.e. to dishearten, frighten, or otherwise discourage someone from doing something or from going on--impling a loss of the will to keep trying) or being *Dismayed* (suggesting a sinking feeling in the pit of the stomach from a sense of hopeless discouragement in the face of obstacles) all the way over to being entangled in a paralyzing fear in the face of a threat. To Terrorize is the deliberate incitement of fear as a method of causing a presupposing a much greater degree of violence. *Intimidation* methods—whether by immediate actions or by implications--manipulate victims to use their own fears or weaknesses against themselves as psychological weapons. The effect is that victims are forced to do something they do not want to do or forced not to do something they want or need to do.

If European Intimidation is analogized to a "Star," then what Black gang members have done is to extract aspects out of the "Halo" of that "Star." Hence, the GUN is the "Street Code's" symbol of intimidation, of power, and of the remedy for disputes in the harsh External environment of "Street" youth. For Black gangs, guns are mainly as intimidators -- not trying to injure or kill anyone for personal reasons but rather to display a sense of willingness to commit a lethal act for purposes of dominance (Stretesky, J. *Contemporary Ethnography, 2007*).

GANG VIOLENCE: Gang violence is a way to express masculinity when opportunities to pursue conventional roles are unavailable. Those with defiant individualism, who are small in number, select into gangs because gangs offer means to achieve paramount goals. Group processes enable gang members to do things—particularly violent things—they would not do alone. Violence plays an important and acceptable role in the subculture of people living in socially isolated environments and economically deprived areas because violence provides a means for a member to demonstrate his toughness, and displays of violent retaliation establish socialization within the gang. In the context of physical violence, it is about facing danger as a result of another's threatening behavior or testing of ones willingness to use physical force when insulted by someone outside of the group. Violence begets violence because an attack on one gang member is an attack against all members. The result is a closed "feedback loop" of retaliation and revenge. Guns often help gang members project their violent identities since it is a symbol and actuality of power as well as a remedy for disputes. Despite the legal restrictions that theoretically limit gun access to most gang members, gun ownership and use is commonplace among gang members.

Guns are typically carried at certain times of the day or week or when there was a perceived threat. The actual use of a firearm is for a situation that most lethally expresses the power of guns within the context of attempting to injure those belonging to rival gangs. One youth said: "When I was younger, we used to do drive-bys. It didn't matter who you were. We didn't go after a specific person. We went after a specific group. Whoever is standing at a particular house or wherever you may be, and you're grouped up and have the wrong color on; just because you were in a rival gang. You didn't have to do anything to us to come get you, it was a spontaneous reaction. There's a lot of brutality, there is a lot of murder around us. There is a lot of violence, period. There are enemies and all. A lot of pressure, you know. If you're not going to do this, then they're going to do it to you. I'd rather get caught with a gun than without. The perceived fear for potential harm caused this female gang member to carry a gun with her outside her home. When she expresses the violence prevalent in her environment, she implies how random threats can often occur, seeing the necessity to harm rivals before they harm her. When a member of this culture feels disrespected or his manhood is challenged, he feels justified in exacting justice through the barrel of a gun. It is this psychology of the survival of the self that causes innocent victims to get caught in cross fires, and young men to lose their lives through death or incarceration. These individuals who are afflicted with this inordinate desire not to be shamed or have their manhood tested make up the larger segment of this factor. The lives of others are of less value than the image they have of themselves. When that image is challenged, confrontation is the consequence, and violence is more than likely the result.

DISRESPECT--"THE STREETS" TRIGGER FOR VIOLENCE: Like Respect, there are Spiritual and Earth World categories of Disrespect. The "Dis-" in "Disrespect" is a prefix that means the opposite of; lack of; not; apart; or away from respect. Because of its effect on the Law of Sympathy, Black people have a lower tolerance for their children--or for anyone--being disrespectful than perhaps in any other culture. African *Spiritual Disrespect is an assault on ones Dignity* and that is anti-Love--whether to God, to human beings, or to other creatures or creations. Earth world Disrespect varies with the group or with the individual and consists of the opposite of what the person or group deems to be respectful. Regardless of its features, Ancient Africans said Earthly Disrespect is "the eating of ones self-esteem." The magnitude of disrespect shown by Europeans to the Slaves and its long term repercussions have been unequalled in world history. One of its ramifications following slavery was intra-Black social dissention (which limited the development of group unity) and perpetual intra-group conflict, jealousy, and mistrust—each of which, in the face of rejection and oppression, bred disrespect for the self and for others like the self. The persistence of this pattern explains much of the envy existing between Blacks and for the acts of Black-on-Black violence. White Americas continue to show Black people a lack of respect; rudeness; impoliteness; and discourtesy on all rungs of the social ladder. Such a subdued savage mindset shown by Europeans is a major cause of their overwhelming fear in daily living. Europeans' disrespectful expressions or deeds related to threats to or disturbances or destructions of Black people's dignity has generated chronic anger, especially in Black "Street" youth. Disrespect (i.e. challenging self-identity or self-image) in gang vernacular—a "loss of face"--invariably leads to retaliatory violence, for any affront to ones or ones gang's self-image spurs the use of the gun in order to "Save Face."

Enslaved African American learned the Secular context of "Honor" from Euro-American captors where it was either a capital offense or a call for a duel for a White man to disrespect or "diss" another. That concept has been culturally transmitted to "Honor of the Streets." Meanwhile, the African definition of Disrespect was replaced--either by more profound versions (as the Slaves properly feeling disrespected by everything having to do with slavery) or by diluted and polluted versions. For example, in the 1970s Black "Street" youth had "Respect" at the heart of their code and loosely defined it as being treated "right" or granted the deference one deserves (Anderson, in Ault--Race and Ethnicity, p203). Yet, the racism and self-defeating Slave Survival forces they faced were so overwhelming as to make unclear to them what constituted "Disrespect." Euro-Americans continue not to treat Black Americans with a sense of fair play; continue not to respect them; and continue to show no significant ability to engage in African Tradition type harmony or unity. These factors, present for almost 500 years in the Americas, have caused many Black Americans to "copycat" European disrespect practices.

Thus, model "Street" youth originally followed is primarily that of Europeans--whose issue of "Manhood Respect" requires the display of a certain amount of violence to convey the message of being able to take care of oneself. Mainly through television and videos Black "Street" youth learn that "might is right," "toughness is a virtue," and similar European social meanings of fighting. Adults of the "Street" subculture perpetuate this by such comments as: "Watch your back"; "Protect yourself"; "Don't punk out"; "If somebody messes with you, you got to pay them back"; and "If someone disses you, you got to straighten them out." These promote the building of "*Nerve*"--i.e. striving to be at a "no fear" state of mind. In other words, to these delusional youth the clear risk of violent "life or limb" destruction is preferable to being "dissed" by another (Bailey, Manhood p217).

The reaction of Black youth to these Background factors caused practically all to be hypersensitive ("like a raw nerve") and to display disrespect and/or not "take disrespect" from anybody in general and Europeans in particular. Yet, the effects of slavery "beat the Spirit" (courage) out of them to the point of not retaliating against White people. So, many have displaced their bubbling over aggressions on each other. Those behaviors of many struggling Black youth are influenced by a "Street Culture Code" that prescribes violent reactions to interpersonal attacks and shows of disrespect (Brezina, Youth Violence and Juvenile Justice, 2004). To lose respect in the ghetto is to be "dissed" (disrespected) and disgraced -- the "kiss of death" to ones self-image. Being "Dissed" is to have ones system of values attacked. Attacks for some occur when another violates ones space (e.g. wagging a finger in ones face); for others, someone continuing to bother them by violating their boundaries when asked not to; and for still others, the lacking of a deserved honor.

Anger bordering on rage happens when rivals *challenged ones "Self-Identity"*--i.e. meaning being Disrespected. Hence, the gang has no tolerance for interpersonal transgressions since this is a display of weakness to others and will likely become the target of further transgressions. Transgressions against the self—even the appearance of transgression—must be avenged. One must demonstrate a taste for violent counterattack; otherwise, one appears weak and runs the risk of being "rolled on" or physically assaulted "by any number of others" (Anderson, 1999, p. 73). Adherence to the "Code" is not simply a reflection of corrupt values or deviant socialization. Rather, it represents in part an adaptation to status insecurity and to the persistent threat of violence that is present in some urban communities. In such communities, many young men believe that enactment of the "Code" is a necessary aspect of "Street" survival whether or not they are personally inclined to physical aggression and whether or not they are completely committed to elements of the "Code" (Anderson). In fact, mainstream people may feel that true "nerve" is displayed by walking away from a fight.

"Street" youth take personally this lack of respect and therefore place "Respect" as an almost external entity that is hard-won but easily lost. The importance of such a reputation is highlighted by the fact that, in certain communities, "there are always people around looking for a fight"—people who actively campaign for respect on the streets by taking it away from others. One youth said: "Violence starts to escalate once you start to disrespect me. Once you start to second guess my manhood, I'll f**k you up. You start coming at me with threats, then I feel offended. Once I feel offended, I react violently. That's how I was taught to react." An extremely serious breach of gang etiquette is to threaten ones masculinity by not recognizing another's status: "When someone disrespects me, they are putting my manhood in jeopardy. They are saying my words are s**t, or putting my family in danger. . . . Most of the time, I do it [use violence] to make people feel the pain or hurt that I feel. I don't know no other way to do it, as far as expressing myself any other way."

Furthermore, most struggling Black communities have no confidence in the ability or desire of the police to provide adequate protection—a reality which has spurred the "Code" embodying a set of informal rules and expectations. The failure to conform to them has severe consequences. Anderson says that unless youth are completely immersed in the "Code" behavior, they "code-switch"—i.e. conform to the expectations of the "Code" in public encounters—where it may be necessary or justified—while conforming to more conventional norms in private settings. Whatever "Respect" they have requires constant surveillance as part of the guarding process and an "Emergency Brain" mindset that is ever ready to defend it. The way of life in "the Streets" seems to be aimed at gaining, enhancing, or maintaining respect--or at least to not lose it.

The Code provides a framework for negotiating respect. Ones clothing, demeanor, "the walk, the talk, and the look" are designed to deter transgressions. Since "Respect" is so scarce in the ghetto, there are continual "dog fights" in the "Streets" to either grab as much as possible (mainly by "Bad Dudes") or to prevent losing the Command Appearance of "manhood" (by "Decent Dudes"). Nevertheless, the bigger picture is gang rivalry, with destruction coming from such old-fashioned conflicts as: "I got to teach you a lesson" or "somebody-done-somebody-wrong" killings -- perhaps over drugs, a girl, or some ill-defined type of disrespect. Any rival who violates the gang's unwritten rules with disrespect has to be made an "example of" by punishing with such cruelty as to attempt to intimidate any would-be rule violators. However, evil actions only make for outrage in the kin of the member "taken down" and in this way a feud may start--and some continue indefinitely (e.g. "Bloods vs. Crips"). The aspects of disrespect and "make an example of" are direct transfers from how slave owners dealt with the Enslaved and how today's courts work. Both are signs that Euro-Americans racists have set up effective self-generating models whereby they can still control a segment of Black People without being physically present.

GANG LIFE'S COURSE VS. POLICE

The Mental Emulsions present in the minds of many Black and White Americans is a reflection of the interactions of the nature of their respective philosophies--philosophies acting like oil and water in that they do not mix. Of significance here is that the philosophy of African Tradition is centered on God, the Metaphysical Realms (including the Spiritual), the Spiritual-Supernatural, and the Spiritual Elements (Unconditional Love, Truth, Reality, and the Natural). What does not mix with this is the Brute ("Aryan") European philosophy that is "Inside-Out" with respect to African Tradition--i.e. in opposite worlds. By being anti-Spiritual Elements oriented means what they think, feel, say, and do makes no sense to the remainder of the world. However, because of the GUN, with an ongoing reality of using it to Kill/Take/Destroy, their Satanists ways dominate and lead astray (e.g. by delusions) peoples of the world by means of "sameness" patterns--a 'big picture' Kill/Take/Destroy/Dominate model dating to their European beginnings. With respect to "Killer" police in a showdown with Black gangs, no gang is a match since Europeans have perfected to an ultimate degree their ability to fight and kill. Nevertheless, there are many Brain/Mind similarities between the police and gangs.

BRAIN/POWER USAGE OF "KILLER" GANGS & "KILLER" POLICE: There is not a great deal of difference between White policemens and Black gangs because they think so much alike but for different reasons. Although the police are not likely to be beatened in physical confrontations with any gang, there are ways a gang can use the police to their advantage as part of the process of becoming untangled from their influence. Such requires understanding in detail how they evolved, what they think, and why they think like they do in order to also be able to better defend and/or get around any police misconduct. Three levels of human power are: (1) Physical; (2) Intellect (occurring among those who compete higher up on the Social Ladder—"the pen is mightier than the sword"); and (3) Spiritual Elements (for those at the top of the Humanity Ladder). Pure Intellect and Spiritual Power come from looking within for answers—and this is what is needed to get back to ones Real Self to start the process of healing. However, gang members are fixated on Physical Power and that comes from gathering and internalizing anti-Spiritual Elements forces in the the External World.

These forms of power derive from specialized portions of a human's brain. The part of greatest concern here is the *Ancient Brain* which includes the Cerebellum, the Brainstem (upper portion of the spinal cord, the Basal Ganglia, the Diencephalon, Medulla, Pons), and parts of the Mid-brain. Three fundamental subdivisions of the Ancient Brain are the Instinct, Omnibus, and Brute portions. Although on all worldly levels of power there are those who use deception and accoutrements to be who they are not, the focus here is on those specializing in *Accouterment GUN Power.* As "Killers," they operate out of the Brute part of their Ancient Brain. Some are socialized to believe they are 'little gods" but are always insecure about having to prove it or maintain their façade appearance.

The majority have personal insecurities but assume a mindset façade that they are "superior" when, in fact they feel just the opposite. Both types have an obsession and compulsion to generate "Excitement" within the context of self-interest purposes—e.g. to "Take" what belongs to others, or to prop up their shakey Self-Esteem beliefs in being "superior' or out of religions reason (e.g. light must destroy the "dark" or "black"). Being chronically and deeply unhappy are Triggers (among others) for them to hate those they select as scapegoats. Whatever cues pertaining to these scapegoats come in from the outside world, does so as 'toned' information passed through tinted (i.e. biased) emotional lens. It enters their brains and influences its brainstem (including its Brute Brain and Medulla Oblongata). However, what is generally overlooked is the *Cerebellum*—which, though normally thought of to be about coordinating the human body's movement, has strong psychological features. What the Cerebellum does for movement (e.g. tells legs to start walking and do it smoothly and in balance), it also does something similar for ones personality, emotions, and intellect—all disturbed by input. For example, because of Cerebellum input one is not introspective, perhaps resulting from the prominence given to ones nonrational thinking and its associated Emotions.

One cannot get into deeper levels of conversations required to build strong personal relationships or deep friendships from not knowing how to show emotions or how to behave in social situations. All of these make more acute Psychological Conditioned Reflex or Response reactions towards perceived enemies. The *Pons* connects the Cerebellum with the cerebral cortex—and all are primarily involved. A function of the *Medulla Oblongata* is its reflex action—i.e. sending a motor impulse to any part of the body before the sensation resulting in that impulse reaches the brain—impulses which enter deep nuclear regions where there are nerve fiber loops within loops. Received there are motor commands formulated in other brain regions which, in turn, are extended down to spinal motor pools to account for motor control. When the brain is stimulated by given psychological factors to which the Brute is sensitive (e.g. "dark" or "black"), the cerebral motor cortex receives instructions from other cortical areas to react in the Cerebellum. Repetition of this psychological input pattern leads to plasticity learning in the Cerebellum's neuronal circuitry.

Once that happens the cerebral motor cortex acts directly through the Cerebellum, via the loop connection existing between the cerebellum and motor cortex as well as loops between the prefrontal cortical area and the Cerebellum. These actions cause sentiments (thoughts, ideas, concepts wrapped in emotions) to be manipulated to make them increasingly automatic and less and less of a conscious nature. Gradually, their Brute Brain forms Philosophical/Psychological Reflex reactions. Whenever certain triggering conditions are in place, Brute Europeans have automatic negative associations with Blacks (or other non-White groups) with stereotypic ways of reacting to them. This is regardless of their focused attention at that moment, or of recent thinking, or of their current goals and attention. Because they are automatic, their early biases— constantly reinforced by "following their leaders"--are inevitable and their influence is nearly impossible to alter. Correction for these problems is with the Sankofa approach or whatever it takes for one to return to ones Real Self. Then, by using the Bridge Method—i.e. establishing Human Ideal goals—proceed to go "straight ahead." Let old ways die.

"KILLER" POLICE vs BLACK GANG ACTIONS: A 'big picture' recognized by practically all Black Americans is that the Police and Black People in general (especially Black males) and Black gangs in particular are enemies. Because of the importance of racial and personal (Self and "Manhood") Identity by those involved, there is a mutual complementary need for Enemies. The background is that European Warriors, Religious people, and Pseudo-Intellectuals are like different waves in the same ocean. This "ocean" represents the primitive European mother womb. Thus, its triplet off-springs share the same "Normal Variant" Philosophy of Life (POL)—all joining forces to generate rip currents (dark paths of calm water) that can "suck in" the naïve and thereafter being in control of the minds of the naïve. A *Rip current* (fig. 21) is a strong and usually narrow surface of water flowing outward from a shore. It results from the return flow of waves and wind-driven water. Surfers often take advantage of rip currents for a ride out to sea. A swimmer caught in a rip current is in much more danger than a surfer because the current flow is faster than a human swimmer can swim. Besides, to swim against the current is exhausting, like being in a vicious cycle.

Since all Black Americans with Ancestors dating to African American slavery have Europeans as their basic 'role models,' the overwhelming majority have imitated the think, feel, express, actions, and reactions of Europeans. This is most spotlighted by Black gang members. The main problem is that these Black Americans are like swimmers caught in a rip current and have no idea how to escape. The most desperate have been beaten down so much by the rip currents as to have turned their POL and thinking patterns "Inside-Out." An expression of this is that despite being told they might be able to escape the rip current by swimming parallel to shore or instructed that floating along the current past the surf line (where the rip current disappears) is also an option, "Inside-Out" victims ignore this advice. Instead, they try to swim against the rip current or give up trying to do anything because they find themselves such a long way from shore that swimming back would require too much time, energy, and effort. They simply accept what happens to them as: "Its my fate!"—and "Make Do."

Still, European Warriors police + Black officers who imitate them + Black gangs share much in common. Both enhance their respective in-groups by spotlighting intolerance expressions for each other and, to a lesser extent, for out-groups on the periphery out-skirts of the spotlight. The weak people in both stem from childhood—the police being conditioned to hate Black People—Black gang members who suffered from childhood deprivation—as well as both having significant Insecurities which cause anxieties about their abilities to perform when their "Manhood" is tested. Once individuals in both groups blame the other out-group for their personal situations, they continue to defend against unwanted internal feelings by maintaining their attack—the police on Black People—Black gangs on other Black gangs andBlack People. Added to Black ethnic intolerance is the ongoing lack of opportunity for social advancement and pressures on them are increased in times of economic distress for both Black and White people.

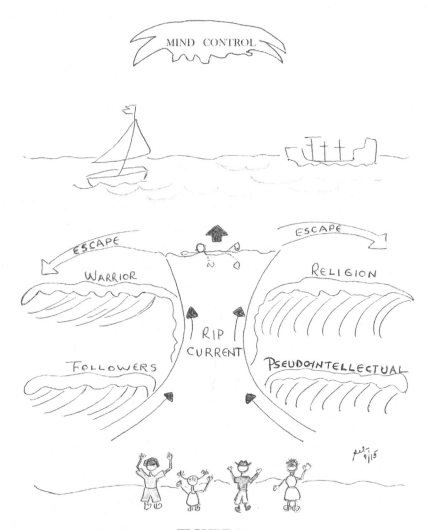

FIGURE 21

European experts explain the European need for enemies to establish their identity—a need arising around 4 to 6 months of age from *"Stranger Anxiety"*. Stranger anxiety is a form of distress that children experience when exposed to people unfamiliar to them (Moore). Symptoms may include: getting quiet and staring at the stranger, verbally protesting by cries or other vocalizations, and hiding behind a parent. It is accompanied by an upsurge of aggression that leads to *Displacement* (an unconscious defense mechanism of transferring emotional reactions from one Thing to another)--the, establishing of a precursor mental Icon Image for the individualized idea of an enemy or a scapegoat. An Effect of Displacement among Brute Europeans is their relieving tension by "taking it out" on an innocent or on a previously Targeted Person(s), as on Black People. A driving force is from the delusional concept of needing to have the courage to preserve their lives and lands (territorialism).

Another is to be a hero, as derived from a sense of obligation they felt from belonging to their ethnic and national groups (ethnic identity). Displacement is manifest among Black gangs similar to what the spanked child does to relieve tension. Since he does not dare strike his mother, he kicks his little brother or breaks a toy instead. Such feigned enemies are needed by weak people as external stabilizers for their own sense of identity and inner control. In gang aggression, ones "Manhood" rests on mental representations, especially when under stress. Similar to the driving force in European males, the defense of territory—'turf wars'--is a motivating factor in gangs.

It has been typical for struggling Black People to express hopelessness regarding the hostile police situation--regarding the police as "bullies in uniform"—all agreeing officers would never see them as anything other than symbolic assailants, even when they were engaged in entirely lawful activity. Compared to Whites, young Blacks had "virtually *no* conception of the police as guardians" and most agree that if the police are called in a problematic situation, they will be worse off. Black youth are angered by frequent and seemingly arbitrary police pedestrian and vehicle stops—some saying they wished officers would generally stay out of their neighborhoods unless called upon. They take particular exception to the way officers verbally abuse them during these encounters, believing officers intentionally use inciting hostile language to provoke them to respond in kind so as to justify an assault or arrest. Even White youth have reported that the officers' uncivil language of the most vile kind (racial slurs, profanity) are reserved for Black males.

Such verbal abuse challenges these males' "Manhood" and thus often causes impulsive destructive reaction which have terrible long-term consequences—practically, behaviorally, and symbolically. Thus, it is usual for Black youth, from ever sensing powerless and expecting antagonism when they encounter sadistic policemen, try their best to avoid them. Black People know there is no one to whom the police are accountable for gross misconduct. I have personally learned that. Yet, a budding trend is a new atmosphere of amplified animosity in which the police are being villifed by a public on Twitter, YouTube, and other social media sites. A routine traffic stop may be recorded by dashboard video, body cameras, or nearby cellphones. Increasing numbers of policemen are being sued, investigated, arrested and indicted, and getting killed, even by ambush. Police are now saying: "These days, if I don't know you, I'm going to be extra guarded around you."

"KILLER" POLICE FORCEFUL ENCOUNTERS WITH "STREET" YOUTH: Police decisions to use force in potentially violent encounters can be crudely analyzed in stages: Stage I is becoming aware of potential suspects by such Trigger factors as: (1) the demographic profile of the youth (male, low social class, from a broken family and deprived neighborhood); (2) the youth's involvement in serious offending and other risky behaviors (e.g. illegal drug use and underage drinking)—especially if persistent; (3) propensity to be visible in public places outside the purview of parents; (4) keeping the 'wrong' company; and (5) most importantly, earlier experience of police contact, both personally and vicariously through others. Once youngsters come under the purview of the police, they then become part of the permanent suspect population and, as a consequence, any of their friends and associates who have not had past experience of adversarial police contact, become suspect too. This cycle of labelling contributes to further and indeed more serious forms of contact by 500% (Mcara, *Criminal Justice, 2005)*. Stage II is an initial stage of anticipation where officers receive information prior to the direct encounter (e.g. over the police radio) concerning brief details of the incident needing a response, information regarding offending behavior, and a history of the person of interest. Stage III is the initial contact where officers gather information directly, as by observing the scene and person of interest—e.g. violent behavior and the presence of deadly weapons. Stage IV involves information exchange between the officer and the person of interest, usually a dialogue but also including nonverbal behaviour.

Stage V is the final decision, or final frame--for example where an officer decides to shoot or not shoot a suspect. Each stage involves information gathering and interpretation by the officers that leads to the final decision, and possible difficulties can arise due to information ambiguity, absence, or error; interpretive bias and prejudices; and a conditioned response. Otherwise, even without a warrant the police generally make an arrest for a crime committed or attempted in their presence as well as when they decide to have reasonable ground to believe the arrested person has committed a felony despite not in their presence. It is typical for an arrest to be made and, in theory, Necessary force may be used to effect the arrest. A legal arrest confers authority upon the arresting officer to search the prisoner thoroughly for weapons. The Black or Brown prisoner is then taken into custody and then to the police station to "make the arrest known" so the prisoner may answer a charge of crime. If suspects cannot pay bail, they are kept in jail without any definite charge or forced to plea guilty in order to get out.

As soon as possible thereafter the prisoner is taken to court for a preliminary arraignment, often called a pretrial hearing—which means a 'loss of control' power for the police since the court system takes control. In general, the more eager a policeman is to perform his duty by arresting criminals, the more tempted he is to ignore, and even violate the suspect's constitutional rights. That stigma of arrest is devastating for community residents who are trying to make a living in an already pre-existing daily struggle. An advantage for Whites is that a criminal records takes away much of the voting power which Black People have used against them—even at the price of getting killed.

Not all potentially violent confrontations include all stages, with options apparently available at the final stage often being influenced or constrained by what has occurred in the previous stages. Yet, these generic stages are useful for assessing the rightness or wrongness of the police having killed someone—but always in conjunction with the Coroner. The investigation questions are to include: if there was--between the police and the deceased at the time of the initial encounter--visual contact, verbal contact, and/or there physical contact. Did the death occur during a custody-related operation; during an attempt to detain the deceased; or as a result of a siege. The Coroner's job includes identifying the deceased; determining the date and place of death; determine the manner and cause of death (including the circumstances surrounding the death); and, if applicable, make recommendations to the appropriate authorities to prevent a death in similar circumstances occurring in the future (Porter *Australian & New Zealand Journal of Criminology, 2013*).

ENDING THE CULTURE OF STREET CRIME

The ending of "Street Culture" Violence involves each individual gang member, each gang, and each community coming to terms with what is in their best interest so that they, as a group, can be as solid voice to advocate policy changes in the local government and in how to deal with the police. Each individual gang member and any given gang can first learn about themselves by doing this in conjunction with analyzing the police, since there are great similarities between them. This starts with the Brain/Mind assessment in relation to Power.

LEADERSHIP FOR ENDING "STREET CULTURE": The leaders of the gang situation are the most influential to pave the 'ending of the violence culture. Also, to be emphasized is those former gang members who left the gang and legitimately succeeded in the marketplace because they know the gang problem from A to Z. In other words, the fastest and most effective way to end or significantly reduce the gang issue are those most acquainted with the "Street" crime culture, who have gone through the transformational process, and who have the cooperation of community members. By sitting at a "round table" they ought to be empowered to use their unique experience and street knowledge to end it. Generalizations are to be shed. For example, gangs are conceived as a violent cultural expression of self-inflicted deprivation; 'gang culture' a sub facet of the 'culture of poverty'. To assume all suspected gang members share the same criminal intent wrongly criminalizes some of the most disadvantaged youth and thus they need to be distinguished. Another misconception is of unemployment being purely the responsibility of unemployed individuals who are unwilling to work when typically there is a willful disregard for the lack of labor market demand. That is the primary cause of youth unemployment today. But it is true that the toxic impact of poverty increases the risk of violent behavior, which can become normalized both in the home and on the street (Cottrell-Boyce *Youth Justice, 2013*).

METHODS FOR ENDING "STREET CULTURE": In the 1990s, since the historical course showed that police brutality functions as 'delegated vigilantism' against perceived social threats by Black People, the rapper Ice-T recommended that Black gangs be "Cop Killers"—and that created a tremendous uproar nation-wide. It is not the answer! What does have a good chance of working is for the gang and the Black community to come together as a solid front for going to the local government with a list of demands. One demand is to weed out those policemen who are not suited for the Black Community. Most of these include European males who have a "culture shock" by being around Black People are not suitable for policing the Black community and the Black policemen who are puppets for the White establishment. The reaction of these policemen is typically being cocky and dismissive of an misconduct on their part, including engaging in senseless killings. They concoct versions for their misdeeds of what will be acceptable for the Network that protects them and the media elaborates on those deceptive comments.

Second is for the gang and the Black community to decide what is likely to work best. Policing interventions and legal instruments targeting gangs and gang membership are inefficient and carry the potential to criminalize and further alienate young people. The criminal justice system would better abandon the term [gang] and focus instead on the problem behaviors--i.e. prolific offending of varying types and seriousness amongst associated networks of individuals. A focus on violent behavior is more meaningful to youth 'who may not have perceived their "gang membership" to be anything more than hanging around with their friends'. It is best for behavior-focused interventions (e.g. the 'Boston model') and the government to invest resources in such strategies which offer clear incentives to desist from violent behavior, as opposed to its current 'drag net' approach targeting gang-membership.

Third, help is needed from mental health specialists about other beneficial organizations and method. Some include: (1) Multi-Systemic Therapy, for example, which takes a whole family approach to youth offending and other issues; (2) improve the quality of education delivered to pupils excluded from mainstream schools; (3) place youth work teams engage with the victims of serious youth violence; (4) provide jobs; (5) recruit volunteers who are in employment to go into schools and 'raise young people's aspirations; and (6) get the help of the young people involved in how 'to exit gang life'. It is more effective and efficient to target specific patterns of violent behavior rather than gang membership for preventative and enforcement attention.

Fourth, seek out organizations dealing with similar issues for advice. For example, the conflicting ideologies advanced by the Coalition in Support of the Gang Truce (CSGT) is illustrative of paradoxes (Pihos, *J. Urban History, 2011*). CSGT, established after a 1992 truce between the Crips and Bloods, endeavors to repair the fault lines pervading South Central Los Angeles. Its familiar "social critique" of contemporary law enforcement measures coexists with its use of Amer-I-Can's "self-help" program. Founded by football Hall of Famer Jim Brown to assist gang members in adapting to the American mainstream, the program seeks personal transformation based on the notion that "individuals' fates are within their own control. . . . Success is . . . a matter of having discipline and perseverance". Amer-I-Can offers a window into how broader ideologies of "individual responsibility" are transported to the ghetto. The "sense of self-worth and agency" that it inculcates might enable political organizing, but it also replicates the individualist ideology underlying state retrenchment. By making success a matter of self-reliance, it disguises the structural inequalities faced by the population it serves and displaces responsibility for inequality from politics onto the individual. Expecting people marginalized by contemporary policies to create expansive solidarities in the face of their exclusion is surely an unfair burden.

Fifth, determine if there a police willing to work with the Black community and Black gang members. If so, despite underlying delusions based upon ongoing world-wide mis-education those Black and White Americans will have aspects of their philosophies which are mutually beneficial, --philosophies capable of acting like water and alcohol blending into a *Solution*. The Background setting for such discussions is that a major difference is White people benefit from racism while Black People are devastated by it, and to such a degree that each take life paths in different directions out of their Mental Emulsions. Some join the flow of White people's ways; some stay on a treadmill; some react badly; some progress far ahead. Each of these is to be dealt with so as to 'level the playing field.' From this information gathering the appropriate people can make the appropriate recommendations by targeting the stage/stages associated with where the keystone problem occurred, followed by dealing with the satellite aspects which make for excessive and unnecessary risks for all concerned.

Perhaps the primary ones concern improvements to police training, including their response to high-risk situations or the prospect of a specialised response unit to teach the officer how to specifically respond to ambiguous situations and to make appropriate decisions. If it is discovered the officer's behaviors have not been in line with proper training or if there were reactions out of panic in a rapidly unfolding, dangerous and unfamiliar situation, then these need to be definitively handled. If re-education and re-training are not feasible, then the officer can be considered for relief of front line duty (e.g. reassigned to a desk job) or dismissed altogether.

MANAGEMENT FOR ENDING "STREET CULTURE":The 'big picture' for how struggling Black People can untangle from their Mental Emulsions is by the *Sankofa approach: (1)* return to African Tradition to learn Principles of how to; (2) Prepare in the present; (3) in order to go forward into a Thriving future. But there are many problems involved in carrying this out. First, time must be made in ones life to apply the energy and effort to do the hard and tedious work. Second, one must use the *Spiritual Energy Package* of dedication, commitment, loyalty, determination, persistence, and perseverance to not give up—to never succumb to attractive distractions--to always give ones best effort—and to achieve the goal in the most efficient and effective manner. Each of these six is like the links in a chain and each is needed to complete any worthwhile task while driving away ones Emotional Energy powered Ego (*False Self*). Third, one must be obsessive and compulsive in seeking the absolute truthfulness that is only found in African philosophy. There can be inclusion of any European information, including no definitions. Truth will not be found in anything written by Europeans, no matter how close it gets to SEEMING right.

Fourth is knowing where to look. There are a small handful of Black scholars who write the best available Black History. Also, since migrating Africans went into all regions of the Earth and carried their philosophies with them, certain cultures modified them but less so than others. Thus, many useful African Tradition concepts can be found in certain Chinese and Indian (both Amerindians and India) sources. However, any thing lacking Order, Regularity, Coherence, Consistency, Compatibility, Balance, Harmony, and Predictability inside the Spiritual Elements is not part of African Tradition. Fifth, it is absolutely essential to clear ones mind of all Emotional Junk (e.g. hate, revenge, envy, blame, con-artistry). For me this is best done by writing it out until there is nothing else to say. The objective is to get to a state of profound peace, even though things may be chaotic and require chronic juggling. Remaining calm helps clear the way for figuring out workable solutions while avoiding more trouble.

In the pursuit of life-changing and life-shaping knowledge, what has never worked for me is to "pick and choose" what I like. Typically, the most 'pearls' have come from the boring, the difficult, and the so hard to understand that I have to wrestle with it and look up words in hopes of getting a different slant on what is trying to be conveyed. For one to say: "I'm too busy" is simply an excuse to hide that one is either too lazy or too fearful (e.g. of what will be discovered; of leaving the familiar; of getting lost along the way). If that works, then stay in the status quo--which is actually likely to get worse as one ages. If one truly loves oneself, then one will want the very best for oneself in this lifetime and thereby do what it takes to get on the path to being happy. For those willing to work, there will be the amazing discovery of realizing how Ancient African Ancestors laid the foundation for all that is great today. At that point one will ask: "Why do I allow others to guide me in wrong directions?" and "Why do I accept information (all flawed) from stupid or evil people and disregard the true Knowledge (Certainty) of my own Ancient African Ancestors?" jabaileymd.com

SUMMARY

Although a given Black gang adopts unique identifying features, they have a certain "sameness" within their gang as well as in relation to other gangs. Black gang generic "sameness" is that members hangs out together, wearing certain colors, types of clothing, hand signals, argot or in-group speech idioms, emblems, and tattoos. They have set clear boundaries of their "territory or turf" (which they do not own) and protect members and turf against other rival gangs through fighting or threats. The "sameness" of all Black gangs is an imitation of the "Halo" of Brute European males' Disaster Star, but not the "Star" itself. Features of the Brute European males Disaster Star include them being drawn to very forms of violence out of being socialized to it; from choosing to have a Brute Brain mindset; because of it being a historical "second nature"; and because it satisfies the way they choose to live life, for there is "sick" pleasure in wallowing in their brutish animal nature and the adventure associated with making that happen. And they will never change.

What dictates all Black gangs "Uniqueness" is the various forms of poverty out of which they arise, and that has significant distinguishing features. Examples may be horrendous problems from living in impoverished homes and neighborhoods that offer them little hope or opportunity for socially acceptable pathways to success. This makes it an easy next step to develop a moral code of behavior outside the flow of the mainstream—e.g. disregard prohibitions against committing antisocial actions, particularly when such actions are associated with the means to obtain financial success (e.g. dealing illicit drugs) or ensuring safety (e.g. joining a gang) or feeling better about themselves. Yet, whether they gain or not, these activities invite moral condemnation from parents, teachers, and others—and the effect may have been for them to temper at least some of their criminal activity. Those restraints are likely to disappear once they join a gang where crime and violence are "what's happening—and it can become addictive based on the material benefits and from a sense of belonging. To be consided for acceptance or even recently initiated as a gang member on the "Streets" or in prison prompts the setting aside of existing moral standards--either unconsciously or deliberately--so that the individual's social way of thinking fits with what one perceive as gang membership requirements to engage in illegal behavior. They then adopt or develop pro-gang, pro-crime patterns.

For this to happen requires the development of a "*Numbness Anti-Compassion Armor*" used to isolate them from the pain and misery they caused others. This becomes layered as they continue to be shaped by their gang membership and that slowly erases any objection to believing that violence is justified. An ability to morally disengage is linked with an increased use of violence. The more they see violence as justified then the more likely they are to use it, even displacing it onto undeserving others to "save face" and maintain/acquire status. But this has a boomerang effect in causing them to know "deep down" that this is wrong and not what their lives are supposed to be about. Meanwhile, the chances for random targeting of any given opposing gang member increases when it is uncertain as who started a given current conflict (e.g. a drive-by shooting situation). Such has a ripple effect in raising the potential that *any and all* members of a rival gang are justified targets of violence since they are all the same. Inter-gang violence even fueled by rivals who look alike all become justifiable targets.

Since at no time in Black American history has there been a focus on achieving the American Dream" because all efforts have simply been on trying to survive day-to-day, in general gang members' School and scholar aspirations are private matters, not to be publicly valued or promoted among gang peers. Furthermore, these are not compatible with the use of their Omnibus Brain dominate usage. Thus, for gang members, school is social rather than academic. Instead, gangs redefine success in the group context, where the acquisition of respect and status enhancement is earned by way of physical prowess, athleticism, "street smarts," wit, and tough banter. Yet, the most salvageable are the "Dreamers" who want to "Be Somebody," those who have been most exposed to the Spiritual God of African Tradition (even in the form of Black American Customs), and those having an incomplete "Numbness Anti-Compassion Armor" (which wears off while having time to be quiet in prison).

A pervading self-defeating gang mindset is one that says: "Since I'm human it is okay to make mistakes—and besides, what difference does it make?" This leads one to personally feel and do things that are about weaknesses, limitations, flaws. They easily and quickly stray off course by the pull of "attractive distractions" or because "I can't do it." Obviously, *a chain is no stronger than its weakest link* Examples include some link being incomplete, deformed, missing, or weak. Correction comes from troubleshooting to discover all the problems and then fixing those problems so as to strive for Perfection. The objective is to get the links of the chain to be complete, strong, and flowing together in the same direction and at the same speed and toward the same destination. A starting process of correction is to get these gang members involved in Nature, for that brings harmony to their Selfhoods and gives them a hint of how great a "Thing" of Nature, including themselves, really is.

What worked for me was the reinforcing of my Nature education by the various kinds of work I did--e.g. household jobs simply from being part of the family (e.g. washing the car; working the flower and vegetable gardens; washing windows every Saturday morning; painting the house); to help elderly neighbors do this or that; to work selling newspapers and magazines, shining shoes, cutting grass, cleaning people's homes, etc.; and, of particular importance, being completely responsible for my dog. These things did not allow me to cater to any whim of "not feeling like doing it" or "doing it when I felt like it." Rather, if I did not do it then it would not get done. In short, success is in the details. Ref: Bailey, Rational Thinking.

CHAPTER XII

DISRESPECTED DIGNITY

EATS

ONES SELF-ESTEEM

WOMEN & VIOLENCE

When children sing 'on-key' their pitch sound matches the tone without being flat or sharp as well as matches the intended interval of the melody or harmony written for the song. If they were to sing the wrong notes as indicated by the music or deviate from the correct tone or pitch, the result would be somewhat irregular, abnormal, or incongruous—a situation called "Off-Key" or "out of tune." There are Mild, Slight, Moderate, and Extreme degrees of being "out of tune"--meaning progressively being inaccurate in pitch; singing one or more "false (or sour) notes"; or being in disharmony. To be ones Real Self in "Life-Living" is to be "On-Key"—in tune with ones Selfhood and life. To be Mildly "Off-Key" is to be in a "Normal Variant" state of Selfhood. Ones Selfhood or "Life-Living" that is in the Slight, Moderate, and Extreme degree is to be "out of tune" or "Off-Key."

Children reared to be their Real Selves are allowed to self-develop with strategic periodic guidance in a safe and congenial environment. However, the way most female children are reared is Mildly "Off-Key" because of being steered into certain roles. The Slight and Moderate ones are "out of tune" when they react negatively to the domination patterns of males that enforces "stay-in-your-place". If those reactions are Extremely "Off-Key" then they are likely to chose a life of violence to themselves and/or directed towards others. By contrast, females may be "On-Key" or "Off-Key" at the time they are abused sexually, physically, emotionally, spiritually, socially, or otherwise.

METAPHYSICAL DISORDER LEADING TO "BADNESS": Metaphysical Disorder per se is of a non-moral nature and yet implies to "go astray," become lost," stray from correct behavior by going outside the boundaries of Ma'at to enter "Badness." The C13 word "Bad" possibly began with a homophobic origin—derogatory terms (e.g. contemptible, worthless, moral depravity) for homosexuals (e.g. 'effeminate males'; hermaphrodites), with overtones of sodomy. This expanded to include "bad money drives out good"—based on the C16 concern that people tended to hang on to coins of a high intrinsic worth, like gold sovereigns, while being happier to spend those of a lower intrinsic worth but of equal face value. This gave rise to the sense that, as with eggs, things are either good or bad. Then a medical contribution referred to those who had a potential for abusive or destructive behavior toward oneself or others. Etiologic factors have included antisocial character, catatonic excitement, panic states, rage reactions, organic brain syndrome, and toxic reactions to drugs.

Defining characteristics encompass aggressive body language, verbalization of hostility, boasting to others about prior abuse, increased motor activity, and overt and aggressive acts. Others are: suicidal tendencies, depression, possession of weapons, history of abuse of controlled substances or "Street Drugs," and an inability to verbalize emotions. However, when similar patterns of behaviors are seen within a given society that can be traced back to their primitive history, then this indicates a "Philosophical" rather than "Psychiatric" or "Psychological" cause. Although mistakes can be made inside the flow of the Spiritual Elements without altering the course of ones life, to step outside—whether one runs away or simply sits down on shore—is like putting "Clouds" over ones "Soul Sunshine". That "*Philosophical Badness*" may be seen at anytime in an individual's life and may vary from Mild, Slight, Moderate, or Extreme degrees (Bailey, African Bible Messages). Regardless of degree, "Clouds" mean one has switched the orchestration of ones Real Selfhood over to being dominated by a False Self (Ego, Imagined Self).

CLASSIFICATION OF TODAY'S BLACK PEOPLE

Ancient African Sages said the 'Self' of a human—meaning ones (Spiritual) Self-Identity or ones absolutely unchanging "sameness" which answers the question of: "Who I Am" + serves as the standard, filter, guide, and measure for how to proceed through life. Because of all of this Enlightenment, the "Self" can be thought of as ones "Soul Sunshine." However, False Self people have "Clouds" covering their "Soul Sunshine". Each of their acquired emotions acts like a "Cloud" placed over their "Self's Soul Sunshine" and thereby generates varying degrees of occlusion and extents of Unknowings about aspects of their Selfhood. Here are some very rough types of "Clouds."

Type I are in the category of featuring a "Cloud with a silver-lining" covering their "Soul Sunshine." A metaphor for this is having "one foot" in the Spiritual Elements flow and "one foot" outside it. They do mild or slight violence to themselves, as in not being all they can be or not pursuing their Mission in life. Otherwise, they are good people. Type I's *Mild Self-Un-knowing* of ones own Self, which violates ones birth-gift Selfhood integrity, is *Denial* (disavowing thoughts, emotions, wishes, or needs) or *Suppression* (the conscious, voluntary elimination of some behavior).

Type II have their "Cloud" completely covering their "Soul Sunshine" which is like 'sitting on the shore' of the Spiritual Elements' stream. They do petty mean things to themselves and to others. Their *Slight Self-Un-knowing* is indicated by *Repression*—mental activities relegated to and maintained in the Unconscious and thereby able to "do its own thing" without ones awareness—"I have no idea why I did that!". A temporary form occurs from engaging in violence since one forgets who one is.

Type III have "Dark Clouds" covering their "Soul Sunshine"—as represented by Black Gang members. Yet, they are familiarized with the Spiritual God spotlighted in African Tradition. A *Moderate Self-Un-knowing* is what Europeans did by enslaving Africans.

Type IV's "Super-Dark Clouds" covering up their "Soul Sunshine possess such force as to push the afflicted into a Supernatural Realm. Such *Extreme Self-Un-Knowing* is seen in all people: (1) who have chosen to adopt a False Self (Ego) to orchestrate their "Life-Living"; (2) who do not know their most remote ancestral origin; and (3) who deny the reality of their ultimate ancestral origins, particularly so as to foolishly self-declare they are 'superior'. As Brutes and Satanists, they fight the Spiritual Elements with the effect that everybody loses. To symbolize them on a BRUTE ARCHERY PAD (fig. 7) implies that their mindset of Indifference/Hate/Evil/Sadism (IHES) Complex features Kill/Take/Destroy/Dominate actions.

Types I, II, and III are not outwardly violent but instead are victims. If those on the Archery Pad can be thought of as "Disaster Stars," then their victims are under the influence of the "Halos" of those "Disaster Stars." Victims who have extremely absorbed the Halo of these Disaster Star Groups have tended to "blank out"—i.e. willfully suspend their consciousness--refuse to think--not see even the obvious. Each of these forms of not wanting to know is self-destructive. They have unfocused their minds and induced Clouds over the

Necessary and Important as an Escape from the responsibility of making tough decisions and engaging in risky solutions. Like a little child putting her hand over her eyes when she wants something bad to go away, these victims believe that the problems they face will not exist if they refuse to identify it. There is a loss of Caring, Curiosity, Courage, Consistency, and self-improvement. Thus, they come late, pick and choose what is there, leave to wander around at moments when vital information is being given, skip sessions or stop coming after one or two time, leave early, and only seek the gist of the topic discussed.

BLACK FEMALE VIOLENCE HISTORICAL REVIEW

Ancient Africans had no known textual indication that women's natures were viewed different from men—nothing like having unpredictable "dual good and bad natures." But they did recognize the human capacity for doing good and evil, which applied to both women and men—rooted in and reflected of the concept of human's Free Wills. The patriarchal cultures of women being dominated, exploited, unrecognized as having dignity, and consistently being disrespected date back to primitive times outside of Africa—most notably those of European, Turkish, and Arabic cultures where women have historically being treated as 'nothings'—simply as pieces of property. Since there has been no possibility for them to retaliate openly with hostility, oppressed women have secretly retaliated, as clearly seen by Enslaved Africans in the USA Southern plantations. Maslow (*J.Humanistic Psychology*, 1963) puts it this way: "The exploiter comes to take for granted the exploitee almost as a kind of character…. The wolf expects that the lamb will continue to behave like a lamb. If suddenly the lamb turns around and bites the wolf, then I can understand that the wolf would not only be surprised but also become very indignant. Lambs aren't supposed to behave that way. Lambs must lie quietly and get eaten up. Just so I have seen human wolves get very angry when their victims finally turn around and strike back. For instance, this is a fairly common reaction in exploitative women who marry themselves a kind of an ox whom thereafter they treat with domination and contempt and so on and whom they regard as a servant or slave while they regard themselves as queens. But the delicate point here is that somehow they come to regard their queenly status as deserved, as an edict of nature somehow, and they feel somehow that it is quite just that they should have a personal male servant who goes to work and who sweats and slaves and so on in order to give comforts and luxuries to his exploiter wife. Such a woman ordinarily becomes extremely angry, very indignant, very surprised when the ox type of husband gets angry at having his blood sucked and makes some kind of retaliation, whether overtly by punching her in the nose or, as is much more usual, covertly by secretly taking up with another woman. Or another example that I have observed and which is usable in this situation is the very frequent conversation that one is apt to hear in older ladies who are wealthy and who always have been wealthy."

ENSLAVED BLACK FEMALES: Although Enslaved females were positioned to be dominate over Enslaved males (as part of the European males' envy of the "Manhood" of Black males), in some respects slavery created patterns of gender equity as slave women worked in the fields with men. They labored for the same periods during the days, and they suffered the blows of the lash. Some Enslaved women assumed authority as preachers; others became noted for their skills as midwives, cooks, and expert field hands. Not only was the degree of equity between Enslaved women and men was mitigated by labor and violence, after leaving the fields in the evenings women cared for their children, cooked and sewed for family members. In the process, they created female networks on some plantations. It was essential for the Enslaved to present themselves in the presence of White people using Masks and Masquerades—i.e. concealing their thoughts and emotions. Even as Enslaved women were repeated raped by slave owners or their sons and visitors--even as Enslaved children and their parents were sold away from each other, Enslaved communities clutched to broad definitions of family that differed from the Euro-American families they served. Household Enslaved females cared for White and Black children as Enslaved parents labored in the fields from "can't see" in the mornings to "can't see" in the evenings. If an owner sold a mother, other Enslaved women assumed responsibility for the orphaned children in the community.

Enslaved rebellions were a major concern among White planters as early as 1642 and a crucial component of Slave Codes was to deter insurrections by imposing harsh punishments. Poisoning and arson were the most prevalent methods Enslaved women used to kill their White oppressors and destroy property unjustly acquired through Enslaved labor. Cases of poisoning typically involved an accusation of poisoning food prepared by Enslaved women for the owner's family, which mostly resulted from a lack of safe food preparation methods rather than intentional acts of harm. Other cases involved the Enslaved unknowingly administering poisonous medicine or unlawfully administering medicines. Enslaved women burned their owner's houses, jails, shops, wheat stacks, and agricultural buildings such as mills and barns. Most female Enslaved insurrections amounted to day-to-day resistance that took on a variety of forms, including "malingering; self mutilation; suicide; destruction of owner's crops, tools, and livestock; running away; or criminal activity like stealing and violent insurrection". Enslaved women also manifested resistance to bondage by assaulting or poisoning overseers and owners, breaking tools, pilfering, and burning barns. To a lesser extent, Enslaved women's resistance included controlling reproductive and maternal functions, such as inducing abortions and committing infanticide. Most other female slave insurrection amounted to day-to-day resistance that took on a variety of forms, including "malingering; self mutilation; suicide; destruction of owner's crops, tools, and livestock; running away; or criminal activity like stealing and violent insurrection".

There were artful and designing women and men found on plantations throughout the Americas who served as conduits of powerful Supernatural forces beyond the comprehension of their contemporaries and were, therefore, believed to be integral to the success of a number of Enslaved Resistance Movements. The mystical powers conjurers claimed to control made them formidable and respected figures among Enslaved Africans. As historian John Blassingame (1972) noted, Conjurers' influence was important, not from having power over the slave owners--which a few did--but rather from possessing powers the slave owners' lacked. By making a big impression on the Slaves the Conjurer often had more control over them than did the slave owner. These *"Black Magic"* practitioners used Superstitions to promote optimism and confidence in their ability to achieve goals. Otherwise, throughout history some Superstitions helped people get on with a better life--either as a way of attempting to regain control over events in each ones life or because simply the presence of the thing reminded them of a good atmosphere from former successes and thereby sets higher goals.

BLACK WOMAN POST-SLAVERY: Whether "On-Key" or "Off-Key," Black American households from slavery onward have had an octopus type image—meaning each reached beyond the household into local and regional communities defined by fellow Black People--the Black Church as their main religion—a diluted and polluted African Tradition ideology—a fragmented culture, and a poverty economics to accomplish goals for themselves and their children. African Americans bequeathed this legacy to following generations who continued to insist on the interdependence of Black communities through the early C20. The Enslaved made extraordinary efforts to maintain families within a social system that frequently attempted to obliterate them (Chirhart *J.Family History, 2003*). White and Black women had issues with the way White men treated them. Some Black women also had issues with how black men treated black women, but not as much because Black women were made dominant over Black men in slavery—a dominance continuing post-slavery since they, but not Black men, could get jobs. Black men resented that they could not show their full "Manliness" and women reacted to males 'ugliness' by down grading men. Lack of "Life-Living" paying jobs were essentially non-existent and this caused so much turmoil with Black males as to spur many to violence inside poverty conditions—itself a stimulus to be violent. All victims of inhumane poverty developed problematic emotions—a situation continuing to the present. Otherwise, Black women in my boyhood days were very tolerant of the turmoil Black men were going through and put up with a lot of "stuff." Meanwhile, White terrorist nightriders drove Black People from towns and entire counties, and riots erupted periodically, including in Atlanta in 1906. Persisting slavery concepts included Black People being thought of as chattel, good only for cheap labor and European male's sexual violence.

CONVICT LEASE PRISON SYSTEM: Before emancipation, southern states rarely incarcerated the Enslaved because slave owners' production needs overrode any Enslaved said to deserve punishment. To overcome the loss of Enslaved labor, southern justice systems quickly passed laws saying any Black person not working would be put in jail but there was no work to be had for pay. This was another source of great riches for Whites. For example, much money was/is to be made from imprisonments--paying off police, judges, product manufacturers, guards, building contractors. After 1865, however, newly freed Black males and women swelled the ranks of southern prison populations, with Black females comprising between 40 and 70% of females committed to southern penitentiaries. The reason for Black female incarceration rates increases was because many of them had significant contact with Whites as domestic servants and housemaids, thus rendering them especially prone to crime accusations. Such particularly came from the fact that the vulnerability of Black women to White male sexual violence was greater in the post-bellum period than it had been during slavery and any problems the females caused led to their imprisonment. White employers beat Black women for "using insolent language," for refusing to call her employer "master," and "for crying because he whipped my mother". Otherwise, although imprisoned Black women committed mostly property crimes, violent crimes were still common among Black females.

This scenario led to fewer Black female executions because of the dramatic increase in Black women prison populations in southern states immediately following the Civil War. The same types of accusations applied to Black males. The imprisoned (for life) Black People were then leased to private and public enterprises where, as part of the Convict Lease System, they were worked to death—I did not find evidence of any living over 10 years once in that system. Black prisoners composed large numbers of leased prison work gangs for mining and railroad interests and prison farms, unprecedented in slavery. Other deceptive methods were part of the Share Cropping System that essential returned Black families to slavery. The point is that again Whites had free labor through such means as the Convict Lease System, Tenant Farming, and the like.

Meanwhile, Blacks developed a 'clannishness' for a number of reasons. Although segregation for Whites was not even an inconvenience, for Black People it made race the supreme fact of life. Personally, I had to think of race in terms of any professional decision I made. Blacks have consistently been portrayed in a negative light where Black crime was on the front page but Black achievements went unnoticed. By Blacks being systematically excluded from "Life-Living" paying jobs and otherwise getting the message of not being wanted it would seem that Whites are clannish and thus making Blacks clannish by default, if nothing else. By being clannish and adhering to that, they feel less haunted by all the problems caused by racism. This makes Blacks have a sense of common identity which, in turn, increases their inter-group interactions and reduces contacts with outsiders.

BLACK FEMALES IN THE 20ᵀᴴ CENTURY: Early in C20 Black females were twice as vocal and bi-ased towards feminist issues and beliefs as their White counterparts. This caused Gloria Steinem, in referring women's fight for gender equality, to say: "I thought that [Black women] invented the feminist movement…I learned feminism disproportionately from Black women." Such caused her to give the floor to other young Black women (whether or not they self-identify as feminists) to address concerns for people of varying socio-economic backgrounds since this helped both races toward getting dignity, autonomy, and freedom. Steinem has continually advocated the importance of equally employing women in the police force to calm racially tense situations as a way of decreasing police brutality saying: "[W]e haven't been raise with our masculinity to prove. All the studies show that if a woman cop arrives on the scene, she de-escalates the situation by her presence and a man cop escalates. So while we're talking as we should about cops looking like the community, how come we don't say they should be half women?"

Women are treated differently in jobs, including being paid less. Callahan (Violence Against Women, 2009) describes how she, as a USA Air Force Academy basic cadet was treated—initially referred to as *Doolies (Slave)*. All civilian clothing is replaced with a uniform; male cadets have their hair shaved. Instead of civilian glasses and contact lenses, all cadets must wear black, horn-rimmed, "birth control glasses". While in Basic Cadet Training, Doolies are not allowed to go anywhere outside the squadron area alone; march at attention at all times; and participate "warrior" spirit activities. Although the stated reason is to create cohesiveness among team members of different socioeconomic statuses, classes, races, and genders, the main reason is designed to break the will of new cadets to remold them into a military image. People, or actors, create social systems by repeatedly interacting with one another. Their interactions are guided by rules and resources that make up the structure of social systems. The heart of structuration theory, however, is that there is a reciprocal relationship between these systems and structures. In the process of interacting with one another, people both consciously and unconsciously create rules and establish power relationships. In turn, these rules and relationships serve as the structures that frame social systems until actors redefine the structures by their continued interactions. This process of creating, maintaining, and redefining structures is called "*Structuration.*"

PREDISPOSITIONS TO FEMALE VIOLENCE

Women who are victims of childhood abuse have violent role models and are more likely to be convicted of violent crime than non-victims. Women who are violent were more likely to be younger, African American, unemployed, and having extensive criminal histories. They were more likely to come from dysfunctional fami-lies with childhood abuse; tend to be highest in "underclass" communities, and women, especially women of color, who live in these communities, are the most likely group to be arrested and convicted of violent crimes. Even in these communities, however, there may be differences in propensity to violence. Whereas boys are acknowledged for acting aggressively, girls are punished. As they grow up, girls learn to suppress and hide any aggressive impulses and avoid violent expressions. Yet, many boys cultivate them for their benefits. Unlike men, women are not exposed to violent role models nor are they reinforced for violent behaviors. This may lead to Passivity in many girls or to "Passive-aggressiveness" in girls and women, as shown by verbal aggres-sion, rejection, manipulation, and enlistment of the help of others. Thus, girls' and women's criminality may be expressed in culturally appropriate venues as, for example, property crime (*J. Interpersonal Violence, 2006*).

CONTINGENT BEING TECHNOLOGY ERODES RELATIONSHIPS: A tens of thousands of year old Ancient African Bible teaching, upon which African Tradition is based is the Cosmic Organism because one has a "ME/WE" Integrity (all in a "Oneness" and not divided within itself) orientation. The bonding Base of all humans' Needy Wants is Unconditional Love which is manifested by Compassion--a manner every human can understand—a connection that imparts a feeling of worth, important, powerful, and belonging—an awareness that the thing to be known and the knower engaging in that awareness are the same. To recognize that there is no separation of the Knower and the Known--to feel a feeling or the experiencing of the experience are the same process means that all real Things, including oneself, are a Oneness entity. As a result, one does not have a choice but to have Compassion for all since in order to save oneself cannot be done alone because one is not alone. An idea of this happening can be gained by a state of no thinking and no self-talk meditation. This enables seeing the world without bringing concepts to it since no concept of it is ever complete or valid. To shed those concepts puts one at the essence of the Base of all that exists—a Base which is consistent, permanent, stationary, and unchanging—a Base called Unconditional Love (i.e. God's inner nature)—a Base that is the Ultimate "Ground of Being" for all real things. However, one has the Free Will of seeing the Cosmos from this perspective and thereby maintaining ones birth gift awareness sense of Selfhood Greatness founded on "ME/WE" or choose to orchestrate ones life by a False Self—i.e. ones interpretations of the monitored feedback one gets from outside influences.

That choice determines what meaning sense of Belonging one values most highly. To choose a False Self means one has no 'ground of being' to build any sound thinking structure. Thus, they are forced to fashion all meaningful Thoughts out of Fantasy Supernatural ingredients they, themselves, supply in order to design their Philosophy of Life (POL)—a POL that necessarily consists of chaotic thoughts featuring Lower (animal) Self passions. From this springs their Life-Living of Confusion, around which they build a lifestyle designed to deceive oneself and others. The main public Illusion is Technology. In its most subtle display, its Deception *erodes* (wear away) and *corrodes* (gnaw away) the "what it is" of ones mental, physical, and emotional health. Basic problems are that many people feel alone in trying to adapt to their False Self "Individualism"; most feel weak and need constant companionship; practically all are bored and cannot stand to be quiet. Contingent Beings (CB) like Flashing Light Gadgets for viewing, hearing and working (e.g. robots) have become necessities of intimacy for companionship without relationships. These CB willingly trick people into thinking they care about them—some even making eye contact with the CB while texting.

However, the deception starts with changing who people are and that spells trouble for how one relates to oneself. In the process of giving CB ones full attention, one denies friends and possible friends their full attention. That makes it hard to recognize or even redefine human connections. By hiding from them prevents them from learning what to do and what not to do for proper interrelating. In this manner, and with images from CB, people learn wrong ways of defining each other—oversimplifying the complex. CB have so allowed the weird to customize their lives that they are now normal controls over where they put their attention—with the objective of wanting to be 'special'. The more one expects from CB, the less one expects of oneself and thus calls on others to do what is essential for ones progress. Some call this "plugged-in" lives. CB become 'crutches,' as in talking on cell phones to relieve depression, and otherwise removes one from the struggle and grief. Crutches take away the trial-and-error struggles need to progress from self-reflection (e.g. about it takes for their needs and values) or wrestling with tough problems that teach transferrable skills.

Technology replaces jobs, like elevator operators who might be mentally challenged. Besides putting them on welfare where they are further ridiculed as only wanting a handout, the riders in the elevators no longer to have anyone to with whom to chit-chat and thereby relief some of their daily stress. Only the mega-rich money-makers benefit.

"BIG BANG" PSYCHIC TRAUMAS

This is like hammering a pattern of thinking into victims to affect their physical, mental, social, financial, and spiritual Selfhood parts. Abuse or any significant psychic trauma may cause one to develop a "Raw Nerve" with its associated mental barriers; become self-absorbed and apathetic; nurse ones self-protected Splintered Selfhood in self-pity; switch to using ones Omnibus Brain which is oriented to the "Here and Now"; engage in chronic juggling; be revengeful, and be driven to frequent "Escapes" from Reality. To deal with "Raw Nerves" coming from some form of abuse or psychic trauma requires detecting as many self-defeating traits as possible over days, weeks, or months. Write them out using the "What's Behind That? Inquiry Process.

CHILD ABUSE: Abuse (ab, away, meaning in the wrong direction + to use) is anything contrary to societal good order--i.e. overuse; immoderate or improper use; the injurious, harmful, offensive; deceitful; mal-aligned; or a departure from reasonable use by word or act. Such includes threats, insults, humiliation, intimidation, isolation, bad name-calling, put-downs, yelling and screaming, being intentionally embarrassed in public, and projection (blaming scapegoats for ones own mental afflictions and bad behaviors). Bad childhoods can come from "Big Bang" and/or Cummulative micro-traumas may cause psychic traumas of Mild, Slight, Moderate, or Extreme degree--either at any given time or at alternating times or in varying combinations. Examples include: neglect; physically, sexually, emotionally, or spiritually abused and/or abandoned or being victims of a war.

DOMESTIC VIOLENCE: Men and women are equally violent in domestic relationships. Similar to racist incidents, domestic violence is usually not a single-event trauma. The violence occurs in multiple violations over time. People living in conditions of domestic violence or in societies where racist incidents occur may not always be able to establish safety first and then seek treatment. They must live with the threat of future violations. Survivors who live with domestic violence live with the expectation that a violation may occur, although they are unaware of the form the violation will take. Similarly, many target group members who live with racism live with the expectation that racism will be felt, yet they are unsure of when the incident will occur or of what type of racism they will face. Knowing neither what will happen nor how devastating the effects will be contributes to hyper-arousal and anxiety. This marriage of expectancy and shock is unique to experiences of trauma such as domestic violence and racism. Black males live under a tremendous amount of pressure as a result of European males being dedicated to their oppression. For example, occupational stressors—such as demotion, job loss, and trouble with superiors—consistently emerge as predictors of men's violence toward their female partners. Moreover, whenever men's reputation and honor are damaged by female adultery, husband-to-wife violence occurs relatively frequently and is viewed as an acceptable response to infidelity. Men, at times, use physical aggression to restore threatened manhood. Low socio-economic status has been shown to increase the risk of both domestic violence and

child neglect occurring in families. Experiencing neglect, and the witnessing of domestic violence have in turn been recognized as key risk factors for future violent offending by young people.
[Ref: Bryant-Davis, *The Counseling Psychologist, 2005*]

RAPE VICTIMS: perpetrators of rape seek to gain power by the perpetuation of myths about those whom they victimize (i.e. globally primarily women): They are promiscuous, enjoy being raped, are liars, are teasers, and are untrustworthy describe self-neglectful and self-destructive behaviors (e.g., substance abuse or failure to secure adequate health care) among African Americans, which are connected to social traumas such as racism.

CUMULATIVE MICRO-TRAUMAS

Whether from "Big Bang" Traumas or Cumulative Micro-traumas, Children, adolescents, and adults tend to react angrily and aggressively when threatened and attacked, especially when they feel the attack was unjustified. How a person reacts to such attacks or to abuse varies with the individual and at different times within the same individual but invariably they leave an impression.

CHILD ABUSE: Words of demeaning nature or those which put needless boundaries on a child's abilities or those used as weapons as well as one being hypersensitive about childhood obesity or skin color problems or being smart compared with peers are each capable of causing mental and emotional problems by way of a "Big Bang" or by cumulative trauma.

BULLYING: Bullying is the behaviors instituted by those with an inferiority complex displaying as a Superiority Complex (the donning of a mask of self-confidence and greatness with a reality of arrogance and aggression to conceal a sense of deep inferiority). Fluck says (*Youth & Society, 2014*) Bullying is an "aggressive behavior normally characterized by repetition and imbalance of power." *Power* is a special kind of instrumental violence that is universal in human beings exercise power occurs when the perpetrator hopes to secure or to enhance his or her position within a social entity. Girls use different kinds of violence than boys. The means they use may be different, but the aims they use them for are the same. Boys as well as girls use violence to maintain or improve their position in the "pecking order" of the class.

The "Bully Group" engages in Mild or Slight forms of the Indifference/Hate/Evil/Sadism Complex whereas Moderate and Extreme forms are done by Brutes. All types always acts dishonorably. Bullying may occur in schools, prisons, or neighborhoods--for *purposes* of revenge or to display power--as direct (A hits/insults B) or indirect (A tells B to punch C; spreads rumors) actions—in the form of physical, verbal, and psychological (or called relational bullying is used to undermine the victim's status within a group or to destroy his or her friendships) displays.

Methods include: harassment—sending offensive messages to the victim; denigration—spreading rumors about someone; impersonation—identity theft; outing and trickery—forwarding embarrassing or private pictures, videos, or messages; exclusion—excluding someone from common activities such as chats or online games--and the "emotional and discreet bullying of other girls (e.g. gossip, manipulation, teasing, and exclusion. Cyberbullying is a medium for the physically weak to take revenge on their real-life bullies. *Medium* embrace bullying by phone, text message, email, picture or video clip, instant messenger, website, chat.

Causes: Victims and offenders give very different reasons for an attack: Offenders say they did not have any other choice but to choose violent means because of being provoked; defending oneself; getting revenge against earlier attacks by the victim; or boredom. Victims say there was no good reason—and offenders reacted out of meanness without the slightest reason or provocation. The truth lies in between. While bullies give revenge as the most common motive, followed by sadism and power, victims reverse this—saying it was done mainly for mean people to have fun. Blackmailing for money or valuables is common in poorer neighborhoods.

Reasons for being selected in the schoolyard are psychological—e.g. low self-esteem, shyness, introversion. Elsewhere, it may be about ethnicity, social status, outer appearance, sexual orientation, religious affiliation, and other obvious traits that distinguish the individual from the majority. The issue for both bullies and victims concerns their Self-Worth. For the bully, hurting others is in contrast to the self-perception of being a nice person, whereas being bullied by others might be contradictory to the picture of oneself as a likable person. Mild and Slight *Sadism* is deriving "sick" pleasure from from watching another person suffer.

JOB VIOLENCE: I have direct experience with teachers telling me they cannot be advocates for Black students for fear of losing their jobs. Such unspoken intimidation is the rule "everywhere." A hypocritical aspect of Republicans is rejecting things to benefit poor and disadvantaged people because they are anti-big government. Yet, they do all they can to tell women what they can do with their bodies.

VICTIM RESPONSES TO PSYCHIC TRAUMAS

How one responds to "Big Bang" Traumas or Cumulative Micro-traumas or Micro-Aggressions depends upon the degree of Private Selfhood Greatness one has. The insecure react in Moderate and Extreme categories. This may show with them have the spoken or unspoken demand on others of: "Your are required to do something acceptable to me but only if you do it voluntarily." If it is not done "just so" or if it has to be asked for, the insecure may exhibit great emotional displays. They also demand conformity, are intolerant, deem others as inferior and thus believe they deserve rudeness. All of this (among others) is because such females and males have mindsets turned "Inside-Out". But this comes from a background of Chronic Rage. The ongoing racist incidents and various types of psychic traumas (e.g. domestic violence) leave survivors feeling shame, self-blame, powerlessness, fear, and confusion. No one should be ashamed of being victimized, but survivors are often made to feel ashamed, as if being violated is their fault. Connected to this issue of shame is self-blame.

Survivor Guilt—first used to describe the guilt people feel when surviving the death of someone close and more recently expanded to refer generally to guilt felt by the advantaged after any unfavorable social comparison—may also occur in survivors of racist. Victims of racist incidents who can survive and even thrive may experience guilt because they are aware that many who share their ethnic or racial identification continue to be limited by oppression while they have managed to acquire education, wealth, status, or fame. Outwardly, these socalled success stories may question their own authenticity as group members or find that others question that authenticity. This perception can create shame, distress, identity confusion, and a feeling of alienation. Survivors of racist incidents who utilize their resources to aid those still struggling with the institutional impact of racist incidents can replace guilt with responsible activism. [Bryant-Davis, *The Counseling Psychologist, 2005*]

SELF-HARM INFLICTIONS: The overwhelming inhumane effects of slavery caused the Enslaved to develop every conceivable mindset—each "Clouded" in various ways and with various degrees of intensity. Harris (*Qualitative Health Research,* 2000) discusses several forms of Self-Harm engaged in by many Black females as a result of "Ugliness" following a significant Trigger Life Event, perhaps intiated by a Trigger Person(s), that resulted in a "Raw Nerve" with its associated emotional/spiritual pain. An example would be a child being raped by her father and/or by several complete strangers—a horrible experience which is internalized. The reaction is to make varied types of attempts to "cut it out." Perhaps what is done is guided by those familiar with the European Bible which says such things as: "If your hand is your undoing, cut it off; it is better for you to enter into life maimed than to keep both hands and go to hell into unquenchable fire" (Mark 9:43). To do self-harm is accompanied by apparent benefits or release of guilt. Afflicted women experience very severe and distressing significant life events prior to commencing self-harm: usually emotional, physical, and/or sexual abuse.

One woman said: At the age of 6 the emotional pain became so great that all I wanted to do was end all the pain. I hit the wall in my bedroom, and all the emotional pain just went. For the first time I had found relief from this kind of pain. I found that physical pain or selfharming became a normal part ofmylife. I found myself at school deliberately hurting myself, falling over in the playground or falling off apparatus in the gym. Doing this I found relieved the emotional pain, and I received the warmth, love and attention that I had been looking for. A second female: "After I have harmed myself, I feel a lot calmer and relaxed as if I've got the bad out. I usually do it at night and bandage myself up and curl up in bed. It helps me to fall asleep. I think it sort of comforts me." A third: When I started to emerge from my anorexia, I needed some other way of dealing with the pain and hurt, so I started cutting instead. It is a way of gaining temporary relief. As the blood flows down the sink, so does the anger and the anguish. It's a way of transferring the scars and wounds inside onto a visible object, in my case my arm (once my leg and once my chest). It's easier to deal with it on the outside and it's a way of communicating the pain within.

Other forms used to eulogize (praise highly) self-harm include assigning a particular symbolic significance to: anorexia, bulimia, and overdosing on prescribed medication. Serving as metaphorical imagery, certain projected Symbols are in the form of using physical pain as a way to cope with emotional pain. For example, the letting of blood signifies the idea of communicating inner distress or rendering it visible as the indicator of the "Self-Released" experience. One woman says: I am totally in control of my life and my self-harm. I am not a danger to either myself or anyone else. To me self-harm is the total opposite of suicide. I have never wanted or attempted to kill myself. It is all about coping. I do want to stop, but to be honest I don't know if I ever will 'cos its been a way of life for so long that I don't know if I could cope without it.

Self-harm is all about emotions and dealing with them--and not about being mentally ill. "When there is no feeling when you're dead inside, the pain, the blood, it proves I am alive. The blood is so red and beautiful and I can feel again." The logic of self-harm states that the release from emotional turmoil can be obtained by cutting the self; that this act is controlled in its extent; that the purpose of the act is to exert control over the body and the environment and to obtain relief; that a further purpose may be to translate emotional pain into physical pain; and that far from being a random and irrational act, cutting can be a means of limiting the damage to the self. The logic I hate myself and I've never felt loved as a child or teen's or even now as an adult.

"INSIDE-OUT" MINDSETS: Being born with Selfhood Greatness and its Disposition to Thrive and Be Happy is the theme of African Traditions' teaching for its youth. The way this lifestyle is lived, within ones Private Self, is by ones *Divine Consciousness* (ones "Self") serving as the Background of all that happens to ones entire Selfhood. To briefly review, on 'the Self's' other side is ones *Spiritual Awareness* (Will)—the Foreground for 'the Self'. At the Divine Spirit level of ones Public Self, ones *Secular Sensory Consciousness* is the Background situated on its near side. On the opposite side, ones *Secular Sensory Awareness*—the Public Self Foreground is in direct contact with the External World, possessing the capacity to have subjective experiences and images (e.g. receiving sensations that are formed into Percepts. The purpose of the Sensory Consciousness is to provide "light" for assessing the Physical Realms.

For whatever reason, Black People who have acquired Bad Conditioned Responses have allowed "Clouds" to form over the "Soul Sunshine" of their Hearts--Group I, self-imposed; Group II, as victims; Group III, as Brutes perpetrators. These "Clouded Soul" Black People used their Free Will to go through life in a non-Spiritual Elements stream. That choice is an automatic replacement of ones Spiritual Divine Conscious with the Supernatural Ego (False Self) which features such Fetters as "Me, Me, Me" Individualism which cleaves into an External World course featuring hatred, arrogance, pride, fear, lies, selfishness, greed, anger, lust, egoism, envy, jealousy, and frustration. Their Self-Absorbed course shows as aggression, passiveness, passive-aggressive, and a 'strained' non-aggression. Both course completely "Cloud-Out" ones Divine Conscious and its powers which result from the "Spark of God"—meaning one loses the Private Self sense of the "5Ss"—safety, security, sureness, strength, and stability. Their False Self "*Extroverts*"—being addicted to people and what people do. They have lost their Courage and thus give up who they are, choosing to do just the opposite of African Tradition and of 'Human Nature' features of taking care of themselves.

They are bonded to and imitate and protect their oppressors while attacking anyone trying to help them. They have no interest in helping themselves—not attending self-help courses or doing assignments—getting angry at those who do not give them enough or give things the way they want. A way to program and activate Consciousness "Inside-Out" Conditional Response Centers is for one to engage in activities which, without ones conscious effort, results in self-defeating Behaviors X, Y, and Z. In the 'big picture' process, those Images of fear, bonding with the oppressor, being against each other and those trying to help them are programmed into ones *Secular Sensory Consciousness Background* and *Foreground* initially formed by some emotional aspect of ones Ego and carried out by ones Will, and Spirit power forces. Between them is the cultivation of a Conditioned Response.

First, displays of ingredients pertaining to self-defeating "black" Characteristics, Traits, and Features are imprinted in long-term memory traces or engrams within the nerves of their developing Conditioned Response. Second, a Disposition is present inside the Icon Image whose emotional power can/does continually activate or enhance ones spirit force generated behaviors within the pattern of the original False Self IHES message. Third, repetition reinforces engram 'conditioning' which gradually expands to operate in the brain's reverberating circuits as a more dynamic engram involving larger numbers of synapses—each growing with every triggere repetition. Fourth, counteracting neurons are weakened or eliminated, spurred by chemical changes resulting from a lack of use. In successful Conditional Response or Unconditional Reflexes, the '*Ideo-motor Action*' stimulative sequence of events begins with merely thinking of its trigger--an act evoking the act itself.

"INSIDE-OUT" DISPLAYS: From their Ancient African and African American slavery past, couple with the present, Black youth carry in their Selfhood a collage of different types of wonderfully formed bonds, reminisces of shattered wonderful bonds, *Deficient* Physical Human Nature Needs (PHNN) bonds, frustrated Selfhood bonds; desperation for *Spiritual Human Nature Needs* (SHNN) bonds (e.g. with ones dad), and the original Mother-Child bond. The very best bonds are Sacred because they fulfill ones PHNN and SHNN. Any other bonds are problematic and relegated to ones sub-awareness for self-defense purposes. To repeat, foundational to today's Black-On-Black Violence is the shattering of ones SHNN--the entity which forms and holds together ones Self-Esteem. *The absence of a supplier of ones SHNN is a disaster and finding one is a youth's central focus, often representing the driving force for joining a gang.* The pertinent Causes for an unfulfilled SHNN or the lack of a SHNN bonding supplier must be understood as essential factors in determining what to do to stop the violence.

Bonding occurs by one feeding--to any degree--another's PHNN and/or ones SHNN. Human *Ideal Bonding* occurs when ones PHNN and ones SHNN are fulfilled. "*Desperate Bonding*" is present when either ones PHNN or SHNN are neglected to any degree. *Desperate Bonding is what characterizes the Selfhoods of gang members--particularly the SHNN since one feels one is dependent on others to supply this.* A feature of each of ones SHNN members is that it is of a Spiritual Boundlessness nature which flows naturally out of ones Spiritual Elements Soul. Thus, "Inside-Out" mindset, by having different proportions of deficits in SHNN, PHNN, and Bonding, have Mild, Slight, Moderate, and Extreme degrees. All degrees are characterized by Blacks with a sense of powerlessness and who have bonded with the oppressors and a mindset that is in agreement with slave owners attitudes, beliefs, and practices as it relates to Black People and how they are defined. They may admire what another Black is doing but are envious because they are not free mentally or from problems. Their emotional hypersensitivity is easily triggered to become angry with those who do not do what the "Inside-Out" Enslaved minded people say do. One way this shows today is they will not work with helpers in order to get community things done. It is apparent that their low self-control, coupled with risky leisure used as an "Escape" from doing the Necessary, produces the most problematic outcomes.

Impulsiveness is a major feature. Originally, the C15 word "Impulse" meant having the effect of reducing ones 'humors' so as to impel an easily moving driving action to move onward. Today, "Impulsive" is a general term used of any sudden incitement to act in accordance with ones Inclination and Temperament—or of the person prone to such acts. It is an unexpected swift action carried out immediately and absent volition or conscious judgment resulting from forethought, foresight, deliberation, or reflection. Such occurs on the mere presentation of a situation, either in perception or in idea gained from a subjective origin. It is an act of emotional "excitement" that the perpetrator intensely desires to repeat whenever the opportunity presents itself. However, the victims of a Trigger Event have an impulsive inclination to respond immediately by fight, flight, or fright. The implication is the advanced stage of "Impulsive Violence" e.g. Killing is dependent on accepting prior compatible destructive beliefs and practices based upon once-neutral persons or situations. Yet, because of a lack of obstruction to being destructively Impulsive, one has become 'conditioned' to doing that act as if it were a reflex (like an eye blink).[Ref: Buchanan, *JUrban History, 2004;* Butler *JBlack Studies 2011]*

CAUSES OF VICTIM RESPONSES TO PSYCHIC TRAUMAS

All of the factors previously discussed about bad happenings to the brain/minds of the Enslaved—e.g. the hellishness of slavery (e.g. the selling away of family members), restrictions from reading, writing, and counting; having nothing to think about; a loss of the Left Brain skills and its powers to discipline its Right Brain partner; constantly inflicted pains and sufferings—all (among others) led to hyperemotionalism among many Enslaved. It persisted following slavery out of custom and because even increased White terrorism. Those Selfhood ruling Emotions are what sparked the Enslaved and Ex-Slaves Consciousness to change from light to darkness and from inertia to movement or vice versa. By often being repressed, there often occurred Selfhood insurrection. An out of Control Right Brain means one is hyper- Emotional, meaning people live by their Emotions, not intellect, and constantly have tantrum like Terrible Two's. Hence they are unreasonable and no one can reason with them and they have no concept of fair play.

In short, the afflicted see only one-side of the "*Assessment Coin.*" This causes them to join forces with those who think like they do so as to create a sense of social solidarity. As a result, members of that group exaggerate, with loud voices, what they believe to be true--as if that is the only way to believe. In what they say there is usually a bit of truth checkered among what is not true, but those truths are not in proper context and are selectively chosen to support their position. This is the same type of mindset present in many Black gangs which must deal with racism oppression (as present during slavery) + daily "Street" survival + daily human needs survival in a hostile world. As a result, they struggle to live life as best they can and do things differently from the norm. Examples include striking out at anyone because they are not respected. The *Respect Platter* is a basic Spiritual Human Nature Need. Being stereotyped into believing they lack Selfhood Greatness, their emotional pain keeps them from knowing what that is about. Thus, they fail to treat themselves with respect and are unable to show others Respect.

MAAFA FIGHT/FLIGHT/FRIGHT/FUNK ENSLAVED MINDSET: The Left Brain skills of most of the Enslaved were removed because it was against the law to provide what it takes to develop them. In other words, educating the Enslaved by means of reading, writing, and counting were not allowed. There was nothing else to think about except how to endure and this caused their Left Brain skills to on hold—like telephone's "call waiting". Since the Left Brain is a "check and balance" for the Right Brain so as to enable its skills to operate for the well-being of a human, removal of the Left Brain resulted in problems. Such was contributed to by the "Brain Switch" discussed previously. An undisciplined Omnibus Brain/Right Brain is unsuited to make decisions about serious business. It is about being in a constant state of Alarm to a hint of a threat, focused only on the "here and now," and having no consideration of thoughts for looking out for what happens in the future or for what is in the best interest of anyone except "Me, Me, Me."

As elaborately discussed in Bailey, Post-Traumatic Distress Syndrome, this "4F" mindset had Chronic Rage at its core. European Brutes who enslaved Africans and treated them with unspeakable cruelties unknown in the history of mankind instituted Chronic Rage (originally meaning "rabies" or madness) in an otherwise generally gentle people. These Brutes ongoing racism practices have added untold layers of Anger. The Ancient African meaning of "Anger" is distress that narrows ones oxygen supply--i.e. breath of life (spirit). An analogy is a head of lettuce, with each leaf covering the core of Rage representing extreme Anger--a combination that makes for a hybrid. To some extent and at varying depths of consciousness or unconsciousness this hybrid is present in all Black Americans--each having an Icon Image with "uniqueness" features for each as well as "sameness" features among all. The most seriously and obviously affected by Chronic Rage/Layered Anger has resulted in Black America males, throughout their history, having their Brain/Mind Anger "Zones" being constantly and excessively stimulated by an accumulation of all they have collectively gone through and all each is now going through. Despite there being overwhelming justification of Icon Images of Rage, it is not in their best Private Self (e.g. health and choices for living) or Public Self (e.g. ways of coping in life and preparations for self-preservation) to continue on that path.

EMOTIONS "OUT OF CONTROL": By emotions lacking morals, no urge to be academic, or any desire to thrive means those involved are guided in life by what they like and dislike. A mindset of "Likes/Dislikes" is one unconcerned about their likes taking them over a cliff as long as they are part of the crowd. Nor are they concerned about their dislikes stopping advantages they are already receiving. Those exhibiting out of control Animalistic Emotions are demonstrated as evilness in humans and "madness" in animals. One of the manifestations of out of control Animal Emotions is popularly called "Broad-Stroking" or "Broad-Brushing." This means painting a race, a group, an individual, a scale of values--with the same paint on the same brush--a stereotyping which says: "all X people look alike and act alike." These practices are not changed by attempts to demonstrate its absurdity or falsity and, in addition, lead to narrow thinking.

Examples: "Are you for me or against me" or "Are you like me and if not there is something wrong and unnatural about you." Any outsider who does not agree with a given stereotype is deemed to be "Against Me"--a concept to which they cling as if they would drop off a cliff if they let it go. It was Enslaved Africans exposure to, and imitation of, such European "Broad-Stroking" type of thinking while in a state of Despair that dismantled their "Humanity Respect" for themselves and gradually their Kinship System, as manifesting out of control in much of the Black Community today. This is a keystone of the Black gang mind and when enraged, the following happens:

RAGE SHORT-CUT: What this shortcut does is to allow the hyper-reactor's emotional response to the threat to assume control before the message gets to the neocortex. The process starts normally whereby impulses triggered by the fearful person's perceptions go as usual to the thalamus. However, a "shortcut" then relays the threatening message across a single nerve synapse and thereby causing that "emotional" message to enter the Amygdala. Once in the Amygdala, the fear and/or rage overwhelm the outraged person's self-control unit in the Left Prefrontal Cortex--i.e. its rational constraints, reasonable rules, and moral conscience. By lacking any constraints, rules, or moral conscience, these emotional impulses in the Amygdala lead to destructive acts and vicious cycles.

EFFECTS OF CHRONIC RAGE: Whether from Childhood psychic trauma (e.g. abuse, neglect), Teen Age ("I'll Show You!"), and Adult forms of Enslaved Minds that have been culturally transmitted and daily reinforced by racism of whatever cause represents the "Seed" which give rise to the "Roots"--i.e. the "4Fs" (Fight, Flight, Fright, and Funk). The Teen Age and Adult sources may indirectly be from Slave Survivals culturally transmitted evolved patterns of the "4Fs"; from the atmosphere created by post-slavery racism; or from personal experiences (e.g. racism, Childhood psychic trauma). Mild forms of Childhood psychic trauma may have sensitized the afflicted to the slavery and post-slavery related indirect forms and/or to ones personal experience forms of racism. Any one of these categories or any psychic trauma form in a given category have the capability of forming Icon Images that radiate in all directions like the spokes out of the hub of a wheel. Time and circumstances may have altered the natural course of "4Fs." For example, the original Fight, Flight, or Fright spoke beginning may have "burnt-out" to cause a state of Funk (see *Amygdala Burn-out Syndrome*).

The destruction of the "5Ss" generates a bottomless pit of worthlessness--a pit whose magnet exerts an overwhelming pull to do anything necessary to feel worthwhile in any manner and no matter how brief--a pull that wipes out all thoughts of any problematic consequences--a pull that is more basic than food. They will go to even the meanest of Brutes who make them feel wanted or needed or lovely or important even though it is only for an hour that one time and even though that is all they will ever get. The price they pay is getting pregnant. Such a scenario occurs in all "Like-Kind" situations with females or males. Boys who feel lost and disserted will join a gang, knowing they are probably not compatible with them for anything long-term, but right this minute that gang can make them feel powerful and valuable--even if it goes against what they know to be "Right." They fail to plan for the long term because, for males, they do not believe they will live past late teens; or for females, realizing it is surely to end in heartbreak. Whatever the situation, the players in it simply live for the "here and now" moment. Any of these created barriers between the Dissociated "Self" but I suspect only an attenuation of the connection between ones "Self" and Spirit occurred. To elaborate, recall that silver cords' (as Ancient Africans called them) are invisible bonds which connect all God's creations and creatures and which connect things within the Selfhood of a given individual. A way to begin handling this problem is to detect what triggers distress and minimize that. Yet, most people form an Icon Image of what powers their Rage.

ICON IMAGES OF RAGE: The Icon Image formed concerning Rage may be about a "Rage Monster" or about the Cause of that Rage or about any of the "4Fs" Effects of that Rage or about any Consequence of the "4Fs" or about the "Big Picture" Results or about the path they are on urged by the Results. For example, a *Passive-Aggressive Icon Image* concerning all Black males may be seen in women who have several "baby's daddies" because they seek to find a bit of connection to whatever or to wherever they can to survive. Hence, their choices of paths to take may SEEM natural but it is not on the Spiritual Elements Track. To persist on that self-made path of what SEEMS natural is a certain way to ensure that one will not get what one wants (e.g. the "5Ss" of Safety, Security, Sureness/Self-Confidence, Strength, and Stability). It also ensures one will get what one does not want (e.g. a needlessly hard life; put in jail; killed), which makes it terribly hard for their loved ones. With them, with their families, with families of my patients, in my family, I have seen "Seeds" of Spiritual Elements flawed or destroyed to the point that everyone involved loses because of unresolved Chronic Rage/Layered Anger on the part of someone in particular. Simply replacing this with its *Practical Ideal* opposite could free ones mind of a major block to ones wholesome progress in life. To do so is a display of Self-Love because than embraces the avoidance of doing anything that causes harm to oneself; to free oneself of needless burdens; and to do all one can to have Happiness in life. However, if Rage remains chronic and at a Moderate or Extreme level, ones mindset may become "Inside-Out."

VIOLENCE CAUSING IN-HOUSE PRISON DEATHS: Whereas in police custody 95.5% of arrest-related deaths are male, the 4.5% of female deaths are half from natural causes or intoxication and half from homicide. In the USA 63% are White and 12% Black, the chance of Blacks dying in a confrontation with police is much, much higher—and so is police violence against Black women (e.g. sexual assault and extrajudicial killings). As happened throughout slavery and thereafter, what has been reported as Black deaths at the hands of terrorist Whites are tremendously small. Still, reported arrested-related deaths of Black women are consistent, expected, and on the rise.

FEMALE GANGS

Girls who join gangs often have a history of being more likely than boys to have mental health problems. In the family domain, important risk factors for girls are a history of physical and sexual abuse, the quality of parent–child relationships, conflicts within the family, parental control, family violence, and having caregivers with a history of substance abuse or crime physical as well as sexual abuse at home by older family males and acquaintances--both reside in extremely disadvantage neighborhoods. While such victimization may lead girls and males to join gangs for protection, they are open to new forms of victimization as a function of exposure to risky lifestyle routines itself + the effect of gang participation + an array of antisocial personalities and antisocial peers. Compared to nongang youth, gang members are more likely to be violently victimized, sexually assaulted (males or females), to suffer serious injuries from fighting and be targeted by rival gangs.

Being on the receiving end of increased victimization may increase members' inclination to justify their violence to others such as rival gang members. School and family relationships + a history of physical and/or sexual assault, though less powerful, are significant predictors of female delinquency (Petersen, *Criminal Justice Review, 2013*). Social vulnerability—especially being Black, having a parent who has been incarcerated, and being unemployed at the time of the arrest—mediate relationships between experiencing violence, using drugs, and believing interpersonal violence contributes to ones imprisonment (Schlesinger, *Sage Open, 2011*).

FEMALE GANG MINDSETS: In dealing with today's Black gang minds, the Primary Cause dates back to their Enslaved Ancestors forming "Clouds" over their *Ultimate Divine Selfhood Background—the "Self"* out of which arose either a Flawed Real Self or a Semi-False Self or a False Self—each changing the nature of the afflicted person's *Ultimate Divine Selfhood Foreground* of ones "Self" and thus ones sense of Self-Identity and ones Self-Meaning—the Spiritual parts of ones Self-Esteem (see Bailey, Teaching Black Youth; Bailey, African Tradition For Black Youth). This meant that the afflicted thereafter lived mainly out of their *Sensory Secular World Consciousness Background* which, in turn, provided ingredients for the performance of their Sensory Consciousness Foreground daily living think, feel, say, and do activities. The degree to which the afflicted have distanced themselves from their Real Self has been to Mild, Slight, Moderate, and Extreme levels. The traumas' Effects were of sufficient magnitude to cause one or more "Raw Nerves" superimposed on their culturally transmitted "Clouded" Ultimate Divine Selfhood Background. That combination thus caused their *Sensory Secular World Consciousness Background* to possess the power to deal effectively with their ongoing 'big bang' and cumulative micro-traumas layered on to their Trigger Trauma. Out of these came a host of like-kind Consequences. The Result is that all of these combined to fashion a like-kind shared *Sensory Secular World Consciousness Background which manifests as Black American Customs.*

A key mindset feature for both Black male and female gang members is *"Numbness"* (Anglo-Saxon, 'take away')—to be destitute of the power of sensation or motion. "Numbness" can be organic, induced (e.g. by anesthesia), or psychological (called Psychosomatic)—the one characterizing most Black gang member so as to have no reaction to doing harm to others or to themselves. Many women feel that childhood sexual violence "damaged" them to the point of no return--leaving them vulnerable to sexual violence in adulthood and in effect, sealed their fate so that they were mentally imprisoned. "I was also sexually assaulted when I got older, and at that point a lot of what I felt was numbness. I felt nothing after a while and also did feel powerless, you know? This all really damaged me and got me to where I am today in the system." Women who have experienced incarceration and who are survivors of physical abuse, especially those who experienced violence at the hands of an intimate partner, report that drug use "numbed out the pain" of the physical violence and helped them to cope with difficult life situations. What seems common to women is when they have hurt emotions and nursing that hurt they are also in the process of internalizing that anger.

The C15 Latin word "*Internal*" (inside, inner, between, among) means to give inward or subjective character to a concept, understanding, custom and done by interweaving the new with ones established Information, Knowledge or even Philosophy of Life in a manner that a given thread goes over a specific aspect of Reality--under the next--over--under, and so on in the manner of forming a Tapestry. The result is what is internalized *is so automatic as for them to flow out of ones Selfhood*. When something flows it is *without rigid rules* (since rigid rules are man-made and thus lacking certainty). The transformed anger acts like an octopus, with several tentacles, like "disappointment, depression, despair, self-pity, self-blame, guilt, rage, and desire for revenge which has no bounds in intensity or duration. The consequence is chronic distress which, in turn, makes her even more hypersensitive to real or perceived 'slights' (e.g. blocked opportunities and cultural messages that devalue women.) Furthermore, women of lower social classes experience greater stress than women in better economic circumstances and have less experience and, therefore, less ability to use anger as coping mechanisms.

BLACK FEMALE GANG COPING MECHANISMS: Long (*Feminist Criminology, 2013*) mentioned that among women's most common sexual victimization and other stressful life events coping mechanism is alcohol and/or drugs—both forms of self-medication. One who faced abandonment by family and community after she killed her rapist and blame when she disclosed it to a romantic partner, described using heroin and alcohol to cope with her multiple victimizations experienced, as well as to numb her pain, explaining: As a result of [those experiences] I started drugging. I started using drugs and doing drugs. I decided to go numb . . . I felt like I was an expert at locking s**t out but I always did it with drugs or alcohol. Several other women described adopting the persona of the *strong Black woman*, and sought to cope with their victimization experiences without assistance. Another believed that if members of her community knew about her sexual victimization she would be looked at differently. Her method of dealing with the victimization was to "get over it," which appears to be a common response among Black women.

Several of the women's lack of access to social support or institutional resources for coping with their victimization, coupled with the accumulation of trauma, resulted in serious mental health problems. One had suffered a mental breakdown and attempted suicide multiple times as a consequence of the abuses she suffered, for which she was hospitalized several times, including one stay of approximately 6 months for depression, Post-Traumatic Distress Syndrome, self-harm, and suicidality. Shared similar traumatic life experiences provided her with much needed social support, which she believed was assisting her to cope with her experiences.

FEMALE GANG MANIFESTATIONS: Once in a gang, the proportionate increase in the odds of violence associated with gangs is statistically similar for males and females--75% of female gang members reported being involved in gang fights, and 37% reported having attacked someone with a weapon. Individual violent offending rates were similar except for hitting someone, general violence, and particularly serious violence, for which boy's rates were significantly higher. As with boys, a small proportion of female gang members are extensively involved in more serious and violent offenses. Females and males share many of the same risk factors for gang involvement, are similarly affected in negative life-course-altering ways, and are most criminally active in coed gangs. Robbery, the epitome of male crime, involving themes of aggression, power, and dominance—overshadows Women's participation in robbery, and is lower than any other violent crime.

With respect to assault, 75% of all violent female offenders commit assault, and in 75% of these cases, their victims were other women—and 66% having had a prior relationship with their victim; 40% while under the effects of drugs or alcohol; 50% taking place at or near the victim's home or school. When women kill, they are much more likely than men to kill someone they know. Violent crimes perpetrated by women are emotionally motivated and impulsive, and the target is generally a family member or acquaintance. There are important differences between these women and other violent female criminals. By carrying around chronic anger in a mindset devoid of Selfhood Greatness results in low rates of aggression by women interspersed with instances of extreme violence. A display is a battered wife who not only kills her husband but also "overkills" him, stabbing him repeatedly or shooting him many times. Hormonal alterations, as occurs in following delivery of a baby create higher-than-normal levels of stress throughout the postpartum period, making instance of homicidal violence more likely.

"KILLER" GANGS & "KILLER" POLICE ENCOUNTERS: Arrest practices are alike for male and female but Black males and Amerindian males dominate over females being murdered by police. In the first 5 months of 2015 an average of 2 unarmed people (females and males) a day were killed by policemen. Within the worlds of males who operate out of their False Self, the spotlight is on their constant competition with those with whom they have more than passing encounters. The object of that contest, when there is a "level playing field," is for each to come out a winner, as clearly shown by the other being a loser. Those who recognize they are losers do so because the winner is the one with the GUN and/or the one with a powerful supporting Network—either or both the Loser Victims have been in an unfair fight. Victims with a chronic sense of "non-power"—whether it was derived from being defeated by ongoing terrorists or by their own sense of inadequacies and personal Shame--have an Inferiority Complex. Either they remain so and build a lifestyle around it or develop a Superiority Complex by joining some Indifference/Hate/Evil/Sadism Complex oriented "Bully or Terrorist Group". That group always acts dishonorably and finds "Excitement" in engaging in Intimidation as well as Kill/Take/Destroy practices. But still remaining uppermost in their minds is their terrible self-image.

For police or gang members, a bad self-image is typically such a great threat to ones Selfhood as to drive one to invoke negative stereotypes of others (scapegoats) as a means of temporarily feeling better about themselves. This becomes an automatic process, featuring the absence of awareness or attention as well as a lack of intention to what they are doing, even when it reaches the stage of uncontrollability. Yet, the intensity of the negative reactions varying from Mild, Slight, Moderate, and Extreme, depending upon the mood of those involved + with respect to their group + to their hated entity. These stereotyped reactions dominate even in non-Brute "Troops," unless they spend more time learning about the feigned enemies' common humanity and unique attributes. The automatic processes eventually becomes a conditioned Response with automaticity actions and reactions that are influenced by the perceiver's motives and Goals—by the thought, appearance, or suggestion from others of the scapegoat--and aspects of the situation enabling them to get away with killings (as when the laws and Network are cheering on the police). When it is clearly demonstrated that such there are no punishments and, in fact many rewards, their Conditioned Reflex effects can advance to "automatic" killings under more controlled mental responses.

RACIST ARREST/INTERROGATION/LEGAL/COURT SYSTEM

Juries are strongly influenced by confession, despite the fact that 25% confess to things they did not do. Since the effects of confession cannot be reversed, they are wrongfully convicted and some are later exonerated by DNA evidence. Much of the problem is the way confessions are obtained. Initially, police focus on behaviors that might indicate a suspect is lying using false clues, demeanor elements like jittery limbs or averted gaze or body language and deceptive leading questioning. The suspect is placed in a small, windowless room, and asked provocative questions designed to reveal deceit. Experienced criminals know to look the questioner in the eye and say they are innocent. With this incredibly fallible Background which often wrongly indicates one is lying, step II is interrogation, focusing on gaining an admission of guilt—and not checking for prior misunderstandings. Here, "good-cop, bad-cop" routine—i.e. maximization and minimization—which is highly coercive, especially with the intellectually challenged, the young, teenagers, and those with mental health problems (usually to to appease interrogators). Individuals are sentenced to prison differentially—issues such as class, competency of attorney, pretrial release or incarceration, county of conviction, and characteristics of the victim all play a part in whether or not any particular offender is sentenced to prison or receives probation. Survivors of racist incidents are told if they are friendly enough, smart enough, work hard enough, dress professionally, speak articulately, avoid the wrong neighborhoods, and stop associating with the wrong types of people, they will not experience racist incidents. The feeling of powerlessness ensues when one attempts to follow the numerous and often arbitrary rules yet continues to be violated. Survivors discover they do not have the power to stop the violations. They develop fear, hyperarousal, and confusion, which may be triggered by the perpetrator, by people who are similar to or who aid the perpetrator, and by areas in which they live. The confused and fearful survivors are unsure whom to trust and may question their own experience.

INSIDE PRISON

Every inhumanity conceivable has been reported as occurring to inmates. Examples include the handcuffing of an inmate without food of 32 hours and without being allowed to go to the restroom; tethering inmates to objects for prolonged periods and in physically uncomfortable positions; restraining inmates naked in an area where visitors to the jail could view them; the common practice brutal beating of inmates, particularly when handcuffed. The mentally ill often receive no special consideration and it is not unusual for medically ill inmates to not be given medicines or females to not be provided with sanitary napkins. Many are put in solitary confinement for frivously reasons and for prolonged periods—a practice that can drive people insane.

WHITE HATE GROUPS

During slavery the overwhelming majority of Euro-Americans qualified as being in Hate groups and the percentage has not decreased much since then. Some of the more prominent ones include: *Type I:* Credit for the idea of the *Ku Klux Klan* is given to Pulaski, Tennessee where a group of school boys at home for the Christmas holidays in 1866 decided to amuse themselves by covering themselves with sheets and parading about the town at night. Superstitious Negroes who saw these "spooks" were terrified, and the effect was noticed by the Whites. Thus, the ideas of the fantastic disguises, some with removable heads, or false stomachs that could consume immense quantities of food and water, and horses with padded hoofs moving silently through the night, were adopted by the Klan social club for former confederate soldiers as the proper regalia for impressing their superstitious victims, as well as for concealing the identity of its members. They sought to dismantle the political power of southern Blacks and Republicans who came into prominence after the Civil War. Some say there are 44 active Klan groups totaling 4,000. Competition with Nazi, Skinheads, and like-kind Hate groups weaken the KKK. Other White nationalists view them as uneducated, live out in the middle of the country, and are movement "do-nothings". Yet, at all times they have been tied in with all facets of USA institutions, particularly the police and Court systems.

Type II: Neo-Nazis date to 1959 by Rockwell who wanted to include many ethnic groups deemed to be "White"—including those excluded by Hitler (e.g the Greeks, Spanish, and Slavic peoples). Now, it is but a shell of its former self—ruined by bad financial management, a lack of charismatic leadership, and petty internal schisms. Whereas the Klan is a specifically Christian association, Neo-Nazis do not endorse a specific religion.

Type III: Skinheads arose in Britain in the 1960s as a reaction against the peace and love hippies, despising trust fund children and people promoting peace signs and long hair. "Instead, their accoutrements symbolized a tough working class--wearing steel-toed boots (part of factory people's uniforms who feared a heavy beam falling on their feet) and shaved their heads to keep their hair from getting eaten up by machinery. In the 1970s they split into racist (joining the White supremacist British National Front) and anti-racist factions. In 1988 the Aryan Fests brought together Skinheads who formed the Hammerskin Nation--a leaderless male/female group who adopted the White Power Skinhead lifestyle," including attacking Blacks and Hispanics, and planning the destruction of Jewish businesses. They, like many Right Wing USA Hate movements, had a temporary growth spurt following the election of the Black President Obama. They meanwhile engage in successful law enforcement operations and the death of important leaders.

Type IV: Christian Identity includes a variety of religious White European sects. They engaged in major conspiracies and violent acts by right-wing extremists in the 1970 through 1990s—e.g. shooting sprees, bombings and bomb plots, and armed robberies. Christian Identity mingle with neo-Nazis, through groups such as Aryan Nations. Perhaps there are 100 Christian Identity groups with 120 preachers—so scattered that an actual church is hard to locate. People leave to do internet activism due to the very high social cost of being a member.

Type V: White supremacist prison gangs are the only thriving formal Hate-Groups—the oldest and most notorious being the Aryan Brotherhood ("The Brand"). They established nation-wide drug-trafficking, prostitution, and extortion rackets in prisons--their leaders often working out of barren cells in solitary confinement and allegedly ordering scores of stabbings and murders. Killing is done primarily to impose a culture of terror to solidify their power—the main driver as opposed to an abstract vision of "White purity". Their numbers are growing because of the USA's booming prison-industrial complex. Private prisons spend huge sums of money and lobby elected officials to send more people to jail for longer sentences so as to ensure the continuing need for more and bigger facilities. Prison gangs are a major source of authority and structure—like an organized crime syndicate. Since gangs are the most efficient creators of order, race is more a recruiting and organizing tool than it is an actual set of political beliefs. By being more interested in money and drugs, they set aside ideological beliefs to work alongside other gangs, other groups, and races.

Type VI is the Racialist Intellectuals--contemporary White nationalists comprised of an amorphous band of "intellectuals" whose written and published works aim to give racialist crusaders a new look of Supernatural academic credibility by spreading their message with more mainstream conservatives. The essence of the message is that "race is an important aspect of individual and group identity; that different races build different societies that reflect their natures; and that it is entirely normal for whites (or for people of any other race) to want to be the majority race in their own homeland. If Whites permit themselves to become a minority population, they will lose their civilization, their heritage, and even their existence as a distinct people."

Type VII: Migration Online is being done by White nationalists and separatists to websites like stormfront. org (which, with 40,000 daily visitors, seems to be the most popular website of its kind in the world) and newsaxon.org (the social networking site for the neo-Nazi movement). People can set up a website with no financial investment; there is no publishing cost. The internet also allows you to keep private and remain anonymous—and that lessens fears of the government and persecution. This group of *Internet Individualists* are able to have a private bath in the well of Hate without engaging in the social and legal risks that come with being a registered, card-carrying member. There is much cross-pollination among Hate groups so that one can go online to extract ingredients for fashioning a philosophy of life whose theme is White supremacist oriented. These are "lone wolves" who are indoctrinated but avoid law enforcement radar by not showing up to Klan rallies.

Being "rogue agents" who take matters into their own hands, duplicate the quasi-mythical element common to many extremist subcultures. This is like some *"Numinous Feelings"* consisting of being filled up with a sensation of a Supernatural Numen presence pertaining to something like a kind of massive conspiracy combined with crushing, invasive power that requires people to act out on their own, as is suggestive of Al Qaeda, ISIS, or the way people are streaming music rather than buying albums. Hence, these "rogue agents" do not join Hate groups but rather are "streaming hate"—not having to embrace the whole dogma of any given one. Their displayed Hate follows patterns similar to what a Nazi, Skinhead, or KKK member might do. And such is encouraged by Satanists, for as long as someone does evil against a minority, it is suggestive of a favorable Hate Numinous power--an Icon Contingent Being which originates out of ones imagination but, by never coming into existence, it contains no natural rhythms capable of stirring a human's emotional reaction. Thus, these "rogue agents" mean there is no "fingerprints" on the crime scene. This pattern of not affiliating with Hate groups directly while being indoctrinated into their dogma—being able to sympathize and support the cause without really having to interact—characterizes present day White supremacists.

LEAVING GANGS

To leave a gang requires that one "be sick and tired of being sick and tired" (a Black American expression) of either what is going on in the gang and/or intensely desiring to be about ones Mission in life. There are very few differences in the gang disengagement process between females and males (O'Neal, *Youth Violence and Juvenile Justice*). Females have continued concerns about threats to their family, while males' focus is on continued police harassment after leaving the gang. In the process of "becoming an ex," individuals gradually transition from one role to another that involves four stages: first doubts, seeking alternatives, turning points, and creating an ex-role. First doubts are experienced when individuals start to question their commitment to a role. This stage is accompanied by considering alternatives and weighing costs and rewards associated with role demands. The second stage, seeking alternatives, involves actively evaluating alternative roles. The third stage involves a "turning point" that facilitates role exit. The final stage includes creating the ex-role which includes accepting the expectations and identity associated with being an "ex" and acknowledging the tension between the past, present, and future.

The process might be different for female and male gang members Whereas status and the importance of membership play a role in some individuals' ex-gang member identity, others focus on new roles such as parenthood. For example, one female ex-gang member, when asked what it meant to no longer be a gang member told us that "To be, like, below the level of, you know, hard, or somebody that would be able to go anywhere and just get respect. Like a nobody." Gang membership was a source of status for this respondent, something that was lost when exiting the gang. For both females and males, tiring of gang life and starting a family were the main sources that influenced their exit from gangs. For example, one female ex-gang member told us that she left her gang after she got pregnant. When asked whether anything else helped her exit the gang she responded, "Just the baby."

Encourage the development of positive prototypes (gists) or images of healthy behaviors and negative images of unhealthy behaviors using visual depictions, films, novels, serial dramas and other emotionally evocative media.

REHABILITATION

The development of ones personality or character was a gradual process, and any alterations to it must likewise be the same. Because ones concept of ones Secular Self is deemed to be essential to the mental and emotional health and well-being of the person, one will subconsciously resist efforts to change when their Self-Concept is challenged. However, European slavers so beat down the Spirits of the Enslaves as for them to have been brainwashed into changing "everything" and being remolded. By the situation being less than extreme compared with slavery, in an attempt to circumvent the powerful defenses fortifying ones personality against change, penologists often use rewards and punishment as if the ego can be bribed or penalized into dropping its safeguards. Because the old model of personal reform through rewards and punishments tends to ignore the realities of the human personality and the development of the self, it has had many more failures than it has had successes.

Even though current rehabilitation models are of this nature, simply because punishments or rewards are held out or alternative information is provided they cannot have any significant long-term change. Nor can one be expected to consciously alter deeply imbedded, subconsciously supported characteristics and behaviors for extended periods of time. Today's Rehabilitation concepts are based on the therapeutic model that suggests that those who commit crimes against society are somehow sick. Thus, they are seen as in need of "scientific treatment" through psychiatric/psychological means, job training, education, and so on. But most important for Black youth is Philosophically directed measures in keeping with African Tradition. It no longer matters about the all the sociological, political, economic, and cultural forces leading them into "Street" crime culture for now ones Rehabilitation is self-determined as to willingness, what is selected, how much and to what degree and to how often one will apply the *Spiritual Energy Package* of dedication, commitment, loyalty, determination, persistence, and perseverance to not give up—to never succumb to attractive distractions--to always give ones best effort—and to achieve the goal in the most efficient and effective manner. Each of these six is like the links in a chain and each is needed to complete any worthwhile task while driving away ones Emotional Energy powered Ego (*False Self*).

After one is on the right track in striving toward self-designed Human Ideal Goals, a major obstacle that must be handled is the temptations to go back to old habits, constantly being faced with environmental wayward enticements, being surrounded by forces which make it difficult to keep going 'straight ahead' and/or wherein the positive changes sought are not reinforced, as is the case in most, if not all prisons. If prison inmates attend therapeutic programs intended to modify their behavior and teach respect for other human beings while residing in a hostile environment wherein they are disrespected, belittled, and perhaps forced to endure daily degradation rituals, then the unreinforced positive instructions may be canceled out entirely by the more powerful negative influences to which they are exposed on a regular basis. This is the dilemma, which sabotages the success of prison rehabilitation measures. They are often contradictory in that one is instructed to evolve while yet rooted in an environment which almost guarantees, perhaps requires, their evolution reversal. The same often happens to Black youth when released from prison to back on the "Streets."

REHABILITATION IN PRISON: Prison treatment programs and therapeutic discussion groups often provide new information knowledge but produce little actual learning that can be practically applied or that lead to permanent behavioral changes. There is little opportunity to practice manners, or even civility, in an antagonistic prison environment. By nothing being done to affect long-term change in behavior, it is very difficult to rehabilitate while punishing someone at the same time—a realism which contributes to high levels of recidivism and the continuation of the culture of crime. Even with apparent successful treatment where prisoners are inspired to change their lives—when they begin to reintegrate into the community and experience the challenges of finding a job, making a living or being accepted, most suffer moral breakdowns and eventually revert to what they know—typically taking on "Street" crime values. The resistance to efforts to change a person's fundamental notions of self and the surrounding world are magnified exponentially when such efforts are made by those outside the individual's trusted peers, elders, and cultural group. Hence, forced change produces little more than temporary modifications in behavior made to increase rewards and decrease punishment until such time as the individual can resume activities more in tune with her/his former "second nature." To this point, Einstein said *the solution to a problem cannot come from the same consciousness as the one that created the problem.* In their attempts to rehabilitate, the afflicted may be momentarily obliged as long as rewards and punishments are proffered. Such is not transformation. Their Selfhoods are not changed, their perceptions remain the same, and their values and principles are left unaltered.

In African Tradition, Spiritual Transformation or *Transfiguration* is of megastar importance in switching from ones False Self to ones Real Self. Its three parts are: (1) *Mystical Dying* of the mortal part of ones Soul (i.e. the "Heart"; (2) *Regeneration* by "re-yoking" ones Selfhood to God; and (3) Rebirth by living and spreading Ma'at Principles (Unconditional Love and Truth). As a result, one is absorbed into the Divine. Rebirth implies the Ba-Soul rejoins the body in the Beyond (the sun at midnight) so as to make new life possible ("born again") into Ma'at principles. For the people, Rebirth is the result of having worked out approaches and methods to buy back ones Soul from Ignorance, the chain of traditional falsehoods, and most of all Delusions (believing what is not real and not believing what is real). [Ref: Bailey, Ancient African Bible Messages].

In keeping with what is practical in the prison system's Transformation, the consciousness of the person must be changed; however, the methods of such change must be made with an understanding of the defense mechanisms designed to prevent such change. Whereas Rehabilitation seeks to change the way a person behaves; transformation changes how one thinks; Rehabilitation looks to the past, transformation is future oriented. Rehabilitation often occurs externally; transformation originates from within from one being empowered to see the world differently. Empowerment differs from inspiration, encouragement, rewards, and so on. These occur externally and are short lived, while empowerment is self-generating. Instead, empowerment means reconfiguring ones way of relating to the world and changing the lens on how one perceives the world. All human characteristics are capable of being culturally transfused and/ or modified. Such is achieved by removing the "Cloud" over ones "Soul Sunshine"—and that does not require any consultant or information for it can be done instantaneously.

However, not all Human Ideal Goal characteristics are viable to all cultures. Associated factors may be that, despite knowing what is right, there may be rebellion if one is advised by a hated or disrespected out-group member and/or if ones own cult does not view favorably those right ingredients. Some are brought to a halt by failing to take into account the idiosyncrasies of the afflicted and the social context wherein they reside. Such speaks to the importance of the offender's peers to be part of the transformation process. In contrast to established social workers, prison officials, and law enforcement personnel, Transformed offenders have strong influence legitimacy among their pre-Transformed peers that do not have. A rehabilitated person need only show selected characteristics deemed desirable; a transformed person. Fundamental changes in personal philosophy, the aim of transformation, are not solely an individual intellectual phenomena and are not complete until they are manifested by personal efforts to transform others ensnared in the "Street" crime lifestyle.

Hence, the transformation process that begins with the "Self," ends with the transformation of others—i.e. the seeking to help reproduce Human Ideal characteristics throughout his or her environment. This is not necessarily so with rehabilitation. The need for returning to ones peers in an effort to transform them culturally is obvious. Only in the process of doing can one truly become and remain ones Real Self. This is more than mere philosophic rhetoric but an essential truth in line with what is presently known about human conditioning. The more practice one has, the greater the likelihood that one perfect the desired changes in personality. Therefore, artists become great artists, not by attending discussion groups about great art but by practicing. Writers become accomplished writers, not by talking to professional writers, but by writing. Moreover, prisoners desiring to learn more socially productive behaviors do so, not by sitting through endless hours of therapeutic group sessions, but by returning to their communities and practicing the socially productive behaviors which they seek to make a part of their lives.

But there is more to one being transformed. One may need help in getting properly oriented to being on the right plane of existence, using the right method, going in the right direction, and being around the right people. The aim of rehabilitation is to restore the individual to some former state that may or may not have worked for the individual in the first place. Transformation, on the other hand, works to completely transform the person's way of thinking as well as that person's self-defeating lifestyle. The focus is not simply on the individual but instead on others and their responsibility to make a contribution to someone else's life. In this context, transformation would be open to all prisoners to raise self-awareness and moral consciousness in a way that brings them in alignment with their innate Real Self human nature.

REHABILITATION OUT OF PRISON: While in prison, inmates have been exposed to a wide variety of philosophy patterns. Some include: *Pattern I* is that emphasized in African Tradition—choosing the Spiritual (the striving to achieve ones Highest Self) to be the orchestrator of their minds, good emotions, bodies into a balanced life of Manliness. Such does not apply if there is the tiniest degree of intentionally being off the Spiritual Elements path. *Pattern II* is the Confusionist Chinese focus on developing the Mind and Good Emotions so as to be smart gentlemen. *Pattern III* are hermit monks who focus on the Spiritual. *Pattern IV* are those who only develop their Emotions. *Pattern V* is that of the European Warrior who spotlights the Physical,

Bad Emotions, and accoutrements (especially the GUN). *Pattern VI* are various combinations, including hypocrites. These generate an Internal Aura of self-greatness if ones Selfhood is harmonious; desperation, if one has a splintered selfhood; or rebellion if one has a False self.

Once released from prison, ones self-directed transformation is refined and expanded to head toward achieving Human Ideal goal; to the proper handling of money and other material necessities; and to getting ones Selfhood sound. Part of the Penal System's plan is theoretically to ensure released offenders from the Department of Corrections (DOC) not only meet the expectation of the Rehabilitation model of being on the way to a thriving life but to also contribute to producing work products that enhance the lives of all—especially those in communities they earlier helped destroy. Such a process, to be effective, must be peer led, directed, and facilitated—on the order of the African Age-Set System heading them to become reacquainted with their Real Self. While internalizing various aspect of this knowledge is motivational for them to stay in the Spiritual Elements flow for self-improvement as well as through the perpetual practice of reforming others who exhibit criminal tendencies or who might be considering it. In this way, one ensures personal climbing as one assists in the efforts to help change others.

REDUCING ARRESTS: The focus here is on educating students about the dangers of gang involvement, the lesson content places considerable emphasis on cognitive–behavioral training, social skills development, refusal skills training, and conflict resolution (Petersen, *Criminal Justice Review, 2013*). A summer activities program can be added to build upon the school-based curriculum. A complementary curriculum is also available to strengthen families by engaging parents/guardians and youth in cooperative lessons designed to improve communication, identify clear and consistent rules and discipline, and establish plans and goals for quality family interaction. Another evidence-based program that appears equally effective for girls and boys in gangs is aggression replacement training (ART). It consists of a 10-week, 30-hr cognitive–behavioral program administered to groups of 8 to 12 adolescents. Although broad goals were established for atrisk females in these programs (e.g., empowerment support groups, promoting cultural awareness, expanding community awareness, promoting employment opportunities, and building spirituality three main components: mediation or conflict resolution, social support, and cultural awareness.

Certain treatment priorities for girls are clearly indicated. One consistent theme in the female gang literature reviewed herein is the dysfunctional family life. Protection of vulnerable girls—especially as they move into the pubescent period—from sexually aggressive boys and exploitative men is paramount. Supervised residential centers serve the purpose of insulating girls from violent community contexts. These centers have three specific objectives: "(1) to shelter and protect girls; (2) to provide job training, and job placement; and (3) to ensure a healthy start for gang girls' children". Social and life skills training (Botvin, Griffin, & Nichols, 2006) should also be provided. In short, these centers would serve as a one-stop resource for a variety of services and sources of assistance.

WOMEN AND VIOLENCE MANAGEMENT OVERVIEW
By Sharon Bingaman R.N.

Violence has been a part of our world since the first European men fought over a piece of raw meat or a woman. It was the violence that was used to settle issues and maintain power and control. From the beginning of early civilizations, women have been exploited, dominated and treated without dignity or respect while living in patriarchal societies. There are cultures where women were and still are thought of as property. In having to survive in those settings, women have learned to retaliate in secret ways much as the Enslaved did on the plantations of the South. Women can become angry and indignant and enter into relationships with a feeling of domination and/or contempt for men. They may take on the demeanor of a queen, if allowed, and feel that they are deserving of that situation with the man in a servant position. A woman with this attitude can become very indignant and surprised when the man doesn't go along with her plans. Believe me, with everything else a man must face in life, he does not need that attitude and women, it isn't serving you well either.

WHO YOU ARE TO YOURSELF

Before we look to see who is at fault in a relationship difficulty, we need to make sure that our own house is in order. Who are we? Do we really know and are we being honest with ourselves? We need to see things as they are, not as we want them to be and then deal with them. There are two points in a woman's life when she is her real self. The first time is when she is born and the second time is with the birth of her children. Think back as far as you can in your youth and remember how you felt and what you were like. You need to focus on those times, write about it, feel it and examine it. When we are born we have all we need to be self- great. We are born with a drop of God, a talent like no one else and the genetics of our brilliant Ancient African Ancestors. You operated freely, creatively and with spontaneity. There was no ego. If you have stayed with these birth gifts then you have stayed on the right path or Truth track. But if you have allowed yourself to stray from that path, developed a false self and are filled with hate, revenge greed, and envy, you will not find a fulfilling life or the right partner. These negatives are fetters and they keep you focused on what someone else has and what you think you don't. To borrow some comments made by Jos. A. Bailey II, MD, about the Ego, "Egos can be vicious and deceptive and they react to bad things by revenge. The Ego can punish through Aggression—e.g. overt abusiveness; passive acts—e.g. silent treatment; passive-aggressive acts – e.g. as a sabotaging sniper; and non-aggressive acts such as failing to help." So take a look at yourself and find out if that Ego of yours is getting in the way of meaningful relationships. If so, it is in your power to get rid of it by mental self-discipline which results in good-self-esteem and self-love. You must replace bad thoughts with good ones and move forward.

By not staying on the Truth tract, you open yourself up to allow harm to come into your life and the lives of others. It's OK to be selfish and take the time to make the best you that you can. Traveling down the wrong road will keep you tied up in knots and struggling and this situation can lead to a life of stress and ill health. Remain strong in yourself. Think back to the time when your children were born. You felt and interacted with your newborn with Unconditional love-no baggage.-full throttle and no holds barred. It was the strongest and purest of bonds. And it was the Truth. That is where we must be as women and in this society it is yet, another struggle. Can I rely on myself to keep my word? Am I trustworthy? Will I stand up for what I know to be right and true? And to what degree of intensity will I stand? Do I withstand the mild push but cave when the going gets tougher? These are all questions that you must ask yourself and answer honestly before moving on to a relationship with another.

WHO WE ARE TO OTHERS

In a culture that has the Ten Commandments as foundational, it is easy to see how women have been viewed since the beginning of time. Women made second to Adam but the first to sin, seen as property to be used and abused at whim, if you believe in the European Bible. If your perspective is Afrocentric, you know that men and women are equals-different but equal. Each has their own unique talents that must be cultivated and then shared for the benefit of others. We are meant to complement each other but not fill a void in others or have them fill a void in us.

But as women, we are usually part of the crowd. That is where we have found our refuge and acceptance by those just like us. However that acceptance is based on how much you conform to their standards, filters, guides and measures. You favorability rating will be based on how much benefit they can get from you. Your unfavorability rating will come from you telling the truth. So, in the crowd there will be those for whom you are very special and on down to those who dislike or hate you. What you must keep in mind is that your first obligation is not to the crowd but to the ME/WE. Their opinion doesn't supersede your Mission in life. If it does matter to you then you still have a problem. If people do not see you clearly, then you need to change the people you hang with- get a new crowd. But the problem may be that you do not have a clear understanding of exactly who you are and if that is the case, you will be looking to something else to give you that identity i.e. the crowd or a partner. And if a man picks up that you are not solid, don't know yourself, well that can be devastating to a relationship.

The experiences I share with you are not offered to tell you what to do in your circumstance but to empower women to formulate the best informed decisions for their particular situation. I am not here to make you feel good with warm fuzzies. I am here to offer pathways to help ease you through problems that might arise and to avoid others. I know women will move at their own pace, moving only when they are ready. I have been there. I will share with you that I have struggled to come to terms with the information I share with you now. As a woman who has endured abuse of a physical, psychological, emotional and spiritual nature, I saw the issue as completely one sided –and that was my side. Coming out the other side of that and returning to my real self has allowed me to see that men are multi-dimensional people too and that there is a part that women can play in escalating abusive relationships. I am aware that this information may be difficult for you to receive as your emotions cloud your perspective and that is why I give detailed steps in each area.

In this chapter, I have included discussions on the woman who is a novice in relationships and what are the issues she should pay attention to before entering into one, the woman already in a relationship with problems and suggestions to handle those and avoid future problems and the woman who is out of a relationship but considering a new partner and what she needs to be aware of. I have also addressed the issues of psychological and substance abuse as I have experienced it in relationships

All you did was ask a question about the how the job interview went and did he know that money was in short supply and, Oh yes, the electric bill was due. When out of nowhere –POW! -came a quick blow to the side of your head. Now where did that come from? There are a number of issues that are contained in this scene and many others growing out of it that need to be considered. I have been on both ends of the relationship scale and have experienced many of the ups and downs that you have. That is why I would like to share some ideas with any women who are wallowing in relationships, thinking about entering a relation- ship, have just come out of one and those who have never been in one. If we, as women, are not prepared before entering a relationship, we will be confused, disoriented and not sure of what to do. I have never been able to fully get behind the idea of women as "victims" of domestic abuse. It is a word that gives away all of our power and control to someone or something else. I want women to be more prepared and aware than I was before entering into a relationship and if anything from this chapter is a help, than my time has been well spent. I am offering this information so that other women may be able to fashion effective approaches for relationship building, measures to avoid situations that foster abuse and construct appropriate responses for themselves.

I would like to talk first in a general sense about our society and the manner in which women are socialized. Women are constantly bombarded with all types of social media about how we can look better thus feel better about ourselves and look better to men." Body Shaming" is devastating and can lead to a tragic end. We need to give women more than beauty and fashion advice. Women are not born with a pink gene, loving dolls and all things soft and cuddly. This is learned behavior. What we need to cultivate in our girls is the idea that they can tackle the difficult problems. We should be teaching them mental toughness and how to take themselves seriously and how to impact others to do the same. And just as we should with our sons, girls should grow up in an environment where they are not afraid to cultivate the feminine side if that is their interest. However, being mannish and wanting to be in charge will not increase your chances of attracting a professional man if that is where your interest lies. When a child is born, they come into the world with everything they need to succeed. They have the drop of God in them along with a talent like no one else and the genes of their superior Ancient African Ancestors. There is no cloud over their Soul Sunshine and they are on a path to live a life within the Spiritual Elements of Unconditional Love, Truth, Reality and the Natural. If she is raised to honor these gifts, this will give women a real sense of power so that they can convey to a partner that she is an equal and interested in sharing harmony.

In his book, Teaching Black Youth, Joseph A. Bailey II, MD says that "When the Private Self is healthy, as a result of Sacred Bonding, then one possesses the "5 Ss" which are Safety, Security, Stability, Strength and Sureness. If any of these are not present then one has a 'broken selfhood' and this is the cause of all self-defeating thoughts, emotions, expressions and behaviors." With a broken selfhood you are not feeling good about yourself, are vulnerable, weak and open to and may actually seek out exploitation. What should be emphasized with our women is that they are perfect in the natural state in which they were born.

First, let's review the definition of violence as set forth by The Violence Prevention Alliance in the World Report on Violence. "Violence is the intentional use of physical force, power, threatened or actual, against oneself, another person or against a group or community that either results in injury or death, psychological harm, mal-development or deprivation". I might add there is also the emotional, spiritual, social, financial, gender, psychological, and parental abuse.

I want to return to the earlier domestic abuse scene. The very first thing I have learned to do, once I get my head clear, is to take a few steps back to consider-what part did I play in that? Have I decided to react outside the realm of the Spiritual Elements? Have I been too critical and demanding? When in a relation-ship, we are to be concerned about what is going on with our partner. Have I treated him like a baby? The fundamental difference between your man and a baby is that you cannot make decisions for a man unless he asks. And women do not know how to deal with issues in a man's world. Did I take a moment to let him know that I support his effort and appreciate just his being there? Did I take the time to consider that he is probably overwhelmed, that his manhood is taking a beating? For couples of color this is very touchy because during slavery the women were put in charge of men and after slavery, women of color were able to find jobs when their men could not.

At this point he may be very insecure and criticizing and challenging him will not have any positive effects. What I have found to work is to try to find out what the specific problems are. Possibly he is looking for work that is really not in his area of interest and he needs to know that I am in his corner as he steps into a new venture or that he is not getting paid enough. However, don't let that pendulum swing too far one way or the other. Don't be accepting what doesn't belong to you. But was what I was complaining about really important? If it was important, was it worth it? I try to focus on the ME/WE as we are in this together. Have I created an atmosphere where the man feels free to discuss what he wants to or have I made it harder because it may not be favorable? Has he been trying to tell me about problems and I haven't been listening, remembering that some men do not have the facility to speak about the core of their emotions clearly which can be so frustrating that they react with anger. And now he is at a point of complete frustration that he felt the only way to get my complete attention was to lash out? Healthy relationships make sure that both parties feel safe to discuss any issues without fear of retaliation.

Again, in the above scenario we are discussing this act as a first time occurrence. If I am taking care of the man's Private Self, which is being supportive in many different ways, such as not underestimating what he does, complimenting him or noticing the things he does for me daily, then I should be able to find out if there is a special problem. Is there an underlying medical problem for example? If not and the abuse occurs again, you then have a decision to make. Do I stay or go? If I decide to stay, then I know what to expect. However, if I decide to go, I realize I need a plan and it needs to be well thought-out before I make the move. At the point when I find I have done what I could, there is no room for self-blame. Be careful who you talk with as your business does not belong on the street which is where it will end up. Nor does it belong on any social media platform. What is important is to start gathering information about groups and organizations that can be of support to you. If possible, you may have to stall plans to leave if you need time to put together enough money, set up a safe place or locate /contact shelters. However, it may be that you will not have time to plan and in that case just get yourself and the kids out. For some women, a restraining order is necessary but it is basically not effective. You may have to involve a trusted friend or relative if a hiding place is needed. Those in whom you confide should know that they may also be in danger. He may interpret their helping you as a rejection of him. Whatever you do, don't try to destroy him when you leave or turn his children against him. Do only enough to be effective in getting safe.

NOVICE

For the novice in the world of relationships, before entering one, I suggest you need to ask yourself "Do I really know myself, what am I about, what do I believe?" You want to be a complimentary equal. When entering a relationship that you want to last, you want to be in charge of yourself, in control of what you do and the situation. Armed with this knowledge you will be strong in yourself. Are you working on fulfilling your purpose in life? Can you be self-supporting? Ladies, please do not enter a relationship when you don't bring anything to the table. Don't expect a free ride and you will not be disappointed. For those considering a relationship for the first time, look passed the handsome face, the great body and great clothes. He may have great style but what does he have under all of that? Is there anything of substance? Take careful note if there is something, anything that bothers you. Don't go in with any expectations, what you see is what you get and what will be. Investigate it. Feel free to check for any police records that might deal with issues you will not be comfortable with and know that he might do the same with you. And for goodness sake, don't go through his pockets or his phone when he is not around. Men are more private than women so don't break a trust. Many people have some secret that they want to remain in that state and that should be honored. The small things that bother you now may grow into something larger later that you will not be able to live with. The small thing should be distinguished from the insignificant. The way to do that is to play it out to its Nth degree. You need to decide if you can live with that or not. Part of that decision is that you might be faced with it every day and can you deal with it?

I had a relationship with a young man who in the early stages of our relationship told me he didn't like saddle shoes because they had the colors of black and white together on the same shoe and he made random jokes about people of color. Now they were, I thought, just passing remarks. However, I later found out he was a flaming racist. It was something I chose to ignore and regretted it. You also need to be aware of the type of people he surrounds himself with as this can be an indicator of his Philosophy of Life. And, by all means, don't rush into anything as you need to be able to see how a person reacts to different situations over a period of time, approximately three years. Again, there could be more to the small thing that bothered you than you realize. A friend of mine has likened this to seeing only the tip of an iceberg and not knowing the full truth of what is not seen. Can you see that he might be trying to isolate you from friends and family? Does he want complete control over your finances and important documents? Is he critical of you in public? Has he destroyed some of your property, made threats to commit suicide if you do not do what he says? Is he trying to control you? The list goes on. Another issue to consider is, has he had a traumatic childhood? Get to know his family and close, long-time friends well. Please don't overlook a discussion about money and child rearing as these are important and major issues to be considered when thinking of a serious relationship. If organized religion plays a large part in your life, this also needs to be discussed along with the expectations that each might have .

THOSE NOT YET IN A RELATIONSHIP

For those not yet in a relationship, you need to think about just how much you want to give. Do you want it to be 50-50 or 80-20? If this man is truly my man I am prepared to give 100%. It is also important for you going into a relationship for the first time to ask friends, separately, for their input about other possibilities that arise in relationships. What is fundamental in any situation is that you make your own decisions after collecting as much information as possible. Never allow others to influence your decisions so that if it goes wrong, you will know where to make corrections and not repeat that mistake. And never put your money together with easy access by both. Be sure you are clear about who you are and what you want.

THOSE WOMEN IN A RELATIONSHIP

For those women who are in a relationship, you know that it takes continued work by both parties but you can be responsible only for what you do. Take an honest look at yourself and ask-Am I too bossy? Am I playing the man? Am I treating my man as a child and not a partner? Am I taking care of his Private Selfhood? Taking Care of his Private Selfhood is sharing the same values and Philosophy of Life. Do I see myself as always right and knowing what is best? I must admit that in the past I have been guilty of being a part of a number of these categories. Showing an interest in something he is doing and taking an active part, when possible, is a great relationship builder. When a disagreement happens, don't forget to take that moment to step back and look at the part you may have played in it. Don't get caught in keeping a score card of what you do for him. What women need to keep in mind is that many times what we do is very visible and in the physical world while what he is doing may be on another plane of existence or unknown but nonetheless important and contributory to the partnership. I might be scrubbing a floor and he could be sitting at the desk figuring out the taxes; both important and needed. His mere presence, in itself, is protective of her.

Any time you have a conflict with your partner, it needs to be discussed then and there and not 6 months later. In the discussion you need to clearly hear what your partner is saying from beginning until the end and not be forming a rebuttal in your mind at the same time. And women should not be telling a man how to live his life. Before making any decisions be sure you are well rested because once you leave you may find out that he was doing more than you knew and an adjustment will be needed. If you find that this relationship is not working and you have discussed it or tried to discuss it with your partner, your options are easy- stay and with no further complaint or go. The "going" decision does require minute detailed planning as does the ability to stay away. First, make sure that there are no guns or other weapons in the home. If there are –remove them.

The second thing I learned was never to threaten to do something without a plan in place and never threaten him. If you are the one to go, make sure you have a place to go. Make sure you have access to your important documents and enough cash by keeping them in a secret place. Try to put enough money together to have enough to cover the transition period from two paychecks to one. Take with you only what is absolutely necessary as "stuff" can be replaced. If your partner is the one to go, don't fight about material things but be prepared to handle them –just let it go. Once he is gone –make sure you change locks if it is your home.

OUT OF RELATIONSHIP-CONSIDERING AGAIN

For those women out of a relationship and thinking about it again, make sure that you write out all the problems and pitfalls you can about the last relationship. Doing some post action judgement will allow you to see where you made mistakes, how to correct them and find out what lessons you learned. Learn your lesson and then write out a plan. And again, I want to emphasize that we ask ourselves about the part we played in the end of the relationship. You may even go so far as to ask your enemies if you have had a hand in bringing about this behavior. Those who are not your friends will be more than happy to tell you where you have made mistakes and their answers may be more truthful than a self- evaluation or from your friends I have tried to learn something from each of the past partners. I many times took a look deep down inside myself to ask-what do I lose or gain with a new relationship-am I willing to love and lose? Examine yourself closely. Are you harboring a hatred of men? If you are, you need to get rid of it or you will continue to fail. Men can pick up that vibe easily and will not show any respect to that woman. I know that it can be very lonely at times but don't rush into anything just so you won't be alone. You know the old cliché that you can be alone in a crowd.

PSYCHOLOGICAL ABUSE

There may be those times when abuse of a psychological nature occurs and you need to be prepared. If you have maintained your sense of Selfhood Greatness then you have fortified yourself against these attacks on self. If you don't have Selfhood Greatness, you are automatically sensitive. If you are sensitive, a compliment will be taken as neutral and a neutral comment will be taken as bad and a bad statement will be exaggerated into something much worse. That will cause you to want to get revenge and women tend not to get enough revenge. If you are in that mental state, empty yourself of all of that by writing out everything you are feeling until there is absolutely nothing left. Later, if anything else should pop up, write that out too. In order to build a solid self, you need to try to get back to your Selfhood Greatness. You need to support yourself mentally and do something good for someone else and particularly anonymously and without finding out if they benefitted from it or appreciated it. If you are successful you can then say Yes, I'm O.K. The reason for doing it anonymously is that the receiver may not appreciate it and/or they may not give you a compliment and chances of all three are good. If you don't know, you can feel like a really good person. Keeping a daily journal is a good place to document how and what you are feeling and to chart your progress and new findings about yourself. Remember to get enough rest.. A third thing is to stay away from negative people. A fourth thing is don't take on the problems of others. A fifth thing is whatever problems you have that belong to someone else, give it back to them. Don't allow anyone to undermine the sense of a workable, self- reliant self that you have built. You must build immunity to this psychological abuse. Don't fight it. If you dismiss the attempts at psychological abuse, it will die from lack of energy. You get to that point by realizing that you are more important than anything anyone says about you. Your decision reigns. If anyone says anything bad about you, then they have the problem. The idea is for you to be in control of yourself and the situation. I knew a couple who were going through some difficult times. The wife woke up one morning to find that her husband had thrown away all her underwear and she was scheduled to go to work that day. She called a friend to make a run to a local store to pick up what she needed. She related to me that she was prepared to make the stop on the way to work if necessary but her friend came through. When she returned home that evening, she made no mention of the incident and that was the end of that. She said she put no thought into making any similar move against her husband as she saw no need to continue a "tit for tat" atmosphere. Keep the perspective that when these episodes of mind games arise, use them as a challenge and don't give way to blaming or complaining. Use it as an opportunity to be creative. The reason for not complaining is not to give your power away to anyone or anything.

I am not in favor of you spending your life having to deal with this type of behavior. This is a point where you need to ask yourself again-Have I played any part in this to bring about this type of behavior? If this is behavior not consistent with the partner you know, you may want to consider that there is an underlying medical condition. If these questions come up negative then you will have to think about bringing up a discussion about the mind games the person is trying to play. Of course this discussion can only occur if the situations allows. My husband would follow me when I left the house but when asked about the reason for it, he would deny it even happened and accused me of making up stories. Unless you are prepared to continue with this behavior, you should be making a plan to get out of the relationship quickly. Do not continue to allow someone to place you in the position of "victim" as it will continue to sap your energies and make you appear weak and not in control. Don't waste time blaming – it gives away your power. You gain nothing by allowing continued harm of any kind to yourself. You could also start a Self-Protection journal where you write out all that happens but using false names for those involved and be sure to put it somewhere it will not be discovered. The idea of being anonymous allows for complete honesty in the journaling.

One of the exercises I use to decide where I am in my level of accepting certain levels of behavior from others is a Thinkers Scale (fig. 22). It looks like a ruler with a zero in the middle and stretching out on both sides of the zero is a scale from 0 to 100. To the left of the zero are negative numbers and to the right are positive numbers. Now I have fashioned that on the negative side 0 -24 is mildly abusive behavior.

Slightly abusive is 25-49, 50-74 is moderately abusive and 75-100 is extremely abusive behavior. I then decide what is contained in each of those categories such as someone shouting at me which would fall in slightly abusive or if someone hit me, it would fall in the extremely abusive category. I then decide what my action, if any, would be and so on for the rest of the categories. When finished putting all items on the scale-add them up to see where you are. This example can let you be aware what behavior you will tolerate and if not, what action you have decided to take. An aspect to keep in mind when doing this is to ask "Am I being too hypersensitive about certain behaviors of my partner "and where am I rating that behavior on the Thinker's Scale? The assessments must be real and true.

It is important to have a model of a good relationship and you can look for those around you. You can also question your friends and family as to what they think is important to keep in mind before entering into a relationship. Be sure to write down all that you are looking for in a partner and add to it each day, if needed, so nothing is missed.

One of the most important images for me to keep in mind after relationship difficulties was the idea of the third candle. That would be the candle that is lit from both the flame of the bride's candle and the flame from the groom's candle in a wedding ceremony. It says that the union is greater than the sum of the parts of you and me. It is the ME/WE that must be uppermost in the mind and not just ME.

I thought I would include some of the things I have learned along the way to impart to those ladies who are interested.

1. Set limits on what you are willing to tolerate-if you don't, the other person may take that as approval for any kind of behavior
2. Just be real, be yourself-trying to project a false self cannot work or last forever
3. Appreciate that the opposite sex is not like you, doesn't think like you
4. You need to laugh every day and especially at yourself
5. Please don't keep a score card- this is not a game
6. Complement each other on a daily basis-fun complements are a good idea such as "I saw that beautiful sunrise you put up for me today, Thank you'"
7. Partners should take care of the other's Private Selfhood and work to enhance the Public Selfhood of each other
8. Be on the look out to see what you can do to make his life easier
9. Have interest in what the other does
10. Volunteer to help him in any way
11. It is important to have a common goal outside the home
12. Always say what bothers you in a manner in which you would like to be spoken to
13. It is important in life to lift others while climbing and never more important than in your personal relationship
14. It is important not to try to impose your values on your partner as long as you are both operating within the Spiritual Elements of Unconditional Love, Truth, Reality and the Natural.
15. Be able to appreciate what unique talents each of you brings to the relationship and do not try to make it a competition
16. Don't be judgmental
17. Give the other person space —don't be up in his face
18. Try to keep your body language and facial expressions neutral during heated discussions
19. Remain calm

20. If possible, allow for a period of silence for both of you to be able to really hear what was said and allow for a cool down
21. Speak little and listen a lot
22. Never go to bed angry-stay up for as long as it takes to voice how you both feel and come to a point of understanding
23. Be aware and comment when decisions he makes, keeps troubles from arising.
24. Don't try to control men and think that you know best in all things-allow the man to make the decision to ask for your help
25. If there are children involved, do not stay in a relationship because of them. You will only expose them to further danger and damage.
26. Don't withhold sex to use as a weapon against your partner

SUBSTANCE ABUSE ISSUES

If drugs, alcohol or any substance is causing a problem in your life please seek help before entering into a relationship. And likewise, be observant of the behavior of another when choosing a partner. Be on the lookout for changes in attitude and personality without identifiable causes, chronic lying, in activities, hobbies or paranoia. There is also the issue of change in personal cleanliness and, of course, track marks. The behavior that was wild, crazy and sometimes exciting will quickly lose its appeal as you try to build a sound relationship. If you are already in a relationship and there are problems existing, arguments could lead to use and abuse of a substance in order to escape, reduce the stress or soften the blow. But that leads then to a vicious cycle as the use of the substance fosters more arguments about that. Many people who use drugs and alcohol do not become abusive but substance use can make abusive situations worse and the substance then becomes the excuse. Your partner may be dealing with issues of shame, fear, remorse, anger. Always be supportive and let your partner know you are willing to participate in the recovery process. If the partner is willing, together, find programs available to help and make sure you also have support. Be mindful of the reality that recovery never ends. Keep in mind that the causes for physiological abuse cannot be changed so support groups such as AA are recommended.

Summary: What I have tried to offer is the suggestion that in a relationship, first make sure that you are in good shape before entering a relationship. Then honor the dignity of the other and treat them with respect for who they are and their many talents. Dignity, in African tradition is part of the substance of God along with Divinity, the image of God. As such, this automatically calls for us to honor each human being. Don't go into the relationship thinking that you will change those things about your partner that you don't like; accept him/her as they are or not. Make sure that your act is together and solid.. Make sure that your support of your partner is 100%. When problems arise, write it out until you are empty and if something comes up later go back and write it out also. Attempt to talk out issues as they arise. If you begin to experience some rough spots and talking doesn't help, between the two of you, you might seek the help of a counselor. If it appears the relationship is over and you are thinking about leaving, make sure you have a solid, safe plan for leaving the relationship. Make sure that you are calm and well rested before making decisions. Own only what is yours. Don't look to friends to give you sound advice because the best they can do is to get you through the moment. What you will get are only opinions and those can be on many planes of existence like the physical or supernatural (fantasy world). What that does is only add to the confusion. There is little chance that any of it is the Truth or the complete Truth. Long term, solid plans must be made by you. And if the relationship goes bad, it is half the fault of each.

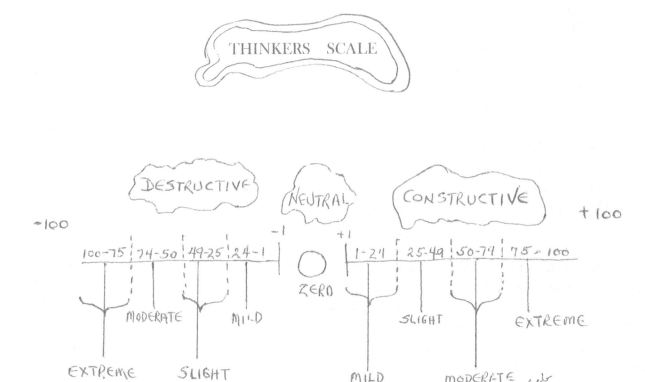

FIGURE 22

Remember, Love creates or enhances harmony and unity within ourselves and others. Egos create and enhance disharmony and separateness.

SUMMARY

The argot of crime is the language of the despondent, the damaged and the traumatized. It is the idiom of the mentally ill. Hope cannot be infused in those for whom hope is foreign. Usually, there is an interlink with impoverished neighborhoods, strongly associated with gang membership, and antisocial behavior. If Circle 1 is on the left, Circle 2 is at the top, and Circle 3 on the right, Circle 4 is where those three Circle interlock, and that is called an "Interchange". The other three Circles impart ingredients out of the nature of each to make for similarities in the somewhat dissimilar Circles. Together there are uniqueness in the similarities as well as the similarities which make up the "sameness" aspects inside the "Interchange (Circle 4). So what is going on inside the "Interchange" is a reciprocal give and take intermingling as well as change of two or more things for another so that any given item takes on the place and/or nature of the other; to become by turns; or items may alternate or move in varied successions in time, order, or space. Put another way, just as there is a certain "sameness" about each day, there distinct differences in each one.

The same applies to gangs and what they do—whether they are male or female. For example, some female gangs, like those of males, adopt identifying features—e.g. spotlighting a particular color, clothing, and tattoos, and use argot, hand signals, and emblems to emphasize their unique identity. The influence of gang membership—or even the potential for membership—may prompt the setting aside of existing moral standards so that ones ways of life come to fit with what one perceives as gang membership requirements. By so doing in adopting what they see as a *unique* identity, the group effectively communicates its character. By joining a gang and adopting that gang's group norms and behavior will mold their social and worldview ways of thinking, feeling, expressing, acting, and reacting. This leads them into things of the wrong type, in the wrong place, in the wrong arrangement or combination or form; or in the wrong place, the wrong time; on the wrong plane of existence, with the wrong people, on the wrong track in the right direction, on the wrong track going on the wrong directions, or on the right track going in the wrong direction. Correction comes from troubleshooting to discover all the problems and then fixing those problems so as to strive for Perfection. The objective is to get their Life-Living links of the chain to be complete, strong, and flowing together in the same direction and at the same speed and toward the same destination. In short, an old truism applying to gang members is: "success is in the details." Ref: Bailey, Rational Thinking.

CHAPTER XIII

TO STOP THE VIOLENCE
RETURN TO
UNCONDITIONAL LOVE

NATURE/MA'AT MANAGING OF VIOLENCE

The theme of my life has been to follow the "skeleton" of Nature using the Principles of Ma'at—both being internalized from my boyhood family and all-Black communities—both emphasizing the necessity for Manners (caring about and taking care of the pre-birth Emotions of others)—both being about the "ME/WE" of staying in contact with my deepest Inner World and displaying it in the External World to do what mutually benefits myself and others. The practicalities started by doing gardening as a boy. I learned principles of Nature and Ma'at by paying close attention to how things grow and what it takes to make them grow and what to do to prevent things which interfere with their growing in order to feed my family and share food with neighbors. In this process I would take off my shoes and socks so as to wiggle my toes in the dirt—and that would carry me into a Sublime realm. During the summers my dog Sandy and I would walk 3 miles to a fishing pond that no one visited and while focusing on the cork to see if it bobbed because of a fish biting at it, I went into some other plane of Cosmic existence. Every year in my early life I would drive up to 17 hours to find a 'non-people spoiled' place in Nature; then sleep for 15 hours; then go to "my Nature spot" and simply be quiet, as if in a sort of Trance. At that time, all of my most significant life's problems would be solved. Subsequently, I would sit on "my Nature rock" with my toes reaching the water's edge and be quiet. In the process, my body assumed the rhythm of Nature and that put my entire Selfhood in order.

The Cosmic organism provides me with a Spiritual Entourage who has guided me through life. This book has been extremely difficult to put together, especially since much is about the Metaphysical and the Supernatural. So, in trying to decide what to say about this chapter, "my Spiritual Entourage" awakened me to say to write about "Nature" as a way to approach the subject of how to help Broken Black People—those who cry outwardly or inwardly to be healed in body, mind, and spirit. That awareness was like finally being able to scratch the bump that itches. But before elaborating, allow me to put a perspective to this complex subject using the SOBMER Process components as it applies to Nature.

LAWS OF NATURE

The Laws of Nature are simply the observance of its regularities—whether behind the Obvious or what is Underlying the hidden of natural events. These regularities are permanent, stationary, unchanging patterns or elements and held together by an unchanging steadfast Spiritual bond internally linking and ruling all things springing from it as well as serving as a Virtual bond with all that is modeled after it or copied from it. For example, the Earth's magnetic resonances vibrate at the same frequency as the human heart rhythm and brain waves. Thus, all God's creatures and creations residing in Nature possess within and among them: (1) Coherence (its hidden internal links and components being consistent with one another); (2) Consistency (standing firmly together within a state of harmony and balance with what makes sense); (3) Compatibility with Reality (practical); (4) Interconnectedness (everything real depends on every other real thing); (5) Order (sharing the "Oneness" of Cosmic Primordial Substance center); (6) Regularity (conforming to the prescribed standard or the established pattern for it kind); (7) Balance (rendering no favorites on either side but conforming to the Ultimate Standard); (8) Harmony (complete adaptation of each part to the Wholistic Circle); (9) Endurance (progressing inside/in tune with the Spiritual Elements); and (10) Predictability.

This means there is Continuity (Unity running through Multiplicity) from all interdependently doing its independent things for the benefit of the whole in the *course* of their *Natural Processes*. To illustrate, every atom is constantly sending out, and receiving, infinite vibrations to and from all other atoms. The same particles of gaseous, liquid, solid substances are circulating through all sorts of living bodies and "Things" throughout such Kingdoms of Nature as the succession of Mineral, Vegetable, Animal, Human, and those Higher. For example, similar thoughts, feelings, desires, volitions can be found in all minds with respect to what constitutes human nature (Das p186).

Nature, said Ancient African Sages, is the home of God's Laws--the source of humans' wisdom—a human's Work in life *is an intensification of the work the God Spirit* does in Nature, but on a tiny scale—and a human is to neither *work simply for others or simply for oneself but rather to do Win-Win work whereby everybody benefits—a "ME/WE" concept.* And that is all one needs to convert from a Brute to having a successful life— i.e. getting what one really, really wants and not getting what one really, really does not want. This can happen because Nature and humans are an indivisible unity, like two sides of a coin. Put another way, humans, in their identity as images of God, belong to the Cosmic Organism Society and, as living Beings, belong to Nature. These three are interactive, interrelated, and mutually affective (Karanga, MAAT, p10). Since its processes of un-wearied power display is reality, Nature is the Cosmic Background and the theater for the stage on which humans, in the Foreground of Earth, Live-Life. Everything begins on a mental level before it manifests in physical results.

The Ancient Egyptian words "*Neter*" (God) and "*Neteru*" (God's manifestations) are the roots for the words "Nature" and "Natural"—later known in ancient Latin as "natural," neutral, and eternity. *Nature means the sum of all real phenomena—together with the Causes which produce them—including all that happens as well as all that has happened and all that is capable of happening--to generate Spiritual Elements Effects and their Consequences.* Nature (African Nebethet, Mistress of the House) is Ma'at (Spiritual Elements in action) Principles. These Principles are an ordered interrelated divine and social binding of all God's creatures and creations within a state of existence. This is why the more one knows about mathematics, the easier it is to follow the flow of the Principles of Nature. Ancient Africans explained this by saying Nature is the model for the cultivation of ones genius, in general. Furthermore, Principles for solving any of ones life-shaping or life-changing esoteric (hidden) projects or problems, in particular, could be found in Nature--because of the *Law of Correspondence*.

LAW OF CORRESPONDENCE

The African Law of Correspondence is a conceptual tool unequaled for gaining insight into the Unknown or to clarify Understanding. *Correspondence* ('to answer') can be likened to an "Echo" (a reproduction of sound caused by sound waves striking an obstacle and being thrown back towards their starting point). Recall having shouted in an empty room and hearing your own voice repeating itself a split second later—*same vibrations, different form*. Such was caused by the sound of your voice bouncing back from a surface, like a rubber ball bouncing back from hitting a wall. Bats use the projection of their vibrations to find out how far away from objects they are—called *Echolocation*. And so do under water submarines' sonar equipment, similar to light reflected from a mirror. In a valley where mountains are all around, a sound may be echoed many times—the echo becoming fainter each time, until it dies away altogether. This is a *Compound Echo, or Reverberation*. Under usual circumstances, an echo cannot be heard separate and distinct from its original sound. Basically, an echo would not exist without the original sound, for that is its "Ground of Being." A "*Ground of Being*" is the essence of a "Thing"—i.e. what that "Thing" was when it came into Being—the ultimate 'ancestor' that by itself, reproduces itself, to become the off-spring "Things" it makes—like ocean waves. And that constitutes a *Genetic Family*—i.e. all the "genes" of each member are derived from a "Ground of Being" center but each has those same genetics in different combinations. Thus, there is individual "Uniqueness" in the "Sameness" of these intimate relationships. "*Intimate*" (C17 inmost, deepest, profound) in African Tradition is sharing the same Spiritual Space while being Spiritually connected. An illustration of that Genetic Family Correspondence is the mother and father's children who all possess the same genetics but in different combinations—a difference that provides to each child various types of "Uniqueness" and yet they share a "Sameness".

The Cosmic Organism Family's (i.e. all God's creatures and creations) Spiritual "Ground of Being" center is the primordial substance. Their Correspondence is provable by Mathematics applied to the *African Subjective Sciences*—i.e. Observation, Reflection, "Pure" Feelings, Productive Imagination, Contemplation, Inductive and Deductive Inferences, and Common Sense. The mathematics is that the "Oneness" of Cosmic Origin in the Spiritual realm is the basis of *Order*. The duplication of that "Oneness"—regardless of the degree of Matter added on any given plane of Cosmic existence--is called Correspondence and it remains in Order because of its natural progression. Put another way, all numbers originate with (1)—the "Ground of Being." All of the numbers that can be brought into the highest human awareness remain related to (1) as well as with each other. To evaporate (1) means no other numbers would exist in their essence or in their ultimate significance. How this came about is Ancient African Sages determined the inactive Primordial Substance (God's androgynic protoplast) as the 'Oneness' foundation of potentiality from which all 'Things' in the Cosmos emerge--*The Path* is what they called it. Thus, any off-spring on any plane of existence that came out of Primordial Substance and remains on the Path contains the "Sameness" of the Spiritual Elements but each with its own "Unique" combination.

The Alphabet invented by Nubians of Very Ancient Africa (consisting of 24 symbols representing vowels and consonants) and Interior Africans invention of writing at least by 77,000 BC can both be used to explain Correspondence. First, Ancient Egyptians modified the original African Nubian alphabet into a hieroglyphic system having two components. One part consisted of alphabetic characters (which communicate with the Left Brain); the other, an Ideogram with a literal or figurative meaning was called "*Determinatives*" which served the purpose of stimulating the Right Brain because they generated mental images in thinking and meditating. By engaging both sides of the brain, this hieroglyphic system established an optimum mental Correspondence condition for learning and understanding. Second, the letters of the Alphabet were formed into words—the words into paragraphs--paragraphs into a book—all having Correspondence. The white paper on which black letters are printed have Correspondence—2 sides of the same coin—meaning both the white paper and black letters are different and yet are inseparable—neither being able to exist without the other.

Similarly, in the Cosmos, there exists an endless combination and repetition of the four Spiritual Elements. Formerly put, The African *Law of Correspondence* says all Cosmic Phenomena are limited and serial—and, in addition, they appear as scales or series on separate planes. But this condition is neither chaotic nor neutral, for the components of one series are linked with those of another in their essence and in their ultimate significance—just like all the numbers are based upon (1). The "Big Picture" is that every natural "Thing" corresponds to and typifies some Spiritual Element or some Cosmic Organism Spiritual Principle or Truth—this being the only key for the fashioning of Ma'at patterns for Life-Living.

Furthermore, what goes on in Nature is also going on in the mind of each Real Self individual. This is because a human is a microcosm of the macrocosm of Nature in the way there is agreement in a human's Soul consisting of a "drop of God" in relation to God being likened to an endless ocean—in the way the "small" is compared to the "large"—in the way the Infinitesimal has conforming agreement with the Infinite. The Laws of Nature apply here as, for example, its principle of Interconnectedness (everything real depends on every other real thing). Hence, if that human completely vanished, then Nature, the Cosmic Organism, the Primordial Substance (God's androgynic protoplast) would be incomplete—i.e. not whole. The very few principles underlying a multiplicity of demonstrable and non-demonstrable Things in the Cosmos can all be reduced to a Unity inside a "Oneness". This is why Ancient Africans said that the first thing to do with any chaotic subject is to put in Order, starting at the beginning. The Archetype Seed is destined to provide a steadfast Spiritual bond internally linking and ruling all things springing from it as well as a Virtual bond with all that is modeled after it or copied from it. For that reason, if one knows something thoroughly about a given thing, one automatically knows a great deal about its "Unseen" or "Unknown" like-kind off-spring or counterparts on other planes of existence.

SECULAR CORRESPONDENCE: Human-made harmonious fittings of parts or character and mutual agreement to conformity is seen in countless aspects of daily living. For Right Life-Living one is to use Nature as a model to form Human Ideals and then use Ma'at for practical application in daily life. Since this process is based upon each individual's assessment of what seems best, only an illustration of what Secular Correspondence is about and how it can be used is given here. One example is the Alphabet Concept, consisting of a system of Writing and printed language. Its essential ingredients are that each of its symbols generally represents one sound, as with 'b' at the beginning of the word 'boat.' *Writing* is symbolic, not only because its characters stand for sounds, but also for words or concepts, all within an agreed, conventionalized code. To look at this printed page, what most people notice is only the printed message and ignore the white background upon which the black ink is printed. What one sees on this page is the result of having learned definite rules about the printed message--e.g. the letters of the alphabet; the formation of words from the alphabet; the meanings given to those words by the creator of the message; the Receiver's connotative interpretations of those words which may or may not be what the author had in mind; and so forth. But behind those rules related to what is printed is the blank white page--a Secular Substance ('stands underneath').

Spoken words are the symbols for objects and ideas. Based upon this background, let us use the Alphabet to serve as a means for penetrating into and elaborating on how to deal with any complex subject as, for example, Rational Thinking. First one must learn the letters (or tools) of the alphabet and they must be *internalized*. Second, after the alphabet is learned and internalized, advance to putting letters formed into words. Third is generating a meaning(s) out of each word (called a Denotation) and when that word is acceptable to society then they give their own meanings (called Connotations). It is essential to know the meanings people give the chosen word. The meanings given to them, as given to oneself, has three fundamental senses--*Intension* (the decision of what one means to do or what is ones purpose); *Significance* (of enduring importance, whether cognitive or affective); and *Effects* (deciding how to be most effective in conveying ones meanings).

Fourth, out of either Denotations or Connotations the sense of what is intended and then arranging and combining appropriate meanings so they have the power in the acceptable words imparted to persuade, inform, entertain, express, share, teach, instruct, educate, or serve as a call to action for decision making and problem solving. One can create new words and either impart a meaning to them or leave them without meaning. Whatever is presented must generate mental pictures and concepts plainly and simply enough for the other to receive the point with clarity and ease.

Fifth is arranging and combining the conveying of paragraphs, pages, chapters, and books for communication in an attractive design. Logic and having a "common touch" with the audience helps determine which word touches the "Heart" or "Head" the best--*the proper selection of which shortens the distance between the message of the messenger and the people's understanding of both.* The degree to which speaking or writing is successful depends on the content, the words chosen, the clarity, the simplicity, the "polishing" of the communication, and how it is received and interpreted. Once there has been an agreed upon plan of what is significant, then it is distributed to various branches of learning—in person or by means of lessons sent by mail (called Correspondence Schools).

NATURE OVERVIEW

Ancient Africans said the Creator of Nature and the *Source* of its Process and the furnisher of a first and continuous supply impregnates Nature with its life giving essence. This starts in the Cosmic Organism which is orchestrated by the Cosmic Mind (i.e. God's Intelligence). The most direct way to know the God orchestrator, said Ancient Egyptians, is to study God's natural manifestations (Ashby, Egyptian Yoga, p. 50). Many aspects of Nature and the Natural can be seen while others are so beyond the powers of the human mind as to require being I*nferred* (to conclude from evidence, or from premises, or by reasoning from circumstances) or *Intuited* (meditating to gain insights above and beyond the realm of the mind's thought processes). According to Natural Law, anything born must be subject to the laws of Nature and ultimately die into a transmuted state. Nature's meaning is first acquired in the commentaries its works provoke.

Notice that Nature is about continual evolution out of the Spiritual Elements while remaining inside them. Nature forms humans to be the Real Self for ME/WE" purposes and not a False Self so as to be with others—to be and do, not to seem to be and do. The orientation is realizing that everything unnatural is imperfect; that the nature of ones Real Self is perfect as it is; and that to deviate from ones Real Self is to deceive oneself. It makes no superior or inferior things—no princess or prince—no rich or poor. Instead, what it makes is for each product to do its job so as to benefit the whole. Its "Heart" core qualities, like the bloom on fruits, are best preserved by the most delicate handling. Nature is read by the practice of Humanity in all parts of the Cosmic Organism. The life of Nature is one of frugality and with few wants but the satisfying of those wants brings deep enjoyment. Nature needs what she asks for, always better understanding her own affairs than any human. Nature tells once her every secret but one must go deep into certain hidden mines and caves to hear it.

To elaborate, the unruffled calmness of clouds in the sky and the halo of the moon—the rhythm of the ocean tides—the sounds of chirping birds—and the *"Voice of the Silence"* which says everything by not saying anything at all while it retains everything by giving away everything—are each tonics to quiet disturbed minds. There is no other door to Knowledge than the door Nature opens into the realm of Wealth (that which is beautiful, calm, and imparts happiness). Such "Wealth" is *Wisdom* (the manipulation and maneuvering of Ma'at Principles), appearing as packaged forms of Nature's principles at work —principles that by themselves, reproduce themselves, to become the Things they make. The ultimate Wisdom deals with the essence which is always in a seed. There it lies, the simplest fact of the Cosmos and at the same time the one which calls forth faith rather than reason. A grain planted in good ground brings forth the fruit of its seed. A Ma'at principle planted into a receptive mind brings forth like-kind creations. That endless combination and repetition of a very few principles is called *Correspondence* and those principles come from an ultimate Creator source.

Thus, to see a Thing of Nature is to have a visible thought about the Spiritual. Part of that thought is that Nature works on a method of all for each and each for all. Understanding Correspondence enabled me to leap into new levels of Understanding. As a product of Nature, every human is given all the essential qualities to equip that human to do all that is needed. What is to be borrowed from Nature is to be devoid of envy or malevolence because one is simply borrowing from oneself and that borrowing is a contribution to bettering oneself. To work with Nature, each human must never desert her/his line of *Talent*. Nothing happens to any human that she/he is not form by Nature to bear.

NATURE USED FOR HEALING: Ones consultant for healing is the works of Nature because nothing is lacking and nothing is superfluous—but it speaks in Symbols and Signs. What is needed for healing are Nature's hidden forces within the Broken because Nature and Humankind are "One." Learn from the birds what food the thickets yield. Learn from the beasts the physic of the field. Learn from the bees the arts of building. Learn from the worm the weaving of a mole. Learn of the little nautilus to sail by spreading the thin oar, and catching the driving wind. There are no "Air Castle" social remedies capable of bringing about any Real Self restoration and nothing can begin to start working until the afflicted have then feet on Cosmic reality soil so as to Understand Nature.

Because of Nature's intimate relationship to all humans, it is the initiator or motivating principle of healing related action. By having more power than education and more knowledge that the masters, Nature does this in humans as it does for the sea--gaining by the flow of the tide in one place what it has lost by the ebb in another—but always in harmony. To explore Nature's mysteries is to have the revealing of plain practical lessons for every-day duty. For example, Nature's Things 'elbow their way' to their rightful place and remain calm once in that place. Within that wholism, at any given moment each Thing is precisely what it is and does what it does while all other parts are what they are and do what they do.

Beginning of Healing (the first part, point, degree, or start of external actions): What triggers the initial internal reaction to start the process that leads to budding, flowering, and fruiting is for the Broken to stop deserting Nature--reconnect with ones own nature--do the daily work of cultivation—and all the while nourishing ones Selfhood with the Spiritual Elements. The Nature in each human, like the realities of flowing water, can break through every obstacle, replace losses, and supply lacks in order to push forward in making herself a way. What cannot be changed must be allowed to take its course. What needs to be replaced is allowed to die from disuse. What is 'okay' must be made excellent as a routine. As naturally as bees swarm and follow their queen to make honey, Nature's forces begin management back to health by gathering up the fragments and refashioning them into ones newborn state of Selfhood Greatness. Start with what delights and enlarges ones Selfhood from the inside out. Then build an orderly Tree Concept type image of oneself that is about excellent, goodness, useful, and benevolent things.

Middle of Nature's Healing. This is concerned with Nature's greatest activity of external actions in order for that human's nature to do all it can do to return to ones birth state). Then to carry out ones birth gift *Mission*—although it is never complete--is to have a successful life. This demands going ones own way, as Nature does, and although that seems an exception, it is really according to order. A requirement of Nature is the imposing of tasks when she presents or makes opportunities happen—not allowing her creations to pause in progress and development. This is because nature is a never idle workshop--never does anything in vain—and never makes excellent things for mean usages. Since nothing takes place all at once, Nature's *Progress* is not made by 'leaps and bounds'—i.e. not done rapidly or in fast progress--but by changing one mind, one group, one institution one step at a time. Part of ones process is to imitate Nature's thriftiness in never wasting or annihilating of anything; in allowing no rest; in giving just enough to everything; and in doing what it has to do to get the job done, regardless of who or what is in the way. Nature is no spendthrift and always goes 'straight ahead' in carrying out its tasks—and without detours or rest periods. There is no unemployed force in Nature.

Nature is ever at work building/pulling down, creating/destroying, being cyclic rhythms/in rhythmical motion, in pulses/keeping everything whirling. There are changes in magnetic fields—in continental plates moving—in water cycles and flowing;—in seasons changing—in life/death—in process/connection. Nature flows through webs of structure and shifting time: from ocean to cloud to rain to river to ocean. Natural rhythms. Nature provides exceptions to every rule As Nature undergoes constant change, inside there is a certain sameness resulting from its essence remaining unaffected. An illustration of what is always present is the ever changing cloud. Every product of Nature has some beauty of its own—a material fact having sheathed within it the Spiritual Elements. To be able to see that is the way to develop *Appreciation* for 'what it is' and how it came about and what its Creator must be like. This is like seeing a World in a Grain of Sand or a Heaven in a Wild Flower.

I. *End*/Ending (where the external actions stop or are stopping): All of Nature's decomposition is re-composition. Death is transmutation, as in changing of bodies into light and light into bodies. Yet, nothing is ever finished and nothing is ever isolated because it has reference to something else and each achieves meaning apart fro that which neighbors it. When one has done the preparation of ones Mission and begins to perform ones Talents, follow the ways of Nature to go into every empty corner—into all forgotten things and nooks—and pour what it takes for them to stop going downward or to start pushing them up or to help them thrive.

I. *Result* is the good, bad, or neutral Effects. The study of every part of ones nature, though it makes no claim to beauty, is the way to become "Alive" about each discovery occupying ones imagination about its infinite power. It is always in the Right and competent and pure in what each well-functioning aspect does.

I. Consequences: In Nature there are neither rewards nor punishments—there are only Consequences. By Nature being inside, surrounding, and outside oneself, in the way the various parts of a spider web is connected, means that to take care of Nature is to take care of oneself and to take care of oneself is take care of Nature and all that is within it.

NATURE AS A TOUGH "TASK MASTER": "It is easier to build strong children than to repair broken men" (Frederick Douglass). Nature shows how this can be done before or after the fact.

Nature has some perfections to show she is the Image of God and some defects to show she is only an Image of God. The ways of Nature are just in a Cosmic sense but some of those, as judged by humans, can be terrible and merciless. Just as Nature's fires will burn the good—and water will drown—and the earth will bury, this is a way the Divine Plan is presented to ones life. For this Plan to be fulfilled, one is to use like-kind difficulties one has in life as tools to force out the divine powers within ones Selfhood so they can be cultivated into flowers and fruit. Although there is no intention by Nature to be mean, what it natural's no nonsense does is to serve as a model for how problematic things work in the world. From understanding these things and fashioning them into reasonable "what ifs," one can then the preparations to avoid them, get around them, or instantly handle them 'head-on' as soon as they appear. These preparations are transferrable workable patterns for problems actually encountered that are in the same categories. There is no forgiveness in Nature.

Notice that Nature does not pamper for to do ones Mission is to see things—no matter how rough or surly (gruff)--as they actually are. Such seeing is done without an opinion as to how one would like or not like them to be. The big fish eat the little fish; the little fish eat the water insects; and the water insects eat the weeds and the mud (Chinese Proverb). Nature recognizes no excuse, regardless of how reasonable, for not doing ones Mission. Nature's rules have no exceptions. This is a survival factor illustrating the necessity for Selfishness as the first law of Nature. What Nature produces is not good or bad per se but rather how it is used, as judged by humans.

HUMANS' VIOLENCE PROBLEMS

The Interchange of the Interlocking Rings of Nature and Ma'at is called Circle 1. Those rings pertain to Circle 2—What is "Right Living" in African Tradition; Circle 3--how to avoid being violent; Circle 4--the disregarding of Nature and Ma'at's principles; and Circle 5--how to get out of a life of violence. However, because the Cosmos and the Cosmic Organism is Based (i.e. what the foundation is situated on and arise out of) on Unconditional Love, by necessity each human has Free Will (Will, the faculty of the freedom to choose). This embraces the capability of choosing to ignore the emotional, instinctive, and/or divine parts of ones Selfhood. The Will is free of emotions and sensuality or from any coercion, impulse, or compulsion from the emotional part of ones Selfhood. Thus, when one arrives at worthwhile accomplishments or chooses to engage in violence, these are volitional (i.e. under ones full control). To choose not to follow Circle 2—"The Way" of "Right Living" in African Tradition—means one is filled with ranging Ignorance displays.

Type I is those believing it is best to Life Live by ones "Heart Feelings" (i.e. ones Emotions)—and that is like sliding down a hill on a sled having no steering wheel or brakes. The ignorance is that one mistakes ones Emotions for ones Instinct (ones true "Feelings") or uses Acquired Emotions instead of pre-Birth Emotions (Bailey, African Tradition for Black Youth p279-81). Some cultures emphasized living by emotions, sensualism, and opinions over living by Truth. A Spanish saying is: If someone got up on a platform to tell the Truth, he would be the only one listening. It is preferable for cultures desiring to control the minds of the public to emphasize the emotional appearance of things and completely ignore the harm it can do.

Type II occurs in those whose thinking is not based on laws but on beliefs or opinions about oneself and ones relationship to the world—a clue to indicate Ma'at has broken down and Isfet ensues. This means the blind forces of emotionalism and sensuality are displayed within the realm of Metaphysical Disorder--"go astray," become lost," stray from correct behavior, and outside the boundaries of Ma'at necessary for humans to recognize the Good, to strive for Perfection, and Plan opposite to it as a life's course. These blind forces de-stabilize, devitalize, and disharmonize ones life-force and thereby causes a host of ills. Ones mind then thinks mechanically. For example, mechanical thinkers believe another human is always the same and unchanging mood with respect to its nature, depth, intensity, and height. Or, that another is hungry to the same degree everyday at the same time. One puts boundaries on the boundless to thereby needless limit ones abilities: "I can't do this" (despite it being in ones capacity). One looks outside oneself to blame—"what I did not receive"; or "the harm my parents did to me" So, people owe me. It is typical for people to claim they had no choice because "I am only human"—this is intellectual rationalization so as to have an excuse for indulging in the act.

Type III is those who choose to live out of their Brute Brains do Life Living with violence. This constitutes an extreme degree of the forces of Disorder, Isfet (abomination of God). The evilness in their Souls will, on Judgment Day, be eaten by a monster. Next, they enter a purgatory in preparation to reincarnate until "Right Living" generates the proper vibration speed to allow rejoining God.

MA'AT CURES VIOLENCE

The Ankh, a symbol of Ma'at, was originally based on the Feminine Principles of Nature, Spirituality, and Peace—the ingredients Ma'at models to cure violence. The C16 Italian word "*Model*" (a small measure) is a representation of something else on a smaller and more manageable scale. It may match the original in most details or be an idealization which seeks to represent only its main features. Nature serves as the model for one to extract principles for fashioning into an individualized Human Ideal—i.e. customized for a given human's life--having correspondence with Ma'at Principles. As stated in "About The Cover," Ma'at (the Spiritual Elements in Action) came into prominence because of its role in Cosmic Creation. Understanding basic African Tradition is fundamental to completely recover from violence as a perpetuator and/or as a victim. The "construction" of all things and the unfolding of all events are based on universal patterns underlying the activities of all Natural forces. For Ancient Africans the creation of the Cosmos was not a physical event (like European's "Big Bang" concept) that just happened but rather was an orderly event pre-planned and executed according to an Divine Law or Order (Maa, to see, insight) that makes all forms and governs the Physical and Metaphysical Worlds. This Plan they called Ma'at (equated to Chinese Tao)—the law that governs all events in the world—electro-magnetic forces, quarks, gluons, atoms, molecules, chemical interaction, gravity, the diet of creatures, and human life. The Divine Law was said to come from the notion of a one Universal High Spiritual God, boundless and an incomprehensible intelligence and Energy. Tehuti's skill in celestial mathematics made proper use of Ma'at laws upon which the foundation and maintenance of the Cosmos rested. The Division of Light from the Darkness—i.e. Ma'at—Truth and Order—was the first manifestation of creation. Light and Darkness were summoned out of undifferentiated Chaos—i.e. the unformed (formlessness), and "non-ordered" (i.e. undifferentiated)--but *not* "*disordered*" to form the Cosmos.

A powerful way to convey to African People these high level and complex "associations of concepts" as well as have them observe these principles (not worshiping them as dumb European Egyptologists say), African Sages metaphorically stated that "*Neters*" resided in the primordial Chaos (a formless, undefined, nonordered, but not disordered eternal duality). Out of this Chaos a number of lesser gods unfolded from God's Substance—each symbolizing a harmonic force in Nature in the form of the shaping forces of Cosmic Order--each possessing various manifestations related to the Cosmos--each interacting with different coupling strengths (Bynum, African Unconscious p136). The metaphorical gods--masculine principle Shu (fire, heat, air = God's Consciousness/Will) and the feminine principle Tefnut (moisture = Energy/Matter) corresponded exactly to what the later appearing Chinese called Yang and Yin (Amen, Metu Neter II:50, 74). In turn, Shu and Tefnut beget the Energies Nut (Sky, the Metaphysical) and Geb (Earth, the Physical) parts of Being--the four pairs of opposite principles of African Creation. In the Ancient Egyptian texts, Shu and Tefnut are described as the Ancestors of all the neteru who begat all beings in the Cosmos. This Trinity ensured a continuous relationship between the Creator and all the subsequent created.

MA'AT IN HUMANS: Since humans are a microcosm of this macrocosm, the same Cosmic Ma'at Principles and their formation apply to human's mental, psychic, and physiological activities. Human thought determines the behavior of the Energy System (Ra, Holy Spirit, Kundalini, Qi) within (Amen, Nuk Au Neter p18). Such thoughts, based upon Natural Laws, generate ones Private Self's "5Ss" (safety, security, self-confidence, strength, and stability), vitality, and harmony within ones life-force. By spiritually staying in ones newborn state means one continues with genius type thinking and Life Living. Ones psychic forces then attract good things and repel needless problems. These mental and psychic force orientations cause ones physiology to create, enhance, maintain, defend, and protect ones health. Together such principles of the Cosmos and the human body are a unity of events—are integral parts of a whole—are each independently contributing to the life of the whole—and their interdependent contributions make up a unit, a mono, one, single, alone. Out of this came the concept of *Monotheism*--the principle of Unity of the involved set of faculties—a "Big Picture" of a unity rather than simply being a label for singularity of existence. Ancient Africans said that how all of this comes about is by the Ma'at faculty in humans. It is deeply buried in the Spirit of the mid-function of the Right Brain with the capability of communicating to one mind the working of the force that maintains Order of ones physiological and mental functions. Ma'at itself is a projection of the forces that inter-relate the various functions of the body into a human's awareness.

The perfect harmony existing between the various functions of the body is Truth and Reality. One can intuit from this faculty and experience the urge to live by the Spiritual Elements of Unconditional Love, Truth, Reality, and the Natural—the Human Ideal in Life Living according to the laws of ones indwelling Divine Consciousness—i.e. the "Soul Sunshine" of ones Private Self. When Ma'at is projected into the mind to guide thinking, then one is led "instinctively" to the apprehension of Truth of a premise; to give Unconditional Love without seeking anything in return; and to have the ability to intuit (without guiding precedents) Divine Laws (relationships and interdependence between things) govering human lives and the world. One can thereby live in harmony with all things because all things in the Cosmos are functions within a system governed by the one Universal High Spiritual God. But Ancient African Monotheism was more than there being only one Universal High Spiritual God. To elaborate, the Cosmos is composed of a web of interdependent systems and all things exhibit an interdependence and mutual relationship with the other functionaries composing the system (whole) to which they belong. Examples are seen in the Plant/Animal food chain, water cycle, oxygen cycle, etc. The master principle governing the relationship between all functionaries and systems is the *Law of Equilibrium*. All functions must be maintained in their proper place in space and time. To illustrate, vibrations are felt via the Senses. Each Sense leads to ones Emotions. If the vibrations are disharmonious, as indicated by abruptness and harshness, the Senses of ones Real Self react by slowly tuning them out and distancing from them.

The "Natural" World works because it is built upon Laws—Laws, as determinal by Science and Mathematics, which govern Energy--Energy which make all activities in the World possible. This is the foundation of understanding the reason for creation (the Divine Plan), the reason for the creation of Humans and other creatures (e.g. deities, animals), and the reason for creating Laws. In contrast to Human-made Laws, Spiritual Laws are what meet the demands for compliance with the Natural purpose of God-made things and their relationships, and interdependence with other things and the whole. Underlying these are the principles of Duality and Equilibrium. For example, humans do not live underwater as fish as a result of the dual relationship between human's biological make-up and the associated living environment.

MA'AT APPLIED TO VIOLENCE: To make assessments for Spiritual Truths that leads one back to ones Real Self means ones Ma'at Faculty must be awakened--ones Ma'at "Soul Sunshine" must not be "Clouded"—and sound intuiting and thinking must be done concerning gaining insight into a given Event (activity), evaluation the presentation of a premise, or in "Knowing Thyself". Such cannot be done by being governed by likes/dislikes, "picking and choosing" what to deal with; by only getting the gist of or no dabbling in whatever is related; or by being on the outside of the fence enclosing the Interchange and merely peering in to make determinations—i.e. and disconnect after it is gone. Instead, one must engage in *Contemplation*—i.e. be in the inner world realm where all of this mental-spiritual interaction is taking place. This is about wallowing (getting in it, around it, like a pig in mud to experience it in every way you can) with it inside so that it is internalize and becomes a part of oneself. This is a way to stay in contact with what is necessary. The detachment of ones identity from oneself enables objectivity needed to consistently and accurately analyze (lysis=destroy) the issues of life. For a human to do Life Living by Divine Law is not simply about morality but rather by manifesting ones Real Self "Soul Sunshine." This has to be Programmed into ones Unconscious by Conscious factors. Ma'at is not about following some list of rules or commandments or dogmatic statements. Rather it is funneled through standards, filters, guides, and measures that allow for assessing whether they are of and have stayed within the Spiritual Elements.

When ones Ma'at "Soul Sunshine" is not "Clouded," it sees in "Knowing Thyself" or in the situation at hand the inner factors that unify things based upon the mutual relationships and interdependence of things with each other and the whole. Those factors consist of what each contributory ingredient was when it came into Being as well as whether its Source was God-made (Reality) or Human-made (unreal) as well as whether they are harmonious or not. Such is expressed through the abstract or metaphoric use of Images. It perceives all the ingredient components underlying things and events, thus enabling one to see the whole—and that is a form of Synthesis. Then one can proceed going across the bridge with the vehicle used to program the animating part of ones Being. Such includes using of ones Pre-Birth Emotions and Intellect interchangebly—e.g. to trace the story of a word in order to learn its nuances. This aids properly defining that word's, determining the "What it is," describing the topic's essence by Affect Symbolic Imagery; pointing out Concepts at each stage of its evolution through the ingredient used (e.g. sensations, memory), Percepts, Notions, Ideas), and Productive Imagination.

WHAT IS "SIGNIFICANT"

Fundamental to every human's determination of "*How Shall I Live?*" is the selection of what is "Significant." The "Significance" of ones life is clearly known on ones death bed. To imagine oneself there—to decide what is the single most "Significant" Thing—and to adjust ones present life to make that one Thing happen is what I call the "*Retrospectoscope*" (fig. 23). The Umbrella term "*Significant*" embraces several variable ideas as to what is absolutely great or terrible. What is great or terrible depends on who is involved; on the intent; and compared to what. A Thing may begin as good or bad and turn out to be the opposite. Such ideas have sprung out of different African and European (among others) contexts. To elaborate, in C14 English, "Significant" was defined as 'the meaning of something' (e.g. force, energy); in 1579, 'full of meaning'; in 1725, Consequence; and in 1761, of Importance. Subsequently, despite a broadening in scope, "Significant" retained the core ideas of being about the qualitative (or "worth") and the quantitative (or things of "value"). Illustrative African examples of "Significance" diversity are: (I) its origin came from the blessed name given to every Ancient African child at birth--a name in keeping with its implied worth and value meaning—a name symbolizing to the child, relatives, and acquaintances that he/she was outstanding--a name serving as a mark or sign which distinguished the child's outstanding deeds done in a prior lifetime (i.e. a good karma). (II) African people who distinguished themselves by great achievements were similarly recognized by members in the villages as 'Significant'. Example: the successful medicine man's therapeutic abilities had special meaning to the sick because they shed the bad + did curing.

(III) In medicine, *Quantitatively* Significant occurs whenever there is a measurable degree *of* change. When one says: "there has been no change in the patient's condition"--meaning the patient is neither measurably better nor worse in degree—such is an "important" indicator but without it being significant. By contrast, to say: "there is no significant change in the patient's condition" either confirms or throws doubt on the earlier prognosis because no meaning--like "better" or "worse"-- exists in comparing the two. Here, "Significance" implies no qualitative change. (IV) Significant humans have Courage to be their Real Selves who keep their word; cultivate what they honor; immediately "rise to the occasion" to handle Things they would rather not; remain undefeated by continuing to try; and influence each other through useful products and not necessarily by direct personal contact. (V) Ancient African children, as like me, saw significance in engaging in *Nonsense*—in being Silly without thinking—since it is fun to participate in "stuff" going 'nowhere'. The same occurs with Dance whereby one executes a pleasurable pattern without going anywhere. Fun does not lead to something else—it 'just is.' (VI) Some things have double (or more) Significance, as in how food is cooked and tastes as well as the extent to which nutrition is provided upon eating it.

(VII) *Contemplation* inside the flow of the Spiritual Elements was, for Ancient Africans, to be in a 'state of Significance'. This required a self-induced Trance by so concentrating as to blend into the topic's Truth which, in turn, displays correspondence with like-kind Cosmic things. To observe Things without inner turmoil, without "looking for" something, and without seeking a mental quest, permits recognizing the significance of what was formerly taken for granted or considered insignificant. It helps better planning. The point: *simply being inside a new realm and experiencing a connection with whatever is in it (e.g. Compassion) and without an opinion* is the way for the Significant to arise in ones mind. I call this MULLING. One progresses from time to timelessness; from space to spacelessness; from multiplicity to unity; from a dynamic mover to an unmoved Mover. At such higher levels of understanding, one has an increased ability to discern more interrelationships between dissimilar and/or similar things which have correspondence. From that alone, one can infer Principles and fashion Base patterns that promote their manipulating and maneuvering--as is vital to making for never ending evolutions of Significant new meanings and/or Forms to design/enhance Visions. This is also the path to *Esoteric Thinking*—i.e. revealing certain of the mysterious things about God; the things belonging to God; and the things revealed by God to humans. jabaileymd.com

PERFECT SOUND THINKING SKILLS

The single most important tool for Ancient Africans was the development and continual perfecting of Real Self Thinking so as to live within Ma'at. Together, this combination was the most important fashioners of Self-Esteem. By contrast, the cause of the basic problems struggling Black People have with thinking is that the sound thinking patterns of their Enslaved Ancestor was shattered by European captors. In addition, European males have never been, are not now, and never will be able to Sound Thinking in a Natural world sense because they pride themselves on the Supernatural "Non-Rational" Thinking they simply made up out of fantasy. Besides Europeans not knowing how to think, they do not care to know, do not want their victims to know, and ensure victims can have no way of knowing how to do Sound Thinking by eliminating access to African Logic. Yet, they claim they have "Logic" but their best was plagiarized from Africans. Other reasons they cannot be logical is that they disregard their Right Brains (which ancient Greeks discarded use of after studying in Africa because they associated it with being "feminine"). African Logic uses both the Left and Right Brain in their reasoning but have their Right Brain orchestrate because of its intuitive faculties that lead one into deeper realms of the Cosmos and thus allows for creativity.

Ancient Africans used the Supernatural within the context of the Spiritual and the Metaphysical—both avoided by Europeans—in order to explain the Truth of African Spiritual concepts. That is how the Ancient African Bible was written—in metaphoric language—which Europeans copied and changed into "Delusional Facts." European para-logical thinkers put out the propaganda of the presumption that modernisation is accompanied by a shift away from Supernatural belief systems to more rational and scientific interpretive frameworks. This is not actually the case. As a result of never having been exposed to the Truth, Black American Custom thinking is flawed in comparison to thought patterns of African Tradition. Fundamental to perfecting ones Thinking skills is to distinguish those which are Self-Defeating (typically Black American Customs) while discovering and internalizing those of African Tradition.

SELF-DEFEATING THINKING

What originally "took down" the sound thinking of African Tradition was being "awed" by the new way of thinking presented to them by Europeans. What Africans did not realize was that this "new way" was situated in another world—a Supernatural World that was completely destructive of Africans Natural Realm thinking. By Europeans only using emotions and their Left Brains means they had/have no basis for knowing what it "Right" (i.e. compatible with the Laws of Nature and their mathematical basis). Thus, their starting Base for a Thought Structure is on "Air" (derived from Non-Rational "Air Castle" Supernatural thinking) and therefore cannot follow any mathematical order. This is why it is essential to challenge the 'major premise' of anything Europeans say. To accept that flawed 'major premise' means that a 'logical' order is followed but on a non-truthful, non-orderly, and non-reality path. Struggling Black People who falsely think European males are simply "lost" or on the wrong track in the Natural Cosmos do not realize there are simply operating out of another world—a Supernatural world they claim to be superior—a realm European males claim to be "superior" simply because they say so. The Effects of their Non-Rational thinking is that it is "6:00" by the clock 180 degrees opposed to the Spiritual Elements—meaning they attack the Spiritual Elements (fig. 24).

Pause to recall if you have ever heard Europeans ever saying anything about Unconditional Love. One would not realize that nothing Europeans say is the Truth if one has never exposed oneself to African Truth and learned that all that African Sages say is mathematically based—not made up Supernature ideas. Nevertheless, the mental Form-Body state Enslaved Africans were forced into led them to start thinking in European flawed patterns. To illustrate with one example: "Disordered Selfhoods" pay attention only to getting the gist of what it takes to get through the moment--sufficient to get an answer that is "good enough" or "Almost" or "SEEMS" right.

As a result, the following sequence occurs: (1) all things in the Background of ones focus on the Foreground are disregarded; (2) disregarding the Background drop aways the supporting reality around what is focused on in the Foreground, making for an unreality; (3) each significant thing detected in the Foreground concerns ones interest and that "Thing" is viewed as an isolated bit of information; (4) studying that isolated "Thing" leads to varied interpretations which are out of context with reality; (5) a "Thought Structure" is built out the interpretation ingredients and those ingredients are arranged or combined into various versions of non-truth; (6) one grasps ideas out of these non-truths by only their external aspects, thereby omitting what makes for the totality of the "Thing"—like its inner underlying relationships, the true height, depth, and scope of the ingredients if all was in harmony; and (7) one convinces oneself of being right while on the wrong track. To talk about Arkansas without knowing about its bordering states will give a wrong idea of the shape of Arkansas. One then forms beliefs about the nature of these types and the picture one presents of them depends upon ones fashioning of combinations and arrangement of relationships. This sheds the reality that all things in the Cosmos are Interconnected.

If one gets good results from the application of these falsities, it is a coincidence but that arrogantly convinces one of being "right" in ones beliefs and methods. But more often the results are bad—which are simply disregarded. Yet, when others err about an area whereby one was accidently correct, one is motivated to wear a Moral or Righteous Indignation "Halo" and be harshly critical. By contrast, if someone makes a success out of what the arrogant one failed in, that same "Halo" of demeaning the achievement may be to hide ones envy at the courage the other showed. The point: one cannot live in non-truth and remain in ones Real Self. The following have been discussed in my other books.

CLASSIFICATION OF SUPERFICIAL THINKING
I. Traumatic
II."Off & On"
III. Broad-Stroke
IV.Patterned
V. Impulsive Omnibus,
VI. "Automatic Pilot,"
VII. Emotional Thinking
VIII *Flawed Critical Thinking*)

IX. There was no place for "Gist" Thinking—scanning some to get a general idea of something—except to help them get the 'big picture' of some for purposes of getting organized. To use it otherwise would lead to conclusions that were *unreasonable* from being flawed in checkered areas—flaws resulting from choosing not to pay attention to detail; or from possessing a perverse bias; or an intent to go wrong so as to not look bad, to make others wrong, out of ignorance or revenge.

X. "PICK AND CHOOSE"

AFRICAN TRADITION THINKING

All thinking done by Ancient Africans was no doubt done by both sides of their brains. However, certain sides dominated for the issue at hand. What is to follow is simply to introduce the subject. However the pursuit to perfect these leads to Wisdom (intuiting the Will of God out of ones own Divine Consciousness)—and its always about "ME/WE" order, unity, and harmony and the ability to do what is best for "ME/WE". It concerns using a Rational Process to draw conclusions for application to formulating a "non-rational" awareness of how to live in the world.

SPIRITUAL ELEMENTS ASSESSMENT: One cannot escape assessing the "Big Picture" of ones Life-Living—how it has been—how it is going—what it might be like. Personally, I like the Causes and Effects of how my life has gone. Yet, with respect to the Consequence Branches, most have gone well while a few have generated personal pain. For example, there are many who have hostility towards me to whom I have never said or done anything. Yet, I could not let them stop me from doing my Mission. Of course, I made as many mistakes as almost anyone because of being involved in many different things and having to take calculated risks and gambles. Still, I never got down on myself from wrong decisions or things that did not go well since I did my best at the time. One can minimize ones bad Consequences by means of proper Foresight and Forethought. Those ingredients are best manipulated and maneuvered by having a Human Ideal situated at the end of ones life. Then one can go through life with a focus centered on developing ones Real Self Intellect so as to achieve that Human Ideal. Ancient Africans had at least 10 forms of thinking they used for different purposes—e.g. different levels of Common Sense, Emotional, Concrete Rational, Abstraction and Abstract, and Spiritual (this necessarily draws on ones intuition) forms of Thinking.

The factors inside and contributory to the issue at hand to be assessed include: (1) what was each ingredient when it came into Being; (2) what was the Source of each ingredient—was it God-made (Reality) or Human-made (unreal); (3) what are the shaping factors of those ingredients; (4) are there mutual relationships and interdependence of the pertinent things with each other and the whole; (5) are those pertinent things harmonious or not; (6) are all of its activities within and developing out of the Spiritual Elements and headed towards a Human Ideal Goal concerns; and (7) to perceive all the ingredient components underlying a given thing/event as being the whole is a form of Synthesis—and Order at its best! A key factor in discovering the Truth is to distinguish Contrary Opposites (e.g. Love, a God-made Spiritual Element vs. Hate, a Human-made package) from Complementary Opposites. Complementary Opposites are halves of a unit and thus complement (complete) each other. Roots are not created without the soil. There can be no deviations or flaws, especially since the essence of the conclusion is expressed through the abstract or metaphoric use of Images. This enables one to transfer the process and the knowledge gained from going through the process and from the conclusion to be transferred to other areas of ones life.

BAILEY'S SECULAR TRUTH CONCLUSION PROCESS: The Spiritual Elements are an unchanging sameness consisting of internal linkages and whose Reality is known by displays of Order, Regularity, Peace, Fellowship, Justice, Righteousness, Straightness, Coherence, Consistency, Compatibility, Balance, Harmony, and Predictability that conform to Truth. A mistake most people make is to assume that the information they gather and that the tools they have and the path they are going on is "Right." At a more profound level, it is the understanding of and staying within the wholistic thinking encompassed in the Spiritual Elements that serves as Standard. What one then looks for is the unifying mutual relationships and interdependence of things with each other and the whole + their shaping factors. If these are in harmony that enables one to *establish the Truth of a premise.*

The Post-Action Judgment of this conclusion must then pass a rigid "Bailey's Test". This means acceptance for proceeding on with ones Plan A, B, or C is to occur *only when all of a subject's components have been examined, researched, reflected upon, and tested// and one finds they "fit" with ones education, training, experience, instincts, intuition, insights, reason, common sense// and one is in its flow// and it "Feels Right"// and without friendship or hearsay input// and not dependent on traditions, customs, beliefs, faith, or "everybody" agreeing.*

PRE-BIRTH EMOTIONS INTELLECTUALIZED

Spiritual Emotional (pre-birth or Congenital) Thinking is Metaphysically irrational and illogical aspects (as opposed to the acquired absurb irrational and illogical resulting from rational constraints) and thus is outside the province of Reason--similar to the way "Normal Variants" are between "Normal" and "Abnormal"--and yet they possess elements of mental activity without the capability of having a reproducible end product. Some types are: (A) Newborn's emotions creator/enhance, maintainer/defender of the Spiritual Elements); (B) Affect Symbolic Imagery (Spiritual Elements mental picture/Image stories); (C) Creative Thinking (arranging/rearranging, combining/recombining "raw materials" into novel forms); (D) Analogical Reasoning (using the familiar to explain the Unknown); (E) "Feel It"; (F) Mulling—"Just Be" (listen to the Voice of the Silence and the Rhythms of Nature to get harmonized).

ANIMATION PROGRAMMING APPROACHES: This involves things like tracing the story of a word so as to properly define it; describe the essence, the "What it is" by Affect Symbolic Imagery; pointing out Concepts at each stage of its evolution through the ingredient used (e.g. sensations, memory), Percepts, Notions, Ideas), and Productive Imagination. Perhaps Syllogistic Logical Thinking may have application. The soundness of the conclusions depends upon the ingredients used to arrive at the conclusion and the soundness of the "Chain Linked" components. This is summarized in the computer saying: "Garbage in, Garbage out". Of greater significance is what one does with the conclusion, like improperly embracing a belief as a truism.

EMOTION/INTELLECT THINKING

Intellectualizing Spiritual Emotions was exemplified by Very Ancient African Subjective Sciences—i.e. Observation, Reflection, "Pure" Feelings, Productive Imagination, Contemplation, Inductive and Deductive Inferences, and Common Sense and they remain powerful tools. Examples of their applications are:

I. Reasoning by Analogy is perhaps the first way children learn to think. It is the comparing of two or more systems similar in structure and then taking the familiar in one to explain the unknown in the other.

Analogies possess the power to bring things to life by evoking images that illuminate the points of comparison the author is trying to make. Analogies have two parts: an original subject and a compared subject (what the original is being likened to). In comparing my love for my dog Titan to a gardenia, the original subject is my love while the compared subject is the gardenia so as to illuminate and express my love for both. The comparison can be either obvious (explicit) or implied (implicit). Emotive language often combines with visual imagery to present extremes of ideas and feelings, as seen in advertising. This is sort of like Ancient African ritual specialists who used ugly masks to personify things—like bringing into a mental picture existence the idea of a destructive evil spirit. By so doing the people could focus on that mask and then take the appropriate action.

II. Perfect being Silly, for it is a way to feel good and develop "raw materials" for creativity.

III. *Common Sense* to be found in the ability to do what is best for (Ma'at "Me/WE" Life Living) — concerns having a "non-rational" awareness of how to live in the world. This necessarily draws on ones intuition.

IV. *Law of Correspondence* thinking (so above so below, so below, so above)

CLASSIFICATION OF AFRICAN TRADITION INTELLECTUAL THINKING

This involves perfecting: (1) Abstract Thinking (association of Metaphysical Ideas); (2) Abstraction Thinking (Big Picture uniting of like-kind material things); (3) Reflection (inner exploring of "Know Thyself" philosophy); (4) Critical Thinking (it is the creator/enhance, maintainer/defender of the Spiritual Elements); (5) African Logic (yolk to the Cosmic Organism/God Source; (6) Rational Thinking (prove/disprove Spiritual Elements point); (7) Inference; (8) Interrelationships; (9) Spiritual Thinking (done in symbols and principles for esoteric knowledge); (10) Circumstantial Truths; (11) Contemplation (dissolving into the Spiritual Elements.

I. Rational Thinking the "Rational" aspect means *Understanding one or more fundamentals of life or essential of the topic at hand;* from the mental structure being built and endowed with sensibleness (i.e. from the ability to harmoniously fit relationships together so as to see its reasonable thought flow); and possessing reasoning power leading to Thoughts of practical or workable usefulness. It is built like a pyramind and each block must be sound. *Rational Thinking* the "Rational" aspect means *Understanding one or more fundamentals of life or essential of the topic at hand;* from the mental structure being built and endowed with sensibleness (i.e. from the ability to harmoniously fit relationships together so as to see its reasonable thought flow); and possessing reasoning power leading to Thoughts of practical or workable usefulness. It is built like a pyramind and each block must be sound. One arrives at unacceptable conclusions from Invalid reasoning By adhering to that makes it impossible to do Rational Thinking (i.e. Logic as originated in African Tradition).

II. Abstract and Abstraction Thinking--the highest form of Rational Thinking. ABSTRACT/ ABSTRACTION: *the virtual in the Metaphysical or Supernatural;* An *Abstract* is ones mind fashioning a "Virtual" (boundary-less) Contingent out of something in the Metaphysical (the Spiritual wrapped in the Ether) or Supernatural realms. An *Abstraction* is ones mind fashioning a "Virtual" (boundary-less) Contingent out of something in the Physical (the Spiritual wrapped in Matter). Both an Abstract and an Abstraction gain their "raw materials" for formation as a result of being an *Attribute* from their respective sources—and thus both are Contingent Primary Qualities (i.e. they do not exist independently) of their sources and can be isolated only conceptually for the purpose of identification. Yet, each carries an impactful 'payload' activating something good or bad in the "Heart" of one(s) touched by it.

III. Critical Thinking uses all of the above ways of thinking to gather and convey a precise and exact rational process in order to synthesize (think cosmologically)--to see the abstract unity and interdependence between all independent real things--and to establish Truth from mathematically determined Spiritual Principles.

IV. High Abstract Thinking (Supra-Rational) on knowledge from Right Brain assessments and then switchs to Rational Thinking in order to expand, elaborate on, and more completely understand the Contextual Thinking so as to arrive at "*Esoteric Knowledge*". To elaborate on the above Consciousness discussion, ones Sensory Consciousness Background can be analogized to a blackboard on which things (e.g. chalk marks) make an impression. These impressions made on the blackboard are the same as the blackboard but a mutual contrast is needed for each to be recognized. When taking a shower, I face a window (serving as a mirror at night) which enables me to see the dog walking in the bedroom behind the shower. But that seeing is only possible at night because the darkness is the background for the window glass that enable me to see what is behind me. The window, whether night or day, grasps nothing for it has no Consciousness to retain the image of the dog. I know the dog because my Conscious retains my dog's image, even though it is only a reflection on the window. Thus, my Conscious (which allows me to 'know') and the image of my dog (the known) are the same even though they necessarily involve differences whose boundaries hold things in common. A fence separating me from my neighbor means we both hold the fence in common. Mine is what is the other and the other is what is mine. Similarly, the 'others' in the External world are the condition of me being myself. Such occurs as a "State" ('way of standing, condition, position') of vibratory energy consisting of wave-like entities, each possessing different dimensions. It can be inferred that ones mind is space (emptiness) containing wavy vibratory energy with different dimensions forming different shapes and colors in the context of vision. This enables ones to know there is Being/Non-Being of both the mind and what is seen—and this is part of reality. Thus, an experience is not an encounter but simply a part of who one is which, when it occurs, represents an expansion of ones mental content, as occurs when the bud expands into the flower

V. Creative Thinking is arranging and combining ingredients into novel forms. This starts with being Silly and Playful.

VI. Spiritual/Metaphysical Thinking uses symbols and principles to deal with Cosmic Principles and Laws (called Sacred Geometry). It draws from one intuiting the will of God. *Supra-Rational* uses symbols and principles to deal with *Spiritual Thinking*. It draws on knowledge from Right Brain assessments and one then switches to Rational Thinking in order to expand, elaborate on, and more completely understand the Contextual Thinking so as to arrive at "*Esoteric Knowledge*".

ORDERED MENTAL PROCESSES TO SHED VIOLENCE

The "Big Picture" understanding is that before meaningful things can be made on any level of existence, a foundation based on Order (Ma'at) must be put in place. A PROCESS is the way in which a thing is done and that can be: (1) mere doing; (2) doing with a purpose; (3) doing which follows a thought-out plan; and (4) idealizing doing which results from vivid imaging. As the fashioner of an Outline of a plan, a Process shows the parts of a discourse in some sort of skeletal form pertaining to *Order* (like rungs on a ladder). The key is to have a well-thought out "ME/WE" goal. My Self-Declaration is to make it perfect for myself in order to be proud and I want to make it perfect, plain, and simple so I can share. A successful goal is for me to "Leave things better than I found them" for this enlarges my thinking skills as well as my observation and creative abilities.

RATIONAL THINKING STEPS

An assessment of this process has been given in my book: Leadership Critical Thinking:

Step I--Clearly define the problem

Step II--Gather pertinent information

Step III--Assess the gathered information and categorize the keystone issues into Pros/Cons

Step IV--Analyze the assessed information, including grading each Pro and Con by means of Measurements for quantitative items (e.g. things seen) and Estimates for qualitative aspects (i.e. things one cannot see)

Step V--Manipulate the analysis into cause and effect; gather all factors for both

Step VI--Maneuver creatively around obstacles so as to arrive at the Truth.

Step VII--by using this insight, one can now Poetically synthesize all existing pertinent high quality aspects involved in the mental activity. A well-known Dialectic law is a *change in quantity beyond a certain point brings about a change in quality*. Or, it gives a different perspective on existing qualities. Either way, pertinent changes are made in that Thing's unique rules and character to thereby bring about changes in the characteristics and the circumstances in which that Thing operates. If changes are great enough and abrupt enough, a *Revolution* transformation into a different mindset occurs. Out of this new mindset comes a higher level insight which carries a *Vision*. A Vision is the art of seeing invisible and unifying essences concerning quantities and qualities underlying the obvious and the hidden that others are unable to see or that they themselves, until now, have been unable to see. This Vision enables one to fashion Options of how to best handle problems by establishing connections of Cause to the Effects and then devising Solutions to handle the Effects.

Step VIII--Prioritized top 3 Options are for Judgments to make them into Plans A, B and C

Step IX--Troubleshoot the Plans A, B, and C

Step X--Post-action judgments of a "check and balance" nature are made after each mental and physical action. Here, one looks for any flaw, weakness, limitation, how can it be made better, what can be eliminated, how to make excellence routine) and follow that with Mulling ("Just Be") whereby one simply gets quiet and not think about anything. In this way glimpses of the peaks of what has been synthesized from the process show themselves quickly before disappearing forever. The point is to take advantage of that opportunity since that one thing along can represent the success path.

CONGENIAL ATMOSPHERE TO RESOLVE VIOLENCE

The whole art of teaching Black youth is to *awaken their natural curiosity for the purpose of generating the enjoyment of learning*. The force, beauty, and intent of a Congenial Learning Atmosphere is the process of paving the way for struggling Black youth to learn how to free their enslaved minds. The C17 European word "*Congenial*" etymologically means kindred, "agreeable, suited to" and sympathetic. Whereas ideas in these words imply a veil existing between those involved, in African Tradition people relationships have no such veils. Instead, the way Afrocentric type of "Congenial" is used in the following discussion is similar to one of my dreams as a boy entitled "*Laughing While Learning*." Its setting is having a big family whose best moments are sitting around the table at meal time engaged in learning things in a fun manner. The atmosphere itself is composed of the *Unconditional Love Platter*--the instinct to Love; to spread Love; to be Loved; and to be Lovable. In turn, the Spiritual Energy in which these flow give rise to an "Aliveness" in each youth. In this setting of sharing the same loving space, there is no sense of Western "win-lose" type competition. Love makes this space sacred and therefore special things can happen, like the Self of each being transformed. Fun Compliments is a "fake it till you make it" tool whereby youth are made to feel good about themselves and that opens up their imaginative investigations and elevates their Thought Ladder perceptions for creating. It and Silliness lets the hyper-protective to feel "safe" to be who they really are inside pleasant atmospheres.

POWERS OF SILLINESS FOR BLACK CHILDREN

"Silliness" in little children consists of "Aliveness" wrapped in "Excitement"—a Real Self manifestation of enjoying life "my way". Such Free Minds, by being in a boundless state of wholeness and in contact with the Cosmic Organism, do not mentally cling to anything. Hence, they abandon themselves to the fullness of whatever they make into an illusion, and without reservation. Ancient Africans' expression: "Enjoyment is the property of the Gods" indicates one is on the path headed toward achieving ones Highest Self divinity—the state human newborns were in at the time of their birth—the realm contents expressed by childhood "Silliness". Such "Silliness" is the product of children investing in the most insignificant "Things"—"Things" imaged into any form they please—"Things" of a Caricature ('overloaded' representation) nature that exaggerates and distorts each "Thing's" most prominent features into a comic effect. Next, their Magical Thinking directs these unrealistic "Things" to bring about changes in a Fantasy world. Each comic creation is "looked at "upside-down" or "inside-out" or in whatever ways they wish to see it that will repetitiously produce giggling and laughter. That is the ultimate in creativity--the essence of Play. But deeper than this Fun are the sure signs little children are bathing in the highest Cosmic (Spiritual) Energy system. Some of these signs include their effervescing *Curiosity*—naturally making them intensely interested in the unfamiliar—their unhesitating readiness and willingness to *Courageously* explore all unknown and especially mysterious realms with complete confidence--and untainted by fears, doubts, worry, or fatigue—as well as their unbounded "Awe" and "Wonder" about things discovered. All of this derives from their "*Aliveness*" (a Spiritual Elements off-spring) which displays as an alertness to, and the living of, Life by defining oneself from the view of always exploring ones potential possibilities rather than from believing oneself to be boxed in by ones limitations.

The fancifulness of "Silliness Aliveness" possesses a titillating (Latin, tickle) or tantalizing fantasy influence amounting to a kind of spell from their Contingent Being creations in the "here and now". The Material World complementary counterpart, "Excitement," promotes "Play and Stay." By contrast, False Self people, from having chosen to disconnect from their Spiritual Selves, can only strive for "Excitement," which is but a shadow of what it is when partnered with "Aliveness." In doing Ma'at "Right" living, one is striving towards ones Highest Self divinity by intertwined Selfhood/Cosmic "Wholeness" practices. Silliness is a real experience Sample (a uniform piece of the whole) of this—a Sample composed of the essences of the Law of Correspondence—i.e. "as without, so within" + "As above, so below; as below, so above". Cosmic/Selfhood *Wholeness* means all of its mutual ingredients are each enfolded (enclosed) within the Spiritual Elements—each is doing its own job—each interpenetrates all others so as to be throughout the whole—and each works in balance and interdependently as part of an interwoven flowing movement.

In short, Silliness is a signal of ones Selfhood participating as a total, natural, and orderly form in the harmonious Wholeness. And this is the ultimate in Selfhood Health! In African Tradition, the word "*Health*" literally means whole or sound in body and mind. These rise to their peak when living begins— i.e. when one really enjoys life. Perhaps this is why the Old English definition of "Silly" is "Blessed by God with Happiness". However, today's Black children are programmed out of displaying silliness from the culturally transmitted effects of slavery. Back then, the God blessing of being "Silly" was beaten out of the adult Enslaved while it was never allowed to develop in Enslaved children. The reason is that as soon as they were able to assume responsibility—perhaps at age 4—European slave owners sent them to do drudgery work in the cotton fields. That established a pattern for all ex-Slaves and their descendants, as indicated by Billie Holiday's (1915-1959) comment: "I never had a chance to play with dolls like other [White] kids. I started working when I was six years old." The atmosphere in USA's hostile society is not conducive to Black youth being silly. Yet, because of its infinite variety of benefits—as in aiding being analytical and inventive—there is an urgent need for Black youth to cultivate their birth gift of "Silliness". jabaileymd.com

FUN COMPLIMENTS: It is typical for boys to be in environments where nothing good about them is ever said. In fact, all they hear is how bad they are and "how you are going to turn out bad just like ...." The question is: "how can they deal with this non-supportive environment? Since the lives of struggling Black boys have been about serious business, and since they know little about fun of a "Fulfilling" type and since they usually cannot escape this environment, what they can do is to cleverly play the hand they are dealt by turning it into a positive. To this end, there are two approaches.

First, is using "Fun Compliments" to create their own pleasant atmosphere. Example: Anytime anybody says something nice about a place, thing, or the weather -- like: "Its a nice day" or "the flowers are so beautiful" or "that is a lovely sunset" -- then the boy can say "thank you." This not only lightens the mood of the atmosphere but on rare occasions it makes a subtle impression on the boy's mind that he just may have had something to do with making it a nice day or whatever. Just to hear himself say: "Thank you" has cumulative beneficial effects that elevates how he thinks about himself. This is like saying smile and you will feel better. There is nothing like a positive word to somebody.

Second, is what the Mentor does several times a day to introduce, enhance, or maintain a pleasant atmosphere that, in turn, causes the boys to feel somewhat pleasant. Example One: A large group of *Fun Compliments*" consists of the playfulness of being an exaggeration of the accentuation of the positive. If a boy says: "it's a hot day," the Mentor could respond: "You are so observant; how can I learn to be like that." Or, "you really did a good job putting water in the dog's water dish." Example Two is being an "expert of the obvious." If a boy says: "I'm hungry, I think I'll eat" -- the Mentor responds: "You're so smart to realize the problem and come up with a solution." Example Three: Make a positive out of a negative as, for example, if a boy is singing off key with all his heart, the Mentor might say: "you are really good to be able to consistently hit all the wrong notes." But here the atmosphere needs to already be pleasant so as to avoid hurting the boy's feelings.

As long as care is taken to not touch on a "Hypersensitive" spot that can cause the boy to feel ashamed, one thing both "Fun Compliments" approaches do is to get the boys to relax (or to stay relaxed); to let down their mindset defenses; to elevate their mood; and to start to recurrently enjoy at least a small piece of life. Not only will both approaches bring a muffled smile from the boy(s) but both are sneaky ways to build self-esteem any time the boy thinks beyond the boundaries of the "Fun Compliment". Such an expansion is likely to happen in Approach Two. For example, because even though the boy knows the Mentor is just kidding, he is not likely to consider the "Fun Compliment" as completely "fake" (like flattery). Such a consideration of expanding beyond the boundaries of the "Fun Compliment" tends to come at a moment when the boy has really relaxed his mental guard (since no one is on high alert guard all the time), and especially while in a pleasant atmosphere.

Instead, one in ten of the "Fun Compliments" carries the possibility of being taken seriously by the boy. If that happens, his unchecked imagination causes him to fashion grandiose ideas about himself being "pretty good" -- and that is a "seed." His resultant "mental stretching" may undergo some modification of the context of the "Fun Compliments" and it go something like this: "Hey, maybe that is true about me"; "maybe I am a good observer" or "maybe I am good at taking care of the dog" or maybe "I am smart at realizing the problem and coming up with a solution."

At the moment when the boy is even considering the possibly of being better than he normally thinks he is, there is the element of hopefulness about him becoming some of who he is really supposed to be. This hope may be the pass that opens the inner recesses of his mind where lies the potential greatness he knows he has. Meanwhile, the "seed" planted by the "Fun Compliment," with its associated imagination "mental stretch," can start the process of leading him toward a self-fulfilling prophecy of his grandiose idea of himself. The point is that both Fun Compliments and respect for every ones Dignity improve the atmosphere in which struggling Black youth interact inside a Common Humanity; build self-esteem props; and are like grease applied to the keys used for unlocking their mental vault. By both Dignity and Fun Compliments being indicators of recognition of something personally and deeply important to these youth, the effect just may contribute to them expanding their sense of importance and personal power. Those improved senses can pave the way to doing more things just outside their comfort zone and familiarity territory and thereby put them on the path that is about success (See Self-Esteem in Chapter V). In short, Compliments, are underrated in their power to soften barriers around and bring about change in resistant minds.

TEACHING BLACK YOUTH

Teaching or Mentoring gang members is to not only bring them back to sound mental health but also to help them discover their Gifts, Genius, and Talent so they can expand the cultivation of the ingredients which are normally only within a given Black youth's reach. I have seen many of these as school "drop-outs" who could easily have become dominant in marketplace and academic circles because of their Talents. Such would involve "Gifting" their Talents (i.e. cultivating them into skilled perfection) while leading them back into their genius. CARING Teachers have an obligation, duty, and responsibility to BOND with these youth; to give great thought to was is to be taught; and to Exposed them to the pertinent. Common sense says this will make things better for all involved.

Since Black American Customs have switched paths from African Tradition onto a chronically struggling path, it is improper for a teacher to say: "this is how I am going to teach Black Youth because this is the way it has always been done". This would have worked well for Ancient Africans in Africa but not for African Americans in the USA. The problem is that "always" only dates to African American slavery--meaning Black American Customs are within the context of slavery and Slave Survivals—and its Non-Rational thinking will not work for thriving in the Americas.

Only the *Sankofa Process*—which has been proven to work in daily living for tens of thousands of years—will work for struggling Black youth. Its steps are: (1) go back to Ancient African philosophy to extract its principles; (2) apply those principles to fashion a Free Mind so as to replace or correct today's Black People's problems; and (3) use African Tradition's entirely new ways of designing solutions to go forward into the future. A Translator who has risen out of the "Don't Care" crowd is needed explain these principles in a form and language to which struggling people can relate.

The Divine Plan for Life Living, said Ancient Africans, is for the "ME/WE" to have the combination of an Unchanging Sameness while, at the same time, each individual does her/his Uniqueness in Patterns in carrying out her/his Mission. In this way, each individual works independently to product Spiritual Elements work products in order to interdependently benefit all. In other words, to proceed with ones Mission, instead of being a milk and water Crowd addiction mix, the "ME" can move with greater sureness and speed by operating like water in oil—meaning ones Mission is carried out as ones primary focus, with the "WE" being secondary.

A way to get started teaching or mentoring is by having Black youth tell their story for they typically have skills in telling complex narratives of many different types. That flexibility in their narratives, varying the narratives according to context, could provide clues to discoveries about what is hampering their Life-Living and/ or what will capture their attention to proceed in a non-violent direction—causing them to think more about "ME/WE" than "ME". This flexibility might also help them in expanding from oral language to the decoding and comprehension of written text.

SELF-HEALING

Fundamental to entering the process of Self-Healing is for one to determine what is a Successful life. This is best determined by the Restrospectoscope Method. The first question is: "*What do I really, really do not want?*" Human beings avoid, said Maslow (*J. Humanistic Psychology, 1963*): Being manipulated, dominated, pushed around, determined by others, misunderstood, a nothing (rather than a somebody), unappreciated, not respected, not feared, not taken seriously, laughed at, deemed to be a ludicrous figure, regulated by others (like an object or machine), treated like a thing rather than like a person, rubricized (i.e. treated like an example of a class rather than as unique), given orders, forced to be "screwed" (used, exploited, raped), controlled, helpless, forced into compliance and deference.

The second question: "*What do I really, really, want?*" Human beings positively seek for: Being a prime mover, Self-determination, Having control over ones own fate, Determining ones movements, Being able to plan, to carry out, and to succeed, achieving Success in something, prestige, respect, dignity, Responsibility (under certain circumstances), (some) activity rather than prolonged passivity, Being a person rather than a thing. An important addition for Black People is to be sociable. Have the youth write or speak on what is paradise for them—how would they describe what they would want to make it a reality and what goes with those things one desires. "Would you want someone pretty/handsome but unable to solve life's problems? And could you live with what you say you want when looked at using the *Box Concept*--an assessment tool referring to the turning of the "Thing" about in all directions in order to: "See" both sides of every side and every angle of that which is observed; "See" how every angle is connected to each side; "See" the advantages and disadvantages of each side and of each angle. Pertinent resultant ingredients extracted can be arranged/rearranged and combined/recombined to come up with different options. Extensively play with one option at a time so that the top 3 that could work the best are labeled Options A, B, and C. Then write all you know and suspect or possibilities about each of the Options and put the subject aside for 2 months during which time aspects of each will ripen in your mind in the way weaving is done to make a tapestry. This is like picking and storing unripe apples so they can ripen.

Upon returning to them 2 months later one will have analogies for them. Rather than using mechanical analogies, select those that come out of Nature to apply to Spiritual and Metaphysical concepts—for that naturally opens up thinking into boundless realms.

SELF-RESPONSIBILITY FOR SELFHOOD GREATNESS: A consistent question that arises in being discussions on healing the violence is the role of the parents. Absolutely parents need to allow their youth to participate in order for the healing process to begin and continue on an ongoing basis. But thereafter, judgment is required. The compentency of parents or a parent ranges from superb to problematic. Once a parent is in the problematic realm, in my view the best way to proceed is to make each youth responsible for him/herself. This is not about excluding parents or the Black community input but it is about working with youth so that they clearly understand what the Spiritual Elements are about. This means letting them know what is within the flow of the Spiritual Elements and that deviating to one side or the other while in that flow is what humans do and is to be immediately corrected. Then assess the flaw responsible for the deviation; correct it; put in a plan for it to never happen again; and apply the lesson everywhere. This process is in contrast to following Rules, for they are like walking a tightrope—a misstep causes one to fall.

Youth must be instructed as to what constitutes stepping outside the Spiritual Elements boundaries—the leaving behind of: "That feels right". To have the sense of it "SEEMS" right or "That's good enough" or "I know this is not right but I'll do it just this one time" each means one is outside the Spiritual Elements. These realizations help one establish the standards, guides, filters, and measures which highlight the Maa--*the Good, the Beautiful, the Beneficial* (nefer)—aspects of the Spiritual Elements and nothing one does is to deviate from them for even a fraction of a degree. In this way, youth are responsible for what they accept, think, feel, say, and do (i.e. act and react). This state of Private Selfhood discipline and control enables one to deal with any type of people. The best circumstance is when a youth is around good parents and inside a good community. An analogy is that ones heart does its own job of pumping blood throughout the body to help all parts of the body and does this independently of the other body parts. Yet, that heart is also working interdependently with all the other body parts to provide the "big picture" of health to the individual.

However, there are variations off this ideal pattern of Life Living. One is to have good parents and a bad neighborhood. A second is to have bad parents and a good neighborhood. A third is having bad parents in a bad neighborhood—the type that causes many Black youth to enter a gang. With any of these three the youth is self-responsible to orchestrate his/her life. However, the way to deal with interrelating with bad people or even good people who give bad advice (i.e. perpetuating Black American Customs instead of African Tradition) is by the Metaphysical Window Concept.

METAPHYSICAL WINDOW CONCEPT: This concept—also called "Window of Right Living Inside Chaos" and "Metaphorical Window"--arose early in my orthopaedic surgical practice when it was necessary for me to get involved in the medical-legal arena. Apart from its interesting and challenging contents, what I really disliked was the Brute-centeredness of this arena, featuring aggressive CT dishonorableness (e.g. telling lies; cheating deserving people out of everything because of being unable to defend themselves). The objective is to generate the confusion that enables one side to win by stomping on and destroying opponents and then celebrating making the loser suffer. "Everybody" is suspicious of everybody else. By arrogantly playing "the game" by their own rules and in defiance of the law which lacks "accountability teeth," they are free to do the least amount of worthwhile work that justifies over-charging. My Orthopaedic involvement enabled me to step into this chaotic amoral arena; be part of what is interesting; and then step back from it without having to sell my soul to the devil.

To handle this situation I carved out a "metaphysical window" in the middle of the chaos. In deciding what to put inside that window, I called on a formula of Algebra where $X = Y$. The equal sign stood for Truth and Reality; the letter X represented my inner chaos from having to conform to the prejudiced written/unwritten rules I disrespected; and Y symbolized being surrounded by overwhelming chaos. Inside the equal sign -- i.e. inside the "window" -- I placed Spiritual Element Standards to live by, applying them as a sound Selfhood foundation to *"Be Right," "Recognize Right," "Do Right," "Make Things Right," and "Defend the Right".* While my Private Self lived safely inside the window, my Public Self operated normally in the world of chaos surrounding me. My sound Selfhood foundation guided my dealings within the chaos of the medical-legal arena in a manner that I maintained my integrity. This is like having one foot inside the window and one foot in the chaos.

Anyone living in a chaotic environment can do the same. Suppose Sankofa stands for the equal sign while X and Y stand for whatever problems one ranks as the keystones. Sankofa is about discovering principles of African Tradition and applying them to ones present situation. Here, one internalizes the Spiritual Elements. Its principles serve as the standard, tools, filter, and guides to establish a sound Selfhood. These same principles are then used to pave a constructive path into a thriving future -- a path whose goals are intended to benefit oneself, loved ones, and possibly others, including the yet unborn. *When ones Spiritual Element lifestyle is part of who one is, it is carried over by ones Public Self into ones underlying dealings with the outside world.* To fashion ones Life Living so as to handle X and Y while maintaining some degree of harmony, connectedness, and balance in interrelationships with non-Brute people is ones own decision—a decision independent of and uninfluenced by others' contrary opinions. This includes humane "Friends of Brutes" despite their imitation of Brutes' non-evil practices. One does what is needed to be part of the crowd so as to "belong" but always while remaining honorable and self-reliant. Still, the key is striving every day and in every way to be better and better. Meanwhile, one must use the Law of Attraction to seek the Truth. Though all this is hard, it is infinitely better than being a fully exposed victim to the hostile world and its consequences.

RELEARNING

Gang members must understand that their present way of thinking is the "Seed" for all of their problems—and not being poor or unsafe or not powerful or being useless or ugly or whatever. The reason is that no matter what problem one has in life, sound thinking and then carrying out that plan can get around or through or go in another direction when one feels Selfhood Great. But then the start of stop going "down hill" in life is to discover a personal Human Ideal and make all daily efforts conform to achieving that end. In the meantime, it is essential to let go of every other non-essential way of thinking and allow those bad habits to die from lack of use. Before one can make wise decisions about what type of Human Ideal Goal to fashion and how to achieve it requires knowing where ones philosophy of life is presently.

BLACK PEOPLE'S PHILOSOPHICAL NATURES: Even a crude idea of Black People's philosophical orientation is helpful in assessing anything having to do with them—e.g. who and who not to spend time with; who and who not to trust; who to call on for help and what type and to what degree; who not to call on for help for any reason; who needs help the most; the kind of obstacles one will face in trying to help the most needy; who to allow ones children to associate with and under what circumstances and what to look out for; who might be destructively deceptive out of ignorance or from being in the Indifference/Hate/Evil/Sadism (IHES) complex mentally and in deeds. Some today's PATTERNS OF BLACK AMERICANS are:

Pattern I—African Tradition is based upon "Harmony with Nature" and "Survival of the the Group"—an interdependency between humans and Nature. The features fashioning proper function and order are Complementary Opposites, Interconnectedness, Synthesis (Senghor, *Diogenes, 1956;* Murove *Diogenes, 2012*).

Pattern II—Black American Customs are fragmented—some at odds with each other (fig. 9, 19). They represent Enslaved Africans coming into contact with a motley collection of diverse customs on the one hand and new situations on the other." Overall, it is not product driven but rather the highest values are about interpersonal relationships, featuring how the group presents itself or sustains itself by strengthening itself—and this is the end in itself. It is not about self-improvement or how fast or how much or how efficient are the efforts to produce. As a result, there is the persistence of the "Make Do" Slave survival custom.

Pattern III are "Oreos" who follow European Trinkets and Trivia and looking for European approval.

Pattern IV are "Black Puppets" to European Puppeteers who work against Black People

Pattern V are Mulattoes who have a hard time fitting into any pattern.

Pattern VI are Gang Members who have combined Patterns I and II within the context of European Brute philosophy and methods. From a lack of organized and stabilized customs for them in congenial American traditions, customs, and institutions in general and family and neighborhood in particular, they seek this in gangs.

Pattern VII—Isolated Individualists Black Americans who combine Pattern I as the Background philosophy for interacting (e.g. offense and defense) in the European marketplace in a manner that they thrive in their Personal and Public Self. The African Tradition pattern of "ME/WE" is directed toward the highest Black American Church Customs aspect of "Lifting others while you Climb"—also a blend of Patterns I and II. These are the Black People most capable of "Uplifting" the race but who are least accepted.

Pattern VIII--Combinations

HUMAN IDEAL GOALS

"Ideal" is a symbol for perfect Truth, Beauty, and Goodness. Striving for ones own Human Ideal is not about absolute Perfection but rather living so as to be on the path to cultivating every potential in ones Selfhood Greatness possession. This does not mean one is "perfect" in everything because that is not humanly possible. What it does mean is living up to the Standards contained in ones Selfhood Greatness--i.e. its "Spark of God" the Absolute Ideal as well as the Human Ideal fashioned by our Ancient African Ancestors. Hence, the necessity for studying Ancient African Philosophy so as to gain more and more insight into each of the "Tree Concept" parts which elaborate on the Human Ideal applicable to ones own life. Meanwhile, one keeps an intention to strive toward the "Spark of God" Absolute Ideal standard which is beyond our Ancient African Ancestors' Human Ideal. This is done by being up on ones Spiritual Elements "toes" in order to mentally "stretch" every day and in every way. African Sages illustrated this by the Scale of Justice used on Judgment Day.

This implied the "Heart" of the Deceased must "balance" Ma'at's feather as a reflection of having lived an overall life of Goodness. If one was "Ideally Perfect" that would not reflect humanness. The process of striving for a lifestyle of overall Goodness is to go with the natural inclinations which are located in ones Selfhood

Greatness and generated by ones Divine Self (Soul). Developing them to the fullest will not concern the following of any established pattern. Instead, one goes with the flow of ones own natural birth gifts. Of course the Absolute Ideal--the Ultimate--is never reached, in the way tomorrow never comes. Yet, in spite of having to settle somewhere short of the Ultimate, simply being on that path is the way to approach achieving the potential of ones Selfhood Greatness. The by-product of that striving toward the Ultimate is Happiness and a successful life. See Consistency; Perfection

GENERATE HUMAN IDEAL "MANILINESS"

Meaningful ideas of what it is for Hu-Mans' (hummus, earth + man) to be made in God's Image come from Metaphorical concepts (since actual images of God are impossible). Ancient Africans said God's visible Spirit is manifested as the Cosmos or Nature. Also, God's Consciousness (the God-Head or Cosmic Mind)--is God's Immaterial nature, perceivable only by humans' Divine Consciousness--the foundational principle upon which Very Ancient Africans connected concepts about Yoga, the human mind (and its consciousness, subconscious, and unconscious aspects), the body, and ones spirit. The 'Roots' gathered for "yoking" humans to God's Consciousness were: the invention of agriculture + its plow (c20,000 BC) + the two oxen plowing together as a unit and fastened (i.e. "*yoked*") by a wooden frame + Egyptians' devised (c10,000 BC) Spiritual path practices to the heaven afterlife. One human "yoking" requirement was/is for ones mental activities to be halted in order for one to experience "Oneness" with God. "Yoking" occurs because God's Consciousness is Immaterial and thus indivisible--implying ones Divine Consciousness experiences are identical experiences of God's Consciousness. Although this linkage is by ones Soul being a Spark of God, its proportions are like a drop of ocean water compared to the ocean. Furthermore, by existing between the realms of heaven and earth, humans are composed of Spirit and Matter--and both are equilibrated into the human newborn. That newborn's Selfhood is composed of two fundamental aspects. One is the "Self"—i.e. pure Divine Consciousness and Will. By the "Self" being devoid of Energy and Matter, it never comes into the world per se but rather projects itself into its human's mind, as the light of a movie projector on to the screen. The other aspect, ones Spirit (divided into 7 subdivisions), is the active Energy and Matter that provides the substance for various forms (e.g. 'Spirit,' Mind, Soul, Life-Force) and forces to manifest as entities in the world.

The "heaven" part which makes a human a Spiritual Being refers to what gives humans the ability to know, to achieve life's Missions, and to thrive with happiness. As long as one has a "ME/WE" (lift others while climbing) approach to life, these 3 are essentially unlimited—with ones Spiritual Entourage instantly manifesting guidance, filters, measures, and standards as needed, like Instincts expressing the will of God. Meanwhile, the "Earth" or Matter part is governed, starting at birth, by the human's two animal brains—the Ancient ("fight-flight-fright") and the Old Mammalian (emotional). Its programmed information enables one to handle personal survival needs and social organization. But these forces are inadequate to guide one into reality's intricate "heaven" realm, as volitional Ma'at Intellects (of the Neocortex) are designed to do. This transformation assumes ones mind is filled with Knowledge of Self and as long as one continues in the Spiritual Elements flow, one automatically expresses Spiritual Human Ideal features (i.e. not Perfect Ideals) of "Manhood".

Sages agreed upon the 'big picture' of Real Self "Manhood" as displaying eternal uprightness so that the necessary consequences head toward grand possibilities of social harmony, order, and well-being throughout ones life's course. It spotlights men with strong minds who see things, whether good or bad, as they really are; have great, gentle "Hearts"; and have ready, willing, able and steady hands. They do not lust for office or fame or status or riches or conquests—are those whom the spoils of office cannot buy—those who love with compassion, have good manners, are honorable, and can be completely trusted; those who help make opportunities for others—who leave things better than when they were found—those who exhibit self-discipline, self-control, justice, and respect for every human, treating women and all races as complementary equals. Good men avoid associating with Bad people (i.e. those against the Spiritual Elements). Nevertheless, each human's possession of a Selfhood Base of Unconditional Love gives that human the Free Will to choose alternate or opposite ways to proceed through life. What is thereby substituted is a False Self and a loss of what is internally *consistent, permanent, stationary, and unchanging*. Hence, whoever one thinks one is (Real or False Self) determines how one will think; how one will use ones imagination, creativity, and act--all are ingredients of ones Fate! [Ref: (Amen, Metu Neter VII:45) jabaileymd.com

SPECIFIC AFRICAN "MANLINESS" GOAL: Ancient Africans said humans' nature arise out of the Primoridal Substance of the Cosmos, consisting of God's androgynic protoplast—a "Oneness". Out of this "Oneness" eminates all God's creatures and creations. Creatures become so by having a binary pattern comprising two opposite phases or aspects integrated within the higher "Oneness" context—phases or aspects that can be either symmetrical (i.e. identical in extent and intensity) or asymmetrical, successive, or simultaneous. Humans' natures are part heavenly and part earthly. Both are based on the counterbalanced forces of two opposite poles consisting of Complementary Opposites as, for example, Masculine and Feminine Principles—the illustration of successive or simultaneous aspects, meaning that on all planes both aspects are present in greater or less degree. The Masculine (the Spirit or Life side) manifestation is the active and positive aspect which acts on the Feminine (the Matter or Form side) or receptive part of ones nature. Hence, a human's Real Self Spiritual Nature ingredients consist of the Higher Mind derived from each ones gift at conception of a "Spark" of God. This "Spark" imparts a "Pure Heart" or "Soul Sunshine" and is at the core of every newborn's Selfhood Greatness. Together, these supplies one with the sense of the "5Ss" and a Talent intended for use in the pursuit of ones Mission in life.

The heavenly part of a human's Higher Mind contains congenitally active First Wisdom (knowledge and power of the Cosmic Organism at the core of the Natural Cosmos) and its Complementary Opposite but successive appearing congenital tarda composition duo of Truth (congenitally active) followed in succession but in the much later appearance of Wisdom from having cultivated Truth; birth Intuition, then Reason; birth Unconditional Love, then Intellect. Thus, inside the Heavenly part of humans there are two distinct lives—one of the Intellect, the other of the Affections—and though separate in the human mind, unite as far as may be—and by their union produce all those Higher Self forms of life which commune with the Cosmic Mind as a means to cultivate ones First Wisdom so as grow the Spiritual Elements inside and outside of a human. One of humans' missions is to evolve within the confines of the "Spark" of God—inferred to be *Immanent* (entirely a mind) which constitutes the "Self" of each newborn—and that evolution concerns expanding ones Higher Mind. To this end, according to Amen, (Metu Neter VII:44), the ingredients are the Self (containing Divine Consciousness and Divine Will called the Ab) and the Spirit (Spiritual Energy/Matter) providing the substance for the forms (spirit, soul, life force, mind) and forces to manifest as an entity in the world. The mind has a Metaphysical (Sahu) faculty to deal with Abstracts as well as an Animal part to deal with and Abstractions and Concrete thinking.

The True (i.e. the unmanifested Self) projects a reflection of itself into the Spirit's Ab in order to program ones mind, the Sahu and a portion of the Ab with the attributes of its divinity. An analogy is the Divine Consciousness/Will projects itself onto the mind as the light of a movie projector on to the screen). So the purpose of the human mind is to serve as a storehouse of the Self's Knowledge of itself. It is the only part of the Spirit where self-knowledge can and has been appointed to take verbal and graphic form. It is where the Divine Self-Image (to serve as the Self's reflection) is constructed.

It takes work to develop the Spiritual Mind and this can only be done by the emergence of the "Soul Sunshine" from within, for it has been there all along, lying deeper than all the corruptions of ones 'fleshly nature.' The chain of the Spiritual Elements and its messages are what lead away from the natural desires of the Animal brain. The development of the Spiritual Mind starts with the masculo-feminine aspect of every human. The virtues of manners can only be tested in a single situation -- that of human interaction. It is by the way a man treats his fellow man, regardless of anyone's station in society that the Hausa will finally evaluate him as meeting the criteria of the good man and fulfilling -- or not. This non-physical form of manhood focuses on the human dignity (i.e. the Spirit of God) residing in the individual.

"MANHOOD" AFRICAN TRADITION MODEL: Ancient Africans used the circumstantial Truth derived from essences of Nature to say that right Manliness is to model its work after *the approaches used in the work done by what the God Spirit* does in Nature to create, enhance, and maintain harmony, balance, and connectedness. For those still burdened today with a problematic "Manhood," the establishment of Maniliness begins by learning to act out of ones Real Self; to shed delusions and replace that with the truth; and to "know" the enslaver—who he is, what he does, and how he appears—so as to create a workable defense and an offense designed to successfully lead to ones mission in life. The envisioning requires realizing what can and cannot be properly Imaged. "Manly" is intended to be a progressive cultivation of a male's Spiritual Mind and what is Spiritual is incapable of having an 'Image'—though it can be symbolized. A proper African Tradition process of maturing is for the "Manly" to successively over-rule ones "Manhood" tendencies. By contrast, for one to have an Image of oneself indicates one is dealing with concepts having "Value" and that may be the result of ignorance or intention.

The switch begins by realizing the human Soul's composition of a Spark of God means the human mind's purpose is to be a storehouse of the divine Self's Knowledge of itself for use in reflecting that Certainty in daily living. Ones duty is to live within and evolve out of the Spiritual Elements—the process for discovering Unconditional Love, Truth, Reality, and the Natural—a process imparting, not pleasure or "excitement," but an "Aliveness," as in overflowing with Curiosity to explore the unknown and seeking its every Spiritual Elements tidbit to use for creating ones life. Such a flow, only possible by Real Self (Ma'at) Life-Living, is maintained by: (1) staying with good thoughts united by the union of the right Intellect, Emotions, and Judgment; (2) imparting good words to encourage or assist; (3) engaging in good "ME/WE" actions that expand beyond finite ends; and (4) staying focused on eternal luminaries (e.g. Unconditional Love and Truth). This process demands Knowing (not Belief or Faith) and meshing Certainty power with Unconditional Love's power.

Out of the resultant Soul Integrity flows what it takes to *"Be Right," "Recognize Right," "Do Right," "Make Things Right," and "Defend the Right"*—and these fulfill every function of Humanity. Guidelines for this process--so as to bring order to ones life and stay in the flow of the Spiritual Elements--include the fact that *Truth can only be known by seeing things the way they are* while disregarding any likes or dislikes about its discovery or where it leads--since one can and ought to live by Truth. Along the path, appreciate the good derived from "living" with Human Ideals so as to evolve into enjoying being about ones Mission.

Ancient Africans said humans' growth patterns are in 3 distinct phases: physical, mental, and spiritual. Adult's Spirituality phase is characterized by the same sense of *Limitlessness*, though modified, as possessed by the Supreme Being: (a) a sense of "Oneness" with all Cosmic creations (omnipresence)—and not having a limited presence, as is the feature of Lower (animalistic) Self people; (b) an *Intuitive* faculty that informs without thinking (wisdom, omniscience)—and not the ignorance of staying ignorant which drives one to seek information from the External World; and (c) ones Will powers acting upon ones Spirit to enable achievements of Human Ideal Goals—and not the impotence at the root of all human dishonorableness, prejudice, and greedy grabbing for the earth's riches. These 3 negatives cause Humankind's problems; these 3 attributes of God solve Humankind's problems, for they are the Substance of claims that humans are made in the likeness of God.

The ultimate human example of perfected God attributes was Tehuti—the African Master of all Masters—a "Man-Godhood" on Earth. Though to lessor degrees, most people know someone who does "a whole lot 24/7" by having unlimited potential thoughts enabling achieving reasonable goals. Partly contributory to their countless achievements is an absolute refusal to accept thoughts limiting their abilities. They have a Mission to which they hone skills of Self-Control and Self-Discipline; constant *Focus* (a key) on handling one thing at a time; of ever striving for Perfection; in efficient precision of Thought Organization into Matter; Matter into Form; and Form into workable effective action. A reason others do not get to be all they can be is because they choose to remain 'un-awakened'. An analogy is the Congenital Tarda genes (e.g. for some great Talent) that are present in each human at birth but do not express themselves until sometime after birth—but only in "Awake and Alive" people. The more that Talent is nourished and cultivated the more it "Fruits."

Primitive Africans' "Manhood" cornerstones were to Provide, Protect, Produce—caring deeply for their children. Later Africans guided children toward their Highest (Divinity) Self. This enables ones sense of Selfhood Greatness to show by realizing the Truth of there being no separation of any human from others; of the identification for all humans with the Universal Self; of eagerly curing ones own follies and false opinions; to give others credit and be happy for others success, to have courage to say: "I was wrong"; "You were right"; "I lost it" (not "It got lost"). Avoid blaming/complaining. African Manhood deals with serious business similar to how a child does it at play. A defining moment in growing up is discovering the surviving core of strength within oneself that overrides very intense hurts and then drives one to instantly face/handle tough problems. jabaileymd.com

GANG VIOLENCE HEALING APPROACH

Self-Improvement cannot happen without a "*Voluntary*" (C14 calling on the sense of ones power of willing) *Volition* ("I will!) to switch to a Spiritual Elements path. This means the switch is done deliberately, intentionally, spontaneously of ones own free will in accordance with desire. Here, again, is where European and African Tradition etymologies do not agree. Europeans say "Spontaneous" is that which is without special premeditation or distinct determination of the will--making it partly voluntary and partly involuntary. African Tradition says Spiritual Spontaneity is what naturally and instinctually flows out of ones Divine Consciousness (Soul). To go along with the European version is to inappropriately apply Rules on the Spiritual Elements and leads the Receiver into a self-contradictory dilemma of how to recognize what is ones SHNN as well as how express what it takes to keep receiving SHNN. Voluntary, as defined by Europeans, opens the door to masks and masquerades in hopes of obtaining SHNN. Hence, the resultant obsession and compulsions prevent most from ever trying to make a proper switch to the Spiritual Elements.

The single most significant factor the prevention, in the stopping, and in the healing of Selfhood violence and/or violence toward others or Things is to satisfy Black youth's Physical and Spiritual Human Nature Needs. Second, for them to reconnect with their Real Self and its associated birth-gift of Selfhood Greatness as well as with its entourage of the "5Ss"—safety, security, self-confidence, strength, and stability. Third is to achieve and maintain a Free Mind that originates in and operates out of the Spiritual Element. All of this is best done within the mental theater of Fun, Appreciation, and an enjoyment of life (e.g. by occasionally being silly). To make all of this happen at its best requires 'the village' but unfortunately Black People, in adopting European ways, have drifted away being devoted to helping each other. They must be shown that all God's creatures and creations are spiritually related and to see each other as separate generates artificial opposites that lead to conflicting opposites engaging in violence. Unless participants committed to helping stop and heal the violence overcome this orientation and other evils European captors brainwashed into the minds of the Enslaved, they will be of no benefit. The same is true if they have not learned the fundamental of African Tradition and are absolutely committed to discarding each and every tiny bit of European teachings, definitions, propaganda, and opinions.

BRING WILLING GANGS/MENTORS TOGETHER: Each of the many links in a long chain symbolizes the organizational and individual efforts—primarily on the part of Black People—to handle the multi-textured problems facing the Black community in general and the Black gangs in particular. Each link represents a different but essential part of every person's daily living, including those that influence criminal behavior. As vital as new standards are for social justice in all institutions of USA culture, Europeans cannot ever be counted on to help make this happen. Thus, a national movement that elevates the moral and community consciousness of every member of society, starting with Black Society, will have to be done by Black People. A collective determination to ensure that the physical, social, and emotional needs of everyone are satisfied would bring about a dramatic reduction in the number of people struggling to simply survive and of criminal offenders so that they can begin doing what it takes to begin thriving.

Nevertheless, the single most difficult job in trying to bring about group and individual change is to both bring people together at the same time and same place and then have them persist together until the job is satisfactorily completed. This is particularly hard for Black People since European slavers were dedicated to generating dissention among all Enslaved and that Slave Survival remains in full force among Black Americans. Today, a tiny few will say they will help but most of those are never heard from again and those who show have so many other obligations (e.g. to social media) that they are 'half-hearted' (a mid-C19 saying for only moderate enthusiasm—the antonym of "with all ones heart"). If those can be overcome, Wood (*Group Processes & Intergroup Relations, 2014*) says the first requirement for Mentors is to be sincerely interested in the gang members as human beings, for that helps design ways to enhance the *attraction* gang members feel towards each other so as for them to desire to do what is in the best interest of each member. Second is to stimulate the *motivation* for a return of each member's Real Self for the purpose of having each participate in the gang's self-improvement activities by eagerly contributing to the group's goals. Third is the *coordination* of gang member efforts to reverse their "them and us" categories and stop using these as a basis to make distinctions that favor their own group. It is fundamental to understand the mindset of the gang members—e.g. the force of competition for power, domination, reputation, respect, and status.

MENTORS: An essential feature of a Mentor is the ability to speak the language of the Receiver--in words, meanings, tones, rhythm. Otherwise, miscommunication is likely to result in conflict and confusion. There must be a congenial atmosphere for gang members to feel safe and to be heard. Mentors, says Lopez-Aguado (*Ethnography, 2013*) are best recruited from the gang's community so that they are familiar with the particular street politics in the neighborhood, and even the families of many of the young people they encounter, and this gives them connections they can develop into mentoring relationships. It is preferable if the interventionists have a comparable histories of gang affiliation, violence, incarceration, substance abuse, and ultimately desistance. These histories make it possible for the interventionists to connect with local youth, as they have struggled through many of the same hardships the youth experience and see affecting their families and communities. Telling their stories is an important way for the interventionists to demonstrate their legitimacy and wisdom and establish themselves as someone youth can relate and listen to.

Oscar is well-known in the neighborhood as an early member of a prominent prison gang, and anytime he meets with youth he recounts stories about prison, shows old pictures, and uses his history to appeal to their interest in or identification with street culture. Jorge explains why sharing this past is important, even necessary: You basically had to come from a messed up background to give back to the street, to do this kind of work. You cannot have a rich kid from Beverly Hills, learn about gangs in college or whatnot, and then do this kind of work. You gotta be a product of the street to do this work. Cuz the kids will read you, they'll know. They'll know, this guy's fake, this guy came from the hood, he's got his scars, he's got his wounds, his history. Those kids can read you man, they will. Lopez-Aguado continues: The interventionists use their stories of enduring street life and the justice system to demonstrate to their cases that they understand their experiences and can relate to their complaints of dealing with criminal stigmas they don't feel are fair.

When a couple of Jorge's cases come to volunteer in the office for community service hours, they begin talking with him about the extra penalties added to criminal sentences for gang members. They complain that these additional punishments are unfair, claiming that one of their friends even had his citizenship application revoked when he was identified in court as a gang member. Jorge nods and replies, 'Courts, police, if you're Black or Mexican they're gonna see you as a thug whether you bang or not.' He then tells them a story about one time when he was arrested, and county sheriffs stripped him naked and laid him down in the street while they posed for photographs standing over him. The teens silently shake their heads for a few moments before finally responding, 'Damn, that's f**ked up.' Jorge nods again, 'That's why you guys gotta stay in school man, it's the only way to avoid all that craziness.' Jorge uses stories about his experiences to relate to the injustices youth experience and offer advice on how to persevere.

In addition to supporting youth in their interactions with the juvenile justice system, the interventionists also serve as advocates for youth seeking social services. As part of a citywide outreach program, it is important to be connected to a network of social service agencies and nonprofit organizations that allowed it to help youth receive services that might otherwise be hard for them to access. These included referrals to programs for tattoo removal, job placement or training, anger management, drug and alcohol rehabilitation, tutoring, school placement or burial assistance for crime victims. On top of referring youth to service agencies, this advocacy also entailed helping them navigate institutional bureaucracies, which was new for many of them. Terence, for example, would spend many of his visits with young people walking them through the steps they had to take to apply for work or social services. This would include coming to their homes to fill out application forms with them line-by-line, or taking them to the DMV so he could help them get a valid ID.

KNOW THE "ENEMY" FOR DEFENSE AND OFFENSE: For Black Americans struggling to find the way to knowledge and self-improvement, a place to get oriented is to know who the enemy is inside their Supernatural realm. This involves discovering what is real about the situation, about oneself, about the enemy, and about a Human Ideal goal fashioned out of African Tradition. A major problem is that gang members are pursuing the "Good Life" façade Europeans present to them without any idea of how untrue that is. The enemy has chosen that realm because its superstar feature is madly doting upon Matter and devoutly worship it as the only Numen. In the Natural world the complement of Spirit is Matter—an aspect of manifestation which receives qualities and takes form—both done from the action of Spirit' energy and order upon it so matter can be actualized or evolved under invariable laws of Nature. Of itself, Matter has no inherent quality and no real being reality. To show that it has no independent existence, it is in a constant state of decaying and also has impermanence. Although Matter is cause of evil, it is itself not evil. The more Matter is pursued, the less that Good can be pursued. The Spirit is replete with all potencies and knowledges from all eternity. But since the Supernatural is of a nonrational nature, none of these comments will have any effect on its Believers. To specify, of itself, money has no worth or value other than what people give it.

AIM FOR A CONSCIOUSNESS OF WISDOM

Consciousness is the phenomenon providing the means for a human's very inner, outer, and Cosmic world existence to be Illuminated so that humans can be Aware of what is Known. But the terminology of Consciousness is so chaotic as to make it difficult to know how to approach the subject. For example, some speak of "Consciousness" as being a single thing while others subdivide it into all sorts of categories. The "Big Picture" of birth gift Consciousness is that it embraces Spiritual and Material phases of Knowing— derived from doing separate things in different directions and yet interdependently working as a unit. A crude terminology understanding of Consciousness is as follows. First, being Aware of the Knowledge in ones Inner World core was so foundational to African Tradition Ma'at (Spiritual Elements in action) Life Living that written on Ancient African temple walls 10,000 years ago was: "*Man, Know Thyself*". This means one has self-illumination: (1) of being a vital part of the Cosmic Organism; (2) being awake to the Awareness of the absence of an isolated center of Cosmic action by realizing one is part of the whole Cosmic Organism, doing what the Cosmos is doing; and (3) of Cosmic Knowledge from having discovered what is natural within oneself and what underlies what is natural is the Cosmic Laws of Nature and Cosmic Laws of Humanity. In other words, a human Spiritual Consciousness Primordial Cosmic interconnection with the deepest Hidden part of that humans' Selfhood, enables her/him to see where she/he came from, is now, and is headed. To do this and to help bud the Divine Consciousness within a human's Unconscious into a *Spiritual Conscious Awareness* in order for it to flower requires highly cultivated meditative skills. That part of a human's faculty to make this happen is what I call the *Supraconscious,* although it is typically lumped into the Unconscious.

Second, Complete and Certain Material World Knowing in a Real Self individual starts with that human's Supraconsciouness having illuminated a state of "Knowing Thyself" of which that individual is Aware. Out of that Background one uses Ma'at Principles (which are Subconscious) to interpret ones Experiences. The C14 word "*Experience*" (try out) means being self-involved in something; actually observing phenomena; or undergoing special events—each to gain first-hand knowledge of a practical nature, as opposed to a speculative way of finding out about a thing. Nevertheless, no Experience is ever sufficiently limited for one to get ones mind around it—meaning the assessment of an Experience is never complete. Still, by staying within the Spiritual Elements flow, one can use the *Law of Correspondence* to infer what it "Right" Life-Living. This requires assessing each life-shaping or life-changing event, problem, situation, or circumstance using the *Box Concept*. This is the process for proceeding to study the Obvious, the Hidden, and the underlying Base/Foundation—for their "big three" of the "what it is," the "what it does," and the "how it appears" of a Thing.

Specifically, the *Box Concept* thoroughly evaluates the "big three" by seeing it on all sides—from top down/bottom up--each angle of each side—both sides of each side/angle—and rating each of all pros/cons. *Making this process routine is the ultimate in Critical Thinking* because it enables one to recognize the Principle contained in the essence, regardless of its varied appearances or situational presentation forms. The objective is to get to the issue's underlying facts, assumptions, or what it is otherwise composed of--breaking down those components into their "bottom-line" parts; evaluating the pros and cons of each bottom-line part; and arriving at a conclusion about or a sense gauging of the good/bad, desirable/undesirable, Worth/Value of the Obvious, Hidden, and Base/Foundation of the "glob" about the something or the someone(s).

Selfhood assessments, grading, prioritizing, and category rankings are made by using *Measurements* for quantitative items (e.g. things one can see); and *Estimates* for qualitative aspects (i.e. things one cannot see). This is the process of establishing a Secular Sensory Consciousness of Wisdom. *Wisdom* is actualized intuition (learning from within)—i.e. providing *direct perceptions of reality* so that its ingredients can be maneuvered and manipulated into Spiritual Elements packages that form options for what is appropriate and most workable for solving the issue.

HOW TO LEARN

Foundational to learning is to realize what is and is not to be learned. What is to be learned at the beginning is Type I—Physical Human Nature Needs (PHNN) Practical Knowledge—that which helps one deal with basic survival problems in the "Here and Now"—e.g. food, safety, a place to sleep. Next is to make sure these PHNN can continue in a manner that does not cause harm to oneself or others. Type II—a Human Ideal Goals for providing ones Private Self with the "5Ss"—and that comes from re-establishing Selfhood Greatness. A good way to start that is to learn to do one thing superbly—something others do not know how to do—something one enjoys—something out of which one can start making money within a week. Type III—is to learn what to stop doing. Here, it helps to make a list of all ones flaws and gets friends and enemies to contribute to what is to be considered (for all of it is not true). Some things will need to be improved; some replaced. Type IV is to learn how to stick with a project until it is completed. This requires replacing ones Emotional Energy with Spiritual Energy Package, which contains "Aliveness" to motivate one into harmonious: *Dedication* (selecting what is cared about); *Commitment* (becoming one with what is cared about); *Loyal* (sticking like glue to a Goal and Purpose no matter what); *Determination* (setting limits within which one will act); *Persistence* (holding fast to ones Purpose and Goal); and *Perseverance* (continuing ruthlessly in the face of opposing forces, set-backs, and momentary failures). These six and Concentration (staying focused on one thing) support each other in completing the task. Together, they over-ride established bad habits like procrastination, being scattered, and working so slowly that little gets done. Make doing this a game to see how doing things can be increasingly Efficient (done quickly), Effective (done right), confidently, and with a sense of urgency.

Type V is about getting on the path to Thriving and being Happy. This involves discovering ones Talent; becoming an entrepreneaur; learning how to make and save and manage money in investments; how to have an excellent product and give excellent service and at a proper marketplace price. This requires getting rid of Black American Customs in all dealing with the marketplace—e.g by being on time, returning phone calls and emails, going to helpful business meetings, reading up on pertinent business practices; and stop wasting time on Flashing Light gadget, including television. Socializing is to be done very sparingly until the business is "safe." Trance develops such learning.

TRANCE: Trance ('go across'), ones only means of making changes and learning, is a temporary alteration of Consciousness accompanied by a loss of sense of identity—a selective focusing on specific aspects of something. Some people volitionally enter a Trance by Meditation or Ritual. Such began for me as a boy without ceremony but simply from getting involved with gardening (with my shoes and socks off so as to wiggle my toes in the dirt). Later it occurred naturally almost every time I went fishing. Still later, I made a conscious effort to concentrate on an imagined scene so as to "Just Be". All of my studies require my thinking deeply in a Calm and very quiet state. By being so engrossed, I lose contact with an awareness of anything around me—seeing, hearing, feeling nothing else—like asking: "where am I"? If someone silently comes into my space and makes any sound, it causes me to jump—like a baby's Startle Reflex. Typically, anyone enters a Trance as a result of experiencing some strong emotions (e.g. rage, fear, excitement, passion, grief, enjoyment, affection). Here, there is intense focus and concentration. Otherwise, practically everybody slips into a trance several times a day—called "Spaced-out," Absorbed," "Absent-Minded," "Daydreaming."

Once in a Trance, ones mind changes to engage in the processes of forming something, transitioning into some where else, or transcend ones present situation or circumstance. These are made possible as a result of being in an atmosphere that heightens receptivity to images, to ones own words, and to ones own imaginations so as to increase ones learning abilities 2 to 50 times greater than normal. Whatever is the effect, it is called *Creative Programming of ones mind*—whether deliberarbly done or not. This is about ideas and images taken in and powered into a heightened state of susceptibility to suggestion from sound, situation, or circumstance. During my boyhood, I used fishing with a cork to challenge my speed against a fish biting. Thus, I focused hard on the cork so as to be able to snatch up the line as soon as the cork bobbed—never realizing this was a powerful way to learn how to focus and concentrate—both carrying me into another worldly realm of trance (contemplation).

Innovative Programming is enhancing what is already programmed in ones mind. In this state, one can easily establish or remove behaviors—either way, modifying physiological functions. Hence, entering Trance is to be avoided when one is filled with negative thoughts and images—as triggered by negative and sensual emotions. *Transcending Programming* of ones mind concerns rising above ones normal mental state (e.g. despair). Visualization requires being in a Trance. Regardless of which type of Trance, instead of being in the Unknown, I am in a mystical (mist) state of whatever is the topic at hand—internalizing with something (e.g. Beauty), healing a "big bang" pain, transcending the "smog" of what I am bathed in; reinforcing the fact that I have what it takes to get through this tough problem.

LEARNING TRANCE STATE: A *Learning Trance* is a withdrawal from the External World while in a calm and peaceful mindset so that ones resultant total receptivity benefits programming of mental events. A Trance aids an Engram with its physiological and emotional functions as part of becoming illogical and irrational memories (simply because they are outside the realm of Reason). That memory retains all that has ever been experienced and they serve as patterns for imitation or cultivation. Though memories may be difficult to recall from being repressed, they still exert powerful influences in shaping ones beliefs and behaviors. Meanwhile, they have been associated on the basis of external qualities and when those qualities are touched upon, they often give recall to prior experiences associated with them. By Trance accelerating learning 2 to 50 times, that enabled ancient Black nations to forge in cultures and civilizations far, far ahead of Western and Eastern nations (Amen, Metu Neter I:168). Trance also helps so to develop ones higher mental and spiritual faculties, thereby enabling the effective coping with and transcending of their emotional dysfunctions. For me, this boundary-less Spiritual Elements state is entered by totally focusing on the issue at hand and continuing to do so while constructing patterns made of dream-like intangibles. But it only works for "ME/WE" purposes. Since Normal people do "Life-Living" out of their Lower (animalistic) Self—e.g. desires, Secular passions, and appetites, both disciplined and undisciplined—and pursue "Emotional Excitement" (a childish trait), they have a False Self.

While in a Trance state characterizing the child's high degree of receptivity and emotionality, the decision to enter ones False Self is to be attracted indiscriminately to and engage in imitation. All imitations of what is External to oneself is off the Real Self learning path. False Self people are in a perpetual state of Trance—as with habitual ways of thinking, emoting, desiring, capabilities. These define ones Secular Self-Identity (i.e. "Personality"). One enters a Trance with each strong emotion, desire, sensation, "spaced out," in "suspense," "absent minded," or devotion to places or things. It is thus that one cultivates or reinforces negative behaviors since one is not mindful of what self-destructive thoughts one takes into the Trance. By being Self-Unknown and not having developed their Intellect within the stream of the Spiritual Elements, their indiscriminate imitation of the "Crowd" + society's Trinkets and Trivia + Flashing Light gadgets destroys thinking skills.

These keep them in the status quo—and showered with problems. Emotional mindsets fail because to recall memories and the external qualities associated with them means emotional colors and exaggerations have been added to both. Hence, they misunderstand more than they understand. That means they deceive themselves in assembling their "*Personality*" (Secular Self-Identity) out of distorted or fantasy entities—most being other people's statements used to define oneself. The same applies to perceptions through the senses. A typical result is: "I'm not good enough"—and that wrongly refers to External World thinking limited to the Physical and Supernatural realms. Attempts to alter life-changing habits fail because ones chronic tension, Emotional Energy, lack of analytical thinking skills, and being pervaded and possessed with ignorant information—most SEEMING alright--is antagonistic to change. The process of awakening to begin the journey to ones Highest Self is to "de-trance" or "dehypnotize" ones Consciousness away from ones "Personality" in order to re-establish with ones Real Self—i.e. ones Self-Identity (Amen, Metu Neter II:88).

Half of what one does in daily life is needless or useless and should be eliminated. It takes volition to cultivate ones divine Self-Image, using reasoned understanding within the Spiritual Elements so as to fashion Selfhood *Order and consistent Patterns underlying ones behaviors*. Then, to promote learning, there are different phases of evolution. *Type I's* evolution is constant repetition reinforcing engrams until they start operating in the brain's *reverberating circuits*—meaning electrical stimulation in isolated brain tissue continues round and round in neuron loops for seconds post-stimulation. This dynamic engram involves a large number of synapses which grow with each repetition of what is triggering it. Counteracting neurons are weakened or eliminated, spurred by chemical changes. Repetition increases a sense of familiarity so that to recognize one spotlighted thing means it is associated with a team, in the way synonyms are naturally associated with a word thoroughly studied.

Type II evolution is by the Memory being 'forgotten' (but merely transformed into a "Repressed" state). Yet, repression implies the retention of a tendency to do certain related things. For example, one might instantly hyper-react to the color red for reasons unknown. But the cause came from riding a red bicycle when it accidently went into a ditch, flipped over, and bad injuries occurred. Instead of this 'red' reaction being a memory, it could be a Conditioned Reflex—the failing to recall but without any harm being done to ones memory. One may otherwise recall perfectly all happenings just before and after that accident. Here, 'red' of Type II (Forgotten Imagination Memory) does not have the same familiarity and therefore associations as would 'red' in Type I (Familiarity Memory). By contrast, Recognition demands seeing an actual object.

To bring this together, Recognition is on one end of a scale (requiring mental effort) and Instinct is on the opposite end (no mental effort involved). Memory and Imagination are alike because both deal with Things which are not present to the senses. Meanwhile, it becomes a 'second nature' response, just short of an Instinct, to form a Conditioned Response. In other words, ones immediate emotional reaction is to a primary reference experience of an object outside oneself but not tied to any sense experience—which makes it a Supernatural reaction. Such extremely destructive and crude practices were present among all the savage European tribes who were continually spurred to fight, rob, and kill anybody--at any time. To put this in a modern context, people were not safe to walk across the street because, by doing so, something bad would happen.

BACKGROUND FUNDAMENTALS OF LEARNING: Ancient Africans' term for "Learning" ('mathesis') came from astrological divination and meant 'Mother Wisdom' (the highest form of Common Sense). The Old English (725) word "Learn" (to get knowledge, be cultivated) carries the underlying notion of gaining experience by following along a track—a track that can be natural, acquired, or a natural one altered by an acquired superimposition. Broadly, learning is present whenever there is relatively permanent change in an organism's behavior resulting from its reaction to environmental influences. This may occur to the developing fetus in the mother's womb (Congenital Learning) or throughout ones lifetime following birth. *"Congenital" Learning* comes about by external influences (e.g. the mother's mood, dietary intake) that fashion a "track". That 'Learning Track' may affect the developing fetus in utero so that its behavior alterations are manifest in utero, at birth in the newborn, or as "Congenital Tarda" displays (congenital/ developmental aspects present before or at birth but that do not flower until sometime after birth). To be distinguished from learning are changes in behavior derived from: (a) maturation from *Inheritance* (genetic parental derived predisposition transmissions)—i.e. normal growth and development which occurs as long as the organism is adequately nourished. A newborn's eyes, for example, cannot follow a moving object but by age 6 months she/he is able to be in control of head turning so as to follow the moving object; (b) from temporary changes such as sensory adaptation or fatigue and warming-up; and (c) miscellaneous factors, as from disease, injury, or by drugs. The complex subject of Natural Learning includes the *"Heritable"*—a term wrongly considered essentially synonymous with 'Genetic' and 'Inherited'--because it includes both. *'Inherited'* implies genes are transferred from parent to child while Mutations, along with the inherited genes, may result in new genes in a *zygote* (the union, yoking, fusion of the male spermatozoon and the female ovum to give a fertilized egg).

This is the foundation upon which all "Genetic" learning of any organism rests. These, termed "Innate," are important for learning in that they are the paths for basic responses + being the started of basic drives for learning + fixing, at least within limits, possible levels of maximum performance. But to aid understanding, let us review two key definitions. First is a *Stimulus* (spur)—a 1684 word originally designating a goad used for driving cattle by pricking them. Today it means spurring to action or effort, as a needle against the skin or a signal acting on ones senses or a printed or spoken word serving as a call to action. Second, ways humans/animal react to a stimulus is called a *Response* (to answer)—i.e. something offered in return, almost as an obligation (hence 'Responsible'). Its Ancient African origin was Griots (story-tellers) participatory audience communication—i.e. "*Call and the Response*"--characterized by the Griot sending out a "call" and the audience acknowledging the message. The audience responded while the speaker spoke--and not afterward--so as to make a fluid harmonious tone of participatory communication. A stimulus response is an act, usually a movement—ranging from Mild (like the twitch of a muscle or the blink of an eyelid) all the way over to the Extreme (e.g. one 'jumping' from a door closing). Innate responses are termed *Reflex* ('turn or bend back') and may be brought about not only by the action of sense organs and the nervous system or by other means (e.g. images).

One innate example is respiration which is, in part, chemically controlled. Some responses are also subject to hormonal control. Type I Innate Responses—i.e. Instincts--are the somewhat undifferentiated mass activity involving a large number of muscles. Babies can be observed twisting, rolling, arching, and waving of the hands and feet. Type II are Reflexes—relatively simple responses to stimuli and are dependent on nerve pathways that develop with the normal growth of the organism. An *Unconditioned Reflex* occurs in the scenario where stimuli trigger responses without any learning. An example is reflexly pulling ones hand away when it touches a hot stove—an instinct reaction helping to keep one alive and healthy. Type III are more complex and integrated types of innate behaviors, as exemplified by combined Instincts and *Tropisms* (the movement of an organism or a part toward or away from an external stimulus, such as light, heat, or gravity). jabaileymd.com

FUNDAMENTALS OF LEARNING: The Innate aspects for Reflexes, Tropisms, Instincts, glandular secretions, and the like are important for learning since they constitute its raw materials. Part of an organism's Innate aspects includes various needs, drives, or urges—so as to acquire, to defend, or to avoid. Also, one will keep reacting to specific problematic stimuli until they are removed. Or, one immediately seeks to acquire food to satisfy hunger but, if not hungry, one does not do so. Learning is information or knowledge gained by "*Education*" ("to lead out what is inside"); "*Teaching*" ("to show" so as to impart knowledge for learning); *Instructing* ("to build in or into"), or "*Training*" (active mind exercising in order to form habits)—in short, by study, reflection, and/or practice--depending upon the topic. For example, *Motor Skills* such as riding a bicycle, can be learned without using words. *Mental Skills* such as playing board games or problem solving require thinking, learning from experience, and an assortment of things which are useful at times and then, to varying degrees (e.g. recognizing shapes, understanding numbers, reading). The core around which such learning occurs might be ones past experiences; the ingredients of Sensation out of ones memory; something going on inside ones Selfhood; something entering a human's senses from the outside world; ones interpretations of the monitored feedback one gets from outside influences; or a combination of these. Then relationships are seen that enable assessments of what is involved in light of ones own experiences. "Connections" are made to form significant meanings which pave the way to expansive learning and the setting of standards. It is more important to learn what not to learn. Part of knowledge is to be ignorant of what is not worth knowing. Just because the "Crowd" or even authorities say something is right does not make it so. They may be 'right' but on the wrong path or going in the wrong direction or what they say may be located on the wrong plane of existences. It is better to learn one thing well before going to the next thing. When learning is at a wisdom level, one has *Vision*.

To learn is: (1) a process of maneuvering and manipulating a number of small independent acts into one or more new arrangements and/or combinations so as to arrive at a new order or a new form (e.g. learning to play a new piece on the piano); (2) performing a familiar act in a new situation (e.g. knowing how to focus a microscope makes it easier to learn how to focus a telescope—or learning how to use a computer makes it easier to instantly learn to use a car radio); (3) the stoppage of doing what is no longer needed (as in forgetting a friend's discontinued telephone number); or (4) not performing a familiar act in its usual setting because it is not worth it or not needed or not in ones best interest. The usages to which learning can apply include: 'learning how to learn' (e.g. taking information to assess and analyze so as to make corrections, and formulate a workable conclusion); correcting mistakes (e.g. spellings of words); classifying anything; predicting; decision making; problem solving; or forming habits. Learning any of these skills allows them to be transferrable to novel like-kind things. Fundamental to acquired learning is that one must be stimulated by a signal alerting one or more of the senses or by a stimulus to peak ones Curiosity. Start learning by correcting or replacing ones most firmly believed but unexamined assumptions (e.g. on religion).

A person then reacts or responds to the stimulus. For instance, to hear a knock on the door (stimulus) causes one to take notice (response). Learning—the going from "nowhere" to "now here"--is the building of new relationships between stimuli and responses so as to design an usually long-lasting change. Much learning is the result of forming habits--pattern acting in a certain way under certain conditions. Approaches used for learning are by: volition; rewards or praise (i.e. *positive reinforcement*); *negative reinforcement* (using criticism or punishment as a way to learn not to do things); and fear. Whether the learning is for good or evil, certain features that enhance the learning process include: motivation; elimination of the non-favored response; discovery of the actual or seemingly most appropriate response; fixation of the desired or intended response so that it becomes "*Second Nature*" (acquired but deeply ingrained). This implies that a given mindset in how to respond has become a mild and possibly beneficial *Obsession* and a *Compulsion*. These principles can be used to fashion a Human Ideal Goal and daily work toward it. jabaileymd.com

AFRICAN TRADITION SANKOFA REHABILITATION

SANKOFA: "We must go back and reclaim our past so we can move forward"; go back "so we can understand why and how we came to be who we are today"; go back to Ancient African Values to rebuilt our philosophy; go back in order to see and embrace a humanity for how to live in the present for the purpose of reaching the heaven Afterlife. Put another way, *Sankofa* is to: *(1)* return to African Tradition to learn Principles of how to; (2) Prepare in the present; (3) in order to go forward into a Thriving future--all staying within the boundaries of Ancient Africans' terminology definitions and descriptions. Its Language and Concepts are the only ones suitable to reflect, represent, and teach Afrocentric People. When African people utilize non-African language and concepts (e.g. Greek, Roman, Anglo Saxon), they unknowingly distort or fantasize the reality essence of African Tradition's Philosophy. The way to get on and proceed down the Wisdom path is by all decisions and solutions remaining within the confines of the African Spiritual Elements of Unconditional Love, Truth, Reality, and the Natural. "Returning to the source" of Ancient African Values is done so as to get ones Selfhood ordered in stability and strength before launching out to "take on the world." These Principles-- known by observation, research, experimentation, and verification--are used as fundamentals to learn and teach Knowledge--Certainty. By returning to philosophical building blocks of African Tradition to derive its wisdom serves as a guide for fashioning a sound present; for correctly building a path into a thriving future; and, in the process, generating Trust in ones Selfhood so that one has confidence in how to acquire the principles for "How Shall I Live?"

SELF-ASSESSMENT FOR REHABILITATON: To apply African Principles to ones present problems and then using the paths laid out by those principles to enter into a thriving future is greatly by having an order of ones strengths, weaknesses, limitations, flaws, and the like. Such is gained by assessing them by a grading system so as to put each of these on the proper place of the Thinker's Scale--i.e. a +1 to +100 Positive Scale ruler and a -1 to -100 Negative Scale ruler, separated by zero. On the negative side of the Thinker's Scale goes what is self-defeating and thus unnatural, as exhibited by humans intentionally doing harm to each other or to oneself and for any reason. On the positive side of the Thinker's Scale, Help is applied to bettering others or things. At the Zero point is put the lessening, stabilizing, or reversing of problems on the negative side.

There are two category of things to start self-assessment are to focus on learning for Oneself--the Necessary, the Important, and the Desires; For Others----the Necessary, the Important, and the Options. The Necessary concerns ones Physical Human Nature Needs (PHNN); ones Spiritual Human Nature Needs (SHNN); what is required for ones Family and for ones Career. The Important is what makes the Necessary happen. The Desires are tended to once the Necessary and the Important are done. If there is not enough time left for ones Desires, then one learns how to make Fun out of hard work. The Necessary for Others is what comes from weighing the benefits and consequences. This requires putting oneself in the shoes of the other to determine how strongly the other considers the issue at hand. Most of today's youth have the concept that they will do what an authority or Elder says when the youth gets around to it--foolishing thinking they have the power to overrule or disregard directions that are inconvenient to them. This is the very attitude that will keep them from succeeding and will prevent receiving "Helping Hands" from those in a power position to provide the missing link for success. It is better to miss a meal or get ones feelings hurt or be rudely treated if it can advance ones Theme Cause.

HUMAN'S MIND COMMITTEE MEETING: Any time one switches a life course path there will be greater than normal mental and "Life-Living" turmoil. When one has made the decision to switch, it is beneficial at the cross-roads before taking the next step for ones mind to have a mental committee meeting to review where one has just come from—the Causes; where one is now; what Effects and Consequences presently demand attention; and where one ought to go so as to select a Human Ideal goal. This is best done by being well-rested and select a quiet place in Nature to think. What will be discovered is one has to give up something nice to get something better as well as one has to pay a high price in order to follow ones Real Self. In preparation to go forward, be aware that there are will be additional and unexpected problems—some appearing as urgencies. There must be time in ones schedule to handle these additions but not lose a step in ones progress towards ones Human Ideal goal. Thus, one must stay focused only on reaching that goal and eliminate all other non-necessities (e.g. watching television, talking for long periods on the telephone.

There are checkered times in my life when I am bogged down about whether I going in a Ma'at direction or from feeling bad about something or by being overwhelmed or simply have to be in a "waiting" period. At those times I have a Selfhood Committee Meeting so as to look at the "Big Picture" of my life—what I have done compared to the best that is within me + what seems best to do and at paying what price, and if I am willing to pay that price. Part of the agenda of the Committed is to decide what is the very best thing to do next that leads to ones Human Ideal Goal. It is time to reassess if the qualities of the philosophical tree I am ingesting has the proper qualities and if I am absorbing its essences and applying all of its those qualities appropriately. By never having done anything intentionally to hurt anyone and by having stayed on course despite not having made the best decisions, my Committee Meeting conclusions is that I did things my way and have no one to blame for any resultant problems; that I am proud of it because it has been the very best I could do with the information available within that particular situation; and, if I had to do those things over again I would gladly pay the price for doing them. A greater price would have been to go against being my Real Self in favor of trying to please others. What I do on my Ma'at course is what has to be done and I find a way to like it, even if other have contrary opinions. Their opinions do not supersede mine.

Experience has taught me that my strength comes from doing what has to be done and without having a like/dislike opinion about it—and having no need to offer apologies if I gave it my all at that time. My own well-thought out values are my standards and never do I rely on the standards or decisions or information of others—no matter how authoritative they are. *Few people are mentally strong enough to look at something for what it is and without a like/dislike opinion.* Nor are many able to do what goes against "the Crowd" and particularly when that involves dealing with people who throw road blocks in the way or who generate rumors which lead to being rejected or abandoned.

A "Waiting Period" occurs for me once I have reached an unexpected goal and have no idea what is the "Ma'at" thing to do next. One of those times was on my 80th birthday. I could not think of another word to add to this book and simply took the day off to celebrate. But from a change of scenary and being in Nature, my Spiritual Entourage filled my head with a variety of things. One is that despite all my daily effort to gain what might help struggling Black People and they rejecting it, I got the "mind flash" that my Mission is to produce it so it is available if and when they decide to use it. Maybe a translator will come along and convey my message. Second, since I have been publishing articles in the Newspaper for 22 years (BlackVoicenews.com) and on my website (the first with 600 Black History articles completely destroyed by a hacker), presently with 550 articles, White people from around the world—reading c4500 pages a day—have sent in glowing comments. This caused me to realize that most White people have never heard the Truth about anything. Also, the Truth may help many Europeans stop hating so much and stop stealing Black People's intellectual property, and start realizing how great Black People are and how their European ancestors are directly responsible for the mess so many Black People are in today. It has taken great courage to publically go against "the Crowd," against "Killer" Police, against the dismantling of the ridiculous "little god" concepts of European males, and against the religious beliefs Black People have that were taught to be self-defeating by Europeans and the Bible they wrote to control people's minds.

Third, all of the ideas presented in this discussion, in the Preface, and the beginning of "About The Cover" came from my birthday thoughts. Fourth, I concluded my life has been "Alive" and full and good and happy and fun without getting involved in the "Trinkets and Trivia" and illusions and delusions of "the Crowd" (who are like 'zombies' and whose "Conditional Love" is given to control the willing). Although something expensive breaks down every day causing me to pay "big bucks" to incompetent people which, in turn makes me irritable, I get out of this mood by appreciating what I have. I believe that ones Mind Committee ought to momentarily meet daily to be thankful for ones health as is, for it can be worse; for the good mate (which also could be worse); for the Ma'at products one produces; for every directed toward self-evolving towards ones Hightest (Divinity) Self; for not being in worse shape than one is in presently; that one already possesses all of what it take to handle the very hardest blows given by life; and appreciate all other blessings one has.

Next, ones Talent must be developed within the context of ones Mission in life, either directly or by way of essential stepping stones leading to it. In the process, one strives to make ones Talent a masterpiece.

PERSONAL FLAWS REHABILITATION

As distinguished from a Spiritual Self-Identity, a Secular Self-Identity nature (see Chapter X) is totally oriented to the External World and is heavily fashioned by the monitored feedback from ones interactions with the outside world. For gang members, Secular Self-Identity is essential to that individual's emotional and psychophysiological well-being. The False Self ego fortifies and protects itself vigorously, employing defense mechanisms designed to shield the identity from attack. For this reason, the sense of ones False Self, developed during ones formative years, is incredibly difficult to alter in ones later years. However, because *the age at which a youth created a "Raw Nerve" is the age that youth stopped maturing*, starting at that "Raw Nerve" age is likely to help in forming a common bond from which maturity can be resumed. It can begin with someone interviewing the youth to give him/her a sense of saying what is felt and having been heard in the process. To stop the violence starts with the individual intensely desiring to switch lifestyle living directions. That starts with reactivating ones birth gift of SELF-TRUST—a concept that is part of an "Association of Self-Awareness Notions" of being Selfhood Great. Although an "Association of Self-Awareness Notions" does not carry a mental image, it does convey the 'payload' message to oneself of: "I bring a system of Spiritual Elements Values to my "ME/WE" orientation to life and all I do." That message is ones standard of behavior—a standard that is within the *Spiritual Elements*—i.e. Unconditional Love (God's inner nature), Truth (the essence of what real things are when they come into existence), Reality (the life of God's outer nature), and the Natural (principles by which the Cosmic Laws operate).

This implies that one does not disregard any aspect of the Spiritual Elements simply because one cannot answer all questions that arise about them. As long as one is flowing in that "ME/WE" Spiritual Elements stream, one has a sense of Selfhood Greatness and that imparts supreme personal Power called Self-Trust—a manifestation of Self-Love. Invariably, while in that stream, losses, lacks, and/or obstructions will occur. But those possessing Self-Trust uses these difficulties tools to force out the divine powers within ones Selfhood Greatness so they can be cultivated along lines that evolve thinking skills and creativity. Yet, when the problems seem overwhelming, solutions will open up from the assistance of "Helping Hands" that come out of nowhere and at just the right time—and without asking for it—but only as long as one refuses to 'give up.' By contrast, Europeans define 'Trust as being in the existential anchoring of reality in an emotional, and, to some degree, in a cognitive sense. This rests on confidence in the reliability of persons, acquired in the early experiences of the infant'.

The 'trust' of infant relationships, they continue, is accompanied here by a 'faith' in the continuity and comprehensibility of ones surroundings; by ones being-in-the-world having sustainable meaning—so that trust, faith and concepts of fate connect. *Networking* is a way of actively sustaining connections in an "Individualized" (European) society. To some extent one can still rely upon established roles, but networking means forming relationships with other people in an active and open way. For Europeans this involves "Active Trust," as in many other sectors of social life today. Networking is quite egalitarian and it evokes the rhetoric of intimacy. . . . It is striking—and extremely rude in many non-European cultures--how many people use first names quickly now, compared to even a few years ago. It is the ability to trust whilst being fully *aware* of the need to trust and consciously *striving* to maintain feelings of trust: 'Active trust is trust that has to be energetically treated and sustained'. This is because it is Secular.

REVERSE "INSIDE-OUT" THINKING: When brainwashing is done to a mind, that mind is turned "Inside-Out" so that one argues against reality and votes against oneself--choosing to live in a Delusional world and wanting something different from "what is." These things occurred with the enslavement of free Africans in Africa so as to not only remove the Selfhood freedom of each but to establish an Un-noble Loyalty of bonding. While the Satanist enslavers totally wiped out the Spiritual, Mental, and Physical aspects of each Enslaved, they provided just enough of the PHNN to maintain bare survival. Since this was all they had and there were no options, bonding with the captors occurred. This meant the Enslaved had been stripped of their Power to get what they needed for PHNN reasons and had no Power characterizing their Self-Worth/Self-Value. Thus, their minds were turned "Inside-Out". Reversing this starts with re-establishing Self-Worth/Self-Value. The first key pertaining to Self-Value and its Self-Greatness determinations is the extent ones Public Self benefits provide favorable reflections on ones Private Selfhood. Second, the extent to which there are benefits for ones Public Self and Private Self determines ones perceived Secular Self-Greatness. If one seeks Respect from people because of material things, then one honors Earth World Respect. Typically, Secular *Self-Value pertains to ones Self-Concept and Self-Image* springing out of dealings in the Material World. Those dealings may be with specific objects or with whatever is associated with objects or with the Symbols for those objects (e.g. money). The degree of Self-Value conveyed depends upon whatever is assessed; how each thing is rated by "authorities" on the priority scale; and by the prevailing standards used for the evaluation.

The degree of Secular Self-Greatness associated with the resultant Self-Value, if any, comes from ones skills and capabilities to get what one wants and to not get what one does not want. The resultant Self-Value refers to the judgment rating concerning ones Self-Respect, Self-Empowerment, Self-Reliance, and Self-Efficacy in relation to ones Self-Concept and Self-Image. Gang members falsely believe that if they have great Secular Self-Value, they will have a great Spiritual Self-Concept and Self-Image.

SHED INTERFERENCES: The prehistoric Germanic word *"Shed"* (separate) originally meant 'divide,' split and in C16 took on the meaning to "cast off," as bark does. Whereas culture provides the tools, institutional racism factors provide the situational characteristics stirring by-products of rage originating during slavery. The Enslaved had lives so terrible that they chose not to think. The way they dealt with their Emotions was by PSYCHIC NUMBNESS. For example, it was extremely upsetting that fellow enslaved were buried without any form of coffin or the common decency of a meaningful funeral. "Nobody cried" after scattering earth over a simple hole and completing this simple burial ceremony. In a society where 25% of the Enslaved perished from 1850 to 1860, African Americans understandably hardened their own sensitivities to the appalling mortality of the sugar country. Following slavery, by the 4th grade, White teachers ignore Black boys—teach them fantasy White Superiority information—and, when they show boredom, respond to them as though they are always the trouble. Thereafter, the resultant disturbed mindsets of these boys are layered with denigration, institutionalized racism, and humiliation. Such causes most to cope by shutting-down their Emotional System and react to their "stay-in-your-place" mental restraint (similar to the Elephant and the Chain story) but replacing their normal "Aliveness" with a self-made Icon collage Symbols of "Manhood."

However Images of themselves are formed, they are self-demeaning and to which they "live down to" as part of fixating a False Self. Living up to the features of that False Self Icon Image is a way of soothing pains from their ever inflamed "Raw Nerve". However, associated with this self-imposed Numbness is an emotional shut-down of all of the afflicted youth's emotions—especially those for pleasure. If the youth have become "Inside-Out" thinkers, even all of their emotions for survival may also be suppressed or repressed—taking with them a moral Conscience. Such is what happens to most gang members and that enables them to fashion a "Manhood" mindset linked to sex, aggression, pride, or violence. Such "Numbness" is endemic to Black males in the prison system.

However, Nandi's survey responses of these prisoners indicated a "thawing" of their "Numbness," as indicated by most having strong desires to perform as fathers, supportive lovers, and productive, autonomous workingmen. Some of their comments included: a good men reaches out to others; upholds morals and principles; learns from his mistakes; has direction; admits when he is wrong; uses failures as tools for achievements; always seeks truth; learns to do without frivolous material things; accentuates the positive and overcomes the negative; regards partner as equal; has self- respect, dignity, and pride; believes in himself; is not afraid of commitment; respects the responsibilities that come with freedom.

SHED "CLOUDS" OVER "SOUL SUNSHINE": Apart from Intergenerational and transgenerational trauma identified in survivors of the Holocaust, internment camps, and reservations, the most pervasive and enduring are associated with African American slavery The Consequences of Black People afflicted by significant psychic trauma are of countless numbers, each being of untold magnitude—most manifesting by self-defeating acts as, for example, by bad actions on children, people, and/or animals as well as by destruction of the environment. The Correction of the Cause of those Consequences involves reconnecting with ones Real Self and Selfhood Greatness. Yet, because a lifestyle was built around them, each of the resultant bad habit must be detected and handled by replacing them with Human Ideal Goals (Bailey, Teaching Black Youth).

SHED BAD BLOOD BONDING: Why would any reasonable person think that going to these same Brute type White people will bring them help? The Spiritual Elements lying deep within their Souls are clouded over with all of the Philosophical and Cultural Collage factors so as to make for a Splintered Selfhood. One part of them knows that what is happening to them in daily living, as orchestrated by the Satanists controlled Society 'at large,' is anti-humanity and that causes ongoing frustration. Another part is the Field Slave Brain/Mindset extension causing them to continue to seek the completion of the Sacred Mother-Child Bonding by expecting the Satanists to supply them with their SHNN, as if this is their only option. To go to them for help is the same as going to Satanists for help. The obsessive-compulsive aspect of this prevents them from knowing there is absolutely no chance of Satanists returning to the ranks of the humane. Prove this to your self by assessing the Legal System and its attorneys; the Government and its politicians; the formal School Systems and what they do and do not teach; the Religious System and their application or non-application of the Spiritual Elements; the Media and its stereotypes; and the Marketplace with its Trinkets and Trivia.

Pause to consider how many honorable people one knows and their degree of caring. When dealing with the effects of what causes violence, one must approach handling it by deciding what to do about the oppressors as well as what is needed to help oneself and the group--what is available--and how much one wants it.

FOUNDATIONAL LIFE THRIVING TOOLS

TRUST: European concepts about the word "*Trust*" date to their Old Testament in general and, in particular, from the Hebrew words that are closely related to "faith" (it will happen but one must wait without effort) and "belief" related to God in two different senses. One sense of trust in God as well as in humans or even inanimate objects involves strong belief and shares the character of faith—both being about "to lean on" or "to have confidence in". In a second sense, trust implies 'to take refuge in'. When applied to humans, "Trust" may be temporary or of a more permanent nature—and may be general or specific. It refers to reliance on another based upon prior experiences that demonstrated credibility and therefore furnishing the assurance that ones trust will not be misplaced or abused. In the interchange of this reciprocal relationship there is reliance upon the integrity, compassion, ability, interest, strength, stability, and efforts to ensure security and safety inside the process of Caring. Such is done in the face of sharing anxieties, contradictory emotions, and secrets.

The involved people, despite associated tensions of doubt, share their intimate stories, gain insight into situations of conflict, and receive guidance and strength for creative living in discovering resources, overcoming difficulties, and learning how to live responsibly going into the future and thereafter. Akin to Hope, trust relies on future possibilities inside the context of current realities and is an essential for worthwhile and sustained progress. Proper Mentor hands-on assistance is a significant part of the mentoring the interventionists could offer youth, as it helps them carry out the advice they give them for desisting from street life and make transformation more attainable. By creating opportunities that will guide them away from street life, the interventionists empower youth to challenge their own criminalization. However, an essential requirement is for Troubled youth to discover Trust among those they seek out as well as having something to Trust particularly when they are having a hard time in life. One reason is that everyone has let them down—Cosmic Order seems to have failed—and confusion, conflict, and chaos gnaw at their spirits.

What they are looking for is some order—some meaning—some insights which impart direction—some relief from loneliness, turmoil. Yet, they do not have experience in whom to trust and do not even know what to look for. Furthermore, there are very few people who are able to generate a situation of trust, know what it is, are ready, willing, and able to do what all is involved in trust (e.g. sacrificing their own ways or preferences, energies, time, effort). Yet, even pure trust is only valid as long as the credibility of someone or some "Thing" is sustained and not broken by betrayal, broken promises, and violated values. Even then, trust can be rebuilt but at a more mature level—e.g. explaining the meanings for why one or oneself is as one is; working with the violator toward a common and higher goal so that one can see "what we did together" as opposed to what you did to me. In African Tradition the key is *Compassion* which alone generates a "5Ss" atmospheric sense loyal, committed, a sense of accountability, and passionate. This allows youth to know they are not alone.

The Mentor takes risks in attempts to establish trust that are first inside the context of self-sacrifice so as to pave the way to the youth feeling safe. Mentors point out the futility of looking for a savior or the blaming of demons because the insight needed to handle all problems is destroyed by hiding behind such things. Some problems can be solved by correcting oneself or ones situation; some by letting go and not clinging as, for example, stop hating for reasons discussed; some by learning to tolerate the unknown—i.e. living with what one will never know. The object is to teach the youth to be a refuge to himself, for this is liberation by ones own power, not by others' input in any way.

SELF-TRUST: Without self-trust, one either fails to do enough to overcome the problem or over-does things from being insecure about ones own competency. Both of these cause a strain in trying to unlock ones creative ideas. Any False Self actions are designed to convey a lack of Self-Trust. Self-Trust is the "5Ss" on display; feeling Selfhood Great; and having ones own best interest at heart. These enable one to first feel safe and on solid ground. Rather that have belief, faith or expectations—each of which hampers experimentations which carry set-backs—one does the planning and preparation for the routine as well as for the "odd" things (and that may give a break-thorough on the seemingly impossible). Self-Compassion makes it okay to venture into the unknown. It does not matter what people think of you for they do not know the situation or know you. Self-Trust automatically means one is not alone for one is doing things for "ME/We" that may manifest in the present or in the future. If one breaks ones Self-Trust, refashion it into a higher level of maturity, as in being able to better tolerate the Unknown. Every success is self-empowering and each serves as a prop to ones Self-Trust.

LIFE'S COURSE STRIVINGS

Metaphysical Order is brought about by Animal Instincts. Animal Instincts act: (1) as a whole rather than by parts; (2) as representatives of a particular part of the brain of humans; (3) enable the human to perform an act without previous experience or observation of the act or its effects; (4) since it is done without thought, there is no knowledge of the Cause, Effects, or Consequences; (5) follows a Metaphysically ordered pattern blindly without any boss, instructions, and doing what is urged to be done without knowing why; and (6) all Selfhood forces are focused on Survival, Self-Protection, and Self-Preservation or to reduce destruction to ones well-being. As used here, *Natural Inclinations* arising out of the Omnibus Brain are the result of having profited from prior Instinct experiences so as to make it available at a Sub-awareness level. This concept was illustrated to me by my roommate at Morehouse College who had been a fighter pilot while in an aircraft that was shot down. Incidentally, this caused him to never get excited about anything happening in daily life.

In his training, he had been shown simulated enemy aircraft presented at fractions of a second--so brief, in fact, that there came a point when he could not perceive the flashes of them. The flash at an "imperceptible shadow" level is a Subliminal message. The 1886 word "*Subliminal*" (sub, under, beneath a limen or sensory threshold) implies it can be seen without being noticed. This is the point of Allegories in African Tradition-- the hidden story within an obvious story which is capable of being mentally seen and understood but is not noticed by those who are un-evolved. Enslaved African Americans used Subliminal messages in Negro Spirituals as a signal or message embedded in another medium, designed to pass below the normal limits of the European mind's perception.

One must decide whether to stay with the Crowd or go off alone on ones mission. The Mission route demands great courage since one will become an Isolated Individualist—meaning self-reliant, foresight and forethought cultivation to keep mistakes to a minimize, organization of the type that allows for the taking advantage of every opportunity as soon as it arises as well as handling emergencies or urgencies immediately with running from them so as to not miss a beat, and be left alone from the crowd. The result is being Happy about doing ones Mission—part of being a genius—regardless of the degree of success or not. Meanwhile, knowing how to do things perfectly will allow for making a lot of money and other displays of thriving—which people will envy, attack, and steal whatever they can. Regardless, one will be able to say one had a good life. By contrast, following the crowd means giving up who one is as person and having to give in to doing things the way the crowd does them, being controlled by and at the mercy of the crowd. In ones old age the crowd will be gone and those remaining will have their own problems and unable to help anyone else. One must be prepared to get along well on ones life's course and that requires periodic Mind committee meetings. Whereas "Steps" are in a sequence, Phases are not. This means that the approach from where one is to the Human Ideal goal one strives to achieve has to be done ones own unique way.

PHASE I--MA'AT SWITCH FROM EVIL TO GOOD: A most enjoyable experience I had as newspaper boy was awakening before daybreak and starting my delivery with my dog Sandy. Greensboro (North Carolina) was very quiet and it seemed as if the world belonged to me because no one had come out of their houses. I felt so good that there were no words for me to express it. So, I would look at the orange colored clouds in the sky and say to myself: "those beautiful clouds express exactly how I good felt". It was like the above mentioned the "Voice of the Silence" which says everything by not saying anything at all while it retains everything by giving away everything. The point is that a successful switch from Evil to Good is like the Silence speaking the impossible--expressing the inexpressible and, in fact, is expressed inexpressibility.

When ones life is based in *Metaphysical Disorder* (going astray and onto anti-Spiritual Elements paths), what the instinct of Metaphysical Order does is to provide messages unrecognizable by the conscious mind to return to the natural flow throughout the stream of the Cosmic's Ocean of Nun. What activates Metaphysical Order is Unconscious (subliminal) learning from Instinct behaviors which have gone through problems, and particularly if there was a struggle. A *Disposition* (fig. 6) is formed and that is a factor in prompting the act to return to the Natural and thereby alter ones method's of performing. For example, each spider weaves its web much as any other of the same species--the similarities being due to instinct. Nevertheless, with gaining subliminally from prior experience, a given spider makes unique modifications. Similarly, each human has reacted to some situation dealing with Right/Wrong. The effects of that reaction had an influence on the lowest neocortical processing areas which, in turn, profoundly altered the pattern of neuronal activation in response to anticipation of the next like-kind experience. That influence occurs on the brain's physical structure (anatomy) as well as its functional organization (physiology) so as to affect a given human's thoughts and emotions at a subliminal level. Thus, the next like-kind experience which required a reaction was some form of improvement within the context of Survival, Self-Protection, and Self-Preservation or to reduce destruction to ones well-being. But the nature of that "improvement" is determined by the mindset of a given human--the designer of her/his brain's neuroplasticity.

What is chosen for guiding ones brain to achieve some end--good, bad, or indifferent--is a reflection of the nature of the owner's existing *Self-Consciousness*. If there are no mental blocks to self-improvement and if there is an intense desire to self-improve, then using this instinctive Metaphysical Order method will automatically cause a Selfhood Understanding that starts correcting the Disorder which leads to Evil actions--a change without any awareness of an intention to shed ones Evil think, emotion, expression, or behavior patterns. By so doing, one gradually recognizes less mental and daily living commotion in ones life and that, in turn, prompts one to recognize this progress was done subliminally. That awareness converts one from a subliminal mindset over to making conscious efforts to consciously continue this climb toward a better lifestyle. Those efforts are done by training or practice. Get past the belief within ones present mindset that corrective actions can be found while following ones typical pattern of *"Socializing Escapes"* (e.g. cell phone, television watch).

Peers do not have the answers to ones problems and will do more harm than good for ones progress. Even more progress stopping is ones way of assessing everything by ones acquired Emotions. An example is hating someone because of being successful or because one is not of the "proper" color. These individuals cling to their fixed ideas and skepticism: "this is the way I do it and it has worked okay for me." They have been educated onto the wrong flow of things and exhibit the same "Bad Stuff" regardless of what rung of the social they are on. The objective is to return to ones birth state of being a Real Self. Then live what one talks about in being in a Ma'at flow.

Acknowledge and learn lessons from and correct "forever" all mistakes and their flawed family members. Have the courage to admit being wrong. Listen to all advice, select the Spiritual Elements aspects, and make ones own decisions. It takes great strength to be ones Real Self and that is so rare as for people to consider it as "weird." The "Crowd" is off-track in using their standards to criticize those following "Ma'at."

PHASE II—DETERMINE MA'AT'S STANDARDS, GUIDES, FILTERS, MEASURES: To determine what qualifies as ingredients for progress is whatever is perfectly inside the Spiritual Elements. "Almost" or "Good Enough" will not work—even if it is 0.000001 degree off. It does not matter how difficult it is to acquire the Right Message or how much one does not want to do it. In studying for my Orthopaedic Surgery Board Examination I needed to go to certain Orthopaedic conferences where they made it clear they did not want me there. And though I really did not want to be around all that hostility, I went anyway because I had, earlier in my life, made the Self-Declaration of not allowing anything to prevent me from becoming an Orthopaedic Surgeon. For that same reason, I was silence White Orthopaedic Surgeons would metaphorically trip me and cause me to fall down stairs. I simply got up, put a band-aid on my wounds, and walked away showing no emotions and saying nothing.

PHASE III--DETERMINE HUMAN IDEAL GOALS BY THE RETROSPECTOSCOPE: Fashioning a Human Ideal Goal is best done out of the Ancient African Bible's philosophy and applying it by means of the Sankofa process (see Preface). This involves determining the Goal by the *Retrospectoscope Method* (fig. 23) of imagining oneself on ones Death Bed. This a conceptual tool done by Visualization for viewing ones life and it has two categories. The intent of Category A is select ones life's goal in a manner that is like selecting the world's MVP (most valuable player) of the All-Star Professional Players. *Category A* concerns getting sound answers to some profound questions: (1) Where Am I?; (2) Where Am I Going?; (3) How Am I going to get there?; (4) What Am I going to do once I get there?. This assessment tells one whether or not one is satisfied with ones life and to what degree. If one is not Happy then the following scenario can be tried—but it only applies to those aspects of ones life that are under ones control. Imagine being on your death bed and looking back over your life. Determine: Q I--"What do I wish I had done with my life that I did not do but was capable of doing?" Q II—What did I do with my life I wish I had not done? Q III--"I'm satisfied with my life because of X, Y, and Z" but something still was not right.

From answering these questions one can design the MVP (most valuable Performance/Program)--meaning what is of ultimate importance to ones life—i.e. the single most important thing that would make one happy. If the answer to Q I would be ones ultimate goal—the MVP or single most importance achievement—then one can stop there. Otherwise, see if an adjustment can be made in the answer to Q II by stop doing something and deciding: if adding A, B, and C would result in the MVP, then that can be the Plan. If, for Q III, the matter was not giving what was done ones best effort, the one may decide is that "what I need to add is E, F, G." After knowing which one of those three is the most meaningful MVP for being content at the end of your life, switch your focus to the other end of the scope which represents: "This is where I am and how do I need to change my life to reach my MVP?" After deciding what it will take to achieve ones

MVP, then lay out stepping stones to it. The point: this MVP is what ones Sacred Dream was at birth and what ones Talent is about.

Then, the first approach is for one to determine the single most significant achievement in ones life and how that could have been made even better and how its excellence could have been made routine. In the second approach, the same assessment is done for what one wishes one would have done that one was capable of doing but did not do—and what would it have taken for that to be done. Then one decides if the two approaches could have been joined and, if not, which achievement would have been the greatest. If they can be joined, then a plan is made how to do this and make that into ones *Human Ideal Goal*. Otherwise, one takes the approach most in keeping with ones Talent and make that into ones Human Ideal Goal.

The next step is to determine where one is at the present time; use the Sankofa method to put oneself if present order; and immediately head to ones Human Ideal Goal—not permitting any Attractive Distractions and avoiding all "Escapes" for each problem must be handled immediately when it appears because its solutions opens doors to how to avoid, get around, or solving even bigger problems which will be met down the line. The only other things to which attention is to be paid is the Necessities for Life-Living—including Enough Money and taking care of Loved ones. This is not the time to get involved with other people's problems, except for emergencies, because the "ME" must be taken care of first before helping the "WE". This is illustrated by the airline stewardess saying to passengers: in case of air shortage, put the oxygen mask on yourself first before putting it on your children. After all, Surivival is the first Law of Nature. Finally, follow the *Bridge Method* (the starting of where one is and going straight ahead to an ideal) or the Check Method (start where one is, go back to clear up problems embracing ones good, bad, and ugly aspects, and then proceed to ones goal) to the Ankh Goal.

Category B is the REVERSE BOWLING PIN CONCEPT: The intent of Category B is to make the application of all efforts concerning ones Talent to be of maximum Efficiency (done quickly), Effectiveness (done right), and confidently with a sense of urgency. Imagine a wooden bowling lane twice as long as normal that goes North and South but divided by 10 bowling pins set in a triangle. The way normal bowling is carried out is by one standing on the South end of the lane and having the front and center lead pin pointing South. Behind the lead pin are 2 pins; behind that 3 pins; and in the back row are 4 pins. The idea of the game is for one to roll a ball down the lane for the purpose of knocking down the lead pin first and having that knock down the 2 pins behind it; and having those 2 pins fall back and knock down the 3 pins behind them; and finally having those 3 pins fall back and knock down the 4 pins in the back row—so that all 10 pins are knocked down to have a "strike."

Now let us suppose the lead pin equates to the MVP that represents the best way you want to live your life. Also imagine going around to the North end of the lane but all else remains the same. So, now the new situation is that you are going to roll the bowling ball to the back row of the triangle of 10 pins. The new idea is to head all of the activities you do in the present so that all of their beneficial effects will be supportive of the MVP lead pin. By standing behind the triangle, let us say that pin 7 in the back row represents your immediate problem that has to be handled right now. To be efficient and effective planning is to be done so as to figure out how to hit pin 7 in order for it to hit pins 8, 9, 10, as well as pins 6 and 3. If I plan well, then pins 6 and 3 will hit pins 4 and 5—and pins 4 and 5, in turn, will hit pin 2--and pin 2, in turn, will hit pin 1.

Put another way, suppose each pin at the base are things to be done now (Sub-goal I); those in the next row up are to be done a little later (Sub-goal II); those closer to the Ultimate Goal are to be done in the distant (Sub-goal III); and the pin symbolizing ones Ultimate MVP Goal is ones achievement on ones Death-Bed. Everything one does on the path to success -- going from Sub-goal I to Sub-goal II to Sub-goal III--is designed to enhance reaching the Ultimate Goal. Next, make a *Self-Declaration* of "I will do these things, come hell or high water". Finally, KEEP YOUR WORD and do it just the way it is planned! The point: everything one does in life ought to head directly toward the Ultimate Goal--a Spirituality display which, in turn, is about Oneness.

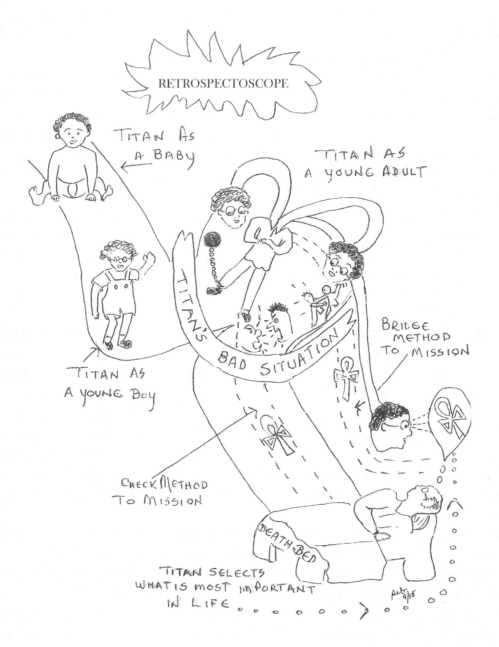

FIGURE 23

PHASE IV—"STAY ON POINT": A problem with those involved in violence is their attention is not focused on the bull's eye which contains the seed of the problem and/or the seed for the solution. Instead, they clutch to some ring around the bull's eye that has nothing to do with either seed and decide if they like it or not—and which has nothing to do with progress while it stops progress. It does matter where concepts of the Spiritual Elements come from—perhaps taking the opposite of what Hitler said and did—put aside judging the one delivering the message and simply ensure that the message has benefit. To help stay on point one can do what it takes in attempting to help "Inside-Out" thinking Black People. Take into account that one will desire to get involved in Attractive Distractions that may permanently take one off course or ones energy may burn out and thereby cause one to "quit." This happens in helping "Inside-Out" others.

Even when exposed to a previously Truth and get "excited" about it, that "excitement" dissolves as soon as they walk out the door and resume "business as usual"—a typical pattern about anything worthwhile (e.g. promising to help the community). In my case, what I say to such groups is overwhelming to what is in their minds—and see no way to completely revamp their lives despite knowing they need to—and therefore many put that information "on-hold"—like a telephone's "call-waiting." Hence it is important to put in reminders that spur staying on the path. An example is that one is related to the "ME/WE" Cosmic Organism and that ones Mission is to "Lift while Climbing." Most find it extremely difficult to accept being "called out" on their resistance or on being on the wrong track." Also, most cannot appreciate scholars whose way of looking and dealing with things is in a completely different world which goes against all they have done and taught and believe up to this point.

PHASE V—HARD WORK. Nothing about Ma'at progress is easy and, actually, ones problems will begin to increase because of going against the IHES forces—forces generated by the "Disaster Star's" hidden teachers of "the Crowd" and, by absorbing effects out of the "Halo" of that "Disaster Star," within "the Crowd" itself where people have direct contact. Both are very limiting and put boundaries on the boundless and on any ones Real Self evolution to as to convert them into False Self with a "Clouding out" of their CreativityThe tool for dealing with these tremendous problems is accessed by stop clinging to ones acquired Emotional Energy which is about "Excitement" so as to automatically return to ones birth gift of Spiritual Energy, which is about "Aliveness." A helpful awareness is that extremely few care about anyone but themselves. Thus, non-Brute mindsets (i.e. those not attacking the Spiritual Elements but neither are they practicing them) are one of Indifference to people except those who would help increase ones money supply or prevent any losses. The White people I have encountered throughout my education, training, and practice in becoming an Orthopaedic Surgeon have always been hostile and that seems normal for them. There, I noticed it was "normal" for them to do IHES deeds and, with the attitude of "What's wrong with that?" What still somewhat surprises me is that they expect their victims to continue welcombing them with open arms. I attribute a worsening of ill-manners and hatred to an increasing focus on greed as well as to social media and its associated Flashing Light gadgets oriented to Trinkets and Trivia. Those who initially knew how to be sociable lost it by the Individualism associated with Social Media and their offspring have never developed it. This makes it easy to anonymously express hated in the comfort of ones own home for average people. These individuals have no effort to make to understand the people they downgrade while engaging in projection as a way to release tension related to their own self-hatred. It is this topic, in its more extreme form of violence, that is the focus of this book. My purpose is simply to focus on the state of affairs of violence and provide suggestions for causes and solutions. This is like discussing the happenings associated with putting ones hand in fire and thereby getting burned. One has the choice of doing that or not.

PHASE VI—SEARCH FOR TRUTHFUL INFORMATION: Those who care about themselves and their family and those they influence will realize the necessity to be certain about the beliefs that shape or change their lives for this orchestrates ones destiny in life. In my lifetime of research in medical and historical and word story fields I have been impressed by the stupidity of "authorities and experts." Egyptologists, for example, claim they know how to decipher Ancient African hieroglyphics. History tells us that their original purpose was to discredit African Bible knowledge. But what they did not/ do not know is that much of Egyptian's 4000 hieroglyphics (each with different levels of meaning that is like an acronym rather than phonetic) creatively contains "Secrets" disguised in figurative or symbolic language + outwardly wrapped in an obvious story. So, getting to the secret story requires Creative Critical and accurate Thinking--i.e. knowing of how to read the hieroglyphic pattern (e.g. right to left or down the right side first) in order to go deeper than the obvious story. After the "Secret" is located, only in-group members can recognize the communication style and its proper interpretation. This is why no Egyptologist fully understands Ancient Egyptian hieroglyphics--and never will-- no matter what they say and no matter how authoritatively it is presented in movies or "documentaries" on television which persuade naïve people. Thus, they are not to be believed. Neither do they know even most of the esoteric aspects of what the Ancient African Bible teaches or the hieroglyphics in which it was written.

A random example of an inappropriate definition that is typical of Europeans is SCHEMA: (C16, form) defined (among others) as: (1) an organized composition of associated and harmonious like-kind ingredients into a transcendental imaginative shape, figure, or form for use as a generalized outline, design, or diagram; (2) as 'general cognitive mental plans, that are abstract and . . . serve as guides for action, as structures for interpreting information, as organized frameworks for solving problems'; (3) as an abstract set of rules that govern discrete movement. It is the rule or relationship that directs decision making when an individual is faced with a movement problem. A schema is developed as a result of combined experiences within a class of actions. Each movement attempt provides the learner with information about the movement, this information is translated into a relationship that will be used to guide future attempts of the movement.

Note with the word "Schema" how practically all European non-concrete definitions are based upon opinions--opinions of different natures (e.g. what it is vs. what it does vs. how it appears)--opinions on different planes of existence (e.g. physical, supernatural)--opinions that by-pass the Spiritual and metaphysical (the specialty of African Tradition). All of this variation causes tremendous confusion, especially when they are in conflict--which they usually are. There is no chance of any of these being the Truth. Depending upon their personal significance (e.g. of a life-shaping or life-changing nature) the opinion one accepts can lead one into distortion or fantasy channels of "no return" and with "no rising above" the dilemma. Such bad stuff have far ranging bad consequences--as in building flawed thought structures to use for decisions and solutions.

VERY FEW PEOPLE TELL THE TRUTH: With the exception of 5 Black scholars, all I have read and heard on "documentaries" are either outright lies or 90% is correct but the 10% is subtle but powerful in leading the ignorant reader out of reality. For example, despite voluminous literature saying Black Americans hate themselves, I have never seen this. The investigative measures European use (e.g. demand characters in assessing if Black children prefer White or Black dolls) are not how Black

People do things—and the same criteria will not work for Blacks and Whites. Black People do not view themselves as Europeans view themselves. Black People, for example, embraces more than skin-color, like ones Spirituality views, in assessing their Self-Concept—which Europeans ignore. Thus, it is wrong to use European definitions, clinical manifestations, and experiences to interpret, diagnose, and explain aspects of Black People. Too often the evilness in this is that those same European definitions, clinical manifestations, and experiences used as a standard for judging Black People influence the types of observations Europeans are directed toward and then the meanings given to them. Rather than Blacks preferring Whites, it is Whites advantages that are attractive. Baldwin (J. Black Psychology, 1979) stated, and I agree: (1) Only suggestive evidence at best shows that some Black People seem to experience what appears to be conflicting color attitudes; some show agreement with negative statements directed towards Black People; and (3) the vast majority respond quite favorably towards self-acceptance. With respect to influencing youth, negative feedback from Black People carries more weight than positive feedback and both supersede whatever Europeans say about them, whether good or bad.

Where problems arise is for Black People to put on a mask to symbolize themselves as being who they are not and they making that mask become their 'face'—living up to that symbol as a lifestyle. Imitation, but modifying, of what Europeans do is a big deal for struggling Black People. They falsely think they can get true information about who they are by books and internet writings by Europeans—the same race that killed 150 million Colored Peoples. Never take anything accepted as truth as the Truth. For example, Nature, the human body, and everything in the Cosmos has a beginning and an end and thus are not absolutely real when compared with the Spiritual's eternity. They appear real to human's limited minds and senses, along with the belief in the mind that they are real. In other words, people believe Matter and physical objects are real even though modern physics has proven that all Matter is not "physical" or "stable." Matter changes constantly and its constituent parts are composed of "empty spaces (Ashby, Book of Life p344).

PHASE VII—WRITE A DICTIONARY "JUST FOR ME": After determining a Human Ideal Goal (Phase III), start a writing a Personal Dictionary in which one puts life-changing and life-shaping definitions and bits and pieces of guiding and meaningful information. This is part of the process of a life of Research which is used to get and remain prepared for dealing with whatever arises in ones Life's Course. The word "Research" is related to the word "Circle." At first, "Search" referred to going round in a circle. Perhaps from this concept came the idea of "search" or "research" or "examination" or "exploring" to locate the circle of the problem at hand, find its center, and determine its essence once all the non-essentials have been removed. The essence is the "seed" of what is real and true. Those and principles are the factors to use in fashioning rational thinking in order to arrive at a solution. Daily spend 5 minutes adding to the Dictionary—elaborating on each "stepping stone" leading to that Goal in a way one can best understand it—perhaps with analogies, metaphors, or personal vignettes of ones life. At least 30 varieties of dictionaries are needed.

For me, simply spending the few moments to look up where to put the new word or add to an established word's meaning serves to give me a glimpse of what I had forgotten about what I thought over a year or two back. Those thoughts, which I had forgotten, were good then but at a different level of where I am presently. I can now revisit that topic and write about it at a higher level or broader scope or into deeper realms—and with even reading what I said two years prior. To elaborate, in my computer collection of articles proposed for publishing in the newspaper I saw on page 550 of 3000 entries an article I had written on the Circle in African Tradition. In up-dating that with new information I had subsequently acquired over the years I was able to come up with new definitions to add to my "Bailey Glossary" Dictionary as well as the making of 5 papers out of that one I rediscovered (whose information was still valid and pertinent. This is how I Spiritually evolve.

PHASE VIII: CORRECT BAD HABITS. The willingness to suffer loss if gained at the expense of others is a prerequisite for the expression of justice. They have no concern for perfection and fall back on "nobody's perfect". "I'll work on that in the future since I have time to make it better." This prevents seeing an interrelationship something new that pops up later—that gives up ones creativity. To live for the moment means let go of what happened and its okay to repeat it.

PHASE IX: RECONCILE WITH ENEMIES. Ma'at is involved the control of differences rather than their elimination. Forgiveness is done so that all the mental turmoil associated with it is removed in order for you to move on with your life. However, real forgiveness of the truly guilty does not come until after the guilty party has been rehabilitated. The point is to let go of all clinging emotions for it saps your energy and serves no purpose.

PHASE X: FIND JOBS FOR BLACK YOUTH. Too many youth do not know how to work and financial poverty spurs many to become gang members. Make a list of jobs a youth can start doing today (e.g. washing cars, shining shoes, cutting grass, raking leaves) and use that as a core around which "ripples" are made (e.g. how to have good Manners in being introduced to potential customers; how to have a superb product; how to give excellent service; how to proper price ones services or products).

PHASE XI: TEACH HOW TO ACHIEVE A GOAL: A Free Mind is needed to do "Right Life-Living" (Bailey, African Tradition for Black Youth) but a place to start learning how to do this is with a small and fairly easily achievable task. Have clear and certain direction as to the most important thing to pursue to reach the goal. That pursuit is done with total focus and ever on the alert to detect pertinent missing pieces that work toward fashioning a perfect product. This requires *Spiritual Energy Package* of dedication, commitment, loyalty, determination, persistence, and perseverance to not give up—to never succumb to attractive distractions--to always give ones best effort—and to achieve the goal in the most efficient and effective manner. Each of these six is like the links in a chain and each is needed to complete any worthwhile task while driving away ones Emotional Energy powered Ego (*False Self*). In decision making and problem solving there is always the eagerness, willingness, and able-ness to search for "the needle in a haystack"—no matter how difficult or how boring.

Ambitions Black youth enter unknown realms where traditional advice does not apply. Instead, they must devise creative solutions for suddenly appearing difficulties one has never seen nor heard of before. An organized approach to go from where one is to where one wants to go so as to do what one has to do has been discussed in my book ("Becoming A Champion Somebody") under the title of the "9Ps" --Preparing to Prepare; Purpose; Plan; Planes of Existence; Preparation; Practice; Performance; Platform; and Post-Action Judgments. This starts by realizing "certain things are the way they are" and there is no point in complaining about them being unfair. Preparation includes having a sound philosophy of life with its right attitudes for dealing with inevitable losses, lacks, or obstacles. At each step, consider possible problems and ask: "what would I do if this bad happens?"

Preparing to Prepare is to ensure, say, the car is in good working order and filled with gas, oil, good tires properly inflated, etc. Though a four cylinder engine is not as powerful nor runs as smoothly as an eight cylinder engine, it will still get you to the destination. Things do not have to be perfect to start. Self-assessments include handling "Problematic Starts or "Problematic Finishes." The *Purpose* of the task is clearly knowing what you need to do once you get to the goal of where you are going. To constructively benefit a tiny piece of the world or yourself is the Motive Force pushing you to complete the task. The *Plan* consists of how you will get to the goal. Always have a Plan A, B, and C. Once that is done, there will be no reason to "give up" unless unexpected dangers arise.

In *Preparing* for the trip, do not expect help from anyone, even those who promised to help for they will "disappear" or have a bunch of excuses when they are needed. There will always be losses, lacks, and obstacles on different *Planes of Existence* (with the car, with people, with the road) that will cause set-backs. Anticipate these and *Practice* creatively figuring out different ways around these problems--and in an honorable manner. To prevent defeats, your greatest chance of success is to know how things (and people) work. For example, in *Performing* your trip you may not have air-conditioning. If your car breaks down while traveling through the desert, to know how its engine works and correcting that might enable you to get to the next city for food or a mechanic.

Once at the destination, you must do the *Platform* work designed to make happen your Purpose. This demands being physically and mentally strong if facing problems never seen or heard of before. Hostile people will try to block your progress but do nothing (like battling them) to let them stop your wholesome progress. Take your opinion of problems you do not want to do; face and handle them immediately; and keep going when you feel as if you cannot take another step. At that time you will receive a "Helping Hand" out of "nowhere" to enable you to get nearer to completing your Purpose. *Post-Action judgments* are assessing what you did to see how it could have been done better. Then do better and better. On your death bed, even though without recognition, say: "I'm proud of what I've done!"

As a boy, it was driven home in my mind by my family that *if a job is worth doing, it must be done right, and ahead of schedule.* The partner of this statement that the reason for doing the job right is because it shows good character and that is a demonstration of Integrity (meaning that one is both sound and complete). But most of all, doing a perfect job (in my eyes) made me feel proud. The implication was that good character only produces the very best of which it is capable. These two statements necessarily mean being self-motivated and with the vow and follow through to start the task right now; to never give up; to not be stopped by overwhelming difficulties; to not allow my attention and focus to be scattered as a result of attractive distractions; and to make a little bit of progress every day, even if I am tired or busy doing things that "Need to be" done or if I simply did not feel like it. At moments like this, having a "ME/WE" orientation spurred me to keep going when I felt "down and out" because "my race" depended on me being successful.

One is not afraid of handling problems as soon as they arise and with no inhibitions on exploring the Unknown— no fear of failure or fear of success—no "I can't" locks and chains on ones capabilities. If such fears are present, then they are to be honestly examined and mentally play them out by saying: "I continue down this path, where and how will it end. One does not cling to anything social, economic, domestic, political, mental, physical, or spiritual because the Right thing to do is simply the natural thing to do—regardless of whether anyone else notices or not—regardless of whether complimented or criticized. As important as socializing is, ones Mission in life is of higher priority. One is free when one sees set-backs as an opportunity to improve or sees a crisis as an opportunity or learns to see what others do not want to or cannot do as an opportunity.

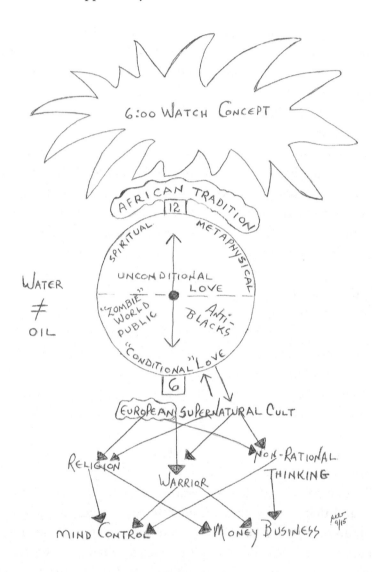

FIGURE 24

For the choose to be their Real Self, prepare them to be Isolated Individualist for they are destined to face countless "alligators" on their path. So to keep going "straight ahead"—despite losses, lacks, or obstructions—requires great Courage, Self-Reliance, and a certainty about their own Selfhood Greatness. Such youth know freedom and what is truly worthwhile is not in the External world, but rather is within. Relying on myself sharpened my personal skills in order to become successful and now enables me to be proud of successes of others. Rather than blaming and complaining, use that as an opportunity to learn how to create better thing out of what was destroyed. I learned in my practice to stop getting anger at Conscious deceivers (i.e. those who were trying to fool me) because I suddenly realized it is not my job to judge, but rather to diagnose and treat--and they have a problem I need to diagnose. I learned to take Take European opinions as a challenge by not using any of it for my Private Self way of living but learning it so as to pass their examinations. Then in practicing medicine, I disregarded most Europeans teaching and relied on African Tradition concepts for treatment. For example, African concepts are to allow ones own body to heal itself (this is not about life threatening problems but rather things like a sore back or neck pain from myofascial causes). By having the body self-correct and stop interfering with it (e.g. with drugs) gave me good results. Historically, Africans have used herbs which is natural. When you use Nature, that is when the body and mind heals.

SPOTLIGHTING A YOUTH'S POTENTIAL

Gifts (from ones mind), Talents (from ones "Heart"), and Genius (from ones "Soul Sunshine") are a continuum of going from the simple to the complex (fig. 25) . In African Tradition, Talents and Gifts are off-springs of ones Genius. African American slavery shattered access to most of Africans' Genius, leaving them to operate out of their Talents and give Gifts to each other. Join me in stepping back to the time of our Enslaved Ancestors and observe inside their minds the hellishness going on mentally, emotionally, spiritually, as well as all the physical traumas they experienced. To get a general concept of this is to gain a crude "big picture" idea of the terribleness today's struggling Black youth are experiences. Again, let us shift focus from all their problems and all that they are not doing that they should be doing over to what they already possess in having the potential to do—a potential that is unlimited—a potential that could lead to return of Black People thriving. The proper setting for a youth's orientation is to see the reality of the societal "Big Picture."

DISTINGUISH AFRICAN AND EUROPEAN TRADITION: Black youth have only been taught the European way and have absolutely no awareness of the super-brilliant processes and practices of their Ancient African Ancestors. African Tradition and European Tradition are symbolized by the *"6:00 Watch Concept"* (fig. 24)--and nothing about them is like a milk and water mix. First, the *"Noon" is deliberately hidden* from Black People (and also the White people crowd). Second, by only being taught to *believe the Supernatural* aspects of Europeans—especially religion, Black youth are not able to stay in the Genius realm because illusions about the greatness of the External World "Cloud out" their Soul Sunshine. These illusions become Delusions and prevent them from returning to their Private Self's "Soul Sunshine." Third, African Tradition and European Tradition are like oil and water. This absolute prevents one from returning to the Spiritual Elements because European information dilutes and pollutes the purity of the Spiritual Elements by Supernatural factors outside the Spiritual or the Metaphysical.

African Tradition's form of Genius is of a Spiritual and Metaphysical nature that stays within and operates out of the Spiritual Elements. By contrast, European Tradition is based upon ignoring the Spiritual and the Metaphysical while placing total focus on the Physical and the Supernatural. They say the Supernatural is so superior to the Spiritual and so far beyond the human mind to conceive of it that the only choice is for people to have Belief and Faith in it. Thus, nothing is reasonable about it—as is readily obvious by listening to Fox News—and therefore European "Genius" is of an entirely different nature than that of African Tradition. This is fundamental for helping to understand the minds of today's struggling Black youth. There can be no place for Black American Customs Thinking patterns (see above). There can be no "picking and choosing" to combine anything about African and European Traditions. And that includes not getting definitions out of European dictionaries. It is either "all-or-none"—meaning one must completely follow African Tradition if one desires to get back to the ways of ones Ancestors. Otherwise, to "pick and choose"—particularly with respect to religion--is to generate more confusion in Black youth's minds.

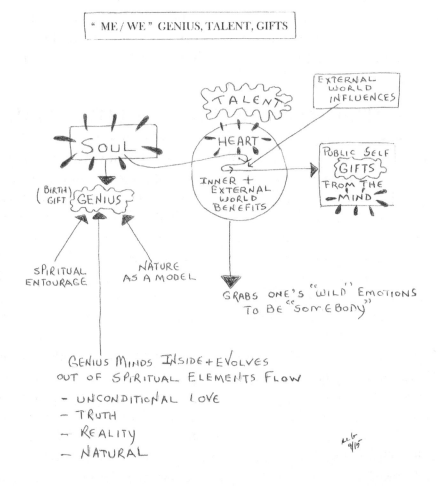

FIGURE 25

DISTINGUISHING GIFTS, TALENTS, GENIUS

    GIFTS (Old English, to give) are something handed over or conveyed to another. First, they may be done from the goodness of ones "Heart". Second, they may be done as a "self-interest" tool—"giving something to get something"—ranging from a favor all the way over to mind control. When one really Cares, there is a great deal that goes into "giving a gift' from which Receivers will benefit. If there is any flaw in that process of developing the gift, then the effect on Receivers will be neutral or detrimental. In Black American Customs, gifts include accepting fellows as they are--spending time with them—and getting involved with their lives. It is extremely important to assess ones Gifts:

    Do you simply give them a fish? Or show them how to fish? Or take them to the lake so they can figure out how to fish? Or put them in contact with fishermen? Or take away the Attractive Distractions keeping them from fishing? Or give them a swift kick in the rear end to motivate them to start helping themselves? Or simply leave them alone so as to give them time to assess and learn from the flawed thinking that got them into their mess? Or support them in the foolish self-defeating things they do? Some people have been socialized to live in a self-defeating way and then live around like-kind people. They have no idea how to change or even that there is such a thing as change. Thus, one approach to dealing with this is to give them a fish while showing them how to fish. Most struggling Black People are so beaten down as to think "*Inside-Out*"—i.e. vote against themselves. Other people are simply lazy and thereby stay in trouble.

GENIUS

African Tradition Genius is based upon Mathematics which gave rise to Certainty about the Spiritual Realm by means of the Law of Correspondence. It is that Certainty, as determined by provable Circumstantial Evidence that serves as the "Ground of Being" from which all of African Tradition derives. *Genius* is a natural and developed endowment (a natural enduring gift) of ones Private Self "Soul Sunshine" (also called "Phosphorescence"—'that light within'). Ancient Africans said that in the very beginning of the formation of every human inside the Cosmic Organism and prior to acquiring a human consciousness, each human is endowed with clairvoyance. That clairvoyance enables each to maintain close rapport with her/his spiritual counterparts in the Cosmic Organism as well as those in the Ancestral World. For a newborn to develop and maintain this connection does (among others) two fundamental things. First, the connection with the Spiritual Cosmic Organism and the Metaphysical world's Living Ancestors allows each human to get the benefits of standards for living, guidance through life, filters to prevent embracing anti-Spiritual Elements, and measures for judging what is morally "Right."

Second, that child can bathe in her/his genius. That birth gift genius is about ones mind being inside of the Spiritual Elements so as to evolve oneself as well as to design work products in a divinely inspired manner. Ones natural genius mind, with its large general powers, has no boundaries and no limits on its abilities. No doubt, this is what my Mother was referring to when she often told me: "Son, you can do anything you put your mind to." I misinterpreted that to mean that I could do "everything" I put my mind to—and for humans that is not the same thing. This means that ones Life-Living "ground of Being"—the Background of ones genius--is not intelligence or imagination but rather Unconditional Love. Ancient Africans said the model for the cultivation of ones genius, in general, and any life-shaping or life-changing esoteric (hidden) subject, in particular, was to be found in Nature. This is because *Nature is the home of God's Laws.* Because of the Law of Correspondence--meaning what goes on in Nature is also going on in the mind of each Real Self individual.

Hence, from start to finish, what is demanded of genius is the arranging and combining of the Spiritual Elements so as to create, enhance, maintain, defend, and protect the indivisible (i.e. Unity) functioning of the "ME/WE" in its Harmony, Coherence, Consistency, Compatibility, Balance, Endurance, and Connectedness.

TALENTS

A child's Talent is the single most significant thing in that child's Selfhood, as indicated by him/her taking a personal interest in discussions about it. Such is explained by youth seeing how their Talent can be developed to "Be Somebody"—like a professional basketball player with all the money, girls, fans, cars, and other USA Materialism features. Besides, each can say: "My Talent belongs to me and nobody can take it away." A human's Talent is a Spiritual Endowment "Seed" consisting of the Spiritual Elements—Unconditional Love, Truth, Reality, and the Natural. That Talent's ingredients may come from ones Private

Self, ones Public Self, or from External World influences. Thus, the nature of its products may range from the Spiritual Elements all the way over to attacking Unconditional Love, Truth, Reality, and the Natural, as is the theme of Satanists. Like Genius, Talent looks at the sides and angles of each "box of life" from views different from the Crowd.

BAILEY'S FARM DREAM FOR BLACK BOYS

Since age 5, I have secretly dreamed of a school located on an isolated 100-acre farm next to a body of water where Bright Black Boys are laughing while learning. On the way to being "Somebody" their eyes beam during heated discussions at morning "Family Talks" on Afrocentric history and Ancient African Tradition. After each boy eagerly advocates his opinion, then with an intense curiosity and desire for learning he argues for the opposite of his former position. Instead of finding fault, everyone supports each other and offers constructive comments. Several buildings provide housing and classrooms. The school's approaches and methods for these residential middle and high schoolers are based on the African Age-set system (Bailey, Manhood). On the farm each boy cleans up the grounds, takes care of his own animals, cultivates his own garden, and gains practical experience in leading, following, and active participation. Physical fitness emphasizes self-discipline and self-control cultivation through martial arts. Non-work time is spent meditating or quietly flowing with, listening to, and enjoying Nature. Television watching and other electronic devices (not including computers), if earned, is only 3 hours a week. Providing help to the elderly and to the truly needy are mandatory. The general curriculum is based upon the realization that far too many struggling Black boys are unconsciously driven by negative inner forces -- forces originating in African American slavery -- forces driving them to believe self-destructive information and disbelieve Truth. What is required is to reverse these forces and their effects; to replace their self-defeating habits with building blocks of Ancient African Philosophy; and to provide productive substitutes for their "Escapes" from the harshness of their lives. Obviously, these must go on at the same time but for mentoring purposes a structural program is needed -- a program sufficiently flexible to meet the uniqueness of each and his situation in a manner to which he can relate.

The *Objective*: Guide boys to be "Somebody";

The *Informational Frame*: Sankofa (return to African Tradition to learn how to prepare in the present in order to go forward into the future and thrive);

The *Bonding* type is the African Age-Set System ("All for one and one for all); The *Tow-rope* is Brief History vignettes of Ancient African brilliance (How Black Boys are like these Ancestors). This requires frequent compliments and Unconditional Love.

Phase I: the way today's struggling Black boys use their brains--i.e. the Emergency Brain on a permanent basis instead of their Thriving Brain--is the foundational base for the "Certain Sameness" present in all of these boys. Also, as a direct result of the impact of slavery the following occurred to each Slave:

(1) A Philosophical Disconnection from the Cosmic Helping Hands and therefore from the Law of Sympathy (all God's creations and creatures are spiritually connected no matter how remote in time or space) and therefore from the Spiritual Energy supplied by God and therefore from the "5Ss" (safety, security, self-confidence, strength, and stability). These disconnections caused their African Philosophical structure and their internalized features of African Tradition to fall into shambles.

(2) From being overwhelmed by the power of the GUN + cruelty from the evil European captors + the lack of Needy Want (Soul) nourishment (Bailey, Unlocking Minds), the Slaves were susceptible to being *Brain-washed*.

(3) From being Brainwashed + the loss of the "5Ss" + the loss of faith in the Law of Sympathy + the loss of belief in the Cosmic Helping Hands, the Slaves developed *Delusions* (believing what is not real and not believing what is real).

(4) From the structure of African Tradition falling into shambles, afflicted Slaves became *Disorderly in Thinking Skills*.

(5) From the Brain Switch + being Brainwashed + Delusions + loss of orderly thinking skills the Slaves developed *Self-Defeating Mindsets*.

(6) The Brain Switch + Philosophical Disconnections + loss of African "5Ss" + brainwashing + a lack of desire to work for the evil captors thereby fashioned in the Slaves a shift from Spiritual Energy powering their daily living activities to Emotional Energy

(7) To avenge the hell to which they were being subjected, the Slaves engaged in Selfhood Armor and Slave Resistance. *Selfhood Armor* is inner avengement (e.g. "White man, you may enslave my body but you cannot enslave the rest of me"). Outer avengement was called *Slave Resistance* (e.g. procrastination, moving and working slowly). Both Selfhood Armor and Slave Resistance worked well for the Slaves but became *Self-Defeating Habits* when culturally transferred out of slavery and on into today's struggling descendants. Another way this shows is Black boys have so much game they do not use. They must open up their power source.

The effects of these seven have been the cause of them being on the negative scale present in all struggling Black Boy both behaviorally and physically (e.g. experiencing an excessive outpouring of hormones which affect the physical body to cause strokes, heart attacks, and premature death).

Phase II pertains to what do to bring about a Brain Switch + how to relieve its associated self-defeating thoughts, feelings, expressions, and behaviors + how to replace the "Escapes" from the hellish lives of struggling Black boys. This collage of problems is discussed in my 38 books on Black Americans. Some must be dealt with privately with each boy while the rest can be dealt with in group sessions. To be spotlighted is Ancient African philosophy (for inner stability and mental toughness) because a sound Philosophy of Life is the foundational mindset to correcting all of the boys' problems and to launch them on the path to a successful destination. Included here is Character; Paradigms, and Self-Esteem development. Next is emphasizing:

The Private Self -- e.g. resolving personal, interpersonal, and society problems by internalizing 25 foundational blocks of Ancient African Philosophy; shedding delusions and anger; self-mastery (personal problems, bad emotions, criticisms and defeats); and developing a free mind, "pure" feelings, concentration, curiosity, creativity, wit and humor (Bailey, Mentoring Black Boys).

The Public Self: Afrocentric academia in a congenial atmosphere; Removal of Slave Survivals

Phase III is discovering how can Phase II information be conveyed to the boys so they will receive and internalize it. My book: Unlocking Minds of Black Boys addresses this.

SHED: Emotional Junk (e.g. chronic anger, worthlessness); loss of Emotional Control; removing mind-trapping Belief Systems through novel applications of Symbols and the Truth; correcting self-defeating Slave Survival bad habits and lifestyles; the part you play in causing your problems. This involves managing your mood (not letting it drop and keeping up intensity from moment to moment) and if it drops, start moving your feet.

FORTIFICATION: Foundational is FOCUS. Then comes Mental Discipline (e.g. Keep Your Word); Rational and Critical Thinking (applied to Personal and Professional Situations); Basic Thinking Tools illustrated with games or by assembling a model (e.g. skyscraper building) applied to each boy's major problem.

TAKING ACTION: Forgiveness; Buy Your Peace; Motivation cultivation by switching to Spiritual Energy from Emotional Energy

Phase IV is stimulating the minds of Black boys by creating, enhancing, and maintaining the Brain Switch reversal back to a Thriving Brain. This is addressed in my book: Mentoring Minds of Black Boys. The introduction starts with Art, Music, Dance, Poetry that expands into the Humanities and African Mathematics. Associated with this are bi-monthly field trips; discussing daily a new word -- for vocabulary building (since this explodes the boundaries for creativity and thought). Besides, learning the stories of words provides the broadest scope, the most interesting, and the greatest amount of information in the fastest way while taking an enjoyable magic carpet ride to wonderful places and cultures inside various nations throughout the ages. Publishing articles opens each student to self expression, to research, and to the free and effective exchange of ideas.

Phase V: The "oil" that smooths the way to Thriving in life is called Life-skills, as elaborated upon in my book: Life-Skills For Black Boys. What is featured is for each boy to discover his SECRET DREAM & TALENT for application to career and legacy life purposes whereby each can find its most productive niche with a high degree of Efficiency and Effectiveness. To these ends the boys need a Life-Skill Worker, counseling and courses. Of equal importance is thorough knowledge concerning Family; Manhood (e.g. a Man's rightful place); Gentleness in dealing with Women, Children, and wherever Compassion is required; Manners; Self-Protection; good health; home maintenance, cooking, parenting; interpersonal skills (e.g. intra-Black social harmony and in listening without an opinion); providing Respect; in honoring Parents; and in choosing a mate and marriage partner;.

Phase VI: Marketplace Success deals with each boy knowing how to work; developing a Business sense and an excellent product; and dealing with the competition. Obviously, Money is major, as in how to make money, how to save money, how to get paid; and how to spend it wisely in business and in life-style stability for immediate, intermediate, and long term needs, wants, and luxuries. Peripheral issues include such personal skills in grooming as haircuts, clothes, eye glasses as well as such work related skills as public speaking, and computer competency. These and other topics have been discussed in my book on the Marketplace.

Working in top gear—whether alone during tough times; as a group to increase cooperation and fun; in helping the slowest catch up; and doing it enthusiastically and urgently -- allows a boy time to help others do their job. Exposure to other's problems improves decision/solution skills. Marketplace success focuses on creating and setting-up jobs (e.g. small appliance repair) and products for sale in the poorest parts of the Black Community.

With profits from selling vegetables, flowers, and dairy products, 60% goes for each boy's college education; 30% to help support him in school; and 10% for spending. Big business is invited to establish contact with a youth and pay for his college education. In exchange, the youth works five years post-college for them.

Once established in life, each graduate is obliged to set up programs to help other struggling youth. The over-all objective is to make excellence routine so as to prepare students for the most outstanding colleges, for the toughest careers, and for being the best family man.

SUMMARY

Primitive Africans apparently interpreted all manifestations of Nature as everything in it is immanent (entirely mind) in it--that all events in Nature are a Willed act (which presupposes an entity source behind it)—and that nothing in the world transcends Nature. Very Ancient Africans extracted principles from Nature and set up a "Trinity-in-Unity Wholism" consisting of God-Nature-Humans—each being aspects of the others since all life runs through its various forms—all being an interdependent Continuity. This implies that Nature is God's Nature, the unchanging Self's ever-changing garment. Ancient Africans rightly regarded every well-proven Law of Nature—since Nature is God's Nature—as one of God's Commandments and converted them into Ma'at Principles. Each Principle is directly and intimately concerned with the healthy conduction of human life—each being inseparably related to all the others.

For any Mentor or teacher to connect with a Black American Customs (BAC) member is very difficult—first because they are the most needy; second because their minds and ways of doing things are turned "Inside-Out"; third because it takes extremely hard work, time, energy, and effort to return to one Real Self; fourth because BAC members are accustomed to ignoring their significant major problems since they feel they will be no worse off regardless as to outcome; fifth, because of great fears about a host of things; sixth, because they have not been taught what most of society takes for granted; seventh, because of a lack of trust; eighth, because of the absence of skills; and so forth.

Thus, in order to get their attention on the first meeting—since they typically will not be seen the second time—is to put a spotlight on each Black youth's unique Talent. The reason is that is "Up close and Personal"—something that grabs the attention of even gang members—each knowing that this personal possession is something nobody can "mess with" and that it is completely under her/his control. One way this is knowable is by recalling from early childhood the Secret (Sacred) Dream that child had. To rediscover it means one has a concept of ones ultimate life's Purpose is about and therefore how to direct ones Talent. Both ones Secret Dream and its matching Talent frame the course of ones Life Living. Failure to do either will lead to a life of mental unrest and personal disappointment. Have them start with doing a superb job on one thing—to help develop focus. Such that they keep thinking of ways how what they are doing can help every one benefit. Teach them how to handle set-backs and failures by being alone and quiet while releasing tensions by writing. The next step is to find each youth a job of any type in general and, if possible, that enhances his/her Talent.

ABOUT THE AUTHOR

If you have been a follower of Joseph A. Bailey, II M.D. and his work, you probably have had chance to read about all of the accomplishments in his life starting out being nourished as a boy from an all-Black community, knowing his Mission from an early age and beginning his life's journey on the path less traveled. You have read about the struggles of a Black man in this society through service to his country and the resistances placed in his way to try to halt his many achievements which at many times meant stealing his intellectual property. He has invented and been an innovator against significant odds. He has set up many organizations in the Black community, endowed a chair at the university level and received many awards for his philanthropy and selfless service over decades. So we are able to see what he has done but what about who he is?

With the realization, as a youngster, that his mission was to help others, he started on a path through life that would find him traveling alone much of the time. Taking the path less traveled by others shaped him into what he likes to call "An Isolated Individualist". When his Sunday school teacher, Mrs. Dobbs, told him that God is Love and God is within you, it shook him to his core. He knew that he would have to find out all he could about Love-how to spread it, how to be lovable and how to be loved.

His decades -long quest to find the answer to his questions led him to study all the world philosophies and religions. When he found the Words and Works of Ancient African Philosophy spread throughout the world and put it together, he knew he had found what he was looking for. He describes it as finally being able to scratch the "bump that itches"----Ahhhhh.

That Spark of God that Mrs. Dobbs spoke about contains the Spiritual Elements of Unconditional Love, Truth, Reality and the Natural. And what Dr. Bailey found was that from his community and family he had absorbed two purposes for humans' transformation during our earthly experiences that sprang from African Tradition. The first purpose is to fulfill the Divine Plan returning to God in the same purified state in which you came into being in this world. Living in this purposeful life meant that there was no room for any negative vibrations- no room for hate, anger etc. which would be destructive to himself and others. There can be no intentional acts of harm to self or others. The idea is for one to work toward perfection in everything you do. Dr. Bailey has found that the only way to live his life is through the Spiritual Elements and that is evident to all who have come in contact with him. He is a Truth seeker and a Truth teller and for many that can be a new experience.

The second purpose human's must fulfill that springs from African Tradition is to develop the tools needed to force out divine powers for self- cultivation in order to handle life's difficulties and be of aid to others in life. When Dr. Bailey left his all-Black community, it was with the admonishment to do well for himself and for his people. Do well in your life so that you can then go back to help the others. That has been an everlasting imprint on his mind. There is no resting on past achievements for him. Daily there is a constant striving to improve and to show those near and far from him, how to be the very best that they can be and the benefits to be had.

My intention has been to paint a picture of a man who is living his life according to the Spiritual Elements of Ancient Africans which for him is a very natural thing to do. To be guided by Unconditional Love is to love without boundaries, to have an open and free mind and not seeking to control. One who is really concerned in helping others while climbing .To live a life of Truth may not always be popular or easy for some to swallow but it indicates a life of Integrity, keeping your word and speaks of a person you can trust. To live in Reality is to be able to see the 'what it is" when a thing came into being and as Dr. Bailey has written "to experience Reality is to shed all that is not Knowledge and see things clearly with the mind's eye". The Natural self has the curiosity that has been maintained since birth, like a child's curiosity and having an open Spiritual Energy Package that operates by being connected to the natural rhythms of the Cosmos.

Living a life with in the guidelines of the Spiritual Elements has led to Dr. Bailey having an over flowing supply of the 5 "Ss" which include Safety, Security, Strength, Stability and Sureness. It also means that when the tough times in life come, one has been able to fashion approaches for handling these "alligators". Coming from this strong life foundation, it is easy to understand why there are so many people who are eager to read his work and find their own way to a thriving and meaningful life.

With this book, Stopping the Violence, Dr. Bailey lays out steps to get off the path of disharmony and destruction and get back on the Truth Track and your Real Self. He continues to study how the minds of Black people have been affected by Slavery and its survival tactics and how that plays out in their lives today. We are in an emergency situation and cannot afford to lose anymore brilliant Black lives.

We have just celebrated the Doctor's 80th birthday and had quite a gathering of folks who wanted to tell their story of how Dr. Bailey has had a positive influence on their lives. The consensus is that he is a scholar for all time and truly an Ancient African and African American Slavery historian. He is a man who actually lives by his motto which says that our duty in the Cosmos is to "Create, Enhance, and Maintain Harmony."

In order to find out more about his work, please visit his website jabaileymd.com

Sharon E. Bingaman R.N.

REFERENCES

Adams, Matthew, Raisborough, Jayne: The self-control ethos and the 'chav': Unpacking cultural representations of white working class. *Culture & Psychology, March 2011; vol. 17, 1: pp. 81-97*

Adegbite, Ademola: **The Concept of Sound in Traditional African Religious Music** *Journal of Black Studies September 1991 22: 45-54*

Aguilar, MI. Divination, Theology. *Feminist Theology, 1994; vol. 3, 7: pp. 34-38.*

Ajani ya Azibo, Daudi: **African-Centered Theses on Mental Health and a Nosology of Black/African Personality Disorder** *Journal of Black Psychology Spring 1989 15: 173-214*

Alderman LA. *Rum, Slaves and Molasses.* New York: Crowell-Collier Press, 1972.

Allen, Brenda A. and Lisa Butler, **The Effects of Music and Movement Opportunity on the Analogical Reasoning Performance of African American and White School Children: A Preliminary Study,** *Journal of Black Psychology* 1996 22: 316;

Allen, Richard L. and Richard P. Bagozzi **Consequences of the Black Sense of Self** *Journal of Black Psychology February 2001 27: 3-28*

Allen, Troy D. **Cheikh Anta Diop's Two Cradle Theory: Revisited** *Journal of Black Studies July 2008 38: 813-829*

Alleyne, Emma, Isabel Fernandes, and Elizabeth Pritchard: Denying humanness to victims: How *gang members* justify violent behavior *Group Processes & Intergroup Relations, November 2014; vol. 17, 6: pp. 750-762.*

Andrejev, V. Art and Religion: *Theology Today, 2004; vol. 61, 1: pp. 53-66*

Amen, RUN. Metu Neter vol. 1, Bronx N.Y.: Khamit Corp., 1990.

Amen, RUN. Metu Neter vol. 2, Brooklyn: Khamit Media Trans Visions, Inc., 1994.

Amen, RUN. Metu Neter vol. 3, Brooklyn: Khamit Media Trans Visions, Inc., 1100 Albemarie Road, Brooklyn, NY 11218: 2003

Amen, RUN. Metu Neter vol. 7, Brooklyn: Khamit Media Trans Visions, Inc., 1100 Albemarie Road, Brooklyn, NY 11218: 2012

Amen, RUN. Tree of Life Meditation System, Brooklyn: Khamit Media Trans Visions, Inc. 1996

Amen, RUN. Maat, THE 11 LAWS OF GOD Brooklyn: Khamit Media Trans Visions, Inc., 2003

Amen, RUN. Maat, Nuk Au Neter, Brooklyn: Khamit Media Trans Visions, Inc., 2008

Anderson E. *The Code of the Streets,* In: Ault A. Race and Ethnicity. St. Paul: Coursewise Publishing, Inc., 2000; 203.

Anderson E. *The Police and The Black Male,* in: Anderson ML and Collins PH. Race, Class, and Gender, 2nd ed., 1995.

Ani M. *Yurugu,* Trenton, NJ: Africa World Press, Inc., 1994.

Arieti S. *Creativity, The Magic Synthesis.* New York: Basic Books, Inc., Publishers, 1976.

Ashby MA. *Egyptian Yoga*, Miami: Cruzian Mystic Books, 1995

Ashby, SM: Redemption of the Criminal Heart. Miami: Selma Institute/Cruzian Mystic Books. 2007

Ashby, MA: The Mystical Journey From Jesus to Christ: Miami: Selma Institute/Cruzian Mystic Books. 1998

Ashby, MA. The Egyptian Book of the Dead. Miami: Cruzian Mystic Books, 2006

Bailey Sr., JA. From Africa to Black Power. Livermore, California: 2008.

Bailey II, JA: African Tradition For Black Youth—Pursuit of a Free Mind. North Charleston, South Carolina: CreateSpace Independent Publishing Platform 2015

Bailey II, JA: Teaching Black Youth—Affect Symbolic Imagery & African Dialectic. North Charleston, South Carolina: CreateSpace Independent Publishing Platform 2014

Bailey II, JA: Post Traumatic Distress Syndrome in Black People. North Charleston, South Carolina: CreateSpace Independent Publishing Platform 2014

Bailey II, JA: Private Selfhood Greatness in Black Americans. North Charleston, South Carolina: CreateSpace Independent Publishing Platform 2013

Bailey II, J.A. (2013): Leadership Critical Thinking in African Tradition. Mira Loma, California: Parker Publishing Inc.

Bailey II, JA. Ancient African Bible Messages. Inglewood, Ca.: Reflections Publishing House 2013

Bailey II, JA. Word Stories Encyclopaedia. Livermore, California: Wing   Span   Press, 2012.

Bailey II, JA. Mentoring Minds of Black Boys. Livermore, California: Wing Span Press, 2011.

Bailey II, JA. Unlocking Minds of Black Boys. Livermore, California: Wing Span Press, 2011.

Bailey II, JA. Black Americans Entering the Marketplace. Livermore, California: Wing Span Press, 2010.

Bailey II, JA. Self-Protection Syndrome In Black Americans. Livermore, California: Wing Span Press, 2010.

Bailey II, JA. Word Stories Surrounding African American Slavery. Livermore, California: Wing Span Press, 2010.

Bailey II, JA. Word Stories Originated by Ancient Africans. Livermore, California: Wing Span Press, 2009.

Bailey, II, JA. Offensive Language Afflicts Black Youth's Psyche. The Western Journal of Black Studies, Vol. 30, No. 3, 2006 p142-154

Bailey II, JA. Afrocentric Critical Thinking, Livermore, California: Wing Span Press 2008.

Bailey II, JA. Freeing Enslaved Minds in Black Americans, Livermore, California: Wing Span Press 2006.

Bailey II, JA. The Foundation Of Self-Esteem. J. Natl. Med. Assoc. 2003; 95: 388-393.

Bailey II, JA. A Classification of Black-American Self-Esteem; J. Natl. Med. Assoc. 2004; 96: 23-28.

Bailey II JA. Echoes of Ancient African Values, Bloomington, Indiana: Authorhouse, 2005.

Bailey II JA. Good Character, Canada: Trafford, 2004.

Bailey II JA. The Handbook for Worker's Compensation Doctors. California: I.C.E. Publishers, 1994.

Bailey II, JA. Afrocentric English and Critical Thinking, Livermore, California: Wing Span Press, 2006.

Bailey II, JA. American Crime From A Black American Perspective, Livermore, CA: Wing Span Press, 2006.

Bailey II, JA. Anger In Black Americans. Livermore, California: Wing Span Press, 2006.

Bailey II, JA. Becoming a Champion Somebody, Livermore, CA: Wing Span Press, 2006.

Bailey II, JA. Black Voice News, Riverside, California: (blackvoicenews.com).

Bailey II, JA. Common Sense Inside African Tradition, Livermore, California: Wing Span Press, 2006.

Bailey II, JA. Creativity, Invention & Discovery, Livermore, California: 2007.

Bailey II, JA. Deceptive Orthopaedic Patients. Unpublished, 1995.

Bailey II, JA. Disproportionate Short Stature -- Diagnosis and Management, Philadelphia: W.B. Sanders Co., 1973.

Bailey II, JA. I Am A Special Somebody, California: wingspanpress.com, 2005.

Bailey II, JA. Manhood in Black Americans; Livermore, CA: Wing Span Press, 2006.

Bailey II, JA. Preparing to Prepare, Teacher's Guide, Lincoln, Ne: iUniverse, 2005.

Bailey II, JA. Rising Above Poverty. Livermore, CA: Wing Span Press, 2007

Bailey II, JA. Managing Emotions. Livermore, CA: Wing Span Press, 2007

Bailey II, JA. Selfhood Mastery. Livermore, CA: Wing Span Press, 2007

Bailey II, JA. Self-Esteem in Black Americans, Livermore, CA: Wing Span Press, 2005.

Bailey II, JA. Self-Esteem Masqueraders in Struggling Black Americans; Accepted for publication in the Journal of Black Studies in the Fall of 2005.

Bailey II, JA. Self-Image, Self-Concept, and Self-Identity Revisited. J. Natl. Med. Assoc. 2003; 95: 383-386.

Bailey II, JA. The Concise Dictionary of Medical-Legal Terms; London: The Parthenon Publishing Group, 1998.

Bailey II, JA. Supreme Thinking—Rational, Poetic, & Visionary—of Ancient Africans, Livermore, California: Wing Span Press, 2008. (Wingspanpress.com)

Bailey II, JA. Rational Thinking. Livermore, CA: Wing Span Press, 2008

Bailey II, JA. Special Minds Among Struggling Black Americans. Livermore, CA: Wing Span Press, 2009

Bailey II, JA. The Purpose of Education: in Smylie MA. Why Do We Educate? Voices From The Conversation. Volume 107, Issue 2 Malden, Massachusetts: Wiley-Blackwell 2008

Baker, David V: Black Female Executions in Historical Context *Criminal Justice Review, March 2008; vol. 33, 1: pp. 64-88.*

Baker, Tom: '… and the Life Everlasting'? Some Personal Reflections *Theology, November 1983; vol. 86, 714: pp. 425-433*

Baldwin, Joseph A: Theory and Research Concerning the Notion of Black Self-**hatred**: A Review and Reinterpretation *Journal of Black Psychology, February 1979; vol. 5, 2: pp. 51-77.*

Baldwin, Debora R. David Jackson III, Ife Okoh, and Rex L.: Cannon **Resiliency and Optimism: An African American Senior Citizen's Perspective** *Journal of Black Psychology February 2011 37: 24-41*

Bengtsson, Tea Torbenfeldt: 'It's what you have to do!': Exploring the role of high-risk edge-work and advanced marginality in a young man's motivation for crime, *Criminology and Criminal Justice, February 2013; vol. 13, 1: pp. 99-115.*

Bernal, Martin: Black Athena. The Afroasiatic Roots of Classical Civilization. New Brunswick, New Jersey: Rutgers University Press. 1991

Billig, Michael: Humour and *Hatred*: The Racist Jokes of the Ku Klux Klan *Discourse & Society, May 2001; vol. 12, 3: pp. 267-289.*

Binder, John J. and Mars Eghigian, Jr.: Gangland Killings in Chicago, 1919-1933 *Journal of Contemporary Criminal Justice, May 2013; vol. 29, 2: pp. 219-232*

Blair, Irene V. The Malleability of Automatic Stereotypes and Prejudice *Personality and Social Psychology Review, August 2002; vol. 6, 3: pp. 242-261.*

Blavatsky, HP. The Theosophical Glossary. Los Angeles: The Theosophy Company 1990

Bingaman, Sharon: Personal Communications

Blassingame JW. The Slave Community. New York: Oxford University Press, 1972

Borders, L. DiAnne and Kathleen A. Archadel: Self-Beliefs and Career Counseling; *Journal of Career Development, December 1987; vol. 14, 2: pp. 69-79.*

Bosson, Jennifer K. and Joseph A. Vandello**:** Precarious ***Manhood*** and Its Links to Action and Aggression *Current Directions in Psychological Science, April 2011; vol. 20, 2: pp. 82-86.*

Bosson, Jennifer K. Joseph A. Vandello, Rochelle M. Burnaford, Jonathan R. Weaver, and S. Arzu Wasti Precarious Manhood and Displays of Physical Aggression *Personality and Social Psychology Bulletin, May 2009; vol. 35, 5: pp. 623-634*

Botkin BA. Lay My Burden Down. Chicago: The University of Chicago Press 1945

Brady PL. *The Black Badge.* Los Angeles: Milligan Books, 2005.

Brezina, Timothy, Robert Agnew, Francis T. Cullen, and John Paul Wright: The Code of the Street: A Quantitative Assessment of Elijah Anderson's Subculture of Violence Thesis and Its Contribution to Youth Violence Research; *Youth Violence and Juvenile Justice, October 2004; vol. 2, 4: pp. 303-328*

Broomé, Rodger E: A Phenomenological Psychological Study of the Police Officer's Lived Experience of the Use of Deadly Force *J.Humanistic Psychology, April 2014; vol. 54, 2: pp. 158-181.*

Brunson, Rod K. and Jacinta M. Gau Officer Race Versus Macro-Level Context: A Test of Competing Hypotheses About Black Citizens' Experiences With and Perceptions of Black Police Officers *Crime & Delinquency, March 2015; vol. 61, 2: pp. 213-242.*

Bryant-Davis, Thema and Carlota Ocampo Racist Incident–Based Trauma; *The Counseling Psychologist, July 2005; vol. 33, 4: pp. 479-500.*

Buchanan, Thomas C. Levees of Hope: ***African American*** Steamboat Workers, Cities, and Slave Escapes on the Antebellum Mississippi *Journal of Urban History, March 2004; vol. 30, 3: pp. 360- 377.*

Buckels, Erin E., Daniel N. Jones, and Delroy L. Paulhus: Behavioral Confirmation of Everyday Sadism, *Psychological Science, November 2013; vol. 24, 11: pp. 2201-2209.*

Butler, Kim D. *Slavery* in the Age of Emancipation: Victims and Rebels in Brazil's Late 19th-Century Domestic Trade *Journal of Black Studies, September 2011; vol. 42, 6: pp. 968-992.,*

Bynum EB. The African Unconscious. New York: Teachers College Press, 1999.

Bynum, EB: Dark Light Consciousness. Rochester, Vermont: Inner Traditions 2012

Callahan, Jamie L. Manifestations of Power and Control: Training as the Catalyst for Scandal at the United States Air Force Academy *Violence Against Women, October 2009; vol. 15, 10: pp. 1149- 1168*

Campbell MD, Robert Jean: *Psychiatric Dictionary 5ᵗʰ ed. New York: Oxford University Press 1981*

Campbell J. *Occidental Mythology*, New York: Penguin Books, 1964.

Candy P, Freke T. *The Hermetica*, New York, J,P. Tarcher/Putman; 1997.

Clairborne, Robert: *Our Marvelous Native Tongue. New York: Times Books 1959*

Carew, Jan: Columbus and the origins of racism in the Americas: part two *Race & Class, July 1988; vol. 30, 1: pp. 33-57*

Carlson, Kelly and Joanne M. Hall Exploring the Concept of Manliness in Relation to the Phenomenon of Crying: A Bourdieusian Approach *Journal of Holistic Nursing, September 2011; vol. 29, 3: pp. 189-197.*

Chandler, Daphne: **The Underutilization of Health Services in the Black Community: An Examination of Causes and Effects** *Journal of Black Studies May 2010 40: 915-931.*

Chirhart, Ann Short :"Better for Us than it was For Her": African American Families, Communities, and Reform in Modern Georgia *Journal of Family History, October 2003; vol. 28, 4: pp. 578-602.*

Chivaura, Vimbai Gukwe: *European* Culture in Africa as Business: Its Implications on the Development of the Human Factor *Journal of Black Studies, November 1998; vol. 29, 2: pp. 189- 208*

Cirlot JE. A Dictionary of Symbols. New York Philosophical Library, 1962.

Costen MW. African American Christian Worship. Nashville: Abingdon Press 1993

Daniel, Makin' a Way Outa No Way; J. Black Studies 1987 17: 482-508).

Decker, Scott H., Charles M. Katz, and Vincent J. Webb Understanding the *Black* Box of Gang Organization: Implications for Involvement in Violent Crime, Drug Sales, and Violent Victimization *Crime & Delinquency, January 2008; vol. 54, 1: pp. 153-172.*

Deme, Mariam Konate: **Heroism and the Supernatural in the African Epic: Toward a Critical Analysis** *Journal of Black Studies January 2009 39: 402-419*

Densley, James A, Tianji Cai, and Susan Hilal Social dominance orientation and trust propensity in street *gang*s *Group Processes & Intergroup Relations, November 2014; vol. 17, 6: pp. 763-779*

Deveau, Jean-Michel: European Slave Trading in the Eighteenth Century *Diogenes, September 1997; vol. 45, 179: pp. 49-74*

Drever J. *A Dictionary of Psychology.* Baltimore: Penguin Books, 1952: 160.

Diamond, Andrew: Rethinking Culture on the Streets: Agency, Masculinity, and Style in the American City; *Journal of Urban History, July 2001; vol. 27, 5: pp. 669-685.*

Diop CA: Civilization or Barbarism. Brooklyn, Lawrence Hall Books; 1991.

Domke, David, David Perlmutter, and Meg Spratt: The primes of our times?: An examination of the 'power' of visual images *Journalism, August 2002; vol. 3, 2: pp. 131-159*

Donkor AE. *African Spirituality.* Trenton, NJ. Africa World Press, Inc., 1997.

Douglass F: My Bondage and My Freedom. New York: Penguin Books 1855: 53

DuBois WEB. *The Souls of Black.* New York: Gramercy Books, 1994.

Elkins M. *August Wilson -- A Casebook.* New York: Garland Publishing, Inc., 1994: 9

Ephraim, C. W. (2003). *The pathology of Eurocentrism: The burdens and responsibilities of being Black.* Trenton, NJ: Africa World Press.

Evans, Art: **Joe Louis as a Key Functionary: White Reactions Toward a Black Champion** *Journal of Black Studies September 1985 16: 95-111*

Fairchild, Halford H. **Black, Negro, or Afro-American?: The Differences Are Crucial!** *Journal of Black Studies September 1985 16: 47-55; K.*

Fandrich, Yorùbá Influences on Haitian Vodou and New Orleans Voodoo J. Black Studies May 2007 37: 775-791).

Franklin, John Hope and Schweninger, Loren: Runaway Slaves. New York: Oxford University Press. 1999

Farley John E. Sociology 3rd ed. Englewood Cliffs, New Jersey: Prentice Hall 1994

Fluck, Julia: Why Do Students Bully? An Analysis of Motives Behind Violence in Schools *Youth & Society, 0044118X14547876, first published on August 29, 2014*

Forbes, Ella: African Resistance to Enslavement: The Nature and the Evidentiary Record *Journal of Black Studies, September 1992; vol. 23, 1: pp. 39-59.*

Foster, Herbert J. African Patterns in the Afro-American Family; *Journal of Black Studies, December 1983; vol. 14, 2: pp. 201-232.*

Fry GM *Night Riders* The University of Tennessee Press 1975: 135-55

Furnas JC *Goodbye to Uncle Tom* New York: William Sloane Associates 1956:127.

Gabbidon, Shaun L., George E. Higgins, and Hillary Potter: Race, Gender, and the Perception of Recently Experiencing Unfair Treatment by the Police: Exploratory Results From an All-Black Sample *Criminal Justice Review, March 2011; vol. 36, 1: pp. 5-21.*

Gadalla, Moustafa: The Ancient Egyptian Roots of Christianity; Tehuti Research Foundation/   PO Box 39406/ Greensboro, NC 27438-9406

Garlick, Steve: What is a Man?: Heterosexuality and the Technology of Masculinity *Men and Masculinities, October 2003; vol. 6, 2: pp. 156-172.*

Garner, Thurman: **Black Ethos in Folktales** *Journal of Black Studies September 1984 15: 53-66.*

Graham, Roderick: **Jazz Consumption Among African Americans from 1982 to 2008** *Journal of Black Studies September 2011 42: 993-1018*

Gaskell GA. Dictionary of All Scriptures and Myths. New York: Arenel Books, 1960.

Good, Michael I. The Reconstruction of Early Childhood Trauma: Fantasy, Reality, and Verification *Journal of the American Psychoanalytic Association, March 1994; vol. 42, 1: pp. 79-101.*

Green, Doris **African Oral Tradition Literacy** *Journal of Black Studies June 1985 15: 405-425*

Greene, Jack R. Geoffrey P. Alpert, and Paul Styles Values and Culture in Two American Police Departments: Lessons from King Arthur *Journal of Contemporary Criminal Justice, August 1992; vol. 8, 3: pp. 183-207.*

Hall, Ronald E. **Rooming in the Master's House: Psychological Domination and the Black Conservative** *Journal of Black Studies March 2008 38: 565-578*

Halperin, Eran Emotion, Emotion Regulation, and ***Conflict Resolution*** *Emotion Review, January 2014; vol. 6, 1: pp. 68-76.,*

Harris, Jennifer: Self-Harm: Cutting the Bad out of Me *Qualitative Health Research, March 2000; vol. 10, 2: pp. 164-173.*

Highwater, Jamake: The Primal Mind—Vision and Reality in Indian America New York: Harper & Row, 1944

Hodge JL, Struckmann DK, Trost LD. *Cultural Bases of Racism and Group Opposition.* Berkeley: Two Riders Press, 1975.

Honeycutt, James M., Loretta Pecchioni, Shaughan A. Keaton, and Michelle E. Pence Developmental Implications of Mental Imagery in Childhood Imaginary Companions *Imagination, Cognition and Personality, September 2011; vol. 31, 1: pp. 79-98.*

Hooke, Alexander E: Training *Police* in *Professional Ethics; Journal of Contemporary Criminal Justice, August 1996; vol. 12, 3: pp. 264-276.*

Huggins NI. *Black Odyssey* New York: First Vintage Books Edition 1977.

Hunter, Andrea G. and James Earl Davis: Hidden Voices of Black Men: The Meaning, Structure, and Complexity of Manhood *Journal of Black Studies, September 1994; vol. 25, 1: pp. 20-40.*

Hunter, Andrea G., Christian A. Friend, S. Yvette Murphy, Alethea Rollins, Meeshay Williams-Wheeler, and Janzelean Laughinghouse: Loss, Survival, and Redemption: African American Male Youths' Reflections on Life Without Fathers, *Manhood*, and Coming of Age *Youth & Society, June 2006; vol. 37, 4: pp. 423-452.*

Irwin, Katherine and Karen Umemoto: *International Journal of Discrimination and the Law, June 2000; vol. 4, 2: pp. 153-172.* Being Fearless and Fearsome: Colonial Legacies, Racial Constructions, and Male Adolescent Violence *Race and Justice, January 2012; vol. 2, 1: pp. 3-28.*

Irwin, Katherine: MANAGING VIOLENCE The *Violence* of Adolescent Life: Experiencing and *Managing* Everyday Threats: *Youth & Society, June 2004; vol. 35, 4: pp. 452-479.*

Ivković, Sanja Kutnjak, Maria Haberfeld, and Robert Peacock: Rainless West: The Integrity Survey's Role in Agency **Accountability** *Police* Quarterly, June 2013; vol. 16, 2: pp. 148-176.

Jalata, Asafa: Revisiting the Black Struggle: Lessons for the 21st Century; *Journal of Black Studies, September 2002; vol. 33, 1: pp. 86-116*

Jalata, Asafa **Being in and out of Africa: The Impact of Duality of Ethiopianism** *Journal of Black Studies November 2009 40: 189-214;*

James GGM. *Stolen Legacy*, Trenton, N.J., Africa World Press, Inc., 1954; 88.

Jerolmack, Colin *and* Tavory, Iddo: Molds *and Totems*: Nonhumans *and* the Constitution of the Social Self *Sociological Theory,* March 2014; vol. 32, 1: pp. 64-77.

Jewell, Sue **Will the Real Black, Afro-American, Mixed, Colored, Negro Please Stand Up?: Impact of the Black Social Movement, Twenty Years Later** *Journal of Black Studies* September 1985 16: 57-75;

Jones RL. *Black Psychology,* 2nd ed. New York: Harper and Row Publishers, 1980.

Joyce, Joyce A. **Semantic Development of the Word Black: A History from Indo-European to the Present** *Journal of Black Studies March 1981 11: 307-312*

Kalunta-Crumpton, Anita: Race in Popular and Courtroom Discourse of Violence *International Journal of Discrimination and the Law, June 2000; vol. 4, 2: pp. 153-172.*

Karenga M: Ma'at. Los Angeles: University of Sankore Press, 2006.

Katz, Donald B. and Joseph E. Steinmetz: Psychological Functions of the Cerebellum. *Behavioral and Cognitive Neuroscience Reviews, September 2002; vol. 1, 3: pp. 229-241.*

King R. *African Origin of Biological Psychiatry,* Hampton, Virginia: U.B. and U.S. Communications Systems, Inc., 1984.

Kittles, Rick **Nature, Origin, and Variation of Human Pigmentation** *Journal of Black Studies* September 1995 26: 36-61

Kofsky, Frank: **The Jazz Tradition : Black Music and its White Critics,** *Journal of Black Studies* 1971 1: 403).

Kouzakova, Mar*in*a, Naomi Ellemers, Fieke Har*in*ck, and Daan Scheepers The Implications of Value *Conflict*: How Disagreement on Values Affects Self-*In*volvement and Perceived Common Ground: *Personality and Social Psychology Bulletin, June 2012; vol. 38, 6: pp. 798-807.*

Kalunta-Crumpton, Anita, Schlesinger, Traci and Jodie Michelle Lawston: Race in Popular and Courtroom Discourse of Violence Experiences of *In*terpersonal Violence and *Criminal* Legal Control: A Mixed Method Analysis *SAGE Open, July - September 2011; vol. 1, 2: 21*

Kennedy, Kathleen A. and Emily Pron*in*: When Disagreement Gets Ugly: Perceptions of Bias and the Escalation of *Conflict*

Lama D. *Mind Science.* Boston: Wisdom Publications, 1991.

Lama, Dalai: *Transforming the Mind. Thorsons:* Hammersmith, London 2000

Lammers, Joris, Janka I. Stoker, and Diederik A. Stapel: Differentiating Social and ***Personal Power***: Opposite Effects on Stereotyping, but Parallel Effects on Behavioral Approach Tendencies *Psychological Science, December 2009; vol. 20, 12: pp. 1543-1548.*

Lawrence-M, Charshee Charlotte: **The Double Meanings of the Spirituals** *Journal of Black Studies June 1987 17: 379-401*

Leidner, Bernhard, Emanuele Castano, and Jeremy Ginges: Dehumanization, Retributive and Restorative Justice, and Aggressive Versus Diplomatic Intergroup **Conflict Resolution** Strategies *Personality and Social Psychology Bulletin, February 2013; vol. 39, 2: pp. 181-192.*

Leonard, Ira M. and Christopher C. Leonard: The Historiography of American Violence *Homicide Studies, May 2003; vol. 7, 2: pp. 99-153*

Leonard, Jacqueline and Marc Lamont Hill: **Using Multimedia to Engage African American Children in Classroom Discourse** *Journal of Black Studies September 2008 39: 22-42*

Long, LaDonna and Sarah E. Ullman The Impact of Multiple Traumatic Victimization on Disclosure and Coping Mechanisms for Black Women: *Feminist Criminology, October 2013; vol. 8, 4: pp. 295- 319.*

Lopez-Aguado, Patrick: Working between two worlds: Gang intervention and street liminality *Ethnography, June 2013; vol. 14, 2: pp. 186-206.,*

Luz Martin J: A Tract for Our Times: Newman, Genet, and the Syntax of Universal Morality. *Irish Theological Quarterly, June 2003; vol. 68, 2: pp. 119-153.*

Macdonald, John and Robert J. Stokes: Race, Social Capital, and Trust in the Police *Urban Affairs Review, January 2006; vol. 41, 3: pp. 358-375.*

Martin, Denise: **Maat and Order in African Cosmology: A Conceptual Tool for Understanding Indigenous Knowledge** *Journal of Black Studies July 2008 38: 951-967*

Martin, Denise: **An Application of Dogon Epistemology** *Journal of Black Studies July 2010 40: 1153- 1167*

Martin, Frank: **The Egyptian Ethnicity Controversy and the Sociology of Knowledge** *Journal of Black Studies March 1984 14: 295-325*

Maslow, Abraham H :Further Notes on the Psychology of Being *Journal of Humanistic Psychology, Spring 1963; vol. 3, 1: pp. 120-135.*

Masud, Sabrina Binte: **Sage Philosophy: Revisiting Oruka's African Ideology** *Journal of Black Studies September 2011 42: 874-886)*

Mattis, Jacqueline S. **African American Women's Definitions of Spirituality and Religiosity** Journal of Black Psychology February 2000 26: 101-122.

Mays, B. Nicholson, J. The Negro's Church, New York, Arno 1969

Mazama, Ama: **The Afrocentric Paradigm: Contours and Definitions** *Journal of Black Studies March 2001 31: 387-405*

Mazama, Ama: **Book Review: T. Tibebu (2011). Hegel and the Third World: The Making of Eurocentrism in World History Syracuse, NY: Syracuse University Press** *Journal of Black Studies July 2011 42: 846-850);*

Mcara, Lesley and Susan Mcvie: The usual suspects?: Street-*life*, young people and the *police Criminal Justice, February 2005; vol. 5, 1: pp. 5-36.*

McMillan, Timothy J. Black Magic: Witchcraft, Race, and Resistance in Colonial New England Journal of Black Studies September 1994 25: 99-117.

Nicolas, Understanding the Strengths of Black Youths; J. Black Psychology 2008 34: 261-280).

Niles, Rhetorical Characteristics of Black Preaching; J. Black Studies 1984 15: 41-52

Murove, Felix:Ubuntu, Munyaradzi *Diogenes, November 2012; vol. 59, 3-4: pp. 36-47*

Modh, Gita Satish: Formulating a New Three Energy Framework of Personality for *Conflict* Analysis and *Resolution* based on Triguna Concept of Bhagavad *Journal of Human Values, October 2014; vol. 20, 2: pp. 153-165.*

Moore, T. Owens: **Revisited Affect-Symbolic Imagery,** *Journal of Black Psychology* 1996 22: 443).

Mowatt, Rasul A. Lynching as Leisure: Broadening Notions of a Field *American Behavioral Scientist, October 2012; vol. 56, 10: pp. 1361-1387*

Moyers B. The Power of Myth New York: Anchor Books 1988.

Mphande, Lupenga and Linda James-Myers, **Traditional African Medicine and the Optimal Theory: Universal Insights for Health and Healing,** *Journal of Black Psychology* 1993 19: 25).

Musanga, Terrence and Anias Mutekwa, **Destabilizing and Subverting Patriarchal and Eurocentric Notions of Time;** *Journal of Black Studies* 2011 42: 1299

Myers DG. Social Psychology 5th ed. New York: Mc Graw-Hill, Inc. 1996 Nandi, M: Re/Constructing Black Masculinity in Prison: *The Journal of Men's Studies, October 2002; vol. 11, 1: pp. 91-107.*

Ogunyemi, Olatunji: **The Implications of Taboos Among African Diasporas for the African Press in the United Kingdom** *Journal of Black Studies July 2008 38: 862-882*

Ogunleye, Tolagbe: **African American Folklore: Its Role in Reconstructing African American History** *Journal of Black Studies March 1997 27: 435-455*

Oliver, William: **"The Streets": An Alternative Black Male Socialization Institution** *Journal of Black Studies July 2006 36: 918-937*

O'Neal, Eryn Nicole, Scott H. Decker, Richard K. Moule, Jr., and David C. Pyrooz :Girls, **Gangs,** and Getting Out: Gender Differences and Similarities in Leaving the Gang: *Youth Violence and Juvenile Justice,*

Osborne, Randall E. and Christopher J. Frost The Anatomy of Hatred: Multiple Pathways to the Construction of Human Hatred; *Humanity & Society, February 2004; vol. 28, 1: pp. 5-23.*

Oshodi, John Egbeazien. **The Place of Spiritualism and Ancient Africa in American Psychology** *Journal of Black Studies November 1996 27: 172-182*

Otto, John Solomon and Augustus Marion Burns **Black Folks and Poor Buckras: Archeological Evidence of Slave and Overseer Living Conditions on an Antebellum Plantation** *Journal of Black Studies December 1983 14: 185-200*

Parker, Karen F. and Scott R. Maggard: Making a Difference: The Impact of Traditional Male Role Models **on** Drug Sale Activity and **Violence** Involving **Black** Urban Youth; *Journal of Drug Issues, July 2009; vol. 39, 3: pp. 715-739.*

Payne, Yasser Arafat: **Site of Resilience: A Reconceptualization of Resiliency and Resilience in Street Life–Oriented Black Men** *Journal of Black Psychology November 2011 37: 426-451*

Peterson, Abby and Sara Uhnoo: *Personality and Social Psychology Bulletin, June 2008; vol. 34, 6: pp. 833- 848.*

Peterson, Abby: Trials of loyalty: Ethnic minority *police* officers as 'outsiders' within a greedy institution *European Journal of Criminology, July 2012; vol. 9, 4: pp. 354-369.*

Petersen, Rebecca D. and James C. Howell :Program Approaches for Girls in **Gangs**: *Female* Specific or Gender Neutral? *Criminal Justice Review, December 2013; vol. 38, 4: pp. 491-509*

Phillips, Frederick B. **NTU Psychotherapy: An Afrocentric Approach** *Journal of Black Psychology Fall 1990 17: 55-74*

Pihos, Peter C: Urban Street **Gang**s *Journal of Urban History, May 2011; vol. 37, 3: pp. 466-473. Ending Gang and Youth Violence*: A Critique Joe Cottrell-Boyce *Youth Justice, December 2013; vol. 13, 3: pp. 193-206*

Poe R. Black Spark White Fire. Rocklin, Ca: Prima Publishing 1997

Prins, Herschel: Coke v. Bumble – comments on some aspects of unlawful **killing** and its disposal; *Medicine, Science and the Law, January 2008; vol. 48, 1: pp. 15-23.*

Pollock, Joycelyn M., Janet L. Mullings, and Ben M. Crouch: **Violent Women**: Findings From the Texas **Women** Inmates Study *Journal of Interpersonal Violence, April 2006; vol. 21, 4: pp. 485-502*

Porter, Louise E:**In**digenous **death**s associated with **police** contact **in** Australia: Event stages and lessons for prevention *Australian & New Zealand Journal of Criminology, August 2013; vol. 46, 2: pp. 178-199*

Ramacharaka Y. Raja Yoga, Chicago: The Yogi Publication Society, 1934

Ramacharaka Y. Fourteen Lessons in Yogi Philosophy, Chicago: The Yogi Publication Society, 1904: 77.

Reber, Arthur S. Dictionary of Psychology. London: Penguin Books 1985

Rhee, Young-hoon **and** Yang, Donghyu: Korean *Nobi* **and American** Black **Slavery**: An Essay **in** Comparison *Millennial Asia, January 2010; vol. 1, 1: pp. 5-39*

Rinpoche, Sogyal: The Tibetan Book of Living and Dying: Harper San Francisco 1993

Rucker, Walter:Conjure, Magic, and Power: The Influence of Afro-Atlantic Religious Practices on Slave Resistance and Rebellion: *Journal of Black Studies, September 2001; vol. 32, 1: pp. 84-103.*

Ruef, Martin and Alona Harness Agrarian Origins of Management Ideology: The Roman and Antebellum Cases; *Organization Studies, June 2009; vol. 30, 6: pp. 589-607.*

Runes DD. *Spinoza Dictionary*, Westport, Connecticut, Greenwood Press Publishers, 1951.

Rycroft C. *Dictionary of Psychoanalysis*. New York: Penguin Books, 1995.

Sarfoh, West African Zongo/American Ghetto; J. Black Studies 1986 17: 71-84

Satter, Beryl :Cops, **Gangs**, and Revolutionaries in 1960s Chicago: What **Black** Police Can Tell Us about Power *Journal of Urban History, 0096144214566985, first published on April 9, 2015 pp1-25*

Sehulster, Frances Harper's Religion of Responsibility in *Sowing and Reaping*; J. Black Studies 2010 40: 1136-1152

Seleem R. Egyptian Book of the Dead. New York: Sterling Publishing Company 2001

Selwyn, E. G.The Life after Death, *Theology, January 1953; vol. 56, 391: pp. 13-19*

Senghor, Léopold Sédar and Elaine P. Halperin African-Negro Aesthetics *Diogenes, December 1956; vol. 4, 16: pp. 23-38.*

Silberman CE. *Crisis in Black and White*, New York, Vintage Books, 1964; 82, 96.

Silcox, Mark: Psychological Trauma and the Simulated Self; *Philosophy of the Social Sciences, June 2014; vol. 44, 3: pp. 349-364*

Senghor, Léopold Sédar and Halperin, Elaine P: African-Negro Aesthetics *Diogenes, December 1956; vol. 4, 16: pp. 23-38. Senghor, Diogenes, 1956*

Shor, Francis: Contrasting *Images* of Reconstructing *Manhood*: Bly's Wild Man versus Spielberg's Inner Child, *The Journal of Men's Studies, November 1993; vol. 2, 2: pp. 109-128.*

Some` MP. *The Healing Wisdom of Africa.* New York: Penguin Putnam, Inc., 1998

Starr-Glass, David: Exploring Organizational Culture: Teaching Notes on Metaphor, Totem, **and** Archetypal ***Images*** *Journal of Management Education, June 2004; vol. 28, 3: pp. 356-371*

Stevenson BE. *Life in Black and White.* New York: Oxford University Press.

Stimpson, George: A Book About A Thousand Things. New York: Harper & Brothers Publishers 1946

Stockhammer M. Plato Dictionary. New York: Philosophical Library 1963

Stretesky, Paul B. **and** Pogreb, Mark R: Gang-Related Gun Violence: Socialization, Identity, **and** Self *in Journal of Contemporary Ethnography, February 2007; vol. 36, 1: pp. 85-114.*

Smith, Michael R. **and** Geoffrey P. Alpert Explaining **Police** Bias: A Theory of Social Conditioning **and** Illusory Correlation *Criminal Justice **and** Behavior, October 2007; vol. 34, 10: pp. 1262-1283.*

Stensrud, Robert: **Personal Power**: a Taoist Perspective Journal of Humanistic Psychology, October 1979; vol. 19, 4: pp. 31-41.

Sugimoto, John D. **and** Kevin Ann Oltjenbruns The Environment of ***Death and*** its Influence on **Police** Officers in the United States *OMEGA - Journal of **Death and** Dying, October 2001; vol. 43, 2: pp. 145-155.*

Taylor, Vincent Life after Death: I. The Modern Situation *The Expository Times, December 1964; vol. 76, 3: pp. 76-79.*

Taylor, The Political Influence of African American Ministers: A Legacy of West African Culture. *J. Black Studies 2006 37: 5-19.*

Taylor, Black Americans' Perceptions of the Sociohistorical Role of the Church; J. Black Studies 1987 18: 123-138

Temple, Christel N. **The Emergence of Sankofa Practice in the United States: A Modern History** *Journal of Black Studies September 2010 41: 127-150*

Testoni, Ines, Dorella Ancona, and Lucia Ronconi The Ontological Representation of ***Death***: A Scale to Measure the Idea of Annihilation Versus Passage *OMEGA - Journal of Death and Dying, May 2015; vol. 71, 1: pp. 60-81.,*

Thomas-Holder, Blacks in Colonial America; J. Black Studies 1991 22: 294-300;

Three Initiates. The Kybalion. Chicago: The Yogi Publishing Society, 1940.

Tibebu, Teshale: **Ethiopia: The "Anomaly" and "Paradox" of Africa** *Journal of Black Studies March 1996 26: 414-430;*

Tillotson, Michael: **A Critical Location of the Contemporary Black Church: Finding a Place for the Word Church Formation,** *The Journal of Black Studies*, Vol. 40, No. 5, May 2010, pp. 1016- 1030.

Tjeder, David: When Character Became Capital: The Advent of the Self-Made man in Sweden, 1850- 1900; *Men and Masculinities, July 2002; vol. 5, 1: pp. 53-79.*

Turner, Jack: Awakening to Race: Ralph Ellison and Democratic Individuality *Political Theory, October 2008; vol. 36, 5: pp. 655-682.*

Vaccaro, Douglas, P. Schrock, and Janice M. McCabe: Managing Emotional *Manhood*: Fighting and Fostering Fear in Mixed Martial Arts *Social Psychology Quarterly, December 2011; vol. 74, 4: pp. 414- 437.*

Valdez, Avelardo, Charles D. Kaplan, and Edward Codina: Psychopathy among Mexican American *Gang* Members: A Comparative Study *International Journal of Offender Therapy and Comparative Criminology, February 2000; vol. 44, 1: pp. 46-58.*

Verharen, Charles C. **Philosophy Against Empire: An Ancient Egyptian Renaissance** *Journal of Black Studies July 2006 36: 958-973*

Verharen, Charles C. **Philosophy's Roles in Afrocentric Education** *Journal of Black Studies January 2002 32: 295-321* Ubuntu, Munyaradzi Felix Murove *Diogenes, November 2012; vol. 59, 3-4: pp. 36-47*

Warren, Howard C.: *Dictionary of Psychology.* Boston: Houghton Mifflin Company 1934

Watkins, Adam M. and Richard K. Moule, Jr. Older, Wiser, and a Bit More Badass? Exploring Differences in Juvenile and Adult *Gang Members' Gang*-Related Attitudes and Behaviors *Youth Violence and Juvenile Justice, April 2014; vol. 12, 2: pp. 121-136*

Watterson B. *Gods of Ancient Egypt,* Godalming, Surrey: Sutton Publishing Company, 1999, 14.

Waytz, Adam, Kelly Marie Hoffman, and Sophie Trawalter A Superhumanization Bias in Whites' Perceptions of Blacks *Social Psychological and Personality Science, April 2015; vol. 6, 3: pp. 352-359*

Weinstein A, Gatell FO, Sarasohn D *American Negro Slavery* 3rd ed New York: Oxford University Press 1979: 230, 246, 248

Wells-Wilbon R, Jackson ND, and Schiele JH. Lessons From the Maafa: Rethinking the Legacy of Slain Hip-Hop Icon Tupac Amaru Shakur J. Black Studies March 2010 40: 509-526

Welsh, Kariamu and Molefi Kete Asante **Myth: The Communication Dimension to the African American Mind** *Journal of Black Studies June 1981 11: 387-395*

Whaley, Arthur L. **Stereotype Threat Paradigm in Search of a Phenomenon: A Comment on Kellow and Jones's (2008) Study** *Journal of Black Psychology November 2009 35: 485-494*

Wiethoff, William E. Enslaved Africans' Rivalry with White Overseers in Plantation Culture: An Unconventional Interpretation *Journal of Black Studies, January 2006; vol. 36, 3: pp. 429-455.*

Wilder, JeffriAnne: **Revisiting "Color Names and Color Notions": A Contemporary Examination of the Language and Attitudes of Skin Color Among Young Black Women** *J Black Studies September 2010 41: 184-206*

Williams C. The Destruction of Black Civilization, Chicago, Third World Press; 1987; 175.

Williams, Walter: The Historical Origin of Christianity. Chicago: Maathian Press 1992

Wood, Jane L:Understanding *gang members*hip: The significance *of* group processes *Group Processes & Intergroup Relations, November 2014; vol. 17, 6: pp. 710-729*

Worgs, Donn C:"Beware of the Frustrated...": The Fantasy and Reality of African American Violent Revolt *Journal of Black Studies, September 2006; vol. 37, 1: pp. 20-45.*

Yelvington, Kevin A, Neill G. Goslin, *and* Wendy Arriaga Whose History?: Museum-making *and* struggles over ethnicity *and* representation *in* the Sunbelt, *Critique of Anthropology,* *September 2002; vol. 22, 3: pp. 343-379*

Yenika-Agbaw, Vivian:Capitalism and the Culture of Hate in Granfield's Amazing Grace: The Story of the Hymn *Journal of Black Studies, January 2006; vol. 36, 3: pp. 353-361*

Yu, Junwei and Alan Bairner: The Confucian legacy and its implications for physical education in Taiwan *European Physical Education Review, June 2011; vol. 17, 2: pp. 219-230*

BOOKS BY DR. BAILEY

I Am a Special Somebody is for anyone having strayed away from his/her destination in life and yet still possesses the intense desire to get back on the path and then head toward happiness.

Self-Esteem in Black Americans presented from a historical perspective, is extensively discussed from the dawn of mankind to the present. Nine major syndromes prominently found in Black people are featured—and with suggestions on how to improve each.

Echoes of Ancient African Values discusses who Ancient Africans were as a people; their genius and creative ways of thinking; their philosophical and spiritual foundations; their world shaping achievements; and how these echo into today's Black Americans.-- $30.00

Preparing to Prepare (iUniverse.com) is about implanting seed ideas of a good character nature. Lesson plans are plentiful to serve as a guideline for stimulating ideas and methods to help youth achieve their dreams and talents for a balanced, mature, and wealthy life.-- $28.00

Good Character explains the history of 50 traits and discusses in practical terms the skills needed to instill or develop good character. These traits are fundamental for achieving a successful and happy life.--$30.00

Becoming a Champion Somebody provides the "nuts & bolts" of choosing ones legacy dream, discovering ones talent, and becoming a successful person. The approach a systematic 9 step process-- called the 9Ps—is based on practical experiences of many people. It is designed to help youth in identifying and pursing their goal in a way that applies to any career or for adults keen on achieving even greater success.

American Crime From A Black American Perspective points out the USA conspiracy against Black males; exposes who the real (non- Black) criminals are; and explores in detail the course of Black males likely to be pushed into and then be destroyed as they go through the unfair prison system.

Manhood in Black Americans classifies the nine broad types of manhood and gives approaches and methods to structuring male children and restructuring the orientation of youth who are off the path that is best for them. Both are mainly directed toward single mothers.

Afrocentric English and Critical Thinking is a book designed for making these subjects more interesting for Black youth from a Yin/Yang perspective. This traces the history of African languages through Europe and on into the Americas up to the present. A full discussion is given on Black English, Ebonics, and the special ways Black Americans use both. The stories of 25 key words required for formal English are given.

Enslaved Minds in Black Americans starts with their origin in slavery and with contributions from "bad" African retentions. Numerous patterns of enslaved minds are then given (e.g. procrastination), with extensive comments on their diagnoses and management.

Common Sense inside African Tradition centers on how it developed and was used by Ancient Africans and how it can be developed and used in Black American children. For this to happen requires the cultivation of pure feelings and poetic thinking of African Tradition. The approaches for teaching are out of mathematics, art, literature, and games.

Anger in Black Americans is the primary emotion related to racism. Though entirely justified, it is self-destructive for daily living. This book points out why and offers a variety of detailed management approaches for a variety of chronic anger types--approach which have a track record of effectiveness.

Creativity, Invention, and Discoveries emphasizes ways to cultivate each in children, re-activate them in those who have fallen into a rigid predictable pattern of living, and remove limitations on those desiring to explore new worlds. Methods are presented for practical application on how to see the uncommon in the common and the common in the uncommon.

Rising above Poverty is about changing the belief system of those who chronically struggle in life. For Black Americans this means switching from an Enslaved Mind belief system to that laid out in African Tradition because its brilliance has stood the test of time. This switch is followed by correcting self-defeating bad habits which are spin-offs from bad beliefs.

Selfhood Mastery inside African Tradition is a guide for creating, enhancing, and maintaining the Inner Strength and Inner Peace that leads to contentment and happiness. It emphasizes stabilizing your inner self and maintaining it by Mental Toughness in order to remain in control and be alert while dealing with life's most difficult problems.

Managing Emotions is a work that has arisen out of experiences from patients in my orthopaedic surgical practice, from personal happenings, and from a lifetime involvement with the struggling poor (whose bad emotional contents differ from the population at large). There are long discussions on Good and Pleasure Emotions. To aid ones understanding of Good and Bad Emotions and to make easier customized management, stories of 116 emotions are presented.

Supreme Thinking of Ancient Africans is presented for the first time and is the result of 25 years of research. It tells how Ancient Africans taught their students; explores the details of the ten steps of Rational Thinking; and gives the steps for becoming a Visionary by means of Poetic Thinking.

Rational Thinking is the result of how the author learned to think over a 40 year period, particularly in the Medical/Legal arena, but is applicable to every aspect of life. It is geared to teenagers and emphasizes pictures helpful for thinking about personal problem solving. It is the author's signature book.

Afrocentric Critical Thinking is any form of Productive Thinking consisting of a collection of mental disciplines that draw on wise and pertinent lessons of the past to achieve a goal in the present and/or the future. The uniqueness of this book is that it mentally guides Black people in maneuvering through the Eurocentric marketplace for offensive and defensive purpose.

Special Minds among Struggling Black Americans discusses what the struggling Blacks need in order to break up their vicious cycles. For them to rise above poverty requires shedding delusions and stubbornness; establishing a sound Ancient African philosophy of life and worldview; and perfecting Left and Right Brain thinking skills (e.g. foresight, forethought) by critical and rational thinking.

From Africa to Black Power by Joseph A. Bailey Sr. traces the history of Black Americans through African American slavery from 1433 to 1964. Emphasized is that of the economic, political, human aspects. It is the best work I have ever read on the subject.

Word Stories Originated By Ancient Africans contains 1000+ life-changing and life-shaping words that are now prominent in the English Language. They give an overview of African Tradition, philosophy, and practices.--$50.00

Word Stories Surrounding African American Slavery contains 2000+ words related to and spoken by Black Americans throughout USA History.--$50.00

Self Protection Syndrome is self-defeating Slave Survivals characterized by "Too Much," "Too Little," or "Just Right" but somehow inappropriate behaviors. Suggestions include helping afflicted Black Americans switch back to using their Thriving Minds; reducing or preventing the need for improper self-protection; and how to feel safe, secure, confident, strong, and stable.

Black Americans Entering the Marketplace speaks to preparing for marketplace success, including essential offensive and defensive practices.--$30.00

Unlocking Minds of Black Boys concerns what it takes to remove the Enslaved Minds of Black boys from their Mental Vaults so as to be mentally free to receive constructive information.$30.00

Mentoring Minds of Black Boys discusses building blocks of Ancient African Philosophy; how to change Belief Systems with Symbols; Art and Music as mind stimulants; Abstract Thinking; Self-Esteem; Ancient African Mathematics; and Diagnosing and Managing Chronic Juggling.--$30.00

Word Stories Encyclopaedia (Afrocentric Vol. III) has 2300 words for teaching youth Word Stories in the easiest, fastest, and most pleasant way in order to learn well-rounded information. These stories generate curiosity, imagination, and an eagerness to learn -- $50.00.

Ancient African Bible Messages spotlights the Spiritual Elements of Unconditional Love, Truth, Reality and the Natural as the standard and filter for "How Shall I live." It gives in-depth African history starting 200,000 years ago; charts the evolution of the world's first Bible; and points out how all the other Bibles of the world evolved out of the African Bible -- $30.00.

Leadership Critical Thinking in African Tradition elaborates on how to orchestrate survival, protection, and preservation under physical, emotional, thoughtful, social, financial, and relationship conditions; on spotlighting standards, filters, and guiding thriving ways for self-help and/or helping others; and on providing mental fun as play, a sport, a dance--$25.00.

Private Selfhood Greatness in Black Americans: The Certainty upon which a human's Base and Foundation rests is their Selfhood Greatness consisting of a "Drop of God," super-brilliant Ancient African Ancestors' Genetics, and one unique Talent. Personal Integrity is maintained by cultivating these three to their greatest potential while remaining inside the context of the Spiritual Elements of Unconditional Love, Truth, Reality, and the Natural--as discussed in this book--$30.00

<u>Post-Traumatic Distress Syndrome in Black People</u>: Those afflicted have allowed a Cloud to cover their birth gift of Selfhood Greatness as a result of deficiencies in their Spiritual Human Nature Needs (e.g. to be loved, to belong). This book gives the diagnosis and management of both in the setting of the Metaphysical aspects which characterized Black People--$30.00.

<u>Teaching Black Youth—Affect Symbolic Imagery & African Dialectic</u>: ASI is Ma'at Supernatural stories for Right living while Dialectic is a means to bring out the Divine Knowledge already in each human. This is designed for teachers and mentors who deal with all Black youth, including those of "the Streets."--$30.00

<u>Bailey II, JA: African Tradition For Black Youth—Pursuit of a Free Mind</u>. North Charleston, South Carolina: CreateSpace Independent Publishing Platform 2015. Humans are born with all they need to have a thriving and happy life. Success is guaranteed by staying within and evolving out of the Spiritual Elements for they provide ones Private Self with the "5Ss" of Safety, Security, Self-Confidence, Strength, and Stability. The "5Ss" underlie what all are searching for in life and their absence causes people to "act ugly." This books discusses ways to make happen the "5Ss"--$30.00

ABBREVIATIONS

CB = Contingent Beings

"5Ss" = safety, security, self-confidence, stability, and strength)

IHES COMPLEX = Indifference to Hate to Evilness to Sadism--the IHES Complex

KTDDO = Kill/Take/Destroy/Dominate/Oppress

PHNN = Physical Human Nature Needs

SHNN: Spiritual Human Nature Needs

"SOBMER" PROCESS = Source, Origin, Beginning, Middle, End, Consequences, and Result

GLOSSARY

"AIR CASTLE": Thought structure having no real Base upon which it rests

ARCHERY PAD CONCEPT: Bull's Eye center surrounded by four ringed spaces, separated by 5 line circles--thus making a total of ten parts.

"AWE": Fear (an emotion excited by threatening evil) + Fright (in actual presence of that which is terrible) + Pain + Distress + Terror (rendering one incapable of defense) + Dread + Apprehension + Fascination.

"BLACK": Designates African Traditions ultimate in Spiritual Perfection and so Ancient Africans proudly called themselves "Black People."

BLACK AMERICAN CUSTOMS: combination of African Tradition bits and pieces + European brainwashing + Enslaved Reactions to being Enslaved were gathered into Collage Patterns of Slave Survivals as a way to endure Life Living.

BOX CONCEPT: an assessment tool referring to the turning of the "Thing" about in all directions in order to: "See" both sides of every side and every angle of that which is observed; "See" how every angle is connected to each side; "See" the advantages and disadvantages of each side and of each angle.

BRAIN SWITCH: At the "Fishnet Moment" that enslaved free Africans there was an instant switch from using their Thriving Brain (i.e. the Cerebral Cortex and the Limbic portions) for normal living over to their Instinct or "Emergency" Brain ("fight, flight, or fright")

CAUSE: Pre-existing, Pre-disposing, Precipitating, and Immediate

CLASSIFICATION: A mental tool for putting "Things" derived from the same "Seed" with "family resemblances" or like-kind "Things" representing "brothers from different mothers" into arrangements or combinations that promote their better understanding and that assist with their prioritizing into a hierarchy of significance. Each entity is a "Class".

CONATIVE ELEMENT: The power for any natural tendency related to purposive behavior directed toward action or change--the power for impulse, desiring, striving, and resolving.

"CONDITIONAL": Applies to anything essential to the occurrence of something.

CONDITIONAL RESPONSE: Begins with Recognition of a stimulus, forming a Disposition about it in the form of an Image; embellishing it with Imagination; committing it to Memory—some parts being of the Forgotten Imagination Memory type and other parts being of the Familiarity Memory type which are constantly repeated until its Icon nature spark increases so as to cause a pre-determine thoughtless reaction.

CONSEQUENCES: the sequel; happenings from what sprang out of the Effects

"DEFLECTION"—draws attention away from ones own "Dark Side Sickness" by putting a floodlight on what is supposedly outrageous about happenings of ones Targeted Scapegoat(s)

DEHUMANIZE: Conversion of humans' Image of God core into a machinelike imbrute—i.e. their rendering into a state of brutishness—impersonal—and unconcerned with human values.

DISRESPECT: "the eating of ones self-esteem"

DOUBLE CONSCIOUSNESS: The sense of being two people—one, the Self they know; the other, the Self they are told by others is the real one

EGO: Narrowed focus of ones Consciousness to ones own Selfhood

EMOTIONAL GLOB: Fear, Fright, Dismay, Consternation, Dread, "Awe," Fascination

ENGRAMS: Neuronal patterns of an acquired skilled act of learning—i.e. permanent memories representing what has been learned

EVIL SAVIOR SYNDROME: In spite of Europeans' cruelty to the Enslaved in body, mind, emotions, and spirit + the inadequacy of the food, clothing, and shelter, many Enslaved bonded with the captors.

EXTROVERTING": Needing the External World for approval as well as gathering what is cherished in the External World as ones own standards, guides, measures, and filters.

FETTERS: extreme selfishness, greed, hatred, anger, egoism, fear, envy, jealousy, frustration, arrogance, pride, lust, conceit.

"FISHNET MOMENT": When the fishnet was thrown over the free African in Africa to thereafter enslave him/her "forever,"

FIRST WISDOM: The original and Divine Intellect--consisting of Spiritual Realm and Cosmic Organism Knowledge from where each human newborn just derived.

FORM-BODY STATE: The presumed state of a newborn's mind or traumatically whipped adult whereby their minds are completely susceptible to being molded by the one feeding it--the "Inside-Out" mindset

GLOB: Personally meaningful emotions, feelings, thoughts, imagination, expectations, desires, symbols, and mysterious 'something' interwoven into a "sticky" tangled ball.

"GROUND OF BEING": The essence of a "Thing"—i.e. what that "Thing" was when it came into Being—the ultimate 'ancestor' that by itself, reproduces itself, to become the offspring "Things" it makes—like ocean waves; or, the mental "home-base" from which ones deals with life.

HUMANITY: *Humanity "Manners" of the Cosmic Organism*—as in having good behaviors toward and good relationships with all God's creatures and creations.

ICON: Symbolizes a Microcosm (a "little world") of a "Macrocosm (a "great world")

ILLUSION POSSSIBLITY: Personified (giving life to the lifeless) into a fantasy reality--called a Contingent Being

IMAGE: The *most primitive unit of thought; a sort of mental pictorial representation of a specific event or object which shows 'highlights of the original*; a pattern of forms and figures endowed with unity, significance, a message having a 'payload,' and an obscureness from its remoteness to impart fascination.

IMAGERY: The mental representation of a sensory experience—visual (e.g. an elephant wearing pink slippers), auditory, gustatory, motor, olfactory, or tactile

INFERRED: to conclude from evidence, or from premises, or by reasoning from circumstances

"INSIDE-OUT": Victims who vote against themselves and their own

INTUITED: Meditating to gain insights above and beyond the realm of the mind's thoughts

LAWS OF NATURE: (1) Coherence (its hidden internal links and components being consistent with one another); (2) Consistency (standing firmly together within a state of harmony and balance with what makes sense); (3) Compatibility with Reality (practical); (4) Interconnectedness (everything real depends on every other real thing); (5) Order (sharing the "Oneness" of Cosmic Primordial Substance center); (6) Regularity (conforming to the prescribed standard or the established pattern for it kind); (7) Balance (rendering no favorites on either side but conforming to the Ultimate Standard); (8) Harmony (complete adaptation of each part to the Wholistic Circle); (9) Endurance (progressing inside/in tune with the Spiritual Elements); and (10) Predictability.

LOVE PLATTER: The instinct to Love; to spread Love; to be Loved; and to be Lovable

MANLINESS: Developing oneself out of ones Spiritual Elements ingredients and using those ingredients to discover, develop, and find just the right niche for ones birth gift Talent.

"ME/WE" Cosmic Organism and that ones Mission is to "Lift while Climbing."

MINSET: An attitude of readiness to respond in a certain way, based upon ones prior experiences or expectations of "what is best for me or against me"

"NORMAL VARIANT": It lies between Normal and Abnormal but is not sufficiently different from either to be called one or the other.

"NUMINOUS FEELINGS: The concept of being filled up with a sensation of Supernatural Numen presence of something both a value and an objective reality—gained from visual experiences.

"PARACOSM": A detailed Imaginary World created inside ones mind.

PARALOGIC: *Non-Rational thinking of the Left Brain and Emotions, passed off as "Logic"*

PHILOSOPHICAL WAREHOUSE: A Subconscious source filled with well-reasoned prior solutions and used for emergency decisions; to refine ones urgent decisions; to serve as a 'light' to guide involuntary/automated behavior activities; and to generally assist in coordinating ones Survival.

PRIMORDIAL SUBSTANCE: God's androgynic protoplast—the 'Oneness' foundation of potentiality from which all 'Things' emerge, called "the Path".

PROJECTION: Hurling onto a scapegoat some "ugly" aspect taken out of ones own bad character in order to make it seem as if it is only the victim who has that "ugly" trait.

QUALITITATIVE JUDGEMENT: The mental act of relating two concepts, accompanied by the belief or assertion of some objective or intrinsic relation between the two.

RAW NERVE: A mental "Raw Nerve" results from a "Big Bang" trauma and/or Cumulative Micro-Traumas. Either or both dismantle the strength of ones philosophy of life and/or of ones psychological safety, security, self-confidence, or stability. One or more of these constituted the cause of the "Switch." The mental "Raw Nerve" acts as if it is "Inflamed" (set on fire or set aflame).

SANKOFA: (1) return to African Tradition to learn Principles of how to; (2) Prepare in the present; (3) in order to go forward into a Thriving future

SECOND NATURE: So frequently repeating something as to make it like its Human Nature

SELF-DECLARATION: A Volitional ('I will') mental decision—i.e. a *Self-Declaration*—which activates Conative (underlying motivation) power to drive how one acts on the Disposition's thoughts and Emotions.

SELFHOOD INTEGRITY: Doing what it takes to "Be Right," "Recognize Right," "Do Right," "Make Things Right," and "Defend the Right"

SEVEN DEADLY SINS: pride (arrogance), covetousness (greed), lust, anger, gluttony, envy, and sloth (lazy)

SLAVE SURVIVALS: ways enabling the Enslave to survive and endure by "Making Do". Reasons for them are now faded but doing them—which are always on the negative scale--are self-defeating outside the Black Community, and particularly defeating in the marketplace.

SPIRITUAL ENERGY PACKAGE: One motivated by "Aliveness" into harmonious: Dedication (selecting what is cared about); Commitment (becoming one with what is cared about); Loyal (sticking like glue to a Goal and Purpose no matter what); Determination (setting limits within which one will act); Persistence (holding fast to ones Purpose and Goal); and Perseverance (continuing ruthlessly in the face of opposing forces, set-backs, and momentary failures)

SUBJECTIVE SCIENCE TOOLS: Observation, Reflection, "Pure" Feelings, Productive Imagination, Contemplation, Inductive and Deductive Inferences, and Common Sense

SUPERNATURAL: Beyond the Natural Cosmos beyond sense experience and entities, beyond identity—and thus 'Super-nature'--referring to the Fantasy, with Supernormal Beings.

SYMBOL: a more abstract unit of thought than Images and may have a number of meanings.

SYNTHESIS: The essence of abstracts or abstractions ingredients coordinated into a whole—a whole whose combined product emerges by means other than through a mere summation of the elements involved—retaining the original ingredients like the egg and the sperm producing a fetus. This whole constitutes a Symbol.

THINKER'S SCALE: A positive and negative ruler separated by a Zero

TOTI-POTENTIAL: a putty dough-like condition able to be modeled in any form

'TREE CONCEPT' for assessment into some order. The natural "Tree Concept" consists of a Seed, Sprouts, Roots, Trunk/Vines, Branches, Leaves, Flowers, and Fruit

VIOLENCE: Any threat to--or disturbance caused by an attack on—or the destruction of the Spiritual Elements—whether in the form of the spiritual, emotional, mental, physical, social, financial, or what is materially meaningful

VISION: The art of seeing invisible essences others are unable to see--enables Intuiting, seeing similarities in the dissimilar and discerning uniqueness in similarities.

VOICE OF THE SILENCE: says everything by not saying anything at all while it retains everything by giving away everything—each are tonics to quiet disturbed minds.

WISDOM: There is no other door to Knowledge than the door Nature opens into the realm of Wealth (that which is beautiful, calm, and imparts happiness). Such "Wealth" is *Wisdom*--the actualized intuition (learning from within)—i.e. providing direct perceptions of reality so that its ingredients can be maneuvered and manipulated into Spiritual Elements packages of Ma'at Principles that form options for what is appropriate and most workable for solving the issue.

INDEX

Made in United States
Orlando, FL
23 September 2023

37206633R00343